John Weale

Rudimentary Dictionary of Terms

John Weale

Rudimentary Dictionary of Terms

ISBN/EAN: 9783741172953

Manufactured in Europe, USA, Canada, Australia, Japa

Cover: Foto ©Andreas Hilbeck / pixelio.de

Manufactured and distributed by brebook publishing software (www.brebook.com)

John Weale

Rudimentary Dictionary of Terms

The doorway on the south side of Great Redisham Church is of a date considerably anterior to the first Edward's reign: it affords a good example of the rude Norman architecture so prevalent in the Suffolk churches.

RUDIMENTARY
DICTIONARY OF TERMS

USED IN

ARCHITECTURE, CIVIL,
ARCHITECTURE, NAVAL,
BUILDING AND CONSTRUCTION,
EARLY AND ECCLESIASTICAL ART,
ENGINEERING, CIVIL,
ENGINEERING, MECHANICAL,
FINE ART,
MINING, SURVEYING, ETC.

TO WHICH ARE ADDED

EXPLANATORY OBSERVATIONS
ON
NUMEROUS SUBJECTS CONNECTED WITH PRACTICAL ART AND SCIENCE.

SECOND EDITION, CORRECTED AND IMPROVED.

London:
EDITED AND PUBLISHED BY
JOHN WEALE, 50, HIGH HOLBORN.
1860.

PRINTED BY
JOHN EDWARD TAYLOR, LITTLE QUEEN STREET,
LINCOLN'S INN FIELDS.

PREFACE.

It was intended that the contents of this work should be comprised within the space of about one hundred and fifty pages, and thus form a single volume of the series of 'Rudimentary Treatises;' but in the course of its compilation it soon became apparent that such confined limits were wholly inadequate to the admission of explanations of terms which, although not immediately connected with the subjects mentioned in the title-page, were yet deemed essential to their further amplification: its utility as a book of reference will therefore, it is hoped, be found commensurate with its necessarily increased extent.

Since the publication, in 1819, of Mr. Peter Nicholson's elaborate 'Architectural Dictionary,' in two quarto volumes, changes of vast import have occurred: the field of practical science has been widely extended, and proportionately occupied by a new generation of professional men and students; important advances have been made in the arts of design and construction; and the extended application of steam as a motive power has not only produced an extraordinary development of the means of internal communication, but surmounted those impediments which considerations of space and time formerly presented to the pursuits of men in quest of business or pleasure,—thus influencing, to a great extent, the various operations by which the wants and luxuries of civilized life are supplied.

In a ratio proportionate to the rapid extension of what may be strictly termed practical knowledge has the study of the more pleasurable sciences also progressed: archæology, architecture, civil and mechanical engineering, geology, etc., have exercised a powerful and captivating influence, which has gradually led to the incorporation of societies or associations devoted to the cultivation and advancement of the several branches of human knowledge; and hence has arisen an extensive class of non-professional men, who, however duly acquainted with scientific principles, may yet be anxious to possess any easily available means of becoming familiar with the nomenclature and the technical language necessarily employed in a series of rudimentary treatises on the practical arts and sciences.

Within the period already adverted to, much professional taste and skill have been displayed in the erection of public buildings, in the construction of engineering works of vast magnitude and importance (both at home and abroad), and in the invention of the improved machinery employed in the arts and manufactures of the country. These and similar causes have combined greatly to augment the ranks of a meritorious and useful class of men, among whom, more especially, new wants may be said to have been created,—a class which comprises no inconsiderable number of ingenious operative engineers, artisans, etc.; and to such this work may become interesting and useful, however insufficient it may prove to those already advanced in their professional pursuits.

Should, however, the paucity of information contained in the following pages induce others more competent to the task, and who have sufficient leisure for the purpose, to devote their talents and time to the production of a more comprehensive and more valuable compilation, some share of useful information will at least have been contributed to the means of supplying the wants of an improving age.

The slender efforts here placed before the reader were accomplished, by the aid of the lamp, after the hours usually devoted to the labours of business, and they are now, with the most humble pretensions, submitted to public approval. It has been well observed, that "the language of truth is simple:" no attempt has here been made to trace the derivations of the scientific or technical terms which have been adopted; they are given and explained as generally written, spoken, and understood at the present period, and care has been taken to avoid surreptitious or unauthorized versions, with the view of correctly guiding the student and the operative workman in the onward path of knowledge.

Some analogous explanations and references may probably appear, at a first glance, as superfluous, and to detract from the merits of the work; but when it is considered how numerous and varied, in the present age, are the ramifications into which the employment of those engaged in the building and constructive arts has been extended, and how earnestly the searchers after technical terms and meanings must desire the acquisition of a knowledge of what may not inaptly be designated as a correct disposition of fine art, any unfavourable impression of this nature, hastily formed, will probably be removed upon mature reflection.

In referring to the series of 'Rudimentary Scientific Works' to which this 'Dictionary of Terms' will, it is presumed, be deemed an appropriate *Companion*, it is proper to mention that the first suggestion as to their publication emanated from the late Major-General Sir William Reid, of the Corps of Royal Engineers, and myself. Sir William kindly contributed, as a commencement, Professor Fownes's 'Rudimentary Chemistry.' This elementary treatise, the first of the series, and to which the recommendation of Sir William Reid was limited, had been printed originally at his own expense, for the laudable and special purpose of adding to the numerous educational and scientific works which he had already distributed among different classes in the West India colonies.

To Major-General Portlock, R.E., E. B. Denison, Esq., Q.C., and to Alan Stevenson, Esq., of Edinburgh, James Peake, Esq., of Keyham (H.M.) Dockyard, Sir R. Macdonald Stephenson, Charles Wye Williams, Esq., of Liverpool, William Bland, Esq., of Hartlip, Kent, Hyde Clarke, Esq., David Gibbons, Esq., Joseph Gwilt, Esq., and to others who have so liberally contributed their aid in the production of the extensive treatises, I have to acknowledge my obligations.

Of the First Edition 10,000 copies have been sold. The present Edition, the second, has been revised with care, and, it is hoped, will be found to be considerably improved.

JOHN WEALE.

59, High Holborn,
    May, 1860.

LIST OF THE WORKS WHICH HAVE BEEN CONSULTED IN
THE COMPILATION OF THIS DICTIONARY.

Adcock's Rules and Data for the Steam Engine, etc. 12mo. 1830.
Aide-Mémoire to the Military Sciences. 3 vols. 8vo.
Architectural Papers. 4 vols. 4to.
Bartol's American Marine Boilers. 8vo. 1851.
Blashfield's Terra Cotta Vases, etc. 4to. 1857.
Britton's Architectural Dictionary. 4to. 1838.
Buchanau's Technological Dictionary. 12mo. 1849.
———————— Practical Essays on Mill-work and on Machinery and Tools.
    2 vols. 8vo. Edited by George Rennie, 1841.
Builder's (The) Dictionary. 2 vols. 4to. 1788.
Bury's Styles of Architecture. 12mo. 1855.
Calmet's Dictionary of the Bible. 8vo. 1848.
Campbell's Text-Book of Inorganic Chemistry. 12mo. 1849.
Castell's Villas of the Ancients. fol. 1728.
Clegg's Essay on the Architecture of Machinery. 4to. 1842.
——————— ———— Manufacture and Distribution of Coal Gas. 4to. 1848.
Dana's Seaman's Vade Mecum. 12mo. 1856.
Dempsey's Practical Railway Engineer. 4to. 1855.
Dictionary of Painters, Sculptors, and Engravers. 8vo. 1810.
Divers Works of Early Masters. 2 vols. imp. folio. 1847.
Dobson's Student's Guide, by Garbett. 8vo. 1858-9.
Dodd's (Ralph) Observations on Water. 18mo. 1805.
Ensamples of Railway Making. 8vo. 1843.
Engineer and Contractor's Pocket-Book for 1859.
Engineering Papers. 6 vols. 4to.
Ewbank's Hydraulics and Machinery. 8vo. New York, 1849.
Fairbairn on Cast and Wrought Iron for Building Purposes. 8vo. 1858.
Fergusson's Rock-Cut Temples of India: plates folio, text 8vo. 1845.
Field's Chromatography. 8vo. 1841.

LIST OF WORKS CONSULTED.

Garbett (E. L.) on the Principles of Design in Architecture. 2 vols. 1852.
Glossary of Architecture. 3 vols. Oxford, Parker. 1845.
Greir's Mechanical Dictionary. 12mo. 1850.
Gregory's Mathematics for Practical Men: large 8vo. 1848.
Gwilt's (Joseph) Encyclopædia of Architecture. 8vo. 1857.
———————— edition of Sir William Chambers's Civil Architecture. 2 vols. imperial 8vo. 1824.
———————— Notitia Architectonica Italiana. 8vo. 1818.
Hamilton on Terms used in the Arts and Sciences. 12mo. 1825.
Haun's Theoretical and Practical Mechanics. 8vo. 1849.
Haun's etc. Theory and Practice of Bridges. 4 vols. in 3; large 8vo. 1850.
Holzapffel's Turnery and Mechanical Manipulation. 3 vols. 8vo. 1848.
Homersham on Water Supply to Manchester and the adjacent Towns. 8vo. 1849.
Hunt's Tudor Architecture. 4to. 1830.
Hutton's Mathematical and Philosophical Dictionary. 2 vols. 4to. 1815.
Jamieson's (Dr.) Dictionary of Mechanical Science. 4to. 1827.
———————— Mechanics for Practical Men. 8vo. 1830.
Leeds's Rudimentary Treatise on the Orders of Architecture. 12mo. 1855.
Meason's Architecture of the Great Painters of Italy. 4to. 1828.
Meteorological Society's Transactions, vol. I. large 8vo. 1839.
National Encyclopædia, by Mr. Charles Knight.
Nicholson's Architectural Dictionary. 2 vols. 4to. 1819.
———————— Mechanical Exercises. 8vo. 1819.
Normand's Parallel of the Orders of Architecture, by Pugin: folio. 1829.
Palladio's Architecture, with Notes by Inigo Jones. 2 vols. folio. 1742.
Pambour's Practical Treatise on Locomotive Engines. 8vo. 1840.
Papers connected with the Duties of the Corps of Royal Engineers. 10 vols. 4to. 1835-1849.
Papers and Practical Illustrations of Public Works, both British and American. royal 8vo.
Pole on the Cornish Pumping Engine. 1 vol. 4to. folio plates. 1844.
Pryce's Treatise on Mines and Minerals: folio. 1773.
Pugin's True Principles of Pointed or Christian Architecture. 4to. 1841.
———— Apology for the Revival of Christian Architecture in England. 4to. 1843.
Reid (Major-General Sir Wm.) on the Law of Storms: large 8vo. 1850.
———————— Variable Winds: crown 8vo. 1857.
Rennie's (Sir John) Harbours, Docks, and Coast Engineering. 2 vols. imp. folio. 1855.
Repton's Theory and Practice of Landscape Architecture: large 4to. 1805.
Rich's Companion to the Greek Lexicon and Latin Dictionary. 8vo. 1849.
Smeaton's Reports. 4to. 1837.

LIST OF WORKS CONSULTED.

Smith's Classical Dictionary: large 8vo. 1849.
Stephenson's (Robert) Report on the Atmospheric Railway System. 4to. 1844.
Stuart's Antiquities of Athens. 4 vols. folio.
Taubert's Use of Field Artillery in Service, translated by Lieut. H. H. Maxwell. 1856.
Templeton's Workshop Companion, 1858.
Thorman's Tannns Railway. 4to. 1846.
Tomlinson's Rudimentary Natural Philosophy. 12mo. 1856.
Transactions of the Institution of Civil Engineers. 3 vols. 4to. 1835–40.
Tredgold on the Steam Engine. 2 vols. 4to. 1838–1849.
———— Strength of Cast Iron. 8vo. 1842.
Tredgold's Elementary Principles of Carpentry. 4to. 1856.
Vitruvius's Civil Architecture, by Wilkins: imperial 4to. 1812.
Watson's Account of Mines. 8vo. 1843.
Wicksteed's Experimental Inquiry into Cornish Engines. 4to. 1845.
———— Work on Cornish and Boulton and Watt Engines. 1846.
Wightwick's Hints to Young Architects. 8vo. 1846.
Williams (Chas. Wye) on Combustion. 2 vols. 12mo.
Willis's (Professor) Architectural Nomenclature. 4to. Cambridge.
———— System of Apparatus for the use of Lectures. 4to. 1841.
And lastly, The Dictionary of Architecture, by the Architectural Publication Society, of which several Parts in folio have already appeared. To this really learned and valuable work I am indebted, and acknowledge with much pleasure and thankfulness the several extracts made from it, and testify to its great utility to the profession at large.

DICTIONARY OF TERMS

USED

IN ARCHITECTURE, BUILDING, ENGINEERING,

NAVAL ARCHITECTURE, ARCHÆOLOGY, ETC.

AARON'S-ROD, an ornamental figure representing a rod with a serpent entwined about it; improperly called the *caduceus* of Mercury.

Abacia, in antiquity, a kind of roll, resembling a bag.

Abaciscus, small tesseræ or square stones, for tessellated pavement.

Abacot, the cap of state, a double crown formerly worn by the sovereigns of England.

Abaculus, a small table or desk.

Abacus, a small tile or covering member of a capital, varying in the several orders: in Grecian Doric, square, without chamfer or moulding; in Roman Doric it has an ogee or fillet round the upper edges; in the Tuscan, a plain fillet and a cavetto under it; in Grecian Ionic it is thinner, with ovolo only; in Roman Ionic, an ogee and ovolo, and fillet above; in the Saxon and Norman styles, and in early English, it varies in form and substance,—flat, chamfered, and hollow, circular and octagonal, with mouldings, latterly decorated.

Abacus (among mathematicians), a table strewed over with dust or sand, on which the ancients used to draw their schemes and figures.

Abacus, a multiplication-table, in form of a right-angled triangle.

Abacus (in old records), a counting-table used for calculations and schemes.

Abacus major, a large trough to wash in.

Abadir (Paul), born at Bordeaux in 1783, a pupil of Bonfin and Percier, built the church of St. André, and other public buildings in that city.

Abaft, towards the stern of a ship.

Abaiser, burnt ivory, or ivory-black.

Abamurus, a buttress or second wall, added to strengthen another.

Abated, sunk or lowered. 'The Marbler' "agrees that all the champes about the letters are to be abated and hatched curiously, to set out the letters."

Abatement, a carpenter's term used by old authors, signifying the waste of a piece of stuff by forming it to a designed purpose.

Abat-jour, a skylight, or aperture for the admission of light.

Abattoir, a building appropriated to the slaughtering of cattle.

Abat-vent, the sloping roof of a tower; a penthouse.

Abat-voix, the sounding-board over a pulpit or rostrum.

Abbey, a building annexed to or adjacent to a convent or monastery, for the residence of the abbot or abbess, and the whole combining a series of buildings for the accommodation of a fraternity under ecclesiastical government.

Abbey gate-house, a lodge for warders or porters at the entrance of an abbey edifice.

Abbot, the superior of a monastery of monks erected into an abbey or priory: there are various classes of abbots, as mitred, crosiered, cardinal, regular, and commendatory abbots.

Abbot's lodgings, in the early times of English ecclesiastical architecture, a complete house, with hall, chapel, and every convenience for the residence of a spiritual baron.

Abbreviate, to contract a word in writing or printing.

Abbreviations, characters or marks over letters to signify either a word or syllable.

Abel (John), an English architect of considerable notoriety, died in 1674, aged 97: built, during the periods of James I. and Charles I., the market-houses of Brecon, Hereford, Weobly, with its school-house, Kingston, and Leominster, and the timberwork of the church at Abbeydore; and being in Hereford when the Scots besieged it in 1645, he constructed mills to grind corn, which were of great use to the besieged, and for which Charles I. afterwards made him one of his carpenters.

Abele-tree, a species of white poplar.

Aber, or *Abber*, the fall or emptying a lesser water into a greater, as of a brook into a river: hence several towns situated on or near the mouth of rivers generally derive the first parts of their names.

Aberration, in astronomy, an apparent motion of the celestial bodies occasioned by the progressive motion of light and the earth's annual motion in its orbit.

Aberration, in optics, the deviation or dispersion of the rays of light when reflected by a lens, by which they are prevented from meeting or uniting in the same point, called the geometrical focus; but spread over a small span, they produce a confusion of images.

Ablactation, in gardening, the method of grafting.

Ablaqueation, the opening of the ground around the roots of trees, for the admission of the air.

Aboard, a nautical term, the inside of a ship, or to go on board.

Abobe, unbaked bricks in Spain, used for the erection of cottages in Castile and Leon.

About-ship, the situation of a ship after she has tacked.

About-sledge, the largest hammer employed by smiths; it is slung round near the extremity of the handle, and generally used by under workmen, called hammer-men.

Abrasion, the effect produced by attrition or rubbing.

Abraum, a red clay, used in England to give a red colour to new mahogany.

Abreast, as when two ships have their sides parallel.

Abreuvoir, a watering-place.

Abreuvoir, in masonry, the interstice or joint between two stones to be filled up with mortar or cement.

Abscissa, a geometrical term for a segment cut off from the straight line by an ordinate to a curve.

Absis, or *Apsis*, the bowed or arched roof of an oven, room, or house.

Absis, or *Apsis*, the ring or compass of a wheel.

Absorbents, in chemistry, those earthy substances capable of uniting, by capillary attraction, a large proportion of water; such are magnesia, lime, and clay, when dry and porous.

Absorbing-well, a shaft or boring for removing either the excess of drainage-waters, or the foul waters produced by manufacturing purposes.

Absorption is the successive and intimate penetration of a gas, or a liquid, into any substance; but familiarly, the taking up moisture, in any material, by capillary attraction.

Absthánes, a lower kind of nobility

formerly in Scotland, but now extinct.

Abstract (To), a term used by artificers and surveyors in arranging and apportioning their work, to explain and price it.

Abstract mathematics, otherwise denominated pure mathematics, that branch of the science which treats of simple properties, magnitude, figure, or quantity, absolutely and generally considered.

Abstraction and absorption of heat is that process under which caloric, or heat, passes from any body to whatever surrounds it, or to any conducting substance with which it is in contact.

Absurd, a term used in demonstrating converse propositions.

Abundant number, a number whose aliquot parts, added together, make a sum which is greater than the number itself.

Abuses: "Architecture," says Palladio, "being an imitatrix of Nature, delights in that which is most consonant with her prototype." Ancient edifices were built with wood, trees forming the columns; and when architects began to build with stone, they made the columns to imitate the trunks of trees, tapering from their bases. Being thus originally of wood, and therefore liable to split when much loaded, they bound them with rings at top and bottom. Thus the bases and capitals in the different orders seem originally derived from these bandages, though they are now become essential ornaments. Thus also in entablatures, the triglyphs, modillions, and dentils represent the ends of those beams and timbers which are employed for the support of the floors and roofs. If therefore all these conditions be duly considered, those practices in building are highly to be reprobated which are in opposition to that analogy which should exist between the original and its imitation, or which depart from Nature and the simplicity observable in all her works.

Consoles or cartouches, which are of a scroll-like form, should never be employed for the apparent support of great weights, in place of columns or pilasters; nor should they ever project from, or spring out of cornices.

Pediments and frontispieces over doors and windows, or elsewhere, should on no account be broken or disconnected in the middle; for the intention of these is to shelter the parts below from the rain, and this result is completely obviated by such a practice.

The projecture of cornices, though for the purpose of sheltering buildings, should not be more than in due proportion to their height, whether or not accompanied by columns; for if too heavy, they seem to threaten with danger those who are under them; and if too small in projection, they do not properly perform their office.

Again, those columns which are feigned to be composed of several pieces, by being jointed together with rings, should be carefully avoided, because the more solid and strong the columns appear, the better they seem to answer the purpose for which they were erected, which is securely to receive the superincumbent loading.

There are many other abuses which the authority of great masters may sanction, but not justify; and such will readily occur to the student, and themselves point out that they ought to be avoided.

Abutment, the solid part of a pier from which the arch springs.

Abutments, the extremities of a bridge, by which it joins upon the banks or sides of a river, etc.; in carpentry and joinery, the junctions or meetings of two pieces of timber, of which the fibres of the one run perpendicular to the joint, and those of the other parallel to it.

Abuttals, the buttings or boundaries of land.

Acacio, a heavy, durable wood, of the red mahogany character, but darker and plainer: it is highly esteemed in ship-building.

Academia, in antiquity, a villa or pleasure-house in one of the suburbs of Athens, where Plato and other philosophers assembled.

Academician, a member of a society or academy instituted for the cultivation of the arts and sciences.

Academy-figure is a drawing or design, done after a model, with crayon or pencil.

Acanthus, the plant *Branca ursina*, in English *bear's-breech*, the leaves of which are imitated in decorating the Corinthian and Composite capitals of columns.

Accelerated motion, a force acting incessantly upon a body; called also a constant or uniformly accelerating force when the velocity increases equally in equal times: the force of gravity near the earth's surface is of this kind; it generates a velocity of 32½ feet in each second of time; that is, a body, after falling one second, acquires a velocity of 32½ feet; after falling two seconds, it will acquire a velocity of 2 × 32½ feet; after three seconds, a velocity of 3 × 32½ feet, and so on.

Accelerating force, in physics, the force which accelerates the motion or velocity of bodies; it is equal to, or expressed by, the quotient arising from the motion or absolute force, divided by the mass or the weight of the body moved.

Accelerative or *retardative force*, is commonly understood to be that which affects the velocity only, or that by which the velocity is accelerated or retarded; it is equal or proportional to the motive force directly, and to the mass or body moved inversely.

Accesses, approaches or passages of communication between the various apartments of a building, as corridors.

Accessible, in surveying, a place which admits of having a distance or length of ground measured from it; or such a height or depth as can be measured by the application of a proper instrument.

Accessories, or *accompaniments*, in painting, secondary objects to the principal one in a picture, introduced as explanatory and illustrative of the scene: sometimes they are considered as solely contributing to the general effect and harmony of the piece.

Accidental point, in perspective, the point in which a right line drawn from the eye, parallel to another right line, cuts the picture or perspective plane.

Acclivity, the slope or steepness of a line or plane inclined to the horizon, taken upwards; in contradistinction to declivity, which is taken downwards.

Accouplement, in carpentry, a tie or brace, or the entire work when framed.

Accretion, in physics, the growth or increase of an organized body.

Accubitus, a room annexed to large churches, in which the clergy occasionally reposed.

Aceric acid, in chemistry, an acid formed from the juice of the maple-tree.

Acerra, in antiquity, an altar erected, among the Romans, near the bed of a person deceased, on which his friends daily offered incense until his burial.

Aces (a sea term), hooks for the chains.

Acesides, the chimneys of furnaces where brass was made; they were contrived to be narrow at top, on purpose to receive and collect the fumes of the melting metal, in order that cadmia might be produced in greater quantities.

Acetate of lead,—sugar of lead,—a compound of acetic acid and lead.

Acetate of potash, a compound of acetic acid and potash, produced by dissolving carbonate of potash in distilled vinegar.

Achievement, the ensigns armorial of a family.

Achleitner (Simon) was master of the works at St. Stephen's, in Vienna, 1481.

Achromatic, a term expressing absence of colour; in optics, applied to telescopes invented to remedy aberrations and colours.

Achromatic, without colour, is applied in decorations to total absence of colour; mere white and black, or white and gold, may be considered in this sense achromatic.

Acids, in chemistry, are sour to the taste, and convert vegetable blues to a red colour; they combine with alkalies, earths, and metallic oxides, and form, with them, the well-known compounds named *salts*.

Acinose, a term applied to iron ore found in masses, and of several colours.

Acisculis, a small pick used by masons, having one end like that of a hammer and the other pointed.

A-cock-bill, in navigation, the situation of the yards when they are topped up at an angle with the deck; the situation of an anchor when it hangs to the cat-head by the ring only.

Acolyte, in the ancient church, a person who trimmed the lamps, prepared for the sacrament, etc.

Acorn, the seed of oak; imitations of it are much used in architecture, and it is sometimes introduced instead of the egg in the Roman ovolo.

Acoumeter, an instrument invented by Itard for estimating the extent of the sense of hearing.

Acoustics, the doctrine or theory of sounds, consisting of diacoustics, or direct sounds, and catacoustics, or reflecting sounds.

Acre, a measure of land, containing, by the ordinance for measuring land in the time of Edward I., 160 perches or square poles of land; and as the statute length of a pole is 5½ yards, or 16½ feet, the acre contains 4840 square yards, or 43,560 square feet. The chain with which land is now commonly measured, invented by Gunter, is 4 poles, or 22 yards, in length; and the acre is therefore just 10 square chains; and as a mile contains 1760 yards, or 80 chains, in length, the square mile is equal to 640 acres. The acre, in surveying, is divided into 4 roods, and the rood into 4 perches.

Acrolithes, in sculpture, statues, the extremities of which are formed of stone.

Acropolis, a building strictly applicable to a Greek city, and usually erected upon a hill, rock, or some natural elevation, and devoted to a magnificent temple; also a tower, castle, or citadel.

Acrostolion, in ancient naval architecture, an ornament of the prow or forecastle of a ship, chiefly of war, most frequently circular or spiral.

Acroteria, small pedestals at the angles and vertex of a pediment; the gate of the Agora at Athens is the only instance in which they appear in Grecian buildings.

Actinometer: Sir John Herschel, at the third meeting of the British Association, submitted an instrument for measuring at any instant the direct heating power of the solar ray: it affords a dynamical measure of the solar radiation, by receiving a quantity of heat per second, or any short space of time, on a surface exposed to the sun. In making observations with this instrument, it should be freely exposed in the shade for one minute, and the variation read; afterwards expose it for the same time to the solar action, and again note it; and lastly, repeat the experiment in the shade: the mean of the two variations in the shade being subducted from the variation in the sun, the excess gives the dilatation per minute due to the sun's rays the quantity subducted being the effect of the other causes at the time.

Action, in painting or sculpture, the posture, attitude, expressive of the passion the painter or carver would convey to the mind of a spectator.

Actus, a Roman measure of length, equal to 120 Roman feet.

Acute angle, in geometry, less than a right angle, and measured by less than 90° or a quadrant of a circle.

Acute-angled cone, that in which the opposite sides make an acute at the vertex, or whose axis, in a right cone, makes less than half a right angle with the side.

Acute-angled section of a cone, an ellipsis made by a plane cutting both sides of an acute-angled cone.

Acute-angled triangle, that in which the three angles are all acute.

Adam (Wm.), an architect of Scotland, died about 1760, designed and built several edifices.

Adam (John), of Edinburgh, son of the above, executed several designs in Scotland.

Adam (Robert), second son of William; he and his brother James executed very many very splendid buildings in England and Scotland, more particularly in London, the Adelphi, Portland-place, Lansdowne-house, and other noblemen's houses.

Mr. Weale purchased several unpublished (and posthumous) plates at the sale of the effects in Albemarle-street in 1822, which he published as a third or supplementary volume to the two volumes sometime previously published.

Adam (James), architect, also a son of William Adam, died in Albemarle-street in 1794, was with his brother Robert the intimate friend of Clerisseau, Zucchi, and patrons of other celebrated French and Italian artists.

Adam (William), architect, another son of the same William, built several houses in Whitehall, died in 1822, aged 84.

Adamant, a very hard stone, used by the ancients for cutting and polishing other hard stones and glass.

Adeling, a title of honour given to the children of princes among the Anglo-Saxons.

Adhesion, the force with which different bodies remain attached to each other when brought into contact.

Adit, the passage or approach to a house; applied also to the horizontal shaft of a mine, driven for the purposes of ventilating, watering, or draining.

Adit-level, in mining, a horizontal excavation through which the water is drawn by the engine.

Adjacent angle, in geometry, an angle immediately contiguous to another, so that one side is common to both.

Adjutage (*Ajutage*), or *jet-d'eau*, a tube fitted to the aperture of a vessel through which water is to be played.

Admeasurement, the measuring or finding the dimensions and quantity of a thing by the application of a standard or rule.

Admeasurement, a process in the art of mensuration for measuring and determining dimensions of work.

Adonia, a festival celebrated in honour of Aphrodite and Adonis in most of the Grecian cities.

Adrift, the condition of a vessel broken from her moorings.

Adytum, the most sacred place in the heathen temples; the Holy of Holies; in Christian architecture, the chancel or altar-end of a church.

Adze, an edged tool used to chip surfaces in a horizontal direction; the axe being employed to chop materials in vertical positions.

Æbrechts (H.) was with Louis Gerbrandt and Klas Huygens, in 1499, to build the town-hall at Gonda, in Holland.

Æcclesiola, in Domesday Book, a chapel subordinate to the mother church.

Ædes, an inferior kind of temple; in Christian architecture, a chapel; also sometimes applied to a house.

Ædicula, a small chapel, house, or building of any kind; not unfrequently applied to the niches of tabernacles in a wall which held statues of the lares or penates.

Ægina marbles: C. R. Cockerell, Esq., visited Athens with Mr. Foster in 1811. In examining the temples of Athens, with their lamented friend and companion, the Baron Haller, some details, of singular interest and novelty, induced them to form the project of excavating the Temple of Jupiter at Ægina, for the purpose of ascertaining how far these might be found common to other remains of Grecian architecture, as well as for the general object of advancing their studies.

The Æginetan statues furnish the only illustrations of the heroic costume and armour, as described by Homer, Æschylus, and the earliest Grecian writers; and the great nicety of execution in the smallest details corresponds perfectly with the exactness which the poets have observed in their description: a minute and scrupulous attention is paid to each tie and fastening; and as if the whole had been offered to the severest scrutiny, the parts never seen were equally furnished with exact resemblance of each particular detail in the most ancient coins of Corinth, Sybaris, Posidonia, and the earliest Greek cities of Italy, as well as of Ionia, which were much earlier proficients in arts than those of Greece Proper; and in the vases of the most archaic style (commonly in black on a red ground) we trace the character which is developed and explained in these statues.

The magnificent statue of Minerva, who, by her action, seems from Olympus to have just alighted to animate the combat by her presence, we have the most antique costume hitherto known to us. The form of the Ægis is singular, nor have we seen it before in sculpture, surrounded with the tassels, the noise of which was said to have dismayed her opponents: we know such a sort of appendage to have been in much earlier use than the more usual one of the serpents. These were undoubtedly of brass, or some metal, which has disappeared; they were fastened by rivets of lead, most of which still remained. The holes by which the Gorgon's head was attached to her breast were evident, and the whole of the Ægis was painted with scales in encaustic; they could not however be discovered.

The lion's head attached to the extreme tile of this temple was found perfect, and in the blocking, which carries the Chimæra, was a sinking, corresponding with the thickness of the plinth, to which the legs were attached.

The whole of the ornaments indicated on the several members of the cornice were painted on the marble in encaustic; as are the extreme tiles, forming the upper moulding of the pediment; and on the stone of which the whole temple was constructed, is a thin coat or varnish of very fine and hard plaster.

Ægricomes, a name given to rams' heads when sculptured on friezes, altars, etc.

Ægyptilla, a species of Egyptian ornament.

Æmasia, a fence, or fence-wall.

Æolipile, in hydraulics, an instrument consisting of a hollow metallic ball with a slender neck or pipe proceeding from it, which, being filled with water, produces a violent blast of wind.

Æolus, a small portable machine for refreshing and changing the air of apartments.

Æolus (in mythology, the god of winds), the name of a ventilator, or a machine used to extract foul air out of rooms.

Ærarium, a treasury among the Romans; the place where public money was deposited.

Aërial perspective, the relative apparent recession of objects from the foreground, owing to the quantity of air interposed between them and the spectator.

Æro, according to Vitruvius, a basket to carry earth in, used by the Romans.

Aëro-dynamics, the science relating to the active powers or forces of gaseous fluids.

Aërology, the doctrine or science of the air.

Aërometer, an instrument contrived to ascertain the mean bulk of gases.

Aërometry, the science of measuring the air, its powers and properties.

Aëronautics, the art of sailing or floating in the air.

Aërostatics, the doctrine of the weight, pressure, and balance of the air and atmosphere.

Ærugo, rust, more especially that of copper,—verdigris.

Æsthetics, the power of perception by means of the senses: the word implies the perception and the study of those qualities which constitute the beautiful and artistic, and form the finer essence of all productions of fine art; it carries with it, therefore, a more exact and philosophic meaning than the word 'taste:' in its adjective form, in which it more frequently occurs, it is particularly useful, as no adequate epithet can be substituted for it. Thus we speak of the 'æsthetic sense,' of 'æsthetic feeling,' or 'study,' or 'principles,' etc.; but we cannot correctly say, the 'tasteful sense,' or 'tasteful study.'

Æstuarium, a description of the ancient baths, to the flue from hypocaustum or stove to chambers.

Æsymnium, a building in Megara; so called from Æsymnius, its founder, who erected that edifice, which consisted of a council-hall round the tomb of his countrymen who died in battle against the Persians.

Æthousa, the portico on the sunny side of the court of a Greek dwelling.

Aëtoma, a pediment,or the tympanum of a pediment.

Affection, in painting, the representation of any passions, whereby they appear to be animated, and swell to the sight.

Affections in general: 1, character, qualities, disposition, nature, spirit, temper, temperament, idiosyncrasy, cast, or frame of mind or soul; 2, personal affections; 3, prospective affections; 4, contemplative affections; 5, extrinsic affections,—social affections, diffusive sympathetic affections, special sympathetic affections, retrospective sympathetic affections, moral obligations, moral sentiments, moral practice, institutions, religious affections, doctrines, sentiments, acts of religion, religious institutions.

Affinity, in chemistry, the power by which the ultimate particles of matter are made to unite, and kept united.

Afflux, a flow of electric matter to a globe and conductor, in opposition to *efflux*, from them.

After, in ship-building, implies a connection, as belonging to the after-body, after-timber, etc.

Agalma, a sculptural ornament or image.

Ager, a Roman acre of land.

Agger, a heap or mound of any kind, formed of stone, wood, or earth.

Agglutination, the cohesion of bodies.

Aggregation, in chemistry, the collection of bodies, solid, fluid, or gaseous.

Agiasterium, the sanctuary, which is the basilica of the Latin Church.

Agnolo (B. D'), born in 1459, excelled in inlaid works, and executed at Florence, besides some coffers in walnut-wood, a large figure-frame, described by Vasari: he was also the most celebrated carver of his time.

Agnolo (D. D'), a son of the preceding, Baccio: was also a wood-carver as well as an architect.

Agnolo (G. D') another son of Baccio: besides wood-carving, he gave more attention to architecture.

Agora, a place of public assembly, in a Greek city, for the transaction of all public business; a market-place.

Agrafe, a French term used by builders for small cramps employed in fixing chimney-pieces, etc.

Agrippa (Camillus), a distinguished Milanese architect of the sixteenth century.

Aguilla, an obelisk, or the spire of a church-tower.

A-hull, the condition of a vessel when she has all her sails furled, and her helm lashed a-lee.

Aile, the wing, the inward portico, on each side of a church or other large building, supported by pillars within.

Air-brick, an iron box used in walls, and usually made to the size of a brick, but with one of its faces formed into a grating.

Air-casing, the sheet-iron casing which surrounds the base of the chimney of a steam-vessel, to prevent too great a transmission of heat to the deck.

Air-drains, cavities between the external walls of a building, protected by a wall towards the earth, which is thus prevented from causing dampness.

Air-escape, a contrivance for letting off the air from water-pipes.

Air-holes, those made for admitting air to ventilate apartments.

Air-machine, in mining, the apparatus used for forcing purer air into or withdrawing foul air from parts badly ventilated.

Air-pipes, in mining, tubes or pipes of iron or wood, for ventilating under ground, or for the conveyance of fresh air into levels having but one communication with the atmosphere, and no current of air; also used for clearing foul air from the holds of ships or other close places.

Air-pump, a pneumatic instrument, by means of which the air is exhausted out of the proper vessels: its effects are produced by the elasticity of the air; and as at each stroke of the pump only a part of the remaining air is withdrawn, an absolute vacuum cannot be obtained, although so near an approximation to it may be had as to remove the general effects of the atmosphere. In steam-engines, the proportion of the air-pump, as given by Watt, is usually about two-thirds of the diameter of the cylinder, when the length of the stroke of the air-bucket is half the length of the stroke of the steam-piston. The area of the passages between the condenser and the air-pump should never be less than one-fourth of the area of the air-pump. The apertures through the air-bucket should have the same proportion; and, if convenient, the discharging flap or valve should be made larger. The capacity of the condenser should at least be equal to that of the air-pump; but, when convenience will admit of it, the larger it is the better.

Air-pump bucket, an open piston, with valves on the upper surface, opening upwards, so as to admit the air and water in the down-stroke, and lift it with the up-stroke of the pump.

Air-pump rod, the rod for connecting the bucket to the beam.

Air-shaft, in mining, a passage made for the air by digging.

Air-tint, in painting, the tint by which the distant parts of a landscape are rendered more distinct, or sometimes giving a misty appearance to the whole: it is generally compounded of a blue-grey, occasionally approaching to purple.

Air-trap, a trap immersed in water, to prevent foul air arising from sewers or drains.

Air-valve, applied to steam boilers

for the purpose of preventing the formation of a vacuum when the steam is condensing in the boiler.

Air-vessel, the closed cylinder connected to the discharge-pipe of a force-pump, and by the action of which the water ejected by the piston or plunger of the pump enters the cylinder and compresses the air within; it acts as a spring during the return stroke, and thus renders the stream constant; also a chamber containing air, attached to pumps and other water-engines, for the purpose of making the discharge constant when the supply is intermittent.

Aisle, the side-passage or division of a church, partially separated from the nave and choir by columns or piers.

Aitre, a hearth or chimney.

Ajambe, the French term for a window: it differs from the usual French window in having four or more casements, with separate hinges and fastenings complete, instead of two upright ones, which they generally have.

Alabaster, a species of gypsum, a mineral substance, chemically termed *sulphate of lime*; also a box or vase for holding perfumes and ointments, so called because originally made of alabaster, and for which the variety called *onyx-alabaster* was usually employed.

Alba, a beacon or lighthouse.

Albarium, white-wash; according to Pliny and Vitruvius, a white stucco or plaster, made of a pure kind of lime burned from marble, and used to spread over the roofs of houses.

Albarium opus, according to Vitruvius, a species of stuccowork.

Alberti (Leone Battista), the son of a noble Florentine, born at Genoa in 1406: an architect of some celebrity, and an author on the subjects of architecture and painting.

Albertolli (G.), the son of an architect, born at Bedana in 1742: was an architect of repute, and published some works on ornament of refined taste.

Alcha, a cellar, pantry, or an apartment for the reception of drinking vessels.

Alchemist, one skilled in the art of alchemy or chemistry.

Alchemy, that branch of chemistry which presumes the transmutation of metals: Lord Bacon calls it the art of distilling or drawing quintessences out of metals by fire.

Alcohol, in chemistry, a pure spirit.

Alcoholometer, an instrument for ascertaining the strength of spirits.

Alcorans, in oriental architecture, high slender towers attached to mosques, in which the Koran is read.

Alcove, a recess in a chamber, or a recess separated from other parts of the room by columns, antæ, and balusters.

Alder, a wood formerly much used. The common alder seldom exceeds 40 feet in height, is very durable under water, and was used for the piles of the Rialto at Venice, the buildings at Ravenna, etc.: it was formerly much used for pipes, pumps, and sluices.

Aldrich (Henry), dean of Christ Church, Oxford, born in 1647: he was distinguished for his architectural attainments, and published a work on its elements.

Aleaceria, a palace, castle, or other large edifice.

Aleatorium, an apartment in a Roman house appropriated to the use of persons playing with dice.

A-lee, a term used to denote the position of the helm when it is put in the opposite direction from that in which the wind blows.

Alembic, in chemistry, a vessel used in distillation.

Alexis, loopholes in the walls of a castle or fortification, through which arrows may be discharged.

Algebra, literal arithmetic, or the science by which quantity, and the operations of quantity, are expressed by conventional symbols.

Alhambra, in Saracenic architecture, the royal palace of the kings of Granada.

Alien priories, cells or small religious houses erected in different countries, and distinguished as *alien* from their dependence on large foreign monasteries.

Alipterion, in ancient Rome, a room wherein bathers anointed themselves.

Aliquot part, such part of a number as will exactly divide it without a remainder; a part as, being taken or repeated a certain number of times, exactly makes up or is equal to the whole; thus 1 is an aliquot part of 6, or any other whole number.

Alkalimeter, an instrument for measuring and determining the quantity and strength of alkalies.

Allette, used to express a small wing of a building; also applied to a pilaster or buttress.

Alley, a passage from one part of a building to another; a passage or court with houses.

Alligation, one of the rules of arithmetic, by which are resolved questions which relate to the compounding or mixing together of divers simples or ingredients.

Allorium, a piazza, corridor, or covered way in the flank of a building.

Alloy, baser metal, commonly mixed with the precious metals.

Alluminate (To), in painting, to wash prints with alum-water, to keep the colours from sinking or running.

Alluminate (To), to enlighten; to give grace, light, and ornament.

Alluvion, the débris occasioned by causes still in operation, as deposits left by the action of rivers, floods, and torrents.

Almacantar, lines parallel to the horizon, and conceived to pass through every degree of the meridian.

Almaria, in old records, the archives of a church; a library.

Almehrab, a niche in the mosques of the Arabs, for praying.

Almond-furnace, a furnace used by refiners, and called a sweep, for separating all sorts of metals from cinders, etc.

Almond-tree, a hard, heavy, oily, or resinous kind of wood, somewhat pliable.

Almonry, a room or place where alms were formerly distributed to the poor.

Almshouse, a house for the reception and support of the poor.

Aloof, in navigation, to keep the ship near the wind when sailing upon a quarter wind.

Alquifore, lead ore found in Cornwall, and used by potters to green-varnish their wares.

Alruna, small images carved out of roots of trees, and anciently held in much veneration by the northern nations.

Altar, an elevated table of either stone, marble, or wood, dedicated to the ceremonies of religious worship. "And Noah builded an altar unto the Lord; and took of every clean beast, and of every clean fowl, and offered burnt-offerings on the altar."

Altar-piece, the ornamental sculpture or painting behind the altar in a Christian church.

Altar-screen, the back of an altar, or the partition by which the choir is separated from the presbytery and lady-chapel.

Altars, among the Greeks, according to Wilkins's 'Vitruvius,' faced the east, and were placed lower than the statues arranged about the cella, in order that those who offered up prayers and sacrifices might know, from their different heights, to what particular deities the several altars were consecrated.

Altare chori, a reading-desk in a church.

Altare farum, the lustre, chandelier, or cresset, suspended over an altar.

Altimetry, the art of taking or measuring altitudes or heights.

Altitude, of a figure, the length of a

line drawn perpendicularly from the vertex to the base.

Altitude of the eye in perspective, a right line let fall perpendicular to the geometrical plane.

Altitude of a figure in geometry, the nearest distance between the vortex or a top of that figure and its base.

Altitude, height.

Alto-rilievo, highly relieved sculpture representing figures either entirely or nearly detached from the background.

Alum, a salt extracted from various minerals called alum ores: of great use to chemists, dyers, and artists; acid and sharp to the taste.

Aluminium is a metal which by uniting with oxide forms the universally distributed earth, alumina, the chief constituent of clay, and an ingredient of many gums and minerals. This metal was originally discovered in 1808, and Mr. Deville, a French chemist, has recently discovered a method of obtaining it in large pieces, and a bar of it has been presented to the Polytechnic Institution in London by the Emperor Napoleon. The metal is coming into very general use by its becoming cheap. Its colour is white, with a faint blue tinge; it is highly malleable and ductile; a perfect conductor of electricity; it melts at a temperature higher than zinc (773° Fahr.), and resists the action of sulphuretted hydrogen, of water, and of oxygen, if not heated. It is of very light weight, its specific gravity being only 2·60, that of gold being 19·26, and of iron 7·79.

Alston Moor, in Northumberland. Mining in this district is of great antiquity; the miners of Alderston had their charter 600 years ago. These mines yielded gold, silver, and lead, but more of the lastnamed, and formerly belonged to Sir Edward Radcliffe, and remained in that family till the confiscation of the estates of James, Earl of Derwentwater, in 1716. It was granted in 1734 to the Royal Hospital for Seamen at Greenwich. In form the manor of Alston Moor nearly resembles a square of about 6¾ miles, containing about 45 square miles, or 29,000 acres. The mines were yielding Greenwich Hospital in 1821 annually £100,000, and the lands £12,000.

Alveus, in hydrography, the channel or belly of a river.

Amausa, such pieces of glass as are used in enamelling.

Amalgam, a mixture of mercury with any other metal, tin, lead, etc.

Ambitus, an enclosure; more particularly applied to the space around a building, as a churchyard, or a castle-yard.

Ambo, Ambone, a rostrum or raised platform.

Ambulatio, walks, or places of exercise, according to Vitruvius, adjacent to theatres.

Ambulatory, a cloister, gallery, or alley.

American wood-boring tools. Some most efficient tools for boring in wood have been invented by Dr. Brown, of the United States, which appear, from the facility with which they may be worked, and the excellent character of their performance, likely to supersede entirely the old-fashioned 'auger' which is now in use in this country. The form of the implements has been borrowed from the boring apparatus with which the tiny insects who make such havoc in timber are provided.

Amethyst, in heraldry, is a purple colour in noblemen's coats of arms.

Ammailare, to enamel.

Ammoniac, a gum used for metallic vessels.

Amphiprostyle, a term applied to a temple with a portico in front and also behind.

Amphitheatre, an edifice formed by the junction of two theatres at the proscenium, so as to admit of seats all round the periphery.

Amphitheatre, in Roman antiquity, a large edifice of an elliptic form, with a series of rising seats or benches disposed around a spacious area, called the arena, in which the combats of gladiators and wild-beasts, and other sports, were exhibited. It consisted exteriorly of a wall pierced in its circumference by two or more ranges of arcades, and interiorly of vaulted passages radiating from the exterior arcades towards the arena, and several transverse vaulted corridors which opened a free communication to the stairs at the ends of the passage and to every other part of the building, the corridors and ranges of seats forming elliptical figures parallel to the boundary wall.

Amphithura, in the Greek Church, the veil or curtain opening to the folding doors, and dividing the chancel from the rest of the church.

Amphora (pl. *amphorae*), an earthen vase or jar, with a handle on each side of the neck: among the ancients, the usual receptacles of olives, grapes, oil, and wine. Hence, in decoration, *amphoral* means, shaped like an amphora or vase.

Amulet, in decoration, a figure or character to which miraculous powers were supposed to be attached, and which particularly distinguished the buildings of Egypt.

Amussium, anciently a carpenter's and mason's instrument, the use of which was to obtain a true plane surface; but the statements of the ancient writers render its construction extremely difficult.

Anabathra, steps to any elevated situation, as the anabathra of theatres, pulpits, etc.

Anabathrum, a pulpit, desk, or high seat.

Anacampteria, the lodgings of persons who fled for sanctuary to privileged religious houses.

Anacamptics, the doctrine of reflected light.

Anachorita, the cell of a hermit.

Anaclastics, the doctrine of refracted light.

Anaglyph, an engraved, embossed, or chased ornament.

Anaglypha, chased or embossed vessels made of bronze or the precious metals, which derived their name from the work on them being in relief, and not engraved.

Anaglyphic work, a species of sculpture wherein figures are made prominent by embossing.

Analemma, a projection of the meridian; used also to designate a wall, pier, or buttress.

Analogium, a tomb over the bodies of saints; also a term formerly applied to pulpits wherein the gospels and epistles were read.

Anamorphosis, a distorted piece of perspective, occasioned by too near a point of view, and from the injudicious altitude or situation of the object, but perfectly true according to the laws of perspective.

Anchor, an instrument used for the mooring of ships; in architecture, a decorative moulding used in the orders, and applied to the echinus; also an ornament in the form of the fluke of an anchor, frequently cut in the ovolo of Ionic capitals, and in the bed-mouldings of Ionic and Corinthian cornices.

Anchor-stock, in ship-building, a method of working planks, by which the abutments are to be disposed near the middle of those planks which are above or below them.

Ancon, in decoration, a carved drinking-cup or horn; an elbow or angle, or corner-stone. The *Ancona* foot measure is 1·282 of an English foot.

Ancone, a console or ornament cut on the key-stone of an arch.

Ancones, trusses or consoles employed in the dressings of apertures; also used to signify the corners or quoins of walls, cross-beams, or rafters, etc.

Andirons, iron bars with legs to support logs of wood in fire-places.

Android, in mechanics, an automaton.

Andron, an apartment, cloister, or gallery, assigned to the male part of a monastic establishment; applied also to the space in a church by which the men were separated from the women.

Anemography, a description of the winds.

Anemometer, an instrument for measuring the force of the wind.

Anemoscope, a machine to denote the changes of the wind or weather.

Angiportum, among the ancients, a narrow lane between two rows of houses.

Angle, in geometry, the mutual inclination of two lines meeting in a point.

Angle-bar, in joinery, the upright bar at the angle of a polygonal window.

Angle-bead, a vertical bead, commonly of wood, fixed to an exterior angle, and flush with the surface of the plaster, etc. of rooms, arches, etc.

Angle-brace, in carpentry, timber fixed to the two extremities of a piece of quadrangular framing, making it to partake of the form of an octagon.

Angle-bracket, a bracket placed in the vertex of an angle, and not at right angles with the sides.

Angle-capital, used in Ionic capitals to the flank columns which have their volutes placed at an angle of 45° with the planes of the front and returning friezes.

Angle-float, in plastering, a float made to any internal angle to the planes of both sides of a room.

Angle-modillion, a modillion placed in a direction parallel to a diagonal drawn through a cornice at its mitring.

Angle-staff, vertical bead, generally of wood, fixed to exterior angles of a building flush with the service of the plaster.

Angle of application, the angle which the line of direction of a power gives the lever it acts upon.

Angle of inclination, the angle an inclined plane makes with the horizon.

Angle of traction, the angle which the direction of a power makes with the inclined plane.

Angular modillions, those which are placed at the return of a cornice in the diagonal vertical plane, passing through the angle or mitre of the cornice.

Angular perspective, a term applied to the horizontal lines, both of the front and end of a building, converging to vanishing points, and terminating in the horizon; it is sometimes called *oblique* perspective.

Anlace, a falchion or sword, shaped like a scythe.

Annealing, the process of softening and restoring the malleability of metals, by heating and allowing them to cool very slowly; and by which means glass, cast-iron, and steel, may be united to other substances.

Annatto, in chemistry, a reddish-yellow vegetable dye, obtained from the seeds of the *Bixa Orellana*, and used for colouring cheese.

Annicut, the Hindostanee term for a weir or dam: it is a stoppage built out in a river from a bank, as a pier or breakwater, and made use of in the Indian rivers to intercept the current of the stream, and divert a portion of its waters into channels or reservoirs for agricultural purposes.

Annular engine, a direct-action marine engine, having two concentric cylinders; the annular space is filled with a piston which is attached to a T-shaped cross-head by two piston-rods; the cross-head is formed by two plates with a space between for the connecting-rod to vibrate, and the lower end slides within the inner cylinder, and is connected to the crank. This arrangement has been patented by Messrs. Maudslay.

Annular vault, a vaulted roof supported on circular walls.

Annulated columns, those clustered together or joined by rings or bands.

Annulet, in architecture, a small square member in the Doric capital; also the name of a small flat moulding.

Anston, a parish in Yorkshire from whence the stone used for the Houses of Parliament have been brought.

Antarala, the inner vestibule of a Hindoo temple.

Antæ, square pilasters terminating the walls of a temple; when a temple had no portico in front, two columns were made to intervene between the antæ, and the aspect of the temple was said to be *in antis*.

Antechamber, a room or passage to an inner chamber, for the accommodation of servants and persons in waiting.

Ante-capitulum, part of a cloister before the door of a chapter-house.

Antefixæ (by some called *Greek tiles*), upright ornamental blocks placed at intervals on the cornice along the side of a roof, to conceal or rather terminate the ridges formed by the overlapping of the roof-tiles; also heads of lions, etc., for waterspouts below the eaves of temples.

Antemural, a term applied to the outward wall of a castle; or that which separates a presbytery from a choir; also to a barbican entrance before a castle.

Antepagmenta, or *Antepagmentum*, the jamb of a door-case.

Ante-parallels, in geometry, lines which make equal angles with two other lines, but in a contrary direction.

Ante-portico, a term sometimes used to denote an outer porch or vestibule; the *propylæum* in classic architecture.

Anterides, buttresses for strengthening walls.

Ante-solarium, a balcony facing the sun.

Ante-venna, an awning or projecting roof of woodwork; a wooden or pent-house before a shop.

Anthepsa, a Grecian vessel used for boiling water or keeping it hot; a cooking utensil.

Anthracite, a coal not bituminous, found principally in South Wales and in the United States.

Antics, in architecture, figures of men, beasts, etc., placed as ornaments to buildings.

Anticum, a porch before a door.

Antilia, an ancient machine similar to the modern pump.

Antimensium, a portable altar or consecrated table, used as a substitute for a proper altar.

Antimeter, an optical instrument for measuring angles.

Antimony, a metal usually found in a crude state combined with sulphur, of a bluish-white colour, crystalline texture, brittle, and easily pulverized: it does not oxidate at ordinary temperatures in the air, but, when heated, it burns with a light flame, producing the oxide; it fuses at 800°, and volatilizes at a white heat.

Antimony yellow, a preparation of antimony, of a deeper colour than Naples yellow, and similar in its properties: it is principally used in enamel and porcelain painting, and is very various in tint; that of a bright colour is not affected by foul air, although blackened by sugar of lead.

Antipagments, ornaments in carved work on the architrave, jambs, posts, or puncheons of doors.

Antiquarium, a repository for antique monuments.

Antoine (J. D.), born in Paris in 1733; became in after-years an architect of a high position; built several noble edifices, in Paris principally; died in 1807.

Antrellum, a small grave or grotto; also a small temple.

Antrum, an early temple for Christian worship.

Antrum tumbale, a sepulchral cave or grotto.

Antwerp blue, light-coloured, and somewhat brighter than Prussian blue, or ferro-prussiate of alumine, having more of the terrene basis, but all the other qualities of that pigment, except its extreme depth. Haarlem blue is a similar pigment.

Antwerp brown, a preparation of asphaltum, ground in strong drying oil, by which it becomes less liable to crack.

Anvil, a large block of iron with a very hard, smooth, horizontal surface on the top, in which there is a hole at one end, for the purpose of inserting various tools, and a strong steel chisel, on which a piece of iron may be laid, and cut through by a blow with a hammer.

A-peek, a nautical term implying that the cable is hove taut, so as to bring the vessel nearly over her anchor: the yards are *a-peek* when they are topped up by contrary lifts.

Aperture, an opening in a wall, doorway, or window.

Apex, the top or highest point of a cone, mountain, pyramid, spire, roof, etc.

Apiary, a place where bees are kept.

Aplome, a mineral of a deep orange-colour.

Aplustre, in early naval architecture, a carved tablet fixed on the extremity of a ship's head, or ensign.

Apodyterium, a dressing-room or anteroom to a bath in Roman villas, contiguous to the laconicum.

Apophyge, in architecture, that part of a column between the upper fillet of the base and the cylindrical shaft, which is usually curved into it by a concave sweep or inverted cavetto.

Apostles (the) of Jesus Christ were his chief disciples, whom he invested with his authority, filled with his spirit, and instructed particularly in his doctrines and services: they were chosen to raise the edifice of his Church, and, after his resurrection, sent into all the world, commissioned to preach, to baptize, and to work miracles. The names of the twelve were: 1, Peter; 2, Andrew; 3, John; 4, Philip; 5, James, major; 6, Bartholomew; 7, Thomas; 8, Matthew; 9, Simon; 10, Jude; 11, James, minor; 12, Judas Iscariot. The last betrayed his master, and having hanged himself, Matthias was chosen in his place.

Apostles (the), in the tables of symbols of the early ages, were represented by twelve sheep or lambs issuing from Bethlehem and Jerusalem, cities of Christ's birth and death.

Apotheca, a place in the upper part of the house, in which the Romans frequently placed their wines in earthen amphoræ; also an apothecary's shop, a cabinet, storehouse, etc.

Apothesis, a recess on the south side of the chancel of a church, fitted up with shelves for books, vestments, etc.

Apparatus, a term denoting a complete set of instruments belonging to an artist or a mechanist.

Appian way, a celebrated road leading from Rome to Brundusium: so named from Appius Claudius.

Appii forum, the forum built by Appius, the Roman consul, about fifty miles distant from Rome, near the modern town of Piperno, on the way to Naples. The uses to which the Romans applied the forum were so various, that it is not easy to ascertain the nature of the building. It might have been a place for the distribution of justice, or for holding a market. The 'Three Taverns' were nearer to Rome than the Appii Forum, as Cicero intimates, who, in going from Rome, a little before he came to the forum of Appius, arrived at the Three Taverns; so that probably the chief number of Christians waited for the Apostle Paul at a place of refreshment, while some of their number went forward to meet him, and respectfully to acquaint him with their expectation of seeing him among them.

Apple-tree, a wood generally hard and close, and of reddish-brown tints, used commonly in Tunbridge turnery, etc.

Apricot-tree, a native wood of Armenia, used by the French in turnery.

Apron, the sill or lower part of a window; a platform or flooring of plank raised at the entrance of a dock: in naval architecture, a piece of curved timber fixed behind the lower part of the stern of a ship.

Apsis, the east end of a church or chancel; sometimes applied to a canopy over an altar; also to a circle about a star or planet.

Apsis gradata, a bishop's throne in cathedral churches.

Aqua fortis, in chemistry, nitric acid diluted: the more concentrated is named spirit of nitre.

Aquamele, a holy-water basin.

Aqua regia, nitro-muriatic acid; a compound of two parts nitric acid and one part muriatic acid.

Aquatinta, in the arts, engraving which resembles drawings in Indian ink.

Aqueduct, a conduit for water: a construction of stone or timber, built on uneven ground, to preserve the level of water, and convey it by a canal from one place to another.

Aquemola, a water-mill.

Aquila, a reading-desk, so called from its shape being that of an eagle with extended wings, supported by a pedestal.

Arabesque, generally applied to a style of ornament for pilasters, friezes, etc., as those painted by Raffaelle in the Vatican.

Arabo-tedesco, a term applied to the Moorish style of buildings in Spain, etc.

Ara dignitalis, an altar at which none but the highest ecclesiastics perform divine rites.

Aræostyle, in architecture, the greatest interval or distance which can be made between columns, that is, eight modules or four diameters; also a species of temple which has its columns placed widely asunder.

Arbor, a spindle or axis upon which a ring or wheel is turned in a lathe.

Arbor Dianæ, in chemistry, crystals formed by the combination of silver and mercury.

Arbores, brass branches for lights suspended from ceilings.

Arboretum, a grove of trees in a park, pleasure-ground, or garden.

Arbor vitæ, a tree which attains to a height of from 40 to 50 feet; its wood is of a reddish colour, very light, soft, and fine-grained, and is much used in house carpentry.

Arc, in geometry, part of the circumference of a circle, or any curve lying between two points; a bow, vault, or arch.

Arca, a place in a vaulted chamber for sepulchral purposes; an excavation before the basement story of a house; an enclosed space; a chest in which the Romans deposited their money: the word is also used to signify a beam of wood which has a groove or channel hollowed in it from one end to the other.

Arcade, a series of recesses with arched ceilings or soffits; a covered passage; in modern appliances, a vaulted avenue, now much in vogue, more particularly in Paris.—Arcades, though less magnificent than colonnades, are of extraordinary beauty when well contrived, affording shade from the sun and shelter from the rain. Though not so magnificent as colonnades, they are stronger, more solid, and less expensive. They are proper for triumphal entrances, gates of cities, of palaces, of gardens, and of parks; for public squares, markets, or large courts in general, and for all apertures that require an extraordinary width.

THEIR ORNAMENTS.—The piers of arcades may be decorated with columns, pilasters, niches, and apertures of different forms. The arch itself may be turned either with rockworked or plain rustic archstones or voussoirs, or with an archivolt properly moulded. The keystone is generally carved in the form of a console, or sculptured with some head, or the like. The archivolt springs from an impost or plat-band, or sometimes from columns; but this is not to be practised except in cases of the most urgent nature, for it makes neither substantial nor beautiful work.

In arches that are of large dimensions, the keystone should never be omitted; its carving, however, may be dispensed with, if expense be an object. When the piers are decorated with disengaged columns, the entablature must break round over the columns; and the columns, whether engaged or not, should stand either on a pedestal or high plinth, by which means they will not only be kept dry, but their bases will likewise be protected from accidental damage.—Arches must always rise from an impost or a plat-band; and if there be no keystone to the archivolt, its summit should be kept down from the under side of the architrave of the accompanying order, at least half the distance that it would be, were a keystone employed, in order that the disagreeable appearance of the acute angle which it would otherwise form with the architrave may be avoided.

THEIR PROPORTIONS. — The height of arches to the under side of their crowns should not exceed twice their clear width, nor should it be much less; the piers not less than one-third the breadth of the arch, nor more than two-thirds; but the piers at the angles should be wider than the other piers by one-half, or one-fourth at least.

Arcæ, in Roman architecture, the gutters of the cavedium.

Arc-boutant, a kind of arched buttress formed of a flat arch, or part of an arch, and abutting against the feet or sides of another arch or vault, to support them, and prevent them from bursting or giving way.

Arcella, in mediæval architecture, a cheese-room.

Arch, the curved part of a building, supported at its extremities only, and concave towards the earth; a vaulted roof, or dome, constructed either with bricks, stone, or other materials: the arch of a bridge is formed of segments of a circle, elliptical or catenarian; in Christian architecture, arches display twenty-two varieties of form. — Arches are used in large intercolumniations of spacious buildings; in porticoes, both within and without temples; in public halls, as ceilings, the courts of palaces, cloisters, theatres, and amphitheatres: they are also used to cover the cellars in the foundations of houses and powder-magazines; also as buttresses and counterforts, to support large walls laid deep in the earth; for triumphal arches, gates, windows, etc.; and, above all, for the foundations of bridges and aqueducts: they are supported by piers, abutments, imposts, etc.—Arches are of several kinds, circular, elliptical, cycloidal, catenarian, etc., according as their curve is in the form of a circle, ellipse, cycloid, catenary, etc. Arches are to be found in the Greek theatres, stadia, and gymnasia, some of them erected probably 400 years before Christ. The most ancient arches of which we have correct data are those of the cloacæ at Rome. The Emperor Hadrian threw a bridge over the Cephisus, between the territories of Attica and Eleusis, on the most frequented road of Greece.

Arch (theory of the). This important subject has exercised the talents and ingenuity of some of the greatest mathematicians in modern times, and many different solutions have been given to the various problems connected with it; but, as the greater part of them are founded on suppositions that have no existence whatever either in nature or practice, they have had a tendency rather to mislead than direct those who are engaged in the operations of bridge-building. Dr. Olinthus Gregory, in the preface to his excellent work on 'Mechanics,' states, that "theoretical and practical men will most effectually promote their mutual interests, not by affecting to despise each other, but by blending their efforts; and further, that an essential service will be done to mechanical science, by endeavouring to make all the scattered rays of light they have separately thrown upon this region of human knowledge converge to one point." Gauthey, speaking of the theory of La Hire, observes that such analytical researches are founded on hypotheses which every day's experience contradicts. The following are the principal writers on the equilibrium of the arch. In 1691, the celebrated mathematicians, Leibnitz, Huygens, James and John Bernouilli, solved the problem of the catenary curve; it was soon perceived that this was precisely the curve that should be given to an arch of which the materials were infinitely small and of equal weight, in order that all its parts may be in equilibrium. In the 'Philosophical Transactions' for the year 1697, it is stated that David Gregory first noticed this identity; but his mode of argument, though sufficiently rigorous, appears not to be so perspicuous as could be desired. In one of the posthumous works of James Bernoulli, two direct solutions of this problem are given, founded on the different modes of viewing the action of the voussoirs: the first is clear, simple, and precise, and easily leads to the equation of the curve, which he shows to be the catenary inverted; the second requires a little correction, which Cramer, the editor of his works, has pointed out. In 1695, La Hire, in his 'Treatise on Mechanics,' laid down, from the theory of the wedge, the proportion according to which the absolute weight of the materials of masonry ought to be increased from the keystone to the springing in a semicircular arch. The historian of the 'Academy of Sciences' relates, in the volume for the year 1704, that Parent determined on the same principle, but only by points, the figure of the extrados of an arch, the intrados being a semicircle, and found the force or thrust of a similar arch against the piers. In the 'Memoirs of the Academy of Sciences' for the year 1712, La Hire gave an investigation of the thrusts in arches under a point of view suggested by his own experiments: he supposed that arches, the piers of which had not solidity enough to resist the thrust, split towards the haunches at an elevation of about 45 degrees above the springings or imposts; he consequently regarded the upper part of the arch as a wedge that tends to separate or overturn the abutments, and determined, on the theory of the wedge and the lever, the dimensions which they ought to have to resist this single effort. Couplet, in a memoir composed of two parts, the first of which was printed in the volume of the Academy for 1729, treats of the thrusts of arches and the thickness of the voussoirs, by considering the materials infinitely small, and capable of sliding over each other without any pressure or friction. But, as this hypothesis is not exactly conformable to experiment, the second part of the memoir, printed in the volume for 1730, resumes the question by supposing that the materials have not the power of sliding over each other, but that they can raise themselves and separate by minute rotatory motions. It cannot however be said that Couplet has added materially to the theories of La Hire and Parent, and none of them treated the subject, either in theory and practice, in such a satisfactory manner as was afterwards done by Coulomb. Subsequently a memoir was published by Bouguer on the curve lines that are most proper for the formation of the arches of domes. He considers that there may be an infinite number of curve lines employed for this purpose, and points out the mode of selecting them. He lays it down uniformly that the voussoirs have their surfaces infinitely smooth, and establishes, on this hypothesis, the conditions of equilibrium in each horizontal course of the dome, but has not given any method of investigating the thrusts of arches of this kind, nor of the forces that act upon the masonry when the generating curve is subjected to given conditions. In 1770, Bossut gave investigations of arches of the different kinds, in two memoirs, which were printed among those of the Academy of Sciences for the years 1774 and 1776: he appears to have been engaged in this in consequence of some disputes concerning the dome of the French Pantheon, begun by the celebrated architect Soufflot, and finished from his designs. In 1772, Dr. Hutton published his principles of bridges, in which he investigated the form of curves for the intrados of an arch, the extrados being given, and *vice versa*. He set out by developing the properties of the equilibrated polygon, which is extremely useful in the equilibrium of structures. Mr. Attwood has written a dissertation on the construction of arches on the same principles as La Hire.

Arch, in architecture, a concave structure raised or turned upon a mould, called the centering, in form of the arc of a curve, and serving as the inward support of some superstructure. Sir Henry Wotton says, "An arch is nothing but a narrow or contracted vault; and a vault is a dilated arch."

Arch, in geometry, a part of any curved line, as of a circle or ellipsis.

Arch, in masonry, a part of a building suspended over a hollow, and concave towards the area of the hollow: the top of the wall or walls which receives the first archstones is technically called the abutment or springing.

Arch, in mining, a piece of ground left unworked.

Arch-band, applied by workmen to that portion of an arch or rib which is seen below the general surface of vaulting.

Arch-brick, a wedge-shaped brick employed in the construction of arches.

Arch-buttress, a piece of insulated masonry usually named a flying-buttress, extending from the clerestory of a church and over the roof of its aisle, where it rests on the buttress of the outer wall.

Arch of equilibration, that which is in equilibrium in all its parts, having no tendency to break in one part more than in another.

Arch, triumphal, a building of which an arch is the principal feature, usually raised to commemorate some great achievement.

Archæology, the study of ancient art, but more particularly that of the middle ages.

Arched, in mining: the roads in a mine, when built with stones or bricks, are generally arched level drifts.

Archeion, a recess in a Grecian temple, for the reception of the treasures of the deity to whom the temple was dedicated.

Archeion, in Athens, the office in which the decrees of the people and other state documents were preserved.

Arches, Norman, semicircular, which form continued to the latest date of this style, and is frequently intermixed with pointed arches, even when other parts had advanced into the next style, of which the Temple Church is an instance.

There are some Norman arches more than a semicircle,—the horse-shoe,—and a few instances of a double arch.

Archelus, a saw for cutting stones: Muratori used the term for a crane or pulley for raising stones to the upper part of a building.

Archimedes screw-propeller, in 1836, was launched by T. P. Smith, patentee. The vessel 232 tons, 125 feet long, 21 feet 10 inches beam, 80-horse power.

Archimedean screw, a machine invented by Archimedes for raising water; also now applied to propel vessels through water.

Archiepiscopal palace, the dwelling of an archbishop.

Architect, a person skilled in the art of building; one who forms plans and designs for edifices, conducts the work, and directs the secondary artificers employed; and whose emoluments are generally 5 per cent. on the amount of money expended.

Architecture, a science applicable to the art of constructing domestic, ecclesiastical, municipal, palatial, or other buildings, and the adornment of the same according to the rules of the several orders, Doric, Ionic, and Corinthian, also the Tuscan and Composite, from Roman models, or other styles, each for its purpose, such as is usually called Gothic architecture, and modes subservient to climate and fashion, or caprice. "Architecture," says Palladio, "being grounded upon rules taken from the imitation of Nature, admits of nothing that is contrary or foreign to that order which Nature has prescribed to all things. An architect is not restrained from departing sometimes from common methods or usage, provided such variation be agreeable and natural."

The public at large has a claim over the architecture of a country. It is common property, inasmuch as it involves the national taste and character; and no man has a right to pass off his own barbarous inventions as the national taste, and to hand down to posterity his own ignorance and disgrace to become a satire and a libel on the knowledge and taste of his age.

Architecture, the Orders of.—Among the ancients, the use of the orders was very frequent; many parts of their cities were provided with spacious porticoes, their temples were surrounded with colonnades, and their theatres, baths, basilicæ, triumphal arches, mausolea, bridges, and other public buildings were profusely enriched with columns; as were likewise the courts, vestibules, and halls of their private villas and houses.

In pure architecture, says A. W. Pugin, the smallest detail should have a meaning or serve a purpose; and even the construction itself should vary with the material employed, and the designs should be adapted to the material in which they are executed.

Strange as it may appear at first sight, it is in pointed architecture alone that these great principles have been carried out: we may be enabled to illustrate them from the vast cathedral to the simplest erection. Moreover, the architects of the middle ages were the first who turned the natural properties of the various materials to their full account, and made their mechanism a vehicle for their art. The wonderful *strength* and solidity of their buildings are the result, not of quantity or size of the stones employed, but of the art of their disposition.

The two following pages contain a synopsis of the proportions of the Orders, and of various examples of each, compiled by Mr. W. H. Leeds for Pugin's edition of Normand's 'Parallel of the Orders.'

Names of the Orders.	Base.			Column.			Capital.			Archi-trave.			Frieze.		
	diam.	mod.	pt.	diam.	mod.	pt.	diam.	mod.	pt.	diam.	mod.	pt.	diam.	mod.	pt.
TUSCAN.															
Palladio	0	1	0	7	0	0	0	1	0	0	1	5	0	0	26
Scamozzi	0	1	0	7	1	0	0	1	0	0	1	2½	0	1	9
Serlio	0	1	0	6	0	0	0	1	0	0	1	0	0	1	0
Vignola	0	1	0	7	0	0	0	1	0	0	0	25	0	1	5
DORIC.															
Parthenon at Athens	.	.	.	5	1	0	0	0	28	0	1	14½	0	1	19½
Temple of Theseus, do.	.	.	.	5	1	0	0	1	0	0	1	20	0	1	25½
Great Temple at Pæstum	.	.	.	4	0	15	0	1	2½	0	1	11½	0	1	3½
Temple of Apollo, at Delos	.	.	.	5	0	25	0	0	29½	0	1	20	0	1	7
Portico of Philip, do.	.	.	.	6	0	20	0	0	10	0	1	0	0	1	14
Temple at Corinth	.	.	.	8	0	10	0	0	25½	0	1	10	.	.	.
Propylæum at Athens	.	.	.	5	1	0	0	0	23	.	.	.	.	.	.
Portico of Augustus, do.	.	.	.	6	0	0	0	0	23	.	.	.	.	.	.
Theatre of Marcellus, Rome	.	.	.	7	1	18	0	1	2½	0	1	1	0	1	10
Doric Order at Albano	.	.	.	7	1	0	0	1	0	0	1	0	0	1	15
Baths of Diocletian	.	.	.	8	0	0	0	1	0	0	1	3	0	1	15
Palladio	0	1	0	8	0	0	0	1	0	0	1	0	0	1	15
Scamozzi	0	1	0	8	1	0	0	1	0	0	1	5	0	1	15
Vignola	0	1	0	8	0	0	0	1	0	0	1	0	0	1	15
Viola	0	1	0	8	0	0	0	1	0	0	1	0	0	1	15
Delorme	0	1	0	8	0	0	0	1	0	0	1	0	0	1	15
IONIC.															
Temple on the Ilissus	0	1	0	8	0	0	0	1	9½	0	1	25	0	1	19
Temple of Minerva Polias, Athens	0	0	25	9	1	0	0	1	13½	0	1	21½	0	1	18½
Temple of Erechtheus, Athens	0	0	23½	9	0	0	0	1	10	.	.	.	.	.	.
Temple of Fortuna Virilis	0	1	0½	8	1	2½	0	0	20	0	1	9½	0	0	28½
Theatre of Marcellus	0	1	0	9	0	0	0	1	1½	0	1	13	0	1	6½
Baths of Diocletian	0	1	0	8	1	0	0	1	1½	0	1	4	0	0	28
Palladio	0	0	22	9	0	0	0	1	1½	0	1	6	0	0	27
Scamozzi	0	0	27	8	1	15	0	0	26½	0	1	18	0	0	28
Vignola	0	0	30	9	0	0	0	1	0½	0	1	7½	0	1	15
Serlio	0	0	20½	7	1	0	0	1	0	0	1	0	0	0	22½
Alberti	0	0	22½	8	0	0	0	1	1½	0	1	0	0	1	0
CORINTHIAN.															
Lantern of Demosthenes, Athens	0	1	0½	10	0	0	1	0	24	0	1	21	0	1	9½
Temple of Jupiter Olympius, do.	0	0	21	9	1	15	1	0	27	0	1	11½	0	0	27½
Incantada at Salonica	0	0	25	9	0	15	1	0	11	0	1	16½	0	1	12½
Arch of Theseus, Athens	0	0	23	9	1	0	1	0	15	0	1	12½	0	1	10
Temple of Jupiter Stator, Rome	0	0	28	10	0	0½	1	0	6½	0	1	13½	0	1	13½
Temple of Jupiter Tonans	0	0	22½	10	0	15	1	0	10	0	1	13½	0	1	13
Portico of the Pantheon	0	0	24	9	1	16½	1	0	7½	0	1	12½	0	1	9½
Interior of the Pantheon	0	0	23½	9	1	4½	1	0	12½	0	1	19	0	1	12
Forum of Nerva	.	.	.	.	.	.	1	0	18	0	1	14	0	1	15
Temple of Antoninus and Faustina	0	0	24	9	1	6	1	0	9½	0	1	13½	0	1	10½
Nero's Frontispiece	0	0	20½	10	0	0	1	0	10	0	1	14½	0	1	14½
Arch of Constantine	0	0	24	9	1	7	1	0	6½	0	1	15	0	1	16
Temple of Mars the Avenger	.	.	.	.	.	.	1	0	9½	0	1	9½	.	.	.
Basilica of Antoninus	0	0	23	10	0	11½	1	0	9½	0	1	13½	0	1	10
Temple of the Sibyl, Tivoli	0	0	16½	9	0	25	1	0	0	0	1	0	0	1	9½
Palladio	0	1	0	9	1	0	1	0	0	0	1	8	0	0	23½
Scamozzi	0	1	0	10	0	0	1	0	0	0	1	12	0	1	3
Vignola	0	1	0	10	0	0	1	0	0	0	1	15	0	1	15
Serlio	0	1	0	9	0	0	1	0	0	0	1	0	0	1	7
Alberti	0	1	0	9	0	0	1	0	0	0	1	0	0	1	0
COMPOSITE.															
Arch of Titus	0	0	23	10	0	0	1	0	14½	0	1	16	0	1	14
Arch of Septimius Severus	0	0	20	9	1	10	1	0	5½	0	1	18	0	0	28½
Baths of Diocletian	0	0	22	10	0	20½	1	0	11	0	1	14½	0	1	14
Palladio	0	1	1½	10	0	0	1	0	0	0	1	10	0	1	0
Scamozzi	0	1	0	9	1	15	1	0	0	0	1	0	0	1	1½
Vignola	0	1	0	10	0	0	1	0	0	0	1	15	0	1	15
Caryatides of the Temple of Pandrosus	.	.	.	5	0	0	0	0	27	0	1	25½	.	.	.

Architecture, qualities of. There is perhaps no subject on which persons are more apt to differ in their opinions than on the beauty of a building. In architecture the creative power of Nature herself is the model imitated. It is an art which appeals directly to the understanding, and has not the means of flattering the senses in the same way as the sister arts: hence its productions are not universally appreciated. The beautiful models of Nature, however, are the index and guide of the painter and sculptor: a successful imitation of these models, even without an advance on the part of the artist towards those higher intellectual beauties which distinguish the historical painter, is capable of affecting us with very agreeable sensations. The object of an artist's inquiry is not so much to investigate metaphysically the cause of beauty in the productions of his art, as to study the effects that flow from those which by the common consent of ages are esteemed beautiful, and thus shorten his road by an *à priori* method. It is in this way that he will more readily obtain information on those qualities which act on the understanding and excite our affections by means of the beautiful result they exhibit. These qualities may be classed as follows:—

MAGNITUDE AND SOLIDITY, as qualities which affect the eye.

ORDER AND HARMONY, as qualities which affect the understanding.

RICHNESS AND SIMPLICITY, as qualities which excite the affections,—in which taste is the principal guide. These qualities answer to the three divisions which those who have written on architecture have usually adopted, namely—

CONSTRUCTION, in which the chief requisites are solidity and strength.

DESIGN OR DISPOSITION, in

which the principal requisites are order and harmony.

DECORATION, whose requisites are richness or simplicity, according to the nature of the composition.

That there are, however, many other circumstances which tend to the production of an agreeable and beautiful result, is sufficiently obvious: one of them should be more particularly noticed, because there can be no doubt of its influence in the excitement of our admiration of the splendid monuments of Grecian art; it is an association with the times and countries which are most hallowed in our imagination. It is difficult for us to see them, even in their modern copies, without feeling them operate upon our minds, as relics of those polished nations where they first arose, and of that great people by whom they were afterwards borrowed.

The business of an architect requires him rather to be a learned judge than a skilful operator; and when he knows how to direct and instruct others with precision, to examine, judge, and value their performances with masterly accuracy, he may truly be said to have acquired all that most men can acquire: there are but few instances of such prodigies as Michael Angelo Buonarroti, who was at once the first architect, painter, geometrician, anatomist, and sculptor of his time.

Vitruvius furthermore observes, that an art enriched with such variety of knowledge is only to be learned by long and constant application; and advises his contemporaries never to assume the title of architects till they are perfect masters of their own profession, and of the arts and sciences with which it is connected; a caution that even in the present times may perhaps not be unnecessary.

Architecture, Naval, the art of constructing ships and vessels to float on the waters. Naval architecture has suffered more than most other sciences by the arbitrary systems of those interested in its improvement. Disregarding the fundamental principles of all floating bodies, and too hastily giving up as hopeless the attainment of a theory combining experiment with established scientific principles, they have contented themselves with ingeniously inventing mechanical methods of forming the designs of ships' bodies, which they did not even pretend to prove had any connection with the properties of the machine necessary to insure the qualities conducive to its intended use. For instance, some invented methods of forming ships' bodies of arcs of circles; others, of arcs of ellipses, parabolas, or of whatever curve they might arbitrarily assume. They did not attempt to show that these curves possessed any property which would render a ship a faster sailer, a more weatherly or safer ship, than any other curves which might have been adopted in the construction of the ship's body.

Architholus, a round chamber, the sudatorium of a Roman bath.

Architrave, the lower of the three principal members of the entablature of an order, being the chief beam resting immediately on the column.

Architrave cornice, an entablature consisting of an architrave and cornice only, without the interposition of a frieze.

Architrave doors, those which have an architrave on the jambs and over the door.

Architrave windows, of timber, are usually an ogee raised out of the solid timber, with a roll over it.

Archivolt, a collection of members in the face of an arch, concentric with the intrados, and supported by imposts.

Archivolt of the arch of a bridge,— the curve line formed by the upper

Archivoltum, a cesspool or common sewer.

Archway, an aperture in a building covered with a vault.

Arcs doubleaux, a French term for arch-band, and employed by English writers from the time of De l'Orme, etc.

Arconio (M.), born in Rome, was both an architect and painter, died about 1640.

Arcula, a small coffer or box.

Arcus, an area in the form of an ancient basilica.

Arcus, an arch; a true arch is formed of a series of wedge-like stones or of bricks supporting each other, and all bound together by their mutual pressure.

Arcus-toralis, in medieval architecture, the lattice separating the choir from the nave in a basilica.

Arculio, a machine consisting of hoops.

Ardeme (John) was clerk of the work at the building of the monument in Westminster Abbey Church to King Henry V., who died in 1422.

Ardesia, a slate used in Italy for covering roofs.

Area, in geometry, the superficial content of any figure.

Areas, in computing the superficial content of land, are generally expressed in statute acres, roods, and perches. The acre is equal to 10 square chains of 66 feet, or 22 yards in length.

Area drain, a narrow area drain not covered, on the basement floor of a building, to remedy or prevent dampness in the connecting walls.

Area wall, the wall which forms the sides of an area.

Arena, the area or floor of an amphitheatre.

Arenarium, an amphitheatre, cemetery, crypt, or sepulchre.

Areometer, an instrument for measuring the density or gravity of fluids.

Areopagus, the court in which the Areopagites, or supreme judges of Athens, assembled.

Areostylos, intercolumniations, when their distance from each other is four diameters.

Arerde, reared, built, or raised up.

Argand lamp, a lamp with a circular wick, through which a current of air passes.

Argyrocopeion, the mint at Athens.

Aristotele (G.F.), architect and sculptor, commenced, from the designs of Raffaelle, the Palazzo Pandolfini at Florence; he died in 1530.

Ark, a shelter, a place of protection from floods: In the time of Moses, a coffer or sort of bark, in shape and appearance like a chest or trunk; also described by Moses as a little wicker basket, in which he was exposed on the Nile. The ancients inform us that the Egyptians used on the Nile barks made of bulrushes.

Ark, a chest used in farm-houses for keeping meal or flour.

Ark (*Noah's*): "And this is the fashion which thou shalt make it of: the length of the ark shall be three hundred cubits, the breadth of it fifty cubits, and the height of it thirty cubits." It is supposed by some authors to have been a mere variation from the ordinary construction of houses for residence, changing its character from that of a house for standing to that of a house for floating. Niebuhr compares it with ordinary houses of the East, the sides of which are constructed of upright supports of timber, plastered over with clay. The application of canes, split and laid across these quarterings, is very like the usage of laths, which are common everywhere. The same may be said of a coating of bitumen,—a substance employed on account of its property of resisting water; and the mode of its application might be similar to our plastering. It is probable however that Noah's ark resembled the Egyptian boats in form; and if we reckon the Hebrew cubit at 21 inches, the ark of Noah was 512 feet long, 87 wide, and 52 high; and the internal capacity of it was 357,600 cubical cubits. If we suppose the cubit to be only 18 inches, its length was 450 feet, its width 75, and its height 45. Its figure was an oblong square, and the covering had a declivity to carry off water. Its length exceeded that of most churches in Europe. The wood used for the ark was called gopher-wood, square pieces of cedar or box, or woods that do not quickly perish: by some it has been supposed to have been constructed of cypress-wood.

Armarium, a niche or cupboard near the side of an altar.

Armenian architecture, the edifices in Armenia, erected previously to the cultivation of a Græco-Roman architecture, supposed A.D. 260–314.

Armilla, an ornament worn by Greek men and women as a bracelet or an armlet.

Armour, a defensive clothing of metal.

Armoury, a storehouse or room in which armour is preserved.

Arnotto (colour), the name of a vegetable substance from the West Indies, of an orange-red colour, soluble in water and spirit of wine, but very fugitive and changeable, and not adapted for painting. It is principally used by the dyer, and in colouring cheese. It is also an ingredient in lacquering.

Aronade, embattled, a junction of several lines forming indentations.

Arragonite, a remarkable form of carbonate of lime, found in different shapes, from hexagonal prismatic crystals of coralloid masses.

Arris, in joinery and masonry, the line of concourse, edge, or meeting of two surfaces.

Arris fillet, a slight piece of timber of a triangular section, used in raising the slates against chimney-shafts, etc.

Arris gutter, a wooden gutter of the V form, fixed to the eaves of a building.

Arris-wise, in bricklaying, tiles laid diagonally.

Arshin, a Russian measure of length, equal to 2¼ feet English.

Arsenal, a building for naval or military stores.

Arsenic, a metal of a crystalline appearance, and very brittle. It sublimes out of the air unchanged at 360°, but in air it is oxidated, and becomes arsenious acid: it is occasionally found alone, but is generally combined with nickel, cobalt, and other metals.

Artesian wells, so called from a mode practised at Artois, in France, in boring for water.

Arthur's oven: According to the testimony of Boethius, we had a specimen of one of the Roman temples in Britain, built in the time of Vespasian, remaining in that singular little structure called Arthur's oven, not far from the Wall of Antoninus. He says, according to tradition, there was an inscription on a stone declaring that the building was erected by Vespasian, in honour of the Emperor Claudius and the Goddess Victory. It had a tessellated pavement. It was 19 feet 6 inches in diameter within, arched towards the top, with a round aperture (like that of the Pantheon at Rome) in the midst of the dome 11 feet 6 inches diameter, and the utmost height to the periphery, or edge of this aperture, from the floor, 22 feet (*query*, within or without, i.e. the lowest or highest periphery of the aperture?).

At a little distance from the top, beneath the circular opening in the midst of the dome, was a small square window on one side, and round the inside, resting on the floor, were stone seats, and against the wall on the south side an altar; the door of entrance, which had a regular Roman arch, being placed under the square window.

Arthur's oven was pulled down about 1743, by Sir Michael Bruce of Stonehouse, near Falkirk, for the sake of the stones; but with little profit to himself, for the stones were used in constructing a mill-dam, which was soon carried away by a flood. See the 'Antiquarian Repertory,' vol. iii. p. 73; also Pennant's 'Tour in Scotland,' pt. i. p. 212, and pt. ii. p. 228; and General Roy's 'Military Antiquities,' pl. 36; and Gordon's 'Itin. Septentr.,' p. 24, tab.

Few Roman arches existing in Britain,—few, it appears probable, were ever erected in it by that people, and those of no great magnificence,—the arch was probably a recent invention when the Romans had possession of this island.

Artificer, one who possesses a superior knowledge as an artist or manufacturer.

Asarotum, a kind of chequered pavement used by the Romans.

Ash, a superior wood, of British growth, of a brownish white with a shade of green: it is tough and elastic, and superior to any other wood exposed to sudden shocks and strains; used for frames of machines, wheel carriages, inside work of furniture, etc.

Ashelcy (Hector), a famous master mason in the times of Henry VII. and VIII.

Ashlar, a term applied to common or freestones as they come out of the quarry. By ashlar is also meant the facing of squared stones on the front of a building; if the work be so smoothed as to take out the marks of the tools by which the stones were first cut, it is called *plane ashlar*; if figured, *tooled ashlar*, or *random tooled*, or chiselled, or boasted, or pointed: if the stones project from the joints, it is said to be *rusticated*.

Ashlar, or *Ashelor*, hewn stone, used for the facings of walls.

Ashlering, in carpentry, the fixing of short upright quarterings between the rafters and the floor.

Ash-pan, in locomotive engines, an iron box, open to the front only, attached to the fire-box to receive the ashes from the fire.

Ashpitel (W. H.), architect and engineer, born in 1776, was extensively employed in some very important public works: his reputation was of a dignified character; he died 20th April, 1852. His son, now in practice, is of equal merit.

Aspect, in architecture, the front situation of a building, or direction towards any point.

Asphalt, native bitumen used with pitch as a substitute for pavement.

Asphaltum, a bituminous substance, used for pavements and as a building material.

Asphaltum, called also Bitumen, Mineral Pitch, etc.; it is a resinous substance rendered brown by the action of the fire, natural or artificial. The substances employed in painting under this name are the residue of the distillation of various resinous and bituminous matters in preparing their essential oils, and are all black and glossy like common pitch, which differs from them only in having been less acted upon by fire, and in their being softer. Asphaltum is principally used in oil-painting: for which purpose it is first dissolved in oil of turpentine, by which it is fitted for glazing and shading. Its fine brown colour and perfect transparency are lures to its free use with many artists, notwithstanding the certain destruction which awaits the work on which it is much employed, owing to its disposition to contract and crack from changes of temperature and the atmosphere.

Assay, to examine and prove metals.

Assay balance, a very accurate balance, used in determining the exact weights of very small bodies.

Assaying, ascertaining the qualities of gold and silver with respect to their purity.

Assemblage, in carpentry and joinery, framing, dovetailing, etc.

Assemblage of the Orders, in architecture, the placing of columns upon one another in the several ranges.

Assembly room, the room or suite of rooms appropriated to the reception of large parties, for balls, etc.

Asser, a term used by Vitruvius for a rafter, carrying the tile of a roof.

Asseris, small rafters immediately beneath the tiles of a roof.

Assize Court, an edifice erected for the accommodation of the officials and the public at the sessions of the judges of the superior courts.

Assula or *Astula*, chippings of blocks of stone, small marble slabs.

Assurance, or *Insurance*, a contract to make good a loss.

Assurance Companies, or *Societies*, afford protection to persons from the chances or hazards to which their property or interests may be exposed.

Assurance on human life is a contract by which a certain amount of capital is secured at the expiration of a stipulated period, either by the payment of a specified sum at the time of *effecting the assurance*, or by the annual payment of a smaller amount, according to the age of a person whose life is assured.

A person, with the view of securing a certain sum of money to his family after his death, desires to effect an assurance, either for a determinate period, as one, three, five, seven, ten, or more years, or for the whole term of his life. In the first case, if the person whose life is assured, die *before* the expiration of the term specified in the policy, his inheritors receive the amount for which the assurance has been effected; but, if the assured live *beyond* that period, they receive nothing, and the assurer reaps the advantage of the contingency. In the latter case,—that is, by assurance for the whole term of life,—the inheritors are entitled to receive the amount named in the policy, upon proof of the death of the person whose life has been assured. To prevent the forfeiture of the policy, it is in all cases essentially important that the conditions upon which it has been granted be strictly complied with.

The calculation as to the amount of premium should be made according to mathematical expectation,—that is, equitably as to both parties, allowing a fair rate of profit to the party granting the assurance. If the terms for assuring £100 be required, for one year, the probability must depend on the age of the person whose life is proposed to be assured; and in equity the sum to be paid should be equal to the value of the expectation, multiplied by the probability of its being obtained. Should the age of the person be 40 years, the probability of death in the course of the year will be, according to the tables of mortality generally adopted, $\frac{174}{10000}$; and this fraction, multiplied by 100, gives the price of the assurance, namely, 1·74 nearly. The result, according to the tables of mortality used in France, is 1·89. This is the rate charged by the 'General Assurance Company' established at Brussels; but the 'Belgic and Strangers' Union Society' charges at the rate of 1·97. Both societies adopt Duhillard's table of mortality, which is deposited in the Bureau of Longitude in Paris.

The profit to the assurer thus appears to be reduced to the interest on the sum paid by the assured; but persons in health being alone accepted, the chance of profit thereby becomes considerable. For a longer term than one year, the calculations are made on an estimate of the probable amount of interest derivable from the premium paid by the assurer.

Assynt marble, a white and greyish-white British marble, found in Sutherlandshire.

Astel, in mining, a board or plank, an arch or ceiling of boards, over the men's heads in a mine, to protect them.

Astragal, a small moulding, whose contour is circular, at the neck of the shafts of columns, next the apophyses: it also occurs in the base of Ionic columns, and below the fasciæ of the Corinthian epistylium.

Astralish (mining), is that ore of gold which lies as yet in its first state or condition.

Assyrian Architecture, of the period of Nineveh and the lower dynasties, see examples of style in the British Museum.

Astronomy, a mixed mathematical science, which treats of the heavenly bodies, their motions, periods, eclipses, magnitudes, etc., and of the causes on which they depend: the knowledge of astronomy is essential in navigation and in measuring the earth's surface: the diameter of this, the third planet in the system, is 7924 miles and 7 furlongs.

Astylar, a term which expresses the absence of columns or pilasters, where they might otherwise be supposed to occur.

Astyllen, in mining, a small ward or stoppage in an adit or mine, to prevent the free and full passage of water, by damming up.

Asylum, in the Greek States, the temples, altars, sacred groves, and statues of the gods; a place provided for the protection of debtors and criminals who fled for refuge.

Atacamite, prismatoidal green malachite, a native muriate of copper.

Athanor, an ancient term for a metal furnace.

Athenæum, a school founded by the Emperor Hadrian, at Rome, for the promotion of literary and scientific studies.

Athwart-hawse, the situation of a ship when driven by the wind or tide across the fore-part of another.

Atlantes, in architecture, male figures, used similarly to the female *Caryatides*, in place of columns.

Atmosphere, the invisible elastic fluid which surrounds the earth to an unknown (exact) height, and partakes of all its motions; the constituent parts are—air, water, carbonic acid gas, and unknown bodies. The atmosphere is measured by a column of mercury of 29·922 inches, which has been adopted in France as the mean height of the barometer at the surface of the sea.

Atmospheric currents, in high latitudes, when undisturbed, are westerly, particularly in the winter season. If storms and gales revolve by a fixed law, and we are able, by studying these disturbing causes of the usual atmospheric currents, to distinguish revolving gales, it is likely that voyages may be shortened. The indications of a revolving gale are, a descending barometer, and a regularly veering wind.

Atmospheric engine, an engine in which the steam is admitted only to the under side of the piston for the up-stroke; it is then condensed, and the top of the cylinder being open, the down-stroke is caused by the pressure of the atmosphere. Marine engines on this principle have three cylinders connected to one crank-shaft, to obtain uniformity of motion.

Atmospheric railway. The conclusions drawn by Mr. R. Stephenson are as follows: 1st, That the atmospheric system is not an economical mode of transmitting power, and inferior in this respect both to locomotive engines and stationary engines with ropes. 2ndly, That it is not calculated practically to acquire and maintain higher velocities than are comprised in the present working of locomotive engines. 3rdly, That it would not, in the majority of instances, produce economy in the original construction of railways, and in many would most materially augment their cost. 4thly, That on some short railways, where the traffic is large, admitting of trains of moderate weight, but requiring high velocities and frequent departures, and where the face of the country is such as to preclude the use of gradients suitable for locomotive engines, the atmospheric system would prove the most eligible. 5thly, That on short lines of railway, say four or five miles in length, in the vicinity of large towns, where frequent and rapid communication is required between the termini alone, the atmospheric system might be advantageously applied. 6thly, That on short lines, such as the Blackwall Railway, where the traffic is chiefly derived from intermediate points, requiring frequent stoppages between the termini, the atmospheric system is inapplicable, being much inferior to the plan of disconnecting the carriages from a rope, for the accommodation of the intermediate traffic. 7thly, That on long lines of railway, the requisites of a large traffic cannot be attained by so inflexible a system as the atmospheric, in which the efficient operation of the whole depends so completely upon the perfect performance of each individual section of the machinery.

Atmospheric vapour. Deluc proves the amount of force and vapour in a vacuum of any given dimensions is equal to its force and quantity in an equal volume of air at the same temperature, or that the temperature of the air will determine the force and quantity of vapour held in it. M. le Roi, however, first observed the temperature at which dew commences to be deposited, as a rule of ascertaining the moisture of the atmosphere. Dr. Dalton investigated the force of vapour of every temperature, from zero to the boiling-point of water (Fahrenheit), and expressed this force by the weight of the mercurial column it could support in the tube of the barometer. Dalton and Le Roi find the clear point by pouring cold water into a glass, and marking the temperature at which it just ceases to deposit dew on the sides of the glass in the open air. The temperature here observed is the point at which dew would begin to be formed. From this Dalton infers not only the force exerted by the vapour, but also its amount in a perpendicular column of the whole atmosphere, and likewise the force of evaporation at the time of observation.

Atomic weights, or *atoms*, are the quantities in which the different objects of chemistry, simple or compound, combine with each other, referred to a common body, taken as unity.

Atramentum, a dye made of soot mixed with burnt resin or pitch, used by the ancients, particularly by painters; used also as a varnish.

Atrium, a term applied by the Romans to a particular part of a private house: the court or hall of a Greek or Roman house entered immediately from the fauces of the vestibulum.

Attal, Attle, Adall, Addle, in mining, corrupt, impure off-casts, found in the working of mines.

Attic base, the base of a column of upper and lower torus, a scotia, and fillets between them.

Attic Order, a low order of architecture, used over a principal order, never with columns, but with antæ or small pilasters.

Attics should not be less than one-quarter nor more than one-third of the order they surmount: they are frequently decorated with small short pilasters, whose breadth ought to be equal to the upper diameter of the column underneath them, and their projection usually not more than one-quarter of their breadth.

Attic story, the upper story of a house when the ceiling is square with the sides, by which it is distinguished from a common garret.

Atticurges, a term applied by Vitruvius to the base of a column, which he describes as divided by a scotia or trochilus, with a fillet above and below, and beneath all a plinth.

Attle, in mining, rubbish, deads, refuse, or stony matter.

Attributes, in architecture, symbols given to figures, or disposed as ornaments on a building, to indicate a distinguished character.

Attrition, the rubbing of bodies one against another, so as to destroy their surfaces.

Auditorium, an apartment in monasteries for the reception of strangers; also, a place where the Roman orators and poets recited their compositions.

Auger, a tool for boring large holes; it consists of a wooden handle, terminated at the bottom with steel.

Aula, an area or open place; in ancient Roman architecture, a court or hall.

Auleolum, a small church or chapel.

Aureola, a crown of glory, given by statuaries, etc., to saints, etc., to denote the victory they have obtained.

Aurificina, a place for melting and refining gold, etc.

Aurum, anciently, gold.

Automaton, an apparently self-acting machine, constructed of weights, levers, pulleys, and springs, by means of which it continues in motion for a definite period.

Autometer, an instrument to measure the quantity of moisture.

Auxiliary, or cushion rafter, a term applied to the raking-piece of the truss in a green post.

Avant mure, an outward wall.

Avenue, a passage from one part of a building to another.

Aviary, an apartment or building for the keeping of birds.

Avilor (A. C. d'), architect, born in Paris in 1653. The companion with Desgodetz as travelling pupil to Rome in 1674; both were captured by Tunisian corsairs; at Tunis Avilor designed and executed a mosque; was ransomed in 1676; published several works, principally of the styles of Louis XIV. and Louis XV.; died in 1700.

Avolta, a place vaulted or arched over.

A-weather, a term applied to the helm of a ship when it is put in the direction from which the wind blows.

Awning, a covering of canvas over the the deck of a vessel, or over a boat, as shelter from the sun or rain.

Axal section, a section through the axis of a body.

Axes, the timbers of a roof which form two sides of a triangle, the tignum being the base; more generally termed Principals.

Axe, or *broad axe*, a tool used in hewing timber.

Axiom, a self-evident truth.

Axis, in architecture, an imaginary line through the centre of a column, etc., or its geometrical representation: where different members are placed over each other, so that the same vertical line, on the elevation, divides them equally, they are said to be on the same axis, although they may be on different planes: thus, triglyphs and modillions are so arranged, that one coincides with the axis or line of axis of each column; in like manner, the windows or other openings in the several stories of a façade must all be in the same respective axis, whether they are all of the same breadth or not.

Axis, in geometry, the straight line in a plane figure, about which it revolves to produce or generate a solid.

Axis, in mechanics, the axis of a balance is the line upon which it moves or turns.

Axis, in turning, an imaginary line passing longitudinally through the middle of the body to be turned, from one point to the other of the two cones, by which the work is suspended, or between the back centre and the centre of the collar of the puppet which supports the end of the mandril at the chuck.

Axis of a circle or *sphere*, any line drawn through the centre, and terminated at the circumference on both sides.

Axis of a cone, the line from the vertex to the centre of the base.

Axis of a cylinder, the line from the centre of the one end to that of the other.

Axis in peritrochio, a wheel and axle, one of the five mechanical powers, or simple machines; contrived chiefly for the raising of weights to a considerable height, as water from a well, etc.

Axis of rotation, of any solid, the line about which the body really revolves when it is put in motion.

Axle bearing, in locomotive engines, the gun-metal, or other metal bearing, under which the axle journal revolves; it is nicely fitted to the journal, and lubricated by a siphon, to reduce, as far as practicable, the friction on the journal.

Axle, in locomotive engines, *journal*, or *neck*, the part of the axle turned and polished for revolving in the axle-box bearing.

Axle, leading, in locomotive engines, the front axle of the engine: eight-wheeled engines have two axles in front of the driving wheel axle, and they are often called leading axles.

Axle, trailing, the last axle of the engine, usually placed under the foot-plate: in Stephenson's and Crampton's patent engines, the driving wheel axle is the last axle.

Axles, in locomotive engines, the iron shafts supporting the engine, and on which the wheels are fixed.

Axles, driving wheel, in locomotive engines, with inside cylinders, this is a cranked axle; with outside cylinders, it is a straight axle; it is called the driving axle because the connecting-rods and eccentric-rods connect this axle to the pistons, slide-valves, and pumps, and by converting the rectilinear motion of the piston into a rotatory one, it propels or drives the engine in the direction required.

Axle-box, in locomotive engines, the box (usually cast iron) fitted up with a metal bearing in it, which rests upon the polished part of the axle.

Axle-box cover, in locomotive engines, the plate of iron (usually lined with leather) fitted to the top of the axle-box to keep the oil clean, and also from shaking out by the motion of the engine.

Axle-box siphon, in locomotive engines, the small tubes fitted into the top of the axle-box for feeding oil on to the axle journal as it revolves: the oil is fed by a piece of cotton or worsted, having one end introduced into these pipes, and the other end lying down amongst the oil in the axle-box.

Axle-guards, or *horn-plates*, in locomotive engines, the parts of the frame in which the axle-box slides up and down, as acted upon by the springs.

Axle-guard stays, in locomotive engines, the iron rods bolted to the frame and to all the ends of the axle-guards, to strengthen them.

Azimuth compass, an instrument used at sea for finding the sun's magnetic azimuth.

Azimuth dial, a dial of which the style or gnomon is perpendicular to the plane of the horizon

Azote, called also Nitrogen, a gas which forms an important constituent of atmospheric air, etc., but which, when breathed alone, destroys life.

Azure, blue colour; in painting, a bright and florid tint of blue, equal in force to ultramarine with the addition of a little white.

B.

BABEL, Tower of, built by the posterity of Noah, after the Flood; remarkable for its great height, and for the disappointment of the builders by the confusion of their language. It was erected in the plain of Shinar, upon the banks of the great river Euphrates, and near the place where the famous city of Babylon subsequently stood. "Let us build us a city and a tower whose top may reach unto heaven."—*Gen.* xi. 4. "The name of it is called Babel, because the Lord did there confound the language of all the earth, and from thence did the Lord scatter them abroad upon the face of all the earth."—*Ib.* xi. 9.

Babylonian architecture takes its appellation from the magnificence and extent of the public buildings of Babylon. This city was founded by Nimrod about 1665 years before Christ; its walls were fifty cubits thick and 200 in height, built of bricks made from the earth dug out of the ditch that surrounded the city. In the walls were 100 gates made of brass; the jambs and lintels were made of the same metal.

Babylonian engine. An engine, to raise water from the Euphrates to supply the hanging gardens of Babylon, was constructed and used in this the most ancient and splendid city of the early age, founded by the builders of Babel and enlarged by Nimrod, extended and beautified by Semiramis. This engine greatly exceeded in the perpendicular the height to which the water was elevated by it. Extensive terraces were formed one above another to the top of the city walls; and to supply them with the necessary moisture, the engine was erected, of which no account is known at the present time.

Bac, in navigation, a praam or ferry-boat.

Bac, in brewing, a cooler.

Baccalaureus, an ecclesiastical apparitor or verger, who carries a staff of office.

Bacca, a light-house, watch-tower, or beacon.

Baccharis, ploughman's spikenard.

Baccio della Porta, called Fra Bartolommeo, born 1469; of the Florentine school; he taught the use of the lay figure.

Back, the back of a lode is the part of it nearest the surface; the back of a level is that part of the lode extending above it to within a short distance of the level above.

Back-board, in turning, that part of the lathe which is sustained by the four legs, and which sustains the pillars that support the puppet-bar: the back-board is only used in the best constructed lathes.

Back centre screw, the screw for setting up the back centre of a lathe, to the work to be turned, after the puppet-head has been fixed.

Backed, a sea phrase, to back an anchor, to carry out a smaller one ahead of the one by which the vessel rides, to take off some of the strain.

Background, in painting, is the space of ground behind the principal objects of the picture.

Back joint, applied by masons to a rebate such as that made on the inner side of the jamb of a chimney-piece to receive a slip.

Back-links, the links in a parallel motion which connect the air-pump rod to the beam.

Back of a hip, in carpentry, is the upper edge of a rafter between two sides of a hipped roof, formed to an angle, so as to range with the rafters on each side of it.

Back of a window, the board or wainscoting between the sash-frames and the floor, uniting with the two elbows in the same plane with the shutters: when framed it is commonly with single panels, with mouldings on the framing corresponding with the doors, shutters, etc., in the apartment in which it is fixed.

Back-painting, the art of painting mezzotinto prints, on plate or crown glass, with oil colours.

Backs, in carpentry, the principal rafters of a roof.

Back-staff, an instrument invented by Capt. Davis for a sea quadrant, so named because the back of the observer is turned towards the sun when using it.

Back-stays, long ropes from the topmast heads to both sides of the ship, where they are extended to the channels.

Back-stay stool, a short piece of plank fitted for the security of the dead-eyes and chains for the backstays, though sometimes the channels are left long enough at the after end for the back-stays to be fitted thereto.

Bac-maker, a cooper who makes liquor-bacs, etc.

Baculometry, the art of measuring either accessible or inaccessible distances or lines, by the help of baculi, staves, or rods.

Baculus, a branch of hazel, used for the discovery of mines, springs, etc.

Badigeon, in statuary, a mixture of plaster and freestone sifted and ground together, used by statuaries to repair defects in their work.

Baguette, a small moulding, like the astragal: when enriched with foliage, it is called a chaplet; when plain, a head.

Bagnio, a bath.

Bagpipe. To bagpipe the mizen is to lay it aback by bringing the sheet to the weather-mizen rigging.

Bailey, an area of ground, a court, within the walls of a fortress; in modern acceptation, frequently applied to a prison.

Baird (Mr.), in 1816, constructed a steamboat in St. Petersburg.

Bakehouse, an apartment with an oven to bake bread.

Baker's central rule for the construction of equations, is a method of constructing all equations not exceeding the fourth degree.

Bal, a term used in mining.

Balance, Hydrostatic, an instrument which determines the specific gravity of fluids and solids by weighing them in water.

Balance, or equilibrium, in a picture, is when the forms of objects, the lights, shades, colours, and expressions, are happily adapted to each other, and no one figure or colour overpowers or obscures the rest. When a building is seen in one corner of a picture, it is frequently balanced by something in the other; even a large bird will produce the effect.

Balance, one of the six simple powers in mechanics, chiefly used in determining the equality or difference in heavy bodies, and consequently their masses or quantities of matter. Balances of various kinds are commonly used—as the common balance, the bent lever balance, the Roman balance, and the Swedish or Danish balance—for the adjustment of differences in weights, etc.

Balance, in hydrostatics, an instrument for determining the specific gravity of bodies.

Balance (The) of a clock or watch, the part which, by the regularity of its motion, determines the beat or strike.

Balance-gates, in hydraulic engineering, may be described by referring to those made for the Compensation Reservoir of the East London Water-works. These gates were designed for the purpose of discharging the body of water collected in the reservoir during the rise of the tide, in order to supply the mills lower down the river Lea, which might otherwise have been injured by the amount withdrawn from the river by the pumping-engines of the Water Company. They differ in construction from common flood-gates, being made to work upon a vertical shaft or spindle as a centre, and having an equal surface of gate on each side of that centre; so that whatever pressure of water there may be on one side of the gate tending to force it open, there is as great a pressure on the opposite leaf to keep it shut.

Balance-reef, a reef in a spanker or fore-aft mainsail, which runs from the outer bead eaving diagonally to the tack; it is the closest reef, and makes the sail triangular.

Balastre, the finest gold-cloth, manufactured at Vienna.

Balcony, a projection in the front of a house or other building, supported by consoles or columns, sometimes applied to the interiors of theatres, and for public convenience in large buildings.

Balcony, the projecting gallery in the stern of large ships.

Baldachin, a canopy supported by columns, and raised over altars, tombs, etc.

Baldachino, in architecture, an open building supported by columns and covered with a canopy, frequently placed over an altar.

Bale: to bale a boat is to throw water out of her.

Balista, in practical geometry, the same as the geometrical cross, called the Jacob's staff.

Balistic pendulum, an instrument used for measuring the velocity of a cannon-ball, i.e. the force of gunpowder. It consists, in its simplest form, of a beam which can swing on a fixed axis at one end, while the ball strikes the other end; and the angle through which that end moves being known, the velocity of the cannon-ball may be computed.

Balistics, the art of throwing missive weapons by means of an engine.

Balistrario, a room in fortified buildings, in which the crossbows were deposited.

Balk, a great beam.

Ball, any spherical body, either natural or artificial.

Ballast, for ships, the materials for which are gravel, iron, or stone, or any heavy substance, to stow away in the hold, to bring a ship to a proper water-line when unladen, to counterbalance the effect of the wind on the masts, and to give stability.

Ball-cock, a hollow globe of metal attached to the end of a lever, which turns the stop-cock of a cistern-pipe by floating on the surface of the water, thereby regulating the supply.

Ball-flower, an ornament like a ball, placed in a circular flower, the petals of which form a cap round it; it belongs to the decorated style of the fourteenth century.

Ball-lever, a lever of metal having a ball affixed at one end as a weight, which assists in closing again the plug or valve of a cistern after it has been pulled up to obtain a supply of water.

Ball of a pendulum, the weight at the bottom of it; sometimes called the bob.

Baluster or *Baluster*, the lateral part of a scroll in the capital of the Ionic column; a little pillar-rail, such as are on the outside of cloisters.

Ball and socket, an instrument made of brass, with a perpetual screw, so as to move horizontally, vertically, or obliquely: used for the managing of surveying and astronomical instruments.

Ballon, is a round globe on the top of a pillar.

Balloon or *Baston*, a mould at the base of a column called a Tore.

Balloon, a spheroidal hollow body, capable of floating in the air by means of its inflation with gas specifically lighter than the air.

Balloon, a globe placed on the top of a pillar or pediment, as an acroter or crowning.

Balls, in electricity, are two pieces of

cork or pith of elder-tree, nicely turned in a lathe to the size of a small pea, and suspended by means of delicate threads.

Balk-staff, a quarter-staff.

Ball-valves, the valves in the force-pumps of a locomotive engine: the balls are turned and ground truly spherical, so as to fit watertight into the valve-seats in every position.

Balneac, in Greek, signifies a bath or bathing-vessel.

Balteum, a band or girdle, according to Vitruvius: this word is used to denote the moulding on the bolsters or sides of the Ionic capital.

Baltei, the bands in the flanks of Ionic pulvinated capitals. Balteum and balteus were generally used by the Romans to signify the belt by which the sword or quiver was suspended.

Baluster, a small column or pillar used in a balustrade. Balusters are generally placed round the gallery in the stern and the quarter gallery of large ships.

Balustrade, a series or row of balusters, joined by a rail, serving for a rest to the arms, or as a fence or enclosure to balconies, altars, staircases, etc.

Balustrades, when intended for use, as against windows, on flights of steps, terraces, and the like, should not be more than three feet six inches, nor less than three feet in height. When used for ornament, as on the summit of a building, their height may be from two-thirds to four-fifths of the entablature whereon they are employed; and this proportion is to be taken exclusive of their zoccolo or plinth, so that from the proper point of sight the whole balustrade may be exposed to view. There are various species of balusters; if single-bellied, the best way is to divide the total height of the space allotted for the balustrade into thirteen equal parts,—the height of the baluster to be eight, of the base three, and of the cornice two of those parts; or divide the total height into fourteen parts, making the baluster eight, the base four, and the cornice two. If double-bellied, the height should be divided into fourteen parts, two of which are to be given to the cornice, three to the base, and the remainder to the baluster.

The distance between two balusters should not be more than half the diameter of the baluster in its thickest part, nor less than one-third of it; but on inclined planes the intervals should not be quite so wide.

Bancalia, cushions or coverings for seats and benches.

Band, in architecture, denotes any flat low member, or moulding, that is broad and not very deep.

Banded column, a support which has its body interrupted at intervals by one or more broad projecting cinctures, etc.

Bandle, an Irish measure of two feet in length.

Bandlet, a small fillet, or flat moulding.

Bandrol, a little flag or streamer affixed to the top of masts.

Bank, a long piece of timber.

Bank, a carpenter's term for a piece of fir-wood unslit, from 4 to 10 inches square, and of any length.

Bank: to double-bank an oar, is to have it pulled by two men.

Banker (The), in bricklaying, a bench from 6 to 12 feet in length, used for preparing the bricks for gauged work.

Banker, a cushion or covering for a seat.

Banker browded, cushions embroidered.

Banneret, anciently a knight made in the field, with a ceremony of cutting off the point of his standard and making it as if it were a banner.

Banquet, the raised footway adjoining to the parapet on the sides of a bridge.

Banqueting house or *room*, a house

or room where public feasts are given.

Bantam-work, painted or carved work, resembling that of japan, only more gaudy.

Baptaterium, a back-mill or fulling-mill.

Baptistery, a place or edifice where baptism is performed. A basin, pool, or place for bathing.

Bar, a barrier, gatehouse; in law, a place where counsellors plead.

Bar, a bank or shoal at the entrance of a harbour.

Bar of ground, in mining, any course of vein which runs across a lode, or different from those in its vicinity.

Bar iron, long prismatic pieces of iron, being rectangular parallelopipeds, prepared from pig iron, so as to be malleable, for the use of blacksmiths for the method of joining bars.

Barberry-wood is of small size, resembling alder, and is straight and tenacious.

Barbacan, or *Barbican*, in the middle ages, a fort at the entrance of a bridge, or the outlet of a city; the part of a fortress where watch and ward was kept.

Barbacan, a long narrow canal or passage for water in Wales, where buildings are liable to be overflowed, likewise to drain off water from a terrace.

Bar-master, among miners, the person who keeps the gauge or dish for measuring the ore.

Bar of the port, a billet thrust through the rings that serve to shut up the portholes of a ship.

Barbarelli (Giorgio), of Castelfranco, known by the name of Giorgione, of the Venetian School of Painting. He died in 1511, at the age of 34.

Barcella, a vessel containing incense.

Barcon, a luggage-vessel used in the Mediterranean.

Bardiglione, a blue variety of anhydrite, cut and polished for ornamental purposes.

Bare poles, the condition of a ship when she has no sail set.

Bari, the portion of a slate showing the gauge, and on which the water falls.

Barge, a large double-banked boat used by the commander of a vessel in the navy.

Barge-board, a front or facing to conceal the barge couples, laths, tiles, thatch, etc. Barge-boards (or, more properly, verge-boards), pendants, pinnacles, and brackets, being the chief decorations of houses in early domestic architecture, should always be made of strong oak, and left to acquire by age a grey hue; and not of slight deal, painted, as is now the too frequent practice.

Barge-couple, in architecture, a beam mortised into another, to strengthen the building.

Barge-course, a part of the tiling or thatching of a roof, projecting over the gable, and filled up with boards, mortar, etc.

Bargh-master, a surveyor of mines.

Bargmote, a court held concerning the affairs of mines.

Barium, a metal that exists in the sulphate and carbonate of barytes; found in nature in great abundance.

Barker's mill, an hydraulic machine much in use.

Barkery, a tan-house; also a sheep-cote.

Bark hert, a seat in large gardens, a resting-place.

Barmkyn, the rampart or outer fortification of a castle.

Barn, a covered farm-building for laying up grain, hay, straw, etc.

Barnacle, a shellfish often found on a vessel's bottom.

Barocci (Federigo), of the Roman school, in the style of Correggio, a style best calculated to reform an age which had neglected the true principles of art, particularly colouring and chiaroscuro.

Barometer and *Sympiesometer*. The barometer is a measure for the weight of the atmosphere, or its pressure on the surface of the globe.

It is well known that it is owing to the atmospheric pressure that water rises in a common pump after the air has been drawn from the barrel, but that the height to which it can be raised by this means is limited, and does not much exceed 30 feet. A little more than 30 feet of water, therefore, balances the atmosphere. Mercury being about twelve times heavier than water, about 30 inches of mercury will also counterpoise the atmosphere. The principle of the barometer is simple. If a tube, about 3 feet long, closed at one end and open at the other, be filled with mercury, and, with the open end stopped by a finger, this tube be reversed, and placed upright in a cup partly filled with the same liquid, the mercury in the tube, in ordinary states of the weather, will descend to 30 inches, measured from the surface of the fluid in the cup, and not much lower. The mercury is sustained in the tube by the pressure of the atmosphere on the surface of the fluid in the cup. Such a tube and cup, so filled, would in fact be a barometer; and if a moveable index were added to it, this simple instrument would indicate the changes which take place in the atmospheric pressure. The Sympiesometer is a more delicate instrument for measuring the atmospheric pressure; but it is also a more complicated one than the mercurial barometer, and it would be best understood by inspection. The upper part of the tube contains hydrogen gas, which is elastic; and the lower part, including the well, contains oil. By this compound construction, whilst the length of the tube is less than that of the mercurial barometer, the index, or scale for measuring the pressure, is increased. Hydrogen gas being very sensibly affected by all changes of temperature, the index, by which the atmospheric pressure is read, requires to be set according to the actual temperature, before the atmospheric pressure can be read off.

Since mercury expands by heat, a correction for temperature is also required for the mercurial barometer, when exact calculations are to be made; and for this reason barometers usually have a thermometer attached to them, in order that the temperature may be read off, and recorded at the same time that the barometer is registered.

The atmosphere is supposed to extend to about the height of 50 miles, and its density to diminish from the surface of the globe upwards, in a geometrical ratio.

Thus, when observations are made on land, above the level of the sea, a correction is required for altitude, since the weight of the atmosphere diminishes as we ascend. It is owing to this that we are enabled to determine the height of mountains by barometers, and that aeronauts compute the altitude to which they ascend in balloons.

The cause of the oscillations of the barometer in a gale of wind was first explained by the late Mr. Redfield, of New York.—A quantity of fluid in a cup, put in rapid circular motion, gives a representation of the form of that portion of the atmosphere which is within the limits of a storm. A whirlwind which sets an extended portion of the atmosphere in a state of rapid revolution, diminishes the pressure over a corresponding portion of the earth's surface, and most of all at the centre of the whirl, where the depth of the compressing column of air will be least.

The principle of the barometer should be explained in all works on navigation, and in all schools where navigation is taught.

The following is a table for the correction to be applied to the observed height of the mercury, to reduce it to the freezing point, at 32° Fahrenheit, or zero of the Centigrade scale.

Reduction of the English Barometer to the Freezing Point, or to 32° on Fahrenheit's Scale.—*Subtractive.* (*From Galbraith's Tables.*)

Temp.		Part I.—For Mercury only. Height of the Barom. in inches.				Part II.—Mercury and Brass. Height of the Barom. in Inches.				Diff. to 2 In.
Fah.	Cent.	28 In.	29 In.	30 In.	31 In.	28 In.	29 In.	30 In.	31 In.	
33	0·00	0·0000	0·0000	0·0000	0·0000	0·0088	0·0091	0·0094	0·0097	2
34	1·11	0·0056	0·0058	0·0060	0·0062	0·0138	0·0143	0·0148	0·0152	5
36	2·22	0·0112	0·0116	0·0120	0·0124	0·0188	0·0194	0·0201	0·0208	7
38	3·33	0·0168	0·0174	0·0180	0·0186	0·0238	0·0246	0·0255	0·0263	9
40	4·44	0·0224	0·0232	0·0240	0·0248	0·0288	0·0298	0·0309	0·0319	11
42	5·55	0·0280	0·0290	0·0300	0·0310	0·0338	0·0350	0·0362	0·0374	12
44	6·66	0·0336	0·0348	0·0360	0·0372	0·0388	0·0402	0·0416	0·0430	14
46	7·77	0·0392	0·0406	0·0420	0·0434	0·0439	0·0454	0·0470	0·0485	16
48	8·88	0·0448	0·0464	0·0480	0·0496	0·0489	0·0506	0·0523	0·0541	17
50	10·00	0·0504	0·0522	0·0540	0·0558	0·0538	0·0558	0·0577	0·0596	19
52	11·11	0·0559	0·0579	0·0599	0·0619	0·0588	0·0609	0·0630	0·0652	21
54	12·22	0·0615	0·0637	0·0659	0·0681	0·0638	0·0661	0·0684	0·0707	23
56	13·33	0·0671	0·0695	0·0719	0·0743	0·0688	0·0713	0·0738	0·0762	25
58	14·44	0·0727	0·0753	0·0779	0·0805	0·0738	0·0765	0·0791	0·0818	26
60	15·55	0·0783	0·0811	0·0839	0·0867	0·0788	0·0817	0·0845	0·0873	28
62	16·66	0·0838	0·0868	0·0898	0·0928	0·0838	0·0868	0·0898	0·0928	30
64	17·77	0·0894	0·0926	0·0958	0·0990	0·0888	0·0920	0·0951	0·0983	32
66	18·88	0·0950	0·0984	0·1018	0·1051	0·0938	0·0971	0·1005	0·1039	34
68	20·00	0·1005	0·1041	0·1077	0·1113	0·0988	0·1023	0·1059	0·1094	36
70	21·11	0·1061	0·1099	0·1137	0·1175	0·1037	0·1075	0·1112	0·1149	38
72	22·22	0·1117	0·1156	0·1196	0·1235	0·1087	0·1126	0·1165	0·1204	40
74	23·33	0·1172	0·1214	0·1255	0·1296	0·1137	0·1178	0·1219	0·1259	42
76	24·44	0·1228	0·1271	0·1315	0·1358	0·1187	0·1229	0·1272	0·1314	44
78	25·55	0·1283	0·1329	0·1375	0·1421	0·1237	0·1281	0·1325	0·1369	45
80	26·66	0·1339	0·1387	0·1434	0·1482	0·1286	0·1332	0·1378	0·1424	47
82	27·77	0·1394	0·1444	0·1494	0·1544	0·1336	0·1384	0·1432	0·1479	49
84	28·88	0·1450	0·1502	0·1553	0·1605	0·1386	0·1435	0·1485	0·1534	51
86	30·00	0·1505	0·1559	0·1613	0·1667	0·1436	0·1486	0·1538	0·1589	53
88	31·11	0·1561	0·1616	0·1672	0·1728	0·1485	0·1538	0·1591	0·1644	54
90	32·22	0·1617	0·1674	0·1731	0·1790	0·1535	0·1590	0·1644	0·1699	56
P. P. for Temp. F. +		0°·4 12	0°·8 24	1°·2 35	1°·6 47	2°·0 59	0°·4 10	0°·8 21	1°·2 31	1°·6 42	2°·0 52

Baroscope, an instrument for finding out the variations of the air, or weather-glass.

Barouche, a coach without a roof.

Barozzi, otherwise Vignola, a distinguished architect and painter, born 1507, died in 1573.

Barque, a three-masted vessel having her fore and main masts rigged like a ship's, and her mizen-mast like the main-mast of a schooner, with no sail upon it but a spanker.

Barra, in the middle ages, a tower or bar at one end of a bridge.

Barracks, buildings for the lodgment of soldiers.

Barrage, a mound or dyke to raise the waters of a river. One of the most remarkable works of this kind is the Barrage of the Nile, for retaining the water of that river at a sufficient height to irrigate the summer crops. The dam consists of a curved quay, 4,500 feet in length; and two sluice-gates are placed at the head of the Delta, one on the Rosetta, the other on the Damietta branch, at a distance of half a league from each other.

Barrel, in machinery, is a term applied generally to anything hollow and cylindrical.

Barrow, in mining, a heap of dead attle, rubbish, etc.

Barrow, in salt-works, wicker cases almost in the shape of a sugar loaf, in which the salt is put to drain.

Barrows, or tumuli, monuments of the greatest antiquity, raised as sepulchres for the interment of the great.

Barry (James), a painter, was born in Cork, October 1741, and died in the 65th year of his age.

Bars, straight pieces of timber or metal that run across from one part of a machine to another.

Bartholomeus (Alfred), architect, born in 1801, published some excellent works for study and use, died in 1844.

Bartisan, a wooden tower; a turret on the top of a house, castle, or church tower; a balcony or platform, within a parapet on the roof of any building; in architecture, bartisans are small overhanging turrets, which project from the angles on the top of a tower, or from the parapet or other parts of a building.

Barton, the demesne lands of a manor, a manor house; the fields, a foldyard, or outhouse.

Barton house, a term used in the southern and western counties to express a farm-building, outhouse, and appurtenances.

Bar wood, an African wood, in pieces four to five feet long. It is used as red dip-wood, also for violin bows, ramrods, and in turning.

Barytes, a heavy mineral, found in copper-mines, and formerly named 'ponderous spar;' it has a caustic, alkaline taste, and is extremely poisonous.

Basalt, a variety of trap-rock, hard and heavy, usually of a dark green or brownish-black colour, composed of augite and felspar, with some iron and olivine; it frequently occurs in a columnar form.

Basanite, a variety of schistose hornstone, called also Lydian stone.

Bascule bridge, a bridge to lift, to accommodate a passing for shipping.

Base of a figure, in geometry, denotes the lowest part of its perimeter.

Base of a conic section is a right line in the parabola and hyperbola formed by the common intersection of the cutting plane and the base of the cone.

Base, in architecture, the lower part or member of a column, on which the shaft stands.

Base-court, the outer or lower yard of a castle, appropriated to stables, offices, etc.

Base-line, in perspective, the common section of a picture and the geometrical plane.

Base-line, in surveying, a line, measured with the greatest possible exactness, on which a series of triangles are constructed, in order to determine the position of objects and places. The measurement of degrees of the meridian, for the purpose of ascertaining the size of the earth, has been undertaken in various countries, with extreme accuracy. The arc measured by the French extended from Dunkirk to the southernmost point of the Balearic Islands, including 120° 22′ 14″, having its centre halfway between the Equator and the North Pole. Another survey of this kind was performed on a part of the shore of Pennsylvania, which happens to be so straight and level as to admit of a line of more than 130 miles being measured directly without triangulation. Very long lines have also been measured (trigonometrically) by order of the English Government, both at home and in India, the mean result of which makes the earth's axis 7898 miles, 5 furlongs, 16 yards, and the diameter of the Equator 7924 miles 7 furlongs.

Basement, the lower story or floor of a building; the story of a house below the level of the ground.

Basements. As an alternative for employing orders upon orders, the ground-floor is made to assume the appearance of a basement, and the order that decorates the principal story placed thereupon: in such cases the basement should not be higher than the order it supports, nor lower than one-half the height of the order; but if a basement be introduced merely for the purpose

BASILICA.

of raising the principal or ground-floor, it may be three, four, five, or six feet high, at pleasure.

These basement stories are generally in rock-worked or plain rustics; and in no case should the height of a rustic course be less than one module of the order resting on the basement, nor should it ever much exceed it: their joints, *if square*, ought not to be broader than one-eighth of the height of the rustic, or narrower than one-tenth, and their depth should equal their breadth; *if chamfered*, the whole joint may be one-quarter to one-third the height of the rustic, the joint being always right-angled. When the basement is high, it is sometimes crowned with a cornice, but a plat-band is more commonly used.—*Gwilt.*

Basenet, a helmet.

Base-plate, the foundation-plate of an engine.

Basevi (George), an architect of considerable taste, born in 1794, accidentally killed in 1845.

Basil, to grind the edge of a tool to an angle.

Basilica, in the time of the Romans, a public hall or court of judicature. After the conversion of the Emperor Constantine to Christianity, these edifices were converted into Christian churches. The *Basilice* of the Romans were the types from which the early Christian places of worship were taken; and the ruins of these buildings were the chief materials used. In several instances the columns that divide the centre part of the church from the aisles have been taken from other edifices, either on account of the want of artists capable of executing anything equal to them, or the haste with which they were erected. The expedient that was adopted tends to show that proportion was not considered; some columns were reduced from their former height, and others mounted on pedestals, to suit the purposes to which they were applied. Besides this total disregard to proportion in the shafts of the columns, capitals and bases were applied without any consideration to their fitness. The heathen basilicæ, generally situated in the forums, were of rectangular form, and divided into three or five parts by rows of columns parallel to the length of the building; another colonnade at the extremity crossed the former at right-angles, and in the middle of the end wall was a semicircular recess, in which was situated the tribune of the judge. These basilicæ had likewise galleries over the aisles, in which commercial or other business was transacted; but in the Christian churches this was appropriated to the women, who (as in the Jewish synagogues) were not allowed to join with the men in the lower parts of the building. These galleries were omitted in the after basilicæ, and one of the aisles was retained solely for their use. Six of the principal churches or basilicæ at Rome are attributed to the zeal of Constantine. The basilicæ of St. John de Lateran, St. Peter, St. Laurentius, St. Paul, St. Agnes, and St. Stephen were built by him, besides the baptisterium that bears his name.

The Christian Basilica may be sketched as follows:—

1. *The Atrium*, or court of entrance, usually surrounded by a columned portico as in the heathen temples. This was an addition to the heathen basilica.

2. *The Portico*, in front of the building, called the Narthex or Scourge—reserved for the catechumens and penitents, the former being confined to its precincts till baptism, the latter till ecclesiastical absolution.

3. In the interior, the central area, or nave, parted from its side-aisles by rows of columns—in the smaller churches single, in the larger double; the rows next the nave

almost invariably supported round arches instead of an unbroken architrave, and upon these arches rested the main walls of the building; the walls were pierced with windows, under which often ran lines of mosaic; both nave and aisles were crowned with a wooden roof, and under that of the aisles Triforia, or galleries, as in their pagan prototypes, were sometimes provided for the women.

4. *The Cancellum, Chancel,* or *Choir*—the upper part of the nave, raised two or three steps, railed off or separated by a low wall, and appropriated to the singers and inferior clergy; within it, sometimes on the same side, more frequently on the opposite, stood the Ambones, or desks, that on the left for reading the Gospel, that on the right for the Epistle; the Paschal candlestick, emblematic of revealed religion, being fixed adjacent to the former. The congregation stood on either side the cancellum, the men to the right, the women to the left, as in the heathen basilicæ.

5. *The Triumphal Arch,* introducing from the central nave into the sanctuary, and thus figurative of the transition through death from the Church Militant on earth to the Church Triumphant in Heaven, respectively symbolized by the nave and sanctuary: subjects allusive to this triumph, the Saviour in glory or the Vision of the New Jerusalem of the Apocalypse, were usually represented on it in mosaic.

6. *The Transept, Presbytery,* or *Sanctuary,* elevated by steps, in the centre of which stood the altar, originally uncovered, but afterwards surmounted by a ciborium or tabernacle supported by small pillars.

7. *The Tribune* or *Absis,* within which, overlooking the church, arose the throne of the bishop, flanked to the right and left by the seats of his attendant clergy. The side-aisles were terminated by similar absides of smaller proportions.

8. Lastly, *the Crypt,* beneath the sanctuary, generally half-sunk below the level of the earth, an open screen or grating admitting a sight of its interior from the nave, and of the Confession, the tomb or shrine containing the relics of the saint or martyr. The theory of a primitive church presumed it to be built over a catacomb. S. Agnes, S. Lorenzo, S. Martino, S. Prassede, and a few others at Rome actually are so; but as this could rarely be the case elsewhere, artificial catacombs or crypts were dug to represent them.

At Rome, the Basilica of San Lorenzo, situated about a mile from the city on the Via Tiburtina.

The Basilica of Santa Croce in Gierusalemme.

The Basilica of San Giovanni in Laterano, the cathedral church of Rome, called the metropolitan church of the Christian world; it is also sometimes named the Basilica Constantiniana.

The Basilica of San Sebastiano fuori le mura.

The Basilica of Santa Maria Maggiore, which is also sometimes called the Basilica Laberiana.

The Basilica of Santa Maria in Trastevere.

The remaining Basilica is either that of San Pietro in Vaticano, or of San Paolo fuori le mura; indeed both of them ought to be included in the number, as they have respectively the Porta Santa.

Basilicula, a shrine, oratory, or cenotaph.

Basins and ewers. In early times, before the cleanly custom of using a fork was practised, the hands were frequently washed during dinner: a basin and ewer were handed for that purpose by an attendant. At the feast given by Henry VIII. to the French ambassadors, there were three ewry boards; one for the king, another for the queen, and the third for the princes, etc.

Basin, a concave piece of metal made use of by opticians to grind their convex glasses in.

Basin, a reservatory of water; a canal; a pond; a dock for repairing ships.

Basset. The basset or outcrop means the emergence at the surface of the different mineral strata from beneath each other.

Basset, or *Outfall*, applied to openings from or into mines to the surface.

Bas-relief, or *Basso-ritievo*, low or flat relief, applied to sculpture connected more or less with a plane surface, and of which the figures do not project in their full proportions.

Bast, lime-tree bark made into ropes and mats.

Bastard stucco, a three-coated plaster, the first generally roughing in or rendering; the second floating, as in trowelled stucco; but the finishing coat contains a little hair besides the sand: it is not handfloated, and the trowelling is done with less labour than in what is called trowelled stucco.

Bastard-toothed file, in smithing, that employed after the rubber.

Bastard wheel, a flat bevel-wheel, or one which is a near approach to a spur-wheel.

Bastide, in the twelfth century, a place of defence, a fortress.

Bastille, a prison; a castle, tower, fortress, or any place of defence.

Bastion, a rampart, bulwark, or earthen mound.

Batardeau, a coffer-dam, or case of piling without a bottom, for building the piers of a bridge.

Batch, in mining, a certain quantity of ore sent to the surface by any pair of men.

Bateau, a light boat, long in proportion to its breadth.

Bateman light, a window in which the sides of the aperture are left to admit light, an upright, and the bottom horizontal.

Bath, a receptacle for water, in which to plunge, wash, or bathe the body. Among the Romans, baths were erected magnificent both in style and purpose, and many of them of great architectural beauty. In later times the bath was always used by the Romans before they went to their supper. The rich generally had hot and cold baths in their own houses; and it was not till the time of Augustus that the baths assumed an air of grandeur and magnificence. The situation chosen for baths ought to be sheltered from the north and north-east. The caldaria and tepidaria should be made to receive their light from the west; or, should local circumstances not admit of this disposition, they may both be made to face the south, because the general time of bathing is from midday until sunset. One thing necessary to be observed is, that the caldaria of that division of the bath which is appropriated to the women should be contiguous to that exclusively used by the men, and have the same aspect; for then the coppers of both may be heated from the same furnace. Three brazen vessels are fixed over the furnace, which are severally called caldarium, tepidarium, and frigidarium: they are so arranged, that whatever heated water is taken from the first, it is replaced by warm water from the second, the deficiency of which is supplied, in a similar manner, from the third. The concave coverings of the small tubes of both baths are likewise heated from the same furnace. The insulated stages of the caldaria are thus constructed: the floor is made inclining towards the furnace, so that if a ball were placed upon any part of it, it would not remain at rest, but take a direction towards the mouth; by which means the flame will more easily pervade the interval between the floors, which is paved with tiles a foot and a half square: upon the floor, earthen props, eight inches each way, are arranged at such intervals as to receive upon them square tiles two feet in length: the props are two feet in height; the tiles which form them are cemented with clay and hair mixed together. The square tiles which they support form the substratum of the pavement of the caldaria.

Bath metal, a mixed metal, otherwise called Prince's metal.

Bath-stone, Bath oolite; minute globules, cemented together by yellowish earthy calcareous matter; it is much used in building, but is not a lasting material. It is soft when quarried, but hardens by exposure to the air.

Batifolium, a movable wooden tower used by besiegers in attacking a fortress.

Batten, in carpentry, a scantling of wooden stuff, from two to four inches broad, and about one thick, principally used for wainscot, on which also are bradded, on the plain boards, also batten doors, those which resemble wainscot-doors, but are not so, for in wainscot-doors the panels are grooved in the framing.

Battens (nautical), thin strips of wood put around the hatches to keep the tarpaulin down; also put upon rigging to keep it from chafing. A large batten widened at the end, and put upon rigging, is called a Scotchman.

Batter, to displace a portion of the iron of any bar or other piece by the blow of a hammer, so as to flatten or compress it inwardly, and spread it outwardly on all sides around the place of impact.

Batter, a term applied to walls built out of the upright, or gently sloping inwards; wharf walls and retaining walls built to support embankments.

Batter, the leaning back of the upper part of the face of a wall, so as to make the plumb-line fall within the base.

Battery, in electricity, a combination of coated surfaces of glass, commonly jars, so connected that they may be charged at once and discharged by means of a common conductor.

Battlement, an open or interrupted parapet on the roof of a building; a parapet with embrasures.

Battory, a name given by the Hans Towns to their country-houses and warehouses in foreign countries.

Baughum, an outhouse or domestic office.

Baulk, a piece of foreign fir or deal, from 8 to 16 inches square, being the trunk of a tree of that species of wood; generally brought to a square for the use of building.

Bawdrick, a cord or thong for the clapper of a bell; a sword-belt; a jewel.

Bawk, a cross-beam in the roof of a house which unites and supports the rafters; a tie-beam.

Bay, a division of a roof or vaulting of a building, consisting of the space between the beams or arches. A part of a window between the mullions is often called a bay or day.

Bay, in plastering, the space between the skreeds, prepared for regulating and working the floating-rule.

Bay of joists, the joisting between two binding joists, or between two girders when binding joists are not used.

Bay of roofing, the small rafters and their supporting purlins between two principal rafters.

Bay-salt, salt obtained by evaporating sea-water in shallow ponds by the heat of the sun; it is of a dark grey colour, and contains iodine.

Bay-tree, a native of Italy and Greece; it grows to the height of thirty feet, and its wood is aromatic.

Bay-window, an oriel window; a window jutting outwards; frequently called a bow-window.

Bayeux tapestry, ordered to be worked by Matilda, the Queen of William the Conqueror.

Bazaar, a market-place.

Beacon, a post or buoy placed over a shoal or bank, to warn vessels off: also a signal-mark on land; a tower placed on an eminence, with a light to warn against the approach of danger.

Beaconage, dues levied for the maintenance of beacons.

Bead, a small globular ornament used in ancient and modern architecture.

Bead and Butt work, in carpentry, framing in which the panels are flush, having beads stuck or run upon the two edges, the grain of the wood being in the direction of them.

Bead and quirk, a bead stuck on the edge of a piece of stuff, flush with its surface.

Bead-butt and square-work, framing with head and butt on one side; and square on the other; used in doors.

Bead-plane, a moulding plane of a semi-cylindric contour, generally used in sticking a moulding of the same name on the edge or on the side close to the arris.

Beak, the crooked end of a piece of iron, to hold anything fast.

Beak, a small pendent fillet, forming a channel behind, to prevent water from running down the lower bed of the cornice.

Beak-head, a small platform at the fore-part of the upper deck in large ships.

Beak-iron, the conic part of the anvil, with its base attached to the side, and its axis horizontal.

Beaking-joint, the joint formed by the meeting of several heading joints in one continued line, which is sometimes the case in folded floors.

Beam, a horizontal piece of iron or timber, used to resist a force or weight, as a tie-beam, where it acts as a string, or chain, by its tension; as a collar-beam, where it acts by compression; as a bres- summer, where it resists a transverse insisting weight.

Beam, in steam-engines, a large lever turning upon a centre, and forming the medium of communication between the piston-rod and the crank-shaft.

Beam of an anchor, the straight part or shank to which the hooks are fastened.

Beams.—FORMS OF BEAMS. In the construction of beams, it is necessary that their form should be such that they will be equally strong throughout; or, in other words, that they will offer an equal resistance to fracture in all their parts, and will, therefore, be equally liable to break at one part of their length as at another.

If a beam be fixed at one end and loaded at the other, and the breadth uniform throughout its length, then, that the beam may be equally strong throughout, its form must be that of a parabola.

This form is generally used in the beams of steam-engines; and in double-acting steam-engines the beam is strained sometimes from one side, and sometimes from the other; therefore, both the sides should be of the same form.

Mr. Emerson gives the load that may be safely borne by a square inch rod of each of the following:

	lbs. avoird.
Iron rod an inch square will bear	76,400
Brass	35,600
Hempen rope	19,600
Ivory	15,700
Oak, box, yew, plum-tree	7,850
Elm, ash, beech	6,070
Walnut, plum	5,360
Red fir, holly, elder, plane, crab	5,000 5,000
Cherry, hazel	4,760
Alder, asp, birch, willow	4,290
Lead	430
Freestone	914

He also gives the following practical rule, viz. That a cylinder, the diameter of which is d inches, loaded to one-fourth of its absolute strength, will carry as follows:—

	cwt.
Iron	$135 \times d^2$
Good rope	$22 \times d^2$
Oak	$14 \times d^2$
Fir	$9 \times d^2$

He also adds, that a cylindric rod of good clean fir, of an inch circumference, drawn in length, will bear at its extremity 400 lbs.; and that a spar of fir, 2 inches diameter, will bear about 7 tons, but not more.

A rod of good iron, of an inch circumference, will bear nearly 3 tons weight.

A good hempen rope, of an inch circumference, will bear 1000 lbs. being at its extremity.

Mr. Barlow gives the following table as a mean derived from his experiments on the strength of direct cohesion on a square inch of the following:—

	lbs.
Box, about	20,000
Ash	17,000
Teak	15,000
Fir	12,000
Beech	11,500
Oak	10,000
Pear	9,800
Mahogany	8,000

TRANSVERSE STRENGTH OF BEAMS, ETC.—The transverse strength of rectangular beams, or the resistance which they offer to fracture, is as the breadth and square of the depth: therefore, if two rectangular beams have the same depth, their strengths are to each other as their breadths; but if their breadths are the same, then their strengths are to each other as the squares of their depths.

The transverse strengths of square beams are as the cubes of the breadths or depths. Also, in cylindrical beams, the transverse strengths are as the cubes of the diameters.

Thus, if a beam which is one foot broad and one foot deep, support a given weight, then a beam of the same depth, and two feet broad, will support double the weight.

But if a beam be one foot broad and two feet deep, it will support four times as much as a beam one foot broad and one foot deep.

If a beam one foot square support a given weight, then a beam two feet square will support eight times as much. Also, a cylinder of two inches in diameter will support eight times as much as a cylinder one inch in diameter.

The following table of data is extracted from tables in Barlow's Essay:—

Teak	2,462
English oak	1,672
Canadian do.	1,766
Dantzic do.	1,457
Adriatic do.	1,383
Ash	2,026
Beech	1,556
Elm	1,013
Pitch pine	1,632
Red pine	1,341
New England fir	1,102
Riga fir	1,108
Mar Forest fir	1,262
Larch	1,127

Beam-ends. A ship is said to be on her beam-ends when she inclines very much on one side, so that her beams approach to a vertical position.

Beam-engine, generally a land engine, which has the top of the piston-rod connected to one end of a lever or beam; by a contrivance called a parallel motion, the beam vibrates upon a central axis, and communicates the motion of the piston to the crank by means of a connecting-rod attached to the other end of the beam, and also gives motion to the various parts.

Beam filling, the brickwork, or masonry, brought up from the level of the under to the upper sides of beams.

Beam gudgeons, the bearings on the

centre of the beam, or the central pivot upon which it vibrates.

Beam of a balance, the horizontal piece of iron from the ends of which the scales are suspended.

Beams, in naval architecture, strong thick pieces of timber stretching across the ship from side to side, to support the decks: they are sustained at each end by thick planks in the ship's side, called clamps, upon which they rest.

Bearer, anything used by way of support to another weight.

Bearer, in turning, that part of the lathe which supports the puppets.

Bearing, the distance that a beam or rafter is suspended in the clear: thus, if a piece of timber rests upon two opposite walls, the span of the void is called the bearing, and not the whole length of the timber.

Bearing, that part of a shaft or spindle which is in contact with the supports.

Bearing, a word used in describing a plaster figure copied from the antique. It is generally said, if the drawing or outline of a figure has not the same bearings or angles of inclination as the original possesses, that it is out in all its bearings.

Bearing, in heraldry, the figures on a coat of arms; a coat of arms in general.

Bearing, the direction of an object from the person looking. In shipping, the bearings of a vessel are the widest part of her below the planksheer; that part of her hull which is on the water-line when she is at anchor and in her proper trim.

Beat away, in mining, to excavate; usually applied to hard ground.

Beating, in navigation, the operation of making progress at sea against the wind.

Beaufet, a cupboard or niche.

Beaufrey, a beam or joist.

Beau idéal, in painting, that beauty which is freed from the deformity and the peculiarity found in nature in all individuals of a species.

Beauty, in architecture, consists of the following qualities: magnitude and strength, order and harmony, richness and simplicity; Construction, in which the chief requisites are magnitude and strength, order and harmony; Decoration, whose requisites are richness or simplicity, according to the nature of the composition.

Beazley (Saml.), an architect of reputation, particularly in the construction of theatres; he also executed with success many other buildings. Born 1786; died in 1851.

Becalm, to intercept the wind by alternate tacks.

Beck, a little river or brook.

Beck, an English weight containing sixteen English pounds, or two gallons.

Becket, a piece of rope, placed so as to confine a spar or another rope; a bundle made of rope in the form of a circle.

Bed of a brick, the horizontal surfaces as disposed in a wall.

Bed, a term used in masonry to describe the direction in which the natural strata in stones lie; it is also applied to the top and bottom surface of stones when worked for building.

Bed, in mining, a seam or horizontal vein of ore.

Beds, of stonework, are the parallel surfaces which intersect the face of the work in lines parallel to the horizon.

Beds and Bedding. Feather-beds, bolsters, and pillows, filled with feathers and down, with mattresses and every other comfort of this kind, seem to have been as well known to, and enjoyed by, the superior orders of society three centuries ago, as they are now. Directions are, however, mentioned as having been given in the reign of Henry VIII. "to examine every night the straw of the king's bed, that no daggers might be concealed."

Beds (Trussing) were beds which packed into chests, for travelling; and, considering the frequent removals, these must have been the most convenient kind. John of Ghent seems to have always slept in such beds, as by his will it appears that he demised to his wife all the beds made for his body, "called in England trussing-beds;" and the "best chambers" of both Master Fermor and Sir Adrian Foskewe had trussing-beds.

Bed-chambers: In Tudor times the furniture of these apartments, in great houses, was of the same gorgeous character as that in the chief rooms; and the paraphernalia of an ancient dressing-table yielded only in the splendour and costliness of plate, to the cupboard of the great chamber, or the altar of the chapel. Like the hall, the state bed-chamber had a high place, on which were placed the 'standing bed' and the 'truckle-bed:' on the former lay the lord, and on the latter his attendant.

Beddern, a refectory.

Bedding-stone, used in bricklaying, a straight piece of marble: its use is to try the rubbed side of the brick; first, to square, to prove whether the surface of the brick be straight; secondly, to fit it upon the leading skewback, or leading end of the arch.

Bed-mouldings. This may be understood as a collective term for all the mouldings beneath the corona or principal projecting member of a cornice, which, without bed-mouldings, would appear too much like a mere shelf.

Bed-plate, the foundation-plate of a marine or a direct-action engine.

Bedsteads: in Tudor times the posts, head-boards, and canopies or spervers of bedsteads were curiously wrought and carved in oak, walnut, box, and other woods, and variously painted and gilt. Ginger-colour, hatched with gold, was a favourite style, but purple and crimson were also used in their decoration.

Bede, among miners, a kind of pick-axe used for separating the ores from the rocks in which they lie.

Bedermen, almsmen who prayed for their benefactors and founders.

Bede-house, an almshouse or hospital.

Beech, a species of timber very much used by artificers: while young, it possesses great toughness, and is of a white colour: the cohesive strength of this timber requires 12,225 lbs. weight to tear asunder a piece one square inch in thickness.

Beech-wood, common in Buckinghamshire and Sussex as the best; about fifty feet high and thirty inches in diameter; white, brown, and black colour: it is used for piles in wet foundations; is used also, for its uniform texture and closeness, in in-door works, as the frames of machines, bedsteads, and furniture; also for planes, tools, lathe-chucks, keys, cogs of machinery, brushes, handles, etc.

Beef-wood, red-coloured wood, generally applied to Botany Bay oak.

Beer-drawing machines are contrivances by means of which beer is drawn from a barrel or cask.

Beer or *Bere stone,* composed chiefly of carbonate of lime, friable and with partial indurations. It is extensively quarried at Bere, or Beer, in Devon.

Bees, pieces of plank bolted to the outer end of the bowsprit, to score the fore-topmast stays through.

Beetle, or *Maul,* a large mallet to knock the corners of framed work, and to set it in its proper position: the handle is about three feet in length.

Beetle, or *Boyle,* a wooden instrument or hammer for driving piles, stakes, wedges, etc.

Before the beam, in naval architecture, is an arc of the horizon comprehended between a line which crosses a ship's length at right angles, and some object at a distance before it; or between the line of the beam, and that point of the compass which she stems.

Behr (Geo. Hen.), published in 1732 a work on Strasburg Cathedral.

Belace, Belage, or to *Belay,* to fasten any running rope when it is haled, that it cannot run forth again; to mend a rope by laying one end over another.

Belandre, in navigation, a sort of Norman vessel.

Belay, to make a rope fast by turns round a pin or coil, without hitching or seizing it.

Belfry, that part of the tower of a church which contains bells.

Bell (Henry), late of Glasgow, who, in 1812, tried Symington's plan for navigating by propulsion a steam-vessel on the Clyde. The vessel ('The Comet') was 25 tons burden, 40 feet long and 10 feet beam, with a steam-engine of four-horse power, which succeeded.

Bell, a metallic instrument rung in the belfry of a church for the attendance of divine worship, and upon occasions of rejoicing; composed of three parts of copper and one of tin, called bell-metal.

Bell : the body of a Corinthian or Composite capital, supposing the foliage stripped off, is called the bell; the same is applied also to the early English and other capitals in Gothic architecture which in any degree partake of this form.

Bell-cage, a timber frame, also called *Belfry,* carrying one or more large bells.

Bell-canopy, a canopy containing a bell in harness.

Bell-chamber, the room containing one or more large bells in harness.

Bell-cot, a structure presenting the appearance of a steeple.

Bell-crank, a bent lever, used for changing a vertical into a horizontal motion.

Bell-gable, a term applied to the gable of a religious edifice, having a plain or ornamental niche for the reception of one or more bells.

Bell-trap, a contrivance, usually air-tight, consisting of an inverted cup, the edges of which dip into a trench, gutter, or canal holding water, and formed at the top of a pipe, for the purpose of preventing foul smells ascending from the drain into the air.

Bellows, the instrument for blowing a fire, with an internal cavity so contrived as to be of greater or less capacity by reciprocating motion, and to draw in air at one place while the capacity is upon the increase, and discharge it by another while upon the decrease. The bellows are placed behind the forge with a pipe, and are worked by means of a lever, called a rocket. Steam machinery is now much used for blowing furnaces.

Bellows, or water blowing-engine, is a machine in which the stream of air is supplied by the flowing of water.

Belly, the hollow part of a compass timber, the round part of which is called the back.

Belt, in building, a string-course and blocking-course; a course of stones projecting from a wall, either moulded, plain, fluted, or enriched.

Belvedere, a turret, lantern, or cupola, raised above the roof of a building. It is sometimes applied in Italy to open galleries or corridors.

Belzoni (G.), an explorer of Egyptian antiquities; died in 1823.

Bema, an ambo, or reading-desk; a raised structure for the seat or throne of a bishop.

Bema, the sanctuary, presbytery, or chancel of a church.

Bema, in Greek, the platform from which the orators spoke in the Athenæum.

Bema, a bishop's throne.

Ben-alive, a Cornish term in mining.

Bench, for carpenters and joiners to do their work on, usually 10 or 12 feet in length, and about 2½ feet in width.

Bench-mark, in surveying, is applied to a mark showing the starting-point in levelling along a line, and to similar marks affixed at convenient distances to substantial or permanent objects, to show the exact points upon which the levelling staffs were placed when the various levels were read, thus facilitating reference and correction.

Bench-planes. The jack-plane, the trying-plane, the long-plane, the jointer, and the smoothing-plane, are called bench-planes.

Bench-table, a low stone seat round the interior of the walls of many churches.

Bend, in mining, indurated clay; a name given by miners to any indurated argillaceous substance.

Bend, the form of the ship from the keel to the top of the side, as the midship bend, etc.

Bends, the strongest parts of a vessel's side, to which the beams, knees, and futtocks are bolted.

Bending-strakes, two strakes wrought near the coverings of the deck, worked all fore and aft, about one inch or one inch and a half thicker than the rest of the deck, and let down between the beams and ledges so that the upper side is even with the rest.

Bending of timber. The process of bending wood to any required curve depends on the property of heat, as its pressure increases the elasticity of the wood.

Benefice, a church endowed with a revenue for the performance of divine service.

Benetier, a vessel to contain holy water; a font, or piscina.

Ben-heyl, in Cornish mining, rich in tin.

Bentick-shrouds, formerly used, and extending from the futtock-staves to the opposite channels of a vessel.

Benzine, the bicarburet of hydrogen, procured by heating benzoic acid with lime.

Bergamo, a coarse tapestry.

Bergmote, a court held on a hill, for the decision of controversies among miners.

Berne machine, for rooting up trees; the invention of Peter Sommer, of Berne.

Berth, the place where a vessel lies; the place in which a man sleeps.

Berth, convenient sea-room to moor a ship.

Berthying a ship, the rising up of the ship's sides.

Beryl, a pellucid gem, of a bluish-green colour, found in the East Indies, Peru, etc.; used by artists.

Bethel's patent for preserving wood. This patent was taken out in 1838, and consists in thoroughly impregnating the wood with oil of tar containing creosote and a crude solution of acetate of iron.

Betty, in mechanics, an instrument to break open doors.

Béton, the French name for concrete; béton is composed by first mixing the proper proportions of lime and sand, either by hand or by a pug-mill, in the same manner as for ordinary mortar.

Bevel, any angle except one of 90 degrees.

Bevel, in bricklaying, is for drawing the soffit-line on the face of the bricks.

Bevel, in joinery; one side is said to be bevelled with respect to another, when the angle formed by these two sides is greater or less than a right angle.

Bevel gear, in mechanics, denotes a species of wheel-work where the axis or shaft of the leader or driver forms an angle with the axis or shaft of the follower or the driven. In practice it is requisite to have finite and sensible teeth in bevel gear: these are made similarly to those of spur gear, except that in the latter they are parallel, while in bevel gear they diminish in length and thickness in approaching the apex of the cone: the teeth are of any breadth, according to the strength required. Bevel gearing is stronger, works smoother, and has superseded the face-wheel and trundle.

Bevelling, in ship-building, the winding of a timber, etc., agreeably to directions given from the mould-loft.

Bevel-wheel, a wheel having teeth formed so as to work at an angle either greater or less than half a right angle.

Bibbs, in ship-building, pieces of timber bolted to the hounds of a mast, to support the trestle-trees.

Bibliotheca, in Greek, the place, apartment, or building where books were kept.

Bicarbide of hydrogen. This gas is known by the names of light carburetted hydrogen, marsh-gas, fire-damp, and gas of the acetates. It is discharged from fissures in coal in large quantities, and from the bottoms of the pools in which there is vegetable matter.

Bice, a blue colour used in painting, prepared from the Lapis Armenius.

Bice, or *Bise*, in painting, a pale blue colour, procured by the reduction of salt to a fine powder.

Bicellum, the dwelling of a tradesman, having under it two vaults, for the reception of merchandise.

Bichoca, a turret or watch-tower.

Bier-balk, the church-road for burials.

Bifrons, in sculpture, double-fronted or faced, usually applied to Janus.

Bigelf, an arch or chamber.

Bigg, to build.

Bigger, a builder.

Bight, the double part of a rope when it is folded, in contradistinction from the ends.

Bilander, a small vessel with two masts, used chiefly in the canals of the Low Countries.

Bilboes, large bars or bolts of iron, with shackles sliding on them, used for criminals.

Bilage, the breadth of a floor of a ship when she lies aground.

Bilge-pump, that which is applied to the side of a ship, to exhaust or pump out the bilge-water.

Bilection-mouldings, those surrounding the panels, and projecting before the face of a door, gate, etc.

Bilge, that part of the floor of a ship which approaches nearer to a horizontal than to a perpendicular direction.

Bilge-pump, the forcing-pump worked by a marine engine, to discharge the bilge-water from the vessel.

Bilge-pump rod, the plunger-rod, or rod connecting the piston of the bilge-pump to one of the side-levers.

Bill, the point at the extremity of the fluke of an anchor.

Billet-moulding, an ornament used in string-courses and the archivolts of windows and doors.

Billiard-room. The apartment prepared for the reception of a billiard table, and therefore requiring to be of specific dimensions.

Billion, in numbers, the sum of a million of millions.

Bills, the ends of compass or knee-timber.

Bimedial line, in geometry, the sum of two medials. When medial lines, equal only in power and containing a rational rectangle, are compounded, the whole will be irrational with respect to either of the two; this is called a first bimedial line; but if two medial lines, commensurable only in power, and containing a medial rectangle, be compounded, the whole will be irrational, and is then called a second bimedial line.

Binary, in arithmetic, double.

Binder, one who undertakes to keep a mine open.

Binding-joists, those beams in a floor which support transversely the bridgings above and the ceiling-joists below.

Bindings, the iron wrought round the dead-eyes.

Binnacle, a box near the helm, containing the compass.

Binocular telescope, one to which both eyes may be applied.

Bins, for wine, open subdivisions in a cellar for the reception of bottles.

Birch-wood, a forest tree, common to Europe and North America; an excellent wood for turning, being of light colour, compact, and easily worked.

Bird (Edward), painter, born at Wolverhampton, April 1772, died November 1819.

Bird's-eye perspective is of two kinds, angular and parallel; it is used in the drawings of extensive buildings having spacious courts and gardens, as palaces, colleges, asylums, etc. The observer is supposed to be on an eminence, and looking down on the building, as from a steeple or mountain.

Bird's-mouth, in carpentry, an interior angle or notch cut in the end of a piece of timber for its reception on the edge of a pole or plate. It signifies also the internal angle of a polygon.

Bireme, a vessel with two banks or tiers of oars.

Birhomboidal, having a surface of twelve rhombic faces, which, being taken six and six, and prolonged till they intercept each other, would form two different rhombs.

Birthing, the working a top side, bulkheads, etc.

Bisection, in geometry, the division of any quantity into two equal parts.

Bishops, prelates holding baronies of the King or of the Pope, and exercising ecclesiastical jurisdiction over a certain extent of territory, called their diocese.

Bismuth. This metal is found native, crystallized in cakes, which generally contain small quantities of silver; it is also combined with oxygen, arsenic, and sulphur.

Bispia, a bishopric or episcopal palace.

Bissextile, or leap-year, a year consisting of 366 days, happening once every four years, by the addition of a day in the month of February, to recover the six hours which the sun spends in his course each year, beyond the 365 days usually allowed for it.

Bistre, a brown pigment, extracted by watery solution from the soot of wood fires, when it retains a strong pyroligneous scent. It is of a wax-like texture, and of a citrine-brown colour, perfectly durable. It has been much used as a water-colour, particularly by the old masters, in tinting drawings and shading sketches, previously to Indian ink coming into general use for such purposes. In oil, it dries with the greatest difficulty.

Bisturres, small towers placed at intervals in the walls of a fortress, forming a barbican.

Bit, an instrument for boring holes in wood, etc.

Bitter (a sea term), a turn of a cable about the timbers called bitts, when the ship lies at anchor. When a ship is stopped by the cable, she is said to be brought up by a bitter.

Bitternut-wood, a native of America, is a large timber wood, measuring 30 inches when squared; plain and soft in the grain, like walnut.

Bitts, in ship-building, perpendicular pieces of timber going through the deck, placed to secure anything to. The cables are fastened to them, if there is no windlass. There are also bitts to secure the windlass, and each side of the heel of the bowsprit.

Bitumen, a name for a number of inflammable mineral substances, known under the names of naphtha, mineral tar, mineral pitch, sea-wax, asphalte, elastic bitumen, or mineral caoutchouc, jet, mineral coal, etc.

Bituminous cement, a factitious substance, used for pavements, for roofs, and other useful purposes.

Bituminous limestone, a limestone of a lamellar structure.

Black, the last and the lowest in the series or scale of descending colours; the opposite extreme from white; the maximum of colour. To be perfect, it must be neutral with respect to colours individually, and absolutely transparent, or destitute of reflective power in regard to light, its use in painting being to represent shade or depth, of which it is the element in a picture and in colours, as white is of light.

Black-band Iron-stone, discovered by Mr. David Mushet, in 1801, while engaged in the erection of the Calder Iron-works. Great prejudice was excited against him by the Iron-masters, in presuming to class the wild coals of the country with iron-stones fit and proper for the blast furnace; yet that discovery has elevated Scotland to a considerable rank amongst the Iron-making nations of Europe, and produces an annual average income of £10,500 to Sir W. Alexander, Bart.

Black Botany Bay wood is the hardest and most wasteful of all woods; some of the finest, however, if well selected, exceeds all woods for eccentric turning.

Black chalk is an indurated black clay, of the texture of white chalk: its principal use is for cutting into the crayons which are employed in sketching and drawing.

Black dye: the ingredients of black dye are logwood, Aleppo galls, verdigris, and sulphate of iron, or green vitriol.

Black Iron, malleable iron, in contradistinction to that which is tinned, called white iron.

Black Jack, in mining, blende.

Black lead, plumbago, or graphite, is a native carburet of iron, or oxide of carbon, found principally at Borrodale in Cumberland; consumed in large quantities in the formation of crayons and black-lead pencils for writing, sketching, designing, and drawing.

Black marble. The marble called in commerce Nero Antico, and Egyptian black, is the most beautiful black marble without any admixture of other colours. In England the chief quarries of uniform colours and texture are at Ashford, Bakewell, Derby, etc.

Black ochre, a variety of the mineral black, combined with iron and alluvial clay.

Black tin, tin ore when dressed, stamped, and washed, ready for melting.

Black wadd, one of the ores of manganese, used as a drying ingredient in paints.

Blade, in joinery, is expressive of any part of a tool that is broad and thin, as the blade of an axe, of an adze, of a chisel, of a square: the blade of a saw is more frequently called the plate.

Blades, the principal rafters or breaks of a roof.

Blanc d'argent, or silver-white. This is a false appellation for a white lead, called also French white. It is first produced in the form of drops, is exquisitely white, but is of less body than flake white, and has all the properties of the best white leads; but, being liable to the same changes, is unfit for general use as a water-colour, though good in oil or varnish.

Blake (William), a poor but meritorious artist, was born in London, in November 1757. The Canterbury Pilgrimage was designed by him. His first work was, however, the Songs of Innocence; his next, the Gates of Paradise. Poverty-stricken as he was, his cheerfulness never forsook him; he uttered no complaint, he contracted no debt, and continued to the last manly and independent.

Blast, the air introduced into a furnace.

Blasting of stone, from rocks and beds of stone, for the purpose of quarrying and shaping stones to be used for building purposes: the ordinary implements used are the jumper or cutting-tool, the hammer, and scraper. For the process and its effect, see Sir John Burgoyne's Rudimentary Volume on Blasting, etc.

Blast-pipe, the waste steam-pipe of an engine, but more particularly applied to locomotive engines: in the latter it leads from the exhaust passages of the cylinders into the chimney, and is of great use for forming the draught through the fire-tubes, as each jet of steam emitted creates a partial vacuum in the chimney, which is immediately filled by a current of air rushing through the fire-grate.

Bleaching, an art divided into branches, bleaching of vegetable and animal substances requiring different processes for whitening them.

Blend, a mineral substance resembling lead.

Blende, in mining, an ore of zinc, composed of iron, zinc, sulphur, silex, and water: on being scratched, it emits a phosphoric light.

Blending and *melting*, in colouring or painting, are synonymous terms. They imply the method of laying different tints on buildings, trees, etc., so that they may mingle together while wet, and render it impossible to discover where one colour begins and another ends. A variety of tints of nearly the same tone, employed on the same object and on the same part, gives a richness and mellowness to the effect; while the outline, insensibly melting into the background, and artfully disappearing, binds the objects together, and preserves them in unison.

Bleontening, mosaic pavement.

Block, a lump of wood or stone.

Blocks, pieces of wood in which the sheaves or pulleys run, and through which the ropes pass.

Block cornices and *entablatures* are frequently used to finish plain buildings, where none of the regular orders have been employed. Of this kind there is a very beautiful one composed by Vignola, much used in Italy, and employed by Sir Christopher Wren to finish the second design of St. Paul's cathedral.

Block-house, a building erected by besiegers for the investment of a castle. Block-houses were erected in the time of Henry VIII. on the south and south-western coast of England.

Blocking-course, a course of masonry or brick-work, laid on the top of a cornice crowning a wall.

Blockings, small pieces of wood, fitted in, or glued, or fixed to the interior angle of two boards or other pieces, in order to give strength to the joint.

Block-machinery, the machinery for manufacturing ships' blocks, invented by the elder Brunel, and adjusted by the late Dr. Gregory.

Block-tin, tin cast into blocks or ingots.

Blondel (F.), architect, was born at Ribemont, in Picardy, in 1617. Principally employed in the construction of fortresses, and published several scientific works.

Blondel (J. F.), architect, son of the preceding, born in Paris, 1705. He published several very beautiful works.

Blondel (J. F.), architecte du Roi, was born at Rouen, in 1683, and stated to be a brother of François. He was extensively employed as an architect and decorator by the Court, and published many beautiful works.

Blondel (J. B.), architect to the city of Paris. Last of the family. He constructed the Temple, Marché St. Germain, etc.

Blood-red heat, the degree of heat which is only necessary to reduce the protuberances on coarse iron by the hammer, in order to prepare it for the file, the iron being previously brought to its shape. This heat is also used in punching small pieces of iron.

Bloom, a mass of iron after having undergone the first hammering.

Bloom (a), in iron-works, is in form a square piece 2 feet long.

Blower, in mining, a smelter.

Blowing, the projection of air into a furnace, in a strong and rapid current, for the purpose of increasing combustion.

Blow-off cock, the stop-cock in the blow-off pipe.

Blow-off pipe, the pipe fixed to the bottom of a boiler, for discharging the sediment, which is effected by blowing through a portion of the water from the boiler.

BLOW-PIPE.

Blow-pipe. The blow-pipe is a most valuable little instrument to the mineralogist, as its effects are striking, rapid, well characterized, and pass immediately under the eye of the operator. The most efficacious flame is produced by a regular, moderate stream of air; while the act of blowing with more force only has the effect of fatiguing the muscles of the cheeks, oppressing the chest, and at the same time renders the flame unsteady.

The student should fill his mouth with air, so as to inflate the cheeks moderately, and continue to breathe without letting the air in the mouth escape; the blow-pipe may then be introduced between the lips, and while the breathing is carried on through the medium of the nose, the cheeks will expel a stream of air through the blow-pipe; and by replenishing the mouth at each expiration, and merely discharging the *surplus* air through the nostrils, a facility will be acquired of keeping up a constant stream of air.

The best flame for the purpose of this instrument is that of a thick wax candle, such as are made for the lamps of carriages, the wick being snuffed to such a length as to occasion a strong combustion: it should be deflected a little to one side, and the current of air directed along its surface towards the point: a well-defined cone will be produced, consisting of an external yellow, and an internal blue flame. At the point of the former, calcination, the oxidation of metals, roasting of ores to expel the sulphur and other volatile ingredients, may be accomplished; and by the extreme point of the latter (which affords the most intense heat) fusion, the deoxidation of metals, and all those operations which require the highest temperature, will be effected. The piece of mineral to be examined must necessarily be supported on some substance; and for the earths, or any subject not being metallic, or requiring the operation of a flux, a spoon or pair of forceps made of platina will be found useful; but, as the metals and most of the fluxes act on platina, the most serviceable support for general purposes, will be a piece of sound, well-burnt charcoal, with the bark scraped off, as free as possible from knots or cracks: the piece of mineral to be examined should not in general be larger than a pepper-corn, which should be placed in a hollow made in the charcoal; and the first impression of the heat should be very gentle, as the sudden application of a high temperature is extremely liable to destroy those effects which it is most material to observe. Many substances decrepitate immediately they become hot; and when that is found to be the case, they should be heated red, under circumstances which will prevent their escape: this may be effected, with the earthy minerals, by wrapping them in a piece of platina foil, and, with the metallic ores, by confining them between two pieces of charcoal, driving the point of the flame through a small groove towards the place where the mineral is fixed, by which means a sort of reverberating furnace may be formed. The principal phenomena to be noticed are, phosphorescence, ebullition, intumescence, the exhalation of vapours having the odour either of sulphur or garlic (the latter arising from the presence of arsenic), decrepitation, fusibility; and, amongst the fusible minerals, whether the produce is a transparent glass, an opaque enamel, or a bead of metal.

Having first made some observations on a particle of the mineral alone, either the residue or a fresh piece should be examined with the addition of a flux, more particularly in the case of the ores, as the nature of the metal may be generally decided by the colour with which it tinges the substance used. The most eligible flux is glass of borax: a piece about half the size of a pea being placed on the charcoal, is to be heated till it melts; the particle of ore being then taken in a pair of forceps, is to be pressed down in it, and the heat applied; or, should the mineral not be inclined to decrepitate, it may be laid on the charcoal, and two or three pieces of glass of borax, about the size of a pin's head, placed over it; and on using the blow-pipe, the whole will form itself into a globular bead.

Blow-valve, the 'snifting valve' of a condensing engine.

Blue, one of the seven primitive colours of the rays of light, into which they are divided when refracted through a glass prism.

Blue-black is a well-burnt and levigated charcoal, of a cool, neutral colour, and not differing from the common Frankfort black. Blue-black was formerly much employed in painting, etc.

Blue carmine is a blue oxide of molybdena, of which little is known as a substance or as a pigment. It is said to be of a beautiful blue colour, and durable in a strong light, but is subject to be changed in hue by other substances, and blackened by. foul air: we may conjecture, therefore, that it is not of much value in painting.

Blue dyes, indigo, Prussian blue, logwood, bilberry, etc.

Bluing, the process of heating iron, and some other metals, until they assume a blue colour.

Blue John, fluor spar, called so by Derbyshire miners.

Blue ochre is a mineral colour of rare occurrence, found with iron pyrites in Cornwall, and also in North America, and is a subphosphate of iron. What Indian red is to the colour red, and the Oxford ochre to yellow, this is to other blue colours. They class in likeness of character: hence it is admirable rather for the modesty and solidity, than for the brilliancy of its colour.

Blue pigments, found in common, are Prussian blue, mountain blue, Bremen blue, iron blue, cobalt blue, smalt, charcoal blue, ultramarine, indigo, litmus, and blue cake.

Blue tint, in colouring, is made of ultramarine and white, mixed to a lightish azure. It is a pleasant working colour, and with it should be blended the gradations in a picture. It follows the yellows, and with them it makes the greens; and with the red it produces the purples. No colour is so proper for blending down or softening the lights into keeping. In pictures of less value, Antwerp blue may be substituted for ultramarine.

Blue verditer is a blue oxide of copper, or precipitate of the nitrate of copper by lime, and is of a beautiful light-blue colour. It is little affected by light; but time, damp, and impure air turn it green, and ultimately blacken it, — changes which ensue even more rapidly in oil than in water: it is, therefore, by no means an eligible pigment in oil, and is principally confined to distemper, painting, and the uses of the paper-stainer, though it has been found to stand well, many years, in water-colour drawings and crayon paintings, when kept dry.

Blue vitriol, sulphate of copper.

Bluff: a bluff-bowed or bluff-headed vessel is one which is full and square forward.

Blunk, heavy cotton cloth; the term is used in Scotland.

Board, a substance of wood contained between two parallel planes; as when the baulk is divided into several pieces by the pit-saw, the pieces are called boards.

Board, in nautical language, the line over which a ship runs between tack and tack. *To board* is to enter a ship.

Boarding-floors are those covered with boards: the operation of boarding floors should commence as soon as the windows are in, and the plaster dry.

Boarding-joists, joists in naked flooring, to which the boards are fixed.

Boarding-pike, a pike used by sailors in boarding an enemy's vessel.

Boasting, in masonry, the paring of a stone with a broad chisel and mallet.

Boasting, in sculpture or carving, is the rough cutting of a stone to form the outline of a statue or ornament.

Boats, small open vessels, impelled on the water by rowing or sailing, having different uses, dimensions, etc., either for river or sea service.

Boat-hook, an iron hook with a sharp point, fixed on a pole, at the extremity.

Boatswain, a warrant officer in the navy, who has the charge of the rigging, and calls the crew to duty.

Bob, the miner's engine-beam.

Bob, of a pendulum, is the metallic weight which is attached to the lower extremity of a pendulum-rod.

Bobstay-holes, those in the fore-part of the knee of the head, for the security of the bobstay.

Bob-stays, used to confine the bowsprit down to the stem or the cut-water.

Bocatorium, anciently a slaughter-house.

Bodium, a crypt, or subterraneous chapel.

Body, in physics or natural philosophy, any solid or extended palpable substance.

Body, or solid, in geometry, has three dimensions, length, breadth, and thickness. Bodies are either hard, soft, or elastic.

Body-plan, in naval architectural drawing, sectional parts showing fore and after parts of a vessel.

Boeria, anciently a manor-house or large country dwelling.

Bog, soft, marshy, and spongy matter, or quagmire. Railroads have been made across bogs in Lancashire and in America, by draining, etc., and in the latter by piling as well as draining.

Bog-iron ore, an iron ore discoverable in boggy land.

Boiler, a wrought-iron vessel containing water, to which heat is applied for the generation of steam. Boilers are made of various forms, according to the nature of their application, and are constructed so as to obtain the largest heating surface with the least cubical content.

Boilers. A boiler for 20-horse power is usually 15 feet long and 6 feet wide; therefore 90 feet of surface, or $4\frac{1}{2}$ feet to 1-horse power; a boiler for 14-horse power, 60 feet of surface, or 4·3 feet to 1-horse power; but engineers allow 5 feet of surface to 1-horse power, and Mr. Hicks, of Bolton, proportions his boilers at the rate of $5\frac{1}{4}$ square feet of horizontal surface of water to each horse-power: Mr. Watt allows 25 cubic feet of space to each horse-power.

Boilers. Iron cement is far preferable to any other material for making iron joints; it has the excellent property, that it becomes more sound and tight the longer it stands, so that cemented joints which at first may be a little leaky, soon become perfectly tight. The following is the best mode of preparing this iron cement: take 16 parts of iron filings, free from rust; 3 parts powdered sal-ammoniac (muriate of ammonia); and 2 parts of flower of sulphur; mix all together intimately, and preserve the compound in a stoppered vessel, kept in a dry place, until it is wanted for use. Then take 1 part of the mixture, add it to 12 parts of clean iron filings, and mix this new compound with so much water as will bring it to the consistence of a paste, having previously added to the water a few drops of sulphuric acid. Instead of filings of hammered iron, filings, turnings, or borings of cast iron may be used; cement, however, made entirely of cast iron is not so tenacious and firm as if of wrought iron; it sooner crumbles and breaks away. It is better to add a certain quantity, at least one-third, of the latter to the former.

BOILERS.

There is but little ground to fear for the soundness of a well-riveted iron boiler; for in time the action of rust and deposit will stop almost any crevices. In order, however, to take all precaution, it is to he recommended that some clammy substance, such as horse-dung, bran, coarse meal, or potatoes, should be boiled in the vessel before it is used. A very small quantity also of the same kind of substance may be put into the boiler when first set to work: this will find its way into the crevices by the pressure within, and, gradually hardening, will soon render the vessel perfectly sound.

Boilers. Copper is more tough and less liable to crack than iron, and is a most excellent material for high-pressure boilers: it has, however, a less cohesive power; and therefore a greater thickness of metal is necessary to produce an equal strength; but since copper boilers never fly in pieces in case of explosion, it is not necessary to be too scrupulous in regard to this point. Even when the metal is thin, especially if the diameter is not great, the use of copper removes all danger of destructive explosion, since at most only a simple tearing asunder of the metal will ensue.

Boiling, or ebullition, the agitation of fluids, arising from the action of fire, etc.

Bole, an argillaceous mineral, having a conchoidal fracture, an internal lustre, and a shining streak.

Bollards, large posts set in the ground at each side of the docks, to lash and secure hawsers for docking and undocking ships.

Bollard timbers, in a ship, two timbers within the stern, one on each side of the bowsprit, to secure its end.

Bolognese School, in painting, a Lombard school, founded by Caracci.

Bolognese School, the great painters of which were,—Francis Agostino, b. 1558, d. 1601; Domenichino, b. 1581, d. 1641; Guido Remi, b. 1575, d. 1642; Gio. Lanfranco, b. 1679, d. 1744; Ludovico Caracci, b. 1555, d. 1619; Annibale Caracci, b. 1560, d. 1609; Francesco Albani, b. 1578, d. 1660; Guercino, b. 1590, d. 1666.

Bolognian stone is derived from sulphate of baryta by calcination and exposure to the rays of the sun.

Bolster, a piece of timber placed upon the upper or lower cheek, worked up about half the depth of the hawse-holes, and cut away for the easement of the cable, and to prevent its rubbing the cheek; likewise the solid piece of timber that is bolted to the ship's side, on which the stantients for the linings of the anchors are placed; or any other small piece fixed under the gunwale, to prevent the main sheet from being rubbed, etc.

Bolster, a tool used for punching holes and for making bolts.

Bolster of a capital, the flank of the Ionic capital.

Bolt, a cylindrical pin of iron or other metal, used for various purposes of fastening, planking, etc.

Bolt-auger, an auger of a large size, used by shipbuilders.

Bolt-rope, the rope to which the edges of sails are sewed, to strengthen them.

Bolt-screwing machine, a machine for screwing bolts, by fixing the bolt-head to a revolving chuck, and causing the end which it is required to screw to enter a set of dies, which advance as the bolt revolves.

Bolts, large iron pins.

Bolts, long cylindrical bars of iron or copper, used to secure or unite the different parts of a vessel; the principal ironwork for fastening and securing the ship.

Bomb-vessel, a strong-built vessel carrying heavy metal for bombardment.

Bomb-ketch, a ship or vessel built with large beams, for carrying and raising of mortars at sea.

Bonarroti (Michelangiolo), born 1474, pupil of Domenico Ghirlandajo,—painter, sculptor, and architect: the most eminent of his country for his very great acquirements in the arts in which he so eminently practised.

Bond, in masonry, is that connection of lapping the stones upon one another in the carrying up of the work so as to form an inseparable mass of building.

Bond, in bricklaying and masonry, is the arrangement or placing of bricks, etc., so as to form a secure mass of building.

Bonders, Bond-stones, Binding stones, stones which reach a considerable distance into, or entirely through, a wall, for the purpose of binding it together.

Bond stones, are placed in the thickness of a wall, at right-angles to its face, to bind securely together.

Bond, in carpentry, a term among workmen,—to make good bond by fastening two or more pieces together, either tenoned, mortising, or dovetailing.

Bond timber, pieces of timber used to bind in brickwork especially. The naked flooring being laid, in carrying up the second story bond timbers must be introduced opposite to all horizontal mouldings, as bases and surfaces. It is also customary to put a row of bond timber in the middle of the story, of greater strength than those for the bases and surfaces.

Bongrace (a sea term), is a frame of old ropes or junks of cables, laid at the bows, sterns, and sides of ships sailing in cold latitudes, to preserve them from damage by flakes of ice.

Bone-brown and *Ivory-brown*, produced by torrefying or roasting bone and ivory, till, by partial charring, they become of a brown colour throughout.

Boning, in carpentry and masonry, the art of making a plane surface by the guidance of the eye: joiners try up their work by boning with two straight-edges, which determine whether it be in or out of winding,

that is to say, whether the surface be twisted or a plane.

Bonnet, in navigation, an additional piece of canvas attached to the foot of a jib, or a schooner's foresail, by lacings, taken off in bad weather.

Bonnets, the cast-iron plates which cover the openings in the valve-chambers of a pump: the openings are made so that ready access can be had when the valves need repairing.

Bonney (mining), a distinct bed of ore, that communicates with no vein.

Bonnington. In landscape his practice was to sketch in the outline and general character, and then make accurate studies of the local light and shade and colour.

Boom, in ship-building, a long pole run out from different places in the ship, to extend the bottoms of particular sails, as jib-boom, flying-jib-boom, studding-sail-boom, etc.

Boomkin, in ship-building, a beam of timber projecting from each bow of a ship, to extend the clue or lower corner of the foresail to windward.

Boor, a parlour, bedchamber, or inner room.

Booth, a stall or standing in a fair or market.

Boot-topping, scraping off the grease, or other matter, which may be on a vessel's bottom, and daubing it over with tallow.

Borax, in chemistry, a salt in appearance like crystals of alum; an artificial salt used for soldering metals.

Borcer, an instrument of iron, steel-pointed, to bore holes in large rocks, in order to blow them up with gunpowder.

Bord, anciently a cottage.

Bore, in hydrography, a sudden and abrupt influx of the tide into a river or narrow strait.

Boreas, the north wind.

Borer, a boring instrument, with a piece of steel at the end, called a boring-bolt.

Boring, the art of perforating or making a hole through any solid body; as boring the earth for water; boring water-pipes, either wood, iron, zinc, or lead; boring cannon, etc.

Boring. Modern steam-engines depend on the improved method of boring their cylinders. The cylinder to be bored is firmly fixed with its axis parallel to the direction in which the borer is to move: the cutting apparatus moves along a bar of iron accurately turned to a cylindrical form.

Boring-bar, a bar of a small horizontal boring-machine: it is used for boring the brasses of plummer-blocks, by means of a cutter fixed in it.

Boring-collar, in turning, a machine having a plate with conical holes of different diameters: the plate is movable upon a centre, which is equidistant from the centres or axes of the conical holes; the axes are placed in the circumference of a circle. The use of the boring-collar is to support the end of a long body that is to be turned hollow, and which would otherwise be too long to be supported by a chuck.

Boring-lathe, a lathe used for boring wheels or short cylinders. The wheel or cylinder is fixed on a large chuck, screwed to the mandril of a lathe.

Boring-machine, a machine for turning the inside of a cylinder.

Boromino (F.), born in Bissano, near the Lago di Lugano, in 1509. He was architect in the service of the family of the Visconti, and was architect of superb taste; many of his buildings are finely portrayed in M. Letarouilly's great work on Rome.

Boron, in chemistry, is an olive-green powder, which, heated out of the air, becomes harder, and darker in colour: it burns brilliantly when heated in air or oxygen, forming boracic acid.

Bosco (Jean de Sacro), a celebrated mathematician of the thirteenth century, who was so called from Holywood, a town in England of that name, which was his birth-place. After studying in the University of Oxford, he went to Paris and acquired great reputation by his knowledge of mathematics. He has left two works, valuable for their time, one entitled, 'De Sphæra Mundi;' the other, 'De Computo Ecclesiastico.' They are printed in one volume.

Boss, a sculptured keystone or carved piece of wood, or moulded plaster, placed at intervals of ribs or groins in vaulted and flat roofs of Gothic structures.

Boss, a short trough for holding mortar when tiling a roof: it is hung to the laths.

Bossage, projecting stones laid rough in building, to be afterwards cut into mouldings or ornaments.

Bosquet, a French expression for a piece of ground in gardens, enclosed by a palisade or high hedgerow of trees, etc.

Botany Bay oak, resembling in colour full red mahogany, is used as veneer for the backs of brushes, turnery, etc.

Bottle-glass, a composition of sand and lime, clay, and alkaline ashes of any kind.

Bottom-captain, a superintendent over the miners in the bottoms.

Bottom-heat, artificial temperature, produced in hothouses.

Bottom-lift, in mining, the deepest or bottom tier of pumps.

Bottom-rail, in joinery, the lowest rail of a door.

Bottoms, in mining, the deepest working parts of a mine, wrought either by sloping, driving, or otherwise breaking the lode.

Bottoms in fork. In Cornwall, when all the bottoms are unwatered, they say, 'the bottoms are in fork;' and to draw out the water from them, or any dippa, or any other particular part of a mine, is said to be 'forking the water;' and when accomplished, such dippa, etc., is 'in fork.' Likewise when an engine has drawn out all the water, they say, 'the engine is in fork.'

Boudoir, a small retiring-room.

Boulders, fragments of rocks transported by water, and found on the sea-shore.

Boulder walls, walls built of the above.

Boultine, in architecture, a convex moulding, whose periphery is a quarter of a circle, next below the plinth in the Doric and Tuscan orders.

Bounds, in mining, signifies the right to tin ore over a given district.

Boulevard, promenades around a city, shaded by avenues of trees.

Bourgeois (Nicolas), an Augustin, was the inventor of the pont-tournant. A reward of 1200 livres a year was offered to him who should invent a movable bridge to be placed over the ditch of the Tuileries.

Bourse, a public edifice for the assemblage of merchants to consult on matters of business or money, an exchange.

Boutant; in architecture, an arc-boutant is an arch, or buttress, serving to sustain a vault, and which is itself sustained by some strong wall or massive pile.

Bova, anciently a wine-cellar.

Bovey coal, wood-coal found at Bovey, in Devonshire.

Bow, the round part of a ship forward.

Bow, anciently an arch or gateway.

Bow-compass, for drawing arches of very large aisles; it consists of a beam of wood or brass with three long screws that bend a lath of wood or steel to any arch. The term also denotes small compasses employed in describing arcs too small to be accurately drawn by the common compasses.

Bow and string bridge, or bow-string or tension bridge; in which the horizontal thrust of the arch, or trussed beam, is resisted by means of a horizontal tie attached as nearly as possible to the chord line of the arch.

Bow and string beam, a beam so trussed that the tendency of the straight part to sag when loaded is counteracted to some extent by the tension upon its two ends, by a bow of wood or metal attached to those extremities.

Bower cables, for ships.

Table showing the different kinds of best bower cables at present employed in the British navy, with the corresponding iron cables, and the proof-strain for each:

Rates of Ships.	Best bower hempen cables, 100 fathoms. Circumf.	Weight.			Number of threads in each.	Breaking strain by experiment.			Diameter and weight of the bolt of the iron cable substituted for the preceding.	Strain for the proof.
	in.	cwt.	qr.	lb.		tons.	cwt.	qr.		tons.
First-rate, large .	25	114	2	7	3240	..			2¼ inches. 210 cwt.	81
middle	24	105	2	17	2988	..				
small .	23	96	2	27	2736	116	0	0		
Second-rate . .	23	96	2	27	2736					
Third, large . .	23	96	2	27	2736					
small . .	22	89	0	12	2520	89	0	0	2 inches. 166 cwt. 2 qrs.	72
Fourth, 60 guns .	21	80	0	22	2268					
58 do. .	19	66	0	21	1872	..			1⅞ inch. 170 cwt. 2 qrs.	63
50 do. .	18½	62	1	14	1764	..				
Fifth, 48 do. .	18	58	2	6	1656	63	0	0	1⅝ inch. 145 cwt. 0 qrs.	55
46 do. } 42 do. }	17½	56	0	1	1584	..				
Sixth, 28 do. .	14½	38	0	21	1080	40	0	0	1⅜ inch. 87 cwt. 2 qrs.	34
Ship, sloop . .	13½	33	0	10	936	..			1¼ inch. 74 cwt. 3 qrs.	28
Brig, large . .	13½	33	0	10	936	..				
Ditto small . .	11	21	2	15	612	..			1⅛ inch. 61 cwt. 1 qr.	23

From the preceding Table the immense advantage of iron cables will be distinctly seen, and particularly when it is considered that a hempen cable, on a rocky bottom, is destroyed in a few months, while the other will sustain no perceptible injury.

Bow and string girder, a wrought-iron bow and string girder, patented by Mr. G. Nasmyth.

Bower, anciently a small enriched chamber for ladies; a private room, or parlour, in ancient castles and mansions.

Bower, a working anchor, the cable of which is bent and veered through the hawse-hole.

Bower, in navigation, two anchors thus named from their being carried at the bow.

Bowerie, in the East Indies, a well descended by steps.

Bow-grace, a frame of old rope or junk, placed round the bows and sides of a vessel, to prevent the ice from injuring her.

Bowge (a sea term), a rope fastened to the middle of the sail, to make it stand closer to the wind.

Bow-line, in navigation, a rope leading forward from the leach of a square sail, to keep the leach well out, when sailing close-hauled.

Bowling-alley, a place where the game and exercise of bowling is carried on.

Bowl, *bowling*, or *bowline* (in a ship), a round space at the head of the mast for men to stand in.

Bowling-green. Bowling, an ancient English game, which was usually attached to the private grounds during the 16th, 17th, and 18th centuries.

Bowls of silver were used as drinking-glasses are now, before the introduction of glass for such purposes; they were of small sizes, in 'nests' fitting one within another. Of the larger-sized bowl, the most distinguished are the mazer and the wassail. Mazer is a term applied to large goblets, of every kind of material; but the best authors agree that its derivation is from *mazer*, which, in Dutch, means maple; and therefore that a mazer bowl was originally one formed of maple-wood.

Bow-saw, a saw used for cutting the thin edges of wood into curves.

Bowse, to pull upon a tackle.

Bowse away, a sea phrase, to pull all together.

Bowsprit, in ship-building, a large boom or mast which projects forward over the stem to carry sail.

Bowtel, the shaft of a clustered pillar, or a shaft attached to the jambs of a door or window.

Box, for mitring, a trough for cutting mitres: it has three sides, and is open at the ends, with cuts in the vertical sides at angles of 45° with them.

Box-drain, an underground drain built of brick and stone, and of a rectangular section.

Box of a rib-saw, two thin iron plates fixed to a handle, in one of which plates an opening is made for the reception of a wedge, by which it is fixed to the saw.

Box-haul, to veer a ship in a manner when it is impossible to tack.

Box the compass, to repeat thirty-two points of the compass in order.

Boxing-off, throwing the head sails aback, to force the ship's head rapidly off the wind.

Boxings of a window, the cases opposite each other on each side of a window, into which the shutters are folded.

Box-wood is of a yellow colour, inclining to orange; is a sound and useful wood, measuring from 2 to 6 feet long, and 2½ to 12 inches in diameter: it is much used by wood-engravers; for clarionets, flutes; for carpenters' rules, drawing-scales, etc. Much of it comes from Box Hill, in Surrey, and from several districts in Gloucestershire, also from other parts of Europe.

Boziga, anciently a house or dwelling.

Brace, a piece of slanting timber, used

in truss partitions, or in framed roofs, in order to form a triangle, and thereby rendering the frame immovable: when a brace is used by way of support to a rafter, it is called a strut: braces in partitions and span roofs are always, or should be, disposed in pairs, and placed in opposite directions.

Brace, an instrument into which a vernier is fixed; also part of the press-drill.

Brace, a rope by which a yard is turned about.

Braces, that security for the rudder which is fixed to the stern-post and to the bottom of a ship.

Bracket plummer-block, a support for a shaft to revolve in, formed so that it can be fixed vertically to the frame of a machine, or to a wall.

Brackets, ornaments: the hair bracket in ship-building is the boundary of the aft-part of the figure of the head, the lower part of which ends with the fore-part of the upper cheek. The console bracket is a light piece of ornament at the fore-part of the quarter-gallery, sometimes called a canting-hose.

Brackets, the cheeks of the carriage of a mortar; a cramping-iron to stay timber-work; also stays set under a shelf, to support it.

Bracket-stairs. "The same method must be observed, with regard to taking the dimensions and laying down the plan and section, as in dogling-stairs. In all stairs whatever, after having ascertained the number of steps, take a rod the height of the story, from the surface of the lower floor to the surface of the upper floor; divide the rod into as many equal parts as there are to be risers; then, if you have a level surface to work upon below the stairs, try each one of the risers as you go on; this will prevent any defect."

Brad, a small nail with a projecting head on one edge.

Brad-awl, the smallest boring tool used by a carpenter; its handle is the frustum of a cone tapering downwards; the steel part is also conical, but tapering upwards, and the cutting edge is the meeting of two basils, ground equally from each side.

Brails, in navigation, ropes by which the foot or lower corners of fore-and-aft sails are hauled up.

Brake, the apparatus used for retarding the motion of a wheel by friction upon its periphery.

Brake, the handle of a ship's pump.

Brake, a machine used in dressing flax.

Brake-wheel, the wheel acted upon by a brake.

Bramah's hydrostatic press consists in the application of water to engines, so as to cause them to act with immense force; in others, to communicate the motion and powers of one part of a machine to some other part of the same machine.

This press was constructed in Woolwich dockyard for testing iron cables, and the strain is produced by hydrostatic pressure; its amount is estimated by a system of levers balanced on knife-edges, which act quite independently of the strain upon the machine, and exhibit sensibly a change of pressure of $\frac{1}{8}$th of a ton, even when the total strain amounts to 100 tons.

This proving-machine was constructed by Messrs. Bramah, of Pimlico, and is doubtless one of the most perfect of the kind which has been executed. It consists of two cast-iron sides, cast in lengths of $9\frac{1}{2}$ feet each, with proper flanges for abutting against each other, and for fixing the whole to sleepers resting on a secure stone foundation. The whole length of the frame is $104\frac{1}{2}$ feet, equal to $\frac{1}{4}$th the length of a cable for a first-rate; so that the cables are tested in that number of detached lengths, which are afterwards united by shackle-bolts. The press is securely bolted down at one end of the frame, and the cylinder is open at both ends.

The solid piston is 5¼ inches in diameter in front and 10¾ inches behind, so that the surface of pressure is the difference of the two, viz.

$$\left(\overline{\frac{21}{2}}\Big|^2 - \overline{\frac{21}{4}}\Big|^2\right) \times \cdot 7854 = 65\tfrac{1}{4} \text{ inches.}$$

The system of levers hung on knife-edges is attached to the other end of the frame, and the cable is attached by bolt-links to this and to the end of the piston-rod. The levers being properly balanced, and the cable attached to a short arm rising above the axis, this draws the other arm downwards; and at a distance equal to twelve times the short arm, is a descending pin and ball, acting in a cup placed on the upper part of the arm of the second lever, and this again acts on a third. The first two levers are under the floor, and pass ultimately into an adjacent room, where a scale carrying weights is conveniently placed, and the whole combination is such that every pound in the scale is the measure of a ton strain; the whole acts with such precision that ⅛th of a pound, more or less, in the scale, very sensibly affects the balance. At the same place is situated a scale, acted upon by the water-pressure from the charge-pipe of the press, and the valve in this pipe is of such dimensions that, together with the lever by which it acts, the power is again such that a pound should balance a ton; but the friction is here so great that it requires several pounds to make a sensible change in the apparent balance, and for this reason this scale is never used. The forcing-pumps are in another adjacent room, and are worked by handles, after the manner of a fire engine. At first, six pistons are acting, and the operation proceeds quickly; but as the pressure and strains increase, the barrels are successively shut off, till at length the whole power of the men is employed on one pair of pumps only, and on this the action is continued till the proofstrain is brought on the cable. A communication is then opened between the cistern and cylinder, and everything is again restored to equilibrium.

Bramley Fall stone, a sandstone of the Millstone Grit formation quarried in the township of Bramley in Yorkshire.

Branch, in mining, a leader, string, or rib of ore, that runs in a lode; or if a lode is divided into several strings, they are called branches, whether they contain ore or not: likewise strings of ore which run transversely into the lode are called branches; and so are all veins that are small, dead or alive, *i. e.* whether they contain ore or not.

Branched-work, carved and sculptured leaves and branches in monuments and friezes.

Branches, anciently the ribs of groined ceilings.

Brandishing or *Brattishing*, a term used for carved-work, as a crest, battlement, or other parapet.

Brandrith, a fence or rail round the opening of a well.

Brass, a factitious metal, made of copper and zinc.

Brass, in the middle ages, a plate of metal inserted or affixed to a flat gravestone.

Brasses (Sepulchral), monumental plates of brass or mixed metal, anciently called *latten*, inlaid on large slabs of stone, which usually form part of the pavement of a church, and represent in their outline, or by lines engraved upon them, the figure of the deceased.

Brattishing, anciently, carved openwork.

Bray, anciently, a bank or earthen mound.

Brazil-wood, the wood of *Cæsalpinia echinata*, which yields a red dye: it is imported principally from Pernambuco: the tree is large, crooked, and knotty; and the bark is thick, and equals the third or fourth of its diameter. Its principal use is for dyeing: the best pieces are selected for violin-bows and turnery.

Braziletto-wood is of a ruddy orange colour, principally used for dyeing, and for turnery and violin-bows.

Brazing, the soldering together of edges of iron, copper, brass, etc., with an alloy of brass and zinc called spelter solder.

Breadth is applied to painting when the colours and shadows are broad and massive, such as the lights and shadows of the drapery; and when the eye is not checked and distracted by numerous little cavities, but glides easily over the whole. Breadth of colouring is a prominent character in the painting of all great masters.

Break, in shipping. *To break bulk*, is to begin to unload.

Break, a projection or recess from the surface or wall of a building.

Break joint, constructively, to disallow two joints to occur over each other.

Breaker, a small cask for water.

Breaking down, in sawing, is dividing the baulk into boards or planks.

Breaking joint, in joinery, is not to allow two joints to come together.

Breakwater, a human contrivance to ward off and diminish the force of waves, to protect harbours, stations, etc., from the violence of tempestuous gales. Some stupendous works have been executed for these purposes, especially that at Plymouth, by the late John Rennie.

Breaming, cleaning a ship's bottom by burning.

Breast, in mining, the face of coal-workings.

Breast-fast, a rope used to confine a vessel sideways to a wharf or to some other vessel.

Breast-hooks, pieces of compass or knee-timber, placed withinside a ship, to keep the bows together. The deck-holes are fayed to the timbers, and placed in the direction of the decks: the rest are placed one between each deck, and as many in the hold as are thought needful; all of which should be placed square with the body of the ship, and fayed on the planks. Breast-hooks are the chief security to keep the ship's bows together; therefore they require to be very strong and well secured.

Breast-knees are placed in the forward part of a vessel, across the stem, to unite the bows on each side.

Breast-plate, that in which the end of the drill opposite the boring end is inserted.

Breast-rail, the upper rail of the balcony or of the breastwork on the quarter-deck.

Breast-rope, a rope passed round a man in the chains, while taking soundings.

Breast-wheel, in mill-work, a form of water-wheel in which the water is delivered to the float-boards at a point somewhat between the bottom and top. Buckets are seldom employed on breast-wheels.

Breastwork, the stantions with rails on the quarter-deck and forecastle. The breastwork fitted on the upper deck of such ships as have no quarter-deck serves to distinguish the main-deck from the quarter-deck.

Breastwork, a mass of earth raised to protect troops from the fire of an enemy.

Breech, the angle of a knee-timber, the inside of which is called the throat.

Breechings, in a ship, are ropes by which the guns are lashed fast or fastened to the ship's side.

Breeze, small ashes and cinders used instead of coal for the burning of bricks.

Breastweall, anciently, a breast-high wall.

Breastsummer, a beam supporting a superincumbent part of an exterior wall, and running longitudinally below that part.

Brest, in architecture, is that column which is called the *thorus* or *tore*.

Bretachiæ, anciently, wooden towers, attached to fortified towns.

Brewhouse, a building specially built and appropriated for the brewing of beer.

Brick. "Let us make brick, and burn them thoroughly. And they had brick for stone, and slime had they for mortar."—*Gen*. xi. 3.

Bricks are a kind of factitious stone, composed of argillaceous earth, and frequently a certain portion of sand, and cinders of sea-coal (called breeze), tempered together with water, dried in the sun, and burnt in a kiln, or in a heap or stack called a clamp. For good brick-making, the earth should be of the purest kind, dug in autumn, and exposed during the winter's frost; this allows the air to penetrate, and divide the earth particles, and facilitates the subsequent operations of mixing and tempering.

The Romans made bricks of various sizes, from 1 foot to 2 feet in length, from 7 inches to 9 inches in breadth, and from 3½ inches to 1½ in thickness. Roman bricks found in the old Roman wall at Verulam, compared with modern bricks, show the superiority of the old to the new, the Roman bricks being lighter and better burnt than the modern.

The brick remains of the period of the Roman empire are more entire than the stone. Bricks were found at Toulouse, quite sharp at the edges, and not altered by time; they measured 14 inches long, 9 inches broad, and 1½ thick. These bricks formed the foundation all around the building. The arches were formed of them for entrances; and round, large, water-worn pebbles of quartz, with mortar, formed the walls of the Circus, resting on the brick arches.

Mr. Layard, in his work on Nineveh, says—"The soil, an alluvial deposit, was rich and tenacious: the builders moistened it with water, and adding a little chopped straw, that it might be more firmly bound together, they formed it into squares, which, when dried by the heat of the sun, served them as bricks. In that climate, the process required but two or three days. Such were the earliest building materials, and as they are used to this day, almost exclusively, in the same country.

"The Assyrians appear to have made much less use of bricks baked in the furnace than the Babylonians, no masses of brickwork, such as are everywhere found in Babylonia Proper, existing to the north of that province. Common clay moistened with water, and mixed with a little stubble, formed, as it does to this day, the mortar used in buildings; but, however simple the materials, they have successfully resisted the ravages of time, and still mark the stupendous nature of the Assyrian structures.

"This mode of brick-making is described by Sanchoniathon: The people of Tyre invented the art of brick-making and of building of huts; after them came two brothers: one of them, Chrysor or Hyphæstus, was the first who sailed in boats; his brother invented the way of making walls with bricks. From the generation were born two youths, one called Technites and the other Genius Autochthon. They discovered the method of mingling stubble with the loam of the bricks, and drying them in the sun; they also invented tiling."

Bricks. Some of Palladio's finest examples are of brick: the cortile of the Carità at Venice is an instance. The interiors of the Redentore and St. Giorgio, in the same city, have but a coat of plaster on them; the beautiful Palazzo Thiene at Vicenza, at least that part which was executed, is left with its rockworked basement in brickwork chipped out. Form alone fastens on the mind in works of art; the rest is meretricious, if used as a substitute to supersede this grand desideratum.

Brick-axe, used for axing off the soffits of bricks to the saw-cuttings, and the sides to the lines drawn: as the bricks are always rubbed smooth after axing, the more truly they are axed, the less labour there will be in rubbing.

Brick groins, the intersecting or meeting of two circles upon their diagonal elevations, drawn upon the different sides of a square, whose principal strength lies in the united force of elevation divided by geometrical proportions to one certain gravity.

Bricklaying, the art by which bricks are joined and cemented, so as to adhere as one body. This art, in London, includes the business of walling, tiling, and paving with bricks or tiles.

Brick-nogging, brickwork carried up and filled in between timber framing.

Brick trimmer, a brick arch abutting upon the wooden trimmer under the slab of a fire-place, to prevent the communication of fire.

Brick-trowel, a tool used for taking up mortar and spreading it on the top of a wall, to cement together the bricks, etc.

Bridge, a constructed platform, supported at intervals, or at remote points, for the purpose of a roadway over a strait, an inlet or arm of the sea, a river or other stream of water, a canal, a valley or other depression, or over another road: it is distinguished from a causeway, or embanked or other continuously supported roadway, and from a raft, by being so borne at intervals or at remote points. Constructions of the nature and general form and arrangement of bridges,—such as aqueducts and viaducts; the former, being to lead or carry streams of water or canals, and the latter, to carry roads or railways upon the same, or nearly the same level, over depressions,—are in practice considered as bridges, although they are not such in the commonly received sense of the term. Taken, however, in the sense which the most plausible etymology that has been suggested of the term would require, the word 'bridge' being formed by prefixing the constructive *be* to *ridge*, a bridge is an elevated construction upon, or over a depression, and between depressed points.

There are bridges built of the materials, stone, brick, iron, timber, wire, and on the principles of suspension; for the explanation of which, see the word *Suspension*.

The bridge across the Zab, at Lizari, is of basket-work. Stakes are firmly fastened together with twigs, forming a long hurdle, reaching from one side of the river to the other. The two ends are laid upon beams, resting upon piers on the opposite banks. Both the beams and the basket-work are kept in their places by heavy stones heaped upon them. Animals, as well as men, are able to cross over this frail structure, which swings to and fro, and seems ready to give way at every step. These bridges are of frequent occurrence in the Tiejari mountains.

Bridges. The principal object to be observed in forming the plan of a bridge, is to give a suitable and convenient aperture to the arches, so as to afford a free vent to the waters of sudden floods or inundations, and to secure the solidity and duration of the edifice by a skilful construction. The solidity of a bridge depends almost entirely on the manner in which its foundations are laid. When these are once properly arranged, the upper part may be erected either with simplicity or elegance, without impairing in any degree the durability of the structure. Experience has proved that many bridges either decay, or are swept away by sudden floods, by reason of the defective mode of fixing their foundations, while very few suffer from an unskilful construction of the piles or arches. This latter defect, however, is easy of correction, nor is it difficult to prevent the consequences that might be expected from it.

In the projection of a bridge, five principal points are necessary to be considered,—first, the choice of its position or locality; secondly, the vent, or egress that must be allowed to the river; thirdly, the form of the arches; fourthly, the size of the arches; fifthly, the breadth of the bridge.

Bridge-board, or notch-board, a board on which the ends of the steps of wooden stairs are fastened.

Bridged gutters are made with boards supported by bearers, and covered above with lead.

Bridge-stone, a stone laid from the pavement to the entrance-door of a house, over a sunk area, and supported by an arch.

Bridging-floors, floors in which bridging-joists are used.

Bridging-joists are the smallest beams in naked floorings, for supporting the boarding for walking upon.

Bridging-pieces, pieces placed between two opposite beams, to prevent their nearer approach, as rafters, braces, struts, etc.

Bridle, the spans of rope attached to the leaches of square sails, to which the bowlines are made fast.

Bridle-cable, in navigation. When a vessel is moored by laying down a cable upon the ground, with an anchor at each end, then another cable attached to the middle of the ground cable is called bridle-cable.

Bridle-port, the foremost part, used for stowing the anchors.

Brig, a square-rigged vessel with two masts.

Brine-pump, the pump in a steamship, used occasionally for drawing off a sufficient quantity of water, to prevent the salt from depositing in the boiler.

Brettingham (M.), an architect of some eminence of more than a century ago; built Norfolk House, in St. James's Square, in 1742; Langley Park, in Norfolk, in 1740-44, etc.

Brittleness, in iron, is a want of tenacity or strength, so as to be easily broken by pressure or impact: when iron is made too hot, so as to be nearly in a state of fusion, or so hard as to resist the action of the file, this is called the disposition of cast iron.

Broach, an old English term for a spire; still in use in some parts of the country to denote a spire springing from the tower without any intermediate parapet.

Broach-to, to fall off so much, when going free, as to bring the wind round on the other quarter, and take the sails aback.

Broadside, the whole side of a vessel.

Broken back, the state of a vessel when she is so loosened as to droop at each end.

Bromine, in chemistry, is found combined with silver in a few ores, also in sea-water and salt-springs; as bromide of potassium, sodium, or magnesium.

Bronteum, in Greek architecture, brazen vessels placed under the floor of a theatre, with stones in them, to imitate thunder.

Bronze, a compound metal, made of from 6 to 12 parts of tin and 100 parts of copper.

Brood, in mining, any heterogeneous mixture among tin or copper ore, as Mundick, Black Jack, etc.

Browning, a process by which the surfaces of articles of iron acquire a shining brown lustre: the material used to produce this is the chloride of antimony.

Brown (Sir Samuel), Captain, R.N. engineer of the chain-pier at Brighton; he was the first to introduce the bar-link.

Sir S. Brown has stated that at Brighton he found the impetus of the waves during heavy gales was "equal to 90lbs. to a foot upon a cylindrical column of 12 inches diameter." The hydrostatical pressure of a wave only 1¼ foot high is equal to 60lb. upon a square foot.

Brown ink. Various compounds were used in sketching by Claude, Rembrandt, and many of the old masters, the principal of which were solutions of bistre and sepia.

Brown ochre, Spruce ochre, or *Ochre de Rue,* a kind of dark-coloured yellow ochre; it is much employed, and affords useful and permanent tints. This and all natural ochres require grinding and washing over, to separate them from extraneous substances; and they acquire depth and redness by burning.

Brown-pink, a fine glazing colour having but little strength of body. In the flesh, it should never join or mix with the lights, because this colour and white antipathize and mix of a warm dirty hue; for which reason their joinings should be blended with a cold middle tint.

Brown-post, a name given by some builders to a beam laid across a building.

Brown spar, a magnesian carbonate of lime, tinged by oxide of iron and manganese.

Bruiser, a concave tool used in grinding the specula of telescopes.

Brunswick green, a pigment composed of carbonate of copper with chalk or lime.

Brush-wheels are used in light machinery, to turn each other by means of bristles or brushes fixed to their circumference.

Buata, anciently an arch of chamber; a crypt.

Bucca, anciently an almonry.

Bucentaur, the name of the once celebrated galley of Venice, used by the Doge on Ascension-day, to celebrate the wedding of the Adriatic, by dropping a ring into that sea.

Buckers, in mining, bruisers of the ore.

Buckets, in water-wheels, a series of cavities placed on the circumference of the wheel, and into which the water is delivered, to set the wheel in motion. By the revolution of the wheel the buckets are alternately placed so as to receive the water, and inverted so as to discharge it, the loaded side always descending.

Bucking, in mining, a term applied to a method of breaking the poor foul copper ore smaller by hand, with small flat irons, called bucking-irons, into order to wash and separate the pure ore from the useless waste: the same term is used in the lead-mines; but Pettus, in his 'Plata Miner,' gives it the signification of washing or wet-stamping ores.

Bucking-iron, in mining, the tool with which the ore is pulverized.

Buckler, a shield of armour, anciently used in war.

Bucklers, in ships, blocks of wood made to fit in the hawse-holes, or holes in the half-ports, when at sea.

Bucranes, in sculpture, the heads of oxen, flayed and lacerated, sometimes represented on friezes.

Buddle, in mining, a pit dug in the earth near the stamping-mill, 7 feet long, 3 feet wide, and 2¼ feet deep, where the stamped tin is curiously washed from its impurities by water constantly running through the buddle, while a boy, called a huddle-boy, is standing in the body of it, and working both with a shovel and with his feet.

Budget, a pocket used by tilers for holding the nails in lathing for tiling.

Buffers, rods with enlarged ends or striking-blocks projecting from the ends of the frame of a railway carriage, and attached to springs, for deadening the shocks received from the engines.

Buffet, a table with long narrow shelves over it; a convenient piece of furniture for a sitting room.

Buhl, unburnished gold.

Buhl-work, ornamental furniture, in which tortoise-shell is inlaid with wood and brass.

Builder, a term applied both in civil and naval architecture: in the former the builder is mostly employed under the superintendence of an architect, by contract, or at measure and value; in the latter, under the naval architect, mostly by contract.

Building, the art which comprises all the operations of an architect in building with stone, brick, timber, iron, cement, etc.

Buildings. Of the aspects best adapted to convenience and health, for the different kinds of buildings, Vitruvius writes: "The principles which should be attended to in allotting to each kind of building an appropriate aspect remain to be explained: the winter eating-rooms and baths ought to face the winter-west, because the use of them requires that they should be light at the time of the sun's setting: besides which, the western sun, being immediately opposite to them, renders their temperature mild at the close of the day. The sleeping apartments and libraries should be made to front the east, because the morning light is necessary for them; and books are better preserved when the air and light are received from that quarter. When libraries have a southern or western aspect, they admit those winds which, at the same time that they carry with them moths, instil also damp vapours into the books, which, in process of time, cause their decay. The vernal and autumnal triclinia should face the east, because the windows being turned from the sun's rays, whose heat increases as the sun advances towards the west, their temperature is cool at the hours they are generally used. The summer triclinia should front the north; because, having that aspect, they will be least exposed to the sun, and the temperature of the apartments will be grateful, at the same time that it is conducive to health. No other aspect possesses equal advantages; for the sun, during the solstice, would render the air of all others sultry. This aspect is necessary for pinacothecæ and the apartments in which the pursuits of embroidery and painting are followed, because the colours used in works of this kind retain their brightness longer when exposed to an equable and regular light." — Wilkins's Vit. p. 220.

Buildings Act, an Act of Parliament passed in the 18th and 19th of Victoria, to regulate the construction of buildings generally, and appurtenances thereto, and to determine their supervision by district surveyors and referees.

Building of beams, the joining of two or several pieces of timber together in one thickness, and of several pieces in one length, by means of bolts, so as to form a beam of given dimensions, which it would be impossible to obtain from a single piece of timber.

Buleuteria, among the Greeks, council-chambers or public halls.

Bulge, that part of a ship which bulges out at the floor-heads, to assist the ship when taking the ground.

Bulge-way, a large piece of timber, or pieces bolted together, making one solid piece, placed under the bulge of a ship, to support her launch. The support of the bulge-ways to lie on is called ways, which sometimes are placed straight and sometimes cumber: but if they do cumber, it should be truly circular; though sometimes the curve is quicker at the lower part, but this is liable to strain the sheer of the ship. Their extreme distance is generally about one-third the breadth of the ship, but this must depend on the form of the midship bend.

Bulk, the contents of the hold of a ship.

Bulker, a beam or rafter.

Bulk-heads, partitions built up in several parts of a ship, to form and separate the various apartments.

Bullantic, so-called ornamental capital letters, used in apostolic bulls.

Bullen-nails, such as have round heads with short shanks, turned and lacquered, used principally for hangings of rooms.

Bullet-wood, from the West Indies, is the produce of a large tree with a white sap; is of a greenish hazel, close and hard; used in the country for building purposes.

Bullet-wood, another species, from Berbice, is of a hazel-brown colour, adapted to general and eccentric turning.

Bull's-eye, a small circular aperture for the admission of light or air.

Bull's-eye, a small oval block of hard wood without sheaves, having a groove round the outside, and a hole in the middle.

Bulwarks, the woodwork round a vessel, above her deck, consisting of boards fastened to stanchions and timber-heads.

Bumboats, those which lie alongside a vessel in port with provisions for sale.

Bumpkins, pieces fitted above the main-rail in the head, which extend nearly as far forward as the fore-part of the knee of the head, and are for the use of hauling down the fore-tack.

Bunch, or *Bunchy*: a mine that is sometimes rich and at other times poor, is said to be *bunchy*.

Bunch, or *Squat*, in mining, a quantity of ore, of small extent, more than a stone and not so much as a course: a mine is said to be *bunchy* when these are found in place of a regular lode.

Bundle-pillar, a column or pier, with others of small dimensions attached to it.

Bunny, in mining, of tin or copper ore; a sombrero in Alonzo Barba; a pipe of ore; a great collection of ore without any vein coming into or going out from it.

Bunt of a sail, the middle part formed into a bag or cavity, that it may gather more wind.

Buntine, thin woollen stuff, of which a ship's colours are made.

Bunt-line cloth, the lining sewed up the sail in the direction of the bunt-line, to prevent the rope from chafing the sail.

Bunt-lines, ropes fastened to cringles on the bottoms of the square sails, to draw them up to their yards.

Buoy, a cask, or block of wood, fastened by a rope to an anchor, to point out shoals or particular spots.

Burden, in mining, the tops or heads of streamwork which lie over the stream of tin, and which must be first cleansed.

Burdon, a pilgrim's staff.

Bureau, a chamber or office for the transaction of state or business affairs.

Burges, the Persian word for Towers, evidently the same as the Gothic *burgh*; a fortified dwelling or enclosed town. *Gird* or *gard* is in Persian a city or fortress, which approximates to *garth*, an enclosure in the Gothic: hence *garden*. But a castle, comprehending towers and walls, is in Persian *calaa*.

Burgundy pitch, a resin collected from the spruce fir.

Burgus, anciently a number of houses protected by a fortress.

Burgward, anciently the custody or keeping of a castle.

Burgwork, anciently applied to a castle or borough.

Burin, an engraver's instrument; a graver.

Burners, for gas-light. Coal gas has now been used for the purposes of artificial illumination nearly fifty years, and the burners sanctioned by the companies at the present day are of several shapes.

Carburetted hydrogen of the specific gravity ·390 (which is about the density of gas when arrived at the point where it has to be burnt) requires two volumes of pure oxygen for its complete combustion and conversion into carbonic acid and water. Atmospheric air contains, in its pure state, twenty per cent. of oxygen,—in populous towns less; but twenty per cent. may be taken as a fair average: 1 cubic foot of carburetted hydrogen then requires for its proper combustion 10 cubic feet of air; if less be admitted on to the flame, a quantity of free carbon will escape (from its not finding a proper volume of oxygen for conversion into carbonic acid), and be deposited in the form of dense black smoke. When the flame from an Argand burner is turned up high, the air which rushes through the interior ring becomes decomposed before it can reach the air on the top of the flame, which consequently burns in one undivided mass, the gas being in part unconsumed, the products unconverted, and carbon deposited abundantly.

If an excess of air is admitted, it would appear at first to be of no consequence, but it will be found that the quantity of nitrogen accompanying this excess has a tendency to extinguish the flame, while it takes no part in the elective affinity constantly going on between the several elementary gases, viz. hydrogen, oxygen, and the vapour of carbon; and also that the quantity of atmospheric air passing through the flame unchanged, tends to reduce the temperature below that necessary for ignition, and therefore to diminish the quantity of light. For the proper combustion of the gas, neither more nor less air than the exact quantity required for the formation of carbonic acid and water can be admitted through the flame without being injurious. It is not possible practically to regulate the supply of air to such a nicety: it is preferred therefore to diminish the quantity of light by having a slight excess of air rather than to produce smoke by a deficiency, the former being unquestionably the least evil.

Burnet (James), a landscape painter: died in 1816, aged 28 years.

Burning-glass, a glass lens, which, being exposed directly to the sun, refracts the rays which fall upon it into a focus.

Burning-house, the furnace in which tin ores are calcined, to sublime the sulphur from pyrites: the latter being thus decomposed, are more readily removed by washing.

Burnisher, a tool used for smoothing and polishing a rough surface. Agates, polished steel, ivory, etc., are used for burnishing.

Burnt Carmine is, according to its name, the carmine of cochineal partially charred till it resembles in colour the purple of gold, for the uses of which in miniature and water painting it excels.

Burnt Sienna earth is, as its name implies, the Terra di Sienna burnt, and is of an orange-russet colour.

Burnt Umber, a pigment obtained from a fossil substance, which when burnt assumes a deeper and more russet hue: it contains manganese and iron, and is very drying in oil, in which it is employed as a dryer. It is a fine warm brown, and a good working strong colour, of great use for the hair of the human head, and mixes finely with the warm shade.

Burnt Verdigris is an olive-coloured oxide of copper deprived of acid. It dries well in oil, and is more durable, and in other respects an improved and more eligible pigment than in its original state.

Burré-stone, a mill-stone which is almost pure silex: the best kind is of a whitish colour.

Burrock, a small weir or dam, where wheels are laid in a river for catching fish.

Burrow, in mining, the heap or heaps of attle, deads, or earth (void of ore), which are raised out of a mine, and commonly lie around the shafts; any heap or hillock of deads or waste.

Burr-pump, a bilge-pump worked by a bar of wood pulled up and down by a rope fastened by the middle.

Bursa, a bag; a purse used in the middle ages for the purposes of a little college or hall for students.

Burser, one to whom a stipend is paid out of a fund set apart for poor students; the treasurer of a college.

Bursary, the treasury of a college.

Burthen, the weight or measure of capacity of a ship. Multiply the length of the keel, the inner midship breadth, and the depth from the main deck, to the plank joining the keelson together; and the product, divided by 94, gives the tonnage or burthen.

Burton, a manor; a manor-house.

Burton, in a ship, a small tackle of two single blocks, named from the inventor.

Bush, in machinery, a piece of metal fitted into the plummer-block of a shaft in which the journal turns. The guide of a sliding-rod also bears the same name.

Bush, a circular piece of iron or other metal, let into the sheaves of such blocks as have iron pins, to prevent their wearing.

Bushel, a dry measure of 8 gallons or 4 pecks.

Bush-harrow, an implement used in harrowing grass lands.

Buskin, a high shoe or boot worn anciently, in tragedy, on the stage.

Bushnell (David), A.M., of Saybrook, in Connecticut, in 1776 invented several machines for the annoyance of shipping; he destroyed a vessel in the charge of Commodore Simmonds, whose report to the Admiralty was published.

Buss, a small sea-vessel used in the herring fishery.

Bust, in sculpture, the head, neck, and breast of human figure.

Bustum, anciently a tomb.

But, the end of a plank where it unites with another.

But-hinges, those employed in the hanging of doors, shutters, etc.

Butmen cheeks, the two solid sides of a mortise varying in thickness.

Butments, the supports on which the feet of arches stand.

Butterfly-valve, the double valve of an air-pump bucket, consisting of two clack-valves, having the joints opposite and on each side of the pump-rod.

Butteris, an instrument of steel set in a wooden handle, used by farriers for paring the hoof of a horse.

Butternut-wood is of large size, and is produced in New Brunswick. The propagation of this tree is very easy, either from the cuttings or from the nut.

Buttery, a cellar in which butts of wine are kept; a place for provisions.

Buttock, the round part of a ship abaft, from the wing transom to the upper water-line, or lower down.

Button (in smithery), a brass knob of a lock serving to open or shut a door.

Button (in carpentry), a piece of wood upon a nail, to keep a door close.

Buttress, in Gothic architectural structures, a pilaster, pier, or masonry added to and standing out from the exterior of a wall. Buttresses are usually divided into several heights, each of which projects less from the wall as they ascend.

Buttress, a piece of strong wall that stands on the outside of another wall, to support it.

By, said of a vessel when her head is lower in the water than her stern; if her stern is lower in the water, she is *by the stern*.

Byard, a piece of leather across the breast, used by those who drag the sledges in coal-pits.

Byzantine Architecture. About the year A.D. 328, Constantine, who had previously resided at Rome, commenced his new capital in the East, which was called after his name, and in May, 330, was solemnly dedicated to the Virgin Mary. He adorned it with so many stately edifices that it nearly equalled the ancient capital itself: he here built a cathedral dedicated to Santa Sophia, or the Eternal Wisdom, and a church to the Apostles. This cathedral, having been twice destroyed by fire, was finally rebuilt about 532 A.D., by Justinian, who had invited the celebrated architect Anthemius to Constantinople for that purpose. It was completed in six years from the time of laying the first stone.

The Emperor, in his admiration of this magnificent edifice, is said to have exclaimed, "I have vanquished thee, O Solomon:" and with justice might he glorify himself, for the dome of St. Sophia is the largest in the world, and the more to be admired in its construction from the lowness of the curvature.

This church, after twelve centuries, remains the same, with the exception of the mode of worship to which it is devoted. It still retains its former name, but the Mahometans, instead of the Christians, possess it.

This is the earliest Byzantine building extant, totally dissimilar in arrangement to the Christian churches in the empire.

The plan of the interior is that of a Greek cross, the four arms of which are of equal length; the central part is a square, the sides are about 115 feet in length. At each angle of the square a massive pier has been carried, 86 feet in height from the pavement, and four semicircular arches stretch across the intervals over the sides of the square, and rest on the piers. The interior angles between the four piers are filled up in a concave form. At 145 feet from the ground is the level of the springing of the dome, which is 115 feet in diameter; the form is a segment of a circle, and the height is equal to one-sixth of its diameter at the base. On both the eastern and western side of the square is a semicircular recess, with domes that rest against the main arches, and assist in resisting the lateral thrust. On the north and south sides of the square are vestibules forming a square on the plan. Above the vestibules are galleries appropriated to women during the performance of worship. The whole church is surrounded by cloisters, and enclosed by walls.

The total cost of St. Sophia has been reckoned at the lowest computation to have exceeded one million pounds; as before the building was four feet out of the ground, its cost had amounted to a sum equivalent to £200,000 sterling.

Besides this cathedral, Justinian is said to have built, at Constantinople, twenty-five churches to the honour of Christ, the Virgin, and the Saints; he also built a church to St. John at Ephesus, and another to the Virgin at Jerusalem: the bridges, hospitals, and aqueducts erected by this emperor were numerously distributed throughout the empire.

Byzanteum artificium, mosaic-work.

C.

CABBLING. The process in the manufacture of iron, which in Gloucestershire is called 'scabbling,' or, more correctly, 'cabbling,' may be thus described. When the cast or pig-iron has been subjected to the influence of a refinery, the product is called 'Finery:' it is then carried to the forge, and smelted in a furnace with charcoal: in a short time, a large ball, about 2¼ cwt., is formed by working with an iron bar; this ball is then taken to a large hammer, and beaten into a flat oval or oblong shape, from 2 to 4 inches in thickness: this is allowed to cool, when 'cabbling' commences, which is simply breaking up this flat iron into small pieces. Men are especially allocated for this operation, and are named 'cabblers.' The pieces of iron obtained by cabbling are then heated in another furnace almost to fusion, hammered down into shape, and ultimately drawn out into bar-iron.

Cabin, a room or apartment in a ship where any of the officers usually reside, and also used in passenger vessels for the residence of passengers.

Cabinet pictures, usually denominated so, are small valuable paintings from the old masters, painted on copper, panel, or canvas. Modern subjects, if painted small in size, should equally be called Cabinet.

Cabinets, in Tudor times, were of massive proportions, carved in oak, ebony, walnut, and other woods, inlaid. Some of them answered the double purpose of depositories and cupboards for plate, from having drawers and recesses, or ambries, enclosed by doors; and broad shelves between the tiers of turned columns were conspicuous objects in these apartments.

Cable, a thick stout rope, made of hemp, etc., to keep a ship at anchor.

Cable-moulding, a bead or torus moulding, cut in imitation of the twisting of a rope, much used in the later period of the Norman style.

Cabling, a round moulding, frequently used in the flutes of columns, pilasters, etc.

Cadmia, a stone, out of which brass is tried; brass ore.

Caduceus, an emblem or attribute of Mercury: a rod entwined by two winged serpents.

Cælatura (Greek), a branch of the fine arts, under which all sorts of ornamental work in metal, except actual statues, appear to be included.

Cæmenticius, built of unhewn stones; large irregular masses laid together without mortar, having the interstices filled in with small chippings.

Caen stone, a peculiar quality of stone used for building purposes, principally for Gothic structures; it is taken from quarries in Normandy.

Cagework, the uppermost carved work of the hull of a ship.

Caisson, a wooden frame or box with a flat bottom, made of strong timbers firmly connected together; used for laying the foundations of a bridge in situations where the coffer-dam cannot be adopted.

Caisson, a name given to the sunk panels of various geometrical forms symmetrically disposed in flat or vaulted ceilings, or in soffits generally.

Cal, in Cornish mining, a kind of iron Gossan stone found in the bryle and backs of lodes, much of the colour of old iron; reckoned a poor brood with tin.

Calcar, a small oven or reverberatory furnace, in which the first calcination of sand and potashes is made for turning them into frit, from which glass is ultimately made.

Calcareous earth, the same as lime, and of which there are various combinations, as marble, limestone, marl, gypsum, etc.

Calcatorium, among the Romans, a raised platform of masonry in the cellar attached to a vineyard.

Calcination, the process of subjecting a body to the action of fire, to drive off the volatile parts, whereby it is reduced to a condition that it may be converted into a powder: thus marble is converted into lime by driving off the carbonic acid and water; and gypsum, alum, borax, and other saline bodies are said to be calcined when they are deprived of their water of crystallization.

Calcium, the metallic basis of lime.

Calcography, writing, engraving, etc.

Calculating machines are of early invention; but recently Mr. Babbage has completed a calculating machine surpassing all previous ones; the machine accomplishes the additions of numbers by the movements of a number of cylinders having on the convex surface of each the series of numbers 1 2 3 4 5 6 7 8 9 0; and the operations are of two kinds: by the first the additions are made, and by the second there is introduced the 1, which should be carried to the ten's place every time that the sum of the two numbers is greater than 10, etc.

Caldarium, the hot bath. The vase which supplied the hot bath was likewise so termed. According to Vitruvius, the thermal chamber in a set of baths.

Calender, a mechanical engine for dressing and finishing cloths.

Calends, in Roman antiquity, the first day of every month.

Caliber or *Caliper compasses;* compasses made with bowed or arched legs, for the purpose of taking the diameter of any round body.

Caliber, an instrument used by carpenters, joiners, and bricklayers, to see whether their work be well squared.

Calico, a cloth made from cottonwool, like linens: the origin of the name is from Calicut, in India.

Calico-printing, the art of applying coloured patterns on a white or coloured ground of linen or cotton.

Calidnets, pipes or canals disposed along the walls of houses and apartments; used by the ancients for conveying heat to several remote parts of the house.

Caligraphy, fair or good writing.

Calin, a mineral, like lead and tin.

Calk, a Cornish term for lime.

Callipers, a species of compasses with legs of a circular form, used to take the thickness or diameter of work, either circular or flat; used also to take the interior size of holes.

Callipers, in turning, compasses with each of the legs bent into the form of a curve, so that when shut the points are united; and the curves, being equal and opposite, enclose a space. The use of the callipers is to try the work in the act of turning, in order to ascertain the diameter or the diameters of the various parts. As the points stand nearer together at the greatest required diameter than the parts of the legs above, the callipers are well adapted to the use intended.

Callys or *Killas* (Cornish), hard, smart; the most common and agreeable stratum in our mine country, usually called killas.

Caloric, the matter and cause of heat.

Caloric (Ericsson's) *ship* has undergone a great experiment in navigation. Wise men have long pondered the idea which Captain Ericsson is working out patiently and hopefully. The need of new motors has become more manifest with the advance of time and commercial prosperity. Electricity has been tried, and has not succeeded. Caloric was something never known in its best sense until now, and the credit is due to Captain Ericsson of directing attention to an old agent of which new applications may produce the most remarkable results. The experiment now making is no ephemeral fancy, but is the work of a quarter of a century of mature reflection and diligent inquiry. The ingenious projector under whose auspices it is carried forward has devoted his best energies to the task, and it will not fail through want of forecast, judgment, or ability.

Calorific, in chemistry, the quality of producing heat.

Calorimeter, an instrument to measure the heat given out by a body in cooling by the quantity of ice it melts.

Calotte, a round cavity or depressure in form of a cap or cup.

Calquing, the process of copying or transferring a drawing. It is effected by rubbing over the back of the original with a fine powder of red chalk or black lead; the smeared side is then laid on a sheet of paper, and the lines of the drawing are traced by a blunt-pointed needle, which imprints them on the paper underneath. Another method is to hold the drawing up to a window with a sheet of paper before it: the outlines will appear through, and may be pencilled off without damage to the original.

Calyon, flint or pebble stone, used in building walls, etc.

Cam, in steam machinery, a plate with curved sides, triangular or otherwise, fixed upon a revolving shaft, for changing the uniform rotatory motion into an irregular rectilinear motion. It is sometimes used for moving the slide-valves.

Camaieu, a term used in painting when there is only one colour, the light and shades being of gold, or on a golden and azure ground. It is chiefly used to represent basso-rilievo.

Camber, the convexity of a beam upon the upper surface, in order that it may not become concave by its own weight, or by the hinder it may have to sustain, in the course of time.

Camber-beams, are those used in the flats of truncated roofs, and raised in the middle with an obtuse angle, for discharging the rain-water towards both sides of the roof.

Camber-slip, a piece of wood, generally about half an inch thick, with at least one curved edge rising about 1 inch in 6 feet, for drawing the soffit-lines of straight arches: when the other edge is curved, it rises only to about one-half of the other, viz. about half an inch in 6 feet, for the purpose of drawing the upper side of the arch so as to prevent it from becoming hollow by the settling of the bricks. The upper edge of the arch is not always cambered, some persons preferring it to be straight. The bricklayer is always provided with a camber-slip, which, being sufficiently long, answers to many different widths of openings: when he has done drawing his arch, he gives the camber-slip to the carpenter, in order to form the centre to the required curve of the soffit.

Cambering, a sea phrase, used when a deck is higher in the middle than at the ends.

Camel, the name of a machine used by the Dutch for carrying vessels heavily laden over the sand-banks in the Zuyder Zee.

Camera (Greek), an arched or vaulted roof, covering, or ceiling, formed by circular bands or beams of wood, over the intervals of which a coating of lath and plaster was spread: they resembled, in their construction, the hooped awnings now commonly in use.

Camera-lucida, and *Camera-obscura*, (the light and dark chamber,) the names given to two methods, similar in principle, of throwing images of external objects upon plane or curved surfaces, for the purpose of drawing or amusement: in the first contrivance there is no chamber; but as it was the last invented, and as its predecessor had been called the 'camera-obscura,' it was termed the 'camera-lucida.'

Camerated, a term applied to the roof of a church.

Cameron (C.), architect; published in 1772 and 1775, editions of the work on the Baths of the Romans.

Cames, the slender rods of metal used by glaziers as turned lead; they are usually cast in lengths which measure 12 or 14 inches.

Caminus, according to Pliny, a smelting furnace.

Campana or *Campanula* or *Gutta*, the drops of the Doric architrave.

Campanile, from the Italian, a bell-tower, principally used for church purposes, but now sometimes for domestic edifices.

Campanini, a species of marble taken out of the mountain of Carrara, in Tuscany; so called because, when wrought, it imitates the sound of a bell.

Campanologia, the art or science of ringing of bells.

Campbell (C.), an architect of his period of some celebrity; erected several of the large mansions of the nobility and gentry of this

CANAL NAVIGATION.

country, and first published his great work, entitled 'Vitruvius Britannicus,' in 1715.

Camphor-wood is imported from China and the Indies in logs and planks of large size, and used in England for cabinet-work and turnery.

Campus Martius, a district outside the walls of ancient Rome, between the Quirinal and Pincian Mounts and the Tiber, dedicated to Mars: there public exercises were performed, and the consuls and other magistrates elected: it was adorned with statues, columns, arches, etc., and much frequented by the citizens.

Camus de Mézières (M. le), born at Paris in 1721, and died in 1789: he was the architect of the Halle au Blé and other buildings, and the author of several valuable professional works.

Cam-wood, the best and hardest of the red dye-woods: it is brought from Africa, and used in ornamental and eccentric turnery.

Can, a term used in Scotland for a chimney-pot.

Canal of the larmier, in architecture, the hollowed plafond or soffit of a cornice, which makes the pendent mouchette.

Canal of the volute, in the Ionic capital, is the face of the circumvolutions enclosed by a listel.

Canal Navigation, or river and inland navigation, or internal communication by water, terms severally expressed.—The origin of inland navigation is involved in great obscurity. The ancient inhabitants of every part of the globe wherewith history has made us acquainted, were alive to the benefits resulting from the adoption of inland navigation: In England, the first on record is the Caerdike, cut by the Romans. Subsequently, very many very important ones, particularly those by Brindlay, under the direction of the celebrated Duke of Bridgewater; and as late as 1829, the science of canal engineering was in active operation. Canals in France for 'grande navigation' are made 33 feet 4 inches wide upon the floor-line, and 49 feet 6 inches upon the water-line, by 5 feet 5 inches depth of water. The locks are 106 feet 8 inches long by about 17 feet wide; the towing-paths 13 feet wide. Canals for 'petite navigation' are made only 33 feet 4 inches wide upon the water-line, and 22 feet on the floor, with a depth of water of 5 feet. The locks are 100 feet long by 9 feet 1 inch wide. Some of the French canals for steam navigation have locks from 26 to 40 feet wide, and of lengths between 150 and 233 feet in clear of gates.—In England, no very definite rule appears to be followed in fixing the dimensions of canals. Those executed for the internal important lines vary from 31 to 48 feet upon the water-line, with an average depth of about 5 feet. The locks are generally 70 feet in length by 14 feet 6 inches to 18 feet wide. Small canals, in the mining districts, have in some cases been executed with a width of not more than 16 feet on the water-line, and they range from that to 28 feet. The locks are made of the same length as for large canals, but of only half the width. Ship-canals have been made of much larger dimensions, such as the Caledonian Canal, which has in part 122 feet upon the water-line, with a depth of 20 feet. The Gloucester and Berkeley Canal has a water-line of 70 feet and a depth of 18 feet. The Thames and Medway had a width of 50 feet by a depth of 7 feet; the Ulverstone, 65 feet by 15 feet: the locks being in proportion to the size of the canals. In the United States the same irregularity occurs in the dimensions of canals as in our own country.

Canal, an artificial watercourse for connecting rivers and lakes; a navigable communication.

Canalis, in Latin, a water-pipe or gutter; used in architecture for any

CANDLESTICKS.

channel, such as the flutings of columns; the channel between the volutes of an Ionic column.

Canary-wood, from South America, is a round, light, orange-coloured wood, used for cabinet-work, musketry, and turnery.

Cancelli, among the Romans, iron gratings and trellis-work; in modern buildings, latticed windows made with cross-bars of wood, iron, lead, etc.

Candela, a candle, made either of wax or tallow; used generally by the Romans before the invention of lamps.

Candelabrum, originally a candlestick, but afterwards used to support lamps.

Candlemas, the popular name for the feast of the Purification of the Virgin Mary, February 2, derived from the lights which were then distributed and carried about in procession.

Candlestick of gold (The) was made by Moses for the service of the Temple, and consisted wholly of pure gold: it had seven branches, upon the extremities of which were seven gold lamps, which were fed with pure olive oil, and lighted every evening by the priest on duty: it was used in the holy place, and served to illumine the altar of incense and the table of shew-bread, which stood in the same chamber.

Candlesticks. The magnificence of these articles was at first displayed in chapels and in domestic apartments, as banquets in early times were given by daylight. We find them, however, of very costly descriptions. In Henry the Eighth's temporary banqueting-room, at Greenwich, the "candlestykes were of amyke worke, which bare little torchetts of white waxe: these candlestykes were polished lyke ambre."

Cangica-wood, from South America, is of a light and yellow-brown colour, used for cabinet-work and turnery.

Can-hooks, strings with flat hooks at each end, used for hoisting barrels or light casks.

Canopy, a covering or hood, the enriched projecting head to a niche or tabernacle. The tablet or dripstone, whether straight or circular, over the heads of doors or windows, if enriched, is so called.

Canopy, in Gothic architecture, an ornamental projection over doors, windows, etc.; a covering over niches, tombs, etc.

Cant, a term used among carpenters to express the cutting off the angle of a square.

Canted, applied to a pillar or turret when the plan is of a polygonal form.

Canterbury (John), born at Tewksbury, was clerk of the works of King's College Chapel, Cambridge, of which College he was a Fellow in 1451.

Canterbury (Michael of), erected in 1291-93, the Cross in Westcheap, London, which was the handsomest, except Charing, of all that were erected to the memory of Queen Eleanor.

Canterii, beams of wood in the framework of a roof, extending from the ridge to the eaves, corresponding to the rafters of a modern roof. The word canterii was also applied to two inclining reeds fixed in the ground some distance asunder and meeting at the top, for the support of vines.

Cantharus, a fountain or cistern in the atrium or court-yard before ancient churches, at which persons washed before they entered the sacred buildings.

Canthus, in Greek and Latin, the tire of a wheel; a hoop of iron or bronze fastened on to the felloe, to preserve the wood from abrasion.

Cantilevers are horizontal rows of timbers, projecting at right angles from the naked part of a wall, for sustaining the eaves or other mouldings.

Cantling. The lower of two courses of burnt bricks, which are placed on the top of a clamp before fire is applied.

Cant-moulding, a bevelled surface, neither perpendicular to the horizon nor to the vertical surface to which it may be attached.

Cantoned, in architecture, is when the corner of a building is adorned with a pilaster, an angular column, rustic quoins, or anything that projects beyond the wall.

Cant-pieces, in ships, pieces of timber fastened to the angles of fishes and side-trees, to supply any part that may prove rotten.

Cant-timbers, in ship-building, those timbers or ribs of the ship which are situated afore or abaft, or at the two ends, where the ship grows narrower below.

Cant-timber abaft, the chock upon which the spanker-boom rests when the sail is not set.

Cantuar. The signature of the Archbishop of Canterbury, is thus abbreviated, the Christian name being usually prefixed.

Canvas, the cloth of which the sails of ships are made.

Caoutchouc, a substance produced by the siphonia elastica, the ficus elastica, and the urceola elastica, and many other American and Asiatic trees. It is often termed Indian-rubber, from its use in removing pencil traces from paper. There are various chemical properties which render caoutchouc valuable in the arts, but elasticity and imperviousness to water are those for which it is most prized. It is worked into a great variety of useful things for dress and for domestic purposes.

Cap, a thick, strong block of wood, with two holes through it, one square and the other round, used in ship-building to confine together the head of a mast and the lower part of that next above it.

Capacity, the same in sense as content or volume in pure mathematics. In physics it generally signifies the power of holding or retaining: thus we speak of the capacity of a body for heat, etc.

Capel, in mining, a stone composed of quartz, schorl, and hornblende, usually occurring in one or both walls of a lode, and more frequently accompanying tin than copper ores.

Capillary attraction and *repulsion.* These names have been given to the properties of matter which cause the ascent above or descent below the level of the surrounding fluid which takes place when a tube of small diameter is dipped into water, mercury, etc.

Capital, in architecture, the head or uppermost part of a column or pilaster. The capitals of the columns constitute the principal and most obvious indicial mark of the respective orders. For those of each of the three classes or orders a certain character conformable with the rest of the order is to be observed; but that attended to, further restriction is unnecessary. Between several examples, all decidedly referable to one and the same order, very great special differences occur, and there might easily be a very great many more. Although the capital itself is indispensable, it is so only æsthetically, and not out of positive necessity. The necessity is only artistic: decoration of the kind there must be, but the express mode of it is one of those matters which should be left to design, to which it properly belongs. Capitals are just as legitimate subjects for the exercise of taste and invention as anything else in decorative design. The capital is only an ornamental head to the column, and therefore admits of being as freely designed as any other piece of ornament, on the conditions of its being accordant in character with the rest of the order, and of forming an agreeable transition from the shaft of the column to the architrave.

Capitolium, a temple or citadel at Rome, on the Tarpeian rock: it was finished by Tarquinius Superbus, and consecrated by the consul M. Horatius,—was burnt in the time of Marius, and rebuilt by Sylla,—destroyed a second and a third time in the troubles under Vitellius and Vespasian, and lastly raised again by Domitian. Its name was derived from the discovery of the head of *Tolius*, during the excavation of the earth for the foundation. Q. Catulus consecrated it to Jupiter Capitolinus, and covered it with gilded brass tiles. The steep ascent of the rock was mounted by 100 steps on the side of the forum. In the temple were statues of gold and silver, vessels of those metals and of crystal, and 3000 brass tables, on which the Roman laws were engraved.

Caple (in Cornwall) *stone* is something like limestone, but will not burn. The walls of most lodes are of this kind, and therefore it is common to call a lode by the name of its caple: those veins which abound with it are termed caples or caple-lodes.

Capreoli, the pieces of timber on a roof which serve to uphold the axes or principals. A fork inclined so as to afford support to anything was formerly called a *Capreolus*.

Capsa or *Capsula*, a box for holding books among the Romans: these boxes were usually made of beech wood, and were cylindrical in form.

Capsize, to overturn.

Capstan, in naval architecture, a strong massive piece of timber let down through the decks of a ship, and resting its foot or axis, which is shod with iron, in an iron socket, called a saucer, fixed on a wooden block or standard, called the step, resting on the beams.

Captain, in mining, an experienced miner; one who directs and oversees the workmen and business of a mine.

Caracol, a term sometimes used for a staircase in a helix or spiral form.

Caradoc formation, the uppermost of the two great divisions of the lower Silurian strata of Murchison, seen principally in Shropshire, Worcestershire, Somersetshire, etc., and on the eastern borders of Wales.

Caravanserai, a building in the East, expressed in our version of the Scripture by the term Inn; in Turkey it is understood to be a place of accommodation for strangers and travellers: they are built at proper distances through the roads of the Turkish dominions, and afford the indigent and weary traveller an asylum from the inclemency of the weather.

Carbon, a non-metallic elementary solid body, which is widely diffused throughout nature. The purest and at the same time the rarest formed which it occurs is that of the diamond; the more common states in which it is met with are those of anthracite, graphite, and coal: another form is that of charcoal.

Carbonate, a salt composed of carbonic acid and a base. The chief varieties are described under their alkaline, earthy, and metallic bases.

Carburet, a compound of carbon with nitrogen, metals, etc.

Carcase (The) of a building is the naked walls and the rough timber-work of the flooring and quarter partitions, before the building is plastered or the floors laid.

Carcase-roofing, that which supports the covering by a grated frame of timber-work.

Career, a prison or gaol. The Roman prisons were divided into three stories, one above the other, each of which was appropriated to distinct purposes.

Card-making machine, an arrangement of wires used in the cotton manufacture, for disentangling the fibres of cotton preparatory to spinning.

Cardo, a pivot and socket, an apparatus by means of which the doors of the ancients were fixed in their places, and made to revolve in opening and shutting.

Careening, the operation of heaving a ship down on one side by the application of a strong purchase to her masts, which are properly supported for the occasion to prevent their breaking with so great a strain, and by which means, one side of the bottom being elevated above the surface of the water, it may be cleansed or repaired.

Carina, according to Cicero, the keel or lowest piece of timber in the framework of a ship.

Carlings, short pieces of timber ranging fore and aft from one deck-beam to another, into which their ends are mortised: they are used to sustain and fortify the smaller beams of the ship.

Carlisle Tables, so called from the more recent mode of making calculations of the value of annuities on lives, based on the average duration of human life, as taken at Carlisle, in Cumberland. The value of a life annuity depends upon the manner in which it is presumed a large number of persons, similarly situated with the buyer, would die off successively. Various tables of these decrements of life, as they are called, have been constructed from observations made among different classes of lives. Some make the mortality greater than others; and, of course, tables which give a large mortality, give the value of the annuity smaller than those which suppose men to live longer. Those who buy annuities would therefore be glad to be rated according to tables of high mortality, or low expectation of life; while those who sell them would prefer receiving the price indicated by tables which give a lower rate of mortality. Hence arise bargains or stipulations according to either the Northampton or Carlisle tabulated rating of the duration of life. In assurances the reverse is the case: the shorter the time which a man is supposed to live, the more must he pay the office, that the latter may at his death have accumulated wherewithal to pay the amount. The Northampton tables, formed by Dr. Price, from observations of burials at Northampton, as compared with all other tables of authority, give too high a mortality at all the younger and middle ages of life, and, consequently, too low a value of the annuity. The Carlisle tables, formed by Mr. Milne, give much less mortality than most of the old tables, and therefore a higher value of the annuities: they have been proved to represent the actual state of life among the middle classes.

Carlovingian Architecture. French authors establish two epochs of art, under the terms Merovingian (from Clovis to Pepin, 481-751) and Carlovingian (from Pepin to Hugh Capet, 751-987).

Carmine (*colour*), a name originally given only to fine specimens of the tinctures of kermes and cochineal, and denoting generally at present any pigment which resembles them in beauty, richness of colour, and fineness of texture; hence we hear of blue and other coloured carmines, though the term is principally confined to the crimson and scarlet colours produced from cochineal by the agency of tin.

Carn, in Cornish mining, a rock; a heap of rocks; a high rock.

Carnagioni (of the Italians), a colour which differs from terra puzzuoli in its hue; in which respect, other variations and denominations are produced by dressing and compounding.

Carol, a small closet or enclosure to sit and read in.

Carpenter's square: the stock and blade are formed, in one piece, of plate-iron, and the instrument is thus constructed:—one leg is 18 inches in length, numbered from the exterior angle; the bottoms of the figures are adjacent to the interior edge of the square, and con-

CARPENTRY.

sequently their tops to the exterior edge: the other leg is 12 inches in length, and numbered from the extremity towards the angle; the figures are read from the internal angle, as in the other side; and each of the legs is about an inch broad. It is not only used as a square, but also as a level, and as a rule: its application as a square and as a rule is so easy as not to require any example; but its use as a level, in taking angles, may be thus illustrated: suppose it were required to take the angle which the heel of a rafter makes with the back,—apply the end of the short leg of the square to the heel-point of the rafter, and the edge of the square level across the plate; extend a line from the ridge to the heel-point, and where this line cuts the perpendicular leg of the square, mark the inches: this will show how far it deviates from the square in 12 inches.

Carpenter's tools: the principal tools used in the rougher operations of carpentry are the axe, the adze, the chisel, the saw, the mortise and tenon-gauge, the square, the plumb-rule, the level, the auger, the crow, and the draw-bore-pin, or hook-pin, for draw-boring.

Carpentry is the art of combining pieces of timber for the support of any considerable weight or pressure.

The theory of carpentry is founded on two distinct branches of mechanical science: the one informs us how strains are propagated through a system of framing; the other, how to proportion the resistance of its parts, so that all may be sufficiently strong to resist the strains to which they are exposed. The one determines the stability of position, the other the stability of resistance. Each of these may be considered in the most simple manner the subject admits of, with the addition of rules and practical remarks.

Timber is wrought into various forms according to the principles of geometry; and these forms are to be preserved in their original shape only by adjusting the stress and strain according to the laws of mechanics. Hence the importance of studying both these sciences is evident, and particularly the latter; for unless the stress and strain be accurately adjusted, the most careful attention to geometrical rules, and the most skilful workmanship, will be exerted in vain. If, for instance, the centre of an arch were to be drawn and worked over so truly to the curve required, what would it avail if the centre changed its form with every course of stone laid upon it? And it must be remarked, that this is not an imaginary case, but one that has frequently happened; and not only to men ignorant of mechanics, but to some of the most celebrated engineers that France ever produced.

The engineers of our own country have been more successful, having succeeded in gradually introducing a better principle of constructing centres than our neighbours. The greatest defect of the English centres is now an excess of strength, which, on principles of economy, it would be desirable to avoid in erections for temporary purposes.

Carpentry, in civil architecture, is the art of employing timber in the construction of buildings.

The first operation of dividing a piece of timber into scantlings, or boards, by means of the pit-saw, belongs to sawing, and is previous to anything done in carpentry.

The tools employed by the carpenter are a ripping-saw, a hand-saw, an axe, an adze, a socket-chisel, a firmer-chisel, a ripping chisel, an auger, a gimlet, a hammer, a mallet, a pair of pincers, and sometimes planes; but as these are not necessarily used, they are described under the head of joinery, in which they are absolutely necessary.

Carr (John), born 1723, at Horbury, near Wakefield, in Yorkshire, commenced his career as a working mason; afterwards settling in York as an architect, in 1750, he executed many fine and expensive buildings; died in 1807.

Carrara marble, a species of white marble: it is distinguished from the Parian or statuary marble by being harder and less bright. It takes its name from Carrara, in Italy.

Carrel, a pew, closet, or desk, with a seat placed under a window, where the monks were engaged in copying writings.

Carriage of a stair, the timber which supports the steps.

Carrick-bend, a kind of knot. Carrick-bitts are the windlass-bitts.

Carrier, the piece of iron which is fixed by a set-screw on the end of a shaft or spindle to be turned in a lathe, to carry it round by the action of the driver of the centre chuck.

Carry away, a sea-term, to break a spar or part a rope.

Carthusian buildings, Charter-house. The characteristic features of these buildings are austere, and to the Benedictine rule. The monasteries of this order had generally two courts: the smaller, next the entrance, contained the priorial residence and the buildings allotted to secular purposes. Females were not only excluded from the court, but from the church.

Cartoon, a distemper-coloured drawing, made on paper, linen, parchment, etc., of the exact pattern of a design intended to be executed either in tapestry, mosaics, or on glass: such are Raphael's divine pictures in Hampton Court Palace.

Cartoon, in painting, a design drawn on strong paper, sometimes afterwards calqued through, and transferred on the fresh plaster of a wall, to be painted in fresco.

Cartouche, the same as modillion, except that it is exclusively used to signify the blocks or modillions on the eaves of a house.

Cartouche, an ornament representing a scroll of paper.

Caracra, or *Chica*, a new pigment, of a soft powdery texture and rich morone colour, first brought from South America by Lieut. Mawe.

Carving and inlaying of woods had become pretty general at the latter end of the sixteenth century. "At Hardwick, in Derbyshire (1570), the wood-work, in several of the principal apartments, is oak, inlaid with ebony ornaments on the panels and stiles. The doors and shutters of 'Mary Queen of Scot's room,' as it is called, are framed in panels of light wood, inlaid with profiles of the Cæsars, and other enrichments; the stiles, of darker coloured oak. In the state-room, the walls are divided, at about half the height, by a stringing, the upper part filled with landscapes, figures, and animals, relieved in plaster, and painted in their proper colours on white ground; and the lower division hung with tapestry. The chimney front is entirely occupied by a large armorial compartment, relieved in plaster and emblazoned."

Caryates or *Caryatides* (Greek), figures used instead of columns, employed in architecture to represent the portraiture of the defeated Persians after the subjugation of the Caryatæ. The male figures are denominated Persians, Telamones, or Atlantides; the female, Caryans or Caryatides.

Caryatides, anthropostylar pillars or human figures (usually female ones) employed instead of columns to support an entablature. Such figures ought always to be perfectly free from all attitudinizing, and to appear to support their burden without any effort. Some very matter-of-fact critics object to caryatides as being at the best only beautiful absurdities; as if statues so applied were particularly liable to be mistaken for living persons subjected to a more severe punishment than that of being posted up in a niche, or on the top of a building.

Casa, according to Vitruvius, a cottage; a small country-house.

Cased tin, in Cornish mining, that which is re-framed by the gentlest current of water, and prevented from running off the frame by turf placed at the bottom.

Case-hardening. The hardness and polish of steel may be united, in a certain degree, with the firmness and cheapness of malleable iron, by what is called case-hardening, an operation much practised and of considerable use.

Casement, a frame enclosing part of the glazing of a window, with hinges to open and shut; also an early English name for a deep hollow moulding.

Casement, the same as 'scotia,' the name of a hollowed moulding.

Casements, sashes or glass frames opening on hinges and revolving upon one of the vertical edges.

Cases, in Cornwall, very small fissures in the strata of the earth, through which small streams of water flow when they are opened by the working underground, greatly to the hindrance of the workmen.

Casing of timber-work, the plastering a house all over on the outside with mortar and then striking it wet by a ruler with the corner of a trowel, or the like instrument, to make it resemble the joints of freestone, by which means the whole house appears as if built thereof.

Casino. The Italian name used at first for a small house, afterwards a pleasure-house in a garden, and then for a place of relaxation in town.

Cassel earth, or *Castle earth*, an ochreous pigment of a brown colour, more inclined to the russet hue.

Cassia Fistula is a native vegetable pigment, though it is more commonly used as a medicinal drug.

Cast, to pay a vessel's head off, in getting under way, on the tack she is to sail upon.

Cast after cast, in Cornwall, is throwing up of tin stuff, etc., from one stage of boards to another, each cast about 5 or 6 feet high.

Castella, square towers in the celebrated Roman wall of Severus, which was raised to separate England from Scotland.

Castellated, built in imitation of an ancient castle.

Castellum, the receptacle in which the water was collected and heated for the public baths of the Romans; a castle.

Casting, among sculptors, the taking casts of impressions of figures, busts, medals, leaves, etc.

Casting of draperies: by this term is implied the distribution of the folds, and draperies are said to be well cast when the folds are distributed in such a manner as to appear rather the result of mere chance than of art, study, or labour. In that manner or style of painting, which is called *the grand*, the folds of the draperies should be great, and as few as possible, because their rich simplicity is more susceptible of great lights; but it is an error to design draperies too heavy and cumbersome, for they ought to be suitable to the figures, with a combination of ease and grandeur. Order, contrast, and a variety of stuffs and folds, constitute the elegance of draperies; and diversity of colours in these stuffs contributes extremely to the harmony of the whole in historic compositions.

Casting or *Warping*, in joinery, is the bending of the surfaces of a piece of wood from their original position, either by the weight of the wood or by an unequal exposure to the weather, or by the unequal texture of the wood.

Cast-iron framing, for mill-work, possesses great superiority over that of timber, for constructing the framing. It is not only much more durable, but, from the uniformity of its texture, may be converted into any shape, so as to give it great advantage in arranging the materials with respect to strength, and proportioning it to the stress it has to sustain.

Cast-iron shoes for roofs. A practice has been recently introduced into the construction of roofs having the beams of wood, of protecting their extremities from the damp and consequent decay to which they are liable, by resting immediately in contact with the brick or stone work of the walls of the building. This is effected by what the workmen call cast-iron shoes, which are attached to the ends of the tie-beams by means of bolts, nuts, etc.

The iron shoe itself, of course, takes various forms, according to circumstances and the situation where it is introduced, and the particular views of the architect who employs it.

In cases where, from the nature of the work carried on, every part is exposed to great heat and moisture, the defence afforded by such an attachment is of great importance; the wood, unless thus protected, being of course very liable to decay in those parts where damp and moisture might accumulate.

Castle, a fortified and strong mansion, situated and constructed and arranged for the purpose of protecting its inmates against the assaults of enemies; in modern use, domestic residences of the nobility and gentry, without the necessity of being garrisoned by armed men.

Cat, the tackle used to hoist the anchor up to the cat-head.

Catacombs, subterraneous vaults or excavations used as burying-places.

Catadrome, a tilt-yard, or place where horses run for prizes; also an engine like a crane, used by builders to draw up or let down any weight.

Catafalco, a decoration of sculpture, painting, etc., raised on a timber scaffold, to show a coffin or tomb in a funeral solemnity.

Catagraph, the first draught of a picture.

Catamaran, a name given both in the East and West Indies to some kinds of rafts, which are used in short navigations along the sea-shore.

Cataract, a contrivance applied to Cornish engines for regulating the number of strokes per minute: it consists of a small pump fixed on a cistern; the piston is raised at each stroke of the engine by a tappet on the plug-rod, and the water rises into the cylinder of the pump; it is then forced through a cock by means of counterweights attached to a cross-head on the pump piston-rod: when the water has been forced back into the cistern, a series of levers, acting on a rising rod, loosen catches which allow weights to act, by means of levers, to open or shut the steam, equilibrium, and exhaust valves.

Cataractes, a cataract, cascade, or sudden fall of water from a higher to a lower level; according to Pliny, a sluice, flood-gate, or lock in a river.

Catch, a contrivance in machinery, acting on the principle of a latch.

Catenary, in the higher geometry, a mechanical curve which a chain or rope forms itself into by its own weight, when hung freely between two points of suspension, whether these points be in the same horizontal plane or not.

Catgut, in turnery, the string which connects the fly and the mandril.

Cat-harpin, an iron leg used to confine the upper part of the rigging to the mast.

Catharpings, small ropes in a ship, running in little blocks, from one side of the shroud to another, near the deck.

Cat-head, in naval architecture, a large square piece of timber, one end of which is fastened upon the forecastle and the other end projects without the bow, so as to keep the anchor clear of the ship when it is being drawn up by a tackle.

Cathedra, according to Horace, a chair without arms; according to Juvenal, a chair with a long deep seat.

Cathedral, the principal church of a diocese, in which the bishop's throne is placed.

Very few of the Gothic cathedrals on the Continent have the tower or spire springing from the centre of the cross, and resting on four pillars, to balance the thrusts of the ranges of arches centering there; nor have those of Strasburg, Ulm, Vienna, Orleans, or Antwerp. "The distribution of light in a Gothic cathedral is admirably adapted to the grandeur of the edifice, and produces that effect which a painter aims at in his picture. At the entrance at the west, the window being placed high, there is a low-toned light on the lower part of the pillars, and a shadow on the pavement, which, as we walk up the nave, graduates into light from the choir. The east window, always the broadest and the highest, pours in a greater body of light than is to be found in any other kind of building. The altar, rather in shadow, surrounded by this strong light, gives additional effect by contrast. The light from the transept windows is softened down by painted glass. The small windows, placed high along the aisles, enlighten their roofs, but the lower part of the pillars and floor remain in shadow."

Cathedral (the very ancient) of Usumbar and other Armenian churches in Georgia have an arcade surrounding the outside of the building, of which the arches are in the flattened Gothic style: the same form prevails in the windows, doors, etc., in the body of the church. These structures are of an earlier date than any Gothic architecture in Italy.

Catherine-wheel, in architecture, an ornament that occurs in the upper part of the north and south transepts of ancient cathedrals.

Catherwood (Frederick), architect, born in London 1799: his travels were extensive; had much to do both in North and South America; was lost in the Arctic in 1854.

Cathetus. The eye of the volute is so termed because its position is determined, in an Ionic or voluted capital, by a line let down from the point in which the volute generates.

Cathinia, a subterraneous mineral vein, out of which gold and silver are dug.

Cat's-paw, a hitch made in a rope.

Cauliculus, the volute or twist under the flower in the Corinthian capital.

Caulking, in naval architecture, the art of driving a quantity of oakum, *i.e.* old ropes untwisted and softened, into the seams of the planks, to keep out the water.

Counter and *Counting*, in Cornish mining, *Contra:* when two lodes run across, the one, with respect to the other, is called a *counter* or *contra* lode.

Caus (S. de), born in France, was drawing-master to Henry Prince of Wales: he published several scientific works. Died in 1614.

Caus (J. de), of Dieppe, brother of the above, hydraulic engineer.

Causeway, a carriage-road.

Cautions in Architectural Construction.—

UNION OF NEW AND OLD WORK.

In attaching any new work to a building, every allowance must be made for the sinking of the footings under pressure, and for the settlement of the masonry into itself. Thus, while it is necessary that a vertical groove, or indent, be made in the old work, to receive a corresponding piece of the new, it is still more essential that a freedom for the downward motion of the latter should be secured: otherwise, if it be tightly toothed and bonded into the old work, the result illustrated in the annexed sketch may be anticipated.

UNION OF ASHLAR FACING WITH BRICK OR RUBBLE BACKING.

The same caution required in the latter case must be here equally observed. The *backing* (composed of small material and much mortar) will settle more than the *face*; and the latter will consequently

bulge. This is easily remedied by computing, and allowing for, the difference of settlement; and by a due regard to the occasional bonding of the ashlar, so as to make the wall *one* substance, instead of *two* differently conditioned. The preceding sketch illustrates the consequence of weight pressing upon unbonded ashlar and upon yielding rubble.

INVERTED ARCHES.

Inverted arches must be used cautiously. Here is an instance,

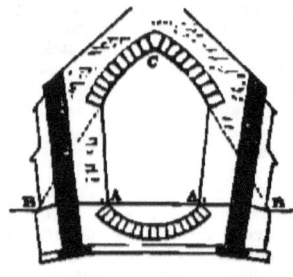

in which the points A and A were prevented by the inverted arch from sinking with the points B B, which latter sunk the more from the pressure of the arch C in the direction of the dotted lines. It is not uncommon for the young architect to *affect* precautionary *science*, without a due consideration of the peculiar circumstances of his case.

DRAINAGE, ETC.

Always endeavour, if possible, to get your water-closet cess-pit outside the building, so that it may be approached for cleaning without disturbing the interior. Be careful in the efficient use of dipdraps to prevent the ascent of rats from the outer sewer into the drains which are under the floors of the house. Rats are destructive in their operations, and if they die in the drain, prove, for a length of time, an unbearable nuisance. Drains may serve every purpose of carrying off soil and water; but the slightest opening in their upper part will allow the escape of effluvia into the space under the ground flooring, and thence into the rooms, unless that space be thoroughly ventilated with grated openings, allowing a thorough draught,—or, at least, a free ingress of fresh air, and equal egress of foul. In the application of covered dry areas round the excavated basements of buildings, on no account omit their entire ventilation. If this be not attended to, the main walling, which they are intended to preserve from damp, may remain even more continually moist than if in immediate connection with the natural ground. Moisture frequently rises up the walling from below its foundation, and, exuding from the face of the masonry, remains confined, unless it evaporate and escape. Without means to this end, a covered area will be merely a receptacle for damp, and may keep the masonry continually wet, even when the ground outside is perfectly dry. Be especially cautious that the water from the rain-pipes of the roofs and flats be not conducted by them into the foundations.

FIRE OPENINGS.

It will save much subsequent trouble and disturbance of masonry, to be assured as to the size and character of the stoves, grates, ranges, etc., which the proprietor will employ. In the kitchen and cooking-rooms, especially, precautionary care should be taken in suiting the openings to the intended apparatus. Do not forget to be prepared for a smoke-jack, etc.

DWARF WALLS.

In constructing these, do not omit the holes, etc., necessary for under-floor ventilation.

PAVING.

Be careful that the bottom, on which fine paving is laid, be dry and free from *staining* material. Common lime mortar is often injurious to pavements. Portland paving is especially liable to be disfigured by it.

WROUGHT STONE-WORK.

In putting wrought stone-work together, *iron* is to be avoided as the certain cause of its subsequent destruction. The stone cornices, architraves, and dressings of many a noble mansion have been brought into premature ruin by the contraction and expansion of iron under the effects of cold and heat. But there are careless contractors who will allow their Corinthian capitals and fluted shafts to be ruined, even before the entablature surmounts them; and the young architect will not, therefore, omit to insert a clause in his specification (and to be peremptory in its enforcement), that all cut stonework be securely preserved, during the progress of the building, with wood casing. It is surprising how grossly indifferent each class of artificers is to the work of the others. It is still more surprising to observe how frequently they seem indifferent to the preservation of their own.

SLATING.

Get rid of the masons and plasterers and plumbers before your slaters begin. The injury done to slating by the afterwork of chimney-tops, etc., is much to be dreaded. The cementitious 'stopping' to a roof will not be efficiently done without close supervision: the ridge, hip, and valley courses will not be properly formed of large cut slates,—nor will every slate have its *two* nails, unless the architect see to it.

PLASTERING.

Clear may be your specification in forbidding salt sand, but, if your work be carried on in the vicinity of any estuary, the chances are (unless you be deemed cruelly strict) that the surface of your internal walls will vary with the weather, from damp to dry, like a seaweed, and throw out salt in abundance.

BEAMS, JOISTS, AND OTHER TIMBERS. LINTELS, BOND, PARTITIONS.

It is the office of walls to carry

beams, etc.; and that of beams to stay the walls from falling outwards or inwards: but it is the duty of architects to see that the wood-work which supplants masonry does not weaken the latter; i. e. that the ends of timbers inserted into walls may not, by compression or decay, leave the superincumbent masonry to loosen downwards. Thus, the beam A, though entering only a *portion* of

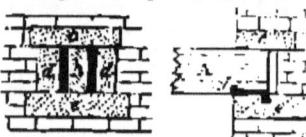

the wall, presses upon the through-stone e, which throws the weight upon the *whole* wall, and has, by means of an iron plate c, a hold to secure its perpendicularity. The cover-stone c presses on the surface of the timber to confirm its security: but should the timber rot, the cover-stone will not sink, because sustained by the side-stones d d. To *prevent* rot, the backing and side-stones are left free of the timber, so that air may traverse round it. The habit of placing the ends of beams on a template, as G, is bad. The only justification of the employment of wood, so built into the walls, is when it forms a continuous plate, that it may act as a bond to preserve the perfect horizontal level of joists, which, however, should ex-

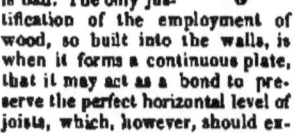

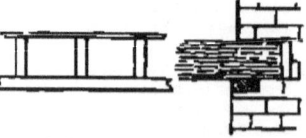

tend a little beyond the plate, so as to have a bearing also on the solid of the wall. Careful inspection will then so manage the construction of the wall in this part, as to leave it but little weakened by the air-hollows required for the plate

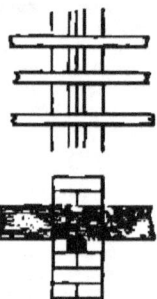

and joists; unless, indeed, it be very thin,—as only one brick, for instance,—when no law of common sense can justify the use of continuous bond. Where joists uninterruptedly cross a thin wall, which is to support another story of masonry, let there only be one plate, thin, and on its edge, in the centre of the wall, so that at least a brick on edge may be placed on each side of it, to fill up the intervals between the joists, and give solid support to the superincumbent masonry. On no account let the upper part of the wall be separated from the lower by a mere layer of perishable wood, or supported by a range of joists on their edge. It has often been seen that iron hooping should be more used than it is as the internal bonding of walls. At the same time it must be remembered that bond timbering is necessary, at intervals, to receive the nails of the battening. When, however, the wall is thin, it may be imperative to avoid its use, employing old oak bats for that purpose. In short, let it be the care of the young architect, so to contrive the union of his masonry and carpentry, as that the entire removal of the latter may leave the former secure in its own strength. In the use of *lintels* especially, he should be cautious. They are useful as bonds to unite the tops of piers, and as means for the fixing of the joinery; but they ought never to be trusted to as a lasting support of masonry,—that support being always really afforded by the relieving segment arch above the lintel. A bressummer may be termed a large lintel; and by its adoption here, at least, the support of the masonry is truly intended. The use of the bressummer, in shop-front openings, is an evil necessity to which an architect must often submit; and all that he can do, is to make the best of a bad job, by *wrought*-iron trussing, which will at least give adequate *strength*, though it may not ensure permanent durability. If *time* spare it, *fire* may destroy it; and the latter evil is not to he met even by iron, which, if wrought, will bend,—if cast, will crack,—with heat. Let the arch, then, or some modification of it, be always used, if possible.

Partitions of wood should not be left to the sagacity of the carpenter. Under all circumstances where they have to support themselves over voids, or to bear, or participate in the bearing of, a pressure from above, they should be considered

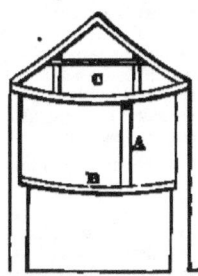

by the architect in his specification, and carefully studied in making the working drawings. It is not enough merely to say, that "they are to be trussed so as to prevent any injury to ceilings by their own pressure;" marginal sketches should be made, showing the disposition of the skeleton framing, with whatever iron-work is necessary to its security. See, for instance, what a carpenter may do, unless well directed: a roof c, bearing partly on the partition A, when it should have borne only on the walls; and, instead of distressing the partition, should have rather held it suspended: the partition A bearing down with its own weight, and that of the roof, on the floor B, instead of being so truss-framed in its length as to leave the floor unconscious of its existence. No ignorance in the young architect is presumed as to the manner of doing these things; he is merely admonished not to imagine that they are so obvious as to be done without his guidance.

In the framing of roofs, give a

maximum strength to the purlins: the undulating surface of a weakly-purlined roof will soon proclaim its defect in this particular. The position of the principals should not be observable from without.

FLOORS; SIMPLE AND FRAMED, ETC.

For permanent and uniform strength, there is no floor so good as one composed of simple joists, stiffened by cross-bonding: but, in very large rooms, there is more economy in the compound floor of binders and joists, or of joists, binders, and girders. There may be particular reasons for girders, etc.; as, when the weight of the floor has to be thrown upon

CAUTIONS.

piers, and not on a continuous wall of uniform strength: but the usual motive to the use of the compound floor, in rooms which exceed 18 or 20 feet in width, is a legitimate economy of materials. It is only necessary to caution the young practitioner on the necessity of considering, that girders have to perform the duty of cross-walls; that they should be trussed to prevent their 'sagging' even with their own weight; that their scantling should allow for the weakening effect of the cuttings made into their substance to receive the timbers they support; that their trusses should be wholly of *iron* (and not partially of oak); and, especially, that the end of each girder, instead of being notched on perishable templates of wood, and closely surrounded with mortar and masonry, should be housed in a cavity with an iron holding-plate; or inserted into a cast-iron boxing, notched into a thorough-stone, leaving a space (however small) for the air to circulate about it,

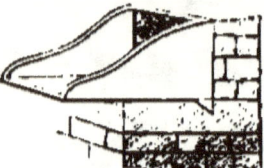

and prevent rot. The failure of a girder sometimes involves the failure of all the rest of the floor: and, though *all* timbers inserted in masonry should have a more careful regard to their preservation from decay than it is usual to bestow, it will be readily admitted, that too much care cannot be given to those leading bearing timbers, without the permanent duration of which the durability of the large remainder is of no avail.

ROOFS.

The same remarks, applying to the extremities of girders, apply also to tie-beams.

CEILINGS.

To procure a good ceiling in single-joist floors it is necessary there should be ceiling-joists crossing below the others: and it is a question whether the ceiling-joists, under double-framed floors, instead of being chase-mortised *into* the binders, should not be in unbroken lengths nailed *under* the binders. Where the ceiling-joists (as under roofs) are likely to be trodden upon, they must be well secured.

SOUND BOARDING.

Always consider whether the occupants of any particular room will be annoyed by noises from the rooms below or above. Sound boarding and pugging considerably increase the weight of the floor, the scantling of whose timbers should therefore be thought upon. Watercloset partitions should be well pugged.

MICE IN PARTITIONS AND SKIRTINGS.

The space behind the skirtings is often a thoroughfare for mice, which also contrive to travel from floor to floor in the hollows of the quarter-partitions, and become in several ways a great nuisance. Plaster or wood stopping is not always so efficacious as the use of broken glass in those secret passages which they are prone to frequent.

COVERINGS TO GUTTERS, CISTERNS, ETC.

The liability of gutters and cisterns to become choked with snow, or filled up with leaves, etc., renders it advisable to protect them with a boarded covering, which may preserve the under-current of water from receiving what may speedily produce a chokage or overflow.

IRON COLUMNS, BEAMS, ETC.

On this most important subject the young architect should not move a step without carefully consulting the experienced knowledge of the engineer. Tredgold's 'Practical Essay on the Strength of Cast Iron' should be well studied, whenever necessity compels the support of heavy and loaded superstructures by iron columns and beams. A careful computation of the weight of the mere building, added to that of its possible burthen, with allowance for theoretical fallacy, and a due estimate of the increased strength of the hollow pillar, as compared with a solid one having the same amount of metal, must be made, examined, and re-examined, before the specification be issued.

Cavædium, one of the courts of a Roman house, most commonly surrounded by a covered passage, having the middle area exposed to the air. There are five kinds of cavædia, which, from their mode of construction, are severally denominated Tuscan, Corinthian, tetrastyle, displuviatum, and testudinatum. They are termed Tuscan when the beams which are thrown across the court have timbers and gutters extending diagonally from the angles made by the walls of the court to those made by the junction of the beams, and the rafters of the eaves are made to incline every way towards the centre of the compluvium. The timbers and compluvia of Corinthian cavædia have a disposition, in all respects, similar; but beams are made to project from the walls, and are supported upon columns arranged around the court.

Cavazion, in architecture, the hollow trench made for laying the foundation of a building; according to Vitruvius, it ought to be one-sixth part of the height of the whole building.

Cavetto, a hollow moulding whose profile is a quadrant of a circle; principally used in cornices.

Cavendish (the Hon. Henry), one of the most learned men in chemistry and the arts of his age. Born 10th October 1731; died 24th February, 1810. An octavo volume, published by the Cavendish Society in 1851, very copiously adduces evidences of Mr. Cavendish's prior claim to the discovery of the theory of the composition of air and water: the volume contains many valuable papers on the life and experimental labours of Cavendish, and the relative merit of Cavendish; on Watt and Lavoisier and others; inquiries of the learned men of the latter end of the last, and the beginning of the present century.

Cawk-stone, a mineral, akin to the white milky, mineral juice of lead mines.

Caya, a key or water-lock.

Cecle, an old English term for a canopy.

Cedar. Cedar-wood was known and used in the earliest times, as in the construction of Solomon's Temple: great varieties are produced in the eastern and western parts of the world: it is used in ship-building, cabinet-work, pencil-making, and for various other purposes.

Cedars of Lebanon, of great age and size, constitute a peculiar and very observable feature in the landscape of the suburbs of London, and are unusually numerous on the west and south-west sides as the adjuncts of stately mansions or elegant villas, along the valley of the Thames.

Poplars (Lombardy) are very freely introduced into the scenery around London. Beeches do not appear at home anywhere along the flat grounds near the Thames; but at Burnham, a little below Slough, there are some celebrated ones, growing on a thin, light, gravelly soil, and Windsor Park contains some superb specimens.

Chestnuts (of Spanish) we shall have some prodigious specimens to notice on a property of the Duke of Devonshire, near Chiswick. In Kensington Gardens, Greenwich Park, and other places, there are some very fine ones. It is a first-rate park tree for the low sheltered tract by the sides of the Thames, and is hardly enough esteemed.

Ceiling, the upper side of an apartment, opposite to the floor, generally finished with plastered work. Ceilings are set in two different ways: the best is where the setting-coat is composed of plaster and putty, commonly called 'gauge.' Common ceilings have plaster, but no hair: the latter is the same as the finishing coat in walls set for paper.

Ceiling, the under covering of a roof, under the surface of the vaulting in vaulted rooms and buildings. Ceilings in buildings of any dimensions at either story are the upper or overhead surfaces of the rooms respectively.

Ceilings. When ceilings are covered, the height of the cove should be regulated by the total height of the room. In proportioning the height of a room to its superficial dimensions, the best proportion for the cove is one-quarter of the whole height.

Celerity is the velocity or swiftness of a body in motion; or that affection of a body in motion by which it can pass over a certain space in a certain time.

Cell, an enclosed space within the walls of an ancient temple; a term applied also to monkish sleeping-rooms in religious establishments.

Cella, the body or principal part of a temple,—anciently written *cela*. It is thought to be derived from *celandus*,—to be concealed or shut out from public view; because in early temple the cella could only be entered by privileged persons.

Cellarino, that part of the capital in the Roman, Doric, and Tuscan orders which is below the annulets under the ovolo.

Cellular beam. A newly introduced application of wrought-iron to the purposes of girders and beams, in which wrought-iron plates are riveted with angle-irons in the form of a series of longitudinal cells with occasional struts.

Cemetery, a place wherein the bodies of the dead are buried; a church-yard or burying-ground.

Cementation is the process of converting iron into steel, which is done by stratifying bars of iron in charcoal, igniting it, and letting them continue in a kiln in that state for five or six days: the carbon of the charcoal is thus absorbed by the iron, and the latter converted into steel.

Cements, natural. When the proportion of clay in calcareous minerals exceeds 27 to 30 per cent., it is seldom that they can be converted into lime by calcination; but they then furnish a kind of natural cement, which may be employed in the same manner as plaster of Paris, by pulverizing it, and kneading it with a certain quantity of water.

There are some natural cements which do not set in water for many days, and some which harden in less than a quarter of an hour: these last are the only ones which have been made use of at present. Though very useful in circumstances where a quick solidification is indispensable, they are far from affording, in ordinary cases, the advantages of hydraulic mortars or cements of good quality. In fact, they merely adhere to the stone, owing to the roughness of its surface, and the entanglement resulting from it; and, however dexterous or experienced the workman may be who makes use of them, he will be unable to connect the different parts of his masonry in one continuous bond by means of them. This statement must be understood to apply only to cements which harden while in contact with bricks *under water*, because the adhesion of such as dry in the open air is well known to be much greater than what would be caused merely by asperities of the surface. It is not uncommon to see from twenty to thirty bricks stuck to one another by Roman cement, and projecting at right angles from the side of a wall, as a proof of the excellence of the composition; and an instance has been mentioned in which thirty-three bricks were successfully supported in this manner. Now, if we assume the weight of a brick and its corresponding joint of cement to be 6 lbs., and their thickness, when the bricks were joined one to another in the manner above alluded to (in which the longest dimension of the brick was placed vertically), to be 2¼ inches, then the cohesive force necessary to unite the first brick to the wall, with sufficient firmness to bear the strain occasioned by the weight of the remaining thirty-two supported by it, must have been nearly 91 lbs. per square inch, or equivalent to a direct load of 3640 lbs. upon its whole surface of about 40 square inches.

That which is in England very improperly termed Roman cement is nothing more than a natural cement, resulting from a slight calcination of a calcareous mineral, containing about 31 per cent. of ochreous clay, and a few hundredths of carbonate of magnesia and manganese. A very great consumption of this cement takes place in London; but its use will infallibly become restricted, in proportion as the mortars of eminently hydraulic lime shall become better known, and, in consequence, better appreciated.

Very recently, natural cements have been found in Russia and in France. They may be composed at once by properly calcining mixtures made in the average proportions of 66 parts of ochreous clay to 100 parts of chalk. It is fair, however, to admit, that no artificial product has yet been proved to equal the English cement in point of hardness.

The pure calcareous substances, when imperfectly calcined, become converted into sub-carbonates, possessed of certain properties. These properties are to afford a powder, which, when kneaded with water in the same way as plaster of Paris, acquires in it, at first, a consistency more or less firm, but which does not continue its progress at the same rate.

The argillaceous limestones, and the artificial mixtures of pure lime and clay in the proportions requisite to constitute hydraulic lime by the ordinary calcination, become natural or artificial cements when they have been subjected merely to a simple incandescence, kept up for some hours, or even for some minutes. This result, which has often occurred in the course of first experiments in burning the artificial hydraulic limestones, has been equally observed in Russia by Colonel Raucourt; and M. Lacordaire, Engineer of Roads, has not only fully verified it with respect to the different argillaceous limestones of the neighbourhood of Pouilly, but has also made a useful and happy application of it in the works which have been erected at the junction of the Burgundy canal; both in transforming these limestones into natural cements, and in turning to account the large quantity of half-burnt lime which is found in the upper layers of the kilns, when the intensity and duration of the heat is so regulated as not to exceed the limit proper for the lower strata of the charge.

The history of these new cements

will not be complete until authentic and multiplied experiments shall have established their power to resist the effects of air and frost, and the degree of adhesion with which they unite to the building-stone.

Cenotaphium, a cenotaph, an empty or honorary tomb, erected by the Greeks as a memorial of a person whose body was buried elsewhere, or not found for burial.

Censitores, surveyors of the Roman aqueducts.

Centaur, poetically, and in ancient mythology, a being represented as half man half horse; the Sagittarius of the Zodiac.

Centering, temporary supports, principally of timber, placed and affixed under vaults and arches to sustain them while they are in course of building. Much ingenuity is displayed in the centering for bridges and tunnels.

Centigrade, the division into grades or degrees by hundredth parts; called also centesimal.

Central forces, the powers which cause a moving body to tend towards or recede from the centre of motion. When a body is made to revolve in a circle round some fixed point, it will have a continued tendency to fly off in a straight line at a tangent in the circle, which tendency is called the *centrifugal force*; and the opposing power by which the body is retained in the circular path is called the *centripetal force*.

Centre, any timber frame, or set of frames, for supporting the arch-stones of a bridge during the construction of an arch.

The qualities of a good centre consist in its being a sufficient support for the weight or pressure of the arch-stones, without any sensible change of form taking place throughout the whole progress of the work, from the springing of the arch to the fixing of the key-stone: it should be capable of being easily and safely removed, and designed so that it may be erected at a comparatively small expense.

In navigable rivers, where a certain space must be left for the passage of vessels, and in deep and rapid rivers, where it is difficult to establish intermediate supports, and where much is to be apprehended from sudden floods, the frames should span the whole width of the archway, or be framed so as to leave a considerable portion of the archway unoccupied. In such cases, a considerable degree of art is required to make the centre an effectual support for the arch-stones, particularly when the arch is large. But in narrow rivers, and in those where the above-mentioned inconveniences do not interfere with the work, the framing may be constructed upon horizontal tie-beams, supported in several places by piles, or frames fixed in the bed of the river; and the construction is comparatively easy.

In large arches, when the arch-stones are laid to a considerable height, they often force the centre out of form, by causing it to rise at the crown; and it is sometimes necessary to load the centre at the crown to prevent such rising; but this is a very imperfect remedy. Notwithstanding the subject has been considered by several very eminent men, their works are not much calculated to instruct the carpenter how to avoid this difficulty: indeed, their object seems to have been exclusively to calculate the strength of a centre already designed, instead of showing the principles on which it ought to be contrived; and even in calculating the strength, they are very imperfect guides, because they have not attempted to find what forces would derange a centre, but only the force that might be supported without fracture.

Centre, in a general sense, denotes a point equally remote from the extremes of a line, surface, or solid: the word signifies a point.

Centre-bit, in joinery, an instrument with a projecting conical point nearly in the middle, called the centre of the bit; on the narrow vertical surface, the one most remote from the centre, is a tooth with a cutting edge. The under edge of the bit on the other side of the centre has a projecting edge inclined forward. The horizontal section of this bit upwards is a rectangle. The axis of the small cone in the centre is in the same straight line as that of the stock; the cutting edge of the tooth is more prominent than the projecting edge on the other side of the centre, and the vertex of the conic centre is still more prominent than the cutting edge of the tooth.

The use of the centre-bit is to form a cylindric excavation, having the upper point of the axis of the intended hole given on the surface of the wood. The centre of the bit is first fixed in this point; then, by placing the axis of the stock and bit in the axis of the hole intended to be bored, with the head of the stock against the breast, and by turning the stock swiftly round by means of the handle, the hollow cone made by the centre will cause the point of the tooth to move in the circumference of a circle, and cut the cylindric surface progressively as it is turned round, while the projecting edge upon the other side of the centre will cut out the cone in a spiral-formed shaving. Centre-bits are of various sizes, for bores of different diameters.

Centre-chuck, a chuck which can be screwed on the mandril of a lathe, and has a hardened steel cone or centre fixed in it; also a projecting arm or driver.

Centre-drill, a small drill used for making a short hole in the ends of a shaft about to be turned, for the entrance of the lathe centres.

Centre of attraction of a body is that point into which, if all its matter were collected, its action upon any remote particle would still be the same as it is while the body retains its own proper form; or it is that point to which bodies tend by their own gravity, or about which a planet revolves as a centre, being attracted or impelled towards it by the action of gravity. The common centre of attraction of two or more bodies is used to denote that point in which, if a particle of matter were placed, the action of each body upon it would be equal, and where it will remain in equilibrium, having no tendency to move one way rather than another.

Centre of a circle, that point in a circle which is equally distant from every point of the circumference, being that from which the circle is described.

Centre of a conic section, that point which bisects any diameter, or that point in which all the diameters intersect each other. This point in an ellipse is within the figure, in the hyperbola without, and in the parabola it is at an infinite distance.

Centre of conversion, a mechanical term, the signification of which may be thus conceived: if a stick be laid on stagnant water, and drawn by a thread fastened to it, so that the thread makes always the same angle with it, the stick will be found to turn about a certain point, which point is called the 'centre of conversion.'

Centre of a curve of the higher kind, is the point where two diameters concur; and when all the diameters concur in the same point, it is called the general centre.

Centre of a dial, that point where the gnomon or style, placed parallel to the axis of the earth, intersects the plane of the dial.

Centre of an equilibrium is the same with respect to bodies immersed in a fluid as the centre of gravity is to bodies in free space; or it is a certain point on which, if a body,

CENTRE OF GRAVITY.

or system of bodies, be suspended, they will rest in any position.

Centre of friction is that point in the base of a body on which it revolves, in which, if the whole surface of the base and the mass of the body were collected and made to revolve about the centre of the base of the given body, the angular velocity destroyed by its friction would be equal to the angular velocity destroyed in the given body by its friction in the same time.

Centre of gravity of any body, or system of bodies, is that point upon which the body or system of bodies acted upon only by the force of gravity will balance itself in all positions; or it is a point on which, when supported, the body or system will be supported, however it may be situated in other respects. Hence it follows, that if a line or plane passing through the centre of gravity be supported, the body or system will also be supported; and conversely, if a body or system balance itself upon a line or plane, in all positions, the centre of gravity is in that line or plane. In a similar manner it will appear, that if a body rest in equilibrio when suspended from any point, the centre of gravity of that body or system is in the perpendicular let fall from the centre of suspension; and on these principles depends the mechanical method of finding the centre of gravity of bodies.

Centre of gyration, that point in a body revolving on an axis, into which, if the matter of the whole body were collected, the same angular velocity would be generated by the same moving force.

Centre of motion of a body is a fixed point about which the body is moved; and the axis of motion is the fixed axis about which it moves.

Centre of oscillation, the point in which the whole of the matter must be collected, in order that the time of oscillation may be the same as when it is distributed.

Centre of percussion, that point of a revolving body which would strike an obstacle with the same force as if the whole of the matter were collected in it.

Centre of position, in mechanics, denotes a point of any body, or system of bodies, so selected that we may properly estimate the situation and motion of the body or system by those points.

Centre of pressure, or metacentre of a fluid against a plane, is that point against which a force being applied, equal and contrary to the whole pressure, it will sustain it, so as that the body pressed on will not incline to either side. This is the same as the centre of percussion, supposing the axis of motion to be at the intersection of this plane with the surface of the fluid; and the centre of pressure upon a plane parallel to the horizon, or upon any plane where the pressure is uniform, is the same as the centre of gravity of that plane.

Centre of spontaneous rotation, that point which remains at rest the instant a body is struck, or about which the body begins to revolve. If a body of any size or form, after rotatory or gyratory motions, be left entirely to itself, it will always have three principal axes of rotation; that is, all the rotary motions by which it is effected may be constantly reduced to three, which are performed round three axes perpendicular to each other, passing through the centre of gravity, and always preserving the same position in absolute space, while the centre of gravity is at rest, or moves uniformly forward in a right line.

Centre phonic, in acoustics, the place where the speaker stands in making polysyllabical and articulate echoes.

Centre phonocamptic, the place or object which returns the voice.

Centre-punch, a small piece of steel with a hardened point at one end.

Centres, in turnery, are the two concs

with their axes horizontally posited for sustaining the body while it is turned.

Centre-velic or *Velic-point*, the centre of gravity of an equivalent sail, or that single sail whose position and magnitude are such as cause it to be acted upon by the wind when the vessel is sailing, so that the motion shall be the same as that which takes place while the sails have their usual positions.

Centrifugal force is that force by which a body revolving about a centre, or about another body, has a tendency to recede from it.

Centrifugal pump, a machine for raising water by centrifugal force combined with the pressure of the atmosphere.

Centripetal force is that force by which a body is perpetually urged onwards to a centre, and thereby made to revolve in a curve instead of a right line.

Ceramics, a term for all the varieties of baked or burnt clay.

Cerium, a metal discovered in 1803 by Berzelius, and named after the planet Ceres. It is brittle, white, and volatile in a very intense heat: it is not acted upon by nitric acid, but is dissolved in aqua regia, nitrohydrochloric acid.

Cesspool, a receptacle, sunk below the level of a drain from a privy or water-closet, for the sediment which would otherwise choke the drain.

Cerceau (A. du), architect: practised in France in 1575, and built several magnificent palaces and mansions for Royalty and for the nobility.

Cerceau (J. A. du), architect: born in 1516, at Orleans; died in 1592. He published valuable books on the architecture of the period.

Chafery, a forge in an iron mill, wherein the iron is wrought into bars.

Chain, in surveying, is a lineal measure, consisting of a certain number of iron links, usually 100, serving to take the dimensions of fields, etc.: at every tenth link is usually fastened a small brass plate, with a figure engraved upon it, or else cut into different shapes, to show how many links it is from one end of the chain.

Chains, strong links or plates of iron, the lower ends of which are bolted through a ship's side to the timbers.

Chain-plates, plates of iron bolted to the side of a ship, to which the chains and dead-eyes of the lower rigging are connected.

Chain-pump, an hydraulic machine for raising water. It is made of different lengths, and consists of two collateral square barrels and an endless chain of pistons of the same form, fixed at proper distances.

Chain-timber, in brick-building, a timber of large dimensions placed in the middle of the height of a story, for imparting strength.

Chairs. Anciently, in most apartments we find "two great chayers:" these were arm-chairs, with stuffed backs and sides, entirely covered, and similar to the lounging-chairs of the present day. Others are described as 'Flemish chairs,' 'scrolled chairs,' and 'turned chairs,' wrought in ebony, walnut, cherry-tree, etc., with high backs, either stuffed in one long upright panel, or filled with wicker-work, etc.

Chalcedony, a precious stone, in colour like a carbuncle; by some translated from the Scriptures as 'emerald.'

Chalcidicum, among the Romans, a large, low, and deep porch, covered with its own roof, supported on pilasters, and appended to the entrance-front of a building, where it protected the principal doorway, and formed a grand entrance to the whole edifice.

Chalcidria, chambers attached to a basilica; they were built at one end when the situation would allow.

Chalcographer, an engraver in copper.

Chalice, the cup used for the wine at the celebration of the Eucharist.

Chalinque, a boat which is almost of a square building, used in Italy.

Chalk, in geology, forms the higher part of the series or group termed cretaceous: it is composed of nearly 44 parts of carbonic acid and 56 parts of lime.

Chamber of a mine, the place where the powder is fixed.

Chambers (Sir William), born in Stockholm in 1725, was an eminent architect of the reign of George III. In the year 1768 was instituted the Royal Academy, to the establishment of which Chambers was principally instrumental. In 1775 he was appointed by the Government to construct the magnificent edifice of Somerset House, which was commenced in the following year. Sir William Chambers had social intimacy with Drs. Johnson, Goldsmith, Burney, and Garrick, and other literary men of his day; he published several architectural works, among them the celebrated work on the decorative part of civil architecture, which Mr. Joseph Gwilt has re-edited and improved. Died in London 1796.

Chambers, according to Palladio, are made either arched or with a flat ceiling: if in the last way, the height from the floor to the joist above ought to be equal to their breadth; and the chambers of the second story must be a sixth part less than them in height.

Chambranle, an ornament in masonry and joiners' work which borders the sides of doors, windows, and chimneys.

Chandry, an apartment in a prince's house, where the candles and other lights are kept.

Chamfer. An edge or arris, taken off equally on the two sides which form it, leaves what is called a chamfer, or a chamfered edge. If the arris be taken off more on one side than the other, it is said to be splayed or bevelled.

Chamfering, the process of cutting the edge or the end of anything bevel or aslope.

Champ, the flat surface of a wall.

Champe, the field or ground on which carving is raised.

Champ de Mars : in French history, the public assemblies of the Franks are said to have been held in an open field, and in the month of March; whence the name.

Chancel, the choir or eastern part of a church appropriated to the use of those who officiate in the performance of the services, and separated from the nave and other portions in which the congregation assemble, sometimes by a screen.

Channel, in hydrography, the deepest part of a river, harbour, or strait, which is most convenient for the track of shipping; also an arm of the sea running between an island and the main, or continent, as the British Channel, etc.

Channelling, in architecture, perpendicular channels, or cavities, cut along the shaft of a column or pilaster.

Channels, broad pieces of plank bolted edgewise to the outside of a vessel, used for spreading the lower rigging.

Chant, Chanting. The word 'chant' is derived from the Latin *Cantus*, which signifies singing; a song, a tune, or melody,—the sound of a trumpet, crowing of a cock (whence this bird is called 'chanticleer'); it also signifies the frequent repetition of the same thing. The word chant is not confined to merely a melody consisting of several notes; it may consist of one only: in this case it is called, in church music, 'Intonation,' although in Gregorian music the word intonation has a somewhat different signification. (See *Gregorian Chant*.) Hence chanting is reciting in a musical tone, and is peculiarly adapted to a dignified utterance of the sublime language of the Liturgy. Chanting or intoning on a monotone, or single sound, is the simplest and easiest method of reading and responding the various prayers, exhortations, litanies, suffrages, Kyrie eleisons, Allelujahs, Gloria Patri, and the Amens, and is eminently more dignified and solemn than when there is neither elevation nor depression of the voice at any one termination. In chanting the greater and lesser Canticles,—the Te Deum, Jubilate, Benedicite, Benedictus, Athanasian Creed, Venite exultemus, Magnificat, Cantate Domino, Nunc dimittis, Deus misereatur, as also the prose Psalms,—the chant may consist of more than one tone, although it is preferable to use a small number. The method of chanting the Psalter in the English church is different from that adopted on the Continent, where it appears to be governed by no rule; whereas the Gregorian chant is governed entirely by rule.

Chantlate, in building, a piece of wood fastened near the ends of the rafters, and projecting beyond the wall, to support two or three rows of tiles, so placed to hinder the rain-water from trickling down the sides of the walls.

Chantry, an ecclesiastical benefice or endowment to provide for the chanting of masses.

Chapel, a small building attached anciently to various parts of large churches or cathedrals, and separately dedicated; also a detached building for divine service: In England chapels are sometimes called *chapels of ease*, built for the accommodation of an increasing population.

Chapelling, wearing a ship round, when taken aback, without bracing the head-yards.

Chapiter, the capital of a column.

Chaplet, in architecture, a small ornament carved into round beads, etc.

Chapman (Admiral), born in the last century, in Sweden, of English descent. His naval architectural works on men-of-war and merchant-vessels are, as examples of principles, to practice the most eminent. The plates are drawn to a large scale, both in English and Swedish measurements.

Chaps, the two planes or flat parts of a vice or pair of tongs or pliers, for holding anything fast, and which are generally roughed with teeth.

Chapter-house, an establishment for Deans and Prebendaries of cathedrals and collegiate churches; the apartment or hall in which the monks and canons of a monastic establishment conduct their affairs connected with ecclesiastical regulations.

Char or *Chare*, to hew, to work charred stone; hewn stone.

Character, in a picture, is giving to the different objects their appropriate and distinguishing appearance.

Charcoal consists mainly of carbon procured from the decomposition of wood by burning. This operation is generally conducted in pits made in the ground, and in iron cylinders. Wood is essentially composed of carbon, oxygen, and hydrogen. Charcoal has the same properties: it is black, lighter than water, and full of pores, occasioned by the expulsion of the bodies volatilized.

Charge, in electricity, is the accumulation of the electric matter on one surface of an electric, as a pane of glass, Leyden phial, etc., whilst an equal quantity passes off from the opposite surface.

Charge, in mining; any quantity of ore put at one time into a furnace to fuse is called a 'charge;' letting it out is called 'tapping.'

Chargers, large dishes, sometimes described as 'flat pieces.'

Châtelet, the common gaol and session-house in the city of Paris.

Cheeks, the shears or bed of the lathe as made with two pieces for conducting the puppets.

Cheeks, the projection on each side

CHEMISTRY.

of a mast, upon which the trestle-trees rest; the sides of the sheet of a block.

Cheeks. Two upright, equal and similar parts of any piece of timber work, as the sides of a dormer-window.

Cheeks (of a mortise) are the two solid parts upon the sides of the mortise. The thickness of each cheek should not be less than the thickness of the mortise, except mouldings on the stiles require it to be otherwise.

Cheerly, quickly; with a will.

Chemistry. The science of chemistry has for its object the study of the nature and properties of the different substances of which the earth, the waters, the air, and their inhabitants (namely, plants and animals), are composed. In a word, it embraces the study of everything under heaven accessible to man. In its highest branches it aims at discovering the laws or rules which regulate the formation of chemical compounds generally; and in its useful applications it has been already exceedingly serviceable in directing and improving the various arts of common life, as agriculture, the working of metals, dyeing, and many other pursuits. It serves also to guide the medical man in the preparation of his remedies, and also occasionally in distinguishing between diseases which are in other respects much alike. There is, indeed, scarcely a situation in life in which a knowledge of chemistry may not prove directly useful. It is a science the study of which, from its simplest beginnings to its highest attempts, is rendered delightful by the constant succession of new and interesting things brought before the eye and the mind.

Cherry-tree, a hard, close-grained wood, of a pale red-brown colour: when stained with lime, and oiled and varnished, it resembles mahogany, and is used for furniture, etc.

Chess-trees, pieces of oak fitted to the sides of a vessel, abaft the fore-chains, with a sheave in them, to board the main-tack to; not much used.

Chest, a piece of furniture for the reception of all kinds of goods, particularly household conveniences, deposited therein for security, and for plate; placed also in churches, for the keeping of the holy vessels, vestments, etc.: the seaman's chest contains all the personalities of a sailor.

Coffers and chests were the general repositories for articles of every kind; writings, apparel, food, and even fuel, were kept within them. Many of these chests which were raised on feet to protect them from damp and vermin, were beautifully ornamented with carving and other sumptuous enrichments. Large trunks, in which clothes, hangings, etc., were packed for removal, were called 'Trussing Chests:' they were substantially made, and bound in every direction with iron straps, wrought into fanciful forms, and secured by locks of artful and curious contrivance. Two "standard chests" were delivered to the laundress of King Henry VIII.; "the one to keep the cleane stuff, and the other to keep the stuff that had been occupied." "In ivory coffers," says Grameo, "I have stuffed my crowns; in cypress chests, my arras, counterpoints, etc." Cypress-wood was selected for its rare properties of neither rotting nor becoming worm-eaten.

Chestnut wood is very durable, and was formerly much used in house carpentry and furniture.

Cheval de frise, a square or octagonal beam of wood, from 6 to 9 feet in length, and pierced by iron rods or wooden pickets 6 feet long, which are pointed at each end, and shod with iron: the pickets are placed 6 inches asunder, and pass through two opposite faces of the beam, in directions alternately at right angles to each other, the cheval resting on the ground at the lower extremity of the pickets.

Chevet, the termination of a church behind the high altar, when of a semicircular or polygonal form.

Chevron, a moulding of a zig-zag character, of the Norman style particularly, but sometimes to be found with the pointed arch.

Chiaro-oscuro, a drawing made in two colours, black and white; also the art of advantageously distributing the lights and shadows which ought to appear in a picture, as well for the repose and satisfaction of the eye as for the effect of the whole together.

Chief point (in do.) is the uppermost part of an escutcheon.

Chiliad, an assemblage of several things ranged by thousands; applied also to tables of logarithms, which were at first divided into thousands.

Chilioëdron, a solid figure of a thousand faces.

Chiliagon, in geometry, a regular plane figure of a thousand sides and angles.

Chimes, a set of bells tuned to the modern musical scale, and struck by hammers acted on by a pinned cylinder, or barrel, which revolves by means of clock-work; also applied to the music or tune produced by mechanical means from the bells in a steeple, tower, or common clock.

Chimney, in locomotive engines. The chimney is regulated in size for each engine so as to act in union with the blast-pipe, to produce a proper blast on the fire. This is done by each exhaust of steam from the cylinders creating a partial vacuum in the chimney: hence a rush of air takes place through the fire and tubes to fill this vacuum; nd these successive rushes of air blow the fire.' This vacuum ranges from 2 to 6 inches of a water-gauge. The mild blast produces the least vacuum and the least consumption of fuel.

Chimney-pieces. The Egyptians, the Greeks, and the Romans, to whom architecture is so much indebted in other respects, living in warm climates, where fires in the apartments were seldom necessary, have thrown but little light on this branch of the science. Palladio only mentions two, which stood in the middle of the rooms, and consisted of columns, supporting architraves, whereon were placed the pyramids or funnels through which the smoke was conveyed. Scamozzi mentions only three in his time, placed similarly. In England, Inigo Jones designed some very elaborate chimney-pieces. The size of the chimney must depend upon the dimensions of the room wherein it is placed: the chimney should always be situated so as to be immediately seen by those who enter: the middle of the side partition wall is the best place in halls, saloons, and other rooms of passage, to which the principal entrances are commonly in the middle of the front or of the back wall; but in drawing-rooms, dressing-rooms, etc., the middle of the back wall is the best situation; the chimney being then farthest removed from the doors of communication.

Chinese architecture, a style peculiar to China, where the material employed is principally wood. It is a style not congenial to English taste or climate: its monstrosity may be seen at Brighton.

Chinese Yellow (colour), a very bright sulphuret of arsenic, brought from China.

Chinse, to thrust oakum into seams with a small iron.

Chisel, a tool with the lower part in the form of a wedge, for cutting iron plate or bar, and with the upper part flat, to receive the blows of a hammer, in order to force the cutting edge through the substance of the iron.

Chisel, an instrument used by carpenters. The large chisels used by millwrights for heavy work are generally composed of iron and steel welded together. Chisels are also employed in turning, and they are driven more or less by blows: those used by the joiners are similar; but those used by cabinet-makers are straight across the end.

Chisels in general. A chisel is an edge tool for cutting wood, either by leaning on it or by striking it with a mallet. The lower part of the chisel is the frustrum of a cuneus or wedge; the cutting edge is always on and generally at right angles to the side. The basil is ground entirely from one side. The two sides taper in a small degree upwards, but the two narrow surfaces taper downwards in a greater degree. The upper part of the iron has a shoulder, which is a plane surface at right angles to the middle line of the chisel. From this plane surface rises a prong in the form of a square pyramid, the middle line of which is the same as the middle line of the cuneus or wedge: the prong is inserted and fixed in a socket of a piece of wood of the same form: this piece of wood is called the handle, and is generally the frustrum of an octagonal pyramid, the middle line of which is the same as that of the chisel: the tapering sides of the handle diminish downwards, and terminate upwards in an octagonal dome. The use of the shoulder is for preventing the prong from splitting the handle while being struck with the mallet. The chisel is made stronger from the cutting edge to the shoulder, as it is sometimes used as a lever, the prop being at or very near the middle, the power at the handle, and the resistance at the cutting-edge. Some chisels are made with iron on one side and steel on the other, and others consist entirely of steel. There are several kinds of chisels, as the mortise-chisel, the ripping-chisel, and the socket-chisel.

Chisel, the firmer, is formed in the lower part similar to the socket-chisel; but each of the edges above the prismoidal part falls into an equal concavity, and diminishes upwards until the substance of the metal between the concave narrow surfaces becomes equal in thickness to the substance of that between the other two sides, produced in a straight line, and meeting a protuberance projecting equally on each side. The firmer chisel is used by carpenters and joiners in cutting away the superfluous wood by thin chips: the best are made of cast steel. When there is a great deal of superfluous wood to be cut away, sometimes a stronger chisel, consisting of an iron back and steel face, is first used, by driving it into the wood with a mallet; and then a slighter one, consisting entirely of steel sharpened to a very fine edge, is used in the finish. The first used is called a firmer, and the last a paring chisel, in the application of which only the shoulder or hand is employed in forcing it into the wood.

Chisel, the mortise, is made exceedingly strong, for cutting out a rectangular prismatic cavity across the fibres, quite through or very deep in a piece of wood, for the purpose of inserting a rectangular pin of the same form on the end of another piece, and thereby uniting the two. The cavity is called a mortise, and the pin inserted a tenon; and the chisel used for cutting out the cavity is, therefore, called a mortise-chisel. As the thickness of this chisel from the face to the back is great, in order to withstand the percussive force of the mallet, and as the angle which the basil makes with the face is about 25°, the slant dimension of the basil is very great. This chisel is only used by percussive force given by the mallet.

Chisel, the ripping, is only an old

socket-chisel used in cutting holes in walls for inserting plugs, and for separating wood that has been nailed together, etc.

Chisel, the socket, is used for cutting excavations: the lower part is a prismoid, the sides of which taper in a small degree upwards, and the edges considerably downwards: one side consists of steel, and the other of iron. The under end is ground into the form of a wedge, forming the basil on the iron side, and the cutting edge on the lower end of the steel face. From the upper end of the prismoidal part rises the frustrum of a hollow cone, increasing in diameter upwards: the cavity or socket contains a handle of wood of the same conic form: the axis of the handle, the hollow cone, and the middle line of the frustrum, are all in the same straight line. The socket-chisel, which is commonly about 1¼ or 1½ inch broad, is chiefly used in cutting mortises, and may be said to be the same as the mortise-chisel employed in joinery.

Chisel, in turnery, is a flat tool, skewed in a small degree at the end, and bevelled from each side, so as to make the cutting edge in the middle of its thickness.

Chock, in navigation, a wedge used to secure anything with, or for anything to rest upon. The long-boat rests upon two large chocks when it is stowed.

Chocolate lead, a pigment prepared by calcinating oxide of lead with about a third of that of copper, and reducing the compound to a uniform tint by levigation.

Choke. An adit is said to be choked when any earth or stone falls in and prevents the current of water through it: the place or part so filled is called 'the choke.'

Chopping-block, a block of wood used for reducing bricks to their intended form by axing them: it is made of any chance piece that can be obtained, and commonly from 6 to 8 inches square, supported generally upon two 14-inch brick piers, if two men are to work at it; but if four men, the chopping-block must be lengthened and supported by three piers, and so on, according to the number: it is about 2 feet 3 inches in height.

Choragic monuments, in Grecian story, monuments in honour of those who had gained a prize as choragus, or leader of the play and choruses.

Choragic monument of Lysicrates, known as the Lantern of Demosthenes, was built in the 111th Olympiad, and is still entire: it is considered the most exquisite and perfect specimen of the orders.

Choragic monument of Thrasycles, etc., now the church of our Lady of the Grotto. It is built against the rock of the Acropolis: above it stand two columns, on which tripods have been placed, and on each side of it the rock has been chiseled away in such form as evidently shows that similar buildings had been erected contiguous to it.

Chord, in geometry, is the right line joining the extremities of any arc of a circle.

Chorobates (Greek), an instrument for determining the slope of an aqueduct, and the levels of the country through which it was to pass. It differed but slightly from a common carpenter's level, which consists of a straight rule supporting a perpendicular piece, against which hangs a plumb-line.

Chorography, the art of making a map of a particular country or province, or of teaching geography.

Chromatics, a division of the science of optics, by which the properties of the colours of light and of natural bodies are illustrated.

Chromascope, or optical chromatics: there are three species of optical effects of colours,—that of refraction of prisms and lenses, that of the transmission of light through transparent media, and that of the reflection of speculas, etc.

Chromate of mercury is improperly classed as a red with vermilion; for though it is of a bright ochreous red colour in powder, it is, when ground, of a bright orange ochre hue, and affords, with white, very pure orange-coloured tints.

Chromatics, the science of the relations of light, shade, and colours.

Chrome greens are compound pigments of which chrome yellow is the principal colouring substance.

Chrome orange is a beautiful orange pigment, and one of the most durable and least exceptionable chromates of lead, but not of iron.

Chrome yellow is a pigment of modern introduction into general use, and of which there are many varieties, mostly chromates of lead, in which the latter metal more or less abounds. They are distinguished by the pureness, beauty, and brilliancy of their colours, which qualities are great temptations to their use in the hands of the painter; they are, however, far from unexceptionable pigments.

Chromium, a very rare metal, found either in the form of chromate of lead or chromate of iron.

Chronometer, a time-keeper, used for determining the longitude at sea, and for other purposes where great accuracy is required.

Chronometrical governor, an improved regulator for rendering the mean velocity of an engine uniform. The mechanism is as follows: a spindle placed vertically has a pulley fixed upon the top, to receive motion from the crank-shaft; below the pulley two bevel-wheels of equal diameters are placed face to face; the upper wheel is fixed to the spindle, and the lower one is free to turn upon it, and has an arm or crank attached to its under side, to act as a driver for the pendulous ball: between the two wheels, and communicating with them, is a third wheel, fixed upon a spindle placed horizontally, and connected at one end with the vertical spindle, so as to turn round it; the other end is supported by a carriage resting upon a plate, and is connected with a spring or counter weight on one side, and on the other side with the throttle-valve; the ball being suspended from a spherical bearing near the top of the rod. The spring is adjusted so that when the velocity of the engine is as required, the upper and lower wheels revolve at the same speed: when the velocity increases, the centrifugal force causes the ball to rise, and retards the motion of the lower wheel; then the intermediate wheel distends the spring, and moves forward upon the lower wheel as a rack, and closes the throttle-valve; when the velocity diminishes, the ball falls, and the lower wheel requires less power, so that the spring pulls back the intermediate wheel and opens the valve. The above is a modification of Mr. James Wood's governor, and is patented by Mr. C. W. Siemens.

Chrysolite, a precious stone, probably the tenth on the high-priest's pectoral, bearing the name of Zebulon: it is transparent, the colour of gold, with a mixture of green, which displays a fine lustre.

Chuck, a piece of wood or metal fixed on the end of the mandril for keeping fast the body to be turned.

Church Music. By this term is commonly understood *all* music set to words of a sacred character: hence we have not only the language of Scripture set to music in the shape of anthems, etc., but also metrical versions and paraphrases thereof, used and considered by many as church music. Indeed it too often happens that these are *adapted* to secular melodies—melodies not originally intended to be applied to words of a sacred character, and yet the music is then termed sacred, probably from an idea that there is no such thing as sacred and profane music. But this is a great error, and arises solely from ignorance of the existence of sacred music,—we mean especially church music. Examine any of the ancient authorized liturgical books, and there will be found an order of music that cannot be mistaken for profane, which is not only sacred in its character, but eminently grand, dignified, noble, and sublime; in short, it is for church purposes so superior to all other music, that it alone can properly be called church music.

Church music is the music of the holy offices,—is that music in which the *whole church*, priests and people, can participate. It is easy to execute, being simple and plain (plain chant). It can be sung by every one, and is always most majestic when sung by all; hence it is also called the full chant (cantus plenus). For a long period, and until very lately, scarcely a remnant of church music was to be found, even in those places where we had a right to expect to find it: the plain chant was banished entirely in some places, and mutilated in others, so that it could scarcely be discerned; but it is now being restored, and we hear the priest intoning his part in the offices of morning and evening prayer, and the people singing, in response, the ancient authorized melodies of the church;—we hear the Psalter chanted to fine old (so called) Gregorian tones;—we hear the Litany chanted to its own proper music, that of the church: we also hear the soul-stirring music in the Communion office, the Gloria in excelsis, the Credo, and Sanctus; the latter moreover in its proper place. We can have also, if so disposed, the church music for the matrimonial, baptismal, and burial offices, as well as an immense variety of tunes for the metrical psalms, of a true church character, unlike any other kind of music, and which is truly church music, inasmuch as it is the church's peculiar property, and would be totally misused in any other place. Our definition of church music is, music which is adapted for the services and purposes of the church, and unfit for any other place or purpose.

Church music, such as is here shortly defined, is unisonous; and harmonized music is not fit for congregational purposes; it is proper only in those parts of divine worship which may be called extra-liturgical, such as the anthem. Singing harmonized chants, canticles, Te Deum, etc., is thrusting out the congregation, that is, the chief part of the church present. The harmonies should be left entirely to the discretion of an intelligent organist, to be executed on the organ alone. Harmonized music requires accomplished and well-informed musicians for its performance, and can be sung only by the few. The anthem, in cathedral worship, is edifying only when it is performed by the choir-men in a masterly manner, not only with correct musical execution, but with care and attention, to develop all the piety, sublimity, grandeur, dignity, and whatever else the music is capable of.

Before the latter half of the 15th century, the liturgy was chanted in unison; and it is from this period we can trace the gradual departure from the rigid church style of music, in the compositions of Josquin de Près especially. In the early part of the 16th century, we find that Adrian Willaert, who was made singing-master at St. Mark's, Venice, was the first who harmonized the psalm melodies for two or more choirs; then followed the motet, or harmonized antiphon, which before had been chanted in unison, as it is done at this day in the Roman Catholic chapels in England, where there are not accomplished singing men to perform the motet. During this century, the use of harmony had not only driven the people away from their part in the performance of the service, but also corrupted the music itself so much, that it was only saved from being wholly forbidden by the grave and devotional motets and other compositions of the renowned Palestrina, whose works were imitated with great success by the disciples of his school, and this in a very eminent degree by the English church musicians. The harmonies used by Tallis, Morley, Gibbons, and the rest of the masters of church music of this age, are truly sublime.

Church ornament consists principally of the painted and stained glass windows of the emblem of the Trinity, of the passion of our Lord, of the evangelists, sacred monograms, statues of the holy apostles, of the holy evangelists, and of the saints commemorated by the church.

Church in rotundo, that whose plan is a perfect circle, in imitation of the Pantheon.

Chymol, a hinge, anciently called a grimmer.

Ciborium, an arch supported by four pillars placed over the high altar.

Cilery, in architecture, the drapery or leavage that is wrought upon the head of pillars.

Cill, the timber or stone at the foot. Ground-cills are the timbers on the ground which support the posts and superstructure.

Cimellare, the vestry or room where plate, vestments, and other rich things belonging to the church are kept.

Cincture, a ring, list, or fillet at the top and bottom of a column, serving to divide the shaft from the capital and its base.

Cinder-frame, in locomotive engines, a wire-work frame placed in front of the tubes, to arrest the ascent of large pieces of ignited coke.

Cinque-cento, a term generally architecturally applied to the Revival of art, co-eval with the early Tudor style in England and the Renaissance style in France.—In 1506 the church of St. Peter's at Rome was commenced by Bramante, the greatest monument of the revived classical or Cinque-cento style of architecture, and on the death of Bramante, in 1514, the great Raffaello continued the building. The Loggia Vaticano is a monument of his fame for its design and ornamentation.

Cinque-cento, literally five hundred, or the fifth Century, generally applied to the period of the Revival of the arts in Italy and even subsequently.—The ornament was of an enriched kind, much applied by the Italians, and since by the French.

Cinque-foil, an ornamental foliation or feathering, used in the arches of the lights and tracery of windows, panellings, etc.

Cinque Ports, the sea-port towns of Dover, Sandwich, Hastings, Hythe, and Romney, to which three others were afterwards added, viz. Winchelsea, Rye, and Seaford. These towns possess peculiar privileges, and are under the government of a Lord Warden.

Cipher, a secret mode of writing.

Cipollino, is a name given by the Italians to an impure marble, which containing veins of schistose, decomposes and falls off in flakes like the coats of an onion.

Cippus (Latin), a low column, sometimes round, but more frequently rectangular, used as a sepulchral monument.

Circinus, a pair of compasses. Those used by statuaries, architects, masons, carpenters, etc., were often represented on their tombs.

Circinus, according to Vitruvius, a pair of compasses employed by architects, carpenters, etc., for describing circles, measuring distances, and taking the thickness of solids.

Circle, a plain figure contained by one line, which is called the circumference, and is such that all straight lines drawn from a certain point within the figure to the circumference are equal to one another, and this point is called the centre of the circle.

The circumference of a circle is known to be about 3·14159 times its diameter, or, in other words, the ratio of the circumference to the diameter is represented by 3·14159; for this number writers generally put the Greek letter π.

Circular sailing, is that which is performed in the arch of a great circle.

Circular saw. Circular saws, revolving upon an axis, have the advantage that they act continually in the same direction, and no force is lost by a backward stroke: they are also susceptible of much greater velocity than the reciprocating saws, an advantage which enables them to cut more smoothly: used principally for cutting mahogany for veneering, and for other woods cut into thin layers.

Circus, an area used by the Romans for chariot-races and horse-races, and for other public sports.

Cissoid of Diocles, in the higher geometry, a curve line of the second order.

Cistern. There were cisterns throughout Palestine, in cities and in private houses. As the cities were mostly built on mountains, and the rains fall in Judea at two seasons only (spring and autumn), people were obliged to keep water in vessels. There are cisterns of very large dimensions at this day in Palestine. Near Bethlehem are the cisterns or pools of Solomon: they are three in number, situated in the sloping hollow of a mountain, one above another, so that the waters of the uppermost descend into the second, and those of the second descend into the third. The breadth is nearly the same in all, between 80 and 90 paces, but the length varies: the first is about 160 paces long; the second, 200; the third, 220. These pools formerly supplied the town of Bethlehem and the city of Jerusalem with water. Wells and cisterns, fountains and springs, are seldom correctly described in Scripture.

Cistern, in the steam-engine, the vessel which surrounds the condenser, and contains the injection water.

Cisterns, an artificial tank or reservoir, sunk in the ground and covered in with a roof, for the purpose of collecting and preserving good water for the use of a household. Near the baths of Titus are nine subterraneous cisterns, 17½ feet wide, 12 feet high, and above 137 feet long.

Citrine, or the colour of the citron, is the first of the tertiary class of colours, or ultimate compounds of the primary triad, yellow, red, and blue, in which yellow is the archeus or predominating colour, and blue the extreme subordinate; for citrine being an immediate compound of the secondaries, orange and green, of both which yellow is a constituent, the latter colour is of double occurrence therein, while the other two primaries enter singly into the composition of citrine; its mean or middle hue comprehending eight blue, five red, and six yellow, of equal intensities.

Citrine lake is a durable and better drying species of brown pink, prepared from the quercitron bark.

City, a town, an incorporated town, a town having had a bishop's see.

Clack, the valve of a pump piston; the can-lead, in Derbyshire.

Clacks, in locomotive engines, the complete valves of the pumps where the ball-valve is enclosed in a frame or cage, to limit its rise, and guide its fall into the steam-tight seat of the orifice of the pipe.

Clack-box, in locomotive engines, the box fitted on to the boiler where a ball-clack is placed, to close the orifice of the feed-pipe, and prevent steam or hot water reaching the pumps. The ball of the clack is raised from its seat by the stroke of the pump-plunger forcing the water against it, which water then passes into the boiler, while the instant fall of the ball prevents egress from the boiler.

Clack-door, a square iron-plate screwed on to the side of a bottom-pump, or small bore for convenience of changing the clack or valve.

Clack-seats, in locomotive engines, two recesses in each pump, for the clacks to fit into.

Clack-valve, in the steam-engine, a flat valve in the cold-water pump, with a hinge joint.

Clamp, a kiln built above the ground, for the purpose of burning bricks in.

Clamp, a piece of wood fixed to the end of a board by mortise and tenon, or by groove and tongue, so that the fibres of the one piece, thus fixed, traverse those of the board, and by this means prevent it from casting: the piece at the end is called a clamp, and the board is said to be clamped.

Clamps, in naval architecture, thick planks in a ship's side, which support the ends of the beams.

Clamping, in joinery: when a piece of board is fitted with the grain to the end of another piece of board across the grain, the first board is said to be clamped.

Clamp-nails, used to fasten on clamps in the building of ships.

Clasp-nails, are such with heads, brought into a little compass, so that they will sink into the wood.

Classic Orders, in architecture: of these there are but *three*,—the Doric, Ionic, and Corinthian: two others, the Tuscan and Composite, are often improperly classed with them, and the whole denominated 'the five orders of architecture.'

Claude Roman, architect of Paris; he designed and executed the grand altar, and, in consideration of the merit of that work, was permitted to be buried before the image of the Virgin, which he had chosen for the place of his interment; he died in 1675, aged 65.

Clausura, brushwood for fences and hedges.

Cleading, in locomotive engines, is usually made of narrow strips of timber, neatly fitted round the boiler and fire-box, to prevent the radiation of the heat. Externally, this is sometimes covered with zinc, and a coating of dry hair felt is commonly placed between the boiler and the timber, for the same purpose.

Clear, in architecture, inside work.

Clearing the deads, a term for clearing a shaft or drift, etc.

Cleat, a piece of wood used in different parts of a vessel to belay ropes to.

Cleavage, in geology, is an indicator of peculiar fossility in certain rocks, which is independent of, and meets at a considerable angle, the surfaces of lamination or deposition. Clay slate furnishes the best examples of this phenomenon.

Cleithral, a covered Greek temple.

Cleithros, an enclosed place; a temple whose roof covers or encloses it.

Clench-bolts, in a ship, clenched at the ends where they come through.

Clench-nails, are such as will drive without splitting the board, and draw without breaking.

Clepsydra, an instrument anciently used by the Egyptians to measure time by the running of water out of one vessel into another; which we call an hour-glass.

Clerestory, an upper story or row of windows in a Gothic church, rising clear above the adjoining parts of the building.

Clew, the lower corner of square-sails, and the after corner of a fore-and-aft sail.

Clew-garnet, a rope for hauling up the clew of a fore-sail or main-sail in a square-rigged vessel.

Clew-line, a rope for hauling up the clew of a square-sail: the clew-garnite is the clew-line of a course.

Clicket, a latch-key; the latch of a door.

Clinch, in navigation, the great ring connected with the mooring-chains.

Clinch, a half-hitch stopped to its own part.

Clinker-bar, in steam-engines, the bar fixed across the top of the ash-pit for supporting the rods used for clearing the fire-bars.

Clinkers, bricks which, by the violence of the fire, are run together and glazed over; hard bricks imported from Holland, so called.

Cloaca, a common sewer. The term cloaca is generally used in reference to those spacious subterraneous vaults, either of stone or brick, through which the foul waters of the city, as well as all the streams brought to Rome by the aqueducts, finally discharged themselves into the Tiber; according to Livy, a large subterranean canal, constructed of masonry or brick-work, for the purpose of carrying off the rain-water from the streets of a town, and the impurities from private houses, which were thus discharged into some neighbouring river.

Cloacarium, the sewers-rate; a tax which was levied in Rome for the expenses of cleansing and repairing the sewers.

Cloister, a covered ambulatory, forming part of a monastic or collegiate establishment. Cloisters are always attached to a college cathedral, and arranged round three or four sides of a quadrangular area, with large windows, not often glazed, looking into the quadrangle.

Close-hauled, a term applied to a vessel sailing with her yards braced up so as to get as much as possible to windward.

Closer, a brick-back inserted where the distance will not permit of a brick in length.

Closet, a small chamber or private room.

Clout-nails, used for nailing clouts on the axle-trees of the carriage.

Clove-hitch, two half-hitches round a spar or other rope.

Clove-hook, an iron clasp, in two parts, moving upon the same pivot and overlapping one another, used for bending chain-sheets to the clews of sails.

Clubbing, drifting down a current with an anchor out.

Club-haul, to bring a vessel's head round on the other tack, by letting go the lee anchor, and cutting or slipping the cable.

Clue garnets, in navigation, tackles fixed to the clews or lower corners of the fore and main sail, to clew them up to the yards.

Clustered column, a pier which consists of several columns or shafts clustered together.

Clutch, an apparatus for engaging or disengaging two shafts: it consists of two pieces of metal formed so that when placed together, projecting pieces on one (made to slide to and fro on the shaft, but turn with it) fit into recesses in the other, which is fixed on the driving shaft, so that the first being pulled back, its shaft will remain at rest.

Coaking, in ship-building, uniting pieces of spar by means of tabular projections, formed by cutting away the solid of one piece into a hollow, so as to make a projection in the other in such a manner that they may correctly fit, the huts preventing the pieces from drawing asunder.

Coal belongs to the third series of the Wernerian principle, viz. carboniferous rocks, coal-measures, carboniferous limestone, and old red sandstone; it is admitted to be of vegetable origin, and comprises —1. Lignites, a species of mineral charcoal or intermediate gradation from wood to coal; 2. Ordinary bituminous coal, of numerous varieties; 3. Anthracite, found generally in connection with the lowest portion of the third series, and sometimes in the primary rocks themselves. Coal, then, appears to have been formed of large vegetable masses, of considerable extent, in strata varying from a few inches to many feet in depth, the strata alternating with rocks wonderfully uniform, and consisting, in most cases, of the following: sandstone, slate clay or shale, fire-clay, ironstone, limestone, etc. Rocks are found participating of both clay and sandstone texture, greatly predominating. The coal-beds are indiscriminately accompanied by rocks either of sandstone or shale, which often rest upon fire-clay. It is in the shale accompanying the coal that the fossil impressions are so numerous; they are seldom found in the sandstones, or in the shales considerably distant from the coal-beds. The organic remains of coal formation consist of many shells of freshwater origin. The fossils, with land plants, occur in great abundance and variety, belonging to extinct species, but bearing considerable analogy to those now growing only in tropical climates. These plants are mostly succulent, and are of enormous growth.

Coal-gas, carburetted hydrogen; coal-gas, when freed from the obnoxious foreign gas, may be propelled in streams out of small apertures, which, when lighted, from jets of flame, and are called gas-lights.

Coal-tar, tar made from bituminous coal.

Coamings, in ships, raised work round the hatches, to prevent water from getting down into the hold.

Coat. Mast-coat is a piece of canvas tarred or painted, placed round a mast or bowsprit where it enters the deck.

Coat, in building, a stratum or thickness of plaster-work.

Cob (Cornish), to break or bruise: a cobber, a bruiser of tin. Cobbed ore is spoiled which is broken out of the solid large stones with sledges, and not put to water, being the best ore: the same as hing ore in the lead-mines.

Cobalt (among miners), the damps of mines, so very fatal to the workmen.

Cobalt. The ancient name for this mineral is not known. Theophrastus mentions its use for staining glass. No cobalt has been discovered in any of the remains of ancient painting. It makes a colour, according to Vitruvius, between scarlet and purple.

In chemistry, a metal, when pure, of a white colour, inclining to bluish or steel gray: at the common temperature its specific gravity is more than 8·5.

Cobalt-blue is the name now appropriated to the modern improved blue prepared with metallic cobalt, or its oxides, although it properly belongs to a class of pigments including Saxon blue, Dutch ultramarine, Thenard's blue, royal blue, Hungary blue, smalt, Zaffre or enamel blue, and Dumont's blue. These differ principally in their degrees of purity, from the nature of the earths with which they are compounded.

Cobalt-green. There are two pigments of this denomination, the one a compound of cobalt-blue and chromic yellow, which partakes of the qualities of those pigments, and may be formed on the pallet.

Caboose, the place where the victuals are cooked on board of merchant and passenger ships.

Cob-wall, a wall built of unburnt clay mixed with straw.

Cochineal is extremely rich in the finest red colouring matter, and has been long employed in scarlet dyeing, and in the manufacture of carmine.

Cochlea, a term used by the ancients to denote something of a spiral form; a spiral pump for raising water, etc.

Cock, or *stop-cock*, a kind of valve contrived for the purpose of permitting or arresting at pleasure the flow of a liquid through a pipe.

Cock-boat, a small boat used on rivers.

Cock-pit, that part of a ship which is appropriated to the use of the surgeon, being the place where the wounded are dressed: it is near the hatchway, and under the lower gun-deck.

Cockle, the skiorl of the Swedes and the schorl of the Germans; a laminated mineral substance of a blackish brown colour, like tin.

Cocoa-wood, the heart of which is seldom sound, is much used in turnery.

Coclitis, according to Pliny, a brick hardened by burning.

Cock-water (among miners), a stream of water brought into a trough to wash away the sand from tin-ore.

Cod-line, an eighteen-thread line.

Co-efficients, in algebra, are numbers or letters prefixed to other letters or unknown quantities, into which they are supposed to be multiplied; and therefore with such letters, or the quantities represented by them, making a product, or co-efficient product.

Coigne, a corner; a wooden wedge.

Coining (in the tin works), is the weighing and stamping the blocks of tin.

Cœlum, according to Vitruvius, a soffit or ceiling.

Cœnobium, anciently a monastary of monks or friars.

Cöfer, in Cornish mining, a small wooden trough which receives the tin cleansed from its impurities or slime.

Coffee-tree, a wood of a light greenish brown, close-grained, and small in stature, sometimes used by cabinet-makers.

Coffer, a deep panel in a ceiling; also applied to a casket for keeping jewels, and sometimes to a chest.

Coffer-dam, a hollow space formed by a double range of piles, with clay rammed in between, for the purpose of constructing an entrance lock to a canal, dock, or basin, or for the piers of a bridge.

Coffin, in Cornish mining, old workings which were all worked open to grass, without any shafts, by digging and casting up the thin stuff from one stall of boards to another.

Coffin, a wooden case in which a dead body is placed, sometimes encased in lead; anciently, stone coffins were used for interment.

Cog, the wooden tooth of a large wheel.

Cog-teeth are formed of a different material from the body of the wheel: a timber tooth on a cog-wheel is one made of wood, when the teeth stand perpendicularly to the plane of the wheel.

Cog-wheel, an iron wheel with wooden teeth or cogs.

Cohesion of fluids. M. Monge and others assert that the phenomena of capillary tubes are referable to the cohesive attraction of the superficial particles only of the fluids employed, and that the surface must consequently be formed into curves of the nature of lintearia, which are supposed to be the results of a uniform tension of a surface resisting the pressure of a fluid, either uniform or varying according to a given law.

Cohesion, the attraction which takes place between the particles of bodies, denoting that force by which the particles firmly cohere.

Cohesion and resistance of fluids, as examined by the force of torsion. Pressure does not augment the friction; on the contrary, the resistance is greater when the immersion is only partial. Greasing wood does not lessen the friction; the friction of oil is 17¼ times as great as that of water. A part of the friction is proportional to the velocity; the constant part is almost insensible. Thus a circle ·195 metre in diameter, turning in water with a velocity equal to ·1·4 m. in 1″, meets a resistance equivalent to a weight of 1 gramme acting on a lever of ·143 m. The portion proportional to the velocity is equivalent to ·042 gr. for a surface equal to twice such a circle moving in its own direction with a velocity of ·01 m.

Cohesive strength of materials. The

force of cohesion may be defined to be that force by which the fibres or particles of a body resist separation, and is proportioned to the number of fibres in the body, or in the area of its section.

Coiling, a serpentine winding of ropes, by which they occupy a small space, and are not liable to be entangled in working the sails of a ship.

Coin, or *quoin,* the angle of a building; used also for the machicolation of a wall.

Coke, charred pitcoal. The most valuable of the secondary products of a gas establishment is coke. The best kind is obtained from coal when carbonized in large masses, in ovens constructed on purpose. In a gas manufactory, the production of coke being of minor importance to the formation of good gas, it is generally of an inferior quality to that made in coke ovens, where it is the primary, and indeed sole object for which the coal is carbonized. But gas-coke is excellent for many purposes in the arts and manufactures, producing as clear a fire as that of the first quality, though it is neither so lasting nor so free from slag: for domestic use, however, it is unobjectionable, and may be burnt both in the drawing-room and kitchen with economy and comfort.

The distinguishing characters of good coke are, first, a clean, granular fracture in any direction, with a pearly lustre, inclining to that exhibited by cast-iron. Secondly, density, or close proximity of its particles, which adhere together in masses, and specific gravity of 1·10, or rather higher. Thirdly, when exposed to a white heat, it consumes entirely away, without leaving either slag or ashes.

It is invariably the case that the quality of the coke is inversely as that of the gas. The manufacturer must not expect to produce *both* of the best quality. The process by which the best gas is made generally leaves the coke light, spongy, and friable, although an increase of quantity is gained; for the simple reason, that the degree of heat and other circumstances required to form perfect coke must be entirely changed when gas of a high specific gravity is to be obtained. Thus large masses of coal exposed to a red heat in close vessels are acted upon by slow degrees, the external portions preventing heat from penetrating into the interior until most of the bituminous portions are given off in condensable vapour, or as charcoal and free hydrogen; the after products being light carburetted hydrogen, carbonic oxide, and carbonic-acid gases. The residue is a carbon of a dense granular composition.

Coke, as prepared for use in locomotive and other steam-engines, may be regarded as *purified* coal, or coal from which the extraneous matters not conducive to combustion have been expelled by the application of heat. It appears from experiments that the heating power of every description of fuel, whether coal, coke, wood, lignite, turf, or peat, is proportional to the quantity of carbon it contains, and that from 83 to 86 per cent. of this element enters into the composition of any given weight of Newcastle, Durham, or Lancashire coal, the other ingredients being hydrogen, azote, oxygen, and ashes. The exact process which takes place in the conversion of coal into coke is not yet thoroughly understood, although the result can be readily estimated, and is found to depend, to a considerable extent, upon the manner in which the process is performed. Thus, by coking in close ovens, Welsh coal loses about 30 per cent. of its weight; but if the coking be effected in uncovered heaps of coarse lumps, as it often is in the Welsh coal and iron districts (where abundance is allowed, as the excuse for extravagance and waste), the loss of weight is from 50 to 55 per cent. While the *weight* is thus *diminished* by coking in close ovens, the *bulk* is *increased* from 22 to 23 per cent. The rapid and complete combustion of the carbon which takes place in the burning of coke has the effect of preventing, to a considerable extent, the emission of that palpable smoke which arises from the combustion of coal; and for this property coke was resorted to for use in locomotive engines, when the non-emission of smoke was imposed as one of the conditions upon which railway companies were empowered by Act of Parliament. The practical advantages since found to be derived from the burning of coke instead of coal are, its greater power in evaporating water and producing steam, and the less rapid destruction of the boiler which ensues from its employment.

Colarin, the little frieze of the capital of the Tuscan and Doric column, placed between the astragal and the annulets.

Cold chisel, a piece of steel flattened and sharpened at one end, which is properly tempered, so that it may be used for cutting metal.

Cold-harbour, an inn; a shelter from the cold; a protection on the wayside for travellers benighted or benumbed.

Cold short iron, iron in an impure state.

Cold-water well and reservoir. To effect the condensation of steam, the water is very commonly raised, by means of the cold-water pump, from a reservoir or well. This absorbs from the engine some portion of its power. Indeed, when the wells are deep, the quantity of power thus expended is so great, that the condensing system can no longer be judiciously applied. This may be known by the following investigation:

Rule.—Multiply the weight of water, in pounds, by the feet through which it passes in a minute, and divide the product by 33,000; the quotient will exhibit, friction excluded, the horses' power expended.

Example.—To condense 103°;
Weight of cold water 10 ℔.
per gallon, at 62° of temperature,
Engine, nominal power .. 4 horses.
Water, per horse power .. 4 gals.
Lift of do., or height
raised, 230 feet per minute.
Hence $\dfrac{4 \times 40 \times 230}{33,000} = 1\tfrac{1}{8}$ h. power.

Cold-water pump, the pump for supplying the water for condensation.

Collar, in ships, an eye in the end or bight of a shroud or stay, to go over the mast-head.

Collar, in turnery, a ring inserted in the puppet for holding the end of the mandril next the chuck, in order to make the spindle run freely and exactly.

Collar, a plate of metal screwed down upon the stuffing-box of a steam-engine, with a hole to allow the piston-rod to pass through.

Collar of a shaft, the timber and boarding used to secure the uppermost part of a shaft in loose rubble from falling in.

Collar-beam, a beam framed across and between two principal rafters.

Collision, in mechanics. Whenever two bodies act on each other so as to change the direction of their relative motions, by means of any forces which preserve their activity undiminished at equal distances on every side, the relative velocities with which the bodies approach to or recede from each other will always be equal at equal distances.

Colliquation, smelting or dissolving anything by heat.

Colluviarium, anciently a well or opening formed at intervals in the channel of an aqueduct for procuring a free current of air along its course, and to facilitate the operation of clearing away foul deposits left by the waters.

Cologne earth is a native pigment, similar to the Vandyke brown in its uses and properties as a colour.

Colonnade, a range of columns, whether attached or insulated, and supporting an entablature.

Colosseum, a name given to the theatre of Vespasian, either from its magnitude or from its colossal statue of Nero; also the name of a fine building in the Regent's Park.

Colossus, a statue of gigantic dimensions, or very much beyond the proportions of nature.

Colour. The term colour being used synonymously for pigment is the cause of much ambiguity, particularly when speaking of colours as sensible or in the abstract; it would be well, therefore, if the term pigment were alone used to denote the material colours of the pallet.

Colouring, in painting, the art of disposing the tints, so as to produce either an imitation of the natural colours of the objects represented, or force and brightness of effect. Although a subject inferior to many others which the painter must study, this is yet of sufficient importance to employ a considerable share of his attention; and to excel in it, he must be well acquainted with that part of optics which has the nature of light and colours for its object. Light, however simple and uncompounded it may appear, is nevertheless made up, as it were, of several distinct substances; and the number and quantity of component parts have been happily discovered by the moderns.

Colours (symbolic), in antiquity, the middle ages, and modern times. The history of symbolic colours is but little known. Colours had the same signification amongst all nations of the remotest antiquity: this conformity indicates a common origin, which extends to the earliest state of humanity, and develops its highest energies in the religion of Persia: the dualism of light and darkness presents, in effect, the two types of colours which become the symbols of two principles, benevolence and malevolence. The ancients admitted but two primitive colours, white and black, whence all others are derived.

The language of colours, intimately connected with religion, passed into India, China, Egypt, Greece, and Rome, and re-appeared in the middle ages; the large windows of Gothic cathedrals found their explanation in the books of the Zenda, the Vedas, and the paintings of the Egyptian temples.

Among the Egyptians, the prophets did not allow metal-founders or statuaries to represent the gods, lest they should deviate from the rules.

At Rome, the penalty of death was incurred by selling or being clothed in a purple stuff. At this day, in China, any one who wears or buys clothes with the prohibited design of the dragon or phœnix, is subjected to 300 stripes and three years' banishment.

Symbolism explains this severity of laws and customs: to each colour, to each pattern, appertained a religious or political idea: to change or to alter it was a crime of apostasy or of rebellion.

Archæologists have remarked that Indian and Egyptian paintings, and those of Greek origin, named Etruscan, are composed of plain tints of a brilliant colour, but without demi-tints; the pattern and the colour had a necessary signification,—it was essentially restrictive: perspective, chiaro-oscuro, and demi-tints, would have led to confusion.

Christianity, in recalling these forgotten significations, restores a new energy to the language of colours: the doctrine taught by Christ was not therefore new, since it borrowed the symbols of ancient religions. The Son of God, in leading back mankind to the truth, came not to change, but to fulfil the law;—this law was the worship of the true God.

The three languages of colours, divine, consecrated, and profane, classify, in Europe, the three estates of society,—the clergy, the nobles, and the people.

The large glass windows of Christian churches, like the paintings of Egypt, have a double signification,—the apparent and the hidden; the one is for the uninitiated, and the other applies itself to the mystic creeds. The theocratic era lasts to the Renaissance; at this epoch, symbolic expressions are extinct; the divine language of colours is forgotten,—painting became an art, and was no longer a science.

The aristocratic era commences; and symbolism, banished from the church, takes refuge at the court: disdained by painting, it is found again in heraldry. Modern painting still preserves its symbolism in church pictures: St. John wears a green robe, Christ and the Virgin are likewise draped in red and blue, and God in white.

Natural philosophy recognizes seven colours, which form the solar ray, decomposed by the prism; namely, violet, indigo, blue, green, yellow, orange, and red. Painting admits but five primitives,—the first and last of which are rejected by natural philosophy,—white, yellow, red, blue, and black. From the combination of these five colours every hue is produced.

According to symbolism, two principles produce all colours, light and darkness.

Light is represented by white, and darkness by black; but light does not exist but by fire, the symbol of which is red: setting out from this basis, symbolism admits two primitive colours, red and white. Black was considered as the negation of colours, and attributed to the spirit of darkness; red is the symbol of divine love; white, the symbol of divine wisdom. From these two attributes of God, love and wisdom, the creation of the universe emanates.

Secondary colours represent different combinations of the two principles; yellow emanates from red and white; it is the symbol of revelation of the love and of the wisdom of God.

Blue emanates likewise from red and white; it indicates divine wisdom manifested by life, by the spirit or the breath of God (air, azure); it is the symbol of the spirit of truth.

Green is formed by the union of yellow and blue; it indicates the manifestation of love and wisdom in action; it was the symbol of charity, and of the regeneration of the soul by works.

Gold and yellow were, in Christian symbolism, the emblems of faith: St. Peter was represented by the illuminators and miniaturists of the middle ages with a golden-yellow robe, and the rod or the key in his hand.

Christianity restored truth to mankind, and reinstated symbolic language in its original purity. In the Transfiguration, the countenance of our Lord became resplendent as the sun, and his vesture shone like the light. Such, in their highest energy, are the symbols of divine love and wisdom. The angel who rolled away the stone from the sepulchre reproduced them in an inferior order,—his face shone like lightning, and his robe was white as snow. Finally, in the last degree, appeared the just, in robes washed white in the blood of the Lamb. The artists of the middle ages preserved their precious traditions, and gave to Jesus Christ, after the resurrection, a white or red costume.

Columbaria, the holes left in walls

for the insertion of pieces of timber; so called from resembling the niches of a pigeon-house. The niches of a mausoleum, made to receive the cineral urns, were likewise termed columbaria. The columbarium was a place of sepulture used for the ashes of the Romans, after the custom of burning the dead had been introduced among them.

Columen, the term applied to the upright timbers of a roof, corresponding to the modern kingposts.

Column, in architecture, a member of a cylindrical form, placed upright for support of buildings, principally wrought in stone, and made decorative in conformity to the order and style of architectural composition. It consists of a base, a shaft or body, and a capital, and differs from the pilaster, which is square on the plan.

Columns, in architecture, according to Vitruvius, were of the three orders. The proportions of Corinthian columns are in every respect, excepting their capitals, similar to those of Ionic; although their form is more graceful and proportionably more delicate, by reason of the greater height of the capitals; for Ionic capitals are a third part only of the lower diameter of the columns, whereas the Corinthian capital is equal in height to an entire diameter. The peculiar character of the capitals, which admits of their being higher than those of Ionic columns by two-thirds of a diameter, gives beauty to them, by permitting an increase of the height without violating the laws of symmetry.

Combustion, the operation of fire upon an inflammable substance, by which it smokes, flames, and is reduced to ashes.

Few or no chemical combinations can take place without a disturbance in the equilibrium of caloric in the substances to be so combined; and when caloric is thereby evolved in sufficient extent and rapidity, and when one or all the bodies engaged may be freely combustible, ignition takes place. When this is unintentional, or is the result of ignorance or carelessness, it is convenient to call it *spontaneous combustion*. Thus we frequently hear of hayricks, etc., on fire; occasionally of carts loaded with quicklime being burned by the rain falling upon the lime. There are also somewhat apocryphal accounts of coal in coal-yards being destroyed in like manner. But the most important instance of this class, as far as regards the preservation of Government establishments, is the combustion that infallibly and rapidly ensues when greasy hemp, flax, or cotton, is allowed to remain loosely heaped together, in any quantity, in a confined unventilated space. Full proof of this has been made by experiment in the dockyards; and there is much reason to attribute many fires in former days to carelessness in the rope-walks and hemp-stores; in consequence of which, rigorous orders have been of late years issued as to the immediate disposal of loose oakum and hemp sweepings—all more or less greased or oiled. The very oil-rags used by engravers in cleaning plates, when heaped together to any amount, will be consumed in a few hours.

The combination in question seems to be between the oil and the oxygen of the atmosphere. Oil has always an affinity for oxygen; though, when the bulk of the former is considerable in proportion to the surface, the action is but feeble, and the results not ordinarily appreciable: but in the case of admixture of such fibrous vegetable bodies as hemp, flax, or cotton with oily matters, where the ratio of surface to solidity is great, and when the conditions for accumulating heat are favourable,

—this accumulation soon produces ignition amongst such inflammable bodies as those just enumerated.

Come. 'Come home;' said of an anchor when it is broken from the ground, and drags. To 'come up' a rope or tackle, is to slack it off.

Commandry, a religious house belonging to a body of knights of the order of St. Bernard and St. Anthony.

Commissure, the joins between two stones, in masonry.

Common pitch, an old term still applied by country workmen to a roof in which the length of the rafters is about three-fourths of the entire span.

Common sewer of Rome: it was near the Senatorian bridge, and was 16 feet in diameter.

Communication valves, the valves in a steam-pipe which connects two boilers to an engine, for cutting off the communication between either boiler and the engine.

Communion table, a piece of church furniture usually placed near the wall of the east end of the chancel, and enclosed by rails, within which the clergyman stands to administer the Sacrament.

Companion, a wooden covering over the staircase to a ship's cabin.

Compartition, the division or distribution of the ground-plan of an edifice into its various apartments.

Compartment of the streets within a city. According to Palladio, regard must be always had to the temperature of the air, and also to the region of heaven, or the climate under which the place is situated; because where the air is cold or temperate, there the streets ought to be made large and noble, since thereby the city will become more wholesome, convenient, and beautiful: it being certain that the less piercing, and the freer the air is, the less will it offend the head; and therefore the more a town is situated in a cold place, or in a piercing air, and the houses are high, the longer ought the streets to be made, that they may be visited by the sun in every part.

Compartment, a division or separate part of a general design.

Compass (Harris's magneto-electric). The inventor's object, in the application of his discovery of the steadying action of the copper ring, "is the combination of great sensitiveness with stability and simplicity of construction; so that while the needle is free to obey the magnetic force of the earth in the most perfect way, it yet remains tranquil amidst the disturbing motions to which a ship is exposed; and this stability is obtained without the aid of friction or other mechanical impediment, which often produce an apparent steadiness or rather sluggishness of the compass (arising from indifference to motion), at the expense of accuracy.

"When the horizontal position of the card is disturbed by any alteration of dip incidental to a change of latitude, it is to be corrected by moving the silver sliders on the needle.

"Should the compass be out of use, care must be taken to let the needle hang freely in the meridian; and if put into a store-room, or otherwise set by, the card and needle should be removed altogether, and placed with the needle downward in the shallow box provided for it,—the north point being on that part of the keeper marked with a cross, thus ×. A good compass is liable to deterioration and damage when stowed away without regard to its magnetic properties, and without due care being taken to preserve the agate and the point of suspension in a perfect state."

Compasses, an instrument with two long legs, working on a centre pin at one extremity; used for drawing circles, measuring distances, setting out work, etc.

COMPOSITION.

Compass-headed, in ancient architecture, circular.

Compass-plane, in joinery, a tool similar to the smoothing-plane in size and shape, but the sole is convex, and the convexity is in the direction of the length of the plane. The use of the compass-plane is to form a concave cylindrical surface, when the wood to be wrought upon is bent with the fibres in the direction of the curve, which is in a plane surface perpendicular to the axis of the cylinder: consequently, compass-planes must be of various sizes, in order to accommodate different diameters.

Compass-roof, a roof in which the braces of the timbers are inclined so as to form a sort of arch.

Compass-saw, in joinery, a tool for cutting the surfaces of wood into curved surfaces: for this purpose it is narrow, without a back, thicker on the cutting edge, as the teeth have no set: the plate is about an inch broad, next to the handle, and diminishes to about one quarter of an inch at the other extremity; there are about five teeth in the inch: the handle is single.

Compass-window, a bay window, or oriel.

Complement (the) of an arch or angle is what it wants of 90 degrees: thus the complement of 50° is 40°, and the complement of 40° is 50°.

Compluvium (Latin), the interval between the roofs of porticoes which surround the cavædium. The rain was admitted through this opening and fell upon the area below, which was termed by some authors the *impluvium*.

Composite Order: by some considered not a distinct order, but a variety of the Corinthian. For its height and proportion, see *Architecture, Orders.*

Care must be taken in Composite as well as in Corinthian capitals, that the feet of the lower leaves do not project beyond the upper part of the column, as at St. Carlo, in the Corso at Rome, and at the Banqueting-house in London; for nothing can be uglier. Neither are these leaves, as they mount, to bend forwards, as in many of the antiques, and in some modern buildings, because they then hide a considerable part of the upper row of leaves, and give a stunted disagreeable form to the whole capital. The different divisions of the acanthus-leaf, and bunches of olive or parsley which compose the total of each leaf, must be firmly marked, and massed in a very distinct manner: the stems that spring from between the upper leaves are to be kept low upon the vase of the capital, while rising between the leaves, then spring gradually forwards, to form the different volutes; and the ornaments, which sometimes are used to adorn the sides of the angular volutes, are never to project beyond the fillets between which they are confined.

Composition of motion, in mechanics, an assemblage of several directions of motion resulting from several powers acting in different though not in opposite directions.

Composition, in painting, is a tasteful and proper distribution of the objects of a picture, in grouping, in the attitudes, in the draperies and the management of the background. In architecture, the several parts which constitute a temple ought to be subject to the laws of symmetry, the principles of which should be familiar to all who profess the science of architecture. Symmetry results from proportion, which, in the Greek language, is termed analogy. Proportion is the commensuration of the various constituent parts with the whole; in the existence of which, symmetry is found to consist; for no building can possess the attributes of composition in which symmetry and proportion are disregarded, nor unless there exists that perfect conformation of parts which may be observed in a well-formed human being.

Compound arch, according to Professor Willis, an arch which has the archivolt moulded or formed into a series of square recesses and angles, on the principle that "it may be resolved into a number of concentric archways successively placed within and behind each other."

Compound pier, a term applied to a clustered column.

Compression, the result of pressing or squeezing matter so as to set its parts nearer to each other, and to make it occupy less space.

Computation, the method of estimating time, weights, measures, etc.

Concamerate, to arch over.

Concameratio, arched work.

Concave, a term denoting the curvilinear vacuity of hollow bodies.

Concentric, having a common centre; as concentric circles, ellipses, etc.

Concha, according to Dr. Whewell, a term for the concave ribless surface of a vault.

Conclave, a private or secret council; an inner room for meeting privately.

Concluding line, a small line leading through the centre of the steps of a rope or Jacob's ladder.

Concrete, a composition of lime, sand, pebbles, or other materials, now commonly used for the foundations of buildings. The general employment of the mixture of lime and gravel, commonly known by the name of concrete, in all foundations where, from the nature of the soil, precautions against partial settlements appear necessary, and the great probability of an extension of its use in situations where the materials of which it is composed are easily and cheaply procured, must of course render it a subject of great interest to the engineer. Much valuable information on this subject will be found in a prize essay by Mr. G. Godwin, published in the 'Transactions of the Institute of British Architects.' In this essay, many instances are brought forward of the employment by the ancients of a mixture analogous to concrete, both for foundations and for walls. Several cases are also mentioned in which, of late years, it has been used advantageously for foundations, by some of the most distinguished architects and civil engineers. In these latter instances, the proportion of the ingredients varies from one of lime and two of gravel, to one of lime and twelve of gravel.—the lime being in most cases Dorking lime, and the gravel, Thames ballast. The proportion, however, most commonly used now, in and about London, is one of lime to seven of ballast; though, from experiments made at the building of the Westminster New Bridewell, it would appear that one of lime to eight of ballast made the most perfect concretion.

Concrete, compounded solely of lime and screened stones, will never assume a consistence at all equal to that of which sand forms a part. The north wing of Buckingham Palace affords an instance of this: it was first erected on a mass of concrete composed of lime and stones, and when subsequent alterations made it necessary to take down the building and remove the foundation, this was found not to have concreted into a mass.

Mr. Godwin states, as the result of several experiments, that two parts of stones and one of sand, with sufficient lime (dependent on the quality of the material) to make good mortar with the latter, formed the best concrete. As the quality of the concrete depends, therefore, on the goodness of the mortar composed of the lime and sand, and as this must vary with the quality of the lime, no fixed proportions can of course be laid down which will suit every case. The proportions must be determined by experiment; but in no case should the quantity of sand be less than double that of the lime.

The best mode of compounding the concrete is to thoroughly mix the lime, previously ground, with the ballast in a dry state; sufficient water being then thrown over it to effect a perfect mixture, it should be turned over at least twice with shovels, and then wheeled away instantly for use. In some cases, where a great quantity of concrete has to be used, it has been found advisable to employ a pug-mill to mix the ingredients: in every case it should be used hot.

With regard to the quantity of water that should be employed in forming concrete, there is some difference of opinion; but as it is usually desirable that the mass should set as rapidly as possible, it is not advisable to use more water than is necessary to bring about a perfect mixture of the ingredients. A great change of bulk takes place in the ingredients of concrete when mixed together: a cubic yard of ballast, with the due proportion of lime and water, will not make a cubic yard of concrete. Mr. Godwin, from several experiments made with Thames ballast, concludes that the diminution is about one-fifth. To form a cubic yard, therefore, of concrete, the proportion of lime being ⅛th of the quantity of ballast, it requires about 30 cubic feet of ballast, and 3¾ cubic feet of ground lime, with sufficient water to effect the admixture.

An expansion takes place in the concrete during the slaking of the lime, of which an important use has been made in the underpinning of walls: the amount of this expansion has been found to be about ⅛ths of an inch to every foot in height; and the size thus gained, the concrete never loses.

The examples from which the above rules are deduced are principally of buildings erected in or about London; the lime used is chiefly from Dorking, and the ballast from the Thames. It is very desirable that a more extended collection of facts should be made, that the proportions of the materials, when other limes and gravels are used, should be stated, in order that some certain rules may be laid down by which the employment of concrete may be regulated under the various circumstances which continually present themselves in practice.

The Dorking and Halling limes are slightly hydraulic. Will common limes, such as chalk, and common stone-lime, answer for forming foundations of concrete, where the soil, although damp, is not exposed to running water? Is it possible, even with hydraulic lime, to form a mass of concrete in running water? If common lime will not answer, may it not be made efficient by a slight mixture of cement? These, and questions similar to these, are of great interest; and facts which elucidate them will be valuable contributions to the stock of knowledge on this subject.

It is a question for consideration, whether a great variety of sizes in the materials used would not form the most solid as well as the hardest wall. The walls of the fortress of Ciudad Rodrigo, in Spain, are of concrete. The marks of the boards which retained the semi-fluid matter in their construction are everywhere perfectly visible; and besides sand and gravel, there are everywhere large quantities of round boulder-stones in the walls, from 4 to 6 inches in diameter, procured from the ground around the city, which is everywhere covered with them.

Condensation, the conversion of vapour into water by cold.

Condenser, in steam-engines, the vessel connected with the exhaust-port of the cylinder of a low-pressure engine, and also with the air-pump, by a passage at the bottom fitted by the foot-valve of the pump: it receives the steam from the cylinder, and condenses it by a jet of cold water, thus forming a vacuum for the return stroke: the water, air, etc., are then drawn off by the air-pump, and discharged into the hot well.

Conditorium, a secret place; a sepulchre; a vault.

Conduction, electrical, a series of phenomena in electricity, giving origin to a classification of substances as conductors of electricity. The substances which properly come under this *conducting* or *non-electric* class are principally as follows:—

LIST OF ELECTRICAL CONDUCTORS.
Every metallic substance known.
Well-burned charcoal.
Plumbago.
Concentrated and diluted acids, and saline fluids.
Water, and moist vegetable matter.
Living animal matter.
Flame — smoke — steam.

The distinctive difference in the conducting and non-conducting property of bodies may be readily illustrated in the following way:— Excite a glass tube and wire, and bring the ball of the wire into contact with any of the *electrics*, as a rod of glass, a stick of sealing-wax, or brimstone rendered perfectly dry: the attractive power of the ball and wire, together with the tube, will not be in any sensible degree impaired. Let the electrified ball now touch the walls of the room or other conducting substance communicating with the ground; the attractive power will instantly vanish.

It is evident from these facts that all electric substances are *non-conductors* or *insulators*, as they are appropriately termed; whilst, on the other hand, *non-electric substances* are transmitters or conductors of electrical action. When, therefore, any conducting substance is placed on an electrical support, such as a rod of glass or shell-lac, it is considered to be insulated, and is termed an *insulated conductor*; when electrified by contact with any excited or other electrified body, it is said to be *charged*. The electrical charge thus communicated to an insulated conductor appears to be collected about its surface, and to be rather dependent on that than on the solid content. Thus, if two metallic spheres or cylinders, the one solid, the other hollow and extremely light, be suspended by silk lines, or placed on dry insulating supports, and be charged by contacts with an excited tube, the attractive energy of each upon any light substance presented to it will be found quite alike in each. In this experiment the insulators must be very dry and perfect.

The best insulating substances are of the vitreous and resinous class, such as shell-lac, brimstone, dry glass rods, vitrified and crystalline bodies: to these may be added silk.

The best conducting substances are principally metallic bodies, saline fluids, and common charcoal.

It should, however, be here understood, that modern researches, especially those of Faraday, lead us to conclude that there are really no substances which perfectly conduct or perfectly obstruct electrical action. The insulating and conducting power is, in fact, a difference of degree only: still, the extreme differences are so great, that if classed in relation to such differences, those at the extremes of the series admit of being considered the one as insulators, the other as conductors; whilst the intermediate terms are made up of substances which may be considered as imperfect, taken as either. Conversely, every substance is capable of excitation by friction; yet the differences in this respect are so great as to admit of some bodies being called electrics and others non-electrics, with an intermediate class between these extremes, which may be termed imperfect electrics.

Series of conductors and insulators.—Metals and concentrated acids are found at the conducting extremity of such a series,—shell-lac, brimstone, all vitreous and resinous bodies, at the other or electric extremity; whilst the imperfect or intermediate substances comprise such matter as common earth and stones, dry chalk, marble, porcelain, paper, and alkaline matter.

The attractive power evinced by any electrical body in a state of excitation, although the first and usually the most evident electrical effect, is yet not the only force which seems to result from this curious condition of common matter. On a closer examination of the phenomena, a new class of facts present themselves, of remarkable interest. If the excitation be considerable, and the attracted body insulated, it will, after being drawn into contact with the electrified substance, rebound from it with great violence, as if repelled by some new power, and will not be again attracted until it has had conducting communication with the earth, or some other mass of matter capable of reducing it to its original condition before the contact.

Conduit, a structure forming a reservoir for water, and from which it is drawn for use.

Cone, a solid body having a circular base, and its other extremity terminating in a single point or vertex. Cones are either right or oblique.

Cone-plate, a strong plate of cast iron fixed vertically to the bed of a lathe, with a conical hole in it, to form a support for the end of a shaft which it is required to bore.

Confessional, a recess or seat in which the priest sits to hear the confessions of penitents.

Conge, another name for the echinus or quarter-round, as also for the cavetto: the former is called the swelling conge, the latter the hollow conge.

Conic sections, the curves formed by the intersection of a circular cone and a plane; the former being either oblique or right.

Conical points, in turnery, the cones fixed in the pillars for supporting the body to be turned: that on the right hand is called the fore centre, and that on the left hand, the back centre.

Coniunctaet, the stone which crowns a pier, or that lies immediately over the capital of the impost, and under the sweep. The bed of it is level below, and curved above, receiving the first rise or spring of the arch or vault.

Conisterium, an apartment in the palæstra, in which sand was kept for sprinkling the athletæ, after they had been anointed.

Connecting-rods, in locomotive engines, the strong iron rods which connect the piston to the driving-wheel axle, and thus give motion to all the machinery.

Connecting-rods, in locomotive engines, *outside* or *side rods*, those which connect together the wheels of good engines. They are seen outside the wheels, making an irregular forward motion, like watermen rowing a boat. By connecting the wheels together, one pair cannot slip without the others, and the greatest practicable adhesion is thus obtained.

Connecting-rod straps, in locomotive engines, strong pieces of iron bent like the letter C, which fit the ends of the connecting-rod, and into which the axle-bearing is fitted in two parts. They are attached to their respective ends of the rod by keys and cotters, which are taken out, and the half of the bearing also, when a connecting-rod has to be put on. The strap and half-bearing are then brought over the axle or cross-head, the other half-bearing put into the strap, the end of the rod brought up against the bearing, and secured by the keys and cotters. Taking off a rod is of course the reverse of putting one on.

Connecting-rod bearings, in locomotive engines, the gun-metal or composition metal bearings fitted into the straps, to suit the particular part they are to work on.

Conning, directing the helmsman in steering a vessel.

Conservation, the ceremony of sanctifying or making holy.

Conservatory, a superior kind of greenhouse, for preserving curious and rare exotic plants. It is made with beds of the finest composts, into which the trees and plants are removed for culture and preservation. Its construction is more capacious than the ordinary greenhouse, and it is furnished in a superior style, provided with a free admission of light, and, in addition, with flues or boiling-water pipes to raise the temperature when necessary, and also contrivances for the introduction of fresh air.

Consideration (the), which one ought to have before he begins to build. Palladio says, "The first thing that requires our consideration, when we are about to build, is the plan, and the upright of the edifice we propose to erect." Three things, according to Vitruvius, are chiefly to be considered, without which a building cannot be of any value. These are, conveniency, solidity, and beauty; for no edifice can be allowed to be perfect, if it be commodious and not durable; or, if being durable, it be subject to many inconveniences; or if having both solidity and conveniency, it has no beauty or uniformity.

Consistory court, a spiritual court, formerly held in the nave of the cathedral church.

Console, a bracket or truss, mostly with scrolls or volutes at the two ends, of unequal size and contrasted, but connected by a flowing line from the back of the upper one to the inner convolving face of the lower.

Constant white, permanent white, or barytic white, is a sulphate of barytes, and, when well prepared and free from acid, is one of the best whites for water-painting, being of superior body in water, but destitute of this quality in oil.

Construction, in architecture: for this the chief requisites are, magnitude and strength, and the art of distributing the different forces and strains of the parts and materials of a building in so scientific a manner as to avoid failure and to insure durability.

Continuous imposts, according to Professor Willis, are the mouldings of an arch which are continued without interruption down the uprights to the ground or base, the impost point having no mark or distinction of any kind.

Contouring (surveying altitudes and levels). This term is applied to the outline of any figure, and consequently to that of any section of a solid body; but when used professionally, in connection with the forms of ground, or of works of defence, the outline of a horizontal section of the ground, or works, is alone to be understood by it.

When the forms of ground, or works, are described by contours, or horizontal sections, these sections are taken at some fixed vertical interval from each other, suited to the scale of the drawing, or to the subject in hand; and the distance of each, above or below some assumed plane of comparison, is given in figures at the most convenient places on the plan. When the scale of the drawing is about 100 feet to an inch, 2 or 3 feet will be found a convenient vertical interval between the contours; and however large the scale of the plan, it will scarcely be found necessary to obtain contours with a less vertical interval than 2 feet. If the scale of the plan be about 250 feet to an inch, or the ordinary special survey scale of 4 chains to an inch, 5 feet will prove a convenient vertical interval; and with a horizontal scale of from 500 to 800 feet per inch, 10 feet may be taken as the vertical interval.

In tracing and surveying the contours of ground, the following process may be adopted: complete the survey of the occupation of the ground, the streams, etc., and determine carefully the altitudes of the trigonometrical points employed above the intended place of comparison; take an accurate trace from the plot of one of the triangles, which, if the distances between the trigonometrical points are properly proportioned to the scale of the plan, will generally be a convenient piece in point of size to contour; take this trace to the ground, and find upon the ground, and mark upon the trace the points where each of the intended contours will cut the boundary lines of the triangle.

Contraction, the effect of cold upon a warm body, causing a diminution in its size by the particles approaching each other.

Contramure, an out-wall built about the wall of a city or fortification.

Convent, a building appropriated to religious persons; a nunnery.

Convocation and *Convocators*, or parliament of tinners. All Stannary laws are enacted by the several convocations, and carry with them all the force and law of acts of parliament.

Coopertorium, the roof of a building.

Co-ordinates, in the theory of curves, any abscissa and its corresponding ordinate.

Cope (to), to jut out as a wall.

Cope (to), to cover over an arch.

Coping, the reversing course of a wall, either flat or sloping on the upper surface, to throw off water.

Coppe-house, anciently a tool-house.

Copper, one of the six primitive metals, and the most ductile and malleable after gold and silver. Of this metal and lapis calaminaris is made brass, which is comparatively a modern invention.

Copper green (colour); the appellation of a class rather than of an individual pigment, under which are comprehended verdigris, verditer, malachite, mineral green, green bice, Scheele's green, Schweinfurt or Vienna green, Hungary green, emerald green, true Brunswick green, lake green, mountain green, African green, French green, Saxon green, Persian green, patent green, marine green, Olympian green, etc. The general characteristic of these greens is brightness of colour, well suited to the purposes of housepainting, but not adapted to the modesty of nature in fine art.

Coral wood is of a fine red colour, hard, and polishable.

Corbel, or *Corbeille*, a short piece of timber or stone let into a wall half its length or more, as the burthen superimposed may require, to carry a weight above it, and projecting from the general face of the work; it is carved in various fanciful ways; the commonest form is, however, that of an ogee.

Corbel, in Gothic architecture, a projecting stone or piece of timber which supports a superincumbent weight.

Corbel-table, a cornice supported by corbels.

Corbie steps, steps up the sides of a gable, found in old houses in Flanders, Holland, etc.

Corbona, in mining, a dropper from a lode in irregular masses.

Corbs, ornaments in architecture.

Cordon, the edge of stone on the outside of a building.

Core, with the Cornish tinmen, is a division of time and labour.

Corinthian Order. The three columns in the Campo Vaccino, supposed remains of the temple of Jupiter Stator, are generally allowed to be the most perfect models of the Corinthian order amongst the antiques at Rome. Palladio, in his fourth book, where he gives the whole profile at large, acknowledges that he never had seen any work better executed, or more delicately finished; that its parts are beautifully formed, well-proportioned, and skilfully combined; all which last qualities are certainly signified by his *benissimo intesi*.

With these favourable sentiments, it is extraordinary that, in his design of the Corinthian order, he should have so very considerably deviated from this excellent original as scarcely to leave the smallest shadow of resemblance.

Vignola, in his Corinthian profile, has chiefly imitated the above-mentioned fragment, and the interior order of the Pantheon, another very perfect model. His composition is uncommonly beautiful, and, without dispute, superior to that of any other master; he artfully collected all the perfections of his originals, and formed a whole far preferable to either of them.

Corinthian Brass. Gold, silver, and copper, casually mixed together at the burning of the city of Corinth, there being a great many statues and vessels melted down and so embodied.

Corner-stones, in architecture, the two stones which stand one in each joint of the chimney.

Cornews, a kind of tin ore, found in black columns, with irregular sides, and terminating in prisms.

Cornice, the projection, consisting of several members, which crowns or finishes an entablature, or the body or part to which it is annexed. The cornice used on a pedestal is called the cap of the pedestal.

Cornish engine, a single-acting beam engine, used for raising water; the steam is worked very expansively, and used for the down-stroke only, to raise an immense weight, fastened to the pump-rod, at the end of the beam: the steam having acted for the down-stroke, and the entrance-valve being closed, a communication is formed between the top and bottom of the cylinder, by lifting a valve in the steam passage, called an equilibrium valve; the pressures on the piston are thus equalized, and the weight acts to force the water up, and raise the piston.

Cornucopia, or horn of plenty; among architects, painters, etc., it is represented under the figure of a large horn, out of which issue fruit, flowers, etc.

Corollary, an inference or deduction.

Coromandel wood, the produce of Ceylon and the coast of India, is shipped in logs and planks from Bombay and Madras; it is of a red hazel-brown colour, handsome for furniture wood, and turns well.

Corona, the members constituting the uppermost of the three divisions of the entablature of a portico, or any other building in which columns are introduced; this division is termed *cornice*.

Corona, that flat, square, and massy member of a cornice, more usually called the drip or larmier, whose situation is between the cymatium above and the bed-moulding below; its use is to carry the water drop by drop from the building.

Corporas cloth, a linen cloth or napkin spread upon the altar, on which the host and chalice are placed at the mass in the Catholic service.

Corpse-gate, a covered place at the entrance to a churchyard, intended to shelter the corpse and mourners from rain.

Correggio (Antonio Allegri); of the Lombard school he acquired the art of modelling. His early style was acquired probably from Andrea Mantegna.

Corridor, a gallery or open communication to the different apartments of a house.

Corrugated Iron, a design for the strength of iron beams or girders, in the employment of corrugated sheet iron. This was the subject of a patent, granted in 1840 to Mr. J. H. Porter, "for an improved mode of applying corrugated iron in the formation of fire-proof floors, roofs, and other structures."

Corsa, the name given by Vitruvius to a platband or square fascia whose height is more than its projecture.

Cortile, a small court enclosed by the divisions or appurtenances of a building.

Cortis, in the middle ages, a court surrounded by edifices.

Corycæum, a room similar to a tennis-court.

Cosecant of an arch, the complement of another to 90 degrees.

Costean pits, in Cornish mining, are shallow pits sunk to trace or find tin.

Costeaning, in mining, the discovering of lodes by sinking pits in their vicinity, and drawing transversely to their supposed direction.

Cot, in nautical phraseology, a bed-frame suspended from the beams of the ship, or otherwise.

Cotangent, is the tangent of any complemental arch, or what the arch wants of a quadrant or 90 degrees.

Cotton, a white woolly or downy substance, found in a brown bud, produced by a shrub, the leaves of which resemble those of the sycamore-tree. The bud, which grows as large as a pigeon's egg, turns black when ripe, and divides at top into three parts; the cotton is as white as snow, and with the heat of the sun swells to the size of a pullet's egg. Scripture speaks of cotton.

Cotton manufactures and *trade*. Cotton was woven by the Hindoos and Chinese many centuries before the Christian era. The Egyptians are supposed to have imported woven cotton before the plant had begun to be cultivated in their country, and the Romans received woven cotton from India long before the cotton-plant was known in Europe. The extension of the manufacture of it has now become enormous. The export of cotton goods from England, in 1846, was £25,600,693 in value.

The distinctive names by which cotton is known in commerce are mostly derived from the countries which produce it; the exceptions are, sea-island cotton, and upland cotton. The former of these was first cultivated in the low sandy islands near the coast of Charleston, in America, while the latter is grown in the inner or upland country. The sea-island cotton is the finest of the several varieties. The upland is often called Bowed Cotton.

The spinning of cotton into the form of yarn or thread requires many preparatory processes; but the inventions and improvements in machinery that have been effected in recent years have rendered the process simple and of great national value.

Cotton and *Calico printing*, the art of staining woven fabrics of cotton with various figures and colours.

Cotton, gun, is prepared with cotton wool, and explodes at 400° Fahr. Gunpowder explodes at 600°.

Couched, laid close, as in a stratum.

Couisinet. (See *Coniusinet*.)

Coulisse, any piece of timber which has grooves in it; also pieces of wood which hold the floodgates in a sluice.

Counter, that part of a vessel between the bottom of the stern and the wing transom and buttock.

Counterfort, a pier, buttress, or oblique wall, built up against a wall to strengthen and support it.

Counter-gauge, in carpentry, a method of measuring joints by transferring the breadth of a mortise to the place on another timber where the tenon is to be made.

Counter-lath, in tiling, a lath placed by the eye.

Counterpoise, any weight which, placed in opposition to another weight, produces an equilibrium; but it is more commonly used to denote the weight used in the Roman balance, or steelyard.

Countersinks, in joinery, are bits for widening the upper part of a hole in wood or iron, for the head of a screw or pin, and have a conical head. Those for wood have one cutter in the conic surface, and have the cutting edge more remote from the axis of the cone than any other part of the surface. Countersinks for brass have eleven or twelve cutters round the conic surface, so that the horizontal section represents a circular saw. These are called rose-countersinks. The conic angle at the vertex is about 90 degrees. Countersinks for iron have two cutting edges, forming an obtuse angle.

Counterview, in painting, a contrast or situation in which two things illustrate or set off each other.

Counters, in ships, two parts of a ship called the upper and lower counter.

Count-house, a reckoning-house, in Derbyshire; a house or room on the mine used for keeping accounts of the products, etc.

Country residences. There are important advantages which deserve to be brought into notice, whether for comfort and convenience, for gratifying taste or fashion. Additional rooms appropriated for new purposes are often requisite. Formerly a gallery, although there were no works of art to fill it, was a necessary part of a mansion; of late years, the billiard-room and the conservatory enter into the arrangements of an architect; and a suit of well-planned nursery-rooms have been made a necessary part of the plan of a country mansion. The gallery is again about to resume its importance, and perhaps we may hereafter imitate the Romans in having covered walks contiguous to the house, in order to enjoy fresh air in the many rainy and snowy days at a country residence in an English winter. The irregular style admits of such additions, and loses nothing of the picturesque effect. The exterior decorations of terraces, parterres, stairs of communication, and different gardens filled with groups of the many flowering shrubs and plants, are admirably in harmony with this style of architecture. While we thus decorate closely around the house, it becomes less necessary to sacrifice so much to the park. The masonry of such irregular architecture requires not the expensive labour bestowed on a Grecian or Roman mansion. The whole should be in rough rubble-work, excepting the parapets, the corners, the windows, and doors. Many very good designs of castellated dwellings have been, in the execution, deprived of their effect, by being built of smooth, hewn freestone. If circular or square towers are introduced in a composition of the irregular style, they should, in every case, be of great dimensions, as much for their being applied to useful rooms, as to produce that grandeur of appearance which bulk in towers always gives.

The Country-seats of the Italians have been copied by most civilized nations of Europe; celebrated by poets, visited and admired by travellers: they have not, however, been described or represented as they deserve. They are so arranged as to produce the best effect, and advantage of the nature of the site has been taken with admirable skill. The regularities of the gardens accompany the decoration, and support the architecture. (See Parker's 'Villa Rustica,' recently published.)

Couple-close, a pair of spars of a roof; also used by heralds as a diminutive of the chevron.

Coupled columns. When, from the extent between columns sometimes necessary for the introduction of doors, windows, niches, or other decorations, neither the eustylos nor the diastylos intercolumniation can be used, coupled columns are frequently introduced. In this case two sistylos intercolumniations are used; the column which would otherwise occupy the middle of the space being brought to the distance of only half a diameter (or sufficient room for the projection of the capitals) from the extreme column. The middle space will then be three diameters and a half. This species has been called aræostylos. When buildings are small, the intercolumniations will not require such particular attention to the foregoing rules, for columns should never be placed nearer to each other than three feet, which will allow for the easy passage of a bulky person.

Coupling, in machinery, is the name given to various arrangements by which the parts of a machine may be connected or disconnected at pleasure, or by which a machine may be disengaged from, or re-engaged with, a revolving wheel or shaft, through which it receives motion from a steam-engine, water-wheel, or other prime mover.

Couplings, in mill-work: it is frequently necessary to convey motion much farther than would be practicable by any one shaft, and therefore often requisite to connect two or more shafts together. These connections are denominated couplings, and may be divided into two classes: 1st, Those having two bearings; 2ndly, Those having one bearing. Couplings having two bearings have been long in use, and before those having one bearing, and are generally more simple in their construction.

Coupling-box, a metal box for joining the ends of two shafts, so that they may revolve together.

Course, a continuous range of stones or bricks, of uniform height, in the wall of a building.

Course, in Cornish mining, is a tin or copper course; a phrase for working of the lode.

Courses, sails that hang from a ship's lower yards: the fore-sail is called the fore-course, and the main-sail the main-course.

Courts of Justice: there were in Rome twelve halls or courts of justice, where causes were heard and tried; they were adorned with statues, fine columns, and porticoes with double rows of columns.

Cove, a cave, a recess; any kind of concave moulding; the concavity of an arch or of a ceiling.

Coved ceiling, the upper surface of an apartment formed in an arched or coved shape at its junction with the side walls.

Covenants of the Old and New Testament (The Two), in the Table of Symbols of the early ages, are represented by the wheel in the middle of a wheel. *Ezek.* i. 16.

Cover, in slating, the part of the slate that is hidden; the exposed part being called the margin.

Cover-way, in roofing, the recess or internal angle left to receive the covering.

Cover, a turret or cupola on the roof of a hall or kitchen, pierced at the sides to let out smoke or steam.

Covie or *Covey*, a pantry.

Coving, the exterior projection of the upper parts of a building beyond the limits of the ground-plan.

Coving, a term applied to houses, etc., that project over the ground-plot.

Coving of a fireplace, the vertical sides, inclining backwards and inwards, for the purpose of reflecting the heat.

Cowl, a cover for the top of a chimney, made to turn round by the wind, and used to facilitate the escape of smoke.

Coxner, an arch part of a ship's stern.

Coxswain, the person who steers a boat, and has charge of her.

Crab, a wooden apparatus, something like a capstan, but not furnished with a drum-head; it is used for similar purposes, with holes made to insert the bars.

Crab, a machine with three claws, used to launch ships, to heave them into the dock, or off the quay.

Cradle, a frame placed under the bottom of a ship, in order to conduct her steadily into the water when she is to be launched, at which time it supports her weight while she slides down the descent or sloping passage, called the Ways, which are for this purpose daubed with soap or tallow.

Craft, a general name for all sorts of vessels employed to load or discharge merchant ships, or to carry alongside or return the guns, stores, or provisions of a man-of-war: such are lighters, hoys, barges, etc.

Cramp, a short bar of iron, with its ends bent so as to form three sides of a parallelogram; at one end a set-screw is inserted, so that two pieces of metal, being placed between, can be held firmly together by the screw.

Crane, a machine used for hoisting and lifting stones, ponderous weights, and heavy goods, principally at wharfs and warehouses, now much employed for hoisting heavy building materials; also as travelling cranes on framed scaffolding, for the assistance of masons, bricklayers, and other artisans in building, saving the time and labour formerly so much prolonged in the execution of the work to be done.

Cranes, pieces of iron or timber at a vessel's sides, used to stow boats or spars upon.

Crank, the condition of a vessel when she is inclined to lean over a good deal, and cannot bear much sail: this may be owing to her construction, or to her stowage.

Crank, the arms projecting from the main shaft of an engine, joined together at the outer ends.

Crank, in mechanics, a square piece projecting from a spindle, serving by its rotation to raise and fall the pistons of engines; it also denotes the iron support for a lantern, and the iron made fast to the stock of a bell.

Crank, in machinery, is a bend in an axle, by which a reciprocating motion in a rod is made to produce a revolving motion of an axle and of a wheel which may be connected with it.

Crank, in turning that part of the axle of the fly which is bent into three knees, or right angles, and three projecting parts: one of the parts is parallel to the axis, and has the upper part of the crank-hook collared round it.

Crank-axle, the driving axle connected to the piston-rods of a locomotive engine.

Crank-hook, in turning, sometimes also called the connecting-rod, as it connects the treadle and the fly.

Crank-pin, the cylindrical piece joining the ends of the crank arms, and attached to the connecting-rod, or, in vibrating engines, to the piston-rod; if the crank has only one arm, the pin projects from the end of it.

Crayon, a chalk; a species of material for drawing. Black chalk, found in Italy, white chalk, found in France, and red chalk, form three of the best varieties of crayons: each has its own peculiar value as a drawing material.

Creazes, in mining, the work or tin in the middle part of the buddle or dressing.

Credence, the small table at the side of the altar, or communion table, on which the bread and wine were formerly placed before they were consecrated.

Creeper, an iron instrument like a grapnel, with four claws, used for dragging the bottom of a harbour or river, to find anything lost.

Cremona school of painting. Boccaccio Boccaccino bears the same character among the Cremonese, as Ghirlandajo, Mantegna, Vanucci, etc., in their respective schools. Camillo Boccaccino was the chief master of this school, grounded in the ancient maxims of his father.

Crenelle, the embrasure of a battlement, or loopholes.

Crepido, according to Pliny, any raised basement upon which other things are built or supported, as of a temple, altar, obelisk, etc.

Crescent, or half-moon.

Cresset, a candlestick or lamp to contain a light.

Crest, a term in heraldry; the ornament of the helmet.

Creste, the ornamented finishing surrounding a screen or canopy of a building.

Crest-tiles, those used to cover the ridge of a roof, upon which they fit on the principle of a saddle.

Creux, a kind of sculpture, when the lines and figures are cut and formed within the face of the plate.

Cringle, a short piece of rope with each end spliced into the bolt-rope of a sail, confining an iron ring or thimble.

Criplings, short spars at the sides of houses.

Crista, a crest; the apex or highest part of a shrine.

Crockets, ornaments of foliage or animals running up the back of a pediment, arch-pinnacle, or spire, from the corbels below to the finial above, in which latter the crockets on both sides appear to merge. Projecting leaves, flowers, or bunches of foliage, used in Gothic architecture to decorate the angles of spires, canopies, pinnacles, etc.

Cromlech, in British antiquity, high, broad, and flat stones, raised upon other stones set on end, apparently for the purpose of an altar.

Crop, ore or tin of the first quality, after it is dressed or cleaned for smelting.

Crosette, a truss, or console, in the flank or return of an architrave of a door, window, or other aperture in a wall.

Crosettes, in decoration, the trusses or consoles on the flanks of the architrave, under the cornice.

Cross-beam, a beam laid across another. In a ship, a great piece of timber so called, crossing two others, called bites, and to which the cable is fastened, when a ship rides at anchor.

Cross-jack, in a ship, is a small yard flung at the upper end of the mizen-mast under the top.

Cross, a gibbet constructed of two pieces of wood placed transversely, whether they cross each other at right angles at the top, like a T, or in the middle of their length, like an X.

Cross, the symbol of the Christian religion.

Cross, cross crusse, cross-bar, cross gaffan, cross lode, either a vein of a metallic nature, or a soft earth, clay, or flookan, like a vein, which unheads and intersects the true lode.

Cross-bars, round bars of iron bent at each end, used as levers to turn the shank of an anchor.

Cross-chocks, pieces of timber layed across the deadwood amidships, to make good the deficiency of the heels of the lower futtocks.

Cross (church), or a Greek cross, that in which the length of the transverse part is equal to that of the nave; so called because most of the Greek churches were built in that form.

Cross (church), or a Latin cross, that whose nave is longer than the cross part, as in most Gothic churches.

Cross-grained stuff, in joinery, wood having its fibres running in contrary positions to the surfaces, and which consequently cannot be made perfectly smooth when planed in one direction, without turning it or turning the plane.

Cross-heads, in locomotive engines,

the part of the motion into which the piston-rod is fitted on the cylinder side and the connecting-rod attached on the driving wheel axle side.

Cross-head guides, in locomotive engines, the parallel bars between which the cross-head moves in a right line with the cylinder and driving wheel axle: they are also called *motion bars*.

Cross-head blocks, in locomotive engines, the parts which slide between the parallel guides. The ends of the cross-head are fitted into these blocks. The cross-head, cross-head guides, and block, constitute what is called 'the motion of the engine.'

Cross-head, in the steam-engine, a cross-bar fixed centrally on the top of a piston-rod, and connected to the beam: its motion is confined to a direct line by guides at each end; or, in the side-lever and beam engines, by an apparatus called a 'parallel motion.'

Cross-jack: the cross-jack yard is the lower yard on the mizen-mast.

Cross-spales, pieces of timber placed across a vessel, and nailed to the frames, to keep the sides together until the knees are bolted.

Cross-somer, a beam of timber.

Cross-springer, in groined vaulting, the rib which extends diagonally from one pier to another.

Cross-trees, pieces of oak supported by the cheeks and trestle-trees at the mast-heads, to sustain the tops on the lower mast, and to spread the top-gallant rigging at the top-mast head.

Cross vaulting is formed by the intersection of two or more simple vaults of arch-work.

Crotchet, a support, or piece of wood fitted into another to sustain it. Also crooked pieces of iron, used on board sloops and long-boats.

Croud, or *Crowde*, a crypt, or undercroft of a church.

Crow, in mechanics, an iron lever, made with a sharp point at one end, and two claws at the other; used in heaving and purchasing great weights.

Crow-foot, a number of small lines rove through to suspend an awning.

Crown, in geometry, a plane ring included between two concentric perimeters, generated by the motion of part of a right line round the centre, to which the moving part is not contiguous.

Crown of an anchor, the place where the arms are joined to the shank.

Crown of an arch, that line or point upon its surface which is the highest or most elevated from its springing.

Crown-post, the middle post of a trussed roof.

Crown-wheels. Circular motion is communicated at right angles by means of teeth or cogs situated parallel to the axis of the wheel. Wheels thus formed are denominated 'crown' or 'contrate wheels:' they act either upon a common pinion or upon a lantern.

Crozier, the pastoral staff of a bishop or mitred abbot, having the head curled round somewhat in the manner of a shepherd's crook.

Crucifix, a representation of our blessed Saviour on the cross.

Crustæ, figures or images in low relief, embossed upon plate.

Crustarius, an artist; an engraver for inlaid work, etc.

Crutch, a knee or piece of knee timber, placed inside a vessel to secure the heels of the cant-timbers abaft.

Cryophorus, an instrument by which the freezing qualities of the atmosphere may be ascertained.

Crypt, a vault beneath a building, either entirely or partly underground, frequently under churches and cathedrals.

Crypta, or *Crypt*, among the Romans, any long narrow vault, whether wholly or partially below the level of the earth.

Crypto Portico, an enclosed gallery or portico having a wall with openings or windows in it, instead of columns at the side.

Ctesibica machina, a double-actioned forcing-pump invented by Ctesibius of Alexandria.

Cuore (Cornish), a quarry of stones.

Cubature, the cubing of a solid, or measuring of the space comprehended in a solid, as in a cone, pyramid, cylinder, etc.

Cube, in geometry, a regular or solid body consisting of six square and six equal faces and sides, and its angles all right and therefore equal.

Cube, or *Hexahedron*, a solid regular body, consisting of six equal square sides.

Cubes, or *Cube numbers* in arithmetic, and the theory of numbers, are those whose cube-root is a complete integer; or they are numbers produced by multiplying a given number twice into itself, or by the multiplication of three equal factors.

Cube-root, of a number, say 8, the number which multiplied into itself twice will produce 8,—namely, 2; or it is that number by which, if you divide a number twice, the quotient will be equal to itself.

Cubic foot of water, what a vessel one foot square and one foot deep will hold.

Cubicule, among the Romans, a bed-chamber, tent, or balcony.

Cubiculum, according to Pliny, a room furnished with a sofa or bed.

Cubile, the ground-work or lowest course of stones in a building.

Cubit, a measure used among the ancients, and which the Hebrews call 'amma,' the mother of other measures. A cubit was originally the distance from the elbow to the extremity of the middle finger; which is the fourth part of a well-proportioned man's stature.

Cubital, a bolster or cushion for the elbow to rest upon, for invalids.

Cuboch, a name for the unit or integer of a power, being the effect produced by one cubic foot of water in one foot perpendicular descent.

Cuckold's-neck, a knot by which a rope is secured to a spar, the two parts of the rope crossing each other and seized together.

Cuddy, a cabin in the fore part of a boat.

Culage, the laying up a ship in the dock, to be repaired.

Cul-de-four of a niche, arched roof of a niche, on a circular plan, a spherical vault.

Cul-de-lampe, for several decorations both of masonry and ironery.

Cullis, a gutter in a roof; any groove or channel.

Culm, stone coal, resembling the Kilkenny coal of Ireland.

Culmen, the roof of a house or church.

Culverhouse, a dove-cot or pigeon-house.

Culvert, an arched drain for the passage of water.

Culvert, an arched passage or bridge beneath a road, canal, or railway.

Culver-tail, to dove-tail.

Cuneus, the wedge.

Cuneus, the division of the audience part of a theatre comprehended between two adjoining scalaria or staircases which lead from one præcinctio to another; so called from its form, which resembles a wedge. The foremost cunei were termed 'cavea prima;' the middle, 'cavea media;' and the uppermost, 'cavea summa.' The whole of the audience part, exclusive of the orchestra, was likewise called 'cavea.'

Cupboards answered in some respects to the sideboards of the present day. They were sometimes mere planched tops, resting on trestles, or fixed with legs against the wall; at others, framed on stages, rising one above another, and movable: these were called 'joined cupboards,' occasionally carved, and, like tables, covered with carpets. At the marriage of Prince Arthur, son of Henry VII., in the hall was a triangular cupboard, five stages high, set with plate, valued at £1200, entirely ornamental; and in the "utter chamber," where the princess dined, was another cupboard, "set with gold plate, garnished with stone and pearl," and valued at £20,000.

Cupola, a small room, either circular or polygonal, standing on the top of a dome: by some it is called a lantern.

Cupola, a spherical or spheroidal covering to a building, or any part of it.

Cup-valve, for a steam-engine: it resembles a conical valve, made to fit a cover in the form of a vase or of the portion of a sphere.

Curia, in architecture; the building in which the highest council of the Roman state assembled, described by Vitruvius as being adjacent to the agora or forum.

Curling-stuff, in joinery, that which is produced by the winding or coiling of the fibres round the boughs of a tree, when they begin to shoot out of the trunk.

Current, a stream or flux of water in any direction. The setting of the current is that point of the compass towards which the waters run; and the drift of a current is the rate it runs per hour.

Curtilage, a term formerly applied to the division or boundary of manorial lands.

Curve, in geometry, a line wherein the several points of which it consists tend several ways, or are posited towards different quarters.

Curvilinear, consisting of curved lines.

Cushion-capital, the capital of a column so sculptured as to resemble a cushion pressed down by the weight of its entablature.

Cushions and *window-pillows* were, in Tudor times, stuffed—not unlike the woolsack of the Lord Chancellor—in round, square, and oblong shapes, covered with carpet-work, velvet, or embroidery; the family arms frequently supplying the device.

Cusp, an ornament generally in Gothic windows or doors; it is to be found in the concave bends of stone-work.

Cusps, projecting points forming the featherings or foliation in Gothic tracery, archery, panels, etc.

Cut, in mining, to intersect a vein, branch, or lode, by driving horizontally or sinking perpendicularly at right angles.

Cutter, a small boat; also a kind of sloop.

Cutting. Cutting instruments act in dividing bodies upon the same principle as the wedge. The blade of the instrument is in general a thin wedge, but the edge itself is usually much more obtuse.

Cutwater, in a ship, is the sharp part of the head under the beak or figure.

Cycle, a round of time; a space in which the same revolution begins again; a periodical space of time. A lunar cycle is a period of nineteen years. A solar cycle is a period of twenty-eight years, after which the days of the month return to the same days of the week.

Cyclograph, or *Arcograph*, an instrument for drawing arcs of circles without centres, used in architectural and engineering drawings when the centres are too distant to be conveniently accessible.

Cycloidal curves are defined as follows: 1. When a circle is made to rotate on a rectilinear basis, the figure described on the plane of the basis by any point in the plane of the circle is called a trochoid: a circle concentric with the generating circle, and passing through the describing circle. 2. If the describing point is in the circumference of the rotating circle, the two circles coincide, and the curve is called a cycloid. 3. If a circular basis be substituted for a rectilinear one, the trochoid will become an epitrochoid, and the cycloid an epicycloid.

Cyclopean Architecture, a class of building supposed to have preceded the invention of the classic orders in Greece, and attributed to the Cyclopes.

Cyclopean wall, the oldest example of mason-work in Italy: in town-walls only has this style of building been used. The history of its origin is obscure. A large irregular mass of stone, having three, four, five, or more sides, hewn only on the irregular sides to be built upon, begins a wall; to this mass others are added, the sides of which are made to fit the irregular sides of the first block; and on these again others of similar forms are built in the same manner.

Cyclostylar, relating to a structure composed of a circular range of columns without a core; with a core, the range would be a peristyle.

Cylinder, a body having two flat surfaces and one circular: for instance, a roller is a cylinder.

Cylinder, a roller used for levelling and condensating the ground in agricultural and other operations.

Cylinders, in steam-engines, hollow cylindrical vessels: within the cylinder the steam exerts its power upon the piston, which, by means of its rod, transmits it to the other parts of the engine. In locomotive engines, hollow vessels, usually made of cast-iron, and bored out accurately, into which pistons are fitted steam-tight, yet easily movable by the pressure of the steam.

Cylinder cocks, in steam-engines, cocks placed in convenient parts of the cylinder for admitting oil to lubricate the piston, or by which to blow out the condensed steam, or any deposit in the cylinders.

Cylinder cover, in steam-engines, the lid bolted to a flanch round the top of a cylinder, so as to be perfectly steam-tight; it has a stuffing-box cast in the centre, through which the piston-rod alternates.

Cylindrical vault, a vault without groins, resting upon two parallel walls.

Cylindrical walling is that erected upon a circular plan, forming a cylinder, or a part less than a cylinder, according as the plan is an entire circumference or a less portion.

Cyling, anciently *ceiling*.

Cyma, called also *cymatium*, its name arising from its resemblance to a wave; a moulding which is hollow in its upper part, and swelling below. There are two sorts,—the *Cyma recta*, just described, and the *Cyma reverse*, whose upper part swells, whilst the lower part is hollow.

Cymatium, a moulding whose section or profile is convex below and concave above, somewhat resembling the letter S.

Cymatium, in sculpture, carved work, resembling rolling waves.

Cymophane, a mineral of a green colour, resembling the chrysoberyl.

Cypress-tree, one of the evergreens; very proper to mix with pines and firs in forming clumps. The wood of the cypress is very valuable, when grown to a size fit for planks, which dimension it attains in as short a time as oak. It was much used by the ancients, and was employed in the original doors of St. Peter's at Rome, which, on being replaced, after six hundred years, by gates of brass, were found to be perfectly free from decay, and within to have retained part of the original odour of the wood.

Cyrtostyle, a circular projecting portico.

Cyzicenus, anciently a hall decorated with sculpture.

D.

Dactylus, a Greek measure of length, the sixteenth part of an English foot.

Dado, a term for the die or plane face of a pedestal. The dado employed in the interior of buildings is a continuous pedestal, with a plinth and base moulding, and a cornice or dado moulding surmounting the die.

Dado, the solid block or cube forming the body of a pedestal, in classical architecture, between the base mouldings and cornice; an architectural arrangement of mouldings, etc., round the lower part of the walls of a room.

Dagger, in ship-building, a piece of timber that crosses all the poppets of the bulge-ways, to keep them together: the plank that secures the heads of the poppets is called the *dagger-plank*.

Dagger knees are lodging knees, with side arms cast down and bolted through the clamp: they are placed at the lower decks of some ships, instead of hanging knees, to preserve as much stowage in the hold as possible.

Daguerreotype, sun drawing; nature's drawing by the aid of light. It was the invention of two Frenchmen, M. Daguerre and M. Niepce. The invention consists of the fixation of the images formed on the focus of the camera-obscura; is made on very smooth surfaces of pure silver plated on copper.

Dairy-house, a place for keeping milk.

Dais, in early domestic architecture, the chief seat at the high board or principal table (cross-table) in a baronial hall; also the principal table itself, and the raised part of the floor on which it is placed.

Dais, a canopy to cover an altar, throne, or tribunal; the chief or upper table in a monastery.

Dam, a bank or obstruction built across a river or stream, for the purpose of raising the level of the water on the opposite side of it. Dams built for the purpose of inland navigation, or for that of securing a water power, may be considered as having a more permanent character.

Damascus steel, a sort of steel brought from the Levant, greatly esteemed for the manufacture of cutting instruments.

Damasquine, a term applied to ornamental work of gold or silver, incrusted on iron or steel.

Damonico or *Monicon*, an iron ochre, being a compound of terra di sienna and Roman ochre, burnt, and having all their qualities: it is rather more russet in hue than the orange de Mars, has considerable transparency, is rich and durable in colour, and affords good flesh tints.

Damper, a valve placed in a chimney, to diminish the draught when the heat is too intense.

Damper, in locomotive engines, a kind of iron Venetian blind, fixed to the smoke-box end of the boiler, in front of the tubes: it is shut down when the engine is standing, and thus stops the draught and economizes fuel; but it is opened when the engine is running.

Damps: various kinds of permanently elastic fluids generated in mines are thus named by the miners: choke-damps consist mostly of carbonic acid gas, and fire-damps of carburetted hydrogen gas.

Dancette, in heraldry, zigzag or chevron fret; seen in Norman buildings.

Dark ages were periods when the monks and ecclesiastics were the only learned persons: when religion, law, politics, and physics were administered and controlled by the clergy, denominated clerks.

Data useful in various calculations of the properties of materials. [The data correspond to the mean tem-

DAT   **DATA.**   **DAT**

perature and pressure of the atmosphere; the materials are assumed to be dry, and the temperature is measured by Fahrenheit's scale.]

AIR. Specific gravity, 0·0012; weight of a cubic foot, 0·0753 lbs., or 527 grains (Shuckburgh); 13·3 cubic feet, or 17 cylindric feet of air, weigh 1 lb.; it expands $\frac{1}{480}$ or ·00208 of its bulk at 32° by the addition of one degree of heat. (Dulong and Petit.)

ASH. Specific gravity, 0·76; weight of a cubic foot, 47·5 lbs; weight of a bar 1 foot long and 1 inch square, 0·33 lbs.; will bear without permanent alteration a strain of 3540 lbs. upon a square inch, and an extension of $\frac{1}{77}$ of its length; weight of modulus of elasticity for a base of an inch square, 1,640,000 lbs.; height of modulus of elasticity, 4,970,000 feet; modulus of resilience, 7·6; specific resilience, 10. (Calculated from Barlow's experiments.)

Compared with cast iron as unity, its strength is 0·23; its extensibility, 2·6; and its stiffness, 0·089.

ATMOSPHERE. Mean pressure of, at London, 28·89 inches of mercury = 14·18 lbs. upon a square inch. (Royal Society.) The pressure of the atmosphere is usually estimated at 30 inches of mercury, which is very nearly 13¾ lbs. upon a square inch, and equivalent to a column of water 34 feet high.

BEECH. Specific gravity, 0·696; weight of a cubic foot, 45·3 lbs.; weight of a bar 1 foot long and 1 inch square, 0·315 lb.; will bear without permanent alteration on a square inch, 2360 lbs., and an extension of $\frac{1}{570}$ of its length; weight of modulus of elasticity for a base of an inch square, 1,345,000 lbs.; height of modulus of elasticity, 4,600,000 feet; modulus of resilience, 4·14; specific resilience, 6. (Calculated from Barlow's Experiments.)

Compared with cast iron as unity, its strength is 0·15; its extensibility, 2·1; and its stiffness, 0·073.

BRASS, cast. Specific gravity, 8·37; weight of a cubic foot, 523 lbs.; weight of a bar 1 foot long and 1 inch square, 3·63 lbs.; expands $\frac{1}{54000}$ of its length by one degree of heat (Troughton); melts at 1869° (Daniell); cohesive force of a square inch, 18,000 lbs. (Rennie); will bear on a square inch without permanent alteration, 6700 lbs., and an extension in length of $\frac{1}{1111}$; weight of modulus of elasticity for a base of an inch square, 8,930,000 lbs.; height of modulus of elasticity, 2,406,000 feet; modulus of resilience, 5; specific resilience, 0·6. (Tredgold.)

Compared with cast iron as unity, its strength is 0·435; its extensibility, 0·9; and its stiffness, 0·49.

BRICK. Specific gravity, 1·841; weight of a cubic foot, 115 lbs.; absorbs $\frac{1}{15}$ of its weight of water; cohesive force of a square inch, 275 lbs. (Tredgold); is crushed by a force of 562 lbs. on a square inch (Rennie.)

BRICK-WORK. Weight of a cubic foot of newly built, 117 lbs.; weight of a rod of new brick-work, 16 tons.

BRIDGES. When a bridge is covered with people, it is about equivalent to a load of 120 lbs. on a superficial foot; and this may be esteemed the greatest possible extraneous load that can be collected on a bridge; while one incapable of supporting this load cannot be deemed safe.

BRONZE. See *Gun-metal*.

CAST IRON. Specific gravity, 7·207; weight of a cubic foot, 450 lbs.; a bar 1 foot long and 1 inch square weighs 3·2 lbs. nearly; it expands $\frac{1}{160000}$ of its length by one degree of heat (Roy); greatest change of length in the shade in this climate, $\frac{1}{578}$; greatest change of length when exposed to sun's rays, $\frac{1}{378}$; melts at 3479° (Daniell), and shrinks in cooling from $\frac{1}{96}$ to $\frac{1}{73}$ of its length (Muschet);

DAT   DATA.   DAT

is crushed by a force of 93,000 lbs. upon a square inch (Rennie); will bear without permanent alteration 15,300 lbs. upon a square inch, and an extension of $\frac{1}{747}$ of its length; weight of modulus of elasticity, for a base 1 inch square, 18,400,000 lbs.; height of modulus of elasticity, 5,750,000 feet; modulus of resilience, 12·7; specific resilience, 1·76. (Tredgold.)

CHALK. Specific gravity, 2·315; weight of a cubic foot, 144·7 lbs.; is crushed by a force of 500 lbs. on a square inch. (Rennie.)

CLAY. Specific gravity, 2·0; weight of a cubic foot, 125 lbs.

COAL, *Newcastle*. Specific gravity, 1·269; weight of a cubic foot, 79·31 lbs. A London chaldron of 36 bushels weighs about 28 cwt., whence a bushel is 87 lbs. (but is usually rated at 84 lbs.) A Newcastle chaldron, 53 cwt. (Smeaton.)

COPPER. Specific gravity, 8·75 (Hatchett); weight of a cubic foot, 549 lbs.; weight of a bar 1 foot long and 1 inch square, 3·81 lbs.; expands in length by one degree of heat, $\frac{1}{78000}$ (Smeaton); melts at 2548° (Daniell); cohesive force of a square inch, when hammered, 33,000 lbs. (Rennie.)

EARTH, *common*. Specific gravity, 1·52 to 2·00; weight of a cubic foot, from 95 to 125 lbs.

ELM. Specific gravity, 0·544; weight of a cubic foot, 34 lbs.; weight of a bar 1 foot long and 1 inch square, 0·236 lbs.; will bear on a square inch without permanent alteration, 3240 lbs., and an extension in length of $\frac{1}{717}$; weight of modulus of elasticity for a base of an inch square, 1,310,000 lbs.; height of modulus of elasticity, 5,680,000 feet; modulus of resilience, 7·87; specific resilience, 14·4. (Calculated from Barlow's Experiments.)

Compared with cast iron as unity, its strength is 0·21; its extensibility, 2·9; and its stiffness, 0·073.

FIR, *red* or *yellow*. Specific gravity, 0·557; weight of a cubic foot, 34·8 lbs.; weight of a bar 1 foot long and 1 inch square, 0·242 lb.; will bear on a square inch without permanent alteration, 4290 lbs. = 2 tons nearly, and an extension in length of $\frac{1}{717}$; weight of modulus of elasticity for a base of an inch square, 2,016,000 lbs.; height of modulus of elasticity, 6,330,000 feet; modulus of resilience, 9·13; its specific resilience, 16·4. (Tredgold.)

Compared with cast iron as unity, its strength is 0·3; its extensibility, 2·6, and its stiffness, 0·1154, = $\frac{1}{7}$.

FIR, *white*. Specific gravity, 0·47; weight of a cubic foot, 29·3 lbs.; weight of a bar 1 foot long and 1 inch square, 0·204 lb.; will bear on a square inch without permanent alteration, 3630 lbs., and an extension in length of $\frac{1}{717}$; weight of modulus of elasticity for a base of an inch square, 1,830,000 lbs.; height of modulus of elasticity, 8,970,000 feet; modulus of resilience, 7·2; specific resilience, 15·3. (Tredgold.)

Compared with cast iron as unity, its strength is 0·23; its extensibility, 2·4; and its stiffness, 0·1.

FLOORS. The weight of a superficial foot of a floor is about 40 lbs. when there is a ceiling, counterfloor, and iron girders. When a floor is covered with people, the load upon a superficial foot may be calculated at 120 lbs.; therefore, 120 + 40 = 160 lbs. on a superficial foot is the least stress that ought to be taken in estimating the strength for the parts of a floor of a room.

FORCE. See *Gravity*, *Horse*, etc.

GRANITE, *Aberdeen*. Specific gravity, 2·625; weight of a cubic foot, 164 lbs.; is crushed by a force of 10·910 lbs. upon a square inch. (Rennie.)

GRAVEL. Weight of a cubic foot, about 120 lbs.

GRAVITY generates a velocity

of 32¼ feet in a second in a body falling from rest; space described in the first second, 16 1/12 feet.

GUN-METAL, *cast* (copper 8 parts, tin 1). Specific gravity, 8·153; weight of a cubic foot, 509¼ lbs.; weight of a bar 1 foot long and 1 inch square, 3·54 lbs. (Tredgold); expands in length by 1° of heat, 1/4900 (Smeaton); will bear on a square inch without permanent alteration, 10,000 lbs., and an extension in length of 1/910; weight of modulus of elasticity for a base 1 inch square, 9,873,000 lbs.; height of modulus of elasticity, 2,790,000 feet; modulus of resilience, and specific resilience, not determined. (Tredgold.)

Compared with cast iron as unity, its strength is 0·65; its extensibility, 1·25; and its stiffness, 0·535.

HORSE, of average power, produces the greatest effect in drawing a load when exerting a force of 187½ lbs. with a velocity of 2½ feet per second, working 8 hours in a day. (Tredgold.) A good horse can exert a force of 480 lbs. for a short time. (Desaguliers.) In calculating the strength for horse machinery, the horse's power should be considered 400 lbs.

IRON, *cast*. See *Cast Iron*.

Iron, *malleable*. Specific gravity, 7·6 (Muschenbroek); weight of a cubic foot, 475 lbs.; weight of a bar 1 foot long and 1 inch square, 3·3 lbs.; ditto, when hammered, 3·4 lbs.; expands in length by 1° of heat, 1/14400 (Smeaton); good English iron will bear on a square inch without permanent alteration, 17,800 lbs.=8 tons nearly, and an extension in length of 1/1500 ; cohesive force diminished 1/1000 by an elevation 1° of temperature; weight of modulus of elasticity for a base of an inch square, 24,920,000 lbs.; height of modulus of elasticity, 7,550,000 feet; modulus of resilience, and specific resilience, not determined. (Tredgold.)

Compared with cast iron as unity, its strength is 1·12; its extensibility, 0·86; and its stiffness, 1·3.

LARCH. Specific gravity, ·560; weight of a cubic foot, 35 lbs.; weight of a bar 1 foot long and 1 inch square, 0·243 lb.; will bear on a square inch without permanent alteration, 2065 lbs., and an extension in length of 1/215 ; weight of modulus of elasticity for a base of an inch square, 10,074,000 lbs.; height of modulus of elasticity, 4,415,000 feet; modulus of resilience, 4; specific resilience, 7·1. (Calculated from Barlow's Experiments.)

Compared with cast iron as unity, its strength is 0·136; its extensibility, 2·3; and its stiffness, 0·058.

LEAD, *cast*. Specific gravity, 11·353 (Brisson); weight of a cubic foot, 709·5 lbs.; weight of a bar 1 foot long and 1 inch square, 4·94 lbs.; expands in length by 1 degree of heat, 1/14400 (Smeaton); melts at 612° (Crichton); will bear on a square inch without permanent alteration, 1500 lbs., and an extension in length of 1/15 ; weight of modulus of elasticity for a base 1 inch square, 720,000 lbs.; height of modulus of elasticity, 146,000 feet; modulus of resilience, 3·12; specific resilience, 0·27 (Tredgold).

Compared with cast iron as unity, its strength is 0·096; extensibility, 2·5; and its stiffness, 0·0385.

MAHOGANY, *Honduras*. Specific gravity, 0·56; weight of a cubic foot, 35 lbs.; weight of a bar 1 foot long and 1 inch square, 0·243 lb.; will bear on a square inch without permanent alteration, 3800 lbs., and an extension in length of 1/75 ; weight of modulus of elasticity for a base 1 inch square, 1,596,000 lbs.; height of modulus of elasticity, 6,570,000 feet; modulus of resilience, 9·047; specific resilience, 16·1. (Tredgold.)

Compared with cast iron as unity, its strength is 0·24; its extensibility, 2·9; and its stiffness, 0·487.

MAN. A man of average power produces the greatest effect when exerting a force of 31¼ lbs. with a velocity of 2 feet per second, for 10 hours in a day. (Tredgold.) A strong man will raise and carry from 250 to 300 lbs. (Desaguliers.)

MARBLE, *white.* Specific gravity, 2·706; weight of a cubic foot, 169 lbs; weight of a bar 1 foot long and 1 inch square, 1·17 lb.; cohesive force of a square inch, 1811 lbs.; extensibility, $\frac{1}{1812}$ of its length; weight of modulus of elasticity for a base of an inch square, 2,520,000 lbs.; height of modulus of elasticity, 2,150,000 feet; modulus of resilience at the point of fracture, 1·3; specific resilience at the point of fracture, 0·48 (Tredgold); is crushed by a force of 6060 lbs. upon a square inch (Rennie).

MERCURY. Specific gravity, 13·568 (Brisson); weight of a cubic inch, 0·4948 lb.; expands in bulk by 1° of heat, $\frac{1}{5550}$ (Dulong and Petit); weight of modulus of elasticity for a base of an inch square, 4,417,000 lbs.; height of modulus of elasticity, 750,000 feet. (Dr. Young, from Canton's Experiments.)

OAK, *good English.* Specific gravity, 0·83; weight of a cubic foot, 52 lbs.; weight of a bar 1 foot long and 1 inch square, 0·36 lb.; will bear upon a square inch without permanent alteration, 3960 lbs., and an extension in length of $\frac{1}{813}$; weight of modulus of elasticity for a base 1 inch square, 1,700,000 lbs.; height of modulus of elasticity, 4,730,000 feet; modulus of resilience, 9·2; specific resilience, 11. (Tredgold.)

Compared with cast iron as unity, its strength is 0·25; its extensibility, 2·8; and its stiffness, 0·093.

PENDULUM. Length of pendulum to vibrate seconds in the latitude of London, 39·1372 inches (Kater); ditto to vibrate half-seconds, 9·7843 inches.

PINE, *American yellow.* Specific gravity, 0·46; weight of a cubic foot, 26¾ lbs.; weight of a bar 1 foot long and one inch square, 0·186 lb.; will bear on a square inch without permanent alteration, 3900 lbs., and an extension in length of $\frac{1}{717}$; weight of modulus of elasticity for a base of an inch square, 1,600,000 lbs.; height of modulus of elasticity, 8,700,000 feet; modulus of resilience, 9·4; specific resilience, 20. (Tredgold.)

Compared with cast iron as unity, its strength is 0·25; its extensibility, 2·9; and its stiffness, 0·087.

PORPHYRY, *red.* Specific gravity, 2·871; weight of a cubic foot, 179 lbs.; is crushed by a force of 35,568 lbs. upon a square inch. (Gauthey.)

ROPE, *hempen.* Weight of a common rope 1 foot long and 1 inch in circumference, from 0·04 to 0·46 lb.; a rope of this size should not be exposed to a strain greater than 200 lbs.; but in compounded ropes, such as cables, the greatest strain should exceed 120 lbs.; and the weight of a cable 1 foot in length and 1 inch in circumference does not exceed 0·027 lb. The square of the circumference in inches multiplied by 200 will give the number of pounds a rope may be loaded with; and multiply by 120 instead of 200 for cables. Common ropes will bear a greater load with safety after they have been some time in use, in consequence of the tension of the fibres becoming equalized by repeated stretchings and partial untwisting. It has been imagined that the improved strength was gained by their being laid up in store; but if they can there be preserved from deterioration, it is as much as can be expected.

ROOFS. Weight of a square foot of Welsh rag slating, 11½ lbs.; weight of a square foot of plain tiling, 16¼ lbs.; greatest force of the wind upon a superficial foot of roofing may be estimated at 40 lbs.

SLATE, *Welsh*. Specific gravity, 2·752 (Kirwan); weight of a cubic foot, 172 lbs.; weight of a bar 1 foot long and 1 inch square, 1·19 lb.; cohesive force of a square inch, 11,500 lbs.; extension before fracture, $\frac{1}{1170}$; weight of modulus of elasticity for a base of an inch square, 15,800,000 lbs.; height of modulus of elasticity, 13,240,000 feet; modulus of resilience, 8·4; specific resilience, 2 (Tredgold).

SLATE, *Westmoreland*. Cohesive force of a square inch, 7870 lbs.; extension in length before fracture, $\frac{1}{1640}$; weight of modulus of elasticity for a base of an inch square, 12,900,000 lbs. (Tredgold.)

SLATE, *Scotch*. Cohesive force of a square inch, 9600 lbs.; extension in length before fracture, $\frac{1}{1713}$; weight of modulus of elasticity for a base 1 inch square, 15,790,000 lbs. (Tredgold.)

STEAM. Specific gravity at 212° is to that of air at the mean temperature as 0·472 is to 1 (Thomson); weight of a cubic foot, 219 grains; modulus of elasticity for a base of an inch square, 14¾ lbs.; when not in contact with water, expands $\frac{1}{480}$ of its bulk by 1° of heat (Gay-Lussac).

STEEL. Specific gravity, 7·84; weight of a cubic foot, 490 lbs.; a bar 1 foot long and 1 inch square weighs 3·4 lbs.; it expands in length by 1° of heat, $\frac{1}{75300}$ (Hoy); tempered steel will bear without permanent alteration, 45,000 lbs.; cohesive force of a square inch, 130,000 lbs. (Rennie); cohesive force diminished $\frac{1}{850}$ by elevating the temperature 1°; modulus of elasticity for a base of an inch square, 29,000,000 lbs.; height of modulus of elasticity, 8,530,000 feet. (Dr. Young.)

STONE, *Portland*. Specific gravity, 2·113; weight of a cubic foot, 132 lbs.; weight of a prism 1 inch square and 1 foot long, 0·92 lb.; absorbs $\frac{1}{17}$ of its weight of water (R. Tredgold); is crushed by a force of 3729 lbs. upon a square inch (Rennie); cohesive force of a square inch, 857 lbs.; extends before fracture $\frac{1}{1117}$ of its length; modulus of elasticity for a base of an inch square, 1,533,000 lbs.; height of modulus of elasticity, 1,672,000 feet; modulus of resilience at the point of fracture, 0·5; specific resilience at the point of fracture, 0·23. (Tredgold.)

STONE, *Bath*. Specific gravity, 1·975; weight of a cubic foot, 123·4 lbs.; absorbs $\frac{1}{12}$ of its weight of water (R. Tredgold); cohesive force of a square inch, 478 lbs. (Tredgold.)

STONE, *Craigleith*. Specific gravity, 2·362; weight of a cubic foot 147·6 lbs. absorbs $\frac{1}{17}$ of its weight of water; cohesive force of a square inch, 772 lbs. (Tredgold); is crushed by a force of 5490 lbs. upon a square inch (Rennie).

STONE, *Dundee*. Specific gravity, 2·621; weight of a cubic foot, 163·8 lbs.; absorbs $\frac{1}{17}$ part of its weight of water; cohesive force of a square inch, 2061 lbs. (Tredgold); is crushed by a force of 6630 lbs. upon a square inch (Rennie).

STONE-WORK. Weight of a cubic foot of rubble-work, about 140 lbs.; of hewn stone, 160 lbs.

TIN, *cast*. Specific gravity, 7·291 (Brisson); weight of a cubic foot, 455·7 lbs.; weight of a bar 1 foot long and 1 inch square, 3·165 lbs.; expands in length by 1° of heat, $\frac{1}{7200}$ (Smeaton); melts at 442° (Crichton); will bear upon a square inch without permanent alteration, 2880 lbs., and an extension in length of $\frac{1}{1200}$; modulus of elasticity for a base of an inch square, 4,608,000; height of modulus of elasticity, 1,453,000 feet; modulus of resilience, 1·8; specific resilience, 0·247 (Tredgold).

Compared with cast iron as unity, its strength is 0·192; its extensibility, 0·75; and its stiffness, 0·25.

DAT DEAD COLOURING. DEA

WATER, river. Specific gravity, 1·000; weight of a cubic foot, 62·5 lbs.; weight of a cubic inch, 252·525 grains; weight of a prism 1 foot long and 1 inch square, 0·434 lb.; weight of an ale gallon of water, 10·2 lbs.; expands in bulk by 1° of heat, $\frac{1}{7171}$ (Dalton); expands in freezing, $\frac{1}{17}$ of its bulk (Williams); and the expanding force of freezing water is about 35,000 lbs. upon a square inch, according to Muschenbroek's valuation; modulus of elasticity for a base of an inch square, 326,000 lbs.; height of modulus of elasticity, 750,000 feet, or 22,100 atmospheres of 30 inches of mercury. (Dr. Young, from Canton's Experiments.)

Water has a state of maximum density at or near 40°, which is considered an exception to the general law of expansion by heat: it is extremely improbable that there is anything more than an apparent exception, most likely arising from water at low temperatures absorbing a considerable quantity of air, which has the effect of expanding it, and consequently of causing the apparent anomaly.

WATER, sea. Specific gravity, 1·0271; weight of a cubic foot, 64·2 lbs.

WATER is 828 times the density of air of the temperature 60°, and barometer 30.

WHALE-BONE. Specific gravity, 1·3; weight of a cubic foot, 81 lbs.; will bear a strain of 5600 lbs. upon a square inch without permanent alteration, and an extension in length of $\frac{1}{717}$; modulus of elasticity for a base of an inch square, 820,000 lbs.; height of modulus of elasticity, 1,438,000 feet; modulus of resilience, 38·3; specific resilience, 29. (Tredgold.)

WIND. Greatest observed velocity, 159 feet per second (Rochon); force of wind with that velocity, about 57¾ lbs. on a square foot.

ZINC cast. Specific gravity, 7·028 (Watson); weight of a cubic foot, 439¼ lbs; weight of a bar 1 inch square and 1 foot long, 3·05 lbs.; expands in length by 1° of heat, $\frac{1}{3410}$ (Smeaton); melts at 648° (Daniell); will bear on a square inch without permanent alteration, 5700 lbs. = 0·365 cast iron, and an extension in length of $\frac{1}{1500}$ = ¼ that of cast iron (Tredgold); modulus of elasticity for a base of an inch square, 13,680,000 lbs.; height of modulus of elasticity, 4,480,000 feet; modulus of resilience, 2·4; specific resilience, 0·34. (Tredgold.)

Compared with cast iron as unity, its strength is 0·365; its extensibility, 0·5; and its stiffness, 0·76.

Data, a term for such facts, things, or quantities as are given or known, in order thereby to find other things that are unknown.

Davit, in navigation, a short boom fitted in the fore channel, to hoist the flukes of the anchor to the bow, which is called 'fishing the anchor.'

David's-staff, an instrument used in navigation.

Day, or *Bay*, in architecture, one of the lights or compartments between mullion and mullion, in the great windows of the pointed style.

Days, in early domestic architecture, the bay or lights of a window; the spaces between the mullions.

Dead colouring is the first layer of colours, consisting usually of some shade of grey. Its design is to receive and preserve the finishing colours; and it is called dead because it is not seen when the work is completed.

Dead doors, in ship-building, fitted to the outside of the quarter-gallery doors, in case the quarter-gallery should be carried away.

Dead eyes, fixed in the channels, with three holes to receive the lanyard of the shrouds.

Dead flat, the name of a midship board

Dead lights, in navigation, wooden

shutters for the cabin windows, which are fastened on when the sea runs high.

Dead-men's-eyes (in a ship), small blocks or pulleys with many holes, but no shivers wherein run the laniers.

Dead-neap, a low tide.

Dead reckoning, the estimation which seamen make of the ship's place, by keeping an account of her way by the log, by the course steered, and by rectifying the whole by allowance for drift, leeway, etc.

Dead rising, is that part of the ship that lies aft, between her keel and floor timbers.

Dead ropes, ropes which do not run in any block or pulley.

Deads (among miners), the earth or other fossil substances which enclose the ore on every side.

Dead shore, a piece of timber worked up in brick-work, to support a superincumbent mass until the brick-work which is to carry it has set or become hard.

Dead water, the eddy water immediately at the stern of a ship while under way.

Dead wood, pieces of timber fayed on the keel to seat the flow-timbers on afore and abaft the floors, and continued as high as the cutting down of the floors.

Deafening sound-boarding, the pugging used to prevent the passage of sound through wooden partitions.

Dearn, a door-post, or threshold; to conceal, or shut up.

Deambulatory, an ambulatory or cloister for exercise; also the aisles of a church, or the porticoes round the body of a church.

Debacle, a great aqueous torrent, a breaking up and transport of massive rocks and gravel by an enormous rush of water.

Debris, fragments of rocks, boulders, gravel, sand, trunks of trees, etc., detached from the summits and sides of mountains by the effect of the elements.

Decade, the sum of ten.

Decagon, in geometry, a plain figure of ten sides.

Decalogue, the Ten Commandments delivered to the Israelites from Mount Sinai, in which the moral law is summarily comprehended. The Jews call these precepts 'The Ten Words.'* In the building of new churches, and in the restoration of those of olden times, a proper and effective style of painting and embellishing the words of the ten commandments in face of the altar has been introduced.

Decanicum, an ecclesiastical prison.

Decastyle, in architecture: a temple is said to be decastyle when its portico contains ten columns in a line.

Decastyle, a portico consisting of ten columns in front.

Decempeda, a ten-foot rod employed by architects and surveyors for taking measurements.

Decemremis, a vessel with ten banks of oars on a side.

Decimal, the tenth part.

Deck, the floor of a ship.

Decoration, the combination of ornamental objects which are employed in great variety, principally for the interior and exterior of all kinds of edifices, and for purposes of art generally. Decoration, when judiciously introduced, becomes in many instances a language, intelligible only, however, when the artist is capable of speaking it correctly and the spectator of comprehending it. It is then a system of hieroglyphic writing, and the building to which it is applied becomes historical, and tells its tale more nobly and appropriately than it can ever do through the undignified medium of mural inscriptions. Nothing can be more judicious or appropriate than the sculpture in the metopes and pedi-

---

* To these the Saviour added another: "A new commandment I give unto you, That ye love one another; as I have loved you, that ye also love one another." (*John* xiii. 34.)

ment of the Parthenon. Ornament here not only creates a variety on the surface of the work, but relates, by the aid of the sculptor, a history intimately connected with the religious and moral destination of the edifice to which it is applied.

Decorative style of Gothic Architecture: first introduced in the reign of Edward I., it was matured in England, and prevailed during the greater part of the 14th century. Its distinguishing features, says Dr. Whewell, are characterized by its window-tracery, geometrical in the early instances, flowing in the later; but also, and perhaps better, by its triangular canopies, crocketed and finialed; its niched buttresses, with triangular heads; its peculiar mouldings, no longer a collection of equal rounds, with hollows like the early English, but an assemblage of various members, some broad, some narrow, beautifully grouped and proportioned. A capital with crumpled leaves, a peculiar base and pedestal, also belong to this style.

Definitions in geometry:—

1. A point is that which hath no parts, or which hath no magnitude.
2. A line is length without breadth.
3. A superficies has length and breadth.
4. A solid is a figure of three dimensions, having length, breadth, and thickness. Hence surfaces are extremities of solids, and lines the extremities of surfaces, and points the extremities of lines.

If two lines will always coincide however applied, when any two points in the one coincide with the two points in the other, the two lines are called straight lines, or otherwise right lines.

A curve continually changes its direction between its extreme points, or has no part straight.

Parallel lines are always at the same distance, and will never meet, though ever so far produced. Oblique right lines change their distance, and would meet, if produced.

One line is perpendicular to another when it inclines no more to one side than another.

A straight line is a tangent to a circle when it touches the circle without cutting, when both are produced.

An angle is the inclination of two lines towards one another in the same plane, meeting in a point.

Angles are either right, acute, or oblique.

A right angle is that which is made by one line perpendicular to another, or when the angles on each side are equal.

An acute angle is less than a right angle.

An obtuse angle is greater than a right angle.

A plane is a surface with which a straight line will everywhere coincide; and is otherwise called a straight surface.

Plane figures, bounded by right lines, have names according to the number of their sides, or of their angles, for they have as many sides as angles: the least number is three.

An equilateral triangle is that whose three sides are equal.

An isosceles triangle has only two sides equal.

A scalene triangle has all sides unequal.

A right-angled triangle has only one right angle.

Other triangles are oblique-angled, and are either obtuse or acute.

An acute-angled triangle has all its angles acute.

An obtuse-angled triangle has one obtuse angle.

A figure of four sides, or angles, is called a quadrilateral, or quadrangle.

A parallelogram is a quadrilateral, which has both pairs of its

DEFINITIONS IN GEOMETRY.

opposite sides parallel, and takes the following particular names:—

A rectangle is a parallelogram, having all its angles right ones.

A square is an equilateral rectangle, having all its sides equal, and all its angles right angles.

A rhombus is an equilateral parallelogram whose angles are oblique.

A rhomboid is an oblique-angled parallelogram, and its opposite sides only are equal.

A trapezium is a quadrilateral, which has neither pair of its sides parallel.

A trapezoid has only one of its sides parallel.

Plane figures, having more than four sides, are in general called polygons, and receive other particular names according to the number of their sides or angles.

A pentagon is a polygon of five sides, a hexagon of six sides, a heptagon seven, an octagon eight, an enneagon nine, a decagon ten, an undecagon eleven, and a dodecagon twelve sides.

A regular polygon has all its sides and its angles equal; and if they are not equal, the polygon is irregular.

An equilateral triangle is also a regular figure of three sides, and a square is one of four; the former being called a trigon, and the latter a tetragon.

A circle is a plane figure, bounded by a curve line, called the circumference, which is everywhere equidistant, from a certain point within, called its centre.

The radius of a circle is a right line drawn from the centre to the circumference.

A diameter of a circle is a right line drawn through the centre, terminating on both sides of the circumference.

An arc of a circle is any part of the circumference.

A chord is a right line joining the extremities of an arc.

A segment is any part of a circle bounded by an arc and its chord.

A semicircle is half a circle, or a segment cut off by the diameter.

A sector is any part of a circle bounded by an arc, and two radii drawn to its extremities.

A quadrant, or quarter of a circle, is a sector having a quarter part of the circumference for its arc, and the two radii perpendicular to each other.

The height or altitude of any figure is a perpendicular let fall from an angle or its vertex to the opposite side, called the base.

The measure of any right-lined angle is an arc of any circle contained between the two lines which form the angle, the angular point being the centre.

A solid is said to be cut by a plane when it is divided into two parts, of which the common surface of separation is a plane, and this plane is called a section.

Definitions of solids:—

A prism is a solid, the ends of which are similar and equal parallel planes and the sides parallelograms.

If the ends of the prism are perpendicular to the sides, the prism is called a right prism.

If the ends of the prism are oblique to the sides, the prism is called an oblique prism.

If the ends and sides are equal squares, the prism is called a cube.

If the base or ends are parallelograms, the solid is called a parallelopiped.

If the bases and sides are rectangles, the prism is called a rectangular prism.

If the ends are circles, the prism is called a cylinder.

If the ends or bases are ellipses, the prism is called a cylindroid.

A solid, standing upon any plane figure for its base, the sides of which are plane triangles, meeting in one point, is called a pyramid.

The solid is denominated from

its base, as a triangular pyramid is one upon a triangular base, a square pyramid one upon a square base, etc.

If the base is a circle or an ellipsis, then the pyramid is called a cone.

If a solid be terminated by two dissimilar parallel planes as ends, and the remaining surfaces joining the ends be also planes, the solid is called a prismoid.

If a part of a pyramid next to the vertex be cut off by a plane parallel to the base, the portion of the pyramid contained between the cutting plane and the base is called the frustum of a pyramid.

A solid, the base of which is a rectangle, the four sides joining the base plane surfaces, and two opposite ones meeting in a line parallel to the base, is called a cuneus or wedge.

A solid terminated by a surface which is everywhere equally distant from a certain point within it is called a sphere or globe.

If a sphere be cut by any two planes, the portion contained between the planes is called a zone, and each of the parts contained by a plane and the curved surface is called a segment.

If a semi-ellipsis, having an axis for its diameter, be revolved round this axis until it come to the place whence the motion began, the solid formed by the circumvolution is called a spheroid.

If the spheroid be generated round the greater axis, the solid is called a prolate spheroid.

If the solid be generated round the lesser axis, the solid is called an oblate spheroid.

A solid of any of the above structures, hollow within, so as to contain a solid of the same structure, is called a hollow solid.

Deflagrator, an instrument for producing intense light and heat.

Deflection, a term applied to the distance by which a curve departs from another curve, or from a straight line.

Deflection, the deviation of a ship from its course.

Degree, the 360th part of the circumference of a circle; 60 geographical miles.

Degree, consisting of three figures of three places, comprehending units, tens, and hundreds.

Delen (Derk Von) painted temples, saloons, and colonnades, and was a perfect master of architectural embellishment.

De l'Orme (Philibert) claims the honour of inventing the volute now most commonly used, and complains that others pretend to it because Palladio and Serlio have spoken of it before him.

Deliquiæ, according to Vitruvius, gutters, or drains.

Delivery valve, the upper valve in the air-pump, or that through which the water is lifted into the hot well; also used when speaking of any sort of pump.

Delphica, a table made of marble or bronze, and resembling a tripod.

Delving, to dig.

Delubrum, a font or baptismal basin. In antiquity, a church, chapel, temple, or consecrated place. Also that part of a Roman temple in which the altar or statue of the deity was erected.

Demesne, lands belonging to the lord of a manor, and which are contiguous to the manor-house.

Demi-relievo, in sculpture, half-raised figures from the plane, as if cut in two, and only half fixed to the plane.

Demi-tint is that shade seen when the sun shines on a house, or any other object, making an angle of nearly 45° on the ground plane, or when it shines more on the front than on the end.

Dendrometer, an instrument for the measuring of trees.

Dendiculus, a member in the Ionic and Corinthian entablatures, occurring between the zophoras and corona, and, properly speaking, a part of the latter: so called because it represents denticuli, or small teeth, placed at equal intervals apart.

Dentils, ornaments resembling teeth, used in the bed-mouldings of Ionic, Corinthian, and Composite cornices.

Departure, in navigation, is the easting or westing of a ship with respect to the meridian from which it departed or sailed; or it is the difference of longitude between the present meridian and where the last reckoning was made.

Depression of the pole, in navigation: so many degrees as you sail from the pole towards the equator, so many you are said to depress the pole, because it becomes so much lower in the horizon.

Derrick, a Cornish word for a miner.

Derrick, in navigation, a tackle used at the outer quarters of the mizenyard; it also signifies a prop or support to sheers, etc.

Derrick. Sheers and Gyn have one object in common,—to find a point or fulcrum in space to which the pulley, in the shape of block and tackle, is to be supplied; and this is effected by the above, on one, two, and three legs, respectively. In the derrick and sheers, stability is given by guys; in the gyn, they are unnecessary. Wherever these guys are used, great attention must be paid to their being well fixed, or being (when requisite) duly eased-off: when accidents occur from neglect in this respect, they are generally very severe.

Describent, in geometry, is the line or surface from the motion of which a surface or body is supposed to be generated or described.

Descriptive geometry: the application of geometrical rules to the representation of the figures and the various relations of the forms of bodies, in accordance to forms applicable to civil, military, and naval architecture, civil and mechanical engineering, and the other arts that require more correct scientific representations than have hitherto been afforded to the student.

Desiccation, the chemical operation of drying bodies, sometimes effected by drying in the air, sometimes in warm chambers, by the air-pump, etc.

Design, a term in the fine arts, is employed first to signify the art of drawing or representing in lines the form of any object; next it expresses that combination of invention and purpose which enables the artist to compose a picture or a group, without reference to the material in which it is executed.

Designing, the art of delineating or drawing the appearance of natural objects by lines.

Destina, according to Vitruvius, a column or pillar to support an edifice.

Detrempe, in painting, in water-colours.

Device, an emblem or ensign formerly borne on shields or embroidered upon banners as a cognizance; contemporary, in the history of heraldry, with coat armour itself.

Device, in heraldry, painting, etc., any emblem used to represent a certain family, person, action, or quality, with a suitable motto, applied in a figurative sense.

Diagonal, a line drawn from angle to angle.

Diagonal rib, a projecting band of stone or timber passing diagonally from one angle of a vaulted ceiling across the centre to the opposite angle.

Diagonal scale. Equidistant parallel lines cut all lines drawn across them into equal parts; consequently a set of equidistant parallels laid down upon a ruler, with oblique lines of various lengths drawn across them, give with the compasses the means of immediately taking off various proportions of those lines.

Diagram, a delineation of geometrical figures; a mathematical illustration.

Diagraphic Art, the art of painting or engraving.

Dial, an instrument for the measuring of time; not mentioned in Scripture before the reign of Ahaz, A.M. 3262. It is not clearly ascertained, even after this time, how the Jews divided the time by hours. The word *hour* occurs first in Tobit, which may confirm the opinion that the invention of dials came from beyond the Euphrates.

Dialling. In all dials, the gnomon represents the axis of the earth; hence its angle with the horizon is the latitude of the place, and it lies in the plane of the meridian. There are a great variety of dials, according to whether they are horizontal, oblique, or vertical, and also depending on their aspect with reference to the sun, etc.

Diamicton, according to Pliny, a term used by the Roman builders to designate a particular manner of constructing walls, the exterior of masonry and the interior of rubble.

Diamond, a genus of precious stones of a fine pellucid substance of great hardness, and never debased by any admixture of earthy or other coarse matter. When pure, it is perfectly colourless. It is the most valuable of all gems, and is found only in the East Indies and the Brazils. It is constituted solely of carbon in its densest form.

Diamond, glaziers', the pencil diamond, used in cutting glass, is a small fractured piece of diamond.

Diaper ornament, of flowers, applied to a plain surface, either carved or painted: if carved, the flowers are entirely sunk into the work below the general surface; they are usually square, and placed close to each other, and are various in their pattern and design: it was first introduced in the early English style in some of the principal Gothic structures in England.

Diaper, a panel or flat recessed surface covered with carving or other wrought work in low relief; a kind of linen cloth, wrought with figures in the process of weaving.

Diastyle, an arrangement of columns in Grecian and Roman architecture, in which the intercolumniation or space between them is equal to three or four diameters of the shaft.

Diathyra, the vestibule before the doors of a Greek house, corresponding with the prothyra of the Romans.

Diatoni, the angle stones of a wall, wrought on two faces, and which, stretching beyond the stones above and below them, form a good band or tie to the work.

Diatoni, according to Vitruvius, the girders or band-stones formerly employed in constructing walls; corner stones.

Diatretum, an enchased or curiously engraved vase or drinking-cup.

Diaulon, a race-course, the circuit of which was two stadia, or 1200 feet; whence it was used to signify a measure of two stadia.

Dicrotum, a boat with two oars.

Die, the cube or dado of a pedestal.

Die or *Dye*, a naked square cube: thus the body of a pedestal, or that part between its base and its cap, is called the die of the pedestal.

Dies, two pieces of hardened steel, which, when placed together, form a female screw (or a screw in a nut) which has cutting edges, used for making a screw on a bolt.

Die-sinking: in the preparation of coined money and of medals, the most important feature is the engraving of the die which is to form the stamp. The piece of steel is prepared with care, and brought to a soft state when about to be submitted to the hands of the engraver. By the aid of small, fine, hardened steel tools, the engraver cuts away the steel until he has produced, in cavity or intaglio, an exact reverse of the design for the medal or coin.

Dieu et mon droit,—'God and my right.'—in heraldry; the motto of the royal arms of England, first assumed by Richard I.

Differential thermometer. This instrument was invented by the same gentleman who contrived the photometer and ætherioscope, and was used by him in his investigations on heat. Its principal use to the meteorologist is to make experiments on the light and heat of the moon, etc., by concentrating its rays, by a lens upon the sentient ball. This can only be done when the moon is on the meridian. It is peculiarly adapted for measuring the effect of radiation.

Digester, a boiler invented by Papin for raising water to a higher temperature than the common boiling point, 212°; this is effected by forming a vessel somewhat resembling a kitchen pot; the mouth is formed into a flat ring, so that a cover may be screwed tightly on; this cover is furnished with a safety-valve, loaded to the required pressure.

Digit, a finger; a term employed to signify any symbol of number from 0 to 9; thus ten (10) is a number of two digits.

Digit, a measure of length, containing three-fourths of an inch.

Diglyph, in architecture, an imperfect triglyph, with only two channels instead of three.

Dilapidation, decay for want of repair; not unfrequently a point of dispute between a party in possession of a house and another party having an interest therein. Where there is a right to use lands or houses, questions will arise as to the manner in which they ought to be used, and by whom dilapidations, whether caused by accident or decay, ought to be supplied. The rights of parties with respect to immovable property so closely border on each other, and the line of demarcation between them is so indistinct, that one man, in the fancied exercise of his right, is continually liable to encroach upon or disregard the right of another. No person, however absolute his property in land, can put it to any use he pleases; his right to use it is restrained by the rights of his neighbour; he is bound to take care that his manner of using does not interfere with the inoffensive and profitable occupation by his neighbour of his land. (See the second edition, just published, of Mr. Gibbons's elaborate work on the 'Law of Dilapidations and Nuisances.')

Dilettante (Italian), an ardent admirer of the fine arts. The Dilettanti Society, consisting of many distinguished noblemen and gentlemen, has done much to rescue the noble monuments of Grecian art from otherwise inevitable ruin.

Dilluing, a Cornish word for a method of washing or finishing the dressing of tin in very fine hair sieves.

Diluvial formation, the superficial deposits of gravel, clay, sand, etc., which lie far from their original sites on hills, and in other situations, to which no forces of water now in action could transport them.

Dilving, in dressing tin ore, shaking it in a canvas sieve, in a tub of water, so that the waste flows over the rim of the sieve, leaving the tin behind.

Dimension, a term used in the same sense as *degree*.

Dimensions. 1. General dimensions: size, magnitude, dimension, bulk, volume, largeness, massiveness. 2. Linear dimensions. 3. Central.

Diminution, a term expressing the gradual decrease of thickness in the upper part of a column.

Diminution of columns. The shafts of columns are diminished in diameter as they rise, sometimes from the foot itself of the shaft, sometimes from one-quarter, and sometimes from one-third of its height. The diminution at top is seldom less than one-eighth or more than one-sixth of the inferior diameter of the column.

Dioptase or *emerald copper*, a crystalized silicate of copper, the primary form of which is a rhomboid. Its colour varies from emerald to blackish green: it is translucent and brittle.

Dioptra, a geometrical instrument employed in measuring the altitude of distant objects, and for taking the levels of a source of water intended to be conveyed to a distance by means of an aqueduct.

Diorama, a mode of scenic exhibition invented by two French artists, Daguerre and Bouton.

Dip, in mining, the greatest inclination of a stratum to the horizon.

Di Palito is a light yellow ochre, affording tints rather purer in colour than the stone ochre, but less so than Naples yellow. Many pleasing varieties of ochreous colours are produced by burning and compounding with lighter, brighter, and darker colours, but often very injudiciously and adversely to that simple economy of the palette which is favourable to the certainty of operation, effect, and durability.

Diphryges, the scorial sediment, a calx of melted copper, gathered in the furnace when the metal was run out.

Diplinthius, according to Vitruvius, two bricks thick.

Dipping-needle, in navigation, a magnetic needle, so hung that one end dips, or inclines to the horizon, and the other is proportionally elevated, forming an angle equal to the dipping of the needle at the place where the experiment is made.

Dipping (among miners), the interruption or breaking off of the vein of ore.

Dipteral, having a double range of columns all round; a dipteral temple usually had eight in the front row of the end porticoes, and fifteen at the sides, the columns at the angles being included in both.

Dipteron, in ancient architecture, a temple surrounded with a double row of columns which form porticoes, called wings or aisles.

Dipteros, in Greek architecture, a temple with a double row of columns on each of the four sides.

Direct-action engine, an engine having the rotatory motion communicated to a crank placed directly over the cylinder, so as to save height, and lessen the weight of the engine: the term applies more particularly to marine engines.

Discharging arch, an arch formed in the substance of a wall, to relieve the part which is below it from the superincumbent weight: it is frequently used over lintels and flat-headed openings.

Discord, a term applied to painting when there is a disagreement of the parts or the colouring; when the objects appear foreign to each other, and have an unpleasing and unnatural effect.

Disembogue, to pour out at the mouth of a river.

Distemper, in painting, the working-up of colours with something else besides mere water or oil. If the colours be prepared with the first, it is called limning; and with the last, painting in oil.

Distemper is a preparation of colours without oil, only mixed with size, whites of eggs, or any such proper glutinous or unctuous substance: with this kind of colour all the ancient pictures, before the year 1410, were painted, as also are the celebrated cartoons of Raphael.

Disti Salvi built the Baptistery of Pisa.

Ditriglyph, an interval between two columns, admitting two triglyphs in the entablature; used in the Doric order.

Dividiculum, in Rome, a tower on an aqueduct, containing a large reservoir.

Diving-bell, a machine contrived for safely lowering a man to any reasonable depth under water, so that he may remain there for a considerable time.

Division of an Order. The general division of an Order being into two parts, namely, the column and entablature, the column is subdivided into three unequal parts, viz. the base, the shaft, and the capital. The entablature consists also of three unequal parts, which are, the architrave, the frieze, and the cornice. Each of these divisions consists of several smaller parts, which by their variety and peculiarity distinguish the Orders from each other.

Dock, a place artificially formed for the reception of ships, the entrance of which is generally closed by gates. There are two kinds of docks,—dry docks and wet docks: the former are used for receiving ships for repair, the latter for the purpose of keeping vessels afloat.

Docks are enclosed artificial receptacles for shipping, and are usually formed by excavation of the soil and constructed walls of masonry, with inlets and gates for admitting the passage of vessels. Docks are usually distinguished as wet docks or basins and dry or graving docks. The former of these are already described under the head *Basin;* the latter may be described as follows:

Graving docks, in which repairs of vessels are effected, are constructed of various dimensions, according to the class of vessel for which provision is intended. Several splendid works of this kind have, within the last few years, been executed in the English dockyards. One of these—the Eastern Dock in Her Majesty's Dockyard at Woolwich—is 282 feet in extreme length, 81 feet in width on the ground level, and 39 feet in the bed. The depth from the ground level to the bed is 27 feet. The inclined sides and curved end of the masonry are formed into a series of steps or altars, by which access is readily obtained to all parts of the dock, and fixing-places obtained for the struts with which the sides of the vessel under repair are maintained in an upright position, when the water is discharged from the dock. The river-wall of this structure was originally constructed of concrete block-facings with rough concrete backings, according to a plan introduced into this country by Mr. Ranger; but these were abandoned, and granite facings substituted, the entire mass of the wall being supported on timber-piling. The whole of the piers, apron, and coffer-dam walls were executed by tide-work, in the following manner: a small space was surrounded by sheet-piling, which was carried up from 6 to 8 feet above the level of low-water: into the enclosure thus formed a pipe from two 18-inch pumps, worked by a steam-engine, was led, and the pumps set to work as soon as the tide fell below the sheet-piling. The subsequent excavation for the dock reached a bed of chalk, which was found to be sufficiently firm to dispense with the inverted arch of masonry usually constructed beneath the bed of these docks, and the floor was consequently constructed of a horizontal paving of blocks of granite 2 feet in thickness, each stone, being joggled to the adjacent stones with dove-tail joggles of Valentia slate bedded in cement. The river water is admitted into the dock through a culvert 5 feet high and 3 feet wide, passing through each pier, and which culverts are worked by sluices of cast-iron. The front of the dock is closed with a caisson formed of plate-iron, fixed with rivets to ribs of angle-iron; the form of the caisson being similar to that of a vessel, namely, with a continuous keel along the bottom and up each end, and a swelling outline tapering towards the end keels, and reduced to a width nearly parallel to the dock-level. This continuous keel, which is of oak, and formed in two pieces, fits into a recess in the masonry at the entrance of the dock, and the admission of water into it is regulated by sluices and pumps.

From the description given of graving docks, it will be understood that their action and efficiency depend upon the command of an adequate depth of water, and a sufficient rise and fall of tide to leave the vessel dry or to float her, as occasion requires. The use of these docks also compels the retention of the vessel during the action of the tide, and thus involves a considerable lapse of time, which sometimes cannot be afforded for trifling repairs or examination of a vessel in active service.

For situations in which no tide exists, a different arrangement becomes necessary, and a construction called a 'slip' is commonly substituted for a graving dock. The slip which has been the most extensively used is that known as 'Morton's slip,' and which was secured by a patent dated March 23, 1819, granted to T. Morton, for a method of dragging ships out of water for repairs, etc. This slip consists of an inclined plane, formed of timber framing laid upon suitable foundations of masonry, or cut in the surface of the rock. Upon this framing longitudinal metal racks are fixed, and a moveable carriage, upon which the vessel is received (by running the carriage to the lower part of the plane, beneath the water, and securing the vessel upon it), is fitted with cog-wheels, or other suitable apparatus for working upon these racks. The moving carriage consists of a succession of small strong blocks or carriages, any number of which may be connected together, according to the length of vessel to be hauled up. Each of these blocks or carriages, which are laid in corresponding pairs on each side of the central line of the slip, so as to leave a continuous intermediate space to receive the keel of the vessel, is fitted with rollers, upon which it may be moved transversely; and thus the distance between the two blocks of each pair, or on each side of the centre, may be adjusted according to the sectional form of the ship. These motions are ingeniously effected with the aid of cross-ropes or lines which are fixed to the blocks, and by which means the entire action of the apparatus is much facilitated. The combined carriage, when loaded with the vessel, is hauled up the slip by cables attached to a drum apparatus, with suitable gearing fixed in a building at the head or upper end of the slip. The power required is of course in proportion to the weight to be hauled up, and to the rate of inclination of the slip, and is usually supplied by a steam-engine.

This principle is susceptible of being extended, so as to provide berths for several vessels with only one hauling-up slip and machinery. For this purpose it has been suggested to construct a series of frames arranged radially round a centre, and capable of motion and of adjustment, with one slip constructed in such a direction as to correspond with a produced radius of the same circle. This arrangement, which would be similar to that of the polygonal engine-houses now erected on several lines of railway, offers great facilities for extended operations in the repair of vessels, but of course requires great space for the construction of the radial frames.

In order to provide for cases in which sufficient tidal difference cannot be had for raising vessels of deep draughts on to a dry dock, *floating docks* have been introduced in North America, and found to act satisfactorily. These floating docks are constructed with a buoyant bed or cradle, capable of supporting a vessel within the dock, with its keel above the surface of the water. This float or cradle is made in a box-like form, composed of strong logs, jointed firmly, and well caulked, so as to make it water-proof. The capacity of the float must be such that when freed from water by pumping, and loaded with the vessel, workmen, etc., it shall sustain the load with safety. The float moves within a recess of masonry, by which its motion is guided and secured. Suitable shores, blocks, struts, etc., are used in making the vessel steady within the float, which is fitted with valves in the lower part. The action of this floating dock is as follows: The cradle or float, being full of water (the valves being open), is sunk so that the vessel may be brought over it, and temporarily secured in position: the valves are then closed, and the pumps set to work to clear the water from the float, which rises in consequence, and brings up the vessel to a dry level. When the ship is again ready for sea, the opening of the valves admits the water, and sinks the float, leaving the vessel free above it to pass out of the dock.

The docks and basins of London and Liverpool comprise some of the largest specimens of works of this kind. Those of the latter port were commenced in 1708, and consist of several docks of great extent. The first public docks for merchant shipping in London were the West India Docks, opened in 1805, the great basin of which is 420 yards in length, and 230 yards in width. This is connected with the river by another basin of about three acres in area. The London Docks were commenced soon after the West India Docks, and opened in the same year, viz. 1805. The principal basin of these docks is 420 yards in length, and 276 yards in width. The East India Dock for unloading inwards is 470 yards in length, and 173 yards in width; and that for loading outwards is 260 yards in length, and 140 yards in width. The St. Katherine's Docks occupy an area of 24 acres.

Dodecagon, in geometry, a figure of twelve angles and sides.

Dodecahedron, in geometry, one of the regular bodies comprehended under twelve equal sides, each of which is a pentagon.

Dodecastyle, a building having twelve columns in front.

Dogs, or andirons, creepers, braziers, etc. Long after the general introduction of chimneys, wood was the ordinary fuel for all sorts of apartments. Coals formed no part of the 'liveries,' but wood was commonly included in them. A 'cradle for sea-coal' is however frequently mentioned as belonging to the chief rooms in superior houses, though the usual way of warming, or rather airing, bed-chambers was with braziers or chafing dishes. Andirons are a larger and higher sort of irons, made to support the wood, and have usually long necks rising up before, to prevent the wood from falling upon the floor. Creepers are smaller and lower irons with short necks, or none at all, which are placed between the andirons, to keep the ends of the wood and the brands from the hearth, that the fire may burn more freely.

Dog-kennel, a lodgement for dogs kept for the purpose of field sports: it is almost as invariable an appendage to the manor-house as it was formerly to the baronial castle. Bishop Percy observes, "that a nobleman in the dark ages, retired within his castle, had neither books, nor newspapers, nor literary correspondence, nor visits, nor cards, to fill up his leisure: his only amusements were field sports; nor did the love for these decline in the Tudor period."

Dog-wood, a small underwood, free from silex: small splinters are used by watch-makers for cleaning out the pivot-holes of watches; it is also used by butchers for making skewers.

Dogger, a ship of about eighty tons burden, with a well in the middle, to bring fish alive to shore.

Dolomite, massive magnesian limestone, used by the ancient sculptors in their best works.

Dolphin, a technical term applied to the pipe and cover at a source for the supply of water.

Dome, a term applied to a covering of the whole or part of a building: the word dome is strictly applied to the external part of the spherical or polygonal roof, and cupola to the internal part.

Dome or *cupola*, a roof, the base of which is a circle, an ellipsis, or a polygon, and its vertical section a curve line, concave towards the interior. Hence domes are called circular, elliptical, or polygonal, according to the figure of the base. The most usual form for a dome is the spherical, in which case its plan is a circle, the section a segment of a circle. The top of a large dome is often finished with a *lantern*, which is supported by the framing of the dome. The interior and exterior forms of a dome are not often alike, and in the space between, a staircase to the lantern is generally made. According to the space left between the external and internal domes, the framing must be designed. Sometimes the framing may be trussed with ties across the opening; but often the interior dome rises so high that ties cannot be inserted. Accordingly, the construction of domes may be divided into two cases: viz. domes with horizontal ties, and those not having such ties.

Dome, in locomotive-engines, the conical part of the boiler, forming a steam-chamber, and terminating the top of the fire-box part. In a locomotive-engine the safety-valves are usually placed on the top of the dome or the body of the boiler.

Dome-cover, in locomotive-engines, the brass or copper cover which encloses the dome, to prevent the radiation of heat.

Dome Cathedral of Pisa, the first model of that Tuscan style of architecture, so solid, grave, and imposing, neither Greek nor Gothic, was begun in the eleventh century; and in the thirteenth was founded the majestic church of Santa Maria dei Fiori at Florence, of which the dome equals in size that of St. Peter's at Rome, and was its model.

Dome of St. Paul's Cathedral (the) is elliptical, and built of wood; it is confined by strong chains, consisting of iron bars: that of the Pantheon at Rome is nearly circular, and its lower parts are so much thicker than its upper parts as to afford sufficient resistance to their pressure; they are supported by walls of great thickness, and furnished with many projections which answer the purpose of abutments and buttresses.

Domes in Asia are probably more ancient than in Italy. At Lankerrood, at Dhay-nain, at Sin-sin, five or six days' journey south of Teheran, in Persia, the towns are all deserted: there are about a hundred large dwelling-houses quite entire, of a very singular construction. Each edifice stands separate, and is constructed of several central arches supporting a pointed dome; while smaller divisions project from the body of the building, also arched, and the whole finished with the greatest neatness, having remains of stucco-painted walls within.

It is probable that the arch and vault and dome were not unknown to the nations in the East, beyond the Indies, in a very remote age; but in Greece and in Asia Minor there are no traces of them before their introduction by the Romans. To the Romans they were familiar at a very early period of their history; a knowledge of which they borrowed perhaps from the Etruscans, or from the supposed extinct people who possessed a city on the site of Rome itself, before the Romans.

Domestic Architecture in England. At the termination of the York and Lancaster wars, the fortified style of architecture was gradually abandoned in England; and as we had no other model of domestic architecture than the gable and the cottage, by the duplication of this simple form, in various positions, was constructed what has been called the Old English Manor-house style. If we take a common two-floored English gable and cottage, add to it one, two, or three cottages side by side, of the same size, and, in order to gain rooms out of the roof on the sides of this double or triple cottage, raise gable ends either projecting from the ground to the top of the roof, or merely raised from the eaves-drop; if we insert broad low windows, divided by simple wooden or stone mullions, in these projecting gable ends, and similar windows at the ends of this double or triple cottage; ornament the inclined sides of the gable ends above the eaves-drop by steps or small pinnacles, or both; then add a parapet, plain or embattled, we have a manor-house in the most florid style. Many such houses came afterwards to be adorned by a centre of architectural decoration, in which Roman, Grecian, and Gothic were strangely mixed. There is, however, a certain degree of antique-like grandeur in such houses, which produces a very striking impression. This step towards a better style took place before the time of Inigo Jones.

"The mansion at South Elmham, when entire, formed a quadrangle, as usual, of which stables and offices made up a part. The domestic and ecclesiastical styles are singularly combined in this building, though the latter seems to predominate; and the occasional discovery of old floor-stones, of a sepulchral character, intimates that the projecting porch led to the chapel of the dwelling, not into the hall; and yet the ceilings of the chambers where the two wings and upper windows are observed, on the right hand of the porch, are flat, divided into small squares by the girders above, and covered with plastered mouldings, in the manner usually seen in dwellings of an early period."

Domestic buildings and *castles.* The towns and ordinary houses of the Normans were entirely built of wood, and, for the most part, are so to this day. Their castles, having but one destination, that of defence, aimed at nothing but strength in their plan or construction. A site was also selected which was already fortified by nature.

The plan of the Norman castles was as nearly the same as the diversity of ground would allow. The principal feature was always the keep, which contained the apartments of the lord of the castle, and was also meant to be the last refuge of the garrison, if the outer works were forced. The keep was usually raised on an artificial monnd, or placed on the edge of a precipice. The walls, strengthened in every way that art could devise, were of immense thickness, and composed of grouting poured in between two solid walls of stone. The facing consisted sometimes of irregular courses, and sometimes of small squared stones, after the Roman manner. Ashler was usually introduced at the angles of the building. The windows were few, and little more than chinks, unless very high up, or turned to the court. The door of entrance could only be reached by a staircase. Under the keep were usually vaults, or dungeons, for the reception of prisoners. The keep was enclosed in two courts surrounded by walls flanked with towers. The tower at the entrance was called the barbican, and served at once for an outwork and post of observation. The whole fortress was defended by a moat.

The remains of the Norman castles which exist scarcely afford any specimens of early Norman construction, almost all these castles having been besieged, destroyed, and rebuilt, over and over again. The keep of Falaise is perhaps the only castellated remnant of early Norman times. The castle of Gizors, which was built by William Rufus, retains nothing of its original construction.

Doorway (Anglo-Norman). The Anglo-Norman builders bestowed much pains and evinced considerable artistic skill in very elaborately ornamenting the portal entrances to churches in their style of architecture, by a profusion of ornamental mouldings and of sculpture. Very many examples are to be met with in great variety in several of the counties of England, particularly in the counties of Norfolk and Suffolk. The example represented in the annexed engraving is a beautiful specimen taken from the church of St. Botolph, at Cove, in the county of Suffolk.

Domus, a private house occupied by a single proprietor and his family.

Doors (Antique). The Greeks in the temple of Minerva Polias, at Athens, and also the Romans in the temple of Vesta, or the Sibyl, at Tivoli, made the doors and windows smaller at top than at bottom: the architrave or dressing always constituted an agreeable decoration when in character with the building. Those of the windows in the Grecian temple have a projection, or what is sometimes termed a knee, at their upper angle; while those of the temple of Vesta, whose apertures have the same form, continue without interruption, and are surmounted by a cornice; but the cornice above the door is separated from the archi-

trave by a frieze, while the cornice of the windows joins the architrave. In the temple of Minerva, the architrave of the windows rests only on a plain socle; those of the temple of Vesta rest also on a socle or support, the face of which is sunk.

Doors (Modern). There are two doors, designs of Vignola, which offer in their profiles and proportions a happy medium between the antique and modern compositions; and all other designs of this kind are either derived from them, or possess a vague character which renders them unworthy of imitation.

There are breaks in the architrave, as in those of the temple of Minerva Polias; and the termination or lower extremity of these breaks determines the length of the consoles, which gives harmony to the arrangement. These consoles are also placed against a second architrave, beyond which the first projects. The design of the door of the church of St. Lorenzo is more regular.

Doorways. In the Gothic, and the architecture of the middle ages, doorways are striking and important features, affording in the character of the mouldings and ornaments the style and period of the edifice.

Doric Order. The Doric order, says Palladio, was invented by the Dorians and named from them, being a Grecian people which dwelt in Asia. If Doric columns are made alone without pilasters, they ought to be seven and a half or eight diameters high. The intercolumns are to be little less than three diameters of the columns; and this manner of spacing the columns is by Vitruvius called Diastylos.

The ancients employed the Doric in temples dedicated to Minerva, to Mars, and to Hercules, whose grave and manly dispositions suited well with the character of this order. Serlio says it is proper for churches dedicated to Jesus Christ, to St. Paul, St. Peter, or any other saints remarkable for their fortitude in exposing their lives and suffering for the Christian faith. Le Clerc recommends the use of it in all kinds of military buildings; as arsenals, gates of fortified places, guard-rooms, and similar structures. It may likewise be employed in the houses of generals or other martial men,—in mausoleums erected to their memory, or in triumphal bridges and arches built to celebrate their victories.

Vitruvius himself makes the Doric column in porticoes higher by half a diameter than in temples; and most modern architects have, on some occasions, followed his example. In private houses, therefore, it may be 16¼, 16½, or 16¾ modules high; in interior decorations, even seventeen modules, and sometimes perhaps a trifle more; which increase in the height may be added entirely to the shaft, as in the Tuscan order, without changing either the base or capital. The entablature, too, may remain unaltered in all the aforesaid cases; for it will be sufficiently bold without alteration.

The height of the Doric column, including its capital and base, is sixteen modules; and the height of the entablature, four modules; the latter of which being divided into eight parts, two of them are given to the architrave, three to the frieze, and the remaining three to the cornice.

In most of the antiques, the Doric column is executed without a base. Vitruvius likewise makes it without one; the base, according to that author, having been first employed in the Ionic order, to imitate the sandal or covering of a woman's foot. Scamozzi blames this practice; and most of the moderns have been of his opinion, the greatest part of them having employed the Attic base in this order.

Dorman tree, a large beam lying across a room; a joist, or sleeper.

Dormer window, a window pierced through a sloping roof, and placed in a small gable which rises on the side of the roof.

Dormitory, a sleeping apartment; a term formerly applied to the sleeping-room of the inmates of monasteries and other religious houses.

Dormond, a large beam lying across a room; a joist, or sleeper: same as Dorman.

Doron, a hand-breadth, or palm: among the Greeks, their bricks or tiles were termed *tetradoron*, four hands' breadth, or *pentadoron*, five hands broad; the word also implies a gift: hence, probably, the origin of the English word dowry.

Dorture, a place to sleep in, a bed-chamber. "He led us to a gallery like a dorture."

Dosel, hangings round the walls of a hall, or at the east end, and sometimes the sides, of the chancel of a church, made of tapestry or carpet-work; used also in churches, and frequently richly embroidered with silks, and gold and silver.

Dosel, ornamental and rich stuff for the back of a chair, a throne, or a screen of ornamental woodwork.

Double-acting pump, a pump which lifts and forces water at the same time, by means of a solid piston, and an entrance and exit-valve communicating with each side.

Double-beat valve, a valve used in Cornish engines and water-works. It has two heats, or seatings, one above the other; the bottom one is similar to an ordinary-circular valve seating; the top one is somewhat less in diameter than the bottom one, and is supported from it by ribs, and forms a cover nearly the size of the inner passage. A shell with two heats to correspond with the seatings shuts the sides; when raised (which requires but little power, as the fixed cover before mentioned bears nearly all the pressure, its diameter being nearly equal to that of the shell) the steam or water escapes at the sides both of the top and bottom beat.

Double-cylinder engine, a marine engine with two cylinders placed at right angles to the crank-shaft, and at a small distance apart, to give space for the vibration of the rod connecting the crank to the long end of a shaped cross-head, which slides in grooves between the cylinders; the upper ends of the cross-head are connected to the piston-rods. This form of engine is patented by Messrs. Maudslay.

Doucine, a moulding, concave above and convex below.

Dove-tail, in carpentry, a method of joining two boards together by letting one piece into another in the form of the tail of a dove, when that which is inserted has the appearance of a wedge reversed.

Dove-tailing, a method of fastening together two pieces of metal or wood by projecting bits cut in the form of dove-tails in one piece, to fit into corresponding hollows in the other.

Dowel. A round dowel or coak is the piece of timber to which the felloes of a carriage-wheel are united.

Dowsing cheeks, in ship-building, pieces fayed across the apron, and lapped on the knightheads or inside stuff above the upper deck.

Drabler, a small topsail.

Drabs, in salt-works, a kind of wooden box for holding the salt when taken out of the boiling pan.

Draft-engine, an engine used for pumping.

Drag-bar, a strong iron rod with eye-holes at each end, connecting a locomotive engine and tender by means of the drag-bolt and spring.

Drag-bolt, the strong bolt coupling the drag-bar of a locomotive engine and tender together, and removable at pleasure.

Drag-hook and chain, the strong chain and hook attached to the front of the engine buffer-bar, to connect it on to any other locomotive engine or tender; also attached to the drag-bars of goods-waggons.

Drag-link, a link for connecting the cranks of two shafts; it is used in marine engines for connecting the crank on the main-shaft to that on the inner paddle-shaft.

Drag-spring, a strong spring placed near the back of the tender. It is attached by the ends to the drag-bar which connects the engine and tender, and by the centre to the drag-bar which connects the train to the tender.

Dragon-beams are two strong braces which stand under a breast-summer and meet in an angle on the shoulders of the king-piece.

Dragon's blood (colour), a resinous substance brought from the East Indies. It is of a warm semi-transparent, rather dull-red colour, which is deepened by impure air, and darkened by light. There are two or three sorts, but that in drops is the best. White lead soon destroys it, and it dries with extreme difficulty in oil. It is sometimes used to colour varnishes and lacquers, being soluble in oils and alcohol; but notwithstanding it has been recommended as a pigment, it does not merit the attention of the artist.

Drainage of marshes and fen lands. The steam-engine is used to raise the water above the level of those lands which lie too low to be drained by natural outfall, and also in situations where the fall is not sufficient to carry off the superfluous water in time to prevent damage to the crops.

Mr. Glynn has applied steam-power to the drainage of land in fifteen districts, all in England, chiefly in Cambridgeshire, Lincolnshire, and Norfolk. The quantity of land so drained amounts to more than 125,000 acres, the engines employed being seventeen in number, and their aggregate power 870 horses; the size of the engines varies from 20 to 80 horses. Mr. Glynn was also engaged in draining by steam power the Hammerbrook district, close by the city of Hamburgh; and in another level near to Rotterdam, an engine and machinery with the requisite buildings have been erected from his plans by the Chevalier Conrad, and the works successfully carried into effect.

In British Guiana the steam-engine has been made to answer the double purpose of drainage and irrigation. Some of the sugar-plantations of Demerara are drained of the superfluous water during the rainy season, and watered during the dry season.

In many of the swampy levels of Lincolnshire and Cambridgeshire, much had been done to carry off the water by natural means, and many large cuts had been made and embankments formed, especially in the Bedford Level, which alone contains about 300,000 acres of fen-land; the Great Level of the fens contains about 680,000, formerly of little value, but now rich in corn and cattle. The general plan is to carry away the water coming off the higher grounds, and prevent it, as much as possible, from running down into the marsh by means of the catchwater drains, leaving the rain alone which falls upon the district to be dealt with by mechanical power. As the quantity of rain falling on the Great Level of the fens seldom exceeds 26 inches in the year, and about two-thirds of this quantity is carried off by evaporation and absorption, or the growth of plants, it is only in extreme cases that 2 inches in depth require to be thrown off by the engines in any one month, which amounts to $1\frac{1}{2}$ cubic foot of water upon every square yard of land, or 7260 feet to the acre.

The standard and accepted measure of a horse's power is 33,000 lbs.

raised 1 foot high in a minute, or 3300lbs. raised 10 feet high in the same time; and as a cubic foot of water weighs 62½lbs., and a gallon of water 10lbs., so one horse's power will raise and discharge, at a height of 10 feet, 330 gallons, or 52$\frac{7}{8}$ cubic feet of water in a minute. Consequently this assumed excess of 7260 cubic feet of water fallen upon an acre of land will be raised and discharged at an elevation of 10 feet in about two hours and twenty minutes. If the quantity of land be 1000 acres of fen or marsh, with the upland waters all banked out, the excess of rain, according to the foregoing estimate, will amount to 726,000 cubic feet. A steam-engine of 10-horse power will throw off this water in 232 hours, or in less than twenty days, working twelve hours a day. This calculation has been found fully supported in practice.

Although the rain due to any given month may fall in a few days, yet in such case much of it will be absorbed by the ground; and the drains must be made of sufficient capacity to receive and contain the rain as it falls; besides, in case of necessity, the engine may be made to work twenty hours a day instead of twelve, until the danger be past.

The main drains have generally been cut 7½ feet deep, and of width sufficient to give them the required capacity to contain the excess of rain, and to bring the water freely down to the engine. In some instances, where the districts are extensive and their length great, it has been found necessary to make them somewhat deeper.

In all cases where it has been requisite to use steam-power, Mr. Glynn has applied scoop-wheels to raise the water. These scoop-wheels somewhat resemble the undershot wheel of a water-mill, but instead of being turned by the impulse of the water, they are used to lift it, and are kept in motion by the steam-engine.

The floats or ladle-boards of the wheels are made of wood, and fitted to work in a trough or track of masonry; they are generally made 5 feet in length, that is to say, they are immersed 5 feet deep in the water, and their width or horizontal dimension varies from 20 inches to 5 feet, according to the power of the engines employed, and the head of water to be overcome. The wheel-track at the lower end communicates with the main drain, and at the higher end with the river; the water in the river being kept out by a pair of pointing doors, like the lock-gates of a canal, which close when the engine ceases to work. The wheels themselves are made of cast-iron, formed in parts for convenience of transport. The float-boards are connected with the cast-iron part of the wheel by means of oak-starts, which are stepped into sockets cast in the circumference of the wheel to receive them.

There are cast-iron toothed segments fitted to the wheel, into which works a pinion fixed upon the crank-shaft of the steam-engine. When the head of water in the river or delivering drain does not vary much, it is sufficient to have one speed for the wheel; but where the tide rises in the river, it is desirable to have two speeds or powers of wheel-work, the one to be used at low rate, the other more powerful combination to act against the rising tide. But in most cases it is not requisite to raise the water more than 3 or 4 feet higher than the surface of the land intended to be drained; and even this is only necessary when the rivers are full between their banks, from a continuance of wet weather, or from upland floods. In some instances, the height of the water in the rivers being affected by the tide, the drainage by natural outfall can take place only during the ebb; and here, in case of long continuing rains, the natural drainage requires the assistance of mechanical power.

It has been stated that the main drains have generally been made 7½ feet deep, or more in larger districts, so that the water may never rise higher than within 18 inches or 2 feet of the surface of the ground, and the ladles or floatboards dip 5 feet below the water, leaving a foot in depth below the dip of the wheel, that the water may run freely to it, and to allow for the casual obstruction of weeds in the main drain, which, if it be sufficiently capacious and well formed, will bring down the water to the engine with a descent of 3 inches in a mile. Suppose then that the wheel dips 5 feet below the surface of the water in the main drain, and that the water in the river into which this water must be raised and discharged has its level 5 feet above that in the drain, the wheel in such case will be said to have 10 feet head and dip, and ought to be made 28 or 30 feet in diameter.

Mr. Glynn has found it practicable to throw out the water against a head of 10 feet with a dip of 5 feet, that is to say, 15 feet of head and dip, with a wheel of 35 feet in diameter; but in another engine, more recently erected, he has made the wheel 40 feet in diameter. The engine that drives this wheel is of 80-horse power, and is situated on the Ten-mile Bank, near Littlepool, in the Isle of Ely. The largest quantity of water delivered by one engine is from Deeping Fen, near Spalding; this fen contains 25,000 acres, and is drained by two engines, one of 80 and one of 60-horse power.

The 80-horse engine has a wheel of 28 feet in diameter, with floatboards or ladles measuring 5½ feet by 5 feet, and moving with a mean velocity of 6 feet per second; so that the section of the stream is 27½ feet, and the quantity discharged per second 165 cubic feet; equal to more than 4½ tons of water in a second, or about 16,200 tons of water in an hour.

It was in 1825 that these two engines were erected, and at that time the district was kept in a half-cultivated state by the help of forty-four windmills, the land at times being wholly under water. It now grows excellent wheat, producing from four to six quarters to the acre. In many districts, land has been purchased at from £10 to £20 an acre, by persons who foresaw the consequences of these improvements, and which they could now sell at from £50 to £70 an acre. This increase in value has arisen, not only from the land being cleared from the injurious effects of the water upon it, but from the improved system of cultivation it has enabled the farmers to adopt.

The fen-lands in Cambridgeshire and great part of the neighbouring counties are formed of a rich black earth, consisting of decomposed vegetable matter, generally from 6 feet to 10 feet thick, although in some places much thicker, resting upon a bed of blue galt, containing clay, lime, and sand.

Draining, as applied to lands, towns, and buildings, is the art of drawing or conveying away refuse liquid and other matters, the accumulation of which would be detrimental to animal and vegetable existence.

In that department which relates to lands, draining comprehends also the methods of *irrigating* or supplying water for agricultural purposes, for which the natural supply is inadequate. Referring to towns, and buildings, this art includes also, for the purpose of thorough cleansing, the artificial supply of water.

According to this comprehensive definition, which will be found to have greater practical convenience than any more limited one, Draining comprises observations of the relative levels of districts and of their geological structure; of the several sources of water, and the amount of their products; and the construction and arrangement of all the artificial appliances required for the supply, conduct, and disposal of water, and for conveying and discharging refuse matters generally.

The sources of water are rains and the ocean. The former passing into the earth, descend along the lower surfaces, and form streams and rivers; or penetrate into some permeable media, and accumulating in subterranean depositories, form springs. An examination of the superficial and structural features of the soil enables us to estimate the quantity of water present in a district, and to determine the means that will be available for supplying the deficiency or discharging the excess. The same observations afford general information required in order to arrange the artificial channels, drains, sewers, etc., by which the supply and refuse matters are to be conducted and disposed of.

Soils are retentive of water in proportion to their density and compactness. Thus, on clay-lands an excess of water is commonly found, while, from the porous texture of gravel and loose sand, water passes rapidly away, and they are thus kept in a dry condition.

The *size* of the channels or *drains*, by which the water is conducted away, will be adapted to the superficial extent to be drained, and the quantity of water due to the district, as computed from its relative position and structure. The *construction* of the drains will depend upon the materials of the soil, and the proximity of those suitable for the purpose. Generally, *covered* drains are far preferable to open ones; and those formed with a duct of *earthen piping* are more durable and economical than any others. The *implements* used are rods and levels, for measuring distances and ascertaining inclinations of surface;—tools for boring the soil, to examine substrata, and detect springs, consisting of augers, chisels, punches, etc.;—spades, shovels, and picks of various forms and dimensions; and hoes, scoops, etc., for clearing out and finishing the form of drains.

For the draining of towns and buildings, including the artificial supply of water, the best available sources—such as rivers and springs—are resorted to, and the advantageous use of these will require a careful consideration of the *qualities* of the water obtained, and its suitability for domestic and manufacturing purposes. Arrangements are required for making the water furnished by rains available to the full extent, and rendering it and all other waters fit for use by subsidence, filtration, and purification.

For discharging the refuse matters from houses and other buildings, and from streets and public thoroughfares, drains and sewers of various forms and materials are to be selected, made of *ample dimensions* and permanent construction, with such vertical inclination, and so arranged, that their contents shall always have a tendency to run off, and never suffer interference from the discharge of other channels.

As a final point to be observed in any system of town-drainage, that of the ultimate disposal of the refuse matters is one of the highest importance in both a sanatory and an economical point of view. Collected in proper reservoirs, and judiciously treated, these matters may be distributed in fertilizing streams over the fields and the gardens of the suburbs, and will thus realize immense value in improved and augmented crops; allowed to accumulate in cesspools beneath human dwellings, they engender malignant and fatal disease, and if finally discharged into a river, by way of getting rid of them, they pollute waters otherwise wholesome, and, in dry seasons, send forth from the banks the most unhealthy gases.

Drana, a drain or watercourse.

Draught, in ship draughting, the drawing or design by which the ship is to be built, which is generally by a scale of one-fourth of an inch to a foot.

Draute-chamber, a retiring or withdrawing room.

Draw-bore, the pinning a mortise and tenon, by piercing the hole through the tenon nearer to the shoulder than the holes through the cheeks from the abutment in which the shoulder is to come in contact.

Draw-bore pins, pieces of steel in the shape of the frustum of a cone, somewhat tapered, and inserted in handles with the greatest diameter next to the handle, for driving through the draw-bores of a mortise and tenon, in order to bring the shoulder of the rail close home to the abutment on the edge of the style; when this is effected, the draw-bore pins, when more than one are used, are taken out singly, and the holes filled up with wooden pegs.

Drawbridge. All drawbridges are composed of two distinct parts, viz. the platform, which revolves on a horizontal axis, acting as a barrier or gate when in a vertical position, and becoming a bridge when in a horizontal position; and the contrivance necessary to balance the platform in every position. The equilibrium should be such that friction is the only force to be overcome in raising or lowering the platform.

The chief difference between drawbridges lies in the arrangement of this latter contrivance; for the platforms only differ in small details of construction, which have very little influence on the qualities which are essential to the arrangement of the balancing apparatus. These qualities remain the same, whether the drawbridges are used for closing communications in fortified works, or merely for forming passages across navigable canals. They are principally as follows:—

1st. The whole system should possess sufficient strength to be perfectly free from danger in all positions and at all times, and should therefore be constructed of solid and lasting materials.

2nd. A small number of men should be able to raise or lower the bridge in a short space of time. This quality requires all the parts to be in equilibrium when friction is not considered.

3rd. The machinery for raising and lowering the bridge should not obstruct the communications either in front or in rear of the buttresses of the gateway where it is placed; and also the space formed by raising the bridge should be as wide as possible, for this space constitutes the chief use of the bridge.

4th. The counterpoise and the machinery attached to it should be raised as little as possible above the platform when vertical, in order that it may not be much exposed to an enemy's fire, and that it may be easily covered by the advanced works; besides that, by raising it, the expense of constructing and the inconvenience of working the machinery are increased, and the strength of the gateway or postern is sometimes diminished.

5th. The counterpoise and its machinery should not be much below the level of the ground, and particularly very little below the level of the surface of the water in wet ditches. At all events, the descending parts should be enclosed in narrow shafts of masonry secure from damp. In order not to weaken the postern walls, they should be at least 3 feet in rear of them.

Drawing is the art of representing objects on a flat surface by lines describing their forms and contours alone, independently of colour or even shadow, although the latter is closely allied with drawing, both in practice and theory.

Drawings in pencil are sometimes required to be fixed: this can be done by using water-starch made to the consistency of that employed by laundresses: it should be applied with a broad camel's hair brush, as in varnishing. Isinglass, size, and rice-water are sometimes used, but are not so good as the first-named substance.

Dredge's Suspension Bridge consists in making the chains of sufficient magnitude and strength at the points of suspension to support with safety the greatest permanent and contingent load to which, under the circumstances of locality, they are ever likely to be exposed; and from thence, to taper or diminish them gradually to the middle of the bridge, where the strain becomes essentially evanescent. The gradual diminution of the chains, however, is not the only peculiarity which characterizes this mode of construction, and marks its utility. The suspending-rods or bars that support the platform, or roadway, instead of being hung vertically or at right angles to the plane of the horizon, are inclined to it in angles which vary in magnitude from the abutments to the middle of the bridge, where the obliquity, as well as the stress upon the chains, attains its minimum value.

Dredging machines, mechanical contrivances placed in the hull of a vessel, and floated in situations for the dredging and clearing away of deposited matter from the beds of rivers, canals, harbours, basins, etc. Some machines for these purposes are to be compared to harrows or shovels, which loosen the deposit preparatory to its removal either by the action of the tide or stream; but for the more general purposes of dredging, vast improvements have been effected. The machinery of the best construction is described in Weale's 'Quarterly Papers on Engineering.'

Dressings, the mouldings and sculptured decorations of all kinds which are used on the walls and ceilings of a building for the purpose of ornament.

Drift, a piece of hardened steel, notched at the sides and made slightly tapering: it is used for enlarging a hole in a piece of metal to a particular size by being driven through it.

Drift, the horizontal force which an arch exerts with a tendency to overset the piers from which it springs.

Drifts, in the sheer draught, are where the rails are cut off and ended with a scroll. Pieces fitted to form the drifts are called driftpieces.

Driftway, in mining, is a passage cut under the earth from shaft to shaft.

Drill, a tool for cutting a circular hole in a piece of metal.

Drilling machine, a machine for cutting circular holes in metal by means of a revolving drill.

Drilling, the art of boring small holes. Drilling may be effected in a lathe. The drill is screwed upon the spindle, so that its point shall turn exactly opposite that of the screw in the shifting head. Various ingenious improvements have recently been made.

Drip, the projecting edge of a moulding channeled beneath, so that the rain will drip from it: the corona of the Italian architects.

Dripstone, called also the 'label,' 'weather moulding,' and 'water table,' a projecting tablet or moulding over the heads of doorways, windows, archways, niches, etc.

Driver, the foremost spur in the bulge-ways, the heel of which is fayed to the foreside of the foremost poppet, and the sides placed to look fore and aft in a ship.

Driver, the bent piece of iron fixed in the centre chuck, and projecting over it to meet the carrier, and drive it forward.

Driving shaft, any shaft which gives motion to another shaft.

Driving springs, the springs fixed upon the boxes of the driving axle of a locomotive engine, to support the weight and to deaden the shocks caused by irregularities in the rails.

Driving wheels, the large wheels of a locomotive engine, which are fixed upon the crank-axle or main shaft of the engine.

Drop, in architecture, is an ornament of the columns of the Doric order, representing drops or little bells under the triglyphs.

Drum, in architecture, the bell-formed part of the Corinthian and Composite capitals.

Drum, a hollow cylinder fixed on a shaft, for driving another shaft by a hand.

Drummond light, a peculiar light invented by the late Captain Drummond, called a heliostat, which reflected the sun's rays in sufficient abundance to render the station which was to be observed visible. This invention obviated the difficulty of distinguishing the stations chosen for the angular points of the triangles in a geodesical survey: where those stations are many miles asunder, it is necessary to have recourse to illuminations even in daytime.

Dry oil, nearly colourless, may be obtained by combining linseed or nut oil with litharge, and triturating them together for a considerable time; this will produce a yellowish creamy substance, which being allowed to rest, soon becomes clear; but if there be not time to wait, this fluid may be filtered through blotting paper; it is then transparent, but with a little colour,

which soon goes off when exposed to the light.

Druxey, timber in a state of decay, with white spongy veins.

Dryness is a term by which artists express the common defect of the early painters in oil, who had but little knowledge of the flowing contours which so elegantly show the delicate forms of the limbs and the insertions of the muscles; the flesh in their colouring appearing hard and stiff, instead of expressing a pleasing softness. The draperies of those early painters, and particularly of the Germans, concealed the limbs of the figures, without truth or elegance of choice; and even in their best masters, the draperies very frequently either demeaned or encumbered the figures.

Dry-rot, a disease affecting timber, and particularly the oak employed for naval purposes. Many contrivances are employed as remedies which have recently been patented, and have been successfully applied.

Dub, to work with the adze.

Ductilimeter, an instrument for comparing the ductility of lead, tin, etc.

Ductility is that property of bodies which admits of their being drawn out in length, while their diameter is diminished, without any actual fracture. Gold, silver, platinum, iron, copper, zinc, tin, lead, nickel, are ductile in the order here given: wire-drawing depends on ductility.

Duns (in Cornish), frames of wood like the jambs of a door or the frame of a window; set in loose ground in adits and places that are weak and liable to fall in or tumble down.

Dungeon, a place of incarceration, formerly the principal tower or keep of a castle: it was always the strongest and least accessible part of a building.

Durbar (Persian), a court or building where the sovereign or viceroy gives audience.

Dutch Pink, *English* and *Italian Pinks*, are bright yellow colours used in distemper and for paper-staining, and other ordinary purposes. The pigment called 'stil,' or 'stil de grain,' is a similar preparation, and a very fugitive yellow, the darker kind of which is called Brown Pink.

Dutch School of Painting.—This school of art cannot be said to possess the perfections that are to be observed in the Flemish school; their subjects are derived from the tavern, the smith's shop, and from vulgar amusements of the rudest peasants. The expressions are sufficiently marked; but it is the expression of passions which debase, instead of ennobling human nature. It must be acknowledged, at the same time, that the Dutch painters have succeeded in several branches of the art. If they have chosen low subjects of imitation, they have represented them with great exactness; and truth must always please. If they have not succeeded in most difficult parts of the chiaro-oscuro, they at least excel in the most striking, such as in light confined in a narrow space, night illuminated by the moon, or by torches, and the light of a smith's forge. The Dutch understand the gradations of colours. They have no rivals in landscape painting, considered as the faithful representation of a particular scene; but they are far from equalling Titian, Poussin, Claude Lorraine, etc., who have carried to the greatest perfection the ideal landscape; and whose pictures, instead of being the topographical representation of certain places, are the combined result of everything beautiful in imagination or in nature.

Dyeing is the art of staining textile substances with permanent colours.

Dyke, in coal mining, the banks of basalt or whin, by which the coal strata are frequently divided.

Dynamics, the science of moving powers, or of the action of forces on solid bodies when the result of that action is motion.

GENERAL DEFINITIONS.

1. The *mass* of a body is the quantity of matter of which it is composed, and is proportional to its weight, or to the *force* which must be applied to the body to prevent its gravitating to the earth, and which, being greater or less as the mass is greater or less, we regard as a measure of the mass itself.

2. *Density* is a word by which we indicate the comparative closeness or otherwise of the particles of bodies, and is synonymous with the term *specific gravity*. Those bodies which have the greatest number of particles, or the greatest quantity of matter, in a given magnitude, we call *most dense;* those which have the least quantity of matter, *least dense*. Thus lead is more dense than freestone; freestone more dense than oak; and oak more dense than cork.

3. The *velocity* with which a body in motion moves, is measured by the space over which it passes in any given time; the unit usually assumed being one *second*.

4. If the body passes over an equal space in each successive unit of time, the body is said to move *uniformly*, or to have a *uniform velocity*, and the measure of such velocity is the space actually passed over by the body in each second.

5. If, however, the body passes over a *greater* space in each successive second than it did in the preceding, then it is said to move with an *accelerated velocity*: when the differences between the spaces moved over in any two successive seconds is the same, at whatever period of the body's motion they be taken, or in other words, when the successive spaces form an arithmetical progression, the body is said to move with a *uniformly accelerated* velocity; but when the spaces passed over in successive

seconds increase according to any other law, the body is then said to have its velocity *variably accelerated*.

6. If, on the other hand, the body passes over a *smaller* space in each successive second than it did in the preceding, then it is said to move with a *retarded* velocity; which, if the successive spaces form a decreasing arithmetical series, is said to be *uniformly retarded*; if otherwise, it is said to be *variably retarded*.

7. The *velocity* of a body whose motion is variable is expressed at any moment by the space which it *would pass over in a second*, if its velocity at the moment spoken of were to continue *uniform for that period*.

8. *Mechanical effect* is measured by the product of the *mass* or *weight* of the body into the space over which it has been moved; no regard being had to the time occupied. The unit of mechanical effect is a weight of one pound raised through a space of one foot.

9. The *momentum* of a body in motion means the mechanical effect which such a body will produce in a *moment* (or second) of time, and varies as the weight of the body multiplied by its *velocity*.

10. The *vis viva* of a body in motion is the whole mechanical effect which it will produce in *being brought to a state of rest*, no regard being had to the time in which the effect is produced, and it varies as the weight of the body multiplied by the *square of its velocity*.

Dynamometer, an instrument which measures anything to which the name of power has been given, whether that of an animal or otherwise.

Dysodile, a papyraceous brown coal.

E.

Early English Architecture, the first of the pointed or Gothic styles of architecture used in England. It immediately succeeded the Norman towards the end of the 12th century, and gradually merged into the Decorated at the end of the 13th. The mouldings consist of alternate rounds and deeply cut hollows, with small fillets, producing a strong effect of light and shadow. The arches are usually equilateral or lanced-shaped, though drop-arches are frequently met with, and sometimes pointed segmented arches: trefoil and cinquefoil arches are also often used in small openings and panelings. The doorways of this style, in large buildings, are often divided into two by a single shaft or small pin, with a quatrefoil or other ornament. The windows are almost universally of long and narrow proportions, and are used singly, or in combinations of two, three, five, and seven: when thus combined, the space between them sometimes but little exceeds the width of the mullions of the latter styles. Groined ceilings are very common in this style. The pillars usually consist of small shafts arranged round a larger circular pier, but others of a different kind are sometimes found. The capitals consist of plain mouldings, or are enriched with foliage and sculpture characteristic of the style.

Earthwork. The patented excavator, an American invention, is capable, it is said, of cutting and levelling earthwork for the making of railways and for other works at a cost considerably below manual labour, and has the additional advantage of saving much time: it forms an important consideration in railway making, but little used in England.

Earth-table, the lowest course of stone that is seen in a building, level with the earth.

Easel, for painters, the frame on which the canvas is laid, stretched for painting.

East Indian Black-wood grows to an immense size, and is much used for making furniture.

Easter, a movable feast held in commemoration of the Resurrection. Being the most important and most ancient in observance, it governs the other movable feasts throughout the year.

Eaves, the lower edge of a sloping roof which overhangs the face of a wall, for the purpose of throwing off the water.

Ebony wood is of several colours, as yellow, red, green, and black. The latter is always preferred, and is much used. It is imported principally from the East, and is used for cabinet, mosaic, and turnery work, for flutes, handles of doors, knives, surgeons' instruments, piano-forte keys, etc.

Eborarius, a term applied by the Romans to a kind of ivory-work.

Eccentric, or *Excentric*, a circular disc revolving within a strap or ring, and having its axis of revolution on one side of the centre. It is used as a substitute for a crank for giving a reciprocating motion to the slide-valve or to the feed-pump of a steam-engine.

Eccentrics are circular sheaves with a hole for the driving-wheel axle, about two inches out of the centre of the sheave of a locomotive-engine, which thus makes it project some four inches more from the centre of the driving axle on one side than on the other. It is this eccentricity of motion which works the slide-valve gear and pumps in a very satisfactory manner. Eccentrics are fitted in two parts, and secured to the axle by a hoop and setbolts.

Eccentric hoops, hoops fitted round the projecting part of the eccentric sheaves of a locomotive-engine, to strengthen them.

Eccentric rod and *strap*, the rod, the strap end of which encircles the eccentric sheave, and the other end connects it with the quadrant, or rocking-shaft, according to the class of a locomotive-engine. In some engines the end is forked to go on the stud of the rocking-shaft, and opens out something like the letter V; or when only one rod is used for both back and forward movements, it resembles the letter X. In other engines it is attached to the quadrants by a bolt, one rod for forward gear, and another rod for backward gear.

Eccentric rod, the rod connecting the eccentric strap to the lever which moves the slide-valve.

Eccentric strap, a brass ring formed by two pieces bolted together, and fixed to the eccentric rod: the ring fits a grooved part in the circumference of the eccentric.

Echinus, the egg and anchor, or egg and tongue ornament found carved on the ovolo, in classical architecture.

Echinus, a member of the Doric capital; so called from its resemblance to the echinus, or large vase, in which drinking-cups were washed.

Ecphora, the projection of any member or moulding before the face of the member or moulding next below it.

Eduction pipe, the pipe from the exhaust passage of the cylinder to the condenser.

Effect is the art of giving to a drawing a striking appearance, or solemnity, awe, sadness, mirth, or tranquillity, by a judicious combination of objects, and by strong light and shadow. It is a faithful representation of the appearance of nature, best seen under certain circumstances and at certain times, such as morning effect, evening effect, twilight effect, and stormy effect, torch-light and candle-light effects, etc.

Effects of buildings. "The site adapted for buildings, and the accompaniments of terraces, gardens, and other decorations to set off their architectural designs, are subjects for consideration in which we are influenced by the desire to raise and extend the theory and practice to what we consider belongs to the art. It was in Italy, when the fine arts were in perfection, that the laying out great villas was practised by artists who often combined the practice of painting and architure; and until it be adopted in England, the designs of the architect never will have justice done to them in the execution. Our parks may be beautiful, our mansions faultless in design; but nothing is more rare than to see the two properly connected. Let the architect by study and observation qualify himself to include in his art the decorations around the immediate site of the intended building, together with its interior adornment, furniture, and upholstery, and the growing taste among the gentry of England will second such laudable efforts."

Egg, in architecture, an ornament of that form, cut in the echinus or quarter round.

Egyptian Architecture had its origin 2222 years before Christ, and advanced and flourished under different dynasties. The first includes the two great dynasties of Theban princes, who governed Egypt during her "most high and palmy state," when Thebes sent forth her armies to distant conquest. In the second period is comprised the erection of the Pyramids. The third includes the reigns of the Ptolemies and earlier Cæsars, under whom Egyptian architecture flourished in a second youth, and almost attained its original splendour. Egyptian architecture, so massive and so sombre, with its vast aisled halls without windows, its close files of gigantic columns, and its colossal statues, owes many characteristic forms and effects to earlier cavern temples in Ethiopia. One of the most striking peculiarities of the style is the pyramidal character of the ascending lines; it is observed in the outline of the portal and the gigantic pylon, in walls, doorways, pedestals, and screens: it pervades the whole system, and must have been occasioned by circumstances connected with its origin. The representations given in ancient paintings show a remarkable love of uniformity of arrangement of their domestic houses and gardens. In an ordinary house a number of chambers were ranged round a rectangular court, as at Pompeii. The larger mansions sometimes consisted of an assemblage of such courts, the whole occupying a square or oblong plot. Sometimes a central group of buildings was surrounded by a narrow court. A spacious area often extended from front to rear, with a chief and side entrances at either end: the exterior had nothing of the ponderous character of temple structures, which would have been ill-suited to the wants and festivities of social life. Houses two and three stories high were common; but large mansions appear to have been low and extensive rather than lofty. The terraced top was covered by an awning or roof, supported on light graceful columns.

Ediograph, an instrument contrived for the purpose of copying drawings.

Ekeing, in ship-building, a piece fitted to make good a deficiency in length on the lower part of the supporter under the cat-head, etc.; likewise the piece of carved work under the lower end of the quarter-piece at the aft part of the quarter-gallery.

Elastic, springy, having the power of returning to the form from which it was distorted.

Elastic force of steam. The French reckon an atmosphere to be equal to a column of mercury ·76 of a metre in height, which is only 29·92 inches, and the boiling point of their thermometer is adapted thereto; whereas, since about the

ELB   ELECTRIC TELEGRAPH.   ELE

commencement of the present century, the English have reckoned it to be 30 inches. This circumstance accounts in some degree for their scale of temperatures differing from Mr. Southern's.

The French account of the occasion of making their experiments on the temperatures corresponding to different elasticities of steam, in 1829, contains the following passage: "Science did not then possess this knowledge, and engineers appointed to superintend the construction of steam-engines had no other guidance than some discordant measures upon the temperatures which correspond to the elasticities between one and eight atmospheres: for higher pressures there was no result of direct experiments, nor any theory which could supply the deficiency."

Elbow, in architecture, an obtuse angle of a wall, building, etc.

Elder-wood. The branches of the elder contain a very light kind of pith, which is used, when dried, for electrical purposes; the wood is also frequently used for carpenter's rules, weavers' shuttles, etc.

Electric Telegraph in India. According to Dr. O'Shaughnessy's Report on the operations of the Electric Telegraph Department in India, the total number of despatches transmitted from 1st February, 1855, to 31st January, 1856, was 9971, of which 8533 were private, and 1438 public service despatches. Of these by far the greater part was between Bombay and Calcutta, and Bombay and Madras, showing that the commercial intelligence received by mail either from Europe or China is what gives the chief employment to the telegraph. Of the paid messages, not less than 2864 were sent by native correspondents. There is every reason to conclude that the future income of the department will increase. While the European community are comparatively a very limited class, the native merchants, bankers, fundholders, and gentry, may be considered as innumerable. The number of native correspondents is accordingly increasing daily. Not only do they use the lines for financial business, but on the most delicate and secret matters affecting family arrangements, betrothals, marriages, and other domestic affairs, of which they treat with an absence of all disguise which is almost beyond belief. The receipts have averaged 10,089-1-2 rupees per month; of this the Calcutta office alone returns monthly 4433-12 rupees. The service despatches being estimated at the same rate, the work done in the year is not less than two lacs of rupees. When the whole line has acquired public confidence by being found punctual and accurate, the business will vastly increase. Terrible as are the thunderstorms which prevail over nearly all India, the precautions taken to prevent injuries to the offices or persons employed have proved completely successful, though the lines have been repeatedly struck.

Electrical state of the atmosphere. The electrical condition of the air in serene and tempestuous weather has been too much overlooked by meteorologists. The atmosphere is generally found to be in an electrical state. The apparatus for these observations is simply a metallic rod, insulated at its lower extremity, elevated at some height above the ground, and communicating with an electroscope. When the amenity of the weather will permit, a kite should be raised, in the string of which a metallic wire should be interwoven; this will collect the electricity of the higher regions of the air. The atmosphere is usually found to be positively electrified, and its electricity is stronger in the winter than in the summer, and during the day than in the night.

ELEMENTARY INSTRUCTION.

Electricity (from *electrum*, amber), was a name given at first to some peculiar effects observed on rubbing that substance, and gradually extended to an immense collection of facts of a similar kind, as well as to the cause of these effects, whatever it may be, and to the science which investigates their laws.

This science is sometimes divided into five or six branches, according to the modes in which electric effects may be brought about. The term *atmospheric* electricity applies to that which is naturally exhibited at nearly all times, but especially in thunderstorms; *common* or *frictional* electricity, to that developed by mere mechanical actions; *galvanism* or *voltaic* electricity, to that developed by chemical action; *thermo*-electricity, by the action of heat; *magneto*-electricity, by that of magnetism; and *animal* electricity, by the will of certain fishes, which use this power as a defence.

A more modern and comprehensive division is into—1. *Electro-statics*, or *tensional* electricity, referring to those effects in which the agency seems to have the equilibrium of its distribution disturbed, so as to be excessive or deficient in certain bodies, making them appear in different *states*. 2. *Electro-dynamics*, or *current* electricity, describing those effects in which the agency appears to be moving from place to place, and displaying *momentum*.

Electrum, from the Greek, a name given to amber, or to a mixture of metals composed of gold and silver.

Electrum, argentiferous gold; an alloy of silver.

Elegance, in a design, is a manner which embellishes and heightens objects, either as to their form or colour, or both, without destroying or perverting truth.

Elementary Instruction. Before entering into practice, it will be necessary to bear the following rules and tables always in mind; and although we are to suppose every one already well acquainted with them, they may yet possibly be found useful and essential here.

SIGNS AND MARKS.

+ Plus, or more: the sign of addition; as $5 + 6 = 11$.
− Minus, or less: the sign of subtraction, as $20 - 5 = 15$.
× Multiply by: the sign of multiplication, as $8 \times 9 = 72$.
÷ Divide by: the sign of division, as $16 \div 4 = 4$.
= Equal to: the sign of equality, as 27 cubic feet = 1 cubic yard.
∷ Proportion: the sign of proportion, as $3 : 6 :: 8 : 16$.
$2\frac{1}{2}$ Fraction.
√ Square root.   ∛ Cube root.

LINEAL MEASURE.

7·92 inches	1 link.
12 inches	1 foot.
3 feet	1 yard.
5½ yards	1 rod, pole, or perch.
4 poles, 100 links	1 chain.
40 poles, 10 chains	1 furlong.
8 furlongs, 1760 yards	1 mile.
80 chains, 8000 links	1 mile.

SQUARE OR SUPERFICIAL MEASURE.

144 square inches	1 square foot.
9 square feet	1 square yard.
30¼ square yards	1 square pole, or perch.
40 perches	1 rood.
4 roods	1 acre.
640 acres	1 square mile.

CUBIC OR SOLID MEASURE.

1728 solid inches	1 cubic foot.
27 solid feet	1 cubic yard.

Proceeding to the various forms of plane surfaces, and the methods

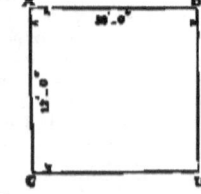

of measuring them, and beginning with the square, which has four equal sides and four right angles, as A, B, C, D,—Rule: Multiply the given side by itself, and the product is the area required. Ex. 12 × 12 = 144.

The next figure will be a parallelogram, or oblong square. Rule: Multiply the length by the breadth,

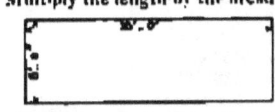

and the product gives the area. Ex. 18' 0" × 6' 0" = 108' 0".

The next figure will be a rhombus, which has four sides all equal, but no right angle. Rule: Multi-

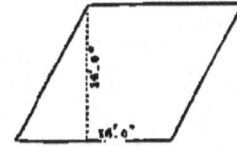

ply the base by the perpendicular height, and the product is the area. Ex. 16' 0" × 14' 0" = 224' 0".

The next figure will be the rhomboid, which has its two sides equal and parallel, but no right angle: it is a long square pushed

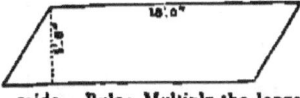

aside. Rule: Multiply the longer side by the perpendicular height or breadth, and the product is the area. Ex. 18' 0" × 5' 6" = 99' 0".

The next will be a right-angled triangle, having one of its angles a true square, or just 90 degrees. Rule: Multiply one of the legs forming the right angle by half the other; the product is the area. Ex. 16'0" ÷ 2 = 8 × 20' 0" = 160' 0".

The next figure will be a triangle. Rule: Multiply the longest side by one-half the perpendicular,

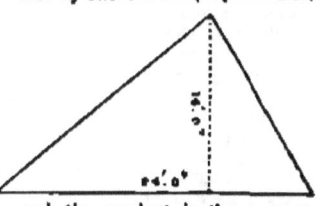

and the product is the content. Ex. 14' 0" ÷ 2 = 7' 0" × 24' 0" = 168' 0", area required.

The next figure will be the trapezium, which consists of four unequal sides, and four unequal angles; it is, indeed, two triangles, and may be measured at twice, as shown in the preceding triangle, or

by this Rule: Multiply the diagonal by one-half the sum of the two perpendiculars. Ex. 8' 0" + 4' 0" = 12' 0" ÷ 2 = 6' 0" × 20' 0" = 120' 0", the area required.

The next figure will be the area of a circle. Rule: Square the diameter, and multiply that pro-

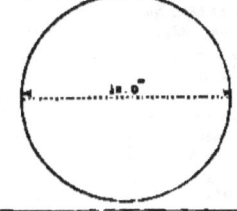

duct by 7854, a decimal, and that product will be the content. Ex. 12' 0" × 12' 0" = 144' 0" × ·7854 = 113·0·76.

The next diagram will be a segment or part of a section of a circle: to measure this, multiply half the sum of the two arches by one of the ends, and the product will give the area. Ex 24' 0" + 18' 0" = 42' 0" ÷ 2 = 21' 0" × 2' 0" = 42' 0", which is the area required.

Where the figure is found of the shape annexed, with two right angles, and the sides not parallel,

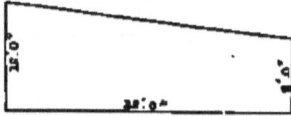

Instead of dividing it and measuring it as a parallelogram and an angle, take the mean of the two perpendiculars, and multiply by the length; the product will give the area required. Ex. 12' 0" + 8' 0" = 20' 0" ÷ 2 = 10' 0" = × 32' 0" = 320' 0".

It is now necessary to take into consideration the methods of measuring solid or cubic bodies; for example, to begin with a cube, viz. a solid bounded by six square sides, similar to a die.

Rule: Multiply the side by itself, and the product by the side again; the last product will be the solid content. Ex. 6' 0" × 6' 0" = 36' 0" × 6' 0" = 216' 0" cubic feet.

The next figure is the parallelopipedon, or oblong cube. Rule: — Multiply the breadth by the depth, and that product by the length; this last product will be the content of it. Ex. 6' 0" × 8' 0" = 48' 0" × 32' 0" = 1536' 0" = the required content of the parallelopipedon.

Next proceed to the prism, to measure which, find the area at the end, multiply that by the length, and that product is the content. Ex. The perpendicular height, 6' 0" ÷ 2 = 3' 0" × 12' 0" = 36' 0" × 32' 0" = 1152' 0".

The inclined plane and wedge may be measured by the same rule as the prism; but the readier way is to multiply one-half of the thickness of the base by its width, and

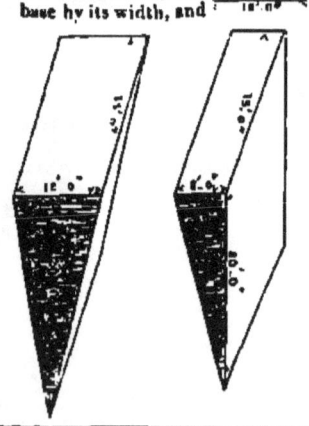

that by the perpendicular or length. Ex. $3' 0'' \times 15' 0'' = 45' 0'' \times 20' 0'' = 900' 0'' =$ content of inclined plane.

This figure will be found in all earth-work, passing from cutting to embankment.

Again, $6' 0'' \times 15' 0'' = 90' 0'' \times 20' 0'' = 1800' 0''$, content of the wedge.

The next figure is a square pyramid, and the one-half of which is a very prominent formation in banks, and is measured by multi-

plying the area of the base by one-third the height or length. Ex. $6' 0'' \times 6' 0'' = 36' 0'' \times 6' 0'' = 216' 0''$ content.

Arriving now at the cylinder, this is measured by multiplying

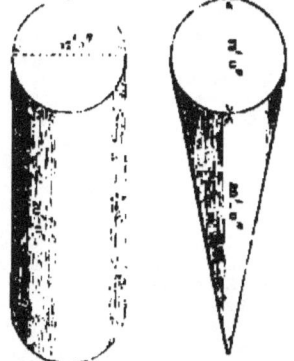

the area of the base or end by the length. Ex. $12' 0'' \times 12' 0'' = 144' 0'' \times \cdot 7854 = 113 \cdot 0976 \times 20' 0'' = 2260' 0''$.

The cone is also measured by multiplying the area of the base by one-third the perpendicular height. Ex. $12' 0'' \times 12' 0'' = 144' 0'' \times \cdot 7854 = 113' 0'' \times 6' 8'' = 753' 4''$.

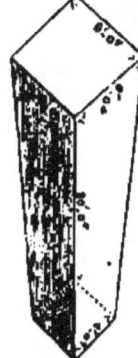

The next figure is the frustum of a square pyramid, which also is a form peculiar in embankments and cuttings. Rule: To four times the area of the mean base add the area of each end, which divide by 6; multiply the product by the length, you will find the contents. Ex. $4' 0'' + 6' 0'' = 10' 0'' \div 2 = 5' 0''$, the mean height of the base or thickness will be $5' 0''$; $5' 0'' \times 5' 0'' = 25' 0'' \times 4' 0'' = 100' 0'' + 36' 0'' = 136' 0'' + 16' 0'' = 152' 0''$; $152' 0'' + 6' 0'' = 25' 4'' \times 20' 0'' = 506' 8''$ content.

The same rule applies to the frustum of a cone.

Elevation, an upright draught of a building, geometrically drawn.

Elizabethan Architecture, the style which prevailed in England at the time of Queen Elizabeth, and immediately subsequent to the Tudor style of Henry VIII.

Ellipse: this curve is one of the conic sections, and next in importance to the circle and the straight line.

Ellipsis, an oval figure generated from the section of a cone by a plane cutting both sides of the cone, but not parallel to the base, and meeting with the base when produced.

Elliptic compasses, a term given to any machine for describing ellipses.

Elliptograph, an instrument for drawing ellipses.

Elm, a timber-tree, of European growth, and of which there are five species: mean size, 44 feet long, 32 inches diameter: it is not liable to split, and bears the driving of nails, bolts, etc.; much used in building; also for the keels of vessels, and for wet foundations.

Elongation, the act of lengthening.

Elutriation, the separation of foul substances from pure, by pulverization.

Elutriation, in metallurgy, the separating the lighter matters from the mixed ores or metals, by means of great quantities of fair water.

Elvan (in Cornish), a hard close-grained stone, said to be a bastard limestone.

Embankments, raised mounds or dykes to preserve the proper and useful course of rivers, etc.; and also for forming a level line of railway.

Embankments (some) executed on the Continent. On the banks of the Po, two sorts of dykes are used to prevent the river from overflowing during the winter, or the flood season. They are called 'in froldi' when immediately upon the banks of the river, and 'in golene' when at any considerable distance, as it is sometimes found advisable to allow the river to spread over a large surface of the adjacent valley, either for the purpose of admitting it to deposit the mud in suspension, or to allow it to lose its torrential character. The maintenance of the works of these dykes is confided to the Government engineers, who are under the control of a syndicate of the proprietors of the property most liable to be affected by inundations. When the river passes from one State to another, as from Piedmont to Modena, a mixed commission is charged with the joint superintendence.

The Haarlem lake, besides the very remarkable steam-engines described by Mr. Dempsey, merits observation for the extensive works executed for the defence of the land, and for the canals reserved for the navigation. The enclosure dyke is 50,000 mètres long, or rather more than 31 miles. It has two outfall dykes, which serve for the navigation, 9000 mètres, about 5½ miles; one-half of which is 40^m (131 ft. 2 in.) wide at the bottom or floor line; the other 43^m 20 (141 ft. 10 in.)

The ordinary tides are, at the flux, 2 ft. 4 in. above the scale or datum line at Amsterdam; at the reflux, 2 ft. 8 in. below the same datum; the difference between high and low water is then, on the average, about 5 feet. With violent winds from the N.W. however, the tides rise sometimes 6 ft. 6 in. above the average. The tides of the Y, near the lake, are + 16^c (or 6¼ in.) and − 23^c (or 9 in.), giving a total variation of 1 ft. 3¼ in.

The estimated cost of reclaiming the 18,000 hectares was 8 millions of florins, or £667,000 English, nearly, about £13 per acre. Previously to undertaking this colossal work, the Zind Plass, of 4600 hectares superficial (nearly 11,500 acres), had been reclaimed at a cost of 3 millions of florins, or £250,000; not far from £22 per acre. The heights of the enclosure dyke are + or − the datum line or mean level of the sea at Amsterdam.

Embankment of the flooded part of the Amsterdam and Haarlem Railway.—The bottom part consists of treble ranges of fascines, tied down by longitudinal poles 1 metre apart from centre to centre, and 0·25 c. diameter; two double stakes at each end of the poles, and two ties in the intermediate distances. The interstices of the fascines and the space between the rows are filled in with sand. The upper part, forming the encasement for the ballast, is made of three rows of treble fascines, well staked, and wattled together.

A core of sand or clay, faced with step fascines, is made up to low-water mark. Upon this a bed of rushes, fastened down by stakes and wattles, is laid; and the upper portion of the bank is faced with fascines of a regular slope of 1 to 1.

Embattled, a term applied to any building with a parapet, and having embrasures to resemble a battery.

Emblema, an emblem, or inlaid ornament of divers colours.

Embolus, in mechanics, a wedge; anciently, among the Greeks, the prow or beak of a vessel, or a body of soldiers in the form of a wedge.

Embolus, the movable part of a pump or syringe, named likewise the piston or sucker.

Embossing, forming work in relievo, whether cast or cut with a chisel; or in modern times, the art of producing raised figures upon wood or other materials by means of pressure, either applied by a sudden blow, as in a stamping press, or in a more gradual manner, as by an ordinary screw or hydraulic press, or by means of revolving cylinders.

Embrasure, the crenelles or interval between the merlons of a battlement.

Embroidery, a mode of working devices on woven substances.

Emerald green is a new colour of copper green upon a terrene base: it is the most vivid of this tribe of colours, being rather opaque, and powerfully reflective of light: it appears to be the most durable pigment of its class.

Emissarium, a sluice, flood-gate, or channel by which an outlet is formed to carry off stagnant or foul water: according to Pliny, an artificial canal, formed for the draining of stagnant waters.

Emplecton, a method of constructing walls introduced by the Greeks and copied by the Roman architects, in which the outside surfaces on both sides were formed of ashlar laid in regular courses, and the central space between them filled in with rubble-work, layers of cross stones being placed at intervals in regular courses, and of sufficient size to extend through the entire thickness of the wall, and so act as girders to bind the whole together.

Emporium, a mart or factory, a large building containing ranges of bonding warehouses, in which foreign merchandise brought by sea is deposited for sale.

Enamelling, the art of using enamel, which is divided into trasparent and opaque. The first is employed for the purpose of ornamenting gold and silver; the second, commonly in the manufacture of watch and clock dials, and of plates for pictures, etc.

Encarpa (*Encarpus*), according to Vitruvius, festoons of carved fruit and flowers, employed as decorative ornaments.

Encaustica, the art of encaustic painting, i.e. in colours mixed with wax, and afterwards hardened by the action of fire.

Encaustic painting, a kind of painting in which by heating or burning in, the colours are rendered permanent in all their original splendour.

Enchasing, the art of enriching and beautifying gold, silver, and other metal work, by some design or figure represented thereon in basso rilievo.

Enclosure, a fence, a wall, or hedge, or other means of protection and security surrounding land.

Endecagon, in geometry, a plane figure of eleven sides and angles.

End-irons, andirons or dogs, articles of household furniture, in earlier times, used in fire-places to sustain the ends of logs of wood.

Engineering, Civil. This profession may be said to have originated in England about the middle of the last century. Before that period, whenever the prospects of great profit induced individuals or bodies to incorporate themselves for the purpose of undertaking extensive systems of drainage, or for the supply of water, requiring the assistance of an engineer, recourse was generally had to those great masters of hydraulic engineering, the Dutch. True it is that some solitary exceptions have occasionally been found; men who, like Sir Hugh Myddelton, combined a speculative turn of mind with some mechanical knowledge, and to these two qualities added an untiring energy of purpose, leading them to persevere in any undertaking, even under the most discouraging circumstances. But these men were rare instances of a peculiar talent, which, though it thus displayed itself occasionally, was far too uncommon a gift to allow the possessors of it to form a class or profession. The case is very different now: a demand for this peculiar talent has been created of late years by the extraordinary development of our system of internal communication, as well as by the application of steam to the purposes of our manufactures; and employment is now found for hundreds where one was sufficient, not fifty years since, for the whole business of the country. So great indeed has been the demand, that the profession may be said to be divided into two distinct bodies, viz. those who turn their attention to subjects which come more particularly within the scope of the duty of a civil engineer, such as docks, bridges, canals, railroads, etc., and those who devote themselves altogether to the manufacture of machinery. The duties which are involved in the practice of these two branches of the profession, though apparently dissimilar in character, are yet founded upon the same general principles; and the acquirements which are necessary to enable the individual of one class to distinguish himself, or even to practise his profession with a moderate chance of success, will be found equally necessary for those of the other class.

These acquirements are partly abstract and theoretical, and partly experimental or practical. A civil engineer should, in addition to the knowledge required to fit him as well as others for the active duties of life, have such a knowledge of mathematics as will enable him to investigate as well as to apply the rules laid down by writers on those branches of the mixed sciences to which his attention will most frequently be drawn. He should be well acquainted with the principles of mechanics, hydraulics, and indeed with all the branches of natural philosophy; and a certain amount of chemical knowledge will be found very valuable: he should be able to draw neatly, and should understand the principles of projection upon which all engineering drawings are constructed: a general knowledge of the principles of architecture will also be essential. Having acquired the requisite amount of theoretical information, the next step is to gain that practical knowledge which is essential in order to the proper application of this information. The best mode of gaining this experience is to enter into the employment of some eminent man in the profession, in whose office there will be every opportunity offered to the young beginner of witnessing the mode in which the various descriptions of work are carried on. He will there be employed, first as a draughtsman, in copying drawings: as he becomes more acquainted with practical details, he will have more responsibility thrown upon him, and be placed in charge of works, at first of small importance, but, by degrees, of those of such magnitude as will require all his theoretical knowledge, and all the practical experience he may have gained, to enable him to carry out the work to the satisfaction of his employers: he should cultivate a habit of observation, and make a point of taking ample notes and sketches of whatever he may see which in any way bears upon his profession. Having thus by degrees acquired a sufficient amount of information to give him a confidence in his own judgment upon any subject which may be submitted to him, and having become known as an active and intelligent agent of others, he will very possibly be called upon to plan and execute a work himself, and then, by degrees, with industry and activity, may work his way upwards in *a profession where merit alone can lead to distinction.*

The course of the man who devotes himself to the machinery branch of the profession differs but little, up to a certain point, from that just described: his theoretical acquirements should be the same, but the practical part of his education will commence at the bench, where he will learn the use of all the tools and machinery by working at them with his own hands: he will then be placed in the drawing room, and go through much the same routine of instruction as before described, and will by degrees work his way up to the position of foreman; then, distinguishing himself by a power of applying general principles to particular cases, he will show himself capable of assuming the direction of an establishment for the manufacture of machinery.

Engineer, Steam-boat. A steam-boat engineer is a person employed for the purpose of keeping the engine or engines of a steam-vessel in as efficient a state as possible, and to superintend their working.

He must set the engines to work, regulate their speed, and stop them, as may be required. His duties while the engines are at work are various. He must take care that every moving part is properly lubricated; that no steam is allowed to pass through valves or joints that ought to be steam-tight; that no air is permitted to enter in any of the parts of the engine where it is essential that a vacuum should be kept up; and that none of the bolts, or pins, or keys, work loose by the vibration, and shift their position, or come out of their places. He must also take care that none of the working parts become overheated by any undue amount of friction, arising from any want of proper lubrication, any excessive tightness, or any other disturbing cause; and if they should become overheated, he must take prompt and energetic measures to remedy the evil, and prevent any serious consequences arising therefrom. He must from time to time carefully observe the effect produced by the gradual wear of the working parts, so that if the truth or accuracy of any of these seems to be materially affected, he may take steps to rectify the defects when lying up in harbour. He must also be careful to observe if the frame of the engine ever begins to move or work in any way, and endeavour to discover the cause, in order that it may be remedied when the engines are at rest. One of the most important of his duties is to take care that the engines are kept clean, and any grit or dirt prevented from getting into the bearings or moving parts: he must wipe away all oil and grease most carefully and completely as soon as they have passed through the bearings, and prevent them from running down the rods or remaining about the engine.

The boiler requires his unremitting and particular attention, in order that the proper supply of steam, neither too much nor too little, may be generated for the engine. To ensure this, the management of the fires must be duly attended to, both in the supply of coal in the proper quantities at the proper intervals, and in the periodical clearing of the fires from the earthy matters of the coal, which may have become vitrified in the furnace, and formed what are called clinkers. By due attention to the former, the smoke in all well-proportioned boilers may be very greatly abated; and, by due attention to both, the consumption of fuel (when the engines are prevented by a strong head-wind, or by the deep immersion of the paddle-wheels on the commencement of a long voyage, from making the proper number of strokes, and thus using the proper amount of steam) may be reduced in an equal or greater degree than has taken place in the consumption of steam. The due and constant supply of water to the boiler, to compensate for the constant evaporation of the water in the formation of the steam, must be assiduously attended to. Another of the most important of the duties of a steam-boat engineer, during the time that the engines are at work on a voyage at sea, is to attend to the degree to which the water in the boilers may become saturated with salt by the continued evaporation which is going on, and in take care that this saturation is not allowed to be carried to such an extent as that a deposition of the salt and other matters contained in sea-water should take place. After the boilers have been in operation for three or four hours in salt water, so that the water in them has become brine, he ought to test the strength of it, that is, he ought to ascertain the degree of saturation to which it has reached, and continue this examination periodically, whether the engines are fitted with an apparatus for the continuous discharge of a portion of the brine, to be exchanged for a portion of sea-water, or whether this system of exchange is left entirely at his discretion, to be attended to by means of the common blow-off cocks. The best test is the common hydrometer, though the thermometer has hitherto been more commonly applied to this purpose, as the brine is considered to be of a proper strength when it boils under atmospheric pressure at a temperature 2° higher than that at which the common sea-water will boil at the same time, under the same circumstances.

Before coming into port, it may occasionally be advantageous to take indicator diagrams, to see whether the action of the valves continues to be correct.

The duties of a steam-boat engineer, on arriving in port after a long voyage, are also various, and equally important with those he has to perform when out at sea. Immediately on coming to anchor, it is a good practice to test the tightness of the steam-valves and pistons, by putting them in such a position that it can be seen if they allow any steam to pass when it ought not to do so. If any imperfections in these the most vital parts of the engines are discovered, he must draw out the valves, or lift the cylinder covers, to get at the pistons, and rectify the defects in the best manner that he can with the means within his power. He should also occasionally examine all the interior parts of the engines, and rectify any incipient defects. He must now also rectify any want of truth in the parallel motion or in any of the shafts or working parts caused by wear, and tighten or make good any of the fastenings of the frame if he has found them to be loose, and put to rights any other such defects. Any parts subject to corrosion should be carefully examined, cleaned, and dried, and painted if need be. The water should be blown off out of the boilers as completely as possible, and all ashes and soot thoroughly cleaned out of the furnaces and flues as soon as possible. The furnaces and flues must then be thoroughly examined, and the slightest leak or defect that can be discovered made good; as it is especially important in a boiler to stop these defects at the first, as otherwise they spread very rapidly. No pains should be spared to discover any suspected leak of steam on the top of the boiler, as nothing tends more to corrode and destroy a boiler than this. Inside the boilers, any scale that may have been deposited from the brine having been allowed to become too strong must be removed, and the whole thoroughly cleaned out from every part of the boiler, from below as well as from the tops and sides of the furnaces and flues. The take-up, the inside of the steam-chests, and of the roofs of the boilers, which are the parts most subject to corrosion from the interior, should be very carefully examined, and after being duly scraped and cleaned and dried, they should be well painted with two or three coats of red lead, or done over with some other preservative.

The paddle-wheels should also be thoroughly examined, and any broken floats or hook-bolts replaced by new ones. The whole of the ironwork should be thoroughly scraped and cleaned, and, when dry, painted with three coats of red lead, or done over with black varnish, once every four months at least. When in harbour, especially if lying in a stream or tideway, the wheels ought to be turned round every three or four days, to change the parts exposed to the action of the water, and thus prevent corrosion. The various kinds of the screw now in use should be well studied, and all circumstances connected with its operations should be closely watched for every incident or change should be considered as a new experiment.

He must now also get his supply of stores made good, so as to be ready for another voyage.

To qualify an engineer to perform these duties, he should be trained as a mechanic, and be a fair workman in iron, brass, and wood. He should be able to work not only at the lathe or vice, but also at a smith's forge. His education should be such as to make him able to keep accounts, and make notes in his log of all that occurs in the engine-room. He should have sufficient knowledge of mechanical drawing to enable him, in the event of any important part of the engines being broken when at a distance from any manufactory, to make such a drawing of it as would enable a manufacturer to replace it. He should have some knowledge of the first principles of mechanics, a general knowledge of the leading principles of hydrostatics, hydraulics, and pneumatics, without which he cannot fully understand many of the principles carried on in the engine, and on which its power depends. Some knowledge of heat, of the theory of combustion, of ebullition, and of evaporation, may also be reckoned as almost indispensable; to which should be added, if possible, an acquaintance with the subject of steam, especially as regards its temperature, pressure, and latent heat.

Engineer, Mechanical, one who is efficient in the invention, contrivance, putting together, and the adjustment of all kinds of machinery; who is acquainted with the strength and quality of the material used, and who also possesses a thorough knowledge of the power of steam and the engine in all its modifications, and the uses for which this motive power is applied: he should also be duly acquainted with millwork of the several kinds, whether impelled by steam, water, or wind.

English School of Painting. This school, which is but of recent date, is connected with the Royal Academy in London, instituted in 1766; and although as a school it did not exist before that period, yet since the revival of the arts, and the consequent encouragement given to them by the sovereigns of Europe, England has possessed portrait-painters of no inconsiderable ability; and it is probably owing to the remarkable partiality of the nation for this branch of the art, that historical painting has been, until recently, comparatively neglected.

Latterly, however, painters of the highest eminence in this superior branch of the art have distinguished themselves, and given earnest of the rise of a school that may, ere long, surpass others of the present age.

English Varnish. When mastic varnish is mixed with drying-oil which holds litharge in solution, the mixture soon assumes the appearance of a firm jelly; which is strong in proportion as a greater quantity of litharge, and a stronger varnish, have been used. This substance holds its place on the palette. This mixture is particularly useful in glazing, for it flows freely under the brush. Instead of using brown drying-oil, it is preferable to use that prepared without fire.

Entablature, those members of a portico which were constructed upon the columns, consisting of the epistylium, zophorus, and corona. Vitruvius uses the words *ornamenta columnarum* to signify these members; and sometimes he includes the three several parts in the term *epistylia.*

Entablature, the superstructure that lies horizontally upon the columns in the several orders or styles of architecture. It is divided into architrave, the part immediately above the column; frieze, the central space; and cornice, the upper projecting mouldings. Each of the orders has its appropriate entablature, of which both the general height and the subdivisions are regulated by a scale of proportion derived from the diameter of the column.

The entablature, though architects frequently vary from the proportions here specified, may, as a general rule, be set up one-fourth the height of the column. The total height thereof thus obtained is in all the orders, except the Doric, divided into ten parts, three of which are given to the architrave, three to the frieze, and four to the cornice. But in the Doric order the whole height should be divided into eight parts, and two given to the architrave, three to the frieze, and three to the cornice. The mouldings which form the detail of these leading features are best learned by reference to representations of the orders at large. Palladio and Vignola, the restorers of genuine architecture, are the authors whose works may be consulted with greatest advantage by those who desire to make any advance in the science, and most particularly by those who wish to obtain further knowledge on the use and abuse of its details.

Entail, a term used in the middle ages to signify elaborated sculptured ornaments and carvings.

Entasis, the swell of the shaft or columns of either of the orders of architecture.

Enterclose, a passage between two rooms in a house, or that leading from the door to the hall.

Entresol, in architecture, a floor between two other floors. The entresol consists of a low apartment usually placed above the first floor: in London, frequently between the ground floor and the first floor.

Ephebeum, an apartment in the palæstra appropriated to wrestling and other athletic exercises.

Epicycle, a little circle whose centre is in the circumference of a greater.

Epicycloid, a curve generated by the revolution of the periphery of a circle along the convex or concave part of another circle.

Epicycloidal wheel, a wheel for converting circular into alternate motion, or alternate into circular.

Episcenium, a division of the scene of a Greek theatre: it sometimes consisted of three divisions made by ranges of columns one above the other; the lower was termed *scena,* and the others *episcenia.*

Epistomium, the cock or spout of a water-pipe, or of any vessel containing liquids to be drawn off in small quantities when required.

Epistylium, the lower of three divisions of an entablature or superstructure upon the columns of a portico, formed by pieces extending from centre to centre of two columns.

Epistylium, the architrave or horizontal course resting immediately upon columns. *Epistylar arcuation* is the system in which columns support arches instead of horizontal architraves and entablatures.

Epitithidas, a term applied by some writers, by way of distinction, to the cymatium on the sloping or *raking* cornices of a pediment, which *superimposed* moulding (as its name implies) was frequently largely developed, and enriched with an ornamental pattern.

Epitithides, the upper members of the corona surmounting the fastigium of a temple, which was also continued along the flanks.

Epotides, in naval architecture, two thick blocks of wood, one on each side the prow of a galley, for warding off the blows of the rostra of the enemy's vessel.

Equation, an equal division: in algebra, a mutual comparing of things of different denominations: in astronomy, the difference between the apparent and mean motion of the sun.

Equilateral, having all sides equal.

Equilibrium, equipoise, equality of weight.

Equilibrium valve, the valve in the steam passage of a Cornish engine for opening the communication between the top and bottom of the cylinder, to render the pressure equal on both sides of the piston.

Era. The year 5611 of the Jewish era commenced September 7, 1850; Ramadân, the month of abstinence observed by the Turks, July 11, 1850; the year 1267 of the Mohammedan era, Nov. 6, 1850; and the Christian era, 1849 since the birth of Jesus Christ, for 1850 years, on the 1st of January, 1850.

Erasement (applied to buildings and cities), entire destruction and demolition.

Ergastulum, a sort of prison or house of correction contiguous to the farms and country villas of the Romans.

Ergata, a capstan or windlass.

Erisma, an arch-buttress, shore-post, or prop, to hold up buildings.

Euripus, an arm of the sea with land on both sides; a canal, a pool, or stand of water; ditch, a trench or moat about a place; a water-pipe of the smaller size, so made that the water therein may mount aloft: also an inlet or small creek.

Escape, the scape of a column in architecture.

Escutcheon, a shield charged with armorial bearings.

Etching, a branch of engraving in which the lines are drawn by a stylus or etching-needle, on copper, steel, or stone, prepared by a chemical process.

Eudiometer, an instrument used to ascertain the purity of air, or rather the quantity of oxygen contained in any given bulk of elastic fluid.

Eurythmy, in architecture, the exact proportion between all parts of a building.

Eustyle, that intercolumniation which, as its name would import, the ancients considered the most elegant, viz. two diameters and a quarter of the column. Vitruvius says, this manner of arranging columns exceeds all others in strength, convenience, and beauty.

Evangelists, The. In the Table of Symbols of the early ages, by the four Mystic Animals, Rev. iv. 7:— The Angel being assigned to St. Matthew, the Lion to St. Mark, the Ox to St. Luke, and the Eagle to St. John; and the four rivers issuing from the Mount of Paradise to enter the earth, Gen. II. 10.

Evaporation, the transformation of a

liquid into a gaseous state by the action of heat.

Evolute, a particular species of curve.

Evolution, in geometry; the equable evolution of the periphery of a circle, or any other curve, is such a gradual approach of the circumference to rectitude as that all the parts meet together, and equally evolve or unbend.

Ewry, an office of household service, where the ewers, etc., were formerly kept.

Examen, the tongue on the beam of a balance, rising perpendicularly from the beam, and moving in an eye affixed to the same, by which it serves to point out the equality or inequality of weight between the objects in the scale.

Excalefaction, heating or warming.

Exedra, an assembly-room or hall of conversation; according to Vitruvius, a large and handsome apartment; also a by-place, or jutty.

Exedra, or *Exhedra*, the portico of the Grecian palæstra, in which disputations of the learned were held: so called from its containing a number of seats, generally open, like the pastas or vestibule of a Greek house.

Exemplar, a pattern, plan, or model; resemblance.

Exhaust-port, the exit passage for the steam from a cylinder.

Exhaust-valve, the valve in the eduction passage of the steam cylinder of a Cornish engine, placed between the cylinder and air-pump, and worked by the tappet motion, so as to open shortly after the equilibrium valve, and admit the steam to the condenser.

Existence, being, entity, subsistence, reality, actuality, positiveness, absoluteness, fact.—Verb: to be, to exist, have being, subsist, live, breathe.

Expansion-joint, a stuffing-box joint connecting the steam-pipes, so as to allow one of them to slide within the enlarged end of the other when the length increases by expansion.

Expansion-valve, an auxiliary valve placed between the slide-valve and the steam cylinder: it is worked by a cam or other contrivance, so as to cut off the steam at a given period, and cause the remainder of the stroke to be performed by expansion.

Expansive steam. The expansive properties of steam are now well understood, and extensively applied to practice in manufacturing districts. In Cornwall, and in some other parts of the kingdom, the application is attended with highly beneficial results. But it should be stated that this system can be introduced with much greater advantage in engines that are employed in raising water, than in those which are entirely devoted to manufacturing purposes. In these last, the power is opposed to a continually varying resistance; while, in the former, the resistance is commonly the same, or of equal intensity.

To pumping engines, the adoption of the expansive system to an almost unlimited extent is recommended, even to the exclusion of any further ingress of steam to the cylinder after the piston has passed through but one-eighth or one-ninth of its stroke.

Expansive steam may be thus explained:—If we allow steam to flow into the cylinder of a steam-engine until the piston be depressed to one-half of the stroke, and then prevent the admission of any further quantity, the piston will, if the engine be properly weighted, continue its motion to the bottom. The pressure of the steam, so long as the supply is continued from the boiler, will be equal, it is presumed, to ten pounds upon the inch. With this force it will act upon the piston until it completes one-half of the stroke: the further supply of steam will then be excluded, and that which is in the cylinder will expand as the piston descends, so that when the stroke is completed it will occupy the entire capacity. The pressure of the steam will then be half of its former amount, or five pounds upon the inch.

During the descent of the piston, the pressure of the steam does not suddenly decrease from ten pounds to five; but it gradually declines, through the successive intervals, until at the final point it yields that force. It is by this gradual expansion and diminution of pressure that the superior action is produced.

Experiments on Brass. Dr. Young made some experiments on brass, from which he calculated the height of the modulus of elasticity of brass plate to be 4,940,000 feet, or 18,000,000 lbs. for its weight to a base of 1 square inch. For wire of inferior brass he found the height to be 4,700,000 feet.

As cast brass had not been submitted to experiment, a cast bar of good brass was procured, with which the following experiment was made:

The bar was filed true and regular; its depth was 0·45 inch, and breadth 0·7 inch; the distance between the supports was 12 inches, and the scale suspended from the middle.

lbs.	inch.	
12 bent the bar	0·01	
23	0·02	
38	0·03	The bar was relieved several times, but it took no perceptible set.
52	0·04	
65	0·05	Relieved, the set was ·01.
110	0·18	
163		slipped between the supports, bent more than 2 inches, but did not break.

Hence 52 lbs. seems to be about the limit which could not be much exceeded without permanent change of structure. It is equivalent to a strain of 6700 lbs. upon a square inch, and the corresponding extension is $\frac{1}{1400}$ of its length. Absolute cohesion above 21,000 lbs. per square inch. The modulus of elasticity according to this experiment is 8,030,000 lbs. for a base of an inch square. The specific gravity of the brass is 8·37, whence we have 2,460,000 feet for the height of the modulus.

Expression principally consists in representing the human body and all its parts in the action suitable to it; in exhibiting in the face the several passions proper to the figures, and marking the motions they impress on the other external parts.

Expression, in painting, consists in the representation of those attitudes of the body, and variations of the countenance which always accompany and indicate the immediate influence of the passions on the mind.

Expression of colour. Every passion and affection of the mind has its appropriate tint; and colouring, if properly adapted, lends its aid, with powerful effect, in the just discrimination and forcible expression of them: it heightens joy, warms love, inflames anger, deepens sadness, and adds coldness to the cheek of death itself.

External thermometer (the) should be a mercurial one, well exhausted of air, and the graduated scale divided to tenths of a degree, or into quarters of a degree, or with whole divisions large enough to be divided into as many parts by the eye. Choose a locality for the instrument, where it will be well exposed to the ambient air,—apart from the reflection of sunbeams, etc.,—and where it may be distinctly read off without inconvenience. It should be read off as quickly as possible. For uniformity

EXT FAHRENHEIT. FAN

of system, it should be read off at stated periods, the same time at which the barometer, etc., are noted, and carefully watched in the interim, to see whenever any remarkable change occurs; before and after storms, during eclipses of the sun and moon, or the passage of dense clouds of vapour, etc.

Extract of gamboge is the colouring matter of gamboge separated from its greenish gum and impurities by solution in alcohol and precipitation, by which means it acquires a powdery texture, rendering it miscible in oil, etc., and capable of use in glazing. It is at the same time improved in colour, and retains its original property of working well in water and gum.

Extrados, the exterior curve of an arch, measured on the top of the voussoirs, as opposed to the soffit or intrados.

Eye, a name given to certain circular parts and apertures in architecture, but more especially to the central circle of the Ionic volute; to the circular or oval window in a pediment; to a small skylight in a roof, or the aperture at the summit of a cupola.

F.

FABER, a name given by the Romans to any artisan or mechanic who worked in hard materials.

Fabrica, according to the Romans, the workshop of any mechanic.

Fabrication, the art of building, construction.

Fabrillia, according to Horace, mechanics' tools.

Façade, the face or front of any considerable building to a street, court, garden, or other place.

Face-piece, in ship-building, a piece wrought on the fore-part of the knee of the head, to assist the conversion of the main-piece, and to shorten the upper bolts of the knee of the head.

Fagg (sea term) the ends of those strands which do not go through the tops, when a cable or rope is closed.

Fagot of Steel, 120 lbs. weight.

Faithful (the), (on the table of symbols of the early ages), represented by sheep, John x. 14; by fish, Matt. xii. 47; by doves eating grapes or ears of corn; by stags, Psalm xlii. 2; by date-trees or cedar-trees, Isaiah i. 13; Jerem. xvii. 8; by little children.

Fahrenheit, a native of Dantzic, was born in 1686; he invented the scale called after his name: he also improved the thermometer by substituting mercury instead of spirits of wine, and formed a new scale for the instrument, founded on accurate experiments, fixing the freezing point of water at 32°, and that of boiling at 212°.

Faldstool, or folding stool, a portable seat made to fold up in the manner of a camp-stool: it was made either of metal or wood, and sometimes covered with rich silk.

False red is a second red, which is sometimes put under the first, to make it deeper.

False stem in a ship, when the stem being too flat, another is fastened to it.

False-roof, the space between the ceiling and the roof above it, whether the ceiling is of plaster or a stone vault, as at King's College chapel, Cambridge, and St. Jacques church, Liége.

Fan-tracery vaulting: this was used in late Perpendicular work, in which all the ribs that rise from the springing of the vault have the same curve, and diverge equally in every direction, producing an effect like the bones of a fan: very fine examples of it exist in Henry the VIIth's chapel, Westminster, St. George's chapel, Windsor, and in King's College chapel, Cambridge.

Fanal, a pharos or lighthouse, or the lantern placed in it.

Fang, in mining, a niche cut in the side of an adit, or shaft, to serve as an air-course; sometimes a main of wood-pipes is called a fanging.

Fanners, vanes or flat discs revolving round a centre, so as to produce a current of air; generally used instead of bellows for forges.

Fanum, a Roman temple or fane, usually consecrated to some deity.

Farm. Vitruvius says,—"The magnitude of the buildings must depend wholly upon the quantity of land attached to them, and upon its produce. The number of courts and their dimensions must be proportioned to the herds of cattle and the quantity of oxen employed. The kitchen should be situated in the warmest part of the court, and the stable for the oxen contiguous to it: the stalls should be made to face the hearth and the east; because when oxen are constantly exposed to light and heat, they become smooth-coated. No husbandman, however ignorant, will suffer cattle to face any other quarter of the heavens than the east. The width of the stables ought not to be less than ten nor more than fifteen feet, their length proportioned to the number of yokes, each of which should occupy an extent of seventeen feet. The scalding-rooms should adjoin the kitchen, in order that the operation of cleaning the utensils may be performed upon the spot. The courts for sheep, etc., should be so spacious as to allow not less than four and a half nor more than six feet to each animal. The granaries should be aboveground, and made to front either the north or the north-east, in order that the grain may not be liable to ferment; but, on the contrary, by exposure to a cold atmosphere, may be preserved a long time: all other aspects encourage the propagation of worms and insects destructive to grain. The stables should be built in the warmest part of the villa most distant from the hearth; because when horses are stalled near fire they become rough-coated. It is likewise expedient to have stalls for oxen at a distance from the kitchen, in the open air: these should be placed so as to front the east, because if they are led there to be fed in winter when the sky is unclouded they will improve in appearance. The barns, the hay-yards, the corn-chambers, and the mills ought to be without the walls; so that the farm may be less liable to accidents from fire."

Farm, in Cornish mining, that part of the lord's fee which is taken for liberty to work in tin-mines only that are bounded, which is generally one-fifteenth of the whole.

Fascia, a flat architectural member in an entablature or elsewhere; a band or broad fillet. The architrave in the more elegant orders of architecture is divided into three bands, which are called fasciæ: the lower is called the first fascia, the middle one the second, and the upper one the third fascia.

Fasciæ, the bands of which the epistylium of the Ionic and Corinthian orders are composed. The antepagments of Ionic doorways were generally divided into three fasciæ or corsæ. Fasciæ were also bands which the Romans were accustomed to bind round the legs.

Fast and loose pulleys, two pulleys placed side by side on a shaft which is driven from another shaft by a band; when it is required to stop the shaft, the band is transferred to the loose pulley.

Fastigium, the pediment of a portico; so called because it followed the form of the roof, which was made like a triangle, the sides being equally inclined, to carry off the water. In architecture, the summit, apex, or ridge of a house or pediment.

Faux, according to Vitruvius, a narrow passage which formed a communication between the two principal divisions of a Roman house,—the atrium and peristylium.

Fay, in ship-building, to join two pieces of timber close together.

Feathering or *foliation*, an arrangement of small arcs or foils separated by projecting points or cusps, used as ornaments in the mouldings of arches, etc., in Gothic architecture.

Feed-head, a cistern containing water and communicating with the boiler of a steam-engine by a pipe, to supply the boiler by the gravity of the water, the height being made sufficient to overcome the pressure within the boiler.

Feed-pipe, the pipe leading from the feed-pump, or from an elevated cistern, to the bottom of the boiler of a locomotive engine.

Feed-pipe cocks, those used to regulate the supply of water to the boiler of a locomotive engine, and the handle of which is placed conveniently to open and shut at pleasure.

Feed-pipe strainer, or *strum*, a perforated half-spherical piece of sheet-iron, after the manner of the rose end of a watering-pot: it is placed over the open end of the feed-pipe in the locomotive tender tank, to protect it.

Feed-pipes, the copper pipes reaching from the clack-box to the pump and from the pump to the tender, to convey water to the boiler of a locomotive engine.

Feed-pump, a forcing-pump, worked by the steam-engine, for supplying the boiler with water.

Feed-pump plunger, the solid piston, or enlarged end of the pump-rod, fitting the stuffing-box of the pump of a steam-engine.

Felling timber, the act of cutting down a full-grown tree, which doubtlessly should be done late in the autumn, when less moisture exists in all trees, and which renders the timber less liable to dry-rot.

Felspar, a mineral of foliated structure.

Felucca, in navigation, a little vessel used in the Mediterranean, capable of going either stem or stern foremost; also a small open boat, rowed with six oars.

Femerell, a lantern, louvre, or covering placed on the roof of a kitchen, hall, etc., for the purpose of ventilation or the escape of smoke.

Femur, in architecture, the long, flat projecting face between each channel of a triglyph; the thigh, or a covering for the thigh.

Fender-piles, those driven to protect work either on land or in water.

Fenders, to vessels or ships, are pieces of old ropes, or wooden billets, hung over the side to prevent injury from collision with other ships.

Fender-bolts are iron pins for the protection of the sides of ships.

Fenestella, the niche at the side of an altar containing the piscina, a vessel for holding water to wash the hands of the officiating priest; also a little window.

Fenestra, a window, an entrance.

Fenestrals: window-blinds, or casements closed with paper or cloth, instead of glass, are so termed.

Fenestration, termed by the Germans *Fenster-architektur*, is, in contradistinction to columniation, the system of construction and mode of design marked by windows. Fenestration and columniation are so far antagonistic and irreconcilable, that fenestration either interferes with the effect aimed at by columniation with insulated columns, as in a portico or colonnade, or reduces it, as is the case with an engaged order, to something quite secondary and merely decorative. Astylar and fenestrated ought, therefore, to be merely convertible terms; but as they are not, that of *columnar fenestrated* has been invented, to denote that mode of composition which unites fenestration with the *semblance*, at least, of the other. Employed as a collective term, fenestration serves to express the character of a building or design with regard to the windows generally: thus it is said, the fenestration is excellent, or the contrary,—ornate or meagre,—well arranged or too crowded,—which last circumstance is a very common fault, and is destructive both of grandeur and of repose.

Feretory, a bier, or coffin; a tomb, or shrine.

Ferrari (Gaudenzio), called by Vasari Gaudenzio Milanese, was ranked among the seven greatest painters in the world.

Ferrule, a metal ring fixed on the handle of a tool to prevent the wood from splitting.

Festoon, an ornament of carved work, representing a wreath or garland of flowers or leaves, or both interwoven with each other; it is thickest in the middle, and small at each extremity, a part often hanging down below the knot.

Festoon, in architecture, an ornament of carved work, in the form of a wreath or garland of flowers, or leaves twisted together.

Fictile, an earthen vessel or other article, moulded and baked.

Pictor, among the Romans, an artist, a deviser, or potter.

Fid-hammer, a tool;—a fidd at one end and a hammer at the other.

Fidd is a piece of iron or wood to open the strands of ropes.

Fife-rails of a ship are banisters on each side of the top of the poop.

Figulus, an artist who makes figures and ornaments.

Filagree, in the arts, a kind of enrichment in gold and silver.

File, a well-known instrument having teeth on the surface for cutting metal, ivory, wood, etc.

File, a strip or bar of steel, the surface of which is cut into fine points or teeth, which act by a species of cutting closely allied to abrasion. When the file is rubbed over the material to be operated upon, it cuts or abrades little shavings or shreds, which, from their minuteness, are called file-dust, and in so doing the file produces minute and irregular furrows of nearly equal depth, leaving the surface that has been filed more or less smooth, according to the size of the teeth of the file, and more or less accurately shaped, according to the degree of skill used in the manipulation of the instrument. The files employed in the mechanical arts are almost endless in variety.

Fillet, a small flat face or band, used principally between mouldings to separate them from each other in classical architecture: in the Gothic, Early English, or Decorated styles of architecture, it is also used upon larger mouldings and shafts.

Finial, sometimes called a pinnacle, but more truly confined to the bunch of foliage which terminates pinnacles, canopies, pediments, etc., in Gothic architecture.

Finite force, a force that acts for a finite time, such as the force of gravity.

Finlayson's Tables of the value of life assurance and annuities differ in several respects widely from either the Northampton or the Carlisle calculated Tables. In framing them for Government annuities, from observations made on the mortality in tontines and amongst the holders of Government annuities, Mr. Finlayson, in his calculations, is inclined to take a favourable view of the duration of human life, and his Tables coincide very nearly with the Carlisle, except that he makes a distinction between males and females,—the latter being considered rather longer lived than the former. As regards annuities, these observations may be thus illustrated: the present value of an annuity of £1 for the life of a person aged twenty-five, calculated at 4 per cent. interest, would be, according to the

        £. s.
Northampton Tables 15 4

Carlisle Tables . . £17 6
Government, Male . . 16 9
Do. Female . 18 1

Fire-bar frame, in a locomotive engine, a frame made to fit the fire-box on which the fire-bars rest: a plan of dropping all the bars at once by a movable frame, acted on by a lever and handle outside the fire-box, has been frequently tried, but the action of the intense heat soon puts it out of working order.

Fire-bars, in a locomotive engine, wedge-shaped iron bars fitted to the fire-box with the thick side uppermost, to support the fire: the ends rest on a frame; they are inclined inwards, with an air space between each, to promote combustion, and are jointed at one end, and supported by a rod at the other, so that the rod being withdrawn, the bars fall, and the fire-box is emptied.

Fire-box, in a locomotive engine, the box (usually made of copper) in which the fire is placed. The outside is of iron, separated from the copper fire-box by a space of about 3 inches all round for water.

Fire-box door, the door opening into the fire-box, facing the locomotive tender, by which coke is supplied to the fire.

Fire-box partition: in large fire-boxes a division is made in the box, into which water is admitted: this division is about the height of the fire-box door, and divides the fire into two parts in a locomotive engine, thereby increasing the heating surface of the fire-box.

Fire-box stays, in a locomotive engine, deep strong iron stays bolted to the top of the copper fire-box, to enable it to resist the pressure of the steam: round copper or iron stays are also used to connect the outside shell to the inside box, in the proportion of about one stay to every 4 square inches of flat surface.

Fire-bricks are used for lining furnaces, and for all kinds of brickwork exposed to intense heat which would melt common bricks. They are made from a natural compound of silica and alumina, which, when free from lime and other fluxes, is infusible under the greatest heat to which it can be subjected. Oxide of iron, however, which is present in most clays, renders the clay fusible when the silica and alumina are nearly in equal proportions, and those fire-clays are the best in which the silica is greatly in excess over the alumina. When the alumina is in excess, broken crucibles, glasshouse pots, and old fire-bricks, ground to powder, are substituted for the common siliceous sand used in the ordinary processes of brick-making, but which, in this case, would be injurious, as having a tendency to render the clay fusible.

Fire-clay being an expensive article, it is usual, when making fire-bricks at a distance from mines, to mix with it burnt clay, for the sake of economizing the clay and diminishing its contraction. Mr. Pellatt states that Stourbridge clay, when carefully picked, ground, and sifted, will bear, for brick-making, two proportions (by weight) of burnt clay to one of native clay.

Fire-clay is found throughout the coal formation, but that of Stourbridge is considered the best. The fire-clays of Newcastle and Glasgow are also much esteemed. Fire-bricks are brought to London from Stourbridge and from Wales; the latter, however, will not stand such intense heat as the Stourbridge bricks.

Fire-bricks are also made at the village of Hedgerly, near Windsor, of the sandy loam known by the name of Windsor loam, and these are much used in London for fire-work, and also by chemists for luting their furnaces, and for similar purposes.

The relative merits of Windsor, Welsh, and Stourbridge fire-bricks are best shown by their value in the market.

FIREPROOF FLOORS.

The following Table shows the constituents of several infusible clays:— iron ores, glass-making, etc., and sometimes for the linings of retort-ovens: for this latter purpose they

Authority	Dr. Ure.	Vauquelin.	Wrightson.
Description.	Kaolin, or porcelain clay.	Plastic clay of Forge-les-eaux.	Sagger clay, from the Staffordshire potteries.
Silica	52	63	54·38
Alumina	47	16	26·55
Iron	0·33	8	8·38
Lime	—	1	—
Carbonic acid	—	—	3·14
Water	—	10	7·28
	99·33	98	99·73
Remarks		Used for making glass-house pots and pottery.	Used for making saggers and fire-bricks.

The following prices are from the 'Contractor's Pocket-Book for 1850.' They include carriage to London and delivery on the works:
Fire-bricks per M. £. s. d.
 Windsor . . . 5 8 0
 Welsh . . . 8 12 0
 Stourbridge . . 11 6 0

Fire-bricks. The parts of furnaces exposed to heat are built of bricks made of a description of clay which is to different extents infusible, the qualities chosen for use being regulated by the degree of heat to which they are to be exposed. They are known in commerce by the names of Bristol, Stourbridge, Newcastle, Welsh, and Windsor bricks. The first of these are composed almost entirely of silex, and are infusible at the greatest heat of the blast-furnace; but they are very costly, and seldom used. The second quality are made from clay found in the neighbourhood of Stourbridge, lying in a stratum of considerable thickness between the upper soil and the coal formations: they are used in the construction of furnaces required to resist great heat, such as those for smelting iron ores, are considered too expensive, except for the arch immediately over the furnace, as the heat is not intense. The third variety are composed of the clay lying above the coal measures in Northumberland, and for the construction of retort furnaces and ovens are the most desirable.

Fire-damp, in coal-mines, is impure carburetted hydrogen.

Fire-place, a space within a chimney-piece for the burning of fuel to warm the temperature of the air, and in communication with a shaft or chimney-flue.

Fireproof floors. When a fire breaks out in London it destroys a whole building in spite of the prompt efforts of the Brigade; this is owing to the materials used in the construction of houses being very inflammable. In an enlightened country like England, so rich in iron, and commanding such powerful means of action, we ought to have got rid altogether of wooden floors and roofs, which are so expensive, so combustible, so apt to wear out.

In Paris there are firms who

manufacture iron roofs and floors. The Exhibition contained numerous samples of this manufacture, especially those exhibited by the Creusot Foundry, consisting of a flooring with its various modes of construction, all worthy the attention of competent judges. The Creusot manufacture girders offering a resistance of 18 to 20 per cent. above that obtained by any other system, independently of the extra strength produced by the peculiar mode in which they are riveted.

The usual price of iron girders in England is from 30 to 40 per cent. cheaper than in Paris, and the timber joists are from 30 to 40 per cent. dearer; the former are generally preferred in Paris on account of their greater durability and their being fireproof.

There are firms supplying rolled iron girders in London; plate girders have been found by several builders more economical than rolled ones, and there is no lack of them.

The Iron girders are prevented from oxidation when imbedded in mortar, and not in plaster.

In all the French systems the wooden floors ('parquets') are laid on small wooden joists, resting on the top of the main girders, which allows the ventilation required for preventing the 'dry rot.'

Fire-tubes, or tube-flues, are those through which the fire passes, for obtaining a large heating surface, fixed longitudinally in the middle compartment of a locomotive engine, between the fire-box and smoke-box.

Fires of the Ancients. Palladio says. —" Finding that this subject about fires of the ancients had not been treated of distinctly by anybody, I resolved to compose something about it. We are ignorant of most things delivered thereupon by the ancients which might give us some light upon the matter: we must have recourse to the inventions of later times, thereby gradually to obtain a more ample knowledge of it. The Romans were sensible that a continual flame and a great heat from live coals were hurtful to the eyes; they therefore went very wisely about finding out a remedy. They found how dangerous it was to carry fire about the house from one room to another. Stoves are an abominable invention; they cause a continual stench, swell the head, and make men drowsy, dull, and lazy. Most people that use them grow tender and weak: some cannot stir out of these rooms all the winter. The ancients used to light their fire in a small furnace under the earth. Thence they conveyed a great many tubes of different sizes into all the different stories and rooms of the house, which tubes or pipes were invisible, but laid in the thickness of the walls and ceilings, just like water-pipes. Each of these opened at that part of the furnace which joined to the very wall of the house, and through these ascended the heat, which was let in whenever they had a mind it should, whether in dining-rooms, bed-chambers, or closets, much in the manner as we see the heat or steam of water contained in an alembic to ascend and warm the parts most distant from the fire-place. The heat in that manner used to spread so equally that it warmed the whole house alike. It is not so with chimneys or hearths; for if you stand near, you are scorched; if at any distance, you are frozen; but here a very mild warm air spreads all around, according as the fire that warms the pipes laid along the wall opposite to the hearth is more or less burning. Those pipes which dispersed the heat did not open into the very furnace, on purpose that neither smoke nor flame should get into them, but only a warm steam should enter, which they let out again; thereby creating a continual moderate heat. The fire needed not to be large, provided it was continual, to supply those confined and enclosed pipes with a sufficient power of warming. They dressed their meat at the mouth of the furnace; and all along the walls were disposed kettles, or other vessels, filled with hot water, to keep the meat warm."

Fir-poles, small trunks of fir-trees, from 10 to 16 feet in length; used in rustic buildings and out-houses.

Fish, a machine employed to hoist and draw up the flukes of a ship's anchor towards the top of the bow, in order to stow it after it has been catted.

Fissure, or *Gulley*, is that crack or split in the strata of the earth which is the receptacle of mineral particles, whose contents are styled a 'lode.'

Fistuca, among the Romans, an instrument used for ramming down pavements and threshing-floors, and the foundations of buildings.

Fistula, a water-pipe, according to Vitruvius, who distinguishes three modes of conveying water: by leaden pipes, by earthen pipes, and by channels of masonry.

Five species of temples (the). There are five species of temples: namely, the pycnostyle, in which the columns are placed far apart; the systyle, in which they are more remote; the diastyle, whose columns are at an ample distance from each other; the aræostyle, in which the intervals between the columns are too great; and the eustyle, whose intercolumniations are justly proportioned. In the pycnostyle species the interval between the columns is equal to one diameter and a half: there is an instance of this in the temple of Julius, and another in the temple of Venus, which is erected in the forum of Cæsar: in all temples of this species the same interval between the columns is observed. In the systyle species there should be an interval between the columns equal to two diameters: this arrangement would leave the space between the plinths of the bases of the columns equal to the extent of the plinths themselves.

Flag, a national colour, a standard.

Flag, a stone for pavement.

Flake-white is an English white lead, in the form of scales or plates, sometimes grey on the surface. It takes its name from its figure, is equal or sometimes superior to crems white, and is an oxidized carbonate of lead, not essentially differing from the best of the above. Other white leads seldom equal it in body; and when levigated, it is called 'body-white.'

Flamboyant Style of Architecture, the decorated and very ornamental style of architecture of French invention and use, and contemporary in France with the Perpendicular style in England. One of the most striking and universal features is the waving arrangements of the tracery of the windows, panels, etc. The foliage used for enrichments is well carved, and has a playful and frequently a good effect.

Flanders varnish: dissolve grain mastic in alcohol: this operation is requisite to detach the impurities in the resin. The proportion of spirit ought to be sufficient to cover the mastic, and ⅓ part more.

Flanning, the internal splay of a window-jamb.

Flaring, in ship-building, over-hanging, as in the top side forward.

Flatting, in house-painting, a mode of painting in oil in which the surface is left, when finished, without gloss. The material is prepared with a mixture of oil of turpentine, which secures the colours, and, when used in the finishing, leaves the paint quite dead.

Flemish bricks are used for paving: seventy-two will pave a square yard: they are of a yellowish colour, and harder than the ordinary bricks.

Flemish School of Painting. This school is highly recommended to the lovers of the art by the discovery, or at least the first practice, of painting in oil. It has been generally attributed to John Van Eyck, who was, it is said, accustomed to varnish his distemper pictures with a composition of oils, which was pleasing on account of the lustre it gave them. In the course of his practice he came to mix his colours with oil, instead of water, which he found rendered them brilliant without the trouble of varnishing. From this and subsequent experiments arose the art of painting in oil; and this wonderful discovery, whether made by Van Eyck or not, soon acquired notice all over Europe. The attention of the Italian painters was soon excited. John of Bruges was the founder of painting as a profession in Flanders. Peter Paul Rubens was the founder of the art.

Fleur-de-Lis, the ancient trophy of France.

Flight, the stairs from one landing-place to another.

Float, a flat piece of stone or other material attached to a valve in the feed-pipe of the boiler of a steam-engine, and supported upon the surface of the water by a counter-weight; used either for showing the height of the water, or regulating the supply from the cistern.

Flookan, in Cornish, an earth or clay of a slimy, glutinous consistence; in colour for the most part blue or white, or compounded of both.

Floor-hollow, in ship-building, an elliptical mould for the hollow of the floor-timbers and lower futtocks.

Flooking, among miners, the interception of ore by the crossing of a vein of earth or stone.

Floors, in early English domestic arrangements, were generally covered with rushes, carpets being seldom used for such purposes even at the close of Elizabeth's reign, although instances occur of tapestry cloths for the feet to rest upon as early as Edward I. It does not, indeed, appear to have been the custom at any time to leave floors bare, whether boarded or paved. Our poets, and particularly Shakespeare, all speak of rushes and other vegetable substances being strewed in the principal apartments.

Floor-timbers, in ship-building, are those placed immediately across the keel, and upon which the bottom of the ship is framed.

Floran, an exceedingly small-grained tin, scarcely perceivable in the stone, though perhaps very rich.

Florentine lake colour is extracted from the shreds of scarlet cloth: the same may be said also of Chinese lake.

Florentine School of Painting. This school is remarkable for greatness; for attitudes seemingly in motion; for a certain dark severity; for an expression of strength by which grace is perhaps excluded; and for a character of design approaching to the gigantic. The productions of this school may be considered as overcharged; but it cannot be denied that they possess an ideal majesty which elevates human nature above mortality. The Tuscan artists, satisfied with commanding the admiration, seem to have considered the art of pleasing as beneath their notice. This school has an indisputable title to the veneration of all the lovers of the arts, as the first in Italy which cultivated them.

Florentine School. Academies in Italy. In 1349 the painters established themselves into a religious fraternity, which they denominated 'The Society of St. Luke.' This was not the first that had arisen in Italy, as Baldinucci affirms.

Florid Gothic, or Florid English or Tudor, is a style of redundant ornamentation. The period is from 1400–1537. There are many churches of the time of Henry VII. in Somersetshire.

Flotilla, a Spanish term for a number of ships, or fleet.

Flower-garden (the) "should be an object detached and distinct from the general scenery of the place; and whether large or small, whether varied or formal, it ought to be well protected from hares and smaller animals by an inner fence: within this enclosure rare plants of every description should be encouraged, and a provision made of soil and aspect for every different class. Beds of bog-earth should be prepared for the American plants; the aquatic plants, some of which are peculiarly beautiful, should grow on the surface or near the edges of water. The numerous class of rock-plants should have beds of rugged stone provided for their reception, without the affectation of such stones being the natural production of the soil; but, above all, there should be poles or hoops for those kinds of creeping plants which spontaneously form themselves into graceful festoons when encouraged and supported by art."

There is no ornament of a flower-garden more appropriate than a conservatory or greenhouse, where the flower-garden is not too far from the house; but amongst the refinements of modern luxury may be reckoned that of attaching a green-house to some room in the mansion.

Fluccan, in mining, a soft, clayey substance, generally found to accompany the cross-courses and slides.

Fluke, in mining, the head of a charger; an instrument used for cleansing the hole previous to blasting.

Fluor or *Fluores*, a soft, transparent kind of mineral concretion.

Flush, a term common to workmen, and applied to surfaces which are on the same plane.

Flutings or *Flutes*, the hollows or channels cut perpendicularly in the shafts of columns, etc., in classical architecture: they are used in the Doric, Ionic, Corinthian, and Composite orders.

Flux, in metallurgy, saline matters which facilitate the fusion of ores and other substances which are not easily fusible in assays; used also in the reduction of ores.

Fly, in mechanics, that part of a machine which, being put in motion, regulates the rest.

Fly-wheel, a wheel with a heavy rim, fixed upon the crank-shaft of a land engine, for the purpose of equalizing the motion by the centrifugal force absorbing the surplus force at one part of the action, to distribute it again when the action is deficient.

Flyers, stairs that go straight and do not wind, the fore and back part of each stair and the ends respectively being parallel to each other.

Focus, among the Romans, an altar, a fireplace or hearth: hence the Latin motto, "Pro aris et focis," "for our altars and firesides."

Fodina, a mine or quarry.

Foye, Cornish, a forge or blowing-house for smelting tin.

Foils, foliation; the spaces between the cusps of the featherings of Gothic architecture.

Fons, a font or a natural spring of water, frequently converted into ornamented fountains by the Greeks and the Romans. The latter also erected edifices of various degrees of splendour over natural springs, such as the grotto of Egeria, near Rome, where the natural cave is converted by the architect into a temple.

Font, the vessel which contains the water for the purposes of baptism. The font is the only relic of our ancient architecture which in its form is at all analogous to the Grecian and Roman vases. The shape which has at different periods been given to it is a subject of some interest. Norman fonts are generally square or circular; the first frequently placed on five legs; but which may be the older form, the square or circle, is not yet known. The circular form continued to be much used during the Early English period; so, occasionally, was the square. Throughout the continuance of the Decorated style, the octagon was generally used, sometimes the hexagon. During the Perpendicular style, the octagon was almost always used. Until the Reformation, and occasionally after, dipping was practised in this country. Pouring or sprinkling was not unusual previous to the Reformation; for as early as the year 754, pouring, in cases of necessity, was declared by Pope Stephen III. to be lawful; and in the year 1311, the Council of Ravenna declared dipping or sprinkling indifferent: yet dipping appears to have been in this country the more usual mode. The Earl of Warwick, who was born in 1831, was baptized by dipping: so Prince Arthur (eldest son of Henry VII.), King Edward VI., and Queen Elizabeth, were all baptized in a similar manner.

Font of the time of Edward II.

Foot, an ancient measure of tin, containing two gallons; now a nominal measure, but in weight 60 lbs.; also a lineal measure of twelve inches.

Foot-pace, the dais or raised floor at the upper end of an ancient hall.

Foot-plate, the platform on which the engine-man and fire-man of a locomotive engine attend to their duties.

Foot-stall, the plinth or base of a pillar.

Foot-valve, the valve in the passage between the condenser and air-pump of an engine, opening towards the air-pump.

Foot-waling, the plank withinside a ship, below the lower deck.

Force of the wind. Air, when in continuous motion in one direction, becomes a very useful agent of machinery, of greater or less energy according to the velocity with which it moves. Were it not for its variability in direction and force, and the consequent fluctuations in its supply, scarcely any more appropriate first mover could generally be wished for; and even with all its irregularity, it is still so useful as to require a separate consideration.

The force with which air strikes against a moving surface, or with which the wind strikes against a quiescent surface, is nearly as the square of the velocity; or, more correctly, the exponent of the velocity varies between 2·03 and 2·05; so that in most practical cases the exponent 2, or that of the square, may be employed without fear of error.

Forceps, tongs used by smiths to take the hot metal from the fire.

Force-pumps, the plunger-pumps for supplying the boiler of a locomotive engine: the plunger-rods are connected to the piston-rods of the steam cylinder.

Forcer, in Cornish, a small pump worked by hand, used in sinking small simples, dippas, or pits.

Forcing-pump (the) differs but little from a syringe: the latter receives and expels a liquid through the same passage, but the former has a separate pipe for its discharge, and both the receiving and discharging orifices are covered with valves. By this arrangement it is not necessary to remove a pump from the liquid to transfer the contents of its cylinder, as is done with the syringe, but the operation of forcing up water may be continuous, while the instrument is immovable. A forcing-pump, therefore, is merely a syringe furnished with an induction and eduction valve, — one through which water enters the cylinder, the other by which it escapes from it. The ordinary forcing-pump has two valves ; the cylinder is placed above the surface of the water to be raised, and consequently is charged by the pressure of the atmosphere : the machine, therefore, is a compound one, differing from that described, which is purely a forcing-pump, the water entering its cylinder by gravity alone.

Forecastle, a short deck at the fore-part of a ship, above the upper deck, on which castles were formerly erected, or places to shelter the men in time of action.

Fore-foot, the foremost piece of the keel of a vessel.

Foreground, the front of a picture.

Foreyn, an ancient term to signify a drain or cesspool.

Forge, a smith's furnace for heating metals, to render them soft and more malleable.

Fork, a short piece of steel which fits into one of the sockets or chucks of a lathe, and is used by wood-turners for carrying round the piece to be turned ; it is flattened at the end like a chisel, but has a projecting centre-point, to prevent the wood from moving laterally.

Fore-locks, in a ship, little flat wedge-like pieces of iron, used at the ends of bolts to keep the bolts from flying out of the holes.

Foreshorten, in painting, is when a head or face in a draught is made to appear shorter before.

Form : 1. General form ; figure, shape, configuration, make, formation, frame, construction, conformation, efformation, mould, fashion.—2. Special form.—3. Superficial form.

Formosity, beauty, fairness, etc.

Form-peys, an ancient term for form-pieces ; the lower terminations of mullions which are worked upon sills.

Forms and motions of tools. The principles of action of all cutting tools, and of some others, whether guided by hand or by machinery, resolve themselves into the simple condition, that the work is the combined copy of the form of the tool and of the motion employed : thus the geometrical definitions employed convey the primary ideas of lines, superficies, and solids ; that is, the line results from the motion of a point, the superficies from the motion of a line, and the solid from the motion of a superficies.

Formula (pl. *Formulæ*), a prescribed rule in arithmetic or mathematics ; a maxim : in law, an action, process, or indictment.

Formulary, a book containing set forms, rules, or models.

Fornax, among the Romans, a kiln for baking pottery.

Fortification, the science of military architecture ; a defensive building.

Forum, a large open space used by the Romans for the sale of merchandise, and for public assemblies ; also a court of justice.

Forum and *Basilica*. The Greeks built their forum with spacious porticoes, two tiers in height, arranged in a square form ; the columns of the porticoes were placed at small intervals from each other, supporting stone or marble entablatures ; and galleries were made over the lacunaria of the lower porticoes, or places of exercise. In Italy, the mode of constructing the forum was different ; because, by a custom sanctioned by its antiquity, the show of gladiators was exhibited there ; and therefore the intervals between the columns surrounding the area were greater.

FOS FOSSES D'AISANCES. **FOS**

The lower porticoes were occupied as the offices of bankers, which situation was calculated to facilitate the management of the public revenue: the upper contained seats for the spectators of the diversions practised in the forum.

Forward, the fore part of a ship.

Fosses d'Aisances: the cesspools of Paris are so called; and they are usually made 3ᵐ·00 long in the clear by 1ᵐ·70, by 1ᵐ·50, to the springing of the semicircular head (9 ft. 10 in. × 5 ft. 7 in. × 4 ft. 11 in. English, nearly): a man-hole, 1ᵐ·00 by 0ᵐ·35 is left for the purposes of emptying and visiting them (3 ft. 3 $\frac{1}{12}$ in. × 1 ft. 2 in.). The walls which surround them, as well as the bottom, are exclusively formed of such materials as are most efficacious in preventing the filtration of the matters contained within them. Of late years the usual custom has been to employ the *meulière*, or mill-stone, bedded in mortar composed of lime and cement, the inside being well pointed, and rendered throughout with this mortar. No cesspool is allowed to be used until after an examination, to be certified by the municipal authority. Any infiltration to a neighbour's property gives a title to damages, and the architect and builder are both responsible for ten years to the proprietor, as also to the neighbours, in case any nuisance arises from defects in the execution of the works.

When the cesspools require cleaning, notice is given to the Board of Public Health ('aux Agents de la Salubrité publique'), who authorize and direct the operations. In winter these are carried on between 10 P.M. and 7 A.M.; and in summer, between 11 P.M. and 6 A.M. The carts, as well as all the other material of the nightmen, are under the inspection of the above-named officers, and must be, as nearly as possible, both water-tight and air-tight. They contain not more than 20ᵐ·00 cube each, or nearly 71 ft. cube English.

The contents of the cesspools are usually (especially in the modern houses) sufficiently fluid to allow of their extraction by pumps. In this case a small furnace is placed over the bung of the cart, to burn the gas as it rises: the bung itself is plastered over directly the cart is filled. When the contents are too solid to be pumped out, they are conveyed from below in small vessels of wrought iron, called 'tinettes,' holding about 3½ feet ($\frac{1}{10}$th of a mètre cube) each; and the lids are plastered over before the vessels are removed from the cesspool.

Of late years a system of what are called '*fosses mobiles*' has been introduced into the better class of houses. It consists of air-tight tubs, placed in a vault (rendered also as air-tight as possible), which receive the ends of the soil-pipes. These tubs are removed at stated intervals, the openings plastered over, and may in that state be transported at any time of the day. This system obviates the terrible infection of the old kind of cesspool, and is gaining rapidly. Indeed, as the French people are fond of gilt ornaments in their dwellings, and the gases from the cesspools turn them black at once, unless great precautions be observed in covering them, whenever a cesspool is opened, it is easy to understand that the '*fosses mobiles*,' which obviate this inconvenience, should become of general use.

Until of late, all the carts were obliged to pass through the Barrière du Combat to deposit their contents at the layatalls of Montfaucon; but some new works have been constructed at Bony, so as to allow the suppression of this gigantic nuisance at the immediate gates of Paris.

The cleaning of the cesspools of Paris is executed by several private companies, the most important of which is 'La Compagnie Richer,' who do at least one-half of this business: their capital was about £200,000, in land, plant, and buildings. They employ 150 horses and 300 men, of whom 60 are for the repairs of the plant. Their charge is 8f., 9f., and 10f. per metre cube (35¼ feet English, nearly), according to the distance.

No cesspool is allowed to be used after being emptied until it has been visited by an 'Agent de la Salubrité,' to ascertain whether it be water-tight.

The laystalls of Montfaucon consist of two large reservoirs, at a high level, into which the carts are emptied. These reservoirs are about 2½ acres superficial, and apparently 12 feet deep, with a dam between them, to allow of one being used when the other is being emptied. An overflow drain, with sluice-gates at each end, allows the liquid matter to run off to a large basin on a lower level, where it deposits anything which may be merely in a state of mechanical suspension. On the banks of this reservoir are some important sal-ammoniac works. In the centre is also a sluice-gate, which allows the surplus liquid matters to pass into two smaller reservoirs, where deposition takes place without any interference from the pumping apparatus of the chemical works. From thence the waters pass off into four other basins, in which any fertilizing properties they may contain are precipitated by means of straw, dead leaves, etc., and the water, comparatively pure, is at length let off into the main sewer, which discharges itself into the Seine, below Paris. The surface of the intermediate basins is about 250ᵐ· by 60ᵐ· (or 3¾ acres); that of the four last basins is about 350ᵐ· by 110ᵐ· (or nearly 9½ acres).

These reservoirs do not belong to the city of Paris, and some difficulties have arisen from the proposal to remove them: all the carts containing the night-soil being obliged to discharge at Montfaucon, the farming of the contents of the basins became a source of considerable profit. They were let on the last occasion for a sum of 500,500 francs per annum (£20,020 sterling); the previous letting having been 166,000 francs (£6640 sterling). The increased rent and the exorbitant wages paid during the republican excitement of 1848 proved injurious to the company. The ground occupied by the town, moreover, is not sufficiently extensive for the operations connected with the manipulation of the 'poudrette,' and the company were obliged to rent about 7½ acres more land for the purpose of spreading and drying the compost. The land necessary for this operation had been taken on lease by the outgoing company, and they succeeded in obtaining a sum of £60,000 for the remainder of their term, as no other land was to be had in the neighbourhood.

The rent and labour in conversion costs the company from £12,000 to £16,000 per annum. The 'poudrette' is sold to agriculturists at 8 francs le setier, a measure equal to 12 bushels English.

In one plan adopted for emptying the cesspools, the carts are made of strong boiler plate; they are placed under an air-pump, and exhausted; the pipes are connected with the carts and the cesspools, and the atmospheric pressure on the latter forces up the liquid contents.

Investigations have been made respecting the general health of the workmen employed at Montfaucon, the reservoir of all the excrementitious matter of a city which contains about 1,000,000 inhabitants, and it has been ascertained, that although they were not affected by the cholera in 1849, they are very short-lived men: acute

FOS   FOUNDATIONS.   FOU

fevers, and gangrene on the slightest accident, carry them off in a frightful manner. Unfortunately the dwellers in the neighbourhood also are subject to the same action, and the mortality from these causes is very great.

The action of the 'poudrette' upon agriculture is somewhat extraordinary. In the time of Henri Quatre, the wines of Suresnes were highly esteemed: the vines produced little, but of a superior quality: since the poudrette has been used to force them, the quantity of their produce has been increased, but the quality has totally changed: from a superior rank, the wines of the neighbourhood of Paris have fallen to that of what is vulgarly called 'du petit bleu.'

Fossatum, a ditch, or a place fenced with a ditch or trench.

Fossil, a mineral, many kinds of which are peculiarly and elegantly shaped.

Fossiliferous, a geological term applied to a district abounding in fossils.

Foundations, according to Palladio, ought to be twice as thick as the walls to be raised upon them, so that both the quality of the earth and the greatness of the building are to be regarded, making the foundations larger in a soft and loose ground, or where there is a great weight to be supported. The plane of the trench must be as level as possible, so that the weight may press equally, and not incline more on one side than the other, which occasions the cleaving of the walls. For this reason the ancients were accustomed to pave the plane with Tivertine; but we most commonly lay planks or beams to build on. The foundations ought to be made sloping, that is to say, to diminish as they rise; but yet in such a manner that the middle of the wall above may fall plumb with the middle of the lowest part; which must be also observed in the diminution of walls above ground, because by that means the building becomes much stronger than by making the diminution any other way.

Sometimes, to avoid charges, (especially in marshy grounds, where there is a necessity to use piles,) foundations are arched like a bridge, and the walls are built upon those arches. In great buildings it is very proper to make vents through the body of the walls from the foundations to the roof, because they let forth the winds and other vapours, which are very prejudicial to buildings: they lessen the charges, and are of no small convenience, especially when there is occasion for winding-stairs from the bottom to the top. If it be necessary to construct vaults below ground, their foundations must be more substantial than the walls of the buildings which are to be raised upon them. The walls, pillars, and columns of the latter must be placed immediately over those below them, so that solid may bear upon solid; for if walls or columns project beyond the substructure, their duration must necessarily be short.

The value of concrete in foundations was rendered obvious in a building erected by Mr. Clegg at Fulham, in 1829. The foundation was a quicksand. After the excavation was got out to the depth of 15 feet, an iron rod sunk, with little more than its own weight, 15 feet more; it was, in fact, as bad a foundation as could possibly occur. In about twelve days after it was built, it had settled bodily down 16¼ inches, without a crack, or deviating in the least from the plumb. It therefore follows, that the only disadvantage attending a bad natural foundation is the expense of making an artificial one. The following extract relates to the erection of an extensive building upon bad ground.

"The building for the Albion

Mills was erected upon a very soft soil, consisting of the 'made ground' at the abutment of Blackfriars' Bridge; to avoid the danger of settlement in the walls, or the necessity of going to a very unusual depth with the foundations, Mr. Rennie adopted the plan of forming inverted arches upon the ground over the whole space upon which the building was to stand, and for the bottom of the dock. For this purpose the ground upon which all the several walls were to be erected was rendered as solid as is usual for building by driving piles where necessary, and then several courses of large flat stones were laid to form the foundations of the several walls; but to prevent any chance of these foundations being pressed down in case of the soft earth yielding to the incumbent weight, strong inverted arches were built upon the ground between the foundation courses of all the walls, so as to cover the whole surface included between the walls; and the abutments or springings of the inverted arches being built solid into the lower courses of the foundations, they could not sink unless all the ground beneath the arches had yielded to compression, as well as the ground immediately beneath the foundation of the walls. By this method the foundations of all the walls were joined together so as to form one immense base, which would have been very capable of bearing the required weight, even if the ground had been of the consistency of mud; for the whole building would have floated upon it as a ship floats in water; and whatever sinking might have taken place,

When the foundation has been properly disposed of, the brickwork may be commenced. The bricks should be well burned, and set with a thin joint, four courses not occupying more depth than 11¾ inches.

Foundations of Temples. In preparing foundations for works of this kind, it will be first necessary to dig down to a regular stratum, if such is to be met with; and upon this the foundations, constructed with great attention to their strength, are to be laid: their solidity must be proportioned to the magnitude of the building in contemplation. The piers above-ground, below the columns, should be thicker than the diameter of the columns they are to support by one-half, that these substructures, which are called stereobatæ, on account of their sustaining the whole weight, may be enabled by their greater solidity to support what is built upon them. The bases of the columns, when fixed, ought not to project before the face of the stereobatæ on either side. The intervals between the piers should either be made solid by means of piles, or arched over, so as to connect the piers.

If no compact stratum is to be found, but the ground, on the contrary, is loose or marshy to a great depth, trenches must be dug, and piles of charred alder, olive, or oak, placed close together, be driven in by means of machines; the intervals between them should be filled up with charred timber, and upon this substratum the foundations should be formed with solid masonry. The foundations being reared to the same level all round, the lumns may be placed at any distance asunder.

Foundations of a Bridge: these consist, properly, of the underground work of the piers and abutments, which it is within the province of a civil engineer to construct: the necessity of firmness and solidity in the execution of such works will be deemed of importance just in proportion to the intended extent and magnificence of the structure they are designed to support.

Foundemaunt, foundation. (*Chaucer*.)

Foundery, in iron works, the space of six days.

Foundry, a place where masses of metal are melted and run into moulds, so as to assume the required form.

Four-way-cock, a cock having two separate passages in the plug, and communicating with four pipes.

Fox-tail wedging, in carpentry. This is done by sticking into the point of a wooden bolt a thin wedge of hard wood, which when the bolt reaches the bottom of the hole, splits, expands, and secures it.

Frame, the strong frame-work, outside the wheels, which supports the boiler and machinery on the axles of a locomotive engine.

Frame, inside, in locomotive engines. Some engines have the supporting frames within the wheels, and are called *inside-framed engines*. Besides this frame, resting on the axles, there are also other strong stays from the fire-box to the smoke-box, called *inside framing* or *stays*, for supporting the works and strengthening the boiler.

Frames, the bends of timbers that are bolted together: in small ships there are two bolts in every shift of timber, and three in large ships. The bolts should be disposed clear of the chain and preventer-bolts, scupper, lodging knee-bolts, and port cells.

Frankfort-black is said to be made of the lees of wine from which the tartar has been washed, by burning in the manner of ivory-black. Fine Frankfort-black, though almost confined to copper-plate printing, is one of the best black pigments we possess, being of a fine neutral colour, next in intensity to lamp-black, and more powerful than that of ivory.

Frater-house, the refectory or hall of a monastic establishment.

Fredstole, a seat near the altar.

Freedom, in drawing, is a bold and spirited manner, with evident liberty of the pencil; *i. e.* where the drawing is apparently accomplished with ease.

Freemason, as applied to ancient architecture: a person learned in the art of building, more particularly in ecclesiastical construction, and who, by his learning in the science and his taste in the construction of edifices, travelled from one country to another, and executed models of everlasting renown. The term may also be applied to a free-stone mason, or a cutter and worker in stone, without reference to the society called Freemasons.

Free-stone, building stone which may be easily cut into blocks and worked with a chisel; so called from having no grain: it may therefore be cut in any direction.

Free-stuff, that timber or stuff which is quite clean or without knots, and works easily, without tearing.

French chalk is an indurated magnesian mineral, employed to remove grease stains.

French School of Painting. This school has been so different under different masters, that it is difficult to characterize it. Some of its artists have been formed on the Florentine and Lombard styles, others on the Roman, others on the Venetian, and a few of them have distinguished themselves by a style which may be called their own. In speaking in general terms of this school, it appears to have no peculiar character, and can only be distinguished by its aptitude to imitate easily any impressions; and it may be added, speaking still in general terms, that it unites in a moderate degree the different parts of the art, without excelling in any one of them.

Fresco, a kind of painting performed on fresh plaster, or on a wall covered with mortar not quite dry, and with water-colours. The plaster is only to be laid on as the painting proceeds, no more being done at once than the painter can despatch in a day. The colours, being prepared with water, and applied over plaster quite fresh, become incorporated with the plaster, and retain their beauty for a great length of time. The Romans cut out plaster paintings on brick walls at Sparta, packed them up in wooden cases, and transported them to Rome.

Fret, an ornament used in classical architecture, formed by small fillets intersecting each other at right angles.

Friars (the orders of) in England and Wales, previous to their abolition, including the Nuns Minoresses, amounted to—

Black or Dominican friars	54
Grey or Franciscan friars	62
Minoresses or nuns of the order of St. Clare	4
Friars of the order of the Holy Trinity for the redemption of captives	12
Order of the Carmelites or White friars	50
Crutched or Crossed friars	10
Austin friars	32
Friars de pœnitentia or of the sac	9
Bethlemite friars	6

Friction, the act of rubbing two bodies together, or the resistance in machines caused by the contact of different moving parts. Friction is proportional to the pressure; that is, everything remaining the same, the friction increases as the pressure increases.

Friction-clutch, a shell or box fixed on the end of a driving shaft, fitted by a conical piece which slides on a feather, or raised part, at the end of another shaft, so that it can be engaged at pleasure by the cone being forced into the shell by a lever or screw. This apparatus is very useful for driving machines, the parts of which are subjected to violent strains, as the pressure upon the clutch can be regulated so as to allow it to slide when the strain is too great to be borne safely by the machine.

Frieze, the middle division of an entablature, that which lies between the architrave and the cornice.

Frigatron, a Venetian vessel, built with a square stern, without any foremast, having only a main-mast and bowsprit.

Frigidarium, the cold bathing-room in the baths of the ancients, as well as the vessel in which the cold water was received.

The cold bath: the reservoir of cold water in the hypocaustum, or stove room, was termed *ahenum frigidarium*.

Frithstool or *Freedstool*, a seat or chair near the altar, for those especially who sought the privilege of sanctuary.

Frontal, or *Frontier*, the hanging with which the front of an altar was formerly covered.

Fronton, a French word to express an ornament over a door or pediment.

Frowy stuff, short or brittle and soft timber.

Frumstall, a chief seat or mansion house.

Fucus, a name given by the Romans to certain false dyes and paints.

Fuel, the matter or aliment of fire.

Fulcrum, the prop or support by which a lever is sustained.

Fullers'-earth, a soft unctuous marl, used by fullers in the process of cleansing cloth, etc.

Fulling-mill, an engine or mill, in which cloth is cleansed by being beaten with hammers.

Fulminating gold or *silver*, in chemistry, ammonia combined with the oxides of gold or silver.

Fumarium, a chimney; an upper room used among the Romans for collecting the smoke from the lower apartments; used also for smoking or ripening wines.

Fuor, among carpenters, a piece nailed upon a rafter to strengthen it when decayed.

Furling, in navigation, the wrapping up and binding of any sail close to the yard.

Furlong, a measure of length, the eighth part of a mile.

Furnace. The furnace is one of the most important parts of the high-pressure engine. The whole action and power of the machine depend on its construction, and on the effect obtained from it, inasmuch as fire is the prime agent. Too much industry, exactitude, and intimate knowledge of the subject, cannot be brought to bear on the construction of the furnace, in order to attain the two great objects of its action; namely, first, to produce as perfect a combustion of the fuel as possible; and secondly, to apply as much as possible of the heat so developed effectively to the boiler. These two requirements for a good furnace are, however, not so easily satisfied. Much remains to be acquired as to the conditions under which the whole of the caloric may be perfectly developed from the fuel, although the best manner of applying the heat to the boiler is well understood.

Furniture: anterior to the Tudor age, household furniture was in general of a rude, substantial character; the tables were formed of boards or trestles, the seats of massive oak benches or stools, and the floors strewed with straw.

Furniture of the hall: this consisted of but few articles, such as clumsy oak tables covered with carpet, benches or joined forms of the same material, and cupboards for plate, pewter, 'treene,' leather jugs, glass, etc., with a reredos or fire-iron in the centre of the floor, against which fagots were piled and burned, the smoke passing through an aperture in the roof; the fender, formed by a raised rim of stone or tile, and a 'fier fork' and tongs.

Furrings, slips of timber nailed to joists or rafters, in order to bring them to a level, and to range them into a straight surface, when the timbers are sagged, either by casting, or by a set which they have obtained by their weight in the course of time.

Fuseli (Henry), born 1741 at Zurich; died April, 1825, aged eighty-four. He painted with little sympathy for repose; he thought there was no dignity without action, no sublimity without exaggeration. He left upwards of eight hundred sketches, besides splendid pictures.

Fusion, a founding or melting, running metals into fluids.

Fust, the shaft of a column from the astragal to the capital.

Fusarole, in architecture, a moulding or ornament placed immediately under the echinus in the Doric, Ionic, and Composite capitals; the shaft of a column, pilaster or pillar, or that part comprehended between the shaft and the capital.

Fustic, a wood of a species of mulberry growing in most parts of South America, the United States, and the West Indies: it is a large and handsome tree, principally used for dyeing greens and yellows, and also in mosaic cabinet-work and turnery.

Futtock, in ship-building. Every single timber is called a futtock, and distinguished by the terms lower, or first, second, third, etc., except the floors, long and half-timbers, top timbers, stern timbers, etc.

Futtocks, the lower timbers raised over the keel, and which hold the ship together.

Futtock shrouds, in ship-rigging, small shrouds that go from the main-mast, fore-mast, and mizen-mast shrouds to those of the top-mast.

G.

Gable, the upright triangular end of a house, from the cornice or eaves to the top of the building, sometimes called a sloped roof; the upper part of a wall, above the level of the eaves. Examples in English and foreign Domestic and Gothic architecture are various, and generally have a most picturesque effect.

Gablets, small ornamental gables or canopies formed over tabernacles, niches, etc.

Gad, in mining, a small punch of iron with a long wooden handle, used to break up the ore.

Gaff, a sort of boom used in small ships to extend the upper edge of the mizen, and employed for the same purpose on those sails whose foremost edges are joined to the masts by hoops or lacings, and which are usually extended by a boom below; such are the mainsails of sloops, brigs, and schooners.

Gage or **Geuge**, an instrument used for measuring the state of rarefaction in the air-pump, variations in the barometer, etc.; a measure, a standard.

Gainsborough, the painter, was born in 1727, in Sussex. His price for a portrait rose from 5 guineas to 8, and until he had 40 guineas for a half and 100 guineas for a whole length. Like Reynolds, he painted standing in preference to sitting; he rose early, commenced painting between 9 and 10, worked 4 or 5 hours, and then gave up the rest of the day to visits and enjoyment. He died in 1788, in the 61st year of his age, and was buried in Kew churchyard.

Gal, in Cornish, rusty iron ore.

Galena, ore of silver and lead, after the silver is extracted.

Galilee, a porch or chapel at the entrance of a church. The galilee at Lincoln cathedral is a porch on the west side of the south transept; at Ely cathedral it is a porch at the west end of the nave; at Durham it is a large chapel at the west end of the nave, which was built for the use of the women, who were not allowed to advance further into the church than the second pillar of the nave.

Gallery, an apartment generally of greater length in proportion to the width, applied for the purpose of exhibiting pictures or sculpture; used formerly in early English Domestic architecture, in large houses, as a place of resort for dancing and other amusements.

Galliot, a Dutch vessel, carrying a main and a mizen mast, and a large gaff main-sail.

Gall-stone (colour), an animal calculus formed in the gall-bladder, principally of oxen. This concretion varies a little in colour, but is in general of a beautiful golden yellow, more powerful than gamboge, and is highly reputed as a water-colour: nevertheless, its colour is soon changed and destroyed by strong light, though not subject to alteration by impure air.

Galvanism comprises all those electrical phenomena arising from the chemical agency of certain metals with different fluids.

Galvanometer, an instrument contrived to measure minute quantities of electricity.

Gamboge, or, as it is variously written, Gumboge, Gambouge, Cambogia, Gambadium, etc., is brought from Cambaja, in India, and is the produce of several kinds of trees. It is, however, principally obtained from the tree called Gokathu, which grows in Ceylon and Siam. From the wounded leaves and young shoots the gamboge is collected in a liquid state, and dried. Gamboge is a concrete vegetable substance, of a gum-resinous nature, and beautiful yellow colour, bright and transparent, but not of a great depth. When properly used, it is more durable than generally reputed, both in water and oil, and conduces, when mixed with other colours, to their stability and durability, by means of its gum and resin. It is deepened in some degree by ammoniacal and impure air, and somewhat weakened, but not easily discoloured, by the action of light.

Gammoning, in navigation, seven or eight turns of a rope passed over the bowsprit, and through a large hole in the stem or knee of the head, alternately, and serving to bind the inner quarter of the bowsprit close down to the ship's stem, in order to enable it the better to support the stays of the fore-mast: after all the turns are drawn as firm as possible, the opposite ones are braced together under the bowsprit by a frapping.

Gammoning hole, a hole cut through the knee of the head, and sometimes one under the standard in the head, for the use of gammoning the bowsprit.

Garboard strake, the strake in the bottom that is wrought into the rabbet of the keel of a ship.

Gardens. The ancient plans of gardens show that the Egyptians were not less fond than our ancestors of mathematical figures, of straight walks, architectural decorations, and vegetable avenues; and that they as thoroughly entered into the idea of seclusion and safety suggested by enclosures within enclosures. It has been remarked, that in some old English places there were almost as many walled compartments without as apartments within doors: the same may be said of Egyptian country-houses. This principle of seclusion and an excessive love of uniform arrangement are remarkably displayed in the plan of a large square garden given in Professor Rosellini's great work.

As a subject for the painter, the materials which form the scenery of a garden are provided by Nature herself: the artist must therefore be satisfied with the degree of expression which she has bestowed, and give the best possible disposition to those scanty and intractable materials. In a landscape, on the contrary, the painter has the choice of the objects he intends to represent, and can give whatever force or extent he pleases to the expression he wishes to convey, as the whole range of scenery is before his eye.

Gargoyle or *Gurgoyle*, a projecting spout used in Gothic architecture, to throw the water from the gutter of a building off the wall.

Garland, an ornamental band used in Gothic work.

Garnet, a hinge, now called a 'cross garnet;' a red gem of various sizes.

Garret, an upper apartment of a house, immediately under the roof.

Garretting, small splinters of stone inserted in the joints of coarse masonry: they are stuck in after the work is built: flint walls are very frequently garretted.

Gas. All substances, whether animal, vegetable, or mineral, consisting of carbon, hydrogen, and oxygen, when exposed to a red heat, produce various inflammable elastic fluids capable of furnishing artificial light. The evolution of this elastic fluid may be perceived during the combustion of coal in a common fire. The coal, when heated to a certain degree, swells and kindles, and frequently emits remarkably bright streams of flame, and after a certain period these appearances cease, and the coal glows with a red light.

The flame produced from coal, oil, wax, tallow, or other bodies which are composed of carbon and hydrogen, proceeds from the production of carburetted hydrogen gas, evolved from the combustible body when in an ignited state.

If coal, instead of being burnt in the ordinary way, be submitted to the temperature of ignition in close vessels, all its immediate constituent parts may be collected; the bituminous part is distilled over, in the form of coal-tar, etc., and a large quantity of an aqueous fluid is disengaged at the same time, mixed with a portion of essential oil and various ammoniacal salts. A large quantity of carburetted hydrogen, carbonic oxide, carbonic acid, and sulphuretted hydrogen, also make their appearance, together with small quantities of cyanogen, nitrogen, and free hydrogen, and the fixed base of the coal alone remains behind in the distillatory apparatus, in the form of a carbonaceous substance called *coke*. An analysis of the coal is effected by the process of destructive distillation; and the products which the coal furnishes may be separately collected in different vessels.

The carburetted hydrogen, or coal-gas, when freed from the obnoxious foreign gases, may be propelled in streams out of small apertures, which, when lighted, form jets of flame, now called *gas-lights*.

Mr. Croll has patented an invention for the purification of gas from ammonia, which is effected by means of dilute sulphuric acid applied between the condensers and the ordinary lime purifiers. The vessels are made either of wood or iron, and lined with lead, having a wash-plate similar to the wet-lime purifiers. The radiating bottom is formed of wooden bars, for the purpose of supporting the wash-plate and distributing the gas. In commencing the process, these vessels are charged with water and sulphuric acid in the proportion of 7 lbs. of the latter to 100 gallons of the former. As the acid is neutralized by the ammonia contained in the gas passing through the vessels, the above proportion is kept up by a continuous dropping or running of acid, regulated according to the quantity of ammonia contained in the gas, from a reservoir placed on the top of the saturator. This mode of supplying the acid is continued until the specific gravity of the solution is at 1170, or near the point of crystallization; after which the supply of acid is discontinued, and the liquor retained in the vessel until neutralized: it is then drawn off and evaporated, and yields a pure sulphate of ammonia.

Gas (distribution of, through mains). There is no branch of science connected with the subject of gas engineering so highly important as that which relates to its conveyance and distribution through pipes; there is none in which theory affords more assistance, and there is hardly any branch to which so little attention has been paid. The interests of a gas company are not best served by simply increasing the quantity of gas from the same quantity of coal, or improving the lime machinery, etc. The laying of street-mains forms the most considerable item in the outlay; and by a judicious arrangement in the first instance, much may be saved both at first and last.

It is for the purpose of rendering this branch of the science, and that of the passage of gas through pipes, perfectly plain, that the following observations are here given.

When it is proposed to light any town, or district of a town, with gas, the first step to be taken is to ascertain the number of lights, both public and private, that will be required, with as much accuracy as circumstances will permit; the length of time such lights will have to burn, and the quantity of gas consumed by them per hour, making allowances for the increase of lamps that will probably be required by the extension of the town. The size of the works themselves may be easily ascertained from this calculation. It will then remain to fix upon a proper situation in which to erect them; the best local position is upon the banks of a navigable river or canal, and at the lowest available level, and the nearest approach to such a situation is advisable for obvious reasons. A map of the town must be obtained, or a survey made of the different streets and thoroughfares: running levels must be taken through them at several points, and their respective heights marked with reference to the level of the works as a datum: upon this map all the mains must be drawn, also their branches, valves, and governors. Their arrangement must be such as to allow of a perfect circulation of the gas, and a nearly uniform pressure at the highest and lowest point. All the pipes upon the same level should be joined into one another, and no valves used but such as are necessary to shut off the gas for repair of mains. To supply a higher level, a governor should be placed at the summit of the lower level, with the lower main leading into it. The pipe or pipes for supplying the higher parts should proceed from the regulating vessel. A cellar may be appropriated for the reception of this vessel. One leading main should be taken direct from the works to an equilibrium cylinder situated at some point from which several streets diverge, and no supply taken from this main until it has reached the cylinder. Branches suitable to the supply of each division of the district should lead from this cylinder. The supply of gas to the cylinder should be so regulated as to cause the gas to flow along the branches at an even pressure of about five-tenths of an inch. If the cylinder be at any considerable distance from the works, a smaller main, with *increased* pressure, may lead to it, its size being sufficient to equalize the discharge.

Supposing a district to be lighted requiring 1000 public or street lamps, and 7000 private burners, it is usually considered that each lamp on an average will consume 5 cubic feet of gas per hour, therefore 40,000 cubic feet will be required to light the district for an hour; and the leading main must be capable of delivering that quantity into the equilibrium cylinder in that time. To determine the size of this main, the probable increase of lamps must be taken into consideration; and as that will depend so much upon circumstances in every instance, the judgment of the engineer alone can serve to regulate the additional area. If the increase should be beyond that which was expected, the gas must be forced through the leading main at a greater pressure.

In the above example, if the diameter of main for a *present* consumption be 12 inches, and to secure an adequate supply at any future period its diameter be increased to 15 inches, the *present* working pressure may be reduced to 1·5 of an inch instead of 3 inches; and as the leakage will also be decreased, the extra-sized main will not be found disadvantageous even in the first instance.

Gasometer, a reservoir of gas, with conveniences for measuring its volume. The simplest and most general in use consists of an iron vessel, open at the bottom, and inverted into a tank of water below the surface of the ground, having perfect freedom to rise and fall, and guided by upright rods fixed at several points in the circumference. The diameters and numbers of the vessels will vary according to the magnitude of the works to which the gasometer is attached, and the space to be occupied by it. If the works are situated in a town, where the ground is too valuable to allow an increased extent, a 'telescope gasometer' is employed.

Gas-tar, commonly called *coal-tar*. When the manufacture of gas from coal was in its infancy, great advantages were expected to be derived from the coal-tar which distilled over with the inflammable gas. It was considered to be a substance possessing even superior properties to the vegetable tar for the preservation of timber and other perishable materials exposed to the influences of the weather.

In the year 1665 a German chemist proposed to distil coal for the sole purpose of obtaining this tar, and in 1781 the Earl of Dundonald took out a patent for collecting the tar which appeared during the formation of coke. Neither scheme answered. After a few years' trial, coal-tar as a substitute for vegetable tar fell into disuse. It was tried in the navy, and was found to give the timber a considerable degree of hardness, but not of durability. Its smell is extremely offensive; and since that time it has been used only in places where that is of little consequence. The exposed part of the machinery of a gas establishment may be protected by being coated with coal-tar.

Gasket, plaited cord fastened to the sail-yards of a ship, and used to furl or tie up a sail firmly to the yard, by wrapping it round both six or seven times, the turns being at a competent distance from each other.

Gatchers, the after-leavings of tin.

Gate-house, or park entrance, a structure designed rather to produce an agreeable and picturesque effect, than to accord with any fixed rules or customs of art; such, indeed, was the practice towards the latter end of the sixteenth century, when it would appear, that most men wished to display their taste and learning in architecture. The gate-house also forms an entrance to a private mansion, to any public, municipal, or collegiate building, or to a palace, etc. In the early English architecture, gate-houses, now sometimes called *Lodges*, were large and imposing structures, of great elegance.

Gates and doors are generally, whether arched or square, twice their breadth in height. The former may be ornamented with columns, pilasters, entablatures, pediments, rustics, imposts, archivolts, etc.; the latter with architraves round the sides and top of the opening, and crowned with a frieze and cornice. The cornice in this case is very frequently supported with a console on each side. Columns, pilasters, and other ornaments are also sometimes employed in the decoration of doors.

Inside doors should not be narrower than 2 feet 9 inches, nor is it needful that they exceed 6 feet in height; entrance doors, 3 feet 6 inches to 6 feet 6 inches broad in private dwellings: but in public buildings, where crowds assemble, they must be considerably enlarged. The smallest width for a gate should be 8 feet 6 inches.

As some general rule for the proportion of the architraves of common dressings to doors may be useful, the following directions may be safely followed: Supposing the height of the aperture to represent the height of a column; then, if an architrave, frieze, and cornice, or the first only, be desired, take them in the proportion that would serve for the order itself, and return the architrave down the sides of the door. The whole entablature over a square-headed door should never exceed one-third the height of such aperture.

Gauge (pronounced *gage*), a measure by which the capacity or contents of a cask or vessel may be ascertained. *Gauging* is a term used in mensuration, and applied by engineers in their several operations. *The gauge*, as applied to railways, became a familiar term during the antagonistic discussions respecting the proper distance between the lines of rail; and the *battle of the gauges*, which raged fiercely and expensively, ended, like many similar contentions, in both parties spending enormous sums of money, without the result of victory on either side.

Gauge, a mixture of fine stuff and plaster, or putty and plaster, or coarse stuff and plaster; used in finishing the best ceilings and for mouldings, and sometimes for setting walls.

Gauge-cocks, two or three small cocks fixed in front of the boiler of a steam-engine, for the purpose of ascertaining the height of the water.

Gauge-glass, in locomotive engines, a strong glass tube, connected with the boiler by two cocks attached to the gauge-cock pedestal. The water is admitted to this tube by the lower cock, the steam by the upper cock. It thus becomes an index to what is going on inside the boiler, exhibiting the height or agitation of the water in it. A small cock is placed below the glass for blowing out any sediment which may be deposited in it.

Gauge-lamp, in locomotive engines, a small lamp placed beside the gauge-glass at night, that the state of the water in the boiler may be seen by the engine-man.

Gauntlet, in heraldry, an iron glove: in challenges, the gauntlet was thrown down in defiance.

Gear, furniture, dress, harness: the term is also applied to the several working parts of a locomotive steam-engine.

Generating surface, the heating surface of a boiler, or that on which heat is applied to generate steam.

Gentese, in early English architecture, cusps or featherings in the arch of a doorway.

Geodesy, the art of measuring and surveying of land.

Geometry, the science of quantity, extension, or magnitude.

Geoscopy, a knowledge of the different kinds of earth.

German School of Painting. In early times, a school of painting can hardly be said to have existed in Germany: it was merely a succession of single artists, who derived their manner from different sources of originality and imitation. There were some German painters of eminence when the art, emerging from its barbarous state, first began to be cultivated in Europe; but as they were totally unacquainted with the ancients, and had scarcely access to the works of their contemporaries in Italy, they copied Nature alone, with the exception of somewhat of that stiffness which forms the Gothic manner. This is by no means the case with their successors, some of whom were educated in Flanders, and others in Italy. But if Mengs or Dietrich were comprehended in this school, there would be nothing peculiar to its manner discovered in their works. Albert Dürer was the first German who corrected the bad taste of his countrymen: he excelled in engraving as well as in painting; his genius was fertile, his compositions varied, his thoughts ingenious, and his colours brilliant. His works, though numerous, were finished with great exactness. For an account of this great man and his productions, see the 'Works of Divers Ancient Masters,' in two vols. folio, 1816.

Geology (a treatise or discourse on the earth) "is a term which admits of a very wide interpretation, and naturally suggests to the mind inquiries,—1st, into the formation and original condition of the earth; 2ndly, into the successive modifications which it has undergone, and the agencies by which they have been effected; and 3rdly, into its present condition, and the agencies by which changes in that condition are still effected. The first object of the geologist is to establish, on the principles of inductive reasoning, the science as it depends on each of these inquiries, and then to apply it to the practical purposes of life. It may be premised that a science is practicably valuable just in proportion as its facts have been discovered, and its laws established and studied; for so long as we are uncertain whether a known result has proceeded from a definite cause, we are unable to apply the fact or circumstance to the elucidation of other facts or circumstances; and so long as we are unacquainted with the properties of any substance under our examination, we cannot declare with certainty what share it may have had in the phenomena we have observed. This may be illustrated by a reference to gunpowder. Its explosive quality is the result of its composition, and we can only depend upon the results when we know that the compound has been accurately formed: to ensure, therefore, certainty in the operations depending on it, we must take care that a proper standard of composition has been adhered to. In a similar manner we can only apply geology as a practical science when we have ascertained and made ourselves familiar with those facts which prove the first principles on which it has been founded to be correct and stable." See Col. Portlock's work in the Rudimentary Series, vol. 3.

Gib and key, the fixed wedge and the driving wedge for tightening the strap which holds the brasses at the end of a connecting-rod in steam machinery.

Gibbons (Grinling), the great carver. The time and place of his birth is unknown: he died 1721.

Gimlet, a piece of steel of a cylindrical form, having a transverse handle at the upper end, and at the other, a worm or screw, and a cylindric cavity, called the cup, above the screw, forming, in its transverse section, a crescent. Its use is to bore small holes: the screw draws it forward in the wood, in the act of boring, while it is turned round by the handle: the angle formed by the exterior and interior cylinders cuts the fibres across, and the cup contains the core of wood so cut: the gimlet is turned round by the application of the fingers, on alternate sides of the wooden lever at the top.

Gin, a machine, a pump worked by wheels.

Giocondo (John) was born at Verona. About the middle of the 15th century he became a Dominican, and acquired great reputation in the sciences, the arts, the knowledge of ancient monuments and architecture. He was called into France by Louis XII., and constructed at Paris the Pont-au-Change and the Pont St. Michel. He also constructed other important works in Italy and other countries. He died at an advanced age in 1530.

Giotto built the exquisitely slender tower of Florence in the 13th century in emulation of the stupendous spires which at that era were erected in Germany and the Low Countries. In Italy not a single spire is now seen.

Giotto of the Florentine School. Painting in his hands became so elegant, that none of his school nor of any other, till the time of Masaccio, surpassed or even equalled him, at least in gracefulness of manner. Giotto was born in the country, and was hired a shepherd.

Girders, the longitudinal beams in a floor. Girders are the chief support of a framed floor; their depth is often limited by the size of the timber, but not always so; therefore the method of finding the scantling may be divided into more than in one case. Girders of wrought and cast iron are now extensively used in the construction of bridges, to girt railroads, canals, etc., and many of them are of considerable span.

Gland, the pressing piece of a stuffing-box of a steam-engine.

Glass: this artificial transparent substance was introduced very early. Hollinshed says, an Englishman named Benedict Biscop, who had taken upon him the habit of a monk in Italy, came here with the Archbishop of Rome, in the year 670, and brought painters, glaziers, and other such curious craftsmen into England for the first time.

Glasses superseded small drinking-bowls; they were of Venetian manufacture, and probably first brought here in the 16th century. Earlier they do not appear to have been used in England; nor to have come into much fashion till the time of Elizabeth.

Glass water-gauge. See *Gauge-glass*.

Glazing, the art of fixing glass to the sashes of windows, casements, etc., for the purpose of admitting the light of day; anciently applied to the affixing to windows decorative, stained, and painted glass. A great many beautiful examples exist in this and other countries, of early designs, and of examples in the cinque-cento style: for the latter, see 'Divers Works of Early Masters,' 2 vols. folio, 1846.

Glazing is also a term applied to the finishing of a drawing with some thin, transparent, and glossy tint, through which the first colours appear, and are heightened in their effect.

Glebe, turf, soil; land possessed as part of the revenue of an ecclesiastical benefice.

Glist, a shining black or brown mineral, of an iron cast.

Glossocomon, a machine composed of several dented wheels with pinions, and used for raising great weights.

Glue, a tenacious viscid matter, which is used as a cement by carpenters, joiners, etc. Glues are found to differ very much from each other in their consistence, colour, taste, smell, and solubility. Some will dissolve in cold water, by agitation; while others are soluble only at the point of ebullition. The best glue is generally admitted to be transparent, and of a brown-yellow colour, without either taste or smell. It is perfectly soluble in water, forming a viscous fluid, which when dry preserves both its tenacity and transparency in every part, and has solidity, colour, and viscidity, in proportion to the age and the strength of the animal from which it is produced. To distinguish good glue from bad, it is necessary to hold it between the eye and the light; and if it appears of a strong dark brown colour, and free from cloudy or black spots, it may be pronounced to be good. The best glue may likewise be known by immersing it in cold water for three or four days, and if it swells powerfully without melting, and afterwards regains its former dimensions and properties by being dried, the article is of the best quality.

A small portion of finely levigated chalk is sometimes added to the common solution of glue in water, to strengthen it and fit it for standing the weather.

A glue that will resist both fire and water may be prepared by mixing a handful of quicklime with four ounces of linseed-oil, thoroughly levigated, and then boiled to a good thickness, and kept in the shade, on tin plates, to dry. It may be rendered fit for use by boiling it over a fire in the ordinary manner.

Glyphs, perpendicular flutings or channels used in the Doric frieze.

Gnomon, in dialling, is the style, pin, or cock of a dial, the shadow whereof points out the hours.

Gobbets, stones; a measure or quantity, so called in the time of Edward III.

God the Father (in the Table of Symbols of the early ages) is indicated by a hand issuing from the symbol of heaven, Ezek. li. 9, viii. 3. God the Son, by a monogram and by the cross (the symbol of salvation); by a rock, 1 Cor. x. 4, Exod. xvii. 6; by a lamb, Isaiah lvii. 7, frequently with a glory and carrying a cross; by a pelican, Psalm cii. 6; by a vine, John xv. 1; by a lamp or candle, as light of the world, John ix. 5; by the piscis, a *vesica piscis*, a glory, shaped like a fish. God the Holy Ghost, by the dove, with usually an olive branch; by water, either from the beak of the dove, or from a vase, John iv. 14; by a lamp or candlestick, seven of which ranged to the right and left of the altar, to signify the gifts of the Spirit, Rev. i. 2, iv. 5.

Gola, the Italian term for *cyma*.

Gold, a well-known valuable metal found in many parts of the world, but the greatest quantity was formerly obtained from the coast of Guinea. The produce of California remains to be determined. Gold seems to be the most simple of all substances. It is spoken of in Scripture, and the use of it among the ancient Hebrews, in its native and mixed state, and for the same purposes as at present, was very common. The ark of the covenant was overlaid with pure gold; the mercy seat, the vessels and utensils belonging to the tabernacle, and those also of the House of the Lord, as well as the drinking-vessels of Solomon, were formed of this metal.

Gold occurs, in the metallic state, mixed with several metals, but more commonly with silver and copper, and sometimes pure.

Golden sulphur of antimony, golden yellow, is the hydro-sulphuret of antimony, of an orange colour, which is destroyed by the action of strong light. It is a bad dryer in oil, injurious to many colours, and in no respect an eligible pigment either in oil or water.

Gold purple, or *Cassius's purple* precipitate, the compound oxide which is precipitated upon mixing the solutions of gold and tin. It is not a bright, but a rich and powerful colour, of great durability, varying in degrees of transparency, and in hue from deep crimson to a murrey or dark purple: it is principally used in miniature painting, and may well be employed in enamel painting.

Gondola, a Venetian barge much ornamented, used in the canals of Venice for the convenience of the inhabitants: the common dimensions are 30 feet by 4 feet; each end is terminated by a very sharp point, which is raised perpendicularly to the full height of a man.

Goniometer, an instrument for measuring angles and crystals.

Gossan, an imperfect iron ore, commonly of a tender rotten substance, and of a red or rusty iron colour.

Gothic Architecture, usually so called. Both Mr. Britton and Mr. Pugin have treated of it by the name of 'Christian Architecture.' It had its rise from the Romanesque: this took its origin from Roman remains at the declension of that empire. It became Saxon, then Norman, and varied in its character with the maturity of years. It was Early English, Perpendicular, Decorated, Flamboyant, etc., till it lost its ecclesiastical and monastic character in the Domestic, which prevailed in the Tudor style (Renaissance), followed by the Elizabethan, etc.

Gouge, in carpentry, an instrument like a round hollow chisel.

Governor, the apparatus for regulating the supply of steam to the cylinder so as to give a constant velocity to the engine. It consists of two balls suspended from a vertical spindle, and revolving with it: the suspending rods are connected by arms to a sliding-piece which fits the spindle and acts upon a lever attached to a throttle-valve in the steam-pipe: the balls rise by the centrifugal force as the velocity increases, and close the valve: when the velocity diminishes, the balls fall, and open the valve.

Governor, a contrivance for equalizing the motion of mills and machinery, as well as being used as above described.

Governor balls, the solid metal balls fixed on the ends of the suspending rods of the governor.

Governor (gas). The governor is a machine for regulating and equalizing the flow of gas from the gasometers to the street-mains, and is much more perfect in its action than any slide-valve applied for that purpose requiring attendance. Its use is nowhere sufficiently appreciated. Had it been a complicated piece of machinery, or expensive in its first cost and after-application, objections to its adoption would not have been surprising, —but it is perfectly simple, its action is certain and unvarying, and its first cost inconsiderable.

The velocity of gas in the mains and pipes of supply is, in the first instance, as various as there are differences in their altitudes and extent. A main at one place will furnish, with a certain pressure of gas, a flame one inch high; while at a different altitude it will furnish a flame double that height. If, again, in the direction of the main there are many bends, angles, or contractions in its diameter, the velocity of the gas through it will vary considerably more than if it were direct and uniform. If the pipe be of any great length, and of uniform bore, but unequally furnished with branches, the burners will be unequally supplied with gas: those which are near its head will be supplied with a fuller stream of gas than those which are situated towards its termination.

Independently of these differences, arising from diversity of local positions, there will always be one great variation in the velocity of the gas, occasioned by the variety of periods during which lights are required by different consumers supplied from the same main or system of pipes: for example, when a certain number of burners is to be supplied, and it happens that one-half are shut off sooner than the rest, the velocity of the gas in the mains will be materially increased, and the remaining lamps should be turned down; but many would not be reduced, and much gas would be lost.

Gowan, decomposed granite; but the term is sometimes applied to the solid rock.

Gozzan, oxide of iron and quartz.

Grace is taken for beauty, graceful form or agreeableness of person; for form, friendship, and kindness; for certain gifts of God, which He bestows freely, when, where, and on whom He pleases: such are the gifts of miracles, prophecy, language, etc.

Grace principally consists in the turn that a painter gives to his objects, to render them agreeable,—even those that are inanimate. It is more seldom found in the face than in the manner; for our manner is produced every moment, and can create surprise. A woman can be beautiful but one way, yet she can be graceful a thousand. Grace is neither found in constrained nor in affected manners, but in a certain freedom and ease between two extremes.

Gradation, in painting and drawing, implies the gradual receding of objects into the remote distance, by a proper strength or due diminution of light, shade, and colour, according to their different distances, the quantity of light which shines upon them, and the medium of air through which they are seen.

Gradient, a deviation from a level surface to an inclined plane.

Graduation, the division of philosophical instruments into degrees and other minute parts.

Grain tin, the finest tin, smelted with

charcoal; also the ore of very rich tin sometimes found in the form of grains or pebbles.

Grange, a monastic farming establishment: in ancient times it was common to attach farm-houses and granaries to the estates of religious institutions.

Granite, a natural stone of great strength, hardness, and durability; much used in building: it is a primary and unstratified rock, consisting of quartz, mica, and felspar, each crystallized and cohering, but without any base or cement.

Grapnel, in navigation, a sort of small anchor with four or five flukes or claws, commonly used for boats and small vessels.

Graunge or *Grange*, a granary or farm belonging to a religious house. (*Chaucer*.)

Gravel, a geological term applied to those sabulous soils, or assemblages of worn and rounded stones, which are found scattered on the surface of the earth.

Graver, the burin of an engraver; a square piece of steel fixed in a handle, and bevelled diagonally at the end: an instrument used for turning iron, after it has been roughed out by the 'heel tool,' is so called.

Gravity is that power or force which causes bodies to approach each other. This universal principle, which pervades the whole system of nature, may be enunciated as follows: the mutual tendency of two bodies towards each other increases in the same proportion as their masses are increased, and the square of their distance is decreased; and it decreases in proportion as their masses are decreased, and as the square of their distance is increased.

Gravity is also the force wherewith a body endeavours to descend towards the centre of the earth: this is called *absolute gravity* when the body tends downwards in free space, and *relative gravity* is the force it endeavours to descend with in a fluid. *Terrestrial gravity* is that force by which bodies are urged towards the centre of the earth, and it is measured by the velocity generated in a second of time. Experiments show that a falling body describes $16\frac{1}{12}$ feet in one second, and it has then acquired a velocity of $32\frac{1}{4}$ feet, which is therefore the true measure of the force of gravity.

Gray colour is the third and last, being the nearest in relation of colour to black. In its common acceptation, gray denotes a class of cool cinereous colours, faint in hue; whence we have blue-grays, olive-grays, green-grays, purple-grays, and grays of all hues, in which blue predominates; but no yellow or red grays, the predominance of such hues carrying the compounds into the classes of brown and morrone.

Graywacke, a coarse slate; in geology, a secondary rock.

Grease-cock, a short pipe fixed in the cylinder cover of a steam-engine, with two stop-cocks inserted at a short distance apart, and a funnel at the top for holding tallow. When the upper cock is opened, the tallow falls into the intermediate space; the cock is then closed, and the lower one opened for the melted grease to enter the cylinder, and lubricate the piston without allowing the steam to escape.

Great Circle sailing, the steering of a ship in the arch of a great circle of the sphere. The nearest course between two places.

Green Cloth, the compting-house of the Kings' households.

Greenhouse, a garden-house for choice flowers, etc.

Green verditer is the same in substance as blue verditer, which is converted into green by boiling it.

Green ebony wood, imported from the West Indies, is used for round rulers, turnery, marquetry-work, etc.; it is also much used for dyeing, and contains resinous matter.

Greenheart wood, from the West Indies, resembles cocoa wood in size and bark, and is used for turnery and other works.

Grees, steps; also a staircase.

Gregorian Chant; Cantus Gregorianus, Cantus Firmus, Cantus Planus or Plenus, in Latin; Canto Firmo, in Italian; Plein Chant, in French; Plain Chant, in English; and Choral, in German. This species of music is the most ancient of all, and is still the only one properly adapted to the ritual services of the Christian churches.

The Gregorian chant consists of a few notes, on which the words of the Liturgies are recited. The earliest specimens in existence consist of only one or two notes, and were used by St. Ambrose, at Milan, in the fourth century. The origin of this chant is traced to the earlier churches of Egypt, Thebes, Palestine, Arabia, Phœnicia, Syria, etc., from whence it was introduced into the church of Constantinople by St. John Chrysostom. St. Ambrose is said to have brought it into use in Milan, "after the custom of the inhabitants of the East," and from Milan it came to Rome "long before the time of St. Gregory." But as, in the course of time, various mutations had taken place, St. Gregory, in order to reform and settle the music for the church, made a compilation of such as was fit for its use, and formed the first ritual book of music, or Roman Antiphonarium. From the order which he gave it, and in consequence of this work of Gregory being afterwards established in the other (the Western) churches, it received the name Gregorian. We have very little of the music ascribed to Gregory himself, a specimen of which is given by Mr. Spencer in his work on the church modes, and is very grand. A portion of the old Gregorian chant is still used in our cathedrals in the so-called 'intoning the service' by the minor canons and also in the responses by the choir, but in a very mutilated form. But in the chanting of the prose Psalms, it is almost entirely abandoned; the only specimen (and that somewhat mutilated) being the grand and well-known 'Tallis's chant.' There is a remarkable difference between the Gregorian melodies for the Psalter and Canticles (and which are called the *eight tones*) and those of a more modern date. No such thing as a double chant exists in Gregorian music, and the 'tones' are formed on one general law; *i.e.* a 'tone' consists of one principal note, called the Dominant, *i.e.* the predominant or reciting note, upon which the principal part of each half-verse is chanted, the remainder being inflected in cadences of one or several notes revolving (as it were) above and below the dominant, or terminating on the final of the mode; and it is a law that the reciting parts are always (when the tone is regular) on the same note, viz. the dominant. There are very few instances of any deviation from this rule. In the modern system there seems to be a total absence of any rule of this sort, and the cadences, both in the middle of the verse and at the end, consist of a greater number of notes, and these of unequal value. Moreover, in the Gregorian chant no attention is paid to time; it is regulated entirely by emphasis and syllabic quantity, not by time and accent, as in modern chanting. On Sundays and the greater festivals it is a rule to commence the 'tone' with a few preliminary notes, called the intonation, which serve as in inchoation, or induction to the dominant, or reciting note; on other occasions, these initial notes are not used. For specimens of the adaptation of these Gregorian tones or chants to the canticles, etc., of the English church, see the 'Hymnal,' by Mr. Spencer.

Gregorian music requires a nobler and more rigid harmony than can be given in the modern system; and its effects in the divine offices, when properly harmonized and performed, are far superior to any other kind of church music.

Greut, or *Grit*, a kind of fossil body, consisting of sandy, rough, hard, earthy particles.

Grey. See *Gray.*

Griddle, a large wire sieve, used instead of a hurdle, for sifting and sorting copper ore as it rises from the mine.

Grimbald, an architect, supposed to have introduced the style of architecture usually called Saxon into England.

Grindstone, a cylindrical stone, on which, being turned round its axis, edge-tools are sharpened by applying their edges to the convex surface.

Gripe, the lower part of the knee of the head that connects with the foremost end of the keel of a vessel.

Grit, coarse sand; rough hard particles of sandstone.

Groin, the angle formed by an intersection of vaults; most of the vaulted ceilings of the buildings of the middle ages were groined, and therefore called groined ceilings. During the early part of the Norman style the groins were left purposely plain, but afterwards they were invariably covered with ribs.

Groins, in coast engineering. A groin is a frame of wood-work, constructed across a beach, between high and low water, perpendicular to the general line of it, either to retain the shingle already accumulated, to recover it when lost, or to accumulate more at any particular point; also to break and check the action of the waves.

The component parts of a groin are piles, planking, land-ties, land tie-bars, blocks, tail-piles, and keys and screw-bolts.

The length of a groin depends on the extent, and the requisite strength of its component parts on the nature of the beach on which it is to be constructed. Those at Eastbourne, on the coast of Sussex, of which the following is more particularly a description, are from 150 to 250 feet in length, and the beach at that place being very rough, consisting of coarse heavy shingle and large boulders, they require to be composed of proportionally strong materials to resist its force.

The piles are from 12 to 25 feet long, and 8 by 6½ inches scantling, shod with iron.

The planking is in lengths of 8, 12, and 16 feet, 2½ inches thick, and with parallel edges.

The land-ties are of rough timber from 20 to 25 feet long, and large enough at the butt-end to receive the bars.

The land tie-bars are 13 ft. 6 in. long, and 12 by 5 in. scantling.

The land tie-bar blocks are about 2 feet long, and of the same scantling as the piles.

The land-tie tail-keys are about 2 feet 6 inches long, and 6 by 2½ inches scantling.

The above materials are of oak or beech.

The screw-bolts are of inch round iron, 2 feet 9½ inches and 2 feet 1½ inch long, in equal proportions.

The relative proportions of the component parts are, four piles, one land-tie with tail-piles and keys, one land tie-bar with two blocks, two long and two short bolts, about 180 square feet of planking, and about 140 six-inch spikes for every 17 feet in length; and the expense of a groin, constructed with materials of the above dimensions, may be calculated at about £30 for the same length.

GENERAL RULES OBSERVED IN THE CONSTRUCTION.

When the object, in constructing a groin, is to recover shingle, or accumulate more, the first pile is driven at the high-water mark of neap-tides, leaving its top level with that of spring-tides. The next is driven at the point on the sands, beyond the bottom of the shingle, to which the groin is to extend, leaving about 4 feet of it out of the beach.

The tops of these two piles may be taken for the general slope of the groin, unless the beach should be very steep, and much curved, in which case it becomes necessary to follow its curvature in some degree.

From the high-water mark of neap-tides, the piles are carried back nearly level to that of spring-tides, and as much further as may be considered necessary.

The piles are driven 4 feet asunder from centre to centre, and so as to admit the planking between them alternately, and they should be sunk about two-thirds of their length.

The longest piles are placed between the high-water mark of neap-tides and the bottom of the shingle, particularly from 20 to 40 feet below the former point.

The planking is, if possible, carried down to about two-thirds from the tops of the piles, and kept parallel with them.

The land-ties are placed about one-third from the top of the planking (supposing the latter to commence from the tops of the piles), and their tails are sunk to the level of the bottom of the planking, or as nearly so as possible.

Grotesque. This term, which is now familiar among all the lovers of the art of painting, was by the Italians appropriated to that peculiar manner of composition and invention observed among the antique monumental paintings which were discovered in the subterraneous chambers that had been decorated in the times of the ancient Romans; and as the Italians apply the word Grotto to express every kind of cave or grot, all paintings which were in imitation of the antique designs discovered in those chambers, which for ages had been covered with ruins, are grotesqued or grotesque, which is now applied to English subjects of a quaint and anomalous character.

Grotesque, a name given to the light and fanciful ornaments used formerly to characterize persons and things.

Grotto, a natural or artificial cavern or cave.

Grouan lode, any tin lode which abounds with rough gravel or sand.

Ground-plate or *ground-sill,* the lowest plate of a wooden building for supporting the principal and other posts.

Grounds, pieces of wood fixed to walls and partitions, with their surfaces flush with the plaster, to which the facings or finishings are attached.

Ground table stones, the projecting course of stones in a wall above the plinth.

Ground-ways, large pieces of timber laid across a ship or dock, and upon which the blocks are placed.

Groundwork, in painting, that colour or part on which all the images are drawn.

Grouping is the combining or joining objects in a picture for the satisfaction of the eye, and also for its repose; and although a picture may consist of different groups, yet those groups of objects, managed by the chiaro-oscuro, should all tend to unity, and one only should predominate.

Guag, Cornish. Tinners, holeing into a place which has been wrought before, call it holeing in guag.

Gudgeon, the iron pins fixed in a beam or wooden shaft for bearings.

Gudgeons, in ship-building, are eyes driven into the stern-post, to hang the rudder on.

Guide-blocks, pieces of metal with parallel sides, fitted on the ends of a cross-head of a steam-engine, to slide in grooves in the side frames, and keep the motion of the piston-rod in a direct line.

Guilloche, an ornament used in classical architecture, formed by two or more intertwining bands.

Gulf of ore; a lode which throws up very great quantities of ore, and proves lasting and good in depth, is so called.

Gum wood, or *blue gum wood*, is the produce of New South Wales, sent over in large logs and planks, similar to dark Spanish mahogany: it is used in ship-building, etc.

Gun-boats were first made in this country with condensing engines, but of late a few have been made with non-condensing or high-pressure engines, which latter kind are found more convenient where fresh supplies of fuel can be readily obtained.

Gundulf of Rochester, 1077-1107. His works are seen at Rochester, Canterbury, and Peterborough.

Gun-metal, a mixed metal, an alloy of copper and tin.

Gunnies, in Cornish, a term applied to breadth or width: single gunnies are 3 feet wide.

Gunter's chain, the chain in common use for measuring land: the length of the chain is 66 feet, or 22 yards, or 4 poles of 5½ yards each; it is divided into 100 links of 7·92 inches each. *See* Acre.

Gunwale, or *gunnel*, in ship-building, the piece of timber which reaches on either side of the ship from the half-deck to the forecastle.—The plank that covers the heads of the timbers between the fore and main drifts.

Gussets, as understood in mechanical construction, are brackets or angular pieces of iron, to strengthen, to keep steady, and support a structure.—In the construction of the rectangular covered openings of the Britannia and Conway iron bridges, gussets are used extensively in the interior, consisting of double triangular plates riveted to the bottom and sides of the plates of the bridge, as a series of brackets (and at the top and either side also), to aid to the strength and durability of these extraordinary works, and as a counter-effort to the tendency of strain on the lower sides to separate or open the joints, and on the upper side to force them closer together.

Gusto, a term used by the Italians, signifying taste in the design of the attitudes, good arrangement, and composition of a picture.

Guttæ, ornaments resembling drops, placed in the epistylium of the Doric order below the triglyphs. They occur likewise in the under face of the mutules in the Doric corona. They are supposed to have originated from the intention to represent drops of water running off the roof, adhered to the under surface of the canterii or rafters of early buildings.

Gybing, in navigation, the shifting of any boom-sail from one side of the mast to the other.

Gymnasium, a public building used by the Greeks for the practice and exercise of gymnastics, or muscular development; also a place, according to Vitruvius, for amusements and scientific recreation.

Gynæceum, in Greek architecture, the apartment of the females in the interior of the house; the nursery.

Gypsoplaste, a cast taken in plaster of Paris or white lime.

Gypsum, sulphate of lime, called also plaster of Paris.

H.

Hade of Veins is the mining-term for that inclination which nearly all veins have from a perpendicular direction. Thus, a vein is said to hade to the north when it inclines further north. In Weardale, the veins mostly hade to the south.

Half-bloom, a round mass of metal,

which comes out of the fluing of an iron work.

Half-pace, or *Haute-pace*, a raised floor in a bay window.

Half-timbered houses: this mode of constructing domestic buildings was practised in England and on the Continent during the reigns of Henry VIII. and Elizabeth. It was peculiarly of a picturesque character; the foundations and principal supports were of stout timber, and the interstices of the fronts were filled with plaster. In many cases the ornamental timber framing was of a dark colour, which, with the barge-board gable, gave the whole an exceedingly interesting appearance. There are yet remaining some very fine examples in England, particularly in the western and north-western counties.

Half-timbers, in ship-building, those timbers in the cant-bodies which are answerable to the lower futtocks in the square body.

Hall, the principal apartment in the domestic houses of the middle ages; a place of assembly; a spacious building attached to inns of court.

Halliards, in navigation, the ropes or tackles usually employed to hoist or lower any sail on its respective mast.

Haly-work folk, people who hold land for repairing or defending a church or tombs, on which account they were freed from feudal and military service.

Hallyings, the hangings of a hall.

Halvans, in Cornish, the refuse ore.

Ham (Saxon), a house, home, farm, or village.

Hamburg lake is a colour of great power and depth; rather purplish, or inclining to crimson; it dries with extreme difficulty, but differs in no other essential quality from other cochineal lakes.

Hamlet, a street or village, a dwelling place.

Hammer-beams, horizontal pieces of timber, frequently used in the roofs of old English buildings, in pairs on the opposite sides of the same roof; often used also in the principals of Gothic roofs, to strengthen the framing and to diminish the lateral pressure that falls upon the walls.

Haunces, in architecture, ends of elliptical arches, which are arcs of smaller circles than the scheme or middle part of the arch.

Hand-brace, a tool for boring, consisting of a cranked spindle, at one end of which a broad head or breast-plate is attached by a swivel, so that it may remain stationary while the crank is turned; at the other end is a socket, into which a drill can be fixed.

Hand-drilling machine, a small drilling machine turned by manual labour.

Hand-gear, in a locomotive engine, the handles of the working gear, placed conveniently to the foot-plate so as to be within reach of the engine-man when he requires to use them for regulating the different parts of the engine.

Hand-hook, an instrument made by smiths to twist square iron.

Hand-pump, in a locomotive engine, the pump placed by the side of the fire-box, to be worked by a hand-lever when the engine has to stand with steam up.

Hand-railing, in a locomotive engine, the railing along the sides of the engine, to protect persons passing to the front of the engine for any necessary purpose.

Hand-saw, a saw from 12 to 16 inches in length, fixed in an iron frame, with a handle at one end; used for cutting wood or metal.

Hand-screw, a jack, an instrument for raising heavy timber.

Hand-spike, a wooden lever for moving heavy things.

Hand-vice, a small vice which is held in the hand.

Harbourage, shelter, or entertainment. "Crave harbourage within your city walls."—*Shakspeare*.

Harmony is the general accordance of the objects in a painting with one another, and their subordination to the principal object; so that all unite to constitute a pleasing whole. It is effected by a due combination of lights and shades, by the union and colour, or by such contrasts as are sufficient to relieve the distant groups.

Harmony of colours. Lessons in colouring have ever been given, notwithstanding it is a part so principal in painting, that it has its rules founded on science and reason. Without such study, it is impossible that youth can acquire a good taste in colouring, or understand harmony.

Harpings, pieces of oak which hold the timbers of the fore-and-aft cant-bodies till a ship is planked.

Hatches, the coverings for the hatchways of a ship, made with ledges, and laid with oak or deal, and caulked.

Hatches, flood-gates in a river to stop the current of the water.

Hatching is shadowing with a blacklead pencil or pen: it is done either in straight lines or zigzag strokes, such as are seen in pencil drawings, or in pencilled backgrounds. It is used by engravers in etching.

Hatchways, places in the middle of the decks of a vessel, for the convenience of lowering down goods.

Haul the wind, in navigation, to direct the ship's course nearer to the point of the compass from which the wind blows.

Haunch of an arch, the part between the vertex and the springing.

Hawker, a vessel built like a pink, but masted and rigged like a hoy.

Haws, in Domesday Book, mansions or dwelling-houses.

Hawse, in navigation, the situation of the cables before the ship's stern when she is moored with two anchors forward from the starboard and larboard bow.

Hawse-pieces, the timbers in the bow of a ship whose sides are nearly parallel to the middle line.

Hawthorn, a wood not much used, is hard, and of a whitish colour, with a tinge of yellow.

Hazel, a small underwood, which is very elastic, used for turning, for the handles of blacksmiths' chisels, for the hoops of casks, etc.

Head-ledges, the thwartship pieces which frame the hatch-ways or ladder-ways of ships.

Head-stocks, the frames which support the centres of a lathe; viz. the mandril-frame and the poppethead, or back centre frame.

Head-tin, a preparation of tin-ore towards the fitting it for working into metal.

Headers, in masonry, stones extending over the thickness of a wall; and in bricklaying, the bricks which are laid lengthwise across the thickness of the wall are called headers.

Heads, tiles which are laid at the eaves of a house.

Healing, the covering a roof with lead, tin, slates, etc.

Health of Towns, a phrase recently coined to express the general purpose of public sanatory measures. These measures are based upon the principles of animal physiology, but had been recognized only in the curative policy of the physician, until the evils of their neglect were traced by statistical inquiries into the causes of disease; and they are therefore now properly regarded as essential objects in the social economy of life.

The human constitution is so formed that its health depends on an adequate supply of pure air, water, and light. Every circumstance, therefore, which vitiates the quality, or reduces the due quantity, of these essentials, is injurious to health, and demands amendment or extinction.

Thus the efficient supply of pure and attemperated air requires proper drainage and ventilation, warming or cooling of all places in which human beings live or congregate: it also limits the minimum of size for the healthy habitations of men.

The plentiful supply of pure water necessitates suitable provision for obtaining and treating it, and the proscription of all arrangements which limit the service or injure its purity. Equally important with these conditions is the third one enumerated, which suggests the necessity of so arranging and constructing streets and buildings, that abundance of light may at all times be admitted into them.

As measures auxiliary to these objects, and of great importance in the combined arrangements of society, public exercising and pleasure grounds, baths and wash-houses, cooking apparatus, medical and remedial establishments, street accommodations, etc., command adoption, and, when adequately carried out, will tend to complete the physical requisites of the health of towns.

Heat, in the ordinary application of the word, signifies, or rather implies, the sensation experienced upon touching a body hotter, or of a higher temperature, than the part or parts which we bring into contact with it; in another sense, it is used to express the cause of that sensation. To avoid any ambiguity that may arise from this double use of the same expression, it is usual and proper to employ the word *caloric* to signify the principle or cause of the sensation of heat. On touching a hot body, caloric passes from it, and excites the feeling of warmth; when we touch a body having a lower temperature than our hand, caloric passes from the hand to it, and thus arises the sensation of cold.

Caloric is usually treated of as if it were a material substance; but, like light and electricity, its true nature has yet to be determined.

COMMUNICATION OF CALORIC.

Caloric passes through different bodies with different degrees of velocity. This has led to the division of bodies into *conductors* and non-conductors of caloric: the former includes such bodies as metals, which allow caloric to pass freely through their substance; and the latter comprises those that do not give an easy passage to it, such as stones, glass, wood, charcoal, etc.

Table of the relative conducting power of different bodies.

Gold	1000
Platinum	981
Silver	973
Copper	898
Iron	374
Zinc	363
Tin	304
Lead	180
Marble	24
Porcelain	12.2
Fire-brick	11
Fire-clay	11.4

With Water as the standard.

Water	10
Pine	39
Lime	39
Oak	33
Elm	32
Ash	31
Apple	28
Ebony	22

Relative conducting power of different substances compared with each other.

Hares' fur	1.315
Eider-down	1.305
Beavers' fur	1.296
Raw silk	1.284
Wool	1.116
Lamp-black	1.117
Cotton	1.046
Lint	1.032
Charcoal	.937
Ashes (wood)	.927
Sewing silk	.917
Air	.576

Relative conducting power of fluids.

Mercury	1.000
Water	.357
Proof Spirit	.312
Alcohol (pure)	.232

RADIATION OF CALORIC.

When heated bodies are exposed to the air, they lose portions of their heat, by projection in right lines into space, from all parts of their surface.

Bodies which radiate heat best, absorb it best.

Radiation is affected by the nature of the surface of the body: thus black and rough surfaces radiate and absorb more heat than light and polished surfaces.

Table of the radiating power of different bodies.

Water	100
Lamp-black	100
Writing-paper	100
Glass	90
Indian ink	88
Bright lead	19
Silver	12
Blackened tin	100
Clean do.	12
Scraped do.	16
Ice	85
Mercury	20
Polished iron	15
Copper	12

Professor Leslie has proved, by a variety of experiments, that the heat which is propagated by radiation from different bodies varies with the nature of their external surfaces; the quantity which flows in a given time from a body with a polished surface being much less than would flow from the same body with a rough surface. It therefore follows that the external surfaces of the steam-pipes of steam-engines and steam-cylinders should be as smooth as possible, and should be covered with any body which is a bad conductor of heat.

Heaven (in the Table of Symbols of the early ages) is symbolized by the segment of a circle, sometimes of blue or of the three colours of the rainbow; the Universe, by a globe of blue.

Heckler (Jean Geo.), born in 1629, became in 1654 architect of the cathedral of Strasburg, and died in 1669.

Heel tool, a tool used by turners for roughing out a piece of iron, or turning it to somewhat near the intended size: it has a very acute cutting edge and an angular base or heel.

Height of columns. The height of a column is measured by its diameter immediately above the base.

	Diameters high.
The Tuscan column	7
The Ionic	9
Corinthian and Composite	10

In the above heights are included the capitals and bases, which are esteemed parts of the columns with which they are used.

Heights and Distances. Trigonometry receives its principal practical application in the operations of surveying, and measuring heights and distances; as, however, the methods of its application (depending on the peculiar circumstances of each case) are exceedingly various, no general rules can be specified.

The instruments employed to measure angles are quadrants, sextants, theodolites, etc., the use of either of which may be sooner learned from an examination of the instruments themselves than from any description independently of them. For military men and for civil engineers, a good pocket sextant and an accurate micrometer (such as Cavallo's), attached to a telescope, are highly useful. For measuring small distances, as bases, 50-feet and 100-feet chains and a portable box of graduated tape will be necessary.

For the purposes of surveying, it is usual to employ a chain 66 feet in length, subdivided into 100 links, each 7·92 inches: the reason for using a chain of this length is, that ten of such square chains are equal to an acre, and therefore the acreage of the several divisions of an estate is found with much greater facility when measured in chains and links, than when the measurements are taken in feet.

Heil, to cover, to tile. Wat Tyler was called Wat the Heiler.

Helix, the small volute under the abacus of a Corinthian capital.

Helix, anything of a spiral form, whether in one plane, as the spiral curve, or in different planes, as the screw.

Hemlock spruce forms a large proportion of the evergreen forests of New Brunswick, and is abundantly multiplied in every favourable situation. The wood of the hemlock spruce is firmer than that of the white pine; although coarser-grained, it gives better hold to nails, and offers more resistance to the impression of other bodies.

Hengin, a prison, or house of correction.

Heptagon, in geometry, a figure with seven sides or angles.

Heraldry is a science intimately connected with the early history of Europe, its chivalry, its conquests, and the bearing of arms: it teaches how to blazon or explain in proper terms all that belongs to arms; and how to marshal or dispose with extreme punctualness divers arms on a field. It is in its archæology and in precedent indisputable. It teaches whatever relates to the marshalling of solemn processions and other public ceremonies, at coronations, installations of Knights of the Garter, Knights Grand Cross of the Bath, Knights Companions, etc.; at the creation of peers, nuptials, christenings of princes, funerals, etc. It is, in fact, an important science, particularly in English history, in tracing the narrative of the families of the nobility and commoners, their holdings, their distinguishing qualifications, in arms, in literature, and in the arts.

Hermæ, statues of which only the head is carved, and sometimes a portion of the bust: square or cubical figures of the god Mercury, without legs and arms, anciently placed by the Greeks and Romans at their cross-ways.

Herring-bone work, masonry in which the stones are laid aslant instead of being bedded flat.

Herse, a portcullis; a frame whereon lighted candles were placed at the obsequies of distinguished persons.

Heterogeneous, opposite or dissimilar in nature, as opposed to homogeneous.

Hewns, in Cornwall, the sides of a calciner or burning-house furnace; so called from their being formerly built with hewn moor-stone.

Hexagon, in geometry, a figure of six sides or angles.

Hexahedron, in geometry, one of the five regular solids, being the same with a cube.

Hexastyle, a portico of six columns in front.

Hexastylos, a frontage of six columns.

Hexeres, a vessel with six banks of oars on each side.

Hiatus, an aperture, a breach or defect.

Hick's mandril, an arbor for turning rings: at the centre of the arbor there is a cone, round which, at equal distances, wedges are fitted into dove-tailed grooves, and are expanded to the bore of the ring by a nut acting on a screw at the end of the cone.

Hickory or *white walnut*, a native of America. The wood of the young trees is exceedingly tough and flexible, and makes excellent hand-spikes, etc.

Hieroglyphic, an emblem, a figure by which a word is implied; the Egyptian art of writing in picture.

High-pressure engine, a non-condensing steam-engine, worked by the excess of the pressure of the steam upon the piston above the pressure of the atmosphere: in this engine, after the steam has acted upon the piston, it passes through the eduction-pipe into the air.

Hiling, the covering or roof of a building.

Hinges, the joints on which doors, gates, etc., turn.

Hinges. The diversity of forms into which door furniture has been resolved is almost endless. Many of the ancient hinges were not only wrought into scrolls and other florid devices, but occasionally further enriched with inscriptions.

Hip, the external angle formed by the meeting of the sloping sides of roofs which have their wall-plates running in different directions.

Hip-knob, a pinnacle, finial, or other similar ornament, placed on the top of the hips of a roof or the point of a gable.

Hippodrome, a large plot of ground laid out for the exercise of horses; among the Greeks, a race-course.

Hogarth (William) was born in London in 1697. During his struggles to quit silver plate engraving and to fit himself for an artist, Hogarth writes: " I had learned by practice to copy with tolerable correctness in the ordinary way, but it occurred to me that there were many disadvantages attending this method of study, as having faulty originals, and even when the pictures or prints to be imitated were by the best masters, it was little more than pouring water out of one vessel into another;" again, " Many reasons led me to wish that I could find the shorter path, fix forms and characters in my mind, and instead of copying the lines, try to read the language, and, if possible, find the grammar of the art, by bringing into one focus the various observations I had made, and then trying by my power on the canvas how far my plan enabled me to combine and apply them to practice. For this purpose I considered what various ways, and to what different purposes, the memory might be applied; and fell upon one most suitable to my situation and idle disposition; laying it down as an axiom, that he who could by any means acquire and retain in his memory perfect ideas of the subjects he meant to draw, would have as clear a knowledge of the figure as a man who can write freely hath of the twenty-five letters of the alphabet, and their infinite combinations."—Hogarth supported himself by the sale of his prints—the prices of his paintings kept pace neither with his fame nor with his expectations. In January, 1745, he offered for sale the six paintings of the Harlot's Progress, the eight paintings of the Rake's Progress, the Four Times a Day, and the Strolling Actresses, and received only £427. 7s. for his nineteen pictures. In June, 1750, the six pictures of Marriage-à-la-Mode were sold by public auction for £110; in 1797 they were sold to Angerstein for £1381. The four Election Pictures, begun in 1755 and finished in 1758, were sold for £200, and subsequently were sold to Sir John Soane for £1732.

Hoggan, in Cornish, a hawthorn-berry, the tinner's pasty.

Hogging, in ship-building, the convex appearance resembling the back of a hog, given to a ship after being first launched, by the dropping of the two extremities.

Hogshead, a measure of 63 gallons.

Hoist, an apparatus for raising bodies from the ground-floor of a building to a floor above.

Holle (Henry), of York, designed in 1612 several buildings. It is conjectured that he designed and completed the garden quadrangle building at Merton in 1610, and the whole of Wadham College cost £11,360.

Hollow newel, an opening in the middle of a staircase, the steps only being supported at one end by the surrounding wall, the ends next the hollow unsupported; also a hollow groin, pier, of brick or stone, made behind the lock-gates of canals.

Holly is a very clean, fine-grained wood, the whitest and most costly of those used by the Tunbridge-ware manufacturers: it is used for painted screens and a great variety of fancy and tasteful purposes.

Holy Trinity (The), in the Table of Symbols of the early ages, by the three-coloured rainbow, encircling our Saviour, the visible form of the Deity, who is sometimes seated on it, Ezek. i. 28, Rev. iv. 3; by the beams of light from the hand of Christ; by the extension of the thumb, fore and middle fingers of the Saviour's hand as held in giving the benediction.

Holy-water vessel, the vessel which contains the consecrated or holy water carried in religious processions; also the receptacle for holy water placed at the entrances of Roman Catholic churches.

Holy-water stone, the stoup on which the holy-water vessel is placed.

Holy-work folk, people who hold lands for repairing or defending a church or tombs, on which account they were freed from feudal and military service.

Homestall, or *Homestead*, a mansion, house, or seat in the country; a farm, with the land adjoining.

Homogeneous, a term applied to various substances, to denote that they consist of similar parts, or parts of the same nature and kind.

Hoodings-ends, the ends of planks which fit into the rabbets of the stem and stern-post of a ship.

Hood-mould, a band or string over the head of a door, window, or other opening, in an ancient building; so called from its enclosing, as within a hood, the inferior mouldings and the opening itself.

Hood-moulding, a name given to the label-moulding.

Hook-pins, taper iron pins, only with a hook head, to pin the frame of a roof or floor together.

Hops, Hop-drying. The art of drying hops has been much improved of late years; emulation amongst landlords and tenant-farmers, in regard to the construction of their oasts, has led to this. Hop-drying is a process of desiccation, of which the object is to drive off the superfluous moisture from the hops. Hot wind generally dries more quickly than a cold one; that which has the highest temperature will absorb moisture from any substance over which it passes more rapidly than the cooler current will. It is not, however, so generally apprehended that the converse of the above proposition is also true, and that, with equal temperatures, that substance over which most air passes in a given time will part with a larger portion of its moisture. The application of the latter principle has been illustrated in low-temperature drying, which has been managed by introducing a considerable quantity of external air into the space beneath the hair, by knocking holes in the external walls. Experiments of this sort have been held to be conclusive as to the superiority of low-temperature drying. This, however, is not exactly the case, because as much heat would pass through the hops as before, so long as the fires were kept up as usual; and the true explanation of the circumstance is that the improved drying is due to the larger quantity of air passed through the hops, rather than to the temperature being reduced. If the fires had been lessened, the temperature might have been lowered as much as was done by the admission of cold air; but in that case the hops, instead of drying better, would have been found not to dry so well as at the higher temperature. The questions which are for consideration are, the quantity of air necessary to be admitted; the mode of its admission; the method of heating the air; the proportion and construction of the kiln necessary to give full effect to the above arrangements. The quantity of air to be admitted is dependent upon the temperature at which the drying is to be conducted, and upon the weight of moisture to be evaporated. Air at various temperatures has an ascertained capacity for moisture. When fully saturated,—

Air at 32 deg. contains 1-160th ⎫
  „   59   „   1-80th   ⎪
  „   86   „   1-40th   ⎬ of its weight of water.
  „ 113   „   1-20th   ⎪
  „ 140   „   1-10th   ⎪
  „ 167   „   1-5th   ⎪
  „ 194   „   2-5th   ⎪
  „ 221   „   4-5th   ⎭

The capacity of air for moisture being doubled by each accession of 27 degrees of Fahrenheit. If, then, we desire to know what quantity of air should be admitted to carry off a given weight of moisture at any of the above-named temperatures, we have only to multiply the weight of moisture by the increased capacity for moisture due to air raised from the temperature of the external atmosphere to that of the kiln. Supposing the weight of water to be evaporated to be 7 cwt., the temperature of the external air 59 degrees, and that of the kiln 113 degrees, 186 cwt. of air would be required to carry off this quantity of moisture. About 13 cubic feet of air weigh a pound, and rather more than 270,000 cubic feet of air must therefore be passed through the kiln during the time of drying. If we suppose this operation to be continued for ten hours, this will give 27,000 feet per hour, or about eight feet per second. To allow of the passage of so large a quantity of air, the openings for its admission must be of a corresponding area; and as it is better to admit too much air than too little, it would be well to adopt something like the following proportions of openings:—

6 ft. superficial for a 16 ft. kiln.
8   „   „   18   „
10 „   „   20   „
12 „   „   22   „

The method of heating the kiln has been generally regarded as the most important point connected with hop-drying. The requisite conditions are, that the heating surfaces should be largely extended, and that the contact of the air-currents with the heated material should be perfect over the whole surface. Where the former of these conditions does not obtain, a larger quantity of air cannot be heated. In an open fire, the heating surfaces are nearly as the area of the fire-bars; in a common cockle they may be estimated as about 2-2½ to 1; and in the improved stove, or evaporator, they are as about 30 to 1. The peculiarities in the construction of the improved stove are:—The situation of the fire in the centre or heart of the stove at a distance from the outer surfaces, which cannot therefore become overheated to the extent that takes place where the fuel is in direct contact with the sides. The exceedingly small size of the fire-grate as compared with the area of the fire bars, either of open fires or of ordinary cockles, and the consequent diminution in the consumption of fuel. It has been stated upon competent authority that the cost of drying hops by ordinary cockles was about 10d. per cwt., as compared with 3s. where open fires and charcoal were used. By the improved stove, the loading of a sixteen-feet kiln might certainly be dried with one cwt. of coals. The more perfect combustion of the fuel effected by lining the furnace with fire-brick and the higher temperature thereby induced have much to do with the efficiency of the stove. The common cockle being heated entirely by radiated heat, absorbs none of the heat from the smoke, which would escape at a very high temperature if a further portion of caloric were not abstracted from it in its circuit of the horizontal flues. The principle of bringing the air as it becomes warmed, in successive contact with still more highly-heated portions of the stove, is pursued throughout. The sides of the stove are surrounded by a brick wall, at a distance of about six inches from the stove at the narrowest part. This wall confines the air in its ascent, pressing it as it were against the sides, which are made to overhang, in order to give more perfect contact. On reaching the upper part of the side channels the current of warmed air is deflected by inclined cast-iron plates, and made to traverse the pyramidal top of the stove, where it receives its last portion of heat, and then escapes upwards through the tubes with which the deflecting plates are perforated. It is desirable in building kilns to use every precaution to prevent the loss of heat by radiation to the surrounding atmosphere. This may be effected by building the external walls hollow, or with hollow bricks. An inner circle answers nearly the same purpose if there is a door to shut off the communication with the shed, and no openings through the external walls. The roofs should also be plastered with lime and hair under the tiles before the inner plastering is done. Attention to this point and to carefully stopping all air-passages at the foot of the rafters, will prevent the condensation of the reek upon the interior of the kiln.

Hornbeam, a very tough and stringy European wood, used by millwrights for the cogs of wheels; also for plumbers' dressers, or mallets, etc.

Hornblende, a conspicuous ingredient in the composition of rocks, divided into common hornblende, hornblende-schist, and basaltic hornblende.

Horn-stone, a conchoidal and siliceous mineral substance, allied in composition to flint, but of a more earthy texture.

Horography, the art of constructing dials.

Horologium, a name anciently given to any instrument for measuring time.

Horse, a large round bar of iron fixed in the head of a ship.

Horse, in navigation, the name of a rope reaching from the middle of a yard to its extremity, on which the sailors stand when they are loosing or reefing the sails.

Horse-chestnut wood is one of the white woods used by the Tunbridge turners; it is close and soft, even in the grain, and is much used for brush-backs, etc.

Horse-power. Although horses are not all of one strength, yet there is a certain force now generally agreed upon among those who construct steam-engines, which force is denominated a *horse's power*, and hence steam-engines are distinguished in size by the number of horses' power to which they are said to be equal.

The measure of a mechanical effect equal to a horse's power has been much disputed: this, however, can be but a matter of little consequence, if the measure be generally understood, since there is no such thing as bringing it into any real measure. Some horses will perform double the work of others, and those of one country will work more than those of another. Desaguliers' measure is, that a horse will walk at the rate of 2¼ miles per hour, against a resistance of 200 lbs., and this gives, as a number for comparison, 44,000; that is, the raising of 1 lb. 44,000 feet in a minute, or, what amounts to the same, the raising of 44,000 lbs. 1 foot in a minute.

Emerson's measure is the same as Desaguliers', and Smeaton's result is 22,916 lbs. under the same circumstances.

James Watt found, from repeated experiments, that 33,000 lbs. 1 foot per minute was the average value of a horse's power: but his engines were calculated to work equal to 44,000 lbs. 1 foot per minute.

H.P., the abbreviation for horse-power.

Hortus, a garden or pleasure-ground.

Hose-pipes, in locomotive engines, elastic pipes made of canvas, saturated with a solution of India-rubber, sometimes galvanized, and forming a good elastic connection between the engine and tender feed-pipes. They are now generally used in preference to ball-and-socket connections for conveying the steam to the tender.

Hospitalia, anciently the doorways in the scene of a theatre on the right and left of the valvæ regiæ or principal doorway; so called because the movable scenes, representing inns or places appropriated for the reception of strangers, were placed near them.

Hospitals were originally designed for the relief of poor and impotent persons, and the entertainment of travellers upon the road, particularly of pilgrims, and therefore they were generally built upon the road-side; in later time they have always been founded for fixed inhabitants; before the spoliation, there existed in England above 358 of these houses of relief.

Hostelry, or *Hostry*, anciently an inn.

Hot-air blast. It was conceived that the presence of sulphur in the air was the cause of blast furnaces working irregularly and making bad iron in the summer months. Subsequently it was stated that one of the Muirkirk iron furnaces, in Scotland, situated at a considerable distance from the engine, did not work so well as the others, which led to the conjecture that the friction of the air, in passing along the pipe, prevented an equal volume of the air getting to the distant furnace as to the one which was situated close by the engine: it was considered also, that by heating the air at the distant furnace, its volume would increase in the ratio of the known law, that air and gases expand to double their bulk at 448° temperature.

Example: If 1000 cubic feet, say at 50° of Fahrenheit, were pressed by the engine in a given time, and heated to 600° of Fahrenheit, it would then be increased in volume to 2104·4, and so on for every thousand feet that would be blown into the furnace. In prosecuting the experiments which this idea suggested, circumstances, however, became apparent which induced a belief, that heating the air introduced for supporting combustion into air-furnaces materially increased its efficiency in this respect; and with the view of putting these suspicions to the test, the following experiments were made.

To the nozzle of a pair of common smith's bellows, a cast-iron vessel heated is attached from beneath, in the manner of a retort for generating gas, and to this vessel the blow-pipe, by which the forge or furnace was blown, was also attached. The air from the bellows having thus to pass through the heated vessel above mentioned, was consequently heated to a high temperature before it entered the forge fire, and the result produced, in increasing the intensity of the heat in the furnace, was far beyond expectation, and so evident as to make apparent the fallacy of the generally received opinion, that the coldness of the air of the atmosphere in the winter months was the cause of the best iron being then produced.

In overthrowing the old theory, new principles in the process of iron-making were established.

Experiments on the large scale, to reduce iron ore in a founder's cupola, were commenced at the Clyde Iron-works. These experiments were completely successful, and in consequence the invention was immediately adopted at the Calder Iron-works, where the blast, being made to pass through two retorts placed on each side of one of the large furnaces before entering the furnace, effected an instantaneous change, both in the quantity and quality of iron produced, and a considerable saving of fuel.

The whole of the furnaces at the Calder and Clyde Iron-works were fitted up on the principle of the hot blast, and its use at these works continues to be attended with the utmost success; it has also been adopted at Wilsontown and Gartshirrie Iron-works in Scotland, and at several works in England and France.

The air as at first raised to 250° of Fahrenheit, produced a saving of three-sevenths in every ton of pig-iron made, and the heating apparatus having since been enlarged, so as to increase the temperature of the blast to 600° Fahrenheit and upwards, a proportional saving of fuel is effected; and an immense additional saving is also acquired by the use of raw coal instead of coke, which may now be adopted. By thus increasing the heat of the blast, the whole waste incurred in burning the coal into coke is avoided in the process of making iron.

By the use of this invention, with three-sevenths of the fuel formerly employed in the cold-air process, the iron-maker is now enabled to make one-third more iron of a superior quality.

Were the hot blast generally adopted, the saving to the country in the article of coal would be immense. In Britain, about 700,000 tons of iron are made annually, of which 50,000 tons only are produced in Scotland: on these 50,000 tons would be saved, in the process of manufacture, 200,000 tons of coal annually. In England the saving would be in proportion to the strength and quality of the coal, and cannot be computed at less than 1,520,000 tons annually; and taking the price of coals at the low rate of four shillings per ton, a yearly saving of £296,000 sterling would be effected.

Nor are the advantages of this invention solely confined to iron-making: by its use the founder can cast into roods an equal quantity of iron in much less time, and with a saving of nearly half the fuel employed in the cold-air process; and the blacksmith can produce in the same time one-third more work, with much less fuel than he formerly required.

In all the processes of metallurgical science it will be found of the utmost importance in reducing the ores to a metallic state.

Hospitium, in old writers, an inn or a monastery, built for the reception of strangers and travellers.

Hot-house, a glass building used in gardening, and including stoves, conservatories, etc.

Hot-water pump, the feed-pump of a condensing engine, for supplying the boiler from the hot well.

Hot well, the vessel which receives the water from the air-pump.

Hour-glass stand, a bracket or frame of iron for receiving the hour-glass. See 'Papers on Architecture,' vol. iii., which contains a good example. "By the side of the pulpit still remains the ancient hour-glass and frame."

House, a place of residence. The purpose of a house being for dwelling, and that of tents being the same, they are called by one name in the Hebrew; on the same principle, the Tabernacle of God, though only a tent, is sometimes called the Temple, that is, the residence of God. The ordinary buildings or houses in the East have continued the same from the earliest ages, without the least alteration or improvement;—large doors, spacious chambers, marble pavements, cloistered courts, with fountains, etc.,—conveniences well adapted to the circumstances of these climates, where the summer heats are generally intense. The streets of these cities, the better to shade them from the sun, are usually narrow, with sometimes a range of shops on each side. On entering one of the principal houses, a porch or gateway will first be seen, with benches on each side, where the master of the family receives visits and despatches business. In houses of better fashion, the chambers are hung with velvet or damask from the middle of the wall downwards, and covered and adorned with velvet or damask hangings of white, blue, red, green, or other colours. The ceiling is generally of wainscot, either very artistically painted, or else thrown into a variety of panels with gilded mouldings, and with scrolls of the Koran, etc. The stairs are sometimes placed in the porch, sometimes at the entrance into the court. When there is one or more stories, they are afterwards continued, through one corner or other of the gallery, to the top of the house, whither they conduct through a door that is generally kept shut, to prevent their domestic animals from daubing the terrace, and thereby spoiling the water which falls from thence into the cistern below the court, etc. Such in general are the manner and contrivances of the Eastern houses; and if it may be presumed that our Saviour, at the healing of the paralytic, was preaching in a house of this fashion, it may, by attending only to the structure of it, throw some light on one circumstance of that history, which has given great offence to some unbelievers. The houses of the poorer class of people in the East are of very bad construction, consisting of mud walls, reeds, and rushes. In Constantinople everything is sacrificed to outside decorative show: built principally of wood, conflagrations are frequent and extensive. In earlier history, magnificence and refined luxury were combined with the highest and most noble examples of decorative art. The interior of the domestic residences and public edifices of Herculaneum and Pompeii surpassed every existing example. The houses of the Roman citizens partook also of the refinement of an age of art; and modern Europe has noble examples of domestic dwellings, coeval with the wealth of the country in which they are still to be found. In England, the domestic residence of the nobleman, the merchant, and the trader are, besides the elegances of their arrangements, models of comfort and health.

Before a house is planned, the proprietor should describe the kind of house he wishes to be built. The architect is to consider what must be had, and what may be dispensed with. He ought to keep his plan as scrupulously within the expense proposed, as within the limits of the ground he is to build upon; he is, in short, to enter into the views, the wishes, and the ideas of the gentleman who will inhabit the house proposed to be erected.

Houses suitable to the different ranks of the community.—Vitruvius instructs us of those parts of private houses which are exclusively appropriated to individuals of the family, and in what manner these ought to be connected with the apartments into which strangers are admitted; for there are several parts of a house which may not be approached by those who are not of the household, unless expressly invited; such as the sleeping-rooms, triclinia, baths, and those apartments which are in general use. The parts which are accessible to all, and into which any person may enter uninvited, are the vestibule, cavædium, peristyle, and whatever others are built for similar purposes.

Of the proportions of private houses, Vitruvius says:—"Nothing ought to engage the attention of an architect more than the proportions of all the parts in the houses be constructs: after having determined upon such proportions as the necessity for the commensuration of the parts with the entire building seems to require, the greatest judgment must be exercised in adapting them to the nature of the spot, the use to which the edifices are designed, and the appearance they ought to assume; and this must be done by making such additions or deductions, that, although the proportions are not strictly what they ought to be, the eye may not be conscious wherein they fail. The same objects appear differently under dissimilar circumstances; if near the ground or at a considerable elevation; if in a confined space or an exposed situation. Under every peculiar circumstance, great judgment is necessary in calculating the effect which will be ultimately produced. The impression made upon the sense of seeing is not always a correct image of the object; for, in painting, columns, mutules, and statues are made to appear projecting and detached, when, in fact, every object represented is in one and the same plane. It becomes necessary, in the first place, to institute laws of proportion, upon which all our calculations must be founded. According to these, the ground-plan, exhibiting the length and breadth of the whole work and the several parts of it, must be formed. When the magnitude of these is once determined, the parts must be arranged so as to produce that external beauty which suffers no doubt to arise in the minds of those who examine it as to the want of proportion in any part."

The Greeks had a different way of building from the Romans; for, as Vitruvius says, "instead of making porticoes or galleries and halls, they made the entry to their houses very narrow, placing on one side the stables, and the porter's lodge on the other. From this first entry one passed into a court, which had piazzas on three sides, and towards that of the south they made anti, or abutments of pilasters, which supported the joists of the ceiling more inwards; because that leaving some space between the one and the other, they had very large places, which they appointed for lodging to the mistress of the house, and to the men and women servants. On the same floor with these abutments there were some rooms which may be called antechambers, chambers and drawing-rooms, being every one just behind the other."

House-bote, an allowance of timber out of the lord's wood, to support or repair a tenant's house.

Housing, a tabernacle, or niche for a statue, was formerly so called.

Hovel. The canopies over the heads of the statues of Richard II. and Queen Anne are called hovels or tabernacles.

Howl, or *To Howle*, when the foot-hooks of a ship are scarfed into the ground-timbers, etc.

Huel, a work, a mine, as huel stones, a tin mine.

Hulk, in Cornwall, an old excavated working; 'to hulk the lode.'

Hulk, or *hull*, the body of a ship.

Hummums (Turkish), a sweating house.

Hungarian machine, an hydraulic engine, a very ingenious application of the Hero jet-d'eau principle.

Hydraletes, according to Strabo, a mill for grinding corn by water-power.

Hydraulic belt, an endless double band of woollen cloth, passing over two rollers, the lower part of the belt being immersed in water: it is driven with a velocity of not less than a thousand feet per minute, and the water contained between the two surfaces is carried up and discharged, as it passes over the upper roller, by the pressure of the band.

Hydraulic ram, a machine contrived to raise water by means of its own momentum.

Hydraulics. The science of hydraulics teaches the method of estimating the swiftness and force of fluids in motion. The science is dignified by the name of hydrodynamics, or the application of dynamics to the

HYDRAULIC PRESS.

impulsion and flow of water and other liquids, as well as the forces with which they act upon bodies against which they strike, or which move in them.

Hydrodynamics, the science of the laws of the motion of fluids, consisting of two branches. The science of hydraulics refers principally to the machinery for conducting fluids; that of hydrostatics, to the pressure, equilibrium, and cohesion of fluids.

Hydrogen. Hydrogen gas is commonly obtained for experimental purposes by the decomposition of water: its name is derived from the Greek words meaning *water* and *to generate*.

Hydrometer, an instrument for measuring the specific gravity of various spirits and other liquids, by floating in them.

Hydroscope, an instrument intended to mark the presence of water in air.

Hydrostatic or *Hydraulic Press*, a machine adapted for giving great pressure in cases where little motion is required. The contrivance of this apparatus is due to the celebrated mechanician, Joseph Bramah, who obtained a patent for it on the 31st of March, 1796, under the title of 'certain new methods of producing and applying a more considerable degree of power to all kinds of mechanical apparatus and other machinery requiring motion and force, than by any means at present practised for that purpose.' The action of this press is founded upon the fundamental principle in hydrostatics, that "when a liquid mass is in equilibrium, under the action of forces of any kind, every molecule or part of the mass sustains an equal pressure in all directions." From this it follows, that a pressure exerted on any portion of the surface of a confined mass of fluid is propagated throughout the mass, and transferred undiminished to the entire surface in contact with the water. The first suggestion of the hydraulic press is considered to have been made by Pascal in the middle of the 17th century; but Bramah was the first to carry this suggestion into practice, by devising and applying apparatus in various forms for the purpose of producing pressure.

Since the date of its invention, the hydraulic press has been extensively used in pressing goods of various kinds. Another of its most useful applications is to the testing

Fig. 1.

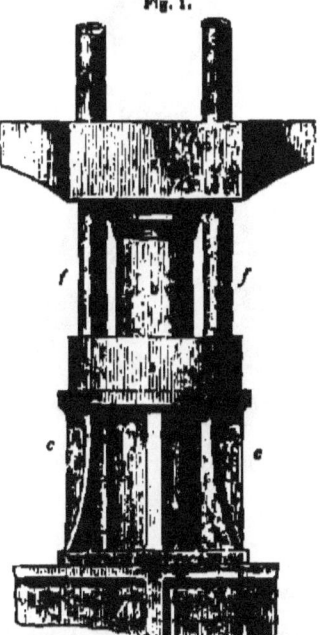

of girders and beams of cast-iron. (See article *Bramah's Hydrostatic Press*.) Its latest and perhaps most remarkable duty is that of lifting the iron-work of tubular bridges *en masse* from the water-level to their final altitude.

Hydrostatic presses consist essentially of two distinct parts, viz. the *press*, or machine in which the force acquired is applied, and the *pumping apparatus*, by which the water is forced into the press; these two parts of the entire machine being connected only by the pipe

Fig. 2.

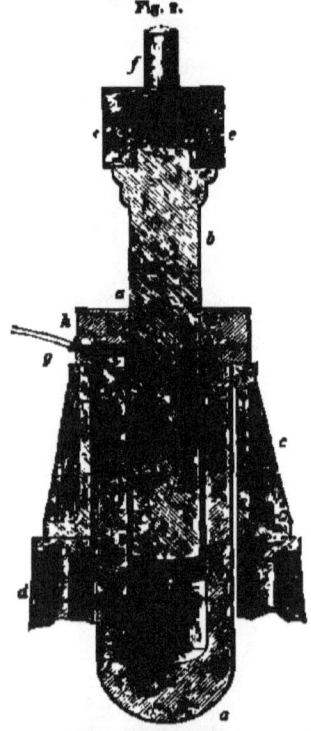

through which the water passes from one to the other. Of the accompanying figures, Nos. 1 and 2 show the main parts of the press, viz. the cylinder, into which the water is admitted; the ram, or solid plunger or piston; and the crosshead by which the pressure at the end of the ram is distributed over a lengthened surface for use. The figures show the cylinder as supported in a frame upon girders, in a manner similar to that adopted in raising the tubes of the railway bridge erected at Conway.

Fig. 3 shows the section of a portable forcing-pump as commonly used for proving castings with the hydraulic press, for which purpose the press is applied horizontally, and mounted on an iron carriage for portability. But, however varied in arrangement for particular purposes, the pump and the press consist of the same essential parts, as follows: the pump comprises a cistern or kind of pail for containing the water, and into which a barrel descends nearly to the bottom. The barrel is fitted with a plunger, by working which, the water is driven through a small tube or pipe into the press. The pump is furnished with a safety-valve, and also with a screw for letting off the water as required. The press consists of a strong hollow cylinder of cast-iron, close at one end, and of a solid ram working through the other end, the water-pipe being inserted through the metal of the cylinder in a water-tight screwed aperture. Fig. 1 is an elevation of the press; fig. 2, a vertical section of the press, taken at right angles to the elevation; and fig. 3, a vertical section of a pump: *a* is the cast-iron cylinder; *b*, the ram; *c*, the casing or frame of the cylinder; *d d* are two cast-iron girders supporting the casing; *e* is the cast-iron cross-head; *f f*, two guide-rods; *g*, the water-pipe from the pump, with a lever-valve at *h*, by closing which the pressure will be retained, should the pipe burst. On fig. 3, *j* shows the other end of the water-pipe, which is at *i* screwed into a stuffing-box on the pump; *k* is the lever of the safety-valve, *s*, which is cylindrical, and finished with a conical end, which fits a seating of similar form; *l* is a standard bolted at *m* to the cover of the cistern, and having an eye-boss at n, for guiding the plunger; o p is a link pinned to the plunger; q is the pail or cistern for holding the water; r, the barrel passing through an opening in the cover, and fixed to it with bolts and nuts; s, the lower valve-seat, and conical

Fig. 3.

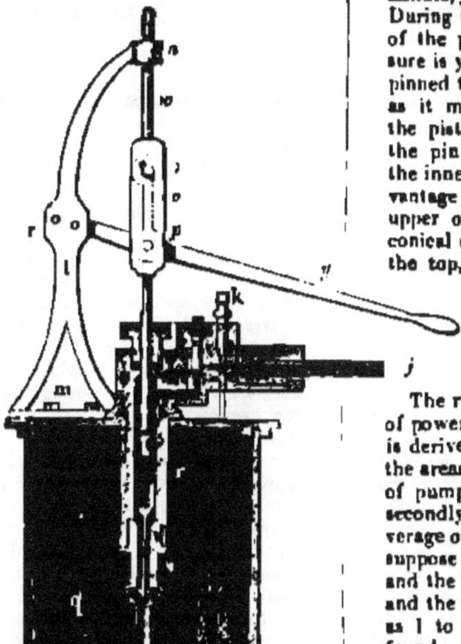

three-sided valve, the former being screwed into the end of the barrel; t, a tube depending from the valve-seat s, and screwed upon it: this tube reaches nearly to the bottom of the cistern, and is perforated at the end with minute apertures, through which the water is admitted without dirt or particles, which would injure the working of the pump; u is the plunger, which works through a stuffing-box on the top of the barrel, and is made with a slot at v, to receive the link o p, which is pinned to it and also to the pump-handle; w is the plunger-rod, screwed into the upper end of the plunger; y, the pump-handle, jointed to the standard at x. During the first part of the action of the pump, while no great pressure is yet produced, the handle is pinned to the outer of these holes, as it makes a larger stroke with the piston, and thus saves time: the pin is afterwards removed to the inner hole, to have all the advantage of the leverage. s is the upper or discharge valve, with a conical end: it is introduced from the top, and covered with a short screw, which likewise regulates the lift of the valve. This valve is formed by being simply filed flat out of the round.

The rule for finding the increase of power commanded by the pump is derived,—first, from the ratio of the areas of cross-section of plunger of pump and ram of press; and, secondly, from the ratio of the leverage of the pump-handle. Thus suppose the plunger to be $\frac{1}{2}$ inch and the ram 6 inches in diameter, and the arms of the lever or handle as 1 to 4, the power will be thus found:—

$$\cdot 5^2 \; : \; 6^2$$
multiplied by $1 \; : \; 4$

$$\cdot 25 \; : \; 144,$$

that is, 1 : 576.

And thus a power equal to 20lbs., applied on the end of the pump-handle, will produce a pressure equal to 11,520lbs. on the ram, or 5 tons 2 cwt. 3 qrs. 12lbs.

Each of the presses applied at Conway was worked by a steam-engine having a horizontal cylinder 17 inches in diameter and 16 inches stroke, with piston-rods working through stuffing-boxes at both ends of the cylinder. The piston-rods worked two forcing-pumps, with plungers 1 7/10 inch diameter and 16 inches stroke. The rams of these presses were each 5 feet 2 inches long and 18¾ inches in diameter, with a space nearly ⅜ inch wide around. The cylinders were 37½ inches diameter externally, and 20 inches internally, the metal being 8¾ inches in thickness: the orifice of the water-tubes ⅜ inch in diameter.

Hydrostatic paradox. This may be explained upon the same principles as the mechanical powers; and an explanation conducted in this manner strips it of its paradoxical appearance.

Hydrostatics, the science which treats of the mechanical properties of fluids; strictly speaking, the weight and equilibrium of fluids. The weight and equilibrium of fluids at rest are the objects of this science. When the equilibrium is destroyed, motion ensues; and the science which considers the laws of fluids in motion is hydraulics.

Hygrometer: this instrument is used to ascertain the quantity of moisture held in the atmosphere. There are several kinds of hygrometers in use, namely, De Luc's, Saussure's, Leslie's, and Professor Daniell's. The latter is considered preferable.

Hypæthral, open above: in temples of this description the cella was in part exposed to the air: they had a double range of columns within the cella, dividing it into three alæ, or aisles. The alæ on either side were roofed, but that in the middle had no covering.

Hypæthrum, a latticed window over the entrance-door of a temple.

Hyperbola, a section of a cone made by a plane, so that the axis of the section inclines to the opposing leg of the cone, which in the parabola is parallel to it, and in the ellipse intersects it.

Hyperthyrum, that part of the frame of a doorway which is over the supercilium. In Greek architecture, a frieze and cornice supported by friezes and consoles.

Hypocastanum, or *chestnut brown,* is a brown lake prepared from the horse-chestnut: it is transparent and rich in colour, warmer than brown pink, and very durable both in water and oil; in the latter it dries moderately well.

Hypocausis, among the Greeks, a furnace with flues running underneath the pavement of an apartment, to increase the temperature.

Hypocaustum, the stove-room of a bath, in which was placed the præfurnium for heating the caldaria.

Hypogæum, in ancient architecture, a name common to all the underground parts of a building.

Hypotrachelium, that part of the capital of a column which occurs between the shaft and the annulets of the echinus.

I.

ICE-HOUSE, a subterranean chamber for preserving ice from the ordinary changes of temperature.

Ich Dien, in heraldry, 'I serve.'

Ichnography, in drawing. The ichnography of a building represents the plan or groundwork; the orthography, the front; and the scenography, the whole building.

Icosahedron, in geometry, a regular body or solid, consisting of twenty triangular pyramids.

Ideas. 1. Formation of ideas, intellect, mind, understanding, reason, thinking principle, nous, sense, common sense, consciousness, capacity, intelligence, intellection. 2. Precursory conditions and operation. 3. Materials for reasoning. 4. Reasoning processes. 5. Results of reasoning. 6. Extension of thought. 7. Creative thought.

Communication of Ideas. 1. Nature of ideas communicated,

meaning, signification, sense, modes of communication, means of communicating ideas.
 Individual Volition. 1. Will, volition, free-will. 2. Prospective volition. 3. Voluntary action. 4. Antagonism. 5. Results of voluntary action, intersocial volition.

Image, a term applied to a statue.

Imbowment, an arch or vault.

Immure, a wall or inclosure. "Within whose strong immures."—*Shakspeare*.

Impages, the horizontal parts of the frame-work of doors, commonly termed rails.

Impetus, in mechanics, violent tendency to any point, violent effort, force, momentum, motion.

Impinge, in mechanics, to fall against, to strike against, to clash with.

Impluvium, the cistern in the central part of the court or atrium of a Roman house, to receive the rain-water.

Impost, the horizontal mouldings or capitals on the top of a pilaster, pillar, or pier, from which an arch springs: in classical architecture the form varies in the several orders. Sometimes the entablature of the order serves for the impost of an arch.

Impost, archivolt, and *key-stone*. The height of the impost should be from one-ninth to one-seventh of the width of the aperture, and the breadth of the archivolt not more than an eighth nor less than a tenth of it. The breadth of the under-side of the key-stone should be the same as the breadth of the archivolt, and its sides, of course, concentric; its length, once and a half its breadth, but not more than double its breadth.

Impulsive force is that which acts during an extremely short time, and is so called because the forces that take place in any impulse, or impact, are speedily exhausted.

Incise, to cut, to engrave, to carve.

Inclined plane (the), in mechanics, is a plane which makes with the horizontal plane any angle whatever, forming one of the simplest mechanical powers. The inclination of the plane is measured by the angle formed by two lines drawn from the sloping and the horizontal plane, perpendicular to their common intersection.

Increment, an increase, produce.

Incrustation. If water, impregnated with calcareous matter, remains long in contact with extraneous substances, an earthy incrustation takes place that soon encloses the incrusted substance, which is then said to be petrified.

Incrusted, in architecture, applied to walls or columns covered with precious marble or stone.

Incumba, that part of a column or pillar on which the weight of a whole building lies.

Indian Architecture consists of two distinct styles,—the Buddhist and the Brahminical,—the former being the earliest, and consisting of topes or tumuli, large domical buildings of brick or stone, either quite solid or containing one or more small chambers, in which are deposited relics, coins, and other similar objects, which the greater number of them were erected to enshrine. The principal topes are now found in Ceylon and Affghanistan, but they also exist in Burmah and in other neighbouring countries.

The next class of Buddhist buildings are the Chaitya halls, similar in plan and use to the early basilicæ: these exist principally in caves in India. And lastly, viharas or monasteries, in which the monks attached to the Chaitya halls resided: these also exist principally as caves in India, and as structural buildings in all countries where Buddhism is still practised.

Brahminical or Hindoo architecture consists mostly of temples, properly so called. These in almost every instance are towers, square in plan, or nearly so, built over the cell or sanctum of the temple. In the south of India, the upper part forms a right-lined pyramid; in the north, the outline is curvilinear, sometimes tapering to a spire.

To these towers are attached porches of greater or less dimensions. In the north there are generally square halls without pillars—in the south, as universally pillared—sometimes attached, at others detached from the temple itself: in the latter case, in the south, some of the porches possess from 500 to 1000 pillars, though this is never the case in the north.

These temples are generally surrounded by a square court; in the south, three, four, and sometimes even seven such enclosures surround the principal cell, the outer one being, in many instances, some miles in circumference.

These Hindoo temples exist sometimes, though rarely, as rock-cut temples; but generally they are structural.

Between these styles comes a third, the Jaina style, being a mixture of the two, possessing some of the characteristics of both, and frequently displaying more elegance than the first, and less tawdriness than the other. By the introduction of domes, whose use was thus brought to great perfection, an element was added which was a great improvement on the other two styles, and from which that of Jaina originated.

The absence of the arch in all constructions of every age is general throughout India, as the principle was quite unknown. The upper parts of the buildings were supported on square piers or pillars, and from all sides of their capitals brackets projected equal to their width, and leaving generally a space equal to three diameters between their greatest projection, thus leaving only one-half of the whole length of the architrave unsupported; but when a greater space was required, a succession of projecting brackets, placed above each other, was adopted, sometimes meeting in the centre, and thus having the effect of the horizontal arch.

Indian Ink: the pigment well known under this name is principally brought from China in oblong cakes, of a musky scent, prepared for painting in water, etc.

Indian red, a colour, is brought from Bengal, and is a very rich iron ore, or peroxide of iron. It is an anomalous red, of a purple-russet hue, of a good body, and valued, when fine, for the pureness and lakey tone of its tints.

Indian yellow is a pigment long employed in India and subsequently introduced generally into painting in European countries. It is imported in the form of balls, is of a fetid odour, and is produced from the urine of the camel. It has also been ascribed, in like manner, to the buffalo, or Indian cow, after feeding on mangoes; but the latter statement is incorrect. Indian yellow resists the sun's rays with singular power in water-painting.

Indicator, the apparatus for showing the force of the steam, and the state of exhaustion in the cylinder during the stroke.

Inigo (Jones), born in London, was first employed at Oxford in 1635; he built the arcades and porticoes of the inner quadrangle of St. John's College with a gallery over; also York-stairs, Strand; and his magnificent design for a royal palace at Whitehall has not yet been surpassed.

Indigo, or *Indian blue*, is a pigment manufactured in the East and West Indies from several plants, but principally from the anil or indigofera.

Inertia, the passiveness of matter: matter has not the power of putting itself into motion, neither has it the power of stopping itself when put into motion by the action of an external force, as it requires as much force to stop a body as it requires to put it in motion.

Inflammable air, hydrogen gas.

Influx, in hydraulics, the act of flowing into any thing, as the tide into a bay or river.

Injection-cock, the stop-cock in the ejection-pipe, for shutting off the supply of cold water used for the condensation of steam.

Injection-pipe, the pipe through which the injection water passes to the condenser; in a steam-vessel the injection-pipe is open to the sea, at the bottom of the vessel.

Inn, or *hostel*, anciently a lodging-house, or a house of lodging and refreshment for travellers: houses for lodging the collegians at Cambridge and Oxford were so called.

Inns of court, houses in which there are many lodgings for the accommodation of students and practitioners at law.

Innate force, in physics, the vis inertiæ.

Inner-post, in ship-building, a piece brought in at the fore-side of the main-post, and generally continued as high as the wing-transom, to seat the other transoms upon.

Insertum opus, according to Vitruvius, a mode of building walls used by the Romans, in which the stones were small and unhewn, similar to what is now called rubble-work.

Insulated columns, in architecture, are those which are unconnected with any wall or building.

Intaglio, in sculpture, etc., anything that has figures engraved on it, so as to rise above the ground.

Intense blue, indigo refined by solution and precipitation, in which state it is equal in colour to Antwerp blue. By this process, indigo also becomes durable, and much more powerful, transparent, and deep. It washes and works well in water; and in other respects it has the common properties of indigo.

Intercolumniation. The space between two columns is called an Intercolumniation. When columns are attached to the wall, this space is not under such rigorous laws as when they are quite insulated; for, in the latter case, real as well as apparent solidity requires them to be near each other, that they may better sustain the entablatures which it is their office to carry.

DIFFERENT SORTS.—The different intercolumniations had the following names bestowed on them by the Greeks, and they still retain their ancient appellations:—

Pycnostylos, when the columns are once and a half of their diameter distant from each other.

Systylos .. when their distance from each other is two diameters.

Eustylos .. when their distance from each other is two diameters and a quarter.

Diastylos .. when their distance from each other is three diameters and quarter.

Aræostylos . when their distance from each other is four diameters.

In the Doric, however, the intercolumniation is regulated by the disposition of the triglyphs in the frieze; for the triglyph ought always to be placed over the centre of a column, and the metope should be square. In the Tuscan interval, the architraves being of wood, the space may be considerably extended.

A strict adherence to the above-named intervals between the columns produces some irregularity in the arrangement of the modillions and dentils of the Corinthian, Ionic, and Composite cornices, which, though not offensive, is better avoided. Vignola therefore has, with some propriety, made his eustylos intercolumniation equal to two diameters and one-third in all but the Doric order.

Intercolumniations. Columns may be said to be either engaged or insulated; when insulated, they are either placed very near the walls or at some considerable distance from them.

With regard to engaged columns, or such as are near the walls of a building, the intercolumniations are not limited, but depend on the width of the arches, windows, niches, or other objects, and their decorations, placed within them. But columns that are entirely detached, and perform alone the office of supporting the entablature, as in peristyles, porches, and galleries, must be near each other, both for the sake of real and apparent solidity.

The ancients had several manners of spacing their columns, which are described by Vitruvius in his third and fourth books. Those practised in the Ionic and Corinthian orders were, the pycnostyle, the systyle, the eustyle, the diastyle, and the arœostyle.

In the Doric order they used other intercolumniations, regulating them by the triglyphs, of which one was always to be placed directly over the middle of each column, so that they were either systyle monotriglyph, of one diameter and a half; diastyle, or arœostyle: the Tuscan intervals were exceedingly wide, some of them being above seven diameters, which, as the architraves were of wood, was practicable.

Vitruvius intended the five intercolumniations, mentioned in his 3rd book, merely for the Ionic and Corinthian orders: the latter of which, according to him, differed from the former only in its capital; for, in the second and seventh chapters of his fourth book, he establishes other intervals for the Doric and Tuscan orders. Nevertheless, they have employed these intercolumniations in different orders. Palladio has used the systyle in the Corinthian and the arœostyle in the Tuscan; by which means the Corinthian peristyle, of which the character should be extreme delicacy and lightness, becomes twice as strong and material as the Tuscan, of which the distinguishing characteristics ought to be extreme solidity.

Interdentals. The space between two dentals.

Interlignium, in ancient architecture, the space between the ends of the tie-beams.

Interpensiva, timbers in the roof of the cavædium, extending in a diagonal direction from the angles made by the walls of the court to the angles made by the junction of the beams supporting the roof.

Intrados, the soffit or under-surface of an arch, as opposed to *extrados.*

In vacuo, a void or empty space.

Invention, in painting, consists principally in three things: first, the choice of a subject properly within the scope of art; secondly, the seizure of the most striking and energetic moment of time, for representation; and lastly, the discovery and solution of such objects, and such probable incidental circumstances, as, combined together, may best tend to develope the story, or augment the interest of the piece. The cartoons of Raphael furnish an example of genius and sagacity in this part of the art.

Inverse, turned back or inverted; opposed to *direct.*

Inverse ratio, when more requires less, or less requires more.

Inverted arch, an arch of stone or brick, with the crown downwards, commonly used in the construction of tunnels.

Iodine scarlet is a new pigment, of a peculiarly vivid and beautiful colour, exceeding even the brilliancy of vermilion. It has received several false appellations, but is truly an iodide or biniodide of mercury, varying in degrees of intense redness. It has the body and opacity of vermilion, but should be used with an ivory palette-knife, as iron and most metals change it to colours varying from yellow to black.

Iodine yellow, ioduret of lead, is a precipitate from an acid solution of lead by an alkaline solution of iodine, of a bright yellow colour, which, from its active chemical affinities, and the little experience of its qualities in painting, is to be employed with doubt and caution.

Ionic capital. The Greek architects must have possessed much science in the formation of curves of every description. We cannot generate the curve of the volute of an Ionic capital but by approximation; but the inventors of the order must have known how to generate this and other curves in Greek architecture, on fixed principles; so must the artist in vases, etc. Mr. Jopling is said to have discovered the true generic curve.

Ionic Order: this, says Palladio, "had its origin in Ionia, a province of Asia; and we read that the famous temple of Diana at Ephesus was built of that order. The column, with its capital and base, is nine modules high; and by a module is understood the diameter of a column below. The architrave, frieze, and cornice, have the fifth part of the height of the column. When the columns are single, the inter-columns are of two diameters and a fourth part, and this is the most beautiful and commodious manner of all inter-columns, which Vitruvius calls eustylos."

Amongst the ancients, the form of the Ionic profile appears to have been more positively determined than that of any other order; for in all the antiques at Rome, the temple of Concord excepted, it is exactly the same, and conformable to the description which Vitruvius has given of it.

Modern artists have likewise been more unanimous in their opinions upon the subject; all of them, excepting Palladio and his imitators, having employed the dentil cornice, and the other parts of the profile, nearly as they are found in the Coliseum, the temple of Fortune, and the theatre of Marcellus.

In Palladio's works we meet with three different Ionic entablatures, all of them very beautiful. The first is the true antique, which he has made use of at the palace of the Porti; and in several doors and windows of the Thiene and Valmarana palaces, in Vicenza. The second is a very judicious imitation of the entablature in the temple of Concord, and is executed by him in the upper arcade of the basilica in the same city. The third, which is an invention of his own, being the same with that in his book, he has employed with some small difference at the Chiericato palace, at the rotunda of Marchese Capra, and in various others of his buildings in the Vicentine, or at Venice.

Iron, the most useful and the most abundant of the metals, is found in various conditions of ore in most parts of the earth. Those ores which are principally worked for the production of the metal for manufacturing purposes, are either oxides or carbonates, that is, they contain the metal in a state of combination either with oxygen, or with oxygen and carbonic acid. The oxides are the best ores, and are found in vast beds in Sweden; the carbonates are inferior in point of strength and ductility, and therefore require an extensive reduction. They form the greater portion of the iron ores of Britain.

The principal varieties of the oxides of iron are,—the magnetic; the massive, found in the north of Europe, and other parts of the world; the micaceous, found in the lava of volcanoes, etc.; and the red and brown hæmatites, found in Great Britain and Europe. The principal varieties of the carbonates are,—the massive, found in Great Britain and Ireland, Europe, and America; and also the argillaceous, commonly known as clay iron-stone, found abundantly in beds and coal deposits in England, Wales, and Scotland.

Besides the oxides and carbonates here enumerated, iron is found in large quantities in combination with sulphur; and the several compounds thus formed are known as pyrites, several varieties of which are found in Norway, Sweden, Germany, America, and in many parts of England.

Various artificial oxides of this metal are applied to medicine, dyeing, and other purposes in the arts.

The tenacity and strength of iron are impaired by its adulteration with foreign matters. Thus, of the oxides and carbonates, those are best in which the proportion of the metal is great. These qualities are further increased by fusion, and by the mechanical process of hammering; and this fact points to the main distinction in the kinds of iron as applied for manufacturing purposes, viz. foundry iron and forge iron.

In the manufacture of iron, the first process is the reduction of the iron-stone or ore, technically called the mine, into the state of a metal. This is done by fusion in a furnace, with coke added to produce combustion, and limestone to act as a flux and assist the fusion of the ore. An artificial current of air is necessary to fuse the ore in these furnaces, which are therefore called blast furnaces, and provided with tubes or tuyères, through the tapered nozzles of which strong currents of air are delivered to the interior of the furnace, the required velocity of the blasts being sustained by steam or other power. Formerly the air was thus introduced at the same temperature as that of the external atmosphere; but a plan has for many years been extensively adopted of previously heating the air for the blasts in separate vessels to a high temperature, by which the fusion of the ore is so powerfully assisted, that the saving of fuel in the furnace is many times greater than the quantity used for the preparatory heating of the air. Furnaces thus supplied are termed hot-blast furnaces, and the product is called hot-blast iron, while that made with unheated air is called cold-blast iron.

The cost of the process of reduction with the hot blast being so much less than of that with the cold blast, the ultimate value of the former is of course also partly dependent upon the quality of the produce. On this head much difference of opinion has often been manifested, and with all the earnestness usually displayed in the advocacy of self-interest. The value of each process must, no doubt, arise from the completeness of the fusion produced, and the separation effected between the iron and the impurities combined with it in the ore. The hot-blast furnace effects the fusion more readily than the cold-blast, but admits a larger combination of cinders with the ore; and the advantage which has been taken of this facility of adulteration, in order to reduce the cost of production, has doubtless led to the introduction into the market of many qualities of hot-blast iron which are inferior in strength to that made with the cold blast. The results of some of the most carefully conducted experiments which have been made upon the strength of cast-iron, and published in the 6th volume of the new series of 'Memoirs of the Literary and Philosophical Society of Manchester,' show that the transverse strength of the cold-blast iron tried was about $2\frac{1}{4}$ per cent. greater than that of the hot-blast. The experiments here referred to were made upon rectangular bars 1 inch square, and 4 feet 6 inches long between the supports. The mean average breaking weights, placed at the middle of these bars, were—

	lbs.
In 21 samples of hot-blast iron	445·5714
In 22 samples of cold-blast iron	456·9090

The metal is allowed to flow from the furnace into rude channels formed on the surface of the ground, where it cools, and is taken up in the form of rough bars about 3 feet long, and each weighing nearly one cwt., which are technically called pigs. In the making of one ton of pig-iron in Staffordshire, the following materials are used:—

Coal, 2 tons 5 cwt.

If coke is used instead of coal, 1 ton 17 cwt.

Charred mine, or ore, 2 tons 5 cwt. to 2 tons 10 cwt.

Limestone, 13 cwt. to 16 cwt.

In the condition of pig-iron, the metal forms the two staple descriptions of foundry iron and of forge iron, according to its qualities, and the proportion of carbon and oxygen which it contains. The several sorts of pig-iron are considered to be six in number, and are thus distinguished: Nos. 1, 2, and 3, foundry iron, of which the first two are never used for forge iron. No. 3, or dark grey, and also the fourth quality known as bright iron, are sometimes used for the foundry, and sometimes for the forge. The fifth and sixth sorts, known as mottled iron and white iron, are never used for the foundry. The order here observed corresponds with that of the proportion of carbon and oxygen mixed with each kind of the iron, and also with that of the fluidity to which the metal is reducible; it also corresponds with the scale of their softness and toughness. Thus, No. 1 has the most carbon and oxygen, and the white iron has the least. No. 1 is the most fluid when melted, and the white iron the least so. Again, No. 1 is the softest, and the white iron the hardest; and No. 1 is the toughest, while the white iron is the most brittle. But white iron is the best adapted for conversion into malleable iron, while Nos. 1 and 2, foundry iron, contain so large a proportion of carbon and oxygen, that they are totally unfit to be manufactured into bars.

The conversion of pig-iron into malleable iron is effected by extended processes, or subsequent to those by which the ore has been reduced to the form of pig. These processes are as follow:—

1. Refining.—2. Puddling, hammering, and rolling.—3. Cutting up, piling, and rolling; the 3rd series of operations being repeated.

The refining is for the purpose of separating a portion of the carbon from the pig, and is performed in furnaces fitted with tuyères for supplying a blast of air to the point of fusion. The metal run from the refining moulds is exceedingly brittle, and is then broken up into small pieces, and committed to the puddling or reverberatory furnace, to undergo a further purification from the oxygen and carbon which remain after the process of refining is accomplished. While in this furnace, the mass into which the pieces of refined metal become clustered is worked and stirred about by the workman or puddler, until its thickness and tenacity are so far increased that it may be formed into lumps, or balls, which the puddler does with tools adapted to the purpose.

The hammering or shingling is performed upon the balls or blooms of puddled iron, with a very heavy hammer, worked by a cam-wheel, and has the effect of improving the solidity of the metal, and reducing the balls into an oblong form, by which they are better prepared for the action of the rollers.

The rolls or rollers are fitted together in pairs, and so formed in the periphery and arranged in size, that open spaces are formed between them, through which the metal is passed while hot; and each succeeding pair of rollers presenting a smaller space, the iron which is drawn through them becomes proportionately reduced in size and increased in length.

The metal has thus been converted from a hard, brittle, and readily fusible substance into a malleable bar, which is soft, tough, and very difficult of fusion; but it is still far from fit for the smith's use, being to a great extent unsound in structure, imperfect in tenacity, and irregular on the surface.

The third set of processes is now commenced by cutting up the puddled bars into lengths with powerful shears. These lengths, of various dimensions, according to the sized bars to be produced, are carefully piled up and heated in another furnace similar to the puddling furnace, and which is called the balling furnace. In this the bars are simply heated to a degree which admits of their becoming welded together in the pile and adapted for reduction to the form of finished bars in the rolls.

The rolling is the last operation in the making of bar-iron. The metal is drawn successively through a series of rollers, that is, between the peripheries of each pair of rollers, and thus gradually reduced in size, increased in length, and freed from the cinder and other impurities which remain after the puddle-rolling has been performed.

The last set of operations is sometimes repeated in producing iron for superior purposes. The processes here described will give a general idea of the manufacture of iron from the native ore into the form of malleable bars; and it may be readily conceived how an extension and variation of the process of rolling may be made to produce the several other forms in which this metal is prepared for the constructions of the engineer, the smith, and the machinist.

As varieties of bar-iron may be mentioned,—L, or angle-iron; T, or tee-iron; and H, or deck-beam iron; which are prepared in several sizes for the construction of roofs, iron vessels, etc. The malleable rails used for railways are also produced by an arrangement of rollers.

Boiler-plate iron, sheet-iron, hoop-iron, and nail rod-iron, are produced from the form of bars by the processes of beating and rolling, or hammering, as required. Boiler-plates require, according to the desired strength and size, several repetitions of heating, hammering, and rolling. Sheet-iron is distinguished from boiler-plate by being thinner; hoop-iron is rolled in the same manner as the bars, but between rollers without grooves in their edges, the requisite thickness being effected by successive passages through the rollers, which are brought nearer to each other at each process, by means of adjusting screws. Nail rod-iron is rolled in thin bars, which are, while still hot, passed between steel cutters that slit them up into the form of small rods, which, although rough, are well fitted to be manufactured into nails.

A very useful form of sheet-iron, which should be noticed, is that of corrugated iron, which is produced by passing the sheets between rollers having grooved peripheries. By this form, the strength or stiffness of the sheet is so much increased, that sheet-iron thus formed may be usefully applied to a great variety of purposes for which it is otherwise, owing to its thinness and pliability, utterly inadequate.

By the combustion of charcoal with the coke, and the adaptation of a peculiar furnace in the process of smelting, Mr. Clay has succeeded in producing malleable iron direct from the ore, and thus materially reducing the series of processes here described. The results thus brought out are of a very interesting character, and promise to acquire a great practical value. Mr. Bessemer has patented most successfully some inventions for making iron and steel without the aid of puddling. See 'Engineer's Pocket Book' for description.

Iron. Moses forbade the Hebrews the use of any stones to form the altar of the Lord, which had been in any manner wrought with iron; as if iron communicated pollution. He says, the stones of Palestine are of iron, that is, of hardness equal to iron, or, being smelted, they yielded iron. "An iron yoke" is a hard and insupportable dominion. "Iron sharpeneth iron," says the Wise Man, "so a man sharpeneth the countenance of his friend:" the presence of a friend gives us more confidence and assurance. God threatens his ungrateful and perfidious people with making the *heavens iron*, and the earth brass; that is, to make the earth barren, and the air to produce no rain. Chariots of iron are chariots armed with iron, with spikes and scythes.

Iron ship building, a new and a most successful mode of construction of ships in the hull of iron, both for merchant and war purposes, and for passenger vessels, upon any scale of dimensions. See vol. 54, John Grantham on Iron Ship Building, in the 'Rudimentary;' also separately, with 'Atlas of Practical Examples' in large engravings.

Iron-stone, iron-bound stone, in colour of a bluish grey: it contains but little iron, and is hard to work.

Iron-stone has the appearance of rusty-black shale, and, when laid together in large heaps, is so combustible that it ignites, leaving a calx of 60 per cent. of iron. It abounds in Scotland. Common iron-stone is also very abundant in connection with coal, and in former times formed the principal supply, which induced the foundation of the Carron Iron-works.

Iron-wood is imported from the Brazils, the East and West Indies, and other countries, in square and round logs, 6 to 9 inches and upwards through. Its colours are very dark browns and reds; sometimes it is streaked, and generally straight-grained; used principally for ramrods, turnery, etc., and is extremely hard.

Iron yellow, jaune de fer, or jaune de Mars, etc., is a bright iron ochre, prepared artificially, of the nature of sienna earth. The colours of iron exist in endless variety in nature, and are capable of the same variation by art, from sienna yellow, through orange and red, to purple, brown, and black, among which are useful and valuable distinctions, which are brighter and purer than native ochres.

Irrigation, watering the ground.

Isochronism, in mechanics, the performing of several things in equal times; such as the vibrations of the pendulum.

Isodomon, a building every way straight.

Isodomos, in Greek architecture, masonry cut and squared to the same height, so that, when laid, the courses were all regular and equal.

Isometrical, projections and drawings so termed.

Isoperimetrical, in geometry, such figures as have equal perimeters or circumferences.

Isosceles, in geometry, a triangle that has only two sides equal.

Isothermal, in chemistry, equal heat.

Italian Architecture, a style now much appreciated, not only in Italy, but in England and France, was first introduced at the revival of classical architecture, and was subsequently much improved, and adapted to modern refinement. The architecture of Venice, Florence, Genoa, Rome and Sicily, afford to the architect a complete library of examples by the possession of the several works published of the architecture of the palaces and mansions of these cities.

Respecting buildings originally erected in Italy, Mr. Jos. Gwilt has thus written:—

The Romans followed the Greeks in the general form of their temples, but added to their splendour by a greater richness of detail, and the employment of other orders. For the simple steps on which the Greek temple was elevated, they substituted pedestals, and added a base to the Doric order. The climate prescribed a more elevated pediment; but the luxury of the people was the cause of the preference given to the richer orders of architecture.

TEMPLES, BRIDGES, AQUEDUCTS, COLUMNS, THEATRES, ETC.

The chief temples of Rome were —the Capitol, built on the Tarpeian or Capitoline mount, by Tarquinius Superbus. (See *Capitolium*.) No traces of it at present remain. The edifice of the Capitol was about 200 feet square, and contained three temples, consecrated to Jupiter, Minerva, and Juno. On the Capitol were also the temples of Terminus and Jupiter Feretrius, and the cottage of Romulus.

The Pantheon, built by Agrippa, the son-in-law of Augustus, and dedicated to Mars and Venus, or more probably, from its name, to all the gods. Pope Boniface IV. consecrated it in honour of the Virgin Mary and All Saints, A.D. 607. It is now generally known by the name of the 'Rotunda;'—its diameter between the axes of the columns is 147 feet; like most of the ancient buildings, it has fallen a prey to the spoiler. The Baldachino in St. Peter's is indebted for its materials to the Pantheon of Agrippa.

The temple of Apollo, on the Palatine hill, was built by Augustus; a temple of Diana stood on the Aventine.

The temple of Janus was supposed to have been built by Romulus; that of Romulus by Papirius. Of those to the Sun and Moon, Fortuna Virilis, Vesta, Minerva Medica, Neptune, Antoninus and Faustina, Concord, Jupiter Stator, and most particularly of the temple of Peace, considerable remains are fortunately still in being. The three magnificent arches nowstanding of that last named, though of themselves majestic, convey but a faint idea of its pristine splendour. Of the temple of Jupiter Stator, whose columns, capitals, and entablatures were a perfect example of the Corinthian order, only three columns are in existence. The remains of the temples of Antoninus Pius, Claudius, Hercules, Jupiter Tonans, Isis, Romulus, and Venus and Cupid, are still interesting.

No vestiges exist of the temples dedicated to Saturn, Juno, Mars his Ultor, in the forum of Augustus, nor of numberless others that adorned the city.

The temples of Balbec and Palmyra are the last of the ancient Roman works that can lay claim to the appellation of classic architecture. In these, invention seems to have found its limits. The reproduction and new adaptation of their detail is all that has been done by following artists.

The Romans, not content with the quadrilateral temple, made use of the circular form, as in the Pantheon, temple of Vesta, and others at Rome, and that of the Sibyl at Tivoli. Except their theatres, and the little work generally known by the name of the Lantern of Demosthenes, the Greeks have left no buildings on a circular plan.

After the time of Diocletian, a new style prevailed in Italy. The basilicæ of Constantine, as they existed previous to their restoration, and, in short, almost all the first Christian churches, were built out of the materials which the old tem-

ITALIAN BUILDINGS.

ples afforded in abundance. The basilica of S. Paolo fuori le Mura still contains a large portion of the columns which had originally belonged to the mausoleum of Adrian. The style of these basilicæ may with propriety be termed Roman-Gothic. This was followed by the Greek-Gothic, of which examples may be found in most of the cities of Italy, as in St. Mark at Venice, the cathedral at Pisa (built by Buschetto da Dulichio, a Greek architect of the 11th century), and in the baptistery and leaning campanile of the same city: specimens abound also in Bologna, Siena, Venice, Viterbo, Rome, etc. They are chiefly the works of Nicola da Pisa and his scholars.

At the time that the famous cathedral of Milan, the perfection of the Lombard-Gothic style, was in hand, Brunelleschi was advancing a step further, and had begun the restoration of classical architecture in the great cupola of Sta. Maria del Fiore at Florence; his prototype seeming to have been the temple of Minerva Medica, to which his work has sufficient resemblance to justify the allusion to it. He succeeded in his enterprise, and thus gave a death-blow to the Italian-Gothic of all sorts. L. B. Alberti, Bramante, and Fra Giocondo restored the use of the orders; Michael Angelo, Raphael, Sangallo, Palladio, and Scamozzi completed the change; the church of St. Peter rose, and every little city began to provide itself with a Duomo.

The fora of the ancients were large squares surrounded by porticoes, which were applied to different purposes. Some parts of them answered for market-places, other parts for the public meetings of the inhabitants, still other parts for courts of justice. The forum also occasionally afforded accommodation for the shows of gladiators. Rome contained seventeen fora, of which fourteen were used for the show and sale of goods provisions, and merchandise, an were called Fora Venalia; the othe three were appropriated for civi and judicial proceedings, and hence called Fora Civilia et Judicialis Of the latter sort was the forun of Trajan.

The forum of Julius Cæsar wa far more splendid than the Forun Romanum: it cost upwards o £800,000 sterling, and stood ii the neighbourhood of the Campe Vaccino, to the east of the temple of Peace and of Antoninus and Faustina.

In the vicinity of that last named was the forum of Augustus: the temple of Mars his Ultor decora ted the centre of it.

The forum of Nerva, called also the Forum Transitorium, begun by Domitian, was decorated by Alex ander Severus with colossal statue of the Emperors, some of whicl were equestrian. Parts of this forun are still in tolerable preservation.

The forum of Trajan, which ha lately been accurately traced by means of very extensive excavations and the demolition of a great num ber of houses, was by far the mos magnificent. The Trajan colum formed one of its ornaments: the architect was Apollodorus, and it situation was between the forum o Nerva and the Capitol.

The basilica (a term now applied to the cathedrals of Rome) wa originally a court of justice. Lik the forum, it was furnished wit shops for the merchants and bank ers. In the place called the Comi tium were four basilicæ, viz. tha of Paulus, the Basilica Opimia Julia (built by Vitruvius), and Por tia; besides these, the most impor tant were those of Sicinius, Sem pronius, Caius and Lucius, Antoni nus Pius, and the Basilica Argen tariorum, or of the goldsmiths Some of less consideration stood in the vicinity of the Forum Ro manum.

The modern halls of Italy in some respects answer the purpose of the ancient basilicæ. Those most worthy of notice are at Venice, Vicenza, Padua, and Brescia.

Near the Tarpeian rock stood the famous prison built by Ancus Martius, which was afterwards called Tullianum, from the additions thereto by Servius Tullius. The Curia Hostilia, where the Senate frequently met, was the Comitium: at its entrance, close to the temple of Saturn, was the Milliarium Aureum, the central point from which all the roads to the different provinces diverged, and near to which ran the gallery constructed by Caligula, which joined the Palatine and Capitoline hills. It was constructed with eighty columns of white marble.

The porticoes of Pompey, Angustus, Domitian, and Nero were the most celebrated of Rome. The first-named afforded a refreshing retreat from the sun's rays. The portico of Augustus was constructed with columns of African marble, and was ornamented with fifty statues of the Danaides. Those of Nero, three in number, each three miles in length, were called Milliariæ, on account of their extraordinary dimensions, forming a part of his palace.

The pyramidal form was generally applied to tombs. In the heroic ages, a cone of earth, whose base was of considerable extent, covered the ashes of the person to be commemorated. This was the practice of the early ages. Men were, however, desirous of triumphing over death, and the Pyramids, as well as numberless other monuments, the names of whose authors are now lost, have proved the vanity of their desires: the memory of man must depend upon "deeds done in the flesh."

The pyramid of Caius Cestius, a trifle compared with those of Egypt, is yet enormous, considering the individual to whose memory it was erected. The tower of Cecilia Metella, called the Capo di Bove, on the Appian way, is a beautiful specimen of art. The Appian, Flaminian, and Latin ways exhibit numberless sepulchres of an interesting nature. Those which are found with the inscription D.M., or Dils Manibus, contain the ashes of the persons whose names they bear; but the others are mostly cenotaphs, the bodies having been deposited elsewhere.

Triumphal arches may be reckoned among the luxuries of the Romans. Nothing which could tend to perpetuate the fame of the conqueror was omitted in the design. Some of them were with two, some with three passages. The richest were on the Triumphal way. Those which also served as gates generally consisted of two openings, one for the carriages passing out of, the other for carriages passing into the city. With the Greeks, a trophy erected on the field of battle was held of equal importance with the triumphal arch of the Romans, and a breach was sometimes made in the walls to admit the entry of the conqueror.

The Roman Senate received the conqueror at the Porta Capena, near the Tiber, which was the entrance to the city from the Appian way.

The arch of Augustus at Rimini has but a single passage, about 33 feet wide: it was crowned with a pediment, contrary to the usual practice. This was a beautiful specimen, but it is much mutilated.

That called the arch of the Goldsmiths at Rome is a curious example. It is very small, with a single opening, whose crowning is a flat lintel.

The arch of Augustus at Susa, a small town just on the Italian side of Mount Cenis, is extremely elegant.

Those of Aurelian and Janus are more singular than beautiful.

The arch of Pola in Istria is only curious on account of its affording a justification of the use of coupled columns, were the authority of the ancients necessary for the purpose: it was erected by Salvia Posthuma in honour of Sergius Lepidus and his two brothers.

The arch of Trajan at Ancona is still in tolerable preservation. It has long since been stripped of its bronze ornaments, but their absence has not impaired its elegant proportions.

The arches of Titus at Rome and Trajan at Benevento bear considerable resemblance to each other. That of Gavius at Verona, called 'del Castel Vecchio,' no longer exists. The precepts of Vitruvius have been confronted with his practice in this arch; but Vitruvius Cerdo, not Vitruvius Pollio, was the architect.

The arches of Septimius Severus and of Constantine are with three openings. The latter is decorated with ornaments shamefully stripped off from the arch of Trajan, which from their absurd application, render the barbarism of the robber more disgusting.

Rome formerly contained eight bridges. The Pons Sublicius, built by Ancus Martius near the Tiber, was of timber, so framed as to require no iron bolts or ties for its security. It stood at the foot of the Aventine, and was that which Horatius Cocles defended. It was replaced by one of stone by Æmilius Lepidus, and then had the name of Æmilianus. Tiberius afterwards repaired it. Finally, Antoninus Pius rebuilt it of marble, whence it obtained the name of Marmoratus.

The Pons Triumphalis, near the Vatican, is in ruins: few vestiges of it exist. Those who triumphed passed over this bridge in their way to the Capitol.

The Pons Fabricius led to an island in the Tiber: it is now called Quattro Capi. That which led from the island to the right bank of the river was called Pons Cestius or Esquilinus: it was rebuilt during the reigns of the emperors Valentinian, Valens, and Gratian.

Pons Janiculi, so called because it led to the Janiculum, and now known by the name of Ponte Sisto (from having been restored by Sixtus IV.), was of marble, and built by Antoninus Pius.

Pons Ælius, built by Ælius Adrianus, is still in existence. It is situated close to the mausoleum of Adrian. This having changed its name into that of Castel St. Angelo, the bridge has acquired a corresponding appellation.

The Pons Milvius, now Ponte Molle, is a little way out of the city, on the road to Florence. On this bridge Cicero arrested the ambassadors of the Allobroges, and in its vicinity Constantine defeated Maxentius.

Pons Senatorius, or Palatinus, is partly remaining, close to the Patine mount.

Ponte Salaro is over the Teverone, about three miles from Rome.

The spans of the arches are generally but small; yet there are some few magnificent exceptions, as in the Ponte del Castel Vecchio at Verona. This consists of three arches, the largest of which is 170 feet span; its two other arches are smaller; they diminish from the city, the left bank of the river being considerably lower than the right. The bridge built by Augustus over the Nar, near Narni, on the Flaminian way, was a single arch of 150 feet span. In the later times of the city, bridges were decorated with trophies, colossal statues, triumphal arches, and the like. Such was the case with the Pons Ælius and the bridge of Augustus at Rimini.

The country round Rome is covered with the remains of aqueducts, some of which conveyed the water to Rome from a distance of more than 60 miles.

The first aqueduct (Aqua Appia) was built, according to Diodorus, by Appius Claudius, in the year of the city 441. The water which it supplied was collected from the neighbourhood of Frascati, and its summit was about 100 feet above the level of Rome.

The second (Anio Vetus) was begun forty years after the last-named, by M. Curius Dentatus, and finished by Fulvius Flaccus: it was supplied from the country beyond Tivoli. Near Vicovaro it is cut through a rock upwards of a mile in length, in which part it is 5 feet high and 4 feet wide. The water of this aqueduct was not good, and therefore only used for the most ordinary purposes.

The third (Aqua Martia) was supplied from a fountain at the extremity of the mountains of the Peligni. The water entered the city by the Esquiline gate. This aqueduct was the work of Quintus Martius.

The fourth (Aqua Tepula) was supplied from the vicinity of Frascati.

The fifth (Aqua Julia) was about six miles long, and entered the city near the Porta Esquilina.

The sixth (Aqua Virginis) was constructed by Agrippa thirteen years after that immediately preceding. Its summit, in the territory of Tusculum, was about eight miles from Rome, which it entered by the Pincian gate. This water still bears its ancient appellation, being called Acqua Vergine.

The seventh (Aqua Alsietina, called also Augusta, from the use to which Augustus intended to apply it for supplying his Naumachia) was brought from the lake whose name it bears.

The eighth (Aqua Claudia), whose summit is about forty miles from Rome, was begun by Caligula, and completed by Claudius. It enters the city at the Porta Nevia, near the Esquiline mount. The quality of the water which this aqueduct supplies is better than that of any of the others.

The ninth (Anio novus, to distinguish it from the second-named water) was begun and finished by the same persons as the last-mentioned. It is the water of the Anio, which, being exceedingly thick and muddy after the rains, is conveyed into a large reservoir at some little distance from Rome, to allow the mud to subside.

The Acqua Felice is modern, and was erected by Sixtus V. in 1581.

The Popes have, from time to time, been at considerable pains and expense in repairing and renewing the aqueducts; but the quantity of water delivered is constantly diminishing. In the ancient city, the total sum of the areas of the different pipes (which were about an inch in diameter) through which the above immense quantity of water was delivered, amounted to about 14,900 superficial inches; but the supply was subsequently reduced to 1170.

The waters were collected in reservoirs called *castella*, and thence were conveyed through the city in leaden pipes. The keepers of the reservoirs were called *castellani*. Agrippa alone built thirty of these reservoirs during his ædileship. There are five modern ones now standing in the city: one at the Porta Maggiore, Castello dell' Acqua Giulia, dell' Acqua Felice, dell' Acqua Paolina, and that called the Fountain of Trevi.

In later times, the bath was always used by the Romans before they went to their supper. The rich generally had hot and cold baths in their own houses; and it was not till the time of Augustus that the baths assumed an air of grandeur and magnificence. They were called Thermæ, that is, hot baths, though the same pile of building always contained cold as well as hot baths. Different authors have reckoned as many as 800 public baths in Rome. The chief were those of Agrippa, Nero, Titus, Domitian, Caracalla, Antoninus, and Diocletian. Their vestiges indicate the amazing magnificence of the age in which they were erected. The pavements were mosaic, the vaulted ceilings were gilt and painted, and the walls incrusted with the richest marbles. Some of the finest and best preserved remains of ancient Greek sculpture have been restored to light from these edifices. It was from these that Raphael took the hint for his fantastic decorations of the Vatican, and the first restorers of art drew their resources.

Dramatic entertainments were first introduced at Rome in the 391st year of the city. In ancient times the people stood during the performance. For a considerable period the theatres were mere temporary buildings constructed of wood. The most splendid of these upon record was that of Marcus Æmilius Scaurus: it was magnificently decorated, and was capable of containing 80,000 persons.

It was in Pompey's second consulship that the first stone theatre was erected: this accommodated 40,000 spectators. To avoid the animadversions of the Censors (for the magistracy did not yet sanction theatrical exhibitions), he dedicated it to Venus.

Several other theatres afterwards arose: that of Marcellus can still be distinctly traced, and part of the circular façade, in tolerable preservation, is singularly elegant. The theatre of Balbus was also of considerable celebrity.

The theatres were open at top to the heavens; but in times of rain or excessive heat, means were provided for covering them with a species of cloth awning, by which the inclemency of the weather might be wholly or partially excluded. Their general form on the plan was that of the letter D. The seats (*gradus*) rose behind each other, like steps. The front row was assigned for the use of the senators and the ambassadors of foreign states. Fourteen rows behind this were reserved for the equites, and the rest were open for the public generally. The beautiful Olympic theatre, by Palladio, at Vicenza, was formed on the model of the ancient Roman theatres, and gives one an excellent idea of their effect.

Like the theatres, amphitheatres were at first constructed of wood, and were only temporary. The first amphitheatre of stone was built by Statilius Taurus, at the desire of Augustus.

Of all the monuments of antiquity, none is capable of creating such sublime sensations in the mind as the stupendous amphitheatre generally called the Coliseum. It was commenced in the time of Vespasian, and completed by Titus. The plan of it is oval, and its accommodation was for 87,000 spectators, who could enjoy the exhibitions therein without crowding each other. The part in which the gladiators fought was at the bottom, and was called the arena, from being usually covered with sand to absorb the blood spilt in the savage conflicts for which it was used. The arena was encircled by a wall, called the podium, which projected at top. The podium was fifteen or sixteen feet in height: immediately round it sat the senators and foreign ambassadors. As in the theatres, the seats rose at the back of each other: fourteen rows in the rear of the podium being allotted to the equites, and the remainder to the public generally, who sat on the bare stone; but cushions were provided for the senators and equites. Though open to the sky, the building was occasionally covered by means similar to those used in the theatres.

The amphitheatre at Verona is still in excellent preservation.

The Naumachiæ, or buildings for the exhibition of sham naval combats, were somewhat similar on their plans to the circi, to which purpose also sometimes these latter were appropriated. The amphitheatres were, moreover, occasionally used for the same sort of display. Those of Augustus and Domitian were the most magnificent.

The circus was a long narrow building, whose length was to its breadth generally as five to one: it was divided down the centre by an ornamented barrier, called the *spina*. These buildings were used for the celebration of games, racing, etc., sometimes also for making harangues to the people.

The first circus of stone is attributed to Tarquin, and was situated between the Palatine and Aventine mounts.

The Circus Maximus was much improved and altered by Julius Cæsar, who supplied it with water for the purpose of occasionally using it as a naumachia. Augustus made great additions to it, decorating it with the famous obelisk which now stands in the Piazza del Popolo, where it was placed by Fontana in the year 1589, during the pontificate of Sixtus V. Being much dilapidated, it was repaired under Antoninus, and afterwards embellished with a second obelisk, which has found a resting-place in front of the church of St. John Lateran, where it was set up by the same Fontana. No vestiges of this circus remain.

The circus of Flaminius, in the vicinity of the Pantheon of Agrippa, was of considerable dimensions, and very magnificent.

The Circus Agonalis occupied the site of what is now known by the name of the Piazza Navona.

The circus of Nero, upon a part whereof some portion of the basilica of St. Peter is seated, was a splendid building. The obelisk now standing in the open circular piazza before St. Peter's belonged to this circus.

Those of Florus, Antoninus, and Aurelian, are no longer even in ruins; but that of Caracalla is sufficiently perfect to trace its plan and distribution. It was 738 feet in length.

The streets, in the time of Augustus, were narrow and irregular. After the great fire in Nero's reign, the city was rebuilt with greater splendour. The streets were then set out straight, and considerably broader than before. Those houses wherein several families dwelt were called *insulæ*. *Domus* was the expression for a house occupied by one family only.

We know little of the form of the Roman houses, though Vitruvius has described at sufficient length the different apartments of which they consisted.

The small houses discovered in the ruins of Pompeii can bear but little if any resemblance to the houses of the opulent inhabitants of Rome. The most celebrated were those of the Gordians, P. Valerius Publicola, Cæsar, Sallust, Mecænas, Cicero, Verres, Augustus, and Lucullus. The Domus Aurea of Nero was probably the most magnificent in Rome. The villa of Adrian, at Tivoli, was so extensive, that it almost deserved the name of a city. Immense ruins of the palaces of the Cæsars are still to be seen.

Rome was decorated with numberless pillars. The most remarkable are fortunately in an excellent state of preservation, namely, those of Trajan and Antoninus.

The column of Trajan stood in that emperor's forum: it is about 12 feet in diameter at its base, and (including the pedestal) is about 125 feet in height. The ascent to the gallery on the top of the abacus of its capital is by 185 steps, each 2 feet 9 inches long, winding round the column, and lighted by 40 openings. A colossal statue of Trajan formerly crowned the top; but St. Peter has long since deposed the Emperor.

The column of Antoninus is 176 feet high, its number of steps 106, with 56 openings for the admission of light. Sixtus V. caused its pedestal to be cased, when, in 1589, the pillar was under repair. It was this pontiff who elevated St. Peter to his situation, as well on this as on the Trajan column.

The great sewers of Rome are reputed to have been the work of Tarquinius Priscus. The Cloaca Maxima, which still carries some of the filth and waste water of Rome into the Tiber, was the work of Tarquinius Superbus.

The public ways were not only some of the most stupendous, but also the most useful of the Roman works.

The first road which the Romans paved was the Via Appia, so called because it was executed by order of Appius Claudius. He carried it as far as Capua, whence it was afterwards continued to Brundusium—in all, a distance of 350 miles. It is still entire in many places, though more than twenty centuries have elapsed since its construction. It was properly called 'Regina Viarum.'

The Via Numicia led to Brindis (Brundusium); the Via Flaminia to Rimini and Aquileia; the Via Aurelia was along the coast of Etruria; the Via Cassia ran to Modena, between the Flaminian and Aurelian ways; the Via Æmilia extended from Rimini to Piacenza.

The smaller ways were, the Via Prænestina to Palestrina (the ancient Præneste); Tiburtina to Tivoli; Ostiensis to Ostia; Laurentina to Laurentum, south of Ostia; Salaria, etc. The cross-roads were called Diverticula.

Italian architecture comprises so many diversities that it is hardly possible to affix to it anything like a precise character, except by limiting it to a particular epoch or school, or to one special class of buildings; and even then the exceptions may be more numerous than the examples referred to as a standard. With many vices and defects, it possesses many excellences and recommendations, and a variety of resources, which render it capable of being turned to far greater account than hitherto has been done. But if on the one hand it affords much scope to the architect, it calls on the other for the exercise of discriminating taste, one that not only rejects what is positively bad, but is capable of re-combining all the better elements of the style, so as to impart to them originality and freshness, without forfeiting what is valuable in and characteristic of the style itself, so that, instead of appearing contrary to its genius, the novel forms and effects that may be produced shall seem to be beauties, which have merely been lying latent, and waiting for a discoverer to bring them to light. A style is to be judged of, not only retrospectively by what it has produced, but prospectively also, according to what it is capable of supplying. Nevertheless, so far from being at all encouraged, such view of the subject is kept out of sight as much as possible; and precedent is allowed to usurp such sway, that any departure from it, no matter in what spirit, is liable to be confounded with and reprobated as capricious innovation, although the one proceeds quite in an opposite direction to the other.

Italian church (the), in the front or façade, is never true to the internal structure; it is always divided into two apparent stories, by two heights of pillars, or pilasters, and by windows, or alcoves; but the greater number of churches in Rome have the outward look of large dwelling-houses, a highly ornamented centre, and wings less so, with two or three ranges of windows, not differing from a habitable house.

Italian varnish, for painting, is prepared by incorporating over a slow fire two parts of linseed or nut oil with one part of litharge, ground fine. The mixture must be frequently stirred to quicken the operation.

Ivory is first mentioned in the reign of Solomon: ivory was used in decorating those boxes of perfumes whose odours were employed to exhilarate the King's spirits. It is probable that Solomon, who traded in India, first brought thence elephants and ivory into Judæa. Cabinets and wardrobes were ornamented with ivory by marquetry-work. These were called 'houses of ivory.'—"Eighty more chests of ivory, for your use and pleasure," are enumerated in the letter which accompanied the very remarkable tribute of the Ethiopian queen, Candace, to Alexander the Great.

Ivory-black and *bone-black*, ivory and bone charred to blackness by strong heat in closed vessels; if skilfully prepared, they are eligible for oil and water painting.

J.

Jack, an instrument for raising a heavy weight through a short distance; it consists of a strong piece of wood, with an iron rack which is moved, by wheels fixed inside the wood, from a handle outside.

Jack, in navigation, a flag or colour; a small union flag.

Jak-wood, a native of India, is imported in logs from 3 ft. to 5 ft. diameter; the grain is coarse and crooked: used in cabinet-work, marquetry, and turning, and also for brush-backs.

Jamb, in building, a supporter on either side, as the posts of a door.

Jambs, the side pieces of any opening in a wall, which bear the piece that discharges the superincumbent weight of such wall.

Janta, a machine extensively used in Bengal and other parts of India, to raise water for the irrigation of land. It consists of a hollow trough of wood, about 15 ft. long, 6 inches wide, and 10 inches deep, and is placed on a horizontal beam lying on bamboos fixed in the bank of a pond or river: one end of the trough rests upon the bank, where a gutter is prepared to carry off the water, and the other end is dipped in the water by a man standing on a stage, plunging it in with his foot.

Janua, among the Romans, the street-door of a private house.

Japanning, the art of painting and varnishing on wood, leather, metal, or paper, after the manner of the Japanese.

Jasper is found along the shores of the Bay of Chaleur, and other localities in the northern part of New Brunswick.

Jaune minéral. This pigment is a chromate of lead, prepared in Paris. The chrome-yellows have obtained other names from places or persons from whence they have been brought, or by whom they have been prepared, such as Jaune de Cologne, etc.

Jesse (the root of), a term applicable to the genealogy of Christ, as affording subjects for the painter, sculptor, or embroiderer.

Jet d'eau, a French expression, signifying a fountain that throws up water to some height in the air.

Jetty, a part of a building that projects beyond the rest, and overhangs the wall below, as the upper stories of timber houses, bay-windows, pent-houses, small turrets at the corners, etc.

Jetty, a projecting erection into the sea, partaking something of a pier, mostly constructed of timber, with open spaces for the sea to play.

Jewry, a district, street, or place or locality, in which Jews formerly resided.

Jib, the overhanging part of a crane, or a triangular frame with a pulley at the end, for the chain to pass over which leads from the crane.

Jib, in navigation, the foremost sail of a ship.

Jib-boom, a spar run out from the bowsprit.

Jigger, a machine consisting of a piece of rope about 5 feet long, with a block at one end and a sheaf at the other, used to hold on the cable when it is heaved into the ship by the revolution of the windlass.

Jigging, in Cornwall, a method of dressing the smaller copper and lead ores, by the motion of a wire sieve in a kieve or vat of water.

Joggle, a term in masonry, the art of joining and fitting the stones together.

Joinery, the art of joining, comprehends all the fixed woodwork intended for ornament or convenience in the interior of a house.

Joint, the interstices between the stones or bricks in masonry and brickwork are so called.

Joists, in carpentry, the secondary beams of a floor; those pieces of timber framed into girders and summers, on which the boards of the floor are laid.

Journal, a bearing of a shaft when it is between the points where the powers and resistance are applied; a bearing subject to torsion.

Jube, anciently, the rood-loft or gallery over the entrance into the choir of a cathedral or church.

Jugumentum, the lintel of a door.

Jumper, a long borer used by one person.

Juniper wood, an aromatic and very durable kind of wood.

Junk, an Indian or Chinese ship.

Junk-ring, a ring fitting a groove round a piston, to make it steam-tight. The ring is turned accurately to the diameter of the cylinder, and slightly hammered all round on the inside to increase its elasticity; it is then cut open, and put in its place; springs are sometimes used for pressing it outward.

Justice (Courts of). These places, according to Palladio, were anciently called Basilicæ, where the judges attended to administer justice, and where, sometimes, great and important affairs were transacted: whence we read, that the tribunes of the people caused to be taken away a column that interrupted their benches, from the Basilica Portia; which was at Rome near the temple of Romulus and Remus, and is now the church of St. Cosmus and Damianus.

K.

KAGE, anciently applied to chantry chapels enclosed with lattices or screenwork.

Kaolin, aluminous earth; the porcelain earth of the Chinese.

Kazer, in Cornwall, a sieve.

Kedging, in navigation, a term used when a vessel is brought up or down a narrow river or over a bar.

Keel (False), in ship-building, a strong thick piece of timber bolted to the bottom of the real keel, which is very useful in preserving it.

Keels, in navigation, small vessels that carry coals down the river Tyne.

Keelson, in ship-building, the piece of timber attached to a ship's keel.

Keep, the chief tower or dungeon of a Norman castle.

Keeping, in painting, is the observance of a due proportion in the general light and colouring of a picture, so that no part be too vivid or more glaring than another, but a proper harmony and gradation be evident in the whole performance.

Kept down is a term implying gloominess of tint, or an object so shaded with fuscous colour that its form can scarcely be determined; which object is not intended to be seen by the spectator until he has regularly observed all the other parts of the painting, but which is necessary to the composition.

Kermes lake, an ancient pigment, perhaps the earliest of the European lakes: the name is probably derived from the Alkermes of the Arabians, from Kerman, the ancient Carmania, on the borders of Persia.

Kerned, a term applied to a heap of mundic or copper ore hardened by lying exposed to the sun.

Ketch, in navigation, a vessel with masts and sails.

Kevels, in ship-building, answer the purpose of timber-heads, and are sometimes fixed to the spirketing on the quarter-deck, when the timber-heads are deficient.

Key, a term applied to a painting when one object, generally the principal one, is so worked up to its proper tone, strength of colour, etc., that the painter is compelled to finish the whole piece in a masterly manner: this is said to have been the practice of Titian.

Key-grooving machine, a machine for cutting the grooves or key-ways in the boss of a wheel to be fixed on a shaft.

Key-screw, a lever used for turning screws.

Key-stone, the stone in an arch which is equally distant from its springing extremities. In a circular arch there will be two key-stones, one at the summit and the other at the bottom thereof: in semi-circular, semi-elliptical arches, etc., it is the highest stone, frequently sculptured on the face and return sides.

Kiabooca-wood, or *Amboyna-wood*, imported from Singapore, is very ornamental, and is used for small boxes and writing-desks.

Kibbal, a bucket in which ore is raised from the mines.

Kieve, a vat or large iron-bound tub for washing of ores.

Kilkenny marble, a fine black marble, full of shells and corolloid bodies.

Killas, a clay slate occurring in different parts of a mine.

Killepe, anciently a gutter, groove, or channel.

Kiln, a furnace for burning bricks and tiles, also limestone or chalk, to make lime; a place for drying malt or hops.

Kilogramme (pronounced *Kilo*), a French weight, equivalent to 2 lbs. 3 oz. 5drs. 13 grs. avoirdupois.

King-at-arms, in heraldry, a principal officer at arms. There are three: Garter, Norroy, and Clarencieux.

King-post, the middle post of a roof, standing in the tie-beam and reaching up to the ridge; it is often formed into an octagonal column with capital and base, and small struts or bases, which are slightly curved, spreading from it above the capital to some other timbers.

Kingston's valve, a flat valve forming the outlet of the blow-off pipe of a marine engine; it opens from the side of the vessel by turning a screw.

King-wood, called also *violet-wood*, is imported from the Brazils; it has violet-streaked tints, and is used in turnery and small cabinet-work.

Kirk, church, a term still used in Scotland, formerly so in England.

Klinometer, or *Clinometer*, an instrument contrived to measure the inclinations of stratified rocks, the declivity of mountains, and the dip of mineral strata.

Knee, a term sometimes used for the return of the drip-stone at the spring of an arch.

Kneller (Sir Godfrey), flourished during Charles II.'s reign.

Knees, in ship-building, are the crooked pieces of oak timber, or iron, which secure the beams to the side of the ship.

Knight-heads or *bollard-timbers*, the timbers on each side nearest the stem, and continued high enough to secure the bowsprit.

Knits, small particles of lead ore.

Knockings, lead ore with spar, as cut from the veins.

Knot or *Knob*, a boss; a round bunch of leaves or flowers, or other ornament of a similar kind.

Knuckle-timber, the foremost top timber in the ship that forms the buck-head; the timbers abaft it, as far as the angle is continued, may be called knuckle-timbers.

Krems, *Cremz*, or *Kremnitz white*, a white carbonate of lead, named from Crems or Krems, in Austria; also called Vienna white.

Kyanizing and *Burnettizing*. Kyanizing is a simple process by means of which timber, canvas, and cordage, etc., may be preserved from the effect of dry-rot, and seasoned in a very short time. It was invented by Mr. Kyan, who obtained a patent for it, which was purchased by a Company called the 'Anti-Dry-rot Company,' constituted and empowered by Act of Parliament.

The timber is prepared as follows: a wooden tank is put together so that no metal of any kind can come in contact with the solution when the tank is charged. The solution consists of corrosive sublimate and water, in the proportion of 1 lb. of corrosive sublimate to 10 gallons of water as a maximum strength, and 1 lb. to 15 gallons as a minimum, according to the porosity or absorption of the timber subjected to the process.

Oak and fir timber absorb nearly alike, but the domestic woods, such as beech, poplar, elm, etc., are more porous.

An hydrometer will mark accurately the strength of the solution, water being 0 (*vide* diagram); then, when the hydrometer sinks to 6°, it denotes that the solution contains 1 lb. of sublimate to 15 gallons of water; when it rises to 17°, 1 lb. of sublimate to 5 gallons.

As a general rule, when it stands midway between 5° and 10°, the solution will be the proper strength.

The corrosive sublimate will dissolve best in tepid water.

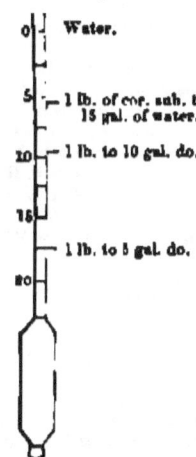

0 — Water.
5 — 1 lb. of cor. sub. to 15 gal. of water.
10 — 1 lb. to 10 gal. do.
15 —
— 1 lb. to 5 gal. do.
20 —

The period required for saturating timber depends on its thickness: 24 hours are required for each inch in thickness, for boards and small timbers.

The timbers, after saturation, should be placed under a shed or cover from the sun and rain, to dry gradually.

In about 14 days, deals and timber not exceeding 3 inches in thickness will be perfectly dry and seasoned, and fit for use. Large timbers will require a proportionate time, according to their thickness.

The solution may be used *ad infinitum*, as its strength is not diminished; but it will be advisable to ascertain occasionally by the hydrometer that it contains the required proportions of corrosive sublimate and water.

Professor Faraday and the late Dr. Birkbeck have, with many other scientific men, testified in the strongest manner to the efficacy of this solution. The former says, with respect to the penetration of the solution by steeping, without pressure, that it may be tested by the application of a drop of hydrosulphuret of ammonia, which will turn black on meeting with the mercury.

In the cube of elm, the corrosive sublimate may be traced by the above test to the depth of from $\frac{1}{4}$ to $\frac{3}{4}$ of an inch; by the test of voltaic action, from $\frac{3}{4}$ to 1 inch.

In the cube of oak, with the same test, it was found at $\frac{1}{4}$ of an inch, but irregular, and apparently following the fissures of the wood; by voltaic action, not quite so far as in the elm.

In the cube of fir, the penetration was the least by the common test, $\frac{1}{4}$ to $\frac{1}{2}$ of an inch: by voltaic action, $\frac{1}{2}$ of an inch, the turpentine in the wood probably being the obstruction to penetration.

From this testimony it is evident that when pressure is not used, the timber should be worked up into the form required before immersion.

The patentees or Company, who have also the means of saturating with hydraulic pressure at their establishment, similar to that at Portsmouth Dockyard, under Sir William Burnett's process, grant licenses at the rate of 5s. per cubic foot, internal dimensions of the tank, and sell corrosive sublimate at 4s. per lb.

1¼ lb. is sufficient to saturate a load of timber of 50 cubic feet, at the rate of 1 lb. of sublimate to 15 gallons of water.

The process has been for several years extensively used for sleepers on railroads.

Several of the sleepers on the South-western Railway, which had been subjected to this process, were taken up, owing to their being decayed, particularly in the chalk districts. It was, however, stated by the engineer that they had been steeped at the Company's works in a hasty manner, and that he did not consider it conclusive against the process; that he had never seen any wood decayed that had been steeped by the patentees. It is also said that neither Kyan's, Burnett's, nor Payne's process, can resist the combined effects of moisture and great heat, say 80° Fahr.

BURNETTIZING.

Burnettizing is the process by means of which timber, felt, canvas, cordage, cottons, and woollens, may be preserved from dry-rot, mildew, moth, and premature decay. It takes its name from its inventor, Sir William Burnett, M.D., K.C.B., F.R.S., of the Navy, who took out a patent for it in 1837.

It consists in immersing the various substances above enumerated in a solution of chloride of zinc and water in a wooden tank, in the proportion of 1 lb. of chloride of zinc to 4 gallons of water for wood, and 1 lb. of the chloride to 5 gallons of water for the remainder of the articles, with the exception of felt, which requires 1 lb. of the chloride to 2 gallons of water.

Three-inch deals require to remain in the tank or cistern six days, and all other woods in the same proportion, or two days per inch. They are then taken out and put under a shed, on their ends, to dry, and require for this purpose from fourteen days to three months, according to the thickness of the wood, when they are fit for use.

The timber should be reduced to the scantling required for use before it is subjected to this process.

Canvas, yarn for cordage, cottons, and woollens, require to be suspended in the solution for forty-eight hours.

The process, however, with respect to timber, is much more expeditiously and effectively done by hydraulic pressure in her Majesty's dockyard at Portsmouth, where large quantities of timber, etc., are prepared for the use of the Royal Navy at the various dockyards in

England, particularly for ships' magazines.

There is a large wrought-iron tank, 52 feet in length and 6 feet in diameter, with a door 2 feet 6 inches × 2 feet at each end for loading.

Timber of all sizes and descriptions is put into this cylinder, which contains about twenty loads. As soon as it is filled, and the doors well secured both against external and internal pressure, the air is exhausted in the cylinder, and also in the timber, by means of an air-pump worked by a small rotatory engine of 10-horse power, on the Earl of Dundonald's principle, until the barometer stands at 27°: the valve leading to the air-pump is then shut, and the cock of a pipe leading from the tank, filled with the solution, to the cylinder, is turned: the solution rushes into the cylinder to fill up the partial vacuum, and about half-fills it, when the cock is turned, and the air-pump again set to work until the barometer stands at 27½°, when the same process is repeated, and the cylinder nearly filled with the solution.

A pressure of 150 lbs. per square inch is then obtained by means of a Bramah forcing-pump, connected with an iron copper or reservoir, filled with the solution, and communicating with the cylinder by means of a pipe. This is worked by hand until a valve placed on the top of the cylinder, and loaded to the required gauge, begins to lift.

The timber is then left in the cylinder, subject to this pressure, for eight hours, which is considered sufficient for the largest logs, even in a rough state. The solution being then drawn off into the tank, and the timber taken out of the cylinder, it is re-loaded, and the process repeated: the same solution is used for two months, when fresh is prepared.

The same process for drying the timber thus saturated is adopted, as before stated. Canvas, felt, and yarn, etc., are not subjected to pressure.

The felt is used as a lining to the magazines of men-of-war, between two thicknesses of wood; also to cover over the steam-boilers of steam-ships: it is said to be rendered much less liable to combustion by the process.

It is stated that in tropical climates, more especially in Africa, the saturated canvas has stood the climate, when the unprepared, under similar circumstances, has rapidly decayed.

Both Burnettizing and Kyanizing offer great advantages to the engineer:

1st. Wood of every kind is rendered more durable, and is rapidly seasoned.

2ndly. It brings into general use larch, poplar, and a variety of other indigenous woods, as well as American pine, etc., which, without the process, from being liable to rapid decay, and being much inferior to Baltic timber, are seldom used in public buildings.

To the military engineer, these inventions offer still greater advantages. He is frequently called on, in distant colonies, to construct block-houses, stockades, bridges, and barracks, where the only material to be had in abundance is the tree standing in the forest: to him a few pounds of either ingredient would be invaluable, by enabling him to season and render durable the timber a few days after it was cut down, and thus provide him with the ready means of rendering a distant post tenable in a short time by a small body of men, with the additional satisfaction of knowing that the work thus hastily erected would be found to be of a permanent nature.

Kyste, a chest or coffin for the burial of the dead.

L.

Laburnum, a small dark-greenish broom-wood, is sometimes used in ornamental cabinet-work.

Labyrinth, a series of hedges, mounds, or walls, with numerous winding passages; intricate and winding walks in a garden.

Lacing, a piece of compass or knee-timber, faved to the back of the figure and the knee of the head of a ship, and bolted to each.

Locker, or **Lacquer**, a varnish applied upon tin, brass, and other metals, to preserve them from tarnishing, and to improve their colour.

Lac lake is prepared from lac, an Indian drug. It resembles cochineal and kermes, being the production of a species of insect. Its colour is rich, transparent, and deep, —less brilliant and more durable than those of cochineal and kermes, but inferior in both these respects to the colour of madder.

Laconicum, among the ancients, the semicircular end of a bath; a circular stove, for the purpose of heating the sudatories, or sweating-rooms of a bath: the use of the dry bath is said to have been prevalent among the Lacedæmonians.

Lacunar, an arched roof or ceiling, more especially the planking or flooring above the porticoes.

Lacunaria, the ceiling of the ambulatory around the cells of a temple or of the portico. The beams, which extended from the walls to the entablature, were intersected by others ranged longitudinally: the square spaces made by these intersecting beams were contracted towards the top, and were sometimes closed with single stones, which might occasionally be removed.

Lacunars, in architecture, are panels or coffers in the ceilings of apartments, and sometimes in the soffits of the corona of the Ionic, Corinthian, and Composite orders.

Lade, a passage of water, the mouth of a river.

Lady-chapel, a chapel dedicated to the blessed Virgin.

Laines, courses laid in the building of walls.

Lake (colour), a name derived from the lac or lacca of India, is the cognomen of a variety of transparent red and other pigments of great beauty, prepared for the most part by precipitating coloured tinctures of dyeing drugs upon alumine and other earths, etc. The lakes are hence a numerous class of pigments, both with respect to the variety of their appellations and the substances from which they are prepared. The colouring matter of common lake is Brazil wood, which affords a very fugitive colour. Superior red lakes are prepared from cochineal, lac, and kermes; but the best of all are those prepared from the root of the rubia tinctoria, or madder-plant. See *Lac lake*.

Lama, in mining, slime or schelm.

Lamina, the extremely thin plates or layers of metal which compose the solid metal.

Laminable, a term applied to metal which may be extended by passing it between steel or hardened (chilled) cast-iron rollers.

Laminated, disposed in layers or plates. When metal can be readily extended in all directions, under the hammer, it is said to be malleable, and when in fillets under the rolling-press, it is said to be laminable.

Lamp-black, a soot of resinous woods obtained in the manufacturing of tar and turpentine. It is a pure carbonaceous substance of a fine texture, intensely black and perfectly durable, which works well, but dries badly in oil.

Lance wood, imported in long poles from 3 to 6 inches in diameter, from Cuba and Jamaica, is of a paler yellow than box-wood: it is selected for elastic works, as gig shafts, archery bows and springs, surveyors' rods, billiard cues, etc.

Landscape. In landscape we find Nature employing broken colours in enharmonic consonance and variety, and equally true to picturesque relations: she employs also broken forms and figures in conjoint harmony with colours, occasionally throwing into the composition a regular form or a primary.

Landscape Gardening. The outline of a wood may sometimes be great, and always beautiful, but the first requisite is irregularity. That a mixture of trees and underwood should form a long straight line, can never be natural; and a succession of easy sweeps and gentle rounds, each a portion of a greater or less circle, composing altogether a line literally serpentine, is, if possible, worse; it is but a number of regularities put together in a disorderly manner, and equally distant from the beautiful, both of art and of nature.

The true beauty of an outline consists more in breaks than in sweeps; rather in angles than rounds; in variety, not in succession. The outline of a wood is a continued line, and small variations do not save it from the insipidity of sameness: one deep recess, one bold prominence, has more effect than twenty little irregularities; and that one divides the line into parts, but no breach is thereby made in its unity: a continuation of wood always remains, the form of it only is altered, and the extent increased: the eye, which hurries to the extremity of whatever is uniform, delights to trace a varied line through all its intricacies, to pause from stage to stage, and so lengthen the progress.

The parts must not, however, on that account, be multiplied till they are too minute to be interesting, and so numerous as to create confusion: a few large parts should be more strongly distinguished in their forms, their directions, and their situations: each of these may afterwards be decorated with subordinate varieties, and the mere growth of the plants will occasion some irregularity: on many occasions more will not be required. Every variety in the outline of a wood must be a prominence or a recess; breadth in either is not so important as length to the one and depth to the other: if the former ends in an angle, or the latter diminishes to a point, they have more force than a shallow dust or a dwarf excrescence, how wide soever: they are greater deviations from the continued line which they are intended to break, and their effect is to enlarge the wood itself.

Every variety of outline hitherto mentioned may be traced by the underwood alone; but frequently the same effects may be produced with more ease, and much more beauty, by a few trees standing out from the thicket, and belonging or seeming to belong to the wood, so as to make a part of its figure.

The materials of natural landscape are ground, wood, and water, to which man adds buildings, and adapts them to the scene: it is therefore from the artificial considerations of utility, convenience, and propriety, that a place derives its real value in the eyes of a man of taste: he will discover graces and defects in every situation; he will be as much delighted with a bed of flowers as with a forest thicket, and he will be as much disgusted by the fanciful affectation of rude nature in tame scenery as by the trimness of spruce art in that which is wild.

Landscape Painting. The best painters in landscape have studied in Italy or France, where the verdure of England is unknown: hence arises the habit acquired by the connoisseur, of admiring the brown tints and arid foregrounds in the pictures of Claude and Poussin; and from this cause he prefers the bistre sketches to the green paintings of Gainsborough. One of our best landscape painters studied in Ireland, where the soil is not so yellow as in England; and his pictures, however beautiful in design and composition, are always cold and chalky. Autumn is the favourite season of study for landscape painters, when all nature verges towards decay, when the foliage changes its vivid green to brown and orange, and the lawns put on their russet hue: but the tints and verdant colouring of spring and summer will have superior charms to those who delight in the perfection of nature, without perhaps ever considering whether they are adapted to the painter's landscape.

Land Steward. A person solely occupied in the management and cultivation of an estate should see to the production, advancement, and value of the land; should be well acquainted with the pursuits and interests of country life; should understand the qualities of the soil and the proper manuring of the same, as well as the different combinations of sand, gravel, loam, clay, chalk; he should be able to show what stock the pasture will maintain, what quantity of grain the arable land will produce, and what quantity of hay may be expected from the meadows; with other requisite knowledge pertaining to farming, he will be able to form a fair estimate of the produce of the farm, to keep accounts, and ultimately acquire a taste for the erection of farm buildings and labourers' rural cottages, and also the arrangement of landscape, flower, and vegetable gardens.

Lanyard, in navigation, a stout piece of line or cord used to fasten and secure the shrouds, stays, or buoys.

Lantern, in architecture, a small structure on the top of a dome or in similar situations for the admission of light, and the promotion of ventilation. It is generally made ornamental, and was much used in Gothic and Tudor architecture.

Lanzi (Abbate Luigi), the author of the 'History of Painting in Italy,' was born in 1732 and died in 1810.

Lapidarius, a lapidary, a stone-cutter.

Lapis lazuli, a mineral which furnishes the valuable pigment called ultramarine.

Lapis lydius, a variety of touchstone; the schistose jasper of Brongniart, containing silica, iron, alumina, and charcoal.

Laque minérale is a French pigment, a species of chromic orange. This name is also given to orange oxide of iron.

Larboard, in navigation, the left-hand side of a ship, standing with face to the head: now the word 'Port' is used.

Larch, a tree, larchwood, much grown by the Duke of Athol, in Scotland. There are three species, one European and two American.

Lardrove, a screen at the back of a seat behind an altar.

Later, a brick or tile. Besides the Greeks and Romans, other ancient nations employed brick for building to a great extent, especially the Babylonians and Egyptians.

Lathe, a machine for turning metals or wood by causing the material to revolve upon central points, and be cut by a tool fixed in a slide-rest, or held by hand.

The lathe is very ancient, and seems to have been known to the Greeks and Romans, but, till within the last half century, was a very rough and almost powerless machine compared with the elegant, very powerful, and well constructed machine now in use. It is used for turning either metal or timber, and varies in size and construction, according to the nature of the work required.

The construction of the present lathe is as follows: a long frame, called the lathe-bed, having a perfectly planed surface, and a slot or mortise from end to end, is fixed at each end upon two short standards, and upon one end of it a frame, called the head-stock or mandril-frame, is bolted: this frame carries the short shaft or mandril, upon which are the driving pulleys. The end of the mandril stands through the inner side of the frame, and is screwed so that a socket or centre chuck may be fixed on it: this chuck acts as a centre for the work to rest upon, and has a projecting arm or driver to carry it round with it. Another frame, called the back centre frame, capable of being fixed upon the lathe-bed at any distance from the front centre, has a cylinder, with a pointed end or centre, at precisely the same height as the other, with two set-screws, one to adjust the centre piece, the other to fix it. The work is placed between these two centres, and caused to revolve by a band passing over a pulley on the mandril, if the lathe is large, and by a treadle and band-wheel, if the lathe is small.

In small lathes, the rest, upon which the tool is held, is fixed in a socket cast on a small slide by a set-screw: the slide is for adjusting its position, and is capable of being fixed at any part of the lathe-bed between the centres.

In large lathes the slide-rest is always used. See *Slide-rest*.

Lathe-bed, that part of a lathe on which the 'poppet-head' slides forward or backward to its required position.

Latitude, breadth, width, extent; in geography, the distance, north or south, from the equator, a great circle, equally distant from the poles, dividing the globe into equal parts, north and south.

Latten, a mixed metal resembling brass. The monumental brasses in churches are called latten.

Lattern-sail, in navigation, a long triangular sail used in xebecs, etc.

Launders, in mining, tubes and gutters for the conveyance of water in mines, etc.

Lavatory, a cistern or trough to wash in, used formerly in monasteries.

Laver, brazen. Moses was directed to make, among other articles of furniture, for the services of the tabernacle, a laver of brass, borne by four cherubim, standing upon bases or pedestals, mounted on brazen wheels, and having handles belonging to them, by means of which they might be drawn and conveyed from one place to another, as they should be wanted. These lavers were double, composed of a basin which received the water that fell from another square vessel above it, from which the water was drawn by cocks. The whole work was of brass: the square vessel was adorned with the heads of a lion, an ox, and a cherub. Each of the lavers contained forty baths, or four bushels, forty-one pints, and forty cubic inches of Paris measure.

Lay figure, a figure made of wood or cork, in imitation of the human body. It can be placed in any position or attitude, and moves at every joint, on the principle of the ball and socket. It serves, when clothed, as a model for drapery and for foreshortening. The dress of the person is generally placed on the lay-figure after the head is taken, by which the painter finishes his entire portrait at leisure, without requiring the person to sit.

Lazaretto, an hospital ship for the reception of the sick.

Lead is a very heavy metal, sufficiently well known. The mode of purifying it from the dross which is mixed with it, by subjecting it to a fierce flame, and melting off its scoria, furnishes several allusions in Scripture to God's purifying or punishing his people. It was one of the substances used for writing upon by the ancients.

Lead spar, sulphate of lead.

Leader, a branch, rib, or string of ore, leading along to the lode.

Leading springs, the springs fixed upon the leading axle-box of a locomotive engine, bearing the weight above.

Leading wheels, the wheels of a locomotive engine, which are placed before the driving wheels.

Lease, holding of land or house for a term of years at a rent.

Leat, a water-course, or level for conveyance of water.

Leaves, a term applied to window-shutters, the folding-doors of closets, etc.

Leaving (in Cornish), or *casualties*, in tin, is the same as *hanaways* of copper or lead ore.

Lectern or *Lettern*, the desk or stand on which the larger books used in the services of the Roman Catholic church are placed. In modern Protestant churches they are now often used, and are very ornamental in appearance, and far more appropriate than the cumbersome reading-desk. Lecterns are made sometimes of stone or marble, but usually of wood and brass, and generally are extremely well executed.

Lectus, a bed or couch.

Ledger, a large flat stone laid over a tomb; horizontal timbers used in forming scaffolding are also called ledgers.

Ledgment, a string-course, or horizontal suite of mouldings, such as the base-mouldings of a building.

Lee, in navigation, the side opposite to the wind; as the lee-shore is that on which the wind blows.

Lely (Sir Peter), flourished in Charles II.'s reign.

Lembus, according to Plautus, a skiff or small boat, used for carrying a person from a ship to the shore.

Lemon yellow, a beautiful light and vivid colour. In body and opacity it is nearly equal to Naples yellow and masticot, but much more pure and lucid in colour and tint, and at the same time not liable to change by damp, sulphurous or impure air, or by the action of light, or by the steel palette-knife, or by mixture of white lead or other pigments, either in water or oil.

Lessee, one to whom a lease is given.

Lessor, one who grants a lease.

Levecel, anciently a pent-house, or a projecting roof over a window, door, etc.

Level, an instrument for determining the heights of one place with respect to another.

Levelling, the art by which the relative heights of any number of points are determined.

The height of a point is the vertical distance to which it is elevated or depressed, as compared with the true general surface of the earth.

The earth is in form a spheroid. On land we can nowhere trace its true geometric surface; but the sea, when at rest, presents everywhere a very near approximation to it, and hence the level of the sea has been assumed as the standard to which all heights are to be referred.

The absolute height, then, of any point is its vertical distance from the level of the sea: the relative height of two or more points, commonly called their difference of level, is the difference of those vertical distances.

A true level is any surface or line which is parallel to the true geometric surface of the earth; every true level must, therefore, necessarily present a curve everywhere perpendicular to the direction of gravity. It is a beautiful property of fluids that in every situation, when at rest, their surface will present a true level.

All points situated within the same true level are evidently at the same height.

One point is said to be higher or lower than another, according as a true level traced through it passes above or below that point; and the vertical distance at which it so passes is the measure of its relative height.

In theory, levelling is extremely simple. It consists in tracing through space a series of level surfaces, and finding their intersections with vertical lines passing through the points whose relative height we wished to ascertain.

Level (Road), a triangular frame of wood with a long straight base, and a plummet suspended by a thread from the vertex of the triangle. When the ground to which it is applied is level, the thread will coincide with a line perpendicular to the base.

A tool similar in principle to the above-mentioned is used by fitters, and is made of a plate of sheet-iron, two sides of which form a right angle, and the thread which suspends the plummet is parallel to the vertical side when the base is level.

Level (Spirit), a glass tube, closed at the ends, and nearly filled with water or spirits, fixed in a piece of wood or metal with a flat base, to which the tube is perfectly parallel. When placed upon a level surface, an air-bubble will be at the centre of the tube.

Lever, the first mechanical power, being an inflexible straight bar, supported in a single point on a fulcrum or prop, called its centre of motion; it is used to elevate a great weight.

Lever-valve, a safety-valve kept in its seat by the pressure of a lever with an adjustable weight. In locomotive engines a spring is used at the end of the lever, instead of the weight; and the pressure is regulated by a screw, and indicated on a brass plate.

Levigation, the process of reducing hard bodies into subtile powder by grinding upon marble with a muller.

Lewis, an instrument used by masons for hoisting, consisting of thin wedges of iron, forming a dovetail, which is indented into a large stone for the purpose of moving it.

Ley, a standard of metal; contents in pure metal.

Libella, a small balance; a level used by carpenters and masons to test flat surfaces.

Libra, a pound weight; a balance, or a pair of scales: one of the twelve signs of the zodiac.

Library, a room or rooms appropriated for the arrangement and keeping of books, fitted up with shelves to hold them, or furniture called book-cases, to which shelves are affixed for the same purpose.

Lick-gate, a gate belonging to church-yards.

Lifting-gear, the apparatus for lifting the safety-valves from within a boiler: it consists of levers connected to the valve and to a screw worked by a handle outside the boiler.

Lifts, in navigation, the ropes at the yard-arms, used to make the yards hang higher or lower, as required.

Light. The meteorological phenomena induced by the action of light are, chiefly, atmospheric refraction, i. e. the temperature of the different strata of the atmosphere; the tints which at certain times spread over the disc of the sun, the moon, and the stars; the various aspects of the waters of the ocean, of seas, and of lakes; the Fata Morgana, the mirage, and all those varied optical appearances which both celestial and terrestrial objects present when seen through atmospheric strata of different degrees of elasticity.

Light red is an ochre of a russet-orange hue; principally valued for its tints. The common light red is brown ochre burnt; but the principal yellow ochres afford this colour best; and the brighter and better the yellow from which this pigment is prepared, the brighter will this red be, and the better flesh tints will it afford with white.

Lignum vitæ, or *Guaiacum*, is a very hard and heavy wood, shipped from Cuba and other adjacent islands. When first cut, it is soft and easily worked; but it speedily becomes much harder on exposure to the air. It is cross-grained, covered with a smooth yellow sap, like box, almost as hard as the wood, which is of a dull brownish-green, and contains a large quantity of the gum guaiacum, which is extracted for the purposes of medicine. The wood is used in machinery, and for rollers, presses, mills, pestles and mortars, sheaves for ships' blocks, skittle-balls, etc.

Limber-boards, short pieces of plank fitted from the limber-strake to the keelson of a ship, butting at the sides of all the bulk-heads, that they may be easily taken up.

Limber-strake, the strake of wood waling nearest the keelson, from the upper side of which the depth in the hold of a vessel is measured.

Lime, or *Quicklime*. When required perfectly pure, lime is obtained by heating to whiteness, in an open platinum crucible, precipitated carbonate: most marbles yield it moderately pure; but as prepared for ordinary purposes, by the calcination of common limestone in a furnace with coal, it is far otherwise.

Limestone becomes lime on being deprived of its carbonic acid and of the water it contains, whether hygrometrically or in combination. The agent employed to effect this is heat.

With the same heat, the calcination is effected with more ease and rapidity, in proportion as the stone is of a less compact texture than the smallness in bulk of the fragments into which it is reduced, or to its being impregnated with a certain degree of humidity.

The contact of the air is not indispensable, but it exercises a useful influence, especially in regard to argillaceous limestone. Moreover, no limestone can be converted into lime in a vessel so close as to render the escape of the carbonic acid impossible.

Limestone which is pure, or nearly so, supports a white heat without inconvenience. Under the intense heat of the hydro-oxygen blow-pipe, this substance affords the brilliant light, the beautiful application of which to the microscope is now so well known. The compound limestone, on the other hand, alloyed in the proportions necessary to form hydraulic or eminently hydraulic lime, fuses easily. Its calcination demands certain precautions: the heat ought never to be pushed beyond the common red heat, the intensity being made up for by its duration.

The compound limestone, when too much burnt, is heavy, compact, dark-coloured, covered with a kind of enamel, especially about the angular parts; it slakes with great difficulty, and gives a lime carbonized and without energy: sometimes it will not slake at all, but becomes reduced, after some days' exposure to the air, to a harsh powder altogether inert.

The pure and compound limestones, when insufficiently burnt, either refuse to slake, or slake only partially, leaving a solid kernel, a kind of sub-carbonate with excess of base.

The calcining of calcareous minerals constitutes the art of the lime-burner. According to situation, either fire-wood, fagots, brush-wood, turf, or coal is used.

Lime-kilns of various kinds have been suggested and tried. The forms of interior most generally adopted are, 1st, the upright rectangular prism; 2nd, the cylinder; 3rd, the cylinder surmounted by an erect cone slightly truncated; 4th, a truncated inverted cone; 5th, an ellipsoid of revolution variously curvated, or an egg-shaped kiln.

The rectangular kilns are in use

in Nivernais, and in the south of France, in which are burnt, at the same time, limestone and bricks. The limestone occupies very nearly the lower half of the capacity. The upper is filled with bricks, or tiles, laid and packed edgewise.

The cylindric kilns are principally employed upon works which consume a large quantity of lime in a short time. They are termed 'field-kilns;' their construction is expeditious and economical, but precarious. Above a pointed oven-shaped vault, is raised, in the form of a tower, a high stack of limestone, which is enclosed by a curtain of rammed earth, and supported outwardly by a coarse wattling, in which care is taken to leave an opening to introduce the fire beneath the vault.

The kilns of the third kind are constructed in a solid and durable manner, like the four-sided kilns: no bricks are burnt in these; the largest stones occupy the lower part of the cylinder; the smaller pieces and fragments are thrown into the cone which surmounts it.

The kilns of the fourth and fifth kind are specially intended for the burning with coal.

The interior wall of the kiln is generally built with bricks, or other material unalterable by heat, cemented throughout a thickness of from 12 to 15 inches with a mixture of sand and refractory clay, beaten together.

In the flare-kilns fed by logs or brushwood, the charge always rests upon one or two vaults built up dry with the materials of the charge itself. Underneath these vaults a small fire is lighted, which is to a distance over every point of the vaults: it insinuates itself by the joints, and is not long in extending the incandescence by degrees to the highest parts.

There are some kinds of stone which the fire, however well regulated, seizes suddenly, and causes to fly with detonation: they cannot, without the risk of spoiling the charge, be used for the construction of the vaults and piers in loading the kiln. In such a case, materials which are free from this inconvenience are employed.

Practice can alone indicate the time proper for the calcination. It varies with a multitude of circumstances, such as the more or less green, more or less dry quality of the wood; the direction of the wind, if it favour the draught, or otherwise, etc. The master-burners usually judge by the general settling of the charge, which varies from $\frac{1}{5}$ to $\frac{1}{4}$. In a kiln of the capacity of from 211·8 to 264·75 cubic feet, the fire lasts from 100 to 150 hours.

In the coal-kilns by slow heat, the stone and coal are mixed. Of all the methods of burning lime, this is certainly the most precarious and difficult, more especially when applied to the argillaceous limestone. A mere change in the duration or intensity of the wind, any dilapidation of the interior wall of the kiln, a too great inequality in the size of the fragments, are so many causes which may retard or accelerate the draught, and occasion irregular movements in the descent of the materials, which become locked together, form a vault, and precipitate at one time the coal, and ficient to lead the most experienced lime-burner into error. In a word, the calcination by means of coal, and the slow heat, is an affair of cautious investigation and practice.

The capacity of a furnace contributes, no less than does its form, to an equable and proper calcination. There are limits beyond which they cannot be enlarged without serious evils.

The bulk of coal burnt to produce a cubic foot of lime necessarily varies with the hardness of the limestone used, but within narrow limits.

The calcination of limestones presents other important problems, which can only be solved by experiment.

Limes, hydraulic (artificial). Already the artificial limes have been applied to a number of important works. In the canals of St. Martin and St. Maur they have been almost exclusively been used, and nearly a thousand cubic mètres have been employed within five years at the harbour of Toulon. These limes have served for the fabrication of the mortar for the foundations of several bridges, and their consumption is increasing daily in Paris and its environs.

The artificial hydraulic limes are prepared by two methods; the most perfect, but also the most expensive, consists in mixing with rich lime, slaked in any way, a certain proportion of clay, and calcining the mixture: this is termed 'artificial lime *twice kilned*.'

By the second process, any very soft calcareous substance is substituted for the lime (such, for example, as chalk, or the tufas), which it is easy to bruise and reduce to a paste with water. From this a great saving is derived, but at the same time an artificial lime perhaps of not quite so excellent a quality as by the first process, in consequence of the rather less perfect amalgamation of the mixture. In fact, it is impossible, by mere mechanical agency, to reduce calcareous substances to the same degree of fineness as slaked lime. Nevertheless, this second process is the more generally followed, and the results to which it leads become more and more satisfactory.

By a proper regulation of the proportions, a degree of energy may be given to the factitious lime, which will render it equal, if not superior, to the natural hydraulic limes.

It is usual to take twenty parts of dry clay to eighty parts of very rich lime, or to one hundred and forty of carbonate of lime. But if the lime or its carbonate should already be at all mixed in the natural state, then fifteen parts of clay will be sufficient. Moreover, it is proper to determine the proportions for every locality. In fact, all clays do not resemble one another to such an extent as to admit of their being considered as identical: the finest and softest are the best.

There is at Meudon, near Paris, a manufactory of artificial lime, set on foot by Messrs. Brian and St. Leger. The materials made use of are, the chalk of the country and the clay of Vaugirard, which is previously broken up into lumps of a moderate size. A millstone set up edgewise, and a strong wheel with spokes and felloes, firmly attached to a set of harrows and rakes, are set in movement by a two-horse gin, in a circular basin of about six feet and a half radius. In the middle of the basin is a pillar of masonry, on which turns the vertical arbor to which the whole system is fixed: into this basin, to which water is conveyed by means of a cock, four measures of chalk are successively thrown, and one measure of clay. After an hour and a half's working, about fifty-three cubic feet (English) of a thin pulp is obtained, which is drawn off by means of a conduit, pierced horizontally on a level with the bottom of the basin.

The fluid descends by its own weight; first into one excavation, then into a second, then a third, and so on to a fourth or fifth. These excavations communicate with one another at top. When the first is full, the fresh liquid, as it arrives, as well as the supernatant fluids, flow over into the second excavation; from the second into the third, and so on to the last, the clear water from which drains off into a cesspool. Other excavations, cut in steps like the preceding, serve to receive the fresh products of the work, whilst the material in the first series acquires the consistency necessary for moulding. The smaller the depth of the pans in relation to their superficies, the sooner is the above-mentioned consistency obtained.

The mass is now subdivided into solids of a regular form by means of a mould. This operation is executed with rapidity. A moulder, working by the piece, makes on an average five thousand prisms a day, which will measure 211·6 cubic feet. These prisms are arranged on drying-shelves, where in a short time they acquire the degree of desiccation and hardness proper for calcination. At Paris a mixture of coke and coal is employed; and the common mode of burning by slow heat rendered necessary by that kind of combustible.

The artificial hydraulic limes are intended to supply the place of the natural ones in those countries where the argillaceous limestone is entirely wanting, and which are commonly sold in Paris.

Lime-tree (the) is common in Europe, attains considerable size, is very light-coloured, fine and close in the grain, and is used in the construction of piano-fortes, harps, etc.; it is particularly suitable for carving, from its even texture and freedom from knots. The works of Gibbons at Windsor Castle, and St. Paul's, London, are of the lime-tree.

Limning, a term formerly applied to portrait-painting, is drawing or painting the body and limbs of the human figure.

Linch-pin, the small pin, in carts, etc., that is put at the ends of the axle-tree to confine the wheels on them steadily.

Linear perspective is that which describes or represents the position, magnitude, form, etc., of the several lines or contours of objects, and expresses their diminution, in proportion to their distance from the eye.

Link-motion, a new apparatus for reversing steam-engines: it is used in locomotive engines instead of the reversing forks, and consists of a link with a slot from end to end, into which a guide-block fits, and is connected to the slide-valve rod: the rods of the two eccentrics are connected one to each end of the link, which is raised or lowered, or held in a central position, by apparatus attached to the centre of it, moved by the reversing lever. When the link is in a central position with regard to the slide-valve rod, the guide-block remains stationary, as it is then at the centre upon which the link vibrates. When the link is up, the guide-block is at the lower end, and the slide receives motion from the backward eccentric. When the link is down, it receives motion from the forward eccentric. See plate 8, elaborately drawn and explained in Vol. 79*, in 'Rudimentary Series.'

Links, in locomotive engines, are flat or round pieces of iron with round holes at each end: they are used to connect together, by bolts, different parts of the mechanism of the engine.

Linseed oil has the fullest body and dries better than any of the three oils (linseed, nut, and poppy) in use with artists; its colour is a strong yellow, but this effect does not arise from the action of the fire in extracting the oil, but from the pellicle which covers the grains, and which contains a strong colouring matter soluble in oil. Linseed oil, cold drawn, is equally coloured with the other sorts, but, like that of wax, this colour is carried off by exposure to the sun.

Lintel, a piece of timber or stone placed horizontally over a doorway or window, to support the superincumbent weight.

Lintel. "And ye shall take a bunch of hyssop, and dip it in the blood that is in the basin, and strike the lintel and the two side-posts with the blood that is in the basin; and none of you shall go out at the door of his house until the morning."—*Exodus* xii. 22.

Liquid rubiate, or *Liquid madder lake*, is a concentrated tincture of madder, of the most beautiful and perfect rose-colour and transparency. It is used as a water-colour only in its simple state, diluted with pure water, with or without gum; it dries in oil, by acting as a dryer to it. Mixed or ground with all other madder colours, with or without gum, it forms combinations which work freely in simple water, and produce the most beautiful and permanent effects.

Lithography, the art of drawing and engraving on stone, and taking impressions from the same at press, similarly to copper-plate printing, but differing in manipulation.

Little winds, in mining, an underground shaft, sunk from the horizontal drift, by which the top of the winds communicates with the side or bottom of the great working-shaft.

Lloyd's Register. Lloyd's rules for British and foreign shipping exert a most essential and powerful influence on the construction and science in the building of shipping of this country as well as those of continental and transatlantic maritime nations. Insurances from loss can only be made at Lloyd's by conforming to the rules laid down by competent surveyors. See Vol. 54° in the 'Rudimentary Series.'

Load water-line, the mark on a ship which the water makes when she is loaded.

Loam, a natural mixture of sand and clay : in the neighbourhood of London, loam consists of fine reddish-grey sand 87 parts, alumina 13 parts = 100.

Local colours are such as faithfully imitate those of a particular object, or such as are natural and proper for each particular object in a picture; and colour is distinguished by the term trial, because the place it fills requires that particular colour, in order to give a greater character of truth to the several colours around it.

Lock, a mechanical contrivance to fasten a door, gate, or any place or thing for security. A vast deal of ingenuity has been exercised to prevent false openings : keys of various kinds are made to fit the wards (interior contrivances), and prevent what is called picking, the key being made only to suit that belonging to the possessor.

Lock, in inland navigation, a portion of a canal confined between a sluice-gate and a flood-gate, to facilitate the passage of boats in ascending or descending planes.

Lockrand, a course of bond stones, or a bonding course, in masonry.

Locks for canal and river navigation. The earliest approximation to what is now known by the name of lock, consisted of a simple dam formed across the bed of a river, so as to raise the water to such a height as to allow vessels to float along it. Where the river had a considerable fall with a strong current, it was necessary to have these dams at short distances from each other, otherwise the requisite depth of water could not be obtained. As the whole space between two of these dams was in fact the lock, it was necessary, in passing from one level to another, to run down the water for the whole of that distance, thereby causing considerable delay, and a waste of water that would now be considered a serious evil. In China these dams are common, and they have also been used on the Continent. See Vol. 121 of the 'Rudimentary Series.'

Locks with a double set of gates, but no chamber-walls, are now of ordinary construction. The evils attendant on the dams formerly constructed were in a great measure removed by the introduction of double sets of gates or sluices, the upper set being constructed so near to the lower as only to leave room enough for the vessel or vessels to float between them. Framed gates were also used instead of separate beams and planks, because the space to be emptied or filled was so small that a very short time was required to pass the water, and there was no stream of sufficient strength to prevent their being easily opened. Where these locks are intended for rivers, it is usual to make a side cut or artificial canal for the purposes of the navigation, and to leave the river-course for the passage of the surplus water. A quick bend of the river is generally chosen for one of these cuts; and to keep the water in the upper part of the river to a sufficient height for navigation, a dam or weir is made across the old river-course at or below the point where the artificial cut quits it. The lock is then built at the most convenient part of the cut, and its fall made equal to the difference in the levels of the water at the top and at the bottom of the dam or weir. When a vessel is going up the river, she floats along the cut, and passes between the lower gates into the lock; the lower gates are then closed, and the valves or paddles of the upper gates being opened, the water flows into the lock, and rises to the level of the upper part of the river; the upper gates are then opened, and the vessel floats out of the lock. The reverse of this operation conducts a vessel down the river.

The abutments for the gates have been made of timber, brickwork, and masonry; but when the double set of gates was first introduced, it was usual to leave the space between the upper and lower gates unprotected by either timber or any kind of building. Of course the agitation of the water in the lock was constantly washing away the earthen banks, thereby causing a risk of their being broken down by such continued weakening; and by enlarging the space between the two sets of gates, it occasioned a loss of time in emptying and filling, as well as a waste of water.

Lock (common modern canal).—The difference of altitude between the upper and lower levels, where the locks are constructed, varies according to local circumstances. Where the ground is longitudinally steep and water plentiful, the locks are generally made of greater lift or fall than where the ground is comparatively flat and water scarce. It is evident, that where the superficial area of locks is the same, one having a rise of 12 feet would require twice the quantity of water to fill it that would be requisite for one of 6 feet. Having many locks, however, of small lifts, instead of a few of greater, increases the expense, as well as the time for passing them.

For narrow canals these locks are generally made about 60 feet long, and 7½ to 8 feet wide in the chamber. On the Caledonian canal they are 180 feet long, 40 feet wide, and 30 feet deep. Locks are also made of every intermediate size. Lock-gates have till lately been made of timber; but in consequence of the difficulty of procuring it of sufficient size for those on the Caledonian canal, cast-iron was partially adopted for the heads, heels, and ribs. Iron gates, cast in one piece, have been used on the Ellesmere canal, as well as others with cast-iron framing and timber planking.

Locks with side ponds.—When water is scarce, it is common to construct side ponds, by which a considerable portion (in general one-half) is saved. The usual number of these ponds is two; for it has been determined by experience, that when a greater number has been made use of, the loss occasioned by leakage and evaporation has sometimes been more than equal to the additional quantity of water thus retained.

Locks for the transit of vessels of different sizes.—Where vessels of different sizes have to pass the same locks, three pairs of gates are sometimes placed instead of two, —the distance between the upper and lower pairs being sufficient to admit the largest vessels, and that between the upper and middle pairs being adapted to the smaller class. By this contrivance, when a small vessel is to be passed through, the lowest pair of gates is not used; and when a large vessel goes through, the middle pair of gates is not worked. Thus it is evident that the quantity of water contained between the middle and lower pair of gates is saved when a small vessel passes, compared with what would be required were the middle set of gates omitted.

Locks (parallel double-transit).— Where the transit is great, much time and water may be saved by a double-transit lock, which is two locks placed close to and parallel with each other, with a communication between them, which can be opened or cut off at pleasure by valves or paddles.

As one of these locks is kept full and the other empty, a vessel in descending floats into the full one: the upper gates are then closed, and the water is run, by means of the connecting culvert, into the empty lock (the gates of which were previously closed), till the water in the two locks is on the same level, which will be when each is half-full: the connecting paddles are then closed, and the remaining half of the water in the descending lock is run into the lower canal. The next descending vessel has to be floated into the lock which remains half-filled, and which consequently requires only half a lock of water to be run from the upper pond to raise it to the proper level, and then that half is transferred to the lock previously used, to serve the next descending vessel; but supposing a vessel to be ascending after the first descent, it will enter the empty lock, and receive a quarter-lock of water from that which remained half-filled: of course, three-quarters of a lock of water is now required from the upper canal to complete the filling. If a descending vessel next follows, it enters the full lock, and its water is run into the lock which was previously left a quarter-full; and when both have arrived at the same level, it is evident they will be each five-eighths full, and the succeeding descending vessel will require only three-eighths of a lock of water from the upper pond or canal. From these observations, it will be seen that the double-transit lock saves nearly one-half of the water which a common single lock would require.

Sometimes the two parallel locks are made of different sizes, to suit the various descriptions of vessels that may have to pass.

Locks connected longitudinally, commonly called a Chain of Locks.— When loss of water is of no consequence, a considerable expense is sometimes saved by placing the locks close together, without any intermediate pond; for by passing from one immediately into the other, there is only required one pair of gates more than the number of locks so connected, besides a proportionate saving of masonry. Thus eight connected locks would only require nine pairs of gates; whilst if they were detached, they would require sixteen pairs. But to show that these cannot be adopted with propriety excepting where water is abundant, it is necessary to observe, that every two alternate ascending and descending vessels will require as many lockfuls of water as there are locks: for instance, if a vessel has just ascended, it has left all the locks full; a descending vessel then enters the upper lock, and when its gates are closed, the water is run down: but all the locks below being previously filled, they cannot contain it, and it consequently passes over the gates or weirs of all of them into the lower canal: the vessel has by this means descended to the level of the second lock, the water in which must also be run into the lower canal, for the same reason as already stated. When the water of all the locks has thus been run down, an ascending vessel will require all these locks to be filled from the upper canal, which, however, will be retained in the locks ready for the succeeding vessel to pass down. From this it will be evident, that where eight locks are connected, a descending vessel draws no water from the upper canal, because the locks are previously all filled, but it empties eight locks of water into the lower canal; an ascending vessel, on the contrary, empties no water into the lower canal, because all the locks were previously emptied, but it draws eight lockfuls from the upper canal, in order to fill them: consequently, the passing of one ascending vessel, and one descending, requires the expenditure of eight lockfuls of water.

Other modes of passing vessels from one level to another, by substituting machinery, either wholly or in part, have been adopted; but these have either failed entirely, or have not been brought into general use.

Locomotive Steam-engines, a class of travelling machines adapted either for railways or common roads, were originally designed for the latter, but did not succeed; and roads were then made for them, called railways, on which they have been most successful. The principle of action being the same in both kinds, a description of the railway variety will explain the manner in which progressive motion is obtained by the agency of steam.

Locomotion or progression is the combined effect of a number of parts in each engine performing separate duties. The principal of these parts and the plan of their co-operation may be thus classed:

1st. The parts which generate the steam.

2nd. The parts which regulate the employment of the steam.

3rd. The parts by which the driver controls the action of the engine.

4th. The parts immediately concerned in producing locomotion.

5th. The parts which excite the rapid combustion of the fuel.

6th. The parts which supply water to the boiler.

7th. The parts which support the engine on the rails.

8th. The manner in which locomotion is produced by these parts.

In explaining them and their effect as thus arranged, we have

1st. The parts which generate the steam, called the boiler, containing internally a fire-box, varying according to the dimensions of the engine from 25 (as in the 'Rocket') to 303 small tubes (as in the broad-gange engines), a regulator, and a steam-pipe. Externally, a chimney and two safety-valves are fixed to the boiler.

2ndly, The parts which regulate the employment of the steam are, two slide-valves (covering the passages to and from the cylinders), attached to two sets of 'valve-gear,' worked by two eccentrics for the 'forward' and two other eccentrics for the 'backward' motion of the engine; but only two of them work at one time, the other two being what is called 'out of gear.' Four rods called eccentric-rods, encircling the eccentric-sheaves at one end, and jointed to the slide-valve gear at the other end, complete the connection of the slide-valves to the eccentrics fixed on the axle of the driving-wheels.

3rdly, The parts by which the driver controls the action of the engine are, three sets of levers and rods connected to the slide-valve, eccentric-rods, regulator-valves, and feed-pipe cocks, whereby he can 'put on' or 'shut off' steam to the cylinders, water to the boiler, or place the slide-valves in a 'forward' or 'backward' position at his pleasure. These arrangements are usually called the 'hand-gear.'

4thly, The parts immediately concerned in producing locomotion are, two cylinders, on which work two steam-tight pistons, fixed on the end of the piston-rods. On the open end of the piston-rods are also fixed T-pieces, called cross-heads, which slide between or round guide-bars, called motion-bars, fixed parallel with the cylinders. By this means the pistons can only move in a right line with the cylinders. Two strong rods, called connecting-rods, attach the cross-heads to the driving-wheels, or to a cranked axle when there is one used. Whether the pistons are connected to a cranked axle or to the arms of the driving-wheels, this connection is always made at an angle of 45 degrees to each other; therefore the one piston is in the centre of the cylinder exerting its greatest power during that part of the stroke when the other piston is at the end of the cylinder exerting no power. (This excellent arrangement was amongst the first improvements introduced by the late Mr. G. Stephenson, in 1814, who thus placed the locomotive in the same high position, as to efficiency, as was previously done for fixed engines by Watt.) The connection being thus completed between the pistons and the driving-wheels, it is evident that any movement of the one must immediately act upon the other.

5thly, The parts which excite the rapid combustion of the fuel required in locomotive engines are, the chimney and a pipe called the blast-pipe, so made as to cover the exhausting passages from both cylinders, and terminating in the centre of the chimney, near the level of the top of the boiler. It is the escape, through this pipe, of each succeeding cylinderful of steam, or that portion of it allowed to escape by the slide-valves, which causes the 'beats' or 'pulsations' so distinctly audible when the locomotive is at work.

6thly, The parts which supply water to the boiler are, two force-pumps, connected by two feed-pumps to the boiler, and to a reservoir of water. The pumps are worked either from the cross-head, or from eccentrics on the axle of the driving wheels.

7thly, The parts which support the engine are, 2, 4, or 6 wheels, besides the driving-wheels, a set of springs, and a strong frame on which the boiler and machinery are securely fixed.

8thly, The manner in which locomotion is produced from the co-operation of these several parts is as follows. The boiler is filled with water until it completely surrounds all the tubes and inside fire-box. Fire is then applied, and in due time steam is generated from the water and collected between the surface of the water and the top of the boiler, until it has reached the pressure required. On the regulator being then opened, and the slide-valves placed in their working position by the driver, the steam passes from the boiler through the steam-pipe to the cylinders, where its force moves the pistons, which, being attached to the driving-wheels (as has been explained), causes them to revolve, and thus produces locomotion. The slide-valves and pumps being wrought from some part set in motion by the piston, regulate the admission of steam to the cylinder, and of water to the boiler. When the steam has moved the piston to the end of the cylinder, a passage is opened for its escape to the atmosphere through the blast-pipe, and the velocity of this escaping steam creates a partial vacuum in the chimney, causing a rush or 'blast' of air through the fire to fill this vacuum; which blast excites the rapid combustion of the fuel, and consequent rapid generation of steam. This completes the duties of one admission of steam to the cylinders, until its escape to the atmosphere; and when this escape has taken place, another admission of steam, to the opposite side of the piston, forces it back to the other end of the cylinder; and by the medium of the crank, the reciprocating motion of the piston is converted into a rotatory one, and the locomotion begun by the first admission of steam to the cylinders is continued by the second and succeeding admissions.

The repetition of these simple operations has amazed and gratified the world, by safely conveying heavy passenger-trains at upwards of 70 miles an hour, and merchandise trains of 600 tons weight at 25 miles per hour !—the mere idea of which, not many years since, would have been regarded as purely fabulous.

Such is the modern railway locomotive,—an illustrative example of the genius of man; but, like other important inventions, it is the joint production of many minds, and many more are still directed to its further improvement. The records of the Patent Office show, that from January, 1840, to the end of September, 1849, no less than 226 patents were enrolled, all of them more or less applicable to the steam-engine and its appendages. Of these 226 patents, 45 were enrolled during the first nine months of 1849. It has been remarked that steam-engines and railways were too matter-of-fact subjects for poets and painters; but from the above record it is evident that they deeply impress themselves upon the inventive intellect of the world; and if the prodigies performed by steam remain unsung or unportrayed, they dare, if not realize, the very sublimity of both poetry and painting; for what more interesting scene to delineate than one of these stately machines moving safely along, at eagle-speed, the very *élite* of the land (including even the Royal Family), through districts rich in the historical associations of past ages, and still teeming with the works of nature and of art! Surely it cannot be that the subject is too lofty a one for poetical or pictorial illustration, for in greatness of idea lies the success of both.

A brief review of the progress of locomotive engines is all that can be here given. It is now about 2000 years since the powers of steam were recorded by Hero of Alexandria, but it is only 200 years (in 1650) since it was first usefully employed by the Marquis of Worcester. The first idea of using it for propelling carriages is generally ascribed to Dr. Robison, in 1759,

LOCOMOTIVE ENGINES.

when it was suggested by him to Watt, who included a steam-carriage in his patents of 1769 and 1784, but never carried them out. In 1786, Oliver Evans, of Philadelphia, had clear perceptions of the advantages of applying steam to waggons, boats, and mills; but the want of friends and means compelled him to confine his exertions to steam-mills. From 1802 to 1805, Trevithick applied steam-carriages to both common roads and railways, with considerable success for first experiments; and his engine, with Stephenson's improvements, is now the modern locomotive. About the year 1803, it appears that a Mr. Fredericks also made a steam-engine for a silver mine in Hanover, which, in 1811, was employed to convey their Majesties and suite of Westphalia over the mineral railway at considerable speed. This was probably the first royal trip on a railway. From 1805 up to 1814, invention was directed to ensure the adhesion of the wheels upon the rails; and many ingenious plans were tried, some of which succeeded well at slow speeds, but were not calculated for high velocities. In 1814, however, Mr. Blackett, of the Wylam Railway, reverting to Trevithick's plan, fully established the FACT, that on a level, or moderately inclined railway, the adhesion of a smooth iron wheel upon a smooth iron rail was sufficient to draw heavy loads. He tried both six and eight wheeled engines. In 1814, Mr. Stephenson introduced two cylinders, or two complete steam-engines, to one locomotive. From this time up to 1829, the powerful opposition of the owners of other modes of conveyance greatly retarded the progress of the locomotive engine; and so strong was the feeling that they were not economical, that both Mr. Walker and Mr. Rastrick reported against them, in 1829. These reports, and one of a doubtful character by Telford, led to the offer of a prize of £500, in 1829, by the directors of the Liverpool and Manchester Railway, for the best locomotive engine, whose weight was not to exceed six tons. This proceeding gave an important impulse to locomotives, and ended in establishing their superiority over all other existing systems of travelling. Five competitors appeared, namely, Messrs. Stephenson, Erickson, Hockworth, Burstal, and Brandreth. The machinery of the two last was not suitable, and did not proceed to trial. Mr. Stephenson's 'Rocket,' Mr. Erickson's 'Novelty,' and Mr. Hockworth's 'Sanspareil,' were all tried, and the prize was fairly won by the 'Rocket,' which, after the trials were over, reached a speed of 35 miles per hour, and the 'Novelty' about 24 miles per hour.

The 'Rocket' embraced the firebox, tubes, and blast-pipe of the modern locomotive.

The 'Novelty' embraced the plan now much used on short lines, of carrying engine, fuel, and water, all on one frame.

The 'Sanspareil' embraced the blast-pipe of the modern engine, with the single returned tube of the older locomotives. From this it will be seen that this competition at once brought out the leading features which have since rendered the locomotive engine so popular throughout the world.

From 1830, up to the introduction of the 7-feet gauge on the Great Western Railway, in 1838, no marked improvement took place in the locomotive, but the rivalry which sprang up between the gauges served greatly to develope their capabilities.

Engines of a novel construction, having the boiler on one frame, and the machinery on another frame, were tried on the Great Western Railway; also engines embracing Trevithick's plan of working the driving-wheels by toothed wheels, fixed on a separate cranked axle, were tried, but all abandoned for engines modelled from one of Stephenson's; and the last new Great Western engines only follow up his latest improvements and Gray's expansive slide-valve motion on a large scale.

A number of patents have been enrolled for improving the locomotive engine, but a few only have been reduced to practice.

Amongst the more conspicuous of them are, Mr. Stephenson's improvements in the slide-valve motion; Mr. Gray's expansive motion; Mr. Crampton's arrangement of wheels; Mr. Bodmer's arrangement of four pistons in two cylinders; Mr. M'Connell's tank engine; Mr. Samuel's express engine; and Mr. Adam's steam-carriage. The improvements in the mechanism of the slide-valve motion, by Messrs. Stephenson and Gray, have been widely adopted. Mr. Crampton has engines of his plan at work both in England and on the Continent, which enable high driving-wheels to be used on the narrow gauge, without raising the centre of gravity. (For popular description and illustration, see Vols. 78* and 79* in ' Rudimentary Series.')

Mr. Bodmer's plan is to admit the steam between two pistons in one cylinder acting on two cranks, so as to compensate the strain on the frame and machinery. His engines work steadily, and are ingenious in construction.

The tank engine carries on the same frame water and fuel, its tank for water being placed on the top of the boiler. This is the plan adopted on the Great Western Railway; but on narrow-gauge lines the tank is usually placed below the boiler and framing,—a better arrangement, where the machinery permits it to be done.

Mr. Samuel's express engine weighed only 25 cwt., and conveyed seven passengers at the rate of 30 miles per hour on the Eastern Counties Railway.

Mr. Adam's steam-carriage is on this plan, with a very handsome carriage for passengers, all on one frame, and has been tried on some of the branch railways of both gauges.

Having thus briefly glanced at the progress of the locomotive engine, it only remains as briefly to notice some important discussions which have agitated the mechanical world regarding them.

From the earliest introduction of locomotives, four, six, or eight wheels appear to have been used, according to the designs of the makers; but about 1840–1–2, an animated discussion of the respective merits of the four and six wheeled engines was carried on in the columns of the railway press. Both classes have their merits, and both classes had able advocates, but public opinion evidently tended in favour of the six-wheeled engine as the safer of the two under all contingencies: hence the greater proportion of the present locomotives have six wheels.

The gauge controversy of 1845–6–7–8 led to the re-introduction of eight-wheeled engines on both gauges, weighing about 36 tons each, which realized speeds of about sixty and seventy miles per hour. The weight of these monster engines, it will be observed, is more than eight times that of the 'Rocket' (4¼ tons), which won the prize in 1829, whilst the speed is only twice that of the 'Rocket' (thirty-five miles) at that time. It is worthy of remark, that in 1829 the existing engines of 10 to 16½ tons were considered as far too heavy, and the Liverpool and Manchester directors bound competitors not to exceed six tons weight. In 1849, the same feeling prevailed, and the injury done to the railway by these 36-ton engines is much complained of, and tank engines and steam-carriages embody this feeling in practice.

A description of the locomotive can scarcely be closed without noticing the death of its great improver, Mr. G. Stephenson, who died in 1848, aged 68 years.

He found the locomotive a very imperfect machine; he left it in that efficient state that even the daring genius of a Brunel could only copy his plans for the 7-feet gauge. This is another testimony to that farseeing intellect which so early grasped the principal requisites for an efficient locomotive, and whose genius coped with and overcame the leading engineers of England, in 1829, by establishing both locomotives and the Liverpool and Manchester Railway against all opposition, and from which sprang that system of railways which has added so immensely to the resources of the nation—ay, of the world.

Civil services, military services, naval services, and no services, have at all times been liberally rewarded by the Crown and Legislature; but there are no such rewards, no ORDER OF MERIT for such men as the Stephensons, Watt, Arkwright, Field, the Rennies, Whitworth, etc., who are the mainstays of our progress, our greatness, and our power. This is wrong—very wrong, and ought to be amended. However, if the Crown forget, and the Legislature neglect such men, it is consolatory to know, that their names will be embalmed in the hearts of the people, whilst the profligacy of honours and rewards to those having no real claim on the gratitude of the nation is universally condemned.

Upon the Taunus Railway, an apparatus is in use, which, from its simplicity and efficiency, cannot easily be excelled. It is attached to the hinder part of the tender, and is used in case of emergency, as well as being constantly used when at the stations, where it is necessary to uncouple the engine and tender from the train, thereby saving great trouble, and with less danger to engine-men and fire-men, as they can disconnect at any speed or at any time, whether the engine and train are in motion or not. (For a better elucidation of this simple and ingenious contrivance, see the work on the 'Taunus Railway,' 4to.)

Locker, a small closet or cupboard: lockers were used in churches to hold sacred relics.

Locust-tree (the) of North America is of a greenish yellow; is tough and durable, and used for trenails for ships, for posts, stakes, paling, etc.

Lode, in mining, a vein of ore.

Loft, a room in the roof of a building; a store-room in a theatre; a depository for hay and corn in a stable: a music-loft; a singing-loft; a rood-loft in a church.

Lofty tin, rich, massive, and rough tin.

Log, in navigation, a small triangular piece of board balanced by a thin plate of lead so as to swim perpendicularly, and, being fixed to a line, measures the ship's way.

Logarithms are the artificial numbers used to facilitate or abridge arithmetical calculations, and may be considered as expressing the relation between an arithmetical and geometrical series of terms, or between ratios and the measures of ratios, and are the indices or exponents of a series of numbers in geometrical progression. The origin and nature of logarithms may be easily explained.

In arithmetical series the quantities increase or decrease by the same difference, but in a geometrical series they increase or diminish by a common measure. The first of the following lines exhibits an arithmetical progression; all the other lines are examples of geometrical progression.

1—0, 1, 2, 3, 4, 5, 6, 7, 8, 9.
2—1, 2, 4, 8, 16, 32, 64, 128, 256, 512.

3—1, 3, 9, 27, 81, 243, 729, 2187, 6561, 25683.
4—1, 10, 100, 1000, 10,000, etc.

Here consider the upper line as the index to all the rest; every term of it is the logarithm of a corresponding term in each of them; and it is evident that an infinitude of other lines, or any one of the same lines, varying the point of commencement, and containing numbers in geometrical progression, might be added, to all of which the same arithmetical series might furnish logarithms. M. Thoman, an ingenious French mathematician employed by the Co. Crédit Mobilier of Paris, has compiled a series of logarithmic tables to calculate the values and interests of moneys at every $\frac{1}{4}$ and $\frac{1}{8}$ per cent.

Logeum, the pulpitum or wooden stage of a theatre, placed upon the proscenium or permanent stage. In the Greek theatre the pulpitum extended into the orchestra beyond the proscenium.

Logium, a hovel or outhouse.

Logwood, from Campeachy, Jamaica, Honduras, etc., is largely used as a purple or dark-red dye-wood.

Lomazzo (Gio. Paolo) of Milan, pupil of Cerva of Milan; he published his treatise on painting in 1584, and which he condensed in his idea of the 'Temple of Painting,' printed in 1590.

Lombardic Architecture, a style which immediately succeeded the decline of the Roman style.

Lombardic School of Painting. The distinguishing characteristics of this school are, grace, an agreeable taste for design, without great correctness, a mellowness of pencil, and a beautiful mixture of colours. Antonio Allegri, called Correggio, was the father and the greatest ornament of this school: he began by imitating nature alone, but as he was chiefly delighted with the graceful, he was careful to purify his design; he made his figures elegant and large, and varied his outlines by frequent undulations, but was not always pure and correct, though bold in his conceptions. Correggio painted in oil, a kind of painting susceptible of the greatest delicacy and sweetness; and as his character led him to cultivate the agreeable, he gave a pleasing, captivating tone to all his pictures.

London and Nottingham whites. The best of these do not differ in any essential particulars materially, nor from the white leads of other manufactories. The latter, being prepared from flake-white, is generally the greyest of the two. The inferior white leads are adulterated with whiting or other substances, which injure them in body and brightness, dispose them to dry more slowly, to keep their place less firmly, and to discolour the oil with which they are applied. All the above are carbonates of lead, and liable to froth or bubble when used with aqueous, spiritous, or acid preparations.

Longitude, length; the distance of any part of the earth, east or west, from London, or any other given place.

Long timbers, in ship-building, those timbers in the cant bodies which reach from the dead-wood to the second futtock-head.

Loobs, tin slime or sludge.

Loof, in navigation, pronounced *luff*, a term applied when a ship going large before the wind, is brought close by the wind; to put the helm towards the lee-side.

Loop, a part of a block of cast-iron, broken or melted off from the rest.

Loop, a rail of bars joined together like a gate, to be removed in and out at pleasure.

Loop, a hinge of a door.

Loop-hole, a narrow opening or crenelle used in the battlements of the castles of the early English.

Lord of the land or tree, in Cornwall, the person in whose land the mine is; therefore the part which he reserves to himself for liberty to work a mine in his land is the one-sixth, one-seventh, one-eighth, or any other proportion, free of expense, and called the 'duem' dish.'

Lorication, the filling of walls with mortar.

Louvre, a lantern; a turret on the roof of an ancient hall or kitchen for the escape of smoke and for ventilation, now made an ornamental and pleasing object.

Low-pressure engine. (See *Steam-engine*.) Low-pressure steam-engine is when the steam-engine is worked at a low pressure of steam, when the steam is drawn off into a condenser apparatus.

Loxodromics, art of oblique sailing by the rhomb, which always makes equal angles with every meridian.

Lozenge, in geometry called a rhomb, and when the sides are unequal, a rhomboid; in heraldry, a four-cornered figure, resembling a pane of glass in old casements.

Lozenge moulding, a name given to the Norman style of mouldings and ornaments, which are shaped like lozenges.

Lubricate, to make smooth or slippery.

Lubricator, an oil-cup or other contrivance for supplying oil or grease to rubbing surfaces, in order to diminish friction.

Lucerna, an oil-lamp. The Greeks and Romans originally used candles; but in later times these were chiefly confined to the houses of the lower classes.

Lugsail, in navigation, a small sail hoisted occasionally on the mast of a boat or small vessel.

Lychnus, a lamp suspended, or a pendent light.

Lysis, some member above the corona of a podium, introduced in temples, and in the scene of a theatre.

M.

MACHINÆ ORGANA, defined by Vitruvius, in his 10th book, as contrivances for the concentration and application of force, which are known by the names of instruments, mechanical powers, machines, engines, etc.

Machinery, a general term applied to mechanical combinations of parts for creating power, or producing works which may otherwise be, more or less perfectly, made with the hands. The first class of these combinations is usually distinguished by the name of engines; the second, by that of machines.

Engines, or machines for creating or accumulating and applying power, are distinguished from each other according to the material employed in the creation of their power, as air-engines, water-engines, gas-engines, steam-engines, electric engines, etc.

Machines employed in the manufacturing arts are named according to their products, as lace-machinery, rope-machinery, paper-machines; or to the processes they perform, as spinning-machinery, printing-machinery, sawing-machinery, etc.

The materials of which machinery is composed are, wood of various kinds, iron, brass, copper, and other metals, with flexible materials for bands, cords, etc., as wool, caoutchouc, and leather.

The several parts of machinery are, frames, plummer-blocks, carriages, bolts and nuts, pins, shafts, wheels, pinions, levers, cranks, springs, screws, pulleys, riggers, bands or belts, and cords, etc., studs, tappets, wedges, rods, cylinders, tubes, pistons, valves, buckets, floats, weights, beams, racks, chains, clutches, winches, etc. (See also Vols. 114 and 115, for popular elucidation, in the 'Rudimentary Series.')

The power of engines, as distinguished from machines, depends upon the nature of the material from which their power is gathered. The mere mechanical effect of every piece of machinery is calculable upon its combinations of certain elementary forms, commonly termed the mechanical powers, with deductions from the effect of these for friction between the parts, for rigidity of parts which are theoretically supposed to be perfectly flexible, and for the elasticity of parts which are supposed to be perfectly rigid.

The mechanical powers, sometimes described as six in number, viz. the lever, the wheel and axle, the pulley, the inclined plane, the wedge, and the screw, are reducible to two only, viz. the lever and the inclined plane, in each of which the effect produced is just as many times greater than the power employed, as the space through which the power moves is greater than the space through which the effect is continued. Thus, if with a lever a weight be raised ten times greater than the weight or power by which it is raised, this weight or power will have to move through ten times as much space as the height through which the greater weight is raised.

Propriety of form in the detail of machinery depends upon two circumstances. The first is, that the parts subject to wear and tear, and influenced by strains, should be capable of motion or adjustment: the second, that every portion should be equally strong, and present to the eye a uniform figure, or one that is consistent with its degree of action: theory, practice, and taste, all must combine to produce such. A great extent of beauty is attainable in all the details, but mathematical reasons cannot be given why a certain arrangement of lines should be preferable to another, provided they are equally strong. Truth does not strike us without the assistance of custom; but so great is the force of custom, that unassisted by truth it has worked the greatest miracles; and it certainly must be this universal Mentor which gives us the power to choose between forms.

Macellum, a market-place for all kinds of provisions.

Maceria, a rough wall.

Machicolations, openings formed for the purpose of defence at the top of castles and fortifications, by setting the parapet out on corbels, so as to project beyond the face of the wall.

Madder carmine, or *Field's carmine*, is, as its name expresses, prepared from madder. It differs from the rose lakes of madder principally in texture, and in the greater richness, depth, and transparency of its colour, which is of various hues, from rose-colour to crimson.

Madder orange, or *Orange lake*, is a madder lake of an orange hue, varying from yellow to rose-colour and brown.

Madder purple, *Purple rubiate*, or *Field's purple*, is a very rich and deep carmine, prepared from madder. Though not a brilliant purple, its richness, durability, transparency, and superiority of colour, have given it the preference to the purple of gold purple, and to burnt carmine.

Madder yellow is a preparation from the madder-root. The best is of a bright colour, resembling Indian yellow, but more powerful and transparent, though hardly equal to it in durability of hue; metallic, terrene, and alkaline substances acting on and reddening it as they do gamboge: even alone, it has by time a natural tendency to change in appearance.

Mæniana, seats in the upper porticoes of the Roman forum, from whence spectators witnessed the combats of gladiators.

Magnese black is the best of all blacks for drying in oil without addition, or preparation of the oil:

it is a colour of vast body and tingeing power.

Mahogany is a native of the West Indies and the country round the Bay of Honduras. It is said to be of rapid growth, and so large that its trunk often exceeds 40 feet in length and 6 feet in diameter. Spanish mahogany is imported from Cuba, Jamaica, Hispaniola, St. Domingo, and some other of the West India Islands, in logs from about 20 to 26 inches square and 10 feet long. It is close-grained and hard. There is also African mahogany. All the species are used for many purposes, more particularly for superior household furniture.

Main links, the links in the parallel motion which connect the piston-rod to the beam of a steam-engine.

Mainmast of a ship, a long piece of round timber, upright in the waist or middle of a ship.

Malleable, in metallurgy, capable of being spread by beating or by rolling,—a distinguishing character of metals, but more especially of gold. When flattened, it is said to be laminable; when drawn as wire, ductile.

Manacaybo is a furniture wood of moderate size, hard, as good as mahogany, and in appearance between that and tulip-wood.

Manchineel, a large tree of the West Indies and South America: it possesses the general character of mahogany, but has a poisonous and unwholesome sap.

Mandril, the spindle which carries the centre-chuck of a lathe, and communicates motion to the metal to be turned ; in small lathes it is driven by a pulley.

Mandril-frame, the head-stocks or frame bolted to the end of a lathe-bed, for the purpose of supporting the mandril.

Mangrove, an aquatic tree, straight-grained, hard, and elastic: much used for ship-building.

Man-hole, an opening in the top of a boiler, used as an entrance when the boiler requires cleaning: it is covered by a strong plate bolted to the boiler plating, so as to be steam-tight.

Man-hole cover, a strong plate of iron, bolted over the man-hole so as to be removable when required.

Manipulation, in mining, the manner of digging silver or other metals ; a term now generally applied to the means by which materials or effects are produced.

Manner is that habitude which painters have acquired, not only in the management of the pencil, but also in the principal parts of painting, —invention, design, and colouring. It is by the manner in painting that a picture is judged to be by the hand of Titian, Tintoret, Guido, the Caracci, and others. Some masters have had a variety in their manners at different periods of life, and others have so constantly adhered to one manner, that those who have seen even a few of them will immediately know them, and judge of them without any risk of a mistake. The variety observable among artists in their manner and taste arises from the practice of the different schools in which they have received their instructions, or of the artists under whom they have studied. Yet there are many instances of great artists who have divested themselves of that early partiality to a peculiar manner, and have altered it so effectually as to fix on one abundantly more refined and better adapted to their peculiar genius, by which means they have arrived at excellence. Thus, for instance, Raphael proceeded, and acquired a much more elevated manner after he had quitted the school of Perugino.

Manneriet, a term applicable to a painter whose pictures have no resemblance to the beautiful varieties of nature, but discover an unpleasing and tasteless sameness.

Manometer, an instrument intended to measure the rarefaction and condensation of elastic fluids in confined circumstances, whether occasioned by variation of temperature or by actual destruction, or generation of portions of elastic fluids.

Mansard roof, of French origin, from the name of the inventor; a curb roof.

Manse, a parsonage-house.

Mansum capitale, the chief mansion, manor-house, or court of a lord.

Mantelpiece, a beam across the opening of a fire-place, serving as a lintel or bressummer to support the masonry above, which is called the chimney-breast.

Maple-wood is considered to be allied to the sycamore or the plane-tree; its colour is pale: much used for picture-frames and Tunbridge ware.

Marble, a kind of stone found in great masses, and dug out of pits or quarries.

Marcus, a large iron-headed hammer.

Margin, or *Lock-rail,* the flat part of the stile and rail of framed work.

Marine engine, a steam-engine to propel a ship. There are various kinds of them, the beam, direct-acting, oscillating, trunk, high-pressure as used in our new gun-boats, etc. (See Murray's work, Vols. 80 and 81, in the 'Rudimentary Series.')

Market. The market or forum in the cities of antiquity was different from the market in our English towns, where flesh meat, merchandise, etc., are usually sold. The Apostle Paul disputed with philosophers in the market at Athens: this and other evidences prove it to have been also a place of disputation and public resort.

Marline, a small line used for winding round ropes and cables.

Marmoration, a building with marble.

Marone is of a class of impure colours, composed of black and red, black and purple, or black and russet pigments, or with black and any other denomination of pigments in which red predominates.

Marone lake is a preparation of madder, of great depth, transparency, and durability of colour: it works well in water, glazes and dries in oil, and is in all respects a good pigment: its hues are easily given with other pigments, but it is not much used.

Marquetry, chequered or inlaid work; work inlaid with variegation, a sort of veneering, representing flowers, birds, and other figures.

Masaccio, of the Florentine School, a very eminent painter, and distinguished for his foreshortenings and colouring. He died in 1443.

Masonry. The early Roman architecture, both in public and private buildings, was of far more durable materials, and of more accurate masonry than such as was executed in the decline of the Empire. It began to be uncemented blocks of stone, passed into the reticular work of the Republic, thence into the travertine, and descended into the mixture of tufo, and brick, and stucco facing.

Marble is polished by being first rubbed with grit-stone, afterwards with pumice-stone, and lastly with emery or calcined tin. Marbles, with regard to their contexture and variegation of colour, are almost infinite: some are black, some white, and some of a dove colour: the best kind of white marble is called statuary, which, when cut into thin slices, becomes almost transparent, which property the other kinds do not possess. Other species of marble are streaked with clouds and veins. The texture of marble is not altogether understood, even by the best workmen; but they generally know upon sight whether it will receive a polish or not. Some marbles are easily wrought, some are very hard, other kinds resist the tools altogether. Artificial marble, or Scagliola, is real marble pulverized and mixed with plaster, and is used in columns, basso-rilievos, and other ornaments.

The chief kind of stone used in London is Portland stone, which comes from the island of Portland, in Dorsetshire; it is used for buildings in general, as strings, window-sills, balusters, steps, copings, etc., but under great weight or pressure it is apt to splinter, or flush at the joints. When it is recently quarried, it is soft and works easily, but acquires great hardness in course of time. St. Paul's cathedral and Westminster bridge are constructed of Portland stone.

Purbeck stone comes from an island of the same name, also in Dorsetshire, and is mostly employed in rough work, as steps and paving.

Yorkshire stone is also used where strength and durability are requisites, as in paving and coping.

Ryegate stone is used for hearths, slabs, and covings.

Mortar is used by masons in cementing their works. (See *Bricklaying, Cements, Mortars*, etc.) In setting marble or fine work, plaster of Paris is used, and in water-works, tarras is employed.

Tarras is a coarse mortar, durable in water and in most situations. Dutch tarras is made of a soft rockstone, found near Cologne, on the Rhine. It is burnt like lime, and reduced to powder by mills, from thence carried to Holland, whence it has acquired the name of Dutch tarras. It is very dear, on account of the great demand for it in the construction of aquatic works.

An artificial tarras is formed of two parts of lime and one of plaster of Paris: another sort consists of one part of lime and two parts of well-sifted coal ashes.

Masques, grotesque faces used to fill vacant places, on friezes, panels of doors, keys of arches, etc.

Mast earlings, in ship-building, large timbers at the side of the mast rooms that are left deep enough to receive the cross-chocks.

Mastic, a cement used for the plastering of walls.

Mastic varnish is easily prepared by digesting in a bottle, during a few hours, in a warm place, one part of dry picked resin with two parts or more of the oil of turpentine.

Materiatio, according to Vitruvius, the timber-work of a roof.

Materiation, felling of timber for building.

Mathematics, a science which teaches to number and measure whatever is capable of it, comprised under lines, numbers, superficies, or solids.

Matter and *Motion*. Quantities of matter in all bodies are in the compound ratio of their magnitude and densities; for if the magnitudes are equal, the quantities of matter will be as the densities; and if the densities are equal, the quantities of matter will be as the magnitudes: therefore, the quantities of matter are universally in the compound ratio of both.

Matter.—1. Matter in general, materiality, corporeity, corporality, materialness, substantiality, physical condition.—2. Inorganic matter, solid matter, density, solidity, incompressibility, cohesion, fluid matter, liquidity, liquidness, vaporization, specific fluids, fluids in motion, organic matter.

Maul-stick, a painter's stick, upon which he leans his hand when at work.

Mauritius, of London—1086-1108 —built the cathedral of Old Saint Paul's.

Mausoleum, a pompous funereal monument, a costly sepulchre.

Maximum and *Minimum*. The extremes of temperature are no less important to the meteorologist than interesting to the general observer. They are obtained by the self-registering thermometer. The first instrument of this kind was suggested by John Bernouilly. Several forms of thermometers were communicated to the Royal Society by Lord Charles Cavendish. The next in point of time were the contrivances of Fitzgerald and Crighton. Six, Rutherford, Keith, Blackadder, and Dr. Trail, greatly added to the

MEASUREMENT OF EARTHWORK.

stock of self-registering thermometers. There are two kinds in general use; Mr. Six's, which is placed vertically, and Dr. Rutherford's, which is suspended horizontally. The latter is preferable on land, and, from its simplicity, has to a certain extent superseded the former.

Mear, thirty-two yards of ground in a vein of ore.

Measurement of earthwork. There are many works and tables published to facilitate the admeasurement of earth-work, which may be reduced in practice to the following geometrical forms, in one or more chains in length, as the case may be. The two chains marked B and C in the section will reduce to the forms in the diagrams that follow. The dotted lines, fig. 1, show the section at the largest end, next to B in the section; and the dotted line, fig. 2, shows the section at the smallest end, next to A in the section.

The bottom piece, C, being re-

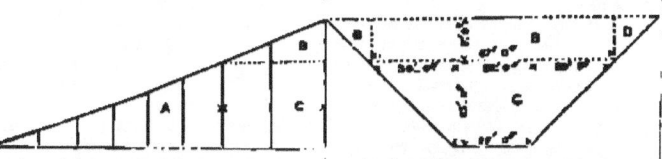

Fig. 1.

duced to a parallel throughout, is measured by multiplying the area of

Slopes 2 to 1.

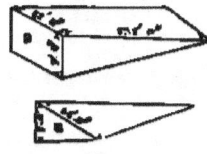

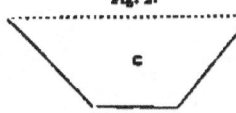

Fig. 2.

Slopes 2 to 1.

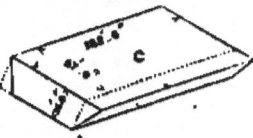

the end by the length; the two banks being equal, it will measure thus: 15' 0" × 57' 0" × 132' 0".

The piece B, the middle or wedge piece, being parallel horizontally only, is measured by taking one-half the vertical height: thus, 3' 6" × 97' 0" × 132' 0".

The two pieces B B form the two halves of a right-angled pyramid, and are measured by multiplying the area of the end by one-third the height: therefore 7' 0" × 14' 0", the slope being 2 to 1, is equal to 98' 0"; the area of the two bases then, 1' 0" × 98' 0" × 44' 0", gives the cube quantity in the two.

Measurement of shipping for tonnage (called the 'new measurement') was regulated in the 5th and 6th of George IV. By this Act certain rules were established for ascertaining the tonnage of ships, as well on shore as afloat, and of vessels propelled by steam; and the account of such tonnage, whenever the same shall have been ascertained according to the rules herein prescribed (except in the case of ships admeasured afloat), it is enacted, shall be deemed the tonnage of such ships, and shall be repeated in every subsequent registry of such ships, unless any alteration shall have been made in their form and burthen, or unless it be discovered that the tonnage had been erroneously computed: and it is considered that the capacity of a ship is the fairest standard by which to regulate its tonnage; that internal measurements will afford the most accurate and convenient method of ascertaining that capacity, and that the adoption of such a mode of admeasurement will tend to the interest of the ship-builder and the owner.

It was enacted that the tonnage of every ship or vessel required by law to be registered shall, previous to her being registered, be measured and ascertained while her hold is clear, and according to the following rule: Divide the length of the upper deck between the after-part of the stem and the fore-part of the stern-post into six equal parts. Depths: At the foremost, the middle, and the aftermost of those points of division, measure in feet and decimal parts of a foot the depths from the under side of the upper deck to the ceiling at the limber strake. In the case of a break in the upper deck, the depths are to be measured from a line stretched in a continuation of the deck. Breadths: Divide each of those three depths into five equal parts, and measure the inside breadths at the following points: at one-fifth and at four-fifths from the upper deck of the foremost and aftermost depths, and at two-fifths and four-fifths from the upper deck of the midship depth. Length: At half the midship depth measure the length of the vessel from the after-part of the stem to the fore-part of the stern-post, then to twice the midship depth add the foremost and the aftermost depths for the sum of the depths; add together the upper and lower breadths at the foremost division, three times the upper breadth and the lower breadth at the midship division, and the upper and twice the lower breadth at the after division, for the sum of the breadths; then multiply the sum of the depths by the sum of the breadths, and this product by the length, and divide the final product by three thousand five hundred, which will give the number of tons for register. If the vessel have a poop or half-deck, or a break in the upper-deck, measure the inside mean length, breadth, and height of such part thereof as may be included within the bulk-head; multiply these three measurements together, and dividing the product by 92·4, the quotient will be the number of tons to be added to the result as above found. In order to ascertain the tonnage of open vessels, the depths are to be measured from the upper edge of the upper strake.

To ascertain the tonnage of steam vessels, it was also further enacted, that in each of the several rules prescribed, when applied for the purpose of ascertaining the tonnage of any ship or vessel propelled by steam, the tonnage due to the cubical contents of the engine-room shall be deducted from the total tonnage of the vessel as determined by the rules, and 'the remainder shall be deemed the true register tonnage of the said ship or vessel. The tonnage due to the cubical contents of the engine-room shall be determined in the following manner: measure the inside length of the engine-room in feet and decimal parts of a foot from the foremost to the aftermost bulk-head, then multiply the said length by the depth of the ship or vessel at the midship division, as aforesaid, and the product by the inside breadth at the same division at two-fifths of the depth from the deck taken as aforesaid, and divide the last product by 92·4, and the quotient is deemed the tonnage due to the cubical contents of the engine-room.

Measurement of standing timber.—Measure from the tree ten, twenty, thirty, etc., feet, and then plant the theodolite level: direct the telescope to the bottom of the tree, and observe the degree and tenth of depression; and to the top of the tree, the degree and tenth of elevation. When the timber has been previously felled, it is customary, in measuring, to girt a string round the middle of the tree, and fold it twice, which will give the fourth part of the girt, and which is considered the true side of the square; then the length is measured from the butt-end of the tree, so far up as the tree will hold half a foot girt, or, more properly speaking, quarter-girt; that is, the line six inches when twice folded. Various tables are published, to assist the timber-measurer in the performance of his duty. All timber is bought and sold by the load, and a load is estimated at forty feet of unhewn or rough timber, and fifty feet of hewn timber, which is supposed to weigh one ton, or twenty hundredweight.

Measurement of base lines, the whole of the operations connected with the execution of a trigonometrical survey of a country, require the most scrupulous care, and a large amount of skill, that the many errors which are inseparable from the instruments that are used, and the several processes that must be followed, may be diminished as far as practicable, and the necessary precautions taken, whereby the corrections to the observations and measurements may be applied, so as to produce the greatest amount of accuracy with the least alteration of the given elements.

Of these processes, the primary is that which consists in the accurate measurement of the distance between two stations A and B, designed to serve as the base, to which the whole extent of country intended to be surveyed, is to be referred.

This measurement is generally expressed in terms of the standard of length of the country in which the operation is carried on, although the actual measurements may in the first instance have been given in terms of some other standard. It is not, however, requisite that the measurement of the base should precede the angular observations, and although generally it is first undertaken, it can be equally well done when every other portion of the work has been completed.

The selection of a site for the base is a matter of considerable importance; a level plain or ground with as little undulation as possible, and a distance varying from five to eight miles is to be preferred; the extremities of the base being sufficiently elevated (either from the nature of the ground or by the use of an artificial stage) above the surrounding country to allow of other stations C and D being seen, and these should be so situated as to form well-conditioned triangles with the base A B, inasmuch as small errors in the measurement of very acute angles would produce large errors in the lengths of the sides deduced from them.

It must not, however, be inferred, that a perfect level is absolutely requisite for the measurement of a base line. That situated on Salisbury Plain has now been twice measured, although there is a difference of level of 428 feet between its two extremities.

Mechanical powers are contrivances by which we are enabled to sustain a great weight or overcome a great resistance by a small force. (See *Machinery*.)

Mechanics, that branch of practical science which considers the laws of equilibrium and the motion of solid bodies; the forces by which bodies, whether animate or inanimate, may be made to act upon one another; and the means by which these forces may be increased so as to overcome those which are more powerful. The term Mechanics was originally applied to the doctrine of equilibrium. It is now, however, extended to the motion and equilibrium of all bodies, whether solid, fluid, or aëriform. The complete arrangement of mechanics is now made to embrace, besides, the pressure and tension of cords, the equilibrated polygon, the catenary curve, suspension bridges, the equilibrium of arches and the stability of their piers, the construction of oblique arches, the equilibrium of domes and vaults with revetments, the strength of materials, whether they be of wood or iron, dynamics (or the science of moving bodies), with hydrostatics, pneumatics, and hydraulics.

Definitions are explanations of terms by means of other terms, the meanings of which are understood: we shall assume that the term *weight* will be accepted without explanation.

Def. Everything which has weight is called *matter*, and *a body* is a portion of matter limited in every direction.

Def. *Space* is that which contains or is capable of containing matter, and is continuous and infinite.

Def. A body is said to be *absolutely at rest* as long as it remains in the same position in space; and to be *absolutely in motion* while it is in the act of changing its position in space.

Def. A body is said to be *relatively at rest* as long as it remains in the same position with respect to some other body with regard to which its state is to be considered; and to be *relatively in motion* while it is in the act of changing its position with respect to this body.

The states of rest and motion which we have generally to consider are relative and not absolute. Thus we have to consider the motion of a locomotive relatively to the surface of the earth, and not the absolute motion made up of this and that of the earth itself, and the motions of the parts of the engine relatively to the frame of the locomotive without regard to the motion of the whole along the road.

Def. *Force* is any cause which produces or tends to produce a change in the state of rest or motion of a body.

Forces are measured by the effects which they produce, and hence in considering effects of different kinds different measures of forces may be introduced.

When a body is acted upon by only a single force, a change in its state of rest or motion will always take place; but two or more forces acting on a body at the same time may counteract each other's effects, so that the body may be in exactly the same state as though these forces were not acting upon it.

Def. Two or more forces which counteract each other's effects are said to be in equilibrium. (From the Course of Mathematics for the use of Students at the Royal Military Academy, Woolwich, vol. iii.)

Medallion, in architecture, any circular tablet on which figures are embossed; busts, etc.

Mediæval, relating to the middle ages.

Member, a moulding; either as a cornice of five members, or a base of three members, and applied to the subordinate parts of a building.

Mensuration is the application of the science of arithmetic to geometry, by which we are enabled to discover the magnitude and dimensions of any geometrical figures, whether solid or superficial. To enable us to express this magnitude in determinate terms, it is necessary to assume some magnitude of the same kind as the unit, and then, by stating how many times the given magnitude contains that unit, we obtain its measure.

The different species of magnitude which have most frequently to be determined are distinguishable into six kinds, viz. 1. Length.—2. Surface.—3. Solidity, or capacity.—4. Force of gravity, commonly called weight.—5. Angles.—6. Time.

Mere, or *Meer*, a name frequently given, in England and the Netherlands, to inland lakes or sheets of fresh water, such as Windermere, Whittleseamere, Ugg-mere, Soham-mere, in England, and the Egmonder meer, Purmer meer, and Haarlemmer meer, etc., in the Netherlands. The term is most frequently used in the latter country, where, prior to 1440, there were more than 150 meers, of which 85 occupied an area of 177,832 acres, since drained and reclaimed, in the provinces of North and South Holland; and where also the Haarlemmer meer, covering an area of 45,230 acres, is now in course of drainage.

As the meers, in fen-lands, serve as reservoirs to hold a portion of the surplus rain-water falling on the district of which they form a part, their being dyked off and drained, where of considerable extent, has most important effects on the neighbouring lands, by contracting the area of the reservoir or catch-water basin of the district. But as these drainages generally oblige improvements in the outfalls, their result is mostly beneficial to the other lands.

The beds of the Dutch meers are from 10 to 20 feet below the level of the lowest point of the natural outfall in their districts; consequently they are always drained by mechanical means. Windmills have been employed to drain the land, in the Netherlands, from time immemorial; but the drainage of the meers was not commenced until 1440, about which period windmills and draining machinery were considerably improved; and as late as 1840, windmills for draining purposes continued in favour with the Dutch engineers, in preference to steam engines; and at that date, 12,000 windmills were employed to drain the polders, in the Netherlands, and only five small steam-engines, the largest not exceeding 30-horse power: the average consumption of fuel was 20 lbs. of coal per horse power per hour.

In the English fens, steam had in a great measure superseded windmills for drainage purposes; but the consumption of fuel was nearly as great as in the Dutch engines.

In 1839, the Dutch States-General decreed the drainage of the Haarlemmer meer, and voted eight millions of florins for that purpose, to which two millions more were subsequently added, making the total sum of £834,000.

The Haarlemmer meer forms part of the great drainage district of Rhynland, which has an area of 305,014 English acres; prior to 1848, this area was occupied by 56,609 acres of meers and watercourses, nearly all in communication with each other, forming what is called the *boezem*, or catch-water basin of the district; the surface of the water being maintained at the lowest level of natural sluiceage, by sluices at Katwyk into the North Sea, and at Sparndam and Halfweg into the Y, or the southern end of the Zuyder Zee.

Above the boezem are 75,357 acres drained into it by natural level; and at depths from 2 feet 6 inches to 4 feet *below* it are 170 polders covering an area of 135,850 acres; and 37,198 acres, divided into 28 polders which were formerly meers, but are now drained, and whose beds are on an average 14 ft. below the level of the boezem.

The surplus rain and infiltration

waters from the 173,048 acres of polder-land are lifted into the hoezem by the united action of 261 large windmills, with an average force of 1500-horse power.

The drainage of the Haarlemmer meer, which forms part of the hoezem or basin, will deduct 45,230 acres from its area, and reduce it to 11,379 acres, or ¼th part of its former size; whilst the land surface drained into it will be increased from 229,657 to 293,735 acres.

The average level of the hoezem is 10 inches below the ordinary low water, and 27 inches below high-water mark in the Y or Zuyder Zee; and 7 inches above low water, and 57 inches below ordinary high water, in the North Sea.

The bed of the Haarlem Lake is 14 feet below the winter level of the boezem; and when drained, the maximum lift will be 16 feet 6 inches to 17 feet, according to the state of the wind, which raises or depresses the surface of the water in the canals very considerably.

The water contents of the Haarlemmer meer to be pumped out, including the additional quantity arising from the surplus rain and infiltration during the draining, are estimated at 800,000,000 cubic mètres or tons.

The greatest quantity of monthly drainage when the meer is pumped out is estimated at 36,000,000 tons, and the annual average surplus of rain-water, etc., at 54,000,000 tons to be lifted, on an average, 16 feet.

The Dutch engineers were generally in favour of windmills, or a combination of windmills and steam-engines, for pumping out the meer; but in 1841, the late king, William II., by the advice of a commission, decreed that steam-engines only should be employed for the purpose; and in 1842, at the suggestion of two English engineers, Mr. Arthur Dean and Mr. Joseph Gibbs, it was determined to erect, and they were directed to prepare the designs for, three steam-engines upon the high pressure, expansive, condensing principle, of the ordinary force of 350-horse power each, but capable of being worked on emergencies up to 500-horse power.

The consumption of fuel was limited to 2¼ lbs. of coal per horse power per hour.

The three engines were named the 'Leeghwater,' 'Cruquius,' and 'Lynden,' after three celebrated men who had at different periods proposed plans for draining the Haarlemmer meer.

The 'Leeghwater' was the first erected, to work eleven pumps of 63 inches diameter, with 10-feet stroke in pumps and steam cylinders; and the 'Cruquius' and 'Lynden' were afterwards constructed, to work eight pumps each, of 73 in. diameter, and with 10-feet stroke; each engine is calculated to lift 66 cubic mètres of water per stroke.

The accompanying sketch is a representation of the interior of the 'Lynden' engine and engine-house, on the upper floor; the 'Cruquius' is on the same model; but the 'Leeghwater' has the inner ends of its eleven pump-beams arranged under the great cross-head, instead of over it.

Each engine has two steam cylinders, placed concentrically, the one within the other, the outer of 12 feet diameter, and the inner one of 7 feet diameter: both are secured to one bottom, and covered by one cover, but the inner cylinder does not touch the cover within 1½ inch: there are two pistons, 26 inches deep, the compartments of which are fitted with cast-iron plates: the outer piston is annular, and has a packing on both sides: beneath this annular piston a constant vacuum is maintained when working: the two pistons are connected by five piston-rods, as shown in the sketch, to a great cross-head or cap, the whole

mass weighing about 85 tons, and by eight connecting-rods the cap pistons are suspended from the inner ends of eight cast-iron balance-beams to the outer ends of which are hung the eight pump-pistons;

the action of the engines is therefore very simple: the steam being applied under the inner piston, lifts both the pistons, the great cross-head, and inner ends of pump balance-beams simultaneously, and the pump-pistons descend at the same time; by an hydraulic apparatus attached to the great cross-head, the dead weight of the pistons, etc., is arrested at the point to which it has been thrown up by the steam, and time is given for the valves of the pump-pistons to close before the down-stroke of the steam-piston is made; then, the equilibrium-valve being opened, the hydraulic apparatus is liberated at the same moment, and the steam passing from beneath the small piston, above both pistons, the pressure on both sides of the small one is equalized, whilst nearly two-thirds of the steam acts upon the annular piston against a vacuum, and in aid of the dead weight helps to make the down-stroke in the steam-cylinder, and the up-stroke in the pumps. The use of the two cylinders enables the engine-man, by judiciously altering the expansion in the small cylinder, to command his work at all times, without stopping the engine to take out, or put in, dead weight, as would be necessary for a single-acting one-cylinder engine, where dead weight only is used for lifting the water. It has frequently occurred that the load of an engine has been added to or diminished by 10 or 12 tons in the course of half an hour, by the action of gales of wind on the surface of the meer and boezem. Each engine has two air-pumps of 40 in. diameter, and 5-feet stroke. The steam is cut off in the small cylinder at from one-fourth to two-thirds of the stroke, according to the load; and after expanding through the remainder of the stroke, it is still farther expanded in the large cylinder.

The anticipated economy in consumption of fuel has been realized: when working with the net power of 350 horses, the average consumption is 2¼ lbs. of best Welsh coals, or 75 millions duty with 94 lbs. of coal; and on a late trial, the 'Cruquius' and 'Lynden' engines were found to do a duty of 87 millions.

The whole cost of machinery, buildings, coals, and wages, to pump out the lake, will not exceed £150,000, whereas, by wind it would have cost £308,000, being a saving of £158,000; and there will also be a further economy upon the works in the bed of the lake, amounting to £40,000 more, so that the total saving by steam over wind will be £200,000, and three years' time.

To compensate the district of Rhynland for the loss of 45,230 acres of the boezem or catch-water basin, a steam-engine of 200-horse power, driving 10 large scoop-wheels, has been erected at Sparndam to lift the boezem water over the tide in the Y, or base of the Zuyder Zee, where the rise is on an average only 17 inches. This engine has discharged 30,000,000 tons of water in fifteen consecutive days. When the state of the boezem permits the 'Leeghwater,' 'Cruquius,' and 'Lynden' engines to work freely, they discharge on an average 2,000,000 tons in twenty-four hours, and they are capable of doing this down to their full depth. In the month of June, 1849, the three engines discharged 60,000,000 tons water, and lowered the meer one foot; between the 1st of May and 1st of December they had lowered the lake 5 feet, and by the autumn of 1850 dry land appeared. (See *Table*.)

The 'Leeghwater,' 'Cruquius' and 'Lynden' engines were contracted for jointly by the Hayle and Perran Foundry Companies, Cornwall, and were manufactured and erected under an able director.

This once formidable meer is now

MERES, DRAINAGE OF.

Table, arranged chronologically, showing the Lakes, Meers, and Water-places which have been drained by mechanical means, and converted into Fertile Lands, in the Provinces of North and South Holland, in the Netherlands.

Date of Drainage.	NORTH HOLLAND. Name of Lake, Meer, or Water-place.	Location near.	Area drained in Eng. acres.	SOUTH HOLLAND. Name of Lake, Meer, or Water-place.	Location near.	Area drained in Eng. Acres.
1440	Nerah Meer	Werverahoofd	50			
1450	Burghorader Do.	Burghorn	684			
1553	The Zyp	Sehagerbrug	19020			
1555	Egmonder Meer	Egmond	10080			
"	Berger Do.	Bergen	194			
1560	Daal Do.	Koedyk	285			
1561	Vroooer Do.	St. Pancras	246			
1566	Achter Do.	Alkmaar	78			
"	Kool Do.	Do.	33			
1567	Zwyne Do.	Oudorp	38			
1590	Hockeier Do.	Akersloot	745			
1607	Wog Do.	Splerdyk	1541			
1609-12	The Beemster	Purmerend	16359			
"	The Weiringerwaard	Colhorn	3072			
1614	" "	" "		Soetermeercsche Meer	Soetermeer	1258
1616	Tjaarlinger Meer	Warmenhuisen	98			
1618-22	Purmer Do.	Purmerend	6250			
1622	" "	" "		The Lisserpoel	Lisse	332
1624	Haaradorper Do.	Berkhout	401	Hem Meer	Sassenheim	140
"	The Enge Wormer	Near Wormer meer	241			
1625	The Hr. Hugowaard	Langendyk	6904			
"	Broeker Meer	Brock & Waterland	650			
1625-23	Belmer Do.	Monnikendam	310			
"	Buikalooter Do.	Buikaloot	772			
1626	The Groot Waal	Berkhout	132			
"	Wormer Meer	Gisp	3786			
1626-32	" "	" "		Diemer Meer	Diemen	1576
1630	Bensing Do.	Abbekerk	245			
"	Harger & Pettemer Polder	Petten	937			
1631	The Tien Meeren	Haring Garspel	4647			
"	The Drie Do.	Oud Garspel	738			
"	Kley Meur	Koedyk	117			
"	Kerk Do.	Do.	48			
"	Dehle Do.	Warmenhuisen	31			
"	Greb Do.	Do.	291			
"	The Vier Meertjes	Medenblyk	680			
"	Braak Meer	Korstwoude	60			
"	Veenhuizer Do.	Veenhuizen	715			
"	Sehals Do.	Knollendam	165			
1632	Schermer Do.	N. & S. Schermer	17000			
1633	The Vier Meertjes	Obdam	142			
1636	Berk Meer	Veenhuizen	390			
1640	Kaik Do.	Lambert Schagen	220			
1642	" "	" "		Slooter Meer		199
1643	Star Do.	Ootgrafdyk	1447			
1644	Noordeinder Do.	Graft	490			
1645	Sap Do.	The Ryp	51			
1646	" "	" "		The Wilde Veneen	Moerkapel	1323
1650	" "	" "		Stom Meer	Aalsmeer	469

MERES, DRAINAGE OF.

	NORTH HOLLAND—continued.			Area drained in Eng. acres.	SOUTH HOLLAND—continued.		Area drained in Eng. acres.
Date of Drainage.	Name of Lake, Meer, or Water-place.		Location near.		Name of Lake, Meer, or Water-place.	Location near.	
1666	..	..	..	..	Wamenarsche Polder	Rhynsaterwoude	2498
1664	..	..	..	..	The Driemans Do.	Sostermeer	2913
1674	..	..	..	..	Horn Meer	Aalsmeer	441
1700	..	..	..	..	Binnenwegsche Polder	Zegwaard	2247
1713	..	..	..	..	H. Groot Polder	Leysloden	394
1713	..	..	..	..	Goger Do.	Alkemade	507
1737	..	..	..	..	Katjes Do.	Zevenhuizen	773
1738	..	..	..	..	The Starrevaarts Do.	Stompwyk	443
1735-43	..	..	..	..	The Vier Ambachts Do.	Esselyherwoude	818
1741	..	..	..	..	Vriesenhoopsche Do.	Vriezekoop	1325
1754-62	..	..	..	..	Endragts Do.	Zevenhuizen	2473
1758-59	..	..	..	..	Damhouder Do.	Stompwyk	942
1759-63	..	..	..	..	Nevider Plas	Hazerswoude	3415
1760-62	..	..	..	..	Palenternsche Polder	Zegwaard	1279
1763-66	..	..	..	..	Ouwendykerbe & Bos Do.	Esselyherwoude	965
1764	..	..	..	..	Bovenkerker Do.	Amstelveen	3413
1767-69	..	..	..	..	Groot and Little Kalkovensche Do.	Oudshoorn	1319
1768-71	..	..	..	..	The Groote Do.	Sostermeer	1666
1772-77	..	..	..	..	Do. Do.	Stompwyk	1179
1772-83	..	..	..	..	Berkelsche Do.	Berkel	2171
1773-84	..	..	..	..	Bleiswykasche Drainage	Bleiswyk	2299
1781-84	..	..	..	..	Schiebrokasche Polder	Shibrock	1457
1782-80	..	..	..	..	Vendsor en Lyker Do.	Alkemade	1373
1785-89	..	..	..	..	Pynaker-eke Do.	Pynacker	1270
1788-91	..	..	..	..	Aarlanderveensche Do.	Aarlanderveen	1171
1789-95	..	..	..	..	Zestienhovensche Do.	Overschie	1664
1790 1810	..	..	..	..	Schievensche Do.	Overschie	834
1797 1809	..	..	..	..	Mydrechtsche Do.	Mydrecht	2622
1798-99	..	..	..	..	Nieuwekoopsche en Zevenhovensche Do.	Niewekoop	1571
1799 1801	..	..	..	..	Onephoek en Vrowe Do.	Oudshoorn	254
1810	..	..	..	..	Bielandsche Do.	Nootdorp	233
1830	..	..	..	..	Kleine Starrevaartsche Do.	Leydschendam	23
1838-40	..	..	..	..	Bylmer Meer	Waamp	1470
1843	..	..	..	..	The Zaid Plas	Rotterdam	14920
1840-60	..	..	..	..	Noorddorpsche Plas	Delft	2500
	..	..	..	98557	Haarlem Lake (not yet completed)	Amsterdam, Haarlem and Leyden	46230
					In South Holland, acres		124566
					In North Do. Do.		98557
					Total Area		223123

a drained district, and is most profitably occupied by industrial agricultural pursuits.

It may be said in this instance, the Dutch have realized the fable of the 'Hare and the Tortoise:'—in 1840, the erection of a steam-engine of 30 or 40-horse power, for drainage purposes, was thought to be a bold step, whereas, under the guidance of English engineers, they have dared, between 1840 and 1842, to erect the most gigantic steam machinery in the world.

The low lands of the Netherlands are divided into large drainage districts, which have been embanked against the inroads of the tides and river floods; and the various parts of a district are connected by what is called the *boezem*, or water-basin, or reservoir, formed by the rivers, lakes, meers, or waterplaces having their origin in the district, and serves to receive the water drained either naturally or artificially from the surrounding lands. The boezem is put into communication with the exterior waters of the rivers or sea by locks and sluices. All lands in a given drainage district above the level of the boezem, and draining naturally into it, are called 'hoezem lands.' All lands lying below the boezem, and drained into it by machinery, are called polders. Of polders there are two kinds: the first are seldom more than 2 or 3 feet below the level of the boezem, which is embanked above the natural surface of the land: of such polders there are upwards of 1000 in the province of South Holland only; and they are kept dry by the aid of an immense number of windmills. Of the second class of polders there are 43 in North Holland and 43 in South Holland, as recorded in the preceding Table, and these are works of a formidable character, being, for the most part, the beds of lakes, or permanent sheets of water, varying in depth from 5 to 20 feet below the boezem, and requiring powerful machinery to pump them out in the first instance, and to maintain them dry afterwards; and as these lakes, etc., always form part of the boezem, or reservoir, of a much larger tract of land, their drainage frequently involves the construction of immense works, and seriously affects the prosperity of the whole district in which they are situate.

The preceding Table will, as an apt illustration of the subject of draining large districts, be found important in engineering history.

By the Table it will be seen that the North Hollanders had effected the drainage of nearly all their lakes, etc., as early as 1645, and they had then recovered 98,557 acres of land forming their beds; whereas the South Hollanders had in 1645 only drained five small lakes, whose area was only 3741 acres. It must be observed that the South Holland drainages are of a much more extensive character than those of North Holland, and the difficulties to be overcome were much greater; and last, but not least, the North Hollanders were much richer than their neighbours. Of the 223,000 acres of lakes, etc., recorded in the Table, upwards of 50,000 acres were formed artificially, by dredging the peat pulp to the depth of 10 or 20 feet, to serve as fuel for domestic purposes, etc.

Meridian, in astronomy, the line drawn from the north to the south, through the zenith, nadir, and poles, which line the sun crosses at noon.

Merlon, the solid part of an embattled parapet, standing up between the embrasures.

Merus, the plain surface between the channels of a triglyph.

Mesaula, a passage, gallery, or lobby; an entry or court.

Messuage, a dwelling-house, with some land adjoining, as garden, orchard, etc., and all other conveniences belonging to it.

Meatling, brass ornaments; candlesticks; sacred utensils used in Anglo-Saxon times.

Metallurgy, the art of working metals, invented by Tubal-Cain, B. C. 3608. "And Zillah also bare Tubal-Cain, an instructor of every artificer in brass and iron." (*Gen.* iv. 22.) In the earliest periods of history, mention is made of the excellence in working metals among the Egyptians. Some specimens of metal-work of an early date exist, and modern fashion has also produced some very elaborate examples.

Metals are elementary bodies capable of combining with oxygen; and many of them, during this combination, exhibit the phenomenon of combustion. Seven metals only were formerly known; but recently a much greater number has been added. Metals are distinguished by their great specific gravity, considerable tenacity, and hardness, opacity, and property of reflecting the greater part of the light which falls on their surface, giving rise to metallic lustre or brilliancy. Metals are the best conductors of caloric: their expansibilities are various, and are probably nearly in the order of their fusibilities. Mercury melts at so low a temperature, that it can be obtained in the solid state only at a very low temperature; others, as platina, can scarcely be melted by the most intense heat which we can excite.

Metals employed in the mechanical arts.—

ANTIMONY is of a silvery white colour, brittle, and crystalline in its ordinary texture: it fuses at about 800°: its specific gravity is 6·712.

BISMUTH is a brittle, white metal with a slight tint of red: its specific gravity is 9·822: it fuses at 476°, and always crystallizes on cooling.

COPPER is the only metal, with the exception of titanium, which has a red colour: it has much lustre, is very malleable and ductile, and exhales a peculiar smell when warmed or rubbed: it melts at a bright red or dull white heat, or at a temperature intermediate between the fusing points of silver and gold = 1996° Fahr.: its specific gravity varies from 8·86 to 8·89,— the former being the least density of cast copper; the latter, the greatest of rolled or hammered copper.

GOLD is of a deep and peculiar yellow colour; it melts at a bright red heat, equivalent, according to Daniell, to 2016° Fahr., and when in fusion, appears of a brilliant greenish colour: its specific gravity is 19·3: it is so malleable, that it may be extended into leaves which do not exceed the $\frac{1}{282000}$th of an inch in thickness, or a single grain may be extended over 56 square inches of surface.

LEAD in colour is bluish-white: it has much brilliancy, is remarkably flexible and soft, and leaves a black streak on paper. When handled, it exhales a peculiar odour: it melts at about 612°, and by the united action of heat and air, is readily converted into an oxide. Its specific gravity, when pure, is 11·445; but the lead of commerce seldom exceeds 11·35. Lead is used, in a state of comparative purity, for roofs, cisterns, pipes, vessels for sulphuric acid, etc.

MERCURY is a brilliant white metal, having much of the colour of silver. It has been known from remote ages. It is liquid at common temperatures, solid and malleable at —40° Fahr., and contracts considerably at the moment of congelation; it boils and becomes vapour at about 670°: its specific gravity at 60° is 13·5. In the solid state, its density exceeds 14. The specific gravity of mercurial vapour is 6·976.

NICKEL is a white brilliant metal, which acts upon the magnetic needle, and is itself capable of becoming a magnet. Its magnetism is more feeble than that of iron and vanishes at a heat somewhat below redness. At 630° it is ductile and malleable: its specific gravity varies from 8·27 to 8·40 when fused, and after hammering, from 8·69 to 9·00. It is not oxidized by exposure to air at common temperatures; but when heated in the air, it acquires various tints, like steel: at a red heat, it becomes coated by a grey oxide.

PALLADIUM is of a dull white colour, malleable and ductile. Its specific gravity is about 11·3, or 11·86 when laminated. It fuses at a temperature above that required for the fusion of gold.

PLATINUM is a white metal, extremely difficult of fusion, and unaltered by the joint action of heat and air. It varies in density from 21 to 21·5, according to the degree of mechanical compression it has sustained. It is extremely ductile, but cannot be beaten into such thin leaves as gold and silver.

RHODIUM, discovered in 1803 by Dr. Wollaston, is a white metal, very difficult of fusion. Its specific gravity is about 11; it is extremely hard. When pure, the acids do not dissolve it.

SILVER is of a more perfect white than any other metal; it has considerable brilliancy, and takes a high polish. Its specific gravity varies between 10·4, which is the density of cast silver, and 10·5 to 10·6, which is the density of rolled or stamped silver. It is so malleable and ductile, that it may be extended into leaves not exceeding a ten-thousandth of an inch in thickness, and drawn into wire much finer than a human hair. Silver melts at a bright red heat, estimated at 1873° Fahr., and when in fusion appears extremely brilliant.

TIN has a silvery white colour, with a slight tint of yellow: it is malleable though sparingly ductile. Common tin-foil, which is obtained by beating out the metal, is not more than $\frac{1}{1000}$th of an inch in thickness, and what is termed 'white Dutch metal' is in much thinner leaves. Its specific gravity fluctuates from 7·28 to 7·6, the highest being the purest metal. When bent, it occasions a peculiar crackling noise, arising from the destruction of cohesion amongst its particles. When a bar of tin is rapidly bent backwards and forwards several times successively, it becomes so hot that it cannot be held in the hand. When rubbed, it exhales a peculiar odour. It melts at 442°, and by exposure to heat and air is gradually converted into a protoxide.

ZINC is a bluish-white metal, with considerable lustre; rather hard; of a specific gravity of about 6·8 in its usual state; but when drawn into wire, or rolled into plates, its density is augmented to 7 or 7·2. In its ordinary state, at common temperatures, it is tough, and with difficulty broken by blows of the hammer: it becomes very brittle when its temperature approaches that of fusion, which is about 773°; but at a temperature a little above 212°, and between that and 300°, it becomes ductile and malleable, and may be rolled into thin leaves, and drawn into moderately fine wire, which, however, possesses but little tenacity. When a mass of zinc which has been fused is slowly cooled, its fracture exhibits a lamellar and prismatic crystalline texture. The pipes of the great organ in the town-hall at Birmingham, and in that of York cathedral, are made principally of sheet zinc.

Aluminium, a newly discovered metal; see p. 12.

Meteorology, the term now used for the purpose of designating the science which observes, registers, classifies, and compares the various and varying phenomena of our atmosphere. It remarks, at the same time, the connection of these phenomena with the heavenly bodies,

METEOROLOGY.

and with the solid and liquid materials of the earth, in reference to their reciprocal and combined influence in determining the character of different climates, and with the view of learning the meteoric history of every region of our globe, of ultimately investigating the laws of atmospheric change, the plan of meteoric action; the theory, in fact, of meteorological phenomena, on which depend essentially the fitness of the various portions of the earth's surface for the production of different vegetable and other substances and for the support of animal life.

Meteorological phenomena are not confined to the inferior regions of the atmosphere, but extend as far as observations have reached. It is possible their influence may extend universally, and therefore it is desirable to know whether there exists throughout space a medium, or conductor, or whether there is such a thing in nature as vacuum. Some have, it is true, endeavoured to reconcile opinions so diametrically opposed to each other, by suggesting that the universe, though infinite, is a plenum and a void! This (the doctrine of Leucippus) a recent author declares to be really true; and some conceive that the Newtonian theory necessarily implies the reality of a void, the astronomical calculations on which that theory rests having been made without any allowance for the resistance to the motions of the planets, which might be experienced from a material medium.

Metoche, the intervals between two denticuli in the Ionic entablature.

Metope, the spaces between the triglyphs of the Doric frieze, which in the Parthenon, for instance, were filled in with sculpture; but in modern porticoes that are *said to be after the Parthenon*, they are mere blanks.

Mètre, a French measure, equal to 39·3702 English inches.

Mezuzoth, a name given to certain pieces of parchment which were anciently fixed on the door-posts of houses.

Mezzanine, a low intermediate story between two higher ones.

Mezzo-relievo, projection of figures between alto- and basso-relievo; demi-relievo.

Mezzotinto, a kind of engraving nearly resembling painting, effected by scraping and burnishing the copper.

Mica, an important ingredient in the composition of rocks, consisting of silica, alumina, oxide of iron, and potash: it is easily divided into laminæ, even to the $\frac{1}{300000}$th part of an inch, and is distinguishable from *talc* by its elasticity: in Russia it is used instead of window-glass.

Micrometer, an instrument for measuring small spaces.

Microscope, an optical instrument for rendering visible minute objects: the *simple* microscope has one lens only, and magnifies by permitting a near view of the object; in the *compound* microscope, a focal image is again magnified by other lenses.

Middle-ground is a term used, not to express the middle of a picture, but generally perspectively so;—sometimes it is the highest part of a picture, and sometimes the second degree of shade. Pictures are divided into three parts: fore-ground, middle-ground, and back-ground.

Middle-rail, the rail of a door which is upon a level with the hand when hanging freely: the lock of the door is generally fixed in this rail.

Midship signifies the middle of a ship.

Midship-bend, the broadest frame in the ship, called the 'dead-flat.'

Milestones. Pliny says, the miles on the Roman roads were distinguished by a pillar, or a stone, set up at the end of each of them, and which was marked with one or more figures, signifying how far it was from the Milliarium Aureum, a pillar in the forum near the temple of Saturn, which had on it the figure I., so that the next pillar to it, which was marked II., was but one mile from the standard pillar, and consequently the XIV. and XI. stones were but thirteen and ten miles from the forum.

Millennium, a thousand years; the term applied to that period of the Christian Church described in Revelation, during which, according to many commentators, it is supposed that Jesus Christ will reign personally on the earth, that the bodies of martyrs and other eminent Christians will be raised from the dead, and in this renewed state constitute the subjects of His glorious kingdom.

Milliare, a Roman mile, consisting of 1000 paces of 5 feet each, and therefore = 5000 feet: taking the Roman foot at 11·6496 English inches, the Roman mile would be 1618 English yards, or 142 yards less than the English statute mile.

Mills for the grinding of grain into flour are of several kinds: windmills, with sails to be impelled by the action of the wind, over-shot and under-shot; and the horizontal or turbine water-wheels. Mill machinery is used for the grinding of tobacco into snuff, impelled by wind, particularly in Holland, where stupendous structures can be seen on the road from Rotterdam to the Hague. Mills are also used, propelled by steam or water, for the grinding of bark, preparing of flax, sawing of timber, and for the many and varied purposes in manufacture. In the 'Papers on Engineering,' vol. vi., will be found an interesting paper by Mr. Fairbairn on 'Water-Wheels with Ventilated Buckets.'

Millwrights' Planing Machine. This machine is similar in principle to the ordinary planing machine (see *Planing Machine*), except in cases where heavy work is required to be planed, when a machine with a movable tool and fixed table is used. The advantage of this arrangement is, that very large and heavy castings are planed, which could not be moved to and fro, as in the ordinary machines, without great loss of power. It is placed over a pit made for the purpose, with steps to descend into it. The two side frames are bolted to the ground, and the table has a series of apertures for bolts to fix the work upon it, and can be raised or lowered to any required height by four strong screws, one at each corner. The horizontal and vertical slides are placed over the work in the usual manner, and are attached to a light frame, which, when the tool is adjusted to the work by the vertical slide, is moved to and fro, carrying with it the slides and tool, and at the end of each backward stroke a lappet, or other contrivance, sets the vertical slide and tool a little further across the table, until the entire surface is planed.

Minaret, in Mohammedan architecture, a spire or steeple.

Mind of Man. For the purposes of anatomy every skeleton may be useful, and may sufficiently tell the tale of the race to which it belongs, but when we come to seek for high beauty and for approaches to perfection, of how infinite a diversity, of what countless degrees, does form appear to be susceptible! How difficult it is to find these, except in mere fragments; and how dangerous does it prove, in dealing with objects, to treat the whole as a normal specimen, simply because parts are fine, or even superlative. When, again, we pass onward, and with the body regard also the mind of man, still greater is the range of difference, and still more rare is either the development of parts in a degree so high as to bring their single excellence near the ideal standard, or the accurate adjustment of their relations to one another, or the completeness of the aggregate which they form. (Gladstone.)

Mineral Black is a native and impure

oxide of carbon, of a soft texture, found in Devonshire.

Mineral Green is the commercial name of green lakes, prepared from the sulphate of copper.

Mineralogy forms one of the three great divisions into which natural history or the knowledge of natural objects has been classified; the other two being botany, devoted to plants, and zoology, to animals. Mineralogy is also distinguished from geology, inasmuch as it regards the characters of minerals in detail, without regard to their formation and general distribution in the crust of the earth, which belong to geology. If the composition of a mineral substance is to be considered, then mineralogy forms a portion of chemistry; but in its more limited sense, mineralogy is the art of distinguishing mineral substances from each other, and the science of accurately describing and arranging them, by what may be termed a natural classification.

Minerva in a speech expresses to Juno her resentment at the restraint put upon her by Jupiter. She accuses him of forgetting the services she had so often rendered to Hercules when he was oppressed by the labours that Eurystheus had laid upon him, and declares that it was she who effected his escape from Hades. (Gladstone.)

Minerva in her capacity of a traditive deity was with perfect consistency worshiped alike among Trojans and Greeks, Hellenic and Pelasgian tribes; there is nothing strange, then, in our finding her the patroness of a Pelasgian people. (Gladstone.)

Mines. Water-springs in mines are wrongly considered to be of great injury. It is true, the lifting of water by machinery from the deep mines is attended with expense, when they are so situated that no level, drift, or watercourse can be obtained for that purpose; but, on the other hand, they are so absolutely necessary in mining, that in the very first process, a judicious miner, in boring down to his mine, previous to his sinking to or working it, even in this simple act, cannot proceed very deep without water to work his bore-rod in; and if the strata of the earth passed through does not produce it, he must pour it down the bore-hole, or he cannot proceed. When all his pits or shafts are sunk, and his mine opened, and ventilation is required to expel inflammable air, fire, or black damp (as it is termed), nothing is superior to water. When this can be obtained, and made to run with facility through the mine and its various workings, it is found superior to air-furnaces of any kind for expelling the fulminating vapours so destructive to the health and lives of the workmen employed.

Mines in Scotland. The general custom of Scotland provides for yielding to the landlord a royalty proportioned upon the net amount of sales at the colliery, in conjunction with a certain or sleeping rent payable half-yearly. The royalty proportion is sometimes so high as one-quarter the amount of sales, but generally one-eighth; of late years many collieries have been let at one-twelfth and at one-fourteenth the amount of sales.

Mining. There is an essential difference between civil and military mining: in the former, the works are frequently carried on at considerable depths below the surface of the earth, and sometimes in solid rock; whereas military mining is what may be termed superficial, and consequently the miner works through the more recent formations of earths and sands, which, from their little tenacity, he has to support as he advances. For the better ventilation of military mines, a machine has been invented by Sergeant Lewis, of the Royal Sappers and Miners; and it has been conjectured that Mr. Haig's patent pneumatic engine, invented for the purpose of purifying the holds of vessels, might also be successfully employed in mining operations.

Minster, a cathedral, anciently a large church. (See *Westminster Abbey*.)

Minute, a proportionate measure in architecture, by which the parts of the orders are regulated; the sixtieth part of the lower diameter of the shaft of a column, written thus, 10′, i.e. ten minutes; in geography and astronomy, the sixtieth part of a degree.

Miserere, projecting brackets in the under side of the seats of stalls in churches; they are always more or less ornamented with carvings of leaves and grotesque subjects.

Mitre, an episcopal crown. In carpentry, the line formed by the meeting of mouldings or other surfaces which intersect each other. If two pieces of wood be formed to equal angles, or if the two sides of each piece form equal inclinations, and thus be joined together at their common vertex, so as to make an angle double to that of either piece, they are said to be mitred together, and the joint is called 'the mitre.'

Mitre-wheel, a wheel having teeth formed so as to work at an angle of 45° to the centre line of the shaft on which it is fixed, to move with another wheel of equal size, fixed on a shaft at right angles to the former one.

Mixed Citrine. There are two principles of combination, of which the artist may avail himself in producing these colours; the one being that of combining two original secondaries, green and orange, in producing a citrine; the other, the uniting the three primaries in such a manner that yellow may predominate in the case of citrine, and blue and red be subordinate in the compound.

Mixed Greys are formed by the compounding of black and white, which yields neutral greys, and of black and blue, black and purple, black and olive, etc.

Mixed Greens, compounds of blue and yellow pigments, which may be formed by compounding them in the several ways of working, or by blending them in the proportions of the various hues required.

Mixed Olive is compounded by uniting green and purple colours, or by adding to blue a smaller proportion of yellow and red, or by breaking much blue with little orange.

Mixed Orange. Orange being a colour compounded of red and yellow, the place of original orange pigments may be supplied by a mixture of the two latter colours, by glazing one over the other; by stippling, or other modes of breaking and intermixing them in working, according to the nature of the work and the effect required.

Mixed Purple. Purple being a secondary colour, composed of blue and red, it follows of course that any blue and red pigments which are chemically at variance may be used in producing a mixed purple of any required hue, either by compounding or by grinding them together ready for use, or by combining them in the various modes of operation in painting.

Mixed Russet. Orange, vermilion, and madder purple afford a compound russet pigment of a good and durable colour.

Mizen-mast, in ship-rigging, the mast next the stern.

Mock lead, wild lead, black lead, or *black jack*, a ponderous black mineral, which does not readily incorporate in the fire; a zinc ore.

Model, a pattern used for moulding; a machine or building executed in miniature.

Modillion, a projecting bracket under the corona of the Corinthian and Composite orders, and sometimes of the Roman Ionic.

Module, a measure of proportion by which the parts of an order or of a building are regulated in classical architecture; considered generally as the diameter or semi-diameter of the lower end of the shaft of the column; in other words, semi-diameter of the column, or 30 minutes.

Molecule, synonymous with *atom*, in physics, a very small mass or portion of any body.

Molybdenum, a brittle and white globulous metal.

Momentum, in dynamics, is the force of a body in motion. When the motion of a body is considered with respect to the mass, or quantity of matter moved, as well as its velocity, it is called its momentum, or quantity of motion. The momentum of a body is therefore in the compound ratio of its quantity of matter and velocity.

Monastery, an establishment for the accommodation of a religious fraternity, who made it the receptacle of benevolence and charity for the poor and the way-worn. A considerable portion of the land was formerly occupied by the monasteries and other religious houses which existed in Britain, and the endowments of these establishments subsequently became the foundation of the great wealth of some of the early aristocracy in England.

Of the ample means enjoyed by the inmates of these cloistered sanctuaries, some idea may be formed from the following historical statement, translated from the preface to the 'Ely Cartulary,' preserved in the Public Library at Cambridge. After the defeat and death of Harold, many of the leading men of the realm, who had strenuously opposed the Bastard, fled for refuge to Ely monastery, together with their friends, "laden with their richest treasures," and withstood, for seven years, the impetuous threatenings of the Normans, until they were unexpectedly surprised. "Then a council being held, it seemed advisable to implore the royal mercy; upon which some were despatched to the king's court, at that time at Warwick, carrying rich treasures to the king, the gift of atonement and compensation of their misconduct; with which the king was satisfied, but on these terms and conditions,—that, during his pleasure, forty royal officers should be lodged at the expense of the monastery. * * The knights are sent for, they arrive, and are present with their household, every one of whom has under him a monk of the first order, as an officer under his earl, or a guest under his host. But the king ordered that the cellarer should dispense provisions to the officers and monks promiscuously in the public hall of the convent. In short, the officers with their earls, the guests with their hosts, the knights with their monks, the monks with their knights, were most grateful to each other; for each and all of them mutually afforded each other the offices of humanity."—After five years passed in this way, the knights were recalled by the Conqueror, to assist in punishing the unnatural wickedness of his son Robert; and "they departed with grief; and our monks, wonderful to relate, lamented the departure of these most illustrious companions, heroic knights, and most pleasing guests, not only in tears, but in dismal howlings and exclamations, and struck their breasts in despair, after the manner of a bride whose husband is unseasonably hurried from her sweet embraces to arms... All the monks accompanied the knights as far as Haddenham, with hymns, crosses, thuribals, processions, and every solemnity, and, when returned, took care to paint the arms of each knight on the walls of the refectory, to the perpetual remembrance of the uncommon humanity of their military guests."—In the cartulary the names of the knights, forty in number, with their companions, are given; and their arms are emblazoned on the margin.

Monkey-wrench, a spanner with a movable jaw, which can be adjusted by a screw or wedge to the size of the nut which it is required to turn.

Monogram, a cipher composed of two or more letters interwoven as an abbreviation of a name: monograms were common as distinctive marks on ancient coins, and were also used as seals.

Monolithic, consisting of a single stone; statues, columns, and pillars were formed by the ancients out of large blocks of stone or marble.

Monopteral, a temple which has no cella, but consists of columns disposed in the form of a circle, covered with a conical roof.

Monota, a vase with one handle.

Monotriglyph, the interval observed between the columns of a Doric portico, where a space is left sufficient for the insertion of one triglyph only between those immediately over two contiguous columns.

Monstrance, sometimes called *Remonstrance*, the vessel in which the consecrated wafer or host is placed while the congregation are blessed with it, in the Roman Catholic Church. In the 'Divers Works of Early Masters,' 2 vols. folio, will be found two of the rarest and most elaborate examples of tabernacles or canopies, in a compartment of either of which the casket or vessel containing the sacred vessel is deposited.

Monton, a heap of ore: a batch under process of amalgamation, varying in different mining districts.

Monument, a mausoleum or tomb. Sepulchral monuments of the middle ages still exist to a considerable extent, both here and on the Continent. Monuments and tombs of modern date are designed from Classical and Gothic architecture, and in many instances are beautiful examples of modern art.

Moor, in Cornish, a root, or quantity of ore in a particular part of a lode, as a 'moor of ore,' a 'moor of tin.'

Moorish, *Mohammedan*, or *Saracenic Architecture*, is a combination of Egyptian, Grecian, and Roman details; first established by the Arabs about the tenth century, and for oriental scenery of a pleasing character: its complicated ornament and lattice-work are rich and peculiar. Many existing examples are interesting; but the style is not adapted to European usages and requirements.

Moot-hall, or *Moot-house*, in Saxon times, a building appropriated to assemblies on public affairs; a *guild-hall* or *town-hall*; *hôtel de ville*, etc.

Mora wood. This tree is 100 feet high, and abundant; it is close-grained, like teak, and superior to oak; esteemed for ship-building.

Moresque, a kind of painting, carving, etc., in the arabesque and grotesque styles of ornament.

Mortar. The materials which are added to lime, in the formation of mortars or calcareous cements, are, 1st, the different kinds of sand, properly so called; 2nd, arenes; 3rd, psammites; 4th, clays; 5th, volcanic or pseudo-volcanic products; and 6th, artificial products arising from the calcination of the clays, the arenes, and the psammites; and the rubbish and slag of manufactories, forges, etc.

INGREDIENTS OF MORTAR.

SAND.—The granitic, schistose, and calcareous rocks, free-stones, etc., reduced to the state of hard and palpable grains, either by the agitation of water, or by spontaneous disaggregation, give birth to the various kinds of sand. We distinguish them from powders by their falling at once to the bottom, when thrown into limpid water, and that without altering its transparency in any sensible degree.

The disaggregation of rocks is often accompanied by a decomposition which produces a powder: this powder renders the sand 'rich,' or, in other terms, susceptible of a certain cohesion, when tempered with water. Washed by rains and currents of water, it is soon freed from the pulverulent particles, and is deposited pure in the beds of rivers. This purity is often changed near the mouths of streams, and in the small rivulets whose tributaries flow over a bed of clay or mould: the sand mixes with vegetable débris and animal matters, and becomes 'loamy.' The particles composing sand faithfully represent those of the rocks whence they are derived. The granitic regions furnish quartz, felspar, and mica; and the volcanic regions, lavas of all kinds. The tabular-shaped sands, whose particles are tender, are furnished by the schistose mountains. It is difficult for them to be transported far without being reduced to powder.

The calcareous sands are the least common, probably arising from the fact that rivers generally take their rise from primitive summits, or such as are composed of primitive elements. The calcareous rocks, besides, are not susceptible of that kind of disaggregation which can be called granitic; for if they be of a soft kind, they produce powder; if hard, scaly splinters.

The partial and secondary revolutions of the globe have occasioned immense deposits of sand in situations where now neither brooks nor rivers flow: these are the fossil sands; and they should be carefully distinguished from the virgin sands, which are still in their original site, and have not been operated on by the waters.

The fossil sands generally exhibit a more angular grain than the sea or river sands; but consist for the most part of the same elements, sometimes pure, sometimes coloured by ochres, etc.

Among the fossil sands is one very remarkable, the arene. Its properties entitle it to attention.

ARENE is a sand, generally quartzose, with very irregular, unequal grains, and mingled with yellow, red, brown, and sometimes white clay, in proportions varying from one to three-fourths of the whole volume.

The arene almost always occupies the summits of the rounded and moderately-elevated hills. It sometimes constitutes entire hillocks; frequently it interposes itself in large veins and seams in the clefts of calcareous rocks: it belongs essentially to alluvial soils.

PSAMMITES is a term applied to an assemblage of the grains of quartz, schist, felspar, and particles of mica, agglutinated by a variable cement. The varieties of these are very numerous: those which in appearance strongly resemble the free-stones and siliceous breccias belong to the class of rocks whose disaggregation furnishes sand, properly so called. But the psammites, which are slaty, of a yellow, red, or brown colour, fine-grained, unctuous to the touch, producing a clayey paste with water, form a distinct species, and one which merits attention.

These last belong to the primitive schistose formations: they do not and cannot exist except *in situ*: they are found in beds or veins, forming part of the schist of which they are merely a decomposition.

CLAYS are earthy substances variously coloured, fine, soft to the touch, which diffuse in water with facility, forming with it a paste, which, when kneaded to a certain consistency, possesses unctuosity and tenacity, and may be drawn out and kneaded in every direction without separating. The clayey paste, when dried, retains its solidity, hardens in the fire, etc.

Clays are essentially composed of silica and alumina: these two substances are adulterated by the presence of the oxide of iron, the carbonates of lime and magnesia, sulphuret of iron, and of vegetable combustible matter partly decomposed.

The clays are separated into four classes; viz. the refractory, which resist, without melting, the heat of the porcelain furnaces (140° Wedgwood); the fusible clays; the effervescing or clayey marls; and, lastly, the ochrey clays, coloured red or pure yellow by oxide of iron.

The position of clays is very varied: they are found as veins in primitive formations; in billocks, on the confines of the primitive chains; in horizontal beds, or layers, in the secondary formations; in threads, thin veins, or infiltrations, in chinks and hollows of calcareous masses; lastly, in volcanic regions, where their formation is attributed to the decomposition of the compact lavas, and perhaps also, with some probability, to miry eruptions.

Mortar. Considered as a plastic material, mortar fit for moulding may be made to take every possible form in moulds or shapes. To give it the appearance of stone, it should be made with fine colourless sand, or rather with fine calcareous powders derived from hard stones.

Mortar contained in a mould may be beaten or rammed in the manner of pisé,—"a mode of building formerly in use, whereby walls were formed by ramming and beating down earth, clay, etc., between upright planks,"—and acquires by that means great compactness; but an increase of resistance does not always result from this.

In order that any material be beaten with effect, it is necessary that it should possess a certain degree of consistency, which is a mean between complete pulverulence and that state of ductility which constitutes a firm paste. No compression is possible when the material escapes from under the rammer; and this is still practised by the builders in pisé, who never employ any but earth slightly moistened. Mortar may always be prepared in this way, leaving it, after it has been worked in the ordinary manner, to undergo desiccation to a proper extent.

The successive approximation of the particles of the compressed material to one another necessarily determines a foliated structure, which, though it may not be perceived, is nevertheless real. Analogy will lead to the conclusion, that, in every possible case, a body thus formed ought to oppose a greater resistance to a tractile force in proportion as its direction forms a smaller angle with the plane of the laminæ; however, experience shows that this in general does not take place. The following has been determined in this respect:—

1st. Beating has the effect of augmenting the absolute resistance of mortars of rich limes and pure sand in every case, but in an unequal manner. The greatest resistance assumes a direction perpendicular to the planes of the laminæ when the mortars are buried in a damp soil immediately after their fabrication. It remains parallel to these same planes when the mortars have been exposed to the atmospheric influence.

2nd. The effect of beating is not constantly useful to mortars of hydraulic or eminently hydraulic limes, and calcareous or quartzose sands or powders, except in the case when these mortars are used under a damp soil. The greatest resistance is then in a direction perpendicular to the planes of these laminæ, as with the mortars of rich limes; but in the air, the superiority of the mortars which have been beaten over those which have not is only exhibited in one direction, and that is parallel to the plane of the laminæ.

3rd. Beating becomes injurious in every case when the hydrates of the hydraulic or eminently hydraulic limes are employed without admixture, and subjected to the influence of a damp soil; and is favourable to it only in the direction parallel to the laminæ when the stuff dries in the air.

Considered as a plastic substance, the numerous casts which have been moulded, both in the bas-relief and alto-relievo, prove that mortar receives and retains impressions well: their hardness is continually on the increase, and a kind of varnish, with which time covers them, gives them a strong resemblance to stone.

One problem remains to be solved, viz. to discover a means of hastening the set of mortar without injuring its future qualities; and this, in order to avoid being obliged to multiply moulds indefinitely for the same casting. This last desideratum appears to be difficult. The natural cements, which harden almost instantly in the air and in the water, when worked up like plaster of Paris, are subject to the inconvenience of being tinged brown. Such as are fabricated artificially, by calcining mixtures of lime and clay free from iron, do not stand the weather.

Mortar of hydraulic lime may be employed as a plastic substance in a multitude of cases, in which the number of moulds is no inconvenience. Such is the case in the preparation of artificial stones bearing mouldings, vases, or ornaments of any kind susceptible of formation by the rectilinear or circular movement of a profile. It is evident that it will then answer to set the mould in a trench, and run the profile along the clayey paste, prepared and arranged for that purpose. The economy which such a process would introduce into ornamental constructions is indeed incredible.

Mortise, in carpentry, a hole cut in a piece of wood, to receive a corresponding projection formed upon another piece.

Mortise and Tenon. The following rules may be referred to as *data* for the workman in ordinary practice.

The tenon, in general, may be taken at about one-third of the thickness of the wood.

When the mortise and tenon are to lie horizontally, as the juncture will thus be unsupported, the tenon should not be more than one-fifth of the thickness of the stuff, in order that the strain on the upper surface of the tenoned piece may not split off the under-cheek of the mortise.

When the piece that is tenoned is not to pass the end of the mortised piece, the tenon should be reduced one-third or one-fourth of its breadth, to prevent the necessity of opening one side of the tenon. As there is always some danger of splitting the end of the piece in which the mortise is made, the end beyond the mortise should, as often as possible, be made considerably longer than it is intended to remain; so that the tenon may be driven tightly in, and the superfluous wood cut off afterwards.

But the above regulations may be varied, according as the tenoned or mortised piece is weaker or stronger.

The labour of making deep mortises, in hard wood, may be lessened, by first boring a number of holes with the auger in the part to be mortised, as the compartments between may then more easily be cut away by the chisel.

Before employing the saw to cut the shoulder of a tenon in neat work, if the line of its entrance be correctly determined by nicking the place with a paring chisel, there will be no danger of the wood being torn at the edges by the saw.

As the neatness and durability of a juncture depend entirely on the sides of the mortise coming exactly in contact with the sides of the tenon, and as this is not easily performed when a mortise is to pass entirely through a piece of stuff, the space allotted for it should be first correctly gauged on both sides. One half is then to be cut from one side, and the other half from the opposite side; and as any irregularities which may arise from an error in the direction of the chisel will thus be confined to the middle of the mortise, they will be of very little hindrance to the exact fitting of the sides of the mortise and tenon. Moreover, as the tenon is expanded by wedges after it is driven in, the sides of the mortise may, in a small degree, be inclined towards each other, near the shoulders of the tenon.

M-roof, a roof formed by the junction of two common roofs with a vallum between them.

Mosaic (The) books, and the other historical books of the Old Testament, are not intended to present, and do not present, a picture of human society, or of our nature drawn at large. Their aim is to exhibit it in one master relation, and to do this with effect, they do it, to a great extent, exclusively. The Homeric materials for exhibiting that relation are different in kind as well as in degree; but as they paint, and paint to the very life, the whole range of our nature and the entire circle of human action and experience, at an epoch much more nearly analogous to the patriarchal time than to any later age, the poems of Homer may be received in the philosophy of human nature, as the complement of the earliest portion of the sacred records. (Gladstone.)

Mosaic-work, the art of picturing with small pebbles and shells of various colours, pieces of glass, marble, etc., cemented on a ground of stucco.

Mosque, a Mohammedan temple.

Motif, that which suggests a hint or idea to an artist; also the hint itself.

Motion. The cross-head, cross-head guides, and blocks, in a locomotive engine, taken as a whole, are called "the motion."

Motion (laws of). A body must continue for ever in a state of rest, or in a state of uniform and rectilineal motion, if it be not disturbed by the action of some external cause. The alteration of motion produced in a body by the action of any external force is always proportional to that force, and in the direction of the right line in which it acts. The action and reaction of bodies on one another are equal, and are exerted in opposite directions.

Motion of bodies on inclined planes. The force of an inclined plane bears the same proportion to the force of gravity as the height of the plane bears to its length; that is, the force which accelerates the motion of a body down an inclined plane, is that fractional part of the force of gravity which is represented by the height of the plane divided by its length.

Mould, the model or pattern used by workmen as a guide in working mouldings and ornaments, in the casting of metal, and models of machinery.

Mouldings, a term applied to all the varieties of outline or contour given to the angles of the various subordinate parts and features of buildings, whether projections or cavities, such as cornices, capitals, bases, door or window jambs, and heads, etc. There are eight sorts of regular mouldings, viz. the Ovolo, the Talon, the Cyma, the Cavetto, the Torus, the Astragal, the Scotia, and the Fillet. These mouldings are not to be used at

MOULDINGS.

hazard, each having certain situations adapted to its reception, to which it must always be applied. Thus the ovolo and talon, from their peculiar form, seem intended to support other important mouldings or members; the cyma and cavetto, being of weaker contour, should only be used for the cover or shelter of other parts; the torus and astragal, bearing a resemblance to a rope, appear calculated to bind and fortify the parts to which they are applied; the use of the fillet and scotia is to separate one moulding from another, and to give a variety to the general profile. The ovolo and talon are mostly placed in situations above the level of the eye; when below it, they should only be applied as crowning members. The place for the scotia is universally below the level of the eye. When the fillet is very wide, and used under the cyma of a cornice, it is termed a corona; if under a corona, it is called a band.

The curved contours of mouldings are portions of either circles or ellipses.

The principal mouldings, and the difference of their profiles in the Grecian and Roman styles, are here exhibited.

GREEK.   ROMAN.

Echinus or Ovolo.

Cyma Recta.

Cyma Reversa.

Scotia.

Torus.

Moulding, the process of forming a cavity in sand or loam, in order to give its form to metal which is applied in a fluid state; an ornamental cavity in wood, stone, or other suitable material.

Mountain-blue. A very beautiful substance of this kind, a carbonate of copper, both blue and green, is found in Cumberland. None of these blues of copper are, however, durable; used in oil, they become green, and, as pigments, are precisely of the character of verditers.

Mountain-green is a native carbonate of copper, combined with a white earth, and often striated with veins of mountain-blue, to which it bears the same relation that green verditer does to blue verditer; nor does it differ from these and other copper-greens in any property essential to the painter.

M. S., an abbreviation commonly used on tomb-stones or monumental tablets for the Latin words *Memoriæ Sacrum*, 'Sacred to the Memory': the letters *I. H. S.* are often similarly applied in sacred edifices, for *Jesus Hominum Salvator*,—'Jesus the Saviour of Men.'

Mud-holes, the covered openings in the bottom of a boiler for discharging the dirt and sediment.

Mud-plugs, in locomotive engines tapered screw-plugs fitted into convenient parts of the boiler, to admit of its being washed out by these plug-holes when necessary.

Mulberry-tree, a wood of great variety, principally from Rio Janeiro, and very suitable for furniture.

Mullion, the division between the lights of windows, screens, etc., in Gothic architecture: the styles or upright divisions in wainscoting are also sometimes called mullions.

Mule-jenny, a machine used in the manufacture of cotton thread.

Mun (Cornish), any fusible metal.

Mundick, an exceedingly ponderous mineral, whitish, beautiful and shining, but brittle. It is abundant in Cornish and Irish mines.

Muniment-house, a strong, properly fire-proof apartment in public or private buildings, for the preservation of charters, deeds, seals, etc.

Munnions, pieces that part the lights in a ship's stern and quarter-gallery.

Munnions, in house-building, upright posts that divide the lights in a window-frame.

Mummy, or *Egyptian-brown*, is a bituminous substance, combined with animal remains brought from the catacombs of Egypt, where liquid bitumen was employed three thousand years ago in embalming, in which office it has been combined, by a slow chemical change, during so many ages, with substances which give it a more solid and lasting texture than simple asphaltum; but in this respect it varies exceedingly.

Mural, pertaining to a wall; a monumental tablet affixed to a wall is a mural monument.

Murometer, an instrument to measure small spaces.

Murus, the wall of a Greek city, in contradistinction to *Paries*, the wall of a house, and *Maceria*, a boundary wall.

Music. This word is derived from the Latin *musica*, and this again from the Greek adjective *mousikos*, which signifies, of or belonging to the Muses. As a substantive, the word *mousikos*, or in Latin *musicus*, a musician, means also a poet or an orator: and in the feminine gender signifies the liberal arts, but especially music, poetry, and eloquence. The ancients, therefore, understood by music far more than has been attributed to it for some ages past. Music is now considered as the language of agreeable sounds, and is both a science and an art. As a science, it teaches the theory of musical sounds, their production by the vibrations of the air, the ratio of these vibrations, and also their times; likewise the various phenomena connected with musical sounds, the causes of discords, beats, etc., as well as the lengths of musical strings and pipes. The mathematical theory of music is part of the science of acoustics, or phonics, and is therefore one of the high mechanical sciences. As an art, music teaches the practical use of the science; the scales or gamuts of sounds in a fixed succession, at fixed intervals from each other; the permutations of their sounds; forming an immense variety of melodies. It teaches also the combination of these sounds according to certain received laws, forming thereby the most agreeable sensations on the ear, by producing a great variety of chords, composed of concordant sounds alone, or of a judicious admixture of concordant and dissonal sounds. Practical music teaches also the use and performance of the several instruments of music, as also their peculiar functions; and herein is embraced the human voice, the most perfect and beautiful of all musical instruments. Music, therefore, is divided into two grand parts, viz. theoretical or scientific, and practical; the former treating of the purely philosophical branch mathematically, the latter being confined solely to the production of musical compositions, and their performance. Practical music consists of several species, the highest of which is the ecclesiastical; then follow the oratorio, opera, military, chamber, and ball-room species; and is divided into vocal and instrumental music, each of these being variously subdivided.

Musnud, in Persia, a throne or chair of state.

Mustaib, a wood from the Brazils, inferior to rosewood, but harder; used at Sheffield for the handles of glaziers' and other knives, etc.

Mutule, a projecting block worked under the corona of the Doric cornice, in the same situation as the modillions in the Corinthian and Composite orders; it is often made to slope downward towards the most prominent part, and has usually a number of small guttæ or drops, worked on the under side.

Mynchery, the Saxon name for a nunnery: nuns were sometimes called Mynchies.

Myoparo, a small piratical craft, employed by the Saxon corsairs.

Myriad, the number of 10,000; proverbially any great number.

Myriamètre, a French measure of 10,000 mètres.

N.

Nails, used in building, are small metallic spikes serving to bind or fasten the parts together. There are several kinds of nails, called by numerous names. In the middle ages, nails were frequently used much ornamented, of which there are several very beautiful existing specimens, particularly in church doors and the gates of large mansions.

Naked, of a column or pilaster, the surface of the shaft where the mouldings are supposed to project.

Naked, of a wall, the remote face whence the projectures take their rise. It is generally a plain surface, and when the plan is circular, the naked is the surface of a cylinder, with its axis perpendicular to the horizon.

Naked flooring, in carpentry, the whole assemblage or contignation of timber-work for supporting the boarding of a floor on which to walk. Naked flooring consists of a row of parallel joists, called floor-joists.

Naos, the chamber or enclosed apartment of a Greek temple. The part of the temple which stood before the naos, comprehended between the wall and the columns of the portico, was called the pronaos; while the corresponding part behind was called the *posticum*.

Naples yellow is a compound of the oxides of lead and antimony, anciently prepared at Naples under the name of Grallolina; it is supposed also to have been a native production of Vesuvius and other volcanoes, and is a pigment of deservedly considerable reputation. It is not so vivid a colour as patent yellow and turbith mineral, but is variously of a pleasing, light, warm golden-yellow tint. Like most other yellows, it is opaque, and in this sense is of good body. It is not changed by the light of the sun, and may be used safely in oil or varnish, under the same management as the whites of lead; but like these latter pigments also, it is likely to change even to blackness by damp and impure air when used as a water-colour, or unprotected by oil or varnish.

Naphtha, a species of mineral oil or fluid bitumen, now commonly used for lamps.

Narthex, a division in the early Christian churches in which the catechisms were said, and penitents admitted; it was near the entrance, and separated from the rest of the church by a railing or screen.

Nasmyth's patent direct-action steam-hammer is employed instead of the old halves or lift-hammers, and is worked by a connected high-pressure steam engine, which raises the hammer to any required height within its vertical range of motion, and in which it is guided by two planed guides. On the escape of the steam, when the valve of the cylinder is opened, the hammer falls on the work that lies on the anvil with the full force due to gravity, without scarcely any loss from friction. The instant the hammer has given its blow, the steam is again let in under the piston, and the same action is repeated with ease and rapidity.

Nasmyth's steam pile-driving engine. There are two grand or important features of novelty in this pile-driving engine, compared with all former contrivances for the like purpose. In the first place, by the employment of the steam-hammer action, the steam is made to act direct in raising up and letting fall the hammer, or monkey, without the intervention of any rotatory motion; while, in the second place, another grand feature consists in the employment of the pile about to be driven, or raised up and planted in its situation by the machine, by means of a windlass worked by a small detached steam engine.

Some conception of the rapidity with which piles are driven by this machine may be formed, when it is stated that a pile measuring 60 feet in length, and 14 inches square, can be driven 45 feet into stiff soil, down to the rock below, in four minutes; and such is the good effect resulting from the blows being given by a great mass of 30 cwt. striking quickly but with small velocity of actual impact, that the head of the pile requires no hoop, and presents, after being driven, a neater appearance than it had when it was first placed under the hammer.

Natural beds of stone are the surfaces from which the laminæ are separated. It is all-important for the duration of stone walls, that the laminæ should be placed perpendicular to the face of the work, and parallel to the horizon.

Natural Philosophy takes an extensive range, embracing the study of the collection of created beings and objects, and of those laws by which they are governed, all of them expressed in the term Nature. Natural objects are separated into two grand classes, the organic and inorganic; the former being distinguished by vital power or life: organic bodies admit of a marked distinction into animals and plants; the science of Zoology describing and classifying the one, and that of Botany the other. These sciences admit of many subdivisions, and collectively with Mineralogy, that of Natural History.

1. Geology, the science which has for its object the observation and description of the structure of the external crust of the globe; Mineralogy taking account only of the

separate items of which the earth's crust is composed. 2. Chemistry, which may be regarded as atomic anatomy, its object being to decompose bodies, to study the properties of their elements, and the laws of combination. 3. Physics, or Natural Philosophy, which considers the general properties of all bodies. Natural philosophy is again subdivided into many distinct sciences. The mutual action of forces and masses of matter produces in the latter either equilibrium or motion, and hence arise those two divisions of sciences, called Statics and Dynamics, which are again divided into Stereo-statics and Stereo-dynamics, as applied to solids; Hydrostatics and Hydrodynamics, as applied to liquids; Electro-statics and Electro-dynamics, as applied to Electricity. The application of statics and dynamics to air and other gaseous fluids is called Pneumatics. The application of dynamics to the arts of life has led to the composition and arrangement of the various machines for assisting the labour of man; this branch is called Mechanics. The construction and performance of the various machines to raise water, or which are driven by the motion of that fluid, belong to hydrodynamics, while the construction of works depending on the equilibrium of liquids belongs to hydrostatics. Those machines which are driven by the wind depend on the application of pneumatics; and all the varied phenomena of the atmosphere arising from the action of heat, light, electricity, and moisture, form the science of Meteorology. The phenomena of heat and electricity also form separate sciences; the latter admitting of five divisions, viz. electricity, magnetism, galvanism or voltaic electricity, thermo-electricity, and animal electricity. The phenomena of light, although included in the term Optics, are varied; namely, perspective, catoptrics, dioptrics, chromatics, physical optics, and polarization; to which may be added actino-chemistry.

Naumachia, among the Greeks, a sea-fight; a spectacle. The term was also applied to a circus encompassed with seats and porticoes, the pit of which, serving as an arena, was filled with water by means of pipes, for the exhibition of sea-fights.

Naupegus, a shipwright.

Nautical, pertaining to ships or sailors.

Naval Architecture, the art of designing and constructing ships and vessels for the purposes of navigation.

Navals, a ship-dock or dockyard.

Navalia, ship-building docks at Rome, where also ships were laid up and refitted.

Navarchus, among the ancients, the name of a commander or admiral of a fleet.

Nave, the body of a church west of the choir, in which the general congregation assemble. In large buildings it consists of a central division, with two or more aisles; and there are frequently, in foreign structures, several small chapels on the sides beyond the aisles. In mechanics, the central part of a wheel.

Navel-hoods, in ship-building, pieces of plank, or thick stuff, wrought above and below the hawse-holes.

Navis, in church furniture, a metal dish or vessel to contain frankincense.

Neap, low, decrescent; a term applied to the tides which happen when the moon is in the middle of her second and fourth quarters. The highest spring-tide is three days after the full or change; the lowest neap-tide is four days before the full or change.

Neapolitan School of painting, which possesses indisputable proofs of having in ancient times ranked among the first in Italy; as in no part of that country do the remains of antiquity evince a more refined taste, nowhere do we find mosaics executed with more elegance, nor anything more beautiful than the subterranean chambers which are ornamented with historical designs and grotesques.

At the restoration of art, it had made little progress in Naples and her territories before *Zingaro's* time. His name was *Antonio Solario*, originally a smith, and commonly called *lo Zingaro*. His history has something romantic in it, like that of Quintin Matsys.

The most celebrated work of Zingaro's was in the choir of S. Severino, in fresco, representing in several compartments the life St. Benedict. He left numerous pictures, and Madonnas of a beautiful form, in various churches of Naples, —in that of S. Domenico Maggiore, where he painted a Dead Christ, and in that of S. Pier Martire, where he represented a S. Vincenzio.

Two eminent artists of the Neapolitan School were Matteo da Siena and Antonella da Messina. The latter is a name so illustrious in the history of art, that he claims notice in the Sienese, Neapolitan, and Venetian Schools.

It has already been observed that at the commencement of the sixteenth century, the art of painting seemed in every country to have attained to maturity, and that every school assumed its own peculiar character. Naples however did not possess a manner so decided as that of other schools in Italy.

A writer has observed that no part of Italy could boast of so many native artists, is seldom found in that school. Nor do we find that it paid much attention to ideal perfection, as most of its professors, following the practice of the naturalists, selected the character of their heads and the attributes of their figures from common life; some with more, and others with less discrimination. With regard to colour this school changed its principles in conformity to the taste of the times.

The modern Neapolitan School is founded on the schools of Raffaello and Michelangiolo.

The chief names are Andrea Sabbatini, Polidoro Caravaggio, Marco da Siena, Corenzio, Ribera Carracciolo, Luca Giordano, and Solimene.

Nebule moulding, an heraldic term. In architecture, an ornament of the zigzag form, but without angles; it is chiefly found in the remains of Saxon architecture, in the archivolts of doors and windows.

Neck of a capital, the space between the astragal on the shaft and the annulet of the capital in the Grecian-Doric order.

Neck-mould, in architecture, a small convex moulding surrounding a column at the junction of the shaft and capital.

Necrology, an obituary formerly kept in churches and monasteries.

Needle, or *Nail*, in mining, a long taper piece of copper or iron, with a copper point; used when stamping the hole for blasting, to make by its insertion an aperture for a fusee or train.

Needlework, a term anciently used for the framework of timber and plaster in old houses.

Neo, a Greek term, to spin or twist a number of separate fibres of wool

Net, or *Neat*, in commerce, that which is pure and unadulterated; the weight of any package after the *tare* has been deducted; sometimes, but improperly, written *nett*.

Newel, the central column round which the steps of a circular staircase wind; the principal post at the angles and foot of a staircase. In the Tudor and Elizabethan residences very beautiful examples exist, adding much to the beauty of the staircase.

Niche, in architecture, a cavity or hollow place in the thickness of a wall, in which to place a figure, a statue, vase, or ornament. Niches are made to partake of all the segments under a semicircle: they are sometimes at an equal distance from the front, and parallel or square on the back with the front line, in which case they are called square recesses, or square niches. Occasionally small pediments were formed over them, supported on consoles, or small columns or pilasters placed at the sides of the niches. Anciently they were used in ecclesiastical buildings for statues and shallow square recesses. The ruins of Palmyra exhibit niches of various kinds. Within the portico of the temple of the Sun there are two niches, etc.

Niche, angular, one formed in the corner of a building.

Niche, in carpentry, the wood-work to be lathed-over for plastering. The usual constructions of niches in carpentry are those with cylindrical backs and spherical heads, called cylindro-spheric niches, the execution of which depends upon the principles of spheric sections.

Niche, ground, that which, instead of bearing on a massive base or dado, has its rise from the ground,—as the niches of the portico of the Pantheon at Rome: their ordinary proportion is, two diameters in height, and one in width. Round or square niches are also formed.

Nigged ashlar, stone hewn with a pick or pointed hammer, instead of a chisel; used principally at Aberdeen for the hewing of the hard granite.

Nitrate of lime, nitric acid in combination with lime for a base, abounding in the mortar of old buildings.

Nitrates, compounds, or salts, formed by the combination of nitric acid, with alkalies, earths, and metallic oxides.

Nitre, common saltpetre; in chemistry, nitrate of potash.

Nodus, anciently, in our cathedrals, a knot, key-stone, or boss.

Nog, in ship-building, a treenail driven through the heel of the shores which support a ship on the slip.

Nogs, blocks of wood cut to the form and size of bricks, and inserted in the nterior walls of apartments as holds for the joinary.

Nogs or *Nays*, in mining, square pieces of wood piled on each other to support the roof of a mine.

Nogging, a kind of brickwork carried up in panels between quarters.

Nogging-pieces are horizontal boards placed in brick-nogging, nailed to the quarters in order to strengthen the brickwork.

Nomades, in antiquity, wandering, rude, or savage tribes.

Nomenclature, the art of naming; a vocabulary or dictionary of technical language peculiar to any art or science.

Nonagon, a figure of nine sides and of as many angles.

Non-condensing Engines are those made without that part of the machine called a condenser, and without those contrivances essential to the ordinary construction of engines that condense the vapour into fluid. In non-condensing engines the steam escapes into the atmosphere, after having acted upon the piston. The effect is measured by the excess of the pressure of the steam upon the piston, less the friction of the engine above the pressure of the atmosphere.

Non-conductors, substances through which the electric fluid passes with considerable difficulty or not at all; such as glass, resin, sulphur, silk, hair, wool, the air, etc.; but these become electric by friction.

Nones, in the Roman calendar, the fifth day of January, February, April, June, August, September, November, December; and the seventh of March, May, July, and October.

Noria, an hydraulic machine, common in Spain for raising water. The engine consists of a vertical wheel of 20 feet diameter, on the circumference of which are fixed buckets, for the purpose of raising water out of wells, etc., communicating with a canal below, and emptying it into a reservoir above, placed by the side of the wheel. The buckets have a lateral orifice, to receive and discharge the water. The axis of the wheel is embraced by four small beams, crossing each other at right angles, tapering at the extremities, and forming eight little arms. This wheel is near the centre of the horse-walk, contiguous to the vertical axis, into the top of which the top beam is fixed; but near the bottom it is embraced by four little beams, forming eight arms similar to those above described, on the axis of the water-wheel. In the movement of the horse or mule, these horizontal arms, acting on cogs, take hold, each in succession, of those arms which are fixed on the axis of the water-wheel, and keep it in rotation.

Norma, a square for measuring right angles, used by carpenters, masons, and other artificers, to make their work rectangular.

Normal line, in geometry, a phrase used for a perpendicular line.

Norman Architecture. In Normandy, in the tenth century, when the Normans occupied Neustria, the churches in other parts of France were in imitation of the Roman style. The plan of the buildings came from Rome, and the round arches, the pillars, and the mouldings, which were employed in their construction, had the same origin. But the corrupt taste of a less civilized people covered the capitals and the portals with a crowd of such appalling images as a wild fancy was likely to suggest, and a rude hand to portray.

The Normans, adopting the habitual plan and the established style, rejected the meretricious accessories, and resolved to trust for success to the two great principles of size and elevation. The oldest of the Norman churches are the plainest, but even these aspire to dimensions which could not fail to command admiration. Their character is severe but sublime. At the same time, the Normans had the boldness to insist upon an addition to their churches, which is admitted to be the grandest feature and the chief ornament of ecclesiastical buildings—the central tower. Towers had, fortunately, become an integral part of churches before the Normans began to build in Neustria, but the few towers which at that time existed in other parts of France only adorned the western end. Size, elevation, simplicity, and strength, together with the central tower, are the architectural peculiarities to which the Normans, as contradistinguished from the Franks, possess undeniable claims.

Norman workmanship was, at first, remarkable only for its solidity. The walls were often built of rubble, faced with small squared stones,—a manner of building which had been copied from the works which the Romans had left behind them in France. The pillars were, of course, composed of larger blocks. By degrees, and in buildings of importance, larger blocks were employed in the walls; but the joints were wide, and the mortar was coarse. In the time of William the Conqueror, greater neatness

NORMAN ARCHITECTURE.

was accomplished; the stones were squared, and the courses regular; but the joints were still rather wide, and the mortar unsifted.

Another mode of construction was with long, narrow stones, which were placed, not in horizontal courses, but alternately inclined to the right and left. This, from the appearance it presented, was called the herring-bone fashion. It did not remain in use much after the eleventh century.

The Norman walls were of great thickness, and were filled up with small stones, amongst which mortar was poured in hot. This was called *grouting*; and in time the whole mass so hardened together as to acquire the consistence and strength of a solid rock. Such walls stood in no need of buttresses, through the means of which more advanced science afterwards obtained an equal amount of power at less labour and less expense. Buttresses, however, appear on the exterior of early Norman buildings, but seem to have been introduced only to relieve the baldness of the surface. They project so slightly that they can add but little support. In early Norman buildings the buttresses never rise above the cornice.

The plan of the early Norman churches is always that of the basilica, with a semicircular recess at the end, which recess formed the choir. The larger churches have transepts and side aisles which are divided from the naves by arcades. The small churches have often neither side aisles nor transepts. The arches of the nave either rest on piers, to which half-pillars are attached, or on single pillars, but hardly ever on those huge cylindrical piers which are commonly seen in the Norman churches of England. Indeed, the thick cylindrical piers of England are scarcely to be met with in all France, except in one or two crypts, where the known superincumbent weight justifies the preference of strength to beauty.

In the churches of France, single pillars preceded piers; the exact reverse of what might have been expected, were it not recollected to what an extent and degree France had become Roman, previous to the inroad of the Northern conquerors. The pillars have always capitals, which, at first, were perfectly plain; but, from the beginning of the eleventh century, were enriched with different kinds of foliage, to a certain degree departing from, but still seeking to imitate, the Roman models. The half-pillars, which are attached to the ends of the piers, are always set back in recesses, or sinks; the same is the case with the small pillars on the outside of the windows, as also with those of the portals. This is a characteristic difference between the Norman style and the Roman, —the Norman pillars are recessed, the Roman project.

The windows are always round-headed and undivided, and, externally, have on each side a small recessed pillar, which supports an impost and moulding.

In the gable, over the entrance door of churches, a small circular window is sometimes introduced.

The windows of castles and of domestic buildings are usually divided by a single shaft.

The portals are round-headed, and were gradually enriched by an increasing number of semicircular mouldings. The most common mouldings are the billet, the nail-head, the chevron, the zigzag or embattled frette, hatchet, nebule, star, rope, beak-head, dog-tooth, and, occasionally, different sorts of foliage, as the vine, the hay, the ivy, etc. (See *Frontispiece*.)

The external cornice, under the eaves of churches, was sometimes a moulding describing a series of semicircles, under a projecting course, and sometimes a series of

ANGLO-NORMAN ARCHITECTURE.

blocks. The ornamented corbels, on the exterior of churches, were adopted by the Normans before imagery was admitted into the interior of the edifice.

The roofs of the early Norman churches were of wood, except the part over the semicircular chancel, which from the first was vaulted with stone. The side aisles were also vaulted with stone; as were, sometimes, the comparatively small naves of village churches. The vaulting was composed either of small stones let into a bed of mortar or of tufa, or of a light calcareous stone, which is found in many parts of Normandy. The most ancient vaulting is without ribs, and the most ancient ribs are without mouldings.

The dome vaulting over the side aisles of the abbey church at Bernay is the only specimen of the kind in Normandy.

The first and purest Norman style prevailed till the latter part of the reign of William the Conqueror, from the early part of the tenth till nearly the end of the eleventh century.

The abbey church of Bernay, begun in the first half of the eleventh century, is the oldest Norman building of any consequence which remains in its primitive form. The architecture of the interior is plain to baldness, but the dimensions are imposing.

The abbey churches of Jumiéges and Cerisy were begun in the first half of the eleventh century. The Norman portions of the cathedral, and of the church of St. Taurin, at Evreux, as also of the church of Mont St. Michel, belong to the same period.

St. Georges de Boscherville, and the two great churches at Caen, are splendid examples of the architecture of the time of William the Conqueror.

In all these buildings the character of simplicity is preserved, but some ornament in the details begins to make its appearance before the close of the Conqueror's reign, as, for instance, in the embattled fretté moulding round the arches of the nave of Matilda's church at Caen, in some parts of St. Georges de Boscherville, and other places.

The florid Norman was already developed in the early part of the twelfth century. Of this style a rich specimen is afforded in the arcade of the nave at Bayeux. The arches are ornamented with a multiplicity and variety of mouldings of intricate design and elaborate execution.

Another specimen of the florid Norman exists in the neighbourhood of Bayeux, in the church of St. Gabriel, built by Robert of Gloucester (1128).

The abbey church of Montivilliers (1117), and the church at Graville, are instances of the florid style in all its exuberance.

Norman Architecture in England. Of the architecture which existed in this country previous to the introduction of the Norman there are no certain vestiges. The most competent authorities have decided that hardly anything which can be proved to be Saxon remains in existence. Parts of a few churches, which have all the marks of a very remote antiquity, and of which the style differs materially from the Norman, may be suspected to be Saxon. Their distinguishing features are a ruder imitation of the Roman, projecting instead of recessed pillars, and the combination of diagonal with perpendicular forms in the external ornaments of towers. Such is the case at the old church of Barton, in Lincolnshire, and at Earl's Barton, in Northamptonshire.

Some persons have imagined that the generality of the Saxon churches were merely timber buildings, but this appears to be a mistake; for in Domesday Book, which takes note of 1700 churches, one, and only one, is specified as being built of wood; and Henry of Huntingdon, speaking of a particular church, says, "It was not built of stone, but of wood, and covered with reeds, as is the custom in Scotland;" demonstrating that it was not the custom in England.

Not only were the Saxon churches not merely timber buildings, but some of them were constructed at a considerable expense, and with much architectural ornament.

In the seventh century, a church was built at Lincoln, which Bede says was of stone, and of good workmanship. The church of the monastery of Wearmouth was erected in 675, by Abbot Benedict Biscopins, a noble Northumbrian, who, at twenty-five years of age, detached himself from the service of King Oswy, and embraced a religious life. He brought over masons from France to build his church in the Roman manner, and, when the building was nearly finished, he procured artificers from the same country, skilled in the mystery of making glass, to glaze the windows.

The conventual church of Ripon, and the cathedral church of Hexham, were both built by Wilfrid, Bishop of York, in the second half of the seventh century; and were both constructed of stone, and supported by pillars and arches. Wilfrid also imported builders and artists from abroad—from Rome, Italy, France, and other countries.

In the eighth century, the monastery of Croyland was built by Ethelbald, King of Mercia; and the church of St. Peter at York was rebuilt by Archbishop Albert, and consecrated just before his death, which took place in 780. Alcuin describes this church as having pillars, arches, and porticoes.

In the ninth century, the progress of the arts was interrupted by the constant incursions of the Danes. All that had been done was destroyed; and little more than repairs, and military works, could be undertaken till the peaceable reign of Edgar, in whose time the abbey of Ramsey was founded, and the church built by Ailwin, then alderman of all England. This church was built in six years, and finished in 974. It was in the form of a cross, and had pillars, arches, and two towers, one of which was supported by four pillars, or piers, in the middle of the building. This appears to have been the first English church that had a tower so situated, or that was built in the form of the cross.

From these descriptions of the Saxon churches, preserved in the early chronicles, it appears that the Saxon style was, like that of every other country, an imitation of the Roman. The abbey church of Ramsey, which was one of the latest, and one of the most celebrated of the works of the Saxons, was completed in six years. The last Saxon work of importance was the abbey church of Westminster, built by Edward the Confessor, and finished and consecrated in 1065, one year before the Conquest. This church is represented to have been of a different character from that of any preceding structure in England, and this difference undoubtedly consisted in an approximation to the Norman method of building. Edward the Confessor had been brought up in Normandy, and was almost reproached for his incessant endeavours to introduce Norman customs and manners.

The churches and monasteries which arose after the Conquest were constructed after a new manner of building. From all this it appears that there must have been a marked difference between the Saxon and the Norman fabrics. But, as both were an imitation of the Roman, the difference must have consisted in the dimensions and the superior workmanship and magnificence of the new structures. It must have been the same style on a grander scale, and executed in a more scientific manner.

At the time of the Conquest the Anglo-Saxons were in every respect a ruder and less civilized race than the Normans had by that time become.

The earliest work of the Normans which exists in this country was conducted by Gundulph, who, after rebuilding his cathedral at Rochester, was employed by William to superintend the construction of the White Tower, in the Tower of London, which contains within its walls perhaps the only ecclesiastical remnant of the Conqueror's time at present in existence.

In the course of the Conqueror's reign, several cathedrals, abbeys, and castles were built, none of which remain in their original state. A remnant of the Conqueror's time existed at Canterbury till within these few years,— the northern tower, at the west end of the cathedral. This was a part of the work of Lanfranc. The stones of which it was built were irregular, and the joints between the courses were wide.

Several castles have the reputation of being of the Conqueror's time, but, on a close investigation, will be found to have been rebuilt in after-years. Such is the case with the castles of Norwich, Rochester, the keep at Conisborough, and many others.

Within less than a century after the Conquest almost all the cathedrals and abbey churches of England, besides innumerable parish churches, were either wholly rebuilt or greatly improved by the Normans, on whom William and his successors conferred all the best ecclesiastical preferments. By the introduction of these Norman prelates, the Norman style was rapidly diffused; at first, however, so much affected by the state of art in this country, as to give to the English building the character of a Norman building of much greater antiquity.

Rufus was a great builder; his principal work was the great hall of his palace at Westminster. This hall, as it now exists, was altered by Richard II., but much of the original work was left, and during the late repairs, portions of this were visible. The lower part of the walls was faced with rubble; the courses were irregular; the joints wide. Remains of a triforium or gallery were discovered, which had been carried along the sides of the hall, halfway up. The capitals of the pillars on which the round arches of this gallery rested were plain cubes. The whole of the workmanship was coarse.

The plan of the churches erected about this time was the same as in Normandy. All were built with the semicircular chancel, which in England afterwards fell into such general disuse that few traces of its existence are to be found in this country. It is, however, to be traced in that of St. Bartholomew-le-Grand, in London (begun in 1123), in the minster at York, at East Ham, Essex, and in other places.

The arches of the nave usually rested on those heavy cylindrical piers which in French churches are hardly ever to be found, except in crypts. Their prevalence in England must be ascribed to the inexpertness of the native workmen, and the probability is, that they had previously been adopted by the Saxons from their inability to imitate the Roman style in a more satisfactory manner. Sometimes, to adorn the cylindrical piers, the Anglo-Normans introduced the spiral groove winding round them, with the net or lozenge-work spreading over them.

The windows and the doors

were the same as in Normandy, and the Norman mouldings were gradually introduced with little alteration.

The walls are remarkably thick, and without prominent buttresses.

Specimens of the time of Rufus are to be seen in the choir, side aisles, and middle transept at Durham; in the walls of the lower part of the western façade of Lincoln; the towers and transept of St. Alban's; the oldest remaining parts of Winchester; and the east end and cross aisle of Worcester.

The walls in this reign were irregularly built, and the joints continued to be wide, as may be seen at Durham, Lincoln, Winchester, and other places.

The style prevailed in the early part of the reign of Henry I., as may be seen by the ruins of St. Botolph's priory, Colchester, which was built by Ernulph, a Norman monk, in the first years of that prince. Here are the same heavy cylindrical piers, the same stumpy proportions, the same poverty of mouldings. But in the course of this reign an impulse was given to architecture by one of those men of genius who affect the character of the age in which they live. Roger Poer, Bishop of Salisbury, a Norman by birth, and combining in himself the offices and the qualities which, in those times of constant commotion, were often united, was much distinguished as a prelate, a warrior, a statesman, and an architect. William of Malmesbury relates, that the walls which were built under the superintendence of Roger of Salisbury were so smooth, and had such fine joints, that they seemed to be made of a single stone. Had fine joints been in use before, their appearance in the works of this prelate would not have been so much extolled. The admiration with which they are mentioned gives us the date of the first introduction of fine joints in the walls of English buildings. From this time progressive improvement took place in other parts of the fabric. Something like decoration was added. The portals began to be enriched. The architecture of England ascended to the level of the architecture of Normandy in the time of William the Conqueror.

Examples of the style of this reign may be seen in the naves at Gloucester, Norwich, Ely, Durham, and Southwell; also in the lateral towers of Exeter cathedral, built by Bishop Warlewast; in St. James's tower, Bury St. Edmund's; in the ruins of the chapter-house at Rochester, built between 1114 and 1125, by the same Ernulph who built St. Botolph's at Colchester, and who, on the death of Gundulph, was promoted to the see of Rochester; in the portal of the round church at Cambridge; in the nave of the church at Dunstable; in Saint Bartholomew-le-Grand, London, which was begun in 1123; in St. Sepulchre's, Northampton, built by Simon de Liz, second earl of Northampton, on his return from the Holy Land, and who died in 1127; and in the abbey church of Tewkesbury, begun by Robert Fitz-Hamon (who died in 1107), and consecrated in 1123.

EXAMPLES.—Portal of the chapter-house at Durham, built by Bishop Galfrid Rufus, between 1133 and 1143; church of Castle Acre priory, Norfolk, consecrated in 1148; church of St. Cross, Hampshire; Ripon minster; St. Fridewide (now Christchurch), Oxford, begun not later than 1150, and finished in 1180.

About this time, or a little later, Domestic architecture began to make its appearance in England, though, from the dimensions and arrangement of some of those buildings which have come down to our time, it is difficult to determine whether all of them were destined for dwelling-houses, or were only halls for public occasions, or for the courts of the feudal lords.

Of these buildings the invariable plan is a parallelogram of two stories; sometimes a double parallelogram. The lower story was vaulted, as we have seen to have been the custom in Normandy, and it had no internal communication with the upper story. The upper story was approached by an external staircase, which probably was movable. The only fixed Norman staircase now extant is the one at Canterbury.

The probability is that the lower story was occupied by the servants, and the upper story by the masters; but in none of the buildings of this time now extant do there exist any traces of subdivisions.

An example of Norman Domestic architecture existed in Southwark till within these few years. It was the hostelry or town residence of the priors of Lewes. The church of St. Olave, Southwark, was confirmed to the prior and convent of Lewes by William, second Earl Warren and Surrey, the son of the founder. Earl William died in 1138. It appears, however, that the priors of Lewes rented a building in 1170 and 1186, for their occupation in London; from whence it may be concluded, that the hostelry in question was not built till after that period. The general features of the portion of the hostelry which remained till lately nearly resembled those of the manor-house of Boothby Pagnel, Moyse's Hall, at Bury St. Edmund's, and the building which is called the Pythagoras School at Cambridge.

In 1826 was still existing at Barneck, in Northamptonshire, a Norman manor-house, which was not built for defence. In this instance the hall, which was the principal feature, was on the ground floor, and had no vaults underneath. The hall consisted of a centre and two side aisles. The fine joints of the walls of this building denoted that it could not have been built much before the middle of the twelfth century.

At Bury St. Edmund's is a Norman domestic building, which goes by the name of Moyse's Hall.

At Boothby Pagnel, in Lincolnshire, is a Norman manor-house on nearly the same plan. In this are a fire-place and a chimney, which indicates that the building of which it forms a part cannot be older than the second half of the twelfth century. This edifice has windows in the ends as well as the sides,—a circumstance which makes it evident that to this building no others could have been attached. It is surrounded by a moat.

At Christchurch, Hants, is a Norman remnant which has also a chimney.

At Lincoln is a Norman domestic building which goes by the name of 'John of Gaunt's Stables,' but which, in fact, was the public meeting-house of a guild. It is so much enriched that it must be placed late in the reign of Henry II.

These examples prove that about the middle of the twelfth century, mansions, distinct from castles for defence, began to be erected in England; and that, independent of colleges, abbots' lodgings, and the habitable parts of convents, instances existed of Domestic architecture. But it was long before dwelling-houses acquired a character bearing any relation to the quality of the proprietor, or were constructed with much regard to convenience.

Examples of the Norman style of the time of Henry II. are to be seen in the abbey gateway, Bristol; in the Galilee, or chapel, at the west end of Durham, built by Bishop Pudsey (1154 to 1197), together with the lateral portals of the nave; in the new nave and great west portal of Rochester, etc.

It was in the latter years of the reign of Henry II. that the struggle between the Round and the Pointed styles, which is called the Transition, began to take place in this country.

Kirkstal abbey, in Yorkshire, was built in the thirty years preceding 1183. The nave arches are pointed, but the pillars are massive, and the windows and portals are round. The church at Roche abbey, though equally in the Transition style, and having round-headed windows above pointed arches, Norman mouldings and capitals, yet is of a less heavy character. Both buildings, however, denote that during those years the new style was only just beginning to be received in England.

About the same time (1170), Archbishop Roger employed the Pointed style in the new crypt of York minster.

But the early examples of the Transition, of which the dates are known with the most undoubted certainty, are the round part of the Temple church, London, which was consecrated in 1185, and the choir of Canterbury cathedral, which was rebuilt after the fire in 1175, and in which the Pointed style was introduced by John of Sens, a French architect. Other instances are to be found in the great tower at the west end of Ely, built by Bishop Ridel, who died in 1189; in the county hall of Okeham, Rutlandshire; in the abbey church of Glastonbury, etc.

But the nave of Rochester and the nave of Peterborough, rebuilt between 1170 and 1194, are proofs that the old fashion was not at once superseded by the new.

Simultaneously with the introduction of the Transition style, hewn stone vaults appear to have been first thrown over the wider parts of English churches, which till then had been habitually roofed with wood. A stone vault was thrown over the new choir of Canterbury, in 1174. It was customary before that time, to roof narrow spaces with plain cross-vaulting, but not to vault wide spaces with stone. Plain cross-vaulting of rubble, with and without ribs, had been adopted before in crypts, side aisles, and chancels. Barrel-vaulting, we have seen, was introduced in the time of William the Conqueror. From the time that the choir of Canterbury was built, which was not long after, it became common to throw stone vaults over the naves of the larger churches of Normandy, and huge stone vaults, plain at first, and gradually enriched, became habitual in England. Prominent buttresses and flying buttresses, as in Normandy, followed in the train of the stone roofs.

From this time, the Round style fell gradually into disuse; but at Fountains abbey, the foundations of which were laid in 1204, and which was in progress during the forty subsequent years, the windows and portals are still round-headed; and an instance of a round portal is to be found at Ketton, in Rutlandshire, as late as 1252.

During the reign of Henry III. the Early Pointed style attained its most perfect condition. Fine examples of this style are to be seen in the chapter-house, the transepts, and part of the choir of Westminster abbey; in the choir of St. Alban's; in the nave of Lincoln; the east end of Durham; nave of Worcester, 1224; nave and spire of Lichfield; south transept of York; and the older part of the choir of Southwell; and in Salisbury cathedral, which was begun in 1221, and carried forward, without interruption, till it was completed.

The establishment of the Pointed style was attended with one remarkable difference in England and Normandy. In Normandy, the semicircular chancel became, generally speaking, polygonal; in England, generally speaking, it became square. Polygonal chancels are as rare in England as square chancels are in the larger churches of Normandy; and this difference of shape in England afforded the opportunity of those magnificent east windows, which are so principal and so splendid a feature of our cathedrals. Another difference to be remarked, is the battlement, which usually forms the parapet of English churches, and which never occurs in the ecclesiastical buildings of France.

It may be said,—1. That the supposed existence of the Pointed style in Normandy, in 1056, is imaginary. 2. That the Normans, adopting the corrupt Roman style, gave it a character of their own. 3. That the Normans greatly contributed to the advancement of the arts in England. 4. That architecture performed exactly the same revolution in England and France, France having, in all the changes, a certain precedence.

Norroy, or *North roy*, in heraldry, one of the two provincial Kings at Arms, whose jurisdiction lies on the north side of the Trent, as does that of Clarencieux to the south.

Northampton Tables, Tables made at the county town of Northampton, formed from the registers of burials of that locality, from which calculations were made of the value of life, for the purpose of its insurance. (See article *Assurance*.)

Nosing, the prominent edge of a moulding or drip; the projecting moulding on the edge of a step.

Nosing of steps, the projecting parts of the tread-board or cover, which stand before the riser. The nosing of steps is generally rounded, so as to have a semicircular section; and in good staircases a hollow is placed under them.

Notch-board, a board notched or grooved out, to receive and support the ends of the steps of a staircase.

Notching, the cutting of an excavation throughout the whole breadth of a substance: by this means timbers are fastened together, or their surfaces, when joined at angles, are made to coincide.

Nozzles, those portions of a steam engine in which are placed the valves that open and close the communication between the cylinder and the boiler and condenser, in low-pressure or condensing engines; and between the cylinder and boiler and atmosphere, in high-pressure or non-condensing engines.

Nucleus, the internal part of the flooring of the ancients, consisting of a strong cement, over which was laid the pavement, which was bound with mortar.

Nuisance, anything tending to hurt, to annoy, or to endanger health. (See the excellent work by Mr. Gibbons on this subject.)

Nullah, in India, a natural canal, or small branch of a river.

Nunnery, a Roman Catholic building for an association of nuns or females devoted to a life of religious seclusion. Previous to the Reformation, there existed in England 127 edifices for the convenient lodging of such pious women, 2 in Wales, and 20 in Scotland; in the whole in Great Britain, 149. But there were many convents and religious houses not specially named nunneries, but which were receptacles also for such purposes.

Nunnery, a term sometimes applied to the triforium or gallery between the aisles of a church and the clerestory; so called from the situation of the nuns' choir in some convents. At the present time, the roomy galleries over the aisles in Westminster abbey are called nunneries, probably from having been used by the nuns of Kilburne, when they visited the abbey, to which they were subordinate.

Nut, a short internal screw, which

acts in the thread of an external screw, and is employed to fasten anything that may come between it and a flange on the bottom of the external screw or bolt.

O

Oak. There are two kinds of this timber common in England, on the Continent, and in America. Oak of good quality is more durable than any other wood which attains the same size: its colour is a well-known brown. Oak is a most valuable wood for ship-building, carpentry, frames, and works requiring great strength or exposed to the weather. It is also much used for carved ornaments, panelling of rooms, pulpits, stalls, and standards for churches. It is likewise used in the construction of all kinds of buildings, for strength and stability. English oak is one of the hardest of the species: it is considerably harder than the American, called white and red Canada oak. African oak is well adapted to the construction of merchant vessels. Italian oak is much purchased for our dockyards, to the prejudice of that which is proudly standing in our several forests.

Obelisk. In architecture, a quadrangular pyramid: those of Egypt may be described as large stones, quadrilateral, diminishing from the base upwards, till, within about a tenth of the height, the sides converge to a point. The width of the base is usually about a tenth of the height, to that part where the sides begin to converge: they are commonly formed from a single stone, mostly of granite. There are, however, two small obelisks in the British Museum, formed of basalt, and one at Philæ, of sandstone. When obelisks were first made in Egypt, it was customary with the patriarchs of the Jews to set up stones to perpetuate the memory of great events. Strabo calls such stones 'books of history:' an epithet which might be applied with propriety to the inscribed Egyptian obelisks. The date of the Flaminian obelisk, which is covered with hieroglyphics, is by some writers supposed to be between 1580 and 1600 B.C. The first obelisk was raised by Rameses, King of Egypt, in the time of the Trojan war: it was 40 cubits high, and employed 20,000 men in building. Phina, another king of Egypt, raised one of 45 cubits, and Ptolemy Philadelphus another of 88 cubits, in memory of Arsinoë, etc. The Romans also erected many, which are well described in Roman history.

Oblate, flattened or shortened; in geometry, a term applied to a spheroid, produced by the revolution of a semi-ellipsis about its shorter diameter. Of this figure is the earth, and probably all the planets, having the equatorial diameter greater than the polar.

Oblique, in geometry, aslant; not direct; not perpendicular nor parallel.

Oblique angle, one that is greater or less than a right angle.

Oblique-angled triangle, one that has no right angle.

Oblique arches, or *Oblique bridges*, are those which conduct high-roads or railroads across a river, canal, etc., in an oblique direction: they are also called *skew arches*.

Oblique line. When one straight line stands upon another, and makes unequal angles therewith, the angles are said to be oblique, the one being greater than a right angle, and the other less: hence a line is only oblique as it relates to another line; otherwise the word would be destitute of meaning.

Oblique sailing occurs when a ship, being in some intermediate rhomb between the four cardinal points, makes an oblique angle with the meridian, and continually changes both its latitude and longitude.

Oblong, a rectangle of unequal dimensions; in geometry, longer than broad.

Observatory, a building erected for the purpose of making observations on the motions of the heavenly bodies. More particularly with reference to the study of Terrestrial Magnetism, observatories have been erected by the British Government in Canada, St. Helena, the Cape of Good Hope, and Van Diemen's Land; by the East India Company at Madras, Singapore, Simla, and Trevandrum; and by the Russian Government at St. Petersburg and other places, in connection with those at Güttingen, etc. The most munificent example of private devotion to the science of Astronomy is the splendid observatory erected by Lord Rosse at Parsonstown, in Ireland.

Obtunding, the blunting or taking away a sharp corner.

Obtuse, in geometry, blunt; in opposition to acute or sharp.

Obtuse angle. In geometry, if the contained angle be less than a right angle, it is called an acute; if greater, it is called an obtuse angle.

Obtuse-angled triangle, a triangle which has an obtuse angle.

Obtuse section of a cone, the hyperbola of ancient geometricians, because they considered it only such a cone whose section through the axis was an obtuse-angled triangle.

Occus, the banqueting-room of a Roman house. There were several kinds of occi, viz. Corinthian, tetrastyle, Cyzicene, and Egyptian. In the Greek houses the occi were spacious apartments, in which the mistress of the family employed herself and servants at the loom.

Ochre, brown, a clay coloured brown by the oxide of iron.

Ochre, red, a clay coloured red by the oxide of iron.

Ochre, yellow, a clay coloured yellow by the oxide of iron.

Octagon, a figure of eight sides and as many angles: when all the sides and all the angles are equal, the figure is called a regular octagon.

Octahedron, in geometry, one of the five regular bodies, consisting of eight equal and equilateral triangles.

Octostylos, a portico which has eight columns in front.

Odeum, a small theatre for the recitation of musical compositions, generally in the neighbourhood of the theatre: the odeum at Athens was contiguous to the theatre of Bacchus; the odeum at Pompeii also joined the theatre.

Odontograph, a very ingenious instrument, invented by Professor Willis, of Cambridge, to enable the millwright, workman, and engineer to measure, draw, and design infinitely in extent, the teeth of wheels.

Odyssey (In the) we have, for example, the case of Castor and Pollux, who enjoyed a peculiar privilege of life after death, and revisited earth in some mysterious manner on alternate days, and this too although they were buried. (Gladstone.)

Œcus, according to Vitruvius, apartments near or connected with the dining-room.

Œillets, or *Oylets*, small openings or loopholes, sometimes circular; extensively used in the fortifications of the middle ages.

Offices, as connected with the domestic purposes of large mansions, palaces, etc., consist of kitchens, sculleries, pantries, breweries, washhouses, etc.; frequently detached or out-houses, and sometimes in cities, underground and vaulted palaces beneath the same roof.

Offices, as connected with business, are apartments for the accommodation of clerks or accountants; merchants' counting-houses, etc.; for law clerks, law agents, etc.

Offing, in navigation, that part of the sea distanced from the shore where there is deep water, and no necessity for a pilot.

Offset, or *Set-off*, the splay or narrow slanting course of stone or brick, serving to connect two portions of a wall, the uppermost of which recedes from the face of that beneath.

Ogee, a moulding consisting of two members, the one concave, the other convex; the same with what is otherwise called cymatium. In Gothic architecture, ogees are very much employed. The term ogee is also applied to a pointed arch, the sides of which are each formed of two contrasted curves.

Ogives, arches or branches of a Gothic vault, which, instead of being circular, pass diagonally from one angle to another, and form a cross with the other arches which make the sides of the squares, whereof the ogives are diagonals. The middle, when the ogives cut or cross each other, is called the key, sometimes carved in the form of a rose. The members or mouldings of the ogives are called nerves, branches, or veins; and the arches which separate the ogives, double arches.

Oliver, a small lift-hammer, worked by the foot. The hammer head is about 2½ inches square and 10 inches long, with a swage tool having a conical crease attached to it, and a corresponding swage is fixed in a square cast-iron anvil-block, about 12 inches square and 6 deep, with one or two round holes for punching, etc. The hammer handle is about 2 to 2½ feet long, and mounted in a cross-spindle nearly as long, supported in a wooden frame between end-screws, to adjust the groove in the hammer face to that in the anvil-block. A short arm, 5 or 6 inches long, is attached to the right end of the hammer axis; and from this arm proceeds a rod to a spring-pole overhead, and also a chain to a treadle a little above the floor of the smithy.

Olympiad, a period of four years, by which the Greeks reckoned their time. The first Olympiad corresponds with the 775th year before the birth of our Saviour, and 22 years before the building of Rome.

Oolite, the Portland stone used in architecture, called also freestone and roestone.

Opa, according to Vitruvius, a bed or cavity in which the head of a tie-beam rests.

Opaque, cloudy, not transparent.

Ophites, a black marble.

Opie (John) was born in Cornwall, 1761, and died April, 1807. Horne Tooke and Sir James Mackintosh speak very highly of his intellectual powers. He sketched out a plan of weekly study, from which pleasure or persuasion seldom wiled him.

Opisthodomos, the enclosed space behind a temple; the treasury at Athens was so called, because it stood behind the temple of Minerva.

Oppidum, according to the Romans, a mass of buildings; an entrance to a town; the façade to a public building, not unlike to the termini on the principal lines of railway.

Opposite angles, those which are formed by two straight lines crossing each other, but not two adjacent angles.

Opposite cones are those to which a straight line can be everywhere applied on the surface of both cones.

Opposite sections, those made by a plane cutting two opposite cones.

Optics, the science of direct vision, including catoptrics, dioptrics, and perspective.

Optostrotum, according to the Greek, a brick-paved flooring.

Opus, Roman reticulated masonry; a mode of workmanship.

Or, in heraldry, gold; it is denoted in engraving by small points all over the field or bearing.

Ora, a Roman hawser.

Oratory, a small private chapel or closet for devotion.

Orb, a mediæval term for a blind window.

Orbs, in Gothic ornament, bosses and

knots of foliage, flowers, or other ornament in cornices.

Orbiculus, according to Vitruvius, a roller or a pulley revolving upon an axis, and having a groove in its circumference for the rope to fit into; employed as a mechanical power for raising or drawing.

Orchestra, the area in the Greek theatre comprised between the lower range of seats and the proscenium. In the Roman theatre, the orchestra was appropriated to the senators; but in the theatres of the Greeks it was the scene of action of the dancers.

Orders of Architecture, usually named the 'five orders,' without reference to other styles of architecture, are thus enumerated by most writers: —1. Tuscan. 2. Doric. 3. Ionic. 4. Corinthian. 5. Composite. (For their proportions, see *Architecture*.)

Ordinates, in geometry and conics, lines drawn from any point of the circumference of an ellipse, or other conic section, perpendicularly across the axis, to the other side.

Ordnance Survey of Great Britain and Ireland: a work of great importance in ascertaining the true geographical position of our islands and of their varied superficial features. This survey originated in the mutual desire on the part of English and French philosophers to determine the precise difference of longitude between the meridians of the Greenwich and Paris observatories. In the pursuit of this object, a meeting was arranged at Dover between three members of the French Academy, MM. Cassini, Mechain, and Legendre, and General Roy and Dr. Blagden, to arrange plans of operation. In the course of the subsequent survey, the officers of the Royal Artillery, to whom the superintendence of the work was entrusted, extended their views and operations, and, under the patronage and at the expense of the Board of Ordnance, proceeded to determine the length of as many degrees on the meridian as came within the limits of the survey. The rules by which the main lines for this and all other extended surveys are obtained, are derived from the principles of trigonometry, or the properties of triangles. By these principles we are enabled to compute the exact form and dimensions of any triangle from the actual measurement of one side only, and of the angles formed at its extremities by the other sides. Upon these principles the true figure and size of our globe have been determined upon the relative lengths of degrees of a meridian in different latitudes.

The exactness of the results of these operations depending upon the correct measurement of the one side, or *base-line*, and of the angles at its ends, formed by the two imaginary sides which have a common meeting point in some distant and conspicuous object, the apparatus for measuring this side and the angle is required to act with extreme delicacy and exactness. For measuring the length, rods of various materials have been used, and endeavours made to obviate the effect of changes of temperature in altering the length of the rods themselves. General Roy commenced the measurement of a base line on Hounslow Heath with rods of deal, each twenty feet long. But these rods, although prepared in the most careful manner, of the best seasoned timber, perfectly straight, and effectually secured against bending, were found to suffer such changes of length, from the varying dryness and moisture of the air, as rendered them utterly unfit for the purpose, and glass tubes were eventually substituted, each of them twenty feet long, and enclosed in a frame of wood, allowing only expansion or contraction in length from heat or cold according to a law ascertained by experiments. With these rods a base of about 5¼ miles in length was measured so exactly, that a remeasurement by Colonel Mudge several years afterwards, made with a steel chain constructed by the celebrated Ramsden, differed only from the original line to the extent of 2¾ in. Steel chains are jointed similar to a watch-chain, and are always used with uniform tension, the differences in length due to temperature being calculated upon the observed fact, that each degree of heat above 62 Fahr. extends the chain ·0076 of an inch.

For determining the angles, the English officers used an excellent theodolite by Ramsden, having both an altitude and an azimuth circle, and a telescope of great power. This instrument, combining the powers of a theodolite, a quadrant, and a transit instrument, is capable of measuring horizontal angles to fractions of a second. It is recorded among the proofs of the accuracy attained in this triangulation, that a testing line, or *base of verification*, as termed in geodesic operations, measured on Salisbury Plain, of which the length exceeded seven miles, differed only *one inch* from the computation carried through the series of triangles from Hounslow Heath to Salisbury Plain.

When the primary triangulation had been thus carefully completed, a further subdivision of each of these great triangles was performed, and each of these again was subdivided into others, so that the entire plot of the country was represented by a complete network of triangles. Each of these divisions and subdivisions being formed independently of the others, and yet the exact accordance of the whole being insisted on and effected, accuracy is secured in all these principal operations, and the filling in of each of these spaces is entrusted to a different class of operators, whose labours in producing the final plan are so divided and arranged that the work of each is a check upon the exactness of his predecessor. Thus the surveyors measure the lines and angles on the ground, but another class of assistants (the plotters) produce the plan from the records of the surveyors, and a third class (examiners) test the plan thus produced by subsequent comparison in the field. One effect of this system, by which the range of operations confided to each operator is thus limited, and the fidelity of these thus severely scrutinized, is, that the bulk of the work after the triangulation may be safely confided to an inferior and cheaply engaged class of assistants, and great comparative economy thus attained.

The Ordnance Survey of Great Britain and Ireland is plotted to different scales.

Organ. This word is derived from the Greek *organon*; *organum* in Latin, *organo* in Italian, *orgue* in French, *orgel* in German. It signifies, generally, an instrument; but is now used for the name of the grandest and most worthy of musical instruments.

The tones of an organ are produced from the pipes only; of these some are of wood, others of various kinds of metal, and even of glass. An organ of full compass may contain all the sounds recognized in the science of music, from the lowest appreciable to the very highest. The largest pipes produce the lowest sounds, and some few are made as long as about 32 feet, while the smallest are about the size of the pipe of a very small key. Organs are of various kinds, viz. for the church, the concert-room, and for the private drawing-room. The church organ should be of a full, deep, and solemn character; while the concert-room organ should be of a lighter and more brilliant kind, with every variety of stop, in order to imitate, not only the full orchestra, but also certain 'solo' instruments. Hence we have the flute-stop; the hautboy, the cremona or krum-horn, the vox-humana, etc. stops; according to the extent of the instrument. These solo, or fancy stops, belong only to the concert-room or drawing-room organ, and are wholly unbecoming in one for the church.

We have not space to give anything like a description of this the noblest of instruments ; and it must suffice to say that it consists of bellows which supply the pipes with wind by means of a wind-chest; the wind being conveyed therefrom, through channels, under the different ranks, or rows of pipes, and thence into the pipes by means of pallets, or valves, opened at the pleasure of the performer, by pressing the proper lever or key.

The organ is a very ancient instrument of the church, and must have been very unwieldy, since we are told of one in the cathedral church at Halberstadt, which had only a few large pipes, and the keys were more than a bandbreadth in width, and were beaten or pressed down by the fist, or elbow ; the wind being supplied by several small bellows. We are also told of the Winchester organ, which required seventy men to supply it with wind ; its compass was of ten notes only, although it had 400 pipes, *i. e.* forty to each note; It was so loud that it could be heard all over the city. The organ is usually described as being of three kinds,—the great, or full chorus organ, the swell organ, and the choir organ: the latter is used to accompany the softer parts of the music, and is such an instrument as was carried in the ancient processions, in the rogation days, and other seasons, to accompany the priests with while chanting the litanies ; the performer, or, more properly speaking, the minister at the organ, being carried also with the instrument, and seated : hence this organ was called the chair-organ, now corrupted into choir-organ, from the difference in its employment. The swell organ is used chiefly to accompany solos ; for interludes, and such like fanciful music, and takes its name from being able to swell out its sounds by openings made by turning a series of boards on their centres, similar to a Venetian blind, these boards being connected by levers under the control of the performer's foot.

The key-board, or row of keys of an organ, are like those of a pianoforte, only they require to be pressed down (not struck like those of the latter instrument), so as to open the pallets before mentioned, and cause the pipes to speak. A complete church organ contains three rows of keys, one for each of the above-mentioned organs; and most organs have also a row of keys called pedals, to enable the organist to play the bass-notes with his feet.

In organs that are played by means of a wind, or handle, the part of the organist is performed by a cylinder, on which are placed a number of wires so contrived as to press upon the levers, and open the pallets or valves ; and hence those instruments are called barrel organs. They are of little or no use for the purposes of the church. It has been the fashion, for some time, to make one organ do the work of two, namely, the full organ and the choir organ : but it is at best but a sorry contrivance ; for in such an organ there can be no good choir organ mixture ; and the full organ is generally too noisy, the fullness being made up of loud-voiced pipes, instead of their being round, mellow, and full-toned. These kinds of organs have not the dignified and solemn character necessary for real church music.

Organ screen, an ornamental stone wall or piece of timber framework, on which a church organ is placed, and which in English cathedrals and churches forms usually the western termination of the choir.

Organum, a name given to a machine or contrivance in aid of the exercise of human labour in architecture and other arts.

Oriel window, a projecting angular window, mostly of a triagonal or pentagonal form, and divided by mullions and transoms into different bays and other proportions. The *oriel* has been discussed by many writers, but there cannot be conceived an architectural charm more cheerful to the interior, or more decorative to the exterior of a building, than an oriel window.

Orlop, in shipping, the middle deck.

Ornithon, an aviary or poultry-house, or the appurtenance to a farm villa.

Orrery, in mechanics, a machine which by many complicated movements represents the revolutions of the heavenly bodies.

Orthography, in architecture, the elevation of a building, showing all the parts thereof in their true proportions: the orthography is either external or internal. The external is the delineation of the outer face or front of a building; the internal is a section of the same.

Oscillating Engine, a marine engine, with a vibrating cylinder, having the piston rod connected to the crank, and the cylinder supported by the trunnions projecting from the sides at or near the centre, cast hollow, and connected to the steam and eduction pipes.

Oscillation, or vibration, in mechanics, the act of moving backward and forward like a pendulum.

Oscillation, the axis of, in mechanics, a right line parallel to the apparent horizontal one, and passing through the centre, about which the pendulum oscillates.

Osterly House. "The opulence and gallantry of Sir Thomas Gresham rivalled the wonders of romance. Queen Elizabeth had visited that superb mansion, and on quitting the window to seek her bed, had remarked aloud, 'How much more gracefully the court-yard would appear if divided in two by a wall.' The words were caught up by Sir Thomas, who instantly, on quitting the royal presence, sent hastily to his masons and bricklayers, assisted them with innumerable labourers, worked all the night, and completed the wall according to the Queen's wishes before she had risen from her bed. The courtiers were chagrined at the knight's abruptness, and one of them consoled himself with a conceit, 'that it was no way strange that one who could build a '*change* could *change* a building.'"

Ostium, an inner door, the door of a chamber.

Outward angle, the same as a salient angle.

Ova, in architecture, ornaments in the form of eggs, carved on the contour of the ovolo, or quarter-round, and separated from each other by anchors and arrow-heads.

Oval, a figure in geometry, bounded by a curve-line returning to itself.

Overshot-wheel, a wheel driven by the weight of water conveyed into buckets, disposed on its circumference so that one part of the wheel is loaded with water while the other is empty.

Over story, the clear story or upper story of a building.

Ovolo, a convex moulding, mostly used in classical architecture; in the Roman examples it is an exact quarter of a circle; in Grecian it is more flat and quirked at the top. It is frequently used in the decorated Gothic style.

Oxidation, rusting; the process of

converting metals and other substances into oxides, by combining a certain portion of oxygen with them.

Oxygen, in chemistry, a gaseous element of great importance in the economy of Nature: it is essential to the maintenance of organic life; hence its original name, 'vital air.'

P.

PACK, a quantity of material, either wood or coals, placed or piled up to support roofs, or for other purposes.

Paddle-shaft, the shaft upon which the paddle-wheel is fixed, placed centrally with, and connected to, the crank-shaft.

Paddle-wheel, the wheel fixed upon the paddle-shaft, for propelling a vessel through the water by the action of a number of paddle-boards fixed at the circumference.

Pagoda, in architecture, a name applied by the Europeans to Hindoo temples and places of worship, but not by the Hindoos themselves, who have no such appellation; they are square stone buildings, not very lofty, crowned with a cupola: the pagodas of China are, however, lofty houses, which sometimes rise to the height of nine stories, of more than twenty feet each. The buildings are depositories of their idols, and used for their worship.

Painted and *Stained Glass*, formerly used exclusively for ecclesiastical purposes,— displaying devotion and spiritual bearing. Latterly painted and stained glass have been used for domestic purposes. The art of painting on glass was known as early as the sixth century, and was applied to the enrichment of the basilica of St. Sophia, and other churches in Constantinople; and in the reign of Charlemagne some progress was made in enriching and beautifying glass with colours. In the tenth century it was much admired, and advanced rapidly: Henry II. patronized this art. In France it progressed in all the magnificence of colour and execution, and was extensively diffused in England. In Canterbury and York some beautiful examples remain, for the admiration and example of modern practice. Of the cinque-cento style, the revival of art under the immortal Albert Dürer, some very fine specimens of the period, picturesquely drawn, are to be found in fine preservation in St. Jacques, at Liége; and of rather a later time, those of the Crabeths, at Gouda, in Holland, are magnificent executions of this art by these brothers. One of these windows, upwards of 70 feet high, was executed by Theodore Crabeth, by command and at the expense of Queen Mary of England, consort of Philip II.: a portion of the picture is magnificently painted, the subject of which is the Queen, with her husband, kneeling at the Lord's table. The upper part of this window has been destroyed by a storm, but the subject referred to remains perfect, and exhibits correct likenesses of these sovereigns.

Painting. The art of painting gives the most direct and expressive representation of objects; and it was doubtless for this reason employed by many nations, before the art of writing was invented, to communicate their thoughts, and to convey intelligence to distant places. The pencil may be said to write a universal language, for every one can instantly understand the meaning of a painter, provided he be faithful to the rules of his art; his skill enables him to display the various scenes of nature at one view, and by his delineations of the striking effects of passion, he instantaneously affects the soul of the spectator. Invention in painting consists principally in three things: first, the choice of a subject properly within the scope of the art; secondly, the seizure of the most striking and energetic moment of time for representation; and, lastly, the discovery and selection of such objects, and such probable incidental circumstances, as, combined together, may best tend to develope the story or augment the interest of the piece.

Architects will often find decorations of a room and its furniture well worthy of their study. In houses recently built, both in town and country, the taste of the architect has been called in, to give designs for the arrangement of curtains, for grates, pier tables, chairs, and sofas; and in many instances the superior chasteness of the designs, and the harmony of the whole with the architectural style of the rooms, may be seen, conformable with the different uses to which the rooms are appropriated.

Painter, in navigation, a sea term for a rope employed to fasten a boat to the ship, wharf, etc.

Palæstra, a building appropriated to gymnastic sports.

Palaces of Persia (the royal country) are at this day castellated, and many villages have towers of defence.

Pale, in heraldry, the third and middle part of the escutcheon.

Palisander, a name used on the continent for rose-wood.

Pall, in heraldry, denotes a sort of cross, representing the pallium or archiepiscopal ornament sent from Rome to metropolitans.

Palls, in ship-building, strong short pieces of iron or wood, placed near the capstan or windlass, so as to prevent their recoiling.

Palladium, a metal found with platina, but in small quantity.

Palladium, in antiquity, a wooden image of the goddess Minerva or Pallas, the possession of which involved the fate of Troy.

Pallium or *Pall*, in church rituals, a pontifical ornament worn by popes, patriarchs, primates, and metropolitans of the Roman church, in the form of a fillet of black silk, over the shoulders, with four red crosses.

Palm-trees, wood of great variety, imported from the East and West Indies, but sparingly employed in England for cabinet and marquetry work, and sometimes for billiard-cues, etc.

Palette (French), in painting, a light board on which the colours are held.

Palsgrave, in heraldry, a count or earl, who has the overseeing of a palace.

Pandation, in architecture, a yielding or bending in the middle.

Pane, the light of a window; formerly applied also to the sides of a tower, turret, spire, etc.

Panel, in carpentry, etc., a square piece of any matter inserted between other bodies; sunken compartments of wainscoting, ceilings, etc., principally employed in Gothic and Domestic architecture for interior fittings.

Panel, a space or compartment in a wall, generally of English or Flemish oak, and on a ceiling, enclosed within a raised margin.

Panel, in mining, a heap of ore dressed and ready for sale.

Panemore, in mechanics, a globular windmill, proposed to be erected in the centre of a ship, for turning wheels and paddles.

Panoply, in heraldry, complete armour.

Panorama (*Full view*), in painting, a picture drawn on the interior surface of a large cylinder, representing the objects that can be seen from one station when the observer directs his eye successively to every point of the horizon.

Pantheon, a temple dedicated to all the gods; one of the most celebrated edifices of Rome.

Pantograph, in mechanics, an instrument contrived for the purpose of copying drawings, so that the copy may be either similar to or larger or smaller than the original. (See *Pentagraph*.)

Para, in Cornish mining, a gang or party of men.

Parabola, one of the conic sections formed by the intersection of a plane and a cone when the plane passes parallel to the side of the cone.

Parabolic Pyramidoid, a solid generated by supposing all the squares of the ordinates applicable to the parabola so placed that the axis shall pass through all their centres at right angles, in which case the aggregate of the planes will form the solid called the parabolic pyramidoid, the solidity of which is equal to the product of the bases and half the altitude.

Paraboloid or *Parabolic Conoid*, the solid generated by the rotation of parabola about its axis, which remains fixed. A frustum of a paraboloid is the lower solid formed by a plane passing parallel to the base of a paraboloid.

Parabolic spindle, the solid generated by the rotation of a parabola about any double ordinate.

Paradise, a private apartment, a study, the private appurtenances to a convent.

Paradromides, hypæthral walks, attached to the Greek palæstra. The Romans called these walls xysta; whereas the xysta of the Greeks were covered porticoes, in which the athletæ exercised in winter.

Parallel, in geometry, is applied to lines, figures, and bodies which are everywhere equidistant from each other, or which, if ever so far produced, would never meet.

Parallel bars, the rods parallel to the centre line of a beam, joining the connecting links at the lower ends.

Parallel motion, the connection between the top of the piston-rod and the beams: a name given to a contrivance, invented by James Watt, for converting a reciprocating circular motion into an alternating rectilinear motion.

Parallel ruler, an instrument consisting of two wooden, brass, or steel, rulers, equally broad throughout, and so joined together by the cross blades as to open to different intervals, and accede and recede, yet still retaining their parallelism.

Parallelogram, in geometry, a quadrilateral right-lined figure whose opposite sides are parallel.

Parallelogram of forces is a phrase denoting the composition of forces, or the finding a single force that shall be equivalent to two or more given forces when acting in given directions.

Parallelopiped, in geometry, a regular solid, contained under six parallelograms, the opposite of which are equal and parallel; or it is a prism whose base is a parallelogram; it is always triple to a pyramid of the same base and height.

Parament, the furniture, ornaments, and hangings of an apartment for a room of state.

Parameter, a constant right line in each of the three conic sections, and otherwise called *latus rectum*, because it measures the conjugate axes by the same ratio which has taken place between the axes themselves, being always a third proportion of them.

Parapet, the upper part of a house, which is above the springing of a roof, and guards the gutter; the upper part of a wall, a bridge, a terrace, or balcony, etc. Parapets around the flat roofs of houses in the East are of most ancient date. "When thou buildest a new house, thou shalt make a battlement for thy roof, that thou bring not blood upon thine house, if any man fall from thence."—*Deut.* xxii. 8.

Parascenium, in ancient theatres, a place behind the scenes to which the actors withdrew to dress and undress themselves.

Parastala, square columns, or antæ; called also parastacles and parastalicæ. Vitruvius uses the term to signify the square posts placed behind the columns of the basilica, for the support of the floors of the upper porticoes.

Pargeting, parge-work, plaster-work, employed exteriorly for timber houses, as an ornament; used also in plain and ornamental work, for both the exterior and interior.

Paries, the walls of a Grecian house, in contradistinction to the wall of a city; a small enclosure, such as a court-yard.

Parlour, a private apartment in a dwelling, usually on the ground floor; a speaking-room in a convent. In the time of Henry VIII. parlours and privy rooms—summer parlours, winter parlours—were well, comfortably, and conveniently furnished; a proof that the gentry of that period were not quite so far behind the present race as might be supposed.

Parsonage-house, a residence of the incumbent of a parish, a building in the vicinity of a church.

Patera, a round dish, plate, saucer, or goblet.

Patina, a basin or bowl of earthenware, rarely of bronze.

Parthenon, in architecture, the temple of Minerva at Athens.

Particle, the minute part of a body, or an assemblage of several atoms of which natural bodies are composed.

Partners, in naval architecture, are thick pieces fitted into a rabbet in the mast carlings, to receive the wedges of the mast; likewise temporary pieces nailed on the deck round the pumps.

Partridge wood is the produce of the Brazils and the West India Islands: it is sent in large planks, or in round and square logs. It was formerly employed in the Brazils for ship-building, and is known in dockyards as cabbage-wood.

Party walls are partitions of brick made between buildings in separate occupations, for preventing the spread of fire. These are made thicker than the external walls; and their thickness, and the necessity of their use, are regulated by Act of Parliament, and specified in some of the clauses of the Buildings Act passed in the reign of the present Queen.

Parvise, a porch: an open area before the entrance of a church.

Paschal, a stand or candlestick, of a large size, used in Roman Catholic worship.

Pasigraphy, the art of universal writing.

Passant, in heraldry, a term applied to an animal in a shield appearing to walk leisurely: for most beasts, except lions, the word *tripping* is frequently used instead of *passant*.

Passion, in painting, implies an emotion of the body, attended with certain expressive lines in the face, denoting an agitation of soul.

Pastici, or *Imitations in Paintings*. Teniers understood the union of colours extremely well, yet Bassan was superior to him in the sweetness and vigour of his tints. De Pile recommends it to all persons who would not wish to be deceived by pastici, to compare the taste of design, the colouring and the character of the pencil, with the originals. Teniers, Giordano, and Don Boulloque are those who have appeared with the greatest reputation for imitating other great masters; and, beside these, many other artists have employed themselves in painting pastici.

Pastoral staff, the official staff of an archbishop, a bishop, or mitred abbot.

Pataud, the bottom plate or sill of a partition of a screen.

Paten, a small plate or salver used in the celebration of the eucharist.

Patents for Inventions are public grants to the inventors of new and useful machinery and processes in the arts, and by which certain privileges are secured to the inventors, for the exclusive use

PATENTS FOR INVENTIONS.

and exercise of their inventions during a limited period. Patents are therefore monopolies of a definite character; but being designed as a security for the reward of those whose ingenious faculties and practical skill have produced improvements of general utility and value, these monopolies, if justly granted and honestly exercised, are not to be decried as injurious to the public interests, but should be conceded with willingness, and command the liberal protection of the community, which is destined to reap a continual and permanent advantage from the improvements thus fostered in their infant development. Patents for inventions should therefore be admitted as bargains between the inventor on the one hand, and the public on the other; and the abuses to which these bargains are liable arise from the common causes of official corruption and individual cupidity and jealousy.

The laws under which patents are granted vary in their form in the several European and American States, and are all, in some degree, imperfect, and ineffective of their proper object.

In the United Kingdom of Great Britain and Ireland patents are granted to the inventor or importer from abroad of "any manner of new manufacture," one grant covering the whole realm with the Channel Islands and the Isle of Man. The colonies were formerly included in the grant for England when applied for, on payment of extra fees; but this practice has been discontinued. Patents are granted in the colony of Victoria, and a law has recently been enacted in India for the same purpose. It is also probable that the patent system will become gradually extended to the colonies generally, in a more definite and practical form than it could be when the grant was merely tacked on to the English patent.

British patents are granted as matters of course, provided certain legal forms are duly complied with, certain stamp duties paid, and the legal advisers of the Crown (the attorney or solicitor-general) are not required by opposing parties to ascertain whether the privilege sought will interfere with any contemporaneous application, or with any existing patent. But the validity of the patent is entirely at the patentee's own risk.

The process of soliciting a patent is as follows:—The applicant has to petition the Crown to grant Letters Patent for the invention, and he accompanies his petition with a declaration of the grounds of his request, and a specification either provisional or final, by which the invention sought to be protected may be identified. The difference between a provisional and a final specification is, that in the former kind of document the details are reserved, while in the latter they are expressed. Every provisional specification is submitted to the law officer, who on being satisfied of its sufficiency, allows a certificate of provisional protection to be issued. The provisional protection lasts nominally six months, but really only four months; because the patent will not be granted unless notice to proceed be given within four months from the date of the original record of the application. The notice to proceed is inserted in the 'London Gazette,' and the public are at liberty, within a period of twenty-one days from the date of the insertion, to enter notice of objections to the granting of the patent. The case is then referred to the law officer, with whom rests the decision between the parties. Should there be no opposition, the patent is granted. Having obtained the Great Seal, the patentee is allowed a period of six months from the original deposit of his papers, to prepare and

PATENTS FOR INVENTIONS.

file his complete or final specification (unless he deposited it at first, which is rarely advisable), with the drawings required to illustrate the invention and to give an accurate idea of the mechanism employed. For this purpose great care and judgment are needed, based on a knowledge of former patents, to frame the specification so that it shall explain with sufficient clearness the precise nature of the improvements, and have that value as property which a good specification of a patent always has. The patent is now complete, and the patentee can safely proceed to practise under it.

The patentee is enabled, under the authority of the attorney or solicitor-general, to amend his title and specification in case of need, and to disclaim part or parts of his claims, which he may have since found to be untenable. He may also petition for a prolongation of his term, of fourteen years, which petition is referred to the Judicial Committee of the Privy Council, who grant the same if the petitioner make out a case, satisfactory to them, of extraordinary losses, delays, or other special reasons for the prolongation.

The property in a patent can be defended from infringement by a bill in equity, or by an action at law. It has been recently found, however, that the ordinary courts of law and equity are incapable of dealing satisfactorily with the science which forms the chief part of the inquiry in a patent case. A special tribunal, to interpret the specification with authority in the first instance, has therefore become a necessity.

The patent may be assigned in whole or part by the patentee to any number of persons: it may also be mortgaged, and licenses may be granted for the use of the patent in a variety of modes. But all assignments and licenses must be registered at the Great Seal Patent Office, in order to give a title to the parties interested.

The cost of obtaining a patent, including fees for agency, if unopposed, is £30. But the patent expires at the end of three years, unless a further stamp-duty of £50 he paid; and at the end of seven years, unless a still further stamp duty of £100 be paid. To these items should be also added the cost of preparing and copying specification and drawings, the charges for which are, of course, very variable, according to length, intricacy, etc.

The expenses and regulations under which the foreign patents are granted vary considerably. The following brief epitome must suffice in this place.

In the United States of America, patents are granted only to the absolute inventor, always for fourteen years, and are granted or withheld at the option of the Government Commissioners of Patents. The amount of official fees payable *depends upon the country of which the applicant is a native.* Thus, a citizen of the United States, or a foreigner who has resided in the States one year next preceding the application, and has made oath of his intention to become a citizen, pays a fee of £30; *a subject of the Sovereign of Great Britain,* £500; *and any other foreigner,* £300. If the application for a patent be rejected by the Commissioner, two-thirds of the fees paid are returnable.

In France, patents for inventions are granted alike to natives and foreigners, and the duration of the privilege may be fixed by the patentee at five, ten, or fifteen years, the amount of tax being proportional to the term, namely, 500 francs for five years; 1000 francs for ten years; and 1500 francs for fifteen years; payable by annual instalments of 100 francs. The patentee thus enjoys the power of relinquishing his invention, if found unprofitable, at any time during the intended term, by ceasing to pay the annual instalment of fees.

In Belgium, patents are granted for five or ten years: imported inventions are patentable, and the Government tax, which is not heavy, is paid annually in small instalments, increasing by 10 francs each year.

In Holland, patents are granted for five, ten, or fifteen years, and may be had for foreign as well as native inventions. The fees for a patent for five years are 150 guilders, or £12. 10s.; and for terms of ten or fifteen years they vary from 300 to 750 guilders, or from £25 to £62. 10s.

In Prussia, Russia, etc., the Governments exercise a discretionary power in granting or refusing patents, and the laws are of a stringent and arbitrary character.

In Austria, patents are granted for terms from five to fifteen years; the taxes must be paid when the application is made, and the invention put in practice within one year from the date of the grant.

The German and Italian States have patent laws peculiar to themselves, but generally similar to those already described.

Patent yellow, Turner's yellow, or *Montpellier yellow,* is a submuriate or chloride of lead, which metal is the basis of the most opaque yellow pigment; it is a hard, ponderous, sparkling substance of a crystalline texture and bright yellow colour, hardly inferior, when ground, to chromic yellow. It has an excellent body, and works well in oil or water, but is soon injured, both by the sun's light and impure air; it is therefore little used, except for the common purposes of house-painting, etc.

Patera, a circular flat ornament, used in Classical architecture; used also in Gothic and Italian architecture.

Patriarchs, the. The chief employment of the patriarchs was the care of their cattle, viz. goats, sheep, camels, horned cattle, and asses. There were no horses nor swine among them. Theirs was a pastoral life, and not a life of tillage. They were always in the field, lying under tents, shifting their abode according to the convenience of pasture.

Paul, the catch which holds a ratchet-wheel, allowing it to turn in one direction only.

Pavilion, in architecture, a detached building; an insulated turret, contained under a single roof, sometimes square and sometimes dome-formed; named from its resemblance to the roof of a tent. The late palatial monstrosity at Brighton was called a pavilion.

Pax, a small tablet, having on it a representation of the crucifixion, or some other Christian symbol, offered to the congregation in the Romish church, to be kissed in the celebration of the mass: it was usually of silver, or other metal, with a handle at the back, but was occasionally of other materials; sometimes it was enamelled, and set with precious stones.

Peach-stone, a bluish-green soft stone.

Pearl-white. There are two pigments of this denomination: one, falsely so called, prepared from bismuth, which turns black in sulphuretted hydrogen gas or any impure air, is employed as a cosmetic: the other is prepared from the waste of pearls and mother-of-pearl, is exquisitely white and of good body in water, but of little force in oil or varnish; it combines, however, with all other colours, without injuring the most delicate, and is itself perfectly permanent and innoxious.

Pear-tree, a native European wood; its colour is a light brown, something of a pale-mahogany or cedar: it is employed by the Tunbridge turners.

Pea-stone, or *pisolite*, in mineralogy, pisiform limestone.

Peat, in mineralogy, a substance consisting of the twigs, leaves, and roots of trees, mixed with grass, straw, plants, and weeds, that have lain long in water, and become converted into a blackish-brown mass that may be cut with a spade, and dried for fuel.

Pedestal, in architecture, the lower member of a pillar, named by the Greeks stylobates and stereobates; also the basis of a statue. In Classical architecture it consists of three divisions: the base, or foot, next the ground, the dado, forming the main body, and the cornice, or sur-base moulding, at the top.

Pediment, the triangular plane or surface formed by the vertical termination of a roof consisting of two sloping sides; consequently it so far corresponds with the *gable*, but in other respects differs widely from it. One material difference between them is, that whereas the gable has no cornices, the pediment is bounded by three, viz. a horizontal one, beneath it, forming its base, and two sloping or *raking* ones, as they are technically termed; and the triangular space or surface included within them is distinguished by the name of the *tympanum* of the pediment. Another marked difference between them is, that the gable may be of any pitch; and being merely a continuation of the wall below, instead of being, like the pediment, separated from it by any horizontal mouldings, its proportions do not at all depend upon the height or width of the front or compartment of the front which it terminates, but may be an equilateral triangle, or even considerably more, as to height, and, besides, is in nowise governed by the height of what is beneath it. The pediment, on the contrary, must be proportioned to the *height* of the order which it crowns; consequently its pitch must be decreased in somewhat the same ratio as its length or base is increased, or, in other words, the greater the number of columns beneath a pediment, the lower must the pitch of the latter be. Hence it is hardly possible to place more than eight, or, at the utmost, ten columns beneath a pediment, without making the pediment either too low in itself, or else too lofty and heavy a mass in comparison with the columns beneath it; thereby not only overloading them—the columns being proportioned to their entablature alone—but also diminishing their importance, and causing the order itself to look almost puny and meagre, while the pediment looks heavy and clumsy. There has been a good deal of mystification about determining the proportion of pediments, and special methods have been devised for that purpose, which, however ingenious in themselves, as such, are anything but artistic, or calculated to secure pleasing proportions. Discarding all such *methods*, it may be laid down as a safe general rule, that the height of the tympanum should accord pretty nearly with that of the entablature beneath the pediment, and not greatly exceed it, under any circumstances. Such is the proportion which Wilkins appears to have observed for the pediment of the London University College; and although that building has a decastyle portico, the pediment does not appear too low, whereas that of the National Gallery is so, the height of the tympanum being there less than that of the entablature, notwithstanding that the portico is octastyle.

The ancients generally made the pediment contribute largely to the embellishment of the structure, by sculpturing its tympanum with figures in high relief, and in some instances by setting it back, and placing entire statues against it;

PEDIMENT.

and for such display of sculpture the pediment eminently recommends itself, both by its conspicuous situation, and by offering a far ampler surface for such purpose than any other part of the edifice; one, moreover, which not only required a higher decoration, for the sake of consistency, but an increased degree of it, in order to produce artistic climax and completion. Yet it must be confessed that if its *situation* marks out the pediment as a very proper place for making a display of decoration, its *shape* is by no means well adapted for a composition of figures, except it be that it compels them to be arranged symmetrically, and the principal one to be directly in the centre. Be the subject what it may, the figures must always be disposed in nearly the same manner, and not only very conventionally but very forcedly, particularly towards the extremities,—an inconvenience that might be easily overcome by confining the figures to the centre of the tympanum, putting there a group of three or five, and either leaving the rest of the triangular space to be quite plain, or else filling it up with mere ornament. While this would certainly be a rather less expensive mode than that now practised, and an equally rational one, its not having been adopted before ought to be itself some recommendation of it, as being a laudable infringement of copyism, conventionalism, and routine.

Besides sculpture within them, pediments are frequently surmounted at their angles and apex with *acroteria*, namely, low pedestals, upon which are placed either single

originated with the Romans, and is somewhat analogous in taste to that of putting them on the summit of monumental columns; for in such situations human figures show only in their general mass as sculptural accessories to the structure, and at a little distance, or seen in a general view of the building, produce scarcely more effect than so many pinnacles, which last are infinitely more characteristic of Gothic architecture than in accordance with the character of a classical portico.

In Italian and modern architecture generally, the pediment is employed as mere decoration in compositions for the dressings of both doors and windows, which practice, like that of applying columns for the same purpose, has been condemned by some in the most unqualified manner; and one writer has vituperated, and endeavoured to bring it into disgrace, by comparing pediments over doors and windows to—cocked hats! The resemblance which he perceives, or fancies, between a cocked hat and a pediment is not a particularly flattering one; but if it exists at all, the injurious comparison holds equally good with regard to a large pediment as a small one; therefore, whether it be that over a portico or over a window, the shape itself is, in either case, the most unfortunate one of a cocked hat; yet, as cocked hats are now gone quite out of fashion, the unlucky resemblance to them is not at all likely to be detected. In matters of decoration, some latitude—some little departure from strict architectural logic—is allowable; otherwise a very great deal in Italian or ones of a roof, to mere openings in the wall; and in like manner, if it be a gross impropriety to flank windows with small columns, it must be as great, if not a greater one, to introduce, merely for the sake of decoration, a large order whose columns are partly buried in the wall, and support nothing but an entablature, or pieces of it, wholly unnecessary in themselves, and put there only that the columns may appear to support something. Again, as to the objection which has sometimes been urged against pediments over doors within a building, namely, those intended to throw off rain, they should be introduced only in external situations,—it partakes of the same kind of hypercriticism as the other; or, if strict *rationality* is to be uniformly enforced in architectural design, we must condemn a great deal in the Gothic style as being exceedingly licentious and irrational; for in that we find a great many members and features originating in forms intended for purposes of actual service externally, converted into mere interior decoration; for instance, *embattlements* on the tops of screens, miniature *buttresses* for ornament instead of strength, miniature *spires*, and miniature blank windows in ornamental panelling.

Pediments are generally placed only over the windows of the principal floor of a building, to which they serve to give distinction and importance. Window pediments are either angular or curved (*i. e.* segmental), and both forms are frequently introduced together, and placed alternately, in which case it is usual to place an angular pediment over the centre window. Sometimes the centre window alone is crowned with a pediment. When all the pediments are alike, they are almost invariably angular, although there are instances of the contrary, as in Bridgewater House, where Mr. Barry has given segmental pediments to all the windows of the principal floor, and has even put them over the centre openings of the triple windows; and it deserves to be further remarked, that he has enriched their tympanums with sculptured ornament—a degree of decoration very rarely indulged in. A far more remarkable instance—perhaps a unique one—may be seen in the house lately erected for Mr. Hope in Piccadilly, large segmental pediments being there placed over windows consisting of *two* openings, consequently forming square, or nearly square, instead of upright compositions. In that instance, too, the pediments are filled in with sculpture; the figures, however, are not exactly confined to the pediments, but come somewhat lower down, the horizontal cornice being partly suppressed for that purpose.

Pedometer, in mechanics, an instrument in the form of a watch, consisting of various wheels, with the teeth catching in each other, and which, by means of a string fastened to anything in motion, numbers the paces gone over from one place to another.

Peek, in navigation, a name given to the upper corners of sails extended by a gaff, or by a yard crossing the mast obliquely, as the mizen-yard of a ship. The upper extremity of those gaffs and yards is also called the peek. To 'peek the mizen' is to put the mizen-yard perpendicular to the mast.

Peek-halyards, the ropes or tackles by which the outer end of the gaff is hoisted.

Peg-tankard, an ancient species of wassail-bowl, used in the time of Queen Elizabeth. It held two quarts, and had generally a row of seven pegs, dividing the height into eight equal parts, each containing half a pint.

Pelasgic Life. In reference to the

Pelasgian people as early settlers in Greece, the Right Honourable W. E. Gladstone, in his recent admirable work, 'Studies on Homer,' says, "For the first agricultural settlers must often be dwellers in woods. It may be said that in the United States, at the present day, the proper name for an agricultural settler is 'backwoodsman.' In British Australia, they who pass beyond the limits of existing settlement, in order to extend it, are said to go into the bush. Thus the idea at the root of the Lycian name is in all probability twin, or rather elder brother to that which properly would indicate the agricultural settler."

Pelasgus. Taken literally, Pelasgus is the son of the Earthborn, and the name given to the Pelasgian race. What the passage signifies evidently is, that by ancient tradition the Pelasgians were the first occupants of the country. Thucydides describes the spot or building called Πελασγικόν, under the Acropolis at Athens, the very situation in which the original town would, in all likelihood, he placed for safety. This historian also sustains, with the weight of his judgment, the opinion that in pre-Hellenic times the prevailing race and name in Greece were Pelasgic (pp. 186-197).

Pendant, an ornament suspended from the roof of a Gothic or Tudor building; the hanging pendants of a vaulted ceiling, uniting solidity with ornament. The most remarkable are those in King Henry VII.'s chapel at Westminster abbey.

Pendentive, the portion of a groined ceiling supported and bounded by the apex of the longitudinal and transverse vaults. In Gothic ceilings of this kind the ribs of the vaults descend from the apex to the impost of each pendentive, where they become united.

Pennyweight, the twentieth part of an ounce.

Pentagon, a figure of five angles and five sides: when these are equal it is called a *regular* pentagon, but otherwise it is *irregular*.

Pentagraph, an instrument whereby designs, prints, etc., may be copied, in any proportion, without a person being skilled in drawing. (See *Pantograph*.)

Pentangular, in geometry, five-cornered or angled.

Pentastyle, in architecture, a work in which there are five rows of columns.

Pentelic marble, in statuary, a beautiful and glossy variety of Parian and Carrara marble, named from Mount Pentelicus, near Athens, where it was quarried. Pentelic marble, from the smallness of the grain, is mistaken for the Parian; but, of the two, the former is of a finer quality. The Pentelic quarries display in a remarkable manner the energies of the ancient Athenians; whole sides of the mountains have disappeared, and present uniformly cut perpendicular cliffs; and holes, still to be traced on the slope of the quarries, made for the insertion of capstans, mark the place of the mechanical descent of the marble; whilst a damaged and rejected cylinder, apparently intended for a part of a column of the Parthenon, interests the traveller on the ascent.

Penthouse, a projection over a door, an entrance, a window, or a flight of steps, etc., for protection from weather.

Peperino marble, in mineralogy, a calcareous stone, something of the nature of travertino. It is supposed he the ancient *Sarum Albanum*, of which the foundations of the capitol at Rome (still to be seen) were built.

Perambulator, in surveying, an instrument for measuring distances; named also the *Pedometer* and *Surveying wheel*.

Perault's Estimation of Architects:—The little estimation in which architects have been held in France has prevented many from embracing a profession to which so little regard has been paid; and those whom the force of strong inclination has induced to adopt it, have led their lives in obscurity, excluded from the company and conversation of men of rank and fortune.

Nor is it regard and honour alone that nourish the arts. The conversation of men of sense, learning, and fortune cannot be dispensed with; for an exquisite taste is rarely formed among the vulgar, and there are a thousand things that cannot be learned in the condition of a simple artisan, nor even in schools, which however are absolutely necessary in order to arrive at excellence in the fine arts.

That haughtiness which sometimes attends the consciousness of superior abilities, and disdain of all mean and vulgar employments, was carried to such excess among the Romans, that many of them put themselves to death rather than work on buildings the structure of which was not so excellent as to render them distinguished. But when good architecture began to be honoured by that people, the art was cultivated with such ardour that in less than forty years it was brought to its highest perfection.

For this it was not necessary to send to Greece for masters. There were many Romans capable of designing and executing the boldest and most magnificent works, and many excellent volumes on architecture were written by Fusitius, Varro, Septimius Celsus, and other learned men. Even the Greeks employed Roman architects, and when King Antiochus completed the Temple of Jupiter Olympus at Athens, it was from the designs and under the conduct of Cossutius, a Roman citizen.

Such was the passion for magnificent buildings, that the expense of a private house was found to amount amount to near two million pounds sterling (50 millions French); and in Edile caused to be built, in less than one year, a theatre adorned with 360 columns, of which those in the lowest order were of marble, and 38 feet high; those of the second order were of crystal, and those of the third order of bronze gilt. It is said that this theatre, which was capable of containing 80,000 persons seated, was also embellished with 3,000 statues of bronze, and that this magnificent building was erected to serve six weeks only.

Historians relate that another Edile built a fountain, upon the aqueduct of which there were 130 towers (*regards* or *châteaux*), and the fountain adorned with 400 columns of marble and 300 figures in bronze. The water, which was poured through 700 pipes, was received into more than 100 basins.

Historians also remark that among the laws made by the Romans to restrain profusion and luxury, some of which were extremely severe, there is not one that controls the expense of buildings. So great was the veneration of this wise people for every art that does honour to merit and virtue, and which can preserve the memory of them to posterity.

In France, as in all other countries which offer sufficient encouragement, a talent for architecture may no doubt be developed. Before the reign of Francis I. the French princes had so little taste for the arts, that they regarded nothing but what related to war.

Perch, a small projecting beam, corbel, or bracket, near the altar of a church.

Perch, or *Pole*, a linear measure of 5½ yards.

Perclose, an enclosure, a railing; sometimes used to protect a tomb, or to separate a chapel from the main body of the church.

Percussion, in mechanics, the striking of one body against another, or the shock arising from the collision of two bodies.

Periacti, the revolving scenes of the theatre, called *scenæ versatiles* by the Romans: they were placed before the *itinera versurarum*, or those entrances to the stage which were in the returns of the permanent scene.

Periactos, a theatrical machine, consisting of three scenes placed in the form of a triangle on a revolving platform; so that, by simply turning the machine, the scene could be changed.

Pericles caused to be erected at Athens the famous statue of Minerva, of gold and ivory. Pausanias says, she stood erect, her garments reaching to her feet; she had a helmet on, and a Medusa's head; in one hand she held a spear, and on the other stood a Victory, of 4 cubits high. Pliny tells us the statue was 26 cubits high (37 ft. 8 in.), in which he perhaps included the pedestal, whereon they both say the birth of Pandora was represented. We are not told whether the ivory was painted; but by what Strabo says, that Panænus, the brother or nephew of Phidias, assisted him in colouring the statue of Jupiter at Elis, which was likewise of ivory and gold, it probably was. The reason why ivory was used in statues of this kind, rather than wood, seems not to have been on account of its colour, but because wood is apt to crack, and to be destroyed by worms: but ivory is not of uniform colour, being yellow near the outside of the tooth, and white in the middle; it therefore would require painting on that account, and likewise to hide the joining of the pieces. Thucydides says the gold about it weighed 40 talents, which, according to the value of gold at that time, was worth about £120,000 sterling.

Peridromus, in ancient architecture, the space of an aisle in a peripteron, between the columns and the wall, used for walks by the Greeks.

Perimeter, the boundary of any figure, being the sum of all the sides in right-lined figures, the same as circumference or periphery in those of a circular form.

Periphery, the circumference of a circle or ellipse.

Peripteral, a temple which had its cella surrounded by columns.

Peristylium, a continued row or series of rows of columns all round a court or building, in contradistinction to porticoes, in which the pillars did not surround a space, but were arranged in one or more parallel lines.

Peritrochium, in mechanics, a wheel or circle concentric with the base of a cylinder, and movable together with it about an axis: the axis, with the wheel and levers fixed in it, to move it, constitute that mechanical power called *axis in peritrochio*.

Perpendicular, in geometry, a line crossing or cutting the horizon or any other line at right angles.

Perpendicular: one line is perpendicular to another when it makes the angles on each side of it equal to each other.

Perpendicular Style of Gothic Architecture, derived from the Decorated about the end of the fourteenth century, and continued till the middle of the sixteenth: it is so called from its tracery consisting of perpendicular lines, and forming one of its most striking features. Many fine examples yet exist in England. The perpendicular character of the style is exhibited in the window tracery, where the transoms cross the mullions at right angles; and in large windows these are occasionally repeated several times: bands, quatrefoils, and other ornaments are more frequently employed than in the other styles, and are often carried across the panellings and vertical lines, creating a rectilinear arrangement, pervading most of the subordinate parts, that gives a peculiar air and stiffness. Panelling is used most abundantly on walls, both internally and externally, and also on vaulting. Some fine examples of this style are drawn in Mr. Parker's 'Glossary,' in 2 vols.

Perpent-stone, a bond-stone; a large stone reaching through a wall so that it appears on both sides of it.

Perpetual motion is that which possesses within itself the principle of motion.

Perron, in architecture, a staircase outside of a building, or the steps in front of a building leading up to the first story.

Persian Architecture. Honahung, the grandson of Kalomurs, the founder of the Paishdadian dynasty, is famous in Persian history as the first who constructed aqueducts. These aqueducts are made by a succession of small wells a few yards from each other, and of such depth as the level and soil require. They are connected with each other at the bottom by a channel, large enough for a man to pass to clear it. These wells commence at a spring, and not only convey its waters, but that of such other springs as are found in the course of the canal. They are common through all Persia: the water they convey is applied to irrigation.

Gushtasp (Darius Hystaspes), in whose reign the Persians became worshipers of fire, ordered 12,000 cowhides to be dressed fine, that the precepts of this new faith might be written upon them. These parchments were deposited in a vault hewn out of the rock at Persepolis. Some vaults answering this description are still seen in the ruins of that city.

The celebrated hall called Chehel Minar, or Hall of Forty Pillars, was built, it is said, by Homai, queen of Persia, the daughter of Artaxerxes Longimanus.

Dara, in Mesopotamia, was 14 miles from Nisibis, and four days' journey from the Tigris. It had two walls at the distance of 50 paces: this space was for the cattle of the garrison. The fortifications were walls or curtains, defended by towers; in the towers and walls were loopholes and galleries for the besieged. It had ditches, which were filled with water at pleasure from the river.

In 638, A.H. 17, the foundations of Bussorah were laid by the Arab chief, Alabah Ghuzwan.

Persian Wheel, a name given to a machine for raising water, which may be turned by means of a stream acting on and turning round the wheel. The buckets, instead of being firmly fastened, are hung upon the wheel by strong pins, fixed in the side of the rim, which must be made as high as the water is intended to be raised above the level of that part of the stream in which the wheel is placed.

Persians, in ancient architecture, male figures employed to support entablatures; the female figures were named *Caryatides*.

Perspective, in painting, etc., the science by which all things are ranged on a plane surface, as in a picture, according to their appearance in their real situation.

Pew, an enclosed seat in a church, introduced since the Reformation. Previous to the Reformation the nave of a church was the part occupied by the congregation. Pews are fixed seats, separated from each other by wainscoting, and varying in height.

Pewter, in metallurgy, a mixed metal, consisting of tin variously alloyed with lead, zinc, bismuth, or antimony. Common low-priced pewter contains 20 parts tin, 3 lead, 1 brass; best pewter, 17 parts antimony, 100 parts tin, and a little copper. Pewter dishes and wooden trenchers were the ordinary services of our ancestors till the time of Elizabeth, when "by reason of sharpe laws provided in that behalf," pewter was compounded of purer metal than before. The splendid services of gold and silver were only used on occasions of ceremony and on festivals.

Pharos or *Pharus*, a lighthouse. The most celebrated lighthouse of antiquity was that situated at the entrance of the port of Alexandria, built by Sostratus on an island, by the direction of Ptolemy, at a cost of 800 talents. Pliny mentions the lighthouses of Ostia and Ravenna. The name of Pharos was given in allusion to that of Alexandria, which was the model for their construction.

Phidias, the great Greek sculptor and director of the works under Pericles.

Phonics, the doctrine of sounds, otherwise named acoustics.

Phosphate of iron is a native ochre, which classes in colour with the deeper hues of ultramarine ashes, and is eligible for all their uses. (See *Blue Ochre*.) Slate-clays and several native earths class with greys; but the colours of some of the latter, which have been tried, are not durable, being subject to become brown by the oxidation of the iron they contain.

Photography, a new art, the production of pictures from nature's image. Photography presents a number of the most interesting phenomena, which have acquired important practical results, in correctly portraying by the light of day all things in nature, whether architecture, drawings of every variable kind, landscape, machinery, pictures in oil, the human form, etc. The aids for the accomplishment of the art is by chemical agency either on glass, paper, ivory, stone, and by the lenses of the camera obscura. Various valuable works have been published descriptive of the whole process. (See Weale's 'Rudimentary Series.')

Physics, the doctrine of natural bodies, their phenomena, causes, and effects, with their various motions, operations, affections, etc. Taken in its most enlarged sense, it comprehends the whole study of nature, and includes physiology and natural history.

Piazza, an open area or square; a covered walk or portico.

Pick, an instrument in common use as well in agricultural as in mining operations.

Pictura (Latin), a painting. The art of imitating the appearances of bodies upon an even surface, by means of light and shade, or colour, was most extensively cultivated by the ancients, but especially by the Greeks, amongst whom it was carried to the highest degree of technical development.

Pier, in architecture, the strong columns on which the arch of a bridge is raised.

Pier, the solid mass between doors, windows, and other openings in buildings: the term is often applied to pillars in Norman and Gothic architecture.

Piers, walls built to support arches, and from which, as bases, they spring.

Pilæ, square blocks placed upon the epistylia, and immediately over the columns in a basilica, for supporting the timbers of the roof. Pilæ were also buttresses built against the walls of a mole, to resist the force of the waters.

Pilaster, in architecture, a square column, sometimes insulated, but more frequently set within a wall, and only showing a fourth or fifth part of the thickness. Pilasters were unknown in Greek architecture, in which only antæ (see *Antæ*) were admitted: they are employed by the moderns as substitutes for an order in engaged columns, and are, perhaps, even preferable to the latter, inasmuch as they combine better and more naturally with the wall to which they are attached.

force of an adequate weight, which was permitted to fall vertically on them from a considerable height. The machinery employed was therefore properly called a *pile-driver*, and consisted simply of a vertical framing, provided with winches and chains, by which the weight or 'monkey' was alternately raised by manual power, and released so as to fall upon the head of the pile; or a gin was applied, and horses used for the same purpose.

Within the last few years a great improvement has been effected in the machinery for pile-driving, by the application of steam power. The earliest invention for this purpose is recorded in a patent granted in 1806, but no practical application appears to have resulted for many years. The patent referred to was dated June 6, 1806, and granted to William Deverell, for "improvements in the mode of giving motion to hammers, stampers, knives, shears, and other things, without the application of wheels, pinions, or any rotative motion, by means of various powers now in common use." The apparatus was designed to consist of a steam-cylinder with piston and rod, and a hammer, raised by admitting the steam below the piston. By the condensation or the escape of the steam, the hammer and the piston were allowed to descend, urged both by their own weight and by the elasticity of the compressed air in the top of the cylinder above the piston. This, therefore, established the *principle* of the steam-hammer: but the most successful application of it to the purposes of driving piles, as well as to those of the smithery, is due to Mr. James Nasmyth, whose steam-hammer consists of a steam-cylinder, which is closed at the bottom, but has openings in the top, to admit the passage of air. The rod of the piston passes through a steam-tight aperture in the bottom of the cylinder, and has the 'monkey,' or driver, weighing 2½ tons, suspended from it. The machine is worked with high-pressure steam, which, entering the bottom of the cylinder, raises the piston and 'monkey.' When the piston reaches the height intended, it shuts the induction and opens the eduction pipe (also at the bottom of the cylinder), by which the steam escapes, and the monkey falls. A heavy iron cap slides between standards and round the head of the pile, and thus guides it in its descent. This machine, as used at Devonport, in driving piles for the steam-dock, made seventy strokes per minute, and drove piles 14 inches square and 18 feet in length.

In the year 1843 (December 5), a patent was obtained by Dr. L. H. Potts, for "improvements in the construction of piers, embankments, breakwaters, and other similar structures." The several objects comprised in this invention were sought with considerable ingenuity, and have been realized with success. The invention includes the application of hollow piles of iron, of a cylindrical or other convenient form, and sinking them by withdrawing the sand, etc., within them by the action of an air-pump. For this purpose the pile is fitted with an air-tight lid, through which a pipe passes to connect the interior of the pile with a receiver. The receiver is connected by a pipe with a three-barrelled air-pump, by working which the air is exhausted from the hollow pile, and the sand and water raised into the receiver, which is emptied as often as necessary. A second purpose proposed in this patent is the use of skeleton frames or cases of cast-iron in connection with the piles, for securing them together, and preserving their relative positions. A third object is the injection, by hydraulic pressure, of such chemical solutions about the feet of the piles as will consolidate the sand upon which they stand, and thus secure the work. And the inventor also proposed to use hydraulic cements in a dry state, delivered at the base of the piles, by the admixture of which cements with the water they would become solidified, and thus materially aid in strengthening the superstructure.

Recently these piles have been successfully used on the Goodwin Sands, by the Trinity Board. Previously, engineers had been baffled in finding a bottom. The piles have now been fairly affixed to the hard bottom, seventy-five feet through the sand.

In connection with Mitchell's, Nasmyth's, and Potts's modes of piling, it is proper to notice also Cram's patent pile-driving locomotive machine, which was successful in its operation in the United States. The volume ('Ensamples of Railway-Making') from which the following extract has been made was edited by the publisher of this Dictionary, with a view to induce a cheaper mode of construction of railways in countries less wealthy than those already intersected by iron roads.

Pile-road.—As a considerable length of the Utica and Syracuse railroad passes through a deep swamp, a foundation of great permanency was required: this gave rise to a modification of the superstructure, and formed that which is known as pile-road. The swamp varied in depth from 10 feet to 60 feet, and was nearly on a dead level throughout: the grude-line closely corresponded with its surface; so that it was necessary to reach the hard bottom before any foundation could be effected. Piles were adopted as the cheapest and most efficacious means to secure a durable and substantial basis: they were driven to their places by a steam pile-driver. This was a machine formed of a platform about 25 feet long and 8 feet broad: at one end were erected two pairs of leaders or guides, in which the hammers moved. Immediately behind the leaders were fixed the rollers, with the necessary brakes and gearing for working the hammers, raising the piles, etc. The rollers were revolved by a small high-pressure steam-engine, occupying the rear of the machine. The arrangement of the leaders was the same as in ordinary piling machines: a curved piece of wood forced open the sheers when the hammers reached their elevation. The hammers were confined to the leaders by a groove: they weighed about 1,000 lbs. each, were made of cast-iron, and at their last blow fell through a space of 27 feet. A pair of piles were driven at one operation by this machine; when driven, cast-iron rollers were placed upon their heads, and the machine, by means of an inverted rail, moved on to the next place. The heads of the piles, sawed off to reduce them to the proper level, were found sufficient to supply the furnace with fuel.

The men employed in operating the machine were,—a foreman, a steam engineer, two brake-men, and two men in front at the saws; also a horse and cart, to furnish water for the boiler. Properly geared in front of the machine, and between the leaders, was a saw that played on a sway-bar and could be pressed against either pile as it was driven home. The machine was manufactured complete for the cost of £400.

Each pile was prepared for being driven by simply sharpening one end to a point, and squarely butting the other; it was drawn up by ropes worked by the engine, secured in position between the leaders, and driven to the hard bottom. Generally the piles manifested no disposition to split: when they did, their heads were encompassed with an iron hoop. When the pile was not of sufficient length to reach the hard bottom, another was dowelled upon its head, and this was repeated as often as necessary. The piles were charred, to increase their durability; and an auger-hole, bored in their heads for the purpose, was filled with salt, and securely plugged up.

Pillar, a kind of irregular column, round and insulate, but deviating from the proportion of a just column. The term pillar is more usually applied to Gothic architecture than to the Classical, the latter being governed by the rules of proportion: not so with the Gothic pillar, it being subject to no fixed rules.

Pillars (monumental), columns raised for the commemoration of events, a practice from remote antiquity. "Jacob set a pillar upon her grave: that is the pillar of Rachel's grave unto this day." (*Gen.* xxxv. 20.)

Pillars, in ship-building, pieces fixed under the middle of the beams, to support the decks.

Pillion, the tin that remains in the slags after it is first melted.

Pinacotheca, a picture gallery. The public gallery at Munich is called the *Pinakothek*.

Pindrill, a drill used for cutting a recess for a bolt-head, or for enlarging a hole.

Pines and *Firs* are cone-bearing timber-trees which thrive best in cold climates: they are of great variety, and the general uses of the wood are innumerable, besides those for ships and house carpentry. Its use in England is most extensive: it is principally imported from America, Norway, the Baltic, Memel, Riga, Dantzic, etc.

Pinion, in mechanics, an arbour or spindle, in the body of which are several notches, into which the teeth of a wheel catch, that serves to turn it round; it is also the name of a lesser wheel that plays in the teeth of a larger one.

Pinite, a micaceous mineral.

Pink, in navigation, a name given to a ship with a very narrow stern.

Pinnacle, an ornament placed on the top of a buttress as a termination to an angle or gable of a house, church, or tower; also a summit or lofty apex.

Pins, in ships, are fixed in the drumheads of capstans, through the ends of the bars, to prevent their unshipping; sometimes put through the bolts to belay a rope, and called belaying pins; and sometimes the main bolts are called bolt-pins.

Pipe, a tube for the conveyance of water, gas, or steam, of various dimensions and uses.

Pipe, in mining, a running vein, having a rock roof and sole.

Piscina. Pliny says the Romans adorned the walls, ceilings, and floors of their baths. It was on the piscina they bestowed the most art. In the baptisterium they dipped their whole body, and this was large enough to swim in; but when they were disposed to swim at large in warmer water, they entered the piscina, a basin so called, as its size bore some resemblance to a pond. When the thermæ were built, they were made to contain lakes of warm water: the water acquired its heat by passing through the fire in a brass pipe, and must have been more or less hot according to the length of its progress.

Piscina, a shallow stone basin, or trough, with a hole in the bottom, formerly placed near to the altar in Roman Catholic churches, and fixed at a convenient height above the floor, to hold the water in which the priest washed his hands; also for rinsing the chalice at the time of the celebration of the mass. It was usually on the right-hand side, on the approach to the altar.

Pisé, a peculiar mode of forming

buildings, particularly those for cottages and farming purposes, with some sort of stiff earthy materials of a loamy quality. The earth so collected, framed, is well rammed until the moisture is driven out, and used to make the walls or sides of the building, instead of bricks. It has been used with much economy and success on the Continent, and in some parts of England.

Pastici, or *Pastici*, a term by which Italians distinguish pictures which cannot be called either original or copies, being the works of some artists who have had the skill to imitate the manner of design and colouring of other eminent masters; sometimes borrowing part of their pictures, sometimes imitating their touch, their style of invention, their colouring, and expression. Several painters, of considerable reputation for their own original performance, have made themselves remarkable in this way; but none of them more than David Teniers, who so successfully counterfeited Giacopo Bassan, as to deceive the most judicious, in many instances, at the first sight; though, upon a closer inspection, his light and easy pencil, and a predominant grey tint, which is observable in the colouring of that master, show a perceptible difference between his pencil and colouring, when they are carefully examined and compared with Bassan's. (See *Pastici*.)

Piston, a movable air-tight division within the steam-cylinder, acted upon by the steam. Pistons are either metallic or packed. Metallic pistons usually have segments of brass or cast-iron, called junk-rings, pressed outward by springs. Packed pistons are surrounded by well-greased hemp.

Piston-rod, the rod fixed to the piston, to communicate its motion to the crank.

Pitch, in building, the vertical angle of a roof, or the proportion between the heights and spans, as when the height is one-fourth, one-third, or one-half, of the breadth of the building. If the height is one-half of the breadth, the inclination of the planes, forming the vertical angle, is a right angle.

Pitching-piece, in staircasing, a horizontal piece of timber having one of its ends wedged into the wall, at the top of a flight of steps, to support the upper ends of the rough strings.

Pitch-wheel. When two toothed-wheels work together, the circles of contact are called the proportional circles, or pitch circles.

Pit-man, one employed to look after the lift of pumps and the drainage.

Pit-work, the pumps and other apparatus of the engine shaft.

Pivot, a stud or small pin on which anything turns.

Pix, in church rituals, a little chest or box, in which the consecrated host is kept.

Plain chart, in navigation, is a sea-chart, wherein the meridian and parallels are straight parallel lines, as in Mercator's projection; consequently the degrees of longitude are the same in all latitudes.

Plain sailing, in navigation, the art of working a ship's motion on a plain chart, which supposes the earth to be an extended plane, or flat, and not globular.

Plan. The plan of a building may be familiarly described as an architectural map; therefore only those who cannot comprehend a geographical or topographical map can be at any loss to understand an architectural one, the latter being precisely of the same nature as the others, with this difference in its favour, that it is much less conventional. To define it more exactly,—a plan is a *horizontal section* supposed to be taken on the level of the floor through the solid parts of the fabric—walls, columns, etc., so as to show their various thicknesses and situations, the dimensions of the several spaces or rooms, the position of the doors by which they communicate with each other, and various particulars that cannot otherwise be explained. Studying buildings without plans, is like studying geography without maps. A plan frequently costs the architect more study than all the rest of his design, and much mistaken are those who suppose that convenience alone has chiefly to be considered. Convenience is, of course, or ought to be, made a *sine qua non*; yet it is not so much a positive merit in itself, as the want of it is a positive defect. Mere convenience is not an artistic quality: from that to beauty of plan,—to striking combinations, and studied effects, and varied play of arrangement,—the distance is very great. A commonplace plan is but a very dull, uninteresting affair; it is no more than what any builder can accomplish; but a plan replete with imagination, piquant play, and well-imagined contrasts, is no everyday matter.

Plancerr, the soffit or underside of the corona of a cornice, in Classical architecture.

Plane, in surveying, a level surface, parallel to the horizon. In carpentry, an instrument by which the surfaces of bodies are smoothed.

Plane, Inclined : in mechanics, this resembles one half of a wedge that has been cut in two parts lengthwise.

Plane, in geometry, a plain level figure, or a surface lying evenly within its boundary lines.

Planing Machine, an invention for diminishing the great labour of planing the surfaces of planks and boards of wood, and for reducing the surface to a true and smooth face, by means of planes, or instruments of a similar nature, which are actuated by the power of the machinery instead of the strength of a man's arm.

Planing Machine. The invention of the 'slide-rest,' which has effected such an important improvement in cylindrical and conical turning, has been of far superior advantage in its application to the planing of surfaces, as the planing machine is but the slide-rest applied to a traversing table. In planing machines of the ordinary construction, the bed or basement frame has two angular ridges from end to end, one on each side, which fit into corresponding angular grooves in a traversing table. This table rests upon the ridges, and is moved backwards and forwards by a screw-rack and pinion, or chain; its surface is accurately planed, and the work being fastened upon it partakes of its motion, and is constrained to move in a perfectly straight line. Over the traversing table, at the centre of the machine, is fixed a slide-rest, which is held fast by being bolted to two upright standards fixed to the bed, one on each side. The horizontal slide has another at right angles to it, which serves to hold the cutting-tool and adjust it to the work, so as to take a cut more or less deep, as required. To the long screw of the horizontal slide, mechanism is connected which causes it to advance the vertical slide and tool a very small distance across the machine, just before the commencement of each forward movement of the table; so that by a repeated series of movements to and fro of the table, the tool is made to traverse the whole surface of the work; and thus, by the perfectly level movement of the table in the one direction, and that of the slide in the other, a perfectly plane surface is obtained. In some machines the table is made to travel backward at a much faster rate than in the forward motion, so as to save time; and in others, the cutting tool acts in both movements, by being turned at the end of each.

Planish, in carpentry, etc., to smoothe, to polish.

Planisher, a thin flat-ended tool, used by turners for smoothing brasswork.

Planisphere, in geometry, etc., a sphere projected on a plane; such are maps of the heavens or of the earth.

Plank, a term applied to all superficial timber which is 4 inches thick and under, except 1-inch, and sometimes 1½-inch, which come under the denomination of *board*.

Plank-sheers, in ship-building, pieces of plank laid over the timber heads on the quarter-deck, forecastle, and round-house.

Plane-tree, a native of Europe; it is also abundant on the banks of the Mississippi and Ohio. This, perhaps one of the largest of the American trees, is sometimes twelve feet in diameter, and is much used in that country for quays. It is used here for musical instruments, and other works requiring a clean, light-coloured wood.

Plasm, in the arts, a mould; a matrix in which anything is cast or formed.

Plaster of Paris, in mineralogy and the arts, gypsum deprived of its water by burning, and reduced to a white powder, which is afterwards mixed with water. It serves many purposes in building, and is used likewise in sculpture, to mould and make statues, basso-relievos, and other decorations in architecture. It is dug out of quarries in several parts of the neighbourhood of Paris, whence its name. The finest is that of Montmartre. It is known also as gypsum.

Plastering, the art of covering the walls and ceilings of a house or other edifice with a composition, of which the groundwork is lime and hair mortar, finished with a coating of finer materials.

Plat, in mining, ground appropriated to ore or deads.

Plat-band, a flat fascia, band, or string, whose proportion is less than its breadth; the lintel of a door or window is sometimes so named.

Plate, and other services for the table. In the time of Henry VIII. and Elizabeth, amongst the numerous costly and magnificent articles for the table, wrought in silver, gold, and other precious materials, were chargers, dishes, plates, porringers, saucers, vases or cups, pots or tankards, flagons, pitchers, pottels, ewers, creuses, bowls, goblets, basins, washing-basins and ewers, horns, cups for caudle cruets, spiceplates, spiceries, salt-cellars, pepper-boxes, spoons and candlesticks.

Plate, a term applied to horizontal timbers, placed on walls, etc., to receive other timberwork: that at the top of a building immediately under the roof is a wall-plate; those also which receive the ends of the joists of the floors above the ground-floor are called the same.

Plate-bending Machine. This invention was contrived for bending plates of metal into any required curve, and is particularly useful in the construction of boilers and the buckets of waterwheels: it consists of two sideframes, which carry three iron rollers and the spurwheels and pinions necessary to communicate motion to two of them, one of which is placed immediately over the other, and can be raised or lowered by screws to the thickness of the plate to be bent. The third roller is placed behind the first two, and it is the height of this roller, with respect to that of the other two, that determines the degree of curvature of the plate: it is therefore made capable of adjustment by setscrews, and being placed to the proper height, and the machine set in motion, the plate is passed between the first two rollers, till, coming in contact with the third, it rises upward and takes the form of a curve.

Platina yellow, is, as its name implies, a preparation from platina, which affords a series of yellow pigments, the deep colours of which resemble the Terra di Siena, but are warmer in tone and richer in colour and transparency, much resembling fine gall-stones, for which they are valuable substitutes. They work well, and are permanent both in water and oil, when carefully prepared; but any portion of palladium in the metal from which they are prepared neutralizes their colour and renders them useless.

Platinum is found in the metallic state alloyed with other metals, but not in large quantities. It is not so white a metal as silver, but is very malleable and ductile, either when hot or cold. No furnace can melt it; but by the oxyhydrogen blow-pipe, or by a voltaic current, it is capable of being fused, and may be dissipated in the air. Alone it is insoluble in nitric acid, but when alloyed with other metals it is soluble.

Plenum, in physics, a term used to signify that state in which every part or space of extension is supposed to be full of matter. It is used in opposition to vacuum.

Plinth, a square member forming the lower division of the base of a column, etc.; also the plain projecting face at the bottom of a wall, immediately above the ground. In Gothic architecture the plinth is occasionally divided into two stages, the tops of which are either splayed or finished with a hollow moulding, or are covered by the base mouldings.

Plinth, the square footing below the bases of Ionic and Corinthian columns. In Grecian architecture plinths do not appear to have been employed, the bases of the columns resting upon the upper step of the building. The Latin word *plinthus* is derived from the Greek, signifying a tile.

Plinthus, any rectangular parallelopiped; a brick or tile.

Pliny, whose villas were by the Romans objects of much attraction for their design and ornament, was a person of excellent judgment in all the useful arts, and, living under Trajan, had an opportunity of seeing the performances of and of advising with Apollodorus, one of the greatest architects that any age produced: whether artists or masters employed by Pliny, or Pliny himself, designed these villas, is not to be determined; but Pliny was perfectly acquainted with the whole that was necessary to be understood in their situation and disposition.

Plotting, among surveyors, the art of describing or laying down on paper, etc., the several angles and lines of a tract of ground surveyed by a theodolite or like instrument, or a chain.

Plotting-scale, a mathematical instrument used in plotting ground, usually of box-wood, sometimes of brass, ivory, or silver, either a foot or a foot and a half long, and about an inch and a half broad.

Plug-rod the air-pump rod of a Cornish engine. The tappets which give motion to the valve are fixed upon these rods.

Plumb, in ship-building, signifies to be perpendicular.

Plumbago forms grey tints of greater permanence and purity than most blacks in general use, and it is now employed for this purpose with approved satisfaction by experienced artists.

Plumb-line, in architecture, etc., a line perpendicular to the horizon, made by dropping a plummet.

Plummer-block, a short carriage or support for a shaft to turn in, with a flat base to bolt on a frame.

Plummet, in carpentry, navigation, etc., a weight of lead hung on a string, by which depths are ascertained and perpendicularity discerned.

Plum-tree, a handsome wood, a native of Europe, used principally in turning, and in Tunbridge works; in the endway of the grain it resembles cherry-tree.

Plus, in algebra, a term commonly used for more, and denoted by the character +, as 6 + 10 = 16, in contradistinction to —, or *minus*, less, as 16 — 10 = 6.

Pluteus, the wall which was sometimes made use of to close the intervals between the columns of a building, and was either of stone or some material less durable. The latter method was adopted only in places under cover, whence that kind of building was called *opus intestinum*. The pluteus was also a kind of podium, intervening between any two orders of columns placed one above the other. The word is used in this sense in the description of the basilica and the scene of the theatre. The pluteus has been adopted between every two orders of columns in the exterior of all the theatres and amphitheatres of the Romans which are known.

Pluviometer, in the arts, a rain-gauge, an instrument to measure the quantity of rain that falls.

Plyers, in mechanics, a kind of balance used in raising or letting down a drawbridge.

Plying to windward, in navigation, the endeavouring to make a progress against the wind.

Pneumatics, the properties of air or fluids; a branch of hydrostatics.

Pnyx, a name given to a place near Athens, at which assemblies were held for oratory, and for the discussion of political affairs of the state; the ancient place of the Athenian parliament. According to Plutarch, who has described the change effected by the Thirty Tyrants in the aspect of the oratory, it was turned from the sea in order to divert the assembled people from being reminded by their orators of maritime affairs, the basis of Athenian dominion. No traveller, it is said, has hitherto remarked the circumstance of the position of the ancient city wall, by which the Pnyx was doubtless enclosed during and after the Peloponnesian war. Plutarch further remarks: "Themistocles did not bring the Piræus into the city, as Aristophanes would have had it; but he joined the city by a line of communication to the Piræus, and the land to the sea." This measure strengthened the people against the nobility, and made them bolder and more intractable, as the power came with wealth into the hands of masters of ships, mariners, and pilots. Hence it was that the oratory in the Pnyx, which was built to front the sea, was afterwards turned by the Thirty Tyrants towards the land, as they believed a maritime power to be inclinable to a democracy, whereas persons employed in agriculture would be less uneasy under an oligarchy.

Podium, in Greek architecture, a continued pedestal, for supporting a row of columns, or serving for a parapet, or forming a sort of terrace, as the podium of a theatre or amphitheatre. It consists of a plinth, base, die, and corona, all which were continued without interruption around three sides of the building. The podium was also adopted in the scenes of theatres; and here, instead of being uninterrupted, it was frequently broken round the basis of the columns, and formed what are commonly called pedestals. Vitruvius seems to consider the podium as a pedestal continued the whole length of a building, and to have been so called both when there were pillars placed on it, or only supported by a wall. When pillars were placed on the sides of buildings, sometimes, instead of having the podium continued the whole length in one line, it was made to break forward under every pillar, which part so advancing was called the stylobate, and that which was betwixt the pillars under the wall, was the podium.

Pointed or *Christian Architecture* had its rise about the twelfth century. Very many beautiful examples exist in England. It was also employed in Germany. Mr. W. Pugin says, that Pointed architecture does not conceal her construction, but beautifies it. A buttress in Pointed architecture at once shows its purpose, and diminishes naturally as it rises, and has less to resist. Here are the true principles of Christian architecture, by the conversion of an essential support of the building into a light and elegant decoration.

Point, in navigation, one of the thirty-two divisions into which the circumference of the horizon and the mariner's compass are distinguished, each comprehending 11° 15'.

Point of horse, in mining, the spot where the vein is divided into one or more branches.

Polacre, in navigation, a merchant vessel of the Mediterranean, having three pole-masts, without tops, caps, or cross-trees, with a bowsprit of one piece.

Polarization. If a round hailstone drop upon the sloping roof of a house, it will act, as regards its rebound, just in the same manner whether the slope be towards the north, south, east, or west. But this will not be the case with an arrow under the same circumstances, because it has a distinction of sides, and its behaviour will vary according as the plane of its barbs is parallel with the eaves or with the rafters of the roof, or inclined to both. A bullet in its flight from a gun has also sides to its motion (though not to its form), because it revolves on an axis, which may be vertical, horizontal, or inclined: but if shot from a rifle, it has no such sides, because, though spinning on an axis, that axis has, by a particular contrivance, been made to coincide with its line of motion, so that it presents the same aspect above, below or on either side. Now if these projectiles were too small or too rapid for us to discover the reason of these differences, we might still observe the differences themselves, and should express them by saying that the motion of the arrow or the gun-bullet possessed polarity, or polarization, which was not the case with that of the hailstone or the rifle-bullet. Polarity, then, means simply a difference of sides. That a ray of light should (in some cases) possess this property is not perhaps so wonderful or unexpected as that man should have been able to detect a fact so refined and remote from common observation, and even to distinguish different varieties of it, and investigate its laws. Indeed, these must be regarded as the very penetralia of physics, the very inmost secrets of Nature that man has been enabled to wrest from her. If the measurable spaces occupied by the waves of light be minute, how far less, in all probability, must be those immeasurable spaces to which its vibrations are confined (which even in sound are mostly inappreciable, though the waves occupy many feet); yet it is to the positions of these inconceivably minute vibrations that the differences of polarization are due.

Poldway, coarse sacking for coal-sacks, etc.

Pole-masts, in navigation, are those made of single trees or spars, in contradistinction to those made of several pieces.

Pole-plate, a small wall-plate used in roofs to receive the pitch of the rafters.

Polroz, in mining, the pit underneath a waterwheel.

Polychromy is the art and practice of painting in positive colours, either on flat surfaces or sculptured forms, and has been referred for its origin to other than æsthetic motives. The object of polychromy is to heighten the effect of architectural decoration, either by causing a more just subordination of the various parts than can be obtained by mere chiaroscuro, or in supplying deficiencies that could not be so well filled up by any other means. Professor Cockerell, who travelled and learned much in Greece, was the first who brought it to light in this country. This very interesting decorative art had its origin doubtless in Egypt; but the Greeks excelled, as in all art, by the existing evidence of the temples of their perfection of architectural art. The interior decorations of Pompeii are also evidences of a refinement of taste, and in Gothic polychromy the designers and operatives have shown some talent. A free and bold style in arabesque prevailed from the time of Henry III. until the close of the reign of Edward III. Bright and lively colours were applied to masses, and the grounds covered with compositions of foliage and birds, animals and human figures; sometimes in one tint, sometimes in varied colours. Many beautiful examples still exist in our cathedrals and some parish churches.

Polyfoil, an ornament formed by a moulding disposed in a number of segments of circles.

Polystyle, having a number of columns. Where columns occur behind columns, as where a portico has inner columns, like that of the Royal Exchange, such portico may be termed *polystyle*.

Pomel, a boss or knob used as an ornamental top of a conical or dome-shaped roof of a turret, etc. A large copper ball or pomel is on the summit of a timber spire of Lincoln cathedral.

Pons (Latin), a bridge. The most ancient bridge upon record is the one erected by Nitocris over the Euphrates at Babylon.

Poon wood, of Singapore, is of a light porous texture, and light greyish cedar colour; it is used in ship-building for planks, and makes excellent spars. The Calcutta poon is preferred.

Poplar wood. There are five species common to England, of which the abele, or great white poplar, and the Lombardy poplar, are most used. The woods are soft, light, easy to work, suited for carving, common turnery, etc.

Poppets, perpendicular pieces that are fixed on the fore and aftermost parts of the bulgeways, to support the ship while being launched.

Poppet-head, that part of a lathe which holds the back centre, and can be fixed on any part of the bed.

Poppy, an ornament representing the poppy-head, used on the tops of the upright ends or elbows which terminate seats, etc., in churches.

Poppy-head, in architecture, a carved ornament at the apex of a standard or open seats in Gothic churches, also carved into an ornamental finial, pomel, or crest, etc.

Porcelain clay, in mineralogy, a substance of great infusibility, derived from disintegrated felspar.

Porch, in architecture, a roof supported on pillars before a door; a kind of vestibule supported by pillars. Any small portico considerably lower than the main structure to which it is attached may be so termed, in contradistinction from one carried up the height of the building, or as high as the principal cornice. Porches were used in Norman architecture, in Early English, and commonly in subsequent dates. When the fashion of building houses on quadrangular plans was discontinued, a porch of at least two stories, and sometimes the whole height of the building, succeeded the gate-house. Low porches had been used as entrances from inner courts from an early date; and of the time of Henry VIII. one may be mentioned at Cowdry, attached to the door leading from the court to the hall.

Pores, small interstices between the solid particles of bodies.

Porisms, in geometry, a name applied by the ancients to certain comprehensive and indefinite problems.

Port, in navigation, the larboard or left side of a ship; as 'a-keel to port' is an inclination to the larboard side.

Ports, the holes in the ship to run the guns out.

Port-lids, shutters to the ports.

Ports and buildings constructed in water. Vitruvius writes: "The opportunity which presents itself of giving some account of ports, and by what means protection may be afforded to ships from the elements, ought not to be neglected. The positions best adapted by nature to such a purpose are bays with capes and promontories at their extremities, from which the shore recedes inwardly in a curved line. Upon shores of this description, docks may be built or porticoes erected, or a channel cut from the port to the emporium, defended by towers on each side, in which machines may be constructed for throwing booms across the passage. If, however, no situation can be found capable by its formation of protecting vessels against the violence of the sea, we must search for a spot where a promontory presents itself on one side, and where no river discharges itself so as to oppose its application to the purposes of a harbour, and supply the want of a corresponding projection on the other by building walls and buttresses. The walls, which it becomes necessary in this case to construct in the water, may be thus formed: sand should first be procured from that part of the coast lying between Carnac and the promontory of Minerva, and mixed with lime in the proportion of two parts to one; then rows of grooved beams must be driven in the water, connected by oaken planks, and bound together by chains. The surface of the ground below the water, on which the wall is to be raised, must then be made even by means of trastilli, and the space comprehended between the beams filled with a composition consisting of rough stone and cement, made in the manner just described. Such is the quality of the sand produced in these spots, that the composition becomes a solid wall."

Port the helm. In navigation this phrase directs a ship's course further to the right, or starboard, by putting the helm to larboard.

Porta (Latin), the gate of a city, citadel, or other open space, enclosed by a wall, in contradistinction to *janua*, which was the door or entrance to any covered building.

Portal, the arch over a door or gateway; an entrance under cover.

Portcullis, a strong defensive framework of timber, hung in grooves within the chief gateway of a fortress, or a castle, or an edifice of safety: it resembles the harrow, but is placed vertically, having a row of iron spikes at the bottom, and is let down to stop the passage in case of assault.

Portico, in architecture, a covered walk supported by columns, and usually vaulted; a piazza or arched pathway. (For the different plans and denominations of porticoes, see 'Rudimentary Architecture,' Part I.)

Porticus (Latin), a walk covered with a roof which is supported by columns. A portico was either attached to temples and public buildings, or it was built independent of any other edifice.

Porticus (*deinde*). In the houses of the Roman citizens, between the atrium (hall, or servants' room) and the inner court, there was usually a room called the *tablinum* (corridor), mentioned by Vitruvius. This porticus lay betwixt the atrium and the cavædiom. The reason for his giving it this round form may be upon two accounts: first, to give a greater grace to its projection, and to make the forepart of it serve for a more beautiful vestibulum to the house; and in the next place, as being designed for a shelter in tempestuous weather, it the better broke the force of those winds that blew on that side than if it had been more square.

Porticus. By the Romans this was a common name given to all buildings that had walks under the cover of a roof or ceiling, supported by pillars or pilasters, though differently called, according to the disposition of the pillars: when placed on the outside of a building, as round some of their temples, it was called *peripterium ;* when these ranges of pillars were within a room, as they were sometimes in their *triclinia, basilicæ, atria,* and temples, the void space betwixt the pillars and the side walls was called *alæ ;* but when pillars surrounded courts, and had walks betwixt them and the walls, these ranges of pillars were called *peristylia,* and the walk betwixt was called a *porticus.*

Portland stone, an alkaline sandstone, of a dull whitish colour, heavy and moderately hard, and somewhat flat texture, and composed of large rounded grit, cemented together by an earthy spar, and intermixed with numerous glittering spangles of pure spar; the grit splits in the cutting of the stone, so that it is capable of being brought to a surface very smooth and equal: it will not strike fire with a steel, and burns to a slight ashen hue. It has been and is much used for all kinds of buildings, particularly in the large structures in London: it is brought from the island of Portland, in Dorsetshire.

Post, an upright timber in a building; those used in modern roofs are called king-posts or queen-posts, according to their number and position.

Post Meridiem (P.M.), after mid-day.

Postern, a small doorway or gateway at the back of a building; a small doorway for private communication with the exterior of a castle or fortress.

Postique, in architecture, an ornament of sculpture superadded when the original plan has been completed.

Pot-metal, a species of stained glass, the colours of which are incorporated within the glass while in a state of fusion.

Poudrette, a French word, signifying powdered dung; but the word is applied, when treating of human excrement, in its meaning to the solid of that soil after the liquid manure has discharged itself. In a vine-growing district near Paris (see article *Fosses d'aisances*) poudrette was used for manure, and, although the application of it produced a great abundance of fruit, yet the wine proved very inferior to that which had been previously made on the same ground.

Power, in mechanics: this denotes a force which, being applied to a machine, tends to produce motion or pressure.

Power, horse, in mechanics, an expression used to denote the power of a steam-engine, that is to say, how many horses' work it will save. If a horse standing still can by his strength keep a weight of 169lbs. from falling, when suspended over a pulley, he will exert 121lbs. at two miles per hour; 100lbs. at three; 81lbs. at four; 64lbs. at five; 49lbs. at six; 36lbs. at seven; 25lbs. at eight; 16lbs. at nine; 9lbs. at ten; 4lbs. at eleven; and 1lb. at twelve miles per hour.

Power-loom, in mechanics, a loom moved by the mechanical force of steam, wind, water, etc., as contradistinguished from handweaving.

Poyhtell, paving formed into small lozenges or squares laid diagonally.

Præcinctiones, the passages or corridors which separated the several ranges of seats in an ancient Roman theatre.

Pressure of fluids consists of two kinds, elastic and non-elastic. The first is comprehended in the science of pneumatics, the second in that of hydrostatics. Both classes of fluids deviate from solid substances in their greater distribution of any pressure to which they may be subjected. Thus solid bodies press downwards only by the force of gravity; all fluids, on the contrary, press not only in this direction, but upwards, sideways, and every way equally. The incompressibility of water renders it serviceable by this principle, in the hydrostatic press.

Preventer bolts, those which are driven at the lower end of the preventer plates, to assist the strain of the chain-bolts.

Preventer plates, in ships, plates of iron below the links of the chains.

Pricker, a thin piece of iron, used to make a hole for the fusee or match to fire a blast.

Prill, a solid piece of ore, a specimen.

Priming, the effect engendered by having too little steam room in the boiler of a steam-engine. Minute particles of water being carried into the cylinder, collect in a body, which obstructs the passage of the piston, and causes a considerable loss of power.

Prince's metal, in metallurgy, an alloy of copper. In imitation of silver, in which the proportion of zinc is greater than in brass.

Principal brace, a brace immediately under the principal rafters or parallel to them, in a state of compression, assisting with the principals to support the timbers of a roof: they are employed in the present roof of St. Paul's church, Covent Garden.

Priory, a monastic establishment for the devotional requirements and maintenance of a religious fraternity, under the government of a prior. Many priories were formerly scattered over Britain.

Prism, in geometry, a body or solid whose two-thirds are any plane figures which are parallel, equal, and similar, and its sides parallelograms.

Prism, in optics, a triangular bar of glass, well known from the effect it produces on a ray of light transmitted through it: this effect is a decomposition of the light into its component emanations, consisting of the three primary colours and the secondary tints arising from their intermixture, which together form what is termed the *solar spectrum*. The lensic prism is a new optical glass, in which the powers of the lens and prism are combined.

Prison, an edifice, unfortunately mostly of large dimensions, for the confinement of persons warring against society.

Profile, the outline of a series of mouldings, or of any other parts, as shown by a section through them.

Profile of an Order, in architecture, an assemblage and arrangement of essential and subservient parts. That profile is preferable wherein the parts are few, varied, and fitly applied. Some member should predominate in each division, which it should appear the office of the other parts to fortify, support, or shelter. In a cornice the corona is supported by modillions, dentils, ovolos, etc., and sheltered and covered from the effects of the weather by its cyma or cavetto.

Projectile, in mechanics, a body put in motion by an external force.

Projectiles, in mechanics, that branch which considers the mass, velocity, range, etc., of a heavy body projected into void space by an external force, and then left to the free action of gravity.

Projection, in geometry, drawing, etc., a plan or delineation; in chemistry, the crisis of an operation.

Projecture, in architecture, the out-jutting or prominence which the moulding and members have beyond the plane of a wall or column.

Prolate, in geometry, an epithet applied to a spheroid produced by the revolution of a semi-ellipsis about its long diameter.

Pronaos, the area immediately before a temple. The term is often used for the portico in front of a building. The porticus in one front corresponds to the pronaos in the other: in some temples, the cella was entered through both. The generality of Grecian temples had two approaches.

Proportion, in architecture, the magnitude of one part as compared with some other. The term 'proportion' is used absolutely in the sense of 'good proportion,' although everything that has shape has proportions of some kind or other. The subject of proportion has been greatly mystified by writers, who have laid down certain fixed proportions as the best of all on every occasion, and as the *ne plus ultra* of artistic taste. But fixed proportions can be followed mechanically by every one alike; whereas it requires ability to deviate successfully from routine measurement, and apply the *poco più* or the *poco meno* as the particular occasion or the particular effect aimed at may require—at least, justify. It is the eye that takes cognizance of proportions; and the architect's own eye ought to be quite as correct as that of other people.

Proportion, that branch of mathematical science which defines the ratio of numbers or quantities to each other.

Proportions of rooms should be suited to the purposes for which they are used; all figures, from the square to one and a half the breadth of the room, may be employed for the plan. Some have extended the plan to a double square. Galleries may be from five to eight times their breadth. The height, if with flat ceilings, is not required to be so great as in those that are covered. The height of square apartments should not exceed five-sixths the side of the square, nor be less than four-fifths; but in rooms that are oblong, the height ought to be equal to the breadth. The height of square rooms that are covered should be equal to one of the sides of the square; but covered oblong rooms require a height equal to the breadth, added to one-fifth, one-quarter, or, at most, one-third of the difference between their length and breadth. The height of galleries should be from one and three-fifths at most, to one and one-third at least, of their breadth. Cornices and dressings in the interior of houses are always to be kept more delicate than those on the outside.

Propylæum, in Greek architecture, the porch of a temple or great hall.

Propylæa: the entrance to a Greek temple, a sacred enclosure, consisted of a gateway flanked by buildings, whence the plural of the word. The Egyptian temples generally had magnificent propylæa, consisting of a pair of oblong truncated pyramids of solid masonry, the faces of which were sculptured with hieroglyphics. The word, however, is generally used to signify the entrance to the Acropolis of Athens, which was the last completed of the great works of architecture executed under the administration of Pericles. Pausanias relates that " there is only one entrance to the acropolis, it being in every remaining part of its circuit a precipice, and fortified with strong walls. This entrance was fronted by a magnificent building, called the propylæa, covered with roofs of white marble, which surpassed for beauty, and the dimensions of the marble, all that he had before seen." The building was commenced during the administration of Pericles, and finished in five years, Mnesicles being the architect, at the expense of 2,012 talents, or nearly £464,000 sterling. There were five gates to the propylæa, and before it stood two lofty piers, on each of which was placed an equestrian statue, supposed to be the sons of Xenophon. On the right of the propylæa was the temple of Victory without wings, whence is a prospect of the sea; and from this place it was said that Ægeus threw himself down headlong, and died. On the left of the propylæa was an edifice adorned with paintings, the work of Polygnotus, of which, says Pausanias, though some were effaced by time, there still remained those of Diomedes and Ulysses, the one bearing off the bow and arrows of Philoctetes from Lemnos, the other, the Palladium from Troy. There were those also of Orestes slaying Ægisthus, and Pylades encountering the sons of Nauplius, who had come to succour Ægisthus; Polyxena, at the sepulchre of Achilles, about to be sacrificed, and Ulysses addressing himself to Nausicaa and her maidens, as described by Homer. Several other pictures in the same place are described by Pausanias. These three contiguous buildings originally formed one front, occupying the whole breadth of the rock from side to side, at its western end, so that the only admission into the acropolis was through the middle building, the five gates of which are still remaining, and prove it to have been the propylæa. It may be supposed that the Hermes Propylæus was here placed, and perhaps the Graces, a piece of Sculpture by the hand of Socrates, in which that celebrated philosopher, deviating from the practice of the sculptors who preceded him, had represented them not naked but clothed.

Other sculptors are also mentioned by Pausanias who seem to have decorated this stately entrance.

Proscenium, the area in front of the scene of a theatre, which was perceived when the pulpitum was removed, and when it is probable the temporary scenes were taken away in order to exhibit the front of the permanent scene.

Prostyle, a temple which has a portico in one front, consisting of insulated columns with their entablatures and fastigium. When the temple had a portico in both fronts, it was termed amphi-prostyle, or prostyle in all parts.

Protractor, in surveying and trigonometry, an instrument by which angles taken in the field with a theodolite-circumferentor are represented on paper.

Prow, in navigation, the head or fore-part of a ship, in opposition to the poop or stern.

Prussian Blue, otherwise called Berlin blue, Parisian blue, Prussiate of iron, cyanide of iron, or, in language more pedantically chemical, per-ferro-cyanate of iron, with alumine, etc., is rather a modern pigment, produced by the combination of the prussic or hydrocyanic acid, iron, and alumine. It is of a deep and powerful blue colour, of vast body and considerable transparency, and forms tints of much beauty with white-lead, though they are by no means equal in purity and brilliancy to those of cobalt or ultramarine, nor have they the perfect durability of the latter.

Prussian Brown is a preparation of Prussian blue from which the blue colouring principle has been expelled by fire, or extracted by an alkaline ley: it is an orange-brown, of the nature and properties of Siena earth, and dries well in oil.

Prussian Green. The pigment celebrated under this name is an imperfect prussiate of iron, or Prussian blue, in which the yellow oxide of iron superabounds, or to which yellow tincture of French berries has been added, but is not in any respect superior as a pigment to the compounds of Prussian blue and yellow ochre. A better sort of Prussian green is formed by precipitating the prussiate of potash with nitrate of cobalt.

Prussiate of Copper differs chemically from Prussian blue only in having copper instead of iron for its basis. It varies in colour from russet to brown, is transparent and deep, but being very liable to change in colour by the action of light or by other pigments, it has been very little employed by artists.

Pryan, in mining, that which is productive of ore, but does not break in large stones, but only in pebbles with a mixture of clay.

Pseudo-dipteral, a temple which has a single range of columns in the flanks, at the same distance from the walls of the cella as though the temple had been dipteral.

Pteroma, the spaces between the walls of the cella of a temple and the columns of a peristyle; called also *ambulatio*.

Puddling, in metallurgy, a process in the refining of iron which consists in stirring it actively about.

Pulley, one of the six mechanical powers. The pulley is a small wheel turning on an axis, with a rope or chain passing over it. The circumference is generally grooved to receive the rope, which is attached on the one end to the moving power, and on the other to the resisting force. Pulleys are of two kinds—fixed and movable. The fixed pulley gives no mechanical advantage, but is of great utility in altering the direction in which it may be applied. The movable, on the contrary, doubles the power, which may be increased in any ratio by adding to the number of pulleys. In a combination of pulleys, the advantage, however, is greatly diminished by the friction of the axles and of the ropes. Too complex a combination therefore would not be of service, as the friction would be increased without a proportional advantage, and from the complexity of the machine would be more liable to be put out of order.

Pulpit, an elevated stage or desk from which sermons are delivered.

Pulpitum, the wooden stage of the theatre upon which the mimic as well as dramatic exhibitions of the Romans were represented. In the Greek theatre, the pulpitum was used only by the histriones, or performers in the drama, and was probably removed before the amusements of the orchestra were exhibited.

Pulvinated. A frieze whose face is convex instead of plain is said to be pulvinated, from its supposed resemblance to the side of a cushion, which swells out when pressed upon.

Pump, an engine for raising liquids, made in various forms, of more or less complexity of parts and effectiveness of action, depending in its simplest form upon the external pressure of the air on the surface of the water, and in other forms deriving its power from the abstraction of the air within the tube or barrel. The simplest form of pump is that of the common lift-pump, which consists of a straight tube with two valves, one of which is fitted to the lower end of the tube, and the other is made to slide air-tight in the cavity of the tube or barrel. Both of these valves are adapted to open upwards only, and thus the water is admitted and lifted from the lower part of the tube to the discharge aperture above. This pump acts by the pressure of the atmosphere upon the external body of water from which the supply is raised, but by the forcing-pump water may be raised above the level to which it is driven by the pressure of the atmosphere. The forcing-pump consists of a barrel fitted with a solid piston or forcer, the barrel being also provided with a branch forcing-pipe. The lower part of the barrel and the branch-pipe are each fitted with a valve opening upwards, and by repeated strokes of the piston, the pressure of the air from above being removed, the fluid is brought up to fill the space between the two valves, and being prevented from returning by the lower valve, it passes through the upper valve of the branch-pipe into a capacious upper vessel, and there accumulating, may be ejected in a constant instead of intermittent stream. The lift-pump, being simple and economical in construction, is well fitted for extensive works in which the quantity of water to be raised is considerable, and is therefore usually employed in works for supplying water for towns. The pumps used at the Metropolitan and other waterworks are of great size, and deliver immense volumes of water at each stroke. Those used at Haarlem are 63 inches in diameter, and the pistons have a stroke of 10 feet in length. Each pump delivers 6 tons of water at each stroke. Pumps of this magnitude are worked by water or steam power. Those at Haarlem, eleven in number, are worked simultaneously by a steam-engine, having two steam-cylinders, one within the other, the larger being 12 and the smaller 7 feet in diameter, with a stroke of 10 ft. (See *Forcing Pump*.)

Pump. Mr. Appold's centrifugal pump for draining marshes, and for other purposes, will discharge 10 gallons of water per minute, cubic contents. From various experiments, it has been found that the larger model with the curved vanes does the most duty, on account of its receiving and delivering the water more obliquely: it will discharge 1,800 gallons per minute, with 607 revolutions, but does the most duty at 535 revolutions, discharging 1,400 gallons; therefore, if a pump 1 inch diameter raise 10 gallons, and another 1 foot diameter 1,440 gallons, it follows that one

	gals. per min.
10 feet diameter, of the best shape, will pump	140,000
20 ditto, ditto . . .	560,000
40 ditto, ditto . . .	2,240,000

To do the above duty, the circumference of the 20-feet pump would be required to travel 560 yards per minute, which would be only 53¼ revolutions, and the 40-feet 26⅝.

From the results of various experiments, it has been found that the loss of power would not be more than 25 per cent. It will be observed, the centrifugal force is not so much in the large diameter, on account of the water moving more in a straight line; but that is compensated for by the force being applied to a greater depth of water, being 10 feet in the 40-feet, and only 3 inches in the 1-foot.

	ft. high.
159 revolutions, with the 1-foot, will raise the water, without discharging any,	1
318 revolutions	4
636 ditto	16
1272 ditto	64

The highest elevation to which

6 tons of water 5 feet 6 inches high per minute, there is no greater strain on any part of the pump than 160 lbs. on the 6-inch drum, which is equal to a leverage of 3 inches. (See the results of various experiments in the following Table.) It will pass almost anything that is small enough to go through, there being no valves. A quantity of nut-galls (about ½ a gallon) were thrown into the 1-foot pump all at once, when it was at full speed, and they passed through without breaking one.

Dimensions of the Pump.

Diameter . . . . . 1 foot.
Width . . . . . . 3 inches.
Contents . . . . . 1 gallon.

Table of Mean Results of various Experiments with Mr. Appold's Centrifugal Pump.

No. of revolutions per minute of 6-inch drum and pump.	Number of gallons raised 5 feet 6 inches high per minute.	Equivalent in lbs. raised 1 foot high per minute.	Strain in lbs., on a drum of 4 ft. diameter driving one of 6 in. diameter, as measured by a dynamometer.	Equivalent strain on the steam-engine, rated in lbs. raised 1 foot high per minute.	Percentage of work done compared with power expended.
400	500	27,500	74	44,400	61·7
412	600	33,000	80	49,440	66·7
427	700	38,500	87	55,723	69·
440	800	44,000	94	62,010	70·9
453	900	49,500	100	67,950	72·8
474	1000	55,000	106	75,366	72·9
481	1100	60,500	113	81,479	74·2
495	1200	66,000	118	87,615	75·3
518	1300	71,500	121	94,017	76·
535	1400	77,000	126	101,115	76·1
563	1500	82,500	134	113,163	72·9
580	1600	88,000	138	120,060	73·3
595	1700	93,500	142	126,733	73·6
607	1800	99,000	150	136,575	72·5

Pump, marine, a machine to draw water out of a ship's hold.

Pump-chain. This consists of a long chain with valves at proper distances, working on two wheels, one above and one below, and passing down through one wooden tube and returning upwards by another.

Pump-cistern, to receive the water from the pumps.

Pump-dales, pipes to convey water from the pump-cisterns through the ship's sides.

Pumping-engine, a steam-engine for raising water.

Punch, in mining, a piece of timber, used as a support for a roof.

Punch, a tool for making an impression, or for forcing a hole through a plate.

Puncheon, a measure of liquids containing eighty-four gallons.

Puncheons, small upright timbers in wooden partitions, now usually called studs or quarters; they are placed upright between two posts whose bearing is too great, serving, together with them, to sustain some large weight.

Punching and Plate-cutting Machine. The operation of punching holes through thick metal plates requires machinery of a very massive description, on account of the violent strains to which it is subjected; and the power of these machines being exerted only at intervals, it is necessary to apply some means of rendering the motion tolerably uniform, and thereby diminishing as much as possible the violence of the strain. This is effected by setting in motion a heavy fly-wheel, so that the power expended in giving a certain velocity to the wheel shall be stored up till the operation of punching commences, which tends to retard the motion: the accumulated power in the wheel will then tend to maintain the speed, and thus an approximation to uniform motion is obtained.

The machine consists of a strong frame, at the front of which is a broad slide, moved vertically up and down by an eccentric fixed on the end of a shaft passing lengthwise through the frame: on this shaft there is a large wheel, which receives motion from a pinion on another shaft carrying the fly-wheel and driving-pulleys. The punches, the number of which varies according to the size of the holes, are fixed in the lower end of the vertical sliding-piece, and immediately under them is fixed a piece of steel, called the dies, which has holes in it to correspond with the punches. The plate in which holes are to be punched is fastened upon a travelling table in front of the machine; and the slide being up, and the surface of the table level with that of the dies, the part where the holes are to be punched is placed between the punches and the dies, so that when the machine is set in motion, the punches are forced through the plate by the action of the eccentric, and the pieces driven out fall through the holes in the dies: after the punches have risen above the surface of the plate, the travelling table is set forward to the required distance by self-acting apparatus, and the operation is repeated by the machine till the required number of holes has been punched.

The plate-cutting apparatus consists of two steel-plates, forming a pair of shears: the lower plate is fixed on the frame of the machine, and the upper one is attached to a slide, as in the case of the punches, acting in a similar manner. The shears are moved by the same shaft as the punches, and act while the punches are being raised; sometimes they are placed at the top of the punching-slide.

Punt, in navigation, a sort of oblong, flat-bottomed, small boat, with a square head and stern.

Purbeck-stone, an alkaline sandstone, harsh and rough, of a disagreeable ash colour, very heavy, and moderately hard; of a texture not very compact, but somewhat porous, and composed of an angular grit, cemented together by an earthy spar. It cuts freely, and with a tolerably even or smooth surface, but will not take a polish; it is used principally in London. The quarries are in the island of Purbeck, Dorsetshire.

Purlins, in carpentry, those pieces of timber that lie across the rafters on the inside, to keep them from sinking in the middle.

Purple, the third and last of the secondary colours, is composed of red and blue, in the proportions of five of the former to eight of the latter, which constitutes a perfect purple, or one of such a hue as will neutralize and best contrast a perfect yellow in the proportion of thirteen to three of surface or intensity. It forms, when mixed with its co-secondary colour, green, the tertiary colour olive, and when mixed with the remaining secondary orange, it constitutes the tertiary colour russet.

Purple Black is a preparation of madder, of a deep purple hue, approaching to black; its tints, with white-lead, are of a purple colour. It is very transparent and powerful, glazes and dries well in oil, and is a durable and eligible pigment, belonging perhaps to the semi-neutral class of marrone.

Purple Lake. The best purple lake, so called, is prepared from cochineal, and is of a rich and powerful colour, inclined to crimson. Its character as a pigment is that of a cochineal lake, already described. It is fugitive both in glazing and tint, but used in considerable body, as in the shadows of draperies, etc., it will last under favourable circumstances a long time. Lac lake resembles it in colour, and may supply its place more durably, although not perfectly so.

Purple Ochre, or *Mineral Purple,* is a dark ochre, a native of the forest of Dean, in Gloucestershire. It is of a murrey or chocolate colour, and forms cool tints of a purple hue, with white. It is of a similar body and opacity, with darker colour than Indian red, which has also been classed among purples, but in all other respects it resembles that pigment. It may be prepared artificially, and some natural red ochres burn to this colour, which has been employed under the denomination of *violet de mar.*

Purple wood is from the Brazils, imported in logs from 8 to 12 inches square, and 8 to 10 feet long, principally used for ramrods, buhl-work, marquetry, and turnery.

Purser, the cashier or paymaster of mines; also the paymaster of a ship.

Pursuivant, in heraldry, a messenger who formerly attended the king in his wars, or at the council table, and ultimately became herald.

Puteal, the enclosure surrounding the opening of a well, to protect persons from falling into it. It was either round or square, from 3 to 4 feet high. There is a round one in the British Museum, made of marble.

Putlogs or *Putlocks,* in building, are short pieces of timber about 7 feet long, used in building scaffolds. They lie at right angles to the wall, with one of their ends resting upon it, and the other upon the poles which lie parallel to the side of the wall of the building.

Putlog-holes, small holes left in walls for the use of the workmen in erecting scaffolding.

Putty, in the arts, a kind of paste used by glaziers, composed of whiting and linseed oil (with or without white-lead), beaten together to the consistence of a tough dough.

Puzzolano, or *Puazzolano,* in mineralogy, a volcanic sand of a violet red colour (the *pulvis Puteoli* of Pliny), brought from Italy, which forms a cement that hardens under water. It appears to be a species of argillaceous earth that probably has been calcined and then ejected from a volcano. Its constituents are silex, alumina, oxide of iron, and a little lime. It was first dug out of the earth by the Romans near the town of Puzzoli, not far from Vesuvius. The environs of Rome furnish it equally. It has been found in France in the extinct volcanoes of Vivarez. There are a few regions exposed to igneous agency which are destitute of it, but it presents itself under very different physical appearances, — sometimes pulverulent, sometimes in coarse grains, often in slag, pumice, tufa, etc. Its colour, which is generally brown, passes to yellow, grey, and black.

The only preparation this material undergoes previous to use is that of pounding or grinding and sifting, whereby it is reduced to powder, in which state it is beaten to a proper consistency with a due proportion of lime. Artificial puzzolano is also much used, and is produced by pulverizing the clay, the psammite, or the arene, which is soluted, and the strewing a layer of it, about four-tenths of an inch, on a plate of iron, heated to a point between a cherry-red and forging-heat. It is left till it be raised to the same degree, for a space of time which varies, for each kind of material, from five to twenty minutes. It must be continually stirred with a small rod, in order that the whole of the particles may be uniformly calcined.

Pycnostyle, that arrangement of Greek or Roman columns, in which the intercolumniations are equal to one diameter and a half of the lower part of the shaft.

Pyramid, in geometry, is a solid figure whose base is a polygon, and whose sides are plane triangles, their several points meeting in one.

Pyrites, in mineralogy, a name given to certain metallic ores containing a large portion of sulphur, native compounds of sulphur with different metals, and more especially with iron. The term is derived from the use to which the stone was formerly applied, that of obtaining sparks by percussion, an application of pyrites mentioned by Pliny.

Pyrites, Copper, in mineralogy, a combination (sulphuret) of copper and sulphur, being the most common ore of copper.

Pyrites, Iron, in mineralogy, a combination (sulphuret) of iron and sulphur, one of the most abundant minerals in nature.

Pyrometer, in chemistry, an instrument for measuring very high temperatures, depending on the uniform and permanent contraction of pure clay.

Pyrometer, a contrivance for ascertaining the temperature of the flues of boilers, by fixing an iron wire at the back of the flue, and connecting it to a lever in front of the boiler, which indicates the degree of expansion and consequently the temperature.

Pyx, Pix, a tabernacle or shrine, a depository for the Host, or consecrated wafer, used in Romish ceremonies. (See *Theoreca*.)

Pyx, in navigation, the box in which the nautical compass is suspended.

Q

QUADRA, in architecture, a name given by Vitruvius to the square piece, commonly called the socle, used to support the pedestals of statutes, vases, and other ornaments.

Quadræ, the bands or fillets of the Ionic base, between which the scotia or hollow occurs; also the plinth, or lower members of the podium.

Quadrangle, a figure having four angles and four sides.

Quadrant, the fourth part of a circle, being bounded by two radii perpendicular to each other, and a quarter of the circumference, or 90 degrees.

Quadrature, the finding a square equal in area to another figure.

Quadrifores, folding-doors whose height was divided into two. Folding-doors which opened in one height were termed *fores valvatæ*, or *valvæ*. Vitruvius directed the doorways to be made wider when these were used, and the height to be increased when the folding-doors were divided in height. The *bifores* of Vitruvius were two single doors.

Quarry, a place underground from

whence are taken marble, freestone, slate, limestone, and other stones proper for building and paving.

Quarry, a pane or piece of glass cut in a lozenge or diamond form.

Quarter, in heraldry: this word is sometimes used for an escutcheon or coat of arms: there are sixteen quarters required to prove nobility.

Quarter (ships), the afterpart of the top-side.

Quarters, in building, those slight upright pieces of timber placed between the puncheons and posts, used to lath upon. These are of two sorts, single and double: the single quarters are sawn to 4 inches thick and 4 inches broad; the double quarters are sawn to 4 inches square. It is a rule in carpentry that no quarters be placed at a greater distance than 14 inches.

Quarter-deck, in ship-building, the short upper deck from the aftermost end of the main chains to the stern.

Quarter-gallery, the projecting convenience and ornament of the top-side which is connected with the stern.

Quarter-pieces, the carved figures at the aftpart of the quarter-gallery which joins to the taffrail, and forms the boundary of the stern.

Quartering, in heraldry, the act of dividing a coat of arms into four or more quarters, by parting, couping, etc., by perpendicular and horizontal lines. The sovereign of Great Britain in the first quarter bears gules, the lions passant, *or*, etc.; in the second, formerly, azure, three fleurs-de-lis, etc.

Quatrefoil, an ornament of frequent occurrence in Gothic architecture, formed by a moulding disposed in four segments of circles.

Quears, in mining, crevices in lodes.

Queen-post, a vertical timber, supporting the rafters of a trussed roof.

Quercitron Lake, or *Quercitron Yellow*, is what its name implies. It is dark in substance, in grains of a glossy fracture, perfectly transparent, and when ground is of a beautiful yellow colour, more durable than the common yellow lakes, although not perfectly permanent.

Quick lime, such lime as is in the caustic or most active state, and which possesses the greatest power of operating upon different substances with which it may come in contact. It is quite the opposite in its qualities and properties to that which has fallen down into a powdery state, in consequence of being saturated with water and carbonic acid gas or fixed air, or, which is slaked and become effete.

Quick-work, the short pieces between the ports withinside a ship.

Quink, in building, a piece of ground taken out of any regular ground-plot or floor: thus, if the ground-plot be oblong or square, a piece taken out of a corner to make a court or yard, etc., is called a quink.

Quirk, a small acute channel or recess, much used between mouldings in Gothic architecture; in Grecian architecture ovolos and ogees are usually quirked at the top, and sometimes in Roman.

Quoins of stone, the corners of brick or stone walls: when they stand out beyond the brickwork, they are called 'rustic quoins.'

R.

RABBET, that part of the keel, stern and stern-post of a ship which is cut for the plank of the bottom to fit into; the edges of plank or deal for bulkheads that are lapped one over the other, and wrought square, making each side of the bulkhead a smooth surface to the distance of two rooms and spaces.

Rack, in mining, an inclined plane on

which the ore and slime are washed and separated.

Rack, a flat bar with teeth on one side, to work into those of a pinion.

Racking, in mining, a process of separating small ores from the earthy particles by means of an inclined wooden frame: the impurities being washed off, the ore remaining near the head of the rock is taken from thence, and undergoes tossing.

Radiant point, any point from which rays proceed.

Radius, in geometry, the semi-diameter of a circle, or a right line drawn from the centre to the line of circumference; in anatomy, a bone of the fore-arm, which accompanies the ulna from the elbow to the wrist.

Radius-rods, the guiding rods in a parallel motion, jointed to the connecting-links, to counteract the vibratory motion communicated by the beam, by guiding the links so that there is a point.

Rafters, in carpentry, the secondary timbers of a house; the timbers let into the great beam.

Rag-stone, in mineralogy. The Kentish rag-stone is a kind of limestone, much preferred to other stones of a similar nature. It is found in beds varying from 6 inches to 3 feet in thickness, and is composed of the following substances: carbonate of lime, with a little magnesia, 92·6; earthy matter, 6·5; oxide of iron, 0·5; carbonaceous matter, 0·4 = 100. This stone is now much used.

Rail or *life guards*, in locomotive engines, strong iron rods reaching down within about 2 inches of the rails, to catch and throw to one side any obstruction which may be on the rails.

Rails, the moulding ornaments in the top-side, likewise in the head and stern of a ship.

Railways; roads in which tracks of iron or other smooth material are laid for the easy passage of wheel-carriages, appear to have been introduced between the years 1600 and 1650, in the neighbourhood of Newcastle, to facilitate the carriage of the coals from the pits, in 'wains' or waggons, to the 'staythes' or discharging-places on the Tyne. In 1676 they were described to be thus formed: "The manner of the carriage is by laying rails of timber from the colliery to the river, exactly straight and parallel; and bulky carts are made, with four rollers fitting those rails, whereby the carriage is so easy, that one horse will draw down four or five chaldrons of coals." These "rails of timber" were laid upon transverse timbers or sleepers, and secured with pegs of wood, the sleepers being embedded in the material of the roadway.

Before the year 1716, it became the practice to preserve the edges of the rails by nailing thin plates of malleable iron upon their upper surfaces in places where the draught was harder than usual. About the year 1767, cast-iron bars were substituted for the wooden rails, and this change is said to have been suggested by the wish of the iron-masters to keep their furnaces at work during a season of unusual depression in the market value of their manufactures. These iron bars were found too valuable to admit of a return to the wooden rails, and improvements of various kinds were introduced. Thus the rails were cast in the form of long narrow plates, with a vertical rim along one side (the transverse section resembling the form of the letter L), and thus the wheels of the waggons were retained in their places without the projecting rims or flanges which were required for wheels running on the plain rails or bars. These rails were called 'tram' or 'plate rails,' and thus distinguished from subsequent forms of iron rails which were introduced to dispense with the longitudinal timbers heretofore required beneath them, by casting the rails of sufficient depth to carry their load, and of reduced width, the flanged-wheels being returned to. Malleable-iron rails were introduced about the year 1815, at coalworks in Cumberland, with a view to remedy the defect of frequent breakage, to which those of cast-iron were liable: these malleable-iron rails were simply bars of iron from 2 to 3 feet in length, and 1 to 2 inches square; but the narrowness of their surface was found to injure the wheels so severely, that the restoration of cast-iron rails appeared likely, when an ingenious invention was made by Mr. Birkinshaw, who obtained a patent in October, 1820, for his improvements, which consisted in passing bars of iron, red-hot, between rollers having indentations in their peripheries, corresponding with the intended shape of the rails. By this mode malleable-iron rails were rolled in lengths of 12 or 15 feet each, and could be formed in any required shape, the section varying throughout the length, so as to give increased depth and width at the points intermediate between the intended bearing places. The rails now generally used are produced in a similar manner, and the permanent way consists of a levelled surface of roadway formed with metalling or suitable ballasting, transverse sleepers, commonly of larch, about 9 feet in length, 8 to 10 inches in width, and about 6 inches deep. These sleepers are laid from 2 feet 6 inches to 3 feet apart, and saddles or chairs of cast iron are fastened upon them with spikes. Two of these chairs are fixed upon each sleeper, at such distance apart that the rails, when placed in them, shall have the intended distance or *gauge* between them, commonly 4 feet 8½ inches. The rails are parallel throughout, and of a form resembling that of the letter $=$ laid on one side, the depth of the rail being about 5 inches, the width over the top and bottom about 2½ inches, and the thickness of the middle vertical rib about ¾ inch; all the angles of the section being carefully removed by rounding the meetings of the several surfaces. For the 'broad gauge,' in which the rails are laid 7 feet apart, continuous longitudinal timbers, about 12 inches square, are employed, and connected by cross-timbers framed to them. The rails are of a bridged or arched section, and rolled with a projecting plate along each side, bolts passing through which secure the rails to the longitudinal timbers.

The theory of a perfect railway requires that it should be level in its vertical position and uniform in direction. Practically, these conditions are sacrificed within certain limits; but the attainment of great speed and safety, upon the present locomotive system, forbids any very wide extension of them. The consequence is, that great and expensive works are required in earthworks, bridges, viaducts, etc., to obtain the required inclination of surface and direction; and although the principles of construction are the same in all, hardly any two railways are alike in details.

In the following Tables, the principal particulars of main lines, branches, amalgamations, date of acts of authority, length of each portion, and total length of each amalgamated line, with amount of cost, or of estimate, or of capital, in round numbers, are arranged with the view of presenting a clear outline of each railway, whether single or combined, arranged as nearly as practicable in a chronological order; the earliest date of the Act for any of the component lines being adopted as the date for determining the chronological place for the amalgamated line in the Table.

RAILWAYS.

Name of Railway, Amalgamation, Main Line, and Branches.	Date of Acts.	Length of each portion.	Total Length.	Estimate, Cost, or Capital.	
		Miles.	Miles.		£.
Severn and Wye . . .	1853			Estimate	37,620
(Originally Lydney and Ledbrook) . . .	1809				
Descending line throughout from Forest of Dean to Lydney Harbour. Steepest grad. 1 in 40.	1853	3¾		Parliam. Estimate .	30,300 48,974
Stockton and Darlington	1842	40			
For Tramroad from River Tees at Stockton to Witton Park Colliery, with branches		On lease 50	90		
Lease of Middlesbro' and Redcar Line .	1847				
Lease of Wear Valley, including Bishop Auckland and Weardale, Wear and Derwent, Weardale Extension, Shildon Tunnel	1847				
Purchase of Middlesbro' Dock, etc. .	1849				
Financial . .	1851				
Financial . .	1852				
Branch to Shildon Tunnel, new Capital, etc. . . .	1854			Authorized Cap. . Received . . .	2,161,972 2,061,329
Monkland.					
Amalgamation of the Monkland and Kirk . . .	1824			Shares . . . . Loans	246,000 82,000
Ballochney . . .	1826			Shares . . . . Loans	110,000 36,666
Slamannan . . .	1835			Shares . . . . Loans	210,000 70,000
Amalgamation . .	1848	36			
Five connecting Lines, viz. with the Edinburgh and Glasgow, Bathgate Mineral Fields, etc. . .	1853	10½	46½	June 30, 1854 . .	73,085 594,446
London and N.-Western	1846				
Amalgamation of the Lond. & Birmingham also of the Warwick and Leamington, and	1833	112¼			5,500,000

Name of Railway, Amalgamation, Main Line, and Branches.	Date of Acts.	Length of each portion.	Total Length.	Estimate, Cost, or Capital.	
Lond. & N.-W. *continued.*		Miles.	Miles.		£.
Peterboro' Branch, amalgamated with the London & Birm.	1843			Amalgamated Cap. .	8,250,000
Grand Junction	1833	86½		Original Capital. .	1,957,800
(with which was amalgamated in 1840 the				Capital at amalgamation of Chester and Crewe . . .	3,098,369
Chester and Crewe)	1837	20½			458,333
Bolton and Leigh .	1825	10			201,750
Huddersfld. & Manch.	1845				
Manchester & Birm.	1837	38½			2,800,000
Leeds, Dewsbury, and Manchester . . .	1845				799,300
North Union . . .	1831	22½			730,000
(joined with Lanc. and Yorksh. and Preston and Wyre)	1835	19½			400,000
West London . .	1836	3			280,000
Manchester, Buxton, Matlock, & Midlds.	1846	11½			421,300
North and South-western Junction .	1851	4			
Birm., Wolverhampt. and Stour Valley	1846				1,110,000
Buckinghamshire .	1846	41½			793,000
Shropshire Union . including the					
Newton and Crewe	1846			⎫ United Capital ⎧	1,500,000
Chester & Wolvrhmpt.	1846			⎬ £3,300,000, ⎨	1,000,000
Shrewsby. & Stafford.	1846			⎭ viz. : . . . ⎩	800,000
Lancaster and Carlisle				Besides loans . .	1,099,999
Bedford	1845	15½			125,000
Branch from Blackwall Line . .	1852				
Besides powers for new Lines, viz.:					
Northampton & Market Harborough	1853	18½		Estimate	250,000
St. Alban's . . .	1853	7½		Ditto	70,000
Shrewsbury & Crewe.	1853	33		Ditto	350,000
Total length in operation, 1854 . .			553½	Total Share Capital.	25,049,592
				Debenture Debt .	9,993,448
				Deb. 3½ p. c. Stock.	402,830
				Grand Total . . .	35,445,870
Newcastle and Carlisle	1829		78½	Capital	1,749,366
Branch to Alston .					
Do. to Swalwell .					

RAILWAYS.

Name of Railway, Amalgamation, Main Line, and Branches.	Date of Acts.	Length of each portion.	Total Length.	Estimate, Cost, or Capital.
		Miles.	Miles.	£.
West Hartlepool.				
Incorporation of the Stockton & Hartlepool	1842	8		
Clarence	1829	37	45	
Hartlepool West Harbour and Dock Co.				Total Capital .. 1,465,037
Dublin and Kingston (Ireland)	1831	6		
Extension to Dalkey		1½		Total Capital .. 290,000
Extension to Bray	1846	7½		
Hartlepool (leased to York, Newcastle, and Berwick	1832	16		Capital authorized . 531,400
London and Greenwich	1833	3¾		993,000
London and S.-Western				
London & Southampt.	1834	76¾		2,100,000
Southampt. & Dorchr. Branches to Hampton Court, Chertsey, Guildford, Farnham, Alton; to Loudon, Brighton, and S. Coast Railway				
Windsor, Staines, and South-western			267	Total Capital .. 8,856,484
North Union (1831, 22½ miles), vested in London and N.-western, and including the Wigan and Preston and Wigan Branch	1834		42	739,201
Great Western.				
London to Bristol	1835	116¼		
Slough to Windsor		3		
Branch from Reading to Basingstoke		15½		
Branch from Reading to Hungerford		25½		
Branch from Didcot to Oxford		10		
Branch from Oxford to Fenny Compton and Birmingham		65¾		
Branch from Swindon to Gloucester		37		
With branch to Cirencester		4		
Branch from Gloucester to Cheltenham		7½		

RAILWAYS.

Name of Railway, Amalgamation, Main Line, and Branches.	Date of Acts.	Length of each portion.	Total Length.	Estimate, Cost, or Capital.
Gt. Western, *continued*.		Miles.	Miles.	£.
Branch from Chippenham to Westbury, Frome, and Warminster . . .		23½		
Branch from Gloucester to Grange-Court (Dean Forest) . .		7¼		
Total mileage now in operation, including the two Shrewsbury lines (77 miles) . .			419	Tot. authorised Cap. 23,927,627
Llanelly Railway & Dock.				
Dock	1828			
Railway	1835	26		
New Branches . .		7½	33½	Authorized Capital 330,000
Arbroath and Forfar .	1836	15½		Capital 230,350
Bristol and Exeter .	1836	75½		
Branch to Clevedon		4		
Do. Weston		1¼		
Do. Yeovil .		19		
Do. Tiverton .		6	105	Total Capital . . 3,535,794
Working (under lease) also the Crediton line 6 miles, and the Somerset Central line 12 miles.				
Total worked by Bristol and Exeter Co. 123 miles.				
Dublin and Drogheda .	1836	31¾		
Branch to Howth .		3¾	35½	
Transfer of Navan Branch . . .	1846			Total Capital . . 835,000
Dundee and Arbroath .	1836	16¾		140,000
Eastern Counties.				
London to Colchester	1836	51		
Northern and Eastern, from Stratford to Newport, with branch to Hertford	1836	44		
Length of Eastern Counties proper .		235		
Norfolk line . . .		96½		
Eastern Union . . .		95		
Total under the united management of the three companies .			426½	
The same Union will work also the—				

Name of Railway, Amalgamation, Main Line, and Branches.	Date of Acts.	Length of each portion.	Total Length.	Estimate, Cost, or Capital.
		Miles.	Miles.	£.
Eastern Counties, *continued*.				
Shepreth & Hitchin		18½		
Newmarket and Cambridge		15		
Newmarket & Bury		14½		
Harwich		12		
Wisbeach Extension		2½		
Hackney branch		2½		
East Anglian		67		
Tilbury		40		
Beccles & Lowestoft		5¾		
				Exp. to June, 1854. 10,471,071
Hull and Selby	1836	30¾		
Branch from Hull to Bridlington			61	
(Rented to York & North Midland)	1845			Capital on which York & North Midland Co. pays 10 p. c. 700,000
Irish South-eastern. Amalgamation	1846			
of the Great Leinster and Munster from Carlow to Kilkenny	1836			
and Kilkenny to Clonmel	1846			
and of the Wexford, Carlow, and Dublin	1846			
Total length first authorized 89 miles, subsequently reduced to			25	Cap. to June, 1854 270,343
London and Blackwall	1836		3½	1,050,000
Midland. Amalgamation of the N. Midland from Leeds to Derby	1846	74½		
Midland Counties, from Derby to Rugby	1836	58½		
Birmingham & Derby, with fork line to London and North-western, at Hampton	1836	48½		
Total amalgamated length, 181½ miles. The following lines are also incorporated:—				
Bristol and Gloucester,				

Name of Railway, Amalgamation, Main Line, and Branches.	Date of Acts.	Length of each portion.	Total length.	Estimate, Cost, or Capital.
Midland, *continued*.		Miles.	Miles.	£.
and Birmingham and Gloucester . .		95½		
Sheffield & Rotherham		9¼		
Leicester & Swannington		16		
Leeds and Bradford .		43		
Total incorporated lines 345½ miles.				
The following extensions have been authorized and constructed since the amalgamation :—				
Syston & Peterborough		48¼		
Nottingham & Lincoln, & Southwell branch		36		
Leicester and Swannington Extension .		23¼		
Erewash Valley . .		21¼		
Nottingham & Mansfield		12½		
Mansfield & Pinxton .		7½		
Total new branches, 149 miles.				
Grand total length open			494½	Total Capital . . 18,685,299
North-Eastern. Comprising the— York, Newcastle, and Berwick.				
Main line . . 151				
Coal branches in Berwick & Durham . . 99½				
Branches to Alnwick, & Warkworth, & Kelso 35				
Branches in Yorkshire . 44½				
			330	Computed Capital . 6,133,000
York & North Midland	1836			
Main line, York, Normanton, & Knottingley . 26½				
Branches to Scarborough and Whitby . . 53				
Hull to Leeds : 50¼				
Short branches . 133				
			263	6,527,66

RAI RAILWAYS. RAI

Name of Railway, Amalgamation, Main Line, and Branches.	Date of Acts.	Length of each portion.	Total Length.	Estimate, Cost, or Capital.
N.-Eastern, *continued.*		Miles.	Miles.	£.
Leeds Northern	1845			
Main line, Leeds to Stockton		61		
Branches		9		
		70	663	Computed Capital . 741,111
				Computed Capital . 12,501,171
Sheffield, Rotherham, Barnsley, Wakefield, Huddersfield, and Goole.				
Sheffield & Rotherham	1836		5½	268,798
Leased to Lancashire and Yorkshire Co. for £13,000 pr. ann.				
South-Eastern.				
South-Eastern original line from Redhill to near Dover	1836	66		
London & Croydon	1835	8½		
Extension into Dover	1843			
Branch to Maidstone	1843			
Bricklayers' Arms br.	1843			
Canterbury, Ramsgate, & Margate Extens.	1844			
Folkestone branch and Harbour	1844			
Tunbridge Wells br.	1845			
Gravesend and Rochester branches	1845			
Minster & Deal, Ashford & Hastings brs.	1845			
Branches from Rye to Rye Harbour, Tunbridge Wells to Hastings, & "North Kent" br. from the junction with the London and Greenwich to Gravesend. Extension to Rochester, over Canal	1846			
Amalgamation of the Reading, Guildford, & Reigate, the Whitstable & Greenwich, & Coal branch at Charlton to Thames	1852			
Total length			289¾	Total Capital . . 10,903,892

RAI   RAILWAYS.   RAI

Name of Railway, Amalgamation, Main Line, and Branches.	Date of Acts.	Length of each portion.	Total Length.	Estimate, Cost, or Capital.
		Miles.	Miles.	£.
Taff Vale	1836	31¼		
Leased in perpetuity, the Aberdare .	1845	8¼		66,600
Junction line with S. Wales at Cardiff .	1852	12		
Rhondda Valleys brs. are completing.				
Thames Haven . .	1836			
Renewed . . .	1846			
Railway from Eastern Counties line at Romford to Docks at Shell Haven . .		16		300,000
Partly abandoned, in favour of the Lond. Tilbury, & Southend	1853			
Ulster.				
Belfast to Armagh .	1836	36		719,590
West London. Incorporated under the title of Birmingham, Bristol, and Thames Junction	1836	9½		294,687
Lancaster and Preston Junctions . . .	1837	20¼		United Capital . . 567,772
London, Brighton, and South Coast. Amalgamation, 1846, of the Croydon and Brighton Cos., viz.				
London and Croydon	1835	8¾		741,000
London and Brighton	1837	41¼		2,400,000
Branches to Mitcham, Epsom, Eastbourne, Hailsham, Horsham, Lewes, Newhaven, St. Leonards, Hastings, Worthing, Arundel, Chichester, & Portsmouth.				
Crystal Palace branch (opened June, 1854)		1¼		
Total length producing revenue (of which 7¾ miles belong to the Southeastern, and 4½ are held jointly with the South-western)			174	Total Capital . . 7,618,626

Name of Railway, Amalgamation, Main Line, and Branches.	Date of Acts.	Length of each portion.	Total Length.	Estimate, Cost, or Capital.	
L. B. & S. C., *continued.*		Miles.	Miles.		£.
United lines in contemplation.					
Wimbledon and Croydon (from Croydon to Mitcham) Act	1853		2¾		
E. Grinstead agreed to	1853		7		
Bognor do.	1853		6		240,000
Maryport and Carlisle	1837		28	Exp. to Dec. 1853.	458,179
Edinburgh and Glasgow	1838		46		1,200,000
Leasing the Stirling and Dunfermline			21		
Polkemmet branch.					
Cowlairs do.					
Bathgate do.					
Campsie do.			11⅝	Total Capital	3,290,849
Ardrossan	1840		12½	Cost (to 1849)	100,950
Amalgamated with Glasgow and South-western	1854				
Norfolk. Amalgamation (1845) of the Yarmouth and Norwich	1842	20½			
Norwich and Brandon	1844	27½			
Wymondham and Dereham		11¼			
Dereham & Fakenham		12¼			
Branch to Halesworth and Lowestoft		9¼	80¾	Total Capital	2,221,163
South Wales Mineral	1843	12¼		Authorized Capital	113,000
Chester and Holyhead	1844	85			
Including the Mold branch (from Chester to Mold)	1847	13½			
Bangor and Carnarvon	1851	7			
From Chester & Holyhead Railway, near Bangor, to Carnarvon, with a branch to port of Dinorwic			105½		4,289,270
Colchester and Stour Valley.					
Leased to E. Union					
East Lancashire.					
Amalgamation (1846) of the Manchester, Bury, & Rossendale	1844	14		Capital Shares	300,000
				„ Loans	100,000
Extension Act	1846	10		Additional Shares	530,000
				„ Loans	277,931

Name of Railway, Amalgamation, Main Line, and Branches.	Date of Acts.	Length of each portion.	Total Length.	Estimate, Cost, or Capital.	
		Miles.	Miles.		£.
E. Lancashire, *continued.*					
Extension Act	1847	6		Additional Shares	300,000
(Besides branches).				,, Loans	100,000
Blackburn & Preston	1844	9¾		Authorized Shares	120,000
				,, Loans	40,000
Branches authorized	1847	6		Additional Shares	30,000
				,, Loans	10,000
Blackburn, Burnley, Accrington, & Colne Extension, with a branch eastward through Burnley to Colne, and Liverpool, Ormskirk, and Preston	1846	36⅝			
Total length authorized (to June 30, 1854, 81¼ miles were in operation)			88	Exp. to June, 1854	3,869,004
Eastern Union.					
Amalgamation, 1847, of the E. Union (From Colchester to Ipswich).	1844	18			
Ipswich and Bury	1846	27			
Extension from Haughley to Norwich		4			
Trowse br. opened (Connecting the Ipswich and Bury with the E. Union.)	1852	2			
Hadleigh branch		7			
Sudbury branch		12			
Total length authorized about Under the management of the E. Counties (which see).			95	Ord. Share Capital	1,206,900
Great Southern and Western From Dublin to Cork, passing near Portarlington, Thurles, Tipperary, and Mallow, with a branch to Carlow.	1844			Capital—Shares Loans	3,602,381 410,606
North British From Edinburgh to Berwick (junction with York, New-	1844	62			

Name of Railway, Amalgamation, Main Line, and Branches.	Date of Acts.	Length of each portion.	Total Length.	Estimate, Cost, or Capital.
		Miles.	Miles.	£.
N. British, *continued*. castle, & Berwick), with branch to Haddington.				
Edinburgh & Dalkeith purchased	1845	14		
Br. to connect same	1845	2		
Edinburgh & Hawick (powers transferred)	1845	43½		
Branches to Selkirk, Jedburgh, Kelso, Tranent, Cockenzie, North-Berwick, and Dunse	1846	42		
Deviation and short extension	1847			
Total length authorized, of which 149 miles are now open			163	
Lancaster and Carlisle	1844		70	Capital 1,613,903
Whitehaven Junction	1844	12		Shares and Loans . 181,196
Shrewsbury and Chester, or N. Wales Mineral from Chester to Wrexham.	1844			
Extended to Ruabon	1845			
Branches to Coal and Mineral Works, nr. Wrexham	1846			
Total about			25	
South Devon	1844			
From Exeter to Plymouth.				
Branches to Torquay and other places	1846			
Extension into Torquay & to Brixham	1847			
Total length authorized			70	Capital 2,101,564
Aberdeen	1845			
From Guthrie (Arbroath and Forfar) to Aberdeen, with branches to Brechin and Montrose.				
Total length, including leased line			72	Total Capital . . 1,760,932
Belfast and Ballymena	1845			
With branches to Carrickfergus and Randalstown			38	Capital 385,000

Name of Railway, Amalgamation, Main Line, and Branches.	Date of Acts.	Length of each portion.	Total Length.	Estimate, Cost, or Capital.
		Miles.	Miles.	£.
Belfast & Ballymena, *cont*. Extension from Randalstown, through Troome, Castle Dawson, Magherafelt, & Moneymore to Cookstown	1853	27		Estimate 192,500
Blackburn. Amalgamation, 1846, of Blackburn, Darwen, and Bolton and Blackburn, Clitheroe, and N. W. Junction	1845			
Total length auth^d.			47	
Caledonian	1845			
Carlisle to Carstairs		73½		
Carstairs to Edinburgh		26¼		
Carstairs to Glasgow		31¼		Total Capital . . 7,877,413
Cockermouth and Workington	1845	8¼		
Branch from Marron Foot to Bridgefoot	1849	¼		
Cork and Bandon.	1845			
Deviation & Extension into Cork	1848	20		
Dublin & Belfast Junction	1845	56		Capital 1,042,365
Dundalk and Enniskillen	1845			Original Capital. Shares . . 750,000 Loans . . 250,030
East Anglian. Incorporation, 1847, of the Lynn and Ely, with branch to Wisbeach	1845	36½		
Lynn and Dereham	1845	26½		
Ely and Huntingdon	1845	22¾		Capital 1,329,745
Furness	1844	11¾		
Total length (of which 20 are in operation)			22	Capital 396,841
Kendal and Windermere	1845	10¼		Capital 215,519
From the Lancaster and Carlisle at Oxenholme to Birthwaite, near Windermere Lake	1845			
Leeds Northern Extended to Junction with the Stockton and Hartlepool	1846			

Name of Railway, Amalgamation, Main Line, and Branches.	Date of Acts.	Length of each portion.	Total Length.	Estimate, Cost, or Capital.
Leeds Northern, *cont.*		Miles.	Miles.	£.
Powers to connect at Melmerby with the extension at Northallerton	1848			
Branches to Harrogate, etc.	1848			
Total length			71	
Amalgamated with N.-E. (which see)	1854			
Manchester South Junction & Altrincham.	1845			Capital—Shares . . 29,000 Loans . . 133,333
Midland Great Western of Ireland	1845			
From Dublin to Mullingar with a branch to Longford				
Extended to Athlone.	1846			
Extension to Port of Galway	1847			
Deviation of Extension to Longford and branch to Cavan	1852			
Total length authorized			181¼	Combined Capital . 2,126,578
Monmouthshire	1845			Total Capital . . . 830,000
Newry and Enniskillen		45		Capital 119,814
North Devon (late Taw Vale).				
Incorporated 1838, & revived	1845			
From Crediton to Barnstaple, with branch to docks at Freemington Pill.				
Total open		32½		Capital 430,377
Branch to Bideford (promoted by the "Bideford Extension Company") in course of construction	1853	6	38½	
Oxford, Worcester, and Wolverhampton.	1845			
From Wolvercot near Oxford junction with Great Western, through Worcester, to Wolverhampton, with branches			91	Cap. to June 1854. 3,437,676

RAILWAYS.

Name of Railway, Amalgamation, Main Line, and Branches.	Date of Acts.	Length of each portion	Total Length.	Estimate, Cost, or Capital.
		Miles.	Miles.	£.
St. Helen's.				
Amalgamation of the Sankey Brook Navigation, and St. Helen's & Runcorn Gap Railway	1845	7½		
Branch from the original line at Widnes to Garston, 4 miles south of Liverpool; and Docks at Garston	1846	7½		
Branches to Warrington and Blackbrook	1847	4½		
Branches to Rainford junction, and to the Eccleston Coal Fields, and minor branches	1853			Total Capital .. 881,131
Scottish Central	1845			
Powers to construct branches to Tillicoultry, Denny, and Crieff, and minor branches ending at Perth	1846			
Total length authorized (of which 50½ miles are opened)			62	Capital. Consolidated Stock 1,020,000 Preference Shares 151,542
Scottish Midland Junct.	1845			
Perth to Forfar		32½		
Branch to Newtyle		2		
Branch from Coupar Angus to Blairgowrie	1853	4½		
Branch from Drumgley to Kirriemuir	1853	3½	41½	Capital 711,230
South Wales	1845			
From Fishguard Bay, Pembroke, and running thence along the northern shore of the Bristol Channel, through Carmarthen, Llanelly, Swansea, Neath, Cardiff, and New-				

Name of Railway, Amalgamation, Main Line, and Branches.	Date of Acts.	Length of each portion.	Total length.	Estimate, Cost, or Capital.
		Miles.	Miles.	£.
South Wales, *continued.* port, to the west bank of the River Wye at Chepstow, with branch from Newport to Monmouth.				
Leased to Gt. West. in Length authorized	1851		169	
Swansea to Chepstow, opened June, 1851.		75		
Grange Court to Chepstow, East; opened 19th Sept. 1851		19¼		
Swansea to Carmarthen, opened 11th Oct. 1852		30½		
Carmarthen to Haverfordwest, opened Jan. 1854		31		
Forest of Dean, converted from Tramway, July 1854		7¼		Total capital.
Total length opened —163½ miles				Shares . . 2,444,230
				Loans, etc. . . . 1,423,997
Extension of Pembroke line, & branch to Swansea Harbour and Junction with Newport and Pontypool	1853			Estimated cost . . 170,000 Power to borrow . 56,600
Waterford & Kilkenny	1845			
From Waterford to Kilkenny with branch to Kells.		31 6¾		
Total length authorized (of which, main line 31 miles are in operation.)			37¾	Shares & Loans . 599,000
Waterford & Limerick Including branches	1845		75	Capital 1,132,538
Wear Valley.				
Whitehaven & Furness	1845			
From Whitehaven to a junction with the "Whitehaven junction" at Whitehaven, and a junction with the Furness				

Name of Railway, Amalgamation, Main Line, and Branches.	Date of Acts.	Length of each portion.	Total length.	Estimate, Cost, or Capital.	
		Miles.	Miles.		£.
Whitehaven, *continued*, at Foxwell, near Broughton.					
Total length		35			
Branch to harbour	1853	¾		Capital authorized	469,933
Ambergate, Nottingham and Boston, and E. Junction	1846				
(Originally 90 miles but reduced to viz.: from Grantham to Colwick.)		23		Total Capital	760,025
Belfast & County Down	1846				
Average cost per mile, £15,520.					
Buckinghamshire. (Leased to London and North-western). Amalgamation 1847 of the Buckingham and Brockley	1846				
and the Oxford and Bletchley	1846	31½			
Extension, north to Banbury. Line from Claydon to a junction with the Great Western, Oxford, & Rugby line, at Banbury		21½	53	Shares and Loans	1,659,600
Caledonian and Dumbartonshire Junction	1846				
Total in operation		8¼		Capital Expended	239,664
Cork, Blackrock, and Passage	1846				
Cork to Passage West		6¼			
Extension to Monkstone Baths (Main line open. Extension in abeyance)		1¼			
Cornwall	1846				
In connection with the South Devon at Plymouth, to Falmouth, with branches to Padstow, to the Liskeard and Caradoc, and to the quays at Truro and Penryn Works in Progress.			83	Expen. to Dec. 1853	540 012

RAILWAYS.

Name of Railway, Amalgamation, Main line, and Branches.	Date of Acts.	Length of each portion.	Total length.	Estimate, Cost or Capital.	
		Miles.	Miles.		£.
Deeside. Originally incorporated	1846				
Re-incorporated	1852	10½		Capital authorized	141,650
Dublin and Wicklow, incorporated, as Waterford, Wexford, Wicklow, & Dublin	1846		135½	Reduced Capital	500,000
Title altered & length etc. reduced	1851				
Dundee & Perth, and Aberdeen Junction	1847		31¾	Capital. Shares	570,000
				Debentures	216,600
General Terminus and Glasgow Harbour	1846	5			
Gloucester and Dean Forest	1846	16		Capital	279,000
Leased to Gt. Western	1854				
Great North of Scotland	1846		138½	Capital	516,232
40 miles between Aberdeen and Huntley completed 19 Sept., 1854.	1846				
Great Northern	1846				
London to Askern, near York. Total powers for 335½ miles, of which 181 are abandoned, leaving a total of			154½	Total Capital	11,128,025
Killarney Junction	1846	41		Capital	247,932
Worked by the Great Southern & Western					
Malton & Driffield Junc.	1846	24		Capital	287,014
Amalgamated with North-eastern.					
Manchester, Buxton, Matlock, & Mid. Jn.	1846			Capital. Shares	453,750
				Loans	151,250
(From Ambergate to Rowsley). Worked by Midland			11½		
Manchester, Sheffield, & Lincolnshire Amalgamation	1846				
Of the Sheffield, Ashton-under-Lyne, & Manchester; the Great Grimsby and Sheffield Junction; the Sheffield and Lincolnshire; the Sheffield and Lin-					

Name of Railway, Amalgamation, Main Line, and Branches.	Date of Acts.	Length of each portion.	Total Length.	Estimate, Cost, or Capital.
		Miles.	Miles.	£.
Manchester, *continued*. colnshire Extension, and the Great Grimsby Dock Companies; and (in 1847) of the Manchester and Lincoln Union . .			171¾	Total Capital . . 8,137,451
Morayshire (from Stotfield to Elgin) . .	1846		11¼	Capital 41,616
Newmarket. From Chesterford Junct. (Eastern Counties) to Newmarket, etc. .	1846	23		
Branch to Bury St. Edmunds single line		14	37	
Newport, Abergavenny, and Hereford . .	1846	33		
Branch to the Taff Vale line	1847	16		Capital 628,245
Powers to make deviations & short bran.	1853			
Newry, Warrenpoint, & Rostrevor . . .	1846	8½		Capital 135,976
North London . .	1846	7¼		
late East and West India Docks, and Birmingham Junct. Branch to Blackwall Extension near Bow	1850			Total Capital . . 1,198,661
North Staffordshire . .	1845			Total Capital . . 5,820,000
Length of Railway (besides 110 miles of canal.)		123		
North-western . .	1846			Capital 1,159,754
Royston and Hitchin	1846	12½		Capital 800,000
Extension to Bedford (leased to G. Nor.)	1848	5		Works cost per mile • 3,500
Shrewsbury & Birmingham with branches to Madeley & Ironbridge . . .	1846	29½		Capital 1,344,787
Amalgamated with Great Western.				
Shrewsbury & Hereford	1846			Capital 600,000
South Staffordshire .	1846			
Amalgamation of the South Staffordshire, junction; and the Trent Valley, Midland, and Grand				

Name of Railway, Amalgamation, Main Line, and Branches.	Date of Acts.	Length of each portion.	Total Length.	Estimate, Cost, or Capital.
S. Staffordshire, *contin.* Junction; besides branches		Miles.	Miles.	£. Capital authorized . 1,260,000
Vale of Neath . . .	1846			
Line from Neath to Merthyr Tydvil, with branches to the Aberdare, etc.			33	Total Capital . . 712,983
West Cornwall . . .	1846			
From Carredas to Penzance, with branch to the Cornwall line Length open . . .			25	Capital 459,253
Birkenhead, Lancashire, & Cheshire Junct.	1847			
Chester and Birkenhead amalgamated	1847			
Re-incorporated	1852			Total Capital . . 2,323,319
Glasgow and S.-Western Amalgamation (1850) of the Glasgow, Paisley, Kilmarnock and Ayr; and the Glasgow, Dumfries, and Carlisle . .			171¼	Total Capital . . 4,090,000
Lancashire & Yorkshire.	1847			
Amalgamation of the Manchester & Leeds; the Manchester, Bolton and Bury; the Liverpool and Bury; the Huddersfield and Sheffield; the Wakefield, Pontefract, &. Goole, and the West Riding Union . .			253½	Total Capital . . 12,308,442
Liverpool, Crosby, and Southport . .	1847		18¼	Capital 300,000
Manchester & Southport	1847			Capital authorized . 1,033,300
South Yorkshire . . .	1847			
Branches to Elescar & Worsbro' . .	1850			Capital 1,085,787
Bangor and Carnarvon. Amalgamated with Chester & Holyhead	1851	7		
East Suffolk. Incorp. as the Halesworth, Beccles,& Haddiscoe Worked jointly with the Norfolk by Act	1851 1852			Capital Shares . . 450,000

RAI   RAILWAYS.   RAI

Name of Railway, Amalgamation, Main Line, and Branches.	Date of Acts.	Length of each portion.	Total Length.	Estimate, Cost, or Capital.	
East Suffolk, *continued*.		Miles.	Miles.		£.
Main line		24	34¾	Loans	150,000
Branches		10¾			
Edinburgh, Perth, and Dundee.					
Re-incorporation . .	1851		90¾	Total capital . .	3,161,263
Total length authord. Length opened 71¾ m.				Capital	274,073
Hereford, Ross, & Gloucester	1851	23			
North & South-western Junction	1851	3¾		Capital	83,810
St. Andrew's	1851	4¼		Capital	25,000
Ulverstone & Lancaster.	1851	19		Capital	293,333
Warrington & Stockport (late Warrington & Altrincham Junct.)	1851	14		Capital	256,000
Waterford and Tramore	1851	17½		Capital	56,343
Waveney Valley (Tivetshall to Bungay) .	[1851]	13½			
Authorized extension to the East Suffolk.	1853	6	19½	Authorized Capital.	155,699
Blyth and Tyne . . .	1852	13			
Branches . . .	1853	8¾	21¾		
Leeds, Bradford, and Halifax Junction .	1852				
Branches to Ardsley and Gildersome, etc. (Worked by G. N.)	1853	7		Capital	241,063
Leven	1852	6			
London, Tilbury, and Southend . . . (Worked by E. C.)	1852	40		Capital (Computed)	500,000
Londonderry and Coleraine. Re-incorp. .	1852	37		Total Capital . .	565,000
Londonderry and Enniskillen. Re-incorp.	1852		60	Total Capital . .	590,849
Middlesbrough and Guisborough	1852	9			
Dr. to Cleveland Hills	1852	3	12	Capital	73,078
Somerset Central . .	1852		12¼	Capital	81,911
In course of construction, 1854.					
Ballymena, Ballymoney, Coleraine and Portrush Junction . .	1853	35		Estimate per mile .	4,000
Banbridge, Newry, Dublin, & Belfast Junc.	1853	6½		Estimate	35,000
Bedale and Leyburn .	1853	11¼		Do.	44,000
Bideford Extension .	1853	6		Do.	48,000

Name of Railway, Amalgamation, Main Line, and Branches.	Date of Acts.	Length of each portion.	Total Length.	Estimate, Cost, or Capital.		
		Miles.	Miles.			£.
Bognor	1853	5½		Estimate		27,000
Boston, Sleaford, and Midland Counties	1853	27½		Do.		200,000
Chard	1853					
Coleford, Monmouth, Usk, and Pontypool	1853	22		Do.		160,000
Crieff Junction	1853	8¾		Do		45,000
Darenth Valley (From Dartford to Farningham)	1853	5¾		Do.		40,000
East Grinstead	1853	6½		Do.		47,000
East Kent (Strood to Canterbury)	1853	31¼		Do.		437,837
Forth and Clide Junct.	1853	29¾		Do.		150,000
Hampstead Junction (Projected as North and South-western, Hampstead, & City Junction.)	1853	6¾		Do.		250,000
Hull and Holderness	1853	18½		Do.		110,000
Limerick and Ennis	1853	24½		Do.		150,000
Limerick and Foynes	1853	26½		Do.		130,000
Llanidloes and Newtown	1853	12¾		Do.		66,000
Londonderry, Enniskillen, and Sligo	1853	51½		Do.		297,000
Londonderry and Lough Swilly	1853	9½		Do.		39,000
Metropol. Subterranean Paddington to Gen. Post Office	1853	4		Capital.	Shares	1,000,000
					Loans	333,000
Norwich and Spalding	1853	15¼				
Branch to Wisbeach	1853	10	25¼	Estimate		170,000
Peebles. From Hawick branch of North British to Peebles	1853	18¾		Capital		93,000
Port Carlisle. (Converted canal)	1853	11¼		Do.		194,477
Portsmouth. Goldaming Station of South-western to Havant Junction with London and Brighton line, and the Fareham Extension of London and South-western and direct to Portsmth.	1853	32¼		Estimate		350,000
Roscrea & Parsonstown Junction	1823	22¼		Do.		100,000

RAILWAYS.

Name of Railway, Amalgamation, Main Line, and Branches.	Date of Acts.	Length of each potion.	Total Length.	Estimate, Cost, or Capital.	
		Miles.	Miles.		£.
St. Ives and West Cornwall Junction	1853	4		Estimate	32,000
Severn Valley	1853	40¼		Do.	560,000
Staines, Workingham, & Woking Junction	1853	22¾		Do.	270,000
Stamford and Essendine	1853	3¾		Do.	46,500
Wellington & Severn Jn.	1853	6		Do.	60,000
West of London and Crystal Palace	1853	9¾		Do.	360,000
Wimbledon & Croydon	1853	5¼		Do.	45,000
Worcester & Hereford	1853	30¼		Do.	560,000
Ayr and Maybole	1854	5¼		Capital	43,000
Bagenalstown and Wexford	1854	42½		Estimate	270,000
Border Counties Hexham to Falstone.	1854	26		Do.	200,000
Bradford, Wakefield, & Leeds	1854	9¾		Do.	180,000
Carmarthen & Cardigan	1854	25½		Do.	247,700
Caterham. To Brighton line	1854	4⅝		Do.	30,000
Chipping Norton	1854	4¼		Do.	24,000
Cork and Youghal	1854			Capital	500,000
Darlington and Barnard Castle	1854	15¾		Estimate	100,000
Dowlais	1854	¼		Do.	7,500
Hertford and Welwyn	1854	7¾		Do.	47,078
Horncastle & Kirkstead	1845	7¼		Do.	45,000
Inverness and Nairn	1854	15¾		Do.	80,000
Leominster and Kington	1854	13¼		Do.	106,000
Mallow and Fermoy	1854	16¾		Capital	133,000
N. York. and Cleveland	1854	29¾		Estimate	160,000
Perth and Dunkeld	1854	8¼		Do.	70,000
Potteries, Biddulph, and Congleton	1854	18¼		Do.	190,000
Rhymney	1854	12		Capital	139,000
Salisbury and Yeovil	1854	40½		Do.	533,333
Selkirk and Galashiels	1854	5¾		Do.	32,000
Shropshire Union Leased to L. & N. W.	1854			Do.	2,255,638
South Devon & Tavistock	1854	17½		Estimate	154,000
Stockport, Disley and Wharley-bridge	1854	10		Do.	150,000
Tralee and Killarney	1854	22		Do.	110,000
Vale of Towy	1854	11¼		Capital	78,000
Wells and Fakenham	1854			Do.	93,000
Westminster Terminus	1854	2½		Do.	640,000
Whitehaven, Cleator & Egremont	1854	6¼		Estimate	48,000

Railway chairs, the pieces of cast-iron which fix the rails to the sleepers.

Rainbow, a meteor in the form of a partly-coloured arch or semicircle exhibited in a rainy sky, opposite to the sun, and caused by the refraction of his rays in the drops of falling rain: it never appears greater than a semicircle, but often much less: it is always double, there being what is termed the superior and inferior, or primary and secondary rainbow: they always exhibit the seven prismatic colours; and the whole of this phenomenon depends upon the rays of the sun falling on spherical drops of water, and being in their passage through them refracted and reflected.

Rain-gauge, an instrument for measuring the depth of rain that falls. A very simple and excellent instrument for this purpose is shown in fig. 1. It consists of a copper funnel, from 5 to 7 inches diameter. The rain being collected in a glass bottle, this bottle should be placed in a small stand near the surface of the ground, to protect the bottle from the action of the sun. The amount of rain fallen in a given time is measured in a graduated glass jar, one-tenth the area of the funnel, similar to that shown in the figure, and so divided that every inch in depth of the tube shall indicate one-tenth of an inch falling in the funnel. The amount of rain falling can be measured by such an instrument to $\frac{1}{1000}$th part of an inch, or even less.

An instrument, fig. 2, is also used for measuring the fall of rain. It consists of a cylinder of copper or other metal, from 5 to 7 inches in diameter, and 30 inches long. A float, just so much smaller as to allow it to rise freely when it becomes filled with water, is placed within the cylinder, and to the centre of the float is attached an upright staff, marked in inches and tenths of an inch, which, rising through a hole at the bottom of the funnel, as shown in the figure, indicates the depth of rain received into the gauge.

This instrument is very simple, and shows the amount of rain collected upon mere inspection: it

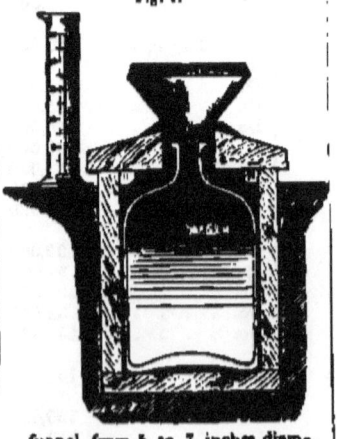

Fig. 1.

Fig. 2.

has, however, been proved that in hilly districts and exposed situations, when the staff rises but a small distance above the receiving surface of the gauge, owing to the rain being carried along with the wind in a slanting, and frequently, on the tops of high hills, almost in a horizontal direction, that the staff, though of small diameter, arrests a large amount of rain, which runs down the staff and causes a much larger quantity to be collected than is properly due to the rain-fall. (Some interesting experiments, showing the incorrect results given by these rain-gauges, will be found in a 'Report on the Supply of Surplus Water to Manchester, Salford, and Stockport,' by S. C. Homersham, Civil Engineer.) When these kind of rain-gauges are used, the rod should be movable, fitting loosely the socket or the float, and only placed in the gauge when the depth of the rain-fall is to be ascertained.

Rainline, a small rope, or line, sometimes used to form the sheer of a ship, and to set the beams of the deck fair.

Rake, in mining, an oblique vein.

Rake, in ship-building, an obtuse angle, such as the stem and sternposts make with the keel of a ship.

Rake of a ship, all that part of the hull which hangs over both ends of the keel.

Raking moulding, in joinery, a moulding whose arrises are inclined to the horizon in any given angle.

Ramp, in hand-railing, a concavity on the upper side, formed over risers, or over half or quarter span, by a sudden rise of the steps above, which frequently occasions a knee above the ramp.

Rampant, in heraldry, a term applied to a lion, leopard, etc., standing on his hind legs, in the escutcheon, with his forefeet reared up in the posture of clawing.

Rampant Arch, one whose abutments spring from an inclined plane.

Ranges, pieces fixed to the inside of a ship to belay the ropes; and sometimes expressed for those between the ports whereon the shots lie.

Rasp, a rough file.

Ratchell, loose stones.

Ratchet-brace, a tool for drilling a hole in a narrow place where there is not sufficient room to use the common brace: a ratchet-wheel is fixed on the drill-socket, and turned by a handle with a strong spring attached to force round the socket on the forward motion, and slips over the teeth on the backward motion.

Ratio is the relation of two quantities of the same kind with respect to quality, and is divided into arithmetical and geometrical.

Ratlines, in ship-rigging, small lines that traverse the shrouds of a ship horizontally, at regular distances, and form ascending ladders to the mast-head.

Rebate, a deep groove, or channel, cut longitudinally in a piece of timber to receive the edge of a plank, or the ends of a number of planks, which are to be securely fastened in it.

Receiver of an air-pump, in pneumatics, a glass vessel placed on the top of a plate, out of which the air is exhausted by the pump.

Recess, a cavity in a wall, left either for ornament or use when it is to receive some furniture, as a sideboard, or to add to the quantity of room; and for ornament when made in the form of a niche, to give beauty and variety to the building.

Reckoning, in navigation, the computation of a ship's way (usually by the log), or the act of estimating the distance run between one part and another.

Reconciles, or *Top Timber-Hollow*, in ship-building, a mould sometimes used to form the hollow in the top-side, which is called the reconciling mould.

Rectangle, a right angle made by the falling of one line perpendicularly upon another.

Rectification, in chemistry, is the repetition of a distillation or a sublimation several times, in order to render the substance purer and finer, or freer from earthy and aqueous particles.

Rectification, in geometry, is the finding of a right line equal to a proposed curve.

Rectilineal, or *Rectilinear*, consisting of right lines.

Rectory, a house for the residence of the rector of a parish, usually situated near the church.

Red is the second and intermediate of the primary colours, standing between yellow and blue, and in like intermediate relation also to white and black, or light and shade. Hence it is pre-eminent among colours, as well as the most positive of all, forming with yellow the secondary orange and its near relatives, scarlet, etc.; and with blue the secondary purple and its allies, crimson, etc. It gives some degree of warmth to all colours, but most so to those which partake of yellow.

Red-lead, *Minium*, or *Saturnine red*, an ancient pigment, by some old writers confounded with cinnabar, and called Sinoper, or Synoper, is a deutoxide of lead, prepared by subjecting massicot to the heat of a furnace with an expanded surface and free accession of air. It is of a scarlet colour and fine hue, warmer than common vermilion; bright, but not so vivid as the biniodide of mercury, though it has the body and opacity of both these pigments, and has been confounded even in name with vermilion, with which it was formerly customary to mix it. When pure and alone, light does not affect its colour; but white-lead, or any oxide or preparation of that metal mixed with it, soon deprives it of colour, as acids do also; and impure air will blacken and ultimately metallize it.

Red Ochre is a name proper rather to a class than to an individual pigment, and comprehends Indian red, light red, Venetian red, scarlet ochre, Indian ochre, redding, ruddle, bole, as well as other absurd appellations, such as English vermilion, and Spanish brown, or majolica.

Reef, in navigation, to contract a sail by tying up a portion of it to the yard.

Refectory, a refreshment-room; the hall or apartment in a monastery.

Refining and Puddling of Iron. The chemical difference between cast-iron and wrought-iron consists principally in the difference of degree in which foreign matters are present in each, which is in larger amount in the former than in the latter. There are many cases in which wrought-iron contains a larger amount of impurities than cast-iron, and is yet malleable; while cast-iron of the same composition may be very hard and brittle. Berzelius detected in a certain kind of bar-iron, 18 per cent. of silex; and yet this iron was still malleable and useful. One-tenth of that amount of silex will make cast-iron brittle. The foreign matters generally combined with pig-iron are carbon, silicon, silex, sulphur, phosphorus, arsenic, zinc, manganese, titanium, chrome, aluminium, magnesium, and calcium. Each of these tends to make iron brittle; therefore, in converting cast into wrought iron, it is necessary, as far as possible, to remove them. Carbon and other foreign matters divide the crude iron into two very distinct classes. In the one, carbon is only an accidental mechanical admixture; in the other, it is in definite chemical combination. To the first belong the white iron of heavy burden, and grey iron; to the latter, the white iron of small burden, or very fusible ores. From the behaviour of the different metals in the refining and puddling process, the presence of silicon and silex appears to exert a similar influence; it is not possible to remove silex from white metal with which carbon is chemically combined. The silex is present in the form of silicon. White metal of small burden may contain from 5 to nearly 6 per cent. of carbon; and, if smelted from pure ore, almost an equal amount of other foreign matter, such as silicon. Upon the presence and form of these its white colour and crystallization in a degree depend. Grey pig-iron seldom contains more than 4·75 per cent. of carbon, and generally only from 3·50 to 4 per cent. When carbon is present to the amount of but 2 to 3 per cent., it becomes white. The more this iron is stretched, the more it forms fibres. Fibrous bar-iron resembles hickory wood, in the fact that it is a combination of fibres and spaces. In bar-iron, these spaces are filled with cinders, and that portion of the iron is proportional to the fluteness of the fibres. That portion of the iron which is not melted, which crystallizes too fast, or whose premature crystallization the workman cannot prevent, is in the condition of cast-metal, and cannot be converted into fibrous wrought-iron. In the puddling furnace it is necessary to prevent crystallization by manual labour. This result, whether in the Catalan forge, the Woolf's oven, or the German forge, is partly accomplished by the blast.

Reflection is the return or regressive motion of a movable body, arising from the reaction of some other body on which it impinges.

Reflex, in painting, denotes those parts of a picture that are supposed to be illuminated by a light reflected from some other body represented in the piece.

Reflux, in hydrography, the ebb, backward course of water, flux, or flowing of the sea.

Refraction, in mechanics, the incurvation or change of determination in the body moved. In dioptrics, it is the variation of a ray of light from that right line in which it would have passed on, had not the density of the medium turned it aside. It is the bending of a ray of light towards the perpendicular when it passes into a denser medium, and from the perpendicular when it passes into a rarer medium.

The law of refraction was first completely established by Snell and Descartes at the commencement of the seventeenth century. The first part of this law is similar to that of reflection, viz. that the angles of incidence and refraction (i. e. the angles which the incident and refracted ray each make with the perpendicular or normal of the surface, or in this case the angles F C D and F' C D'') are both in the same plane. Any ray meeting the surface of a new medium is split into two rays, one reflected and the other refracted; as, for instance, the ray B C into the reflected ray C B', and the refracted ray C B''; or D C into the two rays C D' and C D''. So also a ray B''' C will be partly reflected in the direction C b', and partly refracted into C B; or D''' C will be reflected into C d', and refracted into C D. Now in all these cases the three rays, incident, reflected, and refracted, will be all in one plane, and that plane perpendicular to the acting surface A A.

The angles of incidence and reflection (such as F C D and F C D') are, as already explained, invariably equal; but that of refraction (in this case F' C D'') is different from both, but connected with them by this law, that (at the same surface) the sines of incidence and refraction to the same radius bear a constant ratio to each other, which is always the same in the same two media.

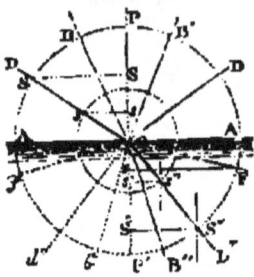

For instance, in passing through the surface A A, at whatever degree of obliquity, and whether upwards from the water into the air, or down from the air into the water, a ray is invariably so bent that the angle it makes with the perpendicular P P in the air may be greater than that in the water; and that the sine of the angle in air may be to that in water (to the same radius) as 4 to 3, which is the ratio that has been determined by experiment. At the surface separating any other two media, a different ratio would be observed with equal constancy.

To find the new direction into which any ray, such as D C, will be bent by this surface, draw a circle round the point c with any radius, such as c s, and the sine of the ray in air (to this radius) will be found to be s s. Therefore the sine in water will be $\frac{3}{4}$ of s s. Draw a line parallel with c P at a distance therefrom equal to $\frac{3}{4}$ of s s, viz. at the distance s′ s″, and as this intersects the circle at s″, the refracted ray must pass through s″ to make its sine in water (s′ s″) $\frac{3}{4}$ of its sine in air (s s), both to the same radius (c s, or c s″). If any other radius be chosen, as c s, it is plain that the same result will be obtained; for, by the property of similar triangles, if s′ s″ be $\frac{3}{4}$ of s s, then s′ s′ is also $\frac{3}{4}$ of s s.

In tracing the course of a ray upwards from the water, as D″ c, then, having found its sine in water to any fixed radius, make its sine in air $\frac{1}{4}$ greater, because the sine in air is always greater than that in water, as 4 : 3; and thus the new direction of the ray will be found to be c D.

In this case a very singular effect takes place if the ray be very oblique to the surface, as F c. It should be remarked that no ray passing from the air into the water, however obliquely, could ever be refracted into the direction c F, for this reason, the sine of no angle can be greater than the radius to which it is drawn, therefore no ray can have its sine to radius c s greater than c s. But its sine in water is only $\frac{3}{4}$ of that in air, and consequently cannot exceed $\frac{3}{4}$ of the radius. Now the sine of the ray c F, viz. F z, is more than $\frac{3}{4}$ of the radius c s, therefore no degree of obliquity of the ray in air will enable it to become so oblique in the water as c F. But a ray may ascend in the direction F c as well as in any other. Now its sine in air must become $\frac{1}{4}$ greater than F z; but this is impossible, for a line $\frac{1}{4}$ longer than F z would be longer than the radius c s, and therefore too long to be the sine of any angle to that radius. As this ray, then, cannot be refracted according to the law, it is not refracted at all but totally reflected in the direction c f, the only known instance of total reflection, for none of the light can penetrate the surface A A, which is, in fact, absolutely opaque to this light. This phenomenon of total reflection may be seen by looking through the side of a tumbler containing water up to its surface, in some such direction as f c, when the surface will be seen to be opaque, and more reflective than any mirror, inasmuch as the images in it are perfectly equal in brightness to the objects themselves.

Now at the surface between any other two media, the ratio of the sines would be different; for though all surfaces reflect alike (as regards the direction of the ray), all do not refract alike. Suppose the ray passed from vacuum into water, the ratio would be rather greater than 3:4, namely 1 : 1·335. In passing from vacuum into air of the common density, the refraction would be much less, and consequently the sines much more nearly equal, viz. as 1 : 1·000294. Now if the sine in any medium be called 1, the corresponding sine *in vacuo* is called the index of refraction of that medium; and is specific for each substance, or as constant as its density, expansibility, specific heat, or any other measurable quality. Thus the refractive index of air of the common density is 1·000294, that of water 1·335, of crown glass 1·52, of flint glass 1·55.

In the case above considered, of refraction from air into water, and *vice versâ*, the sines in air and in water are, strictly speaking, as 1·335 : 1·000294; and generally the sines on each side of any surface are inversely as the refractive indices of the two media.

The refractive indices of a great many media have been measured and arranged in tables. When the density of any substance is increased or diminished, its refractive power is increased or diminished in the same ratio.

The application of the laws of refraction accounts for numerous deceptive effects seen in the atmosphere, and included under the general term *mirage*; the most familiar of which is the distortion of objects seen through a rising current of hot air, which, from its smaller density, has a lower refractive power than the surrounding cold air, and therefore bends the rays in various directions. It is also plain that the rays of the heavenly bodies coming from space into our atmosphere must be refracted, and thus cause the objects whence they come to appear rather above their true place, as the eye at *d* in the figure sees D in the direction *d c* rather above its true place. This forms one of the sources of error to be allowed for in all astronomical observations, and tables are calculated for finding its amount, depending on the object's apparent altitude, and the state of the barometer and thermometer. Owing to the very small refractive power of air, however, this error is hardly sensible when the object is high, but increases rapidly towards the horizon, where it becomes 33', or rather more than the sun's or moon's diameter, so that these bodies may appear just clear of the horizon when they are really completely below it. As the density of the air diminishes gradually upwards, atmospheric refraction is not, like that which has been just considered, a sudden change of direction, but the ray actually describes a curve, being refracted more and more at every step; and this applies equally to the light from a distant terrestrial object which is either lower or higher than the eye, because it must pass through air of constantly increasing or diminishing density. This refraction has therefore to be allowed for in levelling, which is done by assuming that the light from a distant object comes to us in a line arched or curved upwards, the radius of which is about seven times that of the earth.

The application of these laws of Dioptrics has also led to the understanding of the mechanism of the eye, and hence to the imitation thereof by lenses, affording the remedies for its infirmities of long and short sight, and disclosing the wonders of the telescope and the microscope.

Regalia, in heraldry, ensigns of royalty; the apparatus used at a coronation.

Regardant, in heraldry, signifies looking behind, as applied to a lion or any other beast.

Regatta, the name of an aquatic spectacle consisting of gondola races, etc., exhibited at Venice.

Reglet, a flat, narrow moulding, employed to separate panels or other members; or to form knots, frets, and similar ornaments.

Regula, a band below the tænia of the Doric epistylium, extending the width of the triglyph, and having six guttæ depending from it. It also signifies the space between two adjoining canals of the triglyphs.

Regular. In geometry, a regular body is solid whose surface is composed of regular and equal figures, and whose solid angles are all equal. There are five sorts: 1. A pyramid, comprehended under four equal and equilateral triangles: 2. A cube, whose surface is composed of six equal squares: 3. That which is bounded by eight equal and equilateral triangles: 4. That which is contained under twelve equal and equilateral pentagons: 5. A body consisting of twenty equal and equilateral triangles.

Regulator, in mechanics, that part of a machine which makes the motion equable.

Regulator-cock, in locomotive engines, a cock placed to admit oil or tallow to lubricate the faces of the regulator.

Regulator-cover, in locomotive engines, the outside cover, removable when required to examine the regulator.

Regulator-shaft and levers, in locomotive engines, the shaft and levers placed in front of the smoke-box when each cylinder has a separate regulator. A rod connected with the shaft leads to the foot-plate, where a handle is placed conveniently for use.

Regulator-valve, the valve in a steam-pipe of a locomotive engine, for regulating the supply of steam to the cylinders.

Regulator-valve spindle, the spindle for moving the regulator-valve; being fixed to it at one end, the other end of the spindle passes through a stuffing-box joint over the fire-box, and has a handle fixed on the end to turn it.

Relief-valve, a valve belonging to the feeding apparatus of a marine engine, through which the water escapes into the hot well when it is shut off from the boiler.

Relieving tackle, in mechanics, the two strong tackles used to prevent a ship's overturning on the careen, and afterwards to assist in uprighting her.

Repercussion, in mechanics, the act of drawing back; rebound.

Replum, the panel of the impagis, or horizontal rails of a framed door.

Repose, in painting, denotes certain parts in the composition of a picture which seem to tranquillize its aspect.

Reredos, behind the back; the back of a fireplace; also an altarpiece, a screen, or partition wall.

Respond, in Gothic architecture, a half-pillar or piece attached to a wall to support an arch, etc.

Rest, in a lathe, a piece of iron to hold the turning-tool upon, fixed at the end of a slide by a set-screw: the slide can be moved at right angles to the bar of the lathe, and the whole can be fixed at any part of the bed, between the centres.

Reticulated work, a species of masonry or breakwork, formed externally by small square stones, or bricks, placed lozengewise, and presenting the appearance of net-work.

Reticulation is the method of copying a painting or drawing by the help of square threads. An open frame is made similar to a straining frame, and the painting enclosed within it; a number of threads are then strained over at equal distances, like network, which are fastened to the frame by nails. The canvas, or paper, is likewise divided into an equal number of proportional squares, and whatever appears within the square threads in the painting is copied into the corresponding squares on the canvas or paper. The squares of the copy may bear any proportion to those of the original. Painters often adopt this method when they first execute a small design, from which their large and more finished work is copied.

Revels, or *Reveals*, the vertical retreating surface of an aperture, or the two vertical sides of the aperture, between the front of the wall and the windows or door frames, most commonly posted at right angles to the upright surface.

Reversing gear, the apparatus for reversing the motion of a marine or locomotive engine, by changing the time of action of the slide-valve: the eccentric being in advance of the crank for the forward motion will, if turned to an equal distance behind the crank, produce a backward motion.

Reversing handle and guide, the handle placed beside the foot-plate conveniently for use when required. The guide is a quadrant fixed to the foot-plate, notched for the end of the reversing handle for each variation of the expansion gear. To reverse the engine, the handle is removed to any notch past the centre of the guide on the opposite side in which it was before. Expansion is varied by moving the handle from one notch to another notch on the same side of the centre of the guide from which the engine is working. When the handle is on the centre notch, the handle is said to be *out of gear*.

Reversing lever, the lever connected to a crank on the reversing shaft by a rod, and placed at the side of the fire-box, between guide-plates with notches to keep it vertical, or in the forward or backward position.

Reversing shaft, the shaft, with levers on it, connected with the eccentric rods in the rocking-shaft class, but with the slide-valve rod in the expansion-gear class of engines. Both arrangements effect the object of moving the slide-valve so as to admit steam to the contrary side of the piston to which it had previously been admitted, and thus reverse its motion, and with it the motion of the engine also.

Reversing valve. (See *Air-valve*.)

Reynolds (Sir Joshua) was born in 1723, in Devonshire. The price Reynolds first received for a head was five guineas. In 1755 (thirty-two years of age) his charge was twelve guineas. Some years after his price for a head was twenty guineas. In 1758, the account of his studies and distribution of time is curious. He received six sitters daily. In 1760 he raised his price to twenty-five guineas; at this he engaged several subordinate labourers. His study was about 15 feet high; the window was small and square, and the sill 9 feet from the floor. His sitter's chair moved on castors, and stood above the floor 1½ feet. He wrought standing, and with great celerity; the handles of his brushes were 18 inches long. Reynolds again raised his price for a portrait to thirty-five guineas, and finally to fifty guineas.

Rhomb, an oblique angled parallelogram; in geometry, a parallelogram or quadrangular figure having its four sides equal, and consisting of parallel lines, with two opposite angles and two obtuse.

Rhomboidal, approaching the shape of a rhomb: in geometry, used to signify an oblique-angled parallelogram.

Rhumb, in navigation, a vertical circle of any given place, or the intersection of a part of such circle with the horizon. Rhumbs coincide with the points of the world or horizon, and are distinguished like those of the compass. A rhumb-line cuts all the meridians under the same angle.

Rib, in constructive architecture, a moulding on the interior of a vaulted roof.

Rib, an arch formed of a piece of timber.

Rib, a pillar of coal left as a support for the roof of a mine.

Ribs, arch-formed timbers, for sustaining the plasterwork of a vault, or wood ceiling.

Ribband, pieces of fir nailed to the timbers of a square body under which shores are fixed.

Ribbing, the whole of the timberwork for sustaining a vaulted or coved ceiling.

Riders, in ship-building, interior ribs, to strengthen and bind the parts of a ship together, being fayed upon the inside stuff, and bolted through all.

Ridge, the upper angle of a roof: tiles called ridge-tiles are sometimes made very ornamental.

Rigger, a wheel with a flat or slightly curved rim, moved by a leather band.

Right angle, in geometry, is that formed by a line falling perpendicularly on another, or that which subtends an arc of ninety degrees.

Right line, in geometry, signifies the same as a straight line, opposed to curved or crooked.

Ring, in geometry, an annulus.

Ring-tail, in navigation, a quadrilateral sail, occasionally hoisted abaft the after-leech of the boom mainsails, to which the fore-leech is made to correspond.

Rising-rod, a rod in a Cornish engine which rises by means of levers as the cataract piston descends, and lifts catches which release sectors, and allow weights to shut or open the steam, equilibrium, or exhaust valve.

Rivets, short bolts of metal inserted in a hole at the juncture of two plates, and, after insertion, hammered abroad at the ends, so as to keep the plates together. Mr. Wm. Fairbairn invented a riveting machine, which by the aid of steam performs the work rapidly and without noise.

Riveting Machine. The principle of action of the riveting machine is very similar to that of an ordinary punching machine. The work performed by it is usually done by manual labour, which occupies a much longer time, causes great noise, and is much more expensive and less efficient. The machine consists of two strong side-frames forming bearings for the fulcrum for a powerful lever which works between them, and is raised or lowered by a cam acting at the extremity. On one end of the camshaft is a large spur-wheel moved by a pinion on the driving-shaft, which has a very heavy fly-wheel fixed on it, to accumulate power and expend it during the action of the lever. The riveting tool is placed in a guide near the short end of the lever, and directly opposite the end of the tool is another, to form the heads fixed on a pillar called the riveting block. The rivet being made to enter the holes, and placed between the riveting tool and the block, the machine is set in motion, and the cam raises the lever, which presses against the tool and instantly forms the rivet.

Roads are artificially-formed ways between distant places, and being among the first means of personal communication, their formation and treatment, as duties of the engineer, are of the highest importance. The efficiency of roadmaking requires that the surface of the road shall be preserved in a durable condition, and adapted for the kind of traffic to be conducted upon it; and, therefore, the construction of the road, both as regards its superstratum or surface, and substructure, its dimensions and inclination, or declivity, are equally to be determined with reference to the particular kind of wear to which it will be subjected. Thus the weights that will pass over the road will make it necessary that it possess greater or less firmness and solidity, while the rigidity or hardness of its surface affects the power required for moving bodies, or the draught. The vertical inclination of the road has an influence upon the draught, and is also limited by the class of traffic. The old Roman roads, for instance, designed for the passage of animals only, were laid with inclinations of great steepness, and with reference only to the directness of their course. The use of wheel carriages imposes limits to the steepness which cannot be exceeded either with safety or with economy of power. The most improved form of road—the railway—restricts the steepness or inclination still further, the propelling power employed being found to become expensive in a rapid ratio in proportion to the departure of the surface on which it is exerted from a horizontal plane. The qualities of a good road are, solidity of structure,—hardness of surface,—levelness of inclination, and sufficiency of width for all its purposes. To ensure the permanence of these qualities, the formation and the drainage of the road are required to be complete, while the several means to be adopted will be partly determined by the kind of materials at command. Experiments made to ascertain the force of traction on different kinds of roads, have shown that this force is nearly in exact proportion to the strength and hardness of the road. Thus the draught on a well-made pavement is half that upon a broken stone surface, or old flint road, and less than a quarter of the draught upon a gravel road. If the strength or solidity of the foundation be increased, the draught is reduced. Thus, if the broken stone road he laid upon a rough pavement foundation, the draught is reduced one-third, and a similar reduction is effected by laying a bottoming of concrete formed of cement and gravel. The external forces by which the motion of bodies upon roads is retarded, and the draught or power required consequently augmented, are collision, friction, gravity, and the atmosphere. Collision is occasioned by the hard protuberances and irregularities of surface of the road meeting the wheels, and thus diminishing the momentum of carriages. The resistance arising from collision is proportional directly to the load and the height of the obstacle to be surmounted, and inversely to the diameter of the wheels of the carriage in which the load is borne. Professor Leslie has defined the resistance which friction causes to consist "of the consumption of the moving force, or of the horse's labour, occasioned by the soft surface of the road, and the continually depressing of the spongy and elastic substrata of the road." From the formulæ which have been deduced upon the extent of this resistance, it is evident that it is caused by the wheels sinking into the ground, and is proportional directly to the load, and inversely to the width of the wheels. The resistance produced by gravity is evidently in proportion to the steepness of the road, being nothing on a perfectly horizontal plane, and augmenting as the inclination approaches the perpendicular. The force of the air in resisting the motion of loads upon roads may be understood from the experiments which are given in Smeaton's Reports, and from which it appears, that upon a surface of one square foot this force equals 1 lb. when the velocity of the wind is at the rate of 15 miles per hour; and that this force becomes equal to 12 lbs. when the air moves at the rate of 50 miles an hour, constituting a storm.

In designing a road, a correct survey of the proposed line, with the exact relative levels of all parts of its present surface is the first requisite, and upon this the engineer proceeds to consider the propriety of deviating in one direction or another, in order to attain better levels, or to equalize the earthworks, so that the quantity excavated in one part may suffice to embank an adjacent portion, and thus reduce the distances to which the soil must be removed. In determining the inclinations of the surface, facts proved by experience should be consulted, from which the rule may be inferred that an inclination of 1 in 35 is that which admits of horses moving with perfect safety in a fast trot. Valleys are required to be crossed by bridges and viaducts, or solid embankments and hills are excavated with cuttings or with tunnels to reduce the elevation to which it would otherwise be necessary to carry the road. Streams and rivers are also occasionally to be passed over, and thus the design and execution of an extended length of road frequently involves some of the grandest works of engineering art.

Road-making was a principle of employment ingeniously carried out by Napoleon in those countries mastered by his arms; he discovered one element of the mixing of the poorer population by the monopolies and greediness of the rich; his master mind saw clearly that he could not better secure his power than by employing the unfortunate and labouring poor. Road-making zealously occupied his mind; his name to this day, for this simple and important fact, is revered. In those towns on the Continent where a *résumé* existed of the antagonistic principle, it is obvious that pauperism may be staved off by the more wealthy lords of the soil, if they give employment to the poor; and such conduct on the part of Napoleon naturally produced a veneration for his name. These poor people desired no cold charity; they sought for sustenance by the means of useful labour; and one of these was road-making. Many of them cheerfully shouldered the musket for the man who had so cherished them. Among the great projects carried out may be mentioned the Simplon road, from Geneva to Milan, which cost the French Government seventeen millions of livres, about £650,000.

Roasting of Iron Ore is either to produce higher oxidation, or to expel injurious admixtures. In both cases, liberal access of atmospheric air is required. Ore to be roasted should be broken into pieces as small as those usually put into the blast-furnace. The kind of fuel required is wood, and small charcoal, turf or peat, or brown coal, may be used. There are many different forms of ovens used; all of them can be reduced to that of the blast-furnace or the lime-kiln. These ovens are commonly from twelve to eighteen feet high, and contain from fifty to one hundred tons of ore at one time.

Rocking-shaft, the shaft, with levers on it, which works the slide-valves in some steam engines. The eccentric-rod drops on to a stud fixed in one lever, and the links of the slide-valve rod are attached to the opposite lever on the same shaft. This mode of working the slide-valves was generally adopted before the introduction, by Mr. Stephenson, of the direct-action mode of working them.

Rod, or *pole*, a long measure of 16½ linear feet, or a square measure of 272¼ square feet.

Roller, a solid cylinder of metal or wood, used for many purposes.

Rolling Machine, an invention for making the brass mouldings in fenders, and the brasswork in grates.

Rolling Mill, a mill for reducing masses of iron, copper, or other metals, to even parallel bars or thin plates. This is effected by passing the metal, whilst red-hot, between two cylindrical rollers of steel, put in motion by the mill, and so mounted in a strong metal frame that they cannot recede from each other.

Roll-moulding, a moulding used in early English architecture, resembling a roll.

Roman Architecture, in its masonry, both in public and private buildings, was of far more durable character and more accurate workmanship in the earlier periods than at the decline of the empire. It began with uncemented blocks of stone, passed into the reticulated work of the Republic, thence into the travertine, and descended into a mixture of turf and brick, and stucco facing. The polyhœdral wall, or, as it is often named, the Cyclopean, is the oldest example of masonry in Italy; but this style of building has been used in town walls only.

Until about the middle of the last century, Roman architecture was regarded as the Antique and the Classical *par excellence*, and was supposed to exhibit the most refined taste and most perfect artistic propriety. The 'Orders,' as practised by the Romans, were the examples taken up and followed by the Italian masters at the period of the so-called Revival, and still continue to be followed, both in that country and in France, in preference to their Greek prototypes. Among ourselves, however, the Roman style has of late years fallen somewhat into discredit,—at least as far as the orders are concerned,—while some have even gone further, and have censured the style of the Romans as being comparatively rude and coarse in taste, and their system as being radically vicious and inconsistent. Such is the opinion of both Mr. Fergusson and Mr. Freeman; and the latter writer further thinks, that "if the mad desire of imitating Greece had never taken possession of the Roman mind," Rome might, by adhering to her own previous mode of construction with the arch and vault alone, have ultimately wrought out a well-organized style, greatly superior to what she actually did produce, and which he pronounces to be, although not without its merits, "absurd and inconsistent to the last degree." This almost unqualified depreciation errs, perhaps, nearly as much as exaggerated and implicit admiration had done previously.

Nothing, indeed, is to be said in favour of the treatment of the two Greek orders by the Romans; for, strange to say, so far from the Doric acquiring greater energy, or the Ionic greater luxuriance, at their hands, the one was emasculated, the other impoverished, and both of them rendered insipid and characterless. On the other hand, it is to the Romans that we are indebted for almost all that we know of the Corinthian order as a style; and it might, with far greater propriety, be termed the Roman than the Corinthian one; for they not only greatly affected it and stamped it as their own, but frequently treated it with singular gusto.

As to Roman architecture generally, it possesses mechanical advantages and powers of construction unknown to that of the Greeks, and, owing to the adoption of circular and other curved forms of plan, possesses also a degree of variety and piquancy, if not of highly refined beauty, that we miss in the other more polished and correct style. Faulty as the interior of the Pantheon is, in regard to many points of design, Greece could never show anything similar, much less equal to it. The exterior, too, of the same edifice may be quoted as affording an instance of a correct application of a columnar order not introduced as mere decoration between arches, but applied as a portico both for actual use and for the sake of the general effect. If it be a mixed system, that of the Romans possesses this advantage: viz. it allows either arcading or colonnading to be employed as may best accord with circumstances, whether in different buildings or in different parts of one and the same edifice.

Perfect congruity and simplicity are not the only valuable qualities in architecture; for there is also a merit and a charm in complexity, when diverse, if not contradictory, elements of construction and design are combined into an harmonious whole; and the Romans appear to have been far more studious of impressiveness of *ensemble* than of purity of form and elegance of detail. Besides a degree of vastness never aimed at by the Greeks, sumptuousness and picturesqueness may be said to have been the predominant characteristics of their buildings,—at least, of all their principal monuments.

Surely, then, we are at liberty to admire Roman architecture for its better qualities, without either being blind to its faults and defects, or imitating them, as if they were inseparable from its merits. Certain it is, that in all matters of design and decoration, modern taste inclines infinitely more to that of the Romans than of the Greeks. Hardly, too, can we dispense with Roman taste and Roman ideas, unless we can dispense with the Italian style also: yet the latter style, or one founded upon it, must continue to be employed for our secular buildings, both public and private, mediæval architecture being wholly out of the question for buildings generally at the present day.

Roman School (The). It has been doubted whether the Roman school possesses the right to that appellation. Because the schools of Florence, Bologna, and Venice were founded by their respective citizens, and supported through a long course of ages; while the Roman school could boast only of Giulio Romano and Sacchi, and a few others, natives of Rome. The other artists were from other parts of Italy. As the Universities derive their names from the city where they are established, though the professors may be from other states, so with the schools of painting, the name of the country is always attached in preference to that of the master.

The masters of the Roman school are—

Pietro Perugino.
Raffaello, b. 1483, d. 1520.
Barocci, b. 1528, d. 1612.
Caravaggio, b. 1569, d. 1609.
Mola di Como.
Andrea Sacchi, b. 1600, d. 1661.
Nicholas Poussin, b. 1594, d. 1665.
Salvator Rosa, b. 1615, d. 1673.
Claude Lorraine, b. 1600, d. 1682.
Gaspar Poussin, b. 1613, d. 1675.

The characteristic feature of the Roman school consists in a strict imitation of the works of the ancients, not only in sublimity, but also in elegance and selection.

PIETRO PERUGINO is the first most eminent name that occurs in the Roman school. His manner is somewhat hard and dry, like that of other painters of his time; and he occasionally exhibits a poverty in the drapery of his figures. But he atones for these faults by the grace of his heads, particularly in his boys and in his women, which have an air of elegance and a charm of colour unknown to his contemporaries. In the Sistine he has a 'St. Peter invested with the Keys,' and at Perugia the 'Marriage of the Virgin.' This picture is one of the finest objects that noble city affords, and may be considered as containing an epitome of the various styles of Pietro.

It is a remarkable fact that the period of Da Vinci and Buonarruoti embraces not only Raffaello, but Correggio, Giorgione, and Titian, and the most celebrated Venetian painters; so that a man might have seen all these illustrious artists.

RAFFAELLO, born in Urbino, 1483. On settling at Rome, his principal pursuit was the study of the remains of Grecian genius, by which he perfected his knowledge of art. He studied, too, the ancient buildings, and was instructed in architecture for six years by Bramante. He lived among the ancient sculptors, and derived from them not only their contours and drapery and attitudes, but the spirit and principles of the art itself. He also employed artists to copy the remains of antiquity at Pozzuolo and throughout Italy, and even in Greece. Nor did he derive less assistance from living artists whom he consulted on his compositions.

As Michelangiolo had before studied the torso of the Belvidere, so Raffaello also formed himself on this and other marbles.

He was employed nine years on the three chambers in the Vatican.

Raffaello is placed at the head of his art, not because he excelled all others in every department of painting, but because no other artist has ever possessed the various parts of art united in so high a degree.

We stand in amaze at the contours, grace, precision, diligence, and genius which his drawings exhibit. In chasteness of design, he was by some placed on a level with the Greeks, though this praise we must consider as extravagant.

He selected the beautiful from nature, and, as Mariette observes, he copied it with all its imperfections, which he afterwards gradually corrected, as he proceeded with his work. Critics have often wished that his female heads possessed a more dignified character. His children are not so beautiful as those of Titian. The heads of his men are the most perfect.

As to expression, there is not a movement of the soul, there is not a character of passion known to the ancients and capable of being expressed by art, that he has not caught, expressed, and varied, in a thousand different ways, and always within the bounds of propriety.

In regard to colour, Raffaello must yield to Titian and Correggio, although he excelled Michelangiolo.

His frescoes may rank with the first works of other schools in that line; not so his picture in oil.

In composition, he is at the head of his art.

GIULIO PIPPI, or GIULIO ROMANO, was the most distinguished pupil of Raffaello. He resembled his master more in energy than in delicacy of style, and was particularly successful in subjects of war and battles. In style of design he emulates Michelangiolo, and commands the whole mechanism of the human body. His demonstrations of motion are too violent. He generally painted in fresco, and his vast works at Mantua place him at the head of that school.

GIANFRANCESCO PENNI, of Florence, called IL FATTORE, was a principal scholar of Raffaello. Of his works, his frescoes in Rome have perished, and few of his oil pictures remain. He is characterized by fertility of conception, grace of execution, and a singular talent for landscape.

FRANCESCO PRIMATICCIO was a pupil of Giulio.

GIOVANNI DA UDINE was Raffaello's principal assistant in the arabesques of the Loggie.

PERINO DEL VAGA. Vasari considered him the best designer of the Florentine School, after Michelangiolo.

POLIDORO DA CARAVAGGIO, a labourer in the Vatican, distinguished himself in the imitation of antique bassi-relievi painting in chiaro-oscuro. Nothing of this kind was more perfect in composition, mechanism, or design.

BENVENUTO TISIO, called IL GAROFALO, studied under Raffaello. Rome, Bologna, and other cities of Italy abound with his pictures from the lives of the Apostles. They are of various merit, and not wholly painted by himself.

GAUDENZIO FERRARI, assistant of Raffaello in Albano. He never, however, equalled his master in grace, although he had a bolder tone of colour, greater invention, and more vigour of subject. He died in the prime of life. Rome possesses many of his pictures, particularly in fresco, in the churches; and in the Quirinal Palace is 'Joseph found by his Brethren,' which is esteemed a most beautiful piece. There are also many of his pictures to be found in private collections; and in his landscapes, in which he excelled, it is doubted whether the figures are by him.

ANDREA SACCHI was a pupil of Albano. He was the best colourist of the Roman school, and one of the most celebrated in design. Profoundly skilled in the theory of his art, he was slow in execution. His pictures are rare. His compositions do not abound with figures, but every figure appears appropriate to its place. He seems born for the grand style—grave miens, majestic attitudes, draperies folded with care and simplicity; a sober colouring, and a general tone, which gave to all objects a pleasing harmony and a grateful repose to the eye. His picture of 'S. Romualdo surrounded by his Monks' is ranked among the four best compositions in Rome. His 'Transite di S. Anna' at S. Carlo a' Catinari, his 'S. Andrea' in the Quirinal, and his 'S. Joseph' at Corpo alle Case, are also beautiful pictures. He was born in the vicinity of Rome in 1599, and died in 1661.

POUSSIN (NICHOLAS). He studied the Greek statues, and the remains of antiquity afforded him instruction which he could not expect from masters. From the Meleager of the Vatican (a Mercury) he derived his rule of proportion. As a model of composition, he attached himself to the 'Aldobrandini Marriage;' and from that and from basso-relievos he acquired that elegant contrast, that propriety of attitude, and that fear of crowding his picture, for which he was remarkable, being accustomed to say that a half-figure more than requisite was sufficient to destroy the harmony of a whole composition. He remained in Rome twenty-three years.

Of LANDSCAPE PAINTERS, Salvator Rosa, Claude Gellée of Lorraine, and Gaspar Dughet, called Poussin, appeared under Urban.

Salvator Rosa and Gaspar Poussin resembled each other in despatch. Both these artists were accustomed to commence and finish a landscape and decorate it with figures on the same day.

G. Poussin is accused of not having sufficiently diversified his tints, and of adhering too much to a green hue.

Maratta supports the art in its decline.

Roman balance, in mechanics, the steelyard or *statera Romana*.

Romanesque Architecture, a name given to the style of architecture which prevailed after the decline of the Roman empire, from the reign of Constantine till the introduction of the pointed arch.

Roman white is of the purest white colour, but differs from the blanc d'argent only in the warm flesh-colour of the external surface of the large square masses in which it is usually prepared.

Rood, in surveying, the fourth part of an acre in square measure, or 1,210 square yards; a rod; a pole; a measure of 16½ feet, in long measure.

Rood, or *roode*, a cross; a crucifix or image of Christ on the cross, placed in a church. The holy rood anciently was elevated at the junction of the nave and choir, and faced the western entrance to a church.

Rood-loft, a gallery which was generally placed over the chancel screen in parish churches, and was an addition peculiar to the Church of Rome. The rood-loft or gallery had its real support from the tie-beams which connected it with the walls of the building; but in the Decorative construction it appeared to rest on a range of arches or mullions below. Rood-lofts are formed both of stone and wood.

Rood-tower, or *steeple*, a tower or steeple at the intersection of the nave and transept of a church.

Roof, the part above the miner's head; that part of the strata lying immediately upon the coal.

Roofs, or coverings to buildings, are variously formed, both as to materials and construction, although certain essential qualifications are common to all of them. Thus, they are required to effectually exclude the weather, and at the same time impose the least possible weight upon the walls of the buildings over which they are erected; and another purpose which they should be designed to effect is that of aiding the walls in maintaining their position by acting as ties between them at their highest and least stable points. A roof consists mainly of two parts, viz. the framing or trussing, and the covering, the width of most buildings being too great to be spanned with any practicable covering without the support of framing beneath it. In order to avoid unnecessarily loading the walls, the entire roof should be constructed as light as possible consistent with safety and durability, and its several parts so disposed that the weight shall fall *vertically* only upon the walls, and have no tendency to force them asunder. In this respect, therefore, the framing of a roof is required to act entirely together as the supporter of the covering, and cannot be properly designed to act *laterally against* the walls as abutments. Provided this condition is secured, roofs may be formed so as to preserve a level upper surface, or a ridged surface, the adoption of the form depending upon the occasion which may or may not exist for using the exterior of the roof as a place of resort for persons or otherwise. Thus, in the East, and in warm climates, roofs are commonly made flat on the top; while in temperate regions, exposed to rains, they are usually ridged, the surface being unavailable, and the escape of water facilitated by this form.

Flat roofs are generally composed of timber framing, and covered with stone in large slabs, or with artificial cements, or with concrete moulded in rectangular blocks. The timber framing in these roofs consists of main beams which span the roof from wall to wall in one direction, and of rafters of smaller scantling laid transversely to the beams, and notched down upon them; the distance between the rafters being determined by the size of the covering blocks or slabs.

Ridged roofs are composed of framings of wood, malleable iron, or cast-iron, and coverings of tiles of burnt clay in various forms, of slate, of iron in rolled sheets or cast plates, of copper or lead in sheets. Each frame of the roof is termed a *truss*, and consists of several members, according to the width of the truss or span of the roof. The principal of these members, in a wooden truss, are the *tie-beam*, which equals in length the span of the roof, and is laid horizontally across the building, resting at each end upon a wall-plate of timber, a cast-iron shoe, or a stone template;—the *principal rafters*, which are two timbers of equal length, framed into the ends of the tie-beam, and meeting, in the manner of the legs of an isosceles triangle, in a point equidistant from the ends of the tie-beam and at some height above its central point. The apex of the triangle or ridge of the roof is supported by a vertical post, called the *king-post*, properly framed and secured to the heads of the rafters and to the tie-beam. The two triangular spaces thus formed between the rafters, tie-beam, and king-post are filled in with other members, according to the size of the truss, and adapted to assist the rafters in bearing the weight of the covering, and to connect each rafter with the half of the tie-beam below it in a firm and substantial manner. In roofs of small span, these additional members are simply two *struts* fixed in a diagonal position from the bottom of the king-post on either side to the middle of the length of each rafter. In larger roofs the requisite strength is attained, and a space saved in the roof (available as a dormitory or store-room), by introducing two vertical posts, termed *queen-posts*, leaving a space in the centre of the roof between them, these queen-posts being secured by straps below to the tie-beam, and bearing the rafters above. A horizontal beam connects the heads of the queen-posts, and is termed a *collar-beam*, the centre of which is secured to a king-post, which supports the heads of the principal rafters and the ridge of the roof. Diagonal struts are framed in between the rafters and the king-posts and queen-posts, and thus complete the truss. The trusses are fixed at intervals, from 7 to 12 feet apart, throughout the length of the roof, and upon their principal rafters longitudinal timbers, called *purlins*, are notched down, and carry the *common rafters*, which are of minor scantling, fixed parallel to the principal rafters, at small distances apart. According to the kind of covering to be used, thin strips of wood, called *battens*, are secured to the common rafters, and upon these the slates, tiles, etc., are secured with pegs, or copper nails.

Iron roofs, which are much superior to those of timber, especially for large spans, from their lightness and resistance to fire, are composed of the same essential members as those here described, malleable rods or flat bars being substituted for the tie-beams and king-posts, and the rafters and struts made of sufficient stiffness with bars of malleable L or T-iron, or with cast-iron of suitable form and section. In these roofs all the meeting-points of the several parts of each truss or principal are provided with cast-iron shoes, sockets, and connecting-plates, into which the ends of the rafters, struts, and rods are secured with screwed bolts and nuts, or gibs and keys.

Room and space, the distance from the joint or moulding edge of one floor timber to the other, which, in all ships that have ports, should be so disposed that the scantling of the timber of each side of the port, and the breadth of the port fore and aft (the openings between the timbers of the frames, if any, included), be answerable.

Root, in arithmetic and algebra, denotes a quantity which, being multiplied by itself, produces some higher power.

Rope, twisted hemp or wire, used in all kinds of buildings, for the management and control of building, for the construction of bridges, and on board ship; it is a species of tackle inseparable from the arts.

Rope machinery. The simple and beautiful contrivance employed in the dockyards for this most useful material, is contrived by machinery for the spinning of hemp into yarns, and the final preparation of the same into ropes and cables for the navy. The process first employed is separating the fibres from the hemp, and disposing them as nearly as possible into parallel juxtaposition; then the conversion of these bundles of parallel fibres into a flattened ribbon-like form called a sliver, and the spinning of this sliver into a yarn, or simple twist. In a valuable treatise in vol. v. of the 'Papers of the Royal Engineers,' will be found illustrative plates of the machinery employed in this operation in Deptford dockyard, together with an elaborate description.

Rosary, an office in the Church of Rome made up of five or fifteen tens of heads, each ten beginning with a Pater-noster, to direct them to say so many Ave Marias in honour of the Virgin Mary.

Rose Pink is a coarse kind of lake, produced by the dyeing of chalk or whiting with a decoction of Brazil wood, etc. It is a pigment much used by paper-stainers and in the commonest distemper paintings, etc., but too perishable to merit the attention of artists.

Rosetta wood is a good-sized East Indian wood, imported in logs, 9 to 14 inches in diameter; it is handsomely veined. The general colour is a lively red-orange. The wood is close, hard, and very beautiful when first cut, but soon gets darker.

Rose window, a circular window.

Rose-wood is produced in the Brazils, the Canary Isles, the East Indies, and Africa. It is imported in very large slabs, or the halves of trees, that average 18 inches wide. The colours of rose-wood are from light hazel to deep purple, or nearly black; the tints are sometimes abruptly contrasted, at other times striped or nearly uniform. It is very heavy, and most abundantly used for cabinet furniture: large quantities are frequently cut for use in veneers.

Rostrum, the elevated platform or stage in the forum of ancient Rome, from which the orators addressed the people: a platform in a hall or assembly.

Rotary motion, the rotation or motion of any body round an axis or centre; the velocity of this motion of bodies is proportional to their distance from such centre.

Rotunda, in architecture, an appellation given to any building that is round both within and without side, whether it be a church, saloon, theatre, etc. The rotunda at Rome, called the Pantheon, and the chapel of the Escurial, the burying place of Spanish royalty, etc., are of this form.

Rouge. 'The 'rouge végétale' of the French is a species of carmine prepared from safflower, of exquisite beauty and great cost. Its principal uses consist in dyeing silks of rose colours, and in combining with levigated talc to form the paint of the toilette, or cosmetic colours employed by the fair.

Roughcast, in building, a kind of plaster mixed with pebbles, and consequently rough on the surface.

Roundhouse, the uppermost deck in a ship abaft, sometimes called the poop.

Royal Blue is a deep-coloured and

beautiful smalt, and is also a vitreous pigment, principally used in painting on glass and enamelling, in which uses it is very permanent; but in water and oil its beauty soon decays, as is no uncommon case with other vitrified pigments: it is not in other respects an eligible pigment, being, notwithstanding its beautiful appearance, very inferior to other cobalt blues.

Rubble, coarse walling constructed of rough stones, small, irregular in size and shape; a mixture, or the refuse of several kinds of building-stone used for walls exteriorly, or between walls, to fill up.

Rubens' Brown. The pigment still in use in the Netherlands under this appellation is an earth of a lighter colour and more ochreous texture than the Vandyke brown of the London shops; it is also of a warmer or more tawny hue than the latter pigment, and is a beautiful and durable brown, which works well both in water and oil, and much resembles the brown used by Teniers.

Rubric, or *Madder Lakes*. These pigments are of various colours, and are known by the names of rose, rubiate, rose madder, pink madder, and Field's lakes.

Rudder, the principal matter which guides the ship. The main-piece and the bearding-piece are always oak, and the rest generally fir. The rudder should be bearded from the side of the pintles, and the fore-side made to the form of the pintles; but when they are bearded to a sharp edge at the middle line, which is the customary way, it reduces the main-piece more than is necessary, which is easily perceived by having them cut short to work in a socket in the brace, which makes the rudder work easier.

Rudenture, in architecture, the figure of a rope or staff, sometimes plain, sometimes carved, with which the third part of the flutings of columns are frequently filled up.

Ruderation, in building, a term used by Vitruvius for laying of pavement with pebbles. To perform the ruderation it is necessary that the ground be well beaten, to make it firm, and to prevent it from cracking; then a stratum of little stones is laid, to be afterwards bound together with mortar made of lime and sand: if the sand be new, its proportion may be to the lime as three to one; if dug out of old pavements or from walls, as five to two.

Running rigging, in navigation, denotes all that portion of a ship's rigging which passes through the blocks, to dilate, contract, or traverse the sails.

Russet, Rubiate, Madder Brown, or *Field's Russet*, is, as its names indicate, prepared from the *rubia tinctoria*, or madder root. It is of a pure, rich, transparent, and deep russet colour, of a true middle hue between orange and purple, not subject to change by the action of light, impure air, time, or mixture of other pigments. It has supplied a great desideratum, and is indispensable in water-colour painting, both as a local and auxiliary colour, in compounding and producing with yellow the glowing hues of autumnal foliage, etc., and with blue the beautiful and endless variety of aerial greys.

Rustication, the general name for

| SAC | SAFETY-VALVES. | SAI |

what its name literally imports, it is frequently made to show the very reverse of careless rudeness, namely, studied ornamentation, by means of highly finished moulded joints, etc.; and even when the faces of the rustics or stones are *vermiculated*, or otherwise made rough, it is left to be seen that it is done purposely or artificially, more especially when the vermiculation, etc., is made to show a sort of panel surrounded by a smooth border.

S.

SACELLUM, a monumental chapel within a church.

Sacrarium, a small family chapel in a Roman house; a place for the deposit of anything sacred.

Sacristy, a room attached to a church, where the sacred vestments and the utensils belonging to the altars were placed; termed also the sextry, the vestry, etc.

Saddle, in ship-building, a piece fitted on the upper end of the lacing.

Safety-lamp, a wire-gauze lamp, constructed for the purpose of giving light in mines where fire-damp prevails.

Safety-plug, in locomotive engines, a bolt having the centre filled with a fusible metal. It is screwed into the top of the fire-box, that the metal may melt out by the increased temperature when the water becomes too low, and thus admit the water to put the fire out, and save the tubes and fire-box. When the water is allowed to fall below a proper height, there is great risk of spoiling both the fire-box and tubes by the intense action of the fire. This is called 'burning them;' and tubes subjected to such a trial are unfit for use again, as the tenacity of the metal has been destroyed.

Safety-valves, in locomotive engines, two valves placed on the boiler for the escape of steam when it exceeds the pressure limited by the load on these valves. One of them is placed beyond the control of the engine-man, and is usually called the *lock-up valve*. The other is regulated by a lever and spring-balance, at a little lower pressure than the lock-up valve. The apertures for safety-valves require no nice calculation. It is only necessary to have the aperture sufficient to let the steam off from the boiler as fast as it is generated, when the engine is not at work. The safety-valve is loaded sometimes by putting a heavy weight upon it, and sometimes by means of a lever with a weight to move along to suit the required pressure.

Safety-valve lever, in locomotive engines, the lever fixed at one end to a stud, and resting on the valve at a short distance from this stud. Its length is proportioned to the area of the valve, so that the spring-balance may indicate accurately the pressure in lbs. per square inch on the boiler, above the atmosphere.

Sagging, in ship-building, a term the reverse of *hogging*, being applied to the hull of a ship when the middle part of her keel and bottom arch downwards.

Sagitta, in architecture, a name sometimes used for the key-piece of an arch.

Sailing, plain, in navigation, is that which is performed by means of a plane chart, in which the parallels of latitude and longitude are everywhere equal.

Saint Paul's, Old. The tower of old St. Paul's, which had tall lancet windows, was built in 1221. The work of enlargement and restoration proceeded gradually eastward. In the year 1240, the new choir was consecrated (i.e. was begun), for Henry de Lacy and Ralph de Baldoch, who survived to the reign of Edward II., were benefactors to the "new work at the east end, which is no way distinguishable from the rest of the choir." This choir was therefore about forty years in building. Taking this work at a medium between the first and last of these dates, we have a perfect specimen of English architecture in the earlier years of Edward I. Here the false arches of the dado are retained, but instead of the single and slender columns of the former era, they are sustained on pillars more massy and slightly clustered, of which the capitals resemble a rose, while the cusped arch is surmounted by a sweep highly pointed; of these the spandrils are filled with quatrefoils, and a rose appears beneath. The *triforia* remain nearly the same as in the earlier period, but the windows have lost the side columns, the mullions are angular, and the three lights of those in the north aisles surmounted by rich tracery. (*Quar. Rev. of Dr. Milner*, 1811.)

Saints' bell, a small bell used in the Roman Catholic worship, to call attention to the more solemn parts of the service.

Salt-cellars, in Tudor times, were pieces on which the taste and fancy of goldsmiths were severely exercised. These artists were held in high estimation, and ranked with architects and sculptors. Benvenuto Cellini, in the time of Henry VII., was the greatest designer and chaser, or sculptor in gold and silver, in Europe: he visited England at this period, and excited much attention.

Sanctum Sanctorum, or holy of holies, the most sacred part of the temple of Jerusalem, containing the ark of the covenant.

Sanctuary, the presbytery or eastern part of the choir of a church in which the altar is placed.

Sand is the term applied to any mineral substance in a granular state, where the grain is of an appreciable size, and insoluble in water. It is more particularly denominated from the prevailing substance, as siliceous sand, iron sand, etc. Sand is of general use for the mixing of material in building: river sand is far preferable.

Sand-boxes, in locomotive engines, boxes filled with sand, usually placed near the driving wheels, with a pipe to guide the sand to the rails, to be used when slipping takes place.

Sand-stone, a soft porous kind of stone, generally known by the name of free-stone. It is composed of small particles of quartz in rounded grains, united by an argillaceous or calcareous cement.

Sandal wood, a tree having somewhat the appearance of a large myrtle. The wood is extensively employed as a perfume in the funereal ceremonies of the Hindoos. The deeper the colour, which is of a yellow brown, and nearer to the root, the better is the perfume. It is imported in trimmed logs from 3 to 8, and rarely 14 inches in diameter, and the wood is in general softer than box-wood, and easy to cut; it is used for parts of cabinets, necklaces, ornaments, and fans.

Sanitary Precautions, for London in its southern district, were discussed nearly half a century since. Ralph Dodds, an eminent engineer of that period, writes, in his exhortation for a better supply of pure water, the following: "I cannot help noticing that part of the south metropolis St. George's Fields, lies 4 or 5 feet below the flow of high water, and is so badly drained, and I may say, so saturated with filthy water, with other deposits of every species of dirt and filth from the City and Southwark, that it must be the first place to invite pestilence should it ever be generated in this part of the country. I hope this will meet the eye of those who wait only for information to improve its situation."

Sapan wood or *buckum wood*, is a middle-sized tree, indigenous to Siam, Pegu, etc.; for purposes of dyeing it is inferior.

Sap-green, or *Verde Vessie*, is a vegetable pigment prepared from the juice of the berries of the buckthorn, the green leaves of the wood, the blue flowers of the iris, etc.; it is usually preserved in bladders, and is thence sometimes called bladder green; when good, it is of a dark colour and glossy fracture, extremely transparent, and of a fine natural green colour. Though much employed as a water colour without gum, which it contains naturally, it is a very imperfect pigment, disposed to attract the moisture of the atmosphere and to mildew; and having little durability in water-colour painting, and less in oil, it is not eligible in the one, and totally useless in the other.

Sapphire, a pellucid gem, which in its finest state is extremely beautiful and valuable, and inferior only to the diamond in lustre, hardness, and value. Its proper colour is pure blue; in the finest specimens it is of the deepest azure, and in others it varies into paleness, in shades of all degrees between that of a pure crystal brightness and water without the least tinge of colour, but with a lustre much superior to the crystal. The gem known to us by this name differs greatly from the sapphires of the ancients, which was only a semiopaque stone of a deep blue, veined with white, and spotted with small gold-coloured spangles in the form of stars.

Saracenic Architecture is a species of architecture derived by the Europeans from the Arabs, or Saracens, during the crusades.

Sarcophagus, a stone coffin or grave in which the ancients laid those they had not a mind to burn.

Sash, a chequered frame for holding the squares of glass in windows, and so formed as to be let up and down by means of pulleys inserted, or other contrivances. The ordinary sashes are either single or double hung.

Sassafras wood is a species of laurel, and the root is used in medicine; it measures from 4 to 12 inches in diameter. It is sometimes used for cabinet-work and turnery.

Satinwood. The best variety is the West Indian, imported from St. Domingo both in square logs and planks, from 9 to 20 inches wide. The next in quality is the East Indian, logs from 9 to 30 inches diameter. The wood is close, not so hard as box-wood, but somewhat like it in colour, or rather more orange; some pieces are very beautifully mottled and curled. It is much used for internal decorations and furniture. It is also used for many other purposes for its light and agreeable tone.

Saucers, small deep dishes, for sauces, etc., and also used as stands for vases, and other vessels filled with wines, to prevent the liquor being spilt upon the table. In the reign of Elizabeth, dishes and platters, which before her time were quite flat, began to assume their present form.

Saul, or *Sâl*, an East Indian timber-tree. This wood is in very general use in India for beams, rafters, and various building purposes; is close-grained and heavy, of a light brown colour, not so durable, but stronger than teak, and is one of the best timber trees of India.

Saunders Blue (a name corrupted from *cendres-bleu*), the original denomination probably of ultramarine ashes, is of two kinds, the natural and the artificial. The artificial is a verditer, prepared by lime or an alkali, from nitrate or sulphate of copper. The natural is a blue mineral, found near copper mines, and is the same as mountain-blue.

Saw, a toothed instrument which serves to cut into pieces several solid matters, as wood, stone, ivory, etc. The best saws are of tempered steel, ground bright and smooth; those of iron are hammer-hardened: hence the first, besides their being stiffer, are likewise found smoother than the last. They are known to be well hammered by the stiff bending of the blade, and to be well and evenly ground by their bending equally in a bow. The edge in which are the teeth is always thinner than the back, because the hack is to follow the edge. The teeth are cut and sharpened with a triangular file, the blade of the saw being first fixed in a whetting-block.

Saw file, a triangular file for sharpening a saw.

Saw Mills. The very ingenious machinery constructed by the late Mr. Henry Maudslay is employed in the dockyards to saw timber, and for cutting deals and the several kinds of timber used in the navy and in public works, into the several scantlings, sizes, forms, or shapes. In vol. vi. of the 'Papers of the Royal Engineers' will be found a most ample statement of the processes for sawing, and cutting, and hoisting by steam power, in Chatham dock, together with engravings illustrative of every operation in these works.

Saxon Style of Architecture. This is easily recognized by its massive columns and semicircular arches, which usually spring from capitals without the intervention of the entablature. In the first Saxon buildings, the mouldings were extremely simple, the greater part consisting of fillets and plat-bands, at right angles to each other, and to the general surface. The archivolts and imposts were similar to those found in Roman edifices. The general plans and disposition of the latter Saxon churches were as follow: the chief entrance was at the west end and into the nave, at the upper end of which was a cross, with the arms of it extending north and south; the east end, containing the choir, terminated in a semicircular form. A tower was erected over the centre of the cross, and to contain the bells another was frequently added, and sometimes two. The large churches contained a nave and two side aisles, one on each side of the nave, and were divided into three tiers or stories, the lower consisting of a range of arcades on each side, the middle a range of galleries between the roof and vaulting of the aisles, and the uppermost a range of windows. The pillars were either square, polygonal, or circular. Such was the thickness of the walls and pillars, that buttresses were not necessary, neither were they in use. The apertures were splayed from the mullions on both sides. The dressings are generally placed on the sides of the splayed jambs and heads of the arches, and but seldom against the face of the walls; and when this is the case, the projectures are not very prominent. The dressings of the jambs frequently consist of one or several engaged columns upon each side. The imposts, particularly those of the windows, have frequently the appearance of being a part of the wall itself. The doors in general were formed in deep recession, and a series of equidistant engaged columns placed upon each jamb, and were such, that two horizontal straight lines would pass through the axis of each series, and would, if produced, terminate in a point. Each column is attached to a recess formed by two planes, constituting an interior right angle. The angle at the meeting of every two of these recesses formed an exterior right angle, which was sometimes obtunded, and frequently hollowed. The archivolts, resting on the capitals of the columns, are formed on the soffit shelving, like the jambs below. The ornaments of columns and mouldings are of very simple forms. The rudely sculptured figures, which often occur in door cases, when the head of the door itself is square, indicates a Roman original, and are mostly referable to an era immediately preceding the Conquest.

Scabellum, in ancient architecture, a kind of pedestal, commonly terminating in a sort of sheath or scabbard, used to support busts, etc.

Scagliola, in the arts, a composition, an imitation of marble, laid on brick in the manner of stucco, and worked off with iron tools.

Scala, a ladder, a staircase, from Scala Santa, a building at Rome, erected from the designs of Fontana, with three flights of stairs. The building is so called because the middle flight consists of twenty-eight steps, said to have been passed over by our Saviour in his progress to the house of Pilate. They were sent from Jerusalem to Rome by St. Helena, and are objects of reverence to Roman Catholic pilgrims.

Scale, in painting, a figure subdivided by lines like a ladder, which is used to measure proportions between pictures and the things represented.

Scamillus, a small plinth below the bases of Ionic and Corinthian columns.

Scantling, the transverse dimensions of a piece of timber in breadth and thickness.

Scantling, is also the name of a piece of timber, as of quartering for a partition, or the rafters, purlin, or pole-plate of a roof. All quartering under five inches is termed scantling.

Scantling, in masonry, the size of the stones in length, breadth, and thickness.

Scapple: to scapple a stone is to reduce it to a straight surface without working it smooth.

Scarcement, a plain flat set-off in a wall.

Scapus, in architecture, the shaft of a column. In botany, a flower-stalk springing straight from the root, as in the primrose, snowdrop, etc.

Scarf, to lap the ends of plank or timber one over the other, to appear as one solid piece, as keel-pieces, clamps, etc.

Scarfed, in carpentry, signifies pieced or joined, being a particular method of uniting two pieces of timber by their extremities.

Scarfing, the junction of two pieces of timber by being bolted or nailed transversely together, so that the two appear as one.

Scarlet Lake is prepared in form of drops from cochineal, and is of a beautiful transparent red colour and excellent body, working well both in water and oil, though, like other lakes, it dries slowly. Strong light discolours and destroys it, both in water and oil; and its tints with white lead, and its combinations with other pigments, are not permanent: yet when well prepared and judiciously used in sufficient body, and kept from strong light, it has been known to last many years; but it ought never to be employed in glazing, nor at all in peformances that aim at high reputation and durability.

Scarp, in heraldry, signifies the scarf worn by military commanders.

Scena, the permanent architectural front which faced the audience part of a Roman theatre: it sometimes consisted of three several ranges of columns one above another.

Scenography, in perspective, the representation of a body on a perspective plane; a description thereof in all its dimensions, such as it appears to the eye.

Schola, the margin or platform surrounding a bath. It was occupied by those who waited until the bath was cleared. The schola was also a portico corresponding to the exedra of the Greek palæstra, and was intended for the accommodation of the learned, who were accustomed to assemble and converse there.

Schools of Painting. A school in the fine arts denominates a class of artists who have learned their art from a certain master, either by receiving his instruction or by studying his works, and who of consequence discover more or less of his manner from the desire of imitation, or from the habit of adopting his principles. All the painters which Europe has produced since the renovation of the arts are classed under the following Schools: the School of Florence, the School of Rome, the School of Venice, the Lombard School, the French School, the German School, the Flemish School, the Dutch School, the Spanish and the English School.

Schooner, in navigation, a small two-masted vessel whose mainsail and foresail are suspended from gaffs and stretched out below by booms.

Schweinfurt Blue appears to be the same in substance as Scheele's green, prepared without heat, or treated with an alkali. It is a beautiful colour, liable to the same changes, and is of the same habits as blue verditer, and the above ineligible pigment.

Sciography, in architecture, the profile or section of a building, to show the inside thereof. In astronomy, the art of finding the hour of the day or night by the shadow of the sun, moon, or stars.

Sconce, in manufacture, a pensile candlestick, generally with a mirror to reflect the light.

Scotia, the hollow moulding in the base of an Ionic column, derived from the Greek, signifying shade, because, from being hollow, part of it is always in shadow. The scotia is likewise a groove or channel cut in the projecting angle of the Doric corona.

Scovanlode, a lode having no gozzan on its back or near the surface.

Scraper, a piece of iron used to take out the pulverized matter which remains in a hole when bored previous to blasting.

Screen, a movable framework to keep off an excess of light, or heat, or cold; a separation; a partition. In ecclesiastical architecture, a screen denotes a partition of stone, wood, or metal; usually so placed in a church as to shut out an aisle from the choir, a private chapel from the transept, the nave from the choir, the high altar from the east end of the building, etc. Some very beautiful examples exist of screens, especially of those separating the choir from the nave. That of York is of a magnificent character. 'All Saints' Church, Maidstone,' a work published in 4to, is of an interesting description on this head. In modern architecture, a single open colonnade, admitting a view through it, is called a screen of columns: such was that formerly in front of Carlton House. Grosvenor House has a Doric screen in front of it.

Screen bulk-head, in ship-building, that which is under the round-house.

Screw, a spiral groove or thread winding round a cylinder so as to cut all the lines drawn on its surface parallel to its axis at the same angle. The spiral may be either on the convex or concave surface of the cylinder, and it is called accordingly either the screw or the nut. The screw can hardly be called a simple machine, because it is never used without a lever or winch to move it home, and then it becomes an engine of amazing power and utility in pressing together substances that have little cohesion, or in raising to short heights ponderous bodies. The smith, the carpenter, the printer, and the packer, all use screws in their respective occupations. Bales of wool, cotton, hay, etc., may be compressed by means of a screw into packages, the specific gravity of which shall be much heavier than an equal volume of water. Such packages will then sink in the ocean like a cannon-shot. Moreover, many of our domestic operations are performed by means of presses or screws; as the making of sugar, oil, and wine. The screw possesses one great advantage over the inclined plane, from which its principal of action may be said to be derived. The great attrition or friction which takes place in the screw is useful by retaining it in any state to which it has once been brought, and continuing the effect after the power is removed. It is thus the cabinet-maker's cramp, the smith's vice, and all those instruments made by mathematical instrument-makers in which screws act, can be employed with certainty. Screws are made with threads of various forms: some have sharp, others square or round threads.

Screw-jack, a strong screw for lifting or supporting a heavy weight: it rests, by means of a large nut, upon a hollow base or pedestal, and is raised or lowered by turning the nut.

Screw. Screw propellers, for navigation, by means of steam power, have now become objects of importance to all nations, more particularly for those who navigate the broad waters: they are especially applicable for vessels of war, the machinery for propulsion being without the reach of shot. Screw propellers, however variously they may be modified, all derive their power of propelling by being placed on an axis which is parallel to the keel, and by having threads or blades extending from the axis, which form segments of a helix or spiral, so that, by causing the axis to revolve, the threads worm their way through the water, much in the same way as a carpenter's screw inserts itself into a piece of wood. There is, however, considerable difference between the action of a carpenter's screw and of the screw propeller: the latter, acting upon a fluid, cannot propel the vessel without causing the water to recede, while the carpenter's screw progresses through the wood without any such recession. The law which governs the distance which the water recedes is common to the paddle-wheel, and to all bodies moving in the water. The screw propelling is not of recent construction; we find that so early as 1727, Mr. Duquet invented an hydraulic screw machine, which he placed between two boats, connected by transverse bearing, to which the screw was affixed. Mr. Paucton, in 1768, published his 'Theory of the Screw of Archimedes;' other inventions followed, until a recent date, when Mr. George Rennie applied his comprehensive mind to the subject. Sir John Rennie and Mr. George Rennie undertook, when all other engineers declined the order, to construct the engines for the Ship Propeller Company formed in 1836, to work out Mr. J. P. Smith's patent for the application of the screw to propel steam vessels, by placing it in a space to be left for that purpose, in that part called the 'dead-wood;' that is, the solid wood-work between the stern-post and the keel of the vessel. This screw-propeller vessel was at length launched, and the engines, by the Messrs. Rennie, constructed. This vessel, named the 'Archimedes,' of 232 tons and 80-horse power, was brought out in 1840; the success was complete, and the publicity given to her performances by her spirited owners, who took her round Great Britain and showed her powers in every port, rendered the capabilities of the screw no longer a matter of doubt; she was in the first instance fitted with a single-threaded screw, as shown in the accompanying diagram.

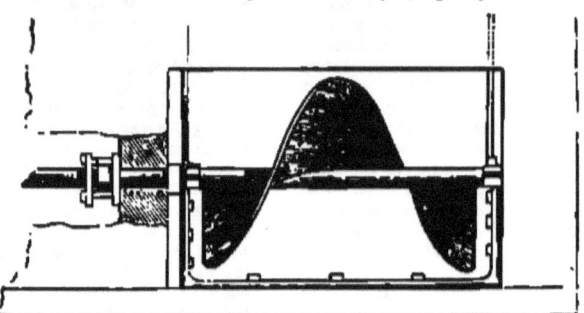

Other patents were subsequently taken out, and many experiments made. In 1836, Mr. Ericsson obtained a patent for a propeller consisting of six blades, a a a a a a, set at equal distances round a cylinder concentric with the axis b: the blades and arms were segments

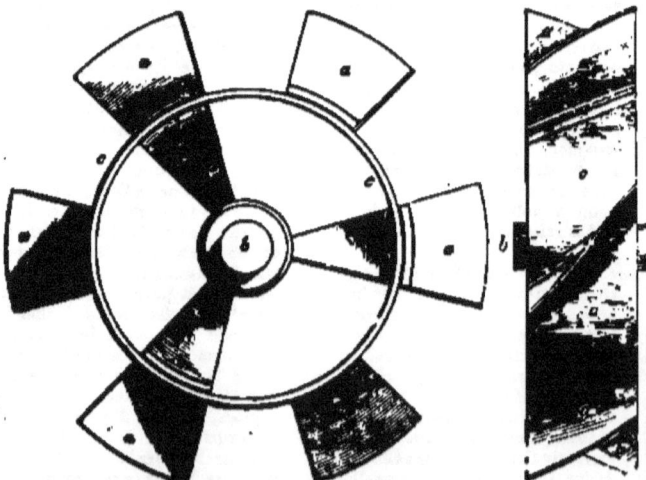

of a screw. The Archimedean screw is a helix, consisting of an inclined plane wound round a cylinder. When such a screw has communicated a retrograde motion to the water equal to its own recession, the further continuance of the thread will not only be useless, but will occasion a friction by its unnecessary surface. Mr. Rennie proposed to make the screw spiral instead of helical; the thread of his propeller would thus be generated by winding an inclined plane round a logarithmic cone or spire.

The accompanying diagram will probably best explain the method adopted.

Various other methods have since been suggested and adopted; one by Mr. Blaxland. This propeller shaft rests upon a bearing in the false stern-post, which is fitted with a stuffing box. There is an open space on the dead-wood, in which the propeller works, similar to that of the 'Archimedes,' but the propeller rests entirely upon the bearing, instead of having an after-bearing like the screw of that vessel. Captain Carpenter's invention was adopted by the Admiralty in the pinnace 'Geyser,' commanded by himself. There are in this case two propellers, which are placed in the quarters. They receive motion by means of a rotatory engine, called the disc engine. The propellers differ from all others, consisting merely of two flat trapeziums attached by arms to the axis: they are therefore not portions of a screw, though this action is helical. In May, 1843, Mr. Bennet Woodcroft was directed by the Lords of the Admiralty to make a screw at his own cost, which they caused to be tried in the 'Rattler.' This screw was made of copper, having four blades; and it corresponded in every respect with a screw of a uniform pitch, also made of copper, in the number of its blades, its diameter, length and pitch, with this exception, that although they each commenced with the same pitch, yet Mr. Woodcroft's screw gradually increased in its pitch throughout, and terminated with an increase of 5 per cent. additional pitch. The trial of Smith's four-bladed Archimedean or true screw took place in the 'Rattler,' on the 18th of March, 1844; and on the 13th of the following month, a trial of Woodcroft's increasing-pitch screw, of four blades, was made with the same vessel. After this trial, Mr. Lloyd, the chief engineer of the Admiralty, who had been present to superintend it, stated to Mr. Woodcroft, who had also been present, that the latter screw was superior to the uniform pitch screw in two important qualities; first, that it propelled the vessel at an equal speed with less power; and, secondly, that it also propelled the vessel at an equal speed with fewer revolutions of the screw, which latter quality he considered superior to the former; but that the difficulty arising from having to drive screws so fast, constituted the greatest obstacle to their introduction in the Royal Navy. Indeed, this is the admitted difficulty in the application of the screw as a marine propeller, and the practical difference between it and the paddle-wheel. The great size of latter enables the speed of the engines to accomplish the required velocity of the boat, whereas the small diameter of the screw renders it necessary that it should perform many more revolutions than the engine makes strokes. Hence the necessity of introducing some multiplying gearing between the engine and the propeller; and this multiplying gear, consisting of cast-iron cog-wheels and pinions, is necessarily liable to frequent breakage and damage. The great object to be now achieved in the application of the screw as a marine propeller, is to introduce an intermediate gearing for multiplying the velocity, which shall not be liable to accident, or to render this gearing altogether unnecessary. Smith's screw, however, with some modifications of his former patent, now

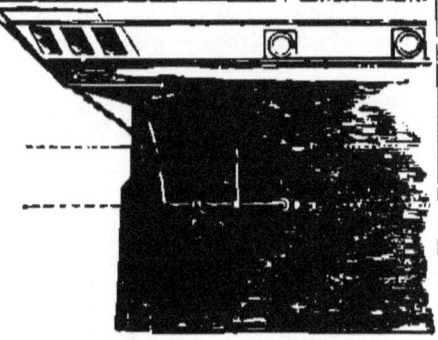

SCR   SCREW.   SCR

diminished to two blades, is used in the navy to some extent, as well as a more recent invention of Mr. Griffiths, whose trials have been generally successful.

Screw-cutting Machine. The machinery adapted to this purpose varies in construction according to the notions of the different makers, but the general principle is the same in all, the difference consisting in the method of carrying it into effect. The machine is a compound of the 'slide-rest' and lathe, with a train of wheels to give motion to the former. The metal to be cut into a screw is placed between the centres of the lathe in the usual manner, and the cutting-tool is fixed upon the slide rest, which has its lower slide made parallel to the centre line; the upper slide is only used for adjusting the cutting-tool. The screw of the lower slide has motion communicated by the train of three or more wheels; the first, or driving wheel, is fixed on the mandril of the lathe, and last of the train is fixed on the end of the slide-screw; the other wheels are intermediate wheels. The pitch of the screw to be cut, or distance between the centres of two consecutive threads, is the space traversed by the tool during one revolution of the work, and is regulated by the sizes of the wheels which must therefore be changed for every difference in the pitch.

The perfection to which screw-cutting has been brought, is mainly attributable to the application of the slide-rest; and the beautiful and accurate screws, of all sizes, produced by the screw-cutting machine, have contributed in no small degree to the perfection of our machinery in general, and more particularly to that of astronomical instruments.

There are also other machines, called screwing machines, for screw-cutting, which perform work of a much rougher description, such as cutting short screws or bolts, for fastening together the flanges of pipes, etc. The machine consists of a strong iron frame, which carries a mandril somewhat similar to that of a lathe, driven by a band passing over a pulley. The head of the bolt to be screwed is held by a clamp at the projecting end of the mandril, so that it revolves with it as in a lathe, the only difference being, that it is held at one end and free at the other. The dies, or two hardened steel pieces, which together form a nut, with the grooves lengthwise for cutting, are placed in a small frame, across the machine, supported by two guides projecting from the machine frame, one on each side, level and parallel with the bolt.

When the machine is set in motion, the small cross frame is brought forward, and the end of the revolving bolt is made to enter the dies, which are pressed upon it by set-screws; and as their cutting edges take effect on the bolt, the frame is carried forward on the guides till it has moved the required length; it is then brought back by reversing the motion of the machine, and the dies are tightened for another cut; this operation is repeated until the screw is of the required diameter. By fixing a tap, or cutting-screw, to the mandril, in place of the bolt, and holding a nut by the screws in the cross-frame, the machine is made to cut internal screws.

Scribing, a term applied to the edge of a board when fitted upon any surface.

Scribing, in joinery, the act of fitting one piece of wood upon another, so that the fibres of both may be perpendicular to each other, and the end cut away across the fibres, so as to fit upon the slide of the other.

Scrin, in mining, a small vein.

Scroll, a name given to a kind of ornament of general use, which resembles a hand arranged in undulations or convolutions.

Sculpture is the art of carving wood or hewing stone into images. It is an art of the most remote antiquity, having been practised, there is reason to suppose, before the Deluge. To this reason is assigned the expedients by which, in the first stages of society, the images of men have everywhere supplied the place of alphabetical characters. These, it is universally known, have been picture writing, such as that of the Mexicans, which, in the progress of refinement and knowledge, were gradually improved into the hieroglyphics of the Egyptians and other ancient nations. To make a distinction between carving and sculpture, the former belonged exclusively to wood and the latter to stone. The latter evinced vast comprehension of mental taste and study of human anatomy as well as that of other animals. In examining the various sculptures of the Egyptians, it is found that a general character prevails throughout their outlines: many valuable specimens remain to attest their greatness in this art. It is to the Greeks that great superiority is due. The art of sculpture probably was influenced by the climate over the human frame, as the violent heats of the torrid zone and the excessive cold of the polar regions are unfavourable to beauty: it is only to the mild climates of the temperate regions that it appears in its most attractive charms. The Romans displayed great talents for statuary; subsequently the Italian masters showed their eminence in the art; and in our own country the works of Westmacott and Chantrey belong to the distinguished English School. Carving in wood exists in the fine and most elaborate works of Flemish masters, and those of Gibbons and others of England are of equal talent in this pleasing art.

The Grecian marbles in the British Museum have given so much grace to British art, and to execution in the art generally, that a short description of them, and their connection with architecture, will not be unacceptable.

We learn from Athenian Stuart, that "the Temple of Minerva, called the Parthenon and Hecatompedon, was built during the administration of Pericles, who employed Callicrates and Ictinus as architects, under Phidias, to whom he committed the direction of all works of elegance and magnificence. It has been celebrated by some of the most eminent writers of antiquity, whose accounts are confirmed and illustrated in the descriptions given us by those travellers who saw it almost entire in the last century. Even in its present state, the spectator on approaching it will find himself not a little affected by so solemn an appearance of ruined grandeur. Accustomed as we were to the ancient and modern magnificence of Rome, and by what we had heard and read, impressed with an advantageous opinion of what we were come to see, we found the image our fancy had preconceived greatly inferior to the real object.

"This temple, the most costly and highly finished example of the Doric order, perhaps the largest octastyle temple of antiquity, had the advantage of the great mind of Phidias. It is to Lord Elgin's enterprise and enthusiasm for art that England owes the unique treasures deposited in the British Museum. Pausanias remarks, 'On entering the temple called the Parthenon, all the works in what are termed the pediments (eagles) seem to relate to the birth of Minerva; those behind represent the contest of Neptune and Minerva concerning Attica; but the statue itself (of the goddess) is formed of ivory and gold.' Pausanias then proceeds to a minute description of the chrys-elephantine statue, notices other monuments of art, describes the Erechtheum, and enlarges on the colossal bronze Minerva by Phidias, called Promachus, etc. The beauty of the marble of the mountains surrounding Athens, particularly that of Pentelicus, from which the temple Parthenon was wrought, must have given a great zest to the Athenians in the cultivation of the refinement of architectural design: with more brilliancy, it is almost capable of receiving the high finish of ivory. According to Pliny, Dio-pœnus and Scyllis, born in Crete about the 50th Olympiad, B.C. 579, were the first sculptors distinguish-ed in working marble, and to them are also attributed the earliest sta-tues of ivory and gold. Of the part Phidias had in the design of the Parthenon temple, and in the production of the sculpture in par-ticular, a diversity of opinion has existed. It has been supposed that the whole of the sculptural deco-rations are the 'undoubted' pro-ductions of that great artist, thus conveying to them a charm, from the association of that great name, which the unequal execution does not entitle portions of them to re-ceive: others assert that he had nothing to do with the works, but that he may have designed the sculpture. However, the words ' skilful sculptor in marble' have been applied by Aristotle to Phidias, in opposition to 'statuary,' given by him to Polycletus, whose works were principally in bronze, in order to strengthen the probability of his having executed the marble sculp-ture of the Parthenon. Pliny states Phidias to have been the first who displayed and perfected the toreutic art, or sculpture formed by the combination of metals and other materials. The fertility of genius of this great sculptor, who was equally skilful in every department of his art, was surprising. He was at the period of the erection of the Parthenon, engaged in so many and such various monuments belonging to the toreutic art, that his atten-tion must have been occupied by them to so great a degree, that any but a general superintendence of the designs of the temple can scarcely be supposed possible. When executing the Minerva of the Parthenon, he had already comple-ted or was engaged on, besides many other statues and groups in ivory and gold, five other statues of that goddess, probably all of them colossal, of which the Mi-nerva Promachus, in bronze, in the Acropolis, must have been up-wards of 50 feet in height, having been seen from the sea. The pas-sage of Plutarch, describing the artists of the structures of Pericles is, 'Phidias directed and superin-tended all the works of him (Pericles), although they had great architects and artificers; for Cal-licrates and Ictinus executed the Hecatompedon, or Parthenon.'"

Sculpture. Mr. Hailes, in 1825, writes the following.—" The introduction of statues of individuals, however eminent and meritorous, into squares and public places, is a no-velty in this our metropolis, which, till of late years, seemed to be re-served for the sovereign and his family. We have, however, two, which, although not contrary to law, at least to any that I know of, are certainly deviations from long-established custom, and a sort of invasion or trespass upon royal prerogative. That of the late Duke of Bedford, the Triptolemus of his time, in Russell Square, is an erect figure, surrounded by the attributes of husbandry; and be-neath it are some smaller figures, equally symbolic. The late Bishop of E——, going with a friend to look at this statue, was asked by him what he thought would be the fittest inscription for it. His an-swer was, ' Bovi Optimo Maxi-

| SCU | SCULPTURE. | SEA |

mo.' It seems extraordinary that his Grace, with these emblems of agriculture about him, has not been made to look towards the country instead of the town. But he looks towards Mr. Fox, the Demosthenes of our day, in Bedford Square, sitting in a lumpish manner in a sort of curule chair, and habited in a toga, *à la Romaine;*—his neck is exposed, and the drapery, passing over one of his shoulders across his breast, might very well give occasion, as it did, to one of his old Westminster constituents, to say, 'So, Charley, you are going to be shaved, I see.' These are two very sharp remarks: one from a very highly cultivated man, and a great scholar; and the other from a very coarse observer, but equally shrewd and comical in their way. They seem to supersede the necessity of any other criterion. We are not happy in this branch of the fine arts; and the only instance in which we can pride ourselves is not of a late date, being the equestrian statue of Charles the First, by a scholar of John de Bologna, at Charing Cross. Our ill success is perhaps the less to be lamented, as works of this sort, exposed to such an atmosphere as we live in, become in a short time so much defaced as to make it very indifferent whether the workmanship be from the hand of a Glycou or a Bacon. All our monuments of this kind seem to represent our chimney-sweepers, a-foot or on horseback, rather than our kings, princes, and other great men." The late Mr. Nash observed, " that these criticisms are unjust as well as impolitic: by running down the best, we open the door to the worst artists. It is a peculiarly English feeling. If Westmacott's bronzes, which one hardly dares (in the face of criticism) to pronounce unrivalled in this country, had received their due praise, the designer of the Duke of Kent, at the top of Portland Place, would never have been suffered to libel the state of English art."

Scumbling is giving a kind of rough dotted shadow to trees, grass, gravel-walks, etc., in a drawing when it is nearly finished. It is performed with a brush having some dark-brown colour in it, but nearly dry. The hairs of the brush are spread apart, then held in a slanting direction, and swept lightly over the foreground, or where the shadows are wanting. This is practised by some artists with considerable effect.

Scuppers, holes cut through a ship's side for throwing off the water from the pump. They should be disposed clear of the guns, standards, the ports below, gangways, etc.

Scutcheon, the shield represented in heraldry.

Scuttles, holes cut in divers parts of the decks, exclusive of hatchways and ladderways; likewise holes cut through the ship's side for air.

Scyricum Marmor, a name given by the ancients sometimes to a white, and sometimes to a yellowish marble; both used in the public buildings of the Romans, but seldom in statuary, not being capable of receiving a high polish.

Sea. The sea covers about three-fourths of the entire surface of the globe. The specific gravity of sea-water is about 1·0277; the water of closed seas into which many rivers fall is lighter, as that of the Black Sea and the Baltic. The water of the Mediterranean is more salt than that of the Atlantic, containing about 4·18 per cent., while that of the Baltic contains only 1·18 per cent. of salt. There are also other mineral substances in sea-water, as iodine, bromine, magnesia, lime, etc., in small quantities. The temperature of the air over the sea has been proved by observation to be more uniform than that of the air over the land; places near the sea have therefore a more uniform climate than those at a considerable distance from it.

Seal, a device or an engraved inscription; also its impression made on wax. Kings, bishops, and prelates were accustomed to use their several devised seals. Cities, towns, corporations, companies, institutions, and public bodies, had their seals. Privy or individual seals were also of frequent use, and some very curious seals exhibit much beauty and ingenuity. That represented in the annexed engraving is the seal of Michael Stanhope, who was Vice-Admiral of Suffolk in the time of Queen Elizabeth.

Seam, in mining, a horse-load.

Seams, the opening between the planks when wrought.

Secant, a true line that cuts another or divides it into two parts.

Section, a vertical plan of the interior of a building, showing it as it would appear upon an upright plane cutting through it. Though rarely shown, sections are almost as indispensable as plans; like which they show the thicknesses of the walls, and, in addition, those of the ceilings and floors; and also heights, both of the rooms themselves, and of doors and windows; —moreover, the forms of the ceilings, whether flat, or coved, or vaulted. In one respect, too, a section partakes of the nature of an elevation, the plane parallel to the line of section being an elevation of the interior, or rather consisting of as many elevations as there are separate rooms or divisions. Sections may be described as either furnished or unfurnished: the latter show only construction and the strictly architectural parts; wherefore, if the side of a room happens to be quite plain, without door, chimney-piece, or other feature, that side or space will be a blank, or little better. Furnished sections, on the contrary, exhibit, besides what strictly belongs to the architecture and its decoration, mirrors, pictures, statues, furniture, draperies, and all other accessories. The number of sections required depends upon the nature of the plan, and what may be worth showing. If the design be worthy of it, there should be as many sections as will suffice to show every side of every principal apartment; though it may not be necessary to repeat the entire section through every floor. Sections are the *deliciæ* of architectural illustration.

Sector, in geometry, an instrument of wood or metal, with a joint and sometimes a piece to turn out and make a true square, with lines of sines, tangents, secants, equal parts, rhombs, polygons, hours, latitudes, etc.

Sedilia, a name for a seat: the term is applied to the seats for the officiating priests, inserted (and some ornamented) in the south wall of a church.

Segment of a circle, a part of a circle bounded by an arc and its chord, and either greater or less than a semicircle.

Segment of a sphere, any part of a sphere cut off by a plane, the section of which, with the sphere, is always a circle.

Sella (Latin), the general term for a seat or a chair of any description. *Sella Curulis*, a chair of state.

Semaphore, in mechanics, a name given by the French to the telegraph, and latterly adopted in England to signify any machine to communicate intelligence by signs or signals.

Semicircle, half a circle, or the area comprehended between a diameter and the semi-circumference.

Semi-ordinate, in conic sections, a line drawn at right angles to and bisected by the axis, and reaching from one side of the section to the other.

Sepia, *Seppia*, or *Æthiops-mineral*. This pigment is named after the sepia or cuttle, which is called also the ink-fish, from its affording a dark liquid, which was used as an ink and pigment by the ancients. From this liquid our pigment sepia, which is brought principally from the Adriatic, may be obtained from the fish on our own coasts; and it is supposed that it enters into the composition of the Indian ink of the Chinese. Sepia is of a powerful, dusky-brown colour, of a fine texture; it works admirably in water, combines cordially in other pigments, and is very permanent. It is much used as a water-colour, and in making drawings in the manner of bistre and Indian ink, but it is not used in oil, in which it dries very reluctantly.

Septuagint, the Greek version of the books of the Old Testament, so called because the translation is supposed to have been effected by seventy-two Jews, who are usually called the seventy interpreters.

Sepulchre, a grave, tomb, or place of interment. Extreme attention to the sepulture of deceased friends characterized nations from remote antiquity, and to be deprived of it was accounted a very degrading circumstance. The Romans were prohibited by a law from burying their dead within the city; and it was a field that the father of the Jews purchased for the sepulture of his wife. "Hear us, my lord: in the choice of our sepulchres bury thy dead; none of us shall withhold from thee his sepulchre, but that thou mayest bury thy dead."—*Gen.* xxiii. 6. The ancient tombs of the East are remarkable for their durability, and, in some instances, their beauty: they are monuments on which the lapse of ages effects no change; in many instances hewn in the solid rock, they are calculated for duration equal to that of the hills in which they have been excavated. In a garden, hewn out of a rock, was the sepulchre of Jesus.

As an instance of a style of modern sepulture, which is rapidly extending, may be mentioned the Cemetery of Père la Chaise, at Paris, which comprehends above 150 acres, thickly studded with chapels, tombs, and monuments, beautified with winding walks, curtained with lofty shady trees, and adorned with plants and evergreens. It contains nearly 16,000 mausolea built of the finest granite, sandstone, and polished Carrara marble, the expense of which has been estimated at about 120,000,000 francs, or £5,000,000 sterling.

Serges, the great wax candles burnt before the altars in Roman Catholic churches.

Serpentine, the *ophites*, or serpent-stone of the ancients. Mona marble is an example of serpentine, and the Lizard Point, Cornwall, is a mass of it.

Serving, in navigation, encircling a rope with line or spun-yarn, to prevent its being chafed.

Set-off, or *Offset*, the part of a wall, etc., which is exposed horizontally when the portion above it is reduced in thickness.

Severey, a bay or compartment of a vaulted ceiling.

Sewers are subterranean passages or channels for the conveyance of waste waters and other matters from towns and buildings. In order that a sewer shall act with efficiency and promote the rapid discharge of the matters committed to it, it is necessary that it be constructed thoroughly impermeable throughout its entire length, that its interior surface be even and smooth, and present no impediments to the sewage, and that its vertical declination be sufficient to prevent any suspension of the current. The sectional area of the sewer should be amply sufficient to contain the entire volume of the sewage, and its form such as will best secure its action with the minimum contents. The form of a sewer should be adapted to resist the utmost pressure to which it may be exposed externally from the surrounding materials in which it is constructed; and ready access should be afforded at intervals for examining its condition from time to time, and detecting and removing any obstruction which may possibly occur to the immediate passage of the sewage. Hence rectangular forms are utterly inapplicable for these works, the section of which should be entirely curvilinear; and theory and experience have concurred in appointing a sectional form, similar to that of the egg, as best fulfilling the conditions of strength to resist external pressure, and (the smaller curve being placed downwards) to produce the most activity in the current when the quantity of sewage is reduced to the minimum. The simplest and best rule for obtaining with circular curves a true egg-shaped or oviform section for sewers is that given in the 'Rudimentary Treatise on the Drainage and Sewage of Towns and Buildings,' belonging to the same series with this work, and which is therefore here quoted.

"Let the greater diameter, or that of the upper part of the section, equal 1; the less diameter, or that of the bed of the sewer, equal ·5; and the entire height of the section equal the sum of these, or 1·5. Then strike a semicircle of 1 diameter for the head or arch of the section, and 120° of a circle of ·5 diameter for the invert; connect the arch and invert with side arcs of 1·5 radius, the centres of these side arcs being on the produced horizontal diameter of the top arch. These arcs will be truly tangential, both to the arch and invert, and will complete a section well adapted for the practical purposes of the sewer, and, being so extremely simple in its construction, peculiarly ready of application by workmen in forming and using templates, and in testing the accuracy of the work as it proceeds. The proper size or sectional area of sewers is determinable upon the quantity of sewage, and the velocity of its passage, which latter element depends jointly upon the rate of declivity at which the sewer is laid, and the volume of water in motion. The quantity of sewage to be conveyed from a town is made up chiefly of the bulk of the water supplied to the population, the excrementitious matters produced, and the quantity of rain-water falling upon the service. The maximum quantity thus accruing during any given period of time will determine the minimum capacity of the sewer, calculated in combination with the rate at which the passage can be effected; while, on the other hand, the minimum quantity thus accruing will limit the proper radius of the invert of the sewer, so that the friction of the water against the surface of the sewer may be reduced in proportion to the total bulk of the sewage. All junctions of one line of sewer with another, and all changes of direction whatever, should be formed with curves of the greatest possible radius, experiment having proved that the current is impeded in proportion as the radius of curvature is reduced, and that angular junctions are still more mischievous in suspending the proper action of the channel. Thus in a sewer 2 feet 6 inches wide, a stream having a velocity of 250 feet per minute suffers a resistance from a rectangular change of direction three times that produced with a curve of 20 feet in radius, and double that produced with a curve of 5 feet radius. The inevitable effect of suspending the motion at these junctions is that the solid particles become deposited, and form a permanent bar, requiring some extraordinary action or force of water to remove it.

"It is usual to distinguish sewers according to their size and functions, as first class, or main sewers; second class, or collateral sewers; and third class, or branch sewers; while the smaller channels for conveying the contributions from individual tenements are termed *drains*. The same rules will apply equally to all of these as far as their proper objects are concerned, although the peculiar construction to be adopted will of course depend to some extent upon the actual size of each channel. For the larger sewers, constructions of brickwork are commonly used. These require careful formation, and to be accurately jointed, and the interior of the invert at any rate smoothly formed with a hard-drying cement. For smaller channels or drains and branch sewers, whole pipes of glazed stoneware are coming into extended employment, and, if truly formed and carefully laid and jointed, these form very superior ducts for the passage of the sewage. By the use of these pipes, the essential qualification of impermeability is better secured than with brick sewers, the repeated joints of which need great labour and care in construction, and if formed with inferior mortar, soon becomes imperfect. As necessary appliances to all sewers and drains, efficient traps or apparatus to prevent the escape of the noxious gases engendered within the channels are really indispensable, and these are required to be simple in construction and unerring in their action. The entire subject of the sewage of towns and buildings is now first receiving the attention due to it as a necessary condition to the public health; and when this important branch of engineering science shall have been thoroughly investigated by qualified public officers, we may hope for the most useful and salutary practice, based upon correct principles, and for corresponding amendment in all that pertains to the subterranean ways of our cities, towns, and dwellings."

Palladio says, "The great common sewer or the general receiver or sink of all the filth of Rome was near the Senatorian bridge, called S. Marca, a performance of Tarquinius Superbus. Authors tell strange things of its largeness, viz. that a full laden hay-cart could drive through it: upon measuring, I have found it to be 16 feet diameter. Into this all other sewers of the city do empty themselves, which is the reason that sturgeons taken between the Senatorian and Subliclan bridges are better than others, feeding on the filth coming out of this great sewer."

Very recently the Legislature have determinately taken up the subject of purifying the Thames and of draining London, and placed funds at the disposal of the Metropolitan Board of Works; so that the task, the great task, is fairly in hand, and likely to proceed satisfactorily and it is to be hoped successfully.

Sextant, in geometry, the sixth part of a circle; in navigation, etc., an astronomical instrument made like a quadrant, but containing only sixty degrees.

Shaft, in architecture, the body of a column or pillar; the part between the capital and base. In mediæval architecture the term is applied to small columns clustered round pillars, or used in the jambs of doors and windows.

Shaft, in mill-work, a large axle, in contradistinction to a small one, which is called a spindle: thus we say, 'the shaft of a fly-wheel,' 'the spindle of a pinion.' Shafts are said to be lying when they are in a horizontal direction, and vertical when they are upright.

Shaft, in mining, a sinking or pit, either in the lode or through the country.

Shafted impost: according to Professor Willis, "those imposts which have horizontal mouldings, the sections of the arch above and of the shaft or pier below such horizontal mouldings being different." The latter point is the distinction between what he terms shafted and banded imposts: "in banded imposts, the sections above and below the impost-moulding are alike, the shaft or pier seeming to pass through its capital."

Shaken, plank or timber which is full of clefts, and will not bear caulking or fastening; generally called *shakey*.

Shambles, stalls on which butchers expose their meat for sale. The shambles, or market-place for the sale of flesh, at Frankfort-on-the-Maine, is a curious and ancient example of early shambles.

Shank, the space between the channels of a triglyph.

Shank-painter, a chain bolted to the top-side abaft the cat-head, to lower the anchor of a ship.

Sheave, in mechanics, a solid cylindrical wheel, fixed in a channel within a *block*, and movable about an axis; being used, in connection with suitable tackle, to raise heavy weights, or to increase the mechanical powers applied to remove any load.

Sheers, in mining, two very high pieces of wood, placed in nearly a vertical position in each side of a shaft, and united at the top, over which, by means of a pulley, passes the capstan rope: this is for the convenience of lifting out, or lowering into the shaft, timber or other things of great length and weight.

Sheers, in ship-building, etc., are masts or large spars set across each other at the upper ends, by which contrivance the heavy bodies, such as frame-timbers, masts, etc., are raised.

Sheer-hulk, in the navy, an old seventy-four cut down to the lower deck, and fitted up with a pair of sheers, for the purpose of taking out the lower masts of ships preparing for sea.

Sheer-strake, the strake under the gunwale in the top side; it is generally worked thicker than the rest of the top-sides, and scarfed between the drifts.

Sheet, in navigation, a rope fastened to one or both corners of a sail, to extend and retain it in a particular situation.

Sheet-Anchor, in navigation, the largest anchor of a ship.

Sheriff's Posts, two ornamental posts or pillars, set up one on each side of the house of a sheriff or chief magistrate.

Shift, the time a miner works in one day.

Shift, of timber or plank, is over launching without either piece being reduced, as the timbers of the frame, or plank in the bottom.

Shingle, coarse sand and pebbles deposited by the surge, accumulating in banks and forming dangerous shoals. Lieut.-Colonel Reid, in the second volume of the 'Professional Papers' of the Corps of Royal Engineers, makes the following observations on the moving of the shingle of the beach along the south coast of England:—

"The prevailing winds being westerly, and the highest seas rolling from the south-west, the pebbles of the beach are gradually carried to the eastward, and a constant supply is furnished by the falling away of the cliffs. On this coast, therefore, groins so constructed as to prevent the moving shingle from pressing to the eastward cause an accumulation of pebbles.

"It has been ascertained, from observation, that the pebbles of the Devonshire coast are forced to the eastward, along the coast of Dorsetshire, as far as the Chesil Bank. The stone pier of Lyme Regis, called the Cobb, does not, as might have been expected, arrest their progress; for, in south-west storms, they are driven over the pier, and the crews in the harbour have had to quit the decks of their vessels, on account of the stones driven over the pier falling on the men. On this account, within a few years, a high wall has been constructed to stop the progress of the shingle at this point. The natural consequence to be expected from this wall is, that the shingle will accumulate on the west side of Lyme Regis pier, until it shall roll round the pier-head, as at the harbour of Dover.

"The Chesil Bank is not composed of calcareous pebbles (as stated in a work of deservedly very high reputation), but mostly consists of siliceous stones, worn to a very remarkable degree of uniformity of shape and also of size (when taken from the same point) by long attrition upon the coast. The largest pebbles have been carried furthest to the east; and the regularity with which they are arranged, according to their size, is very remarkable.

"The progress of the shingle is here first arrested by the Isle of Portland, owing to the projection of that point of land in a line somewhat to the westward of south, and the shingle bank stops just where the land trends in a south-west direction.

"The Chesil Bank, at that part of it nearest the Isle of Portland, is from 20 to 30 feet above the ordinary high-water mark. On the west side it is steep, and the water deep close to the shore; but on the east side it has a gentle slope, with a base of 200 yards, to the above height of 20 or 30 feet.

"This gentle slope on the east side is owing to the accumulation of water on the opposite side during westerly gales, which finds a passage through the gravel bank, washing it into little ravines, and carrying down stones by its current. In very severe storms the sea washes over this bank; and it did so on the 23rd of November, 1824.

"A dangerous shoal of coarse sand, called the Shambles, which lies off the south-east point of the Isle of Portland, is in all probability formed by the tides; but the Chesil Bank is formed by the waves breaking on the shore in south-west gales; and it is important that these two causes, and their resulting consequences, should always be separately considered.

"Siliceous or very hard pebbles only withstand long rolling on the beach, whilst calcareous stones soon become ground into sand. As the silliceous pebbles do not pass round Portland Island, sand only is found on the shore of Portland Roads; and it is calcareous, effervescing strongly with muriatic acid.

"Scarcely any gravel is to be seen between Portland Roads and Weymouth. Within the 'Abergavenny,' an East India ship which sank thirty years ago in the mouth of Weymouth Bay, there is no gravel, and very little sand. East of Weymouth it again begins to collect; but each little headland, acting as a groin, retains much of it in the small bays. Round St. Alban's Head its action has not been observed, but at Christchurch the quantity is considerable, and at Hurst Castle it is very large.

"The Isle of Wight, and the strong current running through the Needles, here again a second time stop its eastward movement; and it forms, nearly in the mid-channel, a shoal called the Shingles, the easternmost end of which (by the action of the westerly winds on one side, and the current of the Needles on the opposite) becomes heaped up above high-water mark into an island, varying in shape and size with every storm, and sometimes disappearing altogether.

"The pebbles coming from the westward must be driven across the north channel to this bank; but they do not pass across the south and principal channel of the Needles to the Isle of Wight, as is evident from local inspection; for those of the Isle of Wight are of a different colour, being black flints from the chalk, whereas those on the side of Hurst Castle are generally yellow.

"The effect of the prevailing wind, in driving the gravel along the coast from west to east, is not less evident on the south of the Isle of Wight than elsewhere. It passes eastward until it reaches Sandown Bay, where the artificial groins, kept up at considerable cost, arrest a certain portion; but the surplus is poured over these groins, and, falling on the east side, continues its course.

"The gravel which passes Portsmouth does not appear to come from the westward of Hurst Castle, for the shores just within the Needles are mud without stones. A new system commences within the Solent. A large quantity of shingle is furnished from the gravelly soil of the south coast of Hampshire; and this shingle is likewise driven eastward, sometimes returning westward when easterly winds prevail, but the balance of its progress is always towards the east.

"Hurst Castle, Calshot Castle, and Blockhouse Fort, Portsmouth, all stand on similar tongues of shingle, formed on the west sides of their respective passages by the prevailing westerly winds.

"At Hurst Castle the gradual additions to the end of the strip of shingle may be plainly seen; for Nature there records her own history in a very visible manner. An ordnance landing-place, 30 feet long, which was constructed in 1806, and stood in the sea, became entirely buried in gravel; and many succeeding lines of high-water mark may be distinctly traced to the eastward of Hurst Castle.

"Similar traces of many former lines of high-water mark are also to be seen near Southsea Castle; and immediately on the west of Fort Monkton, six distinct lines of high water may be counted; and some of these probably belong to very remote periods of time.

"The direction of the line of coast, with reference to the prevailing gales, seems to determine where the shingle will accumulate, or where the sea will be most likely to encroach upon the land; and seems to be one of the most important points to study as regards the subject of opening bar-harbours.

"The south-easterly direction of the beach at Southsea would appear to be one of the causes why the entrance of Portsmouth Harbour is kept as clear as it is, by the current running out of it; for this direction of the land prevents the water from spreading itself on both sides, at the ebbing tide, as it does at the entrance of Langston Harbour, over banks of gravel; and this direction at Southsea appears just sufficient to allow the shingle to be set to the eastward by the prevailing gales.

"It well deserves consideration, whether embankments (on the south coast of England) run out on the eastward of bar-harbours, in a line parallel to the line formed by nature on the east side of Portsmouth Harbour, would not lead to a similar effect as that produced there by keeping open one principal channel. By a proper system of groins on the west side of such harbours, shingle coming from the westward would be stopped, and much of the materials which now form the bars might be arrested in ther course.

"The slope of the beach is flatter after a southerly gale, and its average slope is about 1 foot in 9.

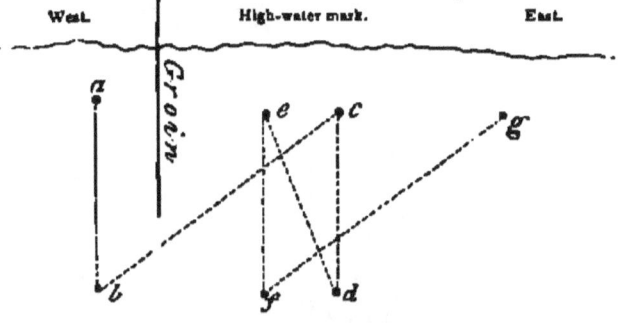

Foot of the slope of gravel.

"If groins are not carried far enough in-land, the sea in south-west storms (on the south coast) will break round and insulate them. If they are not high enough at high-water mark, the gravel will be carried over them to the eastward; and if they are too short, it will pass round the outer end of them.

"During southerly gales, it is frequently said, that the gravel is 'carried into the sea,' because the receding waves draw it down; but it is again driven back, and if the wind is south-west it is set to the eastward.

"The preceding figure, in which a pebble (a) passes to (g), following a course indicated by the alphabetical order of the letters, will explain what is here meant, and show the way in which the gravel passes by groins which are too short.

"From this figure it will also be understood, why a single plank removed from a wooden groin will cause the beach at such place of removal to be carried on forward; and hence the importance of constructing groins of materials not liable to such accidents.

"The point of shingle on which Calshot Castle now stands was once an island, and called, in 1717, Crown Island; since which time the opening has filled in with gravel. The point on the west side of Christchurch Harbour is now lengthening annually; and the mouth of that harbour and its bar become every year more and more removed to the eastward, and if left to nature may continue to be removed eastward until the water from that estuary shall re-open a fresh passage for itself in a more direct line, as the water seems to have done at the harbour of Shoreham.

"At such harbours as Portsmouth it would be desirable, by means of the apparatus for enabling persons to descend and examine the bed of the sea, to observe and determine the precise mode of the action of the shingle at the entrance of harbours.

"The sand being blown by the wind, as well as driven by the surge, it frequently covers the coarser shingle, where it is retained by the *carex arenaria*, a grass which roots at every joint."

(Much valuable information on the subject of encroachments of the sea upon the land will be found in Lyell's ' Geology.')

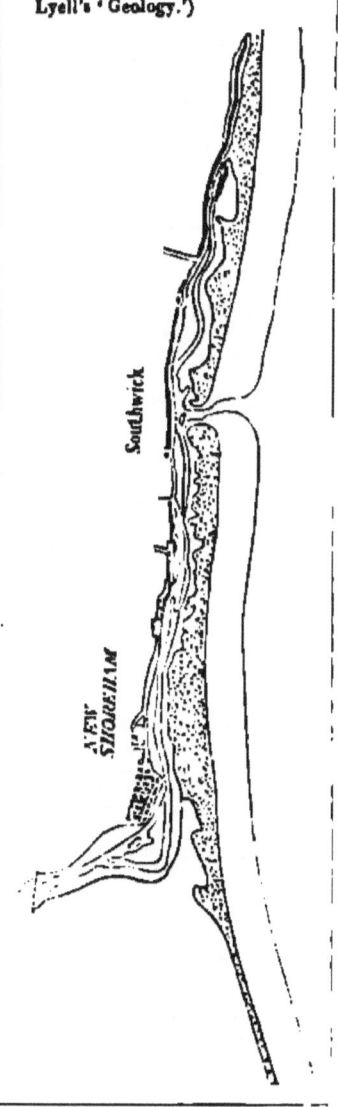

Shingles, in house-building, small pieces of wood sawed to a certain scantling, used in roofing, instead of tiles or slates.

Shittim wood, a valuable kind of timber, of which Moses made the greater part of the tables, altars, and planks, belonging to the tabernacle: it grows in the deserts of Arabia, and is like white-thorn in its colour and leaves, but not in size, as the tree is so large that it affords very long planks: the wood is hard, tough, smooth, without knots, and extremely beautiful; so that the rich and curious make screws of it for their presses.

Shivers, in navigation, the little round wheels, of wood or metal, in which the rope of a pulley or block runs.

Sholes, pieces of plank put under the shores where there are no groundways.

Shores, pieces of timber fixed to support a ship.

Shrines, tombs, or decorated monuments, of ornamental tabernaclework, as they are applied to the entombment of royal and noble persons; several very fine examples exist in the cathedrals and abbey churches: the term is also applied to a cabinet in which sacred things are deposited.

Shunt, a term applicable to the management of railway trains, to remove a carriage or train off the main line. When an engine, carriage, or train is moved off the main line to a siding, it is then said to be 'shunted.' It is most probably derived from the word 'shun:' in the old English Romance 'Mort d'Arthur' we find the word 'schunte' used in this sense, to put off; and in other early works the word 'shunted' may be found, with the meaning, to move from.

Side chains, chains and hooks fixed to the sides of the tender and engine for safety, should the central drag-bar give way.

Sidereal year, that space of time which astronomers compute the sun is moving from any fixed star till it returns to it again, reckoned at 365 days, 6 hours, and almost 10 minutes.

Sienese School, the school of a lively people; and is so agreeable in the selection of the colours and the air of the heads that foreigners are captivated, and sometimes even prefer it to the Florentine. But there is another reason for this preference, viz. the choicest productions of the Sienese painters are all in the churches. In Florence it is otherwise; no picture of Vinci, of Buonarroti, of Rossi, is to be seen in public; none of the finest productions of Andrea or of Frate, and few of the other best masters. The accounts of the early Sienese painters are confused by the plurality of the Guidi, the Mini, the Lippi, the Varni (abbreviations of Giacomo, Filippo, Giovanni). To sum up, the character of the School is not so original as some others, and during its best time some of its artists imitated the style of others. Some of the greatest modern names are Giantonio *Razzi*, surnamed *Il Sodoma*, b. 1479, d. 1554; Domenico *Beccafumi*, called *Mecherino*, b. 1484, d. 1549; Baldassare *Peruzzi*, b. 1481, d. 1536.

Signal lamps, railway lamps, with a bull's-eye glass in front. Each lamp has a recess between the burner and bull's-eye, for dropping in any particular coloured glass, according to the light which is to be shown. The lamp has also recesses for holding these glasses, so that the engineman can at once pick out a red, green, or blue glass, and put it in front as he may require it.

Sill, the lower horizontal frame of a door or window; a threshold.

Silt, in hydrography, etc., mud deposited by rivers, tides, etc., generally in still parts or eddies, and also in lakes or hollows filled with still water.

Silver is sometimes found in the metallic state, and as chloride and sulphide, besides alloyed with gold, copper, and other metals. It is a pure white brilliant metal, of great ductility, capable of being drawn out into very fine wires. It melts at 1873°, and absorbs a large quantity of oxygen, which, disengaging on cooling, gives it a white, frosty appearance; when impure, it does not do so. It is a metal used in great abundance as a coin in all countries, also for plate, for vases, candelabras, cups, etc.

Sinking, in mining, digging downwards; in rising and sinking a shaft, one set of men sink from a certain level, while another set rises from a lower level to meet them.

Siparium, in the time of the Romans, a piece of tapestry stretched on a frame, which rose before the stage of the theatre.

Siphon, or **Syphon**, in hydraulics, a crooked pipe through which liquors are conveyed.

Siphon. The date of the first application of the principle by which water or other fluids may be drawn from one level to another by the exhaustion of the air contained in the limb communicating with the lower level, appears to be very remote. The Egyptians certainly used it for the transvasing of wine: but the first important application of this principle to useful or general practice was in the aqueduct which conducted the springs of Mount Pila to Lyons: the date of this aqueduct is about 40 years after the commencement of the Christian era. Upon the total length of the aqueduct, which with its branches was 15 old French posting leagues, there were three large siphons to carry the water from the upper sides of the same number of valleys to the lower. Of these, the valley of Chaponest was 2400 feet across, measuring in a straight line across the valley; and it was about 200 feet deep. The valley of St. Foy was about 3.192 feet across, by 300 feet deep; that of St. Trenée was 798 feet across, but much shallower.

The pipes of the Chaponest siphon, on leaving the upper reservoir, were 8 inches diameter and 1 inch thick: they were of lead. After running 75 feet of the descent of this dimension, they branched off into two divisions of 6 inches diameter each, in order that the pressure upon the pipes at the lower portion of the siphon might be diminished. They ran over the level bridge in the lower part of the valley of this smaller diameter, and mounted the opposite side for a height of 70 feet, when they reunited into pipes of 8 inches diameter again. The total fall of the Chaponest siphon was 150 feet, the rise on the opposite side was 130 feet, leaving a difference of level of 20 feet to compensate for the friction. The Siphon of St. Foy had a difference of level, from the upper reservoirs to the straight part, of 240 feet.

The Lyons aqueduct had in its total length thirteen common straight aqueduct bridges and three siphons; it delivered very nearly 1,300,000 gallons in the twenty-four hours.

Many writers on hydraulics have failed to notice these extraordinary works, and have expressed their surprise that the ancients were ignorant of the existence of the law by which water finds its own level. The ancients, however, appear to have wisely preferred the more economical system of carrying water in a straight trough, wherever the expense was justifiable. Waterworks were, in early times, Government affairs, and the expense of their maintenance was deliberated. The preceding cases abundantly prove that the ancients applied the well-known law of hydrostatical balance whenever they found such a course advisable; and the details given by Vitruvius remove all doubt upon the subject. His instructions (lib. 8, c. 7) are as follows:—" When the expense of erecting a bridge is too great, a siphon may be used; but this should only be resorted to as a last expedient. The danger of bursting the pipes, and the expense of the repairs, are serious objections to this method, and in the end straight bridges are the cheapest. If, however, it be determined to employ a siphon, it should be laid with a regular curve, and all abrupt elbows avoided. To secure this, a substructure should be raised to fill in any inequalities in the valley where it is to be erected. The last length of the descending pipe and the first of the straight pipe at the level part, as also the last length of the straight pipe and the first ascending one, should be let into a solid stone, which should be carefully fixed and surrounded with ballast, properly rammed." He also gives directions for the construction of air-shafts from the lower parts, which he calls 'columnaria,' and he expressly states that they are necessary to relax the 'vis spiritus in ventris,'—the force of the air in the curves.

Siphon-cups, in steam-engines, cups placed for feeding oil to the working parts of the machinery, trimmed with cotton or worsted, the same as the axle-boxes.

Sissoo is one of the most valuable timber-trees of India, and with the *saul* is more extensively used than any other in north-west India. The ship-builders in Bengal select it for crooked timbers and knees; it is remarkably strong; its colour is a light greyish-brown with dark-coloured veins.

Spindletree, a shrubby tree, with a yellow wood similar to the English boxwood: it is turned into bobbins and common articles.

Site, the situation of a building; the plot of ground on which it stands.

Site, in landscape, signifies the view, prospect, or opening of a country, derived from the Italian word *sito*, situation; and it is in use among painters, as being more expressive.

Sketch, a slightly-made picture, in which the general effect is attended to, but not always the details, and from which more finished works are painted: so also with sketches in architecture, giving the correct outline of a building without filling up with the detail.

Skew, or *Askew*, as applied to masons' work, an oblique arch.

Skirlaw, Walter, when prebend of Fenton, in 1730, took down the middle tower of York cathedral, built by John Romanus, and built the present noble tower in its stead, at his own expense. It was built in six or seven years. "Walter appears to have been a munificent prelate, and an architect of uncommon genius. The tower above-mentioned would have been sufficient to establish this character; but that part of Howden Church, about 19 miles from York and Beverley, shows a richness of fancy and delicacy of taste equally adapted to smaller structures. The Chapter-house struck me as eminently beautiful. A small chapel built by him, called Skinlaw Chapel (which I believe is the name of the village), is worthy of attention for its chaste and elegant style. It is a few miles from Hull and from Beverley. All these I have seen, and can speak of them confidently. Walter Shirton was made Bishop of Lichfield and Coventry, then of Bath and Wells, and afterwards of Durham, where he continued seventeen years. He built the bridges of Shinkley, and Auckland, and Yarrow; also a chapel at Swine, in Holderness (Query, is not this the chapel above mentioned, which is called Skirlaw Chapel?), where he was born. He built also the steeple of Holme, and repaired the church and manor there" (Gent). He bestowed above £800 (a large sum in those days), while Bishop of Durham, towards building the dormitory and cloister of the monastery in that city, and left several sums of money to the churches he had governed, particularly to that of Wells, to buy ornaments for the decent performance of divine service. He was buried in the cathedral of Durham, southward of the choir. From the epitaph we learn that he died 24th March, 1405. Under this prelate Gothic architecture seems to have attained its highest excellence.

Skirting, a narrow board forming a plinth to an internal wall.

Skreens were either of needlework or painted: in the time of Henry VIII. is noticed a skreen as a new year's gift from Luke Hornebound, a painter, to that monarch.

Skylights, glass frames placed in a roof with one or more inclined planes of glass.

Slaking of Lime. Quick-lime, taken as it leaves the kiln, and thrown into a proper quantity of water, splits with noise, puffs up, produces a large disengagement of slightly caustic vapour, and falls into a thick paste. So much heat is produced in slaking, that part of the water flies off in vapour. If the quantity of the lime slaked be great, the heat produced is sufficient to set fire to combustibles: in this manner vessels loaded with lime have sometimes been burnt. When great quantities of lime are slaked in a dark place, not only heat, but light also, is emitted. The specific gravity of pure lime is 3·08.

Slate, an argillaceous stone, readily split, and employed to cover buildings, and also for other purposes: it is quarried in large pieces.

Slating is employed by builders for covering in the roofs of buildings. The slates principally in use in London are brought from North Wales.

Sleepers, pieces of timber employed to support others, and laid asleep, or with a bearing along their own length: sleepers denote more particularly those timbers which are placed lengthwise on walls to support the joists of a floor; they are employed on railroads as longitudinal bearings for the rails to rest upon.

Sleepers, or *Transome-knees*, are fixed withinside a ship abaft, one arm laying on the foot waleing, and the other extended up the transoms.

Stickings, narrow veins of ore.

Slide, a vein of clay, which, intersecting a lode, causes a dislocation vertically.

Slide-rest. This apparatus, the invention of Mr. Henry Maudslay, is of the utmost importance for perfecting and accelerating the construction of machinery. Before its invention, cylindrical turning was a work of manual labour, and was attended with so much difficulty and expense, when the cylinders were either large in diameter or of moderate length, that it was necessary to avoid using them in many cases; and plane surfaces being even still more expensive, in consequence of the very imperfect and laborious operations of chipping and filing them, many very valuable inventions could not be carried into effect on account of the inaccuracy and expense attending their construction. The invention of the slide-rest, forming an all-important part of that of the planing machine, has entirely removed both of these difficulties, and cylindrical turning and planing are now the cheapest and most perfect of mechanical operations.

The office of the slide-rest, as applied to lathes and turning machines, is to *hold, engage, and direct* the turning-tool, and it may be kept in motion either by hand or by self-acting machinery.

When applied to a small lathe, it is generally moved by hand; but in large machines for heavy work, where the time of action is considerable, it is moved by machinery attached to the lathe. The work to be turned being placed in the usual way between the two centre pieces of the lathe, the lower part of the slide-rest is fixed under it on what is called the bed of the lathe: the use of this part of the slide is to move the tool to or from the work, which it effects by means of a slide, at right angles to the work, moved by a screw and handle; this s de has fixed upon it, by a swivel joint, the upper part of the apparatus.

The upper part has also a slide moved by a screw and handle, and generally placed at right angles to the lower slide: the principal use of this upper slide is to move the cutting-tool which is fixed upon it parallel to the centre line of the lathe; but it can be so placed, by aid of the swivel-joint, as to cause the tool to advance at any required angle with the centre line of the lathe. Thus two direct movements are obtained; the first to act the tool to the work, and the second to move it either to the right or left, in a line parallel with the work, or at any given angle with the first.

The slide-rest principle enters largely into the construction of all kinds of machinery, from the most minute to machines of vast magnitude, where by its aid ponderous masses—such, for instance, as railway turn-tables 36 feet in diameter—are operated upon with a precision unattainable by any other means.

Slide-valve, in locomotive engines, the

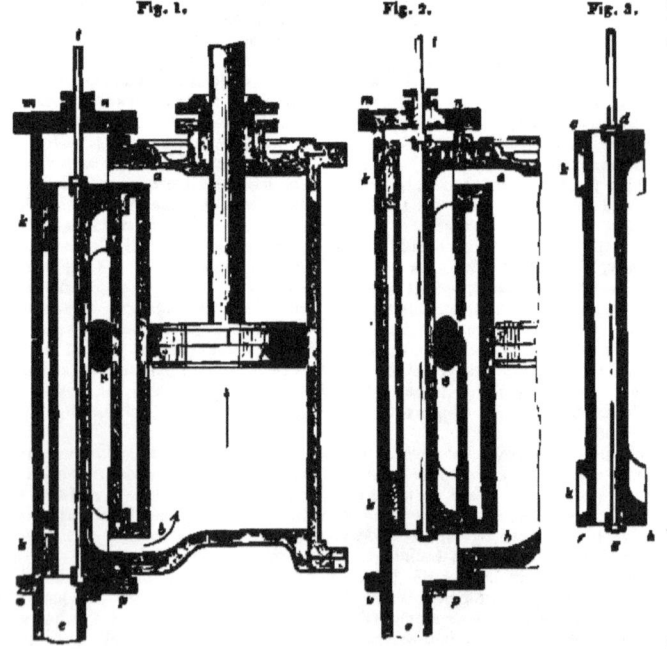

Fig. 1.   Fig. 2.   Fig. 3.

SLIDE-VALVE.

valve placed in the steam-chest to work over the steam-ports. It regulates the admission of steam to the cylinder from the boiler, and the escape of the steam from the cylinder to the atmosphere. Its form is that of an arch in the centre, with a flat face all round to keep it steam-tight on the face of the steam-ports. It is by the arched part that the steam escapes to the atmosphere. It is a very simple valve, and answers its purpose well, with one drawback, namely, the pressure of the steam upon it being unbalanced by any counter-pressure. Numerous attempts have been made to relieve this pressure, some of which it is hoped will be successful. In stationary engines the contrivances differ materially, as shown in the woodcut, Figs. 1, 2, 3.

Fig. 1 represents in section the cylinder, piston, and slide: S is the mouth of the steam-pipe coming from the boiler; e is the pipe leading to the condenser; f is the rod which is attached to the slide, moving through a stuffing-box, m n. This slide is represented in longitudinal section, separately, in fig. 3, and in transverse section in fig. 4. In the position of the slide represented in fig. 1, the steam passing from the boiler enters at S, and passes to the bottom of the cylinder through the opening b, where it acts below the piston, causing it to ascend. The steam which was above the piston escapes through the opening at a, and descending through a longitudinal opening in the slide behind the mouth of the steam-pipe, finds its way to the pipe e, and through that to the condenser.

When the piston has reached the top of the cylinder, the slide will have been moved to the position represented in fig. 2. The steam now entering at S passes through the opening a into the cylinder above the piston, while the steam which was below it escapes through the opening b and the pipe e to the condenser.

Fig. 4. The form of the valve, from which it derives its name of D-valve, is represented in fig. 4. The longitudinal opening through which the steam descends then appears in section of a semicircular form. The packing at the back of the slide is represented at k; this is pressed against the surface of the valve-box.

Slide-valve lap, Outside, in locomotive engines, that portion of valve which would overlap the steam-ports when placed over them. If the steam-ports measure 8 inches over all the ports, and the valve be 10 inches broad, this would be an overlap of 1 inch on each side of the ports, and is called the 'lap' of the valve. Expansion was formerly regulated by the extent of lap only, but it is now regulated by both the lap and the expansion gear, which gives greater scope in doing so. *Inside lap* is the portion of the valve-face which would overlap the inside of the steam-ports when placed over them; for if the steam-ports were 4 inches from inside of the one port to the inside of the other port, and if the arched part of the valve only measured $3\frac{1}{4}$ inches across, this would give $\frac{1}{16}$ of an inch lap on each side, which is called *inside lap*.

Slide-valve lead, in locomotives, the width which the steam-port is opened by the slide-valve when the piston is at the end of the stroke. It varies from $\frac{1}{8}$ to $\frac{1}{4}$ an inch, according to the work required. The lead is obtained by fixing the eccentric on the axle, a little in front of the crank, by which arrangement the steam-port is opened in front of the direction in which the piston is moving before the latter has completed its stroke. By these means the steam-port is thrown quickly open when the piston commences its return stroke, and has at once the full pressure of the steam against it.

Slide-valve travel, the distance which the slide-valve travels in one direction for each stroke of the piston. This is from 4 to 5¼ inches generally, but is reduced by each variation of the expansion gear, and its travel is taken for both the front and back strokes of the piston for each notch where the handle is fixed. The up-and-down quarter-revolutions of the crank do not equally draw the piston the half-length of the cylinder, and this and the expansion gear so far affect the working of the slide, that it is necessary to take the front and back stroke working separately.

Setting the slide-valve: the eccentric is brought as much before the crank as to give the required lead to the slide-valve when the crank is on the centre, that is, in a straight line with a cylinder. The handle is then moved to each separate notch, and the position of the slide and piston carefully taken for each variation. These are then recorded in the following manner:—

Slide-valve and Piston Motions' Register.—Working of expansion gear.

_______________ *Engine*, _______________ 185

	Inches.		Inches.
Diameter of cylinders . .	18	Outside lap of valve . .	1
Length of stroke	24	Inside lap of valve . . .	$\frac{1}{16}$
Size of steam-port . . .	15 × 2	Size of exhaust-port . .	15 × 3½

No. of Notch in reversing handle guide.	Travel of slide-valve.	Lead of slide-valve.	Steam cut off. Front stroke of piston.	Steam cut off. Back stroke of piston.	Exhaust opens. Front stroke of piston.	Exhaust opens. Back stroke of piston.	Compression begins. Front stroke of piston.	Compression begins. Back stroke of piston.	Steam-port opens. Front stroke of piston.	Steam-port opens. Back stroke of piston.	Diameter of blast-pipe.	REMARKS.
	In.	In.	In.	In.	In.	In.	In.	In.	In.	In.	In.	Balance piston for slide-valves.
1	5⅛	$\frac{3}{16}$	19¾	19	22¾	22⅝	22½	22$\frac{5}{16}$	1⅛	1¾	5⅛	
2	4⅛	$\frac{3}{32}$	18$\frac{5}{16}$	18	22$\frac{5}{16}$	21⅛	22	21⅝	1$\frac{5}{16}$	1⅝	,,	
3	4	$\frac{1}{16}$	16⅝	16$\frac{5}{16}$	21⅝	21½	21¼	21	$\frac{15}{16}$	1$\frac{1}{16}$	,,	
4	3⅛	$\frac{1}{16}$	13⅜	13¼	20$\frac{5}{16}$	19$\frac{13}{16}$	20	19½	$\frac{13}{16}$	$\frac{13}{16}$	,,	
5	3⅛	$\frac{1}{16}$	9⅛	10	18$\frac{1}{16}$	18$\frac{1}{16}$	18	17$\frac{9}{16}$	$\frac{9}{16}$	$\frac{9}{16}$	,,	Centre notch.
6	2$\frac{11}{16}$	$\frac{1}{32}$	5$\frac{7}{16}$	6	15⅝	15	15½	15¼	$\frac{11}{32}$	$\frac{11}{32}$	,,	

The above measurements are carefully taken and registered by the mechanic who sets the slide-valves.

Slide-valve rod guide, in locomotive engines, a bracket fixed to the boiler, the lower end of which is fitted for the slide-valve rod to work through. A set-screw is useful in this guide for fixing the rod when the valve has to be disconnected.

Slide-valve rod and frame, in locomotive engines: the frame is fitted on to the top part of the valve, and the rod connects the frame with the slide-block, or rocking-shaft, according to the description of valve-gear of the particular engine.

Slide valve motion, in locomotive engines, a short motion similar to the piston-rod motion, connecting the quadrant to the slide-valve by parallel guides.

Sliding rule, a rule constructed with logarithmic lines, formed upon a slip of wood, brass, or ivory, inserted in a groove, in a rule made to slide longitudinally therein, so that by means of another scale upon the rule itself the contents of a surface or solid may be known.

Slimes, mud containing metallic ores, mud or earthy particles mixed with the ores.

Slit deal, a name for inch and a quarter-inch deal cut into two boards.

Sloop, in navigation, a small one-masted vessel, the mainsail of which is attached to a gaff above and to a long boom below. The word is also applied to any small ship.

Sluice, in hydraulics, a water-gate, a flood-gate, a vent for water.

Smelting, is the process of separating metals from the earthy and other matters with which they are combined in the state of ore. Of this operation, as conducted upon the ores of iron, copper, lead, and tin, the following is a brief description.

Smelting Iron. The reduction of iron ore is effected in a furnace in which, the required intensity of heat being obtained by a current of air driven rapidly into the furnace, has received the name of a blast-furnace. The kind of furnaces employed, the quantity of ore or mine, as it is termed, reduced at each heat, and the peculiar method of conducting the operation, vary widely in different countries and counties, and have some reference in detail to the precise quality and composition of the ore to be treated. Previous to the year 1740, the smelting of ores of iron was, in England, performed solely with the charcoal of wood, the ores operated upon being principally the brown and red hematites, or rich ores, that is, containing a large proportion of metal with a small quantity of earthy materials. In the treatment of this class of ores, it may be observed that very little improvement has yet been effected, the modern process having been chiefly applied to the leaner ores, such as blackband, etc. The expensiveness and comparative scarcity of charcoal as a fuel for the smelting of iron ores, induced those engaged in the art to attempt the substitution of coal for wood-charcoal; and by the year 1788, these attempts had so far succeeded, that there remained only 24 out of 59 charcoal furnaces, while 53 furnaces had been established in which coal, burned into the form of coke, was used for the smelting of the ore. Since that date, the extension of this process has proceeded rapidly, and the total quantity of metal produced has experienced a corresponding augmentation. At the present time, the Backbarrow Iron Company are nearly the only smelters of iron with wood-charcoal in the kingdom. The two principal seats of the iron manufacture in Great Britain are in Staffordshire and South Wales. In the former district, comprising the neighbourhoods of Dudley, Bilston, Wednesbury, etc., the smelting or blast furnaces are constructed almost wholly of bricks. They are usually of a conical form externally, and sometimes pyramidal, the plan being a square or rectangle. In the interior they are mostly circular in form, except in that part called the hearth. The fuel and the ore to be smelted are fed into the furnace from the top, and its height being from 40 to 50 feet, an ascending platform or inclined plane is constructed for wheeling up the barrows in which the materials are conveyed. The pipes through which the air is driven into the furnace (by a steam-engine) are called the tuyères, and are usually two, but sometimes three in number. The relative quantities of coal, ironstone, and limestone, which are put into the smelting furnaces of Staffordshire for the production of each ton weight of iron produced, are about 50 cwt. of coal, 50 cwt. of mine, previously calcined, and from 12 to 16 cwt. of limestone, the latter material being added as a flux to promote the fusion of the mass. The Conegree furnace, near Dudley, may be instanced as a good example of a blast-furnace adapted for the economical smelting of iron ores. It is 54 feet in height, 5 feet in diameter on the hearth, and 12 feet above, widening upward to a diameter of 13 feet 9 inches, and reduced to 8 feet above the platform, on which the charges are delivered. The quantities of materials employed in this furnace to make one ton of pig-iron, are of coal 2 tons and 5 cwt., or of coke 37 cwt., charred mine 2 tons 5 to 10 cwt., limestone 13 to 16 cwt.

Each charge delivered into the furnace consists of 9¼ cwt. of coke, 12 cwt. of charred mine, and 4 cwt. of limestone. At this furnace 115 tons of pig-iron have been made in one week. The cylinder from which the air is blown through the tuyères into the furnace is 72½ in. in diameter, and the stroke is 7 feet in length. Originally there were five tuyères for the introduction of the blast, one muzzle being 2½, two others 2½, and the other two 2 inches in diameter. Subsequently these were changed to four muzzles, of the respective diameters of 3½, 2½, 2½, and 2 inches.

Smelting Copper. Copper ore, as smelted in South Wales and other places, usually consists of pyrites (composed of sulphuret of copper and sulphuret of iron in nearly equal proportions) and vein-stone. The earthy matters combined with the pyrites are commonly siliceous, and the process of smelting consists in alternate roastings and fusions. The first of these operations is, calcining the ore in furnaces in which the heat is applied, and increased gradually, till the temperature be as high as the ore can support without melting or agglutinating, when the ore is thrown into an arch formed under the sole of the furnace. The second operation, or fusion of the calcined ore, is performed in a luted furnace, the ore having been spread uniformly over the hearth, and fluxes, such as lime, sand, or fluor-spar, being added when required, although the necessity for this addition is sought to be obviated by a careful admixture of ores of different qualities, the several earthy components of which shall serve as fluxes in the fusion of the mass. These two processes of calcination and fusion are completed alternately until the ore is completely freed from all the earthy materials, and pure metal is obtained.

Smelting Lead. The ores of lead, after being sorted, cleansed, ground, and washed, are roasted in furnaces, which are without any blast or blowing apparatus, the ores being separable from the metal by its great fusibility. Several of the furnaces are usually connected with one chimney-stalk, to which a series of flues about 18 inches square conduct. The melted lead runs freely from the ore, and is drawn off into the moulds in successive quantities, the ore being repeatedly turned over, and a small quantity of coal added over the burning mass at each drawing.

Smelting Tin. This process consists of the calcining or roasting of the ores after they have been cleaned, sorted, stamped, and washed. The calcining is performed in a reverberatory furnace from 12 to 15 feet long and 7 to 9 feet wide. The hearth of these furnaces is horizontal, and they have only one opening, which is in the front, and closed by an iron door. The sulphureous and arsenical vapours which arise from the ore are conducted by chimneys over the doors of the range of furnaces into horizontal flues, in which the acid is condensed. In the process of calcination, which occupies from 12 to 18 hours, according to the quantity of pyrites contained in the ore, 6 cwt. of ore are treated at once, and the materials are stirred from time to time, to prevent them from agglutinating.

Smoke, Prevention of. There is perhaps no subject so difficult, and none so full of perplexities, as that of the management of a furnace, and the prevention of smoke. Mr. Fairbairn, in his report to the British Association on the Combustion of Fuel and the Prevention of Smoke, observes:—" I have approached this inquiry with considerable diffidence, and after repeated attempts at definite conclusions, have more than once been forced to abandon the investigation as inconclusive and unsatisfactory. They chiefly arise from the constant change of temperature, the variable nature of the volatile products, the want of system, and the irregularity which attends the management of the furnace. Nevertheless, the prevention of smoke and the perfect combustion of the fuel, are completely within the reach of all who choose to adopt measures calculated for the suppression of the one and the improvement of the other.

"On presenting to the British Association an inquiry into the merits of Mr. C. Wye Williams's Argand furnace compared with those of the usual construction, it was found from an average of a series of experiments, that the saving of fuel (inclusive of the absence of smoke) was in the ratio of 292 to 300, or as 1 : 1·039, being at the rate of 4 per cent. in favour of Mr. Williams's plan. Since then a considerable number of experiments have been made by Mr. Heuldsworth, Mr. Williams, and others, which present some curious and interesting phenomena in the further development of this subject."

When these trials were made many of the details of the construction of furnaces were but imperfectly understood and applied, and hence the amount of economy was far short of what has since been realized. Among the more recent experiments, as illustrative of the practicability of effecting perfect combustion of the fuel employed, may be mentioned those made by Sir W. Armstrong, Dr. Richardson, and Mr. Layridge, to whom the inquiry was entrusted by the Colliers' Association of Newcastle. Of these trials an ample report was made, and has since been published, which will well repay examination. Sufficient information is there given of the requirements of furnaces, and the practical details of their relative proportions. These competent judges in this case decided in giving preference to the principles and practice adopted by Mr. Williams, stating their unanimous opinion "That Mr. Williams must be declared the successful competitor, and therefore award him the premium of £500 offered by the Association."

In their Report they state as an

important feature of the successful plan, that "It may be applied under varied circumstances, producing a more complete absorption of the heat generated, with a great increase in the economic value and work done." In this respect the practical result was as near the theoretic value of the fuel, as perhaps will ever be effected.

Mr. Williams's plan, independent of the details of the furnace, relied on the introduction of the required quantity of air through several hundred half-inch orifices inserted in the door-box, and above it. As the entire question of the proper combustion of the fuel depends on the admission and action of the air, it may here be useful to state that each ton of bituminous coal produces, on an average, 10,000 cubic feet of gas; and further, that each cubic foot of this gas requires for its combustion 10 cubic feet of air at atmospheric temperature. That this is independent of the quantity required for the combustion of the coke portion of the coal, and which is estimated at double the quantity required by the gas. Thus, then, 100,000 cubic feet of air are absolutely necessary for the combustion of the gas alone of each ton of coal, and 200,000 for the coke of the same ton weight.

On the question of quantity, then, there is no doubt or difficulty. The next point for consideration is as to the place and mode of introducing this large quantity of air, so that the necessary admixture of the air and the gas may be effected. On these points Mr. Williams, in his treatise on the combustion of coal, states:—"With reference to the place for the admission of the air, it is a matter of perfect indifference, as to effect, in what part of the furnace it is introduced, provided the all-important condition be attended to, namely, that the mechanical mixture of the air and the gas be continuously effected before the temperature of the carbon of the gas (then in the state of flame) be reduced below that of ignition; this temperature, according to Sir H. Davy, being 800°.

With reference to the proportion of the several parts of a furnace, it has been practically ascertained that in the chamber of the furnace there should never be less than 2 feet between the bars and the crown-plate. That an adequate space of at least double the area of the furnace be appropriated behind the bridge as a combustion chamber, in which the process of mixture and chemical union may be effected. Further, that there should be a distance or run between the furnace and the tubes, if any, of not less than ten feet lineals in which the process is continued.

In the experimental furnaces at the Newcastle trial, the area of admission for the air was equal to 4 inches square for each square foot of grate-bars.

The prevention of smoke is so directly connected with the construction of boilers, as to render it necessary to refer to the plan now almost universally adopted, namely, the multitubulous plan. On this point there is a great diversity of opinion among engineers. By numerous improvements made by Mr. Williams, Mr. Dewrance, and others, it has been ascertained that the value of the tubes as heat-absorbing surface has been greatly overrated. It appears, practically, that with the exception of the first 12 or 24 inches of the tubes, the remainder have very little steam-generating effect, and that as a general principle the effective heating surface of tubes should only be estimated at one-tenth of their superficial area. That when coal is used the tubes are seriously productive of smoke, and its accompaniment, soot. Considerable attention has been given of late to this point, since the economy in the use of coal instead of coke in locomotives has been so fully ascertained. With the view of avoiding the nuisance of smoke in locomotives, their construction has of late been much modified. The necessity for a second, or combustion chamber, is now generally admitted, thus assimilating their construction to that of marine boilers, as already described. So insufficient has been the effect of tubes as steam generators, and so injurious are they in the generation of smoke, that an important change will no doubt shortly take place. It is even now found by successful practice on the London and North-western Railway, that while the combustion-chambers are much enlarged, the tubes are no more than 22 inches in length. More recently Mr. C. Wye Williams has proved his complete success in the accomplishment of all that can be desired; his prize at the Society of Arts, and the award of £500 by the Newcastle Association, are proofs of his superiority over his compeers.

Smoke-box, the end of the boiler on which the chimney is placed. Locomotives with inside cylinders have them placed in this box, which keeps both them and the steampipes at a high temperature.

Smoke-box door, the door in front of the smoke-box, by which access is gained to the cylinders or steampipes, and other parts placed in this box.

Snake wood, a kind of speckled wood used in Demerara, Surinam, etc., for the bows of the Indians: the colour of the wood is red hazel, with numerous black spots and marks, which have been tortured into the resemblance of letters, or the scales of reptiles. When fine, it is very beautiful, and is scarce in England: chiefly used for walking-sticks, which are expensive. The pieces that are from 2 to 6 inches in diameter are said to be the produce of large trees.

Snow, in navigation, the largest of European two-masted vessels. The sails and rigging are exactly similar to those of a ship, only behind the mainmast of a snow there is a small spar or mast, fixed into a block of wood on the quarter-deck, which carries a sail resembling the mizen of a ship.

Snying, in navigation, a circular plank edgewise, to work in the bow.

Socle, in architecture, a flat square member under the bases of the pedestal of statues and vases.

Soffit, in architecture, any timber ceiling formed of cross-beams or flying cornices, the square compartments or panels of which are enriched with sculpture, painting, or gilding.

Sol, in heraldry, denotes *or*, the golden colour in the arms of sovereign princes.

Solar month, that space of time occupied by the sun in going through one sign or a twelfth part of the zodiac.

Solar System, in astronomy, the order or supposed disposition of the celestial bodies which move round the sun as the centre of their motion.

Solar year, that space of time in which the sun returns again to the same equinoctial or solstitial point, which is about 365 days, 5 hours, and 50 minutes.

Soldering is the process of uniting the edges or surfaces of similar or dissimilar metals and alloys, by partial fusion. In general, alloys or solders of various and greater degrees of fusibility than the metals to be joined, are placed between them, and the solder, when fused, unites the three parts into a solid mass: less frequently the surfaces or edges are simply melted together with an additional portion of the same metal.

SOL SOUND. SOU

Sole, the seat or bottom of a mine, applied to horizontal veins or lodes.

Solidity, in geometry, the quantity of space contained or occupied by a solid body; called also its solid contents, estimated by the number of solid or cubic inches, feet, yards, etc., which it contains.

Solids are all bodies that have the three dimensions; and among geometricians those that are terminated by regular planes are called regular solids, such as the tetrahedron, hexahedron, octahedron, dodecahedron, and icosahedron.

Sondelets of iron, used for the windows of St. Stephen's chapel, are fastenings and cross-mullions.

Sough, an adit or level for carrying off water.

Sound is produced by a sudden shock or impulse given to the air: these impulses, if quickly repeated, cannot be individually attended to by the ear, and hence they appear as one continued sound, of which the pitch or tone depends on the number occurring in a given time; and all continued sound is but a repetition of impulses.

The motion of sound through the air is at the rate of about 1125 feet per second at the temperature of 62°. At the freezing temperature, when the air is denser, it is only 1089¼ feet per second. The method of determining this velocity is to watch the time that elapses between the flash and the report of a gun fired at the distance of several miles from the observer. As light travels at the rate of nearly 200,000 miles per second, its passage occupies a portion of time too small to be measured in any terrestrial distance. It may, therefore, be supposed to be seen at the distance of several miles from the observer at the very instant of its production. If, therefore, an observer at one station begin to count seconds on an accurate dial, the moment he sees the flash of a gun at another station, say ten miles off, the number of seconds and fractions of a second which elapse between seeing the flash and hearing the report will give a divisor for the number of feet between the two stations, and the quotient will represent the velocity of sound in feet per second.

All sounds, whatever their intensity, whether the noise of a cannon or a whisper,—whatever their pitch, whether from the diapason organ-pipe or the chirping of a cricket,—and whatever their quality, whether the finest music or the most grating noise,—all travel with the same amount of speed.

When sound from any source is propagated in air, waves are formed similar in character to those which may be so beautifully studied when the wind is blowing over a field of standing corn. Now, when it is said that sound travels at the rate of 1125 feet per second, it is not meant that the particles of air move through that distance any more than the ears of corn travel from one end of the field to the other; it is only the form of the wave which thus travels. So with the particles of air: their individual movement is confined within narrow limits; but the effect of this movement is propagated from particle to particle with the rapidity of 1125 feet per second, which, although it would be thought very rapid for a motion or the transfer of a body (being about ten times faster than the most violent West India hurricane), is yet very slow for the communication or transfer of motion; for, if we pull or push one end of a solid rod, or the liquid filling a long tube, the other end appears to move at the same instant: and although this motion must occupy time (unless the body were perfectly incompressible), it is much more rapid in these cases than in air, which, on account of its great compressibility, is one of the slowest conveyers of sound. Every one must have observed that vibration can be diffused through a long mass of metal or wood, so as to be heard at a greater distance than through air; but in this case, if the sound be loud enough to be audible through the air also, it will be heard twice, first through the solid, and then through the air. Iron conveys sound about 17 times faster than air, wood from 17 to 11 times, and water 4½ times faster than air.

When waves of sound meet any fixed surface tolerably smooth, they are reflected according to the law of equal angles of incidence and reflection. In this way echoes are produced. Between two parallel surfaces a loud sound is reflected backwards and forwards, and several echoes are audible. Six may be heard between Carlton Terrace and the Birdcage Walk, in St. James's Park, London; fourteen between the steep banks of the Avon at Clifton, and as many under Maidenhead railway bridge. When the parallel surfaces are much nearer together (as the walls of a room), although a large number of echoes are produced, they follow each other too rapidly to be distinguished; and as they reach the ear after equal intervals, they produce a musical note, however unmusical the original noise may have been. Hence all the phenomena of reverberation. The pitch of the note depends on the distance between the two walls which cause it, and may be calculated therefrom.

A noise may also produce a musical echo by being reflected from a large number of equidistant surfaces receding from the ear, so that the sound reflected from each may arrive successively at equal intervals. If we stamp near a long row of palisades, a shrill ringing will be heard. A fine instance of the same kind is said to occur on the steps of the great Pyramid. If the distance from edge to edge of each step were 2 feet 1 inch, the note produced would be the tenor c, because each echo (having to go and return) would be 4 feet 2 inches later than the previous one, which is the length of the waves of that note. But as the steps gradually diminish in size upwards, the echo, if produced, and heard at the bottom, must gradually rise in pitch.

Sir Isaac Newton discovered a wonderful coincidence which exists between sound and colours, and proves mathematically that the spaces occupied by the colours in the prismatic spectrum correspond with the parts of a musical chord, when it is so divided as to sound the notes of an octave. So this resemblance may now be considered as extending further, for as in music, so likewise in colours, it will be found that harmony consists in distance and contrast, not in similitude or approximation. Two notes near each other are grating to the ear, and called discords: in like manner, two colours very near each other are unpleasing to the sight, and may be called discordant.

The science of acoustics is little understood, consequently not studied in theory. The want of knowledge of the theory of sound (phonics), in architecture, is a positive evil, and ofttimes of grievous complaint made of our public buildings, after the expenditure of considerable sums of money. Sir John Herschel states, that sounds of all kinds agree in the following particulars:—1. The excitement of a motion in the sounding body. 2. The communication of this motion to the air and other intermedium which is interposed between the sounding body and our ears. 3. The propagation of such motion from particle to particle of such intermedium in due succession. 4. Its communication, from the particles of the intermedium adjacent to the ear, to the ear itself. 5. Its conveyance in the ear, by a certain mechanism, to the auditory nerves. 6. The excitement of sensation. The motion of sound has been demonstrated by Chladin on plates of glass and metal, by strewing sand on their surfaces, and observing the forms it assumed when the sound ceased, the sound being produced on the plate by a violin bow. Sound has been used to discover the nature of disease: by the stethoscope, an instrument similar to a flute tube, physicians ascertain the state of pulmonary disorders, by applying it to the exterior surface of the body covering the lungs. In Chladin's theory, it is stated that rooms will be favourable to the transmission of sound when arranged to facilitate its natural progress,—when its intensity is augmented by resonance or simultaneous reflection, so that the reaction is undistinguishable from the primitive sound,—when not too lofty or too vaulted,—when there is not a too extensive surface for the sound to strike against at once, —when the seats are successively elevated. He observes, that when the enclosed space does not exceed 65 feet, any form may be adopted for a room; that elliptical, circular, and semicircular plans produce prolonged reverberation; parabolic plans and ceilings are the best for distinct hearing, and that for concert-rooms, square and polygonal plans should have pyramidal ceilings, and circular plans domed ones, and the orchestra be placed on high, in the centre, to produce the best effect, and avoid echo. Mr. Robert Mills, an American architect, describes the House of Representatives of the United States Congress as the most elegant legislative hall in the world; the plan is a semicircle of 96 feet chord, elongated in its diameter line by a parallelogram 72 feet long by 25 feet wide; the height to the entablature blocking is 35 feet, and to apex of the domed ceiling 57 feet, which is pierced by a circular aperture, crowned by a lantern. Besides additional seats and other improvements, a more important object has been accomplished,—namely, rendering the hall a better speaking and hearing room, in which it was before seriously deficient. The voice is now comparatively distinct, and the ear not sensible, except in a few particular points, of any reverberation of the sound; where the voice before was confused and indistinctly heard, it is now full and clear.

Sounding-board, a canopy over a pulpit, intended to diffuse the sound of a preacher's voice through the church.

Southwark Bridge, this bridge, designed by Mr. John Rennie in 1811, "is admirably suited to the situation, as it will tend to remove the irregularity of shallows in this part of the river, by dividing the stream, and thereby directing the current into three regular channels, and consequently removing those sandbanks so injurious to navigation." The bridge is an iron-work of three arches. The middle arch is 240 feet span; the other two, 210 feet each. The piers are 24 feet each; whole span of the river about 708 feet between the abutments. The abutments are built of stone with dowels introduced into every course of masonry to connect them firmly together, to prevent the possibility of their sliding, and to enable them effectually to resist the lateral thrusts. The foundation for the masonry is formed by *gratings* of strong timber resting upon numerous piles, driven in a slanting direction, forming an angle with base of the abutment. The foundations of the piers are from 9 to 10 feet below the bed of the river, on a strong flooring of timber resting on numerous piles, driven perpendicularly; the courses of masonry are dowelled and laid horizontally. The depth of the foundations were laid thus deep to provide against the deepening of the river should London bridge be rebuilt or altered. The width of the roadway and footways between the parapets is the same as on Blackfriars bridge, 42 feet.

Spalling, in mining, breaking up into small pieces for the sake of easily separating the ore from the rock, after which it undergoes the process of lobbing.

Span, or chord of an arch, an imaginary line extending between its springing on each side.

Spandril, an irregular triangular space formed between the outer curve or extrados of an arch; a horizontal line from its apex and a perpendicular line from its springing; also a space on a wall between the outer mouldings of the two arches, and a horizontal line or string-course above them; likewise between similar mouldings and the line of another arch rising above and enclosing the two.

Spandril bracketing, a cradling of brackets fixed between one or more curves, each in a vertical plane, and in the circumference of a circle whose plane is horizontal.

Spanish and Moorish Architecture. "St. Ferdinand III. of Spain conquered many places from the Moors, and among others that of *Alhamra*, the inhabitants of which retreated to Granada, and settled in a quarter of that city, which took the name of their ancient country. This was about 1226. From hence it appears that the name Alhambra, which Swinburne derives from the red colour of the buildings (the Red House), in fact was derived from their country or city; but where this country or city was I have not discovered, unless it be Alhamra in the kingdom of Granada, about 60 miles from the south-west of the city. It was in the reign of Mahomet II. that the famous palace of Alhambra was begun. Mahomet began his reign in 1273 and died in 1302."

Spanish Black is a soft black, prepared by burning cork in the manner of Frankfort and ivory blacks; and it differs not essentially from the former, except in being of a lighter and softer texture. It is subject to the variation of the charred blacks, and eligible for the same uses.

Spanish Red is an ochre differing little from Venetian red.

Spanshacle, a large bolt driven through the forecastle and forelocked under the forecastle-beam, and under and upon the upper deck-beam; on the forecastle it has a large square ring, for the end of the davit to fix in.

Spar, a piece of timber employed as a common rafter in a roof.

Specific Gravity of a body is the relation of its weight, compared with the weight of some other body of the same magnitude. A body immersed in a fluid will sink if its specific gravity be greater than that of the fluid; but if it be less, the body will rise to the top, and will be only partly uncovered. If the specific gravity of the body and fluid are equal, then the body will remain at rest in any part of the fluid. If the body be heavier than the fluid, it loses as much of its weight when immersed as is equal in weight to a quantity of the fluid of the same bulk. If the specific gravity of the fluid be greater than that of the body, then the quantity of the fluid displaced by the part immersed is equal in weight to the weight of the whole body. Therefore the specific gravity of the fluid is to that of the body as the whole magnitude of the body is to the part immersed. The specific gravities of equal solids are as their parts immersed in the same fluid. The specific gravities of fluids are as the weights lost by the same immersed body.

To form a Table of the specific weights of various substances, it is necessary to select one as the standard of comparison; in practice, pure water is always chosen as the starting point for solids and liquids, and pure atmospheric air for gases, the number 1 (1·000) expressing their specific gravities. The formation of two series is considered to be more convenient than the comparison to all bodies by one standard, on account of the perplexity of the numbers which would result.

Solids and Liquids.

Water	1·000
Platinum	21·5
Gold	19·5
Mercury	13·5
Lead	11·45
Silver	10·5
Copper	8·96
Iron, cast	7·2
Iron, rod	7·7
Steel	7·8
Diamond	3·5
Rock Crystal	2·6
Window-glass	2·52
Wax	0·964
Sulphuric acid	1·84
Oil of Turpentine	0·865
Spirit of Wine (strong)	0·83
Ether	0·72

Gases.

Atmospheric air	1·000
Oxygen	1·106
Hydrogen	0·069
Nitrogen	0·972
Carbonic acid	1·524
Carbonic oxide	0·967
Pit gas	0·558
Light gas	0·985

(For the specific gravities of some other substances, see *Data*, etc.)

Spend, in mining, to break ground, to work a way.

Spere, the screen across the lower end of the hall, in domestic buildings of the middle ages.

Sperver, the wooden frame at the top of a bed or canopy.

Sphere, in geometry, a globe, a solid contained under one uniform surface, every point of which is equally distant from a point within, called the centre of the sphere, and may be conceived to be generated by the revolution of a semicircle about its diameter, which is fixed, and is called the axis of the sphere.

Spherical bracketing, the forming of brackets to support lath-and-plaster work, so that the surface of the plaster shall form the surface of a sphere.

Spheroid, a solid body resembling a sphere, supposed to be generated by the revolution of any oval about an axis.

Spheroidal bracketing, the bracketing prepared for a plaster ceiling whose surface is to form that of a spheroid.

Spice-plate. At the conclusion of Queen Anne Boleyn's coronation dinner, she took wafers and ipocras. "The table was then taken up, and the Earl of Rutland brought up the surnap, and laid it at the boord's end, and the Queen washed; she arose and stoode in the middest of the palace hall: to whom the Earl of Sussex, in a goodlie spice-plate, brought a voïd of spice and comfits."

Spiceries and pepper-boxes were made very large in the Tudor times, and placed on the high table: their shape was that of a tower, castellated and triple-turreted, into which all kinds of spices were placed, of which our ancestors were inordinately fond.

Spinning-jenny, in mechanics, a machine used in the cotton manufactories to turn a great number of spindles, by means of bands from a horizontal wheel.

Spinning-wheel, the wheel formerly employed in the spinning of material for textile fabrics: it consisted of a wheel which gave motion to a spindle, on which the thread spun by the fingers was wound.

Spira (Latin), the base of a column: this member did not exist in the Doric order of architecture, but was always present in the Ionic and Corinthian; and besides the bases properly belonging to those orders, there was one called the Attic, which may be regarded as a variety of the Ionic.

Spiral, in geometry, a curve-line of the circular kind, which in its progress always recedes more and more from its centre. In architecture, a curve that ascends windingabout a cone or spire, so that all its points continually approach its axis.

Spire, in geometry, a line drawn progressively round the same axis, with a distance between each circle; a curve-line; anything contorted or wreathed; a curl, a twist, a wreath. In architecture, it denotes anything growing up taper; a round pyramid, a steeple.

Spirit of wine, or *alcohol*, is weaker than essential oils, and is so volatile as to be of use only as a medium for combining oils with resins, etc., as a powerful solvent in the formation of spirit-varnishes, and in some degree as an innocent promoter of drying in oils and colours. In picture-cleaning it affords also powerful means of removing varnishes, etc.

Spirit-level, a cylindrical glass tube, filled with spirit of wine, except a small bubble of air. In whatever position the tube may be placed, the bubble of air will always tend to the highest part of it; but when placed in a perfectly horizontal position, the bubble will remain stationary at the centre of the tube.

Spirketing, the strake wrought on the ends of the beams of a ship; where there are ports, it is the two strakes worked up to the port-cells; in which case the middle of the planks should not be reduced, unless it occasions the butts to be less than 6 inches.

Spital, a hospital.

Splashers, screws or guards placed over locomotive-engine wheels (usually faced with brass), to prevent any person on the engine coming in contact with the wheels, and also to protect the machinery from any wet or dirt thrown up by the wheels.

Splay, the slanting or bevelled expansion groin, in Gothic and Domestic architecture, to doors, windows, and openings in walls, etc.

Split-pins and cotters, round and flat pins, with a head at one end, and split at the other end. They are used through the ends of bolts, to keep them from getting out of their place, the split end being opened like the letter ≺, to keep the pin or cotter from falling out.

Spoons. In eating, spoons seem to have been almost the only aid to the fingers at a very early period of our history. "Knives (ancient as they are) were first made in England in 1563, by Thomas Mathews, on Fleet Bridge, London," and were therefore only obtainable, in any considerable number, before that time, by the upper classes of society. Horn and wood were the materials of which spoons were made down to Elizabeth's reign, when pewter became common, and was much improved.

Spray, in navigation, the sprinkling of the sea driven from the top of a high wave in stormy weather.

Spring, in mechanics, an elastic body, which, when distorted or compressed, has the power of restoring itself; any active power by which motion is produced or propagated.

Spring, in navigation, a rope passed out at one extremity of a ship, and attached to a cable from the other, to bring her broadside to bear upon an object.

Springs, in locomotive engines, the elastic steel supporters of the boiler and frame upon the axles, named after the particular parts to which they apply; as leading-springs for the leading-axle, driving-springs for the driving-axle, trailing-springs for the trailing-axle, tender-springs, drag-springs, buffer-springs, piston-springs, valve-springs, etc., all proportioned to the particular duty they have to perform.

Springs. Water-springs, top-springs, springs of the deep, etc. In contemplating the origin and utility of water-springs, as dispersed upon the face of the earth, for the use of man and beast, and as far deep in the earth as the miner's art has led,— we find much both to inform and amuse those who have not made this subject their study. All springs take their source from the seas, lakes, and rivers: by the heat from that great luminary of our earth, the sun, they are evaporated into the upper regions, and there rarefied, forming clouds filled with rain, which, by attraction and different causes, is plentifully showered upon the earth. It has been urged by some, that it is impossible for rain to supply the copious springs that arise in stony countries, where there is little appearance of a receiving soil, and that rocky ground is impervious to them. But it must be admitted, that if rocks make a discharge of water, they are also capable of receiving it; and that rocky countries are generally as well supplied with springs as others, is well known to all travellers. One of the most stony countries in Europe is Norway, where there is an abundant supply of pure water. It has also been stated that those places where it never rains, both in Africa and some parts of America, are yet well supplied with springs, and at times have flooded rivers. Whence come their springs? The Nile, Niger, etc., are rivers of magnitude, and drain the greatest part of Africa. They are seldom replenished with rain; but they receive their immense floods from the extensive mountainous country lying above and behind them, where they have all kinds of weather; and some of the hills are annually covered with snow, as well as those districts in America where it seldom rains: but the dews are very prolific, so much so that on walking out in the evening or early in the morning, amongst the herbage, it is nearly the same as in this country after a shower of rain. Hence it may be fairly presumed, that the springs of those countries are fed by the excessive dews, similar to rain in other parts of the world, drawn from seas, lakes, and rivers, from the exhalations by the sun during the heat of the day. In those tropical climates, night and day are nearly equally divided. Nature is thus perfect in all her works, by allowing a sufficient period for the descent of dews to supply the place of rain.

It has been also asserted, that the principal springs come from the sea, and ascend their different chasms in the lower parts of the earth connected with it; that the water is then forced in, divested of its saltness, and made fresh by percolation through the sand or silt in those chasms. It then becomes, the lighter fluid. The superior gravity of the salt then causes it to rise to the height of the highest hills. This hypothesis has proved to be unsound. The water of salt springs, from which so large a portion of salt is made, by evaporation, pumped up from the coal-pits at Butley, in Durham, and at Newcastle, is not sea-water, but is of a redder colour, and contains a far larger portion of natron. But what is still a greater proof that those salt-springs have no connection with the sea, is, that in the middle of the river Wear, between Durham and Bishop's Auckland, during the droughty months of summer, when the waters are low, from a rock bottom arises one of the finest salt-water springs known, many degrees salter than that of the sea, surrounded by copious streams of fresh-water; and this place is between 200 and 300 feet above the level of the sea. What siphon-like power could force it to this altitude, so far within the land, from that fancied source? All these kind of springs receive their saltness from passing through beds or mines of salt, such as those at the Wicke, in Cheshire, etc., or some matter yet unknown, of a less dense body, that will more easily communicate its salter particles to the water running through it. What say the inspired writers?— "There is a multitude of waters in the heavens;" and "He causes the vapours to ascend from the ends of the earth:" "He makes the rain." That is from its seas, its lakes, and rivers, by natural exhalations, the clouds are replenished. "He hindeth up the waters in his thick clouds; and the cloud is not rent under them." "Who hath divided a watercourse for the overflowing of its waters, to cause it to rain on the earth?" The vapours which arise from the sea are much more than sufficient to supply both the surface of the earth and the rivers with water; whilst the mountains, by their particular structure and formation, attract and, as it were, arrest the vapours and the rain that fluctuate about in the atmosphere; and having collected them in their reservoirs, dismiss them again through their sides, either in perpetual or intermitting currents.

Spring-balance, in locomotive engines, a spiral spring weighing-balance, with an index and pointer. This is attached to the end of the lever, by which the pressure upon the safety-valve is adjusted.

Spring-hooks, in locomotive engines, the hooks fixing the driving-wheel spring to the frame. A screw on the end of the hook regulates the weight on the driving wheels.

Spring-pins, in locomotive engines, iron rods fitted between the springs and the axle-boxes, to sustain and regulate the pressure of the axles.

Springing, the bottom stone of an arch which lies upon the impost.

Sprit, in navigation, a small boom or pole which crosses the sail of a vessel diagonally from the mast to the hindermost corner of the sail, to elevate and extend it.

Spritsail, in navigation, the sail that belongs to the bowsprit.

Sprung, in navigation. When a topmast is broken or cracked near the cap, it is said to be sprung.

Spurs, pieces of timber fixed on the bulgeways, and the upper end bolted to the ship's side above water, for security to the bulgeways.

Square, in geometry, a quadrilateral figure with right angles and equal sides. In architecture, an area of four sides, with houses on each side.

Square-rigged, In navigation, an epithet applied to a ship that has long yards at right angles with the length of the deck, in contradistinction to sails extended obliquely by stays or lateen yards.

Square sails are such as are extended by a yard, distinguished from others extended by booms, stays, lateens, and gaffs.

Square tuck, when the planks of the bottom are not worked round to the wing transom, but end at the fashion-piece.

Squaring the circle, in mathematics, is attempting to make a square that shall be equal to a given circle.

Squinch, a term applied to small arches or projecting courses of stone formed across the angles of towers.

Squint, an opening through the wall of a Roman Catholic church, in an oblique direction, for the purpose of enabling persons in the transept or aisle to see the elevation of the Host at the high altar.

Stadium, a Roman measure of length, nearly equivalent to our furlong. The term was also applied to a building, or an enclosed area, in which gymnastic and athletic exercises, chariot-racing, and foot-racing, wrestling, and other public games, were exhibited. The stadium was divided into distances for the racers. Also a Greek structure, of an oblong area, terminated at one end by a straight line, at the other by a semicircle, having the breadth of the stadium for its base. Around this area were ranges of seats rising one above another, erected for the purpose of witnessing the public sports at Olympia and other places.

Staircases. It was in the reign of Elizabeth that staircases first became features in English houses. Hand-rails and balustrades, unlike the rickety contrivances of modern days, were of gigantic proportions, and presented at once a bold, picturesque, and secure appearance; yet so variously and fancifully decorated, that their effect was always pleasing and free from clumsiness. In the middle of Verulam House was a delicate staircase of wood, which was curiously carved; and on the posts of every interstice was fixed some figure, as a grave divine with his book and spectacles, a mendicant friar, etc. In two of the principal chambers of Wressil Castle are small beautiful staircases, with octagon screens, embattled at the top, and covered with very bold sculpture, containing double flights of stairs, winding round each other, after the design of Palladio. The east stairs at Wimbledon House lead from the marble parlour to the great gallery and the dining-room, and are richly adorned with wainscot of oak round the outsides thereof, all well gilt with fillets and stars of gold. The steps of these stairs were in number 33, and 6 feet 6 inches long, adorned with 5-foot paces, all varnished black and white, and chequer-work; the highest of which foot-pace is a very large one, and benched with a wainscot bench, all garnished with gold.

Staircases, in ordinary modern practice, should be light, spacious, and easy, seeming to invite people to ascend. Principal staircases should not be narrower than 4 feet, so that if two persons meet thereon, they may pass each other with convenience; but they may be extended in breadth to 10 or 12 feet, according to the importance of the building. The steps should never exceed 6 inches in height, nor be less than 4 inches; but this latter height is only allowable in very wide staircases. The breadth, or the flat horizontal part, which is called the tread of the step, should not be less than a foot, nor exceed 15 inches.

Stakes, in ship-building, are the regular ranges of planks on the bottom and the sides of the ship, reaching from the stem to the stern.

Stall, a place occupied by a monk, canon, dean, or prebendary, in the choir of a church; sometimes applied also to the sedilia or presbyteries for the officiating ministers in the wall of a chancel.

Stamps, machinery for crushing ores.

Stanchion, in ship-building, a small pillar of wood or iron, used to prop and support the decks, awning, etc.

Stanchion, the upright iron bar between the mullions of a window, screen, etc.

Standards, timbers in the form of knees, with one arm on the deck, and the other fayed to a ship's side.

Stantients, the upright pieces in a bulk-head, breast-work, etc., of a ship.

Starboard, in navigation, the right-hand side of a ship, looking forward, as larboard is the left-hand.

Starlings, in architecture, are large piles placed on the outside of the foundation of the piers of bridges, to break the force of the water and protect the stone-work.

Statics, the science which considers the weight of bodies, or the motion of bodies arising from gravity.

Stations, a generic term applied to fixed points or places, of which a series is included in any extended works or arrangements. Thus we have Post-office Stations, Telegraph Stations, Police Stations, Fire-engine Stations, and Railway Stations.

As applied to railways, the term station is a very comprehensive one, comprising a multitude of buildings and apparatus of an extended and costly character. Terminal stations of long lines of railway usually cover several acres of ground, and include buildings for the assembling of the passengers, and for classifying them in separate compartments, according to the class of carriage they intend to occupy; extended platforms, conveniently arranged for the arrival and departure of the trains, and well protected from the weather, and lighted by night. The level of these platforms is arranged so that persons walk directly into the carriages, without ascent or descent, and their length is sufficient to serve many carriages, or two or more entire trains at one and the same time. A separate department of the station is usually allotted to the receipt, arrangement, and distribution of parcels and goods of all kinds, from bulky bales and ponderous hogsheads down to a packet of such insignificant dimensions that it may hold no more than a half-ounce letter. The goods warehouses belonging to this department are of great size, and fully furnished with cranes and moving and weighing gear of all requisite powers and dimensions, fitted to load and unload the goods-waggons belonging to the line, and all ordinary road vehicles. Besides these purposes, the terminal and first-class stations often include a complete engineering establishment of a practical character, in which the locomotive engines, carriages, trucks, waggons, etc., are repaired and built, and including foundry, smithies, pattern-turning, fitting, erecting, and repairing shops; the latter being provided with rails below for running the engines into the building, and travelling cranes above for lifting them entire when needed, or aiding in their dissection with all the rapidity and delicacy of movement which commonly belong only to operations upon far smaller and easier handled subjects. The station also embraces ample buildings or engine-houses, in which the locomotive engines are ranged like so many post-horses in a road-side stable, ready for immediate action, and in which the raking out of fires and the cleaning and adjustment are daily performed. Complete arrangements are also included for delivering water and coke to the tenders, and in some the necessary buildings and apparatus are comprised for pumping the water from deep wells, for burning the coke, and even for manufacturing the gas to be employed in the lighting of the whole of the buildings and shops. Board-rooms, clerks'-rooms and offices, and residences for the station-master and assistants, besides store-rooms of all kinds, refreshment-saloons, urinals, water-closets, police-rooms, telegraph-rooms, lost-luggage office, etc., etc., are also among the necessary details of a principal railway station. The area of the station is covered with lines of railway for the passage of the engines and carriages, and provided with turn-tables, revolving and traversing, for readily transferring the carriages from one line to another, besides switches and apparatus for connecting the several lines at intervals. Of the extent of some of these works at one of the metropolitan stations, that of Camden Town, on the line of the North-western Railway, the following particulars will convey some idea:—This station, which is chiefly for goods only, covers an area of 30 acres, and has a length of double line of 2500 feet for the goods waggons only, and entirely clear of the main line. The length of single line of railway, exclusive of the main line, exceeds 12 miles. There are 112 sets of points for turning carriages from one line to another, 190 turn-plates, and 110 cranes, varying in power from 1½ to 20 tons. The area covered with goods' sheds exceeds 135,000 superficial feet, and that of the platform is 30,000 feet. The circular engine-house is 160 feet in diameter, and will contain 24 engines and tenders; the central turn-table within it is 41 feet in diameter. The annual consumption of gas exceeds six millions of cubic feet.

In minor or intermediate stations, the works are, of course, of smaller magnitude, and are not required to subserve all the combined purposes of a principal station.

Statuary, a carver of images or representations of life; one who practises or professes the art of sculpture.

Staves, in joinery, the boards that are joined together laterally, in order to form a hollow cylinder, cylindroid, cone, or conoid, or any frustum of these bodies. The shafts of columns, in joinery, are frequently glued up in staves.

Stay, in navigation, a strong rope employed to support the mast in the fore-part: *to stay* a ship, to manage the sails so that she shall not make any way forward, preparatory to her tacking about.

Staysail, in navigation, a sort of triangular sail extended on a stay.

Stays, outside, in locomotive engines, sling-stays binding the boiler and frame together.

Stays, inside boiler, in locomotive steam-engines, rods of iron binding together the flat ends of the boilers. The flat side of the dome is likewise strongly bound together by iron rods. Without these stays, they could not resist the pressure of the steam against so large a surface.

Stays, inside frame, in locomotive engines, strong stays placed below the boiler, firmly fixed at one end to the fire-box, and at the other end to the smoke-box: they support the inside bearings of the driving axle and other parts of the machinery.

Stay-wedges, in locomotive engines, wedges fitted to the inside bearings of the driving axles, to keep them in their proper position in the stays.

Steam, the vapour of hot water at the boiling point of 212 degrees.

Steam-chest, in locomotive engines, a box attached to the cylinders, into which the steam is admitted by the regulator: the slide-valve works in this box over the steam-ports, which open into it from the cylinder.

Steam-chest cocks, in locomotive engines, oil-cups, placed conveniently for lubricating the faces of the steam-ports and slide-valve.

Steam compression. The steam which has performed its duty in the cylinder, but which has not escaped before the slide-valve closes the exhaust-port, is compressed by the advancing piston. This compression begins, according to the lap and travel of the slide, from 2 to 3 inches from the end of the stroke, and is of considerable amount. It is, however, of advantage in checking the momentum of the piston, and relieving the strain on the connecting and piston rods at the end of each stroke, and is not therefore all lost power.

Steam Engine, a machine for deriving power from the expansion which results from the conversion of water into vapour or steam by the application of heat. This expansion is so great that a given quantity of water becomes, when changed into the form of steam, enlarged to about 1,728 times its original bulk; and this expansion takes place with a force that may be termed irresistible. Thus if water be enclosed in a vessel, say of iron or any other strong material, and the water be

STEAM ENGINE.

expanded into steam, and insufficient space left for the expansion, the vessel will be burst by the force of the steam within. A steam engine consists essentially of a vessel into which the steam is admitted, and which is provided with a movable disc, closely fitting the interior and capable of sliding within the vessel. This vessel is made cylindrical, because this form gives the greatest strength and is the most readily fitted with the movable disc. The vessel is termed the *cylinder*, and the disc the *piston*. Supposing the cylinder to be placed upright, and fitted with a close cover, and that while the piston is near the bottom of it steam is admitted to rush in through a pipe below the piston, the piston will be driven up by the steam, and if, when it reaches the upper part of the cylinder, the steam from below is shut off, and admitted through an upper pipe to press upon the top surface of the piston, it will be forced down again. Thus a rectilinear motion up and down is produced, and this constitutes what is called the *principle* of the steam engine. All its other parts are for the purpose of regulating the admission of the steam, and converting the rectilinear motion produced at the cylinder into a rotary motion at the point where the power is required to be applied for working machinery. The steam, when no longer required for that purpose, is allowed to escape into the open atmosphere, or conducted in a pipe to another vessel, which, being cooled by the application of cold water, rapidly condenses the steam, that is, reconverts it into water. If permitted to escape into the air, the steam has to force itself against the pressure of the atmosphere, whereas if conducted into a condenser, this force is not required. Hence steam of less pressure will work what is termed a *low-pressure* or *condensing engine*, while that already described is for distinction called a *high-pressure engine*. A third variety of steam engine is worked by shutting off the steam before it has driven the piston the whole length of the cylinder, or completed the *stroke*, as it is termed, and the subsequent expansion of the steam completes the impulse upon the piston. Engines thus worked are distinguished as *expansive engines*. The principal difference in the mechanism of condensing and expansive steam engines is in the movement of the apparatus which admits and shuts off the steam, or the *valves*, which act as doors within the pipes. The several parts of a condensing engine and its appliances are as follows: 1st, the *boiler*, in which the steam is produced from water by the action of fire in the furnace beneath; 2ndly, the *steam-pipe*, in which the steam is conveyed to the engine; 3rdly, the *steam-chests*, in which the steam is received, and which communicates with the two *induction-pipes* that lead into the upper and lower part of the cylinder; 4thly, the *cylinder* fitted with the *piston*, and having pipes called the *eduction-pipes*, through which the steam passes away when its work in the cylinder is completed, into the condenser; 5thly, the *air-pump*, which abstracts the water formed by the condensed steam, sending it into the boiler, producing a partial vacuum within the condenser, and thus assisting the escape of the steam from the cylinder; 6thly, the *condenser* itself, which is kept cool with water pumped up by the cold-water pump. The piston has a rod fixed to it, which works through a steam-tight opening or *stuffing-box* in the lid of the cylinder, and this *piston-rod* is attached to one end of a *beam*, which turns upon a centre, and the other end of which works a *connecting-rod* attached to a *crank*, to the side of which a rotary motion is thus imparted. In some engines the piston-rod is connected by links directly with the crank, and these are hence termed *direct-action* steam engines, while the former are distinguished as *beam-engines*. In others, again, the piston-rod is attached to the crank without links, and the cylinder, instead of being fixed, is made to vibrate or oscillate: these are therefore termed *vibrating* or *oscillating engines*. *Marine engines* for propelling vessels on the water, and *locomotive engines* for propelling trains of carriages upon railways, are each distinguished by peculiarities of construction and arrangements, fitting them for their especial duties.

Steam exhaust-port, in the locomotive engine, the passage opened below the slide-valve from the cylinder to the atmosphere. It is placed between the two steam-ports, and is nearly twice their area, the more freely to permit the escape of the steam. It is open to the blast-pipe, and is cut off from any communication with the steam in the steam-chest by the slide-valves. The arch part of the slide-valve opens the passage from the cylinder into the central exhaust-port, where, through the blast-pipe and chimney, it escapes to the atmosphere, and by this means produces the draught on the fire.

Steam-gauge, a contrivance to show the exact amount of pressure of the steam; it consists of a siphon-tube with equal legs, half-filled with mercury: one end is cemented into a pipe which enters that part of the boiler which contains the steam; the other end is open to the atmosphere. A stop-cock is usually provided between this gauge and the boiler, so that it may be put in communication with the boiler at pleasure. When the stop-cock is open, the steam acting on the mercury in one leg of the gauge presses it down, and the mercury in the other leg rises. The difference between the two columns is the height of mercury which corresponds to the excess of the pressure of the steam in the boiler above the pressure of the atmosphere; or, in other words, to the effective pressure on the safety-valve. If half a pound per inch be allowed for the length of this column, the effective pressure of the steam, in pounds per square inch, is obtained.

Steam Navigation. This is accomplished by the application of steam power to the *marine engine*, by which vessels of all dimensions are propelled on the waters of the ocean or on the principal rivers. Whether by means of the paddle-wheel, or by the spiral or helix screw, the fluid is displaced and the vessel sent forward at the various speeds consequent upon the skill employed in the making of vessel and engine. Much competition and many controversies have existed upon the best methods to be adopted. Many instances of failures have occurred from the simple circumstance of the builder of the ship and the constructor of the engine not acting in concert. Steam vessels for river passenger-traffic, when in trim and all their parts well constructed, average a speed of 15 miles an hour; in America 16 miles; and sea-going vessels average on their way 12 miles. Cunard's packet from Liverpool to Halifax and Boston have done more. The West India and the Peninsular and Oriental Companies have splendid vessels, which do credit to the companies for their enterprise,—to the builders for the construction of the craft, and to the engineers for the construction of the engines. Other companies exist who deserve their proportion of praise. It is to England and Scotland that the world is indebted for this new element of civilization.

Steam-pipes, in locomotive engines, the pipes which collect and convey the steam to the steam-chest: they commence inside the boiler. In boilers with domes, the receiving pipe is raised as high as possible, and turned back round the edges of the open end, to prevent any water which might rise so high from overlying the pipe. In boilers having no domes, the steam is collected in a horizontal pipe pierced with numerous small holes. After being collected, the steam-pipes are continued outside the boiler to the steam-chest. The internal diameter of the steam-pipe is usually rather more than one-fifth of the diameter of the steam cylinders: the area of the passages through valves, in some of Watt's beam-engines, is nearly one square inch per horse power. This is in some cases too large for steam-passages, but rather too small for the exhausting valve-passages.

Steam-pipe for tender, in locomotives, a small pipe attached to the boiler by a cock, for admitting the spare steam to heat the water in the tender.

Steam-ports, in locomotive engines, two passages from the steam-chest to the cylinder. The steam is admitted to and from these passages by the slide-valve opening the port for the admission of steam to the cylinder, and then by shutting off this port from the steam in the steam-chest, and, opening the same passage by which it entered, it is conveyed to the atmosphere.

Steam-whistle, an apparatus attached to the boiler of a locomotive engine for the purpose of giving warning of its approach when running. The construction of the whistle is shown to one-quarter size in the annexed engravings. It is made of brass, and the foot, A, is cast hollow with a flange, B, at the bottom to bolt it on the fire-box: it has a cock, C, placed in it, with the handle D, and screw E, to keep it tight; the handle projects out, to allow firm hold to be taken of it. The cup F is fixed upon the foot A, by screwing the piece G upon it, and both are turned truly at their outer edges, leaving a very narrow passage, I I, four inches diameter, between them all round. The piece G is hollow, having holes, H, in its sides; and a

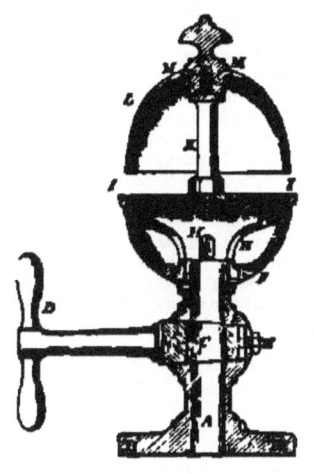

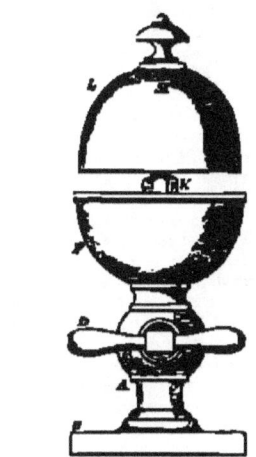

pillar, s, stands upon its centre, on which is screwed the bell, L L, the thin edge of which is brought just over the opening I, and half an inch above it.

When the cock is opened, the steam enters the cup v through the holes H, and rushes out at the narrow slit I, striking the thin edge of the bell, L, in a manner similar to the action in organ-pipes, and producing an exceedingly shrill and piercing sound. Some holes, M, are made in the top of the bell, to allow the steam to pass through, which improves the sound considerably. The size of the concentric part where the steam escapes, and the depth of the bell part, and their distance asunder, regulate the tones of the whistle, from a shrill treble to a deep bass. The cock should be steadily opened, to adjust the quantity of steam, so as to produce the clearest sound. The steam whistle is very effective, and its sound can be heard at a great distance.

Steel is composed chiefly of iron and carbon; yet these alone will produce but a poor and brittle article. Good steel contains a variety of elements, almost all of those, in fact, which are considered impurities of iron when present in excess.

Steel is divided into four distinct classes,—Damascus steel; German steel; Blistered, or blister steel, to which class shear steel belongs; and Cast steel. The first is made directly from the ore, or by welding steel rods and iron rods together; the second from pig metal, by depriving the latter of a portion of its carbon and impurities; the third from bar iron, by impregnating it with carbon; and the fourth class, or cast steel, may be made from either of the others, by melting it in a crucible. Still, blistered steel appears to be the most advantageous, so far as quality is concerned.

Damascus Steel.

This steel derives its name from Damascus, a city in Asia. The swords or scimitars of Damascus present upon their surface a watery appearance, and variegation of streaks of a silvery white, black, and grey colour, and fine and coarse lines, exhibiting regular and irregular figures. The excellent quality of these blades is proverbial; they unite hardness to great elasticity. Genuine Damascus steel is made directly from iron ore; and meagre as our knowledge is concerning the subsequent manipulations, such as forging and hardening, it is known that the steel is smelted, in a kind of Catalan forge, from red oxide of iron, a red clay ore found in transition slate. It is generally believed that the great strength of this steel is to be attributed to a small quantity of aluminum which enters into its composition, and which is derived from the clay of the ore,—an opinion which has this fact in its favour, that no material imparts a greater degree of tenacity to iron than alumina. Great exertions have been made to imitate this steel, in which, of all nations, the French have been the most successful. They have succeeded in imitating not only irregular figures, but arabesques and initials, in the most beautiful manner. Still, the French is far less tenacious and hard than the genuine Damascus steel. The virtue of the latter, therefore, must be sought for in the ore from which it is made.

German Steel.

This steel is made in two different ways, either directly from the ore or by converting the ore into pig-metal, and then into steel. The steel manufactured by the first method is generally crude and irregular, and therefore this method is seldom practised.

The Stück oven, or Wulf's oven,

as well as the Catalan forge, is one of the furnaces employed in the manufacture of steel from ore. In making steel, the blast is directed more upon the fuel than upon the iron: the tuyère is level: the iron is impregnated with carbon. The reverse is the case in the manufacture of iron. In the blue-oven, a kind of pig metal is frequently made, which is almost pure steel; but it is coarse, and never, even after the best refining, makes a good article. All manipulations, the object of which is to make steel directly from the ore, are unprofitable.

To this class belongs the manufacture of wootz, or East Indian steel. This is certainly a good steel, and is partially imitated in America. Wootz is smelted directly from the ore, which is the black magnetic oxide of iron, in furnaces five or six feet in height, of the form of some foundry cupolas. Previously to smelting, the ore is finely pounded and washed, to remove impurities.

The manufacture of steel from pig metal does not depend so much upon the manipulations in the forge as upon the quality of the metal. The ores generally employed are the crystallized carbonate, spathic ore, often mixed in a slight degree with hematite, and the rich red peroxides. Magnetic ores do not answer for such work, and are therefore but seldom used. The same may be said in relation to the hydrated oxides. Pig metal for steel manufacture is smelted with as little lime or other flux as possible. The principal flux to be relied on is manganese; but this always exists in the ore, and is never used as an artificial admixture, though it is possible that an artificial flux might be made of it. Steel metal is in most cases white. It is smelted by rather more ore than that which will make grey iron; but not with so heavy a burden as that which will make white iron containing carbon in small amount. Any ore which contains foreign matter in such large amount as to make the addition of lime as a flux necessary, does not make good steel metal. The only mode of working the furnace is, of course, by means of charcoal and the employment of the cold blast.

The forge fires employed in converting the metal into steel do not differ materially from those in which iron is made. The hearth of the former is generally larger and deeper, and the blast is stronger than that of the latter. Very little iron is connected with it. The bottom is generally formed of sandstone, and the sides of braise, or charcoal-dust mixed with clay. The practical manipulation at these forge-fires varies according to locality, to the form of the furnace, and the qualifications of the workmen. The main principle involved may be generalized under the following proposition:—If it is intended to make steel instead of iron, the metal should be melted before and off from the tuyère; and it should be kept, when melted, always below the blast, and never brought above or into the blast. By due attention to locality, everything else may be easily regulated. A skilful workman will soon ascertain that a flat hearth, an iron lining, and a strongly dipped tuyère will not make steel, though it will make iron, and that a weak blast will tend to produce iron.

The crude steel, the result of the first operation, is generally thrown when red-hot into cold water, then broken and sorted. The most silvery part, of the finest grain, is the best. Fibrous or partially fibrous bars are reserved for iron: they make a superior quality of bar iron. Bluish-looking steel is also thrown aside, for it will become fibrous iron before its impurities can be removed. The crude steel, drawn out into bars an inch or an inch and a quarter square, is placed in piles composed of six or eight pieces then welded, and drawn out into smaller bars. This process, called refining, is repeated three or four times, and each time the number of bars in the pile is increased. The smaller the bars of steel, and the greater the number of them placed together, the more perfect will be the refined steel. The piles are heated in a large blacksmith's fire, by stone coal, which must be sufficiently bituminous to form an arch over the fire. Coal-slack, mixed with loam, is frequently used for this purpose; but it increases the waste of steel. The hammer used for drawing steel should be light, weighing no more than 150 pounds, and ought to make from 300 to 400 strokes per minute. Great skill and dexterity are required to draw steel bars. It is highly important to perform this operation well, as the quality of the steel is, in some measure, dependent upon the manner in which it has been hammered.

In those countries where German steel is made, a remarkable article is manufactured, which deserves notice. It is harder than the best cast iron, but so brittle that it cannot bear any bending when cold. This article is cast steel; it is derived from the remelted steel metal. From 200 to 250 lbs. of this metal are generally melted. When that quantity is melted down in the bottom of the forge-hearth, a small portion of it is let off: it should be tapped as low at the bottom as possible. This mass, which flows like cast iron or cast steel, is broken into small pieces, and pounded into a flat piece of wrought iron, which has a brim drawn up around it: this piece serves as a crucible. It is covered with loam, and exposed to a heat which will melt the cast iron, and unite it firmly with the wrought iron. The former then forms a thin coating of steel over the one side of the iron, of immense hardness. This does not become soft, even though a long time is consumed in tempering it. Wrought-iron plates, furnished with such a coating of steel, are used as draw-plates for wire. The holes for the wire are punched when it is warm; for, when cold, its hardness is so extreme, that no drill-bit can make any impression.

Iron for Blistered Steel.

England is not so celebrated for the production of iron suitable for the manufacture of steel as Sweden and Russia, upon which countries we must depend mostly for our knowledge of the mode of working it, and the kind of materials from which iron for the steel factories is made.

The peculiarities of such iron are so remarkable, that, by means of the most accurate chemical analysis, we cannot detect any difference between a given kind which produces a superior, and another kind which produces an inferior steel. Were it possible to detect this difference, it would prove to exist in the cinders. The iron from which blistered steel is made is a soft, fibrous, often grained, wrought iron, of a peculiar silvery whiteness. It is made from mottled pig iron, smelted from magnetic ore by charcoal and cold blast.

In making pig iron for the manufacture of steel, the ore should be carefully roasted by wood, charcoal, or braise. The height of the blast-furnace must not exceed 35 feet, and the result is still more favourable when it does not exceed 30 feet. The boshes should measure about 9 or 9¼ feet. There ought to be either no hearth at all, as in the Swedish or Styrian furnaces, or one that is very low. Blast of medium strength, and tuyères somewhat inclined into the hearth, are requisite. Hot blast must be rejected altogether. In fact, the operation should be conducted in such a manner as to produce mottled iron of great purity. In fluxing the ore, lime can be employed, but only in such limited quantity as not to cause the furnace to smelt grey or white iron; for neither will be serviceable in the manufacture of good steel.

In converting pig into bar iron, the German forge is generally employed in Sweden, and for this purpose may be considered the most perfect. The refining process resembles the boiling of iron: this is required to make the texture of the iron as uniform as possible. White pig metal will not boil, and it works too fast. Grey pig metal contains a large amount of impurities, and the greatest attention at the forge will not remove them in sufficient amount to answer any practical purpose.

In making blistered steel, it is essential to consider not only the quality, that is, the chemical composition of the iron, but also its form. The bars are generally flat: good qualities are from an inch and a quarter to two inches in width, and half an inch thick. For ordinary steel and for cast steel, the thickness of the bars may be three-quarters of an inch; but in these cases, more time is not only required in blistering, but the heart of the bar is still imperfectly carbonized. Thin bars work faster, and make a more uniform steel than thick and heavy bars: the latter are always more or less raw inside, and contain too much carbon outside. If the iron is very pure, it may be short, that is, without fibres; it may be hard, if it is at the same time strong. Impure iron will not make steel of good quality. As iron void of fibres is generally more impure than that containing fibres, the safest plan is to convert all the iron into fibrous iron. Coarse fibrous iron, whatever may be its strength, does not make good steel; that with black spots or streaks of cinder must be avoided by all means. The indications of a good iron are, a silvery-white colour, short fine fibres, a bright metallic lustre, and an aggregation so uniform, that black spots cannot be detected with a lens. The transformation of bar iron into steel requires no special skill or knowledge. The quality of the steel is determined by the quality of the iron from which it is manufactured.

Blistered Steel.

The furnace for the conversion of wrought iron into blistered steel is from 12 to 15 feet wide, and 20 or 25 feet deep. A conical chimney, 40 or 50 feet high, is designed to lead the smoke above the roof of the factory. The iron is placed in boxes composed of fire-brick or sandstone tiles: these boxes are from 24 to 36 inches square, and from 10 feet to 16 feet in length. Square holes at one end of the furnace serve for the admission of the iron, and the entrance and exit of the workmen. Holes are also made in the ends of the boxes, through which one or more of the bars may be passed, for the purpose of testing the degree of cementation, and the progress of the work. The boxes are enclosed in the furnace, which is provided with a grate and fire-brick arch. The iron, when placed in these boxes, is imbedded and carefully laid edgewise in a cement composed of one part hard charcoal, one-tenth part of wood ashes, and one-twentieth part of common salt. The mixture is ground into a coarse powder under edge-wheels. If the boxes are 10 feet in length, the iron bars may be 9 feet 10 inches. The cement is laid about 2 inches deep in the bottom of the box. The bars of

STEEL, BLISTERED.

iron are then put in edgewise, separated by ⅜ of an inch space, which is filled with cement, and the top of the bars covered to the depth of ¼ an inch. Upon this another layer of bars is set, but in such a manner that the second layer overlies the space which separates the bars of the first layer. In this way the box is filled to within 6 inches of its top. The remaining space is filled with old cement powder, on the top of which, finally, damp sand or fire-tiles are placed. The fire ought to proceed slowly, so that three or four days shall elapse before the furnace and the cement-boxes assume a cherry-red heat. In fact, the fire should be conducted in such a manner that the heat may be slightly increased every day during the whole course of the operation. A diminution of the heat, from the time of starting, occasions a loss both of fuel and time, and is injurious to the chests. A well-conducted heat will finish a small box in four or five days, and a couple of boxes, 3 feet square, in ten or twelve days. The furnace and boxes should be cooled very slowly; for a sudden change of temperature is very apt to break the fire-tiles, or sandstone slabs, of which the boxes are constructed. The trial-bar, which passes through the small hole in one of the ends of the box, and in a corresponding hole in the furnace wall, is somewhat longer than the other bars, so as to be taken by a pair of tongs, and pulled out of the box. There are frequently several of such bars, for a bar that is once pulled cannot be returned; and if, in a case in which there is but one trial-bar in the chest, the bar is pulled too soon, no further opportunity of testing the progress of cementation is afforded. The trial-bars are not sufficiently long to project over the wall of the chest. The trial-hole is closed by a clay stopper. Six days may be considered a sufficient time for blistering bars of common steel, such as spring steel, saw-blades, and common files; eight days for shear steel and steel for common cutlery; and ten or eleven days for the better qualities of steel, and common cast steel. Rods for the finer sorts of blistered, and the finest kinds of cast steel, are returned to the boxes after the first heat, and receive two or three blistering heats, according to the quality of steel wished to be obtained. From eight to twelve tons of iron may be charged in two chests, and from four to eight tons in case the furnace contains but one chest. Two small chests are preferable to one large chest. The smaller the chest, the more uniform will the steel become. The regulation of the fire in the furnace is a somewhat delicate operation. Iron of different qualities requires a different degree of heat; but the heat can be easily managed by recollecting that it should be steadily increased every day. If it is not sufficiently strong, the iron will absorb but very little carbon, and the work will proceed slowly. If the heat is too great, the rod iron will be converted into cast iron, or, at least, into something similar to it; for, after being once overheated, it will not, even with the greatest labour and attention, make good steel. If the heat is carried so far as to melt the blistered iron in the boxes, it is converted into white plate-metal,—the kind from which German steel is manufactured. But this melting cannot well take place, and if it should occur, the slow cooling of the chests, which is equivalent to tempering, will transform the white metal into grey cast iron. The latter is converted into steel with greater difficulty than the white metal.

Blistered steel, taken from the chest, is very brittle: the excellence of its quality is in proportion to its brittleness. The presence of fibres indicates that the cementation is unfinished. A fine-grained, white aggregation, like iron rendered cold-short by phosphorus, indicates that the cementation has not advanced beyond its first stages. A crystalline form of the grains is an indication either of imperfect cementation, or of too low a heat, or bad iron; still, the best kind of iron will exhibit these crystals, and they can be observed by the lens, if the temperature of the chests has not been kept sufficiently high. If a good article be desired, a repetition of the operation is, in such cases, necessary. The grains of good steel appear like round globules, when taken from the chest and broken. After an imperfect cementation, the colour of the steel is white. Good blistered steel should be of a greyish colour, and of a bright lustre; and it should exhibit a coarse grain, as though it were an aggregation of mica or leaves of plumbago. That which exhibits a fine grain, of crystalline form, and which is of a white colour, is always a poor article. But one degree of heat is favourable for each kind of iron; if that degree be hit upon, the operation goes on well; if otherwise, a favourable result cannot be expected. The composition of the cement and the construction of the boxes and furnace have little influence on the quality of the steel. Where the iron is of the best quality, and where the degree of heat is most favourable, the fracture of a bar taken from the chest will exhibit the largest grains or leaves. An indication of good iron is its increase of weight in cementation; while bad iron neither gains nor loses in weight, iron of good quality will gain at the rate of from 15 to 20 per cent. This applies especially to strong and pure iron. The surface of the rods, whatever number of blisters they may have when taken from the chest, must be clean. Bad iron makes but few blisters, or none at all: the surface of the rods is rough. With the quality of the iron the number and size of the blisters increase. Danemora iron draws blister close to blister, and almost all of equal size. Common iron, that is, charcoal iron, raises but few blisters, and these are of irregular size. The best qualities of puddled iron raise but few blisters.

As might be expected, the texture and quality of one bar, as well as the average which a chest contains, cannot be uniform. The interior of a bar, like the interior of the box, will be imperfect, while the external parts will be overdone. The steel should, therefore, be broken, sorted, and refined. Pieces of uniform grain, as well as those including the extremes of quality, are piled, welded, and drawn out into bars. This process must be repeated, if the grain is not sufficiently uniform for the desired purpose. Upon the skill of the hammer-man the quality of the steel, in a considerable degree, depends. Slow and heavy strokes and high heats depreciate its value, while its quality is improved by a low heat and fast work. Rolling steel in a rolling-mill, or welding it in a reheating furnace, makes it brittle, and transforms it into a kind of cast iron. This result, however, can be partially remedied by again bringing the steel to the hammer.

The influence of the tilt-hammer upon the iron is nowhere more observable than in the manufacture of steel. It is impossible to make good steel independently of proper hammer machinery. The temperature at which the hammering should be performed is a matter of considerable importance: the steel will be spoiled equally by a too high as by a too low heat. The secret of success appears to be the prevention of crystallization, which takes place at certain temperatures of the metal. Under favourable conditions, definite compounds of carbon and iron are formed; and these compounds crystallize: this crystallization causes brittleness. The greater the amount of foreign matter which is combined with the iron, the greater the brittleness. Blows of the hammer quickly repeated, and the exposure of the metal a short time to a low heat, appear to be the means of preventing crystallization,—at least, of diminishing its extent. A sudden change of temperature augments the power of crystallization in the highest degree. This makes the iron hard, by giving rise to so strong an affinity between the iron and foreign matter, that the colour occasioned by the carbon disappears. The carbon is enclosed in the particles of iron, which is, in turn, crystallized by means of its strongly cohesive properties. White plate-metal of great purity, containing carbon in large amount, is harder than the hardest cast steel, but the strength of its cohesive properties, and the larger size of its crystals, are the causes of its brittleness. The best steel, if melted at a high heat, similar to that of the blast-furnace, would appear in the same form as plate-metal, and would be quite as brittle. From the facts here stated, a conclusion may be drawn, that the impurities which increase the cohesive power of steel or iron may be retained, and the formation of crystals still be prevented.

Cast Steel.

The irregularity which is exhibited in the texture of common steel gave rise to the invention of cast steel. Common steel is broken into small pieces, and closely packed into a crucible made of good fire-clay. That which is in some degree more highly carbonized than usual is best adapted for cast steel; because, in the melting operation, it loses a portion of its carbon. With the fireclay, plumbago or coke-dust is mixed; but neither of these increases its durability, though diminishing its liability to break on account of sudden changes of heat. This well-mixed mass is firmly pounded in an iron mould, with a movable cone for the interior. The crucible which is thus formed is air-dried and slightly burned before it is employed in the melting of cast steel. For this purpose a crucible 5 inches wide at the top, and 16 or 18 inches in height, is generally employed. Every precaution must be taken to prevent it from cracking; for, in such a case, its contents are generally lost.

The air-furnace for the fusion of the steel is similar in construction to those used by brass-founders: it is 2 feet deep and 12 inches square. The flue at the top is covered by a cast-iron trap-door. The top of the furnace coincides with the plane of the floor of the laboratory. Under the floor of the latter is an arch, into which the grates of the furnace may be emptied: this arch supplies the furnace with air, and in it the ashes accumulate. The crucible is placed on a support composed of two thicknesses of firebrick, and its top is covered with a lid. In many cases, pounded glass and blast-furnace cinders are laid on the top of the steel, as well to prevent the access of air as the oxidation of the carbon; but, if the lid fits well, this precaution is unnecessary; besides, these materials generally tend to glaze, and, as a consequence, to crack the crucible. In large factories, ten or twenty furnaces may be put in one row, each furnace having its own chimney. In England the fuel employed is coke; but anthracite is far superior to coke for this purpose. The more compact the fuel, the better will be the result. In feeding the furnace with coal, great caution must be observed; for a sudden charge of cold fuel is apt to crack the crucible. For this reason, square are preferable to round furnaces. The heat of the furnace must be conducted in such a manner that the melting shall commence from below, and not from the top. This is another reason why the form just described is preferable to any other. All these advantages are increased by the employment of blast, which, of course, is essential where anthracite is used.

The time required to melt steel depends partly upon the draught of the furnace, partly upon the quality of the crude steel, and partly on the quality of the article designed to be manufactured. From one to three hours is generally required for a crucible containing 50 lbs. of metal. The stronger the steel, the greater the length of time consumed. The mass must become perfectly liquid, no matter how long a time is required to produce this result. The liquid steel is then poured into previously heated cast-iron moulds, and cast in the shape of square or octagonal bars, 2 inches thick. Before casting, the steel in the crucible is stirred with a hot iron rod, after which a strong heat is applied for a few minutes. After casting, the top of the steel in the mould is covered with clay, to prevent its blistering, and to prevent the access of air.

The cast rods are exposed to a cherry-red heat, and put, when almost black, to the hammer. The rapid succession of strokes beats ness with which the work is performed. The rods are heated in heating stones, constructed like sheet-iron ovens.

Steeler, the foremost or aftermost plank in a strake, which is dropped short of the stern or sternpost of a vessel.

Steelyard, in statics, a kind of balance having arms of unequal length, in which the weight is moved along the longer arm, and becomes in effect heavier in proportion as it is removed from the fulcrum or port. It was formerly named the *Statera Romana*, or Roman balance.

Steeple, a spire or lantern; the superstructure attached to the tower of a church.

Steering-wheel, a wheel to which the tiller-rope is attached, for the convenience of steering a ship.

Steeving, in navigation, denotes the elevation which a ship's cathead or bowsprit is above the stem, or the angle which either makes with the horizon.

Stem, the foremost piece of timber in a ship.

Stem, in mining, a day's work.

Stemples, in mining, wooden pieces by which to go up and down the mine, instead of steps.

Stemson, a piece wrought on the aft-part of the apron, continued as high as the middle deck or upper deck in small ships, the lower end lapping on or scarfing into the keelson.

Stench-trap, a contrivance for the prevention of the escape of effluvia from sinks and drains. These traps are on the same principle as a gasometer: a cup inverted in water stops the escape of gas. (See the following plan and section of a

that the inverted cup will be immersed in the fluid as high as the dotted lines. If, from neglect, the space intended for fluid only should

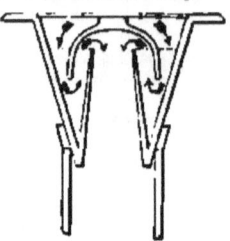

Section of Stench-trap.

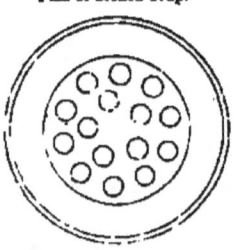

Plan of Stench Trap.

be suffered to become filled with solid matter, the fluid will cease to run in the direction indicated by the arrows, and the utility of the traps will be destroyed; they should, therefore, be kept constantly clear from solid matter.

Some persons, not understanding the principle on which the trap is constructed, remove the inverted cup when the water can no longer flow through it, and then leave it off. The consequence is, that, there being nothing to impede the gas from the drains from rising and flowing into the dwelling-houses, the houses very frequently become filled with noxious air.

Step, in ship-building, a large piece of timber into which the heel of a mast is fixed.

Steps for the masts are large pieces fitted across the keelson, into which the heel of the mast is fixed. The holes for the mast to step into should be cut in proportion to the steps, so as to leave sufficient wood on each side of the hole to answer in strength to the tenon left at the heel of the mast; and if that should be rather too little the hole may be cut more thwartships to answer the deficiency the fore and aft way. There are likewise large pieces called steps of the cupstands; and steps on the top-side, for the convenience of getting on board.

Stereobate, or *Stylobate*, a base; the lower part or basement of a building or column.

Stereographic projection of the sphere; projection.

Stereography, the art of representing solids on a plane.

Stereometry, a science showing how to measure, or to find the solid contents.

Stereotomy, art of cutting solids, or making sections thereof, as walls or other members in profile of architure.

Stereoscope (*The*) has the property of exaggerating the natural effects of perspective and relief. An optical delusion.

The mind judges of the relative position, form, and magnitude of visible objects, by comparing their apparent outlines and varieties of light and shade, with previously acquired impressions of the sense of touch. The knowledge that such and such visual appearances and optical effects are produced by certain varieties of form, position, and distance having been already acquired, it substitutes with the quickness of thought the cause for the effect. The continual repetition of such acts, which are necessarily repeated as often as the sense of vision is exercised, and the extreme rapidity with which all such mental operations are performed, imagination of shape, distance and position are subjects of visual perception.

Exceptional cases, however, are of a class of visual phenomena manifested independent of mere outline and varieties of light and shadow, and which no effort of art can transfer to canvas. Inasmuch, also, as these phenomena are optional effects of distance, form, and position, they become, like the others, indications by which the mind judges of the relative forms and positions of the objects which produce them. Phenomena of this class are manifested, when the objects viewed are placed so near the observer as to have sensible binocular parallax. The aspects under which they are seen in this case by the two eyes, right and left, are different. Certain parts are visible to each eye which are invisible to the other, and the relative positions in which some parts are seen by one eye, differ from those in which the same parts are seen by the other eye. This difference of aspect and apparent position, arises altogether from the different position of the two eyes in relation to the objects. It is a phenomenon, therefore, which can never be developed, in the case of objects whose distance bears a large proportion to the distance between the eyes, because there is no sensible difference between the aspects under which such objects are viewed by the one eye and the other. The phenomenon, therefore, can only be manifested in relation to objects, whose distance from the observer is a small multiple of the distance between the eyes.

It appears that the two eyes, right and left, will have different views of the bust; so that if the observer were to make an exact drawing of the bust with his left eye closed, and another exact drawing of it with his right eye closed, these drawings would not be identical. One of them would show a part of the bust on the extreme right, which would not be exhibited in the other, and the latter would show a part on the extreme left, which would not be included in the former. Moreover, a part of the cheek and the eye would be shown in the drawing made with the right eye closed, which would not appear in the drawing made with the left eye closed.

The stereoscopic pictures are accordingly produced upon daguerreotype plates, photographic paper, or glass. On daguerreotype plates they are necessarily opaque; on glass they are transparent; and on paper may be either opaque or transparent, according to the thickness and quality of the paper.

Since the greater number of stereoscopic pictures represent views of objects which must be so distant from the observer as to have no sensible binocular parallax, it may be asked how it is that stereoscopic effects, so remarkable as those which are manifested by such pictures, can be produced. If the stereoscopic effects be the consequences of binocular parallax, and of that alone, how can such effects be produced by pictures of objects, which have no such parallax?

When the pictures are produced on a small scale they are placed in the stereoscope, the eye-glasses of which will have the effect of causing them to be viewed in lines converging at the same angle, as that formed by the optic axes of the two photographic instruments by which the pictures were produced.

For a full and effective description of this subject see Dr. Lardner's serial work.

Stern, the aft-part of a ship.
Sterne-frame, the frame of timber that is composed of the stern-post, transoms, and fashion-pieces.
Stern-post, the straight piece of timber at the aftermost part of a ship, and to which both sides of the ship unite: the lower end is tenoned into the keel. It is generally worked with the butt-end up-

wards, being most suitable to the conversion of the timber; but in some ships which trade to a hot climate it has been preferred to work the butt-end downwards, because in large ships it requires a piece of such growth whose juices towards the butt are nearly exhausted, and therefore it is supposed to last longer under water; whereas, by the heat of the weather, when the butt is worked upwards, it decays with dry-rot for want of moisture.

Stern-sheets, in navigation, that part of a boat which is contained between the stern and the hindermost seat of the rowers.

Stiff, in navigation, denotes the quality by which a ship is enabled to carry a sufficient quantity of sail without danger of oversetting.

Still-house. Rules are given for building these houses: the first caution is to lay the floor aslope, not flat, where any wet work is to be performed. It should be also well flagged with broad stones, so that no wet be detained in the crevices, but all may run off and be let out at the drains made at the bottom and sides. Stills for wines should be placed abreast on that side of the still-house to which the floor has its current. Fronting the stills, and adjoining to the back of the wall, should be a stage for holding the fermenting-backs; so that these being placed at a proper height, may empty themselves by means of a cock and a canal into the stills, which are thus charged with very little trouble. Near this set of fermenting-backs should be placed a pump or two, that they may readily supply them with water by means of a trunk or canal leading to each back. Under the pavement, adjoining to the stills, should be a kind of cellar, whereon to lodge the receivers, each of which should be furnished with its pump to raise the low wines into the still for rectification; and through this cellar the refuse wash or still-bottoms should be discharged, by means of a hole or other contrivances.

Stilobatum, in architecture, denotes the body of the pedestal of any column. (See *Stereobate*.)

Stone is found in various forms and conditions, embedded in and stratified under the earth's surface. That portion of it which is used for building purposes, is a dense coherent brittle substance, sometimes of a granulated, at others, of a laminated structure; these qualities varying according to its chemical constitution and the mode in which it has been deposited. Sometimes the laminated and granular rocks alternate with each other; at others, a rock of a mixed form prevails, partaking of the characteristics of both structures. Independent of these properties is its power of resistance to compression, which depends chiefly upon its chemical combinations and the pressure to which it has been subjected whilst under the earth's surface from the weight of superincumbent materials. The granite also, and other igneous rocks, owe their hardness to their having crystallized more or less rapidly from a fused mass.

In attempting to ascertain the ultimate powers of resistance of rocks which have been deposited by the action of water, it is necessary to observe the direction in which the pressure is applied, whether in the line of cleavage, or at right angles to it. In nearly all of the following experiments this precaution was attended to, and it will be seen that the strength is far greater when the force is exerted perpendicularly to the laminated surface, than when it is applied in the direction of the cleavage. In building with such stone, it is also important that it should be laid in the same position as that in which it is found in the quarry, as

STONE.

the action of rain and frost rapidly splits off the laminæ of the stone when it is placed otherwise. The strength of the igneous or crystalline rocks is the same in every direction, owing to the arrangement of their particles.

It might have been advantageous to have ascertained, by analysis, the chemical composition of the substances experimented on; but as this varies in almost every locality, and that in accordance with the superincumbent and surrounding strata, this is of less consequence in practice than a knowledge of absolute facts in connection with the properties of the material.

Experiments to determine the force necessary to fracture, and subsequently to crush, 2-inch cubes of sandstone from the Shipley quarries, Bradford. The pressure applied in the direction of the cleavage.

No. of Expt	Weights laid on in lbs.	Remarks.	No. of Expt	Weights laid on in lbs.	Remarks.	No. of Expt	Weights laid on in lbs.	Remarks.
Specimen No. 1. Shipley.			Specimen No. 2. Heaton.			Specimen No. 3. Heaton Park.		
12	31732		11	31732		8	26356	
13	33524	fractured	12	33524	fractured	9	28148	
...	......	......	...	......	......	10	29940	fractured
16	38900	crushed	16	40692	crushed	11	31732	crushed
Specimen No. 4.			Specimen No. 9. Old Whatley.			Specimen No. 10. Manningham-lane.		
This specimen was defective and crushed as the first weight, 28148 lbs., was laid on.			11	31732		8	26356	
			12	33524		9	28148	fractured
			13	35316	fractured & crushed suddenly.	...	......	......
						14	37108	crushed

The results of the experiments 1, 2, 3, 9, 10, fractured and crushed in the line of cleavage, are given in the following Table.

No. of Specimen	Locality.	Size.	Weight at which it fractured.	Weight at which it crushed.
1	Shipley, Bradford.	2-in.cube.	33524	38900
2	Heaton	,,	33524	40692
3	Heaton Park .	,,	29940	31732
9	Old Whatley . .	,,	35316	35316
10	Manningham-lane.	,,	28148	37108
	Mean		32090	36749

Experiments to determine the force required to fracture, and subsequently to crush, 2 inch cubes of sandstone from the Shipley and other quarries, near Bradford. Pressure being applied at right angles to the cleavage.

No. of Expt	Weights laid on in lbs.	Remarks.	No. of Expt	Weights laid on in lbs.	Remarks.
Specimen No. 5. Idle Quarry.			Specimen No. 6. Jegrum's-lane.		
15	38900		18	44276	
16	40692		19	45172	fractured.
17	42484	fractured.	...	......	....
18	43380	crushed.	22	47860	crushed.
Specimen No. 7. Spinkwell.			Specimen No. 8. Coppy Quarry.		
10	29940		14	37108	first fracture.
11	31732	fractured.	...	......	....
...	......	....	16	39796	second fracture.
14	37108	crushed.	...	......	....
			18	41588	crushed.

Specimen No. 11 failed.

Results of experiments on specimens 5, 6, 7, 8, fractured and crushed at right angles to the cleavage.

No. of Specimen	Locality.	Size.	Weight at which it fractured.	Weight with which it crushed
5	Idle Quarry, Bradford	2-in. cube	42484	43380
6	Jegrum's-lane	"	45172	47860
7	Spinkwell	"	31732	37108
8	Coppy Quarry	"	37108	41588
	Mean		39124	42484

By the foregoing experiment it will be observed that the resisting powers of stone to compression, are greatest when the pressure is applied perpendicularly upon the bed or laminated surface, and are in the ratio of 100 : 82 in the force required to fracture, and 100 : 86 in the force required to crush this description of stone. Hence, as already observed, the powers of resistance of every description of laminated stone, are most effective when the beds are placed horizontally or perpendicularly to the direction of the pressure, and this position is the more important when the stone is exposed to the atmosphere, as it partially prevents the absorption of moisture, which in winter tends to destroy the material by the contraction of the stone and the expansion of the water at low temperatures.

Experiments to determine the force required to fracture and crush 1 in., 1¼ in., and 2 in. cubes of stones, from Scotland, Wales, and other places.

No. of Expt	Weight laid on in lbs.	Remarks.	No. of Expt	Weight laid on in lbs.	Remarks.
	Specimen No. 12. Grauwacke. Penmaenmawr, Wales. 2-in. cube.		Specimen No. 14. Granite. Mount Sorrel. 2-in. cube.		

No. of Expt	Weight laid on in lbs.	Remarks.	No. of Expt	Weight laid on in lbs.	Remarks.
16	40692	slight fracture.	19	46068	
...	......	....	20	47860	
29	63988	second fracture.	21	49652	
30	65780		22	51444	fractured, and after a slight rest crushed.
31	67572	crushed.			

Specimen No. 15. Grauwacke. Ingleton. 2-in. cube. | Specimen No. 16. Granite. Aberdeen. 2-in. cube.

No.	Wt.	Remarks	No.	Wt.	Remarks
13	35316	first fracture.	8	26356	
...	......	....	9	27546	fractured.
20	47860	second fracture.	10	28148	
...	....	....	11	28340	not crushed.
25	53236	not crushed.			

Specimen No. 17. Syenite. Mount Sorrel. 2-in. cube. | Specimen No. 18. Granite. Bonaw. 1½-in. cube.

No.	Wt.	Remarks	No.	Wt.	Remarks
17	42484		2	15604	fractured into two nearly equal parts.
18	44276		3	17396	
19	46068		..	....	
20	47264	crushed.	7	24564	crushed.

Specimen No. 19. Furnace Granite. Inverary. 1½-in. cube. | Specimen No. 20. Granite. A. 1½-in. cube.

No.	Wt.	Remarks	No.	Wt.	Remarks
4	19188		4	19188	
5	20980		5	20980	
6	22772		6	22772	fractured.
7	24564	crushed.	7	24564	crushed.

No. of Expt	Weight laid on in lbs.	Remarks.	No. of Expt	Weight laid on in lbs.	Remarks.
Specimen No. 21. Limestone. B. 1¼-in. cube.			Specimen No. 22. Limestone. C. 1¼-in. cube.		
1	13812		2	15604	
2	15604		3	17396	
3	17396	fractured.	4	18292	fractured.
4	19188	crushed.	5	19188	crushed.
Specimen No. 23. Magnesian Limestone. Anston. 1-in. cube.			Specimen No. 24. Magnesian Limestone. Worksop. 1-in. cube.		
1	1258		13	3834	
2	2154	fractured.	14	3946	fractured.
..	....	....	..	....	....
10	3050	crushed.	38	7098	crushed.
Specimen No. 25. Sandstone. 1-in. cube.			Specimen No. 26. Sandstone. 2-in. cube.		
8	2938		11	9770	
9	3050	fractured.	12	10218	fractured.
..	....	....	..	....	....
13	3498	crushed.	20	12228	crushed.

Results of experiments on stone from North Wales and other places. Specimens Nos. 12, 14, 17, 18, 19, 20, 21, 22, 23, 24, 25, and 26.

No. of Specimen.	Description of Stone.	Locality.	Size.	Weight with which it fractured, in lbs.	Weight with which it crushed, in lbs.	Pressure required to crush a 2 in. cube, in lbs.
12	Grauwacke	Penmaenmawr...	2 in. cube.	40692	67572	67572
14	Granite	Mount Sorrel	,,	51444	51444	51444
17	Syenite	,, ,,	,,	47284	47284	47284
18	Granite	Bonaw, Inverary	1½ in. cube.	17396	24564	43669
19	,,	Furnace ,,	,,	24564	24564	43669
20	,,	(A)	,,	22772	24564	43669
21	Limestone	(B)	,,	17396	19188	34112
22	,,	(C)	,,	18292	19188	34112
23	,,	Anston............	1 in. cube.	2154	3050	·12200
24	,,	Worksop.........	,,	3946	7098	28392
25	Sandstone	... ...	,,	3050	3489	13992
26	,,	... ...	2 in. cube.	10218	12228	12228

The Welsh specimen of grauwacke, from Penmaenmawr, exhibits great powers of resistance, nearly double that of some of the Yorkshire sandstones, and about one-third in excess of the granites, excepting only the granite from Mount Sorrel, which is to the Welsh grauwacke as ·7571 : 1. Some others, such as the Ingleton grauwacke, supported more than the granites, but are deficient when compared with that from Penmaenmawr. The specimen No. 23 is the stone of which the Houses of Parliament are built. Specimens Nos. 25 and 26 were broken to show experimentally the ratio of the powers of resistance as the size is changed. The results are sufficiently near to prove that the crushing weights are as the areas of the surface subjected to pressure.

The specific gravity and porosity of the different kinds of rock vary greatly: those from the neighbourhood of Bradford were carefully tested in regard to their powers of absorption; the experiments, which were conducted by Mr. Fairbairn with great precision, gave the following results:—

Experiments to ascertain the amount of water absorbed by various kinds of stone.

No. of specimen.	Description of Stone.	Locality.	Weight before immersion.	Weight after immersion for 48 hours.	Differ'nce of Weight.	Proportion absorbed.
			lbs.			
1	Sandstone	Shipley	5·4687	5·5546	·0859	1 in 63·6
2	,,	Heaton	5·2578	5·3632	·1054	1 in 49·8
3	,,	Heaton Park	5·1718	5·2896	·1171	1 in 44·1
4	,,	Spinkwell	5·2968	5·4726	·1758	1 in 30·1
5	,,	Idle Quarry	5·7179	5·8203	·1016	1 in 56·3
6	,,	Jegrum's-lane	5·5976	5·7187	·1211	1 in 46·2
7	,,	Spinkwell	5·6757	5·7851	·1094	1 in 53·8
8	,,	Coppy Quarry	5·5703	5·6914	·1211	1 in 46·0
9	,,	Old Whatley	5·4726	5·6132	·1406	1 in 38·9
10	,,	Manningham-lane	5·4882	5·6093	·1211	1 in 46·3
11	,,	,, ,,	5·6289	5·7539	·1250	1 in 45·0
12	Grauwacke	Wales	6·4101	6·4140	·0039	1 in 1641·0
13	Granite	Mount Sorrel	5·6875	5·6992	·0117	1 in 485·0
14	,,	,, ,,	5·8007	5·8124	·0117	1 in 495·0
15	Grauwacke	Ingleton	5·7500	5·7539	·0039	1 in 1962·6

From the above table it will be observed that specimen No. 15, the Ingleton grauwacke, is the least absorbent, and No. 12, the Welsh grauwacke, absorbs almost as little, while Nos. 9 and 14 of the sandstones absorb most. The granites, though closely granulated, take up much more water than the grauwackes, but less than the sandstones. The resistance of the grauwacke specimens to the admission of water is four times that of the granite, and thirty-six times that of sandstone, such as is found in the Yorkshire quarries.

STONE.

No. of Specimen	Description of Stone.	Locality.	Size.	Specific gravity.	Pressure to fracture specimen.	Pressure to crush specimen.	Pressure per square inch to crush specimen.	Cubic feet in a ton.	Ratio of powers of absorption.
			cube		lbs.	lbs.	lbs.		1 in.
1	Sandstone	Shipley	2 in.	2·452	35524	39000	9725	14·010	83·6
2	,,	Heaton	,,	2·420	33524	40802	10173	14·801	40·8
3	,,	Heaton Park	,,	2·385	30040	31732	7933	15·027	44·1
4	,,	Spinkwell	,,	2·329	defective			15·388	30·1
5	,,	Idle Quarry	,,	2·434	42484	43390	10846	14·515	56·3
6	,,	Jegrum's-lane	,,	2·401	45172	47860	11965	14·933	46·2
7	,,	Spinkwell	,,	2·450	31732	37108	9277	14·502	53·8
8	,,	Coppy Quarry	,,	2·408	37108	41588	10397	14·833	46·0
9	,,	Old Whatley	,,	2·415	35310	35310	8829	14·810	38·0
10	,,	Manning'm-lane	,,	2·401	28148	37108	9277	14·927	46·3
11	,,	,,	,,	2·421	failed.			14·801	45·0
12	Grauwacke	Penmaenmawr	,,	2·748	40582	07572	10893	13·042	1641·0
13	Granite	Mount Sorrel	,,	2·657				13·480	485·3
14	,,	,,	,,	2·475	51444	51444	12861	13·380	495·0
15	Grauwacke	Ingleton	,,	2·787	35310		not crd	12·860	1962·6
16	Granite	Aberdeen	,,		27540	28840	not crd	—	—
17	Syenite	Mount Sorrel	,,		47284	47284	11821	—	—
18	Granite	Bonaw	1½in.		17390	24564	10017	—	—
19	,,	Furnace	,,		24564	24564	10017	—	—
20	,,	A	,,		22772	24564	10017	—	—
21	Limestone	B	,,		17100	19188	8528	—	—
22	,,	C	,,		16202	19188	8528	—	—
23	,,	Anston	1 in.		2154	3050	3050	—	—
24	,,	Worksop	,,		5046	7088	7008	—	—
25	Sandstone	D	,,		3050	3408	3408	—	—
26	,,	E	2 in.		10218	12228	3057	—	—

On comparing the results of the experiments on the Yorkshire sandstones, it will be seen that the difference of resistance to pressure does not arise so much from the variable character of the stone in different quarries, as from the position in which it is placed as regards its laminated surface, the difference being as 10:8 in favour of the stone being crushed upon its bed to the same when crushed in the line of cleavage; the same may be said of the limestones.

Comparing the strengths indicated by the above experiments, there is found to be a very close approximation in the granites, but considerable difference in the Yorkshire sandstones. Mr. Rennie obtained his specimens from the same district, the valley of the Aire; but the force required to crush the Bromley Fall stone was much less than that required to fracture similar specimens from the Shipley quarries. The following table gives some useful results for comparison.

From the above it is evident that there is a considerable difference between the results of Mr. Rennie's experiments and those in the preceding tables. This may, perhaps, be due to the different methods pursued in the experiments, or from taking the first appearance of fracture as the ultimate power of resistance. Whereas there is in some cases a difference of nearly a third between the weight required to produce the first crack, and that required

STONE.

subsequently to crush the specimen. This is the more remarkable, as all the specimens did not appear to follow the same law, as in some the weight which fractured the specimen by a continuation of the process ultimately crushed it.

Description of Material.	Crushing force in lbs. per square inch.	Authority.
Porphyry	40416	Gauthey.
Granite, Aberdeen	11209	Rennie.
„ mean of 3 varieties ..	11564	Experiments 14, 18, 19.
Sandstone, Yorkshire	6127	Rennie.
„ „ mean of 9	9824	Experiments 1 to 9.
Brick, hard	1888	Rennie.
„ red	905	Rennie.

The necessity of these experiments was more apparent some years since, in the construction of the Britannia and Conway tubular bridges, when fears were entertained of the security of the masonry to support, upon the given area, the immense weight of the tubes, upwards of 1,500 tons, resting on one side of the tower. To ascertain how far the material (Anglesea limestone) was calculated to sustain this load, the following experiments were made :—

BRICKWORK.

No. 1.—9-in. cube of cemented brickwork (Nowell and Co.), No. 1 (or best quality) weighing 54 lbs., set between deal boards. Crushed with 19 tons 18 cwt. 2 qrs. 22 lbs. = 551·3 lbs. per sq. inch.

No. 2.—9-in. cube of brickwork, No. 1 weighing 53 lbs., set in cement, crushed with 22 tons 3 cwt. 0 qr. 17 lbs. = 612·7 lbs. per sq. inch.

No. 3.—9-in. cube of brickwork, No. 3 weighing 52 lbs. set in cement. Crushed with 16 tons 8 cwt. 2 qrs. 8 lbs. = 454·3 lbs. per sq. inch.

No. 4.—9½-in. brickwork, No. 4 weighing 55½ lbs., set in cement. Crushed with 21 tons 14 cwt. 1 qr. 17 lbs. = 568·5 lbs. per square inch.

No. 5.—9-in. brickwork, No. 4 weighing 54½ lbs., set between boards. Crushed with 15 tons 2 cwt. 0 qr. 12 lbs. = 417 lbs. per sq. inch.

Mean of the above experiments = 521 lbs. per sq. inch.

The last three cubes of common brick continued to support the weight, although cracked in all directions; they fell to pieces when the load was removed. All the brickwork began to show irregular cracks a considerable time before it gave way.

The average weight supported by these bricks was 33·5 tons per square foot, equal to a column 583·69 feet high, of such brickwork.

SANDSTONE.

No. 6.—3-in. cube red sandstone, weighing 1 lb. 14¾ oz., set between boards (made quite dry by being kept in an inhabited room). Crushed with 8 tons 4 cwt. 0 qr. 19 lbs. = 2043 lbs. per sq. inch.

No. 7.—3-in. cube sandstone, weighing 1 lb. 14 oz., set in cement (moderately damp). Crushed with 5 tons 3 cwt. 1 qr. 1 lb. = 1285 lbs. per sq. inch.

No. 8.—3-in. sandstone, weighing 1 lb. 15½ oz., set in cement (made very wet). Crushed with

with 4 tons 7 cwt. 0 qr. 21 lbs. = 1085 lbs. per sq. inch.

No. 9.—6-in. cube sandstone, weighing 18 lbs., set in cement. Crushed with 63 tons 1 cwt. 2 qrs. 6 lbs. = 3924·8 lbs. per sq. inch.

No. 10.—9½-in. cubes and stone, weighing 58¼ lbs., set in cement (77½ tons were placed upon this without effect, = 2042 lbs. per sq. inch, which was as much as the machine would carry).

Mean of the above experiments = 2185 lbs. per sq. inch.

All the sandstones gave way *suddenly*, and without any previous cracking or warning. The 3-in. cubes appeared of ordinary description; the 6-in. was fine grained, and appeared tough and of superior quality. After fracture the upper part generally retained the form of an inverted square pyramid about 2½ in. high and very symmetrical, the sides bulging away in pieces all round. The average weight of this material was 130 lbs. 10 oz. per cube foot, or 17 feet per ton.

The average weight required to crush this sandstone is 134 tons per square foot, equal to a column 2351 feet high of such sandstone.

LIMESTONE.

No. 11.—3-in. cube Anglesea limestone, weighing 2 lbs. 10 oz. set between boards. Crushed with 28 tons 11 cwt. 3 qrs. 9 lbs. = 6618 lbs. per sq. inch. This stone formed numerous cracks and splinters all round, and was considered crushed; but on removing the weight about two-thirds of its area were found uninjured.

No. 12.—3-in. limestone, weighing 2 lbs. 9 oz., set between deal boards. Crushed with 32 tons 6 cwt. 0 qr. 1 lb. = 8039 lbs. per sq. inch. This stone also began to splinter externally with 25 tons (or 6220 lbs. per sq. in.), but ultimately bore as above.

No. 13.—3-in. limestone, weighing 2 lbs. 9 oz., set in deal boards. Crushed with 30 tons 18 cwt. 3 qrs. 24 lbs. = 7702·6 lbs. per sq. inch.

No. 14.—Three separate 1-in. cubes of limestone, weighing 2 lbs. 9 oz., set in deal boards. Crushed with 9 tons 7 cwt. 1 qr. 14 lbs. = 6995·3 lbs. per sq. in. All crushed simultaneously.

Mean of the above experiments, 7579 lbs. per sq. inch.

All the limestones formed *perpendicular* cracks and splinters a long time before they crushed.

Weight of the material from above = 165 lbs. 9 oz. per cubic foot, or 13½ feet per ton.

The weight required to crush this limestone is 471·15 tons per square foot, equal to a column 6,433 feet high of such material.

Previously to the experiments just recorded, it was deemed advisable not to trust to the resisting powers of the material of which the towers of either bridge were composed; and, to make security doubly sure, it was ultimately arranged to rest the tubes upon horizontal and transverse beams of great strength, and by increasing the area subject to compression, the splitting or crushing of the masonry might be prevented. This was done with great care, and the result is the present stability of those important structures.

To the consideration of the practical builder the general summary of results on the next page is submitted, obtained from various materials, showing their respective powers of resistance to forces tending to crush them.

Professor Hodgkinson has also experimented on round and square columns of sandstone from Ped Delph, Littleborough, Lancashire, a much harder stone than that found on the banks of the Aire. With regard to these experiments, it appears " that there is a falling off in strength in all columns from

STONE.

General Summary of Results on Compression.

Description of Material.		Crushing force in lbs. per sq. inch.	Authority.
Iron and Steel.	Cast steel		Fairbairn's Experiments on the Mechanical Properties of Metals.—Transactions of the British Association, 1854.
	Blister steel		
	Cast iron (white derived from 14 meltings)	214916	
	Ditto (from 12 meltings)	163744	
	Ditto (from ordinary castings)	89600	
Stone.	Porphyry	40416	Gauthey.
	Graewacke, Penmaenmawr	16893	Experiment No. 12.
	Granite, mean of 3	11565	Ditto Nos. 14, 18, 19.
	Sandstone, Yorkshire	6127	Rennie.
	Ditto, mean of 9 exprmts	9821	Experiments 1 to 10.
	Ditto, Runcorn	2185	Clark.
	Limestone	8528	Experiments 21, 22.
	Ditto, Anglesea	7579	Clark.
	Ditto, Magnesian—mean	5074	Experiments 23, 24.
	Brick, hard	1986	Rennie.
	Ditto, red	805	"
	Ditto, mean of 4 exprmts	1424	Clark.
Timber.	Box	9771	Hodgkinson.
	English Oak (dried)	9509	
	Ash (ditto)	9363	
	Plum-tree (ditto)	8241	
	Beech	6402	
	Red Deal	5748	
	Cedar	5674	
	Yellow Pine	5375	

the shortest to the longest, but that the diminution is so small, when the height of the column is not greater than about twelve times the side of its square, that the strength may be considered uniform, the mean being 10,000 lbs. per square inch or upwards.

"From the experiments on the columns 1 in. square, it appears that when the height is fifteen times the side of the square, the strength is slightly reduced; when the height is twenty-four times the height of the base, the falling-off is from 138 to 96 nearly; when it is thirty times the base, the strength is reduced from 138 to 75; and when it is forty times the base, the strength is reduced to 52, or to little more than one-third. These numbers will be modified to some extent by experiments now in progress.

"As long columns always give way first at the ends, showing that part to be weakest, we might economize the material by making the areas of the ends greater than that of the middle, increasing the strength from the middle both ways towards the ends. If the areas of the ends be to the area of the middle, as the strength of a short column is to that of a long one, we should have for a column, whose height was twenty-four times the breadth, the areas of the ends and middle as 13,769 to 9595 nearly. This, however, would make the ends somewhat too strong, since the weakness of the long columns arises from their flexure.

"Another mode of increasing the strength would be that of preventing flexure, by increasing the dimensions of the middle.

"From the experiments it would appear that the Grecian columns, which seldom had their length more than about ten times the diameter, were nearly of the form capable of bearing the greatest weight when their shafts were uniform, and that columns tapering from the bottom to the top were only capable of bearing weights due to the smallest part of their section, though the larger end might serve to prevent lateral thrusts. This latter remark applies, too, to the Egyptian columns, the strength of the column being only that of the smallest part of the section.

"From the two series of experiments, it appeared that the strength of a short column was nearly in proportion to the area of the section, though the strength of a larger one is somewhat less than in that proportion."

These extracts from Mr. Hodgkinson's paper show the advantages to be derived from proper attention to the construction of columns, not only as regards their resistance to a crushing force, but as to the propriety of enlarging the ends to increase their powers of resistance.

Experimental data cannot always be applied in architectural constructions; but it is, nevertheless, essential that the architect and builder should be cognizant of the facts, in order that they may prepare their plans, as far as possible, in accordance with them, and effect the greatest amount of work with the least waste of material.

Stone-Coal Furnaces — Anthracite Furnaces (American). In eastern Pennsylvania more than sixty blast-furnaces, supplied by anthracite, are most generally in operation. These produce on an average from seventy-five to eighty tons of iron per week. This immense number of furnaces, supplied by stone coal alone, was the result of ten years' industry; and the perfection to which they have been brought is a security that nothing can check their use, or prevent their extension.

Anthracite furnaces resemble, to a greater or less degree, coke and charcoal furnaces. They are seldom so high as coke furnaces, and their horizontal dimensions are usually greater than those of charcoal furnaces. The following are the dimensions of several of the furnaces recently erected in eastern Pennsylvania. One belonging to Mr. Ecket, at Reading, is 37½ feet in height; the top or throat 6 feet in diameter; height of hearth, 5 feet; tuyères, 22 inches above its bottom; the hearth is 5 feet square at the base, and 6 feet at the top; the boshes are inclined 67¼°, or at the rate of 6 inches to the foot, and measure 14 feet at their largest diameter. At the point where the slope of the boshes joins the lining, a perpendicular cylindrical space, 5 feet in height, commences, and from this point the general taper to the throat is continued in a straight line. The hearth, as well as the boshes, is built of coarse sandstone, but the latter are covered with a lining of fire-brick, 9 inches thick. The in-wall consists of two linings, and the interior is the lining which covers the boshes; outside of this is a space 4 inches wide, filled with coarse sand, and this is protected by a rough lining of slate, 2 feet thick. The rough walls of the stack are not heavy, but they are well secured by binders.

Two furnaces erected at the Crane Works, near Allentown, may be considered as the greatest improvement. The stack is 35 feet high, 40 feet square at the base, and at the top 33 feet. This furnace is therefore but slightly tapered.

STONE-COAL FURNACES.

and requires heavy stonework. It generates steam from the trunnel-head gas flame. At most anthracite furnaces, this is done by putting the boilers on the top of the furnace. The hearth is 5 feet high, 4 feet square at the bottom, and 6 feet at the top; the inclination of the boshes is 75°, and the cylindrical part of the in-wall above the boshes is 8 feet high and 12 feet in diameter. From the cylindrical part up to the top, which is 6 feet in width, the in-wall runs in a straight line.

A furnace erected by Messrs. Reeves and Co., at Phœnixville, is 34 feet in height: the hearth is 6 feet high, 4 feet 3 inches square at the bottom, and 5 feet 3 inches at the top: the boshes taper 68°, or at the rate of rather less than 6 inches to the foot; they measure 13 feet at the widest part. Great care is taken that the lining and the boshes form a gradual curve, that sticking and scaffolding in the boshes may be obviated. The top of this furnace is 8 feet square. There is no doubt that the form and construction of these anthracite furnaces have been carried, within the short space of a few years, to so high a state of perfection as to leave but little room for future improvements. Their shape is worthy of imitation, particularly by Western manufacturers; for coal adapted to all of these furnaces is abundant in the western States of America.

Most of these furnaces generate the steam for the motive power of the blast as well as the heat for the hot-blast apparatus at the top of the furnace. In this way expense is not only saved, but a uniform generation of steam and heating of air are produced. The cost of erecting such a furnace cannot be readily estimated, as it must depend greatly upon locality, material, wages, and individual tastes; but it may be laid down as a general rule that a stone-coal furnace costs less than a coke furnace, and that, in most cases, a good charcoal stack can be altered so as to serve for stone coal.

In the Western States, many charcoal furnaces are in operation, and there is no limit to their extension, so far as raw material, wood and ore are concerned. One circumstance, however, will necessitate the introduction of stone-coal furnaces in the West, namely, the price of charcoal iron. Some localities can successfully compete against stone-coal iron; but those which, besides enjoying that advantage, are situated near navigable streams or canals, are very few in number. It is said that the average cost of producing charcoal pig at Pittsburgh is 20 dollars; some furnaces produce it at a cost of 15 dollars: in as many cases, however, 25 dollars is paid for iron. The market price at Pittsburgh varies from 25 to 30 dollars, according to quality; and at this price little profit is left to the owners of the furnaces. How far the stone-coal furnaces are in advance of this will be shown by the following statement of the average result of three years' smelting. This statement was furnished by Mr. Reeves, of Philadelphia.

Amount of material consumed to produce one ton of iron at anthracite furnace No. 1, at Phœnixville.

	Tons.
Iron ore	2·59
Anthracite coal	1·83
Lime	1·14

Amount consumed at furnace No. 2, at the same place.

	Tons.
Iron ore	2·65
Anthracite coal	1·89
Lime	1·15

These furnaces smelt brown hematite, hydrated oxide of iron. The wages for producing one ton of anthracite iron, including all incidental expenses, amount to 2 dollars

50 cents, to which is to be added the interest on capital employed.

Anthracite furnaces require wider tops than coke furnaces, while the latter require far wider tops than charcoal furnaces. This width of the top may be considered the most essential improvement on the blast-furnace which is supplied by anthracite coal. The height of the stack in anthracite is much less than in coke furnaces, and somewhat lower than in charcoal furnaces. Anthracite furnaces vary from 30 to 35 feet in height; charcoal furnaces, from 30 to 40 feet in height; and coke furnaces from 40 to 60 feet. The width of the trunnel-head varies, in the United States, considerably. In Pennsylvania, Ohio, Kentucky, and Tennessee, the width of furnaces at the boshes is 9 and often 10 feet, and at the top from 18 to 20 inches; or in the proportion of 30 square feet at the boshes to 1 square foot at the top. The Cold Spring furnace measures at the boshes 9 feet, and at the top 32 inches: here the proportion is 11 feet at the boshes to 1 foot at the top.

The dimensions of charcoal furnaces in Europe which smelt refractory ores, are generally in the proportion of 5 feet at the boshes to 1 foot at the throat; frequently in the proportion of 4 to 1. In coke furnaces, the proportion of the horizontal section of the boshes to that of the top is seldom less than 4 to 1, though sometimes even 2·5 to 1. In anthracite furnaces, the diameter of the throat is 6 feet, and that of the boshes 12 feet; that is, in the proportion of 1 to 4. But sometimes the boshes measure 13 stead of retarding, it facilitates the vent of the gases. Narrow tops answer where loamy ore and soft coal are used; but, in such cases, to obtain favourable results, weak blast and high stacks should be employed. But these conditions can be observed only where coal and labour are cheap. If any doubt exists concerning the proper dimensions of a furnace, the best course is to commence with a comparatively low stack, wide throat, and with as high a pressure in the blast as the fuel will possibly bear.

Stone ochre. The true stone ochres are found in balls or globular masses of various sizes, in the solid bodies of stones lying near the surface of rocks among the quarries in Gloucestershire or elsewhere. These balls are of a smooth compact texture, in general, free from grit, and of a powdery fracture; they vary exceedingly in colour, from yellow to brown, murrey, and grey, but do not differ in other respects from the Oxfordshire ochre, and may be safely used in oil or water in the several modes of painting, and for browns and dull reds in enamel.

Stools, pieces of plank fastened to a ship's side to receive the bolting of the gallery.

Stopper-bolts, large ring-bolts drove in the deck of a ship before the main-hatch, for the use of the stoppers.

Stopping, in mining, cutting down mineral ground with a pick.

Stories, in architecture. Palladio directs that the height of the story immediately above the principal floor be a sixth part less than that below; and if there be an attic, or third story, it should be nine-

Strake, in ship-building, one range of planks fore and aft.

Strap, in carpentry, an iron plate placed across the junction of two or more timbers, either branched out or straight, as may be found requisite, and each branch bolted or keyed with one or more bolts or keys, through each of the timbers, for the purpose of securing them together.

Strata, in geology, extensive layers of any mineral substance, such as rocks, etc. Secondary strata are nearly all comprised under the heads of sandstone, limestone, and shale.

Streamers, in mining, the persons who work in search of stream-tin.

Stream-tin, in mineralogy, particles or masses of tin found beneath the surface of alluvial ground, and separated from the earthy matter by passing a stream of water over it: hence the name.

Strength and stress of materials. The works of Barlow and Tredgold contain the most useful information on these subjects. Barlow shows that there are four distinct strains to which every hard body may be exposed, and which are,—1st, a body may be pulled or torn asunder by a stretching force, applied in the direction of its fibres, as in the case of ropes, stretchers, kingposts, tie-beams, etc.; 2ndly, it may be broken across by a transverse strain, or by a force acting either perpendicularly or obliquely to its length, as in the case of levers, joists, etc.; 3rdly, it may be crushed by a force acting in the direction of its length, as in the case of pillars, posts, and trussbeams; 4thly, it may be twisted or wrenched by a force acting in a circular direction, as in the case of the axle of a wheel.

Stretching-course, in brickwork and in masonry, a row or course in which the bricks or stones are placed with their longest faces exposed to view. The bricks or stones thus laid are called stretchers; and those disposed with the ends outwards are called headers.

Strigæ, in ancient architecture, what are now called flutings.

String, in mining, a small vein.

String, the strake under the gunwale withinside, generally worked the same thickness as the sheer-strake, and scarfed in the same manner: the string and sheer-strake are bolted through a ship's side.

String-course, a narrow, horizontal, and slightly projecting course of brickwork or masonry in the wall of a building.

Stucco, in architecture, a composition of white marble pulverized and mixed with plaster or lime, but the ingredients vary; it is employed commonly for facing exterior and interior works; it is also sometimes used for floors.

Stück or *Wulf's oven*, a furnace for the reduction of iron, at one time common in Europe, now little employed. The interior of this furnace has the form of two cones united at their bases: it is usually from 10 to 16 feet high, 24 inches wide at bottom and top, and 5 feet at the centre. There are generally two tuyères, both on the same side. The opening called the breast is closed after the furnace is heated, after which, charcoal and ore are thrown in, and the blast introduced. As soon as the ore passes the tuyère, iron is deposited at the bottom of the hearth: when this amounts to a ton, the blast is stopped, the breast wall removed, and the metal lifted out in a solid mass, or *stück*, *wulf*, as it is called by the Germans.

Studding-sails, in navigation, certain light sails extended beyond the skirts of the principal sails in moderate steady breezes; named also 'goose-wings.'

Studies. In painting, these signify works which a painter undertakes, to acquire a practical knowledge of his art and facility of execution. The term is also applied to the parts taken separately, which the artist afterwards transfers to the picture.

Stuffing-boxes, in a locomotive engine, those with recesses for admitting some soft material, such as white spun-yarn, to render steam-tight any rod working through this stuffing or packing. The piston-rods, slide-valve rods, regulator-rods, and pump-plungers, all work through stuffing-boxes of this description.

Stull, timber placed in the backs of bevels and covered with boards, or small piles, to support rubbish.

Sturt, in mining: when a tributer takes a pitch at a high tribute, and cuts a course of ore, he sometimes gets two, three, or five hundred pounds in two months: this great profit is called 'a sturt.'

Styles of early Architecture in England. The several examples, usually denominated Gothic, are as follows: 1. The Anglo-Roman, which existed about 300 years. 2. The Anglo-Saxon, about 450 years. 3. The Anglo-Norman (*which continued in use even on the introduction of the Pointed style*), about 85 years. 4. Early Pointed (*termed also the Lancet style and early English*), about 140 years. 5. The Pointed style (*called by some pure Gothic*), about 110 years. 6. The Florid Pointed (*termed also the Perpendicular*), about 140 years. 7. The Tudor, Elizabethan, and Stuart.

Stylobate, the substructure of a Greek temple below the columns, sometimes formed of three steps, which were continued round the peristyle; and sometimes of walls raised to a considerable height, in which case it was approached by a flight of steps at one end.

Subtangent, in geometry, in any curve is the line which determines the intersection of the tangent in the axis prolonged.

Subtense, in geometry, the chord of an arch; that which is extended under anything.

Sucker, in mechanics, the embolus or piston of a pump. In pneumatics, a round piece of leather, which laid wet on a stone and drawn up in the middle, leaves a vacuum within, which, by the pressure of the atmosphere, makes it adhere.

Sulphate of copper (blue vitriol); in chemistry, metallic salt, a compound of sulphuric acid and copper.

Sulphate of iron (copperas or green vitriol), in chemistry, a metallic salt, a compound of sulphuric acid and iron.

Sulphate of lead, an exceedingly white precipitate from any solution of lead by sulphuric acid, much resembling the *blanc d'argent*, and which has, when well prepared, quite neutral, and thoroughly edulcorated or washed, most of the properties of the best white-leads, but is rather inferior in body and permanence.

Sulphate of lime (gypsum, etc.), in mineralogy, a compound of sulphuric acid and lime.

Sulphate of zinc (white vitriol), in chemistry, a metallic salt, a compound of sulphuric acid and zinc.

Sulphur, a simple combustible substance found native in a loose powder, either detached or in veins. It is met with in the neighbourhood of volcanoes, where it is deposited as a crust on stones contiguous to them. It can be prepared by exposing iron pyrites to heat, when part of the sulphur is driven off in vapour, and may be collected in water: when vaporized, it condenses in small crystalline particles, called flowers of sulphur. It is inflammable, burning slow with a pale blue flame. Sulphur is found in connection with silver, copper, lead, antimony, and iron. Sulphur occurs, in nature, crystallized in acute octohedrons with rhombic bases. It is principally brought to this country from Sicily.

Sulphuret of hydrogen. This gas, commonly known as sulphuretted hydrogen, is invaluable as a re-agent in separating one class of metals from another, is precipitated by it in acid solutions from another gas, and only acted upon by it in alkaline solutions.

Sulphurets of iron.—Iron has a very great affinity for sulphur: there are five definite compounds of these substances. It is very difficult to separate iron from sulphur by heat alone. Of the five different compositions, two only deserve attention,—the white and yellow sulphurets.

White sulphuret of iron (white pyrites) abounds in coal-beds, and in the accompanying strata of clay; also in regular veins, along with ores of lead, copper, and iron, in the transition rocks. Before the flame of the blow-pipe, it becomes red; upon charcoal, the sulphur is evaporated, and oxide of iron remains. It is very liable to decomposition: it is preferable to the yellow kind in the manufacture of copperas, and is, in coal-mines, the most dangerous of any, as it often decomposes so quickly as to kindle the coal-slack. Its composition is, in 100 parts,

45·07 iron.
53·35 sulphur.
9·58 manganese.

99·00 white pyrites.

Yellow sulphuret of iron, yellow pyrites.—This variety becomes red before the blow-pipe; and in the reducing flame it melts into a globule, which continues red-hot for a short time, and possesses, after cooling, a crystalline appearance. In nitric acid it is slowly soluble, with the precipitation of sulphur, but in no other acid. It is composed of

47·30 iron.
52·70 sulphur.

100·00 yellow pyrites.

Yellow pyrites is almost identical with the white pyrites, and the latter appears to be only different in containing more foreign matter: both are widely diffused among the ores of iron, and are found in massive nodules, crystals, and veins, in the coal-beds, clay-slate, grauwacke, greenstone, limestone, and in beds of primitive slate. It is the main material which is used for manufacturing copperas, alum, oil of vitriol, Spanish brown, and sulphur.

Summer, a horizontal beam or girder.

Sump, in mining, a pit sunk in the engine-shaft below the lowest workings.

Sump-shaft, the engine-shaft.

Supercilium, the transverse antepagment of a doorway. The word is also used to denote the small fillets or bands above and below the scotia of the Ionic base.

Superficies, in geometry, the surface of any body or figure, considered as possessing two dimensions, or extension in length and breadth, but destitute of thickness: in mensuration, it is estimated as *area.*

Supporters, in heraldry, figures standing on a scroll and placed by the escutcheon, such as the lion and the unicorn in the British, and the angels in the French arms.

Supporters, in ship-building, the knee-pieces under the cathead.

Surmarks, in ship-building, the stations of the ribbons and harpings which are marked on the timbers.

Surveying is the art of applying the principles of geometry and trigonometry to the measurement of land. The principal operations are laying down or *driving* base lines, and triangles on either side of the base. In large surveys it is desirable to lay down these triangles by measuring each angle with an instrument called the *theodolite,* by which the accuracy of the measurement of the sides may be checked. The theodolite is also available in fixing the true position of points, the distances between which are immeasurable, owing to the intervention of buildings, rivers, or other obstacles. Rectangular or irregular areas of land are similarly reduced to triangles, and their exact position referred to a base line. In driving lines over land, three long poles are requisite: these are ranged in the direction of the intended line at the greatest distance at which they can be seen, either with the naked eye or with the assistance of a telescope, and driven firmly into the ground. Intermediate stakes are then fixed, by which the line is marked out. In proceeding onward to extend the line included between the front and back pole, the latter only is removed, and carried before the front pole to the greatest practicable distance, and being ranged by the two remaining poles, is there driven. Thus the middle pole becomes the back one, and is in like manner removed to the front, and there ranged and fixed: and in this manner, by successively removing the back pole, and conveying it to the front, the line is extended as far as necessary. These poles should be as light as possible, consistent with strength, and shod with iron points, to facilitate driving. On the top of each pole a flag or disk is fixed, to render them conspicuous from a long distance. Distances are measured with a chain formed of wire links, the length of the chain being 66 feet, and formed with 100 links, each link measuring 7·92 inches. The end of each chain is marked by driving a wire pin or arrow into the ground, by counting which the number of chains measured is ascertained. The base line being thus driven and measured, it is recorded in a book, and all intersections of fences, etc., marked, and their relative distances on the base are entered. A distant point on either side of the base is then determined, and a pole erected upon it, and the distance of this point from two fixed points upon the base measured with the chain, and duly recorded. By this means, a triangle is completed, and afterwards correctly filled in with all intervening fences, etc.; and by repeated processes of this kind the survey is extended to any required distance on each side of the base. If the triangles first laid down are of great extent, they should be determined, and the position of their angles ascertained with the theodolite. This instrument consists of a pair of horizontal circular plates, the upper of which is called the vernier plate, turning freely on a centre upon the lower plate, the edge of which is chamfered off, and accurately graduated with degrees and subdivisions. By these plates and their adjusting screws, etc., horizontal angles are measured, the sight of the surveyor being aided by a powerful telescope on the upper part of the instrument, and a microscope to read off the graduations upon the vernier. An upper frame which carries the telescope also supports a vertical arc or semicircle, which is likewise graduated, and with the aid of another microscope the elevation of any high object, as a tower, etc. (observed through the telescope) may be correctly read off. This part of the apparatus thus enables vertical angles to be measured, and by the application of trigonometry, heights or distances may be thus exactly determined without the actual measurement of all the lines in each vertical triangle.

Suspension, in mechanics, as in a balance, are those points in the axis or beam where the weights are applied, or from which they are suspended.

Suspension. Bridges of suspension are of several kinds and of various dimensions, consisting of several iron chains, not formed of small links, like cables, but of whole bars of iron jointed at their ends, passed over a tower, being the access to the bridge on each side of the river, while their extreme ends are firmly attached to large and ponderous stones that are sunk a great depth into the ground on each side of the stream. These masses of masonry are named *abutments*. The chains hang in parallel festoons over the river, between the supporting towers, and carry a number of vertical bars of iron that are attached to and hang down from them for the purpose of suspending beams of wood or iron hanging horizontally in the direction of, or obliquely to, the stream, and serving as joists to support a strong planked platform or roadway that extends across the river: frequently these roadways are paved, or at least gravelled or ballasted over for horses, carriages, and pedestrians. Extraordinary examples exist of this species of building in our own country, viz. that at Bangor, crossing the Menai Strait, by Telford,—that at Hammersmith, by Tierney Clark,—Hungerford, by Brunel; but the most extraordinary structure is the stupendous work of Tierney Clark, uniting Pesth with Buda, in Hungary. Mr. Dredge has constructed several smaller bridges of suspension, according to his arrangement, both in England and Scotland. Suspension bridges have been constructed also with wire as a material at Fribourg, in Switzerland, and at other places.

Sweep, or *Tiller-Sweep*, a circular plank fitted to support the foremost end of the tiller, or handle of a rudder, much improved by conveying the tiller-rope round it, and keeping it always tight.

Swivel, in mechanics, something fixed in another body so as to turn round on it; a kind of ring made to turn round in a staple or other ring. In artillery, a very small cannon, which carries a shot of about half a pound.

Sycamore, a species of *Ficus*, or fig-tree, common in Egypt and other parts of the East; its timber is of little value. The name is also applied to a species of maple, the *Acer Pseudo-Platanus*, a native of the middle and south of Europe, but common in England. The colour of the young wood is silky white, and of the old, brownish white; the wood of the middle age is intermediate in colour, and the strongest. It is used in furniture, pianofortes, and harps, and for the superior kinds of Tunbridge ware. Sycamore may be cut into very good screws, and is used for presses, dairy utensils, etc.

Symmetry, in sculpture, etc., adaptation of parts to each other; proportion; harmony; agreement of one part with another.

Sympiesometer, a barometrical instrument in which the atmospheric pressure is indicated by the ascent of a column of oil in a short glass tube against the elastic pressure of an enclosed volume of hydrogen gas. Its indications require correction for the changes produced by temperature on the gas. The instrument is more compact, but also more complex, than the mercurial barometer.

Synagogue, a word which primarily signified an assembly, but, like the word *church*, came at length to be applied to places in which any assemblies, especially those for the worship of God, met, or were convened. Jewish synagogues were not only used for the purposes of divine worship, but also for courts of judicature. The present ordinary meaning of the term synagogue is a Jewish church.

Syphering, in ship-building. lapping one edge of a plank over the edge of another for bulk-heads, making the edges of the planks and the sides of the bulk-head plain surfaces.

Syphon, a bent tube, having one leg shorter than the other. It acts from the pressure of the atmosphere being removed from the surface of a fluid, which enables it to rise above its common level, and is used for the purpose of emptying liquors from casks, etc.

Syringe, a small hand-pump: in its simplest form, it is provided with a piston and rod, but is destitute of valves, one simple aperture at the extremity serving for the admission and ejection of fluid; those constructed with valves, however, are available, on a smaller scale, for all the purposes of an air-pump.

Systyle, a term applied to a building in which the pillars are closely placed, but not quite so close as in the pycnostyle, the intercolumniation being only two diameters, or four modules, of the columns,

T.

Tabard (Saxon), a jerkin, a coat without sleeves; also, a herald's coat.

Tabernacle, a movable fabric: among the Jews, the name of a portable temple which was constructed in the Wilderness: the term is also applied in Christian architecture to richly ornamented niches.

Table, in architecture, a smooth, simple member or ornament of various forms, but most usually in that of a long square.

Table or *Tablet mouldings*, horizontal bands or mouldings, such as base-mouldings, strings, cornices, etc.

Tables were in the Tudor age usually described as 'bordes,' and were not in any great variety: the sorts were but few, and little distinguished by workmanship; but the splendour of their coverings amply compensated for the rudeness and simplicity of the works so concealed. The most elaborate embroidery, wrought on the finest grounds, velvets and satins fringed with gold and silver, Turkey carpets, and the choicest tapestry, were used as table-covers.

Table-cloths, carpets, which at earlier periods were almost the only coverings for dining-tables and cupboards; *naping* was possessed by the higher orders only. In 1520, Thomas, Duke of Norfolk, bequeathed his *naperie* to Agnes his wife.

Tabling, in ship-building, letting one piece of timber into another, in the same manner as the beams are put together.

Tablinum, an apartment of a Roman house which was entered immediately from the atrium, and in which records were preserved in cases, and the hereditary statues placed.

Tack, in navigation, to change the course or turn about a ship during a contrary wind from the starboard to the larboard, etc.

Tack, in navigation, a rope used to confine the clues of the main and fore courses forward, occasionally in a fixed position: it has a large wall-knot at one end. The word has also various other applications.

Tacks, in navigation, the foremost lower corner of all fore and aft sails.

Tacking, in navigation, signifies a manœuvre by which a ship makes an oblique progression to windward in a zigzag direction, named also 'beating to windward.'

Tackle, in mining, the windlass, rope, and kibble.

Tænia, the band or fillet surmounting the Doric epistylium.

Taffrail, the carved work at the upper part of the stern of a vessel, the ends of which correspond with the quarter-pieces.

Tail-water, the waste water discharged from the buckets of a water-wheel in motion.

Talmud, or *Thalmud*, a book in great veneration among the Jews, containing their doctrines and morality. There are two of these works, the old called the Talmud of Jerusalem, the other, of Babylon; the first, composed by Rabbi Johanan, president of the academy of Palestine, about the 300th year of Christ: this consists of two parts, the Mishna, or the second law, containing the traditions of the Jewish doctors, collected about the year 190 by Rabbi Judah; and the Gemara, or the finishing or completing the whole, which was done by Johanan, and published both together. The Talmud of Babylon contains also the Mishna, and the Gemara of Rabbi Asa, of Babylon, about the year 400: this is much more valued than the other, on account of its great clearness or perspicuity, and also for its extensiveness, though it abounds in fables and ridiculous stories, which the Jews entertain with such eagerness, that they compare the Bible to water, the Mishna to wine, and the Gemara to hippocras, affirming that Moses revealed those traditions and explications to Aaron, to his sons, and the elders, and that he received them from God.

Talus, in architecture, the inclination or slope of a work, as the outside of a wall, where its thickness is diminished by degrees as it rises in height.

Tamping, in mining, the material, usually soft stone, placed upon the gunpowder to confine its force, which would otherwise pass up the hole; also the process of placing the material.

Tamping-iron, a tool used for beating down the earthy substance in the charge used for blasting.

Tangent, in geometry, a right line perpendicularly raised on the extremity of a radius, which touches a circle so that it would never cut it, although infinitely produced, or, in other words, it would never come within its circumference.

Tank, that part of the tender of a locomotive engine which contains the water: tanks vary in size, according to the power of the engine to which they are attached, and are from about 500 to 1600 gallons in capacity.

Tap, in mechanics, a hardened steel screw with a square head, so that it may be turned by a wrench: it is grooved from end to end, and is also slightly tapered; it is used for cutting an internal screw, as that of a nut, etc.

Tap-wrench, the handle for turning a wrench.

Taper, a gradual diminution in the size of a body, so as to form a wedge or cone.

Taper-chain bridge, a suspension bridge invented by Mr. Dredge.

Tapestry, or *Arras*, described as 'hangings,' enriched the walls of superior apartments from very early times: the most ancient tapestry now existing is preserved in the church of Bayeux, in Normandy, and exhibits an entire series of the circumstances attending William the Conqueror's descent in England. The arras was loosely hung in projecting frames, by tenter-hooks, across the walls, which were sometimes not even plastered, covering the whole surface from the floor to the ceiling, and was, like most other furniture, removable from one residence of its owner to another. The most costly materials were employed in the fabrication of the best sort of hangings. The apartment of Henry VIII. at Calais, whither he was accompanied from Boulogne by Francis I. in 1520, was hung with cloth of gold, adorned with precious stones and pearls. In the old inventories, cloth of gold, and cloth of silver, and embroidery, frequently occur, as well as cloth of silk and gold mixed, called baldikin. The walls of the gallery at York House, the residence of Cardinal Wolsey, which was seized by the king, were "hanged with cloth of gold, and tissue of divers makings, and cloth of silver likewise on both sides, and rich cloths of baudikin of divers colours."

Tappet-motion, the apparatus for working the steam-valve of a Cornish steam-engine, consisting of levers connected to the valves, moved at proper intervals by tappets or projecting pieces fixed on a rod connected to the beam.

Tartan, a small coasting vessel of the Mediterranean, with one mast, a bowsprit, and a lateen sail.

Taunt, a sea term, signifying too high or tall, as the mast of a ship.

Teak-wood is a native of the mountainous parts of the Malabar coast, of Java, Ceylon, etc. It grows quickly, straight, and lofty. The wood is light and porous, and easily worked; but it is nevertheless strong and durable. It is soon seasoned, and, being oily, does not injure iron, and shrinks but little in width. Its colour is light brown, and it is esteemed a most valuable timber in India for ship-building and house-carpentry. It has many localities. In twenty-five years the teak attains the size of 2 feet diameter, and is considered serviceable timber, but it requires 100 years to arrive at maturity.

Tegula, a roofing tile: roofing tiles were made by the Greeks, like bricks, of baked clay.

Telamones, or *Atlantes*, statues of men, employed in columns or pilasters in classical architecture.

Telegraph, a machine adapted for communicating intelligence rapidly at a considerable distance by means of various signals previously arranged.

Telescope, a large optical instrument for observing the celestial bodies, whereby several new phenomena have been discovered, and great improvements made in astronomy: by properly grinding and placing the lenses or glasses in a tube or pipe of various lengths, objects at a great distance are brought nearer to the eye, and much more distinctly seen than by the natural eye: there are various kinds of telescopes, which are called by distinct names.

Temperature. The temperature of the surrounding atmosphere exercises a powerful influence in the preservation or decomposition of all organic bodies exposed to it. Thus, while a high temperature hastens the decay of animal and vegetable matter, this is completely arrested at or near the freezing-point of water. Hence, by artificial means, these substances may be preserved for a length of time. A citizen of the United States has thus accomplished the means of preserving meats, fruits, etc. A large apartment is built under the ground, the sides of which are lined with a double wall containing saw-dust: over the ceiling is a room filled with ice, which, gradually melting, filters through the saw-dust, and keeps the temperature of the underground apartment always at $34°$ Fahr., or two degrees above the freezing-point. In this apartment, lemons, oranges, apples, strawberries, flowers, etc., are preserved with complete freshness for any length of time that may be required.

Temperature of different Thermometers. A thermometer is an instrument for measuring the temperature of bodies, or the degree of intensity of their sensible heat. In Europe there are three different kinds of thermometers: 1. Fahrenheit's, which is used chiefly in Great Britain, Holland, and North America, the freezing-point on which is at $32°$, and the boiling-point $212°$. 2. Réaumur's, which was that chiefly used in France before the Revolution, and now generally used in Spain and in some other Continental States: the freezing-point, or zero, is $0°$, and the boiling-point $80°$. 3. The Celsius, or Centigrade thermometer, now almost universally used throughout France, and in the northern and middle kingdoms of Europe: the zero or freezing-point is $0°$, and boiling-point $100°$. Hence, in order to reduce degrees of temperature of the centigrade thermometer, and of that of

Réaumur, to degrees of Fahrenheit's scale, and conversely,—Rule I. Multiply the centigrade degrees by 9, and divide the product by 5; or multiply the degrees of Réaumur by 9, and divide the product by 4; then add 32 to the quotient in either case, and the sum is the degrees of temperature on Fahrenheit's scale. Rule II. From the number of degrees on Fahrenheit's scale subtract 32, multiply the remainder by 5 for centigrade degrees, or by 5 for those of Réaumur's scale, and the product in either case, being divided by 9, will give the temperature required.

In all inquiries into the effects of heat, it is necessary to attend to the following rules respecting the application of the term *Temperature:*—

1stly. If a body subject to no pressure, or to a constant pressure, have at two different times the same bulk, it is said on both occasions to have the same temperature.

2ndly. Two bodies are said to have the same temperature, if, being kept in contact, the temperature of either remains unaltered by the action of the other.

3rdly. When bodies of different temperatures are in contact, the temperature of the hotter body decreases, and that of the colder increases, till they become equal.

4thly. If the bodies be equal in mass or in weight, and of the same substance, the increase of temperature in one will be equal to its decrease in the other.

Hence it will be seen that differences of temperature are measurable and comparable with each other, quite independently of any change of bulk; that is, without using the latter as a measure of temperature, but only as a test by which change of temperature is detected.

In this way it has been discovered that the same increment (not equal increments, as from 40° to 50°, and from 50° to 60°) of temperature causes all masses of the same substance to expand in the same ratio to their whole former bulk; but this is by no means the case with different substances, as is obvious by looking at a common thermometer, an instrument for measuring changes in the bulk of a mass of liquid contained in a glass vessel, of such a form that changes, very small compared with the whole bulk of the liquid, may cause its surface to rise and fall through a considerable space. But this could not be done if the glass and the measuring scale, in undergoing the same changes of temperature as the liquid, experienced also the same change of bulk; for, if such were the case, the liquid surface would always remain opposite the same degree on the scale. The value of this simple instrument therefore depends on the fact that liquids are more expansible than solids.

But it will further be seen that the ratio of the change of bulk to the whole bulk is different for every different substance, when the change of temperature is the same in all. It is necessary, however, to guard against a very common error respecting the relation between temperatures and the numbers by which they are represented; namely, the degrees of the thermometer.

Although the differences of temperatures are known and comparable quantities, yet their ratios are not so: they can be compared by addition and subtraction, but not by multiplication or division. We cannot say, "This temperature is so many times that," because we do not know the real zero of temperature; that is, we do not know what is the smallest bulk into which a given body is capable of being condensed by cold. We cannot, therefore, say, "This body exceeds its minimum bulk by twice as much as that body exceeds its minimum bulk;" or, in other words, "This body is twice as hot as that;" for although the temperature of one body may be 80° and that of another 40°, these numbers are only reckoned from an arbitrary zero or starting-point, adopted because the real zero is unknown. But although we cannot say that A has twice the temperature of B, we can say that the temperature of A exceeds that of B by twice as much as the temperature of C exceeds that of D.

The first question, then, regarding the relation of expansion to temperature, is—"Do equal differences of temperature cause the bulk of a body to vary by equal differences?" This question had to be settled before it could be known whether the common thermometer (the scale of which is divided into equal parts) measured differences of temperature correctly. For this purpose, Dr. Brooke Taylor heated two equal weights of water, one to 200° and the other to 100°, and on mingling them together, he found them to indicate exactly 150°; thereby showing that equal differences of temperature cause equal differences in the expansion of mercury; or rather in the excess of its expansion over that of glass, which is clearly all that the thermometer can measure. More accurate experiments, however, have shown that this rule does not exactly apply to any solid or liquid, but only to gases. When equal masses of the same liquid, at different temperatures, are mixed, their combined bulk becomes a very little diminished. Liquids, therefore, instead of expanding by equal increments of space for equal increments of temperature, expand faster as the temperature increases equably; and it appears that the correctness of the mercurial thermometer observed by Dr. Brooke Taylor was the result of a fortunate coincidence, by which the expansion of the glass, which is very small compared with that of the mercury, exactly compensated the increasing rate of the latter. This however, would not be the case with thermometers constructed with other liquids, for their rates of expansion increase more rapidly than that of mercury. Hence spirit thermometers cannot be depended on for temperatures above the atmospheric range (or above 100°).

Tempering, in metallurgy, the preparing of steel or iron, so as to render them more compact, hard, and firm, or the reverse, more soft and pliant.

Tempering of steel. Nearly every kind of steel requires a particular degree of heat to impart to it the greatest hardness of which it is susceptible. If heated, and suddenly cooled below that degree, it becomes as soft as iron; if heated beyond that degree, it becomes very hard, though brittle; and its brittleness is an indication of the degree of its heat, when cooled off. These are the reasons why, in hardening steel, it is generally overheated, and then tempered. To hit the exact heat required is a matter of extreme delicacy.

The hardening of steel may be perfectly understood by studying its nature. In endeavouring to arrive at the temperature best adapted to a particular case,—a case, for instance, in which a strange kind of steel has to be dealt with, — a practical test, namely drawing the bar into a tapered point or chisel, is applied. This wedge-shaped chisel will, of course be more warm towards the point than at the thick part; and it is evident that this part will, when cooled in the same cold medium, be harder than the thick part. By breaking, and continuing to break off, the point, the difference of grain will show the different temperatures which have been applied. The finest and closest grained is considered the best. In hardening such steel, it is heated with a due relation to the degree of the test-heat. Though this manipulation is very imperfect, careful and intelligent workmen are generally quite successful in arriving at a knowledge of what degree is favourable. The degree of hardness depends, in some measure, upon the heat of the steel, but mainly upon the difference between the heat of the steel and that of the water or medium in which it is cooled. The coldest water will make the hardest steel. Mercury is better adapted to harden steel than water; so is water acidulated with any kind of acid, or containing any kind of salt in solution.

The process of hardening is performed with due relation to the quality of the steel and the purposes for which it is designed. In most instances, the hardening is effected in water or brine. Saw-blades are thus hardened, after being heated in melted lead; and sabres are heated in a choked fire of charcoal, and then swung rapidly through the air. Mint stamps are hardened in oil or metallic compositions. The common method of procedure in hardening is this: The steel is overheated, cooled in cold water, and then annealed or tempered by being so far re-heated that oil and tallow will burn on its surface; or the surface is ground and polished, and the steel re-heated until it assumes a certain colour. The gradations of colour consecutively follow: a light straw-yellow, violet, blue, and finally grey or black, when the steel again becomes as soft as though it had never been hardened.

Templa, certain timbers introduced in the roofs of temples; they were placed upon the canteril, or principal rafters, extending the whole length of the temple from one fastigium to the other, corresponding in situation and use with the common purlins.

Temple, a building set apart for the services of religious worship, especially the Jewish, and those which were dedicated to the heathen deities: the name is not unfrequently applied to Christian sanctuaries, for example, the Temple church, London. The first Jewish temple, built by Solomon, was erected at vast expense; the gold and silver only, which was provided for the purpose, amounting, it is said, to an almost incredible sum. It was built much in the same form as the Tabernacle, only every way of larger dimensions. It was surrounded, except the front or east end, with three stories of chambers, each 5 cubits square, which reached to half the height of the temple, and the front was graced with a magnificent portico, which rose to the height of 120 cubits, so that the shape of the whole was not unlike some churches which have a lofty tower in the front and a low aisle running along each side of the building. This temple was plundered by Nebuchadnezzar, King of Babylon, and the building itself destroyed, according to Josephus, after it had stood between 400 and 500 years. The second temple, erected after the Jews' return from Babylon, stood for 500 years, when Herod rebuilt it in a style of great magnificence. Tacitus, the Roman historian, calls it a temple of immense opulence. This magnificent temple was at length destroyed by the Romans in the same month and on the same day of the month as Solomon's temple was destroyed by the Babylonians. Of the temples of classic history, the most celebrated are those of Greece, consisting of the Parthenon, built under Pericles, the Erechtheum, and others noticed in Stuart's 'Antiquities,' and in the works of the Dilettanti Society, of Cockerell, Donaldson, etc.: of Rome, the chief temples were, the Capitol, the Pantheon (built by Agrippa), the temple of Apollo, the temple of Janus, and others interestingly described by Degodetz, and also by Taylor and Cresy.

Temple of Solomon had no arches. In the Tabernacle, the *Holy of Holies*, where the ark was placed, was a cube of 15 feet. (Exod. xxvi.) The *Holy Place*, where the golden lamps and the table of shew-bread stood, was a double cube of 15 feet. In the Temple, the Holy of Holies was a cube of 30 feet, the *Holy Place* a double cube of 30 feet.

The whole structure was 90 feet long and 45 feet high. The front over the porch seems to have been adorned with a towering edifice of some kind or other, of an elevation of 180 feet.

The *Brazen Pillars*, or two columns standing before the gate of the Temple, seem to have been 6 feet in diameter and 52 feet 6 in. high, or nearly 9 diameters (compare 1 Kings vii. 15, with 2 Chron. iii. 15, although there is in the first passage a proportion of height mentioned which causes some confusion). The capitals were 6 feet in diameter exclusive of their projecting ornaments, and 7½ feet high, or one diameter and a quarter.

The portico of the Temple was 30 feet long and 15 feet wide, in open height 45 feet.

The *Cherubim* on each side of the ark were 15 feet high; their wings, which were extended to meet each other, were 7½ feet, and the *Cherubim* and *Palm-trees* on the wall, which were of carved work covered with gold, seem to have been of just the same proportion.

The greatest part of the cloisters are affirmed to have been constructed of beams of wood laid upon massy pillars. Their outside wall was of stone, 12 feet thick.

The roof was probably flat, according to the general usage of building in Eastern countries, as we know that the Romans stationed a guard of soldiers on the roof of the cloisters to preserve order at public festivals.

Yet as the seditious Jews are said to have set fire to the north-west cloister in order to prevent the Romans from taking the Temple through the castle of Antonia; and afterwards we are told that they filled that part of the western cloister *which was between the beams and the roof* with dry materials and with bitumen and pitch, and setting it on fire the flame burst out on every side. There appears a probability that the roof was not flat, at least it is evident that the interior ceiling was not the floor of the external covering.

Templet, a gauge cut out of a thin piece of metal to the form of the work to be executed.

Templum (Latin), a temple. Temples appear to have existed in Greece from the earliest times; they were separated from the profane land around them, and the entrances were much decorated as architecture advanced.

Tenacity, that quality of bodies by which they resist tension or tearing asunder.

Tender, the carriage which is attached to a locomotive engine, and contains the supply of water and coke.

Tenon, in carpentry, the square end of a piece of wood or metal diminished to one-third of its thickness to be received into a hole in another piece, called the mortise, for the jointing or fastening of the two together.

Tension, a force pulling or stretching a body, as a rod. Animals sustain and move themselves by the tension of their muscles and nerves. A chord, or string, gives an acuter or deeper sound as it is in a greater or less degree of tension, that is, more or less stretched or tightened.

Tension-rod, an iron rod applied to strengthen timber or metal framing, roofs, etc., by its tensile resistance.

Term, a piece of carved work placed under each end of the taffrail of a ship, at the side timbers of the stern, and extended down as low as the foot-rail of the balcony.

Terra Cotta, in the arts, baked earth, bricks, tiles, etc.

Terra di Sienna, or *Raw Sienna Earth*, a ferruginous native pigment, which appears to be an iron ore, and which may be considered as a crude natural yellow lake, firm in substance, of a glossy fracture, and very absorbent. It is in many respects a valuable pigment, of rather an impure yellow colour, but has more body and transparency than the ochres; and being little liable to change by the action of either light, time, or impure air, it may be safely used, according to its powers, either in oil or water, and in all the modes of practice. By burning, it becomes deeper orange and more transparent and drying.

Terre-verte, an ochre of a bluish-green colour; in substance moderately hard, and smooth in texture. It is variously a bluish or grey coaly clay, combined with yellow oxide of iron, or yellow ochre. Although not a bright, it is a very durable pigment, being unaffected by strong light and impure air, and combining with other colours without injury. It has not much body, is semi-transparent, and dries well in oil. There are varieties of this pigment; but the green earths which have copper for their colouring matter are, though generally of brighter colours, inferior in their other qualities, and are not true terre-vertes.

Tessellated, in the arts, variegated by squares; exemplified in the beautiful pavements of the ancients.

Tessera, small cubical pieces of brick, stone, or composition, forming part of an ancient Roman mosaic or tessellated pavement.

Testaceous, consisting of shells; made of baked earth, or of tiles or bricks.

Tetragon, a quadrangle, or a figure having four angles.

Tetrahedron, in geometry, one of the five regular bodies of solids comprehended under four equilateral and equal triangles. It may be conceived as a triangular pyramid of four equal faces.

Tetrantis, the four equal parts into which the area of a circle is divided by two diameters drawn at right angles to each other.

Tetrastyle, a portico, etc., consisting of four columns. A cavædium was called tetrastyle when the beams of the compluvium were supported by columns placed over against the four angles of a court.

Thatch, straw or reeds employed for covering the roofs of buildings; particularly used for cottages.

Thoughts or *Thwarts*, in navigation, the benches or seats in a boat.

Theatres, edifices of various but principally of large dimensions, for dramatic exhibitions.

Theatrum, a theatre. The Athenians, before the time of Æschylus, had only a wooden scaffolding on which their dramas were performed. It was merely erected for the time of the Dionysiac festival, and was afterwards pulled down.

Theodolite, in surveying, a mathematical instrument for measuring heights and distances. (See Heather's work on Instruments.)

Theorem, a term used in mathematics to signify a proposition which states a conclusion and requires its demonstration; as distinguished from a Problem, which leaves the conclusion to be discovered.

Theory, a doctrine which terminates in the sole speculation or consideration of its object, without any view to the practice or application of it. To be learned in an art, the theory is sufficient; to be master of it, both the theory and practice are requisite. Machines often promise very well in theory, but fail in practice. A remarkable circumstance may be instanced of a gentleman of British North America selling his estate and leaving his home to give practical effect to a theory he had, as he considered, beautifully worked out in figures, for an important improvement in steam-machinery. His theory, however, wholly failed on its first application in practice.

Theory, mathematical, the algebraic elucidation of the principles of any physical system, where assumptions are made, in the absence of positive data; the calculated results are expressed in formulæ, which are easily convertible into arithmetical rules. Among others, the ' Theory of the Steam Engine,' by the Count de Pambour, has been found to be most useful for practice; and the following is an explanation of his mathematical investigation, designed for persons not familiar with the algebraic signs, and intended to render clear and easy the use of the formulæ contained in the above-mentioned work, and which may be said to have reference to all mathematical works.

Among persons engaged in the construction or working of steam-engines, there is a great number to whom the algebraic terms are little familiar, and who usually give up the reading of a book as soon as they perceive that it steps beyond the simple notions of arithmetic. When it is intended to make a work profitable to those persons, the usual practice is to annex to each of the definitive formulæ an explanation, in full words, of the arithmetical operations which it represents.

The want of such explanation may be very advantageously supplied, by giving the signification of every sign employed in the formulæ; by explaining what are the arithmetical operations represented by those signs. With the help of a very few rules on this subject, persons will find that the reading of the formulæ is quite as easy in algebraic signs as if they were written in words; since, after all, it is but an abridged way of expressing the same things, and, moreover, the operations to be performed, in order to attain the result, are much more clear, and more easy for the mind to seize. Again, a perfect acquaintance with the signification of the signs in common use can require but a few hours of attention, and when once a person shall have made himself master of them, he will be capable of reading the formulæ of all works.

$A, B, \ldots a, b, \ldots l, m, n, \ldots \alpha, \beta, \ldots$, etc. The letters are an abridged manner of writing the numbers which those letters represent. Thus, when the stroke of the piston has been measured, and found, for instance, to be $17\frac{1}{2}$ inches, it would be inconvenient to write in all the formulæ the number $17\frac{1}{2}$. But if the length of stroke, whatever it might be, has been represented by a letter, as l, for instance, then, every time the letter l occurs, there needs only to recollect that it represents the number $17\frac{1}{2}$, and performing with that number the operations indicated in the formulæ, relative to the letter l, the result sought will be attained.

$= \ldots$ This sign signifies *equal to;* it expresses that a quantity sought is equal to the number resulting from certain operations performed on other quantities known. Thus, for instance, if we find the expression

$$V = 60\,v,$$

this will signify that the quantity V is equal to 60 times the quantity v. Consequently, if we know besides that the letter v represents the number 100, it will follow that the unknown quantity V will

THE THEORY (MATHEMATICAL) EXPLAINED. THE

have for its value 60 times 100, or 6000.

+ .... This sign signifies *plus* (more). Placed between two letters or two numbers, it indicates that they are to be added together. If, for instance, there be in a formula an expression of the form

$$1 + \delta,$$

it means that to the number 1 must be added the number δ. If, then, we know besides that the letter δ represents the number ·14, it follows that the expression $1 + \delta$ will have for its value

$$1 + \delta = 1 + ·14 = 1·14.$$

− ∴ ... This sign indicates *minus* (less). Thus, when an expression occurs of the form

$$P - f - 2118,$$

the expression amounts to saying that, from the number P the numbers f and 2118 are to be successively subtracted. If, then, we know that the letter P represents the number 9360, and that the letter f represents the number 144, the expression will have for its value

$$P - f - 2118 = 9360 - 144 - 2118 = 7098.$$

× .... This sign expresses *multiplied by*. Thus the expression

$$a \times v$$

indicates that the two numbers represented by the letters a and v are to be multiplied one by the other; and the product of that multiplication will be the quantity expressed here by $a \times v$. This multiplication to be performed is equally expressed by a point between the two letters, or by writing the two letters simply together without any sign interposed; so that the expressions

$$a \times v \ldots, a \cdot v \ldots, a v,$$

amount to the same, all three expressing the result of the multiplication of the numbers represented by a and v. If, for instance, an expression occur like the following,

$$a\, r\, v,$$

and it be known that the letter a expresses the number 1·57, the letter r the number 2640·96, and the letter v the number 300, the expression $a\, r\, v$ will have the value

$$a\, r\, v = 1·57 \times 2640·96 \times 300 = 1243800.$$

÷ .... This sign denotes *divided by*. Thus the expression

$$\frac{S}{a}$$

expresses S divided by a, or the quotient resulting from the division of the number expressed by S, by the number expressed by a.
For instance, if we have S = ·67 and a = 1·57, it is plain that the term $\frac{S}{a}$ will have for its value

$$\frac{S}{a} = \frac{67·}{1·57} = ·4268.$$

A fraction may have its numerator or its denominator composed of several numbers, on which divers operations are indicated. In that case, those operations must first be performed, so as to reduce the numerator and the denominator to single numbers, before performing the division of the one by the other, as has just been said.
If, for example, we have the fraction

$$\frac{10000}{1·492 + ·002415\, P},$$

and know besides that the letter P represents the number 9360; we must first perform the multiplication of the number 9360 by the number ·002415, and then add to the product the number 1·492.

486

The result will be the number 24·0964, which will therefore represent the denominator of the fraction. The fraction may then be written under the form

$$\frac{10000}{24 \cdot 0964},$$

and consequently it is reduced to the simple indication of the quotient of two numbers, as in the preceding case.

If two fractions occur, separated by the sign of addition, or that of subtraction, or that of multiplication, the meaning is that, after having sought separately the quotient indicated by each of those fractions, they are either to be added together, or one deducted from the other, or one multiplied by the other. Thus, the expression

$$\frac{8}{a} \cdot \frac{10000}{1 \cdot 492 + \cdot 002415\, P}$$

signifies that, after having sought the quotient indicated by each of the two fractions, the first of these quotients is to be multiplied by the second. Supposing the letters to be of the same numerical value as in the preceding cases, the product of the two fractions would here be the definitive number 176.

It would be the same if we were to find one fraction divided by another. Each of them should be first reduced to a single number by finding the quotient they represent, and then the one of these quotients divided by the other.

( ) or [ ] or { } .... Parentheses indicate that the different quantities contained between them are to be reduced to a single number before performing the other operations indicated in the formula.

Thus, for instance, if we find in a formula the expression

$$(1 + \delta)\, v,$$

this means, that it is the expression $(1 + \delta)$ entire, which is to be multiplied by v. The sum then of $1 + \delta$ is first to be formed, and afterwards multiplied by the number v; whereas, had we only

$$1 + \delta v,$$

this would mean that the product δv is first to be formed, and afterwards the number 1 added to it.

There may occur several parentheses comprised one within the other, but their signification is always the same. The expression

$$\cdot 002415\,[\{(1 + \delta)\,r + f\}]$$

denotes that the sum of $1 + \delta$ is to be formed first, this to be multiplied by r, and the product added to the quantity f, which gives the number represented by the outer parenthesis; and finally, that this number is to be multiplied by ·002415.

Lastly, when there occurs in the formulæ a letter with a small figure or exponent above it, it is the same thing as writing that letter as many times successively as there are units in the figure or exponent.

For instance, the expression

$$v^2$$

is equivalent to the expression $v \times v$, or v written twice; that is to say, it is the product of v by itself. If then v were known to be equal to 300, the quantity represented by v^2 would be

$$v^2 = 300 \times 300 = 90000.$$

These short explanations are all that is necessary, in order to read and perfectly understand all practical formulæ. Replacing each of the signs that are met with in a formula, by the periphrasis which the sign represents, you read the formula such as it ought to be expressed; and effecting the arithmetical operations indicated by those signs, you attain the result sought. A formula is, then, nothing more than an abridged manner of writing the series of operations to be performed, in order to arrive at the result which we want to obtain.

We will subjoin to this explanation some examples, taken from the practical formulæ of high-pressure engines.

I. Suppose we have the formula

$$v = \frac{S}{a} \cdot \frac{10000}{6\cdot6075 + \cdot002415[(1+\delta)r+f]}$$

which is intended to determine the unknown value of v; and let it be supposed that we know, besides, that the other letters comprised in this formula have the following value:—

$$S = \cdot67$$
$$a = 1\cdot57$$
$$\delta = \cdot14$$
$$r = 2641$$
$$f = 144.$$

First form the sum $(1 + \delta)$, indicated in the inner parenthesis, which will be

$$1 + \delta = 1\cdot14.$$

Then multiply this number by r, or 2641, and the result will be

$$(1 + \delta)\, r = 1\cdot14 \times 2641 = 3010.$$

Add to this f, or 144, and the sum will consequently be the quantity indicated by the outer parenthesis, viz.

$$[(1+\delta)\,r+f] = 3154.$$

Now multiply this sum by the number ·002415, and the product will evidently be

$$\cdot002415\,[(1+\delta)\,r+f] = \cdot002415 \times 3154 = 7\cdot6170.$$

Add to this last result the number 6·6075, and you obtain

$$6\cdot6075 + \cdot002415\,[(1+\delta)\,r+f] =$$
$$6\cdot6075 + 7\cdot6170 = 14\cdot2245.$$

This is then the denominator of the fraction which forms the second member of the formula. Performing the division of the number 10000 by the number just obtained, the quotient will be

$$\frac{10000}{6\cdot6075 + \cdot002415\,[(1+\delta)\,r+f]}$$
$$= \frac{10000}{14\cdot2245} = 703\cdot04$$

On the other hand, dividing S by a, or the number ·67 by the number 1·57, you have the value of the fraction $\frac{S}{a}$, viz.

$$\frac{S}{a} = \frac{\cdot67}{1\cdot57} = \cdot4268$$

Finally, then, multiplying this latter quotient by that obtained immediately above, you have definitively

$$v = \frac{S}{a} \cdot \frac{10000}{6\cdot6075 + \cdot002415[(1+\delta)r+f]}$$
$$= \cdot4268 \times 703\cdot04 = 300.$$

Thus it is clear that by effecting successively the series of calculations indicated by the few signs which are explained, and proceeding gradually from the most simple terms to the more compounded ones, we arrive without difficulty at the definitive result.

We will give some other examples of these calculations; but, instead of effecting the operations, we will merely express in words the signification of the formula, which amounts to the same.

II. Suppose we have the formula

$$a\,r = 4140750\, \frac{S}{(1+\delta)v} - \frac{a}{1+\delta}$$
$$(2736 + f);$$

this signifies that the required value of $a\,r$ will be obtained by performing the following arithmetical operations:—

Add 1 to the number represented by the letter δ, and multiply the sum by the number v.

Then divide the number S by the product thus obtained; multiply the quotient of this division by the number 4140750; and write apart this first partial result, which represents the first term of the formula.

Add again to unity the number δ, and by that sum divide the number a.

Similarly add to the number 2736 the number f, and multiply the sum by the last found quotient; and set apart this partial result, which represents the second term of the formula.

Finally, from the first partial result subtract the second, and the difference will be the quantity $a\,r$ sought.

Performing these different operations with the values of S, a, δ, r, and f, given above, and supposing the case wherein the letter v has the value $v = 300$, you find that the quantity $a\,r$ will have for its definitive value

$$a\,r = 4146.$$

III. If we have the formula

$$S = \frac{v\,a}{10000}\left\{6\cdot6075 + \cdot002415\left[(1+\delta)\,r + f\right]\right\}$$

it will amount to the following arithmetical explanation:

To the number 1 add the number δ, and multiply the sum by the number r.

To this product add the number f, and multiply the resulting sum by the number $\cdot002415$.

To the latter product add the number $6\cdot6075$, and keep apart this partial result, which expresses, in one number, what proceeds from all the operations comprised in the great parenthesis.

Then multiply the number a by the number v, and divide the product by the number 10000, which will give you another partial result, expressing the portion of the formula situated beyond the parenthesis.

Finally, multiply the former partial result by the latter, and the definitive product will be the required value of S.

For the values above attributed to the different letters contained in the formula, the result of the calculation will give $S = \cdot 67$.

IV. If we have the formula

$$v' = \frac{S}{a} \cdot \frac{10000}{1\cdot492 + \cdot002415\,P},$$

it will be paraphrased as follows:

Multiply the number $\cdot002415$ by the number P, and add to the product the number $1\cdot492$; divide the number 10000 by the sum thus obtained, and write the quotient apart.

Then divide the number S by the number a, which will give a second quotient.

Finally, multiply the former quotient by the latter, and the resulting product will be the required value of v'.

With the values already indicated for the letters, and, moreover, for $P = 9360$, the result of the preceding formula will give $v' = 176$.

V. In fine, as a last example, we will suppose the formula

$$a\,r' = \frac{a}{1+\delta}(P - f - 2118).$$

It plainly will signify as follows:

From the number P deduct first the number f, and again from the remainder deduct the number 2118.

Then to the number 1 add the number δ, and divide the number a by the sum thus obtained.

Finally, multiply this quotient by the difference before obtained, and the definitive product thus formed will be the required value of $a\,r'$.

The operations thus indicated would, for the case wherein the letters should have the values already given above, produce for the required value of $a\,r'$ the quantity 9777.

Thus we see how easy it is to

replace all the formulæ by their expressions in words; and, consequently, the sight of algebraic formulæ ought in nowise to intimidate persons unfamiliar with algebra.

Theotheca, Monstrance, or *Remonstrance,* sacrament-house in the Roman Catholic Church (the pix), the receptacle of the consecrated host, made generally of the most costly materials, and, in some cases, of expensive and beautiful design. Two magnificent examples are given in the 'Divers Works of Early Masters.' The sacrament-house in the church of St. Lawrence at Nuremberg, date 1510, is 64 feet in height; and another, in the church of St. George at Limbourg, is upwards of 30 feet high.

Thermometer, an instrument used for measuring the degrees of heat. (See *Temperature of different Thermometers.*)

Thesaurus (Greek), a treasure-house. That buildings of this description were required, especially by kings and states, in the earliest period of civilization, is self-evident; and tradition points to subterranean buildings in Greece, of unknown antiquity and of peculiar formation, as having been erected during the heroic period, for the purpose of preserving precious metals, arms, and other property.

Thole, a term used in building: the scutcheon or knot in the midst of a timber vault; also a place in temples where donaries (gifts) were hung up.

Tholobate, a cupola, and a base: that part of a building on which a cupola is placed.

Tholus, an appellation given to all buildings of a circular form. Vitruvius uses it to signify the roof of a circular building.

Thowl, a piece of timber by which oars are kept in their places in rowing.

Throat, in ship-building, the hollow part of knee-timbers.

Throttle-valve, a valve in the steam-pipe of an engine, for regulating the supply of steam to the cylinder. In land engines it is generally connected to a governor.

Thucydides informs us, that the Athenians were first among the Greeks to lay aside the custom of bearing arms, and to cultivate ease and luxury (*Gladstone*).

Thurible, a censer used in some of the services of the Roman Catholic Church, made usually of metal, in the form of a vase.

Thurl, a long adit in a coal-pit.

Thymele, in antiquity, a sort of altar, surrounded with steps, placed in front of the Greek stage or orchestra.

Thyrorea, the doors of a Greek temple or house.

Thyroreum, a passage in the houses of the Greeks, at one end of which was the entrance from abroad, and at the other the doorway leading to the peristyle.

Tiara, an ornament for the head, anciently used by the Persians.

Ticketings, the weekly sales of ores. The adventurers or their agents meet together at noon, and whilst sitting round a table, each buyer gives in his ticket, offering a certain sum per ton for so many tons of ore. The tickets are then read aloud by the chairman, and the persons present note the prices offered, the lots or different samples being sold to the highest bidder.

Tide, the natural fluctuation of the water of the sea and some rivers, whereby it increases and diminishes its quantity at particular times and places, the first being called the tide of flood, the last the tide of ebb: when the tide or flow of water runs against the wind, it is called a windward tide, in which case the sea breaks most, and runs highest.

Tide-gauge. The merit of this invention is due to Mr. Meik, the engineer of Sunderland Harbour, whose attention had been for some time directed to the necessity of having conspicuous tide-gauges erected at all harbours and docks. Entrusted with the management of a tidal harbour with an intricate and narrow channel, and where frequently from 150 to 200 sail of vessels entered or quitted during a single tide, he perceived that the number of vessels that could safely depart on their outward voyage depended not only on the extent of each tide, but also on the knowledge of those in charge as to the rate of its flow, by which alone they would be enabled to form a correct judgment as to the sufficiency of water to enable the vessels to proceed to sea.

It was evidently essential that any tide-gauge for this purpose should be rendered intelligible to seamen of all grades, and so situated as to be seen from all vessels in time to allow the course of those outward bound to be checked, should there not be sufficient depth of water to enable them to pass over the bar; or should the vessel be inward bound, and the depth indicated by the gauge proved insufficient, she might be brought up, or put off again to sea; also if the vessel was at anchor in the roadstead, the captain on board should be able to know, from prominent characters, the earliest time at which he could take the harbour.

The first port provided with a regular set of signals for this purpose was that of Leith. The signals used there are very complete, and, with the assistance of a careful man to work the system according to the rise of the tide, are of essential benefit to the shipping. But few seamen pay sufficient attention to matters of this kind to carry in their memory the exact depth of water corresponding to the signals shown; and before the book is consulted, the vessel may be driven on the shore, or stranded on the bar.

The signals at Leith, although perfect of their kind, are used only during the day; while it is evident that night is the time when they are most required by seamen, to inform them of the state of the tide. By day they generally have some imperfect mode of arriving at the depth of water, by observing when the tide reaches certain points on shore, or covers some known rocks at sea; but at night they cannot guess at the tidal flow even by such inaccurate means, and consequently the gauge-marks or figures should have the property of being clearly distinguished at night as well as by day, otherwise little advantage will be gained, nor will the loss of life be materially lessened.

From these considerations, and for the purpose of exhibiting the advantages to be derived from their adoption at the different ports, a self-acting tidal gauge, combining the above-mentioned properties, as far as relates to outward-bound ships, has been erected at Sunderland Harbour, by Mr. Meik, in conjunction with Mr. Watson, of Newcastle.

The construction of the gauge is as follows: A well, carefully boxed in, and of similar depth to the water on the bar, is sunk below the building which contains the apparatus. Within this well, in an interior pipe or trunk, and rising and falling with the tide, works a float suspended by a copper wire cord, which is carried over a spiral cone fixed in an upper story of the building. By the simple arrangement of a wheel and pinion at the opposite end of the axle to which the cone is fixed, a web of wire gauze works on two rollers fixed at the upper and lower ends of the web. The lower roller is regulated by the movement of this wheel and pinion; the upper one by a balance-weight attached to a copper wire cord, which also passes over another spiral cone, having at the extremity of its axle a second wheel and pinion similar to the first. As the float rises and falls with the tide, the wheels and pinions connected with the cones, over which the cords of the float and balance-weight respectively pass, move the rollers on which the gauze web travels. On this web are painted in large figures the various depths from high to low water, and as the web works, two fixed pointers indicate the number of feet and half-feet on the bar at any hour of the tide.

The web and the figures on it can be made of any size, and to travel 4, 6, 8, 10, or any other proportion to 1 of the float, by regulating the size of the wheels and pinions. By day the figures on the web are shown white on a black ground; by night they appear distinctly lighted up, the ground still remaining dark. A white transparent varnish is used for the figures, and an opaque black for the ground. The illumination by night is so steady and powerful, that the figures, if made large enough, and the apparatus fixed at a sufficient elevation, are visible at a considerable distance at sea, and thus afford vessels the means of knowing the exact depth of water at the mouth of any harbour before entering it. This simple piece of mechanism is applicable to all places where the want of a correct and conspicuous gauge has been felt, not only in harbours and docks, but at railway stations, for signals and such-like purposes. The apparatus used occupies so little space, that it can all be contained and worked in a column or pillar, without any other building.

In the same building is erected, for the Commissioners of the River Weir, a self-registering tide-gauge, to which it is also intended to fix a barometer. The working of this self-registering gauge, which has for some time been in use at a few other ports, is as follows:—

A pencil is fixed in a rack, which registers the variations of the tide, the time of each change being also marked; and immediately under which is a cylinder. On this is fastened a sheet of paper, properly ruled for the purpose, and of sufficient size to receive the variations of the tide, traced by the pencil, for fourteen days. The rack containing the pencil is connected with a wheel, over which a copper wire cord passes, having attached to it a float, which works in a well of similar construction to that already described as used for the new tide-gauge. This float and cord move, by the action of the tide, the rack and the pencil in it, and trace the diagram on the paper below. A dial on one side of the rack is worked by the same machinery, and points out as a clock the hours and minutes of the day, and the number of feet from high to low water.

A time-piece, furnished with a strong minute-hand, gives the revolving movement to the cylinder on which the paper is rolled, and serves to mark the time of the variations of the tide. The float and wheel, in fact, are the means of showing the depths of water; the time-piece, the exact hour and minute of each change of tide.

Tie-beam, a beam which acts as a string or tie, to hold together two things which have a tendency to spread apart.

Tie-rod, a wrought-iron bar or rod for bracing together the frames of steam-engines, roofs, etc.

Tierce, a vessel containing forty-two gallons, or the third part of a pipe. In the Romish Liturgy, it is one of the canonical hours for prayers, viz. eight in the winter, and ten in the summer, at night. At cards, it is a sequence, or three following cards of one sort. In heraldry, it is the division of a shield into three equal parts.

Ties, in navigation, the ropes by which

the yards hang; in mechanics, tension rods.

Tigna, the principal timbers of a roof extending across ancient temples, in contradistinction to the trabes, which were timbers placed upon the columns or walls in the same direction with them. The tigna correspond to our tie-beams.

Tiles, baked clay in thin plates of different shapes, used to cover roofs. Tiles curiously and richly ornamented were formerly used in the early Christian churches for pavements.

Tiller, a piece of timber fitted into the head of a rudder, to which it forms a handle.

Tilt-hammer. The most simple machine by which iron is forged is the German forge-hammer, often called the tilt-hammer. This machine, often of a fanciful form, is very extensively employed. The leading principle sought in its construction is solidity; and various forms have been invented to give permanency to the structure, which is mainly endangered by the action and re-action of the strokes. The cast-iron tilt-hammer varies in weight, according to the purposes for which it is designed, from 50 to 400 pounds. For drawing small iron and nail rods, a hammer of the former size is sufficiently heavy; but for forging blooms of from 60 to 100 pounds in weight, a hammer weighing 300 or 400 pounds is employed. Such a hammer should be cast from the strongest grey iron, and secured by wooden wedges to the helve.

Timber-man, in mining, the man employed in placing supports of timber in the mine.

Timbers, in ship-building, the ribs which branch outwards from the keel in a vertical direction.

Timber-framed roofs. Timber-framed roofs occur in the great halls of castles and palaces. Those at Westminster, Christchurch (Oxford), and Hampton Court, are scarcely inferior in beauty and constructive skill to stone vaults. (Dall. p. 41.)

The fashion of timber-framed roofs originated about the reign of Edward III., as applied to great halls. They are common about 1400 in churches, to which the stone vaulting prior to that date seems to have been peculiar. The first Norman castles had arches of stone in their halls, as had all those built by Edward I. in North Wales. (Ibid.)

The skill in construction is acknowledged to be great in the timber roofs alluded to, but none of them can vie with the best executed roofs of stone in beauty. All the tracery and carving which I have seen in timber roofs are clumsy, ill-formed, and unhandsome. The effect was sometimes grand, but never elegant. The effect of time also on the material produces cracks and chasms, which offend as much as ill workmanship, and indeed destroy that which was once good. In stone the softening of the edges and slight mutilations adds richness and variety without injury to the reputation of the workman, because enough usually remains perfect to attest his skill and taste.

Timbers in the head, in ship-building, pieces with one end bearing on the upper cheeks, and the other extended to the main rail of the head.

Timbers of ermine, a term in armoury or blazon; the rows or ranks of ermine in noblemen's capes.

Tin. This very useful metal is found in small round lumps, in the beds of some rivers near the mines, the principal of which are in Cornwall, but it is generally in nature as an oxide, though occasionally as a sulphate, and associated with many other metals. Tin is a silvery white metal, with a very slight shade of yellow; the purest is the grain-tin, which is prepared from what is found in the river-beds, and known as stream-tin, and is judged by its splitting when a mass is heated till it is brittle and allowed to fall from a height. It is very malleable and soft: it dissolves in hydrochloric acid, evolving hydrogen gas: nitric acid converts it into a hydrated binoxide.

Tin, oxide of. When tin is digested in strong nitric acid, a whitish powder is deposited, which, after being washed, and subsequently fused and pulverized, is known in the arts under the term *putty-powder*, and is used for polishing glass, stones, etc.

Tin white resembles zinc white in many respects, but dries badly, and has even less body and colour in oil, though superior to it in water. It is the basis of the best white in enamel painting. There are various other metallic whites of great body and beauty, such as are those of bismuth, antimony, quicksilver, and arsenic; but none of them are of any value or reputation in painting, on account of their great disposition to change of colour, both by light and foul air, in water and oil.

Tincture, a staining or dyeing; also a term in heraldry, signifying a variable hue of arms.

Tinsel, a kind of cloth composed of silk and silver, glistening like stars or sparks of fire.

Tire, in mechanics, the strong iron hoop that binds the circumference of a wheel.

Tires, of locomotive engines, the outside hoops round the wheels, generally with a flange to keep and guide them on the rails. Stephenson's patent engine and eight-wheeled engines are usually made without flanges on the tires of the driving wheels. Some tires are steeled on the part subjected to most wear, which renders them more durable.

Titanate of iron (Titaniferous iron, Iron sand) is an oxide of iron and titanic acid, and belongs to the class of the magnetic oxides. It is attracted by the magnet, is of a deep black colour, metallic lustre, very hard, and perfectly opaque; melts into a black slag by a high temperature. It is generally found near volcanoes or volcanic rocks, but seldom in quantities sufficient to justify the erection of iron-works; nevertheless the quality is mostly good, and the volcanic regions around the lakes of America may present, in the course of time, encouraging prospects.

Titanium. This metal is found occasionally in the slag of smelting-furnaces, in small cubical crystals of a copper colour: it exists in anatase, and several varieties of titanate of iron, but combined with oxygen.

Ton, a weight which varies in different districts: the common ton is 20 cwts. of 112 lbs., or 2240 lbs.; in Cornwall the miner's ton is 21 cwts. of 112 lbs., or 2352 lbs.

Tontine, a term derived from the name of the inventor, Lorenzo Tonti, a native of Naples, who originated the scheme so called, first adopted in 1653 in France. The subscribers were divided into ten classes, according to their ages, or were allowed to appoint nominees, who were so divided; and a proportionate annuity being assigned to each class, those who lived the longest had the benefit of their survivorship, by the whole annuity being divided amongst the diminished number. Some remarkable cases have occurred in England: a tontine of a recent date consisted of a less number than ten members, all of whom, with the exception of one, died within a very few years from the commencement, leaving this survivor in the receipt of an enormous sum of money annually, derivable from the profits of the undertaking, which are unvarying.

Tools, instruments employed in the manual arts for facilitating mechanical operations, namely, hammers, punches, chisels, axes, adzes, planes, saws, drills, files, etc., by means of percussion, penetration, separation, and abrasion of the substances operated upon; for all of which operations various motions are required to be given either to the tool or to the work. In handicraft work the tool receives motion, but in selfacting or automatic tools, motion may be given to either. In the case of the turning lathe, the tool remains fixed, and the object moves. In that of the planing machine, the tool may remain fixed, or be made to move according to the duty required to be performed. In almost all other machines, such as the slotting, the key-grooving, the punching, the drilling, the nut-cutting, the teeth of wheels cutting, the boring, the screw-cutting machines, the tools receive motion. In the screw, bolt, and nut machines the tool is either movable or fixed. The use of handicraft tools is coeval with the earliest periods of antiquity, and the recent researches of modern travellers have proved the ancients to have been acquainted with almost all the tools now in use. The potter's wheel, the axe, the chisel, the saw, etc., attest the perfection to which the mechanical arts were carried by the Greeks and Romans; and subsequently in the arts of turning exhibited by the Dondi family, in the construction of their clocks and of machines for spinning silk, in the middle of the 13th century, in Italy, and afterwards by Bessoni, De la Hire, De la Condamine, Grand Jean, Plumier, and Morin. The three plates of Bessoni show the different modes of turning and cutting screws of all sorts of fancy work. De la Hire shows how all sorts of polygons may be made by the lathe, and Condamine shows how a lathe may be made to turn all sorts of irregular figures by means of tracers moved over the surface of models and sculptures, medals, etc.; and this is perhaps the first idea of the machine called the *Tour à Portrait*.

The work of Plumier enters most extensively into the art of turning, for he shows the construction of the lathe and its different parts, the art of making, hardening, tempering, and sharpening tools, the different kinds of motions which may be given to the lathe by means of wheels, eccentrics, and models, and the different inventions relative to works of art which have been performed by the lathe, among which may be mentioned the movable or slide rest. In the common rest which supports the tool, the idea of fixing the tool and pushing it in the direction of the parallel bed of the lathe, so as to cause the tool to traverse the work parallel to it, must have been obvious; and as this could have been easily effected by means of the screw and handle, it required little ingenuity to carry out the idea to its fullest extent, by constructing a rest to allow of the slide traversing the horizontal or vertical plane in any direction. The machine described by Plumier is neither more nor less than the slide-rest and planing machine combined; it consists of two parallel bars of wood or iron connected together at both extremities by bolts or keys of sufficient width to admit of the article required to be planed: a movable frame being placed between the two bars, and motion being given to it by a long cylindrical thread, is capable of giving motion to any tool which may be put into the sliding frame, and consequently either causing the screw, by means of a handle at each end of it, to push or draw the point or cutting edge of the tool either way. If also motion be given to the tool by means of guides upwards or downwards, it is evident that any kind of reticulated form can be given to the work, as in the machine described by Plumier, which was intended for ornamenting the handles of knives, and which is called by Plumier, *Machine à Mouche de Couteau d'Angleterre*, from its having been an English invention. The *Machine à Canneler*, described by Bergeron, a mode of grooving columns, is probably derived from the same source, from its resemblance to the English machine. The origin of the planing machine, in more recent times, is said to have arisen from the grooving or fluting of the drawing rollers used in cotton machines, shortly after the introduction of Arkwright's inventions. The patent of Sir Samuel Bentham in 1793, for various new methods for working wood, metal, and other materials, certainly contemplates the working of tools similarly to the tools employed in the planing machine, as it comprehends giving all sorts of motion to tools: and the patent of Joseph Bramah, taken out in 1802, was "for machinery for producing straight, parallel, and smooth surfaces and other materials requiring truth, in a manner more expeditious and perfect than can be performed by the use of axes, screws, planes, and other cutting instruments used by hand in the usual way."

Billingsby, of Birkenshaw, took out a patent in 1802, for boring cylinders in a vertical position, although horizontal machines had their advantages. The boring of large cylinders by horizontal machines had long been practised by Smeaton, Wilkinson, Walker, Darby, and Boulton and Watt, and at Butterley and other great iron-works; but it was many years subsequently that the vertical boring machines came into use.

As respects the introduction of the first planing machines which have been used during the present century, opinions are at variance.

Messrs. Fox, of Derby, the eminent tool-makers, state that the first machine employed for this purpose was constructed by Mr. Fox, senior, in the year 1821, for the purpose of planing the wrought and cast iron bars used in the lace machines: the machine was capable of planing an article 10 feet 6 inches in length, 22 inches in width, and 12 inches in depth: others give the credit of the invention to Manchester, and G. Rennie, Esq., puts in a claim for constructing a planing machine with a movable bed, urged by an endless screw and rack, and furnished with a revolving tool, so early as 1820, having several years previously employed the principle for grooving and planing parallel bars.

Mr. Bramah, in 1811, employed the revolving cutter to plate-iron. Mr. Clement states that he made a planing machine, for planing the sides of weaving looms and the triangular bars of lathes previously to 1820. He afterwards constructed a beautiful machine for planing large and small work with the greatest accuracy. The bed moved on rollers, and the tools cut both ways. The beautiful work executed by this tool, for Mr. Babbage's calculating machine, evinces the perfection of its performance. It is thus by the aid of automatic tools that the greatest precision and identity of parts in machinery is produced; and it is probable that, ere long, the chisel, the file, and the grindstone will be banished from the factory, and that nicety of parts and uniformity and silence of action, blended with the science of construction, will eventually supersede the expensive and imperfect construction of the handicraft system. Subsequently very important tools have been invented by Mr. Joseph Whitworth, of Manchester. For the slide-rest and other tools see second edition of 'Rudimentary Mechanism.'

Toon wood is of a reddish-brown colour, rather coarse-grained, much used all over India for furniture and cabinet-work.

Top and Butt, in ship-building, the general method of working the English plank (except in the topside) to make good work and conversion, which is by disposing of the top-end of every plank within 6 feet of the but-end of the plank above or below it, leaving all the planks to work as broad as possible, so that every other seam is fair.

Top-timbers, in ship-building, the uppermost timbers: the first general tier of timbers that reaches the top of the side are, or should be, called top-timbers; those which scarf on the heads of the upper futtock are called short timbers.

Torricellian tube, in pneumatics, a glass tube named after the inventor, open at one end and hermetically sealed at the other.

Torricellian vacuum. This is produced by filling a tube with mercury, and allowing it to descend to such a height as to be counterbalanced by the pressure of the atmosphere, as in the barometer.

Torsion is that force with which a thread of wire returns to a state of rest after it has been twisted by being turned round on its axis.

Torsion-electrometer, an apparatus for measuring the intensity of electricity.

Torus, the convex member of the Tuscan and Ionic bases. In the attic base there is both an upper and lower torus.

Tossing, Tosing, or *Torlooking,* a process consisting in suspending ores by violent agitation in water: their subsidence being accelerated by packing, the lighter and worthless matter remains uppermost.

Tower, an ancient elongated vertical building, variously formed and constructed in different countries.

Town Hall, Mansion House; in France, Hôtel de Ville; in Italy, Palazzo Publico; in Holland, Stadhaus; an edifice in which all the municipal laws and regulations and the interests of a city are conducted.

Tracery, that species of pattern-work formed or *traced* in the head of a Gothic window by the mullions being continued, but diverging into arches, curves, and flowing lines enriched with foliations.

"Each country," says Mr. Garbett in his 'Rudimentary Treatise on the Principles of Design in Architecture,' "has had its successive styles of tracery, and each has begun with the simple subdivision of one arch into two, and these sometimes into two again, filling up the space between the heads with a *circle*, as at Marburg; a *foiled circle*, as at Salisbury chapter-house, and the aisles of Cologne; or finally a *foil-circle*, as at Westminster, and the clerestory of Cologne, where it is subfoiled: thence proceeding to pack together such forms over an *odd* number of lights, to which the method of continual bisection would not apply, as at the aisles of York; and thus the first kind, which may be called *packed* tracery, became complete. Deviations from the principle of packing led to the general tracery, absurdly called '*geometrical*;' for all Gothic tracery is geometrical, none is hand-drawn. This beautiful purely *unmeaning* tracery was succeeded in all countries by the flowing loop or leaf, and then by the peculiar national After-Gothic. Germany, however, as it had been the first to perfect, was also the last to abandon the 'geometrical' tracery, which continued there, even into the fifteenth century, our Perpendicular Period. England and France, however, in the fourteenth century, abandoned the unmeaning for the flowing leaf-tracery; and this, notwithstanding its beauty, had hardly time to show itself before it was superseded, here by the perpendicular, and in France by the flamboyant. Hence it happens that of the three great classes of tracery,—geometrical, flowing and perpendicular,—while the last is, as every one knows, by far the commonest in England, the most abundant kind in France is flowing (flamboyant), and in Germany geometrical, i. e. unmeaning.

"The unmeaning tracery of Germany is very beautiful, and generally partakes of the packed character; the following forms, which are the elements of German tracery, occurring very abundantly.

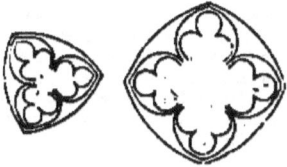

Elements of German tracery.

"The convex-sided triangle and square are placed in all positions indifferently, and the frameless trefoils and quatrefoils are frequently formed on the basis of these figures instead of the circle. The foilings and subfoilings, formed by a very narrow but deep chamfered member, leave their little spandrils (called *eyes* by our workmen) entirely open, thus producing almost the lightness of metal-work.

"The Germans seized on the idea of *growth*, and the budding and sprouting expression; but perhaps the French were most successful in increasing the aspiring expression: by a slight change in the prevailing forms of the flowing tracery, they converted the loops or leaves into flame-like forms, till the flamboyant buildings appeared not vegetating, as in Germany, but *blazing* from the foundation to the bristling finials. The difference between this style of tracery and our own flowing style (exemplified in the west window at York), is, that

English leaf-tracery.

while the upper ends of our loops or leaves are round or simply pointed, i. e. with *finite angles*, the upper ends in France terminate, like the lower, in *angles of contact* (those formed by two curves that have a common tangent). It was necessary to the leafy effect that the *lower* angles should be tangential; but to the flame-like effect, that the *upper* ones should be so, even if the lower were

French flamboyant tracery.

finite; and hence some examples of flamboyant tracery, if turned

TRACTION.

upside down, form a kind of leaf-tracery.

"Our countrymen, however, adopted a method which was less conducive to the aspiring expression, and which conducted them to a style less rich and certainly less

varied than any of the other After-Gothics. Erroneously supposing that an abundance of vertical lines would increase this character, they were led to convert all the flowing lines of the window tracery into vertical ones, to omit the capitals of nearly all the smaller shafts or shaftlets, thus converting what had been blank arcades into mere panels, and then to multiply, diminish, and extend these panels and endless repetition of vertical lines over every part of the interior, and, in florid buildings, even of the exterior."

Traction, in mechanics, is the act of drawing a body along a plane, usually by the power of men, animals, or steam; as when a vessel is towed on the surface of water, or a carriage moved upon a road. The power exerted in order to produce this effect is called the force of traction.

Numerous experiments have been made for the purpose of ascertaining the value of a force so exerted; and when men are employed to draw laden boats on canals, it is found that if the work be continued for several days successively, of eight hours each, the force of traction is equivalent to a weight of $31\frac{1}{4}$ lbs. moved at the rate of 2 feet per second, or $1\frac{1}{4}$ mile per hour (it being understood that such weight is imagined to be raised vertically by means of a rope passing over a pulley, and drawn in a horizontal direction). The force of traction exerted when, without moving from his place, a man pulls horizontally against a weight so suspended, is estimated at 70 lbs. The action of a horse in drawing a vessel on a canal is said to be equivalent to a weight of 180 lbs. raised vertically, as above supposed, with a velocity of $3\frac{1}{4}$ feet per second, or $2\frac{1}{4}$ miles per hour; but this estimate has been considered too high; and from experiments which have been made on the power of horses in waggons, carts, and coaches, on level ground, it is found that the force of traction exerted by a stout horse is equivalent to 80 lbs. raised at the rate of $4\frac{3}{8}$ feet per second, or 3 miles per hour. Tredgold considers that a horse exerts a force of traction expressed by 125 lbs. raised at the rate of $3\frac{3}{8}$ feet per second, or $2\frac{1}{4}$ miles per hour. A man or a horse can, however, double his power of traction for a few minutes without being injured by the exertion; and when the carriage is in motion, so that the friction on the ground is alone to be overcome, a horse can draw, during a short time, on a level road, a weight exceeding 1500 lbs.

The force of traction is found to vary nearly with the term $(w-v)^2$, where w is the greatest walking velocity of a man or horse when unresisted (6 feet per second, or 4 miles per hour, for a man, and 10 feet per second, or $6\frac{3}{4}$ miles per hour, for a horse), and v is the velocity with which the vessel or carriage is moved. From theoretical considerations it has been determined that the greatest effect is produced when the velocity of the object moved is one-third of that with which the man or animal can walk when unresisted.

If a wheel-carriage were situated on a level plane which opposed no resistance, it is evident that, whatever were the diameter of the wheels, the smallest conceivable power of traction applied to the axle would suffice to put the carriage in motion. But when a wheel in moving meets with an obstacle on the ground, that obstacle is pressed at the point of contact by a force acting in the direction of a line drawn to it from the centre of the wheel, and arising from that part of the weight which is supported by the wheel, together with the force of traction; therefore, by the 'resolution of forces,' the ratio between the resistance which is to be overcome by the moving power and the weight on the wheel will become less as the diameter of the wheel is increased: also the most advantageous direction in which the force of traction can be exerted is perpendicular to the line of pressure drawn from the centre of the wheel to the obstacle. But the height of the wheels cannot exceed certain limits, depending on the use to which the carriage is applied; and when the latter has four wheels, the height of those which are in front must be such only as will allow it to be turned round within a given space: also, when a horse is employed to move a carriage, attention must be paid to the conditions under which his power may be advantageously exerted.

It was first observed by M. Deparcieux, and published in the 'Mémoires de l'Académie des Sciences,' 1760, that horses draw heavy loads rather by their weight than by their muscular force. Sir David Brewster has also remarked that when the resistance is great, a horse lifts both its fore-feet from the ground; then, using his hinder feet as a fulcrum, he allows his body to descend by its weight, and thus overcomes the obstacle: and it may be added, that when this action takes place with a two-wheeled carriage, if the loading is disposed so that some portion of it may press on the horse's back, the effect of the animal's weight will thereby be increased. Now, if the traces, or the shafts of the carriage, were attached to the horse's collar, near his centre of gravity, a line imagined to be drawn from the latter point to his hinder feet may represent his weight, and a line drawn perpendicularly from his feet upon a plane passing through the traces or shafts may represent the lever of resistance: but while the former line remains the same, this lever becomes less as the plane of traction (that of the traces or shafts) inclines more upwards from the wheel; and therefore, in order that the power of the horse may be advantageously applied, the diameter of the wheel should be as small as is consistent with other circumstances.

Experiments have shown that when the angle of traction, as it is called, that is, the angle which the plane of the traces makes with the road on which the carriage is moving, is 15 or 16 degrees, a horse pulls with good effect; and the height of the points at which the traces are attached to a horse's collar being about 4 feet 6 inches from the ground, it follows that, in order to obtain this inclination, the lower extremities of the traces or shafts should be 2 feet 3 inches from the ground. In general, however, in two-wheeled carriages the height of these extremities is about 3 feet.

As an example of the force of traction exerted by steam, it may be stated, that on a level line of railway, an engine with an 11-inch cylinder, and having an effective pressure of 50 lbs. per square inch in the boiler, drew 50 tons at the rate of 30 miles per hour, working 10 hours daily; and that the same engine, with an equal pressure in the boiler, drew 160 tons at the rate of 15¼ miles per hour.

Trail, a running enrichment of leaves, flowers, tendrils, etc., in the hollow mouldings of Gothic architecture.

Trail-boards, in ship-building, the carved work between the cheeks; that which is fastened to the knee of the head.

Trailing springs, the springs fixed on the axle-boxes of the trailing wheels of a locomotive engine, which bear slightly against the side frames, so as to leave as much weight as possible upon the driving springs, and to assist in deadening any shock which may take place.

Trailing wheels, the wheels placed behind the driving wheels of a locomotive engine.

Trammel, a rod of iron or wood, with sliding pieces having points, which can be fixed at any distance apart; used for drawing large circles, or setting off distances.

Transept, the transverse portion of a cruciform church; that part which is placed between and extends beyond those divisions of the building containing the nave and the choir.

Transit, a term expressing the passage of a railway train, etc. In astronomy, the passage of any heavenly body over a larger one, as Mercury or Venus over the sun.

Transition, as applied to the architecture of the middle and later ages, the progress of changing from one style to another. There were several periods of transition: Romanesque to Saxon, Norman to Early English, Early English to Decorated, from the Decorated to the Perpendicular to that of the Tudor and to that of the Elizabethan age.

Transom, a horizontal mullion or cross-bar in a window. The most ancient examples are found in the Early English style.

Transom, in carpentry, a thwart-beam or lintel over a door. In shipbuilding, certain timbers extending across the stern-post of a ship, to fortify and strengthen it. In mathematics, the vane of an instrument called a cross-staff, being a piece of wood fixed across, with a square socket upon which this slides.

Transparency, that quality of certain bodies by which they transmit the rays of light, in contradistinction to opacity.

Transparent and Opaque Colours. As a general proposition, the Homeric colours are really the modes and forms of light, and of its opposite or rather negative, darkness; partially affected perhaps by ideas drawn from the metals, like the ruddiness of copper, or the sombre effect of dead blue, whatever the substance may have been; and here and there with an inceptive effort, as it were, to get hold of other ideas of colour; of the transparent and opaque or chiaroscuro, we cannot expect to hear from Homer. (Gladstone, vol. iii. p. 489.)

Transposition, in music, the changing a tune or lesson, and putting it into a higher or lower key or clef.

Transtra, horizontal timbers in the roof of a building. The term is applied to the transverse beams of a gallery which extend from side to side and connect the ribs, in the same manner as those horizontal pieces connect the axis or principals of a roof.

Transverse, in geometry, something that goes across another, from corner to corner, like the diagonals of a square or parallelogram.

Transyle, a narrow or triforial passage.

Trapezium, in geometry, a plane figure contained under four right lines, of which neither of the opposite sides are parallel.

Trapezoid, an irregular figure whose four sides are not parallel, resembling a trapezium.

Traveller, in navigation, a sort of thimble, whose diameter is much larger, in proportion to the breadth of its surface, than the common ones: it is intended to facilitate the hoisting and lowering the top-gallant yards at sea.

Travelling crane, a crab fixed on a carriage which may be moved upon rails across a building, and the cross-rails, together with the carriage, moved lengthwise upon other rails fixed at or near the top of the building.

Traverse sailing, in navigation, is the variation or alteration of a ship's course occasioned by various causes; or it is a compound course in which several different courses and distances are known.

Traverse-table, in navigation, is the same as a table of difference and departure, ready calculated for any distance under 100 miles.

Treadle, a lever or frame connected by a rod to the crank of a foot-lathe, to give motion to the crank-shaft: it is pressed down by the left foot of the turner, and raised by the centrifugal force of the fly-wheel or large pulley which is fixed on the shaft.

Treasury, a building or an apartment where money or valuables are deposited.

Tree-nails or *Trunnels*, in ship-building, long cylindrical wooden pins.

Trefoil, an ornament formed by mouldings so arranged as to resemble the trefoil or three-leaved clover.

Trellis, a gate or screen of open work; lattice-work either of metal or wood.

Trench, a ditch; a defence for soldiers. Trenches, approaches, or attacks, are works carried on by besiegers, with parapets for the men to gain ground and draw near a citadel or fortification: if the ground be hard or rocky, trenches are raised above it with fascines, bags of earth, etc.; but if the earth can be easily dug, then a ditch or way is sunk, and edged with a parapet next to the besieged, the depth being commonly about six or seven feet, and the breadth seven or eight feet.

Trend, in navigation, to bend, to lie in a particular direction.

Trestle-trees, in ship-building, two strong bars of timber fixed horizontally on the opposite sides of the lower mast-head, to support the frame of the top and the weight of the topmast.

Tret, an allowance in weight for waste or impurities.

Triangle, a figure bounded by three sides, and consequently containing three angles. Triangles are of the several kinds, plane or rectilinear, spherical, and curvilinear.

Tribometer, in mechanics, a term applied to an instrument for estimating the friction of metals.

Tribunes, magistrates among the old Romans, chosen to preserve the privileges and secure the liberties of the people against the power and encroachments of the nobles; at first their number was but two, and these afterwards associated three more to them, whose number was in process of time increased to ten. Their authority was so great that they could assemble the people for what purposes they pleased, hinder the deliberations of the senate, approve or annul its decrees, summon the other magistrates before the people, and also their own colleagues and associates: they went so far as sometimes to imprison consuls and fine dictators. At first their jurisdiction reached but a mile out of the city of Rome, but some time afterwards it was extended into the provinces. These officers kept their doors open day and night, to receive such of the common people as sought for shelter with them. The office grew into so much authority and honour, that the greatest men in the state chose it, and by clashing with the consuls and senate occasioned great tumults. There were also military tribunes, but their powers were more limited.

Tribute, in mining, a proportion of the ore which the workman has for his labour. Tributers generally work in gangs, and have a limited portion of a lode set them, called a 'tribute pitch,' beyond which they are not permitted to work, and for which they receive a certain portion of the ore, or so much in the pound as agreed upon in value of what they raise.

Triclinium, the eating-room of a Roman house; so called because in general it contained couches upon which the ancients or their guests reclined at their meals. The term was also applied to the couches themselves.

Triforium, the gallery or open space between the vaulting and the roof of the aisles of a church, generally lighted by windows in the external wall of the building and opening to the nave, choir, or transept over the main arches. In the Temple church it is built around the nave, and has a curious and singular effect.

Triglyphs, in architecture, ornaments repeated at equal intervals in the Doric frieze. Each triglyph consists of two entire gutters or channels cut to a right angle, called *glyphs*, and separated by their interatices, called *fermora*, from each other as well as from two other half-channels that are formed at the sides.

Trigonometry, the art of measuring triangles, or of calculating the sides of any triangle sought, either plain or spherical.

Trim, in navigation, the best posture of a ship's proportion of ballast, arrangement of sails, and position of masts, with a view to her sailing well.

Trimmer, a piece of timber inserted in a roof, floor, wooden partition, etc., to support the ends of any of the joists, rafters, etc.

Tringle, in architecture, a name common to several little square members or ornaments, as regulets, lestets, and platbands.

Tripod, any utensil or article of furniture supported upon three feet.

Triptic, a tablet in three divisions, to open and shut, the two outer folding over the centre one when closed.

Trisection, the division of a line, an angle, etc., into three equal parts.

Trochilus, a hollow moulding; also called *scotia;* constantly occurring in the bases of the classical orders of architecture.

Trochoid, in geometry, a particular description of curve generated by the motion of a wheel.

Tropics, two lesser circles on the globe or sphere; one on each side, distant 23½° from the equator, which are the bounds or limits of the sun's deviation from the equator; at his approach to these circles the sun seems to stand still for a few days, and then returns towards the equator again: that on the north side is called the tropic of Cancer, and, when the sun is there, makes our longest day; and that on the south side is called the tropic of Capricorn, and causes the longest night.

Troubles, in mining, faults or interruptions in the stratum.

Trucks, in navigation, circular flat pieces of elm, with a small sheave on each side, fixed upon the upper end of flag-staffs, and used to reeve the halliards.

Truncated, in geometry, a pyramid or cone, the top or vertex of which is cut off by a plane parallel to its base.

Trunk Engine, a marine steam-engine used for driving a propeller: the cylinder is fixed horizontally.

Trunking, the process of extracting ores from the slimes; the ores subsequently undergo the process of racking and tossing.

Trunnions, knobs of metal in pieces of ordnance which project from the sides and bear the guns on the cheeks of the carriage.

Truss, the collection of timbers forming one of the principal supports to a roof, framed together to give mutual support and to prevent straining or distortion from the superincumbent weight.

Truss, to strain, support or keep tight: a trussed roof is one which, by means of the tie-beams, rafters, king-posts, etc., is strained, or held together in its proper position.

Trussing, in carpentry and ship-building, a series of diagonal braces disposed in triangles, the sides of which give to each other a mutual support and counteraction.

Trussing-beds, in Tudor times, were beds which packed into chests for travelling: in cases of frequent removal, they must have been found very convenient. John of Ghent seems to have always slept in such beds.

Tub, a cast-iron cylinder put in the shaft instead of bricking, for the purpose of heating out the water and making it rise to a level.

Tubes, in locomotive engines, are of brass or iron, about two inches outside diameter. They are of the same length as the boiler, and fixed in it by a ferrule driven in at each end, which makes them steam-tight. They are surrounded with water externally, and internally open to the atmosphere by the chimney. The heated gases and smoke from the fire pass through them, and they are thus the means of rapidly generating steam. The number of tubes in boilers varies from 60 to 70 up to above 200, according to the power of the engine.

Tube Ferrules, in locomotive engines, slightly tapered hoops, one of which is driven in at each end of each tube, to fix it securely in the boiler: formerly they were made of steel and iron; now, cast-iron ferrules are found to answer very well.

Tube plugs, in locomotive engines, are formed of tapered iron or wood, and used for driving into the end of a tube when burst by the steam.

Tube plug-ram, in locomotive engines, a long rod with a socket end, into which the plug fits, and is thus driven into the burst tube, and the plug-ram withdrawn.

Tubular Boilers. Boilers of an angular, prismatic, or indeed any but a cylindrical form,—or even then if not made of wrought metal,—become the peculiar seat of danger in high-pressure engines; and all sorts of safety apparatus, as well for preventing too great a pressure as for avoiding other sources of danger, are but uncertain in their operation, and not to be depended upon. The great object to be sought is so to construct boilers that their explosion may not be dangerous in its result.

This condition has been approximated to by the invention and application of tubular boilers; but it would seem that these have been suggested rather by the necessity of providing, for many technical purposes, and particularly for steam carriages, boilers of less content and weight, than by the desire of removing or lessening danger from explosion. Tubes should have that form which is best adapted to resist pressure, viz. the cylindrical. If they are of small diameter, of not too great thickness, and of suitable material, they may be made to carry out the before-named principle; i. e. they themselves, in case of bursting, will not cause any dangerous consequences to the neighbouring persons or property. This has been amply proved by experience.

Unfortunately, however, there are no tubular boilers which satisfy all conditions required. The subject is often mentioned as one of little difficulty, easy of decision, and unencumbered with practical obstacles; but such is the language only of the prejudiced and the inexperienced. To arrive at the truth, it must be sought with long-continued perseverance, and with no small share of physical knowledge, as the subject is beset with difficulties on every side.

It becomes a most complex problem to construct a tubular boiler for a large supply of steam, by reason of the difficulty of arranging and connecting the great number of tubes it must contain into one convenient whole. The modern English locomotive boilers cannot be legitimately called *tubular* boilers, because they fail altogether in the grand distinguishing quality of all such,—namely, the small diameter of the generating apparatus: the tubes of these boilers are nothing more than a splitting-up or subdivision of the fire-tube of the Trevithick steam-carriage boiler. From their greater outer diameter, locomotive boilers do not avoid the evil of the old capacious form, and therefore do not diminish the objection to it; they have also a defect in the close proximity of the tubes to each other, whereby the water space between them is rendered too confined, and the heated tubes become liable to be laid bare of water. This circumstance gives the key to the well-known fact, that the tubes become so soon destroyed, or at least require constant repair, and add to the mischief occasioned by their expansion, through their connection with the end plates of the cylindrical part of the boiler. It is evident that from the passage upwards of the steam formed among the lower tubes, the upper ones must be most liable to be uncovered with water; while these, being exposed to the hottest part of the fire current, are most likely to receive damage therefrom.

A tubular boiler ought to preserve, as much as possible, the tubular form in all its parts; or, at least, the larger portions ought to be cylindrical, and not of too great diameter, or should be so strongly made that the tubes should form the weakest part of the whole boiler. The tubes themselves should be of such diameter, and be constructed of such metal, that in case of their actual bursting, no dangerous explosion may ensue. This, however, is only possible when their thickness is so small, and the metal of such a kind, that bursting takes place by a comparatively small internal pressure, and is followed by only a ripping open of the tube, and not a scattering about of massive fragments. Under all circumstances, however, the tubes must be the sole generating vessels: they alone must receive the action of the fire, and be exposed to its destructive influence. All other and larger vessels, or parts connected with the tubes, should be most carefully protected from not only this but all other dangerous influences, in order that they may remain in their original proved condition of strength.

Only such a tubular boiler as fulfils all these conditions can be called a safe one. In its use there is no further danger from high-pressure steam, and near it its owner may repose undisturbed by a care for the safety of life or property.

The requisites in the use of the tubes are the following:—They must be placed in such a position with regard to the furnace, that the flame may act upon them in the most favourable manner, and that the heat may be absorbed as completely as possible.—They must have such a proportion between their length and diameter, that neither the ebullition in them may become too violent, and the water be thereby ejected from them, nor that they become warped or made crooked by the heat.—They must properly convey away all the generated steam, and be regularly supplied with water.—They must be connected with the main part of the boiler in such a manner, that in case of a rupture of one of them,

TUBULAR BRIDGES.

the whole content of water and steam cannot suddenly and dangerously discharge itself.—They must lie so deep under the general water-level of the boiler (in the receivers or separators), that some considerable sinking of the water may be allowed to take place without leaving any of them empty; and in case the latter effect should occur, such tubes must first be emptied as are least exposed to the heat of the furnace.—Lastly, they must be connected with each other in such manner that no destructive expansion may be allowed to take place, and that all may be easily and conveniently cleansed of the earthy matters deposited in them.

The larger portions of the boiler, or receiving vessels, may themselves consist of tubes of a larger diameter, or may form flat chambers, constructed of a strength to withstand a very high pressure (say 400 to 500 lbs. per square inch): this involves no difficulty. The diameter of the receivers should not, where it can be avoided, exceed 16 inches, and they should be constructed of plate-iron of at least ½ of an inch thick, securely and exactly riveted together into a cylindrical form. When it is necessary that they should be capacious, their length should be increased, and not their diameter beyond that specified, or their number should be greater. Their covering lids may be flat and of cast-iron, but of considerable thickness (1¼ to 2 inches), and these must be connected to the cylinders securely, and in such a way that they may be easily taken off when cleaning is required. They must, under all circumstances, be entirely removed from all strong action of the fire, and must at most be exposed only to such currents as have discharged the greatest portion of their heat against the generating tubes. In order to preserve them from rust, their internal and external surfaces may be covered with several coats of oil-varnish, and the coating renewed, at least on the inside, every year.

Since these receivers or larger parts of the boiler usually serve as separators, and as means of connection between the generating tubes, they must be perfectly adapted to fulfil these purposes. As separators, they must efficiently separate the steam from the water, so that none of the latter may penetrate into the working parts of the engine; and to this end the water surface in them must be of sufficient extent. In order that the water may not rise to a dangerous height in them by violent ebullition in their tubes, their water space must bear a certain proportion to that of the tubes and the other parts of the boiler. The steam-room in them must also be proportioned to the content of the engine cylinder; so that the pressure may not be too much lessened by the discharge into the engine, and a foaming of the water thereby be caused. Mr. Fairbairn is the great authority for tubular boilers.

Tubular Bridges are those in which the requisite strength and rigidity are obtained by disposing the materials in the form of a horizontal tube, through which the passage is formed for the traffic. They are to be distinguished from trussed bridges, which, when constructed of timber and covered over, as in several of the American bridges, resemble a tube, or two or more parallel tubes, being formed entirely without trussing, and therefore admitting of construction with iron only. Tubular bridges are to be regarded as an original and highly important invention, admirably adapted for spanning wide spaces, and affording all required strength with a positive minimum of depth. In all arched bridges some portion of the space below, or head room for navigation, is sacrificed by the depending haunches; or, on the other hand, if the roadway is made up to correspond with the chord of the arch, the crown is necessarily elevated to a considerable height, and additional weight involved in sustaining and preserving the position of the higher parts of the structure. Hence *flatness*, or the reduction of the total depth has always been a desideratum in the designing of bridges, and scientific skill and boldness have achieved several examples in which this property is attained in a much greater degree than it was once thought safe and prudent to attempt. The wrought-iron tubular bridge, however, is safely constructed with a total depth of $\frac{1}{12}$th of its span, and with sufficient strength and rigidity to sustain great loads, such as railway trains, without sensible vibration or deflection. For bridges of small span, the tubular principle may be adopted in the construction of malleable-iron girders, each of which is itself a rectangular tube of small section, the roadway being thus supported upon two or more of these tubular girders arranged in parallel positions, and at some distance apart. In these bridges a level roadway is formed with a small depth, but the roadway and traffic occupy an additional depth; whereas in the tubular bridge, as constructed for large spans, the depth of the tube itself comprises the entire depth of the structure, and it may therefore be considered as a vast hollow girder, *through* which the roadway is formed. Mr. Robert Stephenson appears to have first suggested the idea of forming tubular bridges; and that over the Conway, erected on the line of the Chester and Holyhead Railway, was completed and opened in 1849. This bridge consists of two tubes, placed parallel to each other over a clear span of 400 feet. Each tube, with its castings, etc., weighs about 1300 tons, and is constructed of plate-iron riveted upon malleable-iron ribs, the section of the tube being a rectangle about 30 feet in height and 15 feet wide. The sides, top, and bottom of the tubes consist of long narrow plates of malleable iron, varying in length up to 12 feet, and in width from 1 foot 9 inches to 2 feet 4 inches: they vary in thickness from $\frac{3}{8}$ to $\frac{3}{4}$ inch. The internal ribs are of T-iron, $3\frac{1}{2}$ inches deep, and placed at intervals of 2 feet. A depth of about 1 foot 9 inches across the tube is occupied at top and bottom with narrow cells formed with plate-iron and L-iron corner pieces, all firmly riveted together. These cells are for the purpose of giving the requisite stiffness to these parts of the tube, and are closer together at the top than at the bottom of the tube, as the tendency of a load is to compress the upper part and distend the lower part of the structure, and wrought-iron is, it appears, much better able to resist extension than compression. In his report to the Directors of the Chester and Holyhead Railway, their engineer, Mr. Stephenson, thus referred to some of the results of the experiments which were made in order to determine the form and proportions for his proposed tubular bridge over the Menai Straits. "The first series of experiments was made with plain circular tubes; the second with elliptical; and the third with rectangular. In the whole of these this remarkable and unexpected fact was brought to light, viz. that in such tubes the power of wrought iron to resist compression was much less than its power to resist tension,—being exactly the reverse of that which holds with cast-iron; for example, in cast-iron beams for sustaining weights, the proper form is to dispose of the greater portion of the material at the bottom side of the beam; whereas with wrought iron, these experiments demonstrate beyond any doubt that the greater portion of the material should be distributed on the upper side of the beam. We have arrived, therefore, at a fact having a most important bearing upon the construction of the tube; viz. that rigidity and strength are best obtained by throwing the greatest thickness of material into the upper side. Another instructive lesson which the experiments have disclosed is, that the rectangular tube is by far the strongest, and that the circular and elliptical should be discarded altogether."

Another tubular bridge, similar to that at Conway, and the Britannia, near Bangor, exceeding these bridges in extent, has just been completed in Canada, over the St. Lawrence.

These grand bridges differ little less in the mode of constructing and erecting them than in their design, from ordinary bridges of stone, timber, or iron. Thus the larger tubes over the water-way are put together adjacent to their final resting-place, and when complete as tubes, they are launched upon pontoons, floated to the piers, and raised to their places complete and entire by hydraulic presses operating at each end. For this purpose of raising, strong temporary frames of cast-iron are fitted to the ends of the tube, and made fast to solid bar-link chains, the upper ends of which are forced upwards by successive lifts of the hydraulic press, each lift being 6 feet, and the ends of the tube being packed up as the raising proceeds. One end of each tube is permanently laid upon cast-iron rollers, to admit of the changes of length produced by variations of temperature. For the purposes of the railway, transverse plates of iron are fixed edgewise on the bottom of the tube, and support longitudinal balks of timber, upon which the rails are laid. The height of the Conway Bridge is 18 feet at the bottom of the tubes above high water; that over the Menai Straits, called the 'Britannia' Bridge, 102 feet above the same level.

Tudor Badges. The badges of the house of Tudor were either assumed or derived from descent or alliance : the red rose was the peculiar distinction of the house of Lancaster, and was borne by Henry VII. as Earl of Richmond. The portcullis was the badge of the Beaufort branch of the same family, assumed by the descendants of John of Ghent, born in the castle of Beaufort; and agreeably to heraldic simplicity, a part of the castle, its most prominent feature, was depicted for the whole. The fleur-de-lis was also a badge of the house of Lancaster, and was introduced, together with the rose, in the border of Henry's arms, as Earl of Richmond. Descended from Cadwallader, the last of the British kings, and deriving from him the name of Tudor, he assumed the badge of the red dragon, Cadwallader's ensign. After the battle of Bosworth Field, Henry took as a badge the hawthorn bush, crowned, in allusion to the circumstance of the crown being found in a hedge, whence it was taken and placed on his head. The red rose, or rose of Lancaster, he placed on the sunbeams, as the white rose had been by the head of the house of York. This monarch assumed the Tudor rose, or the red rose charged with the white, as emblematical of his united claims to the throne by his marriage with Elizabeth, the daughter and sole heir of Edward IV. Upon the marriage of Prince Arthur with Catherine of Arragon, he adopted, in compliment to her, the badges of her house. The castle was an ancient badge of the house of Granada. The sheaf of arrows was assumed by the house of Arragon on the conquest of Granada, which had been achieved by the superiority of the Arragonese archers. The rose dimidiated with the pomegranate was adopted as being symbolical of the junction of England and Spain. The phœnix in flames was assumed by Edward VI., in allusion to the particular nature of his birth, and was granted by him to the family of Seymour. A white falcon, crowned, and holding a sceptre, was assumed by Queen Anne Boleyn as her peculiar badge, and was continued by her daughter, Queen Elizabeth. The harp, an ancient badge of Ireland, was used by Queen Elizabeth. The rose environed by the garter, with its motto, was a badge of several branches of the Tudor family. All these badges were represented crowned, when borne by the monarch, and were occasionally placed between the royal supporters.

Tudor Style of Architecture, a continuation of the Perpendicular Style, merging into a peculiarity in the time of Henry VIII., when it was much applied to domestic purposes and to edifices for collegiate halls, and several foundations for educational and charitable uses, thus appropriating the proceeds of monastic revenues. The mansions of the Tudor period usually consisted of an inner and base court, between which stood the gate-house. The principal apartments were the great chamber, or room of assembly, the hall, the chapel, the gallery for amusements, on an upper story, running the whole length of the principal side of the quadrangle, and the summer and winter parlours. Of quadrangular houses, the seats of the Bishops of Carlisle, Cowdry, Halnaker, etc., may be taken as fair examples. In a work entitled 'Studies of Ancient Houses' (a book of a convenient size and price) are some fine examples in this style, but of a smaller kind. Very many splendid examples of larger dimensions of halls, mansions, etc., still exist scattered over the country.

Tufa, a calcareous earth, composed of broken and concreted shells, or the deposit from water impregnated with lime.

Tugs, in mining, hoops of iron fastened to the covers to which the tackles are affixed.

Tugs, steam, small steam-vessels employed in towing other craft.

Tulip wood, from Brazil, is frequently unsound in the centre, very handsome, but soon fades; it is used in turnery and Tunbridge ware.

Tumbling-home, in nautical language the falling into midships of the top-side above the main breadth, to bring the upper deck guns nearer the centre of the ship.

Tumbril, a machine for the punishment of scolding women, consisting of a chair attached to a long pole; the offender was placed in the chair, swung over a pond, and immersed as often as necessary.

Tummals, in mining, a great quantity or heap.

Tumulus, a heap, or mound of earth, sometimes called a barrow, used for the burial of the dead previous to the Roman invasion of Britain.

Tunnel, a large and subterraneous arch, driven through an elevation or hill, or under a river, for the passage of boats, carriages, etc.

Among the costly and laborious works of a railway, its tunnels occupy the first place. Like mining and all other subterranean operations, the construction of a tunnel can be but little aided by mechanical appliances; it chiefly requires hard manual labour, exercised under circumstances which do not admit of that thorough superintendence which promotes economy, and, moreover, liable to unforeseen interruptions, of surmounting which neither the manner nor the expense can be predetermined. Thus the Kilsby tunnel, on the London and Birmingham Railway, was estimated to cost about £40 per yard lineal; whereas its actual cost was £130 for the same length, owing to its intersecting a quicksand, which the trial borings had escaped. Thus a vast expense was necessarily incurred in setting up and working pumping machinery in order to dry the sand. The pumps brought up nearly 2000 gallons per minute, and were working during a period of nine months. The quicksand extended over a length of about 450 yards of the tunnel. The Box tunnel, on the Great Western Railway, excavated through oolite rock, and being lined with masonry only through a portion of its length, cost upwards of £100 per lineal yard. The Bletchingley tunnel, on the South-eastern Railway, cost £72 per lineal yard; and the Saltwood tunnel, on the same line of railway, cost £118 per lineal yard. This greater cost in the latter work was occasioned by the great body of water in the lower green-sand which the tunnel intersects.

The method of proceeding with tunnelling depends mainly upon the kind of material to be excavated. This having been generally ascertained by borings and trial shafts, the work is commenced by sinking the working shafts, which must be sufficiently capacious to admit readily of lowering men and materials, raising the material excavated, fixing pumps, and also for starting the heading of the intended tunnel when the required depth is reached. Besides the trial and working shafts, air-shafts are sunk for the purpose of effecting ventilation in the works below.

The working shafts are made cylindrical, and from 8 to 10 feet internal diameter; 9 feet is a favourite dimension. They are of brickwork, usually 9 inches thick, and carried up 8 or 10 feet above the surface of the ground, finished with stone coping. These, and all other shafts, rest upon curbs of cast-iron, fitted into the crown of the tunnel, and forming a level base for the shaft. The air-shafts are of similar thickness and form, but usually about 3 feet internal diameter. They should not be allowed to be sunk near to the working shaft, or at a less distance than 50 yards from it. All the shafts are of course sunk on the centre line of the intended tunnel. In the Bletchingley tunnel, the trial-shafts, 6 feet diameter in the clear, 9 inches thick, and 35½ yards deep, cost £6 per yard down through the Weald clay. A similar shaft in the Saltwood tunnel, 25 yards deep, cost £4. 15s. per yard down, in the lower green-sand. Horse gins are usually employed in raising and lowering the materials, etc., and also in drawing the water up the shafts, unless large pumps are used and worked by steam-power. The engineer calculated the expense of horse labour thus exercised at 2¾d. per ton, lifted 100 feet high, and including the boy to drive the horse.

The number of working shafts will depend chiefly upon the rate of speed with which the work is required to be accomplished. With plenty of men, horses, materials, and plant, the work is much facilitated by sinking extra shafts, which will usually well repay their cost. The Watford tunnel, 75 chains in length, on the London and Birmingham Railway, was specified to be worked with six shafts, not less than 8 feet diameter within the brickwork, and 9 inches thick; the brickwork moulded to fit the circumference of the shaft, and laid in two half-brick rings; an air-shaft at a distance of 50 yards on each side of each working shaft, and not less than 3 feet 6 inches diameter inside; the arch and side-walls of the tunnel, usually two bricks thick, and the invert, one and a half brick, except in places where the stratum passed through seemed to require an increased, or admit a diminished thickness. The form of the top of the tunnel is nearly semicircular, supported by curved side-walls standing on stone footings or skew-backs, which rest on the invert forming the base of the tunnel. The ends of the tunnel are formed with wing-walls. The brickwork at the ends of the tunnel is bound by wrought-iron rods 100 feet long, secured at each end in a cast-iron rim or plate built into the brickwork.

The Northchurch tunnel, which is 16 chains in length, on the same line of railway, was worked with two shafts, each 9 feet diameter. In the construction of this tunnel, a heading was driven, 4 feet wide and 5 feet high, throughout the entire length of the tunnel, and between two shafts sunk for this purpose, one near each end of it. It was specified that this heading should be driven through before any part of the tunnel was commenced, and supported and kept open during the execution of the entire work by sufficient timbering.

In commencing the works of the Saltwood tunnel, already referred to, great difficulty was encountered from the great quantity of water in the lower green-sand which the tunnel intersects. The course adopted was to make a heading or adit quite through the hill on a level with the bottom of the tunnel, in which the water was collected and drained off. The size of this, and of the Bletchingley tunnel, is 24 feet wide at the broadest part, 30 feet including the side-walls; 65 feet high in the clear, 30 feet including the invert and top arch, or 21 feet clear above the level of rails. The brickwork in the top arch and walls is from two and a half to four bricks in thickness; the invert three bricks thick.

When water occurs in the sinking of the shafts or the building of a tunnel, the back of the brickwork should be well lined with puddle, and Roman or metallic cement substituted for mortar. The whole of the Kilsby tunnel, on the London and Birmingham Railway, was built in either Roman or metallic cement, and the thickness of the brickwork is chiefly 27 inches. This tunnel is about 2423 yards long, and its length is divided by two ventilating shafts, cylindrical, and 60 feet in diameter. These shafts are 3 feet thick in brickwork, laid in Roman cement throughout. They intersect the line of the tunnel, and thus form curved recesses by that portion of their circumference which extends beyond the width of the tunnel on either side. These shafts were built from the top downwards, by excavating for small portions at a time, from 6 to 12 feet in length and 10 feet deep.

The Box tunnel, on the Great Western Railway, intersects oolite rock, forest marble, and lias marl, with fuller's-earth. Eleven principal shafts, generally 25 feet in diameter, and four immediate shafts 12 feet 6 inches, were sunk for the purpose of carrying on the works of this tunnel, the entire length of which is 3123 yards, or a little more than 1¾ mile. The section of the tunnel was designed to be 27 feet 6 in. wide at the springing of the invert, and 30 feet at a height of 7 feet 3 inches above this; clear height above the rails 25 feet. As a great portion of the tunnel was constructed by mere excavation, and without masonry, these dimensions were in some cases departed from, in order to clear away loose portions of the stone and secure solid surfaces. Where brickwork is used, the sides are seven half-brick rings in thickness, the arch six, and the invert four. During the construction, the constant flow of water into the works, from the numerous fissures in the rock, compelled pumping on a most expensive scale to be adopted. From November, 1837, to July, 1838, the works were suspended, the water having gained so completely over the steam pump then employed, that the portion of the tunnel then completed was filled with water, as also a height of 56 feet in the shafts. A second pump, worked by a steam-engine of 50-horse power, was applied, and enabled the works to be resumed.

When the working shafts are sunk sufficiently deep, a narrow heading is excavated, from 6 to 12 feet in length, 3 or 4 feet wide, and high enough for a man to work in. The top of this heading should be so much above the intended soffit of the tunnel-arch as to admit the thickness of the brickwork, besides the bars of timber and boarding by which the roof of the heading is supported, and several inches should be allowed for the settlement of the timber, which always occurs as the excavation is proceeded with, and before the brickwork can be got in.

This allowance is of the utmost importance, as without it the brickwork will, when the settlement occurs, be forced down, and can only be raised to its proper level by removing the superincumbent earth piecemeal, and at great cost. The bars and polling and packing boards, are introduced in the most convenient manner, according to the nature of soil excavated, and the degree in which it requires support, or may be safely left unsupported.

The heading is extended on either side by first cutting narrow gaps horizontally, or rather dipping downwards in directions following the intended form of the tunnel-arch. Into these gaps, crown bars are laid lengthwise, and supported upon props; and polling boards are put in between them, to retain the earth at the sides of the excavation, when extended. When the heading has thus been widened by excavating right and left, and a sufficient length cleared, the centerings are fixed, and the brickwork is commenced. As this proceeds, the earth is carefully rammed behind it, and all vacancies filled up, to prevent any subsequent settlement of the surrounding earth upon it. The crown bars which are inserted in the heading, and always during the excavations, are not invariably removed. If they can be drawn forward as the heading advances, without disturbing the adjacent ground, and the spaces filled up with broken stone, or other suitable material, no objection can arise; but otherwise they should be allowed to remain, and be built in. The whole of the operations require carefully regulating, so that none of them shall advance too rapidly for those which follow. Contractors are therefore usually restricted to carry the excavation not more than 6 or 8 feet in advance of the brickwork, or less, if so directed by the engineer, should any change occur in the strata which he thinks may require such precaution. When the faces of two contiguous excavations approach within about fifty yards of each other, a heading should be driven quite through the intervening ground, and the workings joined before the whole excavation and brickwork are proceeded with.

Experience has proved that the *quality* of the bricks used in tunnel-work is of the utmost importance. If these contain lime, on which the weather operates injuriously, the face of the work soon decays, and requires extensive repair or restoration. This was the case with the Beechwood tunnel on the London and Birmingham Railway, which in less than three years was considered to be in an unsafe condition, owing to this cause. The remedy adopted was of the most complete character;

it consisted in an entirely new lining of brickwork, 9 inches thick. This tunnel is about 302 yards long, and passes through strata consisting of alternate layers of rock and marl, abounding with springs of water. By judicious arrangement, the lining was completed in forty days. The traffic being diverted to one of the two lines of rails which are laid in the tunnel, and a hoarding erected along the centre, the casing was carried up on one side to the height of 4 feet 6 inches above the springing. At this point a course of York paving, 4½ inches thick, was bonded into the original work, and the new work was securely attached beneath it with wedges of iron; half-brick toothings were also inserted in chases cut 2 feet 3 inches apart in the original work. The traffic was then turned into the line on the side thus cased, and the other wall was similarly treated. Bearers were then fixed 6 feet apart over-head, and a close flooring laid upon them. Upon each bearer a pair of ribs was raised, and keyed stays and laggings were fixed, and the brickwork, in English bond, brought up on each side simultaneously, leaving a central space 2 feet 3 inches wide at the crown. A movable centre of this length was used to close in this space with two half-brick rings. Vertical chases, 4½ inches square, besides those cut for the toothings, were made in the face of the old walls previous to lining. These formed permanent drains, terminating in the culvert beneath the centre of the tunnel. For the extraordinary works now in progress—tunnelling through the Alps—see 'Engineer's Pocket Book' for 1859.

Turbine Water-wheel. The horizontal water-wheel so called, as used in France and Germany, was invented by M. Fourneyron: the water enters at the centre, and, diverging from it in every direction, it then enters all the buckets simultaneously, and passes off at the external circumference of the wheel. The pressure with which the water acts on the buckets of the revolving wheel is in proportion to the vertical column of water, or heights of the fall, and it is conducted into these buckets by fixed curved girders secured upon a platform within the circle of the revolving part of the machine. The efflux of the water is regulated by a hollow cylindrical sluice, to which stops are fixed, which act together between the guides, and are raised or lowered by screws that communicate with a governor, so that the opening of the sluice and stops may be enlarged or reduced in proportion as the velocity of the wheel requires to be accelerated or retarded. Turbines may be divided into high-pressure and low-pressure engines. High-pressure turbines are particularly available in situations such as often occur in hilly districts where high falls of water may be commanded, and the character of the site affords facilities for constructing reservoirs, so that a constant supply may be ensured. In these cases the height of the column of water will compensate for the smallness of its volume, and the high-pressure turbine will be found applicable with great advantage to the grinding of corn, crushing ores, working threshing-machines, or actuating other machinery. The low-pressure turbines produce great effect with a head of only nine inches, and are suitable for situations in which a large bulk of water flows with little fall. The results of an investigation by MM. Arago, Prony, Gambey, and Savary, who were appointed by the French Académie des Sciences to report upon turbines, are given in a treatise by M. Morin on the subject, and are as follows:—

1. That these wheels are applicable equally to great and to small falls of water. 2. That they transmit a useful effect, equal to from 70 to 78 per cent. of the absolute total moving force. 3. That they may work at very different velocities, above or below that corresponding to the maximum effect, without the useful effect varying materially from that maximum. 4. That they may work from one to two yards deep under water, without the proportion which the useful effect bears to the total force being sensibly diminished. 5. In consequence of the last preceding property, they utilize at all times the greatest possible proportion of power, as they may be placed below the lowest levels to which the water surface sinks. 6. That they may receive very variable quantities of water without the relation of the useful effect to the force expended being materially lessened.

The practical value of these machines is most obvious when they are applied to small falls of water. Smeaton's experiments proved that with a high fall in which an overshot water-wheel can be introduced, 80 per cent. of the original moving power may be realized. And there is little doubt, according to Rühlman, whose treatise on turbines has been so well translated and edited by Sir Robert Kane, that where an overshot wheel, or a wheel with tolerably high breasts and overfall sluices, can be erected, they are to be preferred to the turbine, except there is much back-water to contend against, when the turbine may be sunk to a considerable depth in the back-water without any material loss of its power. Even in cases which admit the working of overshot wheels, the peculiar applicability of the turbine, which affords a direct horizontal motion to the working of corn-mills, should command full consideration before it is relinquished in favour of the overshot wheel. In every case of fall, either higher than that suitable for an overshot wheel, or lower than that required for such a breast-wheel as just described, the turbine decidedly deserves the preference. Smeaton proved that undershot wheels realized only 30 per cent. of the original force.

In falls of great height, the velocity of the machine is so rapid that it may be applied to spinning machinery without mill-work, or with very little, to produce the required speed. The turbine in its present form is of comparatively modern date; the experiments of M. Fourneyron, which resulted in its invention, having been commenced in 1823, and the first machine was erected in 1827. In tracing this form of water-motor to its elements, however, the contrivance which is known as Dr. Barker's mill must necessarily be noticed. This machine, which is of very old date, consists of an upright pipe or tube, which revolves on a vertical axis, and is formed with an open funnel-shaped top, and closed at the bottom, from which project two horizontal hollow arms or pipes. These arms are closed at their outer ends, but have each a round hole near the extremity, and so placed that the two holes are opposite to each other. The upright pipe is kept filled with water, which flows into the funnel-shaped top. The issuing of the water from the holes on opposite sides of the horizontal arms causes the machine to revolve rapidly on its axis, with a velocity nearly equal to that of the effluent water, the force being in proportion to the hydrostatic pressure which is exerted by the vertical column, and to the area of the apertures; there being no solid surface at the hole on which the lateral pressure can exert itself while it is acting with its full force on the opposite side of the arm. This unbalanced pressure is, according to Dr. Robison, equal to the weights of a column having the orifice for its base, and twice the depth under the surface of the water in the trunk for its height. If the orifice were closed, the pressure upon it would equal the weights of a column reaching to the surface; but when open, the water issues with a velocity nearly equal to that acquired by falling from the surface, and the quantity of motion which is produced is that of a column of *twice* this length moving with this velocity. The revolution of the machine causes the water, which having descended the vertical pipe moves along the arms, to partake of the circular motion, thus producing a centrifugal force that is exerted against the ends of the arms of the machine. According to the laws of motion, this force increases in proportion to the square of the distance from the centre at which it is developed. Thus the velocity of the efflux is increased, and also the velocity of revolution. But as the circular motion has to be imparted to every particle of water as it enters the horizontal arm, which is done at the expense of the motion already acquired by the arm, there is a limit to the velocity even of an unloaded machine. Barker's mill has been treated of by Desaguliers, Euler, John Bernouilli, and M. Mathon de la Cour, the latter of whom proposed, in 1775, to bring down a large pipe from an elevated reservoir, to bend the lower part of it upwards and attach to it a short pipe with two arms, like Barker's mill reversed, and revolving in like manner upon a vertical spindle; the joint of the two pipes being contrived so as to admit of a free circular motion without much loss of water. By this arrangement a fall of an extended depth may be made available. An improved form of Barker's mill was patented subsequently by Mr. Whitelaw, in which the modifications suggested by M. M. de la Cour were partly included, and a peculiar form given to the horizontal arms, adapted to preserve the centrifugal force from loss or counteraction.

In this mill the two arms form the letter S, the water being emitted from their extremities in the direction of the circle traced by their revolution, the sectional capacity of the arms increasing as they approach the centre of rotation, so as to contain a quantity of water, at each section of the arm, inversely proportional to its velocity at that section.

With a well-made model of this mill, the patentee obtained an effect equal to 73·6 per cent. of the power employed, and nearly equal results are said to have been realized in actual practice. The following particulars of the height of fall and useful effect produced with turbines, already erected on the Continent, will tend to show their increasing value in proportion to the heights of the acting column of water :—

Heights of fall in feet.	Useful effect per cent. of power employed.
7·	71·
63	75
79	87
126	81
144	80

In 1837 a turbine water-wheel was erected by M. Fourneyron, an account of which is here quoted from Mr. Joseph Glynn's Report to the British Association for the Advancement of Science in 1847. This turbine is "erected at St. Blasier, or Blaise, in the Black Forest of Baden, for a fall or column of water of 72 feet

(22 mètres). The wheel is made of cast-iron with wrought-iron buckets; it is about 20 inches in diameter, and weighs about 105 lbs.; it is said to be equal to 56 horses' power, and to give a useful effect equal to 70 or 75 per cent. of the water-power employed. It drives a spinning-mill belonging to M. d'Eichtal. A second turbine, at the same establishment, is worked by a column of water of 108 mètres, or 354 feet high, which is brought into the machine by cast-iron pipes of 18 inches diameter of the local measure, or about 16¼ inches English. The diameter of the water-wheel is 14¼, or about 13 inches English, and it is said to expend a cubic foot of water per second; probably the expenditure may be somewhat more than this. The width of the water-wheel across the face is ·225, or less than a quarter of an inch. It makes from 2200 to 2300 revolutions per minute; and on the end of the spindle, or upright shaft of the turbine, is a bevelled pinion of nineteen teeth, working into two wheels on the right and left, each of which has 300 teeth: these give motion to the machinery of the factory, and drive 8000 water-spindles, roving-frames, carding-engines, cleansers, and other accessories. The useful effect is reported to be from 80 to 85 per cent. of the theoretical water-power. The water is filtered at the reservoir before it enters the conduit-pipes; and it is important to notice this, since the apertures of discharge in the water-wheel are so small as to be easily obstructed or choked."

Turbith or *Turpith mineral* (*Queen's yellow*) is subsulphate of mercury, of a beautiful lemon-yellow colour, but so liable to change by the action of light or impure air, that, notwithstanding it has been sometimes employed, it cannot be used safely, and hardly deserves attention as a pigment.

Turf is generally found in bogs, in horizontal layers from 10 to 30 feet in thickness; sometimes in the form of a blackish-brown mud; sometimes it is a dark peaty mass, and often a combination of roots and stalks of plants: frequently the turf layers interchange with layers of sand or clay. Sea-water is better adapted to the formation of turf than rain or spring water.

Turf is simply dug with spades, and then dried. If too moist, the semi-fluid mass is piled upon a dry spot, and there left until the water leaks off, and until the mass appears dry enough to be formed into square lumps in the form of bricks. In many instances, however, the freshly dug turf is triturated under revolving edge-wheels, faced with iron plates perforated all over their surface; through the apertures in these plates the turf is pressed till it becomes a kind of pap, which is put into a hydraulic press, and squeezed until it looses the greater part of its moisture: it is then dried and charred in suitable ovens.

The charcoal made in this way deserves the notice of the artisan. The component parts of turf differ from those of wood. This difference is owing to the fact of its being decomposed woody fibre. The following is an analysis of several specimens:—

One hundred parts of good turf contained, besides ashes,

	Carbon.	Hydrogen.	Oxygen.
I.	57·03	5·63	31·78
II.	58·09	6·93	31·37
III.	57·79	6·11	30·77

The charring of turf is far more easily effected than the charring of wood, partly on account of its square form, partly on account of its chemical composition. In pits, the charring of turf is not difficult, if the same method is pursued as that adopted in the charring of wood; but channels or draft-holes must be left in the kiln, because the square pieces pack so closely, that, without this precaution, sufficient draught would not be left to conduct the fire. Turf is generally found in considerable masses in one spot; therefore the erection of char-ovens is no object of mere speculation, but affords all the advantages of a permanent establishment.

Turpentine, an oleo-resin procured chiefly from trees of the fir-tribe; spirits of turpentine are obtained from this by distillation, the residue being the substance known as resin, or rosin.

Turnbull's blue (ferricyanide of iron). Professor Graham's account of this variety of Prussian blue is nearly as follows:—It is formed by adding ferricyanide of potassium (red prussiate of potash) to a protosalt of iron; it results from the substitution of three equivalents of iron for three equivalents of potassium. The same blue precipitate may be obtained by adding to a protosalt of iron a mixture of yellow prussiate of potash, chloride of soda, and hydrochloric acid. The tint of this blue is lighter and more delicate than that of Prussian blue. It is occasionally used by the calico-printer, who mixes it with perchloride of tin, and prints the mixture, which is in a great measure soluble, upon Turkey red cloth, raising the blue colour afterwards by passing the cloth through a solution of chloride of lime, containing an excess of lime. The chief object of this operation is to discharge the red and produce white patterns, where tartaric acid is printed upon the cloth; but it has also the effect incidentally of precipitating the blue pigment and peroxide of tin together on the cloth, by neutralizing the chlorine of the perchloride of tin. This blue is believed to resist the action of alkalis longer than ordinary Prussian blue.

Turner's yellow, Cassel yellow, Patent yellow. This is an oxychloride of lead, which may be prepared by different processes: when litharge or the protoxide of lead is acted upon by a solution of common salt, there are formed, soda, which remains dissolved, and a white compound, which is hydrated oxychloride of lead; and this, when heated, loses water, becomes of a yellow colour, and is the compound required. It is composed nearly of one part of chloride and nine parts of oxide of lead; it may also be obtained by heating chloride and oxide of lead together in the requisite proportions, or by heating a mixture of one part of hydrochlorate of ammonia with ten parts of protoxide of lead. In fusing these compounds it is requisite to be extremely careful to avoid any admixture of carbonaceous or combustible matter, as that would reduce a portion of the oxide of lead to its metallic state, and thus injure the colour of the product.

Turning tools. These are of two classes, viz. hand-tools and tools fixed in the slide-rest. Of the former, the principal are the heel-tool, graver, planisher, gouge, and chisel; there are many others which however are but modifications of these, and are required only in particular cases.

The slide-rest tools are distinguished by the same names as the hand-tools, but vary from them slightly in the forms of their cutting parts, which in the hand-tools are in general rather broader, in order that the part to be cut away may be acted on as long as possible before shifting the tool; for forward motion is in their case continuous only for the short period while the cutting edge can be brought to bear on the material without shifting forward the resting point of the tool. The face or front edge of the tool should in every case be nearly perpendicular to the horizontal diameter of the work, but a small difference is required for clearance.

The angle of the cutting edge should be more or less acute, according to the nature of the material to be turned; in general, the softer and more uniform the material, the more acute should be the angle; for wood, it should be very acute, and for iron and steel less acute. The velocity with which the work is made to revolve must also be adapted to the material, and must be such that the tool may take the greatest effect consistent with the preservation of its cutting edge.

The hardening and tempering of turning tools require much experience on the part of the workman; for although they may be of the best possible shape, they are worse than useless unless properly hardened. The general process of hardening and tempering tools is as follows: The cutting end of the tool is slowly heated in a clear fire, and when of a light red heat is cooled quickly in water; it is then very hard and brittle, and requires tempering or reducing to the proper degree of hardness; to effect this, it is necessary to brighten the part, so that a change of colour may be readily observed, and then place it upon a red-hot bar; when it has become heated to a certain degree by contact, the bright part will have a pale straw-colour; this gradually deepens, and when it has arrived at the requisite depth of tint, the tool is removed and again cooled, after which it is fit for use. (See also the article *Tools*.)

Turnsole, a colour used in painting.

Turn-table, a circular table, with cross-rails fixed on its surface, supported by rollers, and capable of being turned on a central pivot: used for moving a railway carriage from one line of rails to another.

Turret, a small tower attached to and forming part of another tower, or placed at the angles of a church or public building, especially in the style of Tudor architecture.

Tuscan Style of Architecture. This originated in the north of Italy, on the first revival of the arts in the free cities, and beyond which it has never yet travelled, except in some examples which were introduced by Inigo Jones in the first church of St. Paul, Covent Garden, and by Sir Christopher Wren in porticoes at St. Paul's cathedral, London. It is a simpler variety of the Doric, with unfluted columns and without triglyphs.

Tuyère. A blast pipe. Before puddling became so generally introduced, the shape and position of the tuyère at a blast furnace received considerable attention. The chief purpose of the metallic tuyère is the preservation of the fire-proof hearthstones; the direction and form of the blast are of minor importance. This protection is accomplished, in some measure, by making a coating of fire-clay in the tuyère-hole which is cut in the hearthstones. By this means, constant attendance, and repeated renewal with clay, the tuyère may be maintained narrow: whether formed of clay or metal, it should never be wider than the nozzle. Where one of the former kind exceeds the width of the nozzle, it burns away, and the earth is exposed to destruction. The preservation of the original dimensions of the earth is the main object which the manager of a furnace seeks to secure; and as the clay tuyère does not effect this object, those made of copper or cast-iron have been substituted in its place. These reach further into the furnace than those of clay, and therefore, as it is decidedly of advantage that the blast should be driven as far as possible into the centre of the hearth, the former are much preferable to the latter. If formed of wrought-iron, they are liable to burn, as the iron, in consequence of its purity, oxidizes, and forms with the clay around it a veryfusible silicate, which is precipitated into the furnace. Grey is preferable to white cast-iron, and also to wrought-iron; the carbon and impurities it contains protect it against oxidation and destruction. Copper is the best metal for tuyères; it is a good conductor of heat, and is kept cool by the blast more easily than iron. Its silicates also are infusible. If copper oxidizes and forms a silicate, the latter will protect it. The advantages derived from the copper tuyère have, in Europe, been acknowledged for more than a century; still the charcoal furnaces in America, at which cold blast is employed, are generally blown by clay tuyères, the result of which is the waste of much coal, and the production of inferior iron. This is mentioned as one of those rare cases in which Americans do not make the best use of the means at their disposal. The copper tuyère is protected against the heat of the furnace by the cold blast, which touches it, and for this reason should not be wider than the nozzle. In this point of view, it may be regarded merely as a prolongation of the nozzle, and is, of course, governed by the rules applicable to the latter. So long as pig-iron is to be made by the charcoal forge, the desire to make white plate-iron in the blast-furnace will exist. It is very difficult, almost impossible, to keep a blast-furnace constantly running upon a certain kind of iron; and therefore the difference which the quality of that in the furnace exhibits is modified to a more or less general standard by means of the position of the tuyère, such as its direction and inclination. Very skilful management is required, in many instances, to produce the desired effect. In some parts of Europe, where cold-blast iron for the forge is manufactured, the copper tuyère is yet in use; but where pig-iron for puddling is made, or hot-blast employed, such close attention is not necessary. In America, the niceties involved in adjusting the tuyère can scarcely be appreciated, not even at the forge fires; but this adjustment is unaccompanied with any practical convenience, as the trouble it requires is never compensated. The advantages which arise from a scrupulous attention are, at best, very small; and such attention would, under the conditions which exist in America, especially the high price of labour, result in loss instead of gain.

At cold-blast furnaces in America, clay or cast-iron tuyères, principally the former, are consequently generally employed. Water tuyères are in use at forges, fineries, hot-blast, and at some cold-blast furnaces. A common one for the Catalan forge, the charcoal forge, finery, and charcoal blast-furnaces,is made of boiler plate. The top part is hollow, while the bottom part, which is generally flat, is solid. A water-pipe, of ¼-inch bore, conducts a current of cold water through the hollow top: this preserves the tuyère, and protects it against burning. The bottom is made flat, so as to serve as a support to the nozzle; and thus the latter may be readily moved to those places where it is most needed. At blast-furnaces and fineries, this precaution is not of much use, as the nozzle remains at the place where it is fixed; but at forges it must be movable. Both of the water-pipes are, in most cases, at the top: but this arrangement can scarcely be considered so advantageous as though one pipe, or the entrance of the water, were nearer the bottom, and the other pipe, or the outflow, at the top.

Tuyères for anthracite, coke, and most of the charcoal furnaces, are perfectly round, and made of boiler plate; seldom of copper or cast iron. The tapering of them does not affect the furnace; and for all the evil this tapering occasions, it may be a perfect cylinder. In using hot blast, it makes no difference how the air is conducted into the furnace, provided the tuyère is kept open, and bright; which is all that is necessary. The nozzle is laid into the tuyère,—how far it reaches into it, is a matter of no consequence,—and the space between them filled up with clay. At a cold-blast furnace, it requires some attention not to push the nozzle too far in, or to draw it too far back. The water-pipes are of lead, ¾-inch, seldom 1-inch bore; one on the lower and the other on the top part of the brim. The lower pipe conducts the water to the tuyère, and the upper one from it. The former is, in many cases pushed as far as possible into its interior, to bring the cold water into the furnace; and the water is thus applied where the heat is greatest. A constant, uninterrupted supply is necessary to prevent the melting of the tuyère. The water must be pure; else it will leave a sediment in it which is sure to cause its destruction. There must, also be a sufficient supply of cold water: if the formation of steam is going on in the interior of the tuyère, the latter is sure to be burned. Copper and brass last longer than iron; but if iron tuyères are well made, and soldered with copper, and if there is no lack of water, they may last a long time. Where there is a deficiency of water, or where there are sediments in the interior of a tuyère, a few hours' heat will destroy it. If it be found that they do not wear well, attention must be directed to the water; and if nothing appears wrong, the application of larger pipes, or higher hydrostatic pressure, will then remedy the evil. Water tuyères are generally from 10 to 20 inches long; those that are too short are liable to be burnt, by the fire working around them, because there is not sufficient room to keep it closed up. Another disadvantage is, that their want of length prevents them from being pushed into the hearth; but length is necessary when the earth is burned out, and when the blast should be carried further into the interior. The external size is also a matter which requires attention in the construction. The total surface determines the amount of water which is necessary. The larger the surface, particularly the diameter, the greater the amount of water necessary, and of course the greater the danger of burning. A tuyère is seldom more than four inches in diameter inside; but the diameter outside is sometimes twelve, and even more inches. With such an increase of the diameter, however, the danger is augmented.

Tuyères may be considered a prolongation of the nozzle or the blast-pipe, and disconnected from it merely for the sake of preservation, and of more convenient access to the interior of the furnace. Those for cold blast should taper more than those for hot blast, because the former clinker in a greater degree, and require cleaning more frequently than the latter. The more acute the angle of the tuyère, the colder it works; and the more tapered it is, the hotter it works. These observations are of practical importance. In most cases the blast is required as far in the interior of the furnace as possible, because fuel is thus saved, better iron produced, and the hearth protected. There is some difficulty in giving cold-blast tuyères a slight taper, because they should be very wide outside; but this difficulty can be overcome by making their interiors more curved. If the extreme end, as far back as the diameter of the mouth, is cylindrical, the same purpose is accomplished as though the whole were cylindrical. If too much tapered, which is shown by its working too hot, the evil is diminished, in some measure, by pushing the nozzle farther into the furnace. This is but a temporary, not a radical remedy; and a tuyère of a proper form must be substituted. If it works too cold, that is, sets on too much cold cinder, the only resource is scrupulously to keep it clean, and to replace it as soon as possible by one more tapered, or with a more obtuse cone. From these considerations, it is evident that different kinds of ore require a tuyère of different taper; but for the exact degree of this taper no general rule can be given. Experience must, in this instance, be the only guide. This will appear more evident on taking into consideration the kind of fuel and the pressure of the blast required. Calcareous ore, as well as the pig-iron made from it, works naturally hot at the tuyère; consequently, those more acute are employed, and serve to drive the blast far into the furnace, by which means they are kept cool. This result can be effected by a water tuyère. Clay ores, which work naturally cold, work better with one that is tapered. These considerations, which have a special bearing upon the working of furnaces and forges, are entirely of a practical nature; and for this reason the management of the furnace or forge is accompanied with such different results. It is evident that the modification of a tuyère cannot, at times, be so quickly accomplished as may be desired: months, and even years, are often consumed, before the required form can be accurately determined; in many cases, this form is never arrived at. The shape is therefore a matter which, as blast-furnaces, generally depends on the decision of the keeper or founder; and as those formed of clay may be altered very conveniently, this may be assigned as one of the reasons why so many of that kind are in use. The whole matter, however, is divested of its mystery, when it is found that an obtuse tuyère tends to work warm, while one more acute produces an opposite effect, and is more advantageous as respects both the quality and quantity of work; but it is more difficult to manage. The form of the nozzle, as well as that of a metal tuyère, is permanent; and as the advantage of either shape can be arrived at, in a more or less perfect manner, by pushing in or drawing back the nozzle, no solid objection exists against those formed of metal. Some difference should be made between the form of the nozzle and that of the tuyère. An obtuse nozzle should work with the latter more acute: a slightly tapered nozzle, with one greatly tapered. The latter form is generally preferred, on account of the facility of cleaning.

In applying hot blast, the form of the tuyère and the nozzle is a matter of indifference; but in their construction it is found desirable to adopt the rules here suggested. The advantages of hot blast are sometimes doubtful; and it is therefore better to unite, by means of perfect forms of apparatus, all the advantages derivable from the cold blast, and thus to regain what is lost in quantity by its employment.

In forge fires there are generally but one tuyère and two nozzles. At refinery fires the tuyères are often all on one side; at other places on opposite sides. All these differences are the result of local causes, originating in the form of the apparatus, the quality of the iron and fuel, the pressure of the blast, and the qualification of the workmen. Their number and their position in the blast-furnace deserve attention. In using cold blast, few should be employed, and in using hot blast as many as possible. Cold-blast tuyères are naturally troublesome; they are apt to become black, and require constant attention, as well in moving the nozzle as in patching them with clay; they also tend to produce white iron, and they cool the lower parts of the hearth. For these reasons their number should be reduced as much as possible, as the hot-blast tuyère works very hot, occasions but little trouble, is much inclined to produce grey iron, and tends to reduce silex, and consequently to produce a poor quality of iron. Therefore, the use of as many hot-blast tuyères as can be conveniently employed is recommended. The position of tuyères is most favourable when placed on both sides of the hearth. The timp is that part of the hearth which is first burnt out; and if the tuyère is in the back part of the hearth, the distance from it to the opposite timp is unnecessarily increased.

Tying, in mining, the term for washing ores.

Tympan of an arch, a triangular space or table in the corners or sides of an arch, usually hollowed, and enriched with branches of laurel, olive, oak, etc., and sometimes with emblematical figures.

Tympanum, the triangular panel of the fastigium of any building, comprehended between its corona and that of the entablature: the panels of a framed door were called *tympana* by the Romans.

Typhoon is a name frequently applied to a tropical storm: it is also given to the hot winds which occasionally blow with great violence in Africa, Syria, Arabia, and Persia; and which are felt, though rarely and with much diminished force, in the southern parts of Italy and Spain. The sirocco of Egypt and the coasts of the Mediterranean, the simoom of Arabia, and the harmattan of the coast of Guinea, are understood to be so many designations of the typhoon; all of them being supposed to originate in the same cause, with modifications depending merely on the nature of the particles exhaled from the ground in the different countries. They are also said to cause water-spouts at sea.

U.

ULTRAMARINE, *Lazuline*, or *Azure*, is prepared from the *lapis lazuli*, a precious stone found principally in Persia and Siberia. It is the most celebrated of all modern pigments, and, from its name and attributes, is probably the same as the no less celebrated Armenian blue, or *cyanus* of the ancients. Of the latter, Theophrastus informs us that the honour of inventing its factitious preparation (by perhaps a very singular chemico-mechanical process still used for ultramarine) was ascribed in the Egyptian annals to one of their kings; and it was so highly prized, that the Phœnicians paid their tribute in it, and it was given in presents to princes; hence it was a common practice, in those times, to counterfeit it.

Ultramarine ashes (mineral grey) are the residue of *lapis lazuli* from which ultramarine has been extracted, and vary in colour from dull grey to blue. Although not equal in beauty, and inferior in strength of colour, to ultramarine, they are extremely useful pigments, affording greys much more pure and tender than such as are composed of black and white, or other blues, and better suited to the pearly tints of flesh, foliage, the greys of skins, the shadows of draperies, etc., in which the old masters were wont to employ them. Ultramarine broken with black and white, etc., produces the same effect, and is thus sometimes carried throughout the colouring of a picture. The brighter sorts of ultramarine ashes are more properly pale ultramarines, and of the class of blue; the inferior are called mineral grey.

Umber, commonly called *Raw Umber*, is a natural ochre, abounding with oxide of manganese, said to have been first obtained from ancient Umbria, now Spoleto, in Italy. It is found also in England, and in most parts of the world; but that which is brought from Cyprus, under the name of Turkish umber, is the best. It is of a brown citrine colour, semi-opaque, has all the properties of good ochre, is perfectly durable both in water and oil and one of the best drying colours we possess: it injures no other good pigment with which it may be mixed.

Undecagon, a polygon of eleven sides.

Undercroft, a subterraneous apartment or crypt.

Underlay. When a vein in a mine hides or inclines from a perpendicular line, it is said to underlay.

Underlay shaft, a shaft sunk on the course of a lode.

Underlayer, in mining, a perpendicular shaft sunk to cut the lode at any required depth.

Undershot wheel, in hydraulics, a wheel with a number of flat boards, which receive the impulse of the water conveyed to the lowest part of the wheel by an inclined canal.

Uniform motion. The velocity of a moving body is said to be uniform when the body passes over equal spaces in equal times.

Union screws or *joints*, in locomotive engines, the brass unions for connecting the elastic bore-pipe of the tender to the feed-pipe of the engine; smaller ones also connect the tender steam-pipe with the feed-pipe and with the boiler. The feed-pipe is likewise attached to the lower end of the pump by a large union screw.

Unit of work. The measure of any amount of work is the work done where a pressure of 1 lb. is exerted through 1 foot, the pressure acting in the direction in which the space is described. If instead of 1 lb. being moved through 1 foot, it be moved through 2 feet, it is clear that the work is doubled, or that two units of work have been done. The difference between the aggregate work done upon a machine during any time by those forces which tend to accelerate the motion, and the aggregate work, during the same time, of those which tend to retard the motion, is equal to the aggregate number of units of work accumulated in the moving parts of the machine during that time, if the former aggregate exceed the latter, and lost by them during that time, if the former aggregate fall short of the latter.

In reference to the unit of time, the unit of mechanical power has been assumed to be 1 lb. raised 1 ft. high, and 1 minute as the unit of time: the unit of work will therefore be represented by 1 lb. raised 1 foot high in 1 minute. Now, it is assumed that a horse is capable of doing 33,000 such units of work, *i. e.* that he is capable of raising 33,000 lbs. 1 foot high in a minute, or 1 lb. 33,000 feet high; and this is called a *horse's power*, and is the unit of work in reference in the unit of time commonly used in this country.

Universal chuck, a circular plate to screw on the mandril of a lathe, and hold a nut or any small piece of metal to be bored; in the plate are two or more radial slots, fitted by the jaws or pieces which project from the face of the chuck, moved by screws towards the centre and tightened upon the nut.

Unmoor, in navigation, to reduce a ship to the state of riding by a single anchor and cable.

Unship, to remove anything out of a ship.

Urn, an ancient utensil, used for a variety of purposes; sometimes as the receptacle of lots or for votes at the public election of magistrates; but its greatest and most frequent use was as a receptacle for the ashes of the dead after their bodies were burnt. These urns were sometimes kept in houses, and also put under tombstones, or within vaults or graves. Urns and similar vessels have been found in the burial places of the ancient Britons. In modern times, the urn is an utensil of domestic use.

V.

Vacuum, a vacuity or space unoccupied by matter; in pneumatics, the vacuum caused by an airpump, which is a degree of rarefaction sufficient to suspend the ordinary effects of the atmosphere.

Vacuum-pump, a pump connected to the boiler of a marine engine, for charging the boiler with water from the sea by discharging the air, causing the water to rise within the boiler, from the pressure of the atmosphere without; by this means much labour and time are saved, which would otherwise be expended in lifting the vats.

Vair, a term in heraldry, being a fur composed of four distinct colours; argent, gules, or, and sable.

Valve, in hydraulics, etc., a lid contrived to open one way, to admit a fluid into a tube, but which shuts when pressed from the other, to prevent its return. In anatomy, a kind of membrane which opens in certain vessels to admit the blood, and shuts to prevent its regress.

Valves, in blast machines, are essential in blast-conducting pipes; first, for shutting up the blast entirely; secondly, for diminishing and increasing it at pleasure. The first kind is needed where the blast is generated, for various purposes, by the same blast machine. The valves in use are, the sliding, the conical, and the trundle. The two first-named are but little employed. If well made, the latter kind of valve is very useful. At one end it has a handle, and, in many instances, a graded scale, which indicates the amount of air which passes through the valve, or, in other words, it shows the opening of the valve. At each tuyère or nozzle a valve is required, which serves either to shut off the blast entirely, or to regulate the passage of whatever amount is needed. At the nozzle-valve, a scale is very useful, partly for the purpose of adjusting the blast, and partly for that of fastening the handle of the valve, and keeping it in a certain position.

The laws which govern the construction of blast-pipes, valves, and tuyères, are summarily as follows: The interior of the blast conductors should be as smooth as possible, as an uneven surface causes great friction. The friction of the air is proportional to the length of the pipe, and to the density of the air which passes through it. It is proportional to the square of the speed of the air, and the reverse of the square of the diameter of the pipe. Obstructions caused by short bends in such pipes are inversely proportional to the angle of the bend, and are governed by the laws of hydrostatics. Sudden contractions and expansions of the pipe occasion a whirling disturbance in the current of the air—a loss of power, or, what is the same, of blast.

Valve, safety, a valve in a steam-engine, to obviate the danger of explosion, by allowing the steam to escape when the pressure is raised beyond a certain weight.

VAL VAPORIZATION. VAP

Valve-seat, the flat or conical surface upon which a valve rests.

Vandyke Brown, a pigment hardly less celebrated than the great painter whose name it bears, is a species of peat or bog-earth, of a fine deep semi-transparent brown colour. The pigment so much esteemed and used by Vandyke is said to have been brought from Cassel; and this seems to be justified by a comparison of Cassel earth with the browns of his pictures. The Vandyke browns in use at present appear to be terrene pigments of a similar kind, purified by grinding and washing over: they vary sometimes in hue, and in degrees of drying in oil, which they in general do tardily, owing to their bituminous nature, but are good browns of powerful body, and are durable both in water and oil.

Vane, or *Wind-vane*, in navigation, a thin slip of bunting; a string of feathers, etc., stuck up to windward, to show the direction of the wind.

Vanes. In Europe, the custom of placing vanes on church steeples is very old; and, as they were made in the figure of a cock, they have been thence denominated weathercocks.

Vanning, removing the impurities from tin ore.

Vaporization. The presence of moisture in the air is accounted for by a modification of the process of vaporization. Water evaporates, or is converted into steam (by steam we here mean the elastic vapour of water, which is always invisible; what is commonly called steam, but properly cloud, is liquid water in a finely divided or powdered state, wafted like dust by currents of air, or of steam properly so called) at all temperatures, until the whole space above it, whether containing air or not, is pervaded with watery vapour of a certain fixed density and elasticity, depending on the temperature, and connected therewith by certain laws. The elasticity or expansive tendency of a fluid is estimated by the number of pounds or ounces with which it presses on each square inch of surface that it touches; or by the number of inches of mercury that it will support, as on a barometer.

Steam can exist at any given temperature, and of such density as to have a certain fixed pressure, and no more; and (if there be water enough present) steam will be accumulated till it has this density; but no more can then be accumulated without raising the temperature: and if the temperature be lowered, a portion of the steam will immediately become water, so that (occupying in this state some thousands of times less space than before) it may leave room for the remaining vapour to expand, till its expansive force is reduced to that which the new temperature can support. The pressure of steam is therefore always the same at the same temperature. At 212° its elastic force is equal to that of the atmosphere, and it will support a column of mercury 30 inches high, which is the reason that boiling requires this temperature in the open air, when the barometer is at 30 inches; but rather less or more, when the barometer stands lower or higher. Above this temperature it becomes high-pressure steam, which at 220° will support nearly 33 inches of mercury; at 230°, nearly 42 inches, and so on. But the steam which is thrown off from the waters of the earth, from damp soil, from the foliage of plants, and even from ice and snow, has but a very small pressure. Steam at 32° will support only 0·200 of an inch of mercury; at 40°, 0·263 of an inch; at 50°, 0·375 of an inch; at 60°, 0·524, or rather more than half an inch of mercury; at 80°, it will support one inch, and so on. When the air contains as much vapour as can exist at the existing temperature, it is said to be saturated. If in this state it experience the smallest reduction of temperature, some of the vapour must immediately become liquid, assuming the form of cloud, fog, or rain. These effects depend on the cooling of the air below the temperature necessary to retain all its vapour. But when a solid body is cooled below this temperature (the air remaining above it), a different kind of deposition occurs, called dew, which does not fall in drops from the air, but grows, as it were, on the solid. Dr. Wells proved, by a most complete investigation of this subject, that instead of dew cooling bodies, as commonly supposed, it is their cooling which causes dew; and its formation even mitigates the cold, by the heat previously latent, which the steam gives out on condensing into water. The degree of heat at which dew begins to be formed is called the dew-point, and instruments called hygrometers have been invented to measure it. The difference between the temperature of the dew-point and the temperature of the atmosphere indicates the degree of dryness, which in this country seldom reaches 30°; that is, the temperature of the earth necessary to condense the vapour of the air is seldom 30° below the temperature of the air. In India it has been known to be 61° below it, and in Africa probably lower still.

If, while dew is forming, the earth continues to cool down until it reaches the freezing-point, hoar-frost is formed. The beautiful figures seen in winter on the inner surface of window panes, cooled by the external air, are produced by these cold surfaces condensing the moisture of the warmer air within.

Varry, a term in heraldry, denoting the mixture of argent and azure together.

Varry, cuppy, a term applied to a fur of cups.

Vat, a wooden tub, used to wash ores and mineral substances in; a working-tub of any kind.

Vault, in architecture, an arched roof, so contrived as that the several stones by their disposition shall support each other.

Veering, or *Wearing*, in navigation, the operation to which a ship, in changing her course from one board to the other, turns her stern to windward/ in opposition to tacking, wherein the bow is turned to the wind and the stern to leeward.

Vein, a course of metal in a mine: a rake vein is perpendicular or nearly so; a pipe vein, nearly horizontal.

Vein, in mining, to wash or cleanse a small portion of ore in a shoal.

Velocimeter, an apparatus for measuring the rate of speed of machinery. When the velocity is uniform, the instrument is merely a measurer of distance; but this is not the case with a variable velocity, which requires a much more elaborate contrivance for its estimation. Such a velocity-measurer was constructed by Breguet, of Paris, under the direction of M. Morin, the principle of which may be briefly explained as follows: A circular disc, covered with card or paper, is made to revolve with a *uniform* motion by means of clock-work, regulated by air-vanes: upon this disc, a revolving pencil, whose motion is caused by and corresponds with that of the body whose *variable* velocity is to be measured, describes a curved line; and from this curve, which results from a combination of the variable with the uniform motion, the velocity may be easily ascertained by processes and formulæ adapted to the purpose. One of these cards, with the curve traced on it by the piston of the Cornish steam-engine at Old Ford, is engraved in the 'Transactions of the British Association for the Advancement of Science.' This beautiful and ingenious contrivance, by which spaces described in the ten-thousandth part of a second may be easily discerned, is the invention of M. Poncelet, and was carried into execution by M. Morin.

The instrument, when put in order, was first tried at King's College, London, a variable motion being given by a small carriage made to descend an inclined plane. The correspondence of the velocity shown by the machine with that deduced by the known laws of dynamics, was such as to give great confidence in its accuracy. After a few minor alterations, suggested by frequent trials, it was removed to the East London Water-works, and attached to the Cornish engine at work there, from which several diagrams were taken; and the velocities calculated from these have been expressed in the form of geometrical curves, whose abscissae represent the spaces passed over by the piston of the engine, and whose ordinates indicate the corresponding velocities at the different points of the stroke.

Velocipede, a carriage which is capable of being propelled along a road by the muscular power of the rider acting upon treadles and levers which communicate with a cranked wheel axle.

Velocity, in dynamics, is the ratio of the quantity of linear extension that has been passed over in a certain portion of time; or it is the ratio of the time that has been employed in moving along a determinate extension.

When a man ascends vertically, his velocity is reduced to about one-half of his horizontal velocity, indicating that he acts against a double resistance; therefore, when a man ascending a ladder carries a load, the maximum effect will take place when his ascending velocity is about one-fourth of the velocity he can walk horizontally without a load.

A man of ordinary strength will not be able to walk, unloaded, at a quicker rate than 3½ miles an hour, if this exertion is to be continued for 10 hours every day. Indeed, those who examine the subject with a view to a fair average, will find this to be about the extreme velocity that can be continued, without injury, for any considerable time; therefore a man ought to move with half this velocity to produce a maximum effect; that is, at the rate of 1¾ mile an hour, which is about 2½ feet per second.

But this supposes the whole load to be the useful effect, whereas part of it must consist of the apparatus employed to carry it, or the friction of the intermediate machine, or other circumstances of a like nature. About one-fifth of the velocity may be considered equivalent, at an average, to the force lost in friction, etc., in all cases; in many it will exceed one-fifth. Hence the maximum of useful effect will take place when the velocity is 2 feet per second, or about 1½ furlongs an hour, continued for 10 hours each day.

Smeaton is said to have made numerous comparisons, from which he concluded that the mechanical power of a man is equivalent to 3750 lbs. moving at the velocity of one foot per minute; and taking this average to be near the true one, as there is reason to conclude it is, we have

$$\frac{3750}{2 \times 60} = 31 \cdot 25 \text{ lbs.}$$

Therefore, we make the average mechanical power of a man 31·25 lbs. moving at the velocity of 2 feet per second, when the useful effect is the greatest possible; or half a cubic foot of water raised two feet per second; a very convenient expression for hydrodynamical inquiries.

If a man ascend a vertical ladder, according to a preceding remark, the velocity which corresponds to the maximum of useful effect will be 1 foot per second, and the load double that which he carries horizontally; consequently the average of useful effect is 62·5 lbs. raised one foot per second.

Bricklayers' labourers in London ascend ladders with a load of about 80 lbs. besides the hod; sometimes at the rate of one foot per second, but more frequently about 9 inches per second.

Ascending stairs is more trying to the muscles of the legs than ascending a ladder; and therefore the useful effect is less, till a person has become accustomed to this kind of labour; and it is also to be observed that the space moved over is increased, unnecessarily, except where the horizontal distance is part of the path over which the load is to be moved.

The force of a horse is, at an average, about equal to that of six men, according to various estimates; and the rate of travelling about the same, perhaps rather less than that of a man, when his exertion is continued for 8 hours: consequently the velocity corresponding to the maximum effect will be about 2¼ feet per second. Whence, the average mechanical power of a horse may be estimated at 187½ lbs. moving with a velocity of 2½ feet per second, or 3 cubic feet of water raised 2½ feet per second; the day's work being 8 hours.

Velocity of motion. The following is a list of the velocities of moving bodies, extracted from Peschel's 'Elements of Physics,' etc.

	Feet per second.
Rivers	3–4
A very rapid stream	13
Wind (ordinary)	10
Storm	54
Hurricane	80–120
Sound (through air)	1100
Sound (through metal)	12,000
Air into a vacuum	1280
Ball from air-gun (air condensed 100 times)	697
Musket-ball	1280
Rifle-ball (at most)	1600
Cannon-ball (24-pounder)	2450
Earth's rotation (at equator)	1525
,, centre (in its orbit)	101,061

	Miles per hour.
Race-horse	60
Pigeon	20–30
Peregrine falcon	120
Ocean steamer	12
River steamers	22
Railway train	80
Sailing vessel	10
Malay proa	20

	Miles per second.
Light	200,000
Electricity	576,000

Velvet painting is the art of colouring on velvet with transparent liquid and other ready diluted colours, compounded and made up with various acids, alkalies, etc., according to their nature and qualities.

Venetian school. This school would have required no further illustration from any other pen had Signor Antonio Zanetti, in his work upon Venetian painting, included a more ample consideration of the artists of that State. Ridolfi and Boschini also furnish copious materials.

It is said that Antonello da Messina having been instructed in the secret of colouring in oils by Giovanni Van Eyck, in Flanders, *received a public salary,* and then he divulged the method of painting in oils to the Venetian professors; this appears from superscriptions attached to his pictures to have taken place about the year 1474.

The colours of these artists (those preceding Titian and Giorgione) are simple and natural, though not always in union, more especially with the ground, nor sufficiently broken by the chiaroscuro.

In seeking the cause of their superiority it is to be remarked that it was a common practice in Titian's time, to prepare with a chalk-surface the altar-pieces and pictures which were to be executed; and that white ground, favourable to every variety of tint the painter could lay upon it, equally favoured the production of a certain polish, floridity, and surprising transparency.

The harmony of colours was not better understood by any other artists, insomuch that the mode of assimilating and of contrasting them, may be considered as the second source of the delightful and lively, so predominant in their works, and more especially in those of Titian and his contemporaries.

Such skill was not merely confined to the fleshy parts, in whose colour the disciples of Titian have so far excelled every other school, it extended also to the drapery. For, indeed, there are no pieces of velvets, of stuffs, or of crapes, which they did not imitate to perfection.

Titian is universally considered the founder of the Venetian school of painting. Some of the principal masters of this school are—

Giorgione	b. 1477, d. 1511.
Sebastiano del Piombo	b. 1485, d. 1547.
Pordenone	b. 1484, d. 1540.
Titian	b. 1477, d. 1576.
Tintoretto	b. 1512, d. 1594.
(Jacopo da Ponte) Bassano	b. 1510, d. 1592.
Paul Veronese	b. 1528, d. 1581.
Tiepolo	b. 1693, d. 1769.

Venetian Red or *Scarlet Ochre.* True Venetian red is said to be a native ochre, but the colours sold under this name are prepared artificially from sulphate of iron, or its residuum in the manufacturing of acids. They are all of redder and deeper hues than light red, are very permanent, and have all the properties of good ochres. Prussian red, English red, and rouge de Mars, are other names for the same pigment.

Ventilation and warming of buildings is a twofold purpose that should enter into the constructive design of all edifices intended for the residence or occasional congregation of human beings. The necessity for this purpose arises from the fact that the breathing of air (as one of the functions of animal life) renders it unfit for re-inspiration, the lungs retaining the vital properties and emitting the remainder, which consists of ingredients detrimental to health, and even destructive of life itself. In order to keep an apartment in a healthy and pleasant condition, fresh air should be constantly supplied at a temperature from 60° to 65°, and the vitiated air should be as constantly removed; and all the varied schemes which have been propounded for ventilating buildings have this common purpose of constant supply and removal. The vitiated air, on being emitted from the mouth, has a temperature between 80° and 90°; and as the universal effect of heat, manifested in the increase of temperature of the supply, 60° or 65° to 80° or 90°, is to expand and enlighten, the vitiated air has a natural tendency to rise to the upper part of the room. To allow this action to proceed, it is evidently necessary that means for its escape to the top should be provided, and also that fresh air should be introduced at the lower portion of the apartment. The operation would, however, be nullified if the heated air, on emerging from the top of the room into a shaft or chimney intended to conduct it away, were met by a downward current of cold air; and it has therefore been deemed advisable to provide not only such a shaft or chimney, but also some means, by stoves or other apparatus, of artificially heating the air in the shaft and thus assisting the escape of the foul air. And further, in order to secure the constant accession of fresh air and give sufficient impulse to it to overcome any tendency that might be created to oppose its introduction by a retrograde movement of the atmosphere of the building, means have been adopted of forcing this fresh air in with fans or bellows. But these two sets of apparatus have been seldom combined. Those who have adopted the shaft have usually contemned the fan, trusting to the sucking action of the former to draw off all the vitiated air, and concluding that fresh air must enter as rapidly to fill its place; and, on the other hand, the adopters of the fan decry the addition of the heating apparatus in the shaft, and contend that its only effect is to draw down foul air for its own supply, and to impede the upward current created by this fan. This effect should be obviated in a well-acting apparatus, which would then doubtless assist the fan in promoting the continual passage of pure air throughout the building. The objection which has been entertained against the use of the shaft without the fan, or some other adequate forcing apparatus, is well-founded on the well-known elasticity of the atmosphere, by which it is susceptible of rarefaction to a considerable extent. The heated shaft consequently acts as a pump in sucking the warmed air upwards, and if no force is in action from below to drive this air upward by the pressure of fresh air entering the apartments, the atmosphere becomes rarefied to a degree which is both unpleasant and prejudicial to sentient existence. It is therefore essential that the two processes of exhaustion and supply shall proceed simultaneously, and be so regulated that no rarefaction shall be suffered in the air to be breathed. The purpose of warming the air in winter, and of cooling it in summer, that is, more properly, of attemperating it, should be sought, and may be attained conjointly with that of ventilation; and one of the best arrangements yet carried out for these combined objects is presented in the system adopted at the Reform Club-house in London. The supplying apparatus there employed consists of a large fan which revolves rapidly in a cylindrical case, and is adapted to throw 11,000 cubic feet of air per minute into a spacious subterranean tunnel under the basement story of the building. This fan is driven by a steam-engine of 5-horse power, working expansively. It is placed in a vault in front of the building, and as it burns anthracite coal and cinders from the house flues, is not productive of any nuisance or offensive smoke. The steam of condensation supplies three chests, constructed of cast-iron, with the heat requisite for warming the building. Each of these chests is a cube in form, and measures 3 feet externally, and is internally divided into seven parallel cases, each 3 inches wide, and separated by alternate parallel spaces of similar width, for the passage of the air as it is impelled by the fan. By this economical arrangement, which thus makes good use of the steam of condensation, 2 cwt. of fuel is sufficient for working the engine during twelve hours, the engine being besides available for pumping water for the purposes of the establishment, and raising coals to the several apartments on the upper stories. The air in passing through the cells between the steam cases is heated to a genial temperature of from 75° to 85°, and thence enters a chamber of brickwork in the basement, from which it is admitted into several distinct flues, regulated by dialled valves or registers, and thus conducted in any required quantities to the several apartments of the building. A stove is placed in the top story, and is formed as a rectangular chest of cast-iron, contracted above into a round pipe, which discharges the burnt air and smoke into a series of horizontal cast-iron pipes, about 4 inches in diameter, which traverse the room beneath the ceiling and terminate in a brick chimney. One advantage of such an apparatus as is here described would be that of introducing cool air during sultry weather, for which purpose it might be readily adapted.

Ventilator, a machine made to turn with the wind, and placed in a wall or roof, in order to throw a due quantity of fresh air into a close apartment.

Verdoy, a term in heraldry, applied when a border is charged with leaves, fruits, and flowers, and like vegetables.

Verge, a rod, wand, or serjeant's mace; also the compass about the king's court that bounds the jurisdiction of the lord steward of the king's household, and of the coroner of the king's house, and is accounted 12 miles' compass; also a rod whereby one is admitted tenant, holding it in his hand and swearing fealty to the lord of the manor, and for that cause called tenant by the verge.

Verge, a small ornamental shaft in Gothic architecture.

Vermiculated, chequered; continuous; embroidered with several colours.

Vermile, a cloth or napkin on which the face of Christ is depicted, derived from the incident related of St. Veronica.

Vermilion, a sulphuret of mercury, which, previous to its being levigated, is called cinnabar. It is an ancient pigment, and is found in a native state, and produced artificially. Vermilion probably obtained its name from resemblance to or admixture with the beautiful though fugitive colours obtained from the vermes, or insects which yield carmine.

Vernier, a graduated movable index, used for measuring minutely the parts of the space between the equidistant divisions of a graduated scale.

Versed sine of an arc, in geometry, the position of the diameter intercepted between the sine and the commencement of the arc.

Vert, in heraldry, a green colour; in the ancient forest laws, everything that grows and bears a green leaf within the forest that may cover and hide a deer.

Vestiary, a wardrobe, or place to lay clothes or apparel in.

Vestibule, in architecture, the porch or the first entrance of a house.

Vestibulum, part of the andrositis of a Greek house, similar, probably, to the prostas of the first peristyle or court.

Vestment, a set of hangings for the service of an altar; and also a suit of robes for a priest.

Via (Latin), by way of; in the time of the Romans, a road or a right of road. Two shallow trenches were commonly dug parallel to each other, marking the breadth of the proposed road: this in the great lines, such as the Via Appia, the Via Flaminia, the Via Valeria, etc., is found to have been from 13 to 15 feet, on the Via Tusculana 11; while those of less importance, from not being great thoroughfares, such as the via which leads up to the temple of Jupiter Latialis, on the summit of the Alban Mount, and which is to the present time singularly perfect, seems to have been 8 feet wide.

Viaduct, a term applied to extended constructions of arches or other artificial works to support a roadway, and thus distinguished from *aqueducts*, which are similar constructions to support waterways. This term has become much more

VIADUCT.

familiar within the present century, in consequence of the great number of vast structures so designated which have been erected in various parts of Great Britain for the purpose of carrying railways over valleys and districts of low level; but the general name of viaduct is now recognized as applicable to all elevated roadways for which artificial constructions of timber, iron, bricks, or stonework are established; and accordingly among the principal railway-works are to be enumerated viaducts of all these materials. The vast dimensions of some of these structures are not more striking to the casual observer, than their great strength, as particularly adapted to railway traffic, is apparent upon a careful study of their construction. The several members of a viaduct are the same as those of a bridge; indeed the former structure may be considered as an extended bridge, frequently resorted to in situations where no water is to be crossed. The necessity which is imperative in the construction of railways for preserving a horizontal level for the roadway, or at least departing from this level within very restricted limits, imposes the raising of the railway surface in many places, and to a considerable extent above the natural level. Various considerations arise as to the preferable mode of effecting this raising, whether by solid embankments of earthwork or by an open or arched structure of other materials. Embankments of earthwork are often liable to subsidence from want of cohesion in the materials, or the effect of long-continued rains; and if free from actual danger arising from these liabilities, they are always sources of much constant expense in making up the surface to the required level, to compensate for the continual depression caused by the passage of heavy loads over them. As a question of economy, therefore, viaducts are often to be preferred, since their repairs involve less expense than those of embankments. It must also be considered that the latter, owing to their necessary extension of base, cover a much wider portion of ground than viaducts, and at the same time cover it in a more absolute and objectionable manner. A solid embankment, like a black line across a picture, spoils a beautiful landscape, and often precludes all view beyond it from sites which otherwise would command an extended range. If the sub-formation of the valley be of a very loose and boggy nature, embankments are scarcely admissible, nor, if the height to be raised exceeds 30 or 40 feet, can they be entertained. Indeed, in the majority of cases, valleys, whether having rivers of magnitude or not, are more economically crossed upon viaducts than embankments.

Whatever the materials of the structure or its finished design, the same points are to be observed in the construction; and the first of these is the strength and durability of the foundations. A substantial and permanent character should always be secured for these, even if the superstructure is intended to aim at cheapness rather than solidity. It is often requisite that piers and abutments be constructed upon piling,—a form of foundation adapted, if thoroughly executed, to afford the most secure basis; but if done carelessly and insufficiently, liable to involve the most destructive failures. The citation of a few of the most extended works of this class, of modern date, will best show the details of the present approved kinds of construction.

Of timber viaducts, two fine examples of similar construction are presented on the line of the Newcastle, North Shields, and Tynemouth Railway. One of these works, which crosses the Ouse bourn, besides a public roadway, a mill race, and the adjacent valley, consists of five spans or arches of timber-work, and four end arches of masonry. Of the former arches, three are 116 feet wide in the clear, and two 114 feet. Two of the end arches are 43 feet span, and the other two 36 feet. The height of the rails above the bed of the bourn is 108 feet. The width of the structure allows 26 feet for a double line of rails, and 5 feet for a footway. The total length of the viaduct is 918 feet, and the two middle piers are erected upon piles, from 21 to 27 feet in length. All the piers are of masonry, and tapered upwards, the principal being 21 feet wide above the footings, and 15 feet at the springing of the arches. The piers are continued upwards, of reduced dimensions, to the level of the roadway, the whole of the five main arches, spandrilling, and superstructure, being formed of timber. The radius of these arches is 68 feet, and their rise or versed sine about 33 feet. The ribs forming the arches are composed of planks of Kyanized Dantzic deal, the lengths of which vary from 20 to 46 feet, by 11 inches wide, and 3 inches thick. These planks are so arranged, that the first course of the rib is two whole deals in width, the next is one whole and two half deals, the joints being crossed longitudinally, as well as in the depth. The thickness of each rib is made up of fourteen deals, which are bent over a centre to the required form, and fixed together with oak trenails, 1¼ inch in diameter, placed 4 feet apart, and each trenail perforating three of the deals. Between the joints a layer of strong brown paper is placed, previously dipped in boiling tar. The spandrils are formed of trussed framing; and the platform of the roadway, which is composed of 3-inch planking, is supported upon transverse beams laid 4 feet apart. The platform is covered with a composition of boiling tar and lime, mixed with gravel in applying it, thus forming a coating impervious to water.

There are several other modes of constructing timber viaducts, without introducing the arches, composed of planks curved into proper form, and which, being laid together like leaves, as just described, have obtained for this kind of construction the name of the 'laminated bridge.' In other forms of timber viaducts, the requisite strength is obtained by trussing, the peculiar description and complication of which depends, of course, mainly on the extent of the span or width of each lay of which the entire structure consists. Where a great width of clear opening is required, a system of diagonal bracing offers peculiar advantages, being susceptible of any desired strength and rigidity. A viaduct of great extent, built upon this principle, is on the line of the Richmond and Petersburg Railway, North America. The length of this structure is 2,900 feet, and the trusses are supported upon eighteen granite piers, the distances between which vary from 130 to 153 feet. They are founded on the granite rock, and are 40 feet high above the water. The depth of the truss frames (which are horizontal on top and bottom) is 20 feet. Another work of the same kind crosses the Susquehannah, and is 2,200 feet in length, divided into spans of 220 feet each.

Of viaducts formed of brickwork and masonry, that named the 'Avon viaduct,' on the line of the North-western Railway, may be mentioned. This consists of nine semi-elliptical arches, 24 feet in span, and 7 feet 6 inches rise, and three semicircular arches at each end of 10 feet span. This viaduct is entirely faced with stone, the interior of the work being of brick. The end arches have brick invert between the piers above the foundations, which are laid uniformly in a solid bed beneath these arches, with steps according to the nature of the substratum. An invert of brickwork is built to the three middle arches, forming an artificial channel for the river, and faced at each end with a row of sheet piling, driven through the loam into a bed of strong gravel beneath. All the foundations which do not reach the gravel are laid upon beds of concrete, and a layer of the same material covers the extrados of the arches, and forms a level bed for the gravel in which the sleepers of the railway are bedded. Many similar works of much more extended dimensions have been erected for railway communication. One of these, of peculiarly light appearance, is known as the 'Victoria Bridge,' and built over the valley of the river Wear, on the line of the Durham Junction Railway. This work consists of two main arches, one 160 feet span, the other 144 feet, two others, each 100 feet span, and six end arches of 20 feet span. The height of the parapet above the high-water level at spring tides is 125 feet, and all the arches are semicircular. The central pier is 23 feet 9 inches in width, and 69 feet high from bottom of footings to springing of arches. The two contiguous piers are 21 feet wide, one 50 feet, the other 52 feet high. The height of the parapet above the springing line of the two main arches is 78 feet. A viaduct, recently constructed over the Moine, at Clisson, near Nantes, in Brittany, is worth notice, for a peculiarity in its construction, which, although not strictly new, is to be found in very few examples. This peculiarity is, that the piers are pierced with a pointed arch, which intersects the cylindrical soffit of the main arches in the direction of the length of the viaduct, so that the roadway is supported upon a groined vault, which, seen from the abutments, has the appearance of the aisle of a Gothic cathedral. This viaduct consists of fifteen arches, and is 348 feet in length. The abutments rest upon a granite foundation, the structure itself being constructed of a fine white granite, and the stones of large size. The foundations are 6 feet below the bed of the river, the height from which to the springing line of the arches being 33 feet, and the total height from the foundation to the top of the parapet 61 feet.

Vibration, the regular reciprocating motion of a body, as a pendulum, musical chord, etc.

Vice, a tool for holding a piece of metal, while operating upon it, by placing it between two jaws or nippers, and screwing them towards each other.

Vice-bench, the bench to which a vice is fixed.

Villa, among the Romans, a farm or country house.

Villa rustica, a tasteful country residence. See Parker's work, in 4to.

Villa urbana, a residence so called by the Romans, because its interior arrangements corresponded principally with those of a town house.

Villas of the ancients. Varro Columella says, "An estate should be in a wholesome climate and fruitful country; one part champaign, and the other hilly, with easy descents either to the east or south; some of the lands cultivated, others wild and woody; not far from the sea or a navigable river, for the easier exportation of the produce of the farm, and the importation of necessaries. The champaign lying below the house should be disposed into grounds for pasture and tillage, osiers and reeds; some of the hills should be naked and without trees, that they may serve best only for corn, which grows in a soil moderately dry and rich, better than in steep grounds; wherefore the upper corn-fields should have as little declivity as possible, and ought to resemble those in the plain: from thence, the other hills should be laid out into olive grounds and vineyards, and produce trees necessary to make props for those fruits, and, if occasion should require building, to afford timber and stone, and also pasture for cattle. Moreover, constant rivulets of water should descend from thence upon the meadows, gardens, and osier-grounds, and also serve for the convenience of the cattle that graze in the fields and thickets, but such a situation is not easily to be met with; that which enjoys most of these advantages is certainly most valuable; that which has them in a moderate degree, is not despicable. The natural good qualities of a situation mentioned by Palladio are, a salutary air, plenty of wholesome water, a fruitful soil, and a commodious place: we may hence conclude that those places are healthy that are not located in deep valleys, or subject to thick clouds, where the inhabitants are of a fresh complexion, have clear heads, good sight, quick hearing, and a free distinct speech; for by these things is the goodness of the air distinguished; and the contrary appearance proclaims that a climate is to be noxious. The unwholesomeness of water may be thus discovered: in the first place, it must not be conveyed from the ditches or fens, or rise from minerals, but be very transparent, not tainted either in taste or smell, without settlement, in winter warm, in summer cold; but because nature often conceals a more lurking mischief, in these outward appearances, we may judge whether water is good by the health of the inhabitants; if their cheeks are clear, their heads sound, and little or no decay in their lungs and breasts; for generally where the distempers in the upper part of the body are transmitted down to the lower, as from the head to the lungs or stomach, there the air is infectious: besides, if the belly, bowels, sides, or veins, are not afflicted with aches or tumours, and there is no ulcer in the bladder; if these or the like are apparently in the major part of the inhabitants, there is no cause to suspect the unwholesomeness of the air and water. The fatal consequences proceeding from bad air, Varro tells us, are in some measure to be alleviated, if not prevented, by the skill of the architect. His words are: That land which is most wholesome is most profitable, because there is a certain crop; whereas, on the contrary, in an unhealthy country, notwithstanding the ground is fertile, yet sickness will not allow the husbandman to reap the fruits of his labour; for where one exposes his life to certain dangers, for uncertain advantages, not only the crop, but the life of the inhabitant, is precarious; wherefore, if it is not wholesome, the tillage is nothing else but the hazard of the owner's life and his family: but this inconvenience is remedied by knowledge, for health, which proceeds from the air and soil, is not in our disposal, but under the guidance of nature; yet, nevertheless, it is as much in our power to make that burden easy by our own care; for, if upon account of the land or water, or some unsavoury smell, which makes an irruption in some part of it, the farm is made unwholesome, or upon account of the climate, or a bad wind that blows, the ground is heated, these inconveniences may be remedied by the skill and expense of the owner, which makes it of the last concernment where the villas are placed, how large they are, and to what quarters their porticoes, gates, and windows are turned. Did not Hippocrates the physician, in the time of a great plague, preserve not only his own farm, but many towns, by his skill? When Varro and his army and his fleet lay at Corcyra, and every house was filled with sick persons and dead bodies, by his care in making new windows to the north-east, and obstructing the infection by altering the position of the doors, he preserved his companions and family in good health. As a house should be built in a wholesome country, so it should be in the most wholesome part of a country; for an open air and at the same time infected, causes many distempers."

Villas (Roman). The term villa was applied to a cluster of buildings in the country for the accommodation of the family of a wealthy Roman citizen. Very extensive villas were divided into three parts, the Urbana, the Rustica, and the Fructuaria. The first contained the eating-room, bed-chambers, baths, covered porticoes, walks, and terraces. The villa rustica was the division for the servants, stables, etc.; and the fructuaria for wine, oil, and the produce of the farm. Although the Roman villas were the boast and delight of poets and philosophers whose works have fortunately reached us, yet no description has been conveyed of their external architecture. From the magnificent style of public buildings at Rome, moderns were led to suppose that the villa architecture bore some analogy in splendour of outward appearance; but from inspection of their remains, and from the late disinterment of one on the outside of the walls of Pompeii, little doubt now remains on the subject. It is true that the extensive remains of Adrian's villa, and that of Mæcenas, covered ground equal almost to a small town, but no regular plan of architectural elevation can be traced with all the ingenuity of even a Roman antiquary. The Pompeian is certainly the most complete example of an ordinary-sized Roman villa: situated on a sloping bank, the front entrance opened, as it were, into the first floor, below which, on the garden side, into which the house looks (for the door is the only aperture on the road side), was a ground floor, with extensive arcades and open rooms, all facing the garden; and above were the principal rooms. It was spacious, and near the entrance was a bath with all the necessary appendages; in the rear the best rooms opened upon a terrace, running the whole width of the house, and overlooking a garden about 30 yards square, surrounded by a covered walk or portico continued under the terrace. The lower apartments under the arcade were paved with mosaic, coved and beautifully painted. One of the rooms had large glazed bow windows; the glass was thick, of a green colour, and set in lead like a modern casement. The walls and ceilings of the villa were ornamented with paintings of elegant design, all of which had relation to the uses of the respective apartments. In the middle of the garden was a reservoir of water, surrounded by columns. The cellars extended under the whole of the house and the arcades.

Pliny tells us that the size of the villa urbana, and its number of parts, were determined by the pleasure or quality of the master, but those parts belonging to agriculture, by the bulk of the farm and the number of cattle. The servants that in most great men's houses were more immediately for the master's use, and may be said to have belonged to the villa urbana, were the *atrienses*, which included all those we call livery servants, and those belonging to the bed-chamber; and the *topiarii*, which were

VILLAS, ITALIAN.

gardeners belonging to the pleasure-garden; with comedians, musicians, and the notaries or secretaries. The principal person over the other parts of the villa was the procurator or bailiff; then the *villicus*, or husbandman, who had under his care the tillage of the land, and the disposal of the produce of the earth about the villa; next was the *villica*, or house-keeper, to whose care everything within doors belonged, and who had immediately under her command the women servants that were employed in those affairs, but particularly those belonging to the feeding and clothing of the household. The master of the cattle may take the next place, and under his command were all the herdsmen, shepherds, goatherds, swineherds, and grooms. The care of all those fowls that were within the bounds of the villa was committed to the poulterer. In great villas it was thought necessary to keep within the family useful mechanics, as smiths, carpenters, etc. The cattle within the villa were horses and mules, etc.; and to make provision for the several persons and animals, and also for corn and the necessary offices of the house, was the architect's care; and the disposition of each part was governed by rules that may be collected from Cato, Vitruvius, Varro, Columella, and Palladius.

Of the Greek villas, no description has been transmitted to us; In villa gardening, however, considerable progress at that time was made, borrowed probably from Asia Minor: myrtles and roses adorned them; the box and lime tree were planted for topary works; and Theophrastus tells us, that flowers and fruits were cultivated in the winter; and the violet more particularly was in profusion in the market of Athens while snow was on the ground.

Villas (Italian). The description of an Italian villa built in the time of Michael Angelo, Raphael, Julio Romano, Domenichino, Paul Veronese, and Pietro da Cortona, deserves the notice of architects. "The palace of Caprarola is situated on the summit of Mount Camino, near Viterbo: below is the village of the same name, of which the principal street runs in a direct line down the descent from the front of the building, but with a sufficient space between them. A double stair, partly direct, partly curved, with terraced landing-places decorated with balustrades, leads to the palace. Entrances under the terraces of the stairs conduct to the underground parts of the building. The form of the palace is a pentagon flanked by five bastions, surrounded by a sunk area. Hence there is a mixture of civil and military architecture that has a good effect. The palace is built in two orders of architecture; the one, Ionic, with semicircular-headed windows; the upper Corinthian, comprehending both the first floor and the mezzanine above. Within the pentagonal figure is included a circle, comprehending the court, the porticoes, the offices, and stairs. The decorations of the whole and the parts are executed with much skill. Although the entire edifice is not great, yet the parts are on a great scale, apparently."

Virtuoso, a man skilled in antique or natural curiosities, studious of painting, statuary, or architecture.

Vis absoluta, absolute force.

Vise, a spiral staircase, the steps of which wind round a perpendicular shaft or pillar, called the newel.

Vis inertiæ, the propensity of nature to remain in its actual condition, whether of motion or rest, and to resist change.

Vis insita, the power or innate force essentially residing in any body, and by which it endeavours to preserve its present state, whatever that be.

Viscount, in law, signifies as much as

VIS   VOLUTE.   WAL.

sheriff; in heraldry, it signifies a degree of nobility next to an earl.

Vis viva (work). The vis viva of a body is its mass multiplied by the square of its velocity: work, or dynamical effect, supposes a body moved, and a resistance overcome; and either of these, without the other, is insufficient to constitute work. The work produced by a pressure moving a body through a certain space is defined to be the product arising from multiplying the pressure by the space through which this pressure acts.

Vitreous, glassy; consisting of or resembling glass.

Vitrification, the act of changing into glass.

Vitriol, oil of, sulphuric acid.

Vitruvian Scroll, a peculiar pattern, consisting of convolved undulations, used in classical architecture.

Viz. to wit, that is; a contraction of *videlicet*.

Voider, in heraldry, a gentlewoman's armory, consisting of an arch line, moderately bowing from the corner of the chief toward the nombril or centre of an escutcheon.

Voiding, a term in heraldry, signifying exemption of some part of the inward substance of things voidable, by reason whereof the field is transparent through the charge.

Volant, in heraldry. When a bird is drawn flying, or having the wings spread out, it is said to be volant.

Volute. The characteristic ornaments and indicial marks of the Ionic capital formed by circumvolving spiral mouldings are termed volutes. The small circle in which the spiral or springs terminate is called the eye of the volute. The introduction of volutes is said by Vitruvius to have arisen from an imitation of the mode in which women were formerly accustomed to ornament their hair; but they are thought, with greater probability, to have represented the horns of the Ammonian Jupiter.

Voussoirs, in architecture, vaultstones, or those that immediately form the arch of a bridge, vault, etc., and are always cut more or less in the shape of a truncated pyramid.

Vugh, in mining, a cavity.

W.

WAGGONS, vehicles for the conveyance of merchandise, etc., varying in form according to their use, and dating in their origin from the remotest antiquity: "Joseph gave them waggons, according to the commandment of Pharaoh, and gave them provision for the way."

Waggon-boiler, a low-pressure boiler, having the form of a waggon, with arched top and incurvated sides.

Wainscot, a name given to boards employed to line the internal walls of an apartment, so called from foreign species of oak named wainscot being first used for such a purpose. Wainscoting, as it is called, both of Flemish and English oak, was commonly used for interior linings in Tudor, Elizabethan, and Stuart times.

Waist, in a ship, the uppermost part of the top-side.

Wake, in navigation, denotes the print or track of a ship on the surface of the waters. Two distinct objects seen at sea are said to be in the wake of each other when the view of the furthest is interrupted by the nearest.

Wales, in ship-building, are an assemblage of strong planks extending along a ship's side, serving to reinforce the decks and form the curves of the vessel.

Wall-plate, a piece of timber placed along the top of a wall, to receive the ends of the roof timbers, or so placed on a wall as to receive the joists of a floor.

Walnut wood. The royal or common walnut is a native of Persia

| WAR | WATER. | WAT |

and the north of China: it was formerly much used in England before the introduction of mahogany. The heart wood is of a greyish brown, with black-brown pores, and often much veined with darker shades of the same colour. Some of the handsome veneers are now used for furniture, frames of machines, gun-stocks, etc.

Wardrobe, a place where the garments of kings or great persons used to be kept; and he that keeps the inventory of all things belonging to the king's wardrobe is called Clerk of the King's Wardrobe.

Wards, and *Liveries*, a certain court erected in the time of Henry VIII.

Warp, in navigation, to change the situation of a ship in harbour, etc., by means of ropes or warps attached to buoys, posts, rings, trees, etc.

Washing, in painting, to lay a colour, such as Indian ink or bistre, over a pencil or crayon drawing, to render it more natural, and add to the shadow of prominences, apertures, etc.

Wassail, a term which is said to have had its origin at the meeting of Vortigern and Rowena, the daughter of Hengist. Geoffrey of Monmouth states, that the lady knelt before the king, and presenting him with a cup of wine said, 'Waes-hæl,' which in Saxon means 'Health be to you.' Vortigern, as he was instructed, replied, 'Drinc-hæl,' i.e. 'drink the health;' Rowena drank, upon which Vortigern took the cup and pledged her. Hence the term and custom.

Waste steam-pipe, in steam-engines, the pipe leading from the safety valve to the atmosphere.

Waste water-pipe, in steam engines, the pipe for carrying off the surplus water from the hot well.

Water is the most abundant and important fluid in nature; it is proved to be composed, by weight, of 8 parts of oxygen and 1 part of hydrogen, and is resolvable into both these gases by voltaic action, and by intensely ignited platinum: other heated metals combine with its oxygen, and liberate the other gas. When hydrogen and oxygen are mixed in the proportion given, and ignited, they unite with explosion, and water alone is produced. The purest water in nature is that which descends from the atmosphere; that of springs, rivers, and the sea being more or less charged with mineral matter. When the foreign substance is not volatile, the water is easily separable by distillation in the form of a pure vapour or steam, while the fixed substance remains. In nature, the solar heat produces this effect on a vast scale, evaporating enormous quantities of water into the atmosphere, whence, by cooling to various degrees, it falls again in the form of rain, hail, or snow; this, in its passage through different strata towards its lowest level, dissolves any soluble matters which it may encounter, of which salt is the most conspicuous, conveying them ultimately into the ocean. This process, operating for ages, is fully sufficient to account for the prevalence of so soluble a mineral as common salt in sea-water, and the comparative purity of that of rivers.

When water runs through beds of chalk or selenite, it acquires both an acid and alkaline quality in a small degree. The acid is discovered by a few drops of solution of oil of tartar: this alkali will seize the acid, and descend with it in a cloud to the bottom of the glass, where, if permitted to stand a sufficient period, it will concrete into a neutral salt. The alkaline part is discoverable by a few drops of the solution of oxalic acid. This acid has so strong an affinity to calcareous earth, that the smallest quantity in water is detected by it. There are numerous tests which discover acid and alkali in water;

as the syrup of violets, tincture of turnsole, ash-bark, logwood, etc. Strictly, philosophically speaking, sea-water is not salt, because if a given quantity is put into a glass retort, by sand heat from material fire it will pass over perfectly fresh, and the marine salt it contained will be left behind. Snow and rain water, when collected at a distance from smoky towns or cities, if collected and kept in a stagnated state, go repeatedly into a state of fermentation, and sometimes become putrid, by the extraneous matters they receive in passing through the lower atmosphere, previous to their reaching the earth. If the specific gravity of water is considered at 1000 ounces the cubic foot, common air will be $1\frac{2}{3}$, fine gold will be $\frac{1}{19640}$, and pure platina $\frac{1}{23000}$; or if a datum is taken of 1 for water, gold will be 20, and refined platinum 22. Water is incompressible, as experiment proves. It has been put into a gold globe, and great power applied in vain to press it into a smaller compass; it passed off by oozing or sweating through the pores of gold. It will rise in some cases above its own level. In a small degree, by capillary attraction. If a piece of dry loaf-sugar or sponge is put into a shallow vessel of water, and have part of it unimmerged, the fluid will be seen to ascend above its level. Water will also ascend to the height of 32 or 33 feet above its level in a vacuum, as in pumps, by the pressure of the atmosphere, which varies more or less according to its density, that is, calculating on the pressure of the atmosphere, at the height of 15 miles. The pressure of water on the base of the vessel in which it is contained is as the base and perpendicular altitude, whatever be the figure of the vessel that contains it. A body immersed in water loses as much weight as an equal bulk of the water weighs, and the water gains the same weight. Thus, if the body be of equal density with the water, it loses all its weight, and so requires no force but the water to sustain it: if it be heavier, its weight in the water will be only the difference between its own weight and the weight of the same bulk of water, and it requires a force to sustain it just equal to that difference; but if it be lighter, it requires a force equal to the same difference of weight to keep it from rising up in the fluid.

Water of great rivers may certainly be deemed the most pure and wholesome for all culinary and domestic concerns, independent of its superior fertilizing powers when used for the purpose of agriculture or the growth of plants; and when thrown into reservoirs, and cleared of its sediment, it becomes clear and equally transparent with the brightest water proceeding from the hardest rock; for, previous to its being thus deposited, while swiftly gliding within its banks, it deposits large portions of its bituminous, calcareous, argillaceous, and chalybeate qualities.

Water is a conductor of atmospheric air, as well as sound. In Ralph Dodd's 'Civil Engineer' an accident is mentioned, by which one of his workmen was buried, by the falling of 40 feet of a shaft, the bottom of which approached to a sand highly charged with water. He remained from Friday evening till Tuesday morning. The workmen were this considerable time before they came to him, conversing together and excavating over his head, which considerably increased his hope of being released from his horrid captivity; for he became aware of their endeavours for his release as soon as the workmen had entered the sandy stratum, through which the water filtered downward,—a strong evidence of its conveying sound,

WATER-COLOUR PAINTING.

as well as atmospheric air, or, doubtless, he could not have existed.

Day-springs, either lying near the surface of the earth, or finding fresh passages thither, break forth into open air on their own account; while those of a deeper nature are sunk down so low as to require hydraulic machinery to bring them up again. Next, they are called top-springs, inasmuch as they appear either above the rock which severs the soil from the mine, or underneath it. Top-springs differ from deep or other springs, in that they stagnate between the superficies of the earth and the surface of the parts confining them, till they are opened by the miner; and those springs that can be let off by drifts, headings, soughs, and trenches, are distinguished from those from a great depth, the draining of which by such means is altogether impracticable or absolutely impossible. In the search after the original source of those currents of water which issue out of the earth, and are commonly called day-springs, the first consideration that arises is, that their natural course, as consisting in motion, is merely local, and caused by the propension of their own weight, still drawing them downward, towards the centre of the earth; their course must always be upon a constant descent from a higher situation to a lower, and so must proceed originally from rain, distilled from the clouds. And if it happen, that at their emersion out of the earth, their spring rises upwards, it is caused by the curvity of their passage, that (siphon-like) points the way; while the preponderance of the water contained in its other arm, descending from a greater height, forces it to rise contrary to its natural inclination.

The specific gravity of rain-water is 1000; weight of a cubic foot 62¼ lbs.; weight of a column, one inch square and a foot in height, 0·434 lbs.; of an ale gallon 10·2 lbs.: expands 1/11 of its bulk in freezing, and 1/1111 for every degree of heat; boils at 212° under the ordinary pressure of the atmosphere: maximum density 39°·38 of Fahr. The specific gravity of sea-water is 11·0271.

Water-colour painting is the art of making a picture with colours ground up with various kinds of aqueous gums or sizes, then called transparent colours. These drawings are executed on various kinds of paper, and are generally termed tinted drawings. The following are the most permanent colours, and therefore most valuable to the water-colour painter: *blues*—ultramarine, French ultramarine, cobalt, indigo, and smalt: *reds*—Indian red, light red, Venetian red, scarlet, vermilion, carmine, pink madder, rose madder, purple lake, and red orpiment: *yellows*—cadmium yellow, gamboge, yellow ochre, Indian yellow, Mars yellow, lemon yellow, Roman ochre, brown ochre, Mars orange, raw sienna, Italian pink, gallstone, and king's yellow: *purples*—purple madder, Indian purple, and burnt carmine: *browns*—burnt sienna, brown pink, burnt umber, Vandyke brown, sepia, Mars brown, Cologne earth, bistre, and madder brown: *greens*—emerald green, olive green, and green oxide of chromium: *blacks*—ivory black, blue black, neutral tint, and British ink: *whites*—oxide of zinc or Chinese white, and sulphate of barytes or constant white.

Water-crane, an apparatus for supplying water from an elevated tank to the tender of a locomotive engine.

Watering the streets of Paris (the contract for). The contractor for this service receives 105,000 francs per annum, or £4200 sterling. It lasts from March 15th to October 15th.

WATER SUPPLY.

He is bound to hold at the disposal of the engineers who are charged with the direction of the roads, twenty-five carts during the first month of the season; during the second, the number is fixed at fifty-five; during the remainder at ninety, with fifteen others in reserve. These carts can only be used for the service of the town; and they are repainted every year. They contain 1 mètre cube, or 1 ton each, and are drawn by one horse. They have a double discharge hose, at the front and at the back. At half-play they water 1000 mètres superficial. At full play they water 700 mètres superficial. In the first case, they are emptied in 10 minutes; in the second, in 6 minutes. Each cart costs 800 francs, or £32; of which 200 francs, or £8, are for the machinery necessary for the distribution of the water.

The Avenue de Neuilly in the Champs Elysées forms a special service, on account of the immense number of carriages which traverse it. The total surface is 32,000 mètres superficial, or nearly 8 acres English (7·976 a). The cost per day in the summer months is as follows:—

2 water-carts, horse and driver included, each at 11·10 f. = . . .	22·20
84·00^m cube water (a mètre cube = 1 ton) at 0·137 f. = . . .	11·50
Turncock (portion of his time)	2·00
Total	35·70

or 0·001116 f. per mètre superficial.

It has been found that the streets of Paris require to be watered 135 days on the average; the numbers are between 107 in the wettest season, and 147 in the driest. On the above average of 135, 100 days require a double watering. The quantity consumed is about 1 litre (1·760773 pints English) per mètre superficial; 1¼ litre, when the roads are so very dry as to require a more abundant watering; and 1·60 litre (or 2·82 pints English) in the Avenue de Neuilly. The water-columns are spaced so as to avoid any useless movements of the carts; in fact, in such a manner as to allow of their being emptied between one column and the other. The usual distance is 500 mètres (about 550 yards).

Water-sail, in navigation, a small sail spread occasionally under the lower studding-sail or driving-boom, during a fair wind and smooth sea.

Water-spout, a strongly agitated mass of air, which moves over the surface of the earth, and revolves on an axis, of which one extremity is on the earth and the other in a cloud. From this cloud a continuation proceeds downwards, which forms the upper portion of the water-spout; while the lower portion, besides air, consists sometimes of water, sometimes of solid portions, according as the water-spout passes over land or over water. Some have separated water-spouts over the land and over the water from each other; but this creates confusion, for water-spouts have been observed which were formed over water, and advance over land; and *vice versâ*, we have accounts of water-spouts which were formed over land, and afterwards suspended over the surface of water.

Water supply for towns. A plentiful supply of water fitted for drinking, culinary, and detergent purposes, is so essentially an article of every-day use, that in all ages, wherever a quantity of human beings have been congregated together, contrivances have necessarily been resorted to, to procure a supply: in some situations wells are sunk to a considerable depth, from which water is lifted by means of buckets, pumps, or like contrivances; in others, the rain-water falling on the roofs of houses is caught and husbanded in suitable receptacles, or, —as was much practised in ancient times, where large populations existed,—rivers are diverted for their use from their natural channels, and conducted over valleys and through mountains in artificial courses having a small but continuous decline.

Much has been written and said of the plentiful supply of water brought into ancient Rome and towns in Italy, Spain, and other places, by means of aqueducts; but the streams supplying these aqueducts would yield but little water in the dry summer and autumn weather, as is proved from the number of sources from which water was frequently brought to a town. Ancient Rome, according to some writers, was supplied from no less than twenty aqueducts, all deriving their water from different sources. These aqueducts were built at separate times, and they were doubtless made to supply a pressing want; for although in wet and moderate seasons, probably one-third this number would have yielded a supply adequate to the demand, it is much to be doubted if this was the case in seasons of drought; especially as the ancients made no provisions by means of impounding reservoirs to store a supply from wet to dry seasons.

In ancient times, water was brought to a town from rivers or springs more elevated than the town itself, and was distributed through fountains to the inhabitants, who fetched it in vessels to their houses.

In modern times, excessive floods are frequently stored in large reservoirs, to yield a supply to our towns in seasons of drought; or water from a neighbouring river, or from deep wells sunk in a subterranean reservoir, or water-bearing stratum situated below the level of a town, is frequently lifted by means of pumps, worked by steam or water power, through a line of cast-iron pipes into a reservoir of sufficient altitude to admit of its being conducted from thence through other pipes to the highest house in a town; and it is no uncommon thing at the present time to lift water from 200 to 300 feet in elevation for this purpose.

But the greatest improvement lately made for supplying towns with water consists in the arrangements for conveying it, when raised to a sufficient altitude, in cast iron or lead pipes, into the house of every inhabitant, even to the upper story, so that this necessary article can always be secured by the turning of a cock; it is also distributed in the same manner for watering roads, and for use in case of fire; and it is principally in the excellent system of distribution, which perfection in the art of making the pipes has induced, that renders modern water-works superior to those of ancient times.

It is of the utmost importance to every house to be supplied plentifully with wholesome soft-water, and there are now few places in which this cannot be accomplished at a cheap rate.

The modern cost of supplying water to a large town may now be taken at a low estimate per head of the population supplied, according to the facilities or difficulties that exist for procuring and distributing the supply: as a general rule, river-water, when unpolluted with the drainage of a town, or the rain-water flowing down the sides of steep hills of a retentive character, when properly filtered, is superior in quality, and better adapted for most domestic uses than the brightest spring water, owing to its freedom from saline matter, which is usually denominated softness.

All rain and surface water should, however, be carefully filtered before it is applied for domestic uses, not only to free it from earthy mechanical impurities, but to rid it of organic matter, which in summertime and warm weather is always mixed with such water in a greater or less degree, and the presence of which renders it unwholesome for drinking or culinary uses. It is principally owing to its freedom from organic matter that springwater, though usually hard, is preferred to river-water as a beverage.

London is supplied with water chiefly by eight companies, the New River, East London, West Middlesex, Chelsea, Grand Junction, Lambeth, Vauxhall, and Southwark.

Water-ways, in ship-building, the planks of the deck which are close to the timbers.

Water-wheel, a wheel turned on its axis by the weight of water falling upon its circumference, and thus adapted as a machine for deriving power wherever a fall of water can be commanded. For this purpose the wheel is erected in a vertical position upon a horizontal shaft or axis, and the periphery of the wheel is so formed that the greatest possible effect shall be received from the weight or gravity of the falling water. To obtain this effect, the rim of the wheel is provided with small troughs or buckets in which the water is received, and its weight made active in carrying down that part of the periphery on which the loaded buckets are situated. As they approach the lowest position, they become emptied, and are thus prepared to be carried upward during the revolution of the wheel, while the descending buckets are successively receiving their supply from the fall of water. Water-wheels are commonly distinguished according to the height of the fall in comparison with the diameter of the wheel, and the position at which the water acts upon the buckets. Thus if the depth of fall equals the diameter of the wheel, (besides allowing a little declivity below the wheel, for the ready escape of the back-water,) so that the water falls on the highest point of its periphery, the wheel is said to be an 'overshot' waterwheel. If the depth of fall is less, so that the water falls upon the wheel, only a little above the level of its centre, the wheel is called a "breast" wheel. And if the depth of fall is so little that the water acts by impulse only against the lower parts of the wheel, it is called an 'undershot' water-wheel. Waterwheels are now made in the most improved manner of iron, the arms being of wrought iron, the centres of cast iron, and the buckets of plate iron. A water-wheel thus constructed consists of a centre boss, and shaft, arms, buckets, and shrouding, the latter being the term applied to the rims of the wheel, between which the buckets are enclosed. In order to derive the greatest working effect from a given fall of water, the principal object is to shape the buckets so that they shall retain the water during the longest possible period. One great difficulty experienced in seeking this object has been the opposition exerted by the air to the admission of the water into the buckets; and, to counteract this evil, several methods have been devised. The only efficient remedy yet introduced is that invented by Mr. Fairbairn, and which he denominates the 'Ventilating Waterwheel,' the general object of which is to prevent the condensation of the air, and to permit its escape during the filling of the bucket with water, as also its re-admission during the discharge of the water into the lower mill-race. Several wheels erected and fitted upon this principle have proved entirely successful in realizing a maximum useful effect from a given fall of water. All these wheels are formed with wrought iron arms radiating from cast-iron centres to the periphery, and so disposed that the entire structure is in a state of tension, and the motion of the wheel being communicated from internal toothed wheels fixed to the shrouding. As applied to common breast-wheels adapted for falls not exceeding 18 or 20 feet, these ventilating buckets effect so great an improvement, that if the wheel is plunged in back-water to the depth of 5 or 6 feet, its uniform speed is not impeded. In these wheels the sole of the buckets is close, and the tail end of them being turned up at a distance of 2 inches from the back of the sole-plate, and running parallel with it, terminate within about 2 inches of the bend of the bucket, immediately above it. The water in entering the bucket drives the air out through the aperture into the space behind, and thence into the bucket above, and so on in succession. The converse occurs when the buckets are emptied, as the air is enabled to enter as fast as the wheel arrives at such a position as to permit the water to escape. (For a more copious description, see *Water-wheels with ventilating buckets*, by Fairbairn.)

There are many cases in which it is of importance to know the proportion of power necessary to give different degrees of velocity to a mill; but as the construction of mills and the purposes they serve are various, it is perhaps impossible to find any law of universal application. Mr. Banks, in his 'Treatise on Mills,' has drawn a conclusion which he appears to consider invariable, namely, that "when a wheel acts by gravity, its velocity will be as the cube root of the quantity of water it receives."

But supposing a wheel to raise water by means of cranks and pumps on Mr. Banks's principle, Buchanan thought it might easily be demonstrated, that by reducing the velocity of the wheel to a certain degree, the wheel would raise more water than would be necessary to move it at that velocity,— a thing evidently impossible.

In this view it would seem that there is no actual case in which Mr. Banks's conclusions will hold true. But, however they may apply to other mills, the experiments of Buchanan seem to prove at least that they do not apply to cotton-mills. On the ground of some experiments made at different times, and with all the attention possible, did he presume to call in question an authority for which the highest respect is entertained.

In January, 1796, he measured the quantity of water the Rothesay old cotton-mill required; first, when going at its common velocity, and secondly, when going at half that velocity. The result was, that the last required just half the quantity of water which the first did. It is to be observed, that in these experiments the quantities of water were calculated from the heads of water and apertures of the sluices.

From these experiments he inferred, "that the quantity of water necessary to be employed in giving different degrees of velocity to a cotton-mill must be nearly as that velocity."

He was satisfied with this experiment, and the inference drawn from it, till some gentlemen well acquainted with the theory and practice of mechanics expressed their doubts on the subject. He had then recourse to another experiment, which he considered less liable to error than the former.

The water which drives the old cotton-mill falls a little below it into a perpendicular-sided pond, which serves as a dam for a corn-mill at some distance below it. To ascertain, therefore, the proportional quantities of water used by the old mill, nothing more was necessary than to measure the time the water took to rise to a certain height in that pond; and accordingly, on the 1st of May, 1798, he made the experiments noted in the following Table:—

Number of experiments	1	2	3	4
Revolutions of one of the upright shafts per minute	45	45	24	23
Rise of water in the pond in inches	5	5	5	5
Time in minutes and seconds	6.58	6.57	14.45	15.0

The first and second experiments were made with the mill at its common velocity; the third and fourth at nearly half that velocity.

The time which the mill required to use the same quantity of water in these experiments may be taken, in round numbers, as follows:—the proper velocity at 7 minutes, and half that velocity at 15 minutes.

The result of these experiments approaches very nearly to that of 1796. The difference may be accounted for by the small degree of leakage which must have taken place at the sluices on the lower end of the pond; and the time being greater in the third and fourth experiments, the leakage would of course be greater.

Smeaton and others have proved in a very satisfactory manner, that "the mechanical power that must of necessity be employed in giving different degrees of velocity to the same body, must be as the square of that velocity." But it appeared to Buchanan that the result of the above experiments may be easily reconciled to this proposition, by considering what Smeaton says immediately afterwards:—"If the converse of this proposition did not hold true, viz. that if a body in motion, in being stopped, would not produce a mechanical effect equal or proportional to the square of its velocity, or to the mechanical power employed in producing it, the effect would not correspond with its producing cause." It is to be observed, that Smeaton's experiments were made on the *velocity* of heavy bodies, free from *friction* and *other causes of resistance;* but in mills there is not only friction, but obstacles, to be removed; and experiments made on friction have proved that the friction of many kinds of bodies increases in direct proportion to their velocity. But the velocity of a cotton-mill at work may be considered as a mechanical effect; and, if so, must correspond with its producing cause.

The preceding experiments on the Rothesay mill are undoubtedly correct and consistent with the principles of motion and power, and also with the experiments of Smeaton on mills and mechanical power.

The mechanical power is as the quantity of water on the wheel, multiplied into its velocity when the wheel, fall, and other circumstances remain the same; and since the mechanical effect is measured by the resistance multiplied into the velocity of the working point when the friction is constant, if the quantity of water be diminished by its half, either half the resistance, or half the velocity with which it is overcome, must be taken away, otherwise there will not be an equilibrium between the power and effect. But at the same time it is to be observed, that an increased velocity lessens the friction of the intermediate machinery, and consequently a greater effect would be produced by the greater velocity, as appears to be the case by the experiments. There is not, however, in the detail of these experiments, sufficient data by which it becomes easy to arrive at any any useful conclusion.

Roberton, an engineer of some eminence, made observations on these experiments, alleging that the conclusions of Banks give most satisfactory evidence that particular care and judgment are necessary in making such trials. It appeared to Roberton, that the wrong conclusions which have been drawn by many writers on this subject, have wholly arisen from misapprehending some of Sir Isaac Newton's fundamental principles of mechanics, and from a love of establishing theoretical expressions rather than strict observations of the invariable laws of nature, expressions such as these, viz. *quantity of motion, instantaneous impulse.*

Taking a constant portion of time (viz. a second) to be the measure of a body, and an instant to be the measure of the effect it produces; or by taking time as the measure of the cause, and space as the measure of the effect,—as to an *instantaneous* effect, Roberton argues that it is an absurdity in itself, as well as in mechanics,— we can form no idea of a body put into motion without the acting power or body act upon the body put into motion for some *time*, and also over some *space*; and to suppose otherwise, leads us entirely out of the sound principles of mechanics.

In mechanics every effect is equal to its producing cause. In the case of a power acting on a body producing motion, and also this body acting against another power which retards its motions, if the causes of action and resistance are each measured by the *time* the motions are produced and retarded, the result will be equal.

If they be measured by the *space* over which they act, the results will be equal; and this is a universal principle, whether applied to accelerating power and motion, as gravity, etc., or to machines, which act constantly and uniformly. Yet, in the case of uniform motion, space or time may be used at pleasure; as from the uniformity of space and time they become a common measure.

To illustrate this, suppose the body A acted upon by the power of gravity through the space A B, in a portion of time which we will call one. When it arrives at B, it meets with another medium of resistance, which is ten times greater than the former; the body A will be resisted in proportion to the cause of action and resistance; that is to say, if the *time* of action were one second, the *time* of resistance will be one-tenth of a second, and the distance A B will be to the distance B C as ten to one; so that whether *space* or *time* be taken as the measure of action, the same must be taken for the measure of the effect to have the results proportionate and equal. But if the cause be measured by *time*, and the effect by *space*, the results will be as the squares of the time, or, which is the same thing, as the squares of the velocity.

Thus, suppose a body in motion, with a velocity of one, has a power to penetrate into a bank of earth 1 foot: if the same body, with a velocity of two, strike the bank, will penetrate to the depth of 4 feet; for the velocity is double, and the time of action is double, and therefore the results will be compounded of both, that is, as the square of the velocity.

From the above it may be inferred that if equal bodies be acted upon by unequal powers, the time requisite to produce an equal motion will be reciprocally proportionate to the powers; that is to say, if a power of ten act upon a body for one second of time, and the power of one act upon an equal body for ten seconds, they will produce equal velocities. But the spaces through which the bodies are carried are very unequal, being as ten to one; and if the square roots of the powers producing the effects be taken, that will give the times they take in carrying the body acted upon through equal spaces.

But it is obvious this doctrine has no more to do with the operation of machines than to supply their first starting from rest to the motion necessary for working. When this is acquired, the power applied and the power of resistance balance each other, and whatever be the motion the machine moves at, the same power will carry it on, (if it be upheld,) provided the machine act in such a manner as not to accumulate resistance by the accumulation of motion, which is the case in forcing fluids through pipes, etc. In cases of this kind, the nature of the machine must be particularly kept in view, and no law whatever adopted to explain the resistance the acting body meets with, but what is simply deduced from the very machine which is under consideration; but, in most cases, any machine may be considered as acting purely on a statical principle. The raising of weights, or overcoming friction, Roberton considers purely as acting on that principle; and when the power of action is equal to the resisting power, the machine is indifferent to motion or rest. If the machine be at rest, the power will not move it, being a balance to the resistance. If the machine be set in motion, the power will keep it in the same motion, (provided the power be upheld,) the same as equal weights hung over a pulley, or in the opposite scales of a beam. If they be at rest, they will remain so; and if they be put in motion, they will endeavour to persevere in the same.

The above doctrine of a statical principle is proved in the most satisfactory manner by the experiments made at the old mill of Rothesay, the motion of the water-wheel being exactly proportional to the quantity of water expended, and therefore an exact and equal load upon the wheel; that is to say, the *buckets were equally full* when the mill moved at its *ordinary motion*, or at *half that motion*. The effect therefore of letting more water on a wheel is not to lodge a greater quantity in the buckets, but to supply the same quantity when the wheel is in a greater motion.

Banks, however, made his experiments agree with his theory, yet Roberton took no trouble in inquiring into them, alleging it would be to little purpose to have done so.

"Suffice it to say," he adds, "that the very small quantities of water which Banks made use of, and the slowness of the motion of his wheel in his experiments, give no ground for placing the smallest dependence on them; and when compared with the more judicious and accurate experiments of Smeaton, they dwindle into contempt."

Roberton further says, that "Smeaton, in running his wheel at nearly 3 feet in the second, brought it nearly to a maximum, and lost but about one-fourth or one-fifth of the original effect (alluding to his *overshot* wheels). Banks, at his highest motion, ran his wheel about 1 foot in the second, and reducing it to one-half of that motion, the same quantity of water then expended was capable of performing four times the work; and by deduction from thence, it appears plain that his wheel (from his own theory) would perform about twenty times the quantity of work which Smeaton's could perform with the same quantity of water, and about sixteen times more than nature; so that the observation (alluding to the theory of Banks) is very just in saying that, by reducing the motion of the wheel, it is demonstrable it would raise more water than supply itself."

Water-wheel (Overshot). The best water-wheel is that which is calculated to produce the greatest effect when it is supplied by a stream which furnishes a given quantity of water with a given fall. The mechanical effect depends on the proportion of the wheel's diameter to the height of the fall, and on the velocity of the circumference of the wheel. These are the two principal parts to be considered in the theory of wheels, but there are also some other points which ought to be attended to, because the effect is much decreased when they are neglected.

Of the proportion of the radius of the water-wheel to the height of

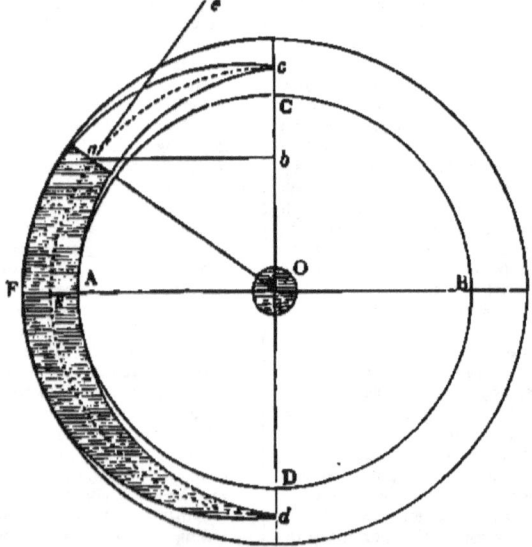

the fall.—Let A B C D be the wheel, and B A the depth of the buckets; then, according to experiments on water-wheels, it appears that the rotatory form of the water in the buckets is nothing at c and d, and that it increases nearly, if not accurately, in the direct ratio of the distance from c or d, and is greatest at A. That is, the force at any point a in a direction e a, or perpendicularly to the radius, is as a c.

A slight consideration of the figure is sufficient to demonstrate that the wheel will not produce the greatest effect when it receives the water at the upper point c, and that there must be considerable advantage in making the wheel of a greater diameter, so that it may receive the water at the same point between A and c, the point

WAT WATER-WHEEL, OVERSHOT. WAT

which will ensure the greatest effect thus calculated.

Let c = that portion of the circumference which is to be loaded with water; and x = the arc comprehended between the point where the water flows upon the wheel and the horizontal line ε A; also make b = the area of the stream supplying the buckets. Then the solid which represents the effective force will be

$$\tfrac{1}{2} b \times \left(\frac{c^3 - 2x^3}{c - x} \right),$$

which is to be the greatest possible; or

$$\frac{c^3 - 2x^3}{c - x}$$

= a maximum. By the principles of maxima and minima this takes place when

$$x = c(1 - \sqrt{\tfrac{1}{3}}) \text{ or } x = \cdot 2929 \, c.$$

Accordingly the arc $c - x$ must be the quadrant dg or 90°, and the arc $x = 37\cdot27°$.

Hence we have this important practical maxim. A water-wheel will produce the greatest effect when the diameter of the wheel is proportioned to the height of the fall, so that the water flows upon the wheel at a point about 52⅔° from the summit of the wheel.

If r be the radius of the wheel to the extreme part of the bucket, and h the effective height of the fall, then $h = r(1 + \sin.37\tfrac{1}{2})$, or $h = 1\cdot605\,r$; for the sin. 37½ = ·605. Also $\cdot623\,h = r$. Therefore, when the effective height of the fall is determined, the radius of the wheel is easily calculated. When the effective fall is eight-ninths of the whole fall, if we make h the whole fall, $r = \cdot554\,h$, or $1\cdot108\,h$ = the diameter of the wheel.

The effective height of the fall is less than the true height by as much as is necessary for giving the water the same velocity as the wheel before it flows upon it.

In low falls a wheel would work with advantage in a considerable depth of tail-water, provided the buckets were of a suitable form for moving through the water, and the effective fall made through a very accurate sweep, so that the sweep, and not the form of the bucket, should confine the water upon the wheel.

Of the velocity of the circumference of the wheel to produce a maximum effect.—It is necessary to premise, that the velocity with which the water flows upon the floating boards or buckets is considered to be equal to the velocity of the wheel, and to strike against the floats as nearly as possible in the direction of the motion of the wheel.

Let x be that part of the fall which gives the necessary velocity v to the water, when the effect is a maximum; v will then be the velocity of the circumference of the wheel. Also, make a = that part of the fall which would correspond to the velocity of the circumference of the wheel when the power would be equal to the friction of the loaded machine only; or when the useful effect would be nothing. Now if h be the whole fall, the effective force of the water on the wheel will always be proportional to $h - x$, when the effect is a maximum; and to $h - a$, when the useful effect, or work done, is nothing.

Hence $v(\overline{h - x} - \overline{h - a})$ must be a maximum; or $v(a - x) =$ a max.; but $v = x^{\tfrac{1}{2}}$, therefore $x^{\tfrac{1}{2}}(a - x) =$ a max., which, according to the rules of maxima and minima, takes place when $a = 3x$.

It is evident that the value of a must entirely depend on the nature of the machine; for if there be many moving parts between the power and the resistance, the friction will be greater, and consequently a will be less. The machine must be very simple indeed, if the friction be less than one-half the moving power, and it will often amount to two-thirds of it. If we suppose it to be two-thirds, then

$$a = \frac{h}{3},$$

and consequently

$$x = \frac{h}{9}$$

and

$$v = \sqrt{\frac{64\frac{1}{3}h}{9}} = 2.67 \sqrt{h}.$$

Hence, when the friction amounts to two-thirds of the moving power, the velocity of the circumference of an overshot wheel in feet per second, should be 2.67 times the square root of the whole height of the fall, in feet.

Again, that part of the fall is to be determined, which will give the water the same velocity as the wheel; and since

$$a = \frac{h}{3}, \text{ and } 3x = a,$$

we have

$$x = \frac{h}{9}.$$

Hence, when the friction is two-thirds of the power, that part of the fall which will give the water the proper velocity is one-ninth of the whole height.

These results may, then, be usefully compared with the experiments of Smeaton; at the same time it is obvious that his experiments were not adapted for arriving at general conclusions, because the water was always delivered upon the same wheel; for it is clear, from the preceding investigation, that every particular wheel must have its particular maximum.

In Smeaton's experiments on overshot wheels, the wheel was 2 feet in diameter; therefore the height of the fall should be 2¼ feet. Now the square root of 2¼ is 1.5; and $1.5 \times 2.67 = 4.005$, that is, the velocity of the wheel should be 4 feet per second; or it should make 38 turns per minute. Smeaton infers that "the best velocity for practice" will be when a wheel of 2 feet diameter makes 30 revolutions per minute. (Miscellaneous Papers, p. 51.) But his model had much more friction in proportion to the effective force of water on the wheel than two-thirds, here calculated upon. When, however, the calculation is made according to the friction of Smeaton's model,

$$v = 2.4 \sqrt{h};$$

and the velocity of the model wheel would come out 3.6 feet per second, or 34 turns per minute. This velocity will perhaps apply correctly enough to overshot wheels, where the water flows on at the summit, and to rough-made machinery; but the former calculation is that which appears to be most correct for the improved kind of wheels here pointed out. It is to be understood, that the friction allowed for includes all the kinds of resistance and loss of force which lessen the useful effect, as well as the resistance of the rubbing surfaces, properly called friction. Many persons may think that two-thirds of the effective force is greatly too much to be lost; it will be well if it draw their attention to lessening the stress on every part of the machinery, and to the importance of having few rubbing surfaces, and other causes of resistance.

On computing the power of overshot water-wheels.—In determining the proportion of the radius of the wheel to the height of the fall, an equation is given for the effective force. Resuming that equation, we have

$$\tfrac{1}{4} b \left(\frac{c^2 - 2r^2}{c - x} \right)$$

= the effective force of the water, and

—its mechanical power. But the quantity of water expended in maintaining this power will be bv. Hence, the quantity of water expended is, to its mechanical power, as

$$1 : \tfrac{1}{2}\left(\frac{c^2-2x^2}{c-x}\right).$$

When the wheel is supplied at the summit, $x = \tfrac{1}{2}c$; and therefore the quantity of water expended is to its mechanical power as $1 : \tfrac{1}{2} c$. Or the power is equal to half the weight of water supplied to the wheel.

The same relation takes place when $x = 0$; that is, when the wheel is supplied at the height of the axis. Hence, when the radius of a breast-wheel is equal to the effective height of the fall, its power will be the same as that of an overshot wheel supplied at the summit.

When the wheel is supplied at the point which produces the greatest effect, $x = \cdot 2929\ c$; and consequently the quantity of water expended is to its mechanical power as $1 . 0\cdot5857\ c$: this effect is greater than when the wheel is supplied at the summit in the ratio of $1\cdot1714 : 1$.

These comparisons will convey some useful information to many readers; and they may sometimes suggest to scientific writers the advantage of studying the actual nature of machines; for relations so extremely obvious and simple could never have been overlooked by any one who might have condescended to apply himself to an examination of the subject.

The power of a water-wheel may be considered under two points of view; each of which has its peculiar use. If we wish to compare it with any other first mover, then we shall have to calculate its mechanical power. But when it is desirable to compute the resistance it will overcome at the working point, the effective force should be calculated.

When the water flows upon the wheel, either at or above the axis, the mechanical power is

$$\tfrac{1}{2} bv \frac{c^2 - 2x^2}{c - x}$$

cubic feet of water, or

$$31\cdot25\ bv\frac{c^2-2x^2}{c-x}\text{ lbs.;}$$

where bv is the quantity of water expended in a second, in cubic feet; c the part of the circumference between the lowest point of the wheel and the place where the water flows upon it, in feet; and x the part of the circumference between the point which is level with the axis, and that where the water flows upon the wheel, in feet.

Suppose the mechanical power of a horse is estimated at 200 lbs., moving with a velocity of $3\tfrac{2}{3}$ feet per second, then a water-wheel will be equal

$$\frac{31\cdot25\ bv\ (c^2-2x^2)}{200\times 3\tfrac{2}{3}\ (c-x)}\text{ horses ;}$$

$$= \frac{\cdot00426\ bv\ (c^2-2x^2)}{c-x}\text{ horses.}$$

When the water flows on either at the summit or at the level of the axis, the mechanical power is $31\cdot25\ bvc$ lbs., or it is $= 0\cdot00426\ bvc$ horses.

When the water flows on at $52\tfrac{1}{2}$ degrees distant from the summit, the mechanical power is $37\cdot192\ bvc$ lbs., or $= \cdot005\ bvc$ horses. Since in this case $c = 127\tfrac{1}{2}$ degrees of the circumference, we have $c = 127\tfrac{1}{2} \times \cdot0174533\ r$; and as $r = \cdot554\ h$; and $v = 2\cdot67\ \sqrt{h}$; by substituting these quantities, we have $122\cdot176\ b\ h^{\tfrac{3}{2}}$ lbs. = the mechanical power; or $\cdot0164\ b h^{\tfrac{3}{2}}$ = the number of horses, where $h =$

the whole height of the fall, in feet, and $b=$ the area of the aperture through which the water flows upon the wheel, in feet.

The effective force is $31\cdot25\,b\,c$ lbs. when the water flows on either at the summit or at the level of the axis.

When the water flows on at $52\frac{1}{4}$ degrees distant from the summit of the wheel, the effective force is $37\cdot192\,b\,c$ lbs. or $45\cdot746\,b\,h$ lbs.

Of the power of breast-wheels.—When the water flows on below the level of the axis of the wheel, it may be termed a breast-wheel.

Let y be the distance below the axis measured on the circumference, then

$$\frac{c^3\,b\,v}{2\,(c+y)}$$

equal the mechanical power in cubic feet of water, or

$$\frac{31\cdot25\,c^3\,b\,v}{c+y}\text{ lbs.}$$

When $y=c$ the power will be reduced one-half, and when $y=2\,c$ it will be reduced two-thirds, and so on.

If we assume that the mechanical power of an undershot wheel is half that of an overshot one "under the same circumstances of quantity and fall;" then it will be an advantage to employ an undershot wheel whenever the fall is less than three-tenths of the radius of the wheel. But since the radius of the wheel may in many cases be diminished, it does not appear to be desirable to employ an undershot wheel in any case, except where the quantity of water is great and the fall inconsiderable.

Water-wheel with ventilated Buckets.
Since the time of Smeaton's experiments in 1759, little or no improvement has been made in the principle on which water-wheels have been constructed. The substitution, however, of iron for wood, as a material for their construction, has afforded opportunities for extensive changes in their forms, particularly in the shape and arrangement of the buckets, and has given altogether a more permanent and lighter character to the machine than had previously been attained with other materials. A curvilinear form of bucket has been generally adopted, the sheet iron of which it is composed affording facility for being moulded or bent into the required shape.

From a work entitled 'Mécaniques et Inventions approuvées par l'Académie Royale des Sciences,' published at Paris in 1735, it appears, that previous to the commencement of the last century, neither the breast nor the overshot water-wheels were much in use, if at all known; and at what period and by whom they were introduced, is probably equally uncertain. The overshot wheel was a great improvement, and its introduction was an important step in the perfecting of hydraulic machines; but the breast-wheel, as now generally made, is a still further improvement, and is probably better calculated for effective duty under the circumstances of a variable supply of water, to which almost every description of water-wheel is subjected. Improvements have taken place during the last and the present centuries. The breast-wheel has taken precedence of the overshot wheel, not so much from any advantage gained by an increase of power on a given fall, as from the increased facilities which a wheel of this description, having a larger diameter than the height of the fall, affords for the reception of the water into the chamber of the bucket, and also for its final exit at the bottom.

Another advantage of the increased diameter is the comparative ease with which the wheel overcomes the obstruction of backwater. The breast-wheel is not only less injured from the effects of floods, but the retarding force is overcome with greater ease, and the wheel works for a longer time and to a much greater depth in back-water.

The late Dr. Robison, Professor of Natural Philosophy in the University of Edinburgh, in treating of water-wheels, says, "There frequently occurs a difficulty in the making of bucket-wheels, when the half-taught millwright attempts to retain the water a long time in the buckets. The water gets into them with a difficulty which he cannot account for, and spills all about, even when the buckets are not moving away from the spout. This arises from the air, which must find its way out to admit the water, but is obstructed by the entering water, and occasions a great sputtering at the entry. This may be entirely prevented by making the spout considerably narrower than the wheel; it will leave room at the two ends of the buckets for the escape of the air. This obstruction is vastly greater than one would imagine; for the water drags along with it a great quantity of air, as is evident in the water-blast as described by many authors."

In the construction of wheels for high falls, the best proportion of the opening of the bucket is found to be nearly as five to twenty-four; that is, the contents of the bucket being 24 cubic feet, the area of the opening, or entrance for the water, would be five square feet. In breast-wheels which receive the water at the height of 10° to 12° above the horizontal centre, the ratio should be nearly as eight to twenty-four, or as one to three. With these proportions, the depth of the shrouding is assumed to be about three times the width of the opening, or three times the distance from the lip to the back of the bucket, as from A to B, fig. 1, the opening being 5 inches, and the depth of the shroud 15 inches.

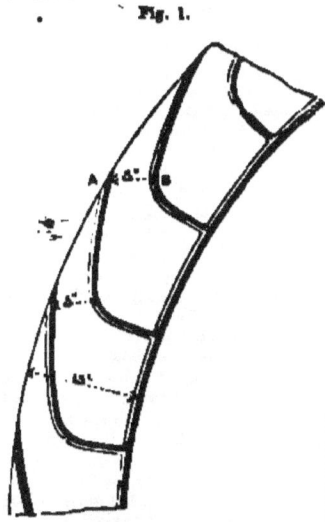

Fig. 1.

For lower falls, or in those wheels which receive the water below the horizontal centre, a larger opening becomes necessary for the reception of a large body of water, and its final discharge.

In the construction of water-wheels, it is requisite, in order to attain the maximum effect, to have the opening of the bucket sufficiently large to allow an easy entrance and an equally free escape for the water, as its retention in the bucket must evidently be injurious, when carried beyond the vertical centre.

Dr. Robison further observes, "There is another and very serious obstruction to the motion of an overshot or bucketed wheel. When it moves in back-water, it is not only resisted by the water when it moves more slowly than the wheel, which is very frequently the case, but it lifts a great deal in the raising buckets. In some particular states of back-water, the descending bucket fills itself completely with water, and in other cases it contains a very considerable quantity, and air of common density, while in some rarer cases it contains less water, with air in a condensed state. In the first case, the rising bucket must come up filled with water, which it cannot drop till its mouth gets out of the water. In the second case, part of the water goes out before this; but the air rarefies, and therefore there is still some water dragged or lifted up by the wheel, by suction, as it is usually called. In the last case, there is no such back-load on the rising side of the wheel, but (which is as detrimental to its performance) the descending side is employed in condensing air; and although this air aids the ascent of the rising side, it does not aid it so much as it impedes the descending side, being (by the form of the bucket) nearer to the vertical line drawn through the axis."

These were the difficulties under which the millwrights of Dr. Robison's time laboured; and the remedy which they applied (and which has since been more or less continued) was to bore holes in what is technically called the 'start' of the bucket. This was the only means adopted for removing the air from the buckets of overshot wheels, in order to facilitate the admission and emission of the water. In lower falls, where wheels with open buckets were used, or straight float-boards radiating from the centre, large openings were made in the sole-planking, exclusive of perforations in each bucket, in order to relieve them from the condensed air. The improved construction of the present time is widely different, the buckets being of such a shape as to admit the water at the same time that the air is making its escape.

During the early part of 1825, and the two succeeding years, two iron water-wheels, each of one hundred and twenty horse power, were constructed in Manchester for Messrs. James Finlay and Co., of the Catrine Works, under the auspices of the late Mr. Buchanan, and also for the same Company at Deanston, in Perthshire, of which firm Mr. James Smith (Deanston) was then the resident partner. These wheels are still (1850) in operation; and taking them in the aggregate, they may probably be considered as some of the most powerful and the most complete hydraulic machines in the United Kingdom. The construction of these wheels, and others for lower falls, first directed attention to the ingress and egress of the water, and led to the improvements which have since been introduced.

The object of these modifications may be generally stated to have been for the purpose of preventing the condensation of the air, and for permitting its escape, during the filling of the bucket with water, as also its re-admission during the discharge of the water into the lower mill-race.

Shortly after the construction of the water-wheels for the Catrine and Deanston Works, a breast-wheel was made and erected for Mr. Andrew Brown of Linwood, near Paisley. In this it was observed, when the wheel was loaded, and in flood-waters, that each of the buckets acted as a water-blast, and forced the water and spray to a height of six or eight feet above the orifice at which it entered. This was complained of as a great defect, and, in order to remedy it, openings were cut in the sole-plates, and small interior buckets were attached to the inner sole, as shown at b, b, b, fig. 2. The air in this case made its escape through the openings a, a, a, into the inner bucket, and passed upwards, as is shown by the arrows, through b, b, b,

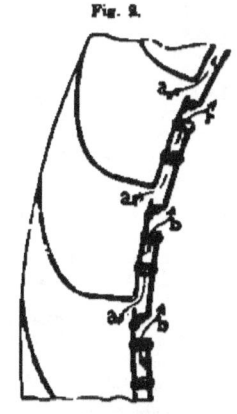

Fig. 2.

into the interior of the wheel. By these means it will be observed that the buckets were effectually cleared of air whilst they were filling, and that during the obstructions of back-water, the same facilities were afforded for its re-admission, and the discharge of the water contained in the rising buckets. The effect produced by this alteration could scarcely be credited, as the wheel not only received and parted with the water freely, but an increase of nearly one-fourth of the power was obtained, and the wheel, which still remains as then altered, continues, in all states of the river, to perform its duty satisfactorily.

The amount of power gained, and the beneficial effects produced upon Mr. Brown's wheel, induced a new and still greater improvement in the principle of construction; the first wheel erected on this, which has been called the 'ventilated' principle, was one designed for Mr. Duckworth, at the Handforth Print-Works, in the neighbourhood of Wilmslow, in Cheshire.

Close-bucketed wheels labour under great difficulties when receiving the water through the same orifice at which the air escapes, and in some wheels the forms and construction of the buckets are such as almost entirely to prevent the entrance of the water, and to deprive the wheel of half its power. These defects may be easily accounted for where the water is discharged upon the wheel in a larger section than the opening between the buckets; under such circumstances the air is suddenly condensed, and, re-acting by its elastic force, throws back the water upon the orifice of the cistern, and thus allows the buckets to pass without their being more than half-filled. Several methods have been adopted for relieving them of the air: the most common plan is, by cutting holes in the sole-plates, close to the back of the buckets, or else making the openings between them much wider, in order to admit the water, and at the same time to allow the air to escape. All these remedies have been more or less effective; but they labour under the objections of a great waste of water and much inconvenience, by the water falling from the openings down upon the lower part of the wheel, exclusive of the puffing and blowing when the bucket is filling.

Other remedies have been applied, such as circular tubes and boxes attached to the sole-plates, which, extending upwards, furnish openings into the interior of the wheel for the air to escape; but these, like many other plans, have been, to a certain extent, unsuccessful, owing to the complexity of their structure, and the inadequate manner in which the objects contemplated were attained. In fact, in wheels of this description it has been found more satisfactory to submit to acknowledged defects, than to incur the trouble and inconvenience of partial and imperfect remedies.

In the improvements made by

Mr. Fairbairn, these objections are to a great extent removed, and a thorough system of ventilation has been effectually introduced. Before entering upon the description of this new principle of ventilation, it is necessary to remark, that in climates like Great Britain and Ireland, where the atmosphere is charged with moisture for six or seven months in the year, it is no uncommon occurrence for the rivers to be considerably swollen, and the mills depending upon water are either impeded or entirely stopped by back-water; while at other times a deficiency of rain reduces the water-power below what is absolutely required to drive the machinery. On occasions of this kind, much loss and inconvenience are sustained, particularly in mills exclusively dependent upon water as a motive power, and where a number of work-people are employed.

On the outskirts of the manufacturing districts, where the mills are more or less dependent upon water, these inconveniences are severely felt; and in some situations these interruptions arise as frequently from an excess of water as from a deficiency in the supply. To remedy these evils, reservoirs have been formed, and wheels have been constructed to work in floods; but although much has been accomplished for diminishing these injurious effects, and giving a more regular supply in dry seasons, yet the system is still imperfect, and much has yet to be done, before water can be considered equal, as a motive power, to the steam engine, which is always available where the necessary fuel is at hand. It is therefore obvious, that any improvement in the construction of water-wheels, whereby their forms and requirements may be better adapted to meet the exigencies of high and low waters, will contribute much to the efficiency and value of mills situated upon rivers subjected to the changes alluded to.

Water-wheels (Ventilated) as adapted to low falls.—The first wheel constructed upon the ventilated principle was erected at Handforth, in Cheshire, in the summer of 1828: it proved highly satisfactory to the proprietors, Messrs. Duckworth and Co., and gave such important results as to induce its repetition, without variation, in cases where the fall did not exceed the semi-diameter of the wheel.

In the earlier construction of iron suspension wheels by the late Mr. J. C. Hewes, the arms and braces were fixed to the centres by screws and nuts upon their ends, as shown in fig. 3. The arms *c, c*, passed through the rim *b, b*, and

Fig. 3.

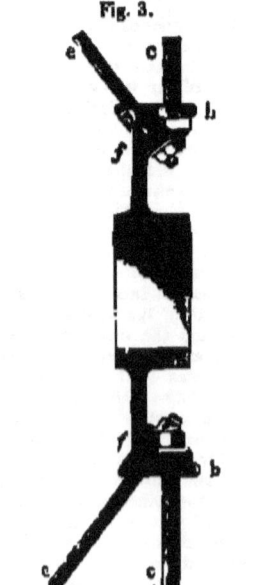

the braces *e, e*, which traverse the angle of the rim *f, f*, are, as nearly as possible, in the position and form adopted by Mr. Hewes. This arrangement, although convenient for tightening up the arms and braces, was liable to many objections, arising from the nuts becoming loose, and the consequent difficulty of keeping the wheels true to the circle, and the arms and braces in a uniform state of tension; gibs and cotters were therefore substituted for the nuts and screws, and since their introduction into the large wheels of the Catrine Works, Ayrshire, the objections have been removed, and the arms and braces are not only perfectly secured, but the periphery of the wheel is retained in its true and correct form.

Having noticed the obstructions offered to the entrance of the water into buckets of the usual form, and the consequent loss which ensues from its retention upon the wheel, after its powers of gravitation have ceased, it is now necessary to show the means whereby those defects were removed, and also to exhibit the relation existing between the breast and the undershot wheels. These terms have, however, become nearly obsolete, as every description of water-wheel may now be properly called a breast-wheel; and in every fall, however low, it is generally found advantageous for the water to act by gravitation, and not by impulse, as during the early periods of the industrial arts.

Water-wheels (Breast), with close Soles and ventilated Buckets. The preceding statements have been principally confined to the form of buckets and description of water-wheel adapted for low falls. It is therefore necessary to describe the best form of breast-wheels for high falls, or those best calculated for attaining a maximum effect on falls varying from one-half to three-fourths of the diameter of the wheel. This is a description of water-wheel in common use, and is generally adopted for falls which do not exceed 18 feet in height, and, in most cases, is preferable to the overshot wheel. It possesses many advantages over the undershot wheel, and its near approximation to the duty, or labouring force, of wheels of the former description, renders it applicable in many situations, especially where the fall does not exceed 19 or 20 feet, and where the wheel is exposed to the obstructions of back-water. In the latter case, wheels of larger diameter are best adapted; and provided sufficient capacity is left in the buckets, such wheels may be forced through the back-water without diminution of speed. Every wheel of this kind should have capacity in the buckets to receive a sufficient quantity of water to force the wheel, at full speed, through a depth of 5 or 6 feet of back-water; and if these provisions are made, a steady uniform speed, under every circumstance of freshes and flood-waters, may be attained.

Irrespective of the advantages of clearing the buckets of air, additional benefit is obtained by the facility with which the water is discharged, and the air again admitted, at the bottom of the fall, during the period of the emptying of the bucket into the tail-race. This is strikingly illustrated where the wheels labour in back-water, as the ventilated buckets rise freely above the surface, and the communication being open from one to the other, the action is rendered perfectly free, at almost any depth to which the wheel may be immersed.

In breast-wheels constructed for falls of 25 feet or upwards, the stone-breast is not required, as the buckets are formed with narrow openings, and the lip being extended nearer to the back of the following bucket, the water is retained much longer upon the wheel. Under these circumstances, a stone-breast is of little or no value, when attached to a wheel with close buckets, on a high fall.

The construction of the breast-wheels, as above described, is almost exactly similar to that for the lower falls; malleable iron arms and braces being common to both, as also the axle, shroud, and segments. These, when duly proportioned and properly fitted to each other, form one of the strongest, and probably the most permanent structures, that can be attained in works of this description.

Water-wheel (common Breast, not ventilated), as constructed by Messrs. Fairbairn and Lillie, between the years 1825 and 1827. These wheels were executed upon the plan of the overshot or breast-wheel, taking the water at an elevation nearly equal to that of its height. Four wheels of this description were constructed for Messrs. James Finlay and Co., for a fall of 32 feet, at Deanston, in Perthshire, and two others, for the same firm, at the Catrine Works, in Ayrshire, on a fall of 48 feet. Taking into consideration the height of the fall, the Catrine waterwheels, both as regards their power and the solidity of their construction, are, even at the present day, probably among the best and most effective structures of their kind in existence. They have now (1850) been at work upwards of twenty years, during which time they have required no repairs, and they remain nearly as perfect as when they were erected.

It was originally intended to have erected four of these wheels at the Catrine Works, but only two have been constructed; preparations were, however, made for receiving two others, in the event of an enlargement of the reservoirs in the hilly districts, and more power being required for the mills. This extension has not yet been wanted, as these two wheels are equal to 240 horse-power, and are sufficiently powerful, except in very dry seasons, to turn the whole of the mills.

These water-wheels are 50 feet in diameter, 10 feet 6 inches wide inside the bucket, and 15 inches deep on the shroud; the internal spur-segments are 48 feet 6 inches diameter, 3¼ inches pitch, and 15 inches broad on the cog; the large spur-wheels are 18 feet 2¼ inches in diameter, 3¼ inches in the pitch, and 16 inches wide on the cog; and the pinions are the same width and pitch, but are 5 feet 6 inches in diameter; the large bevel-wheels are 7 feet in diameter, 3¼ inches in the pitch, and 18 inches broad on the cog, their proportions being calculated to convey the united power of all the four water-wheels, should the original design ever be completed.

The water for the supply of the wheels is conveyed from the river Ayr in a canal and tunnel, and from thence, along the side of a rising bank, to the wheel-house. From this point it is conveyed to the water-wheels by a large sheet-iron trough, supported on iron columns.

When viewed from the entrance, the two wheels already erected have a very imposing effect, each of them being elevated upon stone piers; and as the whole of the cisterns, sluices, winding apparatus, galleries, etc., are considerably elevated, they are conveniently approached in every part. Under the wheels is a capacious tunnel, terminating at a considerable distance down the river.

Water-wheels on a principle introduced by M. Poncelet, have attained some considerable reputation on the Continent; and as Mr. Fairbairn has constructed one of them for Mr. De Bergue, it is necessary to allude briefly to the peculiarities it possesses.

The buckets are of a curvilinear

form, and are quite open at the back, without any sole-plate; so that they are perfectly ventilated. The water impinges upon them at nearly the lowest point of the wheel, the shuttle being arranged to draw upwards; and as the water enters, it follows the inside cavity of the bucket, rises and falls over into the next in succession, and so on. By this system the force of the water is expended on the wheel itself, instead of losing much of its power in rushing along through the wheel-race, as generally occurs in even well-made undershot wheels.

M. Poncelet has treated this subject at much length in his able work on water-wheels; but it may be observed, that a practical improvement might be effected by terminating the lower stone platform of the race somewhat short of the vertical line of the centre of the wheel, as the escape of the water would be facilitated, and the ascending buckets would be more easily relieved of their contents: this is a point of such importance for all wheels, that it must equally apply to this form.

Mr. De Bergue obtained nearly seventy-eight per cent. of power from a breast-wheel, with a good fall, when the periphery was travelling at a velocity of 6 feet per second.

He has erected several of Poncelet's wheels, and thought well of them; indeed, for certain situations it was thought they were preferable to any other form, although M. Poncelet had never yet been able to obtain very superior results from wheels erected under his own superintendence.

Mr. De Bergue has explained the construction of a wheel, on this principle, erected at the Loubregat, near Montserrat, in Catalonia; one of the same kind having been already erected by him at Gerona, between Barcelona and Belgrade.

The diameter was 16 feet 8 inches, and the width was 30 feet, which, with a fall of 6 feet 6 inches, passed 120,000 cubic feet of water per minute, when the periphery travelled at a velocity of 11 to 12 feet per second. An ordinary breast-wheel would require to be 60 feet wide, to use advantageously that quantity of water. It was found that the velocity of the periphery should be about 55 per cent. of that of the water flowing through the sluice; and upon these data the power of the wheel would be about 180-horse power.

The buckets were of a curved form, and made of wrought iron, ⅛th of an inch thick; and it should be observed that there was a larger number of buckets than usual, and that the water came upon them at a tangent, through an orifice of such a form and dimensions as to allow the buckets to fill easily, at the rapid speed at which the periphery passed before the sluice. This great primary velocity was very important, as it caused a considerable saving in the gearing of the mill.

The main shaft was formed by a hollow cylinder of cast iron, 4 feet 6 inches diameter, in short lengths, bolted together; and the arms were of wrought iron, made very light, and of the same form as those of a paddle-wheel of a steamer, and placed very close together. The strain was brought entirely upon the main shaft, and the weight of the wheel was thus reduced to about thirty tons, which was very little for so powerful a machine.

The sluice was formed of cast-iron plates, with planed joints, bolted through the flanches, to form one large shuttle of the entire breadth of the wheel, and its motion was regulated by radial tie-rods, between the stone apron and the back of the sluice, which could thus be raised with great facility

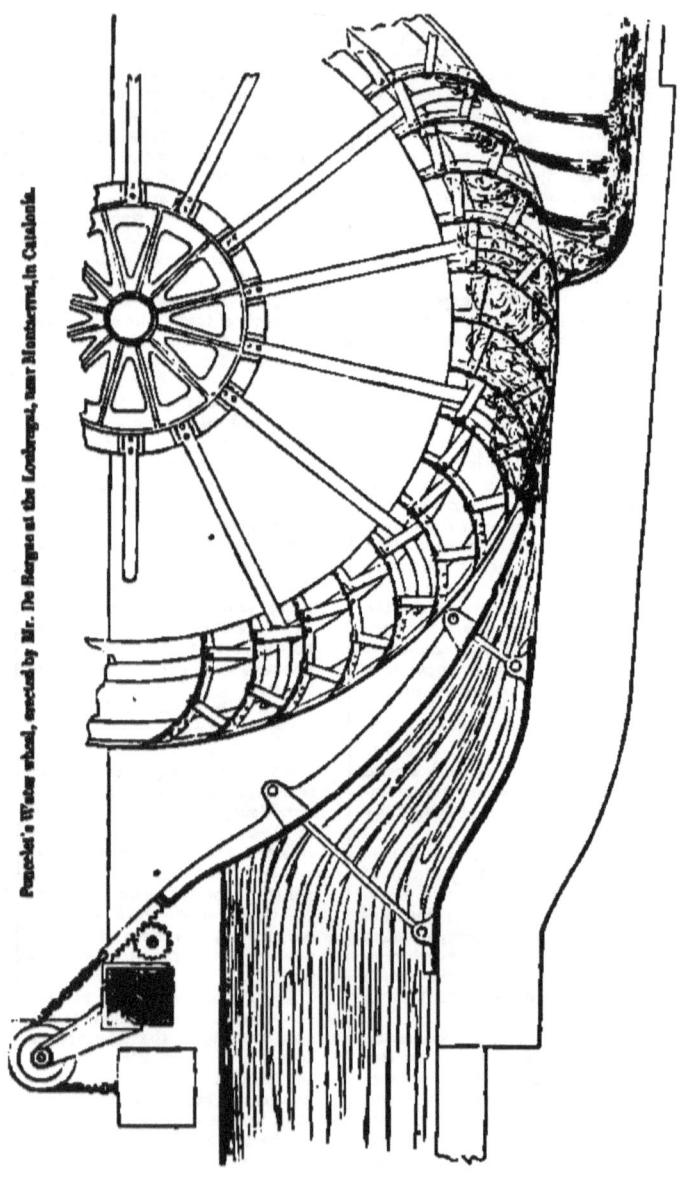

Poncelet's Water wheel, erected by Mr. De Bergue at the Lockerpel, near Monterent, in Catalonia.

by racks and pinions, and be regulated by the ordinary governor, the weight of the sluice being in a great degree supported by the water flowing beneath it on to the wheel. It moved very accurately between the side walls of the pen-trough, and cup-leathers at each side prevented any waste of water.

This kind of wheel was less affected by back-water than any other form, and the water acted upon it with its full power of velocity, without any impediment from the air in entering, as there was no sole-plate; the buckets filled and emptied with great facility. It is therefore most satisfactory for all falls under 8 feet in height, though the principle differs essentially from that generally taken as the basis of construction of water-wheels.

Waved, in heraldry, an indented outline, indicating honours originally acquired at sea.

Way-shaft, in steam engines, the rocking-shaft for working the slide-valve from the eccentric.

Wax, the substance of which the honeycombs of bees are composed, and which is of considerable use in branches of art.

Wealden. Beneath the two great divisions of the Cretaceous system, and consequently of very ancient date, there occurs in England an important series of beds, chiefly of lacustrine or fluviatile origin, known as the Wealden. Before the submergence of what are now the south-eastern parts of England, first beneath the comparatively shallow greensand, and then beneath the profounder depths of the ocean of the chalk, a mighty river, the drainage of some unknown continent, seems to have flowed for many ages along those parts of Kent, Surrey, and Sussex, known as the Valley of the Weald. The banks of this old nameless river were crossed with forests of coniferous trees of pine and araucarian families, with cycadeæ and ferns, and were haunted by gigantic reptiles, herbivorous and carnivorous, some of which rivalled in bulk the mammoth and the elephant; its waters were inhabited by amphibia of the same great class, chiefly crocodiles and chelonians of extinct species and type, —by numerous fishes too of the old Ganoid order, and by shells whose families, and even genera, still exist in our pools and rivers, though the species be all gone. Winged reptiles too occasionally flitted amid its woods, or sped over its broad bosom; and insects of the same family as that to which our dragon-flies belong, spent the first two stages of their existence at the bottom of its pools and shallows, and the terminal one in darting over it on their wings of delicate gauze, in quest of their prey. It is stated by Dr. Mantell, our highest authority on the subject of the Weald, that the delta of this great river is about two thousand feet in thickness,—a thickness which quadruples that of the delta of the Mississippi. The American "Father of Waters" is a very ancient river; and yet it would seem that this river of the Wealden, which has now existed for myriads of ages, is but its fossilized remains, hidden under the wolds of Surrey and Kent. This old river, which flowed over where the ocean of the Oolite once had been, and in turn gave place, and was overflowed by the ocean of the chalk, continued to roll its downward waters amid forests as dense and as thickly inhabited as those of the great American valley during a period perhaps four times as extended.

Weathercock, a vane made in the shape of a cock.

Weather-gage, in navigation. When a ship is to windward of another, she is said to have the *weather-gage* of her.

Weather-moulding, a label, canopy, or drip-stone, over a door or window, intending to keep off water from the parts beneath.

Wedge. The wedge is a solid piece of wood or metal, generally made in the form of a triangle prism, of which the two ends or bases are equal and similar plane triangles, and the three sides rectangular parallelograms: and it is called rectangular, isosceles, or scalene, according as its equal and similar bases are composed of right angles, isosceles, or scalene triangles. As a mechanical power, the wedge performs its office, sometimes in raising heavy bodies, but more frequently in dividing or cleaving them; hence all those instruments which are used in separating the parts of bodies, such as axes, adzes, knives, swords, coulters, chisels, planes, saws, files, nails, spades, etc., are only different modifications that fall under the general denomination of the wedge.

Weighboard, in mining, clay intersecting a vein.

Weight and power, when opposed to one another, signify the body to be moved and the body that moves it. That body which communicates the motion is called the power, and that which receives it the weight.

Weights and Measures. The system of weights and measures used in France at present, in all legal transactions, is called the 'metrical system,' from the fact of its being based upon the unity of length, which is designated 'the mètre.'

Before the great revolution of 1793, the separate provinces of the French kingdom had their different systems of measures: just as in England the different counties had theirs, before the introduction of the Imperial measures. There was, consequently, the same confusion attached to the meanings of the different terms employed, which led our own Government to simplify the question. An acre in Normandy did not mean the same as an acre in Picardy; a pound in Paris differed from a pound elsewhere. But here the analogy between the conduct of the two Governments ceases. That of France reformed the whole system of weights and measures, and based the new one upon natural and easily verifiable principles,—whilst our own retained the arbitrary and illogical system of the middle ages, contenting themselves with merely fixing a sort of uniformity in the definitions of the several terms.

The merit of having originated the metrical system is due to the government of Louis XV., who named a commission to pursue the investigations necessary to decide the principles upon which it was to be carried out. After a very serious consideration of the case, and a numerous series of observations carried on during the reign of Louis XVI. and under the Convention, the Academy of Sciences decided that all the different weights, measures, and coinages should be established according to certain definite relations to the dimensions of the globe itself. These are, to all human perception, invariable. If therefore the standard were lost, it is always possible to refind it, by a repetition of the same sort of observations which gave rise to the fixing it in the first instance. The beat of a pendulum, chosen by our own Astronomical Board, is a very uncertain base for such calculations; for the conditions of the vacuum, the temperature of the atmosphere, the specific gravity of the pendulum, nay, perhaps, even the magnetic currents, may affect the length of the space it goes through, in a manner able to affect calculations which require such mathematical exactitude as those connected with ascertaining the standard of a perfect system of measures.

The length of the earth's meridian was ascertained by Messrs. Delambre and Méchain, in the portion between Dunkerque and Barcelona; and by Messrs. Arago and Biot, in the portion between Barcelona and Formentera. The length of the meridian from the pole to the equator, passing through Paris, was then divided into ten million parts; and one of these parts, called the mètre, became the basis of the new system of weights and measures. Maupertuis had previously, in the year 1736, measured a portion of the arc of a meridian passing through the North Cape, and his observations were combined with those of the second commission. In spite of all this care, however, an error was made in fixing the length of the mètre; for the distance from the equator to the pole is really 10,000,738 mètres, instead of 10,000,000. For any practical purpose, however, this error is inapplicable; but it is very unfortunate.

The length of the mètre once ascertained, the other measures were derived from it. All the multiples and sub-multiples were formed on the decimal system, and respectively designated by Greek and Latin prefixes to the name of the unities. Thus, the multiples of the mètre are the *deca*-mètre, ten mètres; the *hecto*-mètre, a hundred mètres; the *kilo*-mètre, a thousand mètres; the *myria*-mètre, ten thousand mètres. In deference to old customs the term 'league' has been retained, and a legal value of four kilomètres affixed to it.

The sub-multiples of the mètre are: the *deci*-mètre, the tenth part of a mètre; the *centi*-mètre, the hundredth part of a mètre; and the *milli*-mètre, the thousandth part of a mètre.

The same prefixes are, of course, applicable to all the other unities.

The unities of length in use for ascertaining the distances of places, are, as said before, the mètre (the kilomètre and the myriamètre) and the league.

The unity of surface is the 'are,' which is a square of ten mètres on a side, or one hundred superficial mètres. The usual multiples and sub-multiples are, the *hect*-are, a square of one hundred mètres on a side; and the *centi*-are, the mètre superficial. The terms usually employed in the sale of land and in agricultural discussions, are simply those named above.

The unity of weight is the 'gramme,' which is the equivalent of a cube of distilled water (at a temperature of 4° above the 'ice-melting point' of the centigrade scale), measuring a centimètre every way. The multiples and sub-multiples are, as before: the deca-gramme, ten grammes; the hecto-gramme, a hundred grammes; the kilogramme, a thousand grammes; the decigramme, a tenth part of a gramme, etc. A thousand kilogrammes, then, would form a cube equal to one measuring a mètre on every side; and it is made the legal ton for heavy weights.

The unity of capacity is the 'litre,' which is the equivalent of a cube measuring one-tenth part of a mètre, or a decimètre, every way. The multiples and sub-multiples are formed as before. They are, the decalitre, the hectolitre, the kilolitre, the decilitre, and the centilitre, etc. The litre is usually employed in expressing the quantities of liquids; the hectolitre in expressing those of grain.

A thousand litres of water thus are equal to a mètre cube every way, and are one ton in weight. Another advantage in this system is, that the tables of specific gravity serve at once to ascertain the weights of the different substances. Thus, inasmuch as the specific gravity of cast iron is 7202, the weight of a mètre cube is at once

WEIGHTS AND MEASURES.

7202 kilogrammes, or 7 tons 202 kilogrammes.

The 'franc,' the unity of the French coinage, is 5 grammes in weight of an alloy containing nine parts of pure silver to one of alloy, being thus connected with the whole metrical and decimal system.

As investigations connected with the supply of water are of great importance, it may be added, that the quantity reckoned as the unity in such calculations is the module or 20 cubic mètres; being nearly the equivalent of the old 'ponce fontanier,' or the quantity usually delivered by a hole of one inch diameter in the 24 hours.

The law promulgating the metrical system was dated in the year 1795. The forced application of it in legal transactions did not take place till nearly 50 years afterwards.

A Table is subjoined of the different French weights and measures, with the corresponding English equivalents.

Weights and Measures—French, with their English equivalents.

FRENCH.	WEIGHT.	ENGLISH.
Gramme	a cube of one-hundredth of a mètre on a side	15·438 grains troy
Kilogramme	a thousand grammes, or a cube of water one-tenth of a mètre on a side.	2·68026 lbs. troy / 2·20549 lbs. avoirdupois
La tonne	1000 kilogrammes, or a cube of water 1 mètre on a side	1·015649 ton ,,

ENGLISH TROY.	RECIPROCALLY.	FRENCH.
Grain	equal to	0·06477 gramme
Pennyweight	,,	1·55456 ,,
Ounce	,,	31·0913 grammes
Pound Troy (Imperial)	,,	0·3730750 kilogramme

AVOIRDUPOIS.		
Drachm	equal to	1·7712 gramme
Ounce	,,	29·3384 grammes
Pound	,,	0·4534148 kilogramme
Hundredweight	,,	50·7896 kilogrammes
Ton	,,	1015·649 ,,

To convert pounds avoirdupois into kilogrammes, or English tons into French tons, or vice versâ, multiply or divide as follows:

For pounds, by . . . . . 0·4534148
For tons, by . . . . . 1·015649

FRENCH.	LENGTH.	ENGLISH.
Mètre	about 40,000,000 th part of circumference of the globe, or 10-millionth part of a quarter of do.	3·2909992 feet / 1·093633 yard
Kilomètre	one thousand mètres	1093·633 yards
Myriamètre	ten thousand mètres	10936·33 yards
Centimètre	one-hundredth of a mètre	0·393708 inch
Millimètre	one-thousandth of a mètre	0·0393708 inch

ENGLISH.	RECIPROCALLY.	FRENCH.
The inch	one-twelfth of a foot English	2·539954 centimètres
,, foot		3·047949 decimètres
,, yard	3 feet	0·9143819 mètre
,, furlong	220 yards	201·15437 mètres
,, mile	1760 yards	1609·3149 mètres

To reduce English measure into French, multiply by; and to reduce French measures into English, divide by:

Inches to centimètres . . 2·5400
Feet to mètres . . 0·3047945—practically 0·3048
Miles to kilomètres . 1·6093
Feet square to mètres square 0·09290
,, cube to mètres cube . 0·028314   { A yard cube equals 0·76436 mètre cube

WEIGHTS, COMPARATIVE.

FRENCH.	SURFACE.	ENGLISH.
Centiare	a mètre superficial	1·196033 yards superficial
Are	a square of 10 mètres every side	0·098845 rood
Hectare	,, 100 ,, ,,	2·471143 acres

RECIPROCALLY.

A yard square	contains	0·83607 mètre square
The rod, or	perch square	25·291630 mètres square
,, rood	1210 yards square	10·116775 ares
,, acre	4840 do. do.	0·404671 hectare

In round numbers, the hectare may be taken as equal to 2½ acres.

FRENCH.	CAPACITY.	ENGLISH.
Litre	a cube of one-tenth of a mètre on a side	1·760773 pint / 0·220097 gallon
Decalitre	ten litres	2·200968 gallons
Hectolitre	one hundred litres	22·00968 ,,

ENGLISH.	RECIPROCALLY.	FRENCH.
Pint	equal to	0·567932 litre
Quart	,,	1·135864
Gallon Imperial	,,	4·543458794 litres
Chaldron	,,	13·085150 hectolitres

To turn pressure calculated in pounds per inch superficial into their equivalents calculated in kilogrammes per centimètre superficial, or vice versâ, multiply, or divide, by 0·0703774.

Weight in pounds of one cubic foot of the following substances:

Cast iron	450·	Water		62·5
Wrought iron	486·	Air		0·075
Steel	489·	Steam		0·036
Pine wood	29·5			

Weight of a Superficial Foot of Plate or Sheet Iron.

No. of the wire-gauge.	Thickness in inches.	Weight in pounds.	No. of the wire-gauge.	Thickness in inches.	Weight in pounds.
	1	40·	12		4·38
	⅞	35·	13		3·75
	¾	30·	14		3·12
	11⁄16	27·5	15		2·82
	⅝	25·	16	1⁄16	2·50
	9⁄16	22·5	17		2·18
	½	20·	18		1·86
	7⁄16	17·5	19		1·70
	⅜	15·	20		1·54
1	5⁄16	12·5	21		1·40
2		12·	22	1⁄32	1·25
3		11·	23		1·12
4	¼	10·	24		1·
5		8·74	25		0·9
6		8·12	26		0·8
7	3⁄16	7·5	27		0·72
8		6·86	28	3⁄64	0·64
9		6·24	29		0·56
10		5·62	30		0·50
11	⅛	5·			

Weight of Rod Iron 1 foot in length, of the following Dimensions.

SQUARE IRON.		ROUND IRON.		FLAT IRON.	
Inch.	Pounds.	Inch.	Pounds.	Inch.	Pounds.
1/8	0·2	1/8	0·14	1/4 × 1	0·8
3/16	0·5	3/16	0·4	3/8 × 1	1·3
1/4	0·8	1/4	0·7	1/2 × 1	1·7
5/16	1·3	5/16	1·	5/8 × 1	2·1
3/8	1·9	3/8	1·5	3/4 × 1	2·5
1/2	2·6	1/2	2·	1/4 × 2	1·7
1	3·4	1	2·7	3/8 × 2	2·5
1 1/8	4·3	1 1/8	3·4	1/2 × 2	3·4
1 1/4	5·3	1 1/4	4·5	5/8 × 2	4·2
1 3/8	6·4	1 3/8	5·	3/4 × 2	5·1
1 1/2	7·6	1 1/2	6·	1/4 × 3	2·5
1 5/8	8·9	1 5/8	7·	3/8 × 3	3·8
1 3/4	10·4	1 3/4	8·1	1/2 × 3	5·1
1 7/8	11·9	1 7/8	9·3	5/8 × 3	6·3
2	13·5	2	10·6	3/4 × 3	7·6
2 1/4	17·1	2 1/4	13·5	1/4 × 4	3·4
2 1/2	21·1	2 1/2	16·7	3/8 × 4	5·1
2 3/4	25·6	2 3/4	20·1	1/2 × 4	6·8
3	30·4	3	23·9	5/8 × 4	8·4
3 1/2	41·4	3 1/2	32·5	3/4 × 4	10·1
4	54·1	4	42·5	1/4 × 5	4·2
5	84·5	5	66·8	3/8 × 5	6·3
6	121·7	6	95·6	1/2 × 5	8·4
7	165·6	7	130·	5/8 × 5	10·6
8	216·3	8	169·9	3/4 × 5	12·7

Welding, the operation of combining or joining two pieces of iron or steel, by bringing the surface to be joined to a heat nearly equal to that of fusion.

Well, in ship-building, a partition to enclose the pumps, from the bottom to the lower decks, to render them accessible, and prevent their taking damage.

Wells. The practice of boring for water, adopted in the province of Artoise, in France, has given the denomination to those wells which are termed *Artesian*. Wells on this principle are very applicable in low level districts covered with alluvial deposit or clay; in such situations springs are seldom found, and water cannot be obtained by sinking an ordinary well, unless at a disproportionate cost. The eastern part of Lincolnshire, which lies between the chalk range called the Wolds, and the sea, is a case in point. It was discovered, perhaps accidentally, in sinking through the clay to the subjacent chalk, that water rose to the surface in a perpetual fountain, and an ample supply was obtained over the whole of that district by the simple operation of boring.

A number of wells of this description have also been executed in the neighbourhood of London by performing the London clay into the porous bed of the plastic clay formation, and into the chalk.

The principle of operation is simply this. The hole is bored through impervious strata that do not contain water, into lower strata that are fully charged with it, and the water rises by hydrostatic pressure. The height to which it will

WELL-SINKING.

rise obviously depends upon the inclination of the strata, and other causes which affect the relative levels of the hole that is made, and the subterraneous body of water that has been tapped.

Under most circumstances it is necessary to protect the perforation that is made by sinking iron pipes. The boring is thus secured against the accident of the sides falling in, and another advantage, which is of some importance, is obtained: it may chance that the object is to obtain a supply of soft water which has been ascertained to exist at a certain level, and that the strata which have to be pierced to get to it contain hard or impure water; in such a case the boring would be continued down to the proper depth, and the pipes being plunged into the soft water, it would rise through them, and any water or impurity which might be found in the strata through which they passed would be effectually excluded. If it so happened that at a certain depth below the soft water a mineral water could be obtained, instead of going to the expense of a fresh bore from the surface, it would only be necessary (supposing that both would flow to the same level) to bore through the pipes already fixed, to the mineral water, and insert smaller pipes within the larger ones, for bringing it up to the surface.

The history of the great Artesian well which was completed at Grenelle is one of the most remarkable instances of confidence in the principle, and of perseverance in execution, that is on record. The facts are believed to be substantially as follows:—A person suggested to the authorities, that an Artesian well would supply water in a situation where it was greatly required; and after some discussion it ended in his undertaking the work on the stipulation, "No water, no pay." He bored down far beyond the point at which he expected to have terminated his labours; but no signs of water appeared: he persevered, however, till he found that the expenses had ruined him. Under these circumstance, he consulted the celebrated Arago, who encouraged him to proceed. Again he went to work, and after unparalleled difficulties, at the expiration of six years, and at the depth of 1800 feet, the superincumbent mass was bored through, and the water came boiling up in such quantities, and with such force, as to flood the whole district.

The water, when first obtained, was extremely foul; the partial introduction of an Indian-rubber hose is said to have remedied this, and the water thus procured from the main spring was quite pure, and at a very high temperature.

Well-sinking. The process of boring may be thus briefly described:

The auger, the chisel, or any of the great variety of implements which are required to meet different circumstances and overcome the numerous difficulties which are experienced, are screwed to iron rods, which are usually from 2 to 2½ inches square.

The first rod which is attached to the tool is generally about 6 feet long, and the others are of the uniform length of 20 feet. Each rod has a screw at one end, and a tapped socket to receive a screw at the other, and they fit universally; there is also a 'middle knob' in the centre of each rod, which is used for suspending the rods already fixed, whilst others are being added or detached, as the implement is lowered into the bore, or drawn out of it.

In commencing operations, a stage about 8 or 10 feet square, and 20 feet high, is erected, when the boring takes place from the surface. The men who work the tool stand upon this stage, and a windlass or crab is fixed, chiefly for hoisting and lowering the rods, but mechanical power is also required for assisting in the working when the depth is very great.

A boring handle is attached to the rod, which is used for turning the tool round in boring with an auger, or in 'jumping,' as is required when cutting through rock or indurated clay with the chisel. When the boring has proceeded till it is found difficult to turn the rods, or at such times as practical experience dictates, it is necessary to draw out the implements and to bring up the loose material that may be at the bottom of the bore.

Under ordinary circumstances a common windlass, or a small crab, gives sufficient power to work, hoist, and lower the rods; but when the bore is of great depth, or the instruments of unusual size, an increase of mechanical power is necessary. This may be conveniently obtained by placing a second crab on another stage; or, in extraordinary cases, horses may be applied on the surface.

An economical mode of boring has been adopted with success on some parts of the Continent by using a heavy cast-iron bar, 2 cwt. or more, armed with a chisel at the lower end, and surrounded by a cylinder or hollow chamber, which receives through valves and brings up the detritus of the perforated stratum. This implement is suspended over a wheel or pulley fixed above the spot in which the hole is made, and is raised up and let fall by manual labour.

As the rope is raised up and down, its tortion gives the chisel a circular motion, which varies the place of cutting at each descent. When the chamber is full, the whole apparatus is raised quickly to the surface, and the material it contains discharged.

In cutting through a hard stratum, or under circumstances where iron pipes could be dispensed with, this plan of boring a hole would doubtless answer; but it is conceived that the bore could scarcely be made sufficiently straight to admit of pipes being inserted. It is, however, a much less costly method of executing the work where it can be made to apply, and is well worth attention.

Well-staircase, a winding staircase of ascent, or descent, to different parts of a building, so called from the walls enclosing it resembling a well, called frequently a geometrical staircase.

Weold, or *Weald* (Saxon), a forest.

Wharf, a levelled surface, terrace, or embankment, formed on a river or canal bank, or sea-coast, to facilitate the landing and embarkation of persons and goods, and protected by an artificial frontage or structure of masonry or other materials. The natural form of banks and coasts, unless defined by masses of rock, is usually shelving or inclined, so that the depth of water is gradually reduced, and thus prevents the close approach of floating vessels. By the construction of wharf-walls, which are either extended into the deep water, or the foundations of which are sunk so as to permit of the subsequent removal of the bank, and thus bring deep water into contact with them, vessels are enabled to come close alongside, and thus discharge or receive their cargoes directly from the wharf. Wharf-walls are constructed of various materials, but are always formed with a slope or batter outwards towards the base, in order to give greater stability to them, and to resist the action of the tide and the waves. Much theory has been expended in attempts to determine the precise forms which should be given to these structures, and, accordingly, some engineers approve of plane-faced walls, while others prefer curved faces; and another theory has been started to explain that a perfectly vertical face is the best of all adapted to resist the influence of waves. Whether this position be theoretically correct or not, however, the value of an extended base, in giving stability, is too well known to need demonstration, and derives support from that intuitive kind of feeling which proceeds directly from the evidence of our senses. Adopting the inclined plane face as a good practical one for wharf-walls, the rate of inclination or batter may be determined from 1 in 6 to 1 in 12, that is, with a total divergence from the perpendicular of $\frac{1}{8}$ or $\frac{1}{12}$ of the total height, being from 1 to 1$\frac{1}{2}$ inch, in a foot. The front of the wall, if of masonry, may be protected by a row of sheet-piling, either of timber or iron. In the former case, the piles are driven close together, and bound along the top with a horizontal tie or waling firmly bolted to the piles. If iron piling is used, the piles are driven at intervals of from three to five feet, and cast-iron plates fitted in between them, being secured within grooves formed in the sides of the piles. The Brunswick Wharf, at Blackwall, affords a good example of this description of piling. The masonry of the wall is founded upon the piling, the length and closeness of the piles being determined with reference to the nature of the subsoil, and the whole of them are driven to a firm bottom and levelled on the heads, being strongly secured in their position by means of longitudinal and transverse ties or beams, on which the first course of footings was built. The durability of these walls is known to depend greatly upon the kind of mortar or cement used in connecting the masonry or brickwork. Cements known as water-cements, formed with lime which has the property of hardening under water, should be preferred to all others. The thickness of the wall must depend upon its height and the nature of the materials behind it. If these are likely to press severely against the wall, such as clays liable to hold great quantities of water, etc., the thickness of the wall will be required to be greater than if gravel, or other non-retentive material, forms the backing. Strong ties of iron should in all cases be secured to the front of the wall, passing through it, and being secured by plates and keys in the front, and extending backward to a considerable distance, and secured to a row of piling driven into the solid ground. These land-ties will also considerably assist the wall in resisting the forward pressure of the soil behind it. Immediately at the back of the wall a firm body of concrete, or at least well-puddled clay, should be introduced. Whichever of these is used as a backing, it should be consolidated as much as possible, and it will thus resist the admission of moisture behind the wall which is indispensable to secure its permanent durability. The concrete should be cast in from a height above its intended position, and allowed to set before it is filled in; and if clay be substituted, it should be thoroughly well rammed in, and made as solid as possible.

Wheal. The ancient Cornish called a mine *huel,* which has been corrupted into *wheal.*

Wheel and axle. This machine is so named by reason of its consisting of a wheel and cylinders, having a common axis with pivots fixed in its extremities, on which the whole may revolve. This very simple and useful contrivance, although usually designated a second mechanical power, requires the consideration of no other principles than those adduced for the lever; it is nothing but a lever, having the radius of the wheel for one arm, and that of the cylinder or axle for the other, the fulcrum being the common centre of both. This machine is also termed the 'Perpetual Lever;'

for since the power and the resistance operate respectively at the circumference of a circle revolving about an axis, it is obvious that the rotation must maintain the continuity.

Wheels, in locomotive engines: the well-known invention for obtaining a rolling progressive motion. They receive names corresponding to the part of the engine or tender they support; as leading, trailing, etc. Driving wheels vary in size from 4 feet 6 inches up to 10 feet diameter. Leading and trailing wheels vary from 3 feet up to 4 feet 6 inches in diameter. Tender wheels are usually about the same size as the leading and trailing wheels of the engines they are attached to.

Wheel-cutting machine, a machine for cutting out the teeth of wheels. The most perfect machines for shaping the teeth of wheels are those invented by Mr. Lewis, of Manchester, which are adapted for cutting the teeth of spur, bevel, and worm wheels, of either metal or wood. The principal working parts of these machines and the mode of action is as follows:

Two side-frames have angular ridges from end to end, to fit into corresponding grooves in the bottom of a travelling frame: this frame can be adjusted by a screw moved by a hand-wheel at the back of the machine: at the front of the machine is a strong spindle, placed vertically, to carry the work which is fixed on the top of it, and at the lower part is a large worm-wheel moved by a screw, to which is connected a train of three wheels: the sizes of the first and third wheels must be such that half a revolution of a handle, which falls into a notch after each half-revolution, shall turn the work so that any point in the pitch-line of it will move through a distance equal to the pitch. To the travelling frame a slide is attached by bolts and joints, in such manner that it may be fastened to act vertically, or at an angle in the direction either of the length or breadth of the machine. The cutter, and its wheels for diminishing the speed and pulley for communicating motion to it, are carried by the slide. The cutter is a circular piece of steel notched like a saw, and shaped to fit the spaces between the teeth of the wheel, and is raised or lowered by a rack at the back of the slide, worked by a pinion and handle. The travelling frame and slide being adjusted to the work, and the suitable wheels arranged for turning it the given distance, the machine is set in motion and the revolving cutter pressed down upon the rim of the wheel by the handle and rack till the space has been cut; the cutter is then raised, and by giving half a revolution to the handle attached to the worm-wheel apparatus, the spindle and work are turned so that the latter is in proper position for the cutter to act again. For a spur-wheel the slide acts vertically, for a bevel-wheel it acts at the requisite angle in the direction of the length, and for a worm-wheel at an angle in the direction of the breadth of the machine.

Whim, a machine used for raising ores, etc., worked by horses, steam, or water.

Whim-shaft, in mining, the shaft by which the stuff is drawn out of the mine by the horse or steam whim.

Whispering gallery, a curvilinear corridor or balcony within the cupola of St. Paul's cathedral, London, and in other ecclesiastical buildings.

White Chalk is a well-known native carbonate of lime, used by the artist only as a crayon, or for tracing his designs; for which purpose it is sawed into lengths suited to the port-crayon. White crayons and tracing chalks, to be good, must work and cut free from grit. From this material both whiting and lime are prepared, and are the bases of many common pigments and colours used in distempering, paper-staining, etc.

Wicker-work, at an early date, was occasionally employed for the roofing, if not for the entire construction, of churches.

Wicket, a small gate or door within, or a part of a massive or larger door or gate for the passage of pedestrians.

Wilkie (Sir David). The works of the late Sir David Wilkie left by him at his decease consisted of water-colour drawings, portfolios of studies and sketches, sketches in oil colours and incomplete pictures. There were many works finished: nearly all of them were works done when from home: some in Ireland, some in Spain, most on his journey to the Holy Land. They are proofs of unremitting industry; nothing escaped him, all that met his eye formed subjects for his pencil,—whether a distant landscape, a pipe or a sword, an eastern street, a girl at a window, Mehemet Ali, or a scene near the birthplace of Homer. Proofs indeed these works are of his practice being a work of love; it cannot but be supposed that all this labour must have been the occupation of his leisure hours as well as his working hours. Well might Sir Robert Peel, at the meeting for erecting a monument to Wilkie, bring into notice such untiring industry. Anything of the slightest interest was committed to paper. Numbers of the subjects would not form finished pictures, nor enter into the composition of pictures, though possibly any might be subservient for such purpose; but seemingly without looking forward to any further use, he committed everything to canvas, or rather to paper. Similarly may it be said of Wilkie in his art; he reduced to design whatever entered his eye, and design came to him by nature spontaneously. The collection also contained a number of the works of Fuseli. Fuseli and Wilkie, what a contrast! The one all imagination, the other all reality. Sin and Death, A Griffin pursuing an Arimaspian, The Nightmare (sketch for), Macbeth and the Witches, The Walpurgis Night, were some of the subjects Fuseli had selected.

Wilkie's practice does not appear uniformly the same; he varies much in the materials of his studies and sketches. There is a distinction to be remembered between works executed at home and abroad. The facilities in the one case and the difficulties in the other, lead to selecting different materials. There is one, 'A Village School:' the heads and figures are all put in with their expressions, but not finished. Colour is also put in, but unfinished in the back and foreground; the canvas is covered, or rather the panel, for though it is, I should say, the size of a half-length, the painting is on a panel, and the ground pure white. There is much humour in the Dominie, and in the several groups. There is a right good spirit about it, that shows how at home Wilkie was in the subject. For such excellence people don't like to receive his other works. There is much to be said on this question.

His works are evidences of the great care and neatness of hand in the progress of his pictures. There is nothing to undo or to amend, and only the part that he intends to finish appears touched. There is no experimental uncertain painting put in one day to be expunged another. Wilkie advised Haydon to use dark background colours with economy in an early stage, and he practises his precept, though he puts in freely a dark that in chiaroscuro is to stand as such.

The other picture is 'Knox administering the Sacrament;' this too is upon panel, the ground pure white. The heads more—perhaps quite finished. It is less in size; beside it, is a small rough sketch upon paper of the principal figures; the others are uncertain. There is also a smaller sketch in oil made with great precision, the surrounding groups still not the same as appear in the picture. There is too a study in black chalk of Knox, and two of the principal heads very carefully and effectually drawn. The heads are probably painted from these with nature present as a guide. It appears that Wilkie must have made use of his studies and sketches for painting from, because, as in this instance, if he used nature this highly finished chalk study would be useless. Haydon remarked what a strange practice Wilkie had observed in the Knox. On a milk-white panel he had painted in the heads and half-figures into a glaze of asphaltum as it appeared, the MacGuelp just tinged. No other part of the picture was worked upon, a few slight pencil lines only indicating the lower part of the figures in the foreground. The leading part of the picture reminded one of Da Vinci's 'Last Supper.' The background, which was untouched and for which I saw no arrangement in any sketch, was staring him in the face during the time of completing the heads, and from its pure whiteness blinding him while painting. In effect too it was injuring the finished parts, which had a yellow glaze which looked sickly. There is something of this unpleasing effect constantly about Wilkie's painting. It is not from painting into a glaze, I think, that this occurs, but from passing a glaze over finished work, for there was a portion of the armour in the upper portion of one figure which was free from this stain. The white background could not be for a key; it was very dazzling and disagreeable next the finished work. There was one hand left, I suppose, in dead colouring, for it was quite pallid, though it had a finished look, like being worked up in brown and white. Haydon said, "Oh! but the next thing he'd go over the background with colour;" and there was more probability, I think, of his completing the figures before such process. Haydon commended highly Wilkie's mode in 'The School' of getting in the subject: this is what I have before mentioned and admired. There is much cautious treatment, like the process in water-colours. It has more of the neatness and precision of the Dutch masters than the impasto of the Italian. In the catalogue of his effects connected with 'The School,' the following. It is to be remembered there are 36 figures in the composition. No. 84, Study (in chalk) for 'The School.' 150, 'Hedge School;' this probably might suggest the work. 183, 'The School,' group of hands. 184, Do. 185, Do. 186, Do. two studies. 303, Sketch (chalk) for 'The School.' 304, Do. 385, 'The Schoolmaster.' 318, Study for the School. 319, Do. Study of hands and a head for the School. 'The School' brought 720 guineas, and was bought by Moon. For the Knox picture the following are in the catalogue:—

60. 'John Knox administering the Sacrament,' in pen and ink, slightly washed. 191. 'John Knox administering the Sacrament.' 245. 'Knox presenting the Cup,' study of hands. 246. Do., two hands. 247. Do., gauntlets. 248. Do., with the cup and a lady: from same. 249. Do., preaching, and one other. 'The Letter Writer' sold, price 425 guineas. 'The Tartar relating the Capture of Acre' sold for only 175 guineas. Both very unfinished, the latter most so. 'The Letter Writer' was very effective and very pretty. It represents a girl consulting a letter-writer in the streets of Constantinople; a female head

in the foreground forms the group. The old Turk has his pipe, and an old chest beside him, containing his writing materials, I suppose; a dog lies in one corner. Painted upon panel. In the catalogue was found 446. First sketch of the 'Letter Writer,' a tinted drawing; the colouring was very little. This, I think, was probably the the first—whether taken on the spot, or immediately on reaching home, is doubtful. There is another sketch at the Royal Academy which may be for the arrangement of colour: some parts are in pencil, some in red chalk, and water colour. From this probably the oil painting was taken. 680. Study of an old chest. This I did not see, but probably this may be for the 'Letter Writer.' Examples of Eastern costume Wilkie brought with him. A male and female lay figure were dressed in them. From Spain too he brought some. Haydon bid for a Spanish cloak. 498. 'Bargaining for a Circassian Slave,' a tinted drawing. In this sketch, or rather composition, I recognized the figure of the Circassian slave as that of one who before passed as 462. 'A Circassian Lady.' In this way Wilkie may have made figures do duty frequently. 'The Tartar relating the capture of Acre' may have been composed in this way. It is of great interest to trace the history of a great man's works. With this view I examined Wilkie's sketches to trace *their* history if possible, and *his* practice. In this way he may have composed the last-mentioned picture. There was his picture of 'Chelsea Pensioners listening to the News of the Battle of Waterloo,' to suggest the subject; and a great sensation at the time was created by the siege of Acre. Several views of the place he had himself taken. In the East particularly such an event as the siege would form a subject of conversation for the common people; and without seeing the incident he represents there is enough in the following sketches to make up the picture. 447. 'A Barber's Shop, Constantinople.' I mention this, because in the picture is a sketch of a barber shaving a man, with the basin up to his neck. The metal basin is placed with the outside next the throat. It always reminds one of Mambrino's helmet. 482. A 'Turkish Coffee House.' 487. 'A Coffee Shop.' 483. 'Interior of a Café.' From recollection I should say that 444, 'A Post Rider,' a capital finished sketch, was very like the Tartar relating the news, and perhaps was the man, some of their equipments were the same—the position was different. 589 is 'The travelling Tartar, or the Queen's Messenger.' The scene appears in a Turkish coffee-house, where the company are seated, smoking, eating, drinking, being shaved, while the Tartar is relating the news.

Referring again to nature. In works possessing such truth and nature as Wilkie's, a figure can never successfully be turned to a particular use without such being originally in contemplation of the artist. And again, in composition, a figure borrowed from a sketch will not compose without alteration, and with alteration you want nature. Painting from studies that are sketches with design and light shade, where they are taken for one certain intention, and have merely to be copied in colours on canvas, can readily be understood.

William of Wykeham. History has only taken care of the fame of one of our early Gothic artists,—the architect of Winchester Cathedral, Windsor Castle, and New College, Oxford. He was born 1324, the eighteenth of Edward II. Of Windsor Castle little remains of Wykeham's workmanship, save the Round Tower.

Willow wood is of many varieties: it is perhaps the softest and lightest of English woods; it is planed into chips, and used for many simple purposes.

Wilson (Richard) was born 1713, in Montgomeryshire. At first he pursued portrait painting, but in his thirty-sixth year, on going to Italy, relinquished that department of art for landscape painting. He found no market for his productions, gradually fell into distress, and was rescued from utter starvation by the salary of librarian of the Royal Academy. Finally he succeeded to a small estate in Wales, which was sufficient for his comforts, and where he died. Wilson's landscapes are in general productions of fancy, rather than of existing reality—scenes pictured forth by the imagination, rather than transcribed from Nature,—yet there is enough of nature in them to please, and enough of what is poetic, to charm the most fastidious fancy. He sometimes painted fac-similes of scenes.

Wimple, a plaited linen cloth which nuns wear about their necks; also a flag or streamer.

Winch or *Wince*, in mining, the wheel or axle frequently used to draw water, etc. in a kibble by a rope.

Winch and Axle, a machine constituting a small windlass, and consisting of a cylinder of wood which is capable of turning on its axis between two upright posts of the same material, or between the ends of a cast-iron frame: a lever at one or at each extremity of the cylinder is attached to an iron axle passing through the latter at right angles to its direction, and is furnished with a handle, which is parallel to that axle. The name winch is given to a lever or handle of this kind, and the word is supposed to be derived from the verb *guincher*, signifying, in old French, to turn, or bend in a curvilinear manner. The machine is used to raise a weight vertically, or to draw an object towards it; for which purposes the object is connected with it by a rope or chain which continually passes over the curved surface of the cylinder as the latter is made to turn on its axis by a man acting at the handle. Since the cylinder revolves once while the handle, or the extremity of the lever to which it is attached, is made to describe the circumference of a circle, it is evident that the mechanical power of the machine is precisely that of the wheel and axle. When of a simple form, it is employed to raise water from a well, and earth or some other material from the shaft of a small mine; and one of a complex nature is used, by means of a crane, to raise casks or heavy packages from the ground to the upper part of a building.

When great weights are to be raised, the machine is usually fixed in a frame of cast iron, which is rectangular on the plan, but its extremities or faces have the form of a triangle, or of the letter A. The axle of the cylinder is supported on a horizontal bar at the middle of each end of the frame, and to the cylinder is attached a toothed wheel which turns with it on the common axis: above this wheel, and parallel to the cylinder, is an iron axle which carries a pinion with teeth working in those of the wheel, and causing the latter to revolve; the pinion itself being turned by means of the lever and handle at one or at each extremity of the frame. A machine of this kind is called a *crab*; and when a weight is to be drawn horizontally or raised above the cylinder, the machine must of course be bolted to the floor or firmly fixed in the ground, in order to prevent it from being moved from its place. In such machines there is generally, at one extremity of the cylinder, a wheel having on its circumference teeth like those of a saw; and a *click* or catch, which turns freely on a pin, is attached by that pin to the side of the frame in such a manner that it may fall between the teeth. By this contrivance, if the handle should break, or the moving power be taken off while the weight is suspended in the air, the latter is prevented from descending.

Machines of this kind are occasionally constructed, which have the power of holding the weight in any part of its ascent or descent without a ratched-wheel and catch. The only disadvantage attending the machine, when compared with an ordinary winch or capstain, is, that it requires a much greater quantity of rope to raise or move the object through any given distance. It was first proposed in Europe by Mr. George Eckhardt, but machines of a like kind have, it is said, long been in use in the East.

The winch is employed in the common jack, which is used to lift great weights, or to move them through small distances. The handle turns a pinion with teeth, which act on others at the circumference of a small wheel; and on the axle of this is a pinion with teeth, which work in those of a rack-rod. The axles of the wheel and pinions being let into the sides of a case of wood or iron, the revolution of the wheel produces a rectilinear motion of the rack; and one end of the case being fixed to the ground, or against an immovable object, the extremity of the rack at the opposite end forces forward the body which is to be displaced. Sometimes, instead of a rack, the machine is furnished with a wheel whose axle is hollow, and cut in the form of a concave screw: within this screw is one of the convex kind, which by the revolution of the wheel and its axle is made to move in the direction of the latter, and thus to press before it the object which is to be removed. This machine has, however, considerable friction.

The force exerted by a man in turning a winch vertically, varies according to the position of the lever with respect to the horizon. When the lever, or that part which is perpendicular to the axle, is perpendicular to the ground, and the handle is at the highest or lowest part of the circle described by the end of the lever, the man either pushes the handle directly from him or pulls it directly towards him; and in each case he exerts a power which is estimated at 27 or 30 lbs.; but when the lever is in a horizontal position, the man either throws a great portion of his weight on the handle to press it down, or he exerts his muscular force in a direct manner to pull it upwards; and the force exerted in these positions is estimated at 140 or 160 pounds. The force exerted must very evidently have different values between these quantities in other positions of the winch; and the practice is to cause two men to work at the same time to turn the machine, one being at each extremity of the axle of the cylinder. The levers of the two winches are placed at right angles to one another; consequently, when one man is pushing or pulling horizontally, the other is pressing or pulling vertically, and thus the operation of turning goes on with nearly uniform intensity; the first man working in the least favourable position when the other is working in that which is most so.

Wind, instrument for measuring the force and velocity of: a fly (resembling that of a revolving ventilator, or the sails of a wind-mill) is fixed to the small end of the vane of a weathercock so as to be turned with its circular disc to the wind; and it consequently revolves by the action of the wind with a rapidity increasing as the force of the wind increases. The revolutions of the axis of this fly are converted by a train of toothed wheels and screws into a vertical motion, by which a pencil is carried downwards, touching the surface of a vertical cylinder the cylinder having the axis of the weathercock for its axis. As the vertical rod on which the pencil slides is attached to the vane of the weathercock, the point of the compass from which the wind blows is recorded on the sides of the cylinder on which the mark is made; while the *quantity* of the wind is represented by the extent of the *descent* of the pencil.

Wind beam, in ancient carpentry, a cross-beam used in the principals of many ancient roofs, occupying the situation of the collar in modern king-post roofs.

Winding, in ships, twisting on an uneven surface.

Winding engines. In winding engines for drawing coals from a pit, where a given number of strokes are required in drawing a corf, the diameter of the roll at the first lift must be ascertained. In this case the engine is supposed to have flat ropes, such as are generally used, and which lie upon each other. To find the diameter of a rope-roll at the first lift, it is necessary to know the depth of the pit, the thickness of the rope, and the number of strokes which the engine is intended to make in drawing up a corf or curves; then, the thickness of the rope being known and the number of strokes, the thickness of the ropes upon the roll can be determined, let the diameter of the roll be what it may. Suppose the thickness of the rope to be 1 inch, and the number of strokes 10; then the radius of the roll is increased 10 inches, or the diameter is increased 20 inches, whatever the diameter may be.

Windlass, in mechanics, a machine by which a rope or lace is wrapped round a cylinder; in navigation, a horizontal machine of strong timber, used in merchant ships for heaving up the anchor, instead of a capstan.

Wind-mill, a mill which derives its motive power from the impulse of the wind. The building containing the mill-work is usually lofty, and placed on elevated ground. The machinery consists of a shaft, upon one extremity of which arms radiate at right angles, similarly to the spokes of a wheel: upon these, vanes or sails are set at a small angle (about 22°). By this means the wind, blowing directly upon the area occupied by the vanes, acts obliquely upon the whole of them, causing them all to move in a direction transversely to that of the wind. Suitable means are provided for bringing the sails into a position to confront the current of the wind. The motion of the sails is transferred by gearing to any machinery required to be driven, which is most commonly mills for grinding corn. Windmills were formerly extensively employed, in Holland, to give motion to pumps for the drainage of land. The power of the wind is uncertain and variable in its intensity, and its application as a prime mover for mechanical purposes is consequently limited.

Windows were almost unknown in the religious and other monumental structures of the Egyptians, Greeks, and Romans, but they constitute an essential and distinguishing feature of the Gothic, to which style they stand in the same relation as Orders do to the temple architecture of antiquity.

Windows admit of very rich and varied decoration, and those in Beccles church, Suffolk (represented on the opposite page), are beautiful examples. The varied exuberance of fancy displayed in the tracery may possibly be accounted for by supposing each to

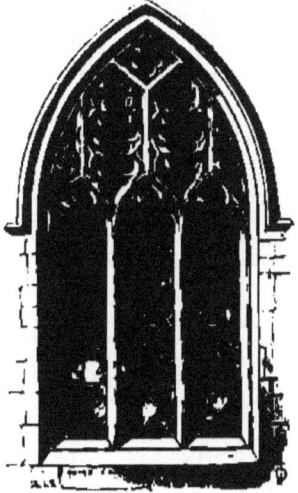

have been the gift of some pious individual, who, while he perpetuated his munificence, marked also his taste and ingenuity.

The practice of window tracery everywhere had its origin in window-*grouping*, placing two or three lancet windows beside each other, and one or more foil or rosette windows above and between their heads, in order to fill out the arched cell of the vaulting, which then necessarily gave the whole group an arched outline; and this was indicated by a general dripmould or label. It then became desirable to lighten the irregular shaped masses of stone left between the perforations, and this was done by piercing these masses, or spandrils, and reducing the solid frame of each foil or rosette to an equal thickness all round, as if several such frames or rings were packed into one great arched opening, which henceforth was regarded as *one* window instead of several. (For further illustration, see art. *Tracery*.)

Wind-sail, in navigation, a sort of ventilator, consisting of a wide tube of canvas shaped like a funnel, to convey a stream of fresh air downwards to the hold and lower deck of a ship.

Wing transom, in ships, the uppermost transom of the stern-frame

Winze, in mining, a sinking in a lode communicating with one level, for proving the lode or ventilating the drivings.

Wipers, the cogs of a horizontal wheel.

Wood, in its raw state, contains a large amount of water. This water contains more or less soluble minerals, and is called *sap*. By drying wood, a great part, but not all, of this water is evaporated. If wood is dried in a closed vessel, and then exposed to the atmosphere, it quickly absorbs moisture; but the moisture thus absorbed is much less than the wood originally contained.

The amount of water varies in different kinds of wood, and also varies according to the season. Wood cut in the month of April contains from 10 to 20 per cent. more water than that cut in the month of January.

The following Table shows the percentage of water in different kinds of wood dried as far as possible in the air:—

Beech	18·6
Poplar	26·0
Sugar and common Maple	27·0
Ash	28·0
Birch	30·0
Oak, red	34·7
Oak, white	35·5
Pine, white	37·0
Chestnut	38·2
Pine, red	39·0
Pine, white	45·5
Linden	47·1
Poplar, Italian	48·2
Poplar, black	51·8

Wood cut during the months of December and January is not only more solid, but it will dry faster than at any other period of the year, because the sap by that time has incorporated a great part of its soluble matter with the woody fibre; what remains is merely water. When the sap, during the months of February, March, and April, rises, it partly dissolves the woody fibre; and the drying of the wood is not only retarded, but the wood is weakened, in consequence of the solid matter thus held in solution.

The difference in chemical composition of the woody fire, in most kinds of wood, is but slight, as the following analytical Table shows:—

	Carbon	Hydrogen	Oxygen
Sugar Maple	52·65	5·25	42·10
Oak	49·43	6·07	44·50
Poplar, black	49·70	6·31	43·99
Pine	50·11	6·31	43·58

Wood is generally bought by admeasurement, and its specific gravity is directly in proportion to its amount of carbon, hydrogen, and oxygen. The following Table shows the specific gravity of wood. Water = 1000:—

	Green.	Air-dried.
Oak, white	1·0754	0·7075
Oak, red	1·0494	0·6777
Poplar	0·9859	0·4873
Beech	0·9822	0·5907
Sugar Maple	0·9036	0·5440
Birch	0·9012	0·6274
Pine, red	0·9121	0·5502
Pine white	0·8699	0·4716
Ebony	"	1·2260
Guaiac (lignum vitæ)	"	1·3420

Woolf's engine, a steam-engine so called from its inventor's name, with two combined cylinders of different diameter, the eduction passage of the smaller cylinder communicating with the steam passages of the other; high-pressure steam being used in the small cylinder, and made to act expansively in the large one, the steam being afterwards condensed in the usual manner. By this arrangement steam is economized, and a considerable saving of fuel is effected.

Work, in mining, ores before they are cleaned and dressed.

Working big, in mining, signifies sufficiently large for a man to work in.

Working drawings consist of plans, elevations, sections, and details in full, of the whole, and of all the parts of an edifice, to as large a scale as may be found convenient; generally made in outline, excepting the sectional parts, which are mostly shadowed, in order to make them more obvious to the workman, for whose use these drawings are made.

Worm-wheel, a wheel having teeth formed to fit into the spiral spaces of a screw, so that the wheel may be turned by the screw.

Wreath, in heraldry, that which is between the mantle and the crest, called also a torce; also a boar's tail, so termed among hunters.

Wren (Sir Christopher), born in 1631 or 1632. The Monument, by Wren, was begun 1671, and completed 1677. It is of the Doric order, rises from the pavement 202 feet. The plinth is 21 feet square, and ornamented with sculpture by Cibber, representing the flames subsiding on the appearance of King Charles; beneath his horse's feet a figure, meant to personify religious malice, crawls out, vomiting fire. The shaft is 15 feet in diameter at the base. The Royal Exchange of London, and Temple Bar, were among his earliest works. St. Paul's was his great work. The Church of St. Peter's, at Rome, had twelve architects, and took 145 years to build; that of St. Paul's was built in thirty-six years, and had but one architect. On the artists of the Roman fabric honours and wealth were showered; on the architect of St. Paul's the king bestowed £200 per annum, and the clerical and lay commissioners harassed him with criticisms, and persecuted him with ridiculous and groundless charges.

To describe all Wren's churches would require volumes at least. The church of St. Mary-le-Bow, Cheapside, has been praised for the incomparable beauty of its spire. The church of St. Stephen's, Walbrook, is reckoned by many the masterpiece of the architect. The church of St. Bride's, Fleet Street, is worthy of being named after that of St. Stephen's, and the many churches in the city of London, St. James's, Westminster, show the greatness of his mind.

Wrought iron. The chemical difference between cast iron and wrought iron consists principally in the degree in which foreign matters is present in each; which is in larger amount in the former than in the latter. this rule is applicable only to a given cast iron, and to the wrought or bar iron which is made from it. There are many cases in which wrought iron contains a larger amount of impurities than cast iron, and still continues malleable; while cast iron of the same composition may be very hard and brittle. Berzelius detected 18 per cent. of silex in a certain kind of bar iron, which was still malleable and useful. One-tenth of that amount of silex will make cast iron brittle. The foreign matters generally combined with pig iron are, carbon, silicon, silex, sulphur, phosphorus, arsenic, zinc, manganese, titanium, chrome, aluminium, magnesium, and calcium. Each of these tends to make iron brittle; therefore, in converting cast into wrought iron, it is necessary, as far as possible, to remove them.

The main difference between pig and wrought iron consists in their mechanical structure, or aggregate form. Pig iron is a homogeneous mixture of impurities and metal. Wrought or bar iron is a mixture of iron more or less pure with a mass of homogeneous impurities, or cinder, the latter filling the crevices between the crystals of the iron. Iron being fusible in proportion to the carbon it contains, if pig metal is melted, and the cinder surrounding it exposed to the atmosphere, the carbon will be volatilized in the form of carbonic acid, and iron of greater or less purity will remain. To keep this iron liquid, a higher temperature is required: unless the temperature is raised, it will crystallize. In this state of metamorphosis its infusibility will increase, and after the expulsion of the carbon, it will contract into a solid mass in opposition to the highest possible heat. By stirring and mixing the pasty iron, small crystals are formed; at first, on account of the partial fusion of the iron, in small particles; but, as the fusibility diminishes, these particles unite by the force of cohesion; and the bodies thus formed may, by exposure to a higher heat, be welded together. The mixing of cinder and iron will prevent the latter from forming large crystals: this result, of course, will be more easily prevented by diligent than by tardy manipulation. Where the pig iron is of such a nature as to keep liquid while the work goes on slowly, still better results will be obtained. This process is analogous to that of salt boiling, in which, by stirring the brine, the formation of large crystals is prevented. If the crystals of iron thus formed cohere, they produce under the influence of motion, a porous, spongy mass, whose crevices are, if not filled, at least coated, with cinder. If these masses, which are the loups or balls at the puddling furnaces, are shingled or squeezed, the crystals of iron will not unite, but form coated cells with a film of cinder, of greater or less thickness, according to the fusibility of the cinder. Iron in a connected form and cinder in separate cells, are thus blended in one homogeneous mass. The more this iron is stretched, the more it forms fibres. Fibrous bar iron resembles hickory wood, in being a combination of fibres and spaces. In bar iron, these spaces are filled with cinder. When other circumstances are equal, the strength of the iron will be proportional to the fineness of the fibres. That portion of the iron which is not melted, which crystallizes too fast, or whose premature crystallization cannot be prevented, is in the condition of cast metal, and cannot be converted into fibrous wrought iron. In the puddling furnace it is necessary to prevent crystallization by manual labour.

If the characteristic between wrought and pig iron consists only in a well-regulated mechanical mixture of cinder and iron, fibrous iron should be producible from any cast iron, whether purified or not: this is actually the case. Very fibrous bar iron, which is strong and malleable, is made from very inferior cast metal, from which no impurity has been removed. At Hyanges, in France, very inferior metal is converted by a cheap and skilful puddling process, into a very fibrous bar iron, of great strength and ductility. But this iron is puddled and re-heated at the lowest possible heat; it is then rolled, and is ready for the market. For hoops, rails, and nails, it is a very useful article, but it is of no use to the blacksmith. Heated to any temperature above that of the puddling and re-heating furnaces, it returns to its primitive state, in which condition it becomes worse than the cast iron from which it was originally made. None but a very skilful blacksmith can weld it; for, when slightly re-heated, it falls to coarse sandy pieces, or melts like pig iron. That which thus loses its fibrous texture in heating, the smith calls 'burnt iron.'

The philosophy of the improvement of metal consists in the circumstance that a part of its impurities which are originally in chemical combination, are converted into mechanical admixtures. Iron, containing a small amount of carbon, silicon, or phosphorus, is always more hard and strong than pure iron. Pure iron is quite soft. Impure iron has the property of crystallizing, or being suddenly cooled: the size of these crystals is proportional to the amount of carbon in chemical combination with the iron, in proportion to other matter. Between the crystals minute spaces are left, which serve for the absorption of oxygen. By this means, silicon and calcium may be oxidized, but not carbon, phosphorus, and sulphur. The metal improves in quality in proportion as oxygen finds access to its impurities.

The absolute cohesion or strength of wrought iron is not dependent upon the degree of purity of the metal, but upon a given mixture of cinder and iron. Pure iron, which is always soft, may be required for various purposes, as in the manufacture of cast steel; but, in most cases, an impure but fibrous iron is preferable. In making wrought iron, the main difficulty consists, not in producing fibres in the first stages of the operation,—for this may be accomplished by almost every experienced manufacturer,—but in retaining these fibres through every subsequent stage of the operation.

Wrought iron of good quality is silvery white and fibrous; carbon imparts to it a bluish, and often a gray colour: sulphur, a dark, dead colour, without a tinge of blue; silicon, phosphorus, and carbon, a bright colour, which is the more beautiful the more the first two elements preponderate. The lustre of iron does not depend principally upon its colour; for pure iron, although silvery white, reflects but little light. A small quantity of carbon in chemical combination, phosphorus, or silicon, increases its brilliancy. Its lustre is diminished by silex, carbon in mechanical admixture, cinder, lime, sulphur, or magnesia. Good iron should appear fresh, somewhat reflex in its fibres, and silky. A dead colour indicates a weak iron, even though it is perfectly white. Dark but very lustrous iron is always superior to that which has a bright colour and feeble lustre. Coarse fibres indicate a strong, but, if the iron is dark, an inferior article. Where the iron is of a white, bright colour they indicate an article of superior quality for sheet iron and boiler-plate, though too soft for railroad iron. For the latter purpose, a coarse, fibrous, slightly bluish iron is required. Iron of short fibre is too pure; it is generally hot-short, and, when cold, not strong. This kind of iron is apt to result from the application of an excess of lime: its weakness is the result of the absence of all impurities. The best qualities of bar iron always contain a small amount of impurity. Steel ceases to be hard and strong, when deprived of the small amount of silicon it contains, or if the silicon is oxidized by repeated heating. This is the case with bar iron. If deprived of all foreign admixture, it ceases to be a strong, tenacious, and beautiful iron, but becomes a pale, soft metal, of feeble strength and lustre. Good bar or wrought iron is always fibrous: it loses its fibres neither by heat nor by cold. Time may change its aggregate form; but its fibrous quality should always be considered the guarantee of its strength. Iron of good quality will bear cold hammering to any extent. A bar an inch square, which cannot be hammered down to a quarter of an inch, on a cold anvil, without showing any traces of splitting, is an inferior iron.

X.

Xebec, in navigation, a small three-masted vessel, without a bowsprit, principally used in the Mediterranean.

Xenodochium, a room in a monastery for the reception and entertainment of strangers, pilgrims, and the relief of paupers.

XP. I., the initials of the Greek names of Christ; a monogram, represented in paintings and mosaics by the Greek Christians.

Xylography, the art of engraving on wood.

Xystos, in ancient architecture, a large portico in the gymnasium, for the accommodation of the wrestlers; a sheltered walk.

Y.

Yacht, in navigation, a small ship for carrying passengers.

Yard, a court enclosed by walls and other buildings; also a measure of 3 feet; a yard or yerd was anciently a spar or rafter in a timber roof.

Yardland, a certain quantity of land, called, in Saxon, gyrdlander; in Latin, virgata terræ; in some places it is 20 acres of land, in others 24 or 30.

Yellow is the first of the primary or simple colours, nearest in relation to and partaking most of the nature of the neutral white: it is accordingly a most advancing colour, of great power in reflecting light. Compounded with the primary red, it constitutes the secondary orange and its relatives, scarlet, etc.; and other warm colours.

Yellow Lake. There are several pigments of this denomination, varying in colour and appearance, according to the colouring substances used and modes of preparation. They are usually in the form of drops, and their colours are, in general, bright yellow, very transparent, and not liable to change in an impure atmosphere,—qualities which would render them very valuable pigments, were they not soon discoloured and even destroyed by the opposite influence of oxygen and light, both in water and oil, in which latter vehicle, like other lakes in general, they are bad dryers, and do not stand the action of white lead or other metallic colours. If used, therefore, it should be as simple as possible.

Yellow Ochre, called also *Mineral Yellow*, is a native pigment, found in most countries, and abundantly in our own. It varies considerably in constitution and colour, in which latter particular it is found from a bright but not very vivid yellow to a brown yellow, called spruce ochre, and is always of a warm cast. Its natural variety is much increased by artificial dressing and compounding.

Yellow Orpiment, or *Yellow Arsenic*, is a sulphurate oxide of arsenic, of a beautiful, bright, and pure yellow colour, not extremely durable in water, and less so in oil. In tint with white lead, it is soon destroyed. It is not subject to discoloration in impure air.

Yew. The yew-tree is common in Spain, Italy, and England, and is indigenous to Nottinghamshire. The tree is not large, and the wood is of a pale yellowish-red colour, handsomely striped, and often dotted like amboyna. It has been long famed for the construction of bows, and is still so employed. The English species is a hard, tough, and durable wood, and lives to a great age. It is also used for the making of chairs, the handles of articles of furniture, etc.

Z.

Zebra wood is the produce of the Brazils and Rio Janeiro; it is sent in logs and planks as large as 24 inches. The colour is orange-brown and dark-brown variously mixed. Its beautiful appearance fits it for cabinet-work and turnery.

Zero, the commencement of a scale marked 0, or nothing. It usually denotes the point from which the scale of a thermometer is graduated.

Zeta, presumed to be a room over the porch of a Christian church.

Zigzag, a moulding by lines arranged in the manner of the heraldic chevron. Zigzag is found frequently used in Norman and Anglo-Norman architecture. Very many beautiful specimens of this ornament exist in doors and windows of the Anglo-Norman Gothic in England. (See *Doors*, and the *Frontispiece* for an early specimen.)

Zinc. This metal exists in abundance, and is employed for many purposes. It is commonly combined with sulphur in zinc blende, and with carbonic acid in the mineral calamine, which is the most valuable of all its ores. Zinc may be obtained pure by redistilling in a porcelain retort, which is sold in commerce. It is obtained from the ores as follows: they are first washed and mixed with powdered coke or charcoal, are distilled from an earthern close vessel, with an iron tube passing through its bottom, the upper end of which is open, and the lower end entering a vessel of water. At a bright red heat zinc volatizes, and is condensed in the water, gases passing off along with it. It is a bluish-white metal, which slowly tarnishes in the air. It is brittle at ordinary temperatures, but at about 300° it is malleable, and may be rolled or hammered into sheets, and retains its ductility when cold. At 400° it may be reduced to powder: it melts at 773°.

Zinc white is an oxide of zinc which has been more celebrated as a pigment than used, being perfectly durable in water and oil, but wanting the body and brightness of fine white leads in oil; while, in water, constant or barytic white and pearl white are superior to it in colour, and equal in durability. Nevertheless, zinc white is valuable as far as its powers extend in painting, on account of its durability both in oil and water, and its innocence with regard to health; and, when duly and skilfully prepared, the colour and body of this pigment are sufficient to qualify it for a general use upon the palette, although the pure white of lead must merit a preference in oil.

Zocle, to name given to a low, plain, square member or plinth supporting a column.

Zoophorus, in architecture, a part between the architraves and cornice, so called on account of the ornaments carved on it, among which are the figures of animals.

Zyghyr, or *Sigger*, in mining. When a slow stream of water issues through a cranny, it is said to sigger, or zyghyr.

ADDENDA.

ELECTRIC TELEGRAPH.

Electric Telegraph. The employment of electricity in the transmission of intelligence originated at an early period of the history of electrical science. Plans to this effect had been brought before the public; but all wanted a simplicity of principle and of construction. In 1837, Messrs. Cooke and Wheatstone obtained their first patent for an electric telegraph, applicable to general purposes. This patent has been subsequently followed at short intervals by others, in which the invention has been gradually brought to its present form; the principles originally employed have been progressively rendered more varied and general in their application, and the apparatus more simple in its details. By these improvements the number of wires necessary for the conveyance of intelligence has been reduced, and the construction has been rendered cheaper and more perfect.

The electric telegraph involves in its construction two essential principles. First, that a magnetized needle, which is free to rotate about its centre, being brought near to a wire, through which an electric current is passing, has a tendency to place itself at right angles to that wire; the direction of its motion following a certain invariable law. This fact was the discovery of Prof. Œrsted, of Copenhagen, in 1819. Secondly, that a piece of soft iron, not being permanently magnetic, is rendered temporarily so during the transmission of an electric current along a wire coiled spirally around it.

The figures to which reference is here made, in the brief description of the apparatus, are, 1. A view of the interior of the single-needle instrument, showing the position of the coil and of the battery connections. A vertical section of the same, through the coil and handle. 3. The handle or key, in the position for giving a signal, part being removed, to render the battery connections more distinct. 4. Plan of the same. The double-needle instrument differs from the single-needle only in the duplication of all the parts.

The coil A, figs. 1 and 2, consists of a light hollow frame of brass or wood, around which are wound, in two portions, about 200 yards of fine copper wire, covered with silk or cotton. This length of wire renders the indications of the needle distinct and prompt, even with a low-battery power, or when forming part of a very extended circuit. The resistance which would be offered by the fine wire of the coil (its diameter being about $\frac{1}{70}$th of an inch) to the passage of a current of electricity, derived from an ordinary battery of a few cells only, is overcome by using a battery arrangement of considerable intensity, but which developes the electrical fluid only in small quantity.

ELECTRIC TELEGRAPH.

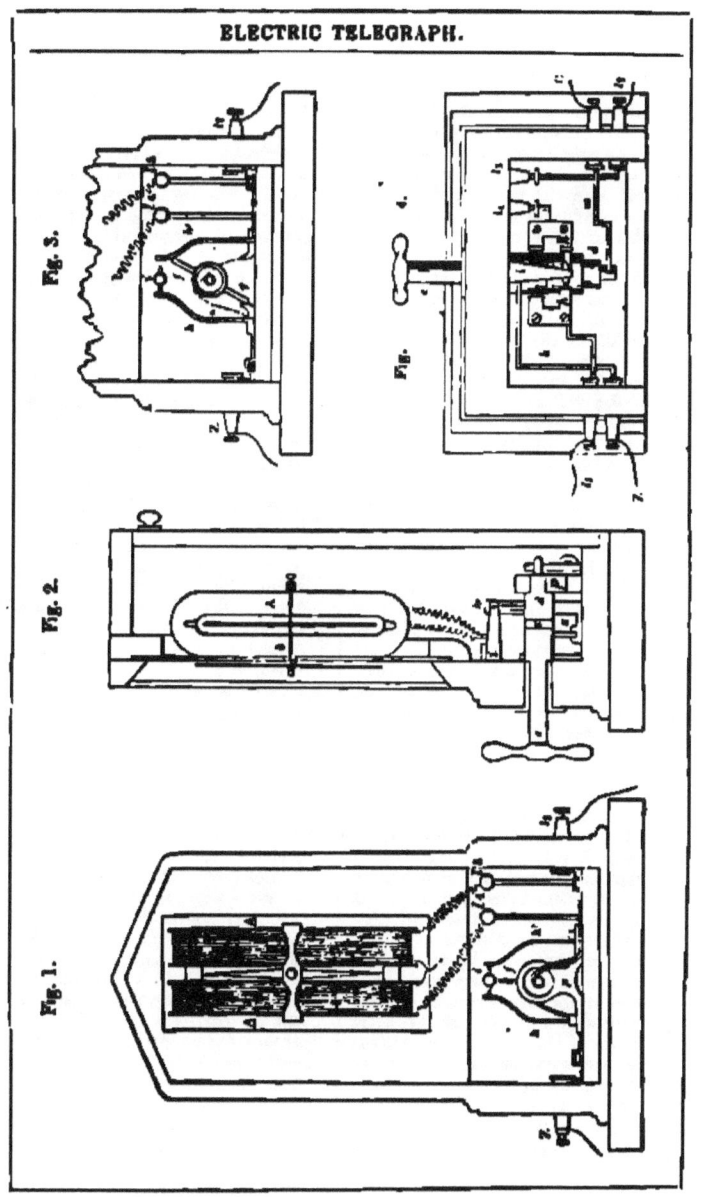

ELECTRIC TELEGRAPH.

Or, speaking rather more correctly, we should say, that the electro-motive resistance, both of the battery and also of the ordinary circuit, being very considerable, the introduction of the resistance of the coil into the latter produces but little influence upon the transmission of the current. Within the brass frame, and therefore interior to the coils of wire, is suspended a magnetic needle, upon a horizontal axis b, which passes across the middle of the frame, and turns on fine pivots at the back and front of the coil. In front of the frame and of the dial of the instrument is fixed on the same axis b, a second needle having its poles oppositely placed to those of the first. This outer needle serves as the indicator or pointer, by which the signals are made, and at the same time is acted upon by the coil, though in a less degree than the inner needle. The combination of the two needles being thus rendered astatic, it is necessary to give a slight preponderance to their lower ends, in order that they may recover their vertical position, after having been deflected; and the action of gravity has been found more effectual, in bringing the needle to rest without oscillations, than either springs applied at the sides, or the directive influence of permanent magnets. With the coil and needles thus arranged, it is evident that signals may be given by the combination of successive deflections to one side or the other; the extent of such deflections being limited to any degree that may be found convenient, either by pins fixed on the dial of the instrument, or by stops placed at the sides of the brass frame of the coil. In fact, all that is necessary for rendering these movements of the needle available for the transmission of intelligence, is a contrivance for reversing with ease and rapidity the connection of the battery with the ends of the two conducting wires. This expedient is provided by the handle or key of the instrument.

The conductor through which the electrical current is to circulate must be absolutely complete in all parts. It is not necessary that the material of the circuit be the same throughout, but only that its conductibility be maintained from the one pole of the battery to the other; the slightest want of continuity of the conducting matter, at any part of the circuit, being fatal to the passage of the fluid. So long as the wires for telegraphic purposes were extended between the two points of communication, by being laid within tubes buried in the earth, a second wire was requisite to enable the current to return from the distant station to the point whence it set out. It was well known that the earth itself afforded such a means of return; but the insulation of the wires in the tubes from the earth could not be rendered sufficiently perfect to make the use of the earth, as a portion of the circuit, either prudent or desirable. When, however, the wires were suspended in the air, according to Mr. Cooke's patent of 1842, the earth was advantageously employed as half the circuit. All that was found necessary, was to connect the extreme ends of the conducting wire with plates of copper or other metal of two or three feet of surface, buried at some depth in the ground; or with any system of gas or water-pipes, which might afford a continuous metallic path for the fluid to the earth. In either case, the depth of the connection beneath the surface must be sufficient to ensure certain contact with moist earth or with water, provided that this latter be not confined within any cistern or reservoir. When all these precautions have been taken, the passage of electricity is readily effected, the earth

ELECTRIC TELEGRAPH.

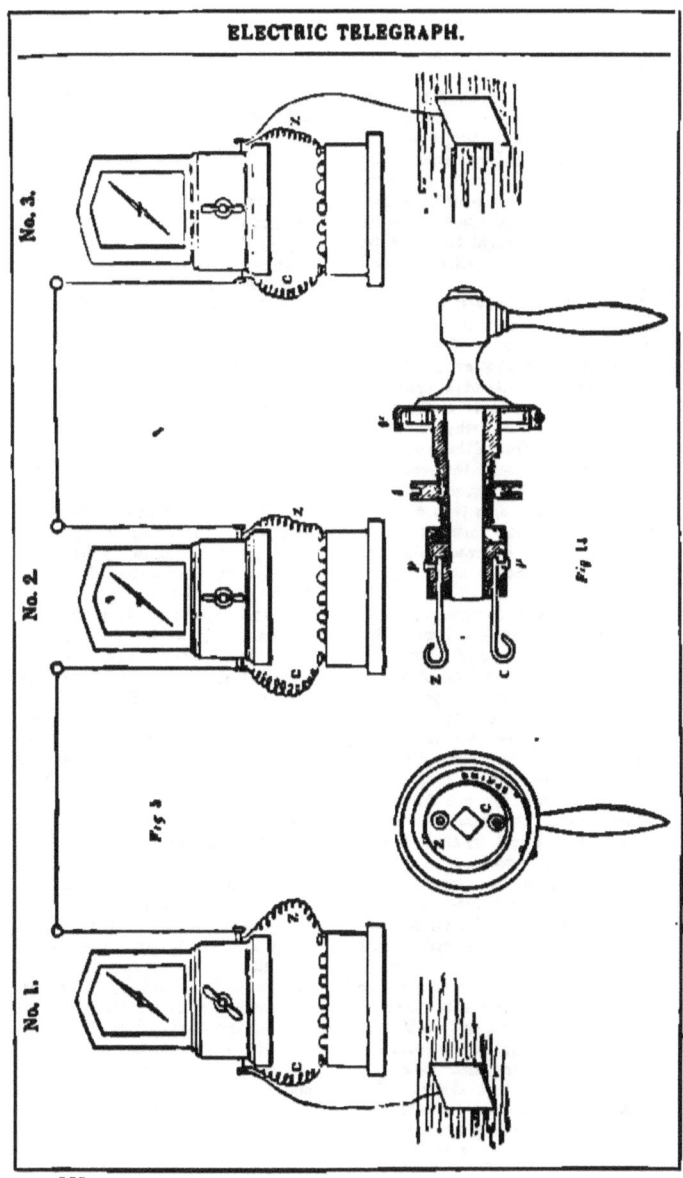

appearing to offer little or no resistance to its progress. According to the law established by Ohm, the resistance of any conductor varies directly as its length, and inversely at its sectional area. The earth may evidently be regarded as a conductor, of which the diameter is infinite, compared with its length, and we might therefore be led to expect the result mentioned above.

To return, however, to the description of the apparatus, the key or handle by means of which the connection of the battery is effected and varied, consists of a cylinder, in which is a middle zone, e, of hard wood or ivory, while the ends are of metal. One of these ends, c, extending through the case in front, forms the actual handle; while the other, d, is turned down to a shoulder and forms a pivot, which rests in a brass collar, p. The end d carries a steel pin, f, projecting upward, and e, a similar pin g, directed downward. The battery being connected with the terminals z and c, and thence by the brass strips k and m, of which the extremities rest as springs on the metallic ends of the cylinder, may in fact be considered as having its poles at the two pins, f and g, which are fixed in those ends. Two springs, h and h', are fixed by broad feet to the base of the instrument, and rest by their upper extremities on two studs or points projecting from a brass rod, i, screwed into the case in front. These springs form the circuit between the terminal $l\,1$, with which one end of the conducting wire is connected, and $l\,4$. Between this latter terminal and the external connection, $l\,2$, the coil itself, and the brass strip extending from $l\,3$ to $l\,2$, are interposed. When a signal is being sent through the instrument (supposed to hold the place of No. 2 in fig. 5), the current from No. 1 being considered to enter from the long wire on the line, by the terminal $l\,2$, passes along the brass strip to the terminal $l\,3$, thence through the coil to $l\,4$; then to the spring h, across the pin i, down the spring h', and to the terminal $l\,1$ in connection with the wire leaving the station. Were the instrument in question situated as No. 1 or No. 3, it will be seen that one of the terminals, $l\,1$ or $l\,2$, according to its position, would be joined to the wire coming from the earth-plate.

When a signal is to be given by the instrument, the handle being turned as in figs. 3 and 4, one battery-pin, f, is brought in contact with the spring h', which is bent back and released from its contact with i, while the other battery-pin g, is pressed against the foot of the other spring h, which at this part is turned up to act as a stop. The current being then supposed to start from the pole f, proceeds down the spring h', to the coil and terminal $l\,2$, as before; thence along the line through the other instruments, and into the earth at the further extremity of the line. Re-ascending from the earth by the wire connected with the terminal $l\,1$, it gains the foot of the spring h, with which the second battery pole g, is in contact. It will be seen that the direction of the current is different, according as the key is turned to the right or left. The position of the battery wires is such, that the needle shall be deflected in parallelism to the handle. A comparison of fig. 5, in which three instruments are shown in series, with the figures 1, 2, 3, and 4, will render the method of connection, both of the two terminal and of the intermediate instruments, sufficiently obvious. The wires on entering a station are designated as 'up' or 'down' wires, according to the portion of the line from which they come. Care must be, of course,

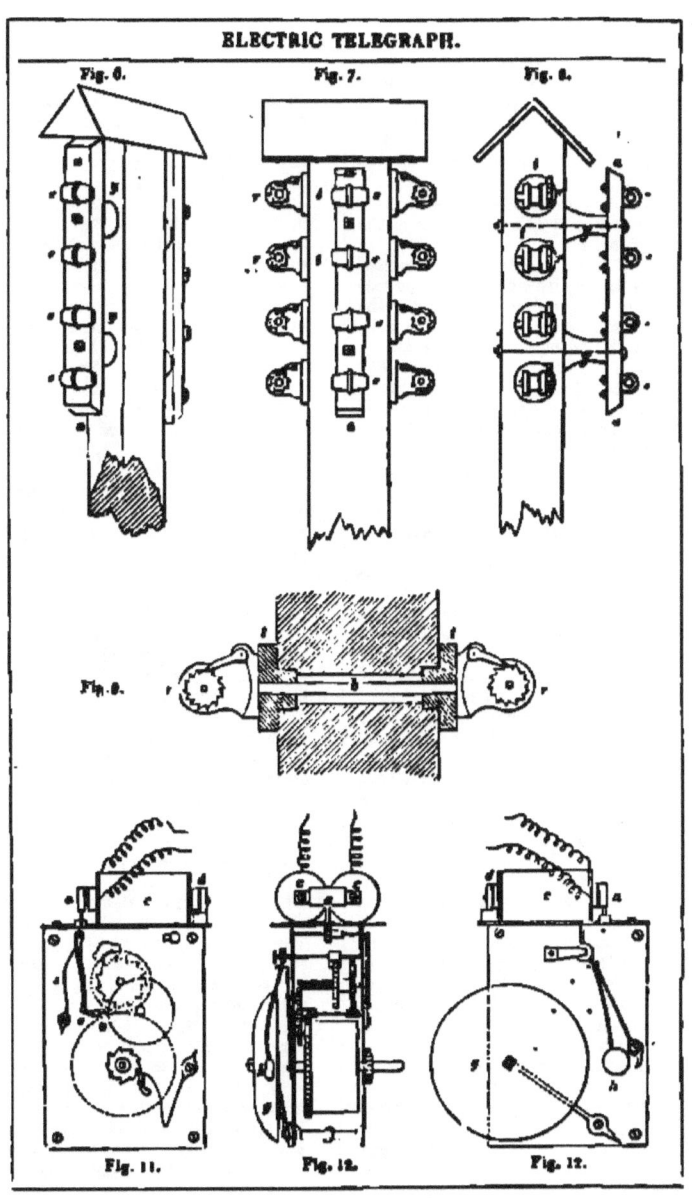

taken that all the instruments in one series are similarly joined to the up and down wires, so that the course of the current may be alike in all. At the extreme 'up station' the earth connection becomes the 'up wire,' and at the opposite terminus it takes the place of the 'down wire.'

The electric fluid is represented as starting from one pole of the battery only, and, after traversing the circuit, returning to the other pole. It is, however, more consonant with the theories deduced from the observation of electrical phenomena, to suppose that force is developed equally at both poles of the battery.

The second principle is that of the temporary magnetization of soft iron by the electric current, applied for the purpose of sounding an alarum at a distant station, in order to summon the attendant to his instrument. The same principle has been employed from an early period of the invention, both by Mr. Cooke and by Prof. Wheatstone, to transmit visible signals by causing the rotation of a disc, bearing letters or figures, or of a hand or index pointing to characters on a fixed dial; but in England the needle telegraph has been universally adopted, in preference to any other form. Many improvements have, however, been effected within the last few years by Prof. Wheatstone in the construction of the mechanical telegraph, as it has been named in contradistinction to the needle instrument. The same gentleman has also succeeded in substituting for the voltaic battery in the working of this telegraph, the magneto-electric machine, in which the current is derived by induction from a permanent magnet. The improvement which was effected by this adoption of a source of power, alike energetic and unalterable, will be immediately perceived. Telegraphs on this plan of construction have been erected in Prussia and France, and, were it not for some very marked advantages connected with the use of the needle signals, they could hardly fail to become general.

The ringing of the alarum was originally effected by the direct action of the voltaic magnet upon the hammer of the bell; but this method has been long superseded. The apparatus generally in use for this purpose is shown in a front and back view in figs. 11 and 13, and in a side view at figure 12. An electro-magnet is formed by coiling fine insulated copper wire around two cylinders of very soft pure iron. These coils, $c\ c$, are then connected by two of their ends, in such a manner that the direction in which the wire is wound about the iron cores may be alike in both. The iron cylinders are joined together at one end by a cross-piece d, likewise of soft iron, so that the whole then forms a horse-shoe magnet, having however its two sides parallel. In front of the free ends or poles of this magnet, which is fixed on the top of the plates of the alurum, an armature a, of soft iron, is placed at such a distance that it may be strongly attracted by the electro-magnet when the circuit is completed through its coils. The armature moves on an arbor, upon which a detent or catch e, is fastened, and so arranged that it is disengaged from a small fly v, whenever the attraction takes place. This disengagement allows a train of clock-work, impelled by a spring or weight, to run down, and by the action of a scape-wheel and pallets, seen in fig. 11, a hammer, h, rapidly strikes a small bell g. Immediately, however, that the current ceases to flow through the coils, the iron within them loses its magnetism, a small re-acting spring, s, draws back the armature, and interposes the detent so as to

ELECTRIC TELEGRAPH.

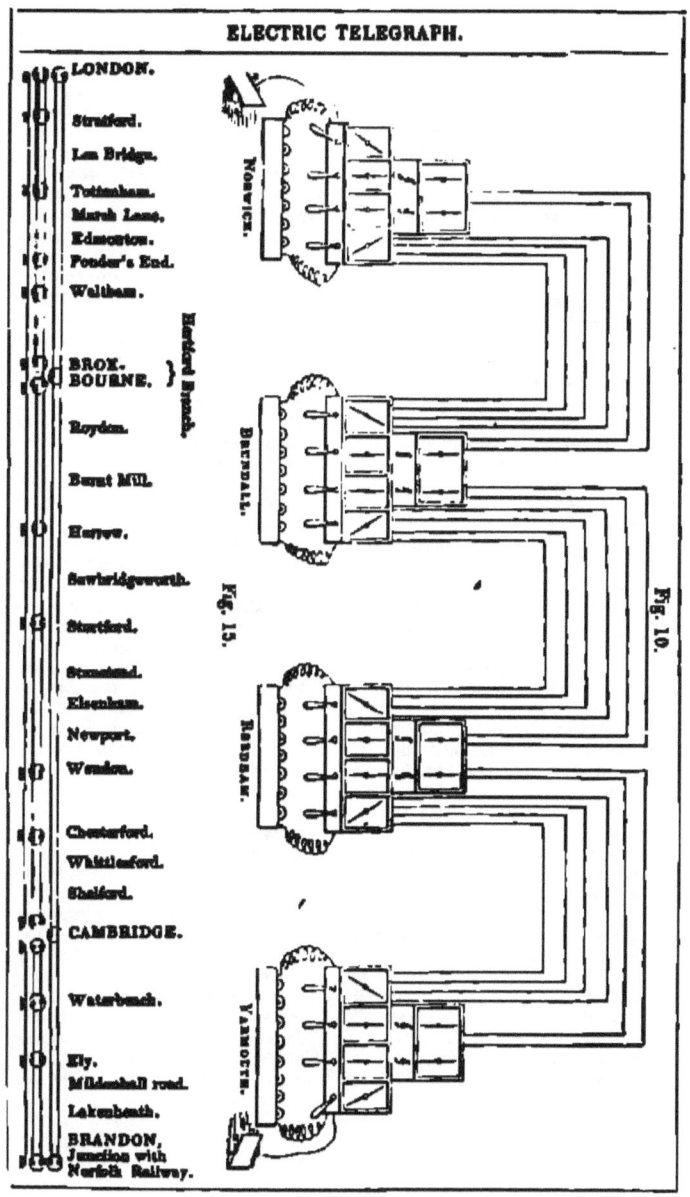

Fig. 15. Fig. 10.

ELECTRIC TELEGRAPH.

stop the clockwork. It is necessary that the iron of the magnet should be quite pure and soft, as otherwise the magnetization is to a greater or less degree permanent; and this may be the case to such an extent as to keep the armature attracted, even after the cessation of the electric current. The bell would then continue to ring until the disengagement of the armature were caused by the hand of the attendant.

The bell or alarum may form part of the telegraphic system in two modes. In the first, and most economical, its coil is made to form part of the circuit of one of the needle wires, in conjunction with a key or rheotome. In the second and more complete method of introducing the alarum, a distinct wire is employed for it, in the course of which the magnet coils at the several stations are interposed. A key of different construction (shown in section at fig. 14) is then employed. The body is of brass, but two stout wires, z and c, are conducted through ivory tubes, and terminated in studs, p p, at the top and bottom of the cylindrical end of the key; the wires and studs being insulated from each other, and from the key, by the ivory in which they are fixed. The collar t', and nut, f, serve to secure the key to the side of the case or box in which it is placed, the former, t', also containing the spring, by which, after use, the key is brought back to its quiescent position. Two springs, not shown in the figure, then rest against the metal of the end, one on each side, and while in this position, merely complete, by the intervening metal, the circuit of the bell-wire which is connected to the foot of one spring directly, and to the foot of the other by the intervention of the bell coil. The wires, z and c, are joined to the two poles of the battery by pieces of thin wire, which will offer no resistance to the revolution of the key on its axis. In the quiescent position, the course of a current entering from a distant station would be, from the line-wire on one side, along one spring, across the body of the key to the other spring, and thence through the alarum coil to the continuation of the line-wire, or to the earth connection. When, however, the bell is to be rung to call the attention of the clerk at another station, the key is for a moment turned one-quarter round. This brings the battery studs, p p, into the circuit, instead of the body of the key; and the current then proceeds from the battery of the ringing station by the spring and wire on one side, passes along the line, and returns by the earth through the other spring again to the battery.

The relative advantages of these two methods may be briefly stated. The first has the recommendation of economy, inasmuch as no additional wire is necessary for the bell. If, however, the clerk in charge of an instrument, after turning off his bell preparatory to sending or transmitting intelligence, should chance to leave his telegraph, and omit to turn the key so as to replace the bell in the circuit, no means are left to other stations of calling his attention, except by working the needles, with the chance of their movement meeting his eye. By the adoption of the second method, the expense of an additional wire is incurred, but the bells at all stations are constantly in a position to be rung if necessary. In addition to this, it may be remarked, that by keeping the bell and needles distinct from each other, no derangement of the one is to be feared from injury to or derangement in the other.

Mr. Cooke's first plan, in the extension of the conducting wires between distant points, was, as has

ELECTRIC TELEGRAPH.

been already stated, to cover each wire with cotton or silk, and then with pitch, caoutchouc, resin, or other non-conducting material, and to enclose them, thus protected, in tubes or pipes of wood, iron, or earthenware. Excepting in those localities where the suspension of wires is impracticable, as in streets, towns, or on public roads, the early plan has given place to more recent inventions. In 1842, a patent was obtained by Mr. Cooke, for a means of suspending and insulating the wires in the air, and the method described in his specification has been since adhered to, with little variation. The wires are generally of iron, which is galvanized, to protect it from the action of the atmosphere. They are of about one-sixth of an inch in diameter, corresponding to No. 8 of the wire-gauge. Being obtained in as great lengths as possible in the first place, successive pieces are welded together, until a coil of about 440 yards is formed. These rings or bundles weigh about 120 pounds each. The wires are suspended on the line, from stout squared posts or standards, of Dantzic or Memel timber. At each quarter-mile, a stronger post is fixed, from which the succeeding lengths of wire on either side are strained or tightened up. Intermediate to these principal posts, are placed smaller standards at from 45 to 55 yards asunder, for the purpose of supporting the wires. The straining apparatus is very simple, consisting merely of a reel or pulley, turning between two cheeks of cast iron, and carrying upon its axis a ratchet-wheel, into the teeth of which a click or catch falls. These winding heads, shown at *r r*, figs. 7 and 9, are connected through the post by a bolt of wrought iron, *b*, tapped into each head. This bolt not only bears the strain of the wires, but also forms the metallic communication between their ends wound on the two reels. In order to insulate the bolt from the wood of the post the hole in this latter is bored very large, and collars of earthenware, *t t*, are inserted at each side, in which the bolt rests, and against their outer surfaces the winding heads are screwed up tight. Fig. 9 is a section through the post and collar, showing this arrangement. Fig. 7 is a front, and 8 a side view of the head of a straining or quarter-post. The wires are usually arranged in two vertical planes, at the back and front of the standards, or intermediate posts. They are not strained at each quarter-mile, but at intervals of half a mile alternately; those in the front plane at one post, and those in the back plane at the next. The standards or supporting posts have merely to sustain the weight of the wires without relation to their tension. They have on each side two stout arms of oak or ash, secured by bolts, passing from one to the other, and resting in collars of earthenware, *x x*, where they pass through the standard. The wires pass through pieces of earthenware, of a double cone shape, *e e*, fastened to the outside of the arms by staples or clips, having a nut and screw at the end. These staples embrace the cones at a groove in the middle of their length. An arm similar to those on the standards is fixed to the back and front of each post alternately, to support that plane of wires which passes without being strained. The insulating earthenwares between the arm and post, *y y*, are, however, different in shape from those used with the standard arms, as greater length is requisite.

In passing through tunnels and bridges, or in front of walls or buildings, where posts cannot be conveniently fixed in the ground, the wires are supported on octagonal standards of oak or ash, fixed

ELECTRIC TELEGRAPH.

at about six inches from the wall by holdfasts of galvanized iron.

The following are the principal dimensions of the posts and poles:

LENGTH.	AT BASE.		AT TOP.	
	Posts.	Standards.	Posts.	Standards.
ft.	in. in.	in. in.	in. in.	in. in.
18	9 × 8	6 × 6	7 × 6½	5¼ × 4½
22	10 × 8	7 × 6	do.	do.
28	11 × 10	8 × 7	do.	do.

The batteries employed are in the form of a Wollaston's trough, in which are arranged plates of copper and amalgamated zinc, each cell being filled with dry and clean sand. When about to be used, the sand is just moistened with dilute sulphuric acid. These batteries are singularly constant, having been known to remain in action during a period of from two to five months, with only the occasional addition of a little more acid solution, to supply the waste by evaporation and saturation. The effect of the sand appears to be, the prevention of too rapid an action, and, at the same time, the separation of the sulphates of copper and zinc. No copper is therefore deposited on the zinc plate. The points necessary to be observed are the perfect amalgamation of the zinc, the absolute freedom of the sand from lime or other alkali, from carbonates or muriates, and the purity of the sulphuric acid. The zinc is about ⅛ or 1/16 of an inch thick, and is in pieces of 4½ inches by 3 inches. These plates will last with care for five or six months in almost constant action. A battery series of from 12 to 60 pairs is required, according to the length and nature of the line and the number of instruments in connection.

Six wires are extended along the whole length of railway, of which the upper pair are used with a special double-needle instrument, for verbal communication, between the main stations, which are Norwich, Brundall, Reedham, and Yarmouth. Each of the other four wires includes at every station a coil and single needle. On the dials connected with the first wire of these four, is engraved the name Norwich at all the stations; with the second, that of Brundall, with the third Reedham, and with the fourth Yarmouth. The distinct telegraphic system belonging to each station has, therefore, its representative at all the other stations. Each needle or pointer represents the state of the portion of line under the control of the station the name of which it bears. The alarum of each instrument is connected only with the wire of its own station, so that on moving either of the needles, the alarum will be rung at the place corresponding to the name of the needle, but at no other point, although the movement of the pointer will be visible throughout.

The electric telegraph is now the chief mode of transmitting all the news of the Government, and the important correspondence of merchants and of the public generally. Its influence is now all-important; its extension to the several civilized and commercial countries, across the seas, by means of the submarine cable, is one of the great aims of science in the present day.

RENAISSANCE.—This term is applied to a style which arose in all the arts of design, from the introduction of antique features, consequent on the revival of classical learning, and the admiration of everything classical after the fall of the Gothic system.

In Italy, where the arts had never become thoroughly Gothic, the renaissance of classical taste commenced as early as the 13th century, but in the rest of Europe the Gothic had then hardly arrived at its complete development, or had hardly begun to display its luxuriance; and two centuries were required to explore its capabilities, to work out its resources in all their wondrous variety, and to push on its suggestions so far in complication and absurdity, as to render a change of style necessary; and accordingly the arts of Germany, the Netherlands, France, and England, were not ripe for this change, called the 'renaissance,' till the end of the 15th or beginning of the 16th century; *i. e.* not till after the invention of printing, the great change of society resulting from which rendered easy the introduction of classic taste into these countries.

In architecture, renaissance of classical forms and principles first distinctly shows itself in the works of Brunelleschi, the great Florentine architect, who lived from 1375 to 1444. His most famous work, the cupola of the cathedral, exhibits a bold emancipation from Gothic complexity, and return to classic simplicity. Contemporary were Michelozzo, and L. B. Alberti, the first modern writer on the art. They were succeeded by Cronaca and Bramante, the latter of whom re-introduced detached colonnades and hanging architraves. His successor, Michael Angelo, with his genius for seizing whatever was grand rather than beautiful, returned (in the Capitoline Museum) to the classic simplicity of a single order, and an entablature unbroken from corner to corner: the renaissance was thus complete. Sanmicheli of Verona (1484–1649) originated the fanciful and luxurious school which characterized the renaissant architecture of Venice, and became the favourite model for the schools of all transalpine countries, especially England.

In this country, the way was prepared by certain tendencies of our After-Gothic, the florid Perpendicular, and Tudor; as (I.) the tendency to subordinate the arch and archlet to the framework of vertical and horizontal lines. (II.) By these horizontal masses of moulding beginning almost to approximate the effect of classic entablatures, in their division into two groups, like cornice and architrave. (III.) By the roofs being reduced in pitch, and by towers being finished without spires. (IV.) By the depression of the arch, and the diminishing importance attached to its *point*. (V.) By the introduction of a large and bold scale of carved ornament, and by the introduction of *attached* ornament, contrary to the Gothic principle of decorating by the *removal* of superfluous material, and not, as in classic architecture, by *addition*.

These several predisposing tendencies of our debased After-Gothic rendered it easy to engraft thereon those Italian details which distinguish the works of the reign of Henry VIII. The chantries of Bishops Fox and Gardiner, at Winchester, are instructive examples of this process; and so are the tomb of Henry VII., the woodwork of King's College chapel, and much of the architecture of Cambridge.

MR. WEALE'S
PUBLICATIONS FOR 1861.

RUDIMENTARY SERIES.

In demy 12mo, cloth, price 1s.
RUDIMENTARY.—1.—CHEMISTRY, by Professor FOWNES, F.R.S, including Agricultural Chemistry, for the Use of Farmers.

In demy 12mo, with Woodcuts, cloth, price 1s.
RUDIMENTARY.—2.—NATURAL PHILOSOPHY, by CHARLES TOMLINSON.

In demy 12mo, with Woodcuts, cloth, price 1s. 6d.
RUDIMENTARY.—3.—GEOLOGY, by Major-Gen. PORTLOCK, F.R.S., &c.

In demy 12mo, with Woodcuts, cloth, price 2s.
RUDIMENTARY.—4, 5.—MINERALOGY, with Mr. DANA'S Additions. 2 vols. in 1.

In demy 12mo, with Woodcuts, cloth, price 1s.
RUDIMENTARY.—6.—MECHANICS, by CHARLES TOMLINSON.

In demy 12mo, with Woodcuts, cloth, price 1s. 6d.
RUDIMENTARY.—7.—ELECTRICITY, by Sir WILLIAM SNOW HARRIS, F.R.S.

In demy 12mo, with Woodcuts, cloth, price 1s. 6d.
RUDIMENTARY.—7*.—ON GALVANISM; ANIMAL AND VOLTAIC ELECTRICITY; by Sir W. SNOW HARRIS.

In demy 12mo, with Woodcuts, cloth, price 3s. 6d.
RUDIMENTARY.—8, 9, 10—MAGNETISM, Concise Exposition of, by Sir W. SNOW HARRIS, 3 vols. in 1.

In demy 12mo, with Woodcuts, cloth, price 2s.
RUDIMENTARY.—11, 11*.—ELECTRIC TELEGRAPH, History of the, by E. HIGHTON, C.E.

In demy 12mo, with Woodcuts, cloth, price 1s.
RUDIMENTARY.—12.—PNEUMATICS, by CHARLES TOMLINSON.

In demy 12mo, with Woodcuts, cloth, price 4s. 6d.
RUDIMENTARY.—13, 14, 15, 15*.—CIVIL ENGINEERING, by HENRY LAW, C.E., 3 vols.; and Supplement by G. R. BURNELL, C.E.

In demy 12mo, with Woodcuts, cloth, price 1s.
RUDIMENTARY.—16.—ARCHITECTURE, Orders of, by W. H. LEEDS.

In demy 12mo, with Woodcuts, cloth, price 1s. 6d.
RUDIMENTARY.—17.—ARCHITECTURE Styles of, by T. BURY, Architect.

John Weale, 59, High Holborn, London, W.C.

MR. WEALE'S RUDIMENTARY SERIES.

In demy 12mo, with Woodcuts, cloth, price 2s.
RUDIMENTARY.—18, 19.—ARCHITECTURE, Principles of Design in by E. L. GARBETT, Architect, 2 vols. in 1.

In demy 12mo, with Woodcuts, cloth, price 2s.
RUDIMENTARY.— 20, 21. — PERSPECTIVE, by G. PYNE, Artist, 2 vols. in 1.

In demy 12mo, with Woodcuts, cloth, price 1s.
RUDIMENTARY.—22.—BUILDING, Art of, by E. DOBSON, C.E.

In demy 12mo, with Woodcuts, cloth, price 2s.
RUDIMENTARY.—23, 24.—BRICK-MAKING, TILE-MAKING, &c., Art of, by E. DOBSON, C.E., 2 vols. in 1.

In demy 12mo, with Woodcuts, cloth, price 2s.
RUDIMENTARY.—25, 26.—MASONRY AND STONE-CUTTING, Art of, by E. DOBSON, C.E., 2 vols. in 1.

In demy 12mo, with Woodcuts, cloth, price 2s.
RUDIMENTARY.—27, 28.—PAINTING, Art of, or a GRAMMAR OF COLOURING, by GEORGE FIELD, 2 vols. in 1.

In demy 12mo, with Woodcuts, cloth, price 1s.
RUDIMENTARY.—29.—PRACTICE OF DRAINING DISTRICTS AND LANDS, Art of, by G. D. DEMPSEY, C.E.

In demy 12mo, with Woodcuts, cloth, price 1s. 6d.
RUDIMENTARY.—30.—PRACTICE OF DRAINING AND SEWAGE OF TOWNS AND BUILDINGS, Art of, by G. D. DEMPSEY, C.E.

In demy 12mo, with Woodcuts, cloth, price 1s.
RUDIMENTARY. — 31. — WELL-SINKING AND BORING, Art of, by G. R. BURNELL, C.E.

In demy 12mo, with Woodcuts, cloth, price 1s.
RUDIMENTARY. — 32. — USE OF INSTRUMENTS, Art of the, by J. F. HEATHER, M.A.

In demy 12mo, with Woodcuts, cloth, price 1s.
RUDIMENTARY. — 33. — CONSTRUCTING CRANES, Art of, by J. GLYNN, F.R.S., C.E.

In demy 12mo, with Woodcuts, cloth, price 1s.
RUDIMENTARY. — 34. — STEAM ENGINE, Treatise on the, by Dr. LARDNER.

In demy 12mo, with Woodcuts, cloth, price 1s.
RUDIMENTARY.—35. — BLASTING ROCKS AND QUARRYING, AND ON STONE, by Lieut.-Gen. Sir J BURGOYNE, Bart., G.C.B., R.E.

In demy 12mo, with Woodcuts, cloth, price 4s.
RUDIMENTARY.—36, 37, 38, 39.—DICTIONARY OF TERMS used by Architects, Builders, Civil and Mechanical Engineers, Surveyors, Artists, Ship-builders, &c., vols. in 1.

In demy 12mo, cloth, price 1s.
RUDIMENTARY.—40.—GLASS STAINING, Art of, by Dr. M. A. GESSERT.

John Weale, 59, High Holborn, London, W.C.

MR. WEALE'S RUDIMENTARY SERIES.

In demy 12mo, cloth, price 1s.
RUDIMENTARY.—41.—PAINTING ON GLASS, Essay on, by E. O. FROMBERG.

In demy 12mo, with Woodcuts, cloth, price 1s.
RUDIMENTARY.—42.—COTTAGE BUILDING, Treatise on.

In demy 12mo, with Woodcuts, cloth, price 1s.
RUDIMENTARY.—43.—TUBULAR AND GIRDER BRIDGES, and others, Treatise on, more particularly describing the Britannia and Conway Bridges.

In demy 12mo, with Woodcuts, cloth, price 1s.
RUDIMENTARY.—44.—FOUNDATIONS, &c., by E. DOBSON, C.E.

In demy 12mo, with Woodcuts, cloth, price 1s.
RUDIMENTARY.—45.—LIMES, CEMENTS, MORTARS, CONCRETE, MASTICS, &c., by G. R. BURNELL, C.E.

In demy 12mo, with Woodcuts, cloth, price 1s.
RUDIMENTARY.—46.—CONSTRUCTING AND REPAIRING COMMON ROADS, by H. LAW, C.E.

In demy 12mo, with Woodcuts, cloth, price 3s.
RUDIMENTARY.—47, 48, 49.—CONSTRUCTION AND ILLUMINATION OF LIGHTHOUSES, by ALAN STEVENSON, C.E., 3 vols. in 1.

In demy 12mo, with Woodcuts, cloth, price 1s.
RUDIMENTARY.—50.—LAW OF CONTRACTS FOR WORKS AND SERVICES, by DAVID GIBBONS, S.P.

In demy 12mo, with Woodcuts, cloth, price 3s.
RUDIMENTARY.—51, 52, 53.—NAVAL ARCHITECTURE, Principles of the Science, by J. PEAKE, N.A., 3 vols. in 1.

In demy 12mo, with Woodcuts, cloth, price 1s.
RUDIMENTARY AND ELEMENTARY.—53*.—PRACTICAL CONSTRUCTION concisely stated of Ships for Ocean or River Service, by Captain H. A. SOMMERFELDT, N.R.N.

In royal 4to. with Engraved Plates, cloth, price 7s. 6d.
RUDIMENTARY.—53**.—ATLAS of 15 Plates to ditto, drawn and engraved to a Scale for Practice.—For the convenience of the Operative Ship Builder the Atlas may be had in three separate Parts. Part I., 2s. 6d. Part II., 2s. 6d. Part III., 2s. 6d.

In demy 12mo, with Woodcuts, cloth, price 1s. 6d.
RUDIMENTARY.—54.—MASTING, MAST-MAKING, AND RIGGING OF SHIPS, by R. KIPPING, A.

In demy 12mo, with Woodcuts, cloth, price 2s. 6d.
RUDIMENTARY.—54*.—IRON SHIP BUILDING, by JOHN GRANTHAM, N.A. and C.E.

In demy 12mo, with Woodcuts, cloth, price 2s.
RUDIMENTARY.—55, 56.—NAVIGATION; THE SAILOR'S SEA-BOOK.—How to Keep the Log and Work it Off—Latitude and Longitude—Great Circle Sailing—Law of Storms and variable Winds; and an Explanation of Terms used, with coloured illustrations of Flags.

John Weale, 59, High Holborn, London, W.C.

MR. WEALE'S RUDIMENTARY SERIES.

In demy 12mo, with Woodcuts, cloth, price 2s.
RUDIMENTARY.—57, 58.—WARMING AND VENTILATION, by CHARLES TOMLINSON, 2 vols. in 1.

In demy 12mo, with Woodcuts, cloth, price 1s.
RUDIMENTARY.—59.—STEAM BOILERS, by R. ARMSTRONG, C.E.

In demy 12mo, with Woodcuts, cloth, price 2s.
RUDIMENTARY. — 60, 61. — LAND AND ENGINEERING SURVEYING, by T. BAKER, C.E., 2 vols. in 1.

In demy 12mo, with Woodcuts, cloth, price 1s.
RUDIMENTARY AND ELEMENTARY.—62. —PRINCIPLES OF RAILWAYS, for the Use of the Beginner in his Studies; with Sketches for Construction. By Sir R. MACDONALD STEPHENSON. Vol. I.

In demy 12mo, with Woodcuts, cloth, price 1s.
RUDIMENTARY.—62*.—RAILWAY WORKING IN GREAT BRITAIN, Statistical Details, Table of Capital and Dividends, Revenue Accounts, Signals, &c., Vol. II.

In demy 12mo, with Woodcuts, cloth, price 3s.
RUDIMENTARY.—63, 64, 65.—AGRICULTURAL BUILDINGS, the Construction of, on Motive Powers, and the Machinery of the Steading; and on Agricultural Field Engines, Machines, and Implements, by G. H. ANDREWS, 3 vols in 1.—John Weale, 59, High Holborn, London, W.C.

In demy 12mo, cloth, price 1s.
RUDIMENTARY.—66.—CLAY LANDS AND LOAMY SOILS, by Professor JOHN DONALDSON, A.E.

In demy 12mo, with Woodcuts, cloth, price 3s.
RUDIMENTARY. — 67, 68. — CLOCK AND WATCH-MAKING, AND ON CHURCH CLOCKS AND BELLS, by E. B. DENISON, M.A., 2 vols. in 1, considerably extended. Fourth Edition.

In demy 12mo, with Woodcuts, cloth, price 2s.
RUDIMENTARY.—69, 70.—MUSIC, Practical Treatise on, by C. C. SPENCER, Mus. Dr. 2 vols. in 1.

In demy 12mo, cloth, price 1s.
RUDIMENTARY. — 71. — PIANOFORTE, Instruction for Playing the, by C. C. SPENCER, Mus. Dr.

In demy 12mo, with Steel Engravings and Woodcuts, cloth, price 5s. 6d.
RUDIMENTARY.—72, 73, 74, 75, 75*.—RECENT FOSSIL SHELLS (A Manual of the Mollusca), by SAMUEL P. WOODWARD, of the Brit. Mus. 4 vols. in 1, with Supplement.

In demy 12mo., with Woodcuts, cloth, price 2s.
RUDIMENTARY. — 76, 77. — DESCRIPTIVE GEOMETRY, by J. F. HEATHER, M.A. 2 vols. in 1.

In demy 12mo, with Woodcuts, price 1s.
RUDIMENTARY. — 77*. — ECONOMY OF FUEL, by T. S. PRIDEAUX.

In demy 12mo, 2 vols. in 1, with Woodcuts, cloth, price 2s.
RUDIMENTARY.—78, 79.—STEAM AS APPLIED TO GENERAL PURPOSES.
John Weale, 59, High Holborn, London, W.C.

MR. WEALE'S RUDIMENTARY SERIES.

In demy 12mo, with Woodcuts, cloth, price 1s. 6d.
RUDIMENTARY.—78*.—LOCOMOTIVE ENGINE, by G. D. DEMPSEY, C.E.

In royal 4to, cloth, price 4s. 6d.
RUDIMENTARY. — 79*. — ATLAS OF ENGRAVED PLATES to DEMPSEY'S LOCOMOTIVE ENGINES.

In demy 12mo, with Woodcuts, cloth, price 1s.
RUDIMENTARY.—79**.—ON PHOTOGRAPHY, the Composition and Properties of the Chemical Substances used, by Dr. H. HALLEUR.

In demy 12mo, with Woodcuts, cloth, price 2s. 6d.
RUDIMENTARY. — 80, 81. — MARINE ENGINES AND ON THE SCREW, &c., by R. MURRAY, C.E. 2 vols. in 1.

In demy 12mo, cloth, price 2s.
RUDIMENTARY.—80*, 81*.—EMBANKING LANDS FROM THE SEA, by JOHN WIGGINS, F.G.S. 2 vols. in 1.

In demy 12mo, with Woodcuts, cloth, price 2s.
RUDIMENTARY. — 82, 82*. — POWER OF WATER, AS APPLIED TO DRIVE FLOUR MILLS, by JOSEPH GLYNN, F.R.S., C.E.

In demy 12mo, cloth, price 1s.
RUDIMENTARY.—83.—BOOK-KEEPING, by JAMES HADDON, M.A.

In demy 12mo, with Woodcuts, price 3s.
RUDIMENTARY. — 82**, 83*, 83 (bis) COAL GAS, on the Manufacture and Distribution of, by SAMUEL HUGHES, C.E.

In demy 12mo, with Woodcuts, cloth, price 5s.
RUDIMENTARY.—82***.—WATER WORKS FOR THE SUPPLY OF CITIES AND TOWNS; Works which have been executed for procuring Supplies by means of Drainage Areas and by Pumping from Wells, by SAMUEL HUGHES, C.E.

In demy 12mo, with Woodcuts, cloth, price 1s. 6d.
RUDIMENTARY.—83**.—CONSTRUCTION OF DOOR LOCKS.

In demy 12mo, with Woodcuts, cloth, price 1s.
RUDIMENTARY. — 83 (bis) — FORMS OF SHIPS AND BOATS, by W. BLAND, of Hartlip.

In demy 12mo, cloth, price 1s. 6d.
RUDIMENTARY.—84.—ARITHMETIC, with numerous Examples, by Prof. J. R. YOUNG.

In demy 12mo, cloth, price 1s. 6d.
RUDIMENTARY. — 84*.— KEY to the above, by Prof. J. R. YOUNG.

In demy 12mo, cloth, price 1s.
RUDIMENTARY. — 85. — EQUATIONAL ARITHMETIC, Questions of Interest, Annuities, &c., by W. HIPSLEY.

John Weale, 59, High Holborn, London, W.C.

MR. WEALE'S RUDIMENTARY SERIES.

In demy 12mo, cloth, price 1s.

RUDIMENTARY.—85*.—SUPPLEMENTARY VOLUME TO HIPSLEY'S EQUATIONAL ARITHMETIC, Tables for the Calculation of Simple Interest, with Logarithms for Compound Interest and Annuities, &c., &c., by W. HIPSLEY.

In demy 12mo, cloth, price 2s.

RUDIMENTARY. — 86, 87. — ALGEBRA, by JAMES HADDON, M.A. 2 vols. in 1.

In demy 12mo, in cloth, price 1s. 6d.

RUDIMENTARY.—86*, 87*.—ELEMENTS OF ALGEBRA, Key to the, by Prof. YOUNG.

In demy 12mo, with Woodcuts, price 2s,

RUDIMENTARY.—88, 89.—ELEMENTS OF GEOMETRY, by HENRY LAW, C.E. 2 vols. in 1.

In demy 12mo, with Woodcuts, cloth, price 1s.

RUDIMENTARY.—90.—GEOMETRY, ANALYTICAL, by Prof. JAMES HANN.

In demy 12mo, with Woodcuts, cloth, price 2s.

RUDIMENTARY. — 91, 92. — PLANE AND SPHERICAL TRIGONOMETRY, by the same. 2 vols. in 1.

In demy 12mo, with Woodcuts, cloth, price 1s.

RUDIMENTARY.—93.—MENSURATION, by T. BAKER, C.E.

In demy 12mo, cloth, price 2s. 6d.

RUDIMENTARY. — 94, 95. — LOGARITHMS, Tables for facilitating Astronomical, Nautical, Trigonometrical, and Logarithmic Calculations, by H. LAW, C.E. New Edition, with Tables of Natural Sines and Tangents, and Natural Cosines. 2 vols. in 1.

In demy 12mo, with Woodcuts, cloth, price 1s.

RUDIMENTARY.—96.—POPULAR ASTRONOMY. By the Rev. ROBERT MAIN, M.R.A.S.

In demy 12mo, with Woodcuts, cloth, price 1s.

RUDIMENTARY.—97.—STATICS AND DYNAMICS, by T. BAKER, C.E.

In demy 12mo, with 220 Woodcuts, cloth, price 2s. 6d.

RUDIMENTARY. — 98, 98*. — MECHANISM AND PRACTICAL CONSTRUCTION OF MACHINES, by T. BAKER, C.E. and ON TOOLS AND MACHINES, by JAMES NASMYTH, C.E.

In demy 12mo, with Woodcuts, cloth, price 2s.

RUDIMENTARY.—99, 100.—NAUTICAL ASTRONOMY AND NAVIGATION, by Prof. YOUNG. 2 vols. in 1.

In demy 12mo, cloth, price 1s. 6d.

RUDIMENTARY. — 100*. — NAVIGATION TABLES, compiled for practical use with the above.

In demy 12mo, cloth, price 1s.

RUDIMENTARY. — 101. — DIFFERENTIAL CALCULUS, by Mr. WOOLHOUSE, F.R.A.S.

John Weale, 59, High Holborn, London, W.C.

MR. WEALE'S RUDIMENTARY SERIES.

In demy 12mo, cloth, price 1s. 6d.
RUDIMENTARY. — 101*.—WEIGHTS AND MEASURES OF ALL NATIONS: Weights, Coins, and the various Divisions of Time, with the principles which determine Rates of Exchange, by Mr. WOOLHOUSE, F.R.A.S.

In demy 12mo, in cloth, price 1s.
RUDIMENTARY. — 102. — INTEGRAL CALCULUS, by H. COX, M.A.

In demy 12mo, in cloth, price 1s.
RUDIMENTARY. — 103.— INTEGRAL CALCULUS, Examples of, by Prof. JAMES HANN.

In demy 12mo, cloth, price 1s.
RUDIMENTARY. — 104. — DIFFERENTIAL CALCULUS, Examples of, by J. HADDON, M.A.

In demy 12mo, with Woodcuts, cloth, price 1s. 6d.
RUDIMENTARY. — 105.— ALGEBRA, GEOMETRY, AND TRIGONOMETRY, Mnemonical Lessons, by the Rev. T. PENYNGTON KIRKMAN, M.A.

In demy 12mo, with Woodcuts, cloth, price 1s. 6d.
RUDIMENTARY.—106.—SHIPS' ANCHORS FOR ALL SERVICES, by Mr. GEORGE COTSELL, N.A.

In demy 12mo, with Woodcuts, price 2s. 6d.
RUDIMENTARY. — 107. — METROPOLITAN BUILDINGS ACT in present operation, with Notes, and the Act dated August 28th, 1860, for better supplying of Gas to the Metropolis.

In demy 12mo, cloth, price 1s. 6d.
RUDIMENTARY. — 108. — METROPOLITAN LOCAL MANAGEMENT ACTS. All the Acts.

In demy 12mo, cloth, price 1s. 6d.
RUDIMENTARY. — 109. — LIMITED LIABILITY AND PARTNERSHIP ACTS.

In demy 12mo, cloth, price 1s.
RUDIMENTARY.—110.—SIX RECENT LEGISLATIVE ENACTMENTS, for Contractors, Merchants, and Tradesmen.

In demy 12mo, cloth, price 1s.
RUDIMENTARY. — 111. — NUISANCES REMOVAL AND DISEASE PREVENTION ACT.

In demy 12mo, cloth, price 1s. 6d.
RUDIMENTARY.—112.—DOMESTIC MEDICINE, PRESERVING HEALTH, by M. RASPAIL.

In demy 12mo, cloth, price 1s. 6d.
RUDIMENTARY. — 113. — USE OF FIELD ARTILLERY ON SERVICE, by Lieut.-Col. HAMILTON MAXWELL, B.A.

In demy 12mo, with Woodcuts, cloth, price 1s. 6d.
RUDIMENTARY.—114.—ON MACHINERY: Rudimentary and Elementary Principles of the Construction and on the Working of Machinery, by C. D. ABEL, C.E.

In royal 4to, cloth, price 7s. 6d.
RUDIMENTARY.—115.—ATLAS OF PLATES OF SEVERAL KINDS OF MACHINES, 17 very valuable Illustrative plates.

John Weale, 59, High Holborn, London, W.C.

MR. WEALE'S RUDIMENTARY SERIES.

In demy 12mo, with Woodcuts, cloth, price 1s. 6d.

RUDIMENTARY. — 116. — TREATISE ON ACOUSTICS: The Distribution of Sound, by T. ROGER SMITH, Architect.

In demy 12mo, with Woodcuts, cloth, price 2s. 6d.

RUDIMENTARY.—117.—SUBTERRANEOUS SURVEYING, RANGING THE LINE WITHOUT THE MAGNET. By THOMAS FENWICK, Coal Viewer. With Improvements and Modern Additions by T. BAKER, C.E.

In demy 12mo, with Plates and Woodcuts, cloth, price 3s.

RUDIMENTARY.—118, 119.—ON THE CIVIL ENGINEERING OF NORTH AMERICA, by D. STEVENSON, C.E. 2 vols. in 1.

In demy 12mo, with Woodcuts, cloth, price 3s.

RUDIMENTARY. — 120. — ON HYDRAULIC ENGINEERING, by G. R. BURNELL, C.E. 2 vols. in 1.

In demy 12mo, with 2 Engraved Plates, cloth, price 1s. 6d.

RUDIMENTARY. — 121. — TREATISE ON RIVERS AND TORRENTS, from the Italian of PAUL FRISI.

In demy 12mo, by PAUL FRISI, in cloth, price 1s.

RUDIMENTARY.—122—ON RIVERS THAT CARRY SAND AND MUD, and an ESSAY ON NAVIGABLE CANALS. 121 and 122 bound together, 2s. 6d.

In demy 12mo, with Woodcuts, cloth, price 1s. 6d.

RUDIMENTARY. — 123. — ON CARPENTRY AND JOINERY, founded on Dr. Robison's Work.

In demy 4to, cloth, price 4s. 6d.

RUDIMENTARY.—123*.—ATLAS of PLATES in detail to the CARPENTRY AND JOINERY. 123 and 123* bound together in cloth in 1 vol.

In demy 12mo, with Woodcuts, cloth, price 1s. 6d.

RUDIMENTARY. — 124. — ON ROOFS FOR PUBLIC AND PRIVATE BUILDINGS, founded on Dr. Robison's Work.

In royal 4to, cloth, price 4s. 6d.

RUDIMENTARY.—124*.—RECENTLY CONSTRUCTED IRON ROOFS, Atlas of plates.

In demy 12mo, with Woodcuts, cloth, price 3s.

RUDIMENTARY.—125.—ON THE COMBUSTION OF COAL AND THE PREVENTION OF SMOKE, Chemically and Practically Considered, by CHARLES WYE WILLIAMS.

In demy 12mo, cloth. 125 and 126 together, price 3s.

RUDIMENTARY. — 126. — ILLUSTRATIONS to WILLIAMS'S COMBUSTION OF COAL. 125 and 126, 2 vols. bound in 1.

In demy 12mo, with Woodcuts, cloth, price 1s. 6d.

RUDIMENTARY. — 127. — PRACTICAL INSTRUCTIONS IN THE ART OF ARCHITECTURAL MODELLING.

John Weale, 59, High Holborn, London, W.C.

MR. WEALE'S RUDIMENTARY SERIES.

In demy 12mo, with Engravings and Woodcuts.

RUDIMENTARY.—128.—THE TEN BOOKS OF M. VITRUVIUS ON CIVIL, MILITARY, AND NAVAL ARCHITECTURE, translated by JOSEPH GWILT, Arch. 2 vols. in 1.

In demy 12mo, 128 and 129 together, cloth, price 5s.

RUDIMENTARY.—129.—ILLUSTRATIVE PLATES TO VITRUVIUS'S TEN BOOKS, by the Author and JOSEPH GANDY, R.A.

In demy 12mo, cloth, price 1s.

RUDIMENTARY.—130.—INQUIRY INTO THE PRINCIPLES OF BEAUTY IN GRECIAN ARCHITECTURE, by the Right Hon. the Earl of ABERDEEN, &c. &c.

In demy 12mo, cloth, price 1s.

RUDIMENTARY.—131.—THE MILLER'S, MERCHANT'S, AND FARMER'S READY RECKONER, for ascertaining at Sight the Value of any quantity of Corn; together with the approximate value of Millstones and Millwork.

In demy 12mo, with Woodcuts, cloth, price 2s. 6d.

RUDIMENTARY.—132.—TREATISE ON THE ERECTION OF DWELLING HOUSES, WITH SPECIFICATIONS, QUANTITIES OF THE VARIOUS MATERIALS, &c., by S. H. BROOKS, Architect. 27 Plates.

RUDIMENTARY SERIES.—ON MINES, SMELTING WORKS, AND THE MANUFACTURE OF METALS, as follows.

In demy 12mo, with Woodcuts, cloth, price 2s.

RUDIMENTARY.—Vol. 1.—TREATISE ON THE METALLURGY OF COPPER, by R. H. LAMBORN.

In demy 12mo, to have Woodcuts, cloth.

RUDIMENTARY.—Vol. 2.—TREATISE ON THE METALLURGY OF SILVER AND LEAD.

In demy 12mo, to have Woodcuts, cloth.

RUDIMENTARY AND ELEMENTARY.—Vol. 3.—TREATISE ON IRON METALLURGY up to the Manufacture of the latest processes.

In demy 12mo, to have Woodcuts, cloth.

RUDIMENTARY AND ELEMENTARY.—Vol. 4.—TREATISE ON GOLD MINING AND ASSAYING PLATINUM, IRIDIUM, &c.

In demy 12mo, to have Woodcuts, cloth.

RUDIMENTARY AND ELEMENTARY.—Vol. 5.—TREATISE ON THE MINING OF ZINC, TIN, NICKEL, COBALT, &c.

In demy 12mo, to have Woodcuts, cloth.

RUDIMENTARY AND ELEMENTARY.—Vol. 6.—TREATISE ON COAL MINING (Geology and Means of Discovering, &c.)

In demy 12mo, with Woodcuts, cloth, price 1s. 6d.

RUDIMENTARY.—Vol. 7.—ELECTRO-METALLURGY.—Practically treated by ALEXANDER WATT, F.R.S.A.

John Weale, 59, High Holborn, London, W.C.

MR. WEALE'S CLASSICAL SERIES.

In demy 12mo.
CICERO.—13.—De Officiis.

In demy 12mo, boards, price 2s.
CICERO.—14.—De Amicitiâ, de Senectute, and Oratus, with English Notes.

In demy 12mo.
JUVENAL AND PERSIUS.—15.—(The indelicate parts expunged.)

In demy 12mo, boards, price 3s.
LIVY.—16.—Books i. to v. in two vols., with English Notes.

In demy 12mo, boards, price 1s.
LIVY.—17.—Books xxi. and xxii., with English Notes.

In demy 12mo.
TACITUS.—18.—Agricola; Germania; and Annals, Book I.

In demy 12mo, boards, price 2s.
SELECTIONS FROM TIBULLUS, OVID, and PROPERTIUS.—19.—With English Notes.

In demy 12mo.
SELECTIONS FROM SUETONIUS and the later Latin Writers.—20.

GREEK SERIES, ON A SIMILAR PLAN TO THE LATIN SERIES.
Those not priced are in the Press.

In demy 12mo, boards, price 1s.
INTRODUCTORY GREEK READER.—1.—On the same plan as the Latin Reader.

In demy 12mo, boards, price 1s.
XENOPHON.—2.—Anabasis, i. ii. iii., with English Notes.

In demy 12mo, boards, price 1s.
XENOPHON.—3.—Anabasis, iv. v. vi. vii., with English Notes.

In demy 12mo, boards, price 1s.
LUCIAN.—4.—Select Dialogues, with English Notes.

In demy 12mo, boards, price 1s. 6d.
HOMER.—5.—Iliad, i. to vi., with English Notes.

In demy 12mo, boards, price 1s. 6d.
HOMER.—6.—Iliad, vii. to xii., with English Notes.

In demy 12mo, boards, price 1s. 6d.
HOMER.—7.—Iliad, xiii. to xviii. with English Notes.

In demy 12mo, boards, price 1s. 6d.
HOMER.—8.—Iliad, xix. to xxiv., with English Notes.

John Weale, 59, High Holborn, London, W.C.

MR. WEALE'S CLASSICAL SERIES.

In demy 12mo, boards, price 1s. 6d.
HOMER.—9.—Odyssey, i. to vi., with English Notes.

In demy 12mo, boards, price 1s. 6d.
HOMER.—10.—Odyssey, vii. to xii., with English Notes.

In demy 12mo, boards, price 1s. 6d.
HOMER.—11.—Odyssey, xiii. to xviii. with English Notes.

In demy 12mo, boards, price 1s. 6d.
HOMER.—12.—Odyssey, xix. to xxiv.; and Hymns, with English Notes.

In demy 12mo, boards, price 2s.
PLATO.—13.—Apology, Crito, and Phædo, with English Notes.

In demy 12mo, boards, price 1s. 6d.
HERODOTUS.—14.—i. ii., with English Notes.—Dedicated to His Grace the Duke of Devonshire.

In demy 12mo, boards, price 1s. 6d.
HERODOTUS.—15.—iii. iv., with English Notes. Dedicated to His Grace the Duke of Devonshire.

In demy 12mo.
HERODOTUS.—16.—v. vi. and part of vii. Dedicated to His Grace the Duke of Devonshire.

In demy 12mo.
HERODOTUS.—17.—Remainder of vii., viii., and ix. Dedicated to His Grace the Duke of Devonshire.

In demy 12mo, boards, price 1s.
SOPHOCLES.—18.—Œdipus Rex, with English Notes.

In demy 12mo.
SOPHOCLES.—19.—Œdipus Colonæus.

In demy 12mo.
SOPHOCLES.—20.—Antigone.

In demy 12mo.
SOPHOCLES.—21.—Ajax.

In demy 12mo.
SOPHOCLES.—22.—Philoctetes.

In demy 12mo, boards, price 1s. 6d.
EURIPIDES.—23.—Hecuba, with English Notes.

In demy 12mo.
EURIPIDES.—24.—Medea.

In demy 12mo.
EURIPIDES.—25.—Hippolytus.

John Weale, 59, High Holborn, London, W.C.

MR. WEALE'S CLASSICAL SERIES.

In demy 12mo, boards, price 1s.
EURIPIDES.—26.—Alcestis, with English Notes.

In demy 12mo.
EURIPIDES.—27.—Orestes.

In demy 12mo.
EURIPIDES.—28.—Extracts from the remaining Plays.

In demy 12mo.
SOPHOCLES.—29.—Extracts from the remaining Plays.

In demy 12mo.
ÆSCHYLUS.—30.—Prometheus Vinctus.

In demy 12mo.
ÆSCHYLUS.—31.—Persæ.

In demy 12mo.
ÆSCHYLUS.—32.—Septem contra Thebas.

In demy 12mo.
ÆSCHYLUS.—33.—Choëphoræ.

In demy 12mo.
ÆSCHYLUS.—34.—Eumenides.

In demy 12mo.
ÆSCHYLUS.—35.—Agamemnon.

In demy 12mo.
ÆSCHYLUS.—36.—Supplices.

In demy 12mo.
PLUTARCH.—37.—Select Lives.

In demy 12mo.
ARISTOPHANES.—38.—Clouds.

In demy 12mo.
ARISTOPHANES.—39.—Frogs.

In demy 12mo.
ARISTOPHANES.—40.—Selections from the remaining Comedies.

In demy 12mo, boards, price 1s.
THUCYDIDES.—41.—I., with English Notes.

In demy 12mo.
THUCYDIDES.—42.—II.

John Weale, 59, High Holborn, London, W.C.

MR. WEALE'S CLASSICAL SERIES.

In demy 12mo.
THEOCRITUS.—43.—Select Idyls.

In demy 12mo.
PINDAR.—44.

In demy 12mo.
SOCRATES.—45.

In demy 12mo.
HESIOD.—46.

MR. WEALE'S PUBLICATIONS OF WORKS ON ARCHITECTURE, ENGINEERING, AND THE FINE ARTS.

In 1 large Atlas, folio Volume, with fine Plates, price £4 4s.

"**BRITISH GOVERNMENT WORK."**—THE ARCHITECTURAL ANTIQUITIES AND RESTORATION OF ST. STEPHEN'S CHAPEL, WESTMINSTER (late the House of Commons).

Fine Plates and Vignettes, Atlas folio, price £3 10s.

"**NORWEGIAN GOVERNMENT WORK.**"—THE CATHEDRAL OF THRONDHEIM, IN NORWAY. Text by Professor MUNCH; drawings by H. E. SCHIRMER, Architect.

Large Atlas folio, 4 livraisons, published in Madrid, at 100 reals each, or £1 in England. Illustrated by beautifully executed Engravings, some of which are coloured.

"**SPANISH GOVERNMENT WORK."**—MONUMENTS ARCHITECTONIQUES DE L'ESPAGNE, PUBLIÉS AUX FRAIS DE LA NATION.—PART I Provincia de Toledo, Granada, Alcalá de Henares.—PART 2. Catedral Toledo, Detailles.—PART 3. Granada, Segovia, Toledo, Salamanca.—PART 4. Santa Maria de Alcalá de Henares, Casa Lonja de Valencia, Toledo, Segovia, &c.—This work surpasses in beauty all other works.

Colombier folio plates, with text also uniform, with gold borders, and sumptuously bound in red morocco, gilt; gilt leaves, £12 12s., Colombier folio plates, with text also uniform, with gold borders. and elegantly half-bound in morocco, gilt, £10 10s.; Plates in Colombier folio, and text in Imperial 4to, half-bound in morocco, gilt, £7 7s.; Plates in Colombier folio, and text in Imperial 4to, in cloth extra, boards and lettered, £1 14s. 6d.

THE VICTORIA BRIDGE, AT MONTREAL, IN CANADA. — Elaborately illustrated by views, plans, elevations, and details of the Bridge; together with the illustrations of the Machinery and Contrivances used in the construction of this stupendously important and valuable engineering work. The whole produced in the finest style of art, pictorially and geometrically drawn, and the views highly coloured, and a descriptive text. Dedicated to His Royal Highness the Prince of Wales. By JAMES HODGES, Engineer to the Contractors. Engineers: ROBERT STEPHENSON and ALEX. M. ROSS. Contractors: Sir S. MORTON PETO, Bart, M.P., THOMAS BRASSEY, and EDWARD LADD BETTS, Esqrs.

John Weale, 59, High Holborn, London, W.C.

MR. WEALE'S WORKS ON ARCHITECTURE, ENGINEERING, FINE ARTS, &c.

In one Imperial folio volume, with exquisite illustrative Plates from costly Drawings made by the most eminent artists, half-bound very neat, price £5 5s. Only 150 copies printed for sale.

PROFESSOR COCKERELL'S WORK.— THE TEMPLES OF JUPITER PANHELLENIUS AT ÆGINA, AND OF APOLLO EPICURIUS AT BASSÆ, NEAR PHIGALEIA, IN ARCADIA.

It is proposed to publish the Life and Works of the late

ISAMBARD KINGDON BRUNEL, F.R.S., Civil Engineer.—The genius, talent, and great enterprise of the fame Mr. Brunel has a world-wide fame, his whole life was devoted alone to the science of his profession, not in imitation or copying others, but in invention. In finding out new roads to the onward advancement of his Art, the lifting up from the slow and beating path of Engineering Art, new ideas and realities, and which has or have given to England a name for reference and of renowned intelligence in this Art.

Just published, in 4to, with 100 Engravings, price, bound, 21s.

THE PRACTICAL HOUSE CARPENTER.— More particularly for country practice, with specifications, quantities, and contracts: also containing—1. Designs for the Centering of Groins. Niches, &c.; 2. Designs for Roofs and Staircases. 3. The Five Orders laid down to a scale; 4. Modern Method of Trussing Girders, Joints of Carpenters' work; 5. Designs for Modern Shop Fronts with their details; 6. Designs for Modern Doors with their details; 7. Designs for Modern Windows, with their details, and for Villa Architecture. The whole amply described, for the use of the Operative Carpenter and Builder. Firstly written and published by WILLIAM PAIN. Secondly, with Modern Designs, and Improvements, by S. H. BROOKS, Architect.

In 1861 will be published a volume in 12mo, entitled

A DIGEST OF PRICES of Works in Civil Engineering and Railway Engineering, Mechanical Engineering, Tools, Wrought and Cast Iron Works, Stone, Timber and Wire Works, and every kind of information that can be obtained and made useful in Estimating, Specifying, and Reporting.

In 4to, 2s. 6d.

AIRY, ASTRONOMER ROYAL, F.R.S., &c.— Results of Experiments on the Disturbance of the Compass in Iron-built Ships.

In a sheet, 3s., in case, 3s. 6d.

ANCIENT DOORWAYS AND WINDOWS (Examples of). Arranged to illustrate the different styles of Gothic Architecture, from the Conquest to the Reformation.

In 1 vol. imperial 4to, with 20 fine Plates, neatly half-bound in cloth, £1 5s.

ANCIENT DOMESTIC ARCHITECTURE.— Principally selected from original drawings in the collection of the late Sir William Burrell, Bart., with observations on the application of ancient architecture to the pictorial composition of modern edifices.

The stained glass fac-simile, 4s. 6d., in an extra case, or in a sheet, 3s. 6d.

ANGLICAN CHURCH ORNAMENT.— Wherein are figured the Saints of the English calendar, with their appropriate emblems; the different styles of stained glass; and various sacred symbols and ornaments used in churches.

John Weale, 59, High Holborn, London, W.C.

MR. WEALE'S WORKS ON ARCHITECTURE, ENGINEERING, FINE ARTS, &c.

In 4to, 1s. 6d.

ARAGO, Mons. — Report on the Atmospheric System, and on the proposed Atmospheric Railway at Paris.

In 4to, with about 500 Engravings, some of which are highly coloured, 4 vols., original copies, half-bound in morocco, £6 6s.

ARCHITECTURAL PAPERS.

2 Engravings, in folio, useful to learners and for schools, 7s. 6d.

ARCHITECTURAL ORDERS (FIVE) AND THEIR ENTABLATURES, drawn to a larger scale, with Figured Dimensions.

4to, 1s.

ARNOLLET, M. — Report on his Atmospheric Railway.

In 4to, 10 Plates, 7s. 6d.

ATMOSPHERIC RAILWAYS. — THREE REPORTS on Improved methods of Constructing and Working Atmospheric Railways. By R. MALLET, C.E.

In 8vo, 1s. 6d.

BARLOW, P. W. — Observations on the Niagara Railway Suspension Bridge.

In large 4to, very neat half-morocco, 16s., with Engravings.

BARRY, SIR CHARLES, R.A., &c. — Studies of Modern English Architecture. By W. H. LEEDS; The Travellers' Club-House, illustrated by Engravings of Plans, Sections, Elevations, and details.

In 1 Vol., large 8vo, with coloured Plates, half-morocco, price £1 1s.

BEWICK'S (J. G.) GEOLOGICAL TREATISE ON THE DISTRICT OF CLEVELAND IN NORTH YORKSHIRE, its Ferruginous Deposits, Lias and Oolites; with some Observations on Ironstone Mining.

In 8vo, with Plates. Price 4s.

BINNS, W. S. — Work on Geometrical Drawing, embracing Practical Geometry, including the use of Drawing Instruments, the construction and use of Scales, Orthographic Projection, and Elementary Descriptive Geometry.

In 4to, with 105 Illustrative Plates, cloth boards, £1 11s. 6d.

BLASHFIELD, J. M., M. R. Inst., &c. — SELECTIONS OF VASES, STATUES, BUSTS, &c, from TERRA COTTAS.

In 8vo, Woodcuts, 1s.

BLASHFIELD, J. M., M. R., Inst., &c. — ACCOUNT OF THE HISTORY AND MANUFACTURE OF ANCIENT AND MODERN TERRA COTTA.

In 4to, 2s. 6d.

BODMER, R., C.E. — On the Propulsion of Vessels by the Screw.

15s.

BRIDGE. — A large magnificent Plate, 3 feet 6 inches by 2 feet, on a scale of 25 feet to an inch, of LONDON BRIDGE; containing Plan and Elevation. Engraved and elaborately finished. The Work of the RENNIES.

John Weale, 59, High Holborn, London, W.C.

MR. WEALE'S WORKS ON ARCHITECTURE, ENGINEERING, FINE ARTS, &c.

10s.

BRIDGE. — Plan and Elevation, on a scale of 10 feet to an inch, of STAINES BRIDGE; a fine Engraving. The work of the RENNIES.

In royal 8vo, with very elaborate Plates (folded), £1 10s.

BRIDGES, SUSPENSION. — An Account, with Illustrations, of the Suspension Bridge across the River Danube, by Wm. T. CLARK, F.R.S.

In 4 vols., royal 8vo, bound in 3 vols., half-morocco, price £4 10s.

BRIDGES. — THE THEORY, PRACTICE, AND ARCHITECTURE OF BRIDGES OF STONE, IRON, TIMBER, AND WIRE; with Examples on the Principle of Suspension; Illustrated by 138 Engravings and 92 Woodcuts.

In one large 8vo volume, with explanatory Text, and 68 Plates comprising details and measured dimensions. Bound in half-morocco, uniform with the preceding work, price £2 10s.

BRIDGES. — SUPPLEMENT TO "THE THEORY, PRACTICE, AND ARCHITECTURE OF BRIDGES OF STONE, IRON, TIMBER, WIRE, AND SUSPENSION."

1 large folio Engraving, price 7s. 6d.

BRIDGE across the Thames.—SOUTHWARK IRON BRIDGE.

1 large folio Engraving, price 5s.

BRIDGE across the Thames. — WATERLOO STONE BRIDGE.

1 very large Engraving, price 5s.

BRIDGE across the Thames. — VAUXHALL IRON BRIDGE.

1 very large Engraving, price 4s. 6d.

BRIDGE across the Thames.—HAMMERSMITH SUSPENSION BRIDGE.

1 large Engraving, price 4s. 6d.

BRIDGE (the UPPER SCHUYLKILL) at PHILADELPHIA, the greatest known span of one arch, covered.

1 large Engraving, price 3s. 6d.

BRIDGE (the SCHUYLKILL) at PHILADELPHIA, covered.

1 large Engraving, price 3s. 6d.

BRIDGE. — ON THE PRINCIPLE OF SUSPENSION, by Sir I. BRUNEL, in the ISLAND OF BOURBON.

1 large Engraving, price 4s.

BRIDGE. — PLAN and ELEVATION of the PATENT IRON BAR BRIDGE over the River Tweed, near Berwick.

34 Plates, folio, £1 1s., boards.

BRIGDEN, R. — Interior Decorations, Details, and Views of Sefton Church, Lancashire, erected in the reign of Henry VIII.

John Weale, 59, High Holborn, London, W.C.

MR. WEALE'S WORKS ON ARCHITECTURE, ENGINEERING, FINE ARTS, &c.

1 large Engraving, price 2s. 6d.

BRITTON'S (John) VIEWS of the WEST FRONTS of 14 ENGLISH CATHEDRALS.

1 large Engraving in outline, price 2s. 6d.

BRITTON'S (John) PERSPECTIVE VIEWS of the INTERIOR of 14 CATHEDRALS.

In 4to, 2s. 6d.

BRODIE, R., C.E. — Rules for Ranging Railway Curves, with the Theodolite, and without Tables.

1 large Engraving, price 4s. 6d.

BROWN'S (Capt. S.) CHAIN PIER at Brighton, with Details.

The Text in one large volume 8vo, and the Plates, upwards of 70 in number, in an atlas folio volume, very neatly half-bound, £2 10s.

BUCHANAN, R. — PRACTICAL ESSAYS ON MILL WORK AND OTHER MACHINERY; with Examples of Tools of modern invention; first published by ROBERT BUCHANAN, M.E.; afterwards improved and edited by THOMAS TREDGOLD, C.E.; and re-edited, with the improvements of the present age, by GEORGE RENNIE, F.R.S., C.E., &c., &c. The whole forming 70 Plates, and 103 Woodcuts. John Weale, 59, High Holborn, London, W.C.

Text in royal 8vo, and Plates in imperial folio, 18s.

BUCHANAN, R. — SUPPLEMENT. — PRACTICAL EXAMPLES ON MODERN TOOLS AND MACHINES; a Supplementary Volume to Mr. RENNIE'S edition of BUCHANAN "On Mill-Work and Other Machinery," by TREDGOLD. The work consists of 18 Plates.

In 8vo, with Plates, 2nd Edition, 1s. 6d.

BURN, C., C.E.—On Tram and Horse Railways.

In one volume, 4to, 21 Plates, half-bound in morocco, £1 1s.

BURY, T., Architect. — Examples of Ancient Ecclesiastical Woodwork.

7s. 6d.

CALCULATOR (THE): Or, TIMBER MERCHANT'S AND BUILDER'S GUIDE. By WILLIAM RICHARDSON and CHARLES GANE, of Wisbeach.

In 8vo, Plates, cloth boards, 7s. 6d.

CALVER, E. K., R.N.—THE CONSERVATION AND IMPROVEMENT OF TIDAL RIVERS.

In 8vo, Woodcuts, 1s. 6d.

CALVER, E.K., R.N.—ON THE CONSTRUCTION AND PRINCIPLE OF A WAVE SCREEN, designed for the Formation of Harbours of Refuge.

In 4to, half-bound, price £1 5s.

CARTER, OWEN B., Architect.—A SERIES OF THE ANCIENT PAINTED GLASS OF WINCHESTER CATHEDRAL, Examples of. 29 Colored Illustrations.

In 4to, 17 Plates, half-bound, 7s. 6d.

CARTER, OWEN B., Architect.—ACCOUNT OF THE CHURCH OF ST. JOHN THE BAPTIST, at Bishopstone, with Illustrations of its Architecture.

John Weale, 59, High Holborn, London, W.C.

MR. WEALE'S WORKS ON ARCHITECTURE, ENGINEERING, FINE ARTS, &c.

In 4to. with 19 Engravings, £1 1s.

CHATEAUNEUF, A. de, Architect.—Architectura Domestica; a Series of very neat examples of Interiors and Exteriors of residences in the Italian style.

Large 4to, in half-red morocco, price £1 8s.

CHIPPENDALE, INIGO JONES, JOHNSON, LOCK, and PETHER.—Old English and French Ornaments: comprising 244 designs on 105 Plates of elaborate examples of Hall Glasses, Picture Frames, Chimney-pieces, Ceilings, Stands for China, Clock and Watch Cases, Girandoles, Brackets, Grates, Lanterns, Ornamental Furniture, Ornaments for brass workers and silver workers, real ornamental iron work Patterns, and for carvers, modellers, &c., &c., &c.

4to, third Edition with additions, price £1 11s. 6d.

CLEGG, SAM., C.E.—A PRACTICAL TREATISE ON THE MANUFACTURE AND DISTRIBUTION OF COAL GAS, Illustrated by Engravings from Working Drawings, with General Estimates.

In 4to, Plates, and 76 Woodcuts, boards, price 6s.

CLEGG, SAM., C.E.—ARCHITECTURE OF MACHINERY. An Essay on Propriety of Form and Proportion. For the use of Students and Schoolmasters.

In 8vo, 1s.

COLBURNS, Z.—On Steam Boiler Explosions.

One very large Engraving, price 4s. 6d.

CONEY'S (J.) Interior View of the Cathedral Church of St. Paul.

In 4to, on card board, 1s.

COWPER, C.—Diagram of the Expansion of Steam.

In one vol. 4to, with 20 Folding Plates, price £1 1s.

CROTON AQUEDUCT.—Description of the New York Croton Aqueduct, in 20 large detailed and engineering explanatory Plates, with text in the English, German, and French languages, by T. SCHRAMKE, C.E.

In demy 12mo, cloth, extra bound and lettered, price 4s.

DENISON.—A Rudimentary Treatise on Clocks and Watches, and Bells; with a full account of the Westminster Clock and Bells, by EDMUND BECKET DENISON, M.A., Q.C. Fourth Edition re-written and enlarged, with Engravings.

In royal 4to, cloth boards, price £1 11s. 6d.

DOWNES, CHARLES, Architect.—Great Exhibition Building. The Building erected in Hyde Park for the Great Exhibition, 1851; 28 large folding Plates, embracing Plans, Elevations, Sections, and Details, laid down to a large scale, and the Working and Measured Drawings.

DRAWING BOOKS.—Showing to Students the superior method of Drawing and Shadowing.

DRAWING BOOK.—COURS ELEMENTAIRES DE LAVIS APPLIQUÉ À L'ARCHITECTURE; folio volume, containing 40 elaborately engraved Plates, in shadows and tints, very finely executed, by the best artists in France. £2. Paris.

John Weale, 59, High Holborn, London, W.C.

MR. WEALE'S WORKS ON ARCHITECTURE, ENGINEERING, FINE ARTS, &c.

DRAWING BOOK.—COURS ÉLÉMENTAIRES DE LAVIS APPLIQUÉ À MÉCHANIQUE) folio volume, containing 50 elaborately engraved Plates, in shadows and tints, very finely executed, by the best artists in France. £2 10s. Paris.

DRAWING BOOK.—COURS ÉLÉMENTAIRES DE LAVIS APPLIQUÉ À ORNEMENTATION; folio volume, containing 20 elaborately engraved Plates, in shadows and tints, very finely executed, by the best artists in France. £1. Paris.

DRAWING BOOK.—ÉTUDES PROGRESSIVES ET COMPLÈTES D'ARCHITECTURE DE LAVIS, par J. D. TRITON; large folio, 24 fine Plates, comprising the Orders of Architecture, mouldings, with profiles, ornaments, and forms of their proportion, art of shadowing doors, balusters, parterres, &c., &c., &c. £1 4s. Paris.

In 12mo, cloth boards, lettered, price 5s.

ECKSTEIN, G. F.—A Practical Treatise on Chimneys; with remarks on Stoves, the consumption of Smoke and Coal, Ventilation, &c.

Plates, Imperial 8vo, price 7s.

ELLET, CHARLES, C. E., of the U. S.—Report on the Improvement of Kanawha, and incidentally of the Ohio River, by means of Artificial Lakes.

In 8vo, with Plates, price 12s.

EXAMPLES of Cheap Railway Making, American and Belgian.

In one vol. 4to, 40 Plates, with dimensions, extra cloth boards, price 21s.

EXAMPLES for Builders, Carpenters, and Joiners; being well-selected Illustrations of recent Modern Art and Construction.

With Engravings and Woodcuts, price 12s.

FROME, Lieutenant-Colonel, R.E.—Outline of the Method of conducting a Trigonometrical Survey for the Formation of Topographical Plans; and Instructions for filling in the Interior Detail, both by Measurement and Sketching; Military Reconnaissances, Levelling, &c., &c., together with Colonial Surveying.

In 4to, with Plates, price 7s 6d.

FAIRBAIRN, W., C.E., F.R.S.—ON WATER-WHEELS, WITH VENTILATED BUCKETS.

In royal 8vo, with Plates and Woodcuts, Second Edition, much improved, price, in extra cloth boards, 16s.

FAIRBAIRN, W., C.E., F.R.S.—ON THE APPLICATION OF CAST AND WROUGHT IRON TO BUILDING PURPOSES.

In imperial 8vo, with fine Plates, a re-issue, price 16s., or 21s. in half-morocco, gilt edges,

FERGUSSON'S (J.) Essay on the Ancient Topography of Jerusalem, with restored Plans of the Temple, &c.

In 8vo, sewed in wrapper, price 2s.

GILL, J.—ESSAY ON THE THERMO DYNAMICS OF ELASTIC FLUIDS, by JOSEPH GILL, with Diagrams.

John Weale, 59, High Holborn, London, W.C.

MR. WEALE'S WORKS ON ARCHITECTURE, ENGINEERING, FINE ARTS, &c.

Plates, 8vo, boards, 5s.

GWILT, JOSEPH, Architect.—TREATISE ON THE EQUILIBRIUM OF ARCHES.

In 8vo, cloth boards, with 6 Plates, 4s. 6d.

HAKEWELL, S. J.—Elizabethan Architecture; illustrated by parallels of Burton House, Hatfield, Longle, and Wollaton, in England, and the Palazzo Della Cancellaria at Rome.

8vo, with a Map, 1s.

HAMILTON, P. S., Barrister-at-Law, Halifax Nova Scotia—Nova Scotia considered as a Field for Emigration.

In Imperial 8vo, Third Edition, with additions, 11 Plates, cloth boards, 8s.

HART, J., On Oblique Bridges.—A Practical Treatise on the Construction of Oblique Arches.

In 4to, with Woodcuts, 3s. 6d.

HEALD, GEORGE, C.E.—System of Setting Out Railway Curves.

Royal 8vo, Plates and Woodcuts, price 13s. 6d.

HEDLEY, JOHN.— Practical Treatise on the Working and Ventilation of Coal Mines, with Suggestions for Improvements in Mining.

Two Vols., demy 12mo, in cloth extra boards and lettered, price 12s. 6d.

HOMER. — The Iliad and Odyssey, with the Hymns of Homer, Edition with an accession of English notes by the Rev. T. H. L. LEARY, M.A.

In 8vo, with Engravings, cloth boards, Third Edition, 10s. 6d.

HOPKINSON, JOSEPH, C.E.—The Working of the Steam Engine Explained by the use of the Indicator.

In 8vo, in boards, 18s.

HUNTINGTON, J. B., C.E.— TABLES and RULES for Facilitating the Calculation of Earthwork, Land, Curves, Distances, and Gradients, required in the Formation of Railways, Roads, and Canals.

Separate from the above, price 3s.

HUNTINGTON, J. B., C.E.— THE TABLES OF GRADIENTS.

10 Plates, 8vo, bound, 5s.

INIGO JONES.—Designs for Chimney Glasses and Chimney Pieces of the Time of Charles the 1st.

In a sheet, 8s.

IRISH.—Plantation and British Statute Measure (comparative Table of), so that English Measure can be transferred into Irish, and vice versâ.

In 4to, with 8 Engravings, in a wrapper, 6s.

IRON. — ACCOUNT OF THE CONSTRUCTION OF THE IRON ROOF OF THE NEW HOUSES OF PARLIAMENT, with elaborate Engravings of details.

In imperial 4to, with 50 Engravings, and 2 fine Woodcuts, half-bound in morocco, £1 4s.

IRON. — DESIGNS OF ORNAMENTAL GATES, LODGES, PALISADING, AND IRON-WORK OF THE ROYAL PARKS, with some other Designs.

John Weale, 59, High Holborn, London, W.C.

MR. WEALE'S WORKS ON ARCHITECTURE, ENGINEERING, FINE ARTS, &c.

In 4to, with 10 Plates, 12s.

JEBB'S, Colonel, Modern Prisons.—Their Construction and Ventilation.

In 3 vols. 8vo, with 26 elaborate Plates, cloth boards, £2 2s.

JONES, Major-Gen. Sir John, Bart.—Journal of the Sieges carried on by the Army under the Duke of Wellington in Spain, between the years 1811 and 1814, with an Account of the Lines of Torres Vedras. By Major-Gen. Sir JOHN T. JONES, Bart, K.C.B. Third Edition, enlarged and edited by Lieut.-General Sir HARRY D. JONES, Bart.

16mo, cloth boards, 2s. 6d.

KENNEDY AND HACKWOOD'S Tables for Setting out Curves.

In 4to, 37 Plates, half cloth boards, 9s.

KING, THOMAS.—The Upholsterer's Guide; Rules for Cutting and Forming Draperies, Valances, &c.

Illustrated by large Draughts and Engravings. In 1 volume 4to, text, and a large atlas folio volume of Plates, half-bound, £6 6s.

KNOWLES, JOHN, F.R.S.—The Elements and Practice of Naval Architecture; or, A Treatise on Ship Building, theoretical and practical, on the best principles established in Great Britain; with copious Tables of Dimensions, Scantlings, &c. The Third Edition, with an Appendix, containing the principles of constructing the Royal and Mercantile Navies, by Sir ROBERT SEPPINGS.

41 Plates of a fine and an elaborate description in large atlas folio half-bound, £2 12s. 6d.; with the text half-bound in 4to.

LOCOMOTIVE ENGINES.—The Principles and Practice and Explanation of the Machinery of Locomotive Engines in operation.

In 12mo, sewed, 1s.

MAIN, Rev. ROBERT,—An Account of the Observatories in and about London.

4to, in boards, 15s.

MANUFACTURES AND MACHINERY.—Progress of, in Great Britain, as exhibited chiefly in Chronological notices of some Letters Patent granted for Inventions and Improvements, from the earliest times to the reign of Queen Anne.

18mo, 2s. 6d.

MAY, R. C., C.E.—Method of setting out Railway Curves.

Imperial 4to, with fine Illustrations, extra cloth boards, £1 5s., or half-bound in morocco, £1 11s. 6d.

METHVEN, CAPTAIN ROBERT.—THE LOG OF A MERCHANT OFFICER, Viewed with Reference to the Education of Young Officers and the Youth of the Merchant Service. By ROBERT METHVEN, Commander in the Peninsular and Oriental Company's Service.

In royal 8vo, 1s. 6d.

METHVEN, CAPTAIN ROBERT.—NARRATIVES WRITTEN BY SEA COMMANDERS, ILLUSTRATIVE OF THE LAW OF STORMS. The "Blenheim" Hurricane of 1851, with Diagrams.

Part 1, large 8vo., 5s. Part 2, in preparation.

MURRAY, JOHN, C.E.—A Treatise on the Stability of Retaining Walls, elucidated by Engravings and Diagrams.

John Weale, 59, High Holborn, London, W.C.

MR. WEALE'S EDUCATIONAL SERIES.

In demy 12mo, cloth, price 1s.

DICTIONARY OF THE FRENCH AND ENGLISH LANGUAGES.—25.—By A. ELWES. Vol. I.

In demy 12mo, cloth, price 1s. 6d.

DICTIONARY OF THE ENGLISH AND FRENCH LANGUAGES.—26.—By A. ELWES. Vol II.

In demy 12mo, cloth, price 1s.

GRAMMAR OF THE ITALIAN LANGUAGE. —27.—By A. ELWES.

In demy 12mo, cloth, price 2s.

DICTIONARY OF THE ITALIAN, ENGLISH, AND FRENCH LANGUAGES.—28, 29.—By A. ELWES. Vol. I.

In demy 12mo, cloth, price 2s.

DICTIONARY OF THE ENGLISH, ITALIAN, AND FRENCH LANGUAGES.—30, 51.—By A. ELWES. Vol. II.

In demy 12mo, cloth, price 2s.

DICTIONARY OF THE FRENCH, ITALIAN, AND ENGLISH LANGUAGES.—32, 53.—By A. ELWES. Vol. III.

In demy 12mo, cloth, price 1s.

GRAMMAR OF THE SPANISH LANGUAGE. —34.—By A. ELWES.

In demy 12mo, cloth, price 4s.

DICTIONARY OF THE SPANISH AND ENGLISH LANGUAGES.—35, 36, 37, 38.—By A. ELWES. 4 vols. in 1.

In demy 12mo, cloth, price 1s.

GRAMMAR OF THE GERMAN LANGUAGE. —39.

In demy 12mo, cloth, price 1s.

CLASSICAL GERMAN READER.—40.—From the best Authors.

In demy 12mo, cloth, price 3s.

DICTIONARIES OF THE ENGLISH, GERMAN, AND FRENCH LANGUAGES.—41, 42, 43.—By N. E. HAMILTON, 3 vols., separately, 1s. each.

In demy 12mo, cloth, price 7s.

DICTIONARY OF THE HEBREW AND ENGLISH LANGUAGES.—44, 45.—Containing the Biblical and Rabbinical words, 2 vols. (together with the Grammar, which may be had separately for 1s.), by Dr. BRESSLAU, Hebrew Professor.

In demy 12mo, cloth, price 3s.

DICTIONARY OF THE ENGLISH AND HEBREW LANGUAGES.—46.—Vol. III. to complete.

In demy 12mo, cloth, price 1s.

FRENCH AND ENGLISH PHRASE BOOK. —47.

John Weale, 59, High Holborn, London, W.C.

Mr. Weale's Works on Architecture, Engineering, Fine Arts, &c.

On a large folio sheet, price 2s. 6d.

NEVILLE, JOHN, C.E., M.R.I.A. — OFFICE HYDRAULIC TABLES: for the use of Engineers engaged in Water Works, giving the Discharge and Dimensions of River Channels and Pipes.

In 8vo, Second and much Improved Edition, with an Appendix, cloth boards, price 10s.

NEVILLE, JOHN, C.E., M.R.I.A.—HYDRAULIC TABLES, COEFFICIENTS, AND FORMULÆ; for Finding the Discharge of Water from Orifices, Notches, Weirs, Pipes, and Rivers, with Extensive Additions, New Formulæ, Tables, and General Information on Rain-Fall Catchment-Basins, Drainage, Sewerage, Water Supply for Towns and Mill Power.

On 23 folio Plates, 12s.

ORNAMENTS. — Ornaments displayed on a full size for Working, proper for all Carvers, Painters, &c., containing a variety of accurate examples of foliage and friezes.

Plates, 8vo, 2s. 6d.

O'BRIEN'S, W., C.E. — Prize Essay on Canals and Canal Conveyance.

In demy 8vo, cloth, boards, 12s.

PAMBOUR, COUNT DE — STEAM ENGINE; the Theory of the Proportions of Steam Engines, and a series of practical formulæ.

In 8vo, cloth, boards, with Plates, a second edition, 18s.

A PRACTICAL TREATISE ON LOCOMOTIVE ENGINES UPON RAILWAYS. — With practical Tables and an Appendix, showing the expense of conveying Goods by means of Locomotives on Railroads. By COUNT F. M. G. DE PAMBOUR.

4to, 72 finely executed Plates, in cloth, £1 16s.

PARKER, CHARLES, Architect, F.I.B.A. — The Rural and Villa Architecture of Italy, portraying the several very interesting examples in that country, with Estimates and Specifications for the application of the same designs in England; selected from buildings and scenes in the vicinity of Rome and Florence, and arranged for Rural and Domestic Buildings generally.

Price, complete, £2 2s. In 4to.

POLE, WILLIAM, M. Inst., C. E. — CORNISH PUMPING ENGINE; designed and constructed at the Hayle Copper House in Cornwall, under the superintendence of CAPTAIN JENKINS; erected and now on duty at the Coal Mines of Languin, Department of the Loire Inférieur, Nantes. Nine elaborate Drawings, historically and scientifically described.

With Plate. 10s. 6d.

AN ANALYTICAL INVESTIGATION OF THE ACTION OF THE CORNISH PUMPING ENGINE. — This Third Part sold separately from above.

28s. bound in 4to size.

PORTFOLIO OF ENGINEERING ENGRAVINGS. — Useful to Students as a Text Book, or a Drawing Book of Engineering and Mechanics; being a series of Practical Examples in Civil, Hydraulic, and Mechanical Engineering. Fifty Engravings to a scale for drawing.

John Weale, 59, High Holborn, London, W.C.

MR. WEALE'S WORKS ON ARCHITECTURE, ENGINEERING, FINE ARTS, &c.

50 Plates, 28s., boards.

PORTFOLIO OF GREEK ARCHITECTURE.—Or, Dilettanti Drawing Book; Architectural Engravings, with descriptive Text. Being adapted as studies of the best Classic Models in the Grecian style of Architecture.

50 Plates, £1 8s., bound.

PORTFOLIO OR DRAWING BOOK OF GOTHIC CHURCH ARCHITECTURE.—Of the periods of the 14th, 15th, and 16th centuries. Useful to Architects, Builders, and Students.

25 Plates, folio. 25s.

PORTFOLIO OF ARCHÆOLOGICAL COLLECTIONS.—Of curious, interesting, and ornamental subjects and patterns for stained glass windows, from York.

18 Plates, 10s. 6d. Small folio.

PORTFOLIO OF ANCIENT CAPITAL LETTERS, MONOGRAMS, QUAINT DESIGNS, &c.—Beautifully Coloured and Ornamented.

159 Plates, folio, half-bound in morocco, very neat, £4 4s.

PUBLIC WORKS OF GREAT BRITAIN.—Consisting of Railways, Rails, Chairs, Blocks, Cuttings, Embankments, Tunnels, Oblique Arches, Viaducts, Bridges, Stations, Locomotive Engines, &c.; Cast-Iron Bridges, Iron and Gas Works, Canals, Lock-gates, Centering, Masonry and Brickwork for Canal Tunnels; Canal Boats; the London and Liverpool Docks, Plans and Dimensions, Dock gates, Walls, Quays, and their Masonry; Mooring-Chains; Plan of the Harbour and Port of London, and other important Engineering Works, with Descriptions and Specifications.

In two Parts. Imperial folio.

PUBLIC WORKS OF THE UNITED STATES OF AMERICA.

And the text in an 8vo Volume, price together £2 6s.

REPORTS, SPECIFICATIONS, AND ESTIMATES OF PUBLIC WORKS OF THE UNITED STATES OF AMERICA; explanatory of the Atlas Folio of Detailed Engravings, elucidating practically these important Engineering Works. The Plates are Engraved in the best style.

Imperial 8vo, 50 Engravings, £1 5s.

PAPERS AND PRACTICAL ILLUSTRATIONS OF PUBLIC WORKS OF RECENT CONSTRUCTION—BOTH BRITISH AND AMERICAN. Supplementary to previous Publications, and containing all the details of the Niagara Suspension Bridge.

Half-bound in morocco, finely coloured Plates, price £3 3s.

RAWLINSON'S, ROBERT, C.E.—Designs for Factory, Furnace, and other Tall Chimney Shafts. Tall chimneys are necessary for purposes of Trade and Manufactures. They are required for Factories, for Foundries, for Gas Works, for Chemical Works, for Baths and Wash-houses, and for many other purposes.

Third Edition, in royal 8vo, boards, with 18 Charts, &c., 12s.

REID, Major-General Sir W., F.R.S., &c.—AN ATTEMPT TO DEVELOP THE LAW OF STORMS by means of facts arranged according to place and time; and hence to point out a cause for the variable winds, with a view to practical use in navigation.

John Weale, 59, High Holborn, London, W.C.

Mr. Weale's Works on Architecture, Engineering, Fine Arts, &c.

In royal 8vo, uniform with the preceding, 8s., with Charts and Woodcuts. The work together in 2 vols., £1 1s.

REID, Major-General Sir W., F.R.S., &c. — THE PROGRESS OF THE DEVELOPMENT OF THE LAW OF STORMS AND OF THE VARIABLE WINDS, with practicable application of the subject to navigation.

Illustrated with 17 Plates, Third Edition, 8vo, cloth, 7s. 6d.

RICHARDSON, C. J., Architect. — A Popular Treatise on the Warming and Ventilation of Buildings; showing the advantages of the improved system of Heated Water Circulation. And a method to effect the combination of large and small pipes to the same apparatus, and ventilating buildings.

Bound in 2 vols., very neat, half-morocco, gilt tops, price £18.

RENNIE'S, Sir JOHN, F.R.S., Work on the Theory, Formation, and Construction of British and Foreign Harbours, Docks, and Naval Arsenals. This great work may now be had complete, 20 parts and supplement, price £16.

In 8vo, 8s.

RÉVY, J. L., C.E. — THE PROGRESSIVE SCREW AS A PROPELLER IN NAVIGATION.

12mo, cloth boards, 3s. 6d.

SIMMS, F. W. — Treatise on the principal Mathematical and Drawing Instruments employed by the Engineer, Architect, and Surveyor; with a description of the Theodolite, together with Instructions in Field Works.

4to, with fine Plates, a New Edition, extended, sewed, 5s.

SMITH, C. H., Sculptor. — Report and Investigation into the Qualifications and Fitness of Stone for Building Purposes.

In 1 vol. 8vo, in boards, 7s. 6d.

SMITH'S, Colonel of the Madras Engineers, Observations on the Duties and Responsibilities Involved in the Management of Mines.

8vo, cloth boards, with Index Map, 5s.

SOPWITH, THOMAS, F.R.S. — THE AWARD OF THE DEAN FOREST COMMISSIONERS AS TO THE COAL AND IRON MINES.

16 large folio Plates, £1 4s. Separately, 2s. each.

SOPWITH, THOMAS, F.R.S. — SERIES OF ENGRAVED PLANS OF THE COAL AND IRON MINES.

12 Plates, 4to, 6s. in a wrapper.

STAIRCASES, HANDRAILS, BALUSTRADES, AND NEWELS OF THE ELIZABETHAN AGE, &c. — Consisting of — 1. Staircase at Audley-end Old Manor House, Wilts; 2. Charlton House, Kent; 3. Great Ellingham Hall, Norfolk; 4. Dorfold, Cheshire; 5. Charterhouse; 6. Oak Staircase at Clare Hall, Cambridge; 7. Cromwell Hall, Highgate; 8. Ditto; 9. Catherine Hall, Cambridge; 10. Staircase by Inigo Jones at a house in Chandos Street; 11. Ditto at East Sutton; 12. Ditto, ditto. Useful to those constructing edifices in the early English domestic style.

Large atlas folio Plates, price £2 2s.

STALKARTT, M., N.A. — Naval Architecture; or, The Rudiments and Rules of Ship Building; exemplified in a Series of Draughts and Plans. No text.

John Weale, 59, High Holborn, London, W.C.

MR. WEALE'S WORKS ON ARCHITECTURE, ENGINEERING, FINE ARTS, &c.

With Illustrative Diagrams. In 8vo, 7s. 6d.

STEVENSON'S, THOMAS, C.E., of Edinburgh,
Description of the Different kinds of Lighthouse Apparatus.

8vo, 2s. 6d.

STEVENSON, DAVID, C.E. of Edinborgh.—
Supplement to his Work on Tidal Rivers.

Text in 4to, and large folio Atlas of 75 Plates, half-cloth boards, £2 12s. 6d.

STEAM NAVIGATION.— Vessels of Iron and Wood; the Steam Engine; and on Screw Propulsion. By WM. FAIRBAIRN, F.R.S., of Manchester; Messrs. FORRESTER, M.I.C.E., of Liverpool; JOHN LAIRD, M.I.C.E., of Birkenhead; OLIVER LANG, (late) of Woolwich; Messrs. SEAWARD, Limehouse, &c. &c. &c. Together with Results of Experiments on the Disturbance of the Compass in Iron-built Ships. By G. B. AIRY, M.A., Astronomer Royal.

10s.

ST. PAUL'S CATHEDRAL, LONDON, SECTION OF.— The Original Splendid Engraving by J. GWYN, J. WALE, decorated agreeably to the original intention of Sir Christopher Wren; a very fine large print, showing distinctly the construction of that magnificent edifice.

Size of Plate 4½ feet in height, 10s.

ST. PAUL'S CATHEDRAL, LONDON, GREAT PLAN.— J. WALE and J. GWYN'S GREAT PLAN, accurately measured from the Building, with all the Dimensions figured and in detail, description of Compartments by engraved Writing.

Second Edition, greatly enlarged, royal 8vo, with Plates, cloth boards, price 16s.

STRENGTH OF MATERIALS.—FAIRBAIRN, WILLIAM, C.E., F.R.S., and of the Legion of Honour of France. On the application of Cast and Wrought Iron to Building Purposes.

With Plates and Diagrams. New Edition. The work complete in 2 vols., bound in 1 vol., price, in cloth boards, 16s. The second portion of the work, containing Mr. Hodgkinson's Experimental Researches, may be had separately, price 9s.

STRENGTH OF MATERIALS.—HODGKINSON, EATON, F.R.S. AND THOMAS TREDGOLD, C.E. A PRACTICAL ESSAY ON THE STRENGTH OF CAST IRON AND OTHER METALS; Intended for the assistance of engineers, ironmasters, millwrights, architects, founders, smiths and others engaged in the construction of machines, buildings, &c. By EATON HODGKINSON, F.R.S.

To be published in 1861, in crown 8vo, bound for use.

STRENGTH OF MATERIALS.—POLE, WILLIAM, C.E., F.R.S.—Tables and popular explanations of the Strength of Materials, of Wrought and Cast Iron with other metals, for structural purposes; developing in a systematic form, the strengths, bearings, weights, and forms of these materials, whether used as girders or arches, for the construction of bridges and viaducts, public buildings, domestic mansions, private buildings, columns or pillars, breastsummers for warehouses, shops, working and manufacturing factories, &c. &c. &c. The whole rendered of easy reference for architects, builders, civil and mechanical engineers, millwrights, ironfounders, &c. &c. &c., and forming Ready Reckoner or Calculator.

John Weale, 59, High Holborn, London, W.C.

MR. WEALE'S WORKS ON ARCHITECTURE, ENGINEERING, FINE ARTS, &c.

30 very elaborately drawn Engravings. In large 4to, neatly half-bound and lettered, £1 1s. A few copies on large imperial size, extra half-binding. £1 11s. 6d.

TEMPLE CHURCH.—The Architectural History and Architectural Ornaments, Embellishments, and Painted Glass, of the Temple Church, London.

Part I., with 20 Engravings on Wood and Copper, in cloth boards, 4to, 10s.

THAMES TUNNEL.—A Memoir of the several Operations and the Construction of the Thames Tunnel, from Papers by the late Sir ISAMBARD BRUNEL, F.R.S., Civil Engineer.

Fourth Edition, with a Supplementary Addition, large 8vo, 12s. 6d.

THOMAS (LYNALL), F.R.S.L.—Rifled Ordnance.—A Practical Treatise on the Application of the Principle of the Rifle to Guns and Mortars of every calibre; to which is added a New Theory of the Initial Action and Force of Fixed Gunpowder plates.

In 4to, complete, cloth, Vol. I., with Engravings, £1 10s.; Vol. II., ditto, £1 6s.; Vol. III., ditto, £2 12s. 6d.

TRANSACTIONS OF THE INSTITUTION OF CIVIL ENGINEERS.

8 vols., numerous Engravings of Sections of Coal Mines, &c., large folding Plates, several of which are coloured, in large 8vo, half-bound in calf, price £1 1s. per volume.

TRANSACTIONS OF THE NORTH OF ENGLAND INSTITUTE OF MINING ENGINEERS.—Commencing in 1852, and continued to 1860.

A New Edition revised by the translator, and with additional Plates, in demy 12mo, India proof Plates and Vignettes, half-bound in morocco, gilt tops, price 12s. Only 25 printed on India paper.

VITRUVIUS. — The Architecture of Marcus Vitruvius Pollio in 10 Books. Translated from the Latin by JOSEPH GWILT, F.S.A., F.R.A.S.

In 4to, with Plates, 7s. 6d.

WALKER'S, THOMAS, Architect.—Account of the Church at Stoke Golding.

£1 10s.

WEALE'S QUARTERLY PAPERS ON ENGINEERING.—Vol. VI. (Parts 11 and 12 completing the work.) Comprising, "On the Principles of Water Power," Plates. Experiments on Locomotive Engines. Coloured Plates. On Naval Arsenals. On the Mode of Forming Foundations under water and on bad ground. Plates. On the Improvement of the River Medway and of the Port and Arsenal of Chatham. On the Improvement of Portsmouth Harbour. An Analysis of the Cornish Pumping. Plates. On Water Wheels. Plates.

Text in 8vo, cloth boards, and Plates in atlas folio, in cloth, 16s.

WHITE'S, THOMAS, N.A., Theory and Practice of Ship Building.

In 8vo, with a large Sectional Plate, 1s. 6d.

WHICHCORD, JOHN, Architect.—OBSERVATIONS ON KENTISH RAG STONE AS A BUILDING MATERIAL.

John Weale, 59, High Holborn, London, W.C.

MR. WEALE'S WORKS ON ARCHITECTURE, ENGINEERING FINE ARTS, &c.

4to, coloured Plates, in half-morocco, 7s. 6d.

WHICHCORD, JOHN, Architect.—HISTORY AND ANTIQUITIES OF THE COLLEGIATE CHURCH OF ALL SAINTS, MAIDSTONE.

In 4to, 6s.

WICKSTEED, THOMAS, C.E. — AN EXPERIMENTAL INQUIRY CONCERNING THE RELATIVE POWER OF, AND USEFUL EFFECT PRODUCED BY, THE CORNISH AND BOULTON & WATT PUMPING ENGINES, and Cylindrical and Waggon-Head Boilers.

In 8vo, 1s.

WICKSTEED, THOMAS, C.E. — FURTHER ELUCIDATION OF THE USEFUL EFFECTS OF CORNISH PUMPING ENGINES; showing the average working for long periods, &c., &c., &c.

£2 2s.

WICKSTEED, THOMAS, C.E.—THE ELABORATELY ENGRAVED ILLUSTRATIONS OF THE CORNISH AND BOULTON & WATT ENGINES erected at the East London Water Works, Old Ford. Eight large atlas folio very fine line engravings by GLADWIN, from elaborate drawings made expressly by Mr. WICKSTEED; folio, together with a 4to explanation of the plates, containing an engraving, by LOWRY, of Harvey and West's patent pump-valve, with specification.

With numerous Woodcuts.

WILLIAMS, C. WYE, Esq., M. Inst. C. E.— THE COMBUSTION OF COAL AND THE PREVENTION OF SMOKE, chemically and practically considered.

Imperial 8vo, with a Portrait, 2s. 6d.

WILLIAMS, C. WYE, Esq., M. Inst. C. E.— PRIZE ESSAY ON THE PREVENTION OF THE SMOKE NUISANCE, with a fine portrait of the Author.

With 3 Plates, containing 51 figures, 4to, 5s.

WILLIS, REV. PROFESSOR, M.A.—A system of Apparatus for the use of Lecturers and Experimenters in Mechanical Philosophy.

In 4to, bound, with 26 large plates and 17 woodcuts, 12s.

WILME'S MANUALS. — A MANUAL OF WRITING AND PRINTING CHARACTERS, both ancient and modern.

Maps and Plans, in 4to, plates coloured, half-bound morocco, £3.

WILME'S MANUALS. — A HANDBOOK FOR MAPPING, ENGINEERING, AND ARCHITECTURAL DRAWING.

Three Vols., large 8vo, £3.

WOOLWICH. — COURSE OF MATHEMATICS. This course is essential to all Students destined for the Royal Military Academy at Woolwich.

8vo, 1s.

YULE, MAJOR-GENERAL—ON BREAKWATERS AND BUOYS of VERTICAL FLOATS.

John Weale, 59, High Holborn, London, W.C.

FOREIGN WORKS, KEPT IN STOCK AS FOLLOWS:—

Large folio, 82 plates, some coloured, and 12 woodcuts, 50 francs. £2 10s.

ARCHITECTURE SUISSE.—Ou Choix de Maisons Rustiques des Alpes du Canton de Berne, par GRAFFINRIED et STÜRLER, Architectes. Berne, 1844.

Small folio, 52 most interesting and explanatory plates of Public Works, Bridges, Iron Works, &c., &c., &c., very neatly halfbound in morocco, £1 10s.

BAUERNFEIND, CARL MAX.—VORLEGEBLAETTER ZUR BRUCKENBAU KUNDE. München.

Large folio, 36 plates of Byzantine capitals, 12s.

BYZANTINISCHE CAPITAELER.—München.

Second edition, 126 plates, large folio, best Paris edition, 100 f., printed on fine paper, half-cloth boards, £4 4s.

CALLIAT, VICTOR, ARCT.—Paralèlle des Maisons de Paris, construites depuis 1830 jusqu'à nos jours.—1857.

Large folio, 60 francs, 60 plates, and several vignettes, £2 8s.

CANÉTO, F.—Sainte-Marié d'Auch. Atlas Monographique de Cette Cathédrale. The Plates consist principally of outline drawings of the Painted Glass Windows in this Cathedral.

120 plates, elegant in half-morocco extra, interleaved, £5 15s. 6d.

CASTERMAN, A.—PARALÈLLE des MAISONS de BRUXELLES et des PRINCIPALES VILLES de la BELGIQUE, construites depuis 1830 jusqu'à nos jours, représentés en plans, élévations, coupes et détails intérieurs et extérieurs. —Paris.

Small folio, 48 plates of edifices, £1 1s.

DEGEN, L.— LES CONSTRUCTIONS EN BRIQUES, composées et publiées. 8 livraisons.—1856.

Small folio, 48 plates of houses, parts of houses, details of all kinds of singularly beautiful woodwork, coloured plates in imitation of the objects given, £1 1s.

DEGEN, L.—LES CONSTRUCTIONS ORNAMENTALES EN BOIS, 6 livraisons.

In 5 very large folio parts, 35 fine plates, £1 11s. 6d.

GAERTNER, F. V.—The splendid works of M. GAERTNER of Munich, drawn to a very large size, consisting of the library in plans, elevations, interiors, details, and sections, and coloured ornaments. The church, with details, ornaments, &c.—München.

Small folio, 36 fine plates of the Architecture, ornament, and detail of the houses and churches of Germany during the middle age, very neatly half-bound in morocco, £2 12s. 6d.

KALLENBACH, C. C.—Chronologie der Deutsch-Mittelalterlichen Baukunst.—München. Fine Work.

The works of the great master KLENZIE of Munich, in 5 parts very large folio, 50 plates of elevations, plans, sections, details and ornaments of his public and private buildings executed in Munich and St. Petersburg, £2 2s.

KLENZE, LEO VON.— Sammlung Arthitectonisher Entwürfe, für die Ausführung bestimmt oder wirklich ausgeführt. Published in Munich.

John Weale, 59, High Holborn, London, W.C.

FOREIGN WORKS KEPT IN STOCK AS
FOLLOWS:—

Upwards of 100 plates, large 4to, £7 12s. 6d.
PETIT, VICTOR.—CHATEAUX DE FRANCE.
Architecture Pittoresque, ou Monuments des quinzième et
seizième siècles. Paris.

Livraisons 1 à 18, very finely executed plates, large Imperial folio,
£5 8s.
CHATEAUX DE LA VALLÉE DE LA
LOIRE DES XV, XVI, ET COMMENCEMENT DU XVII
SIECLE.—Paris, 1857—60.

4to, 90 plates, 72f.; £2 10s.
RECUEIL DE SCULPTURES GOTHIQUE.—
Dessinées et gravées à l'eau forte d'après les plus beaux monuments construits en France depuis le onzième jusqu'au quinzième siècle, par ADAMS, Inspecteur des travaux de la Sainte Chapelle. Paris, 1856.

4 parts are published, price 14s.
RAMÉE.—HISTOIRE GÉNÉRALE DE L'ARCHITECTURE. L'Histoire générale de l'Architecture, par DANIEL RAMÉE, forme 2 vol. grande in 8vo, publiés en 8 fascicules.

5 vols., large 8vo, numerous fine woodcuts, half morocco.
VIOLET-LE-DUC. — DICTIONNAIRE RAISONNÉ, de l'Architecture Française du quinzième au seizième siècle. Paris, 1854-8.

2 vols., extra imperial folio, price £6 10s. 6d.
BADIA D'ALTACOMBA.—Storia e Descrizione della Antico Sepolchro dei Reali di Savoia, fondita da Amedio III. rinnovata da Carlo Felice e Maria Christina.

79 livraisons in large 4to, 200 engravings, £8 18s. 6d.
BELLE ARTI.—Il Palazzo Ducale di Venezia,
Illustrato da Francesco Zanotto. Venezia, 1846—1858.

2 vols. large 4to, 62 very neatly engraved outline Plates, £1 5s.
CANOVA.—Le Tombe ed i Monumenti Illustri
d'Italia. Milano.

2 vols. 4to, 67 elaborate Plates, £1 16s.
CAVALIERI SAN-BERTOLO (NICOLA).—
ISTITUZIONI DI ARCHITETTURA STATICA E IDRAULICA. Mantova.

2 vols. imperial folio, in parts of eight divisions, &c., New and much Improved Edition, comprising 259 Plates of the Public Buildings of Venice, plans, elevations, sections, and details, £8 18s. 6d.
CICOGNARA (COUNT).—Le Fabbriche e i Monumenti Cospicui di Venezia, illustrati da L. Cicognara, da A. Diedo, e da G. A. Selva, edizione con copiose note ed aggiunte di Francesco Zanotto, arricchita di nuove tavole e della Versione Francese. Venezia nello stab. nas. di G. Antonelli a spese degli edit. G. Antonelli e Luciano Basadonna, 1858. The elaborately descriptive text is in French and Italian, beautifully printed.
Copies elegantly half-bound in morocco, extra gilt, library copy and interleaved, £12 12s. Venezia, 1858.

Folio, Portrait, and 147 Plates, consisting of subjects of public buildings, executed at Verona, plans, elevations, sections, details, and ornaments, with some executed works at Venice, &c., £4 4s.
FABBRICHE.—CIVILI ECCLESIASTICHE
E MILITARI DI MICHELE SAN MICHELE disegnate
ed incise da BONZANI FRANCESCO e L.
GIROLAMO.

John Weale, 59, High Holborn, London, W.C.

FOREIGN WORKS KEPT IN STOCK AS FOLLOWS.

Large folio, containing a profusion of Plates of the palaces, theatres, hôtel de villes, and other public buildings in several parts of Italy. Elegantly half-bound in red morocco, extra gilt and interleaved, £8 8s.

FABBRICHE.—E DISEGNI D'ANTONIO DIEDO, NOBILE VENETO. Venezia.

26 livraisons, price £13 12s.

GALLERIA DI TORINO (LA REALE).— Illustrata da R. D'AZEGLIO, Memb. dell' Accad., &c. &c. Copies, Indian proofs, £18 18s.
*** Bound copies in elegant half-morocco binding, India proof, £23 2s.

9 vols. folio, complete, 177 Plates of outline elevations, plans, interiors, details, &c., first impression, 150 francs, half-bound. £6 6s.

GAUTHIER, M.P., Architecte.— Les PLUS BEAUX ÉDIFICES de la VILLE de GENES et des sas ENVIRONS. Paris, 1830-2.

Folio, 109 Plates of plans, elevations, sections, and details, £2 8s.

GRANDJEAN de MONTIGNY et A. FAMIN. — ARCHITECTURE TOSCANE, ou palais, maisons, et autres édifices, de la Toscane. Paris, 1815.

Oblong folio, containing a profusion of picturesque views of palaces and public buildings and scenes of Venice, executed in tinted lithography, with full descriptions attached to each. Elegant in half extra morocco, interleaved, £4 14s. 6d.

KIER, G.—VENEZIA MONUMENTALE PITTORESCA. Venezia.

Large folio, 61 livraisons or 3 vols., with 3 vols. of text in 4to, £18 18s.

LETAROUILLY, P.— Édifices de Rome Moderne. Paris, 1825-55.

Fine Plates of the New Palace of Justice, Senate House, &c., plans, elevations, sections, doors, &c., details of the several parts, &c., £1 1s.

MICHELA, IGNAZIO.—DESCRIZIONE e DISEGNI del PALAZZO del MAGISTRATI SUPREMI di TORINO. Torino.

Large folio, 94 Plates, bound in extra half-morocco, gilt and interleaved, price £6 10s.

REYNAUD, L.—Trattato di Architettura, contenente nozioni generali sul Principii della Construzione e sulla storia dell' Arti, con annot. per cura di Lorenzo Urbani. Venezia, 1857.

4 imperial bulky 8vo volumes, printed and published under authority, and treats of the early foundation of Venice and establishment as a kingdom, its wealth and commerce, and its once great political position, with Plates, £3 3s.

VENEZIA—E le sue Lagune. Venezia, 1847.

VENEZIA.—Copies elegantly bound and gilt, £4 14s. 6d. Venezia, 1847.

In 2 large folio volumes, numerously and elaborately drawn Plates, very well executed in outline, altogether a very fine work. Very elegantly half-bound in morocco, extra gilt and interleaved, £19 12s.

ACCADEMIA DI BELLI ARTI.— Opere dei Grandi Concorsi Premiale dall' I. R. Accademia delle Belle Arti, in Milano, e pubblicate, per cura dell' Architetto, G. ALUISETTI— per la Classi di Ornato—per le Classi di Architettura, figura ed Ornato. Milano, 1825-29.

John Weale, 59, High Holborn, London, W.C.

FOREIGN WORKS, KEPT IN STOCK AS FOLLOWS:—

Atlas folio, very fine impressions, complete in 8 parts, Columbier folio, £3 13s. 6d. Elegantly half-bound in extra morocco and interleaved, £5 15s. 6d.

ALBERTOLLI, G.—Alcune Decorazioni di Nobili Sale ed Attri Ornamenti. Milano, 1787, 1821, 1838.

To be had separately, £1 8s.

ALBERTOLLI, G.—Part III., very frequently required to make up sets.

2 vols., folio, 80 Plates of the most exquisite kind in colours, far superior to any existing work of the present day, £7 10s.

HOFFMAN, ET KELLERHOVEN. — Recueil de Dessins relatifs à l'Art de la Décoration chez tous les peuples et aux plus belles époques de leur civilisation, &c., destinés à servir de motifs et de matériaux aux peintres, décorateurs, peintres sur verre, et aux dessinateurs de fabriques.

Price £1 1s.

HOPE, ALEXANDER J. BERESFORD, Esq.—Abbildungen der Glasgemälde in der Salvator-Kirche zu Kilndown in der Grafschaft Kent. Copies of paintings on glass in Christ Church, Kilndown, in the county of Kent, executed in the Royal Establishment for Painting on Glass, Munich, by order of ALEXANDER J. BERESFORD HOPE, Esq., published by F. Eggert, Painter on Glass, München. The work contains one sheet with the dedication to A. J. B. HOPE, Esq., and fourteen windows; in the whole fifteen, beautifully engraved and carefully coloured.

In large folio, 80 Plates, containing a profusion of rich Italian and other ornaments. Elegant in half-morocco, gilt, and interleaved, £6 6s.

JULIENNE, E.—Industria Artistica o Raccolto di Composizioni e Decorazioni Ornamentali, come suppellettili, tappezzerie, armature, cristalli, soffitti, cornici, lampade, bronzi, ec. Venezia, 1851-1858.

Prix 50f., in folio, £2.

LE PAUTRE.—Collection des plus belles Compositions, gravées par DE CLOUX, Archte. L'Ouvrage contient cent planches. Paris.

This unique collection is in 2 Vols. 4to, had its commencement in 1812, and contains upwards of 500 rich Designs. Price £3 5s.

METIVIER, MONS., Architect.—The original Sketches, Drawings, and Tracings, in pencil and pen and ink, of executed Works and Proposals, displaying the genius of Mons. Metivier, as an architect of high attainments, whose recent death was much regretted in Bavaria. He was a native of France, and was induced to settle in Munich by the late Duke of Leuchtenberg, under whose patronage he was much employed in the construction of private edifices for the Bavarian nobility and gentry; and for decoration and fittings of them; his interiors are still much in admiration. He built a mansion for Prince Charles, in a most simple and elegant style (in Briener Street), which is still now considered one of the purest buildings of Munich. The above Sketches are his professional life and practice.

Twelve Parts, in small oblong 4to, 60 coloured Plates of 90 elaborately coloured and gilt ornaments. £1 1s.

ORNAMENTENBUCH.—Farbige Verzierungen für Fabrikanten, Zimmermaler und andere Bangewerke. München.

John Weale, 59, High Holborn, London, W.C.

FOREIGN WORKS, KEPT IN STOCK AS FOLLOWS:—

410 Plates, in two thick large 4to. Vols., designed and engraved by MM. Raister Arger, d'Hantel, de Wailly, Wagner, L. Feuchère et Regnier, &c. £5 5s.

ORNEMENTS.—Tirés ou imités des Quatre Écoles. Paris.

Six Parts, large folio, Plates beautifully coloured, in fac-similes of the Interiors, Ornaments, Compartments, Ceilings, &c. £3 12s. 6d. Also, elegantly half-bound in morocco gilt, £4 4s.

ROTTMANN, L.—Ornamente aus den vorzüglichsten Bauwerken Münchens. München.

Very elegant, in half red morocco, gilt, and interleaved, £7 17s. 6d.

ZANETTI, G.—STUDII ARCHITETTONICO ORNAMENTALI, dedicati all' J. R. Accademia Veneta delle Belle Arti, seconda edizione con aggiunte del Prof. L. URBANI, 56 livraisons, in imperial folio, about 200 of most elaborately designed subjects of Architecture and Interior Fittings, Designs for Chimney Pieces, Iron Work for Interiors and Exteriors, Gates and Wooden Gates, Garden Decorations, &c., &c., including the Appendices. Venezia.

A Catalogue, of 40 pages, to be had gratis; printed in demy 8vo.

Export Orders executed either for Principals abroad, or Merchants at home.

In Atlas of Plates and Text, 12mo, price 25s. together,

IRON SHIP BUILDING.

WITH

PRACTICAL ILLUSTRATIONS.

BY

JOHN GRANTHAM, N.A.

DESCRIPTION OF PLATES.

1. Hollow and Bar Keels, Stem and Stern Posts.
2. Side Frames, Floorings, and Bilge Pieces.
3. Floorings continued — Keelsons, Deck Beams, Gunwales, and Stringers.
4. Gunwales continued — Lower Decks, and Orlop Beams.
5. Angle-Iron, T Iron, Z Iron, Bulb Iron, as rolled for Iron Ship-Building.
6. Rivets, shown in section, natural size, Flush and Lapped Joints, with Single and Double Riveting.
7. Plating, three plans, Bulkheads, and modes of securing them.
8. Iron Masts, with Longitudinal and Transverse Sections.
9. Sliding Keel, Water Ballast, Moulding the Frames in Iron Ship-building, Levelling Plates.
10. Longitudinal Section, and Half-breadth Deck Plans of large Vessels, on a reduced scale.
11. Midship Sections of Three Vessels of different sizes.
12. *Large Vessel*, showing details.— Fore End in Section, and End View, with Stern Post, Crutches, Deck Beams, &c.
13. *Large Vessel*, showing details.— After End in section, with End View, Stern Frame for Screw, and Rudder.
14. *Large Vessel*, showing details.— Midship Section, Half breadth.
15. *Machines* for Punching and Shearing Plates and Angle-Iron, and for Bending Plates; Rivet Hearth.
16. *Machines.*— Garforth's Riveting Machine, Drilling and Counter Sinking Machine.
17. *Air Furnace* for Heating Plates and Angle-Iron; various Tools used in Riveting and Plating.
18. *Gunwale*, Keel, and Flooring; Plan for Sheathing Iron Ships with Copper.
19. Illustrations of the Magnetic Condition of various Iron Ships.
20. Gray's Floating Compass and Binnacle, with Adjusting Magnets.
21. Corroded Iron Bolt in Frame of Wooden Ship; Caulking Joints of Plates.
22. *Great Eastern*—Longitudinal Sections and Half-breadth Plans.
23. *Great Eastern*—Midship Section, with details.
24. *Great Eastern*—Section in Engine Room, and Paddle Boxes.

This Work may be had of Messrs. LOCKWOOD & Co., No. 7, Stationers' Hall Court, and also of Mr. WEALE; either the Atlas separately for 1*l*. 2*s*. 6*d*., or together with the Text price as above stated.

Bradbury and Evans, Printers, Whitefriars.

www.ingramcontent.com/pod-product-compliance
Lightning Source LLC
Chambersburg PA
CBHW021221300426
44111CB00007B/390